AF576419

SAILORS' WISDOM

DAY BY DAY

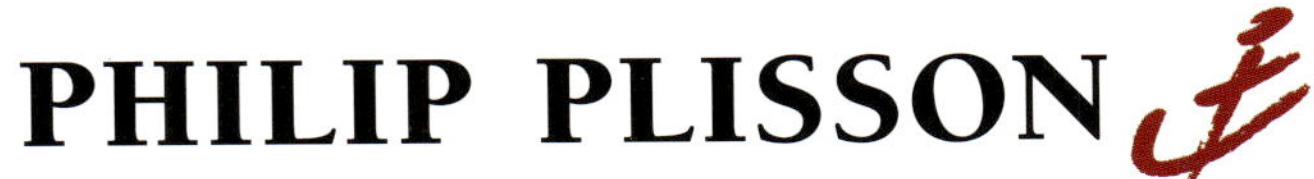

SAILORS' WISDOM

DAY BY DAY

ABRAMS, NEW YORK

JANUARY I

The sea, the sea,
forever starting and re-starting...

Paul Valéry,
from "The Graveyard by the Sea," 1920

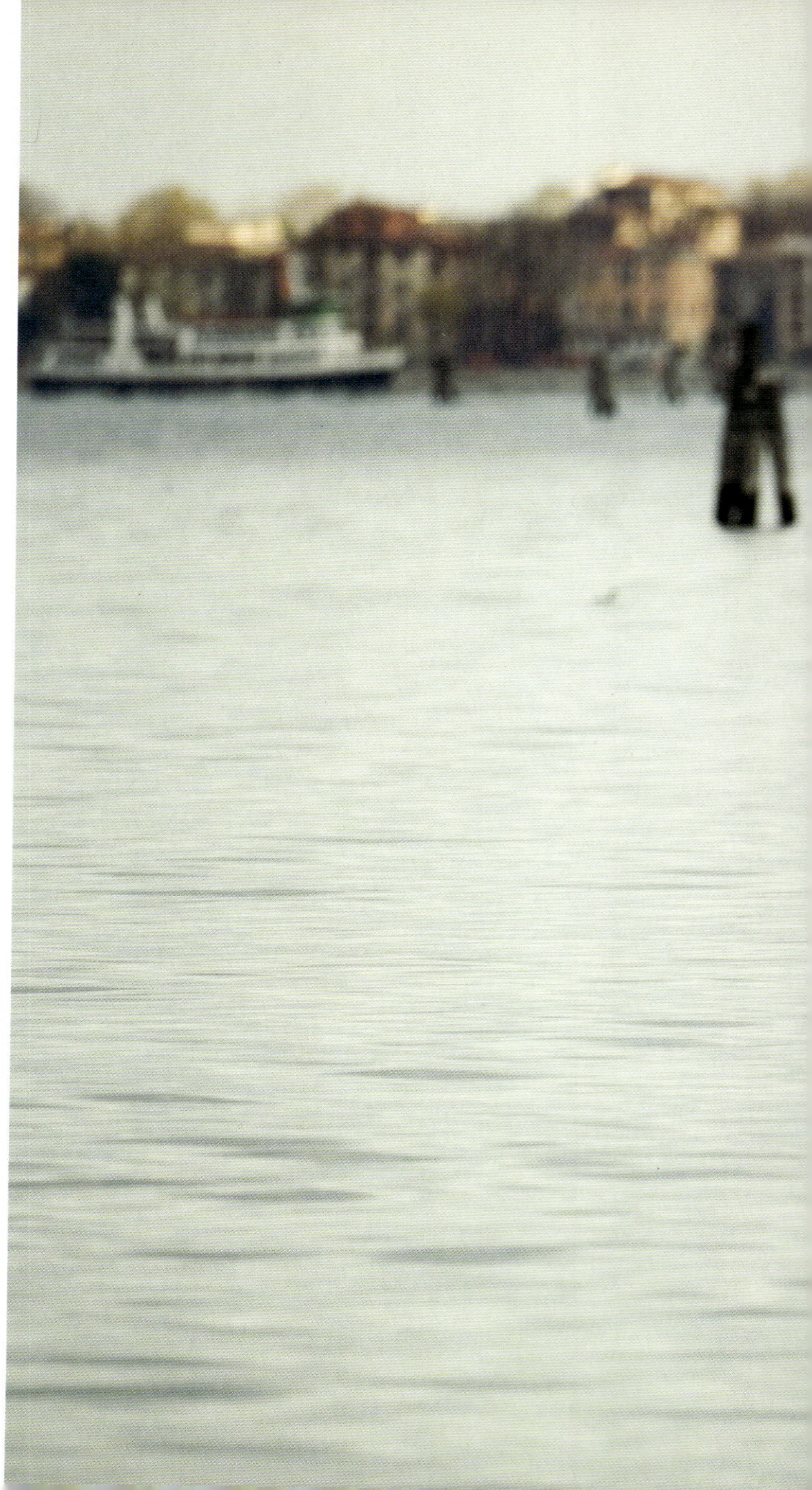

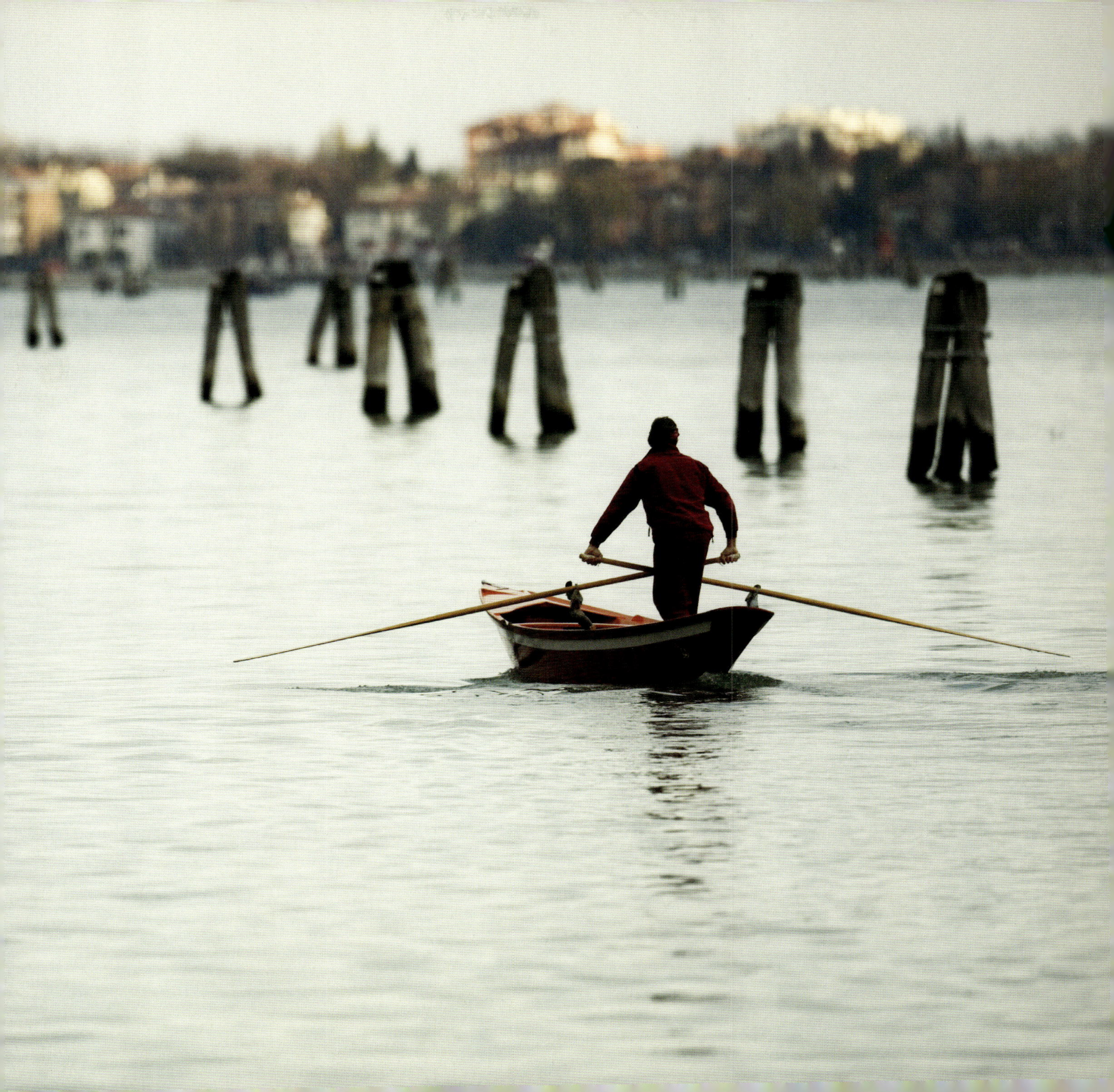

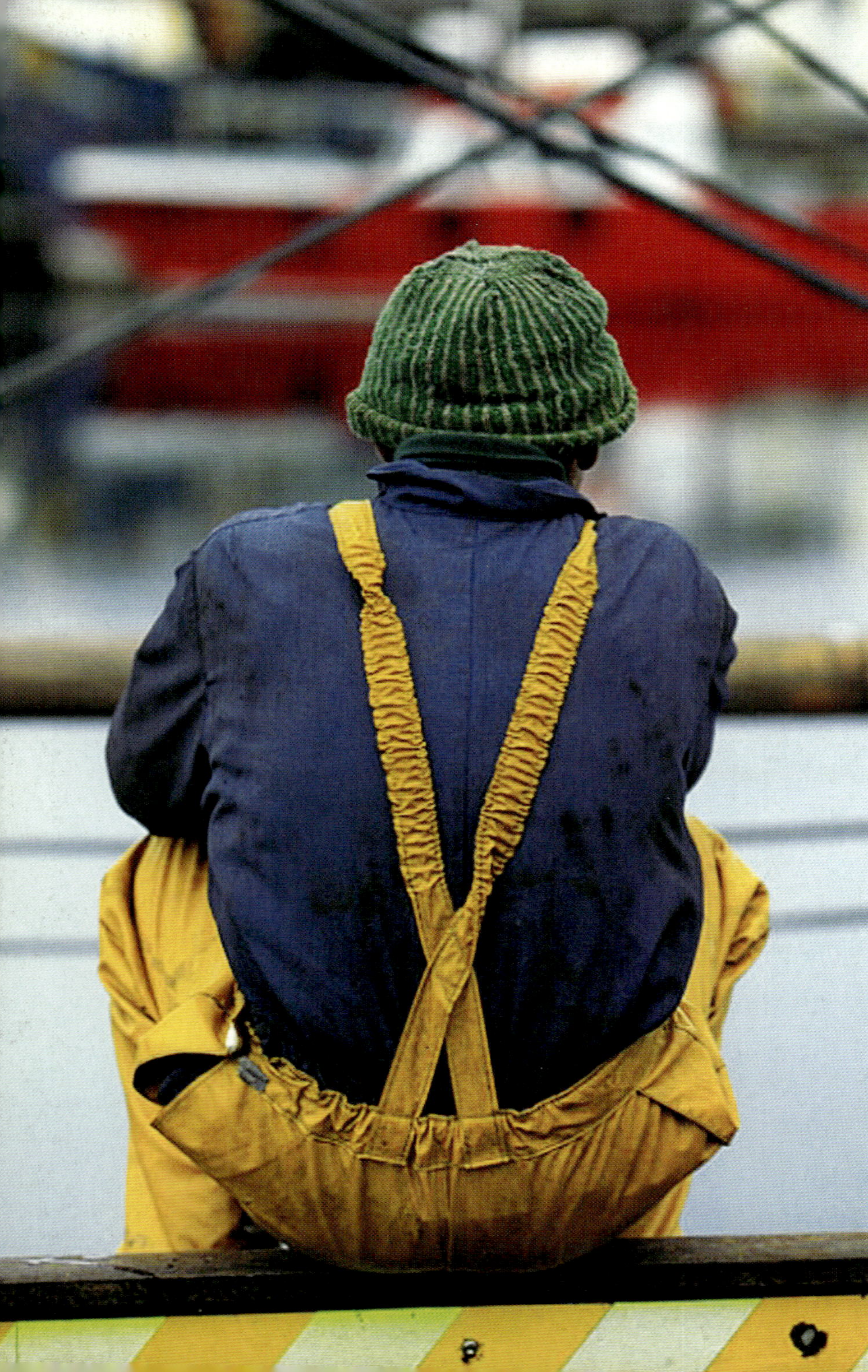

JANUARY 2

The sea drives truth
into a man like salt.

Hilaire Belloc,
from *First and Last,* 1911

JANUARY 3

The person who goes farthest
is generally the one who is willing
to do and dare. The sure-thing
boat never gets far from shore.

Dale Carnegie

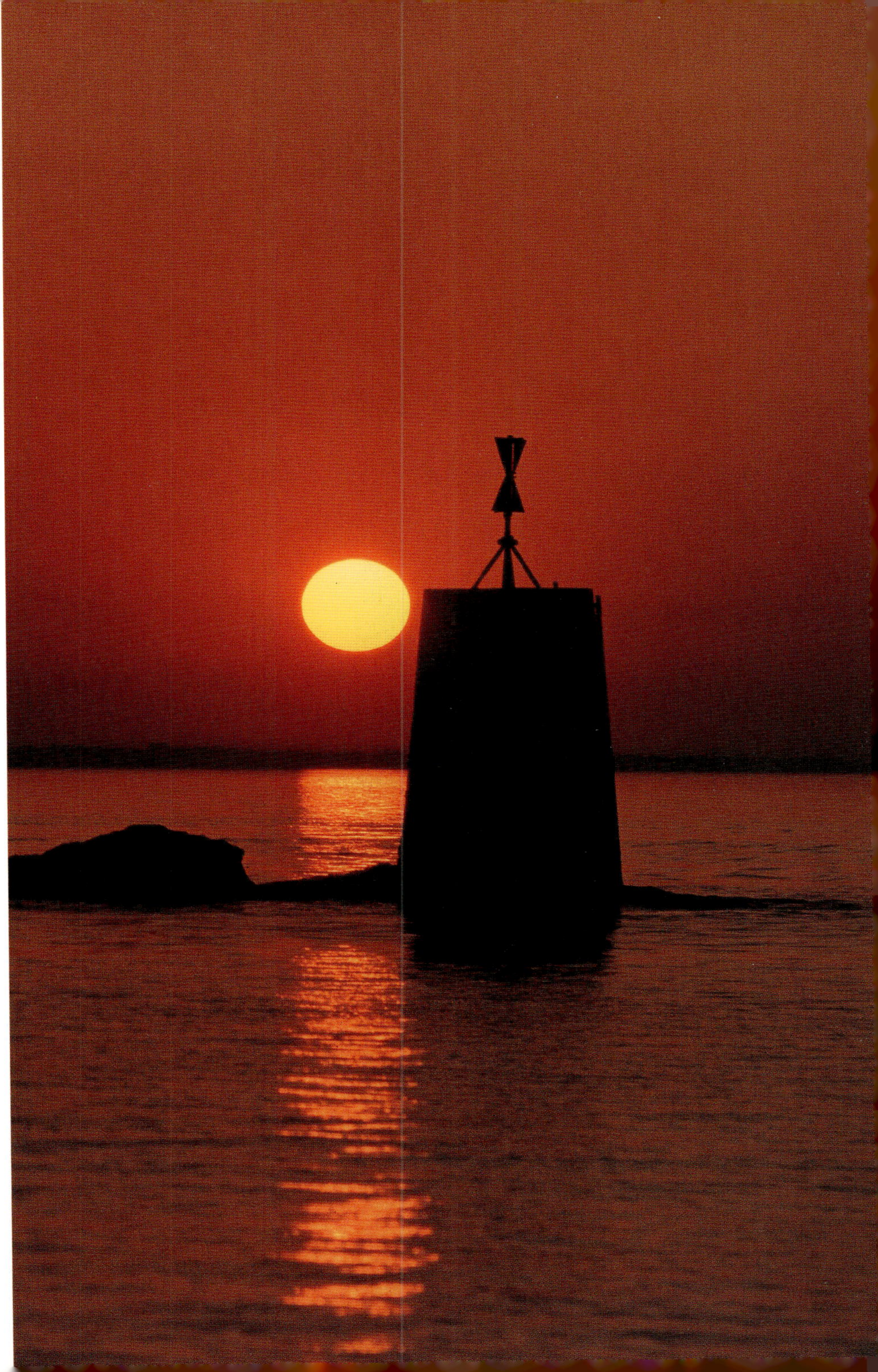

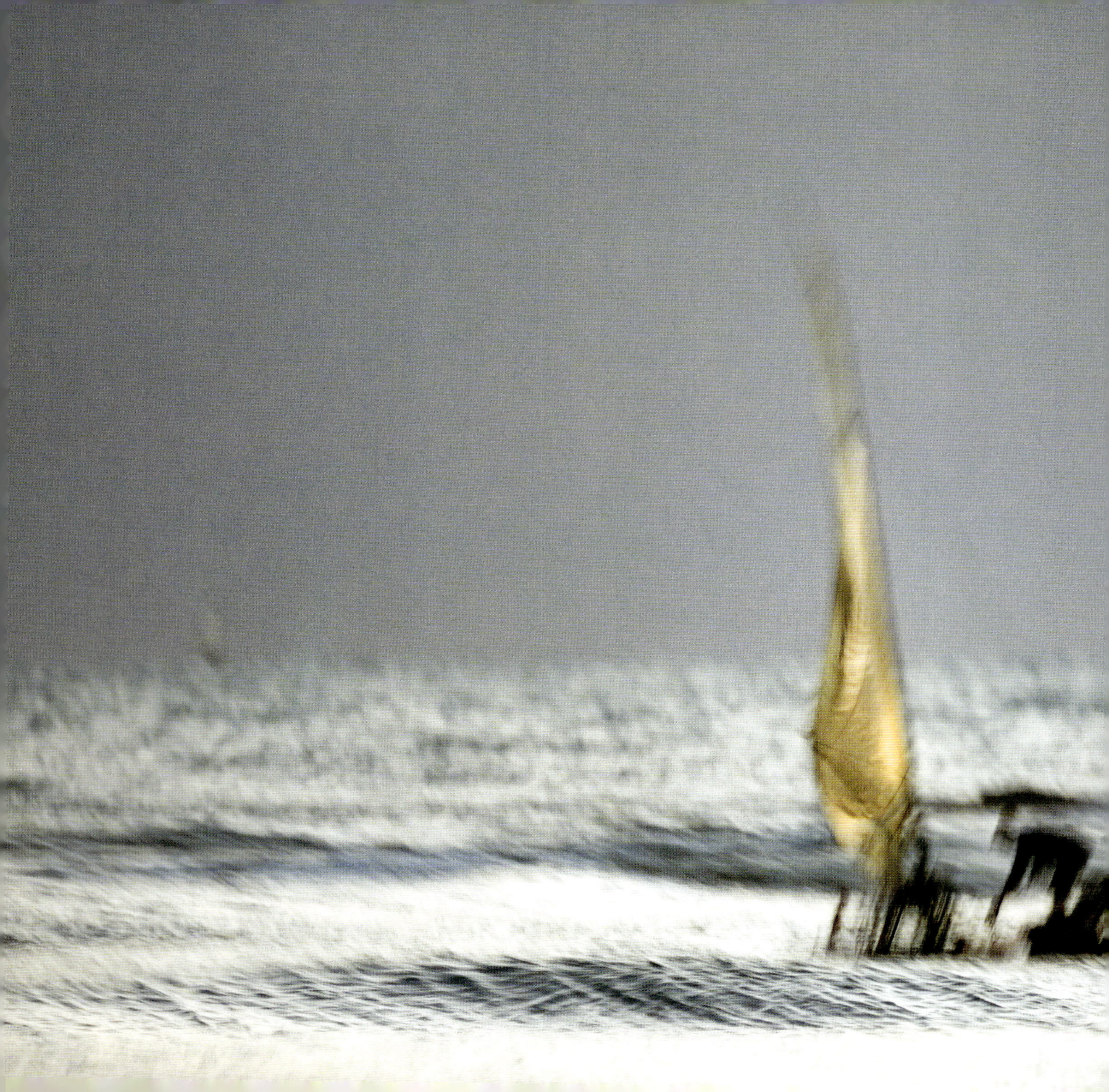

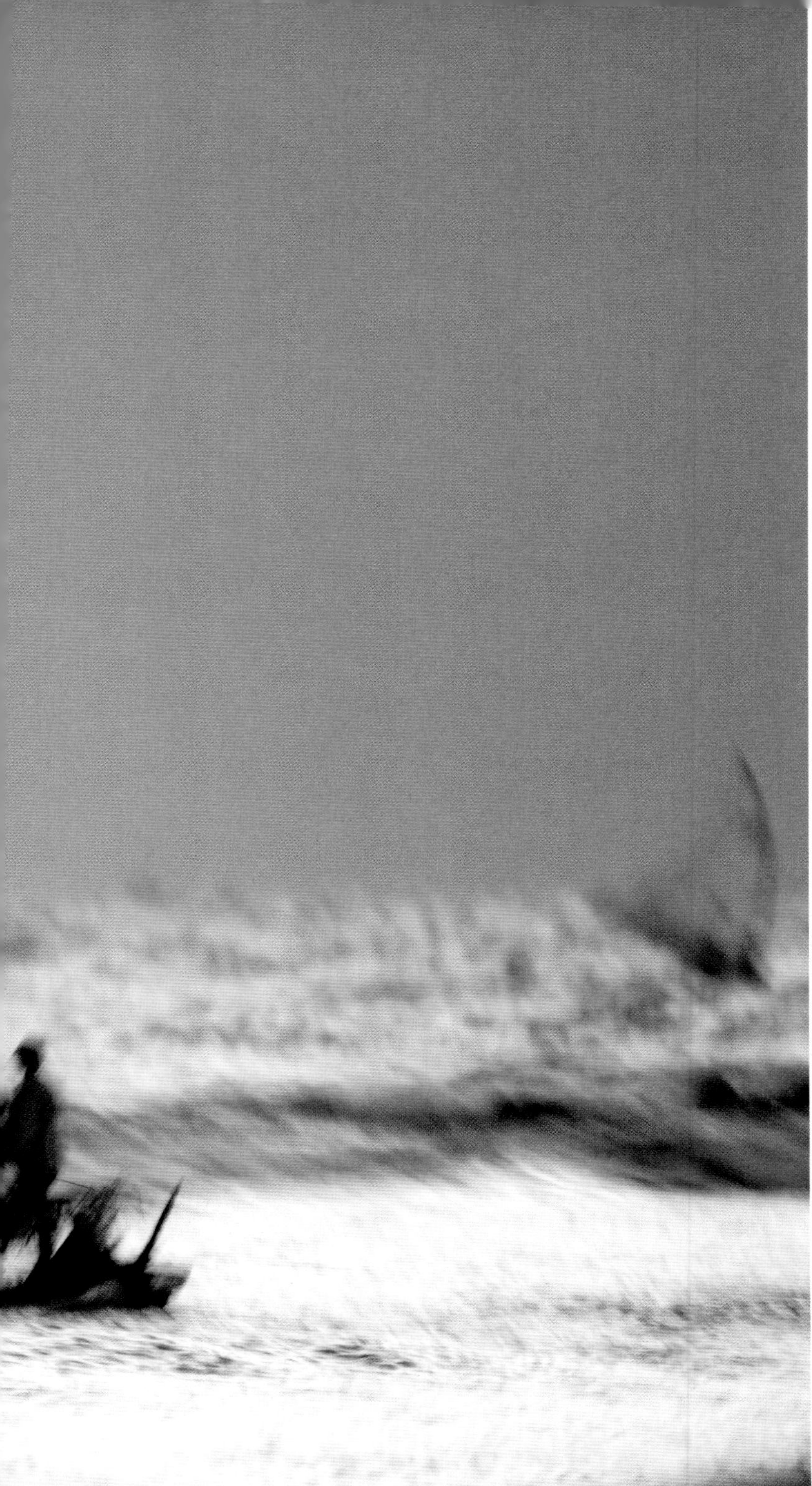

JANUARY 4

One day I saw,
standing at the edge of the rising tide
Passing, filling its sails,
A fast ship enveloped in wind,
And waves and stars.

Victor Hugo, from "The Past,"
Contemplations (Book I) 1856

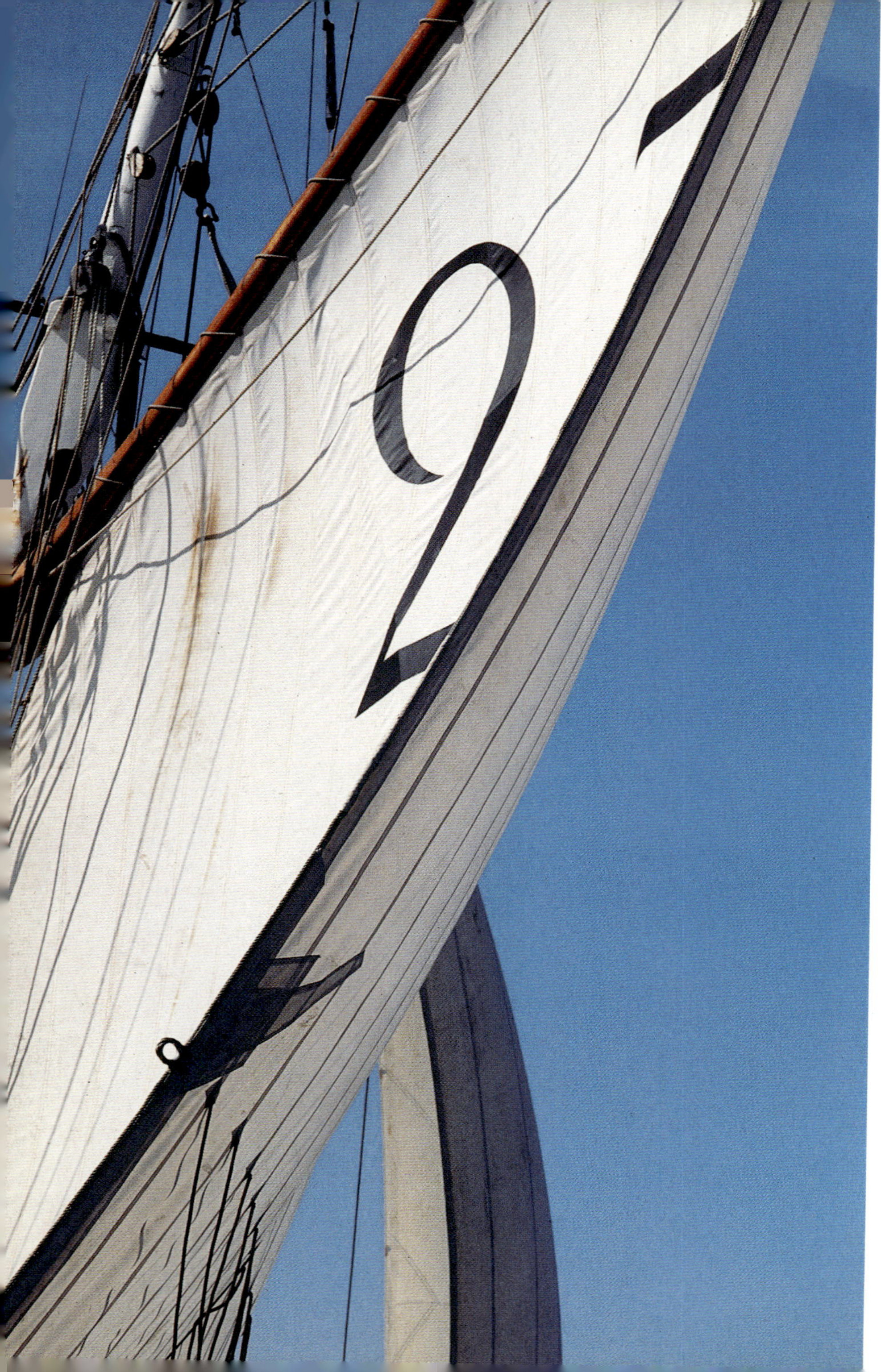

JANUARY 5

He that would learn to pray,
let him go to sea.

George Herbert,
from "Jacula Prudentum," 1651

JANUARY 6

The thing about rigging is,
you can learn it if you become a
master rigger, but there's no book
on rigging.

Richard Serra

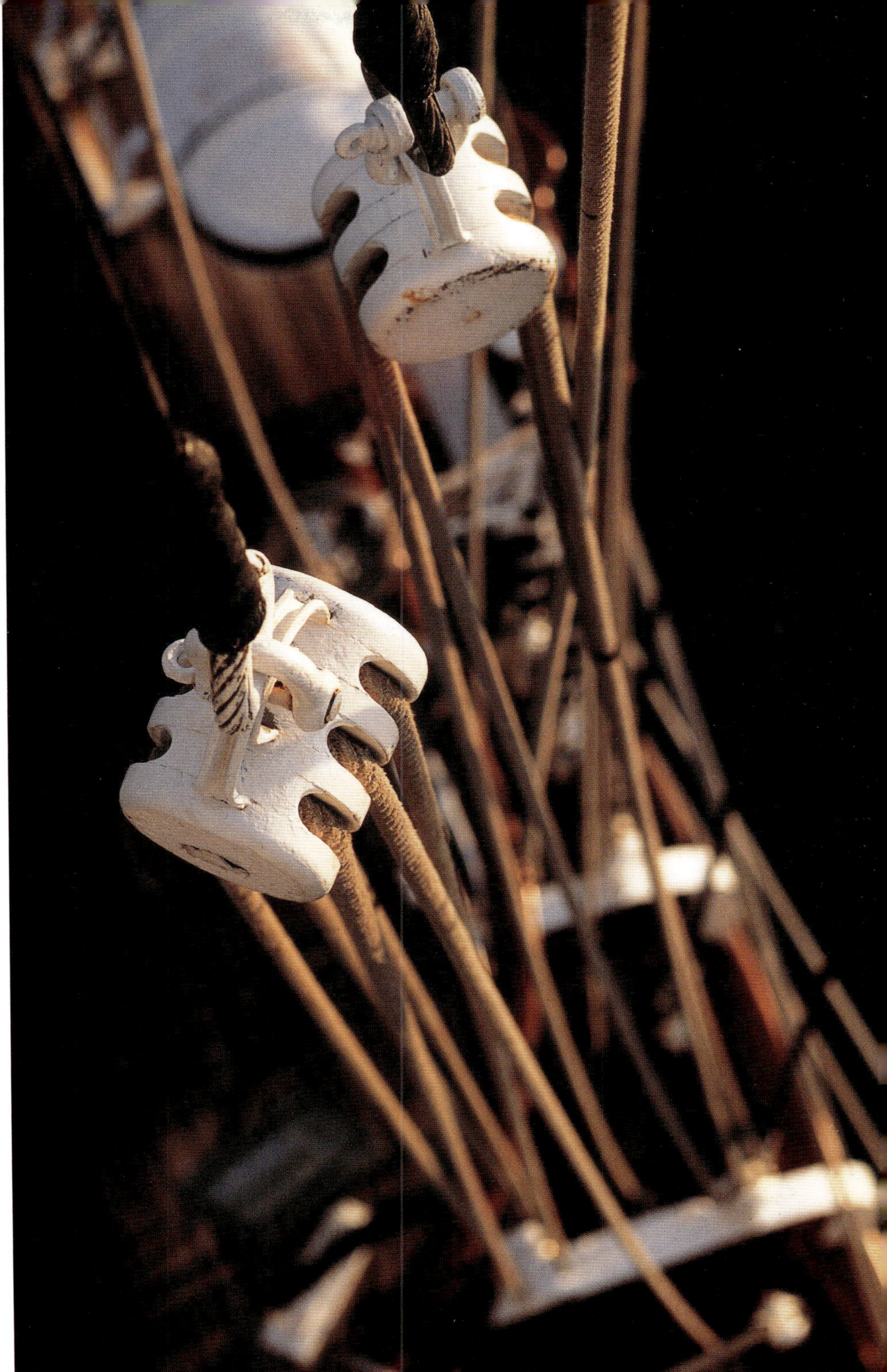

JANUARY 7

It is no use to wait for your ship to come in unless you have sent one out.

Belgian proverb

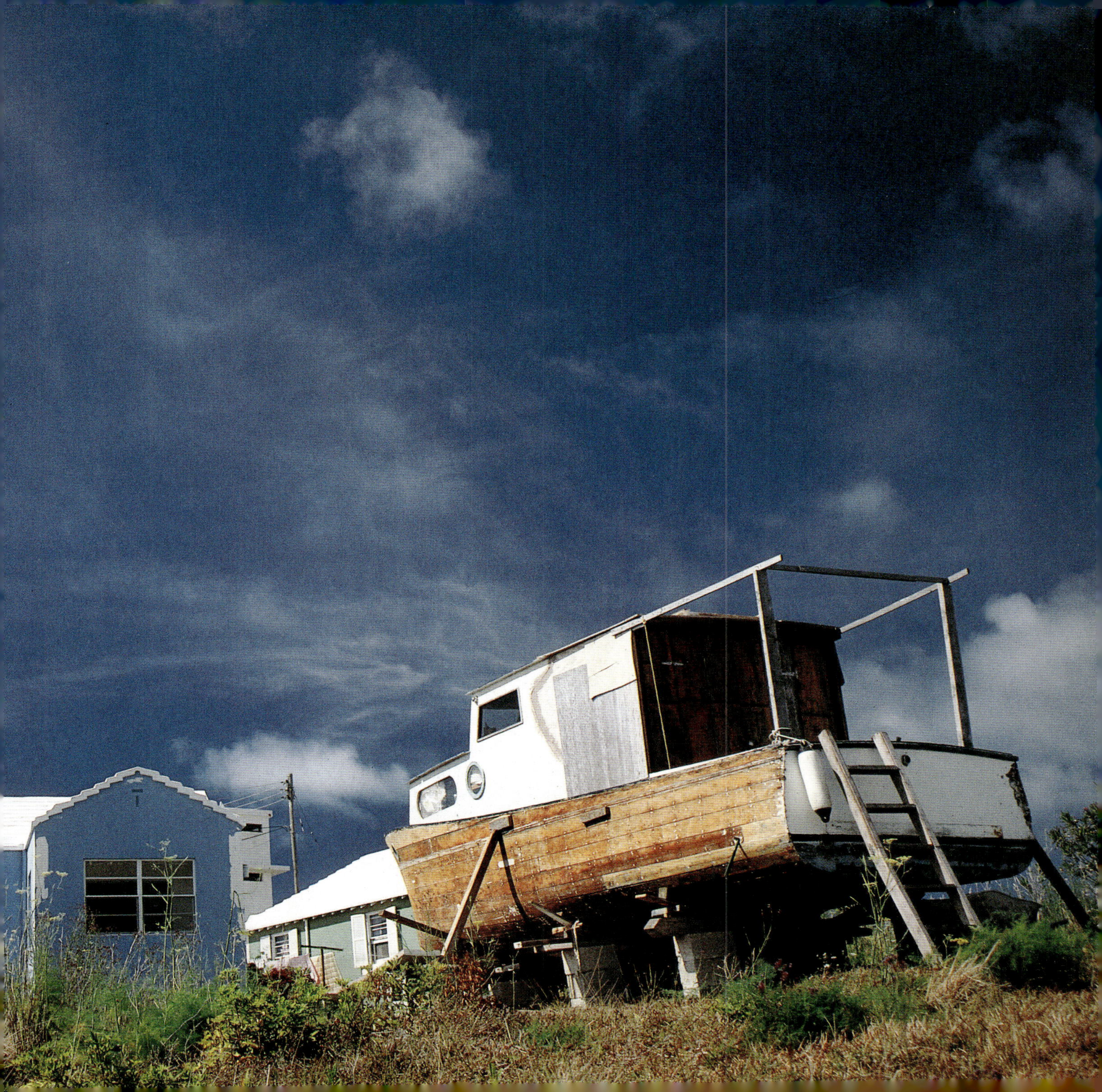

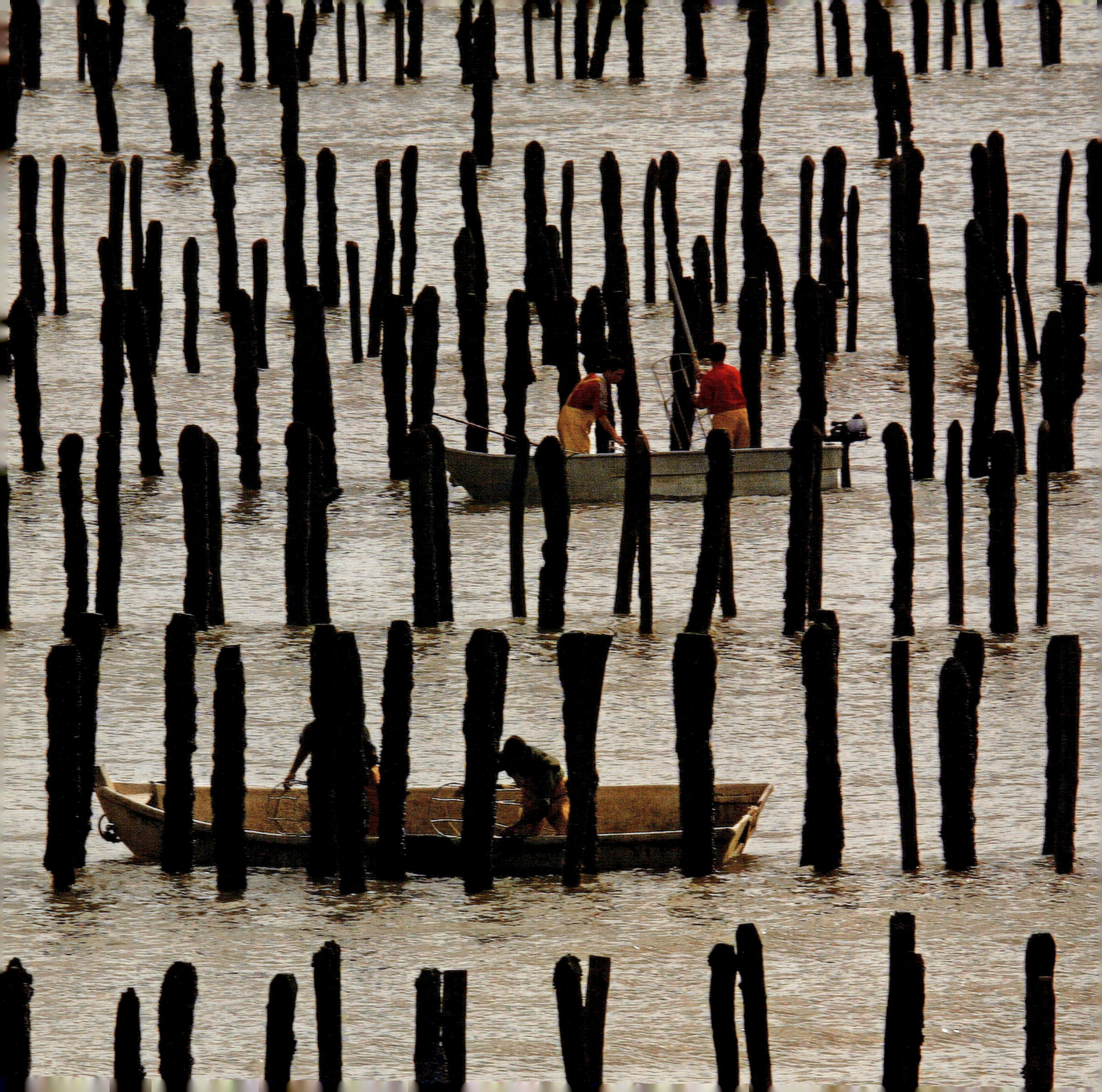

JANUARY 8

Fifteen men on a dead man's chest
Yo ho ho and a bottle of rum
Drink and the devil have done for the rest
Yo ho ho and a bottle of rum

Traditional chantey

JANUARY 9

It is unlucky to kill a gull, as these birds are said to carry the souls of sailors lost at sea.

Traditional wisdom

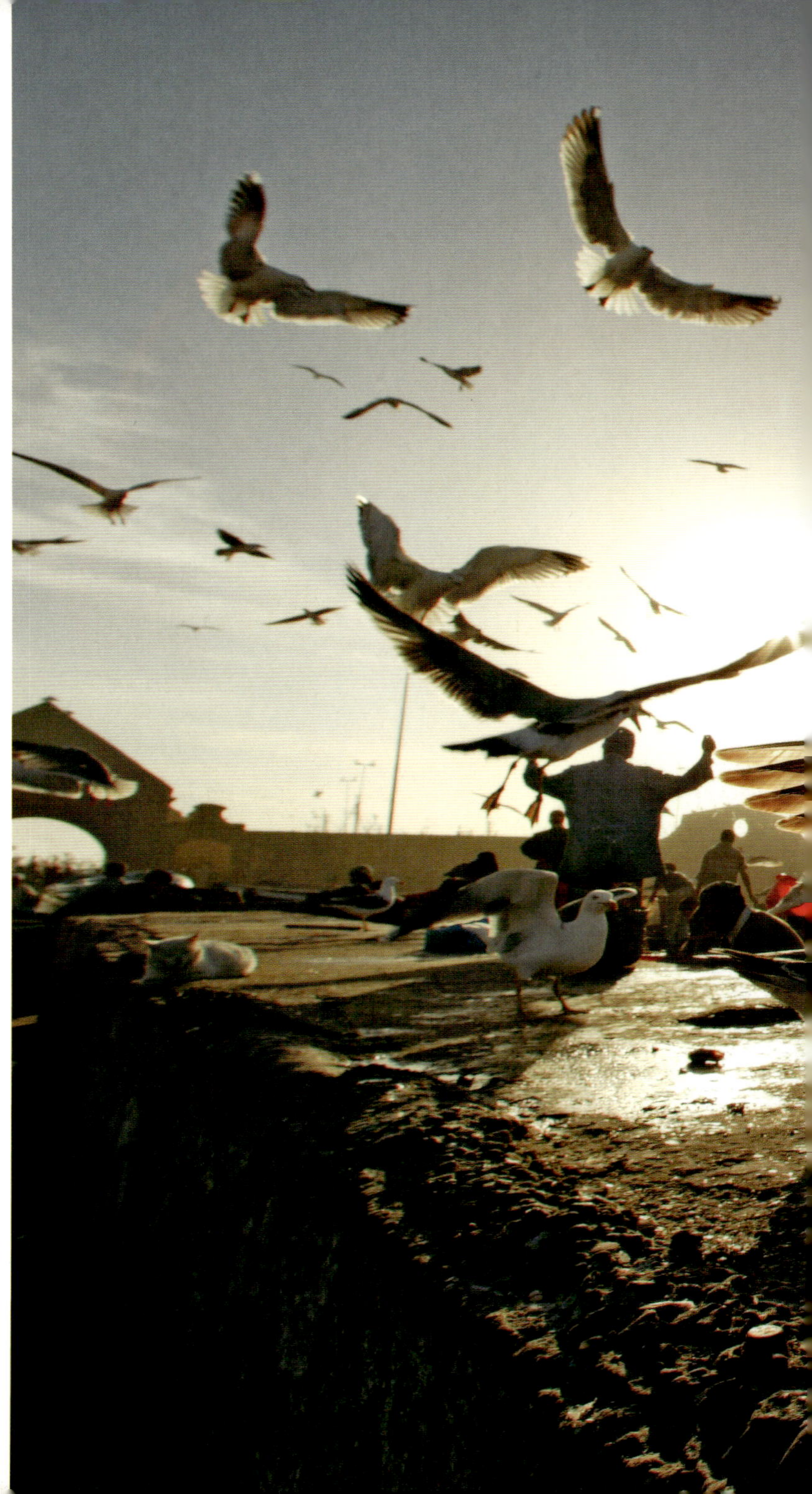

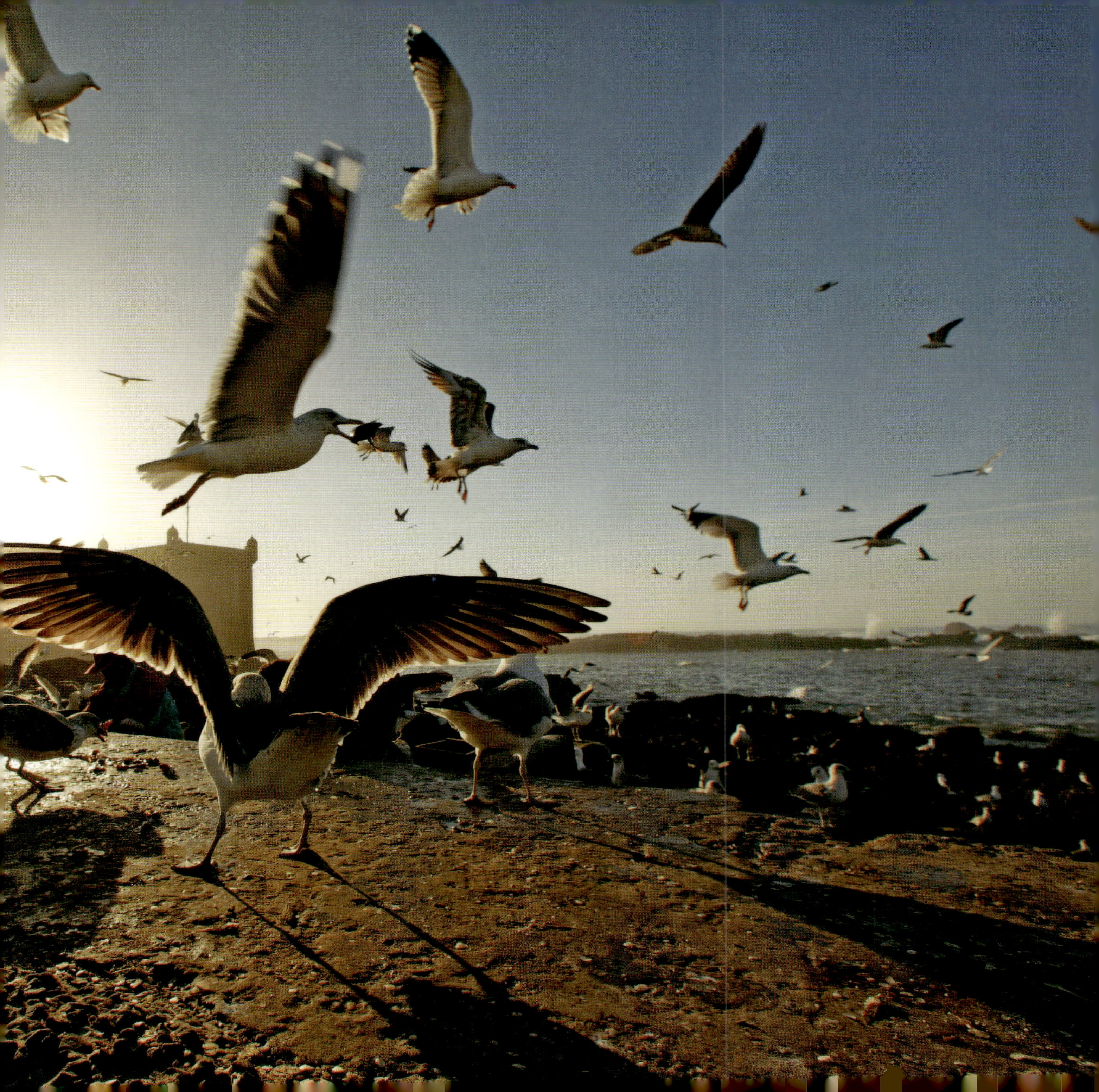

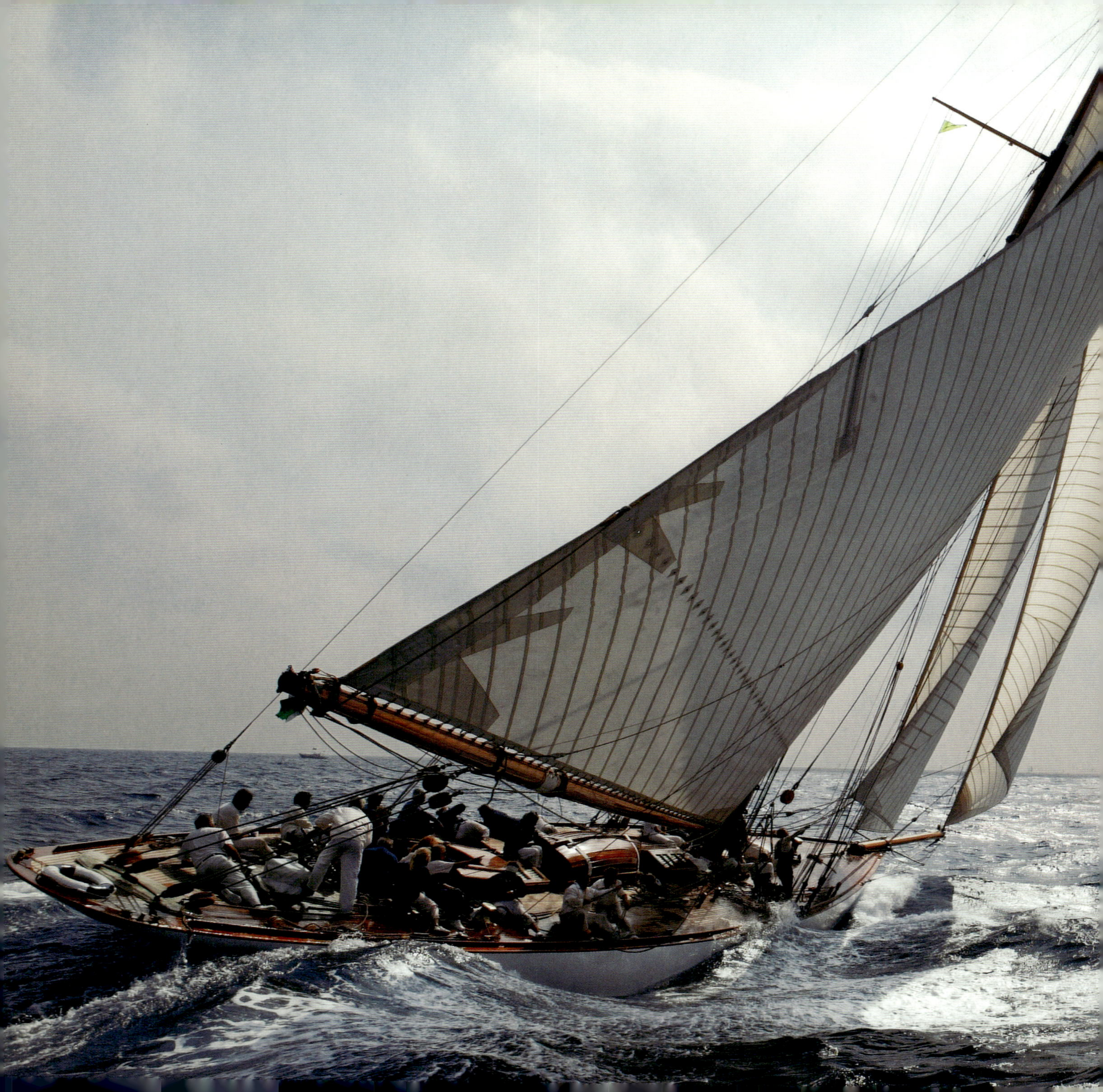

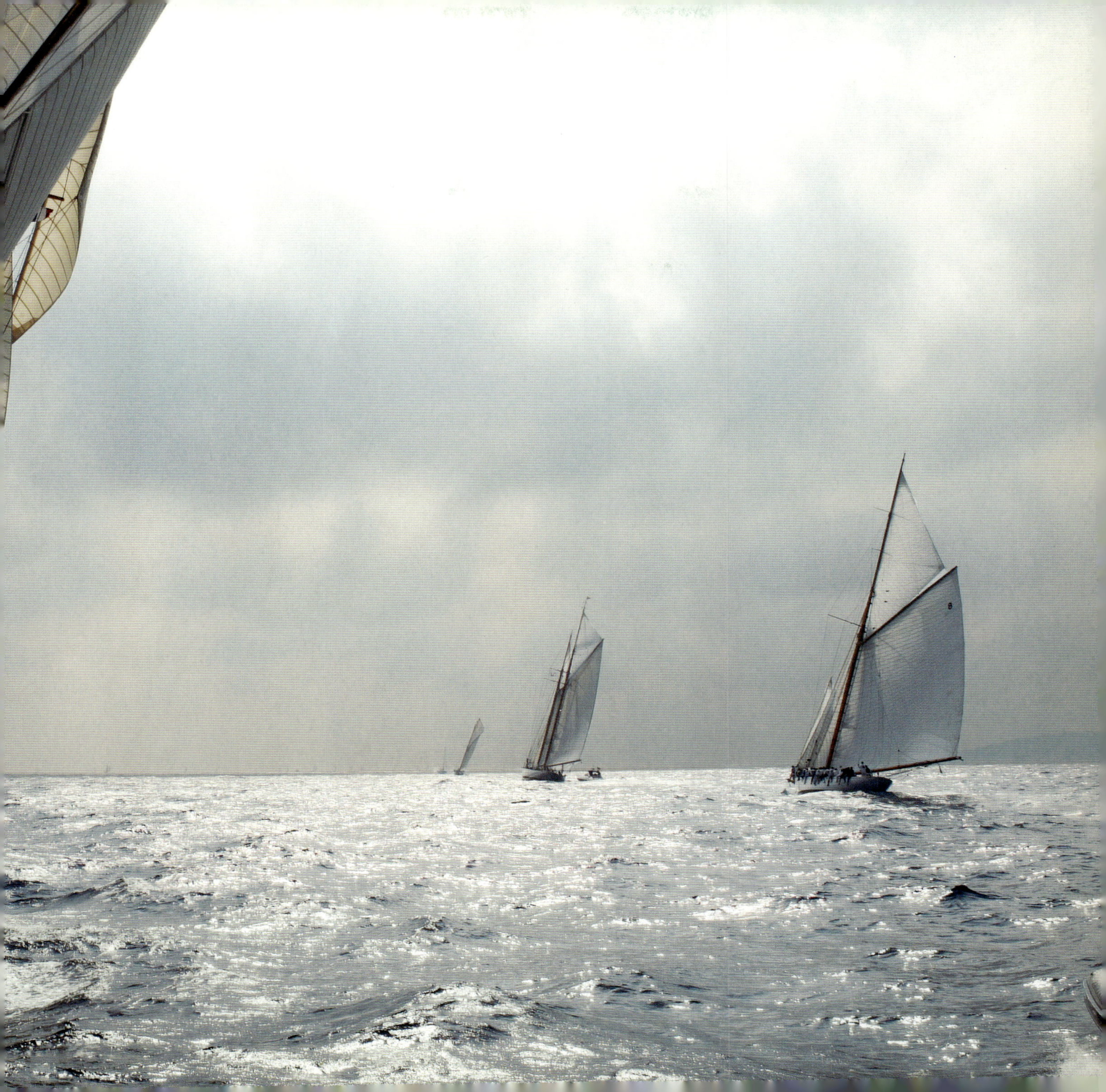

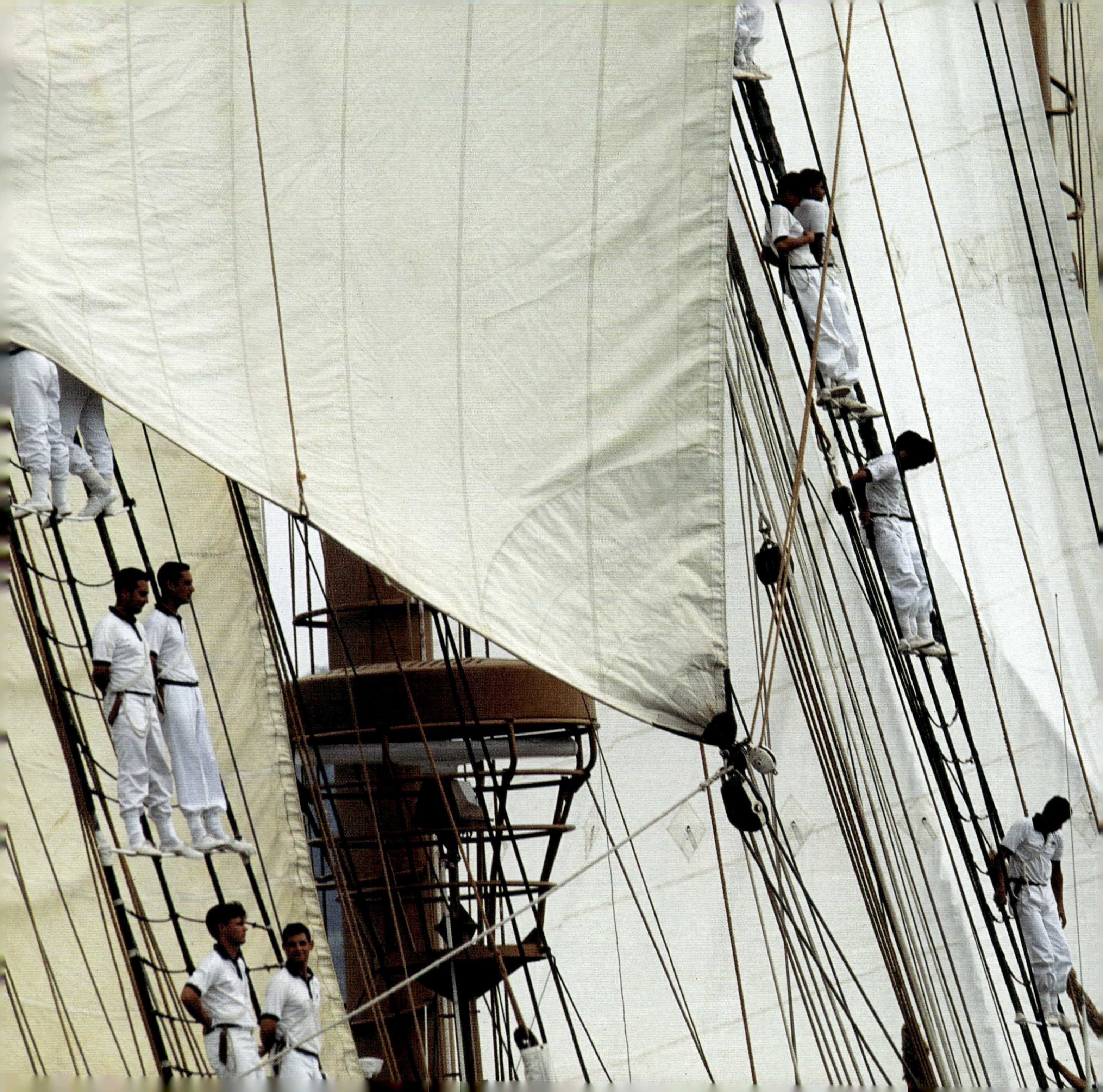

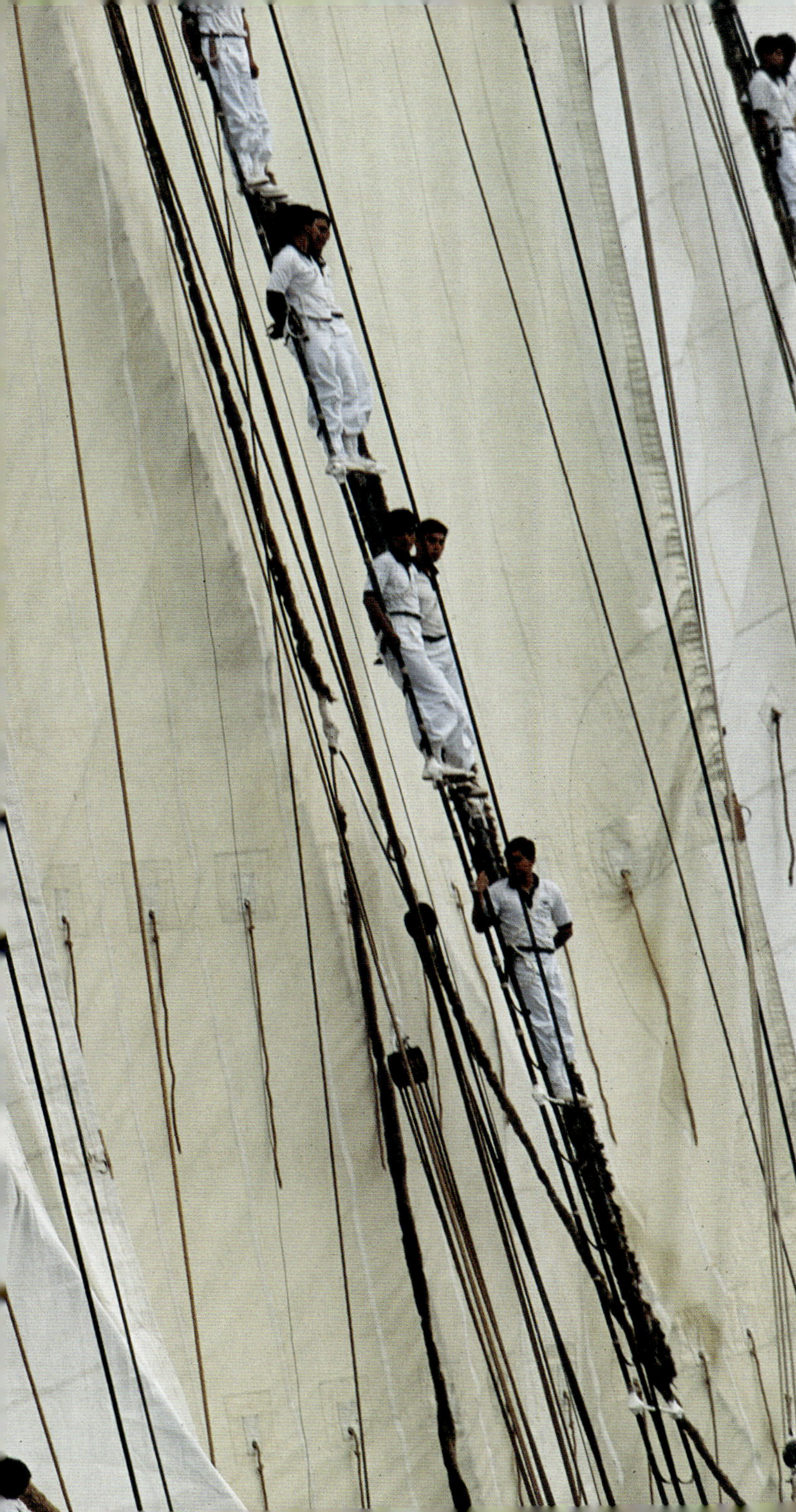

JANUARY 10

Haul the bowline! Now veer the sheet!
Yo ho! Furl'em! Haul in the brails!
Oh, see how well our good ship sails.

Geoffrey Chaucer, 1378

JANUARY 11

On the channels and streams
See each vessel that dreams
In its whimsical vagabond way,
Since it's for your least whim
The oceans they swim
From the ends of the night and the day.

Charles Baudelaire,
from "The Voyage," *Les Fleurs du mal,* 1857

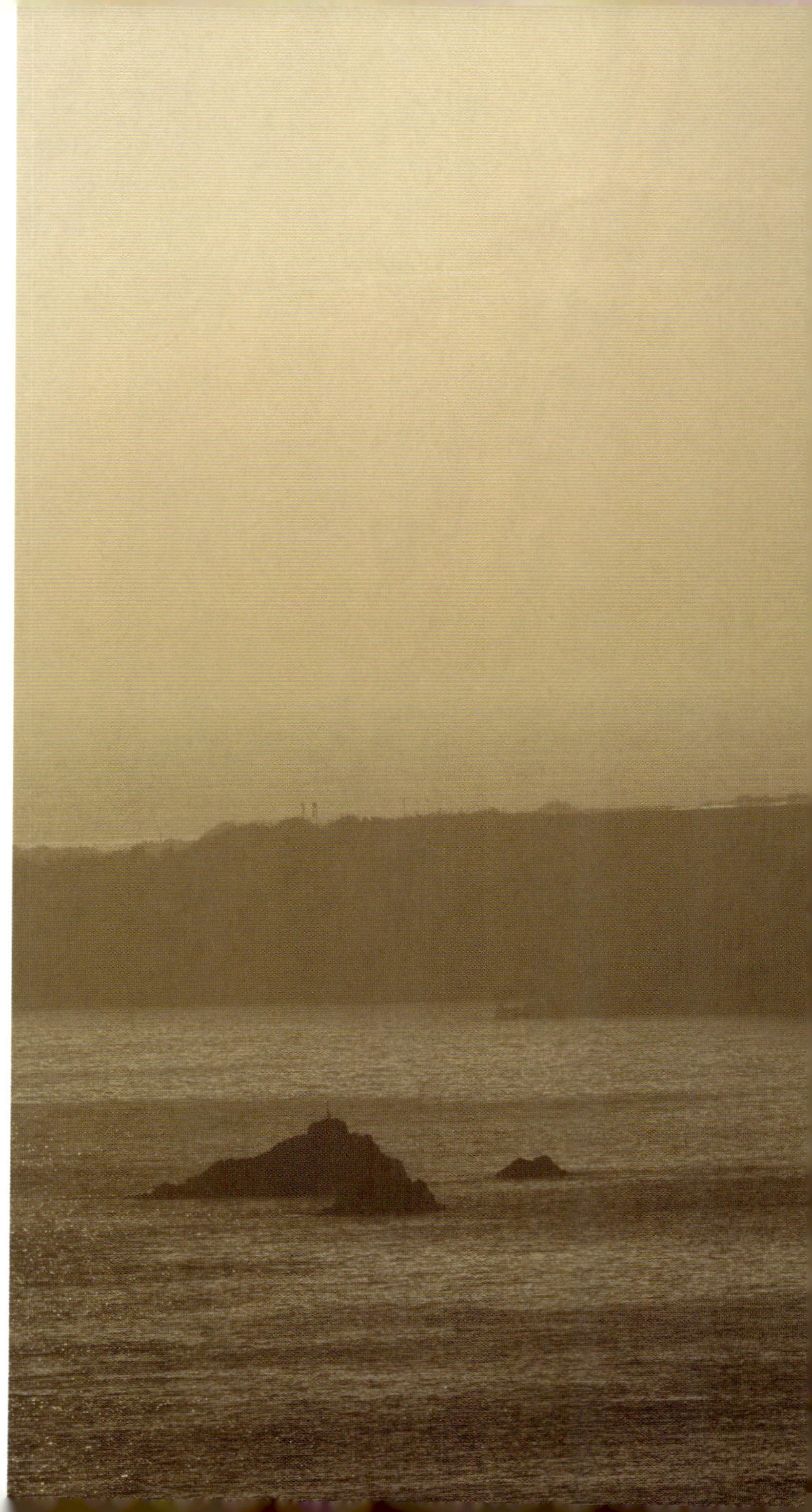

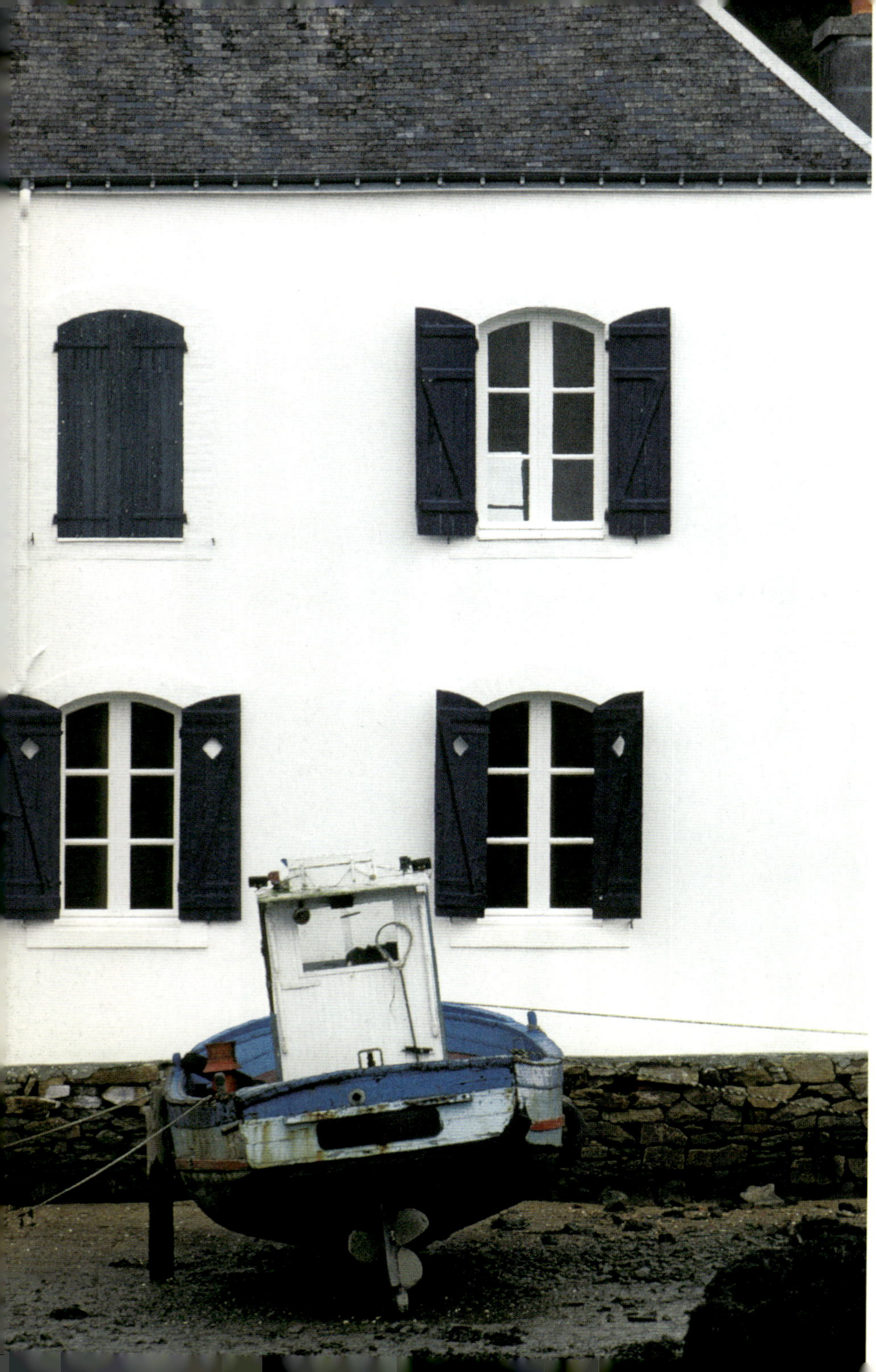

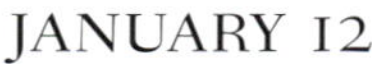

JANUARY 12

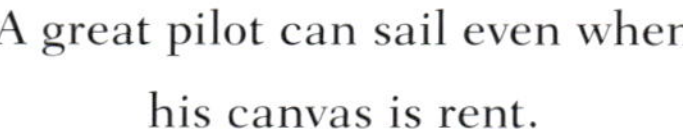

A great pilot can sail even when his canvas is rent.

Seneca

JANUARY 13

A cathedral, a wave of a storm,
a dancer's leap, never turn out to
be as high as we had hoped.

Marcel Proust

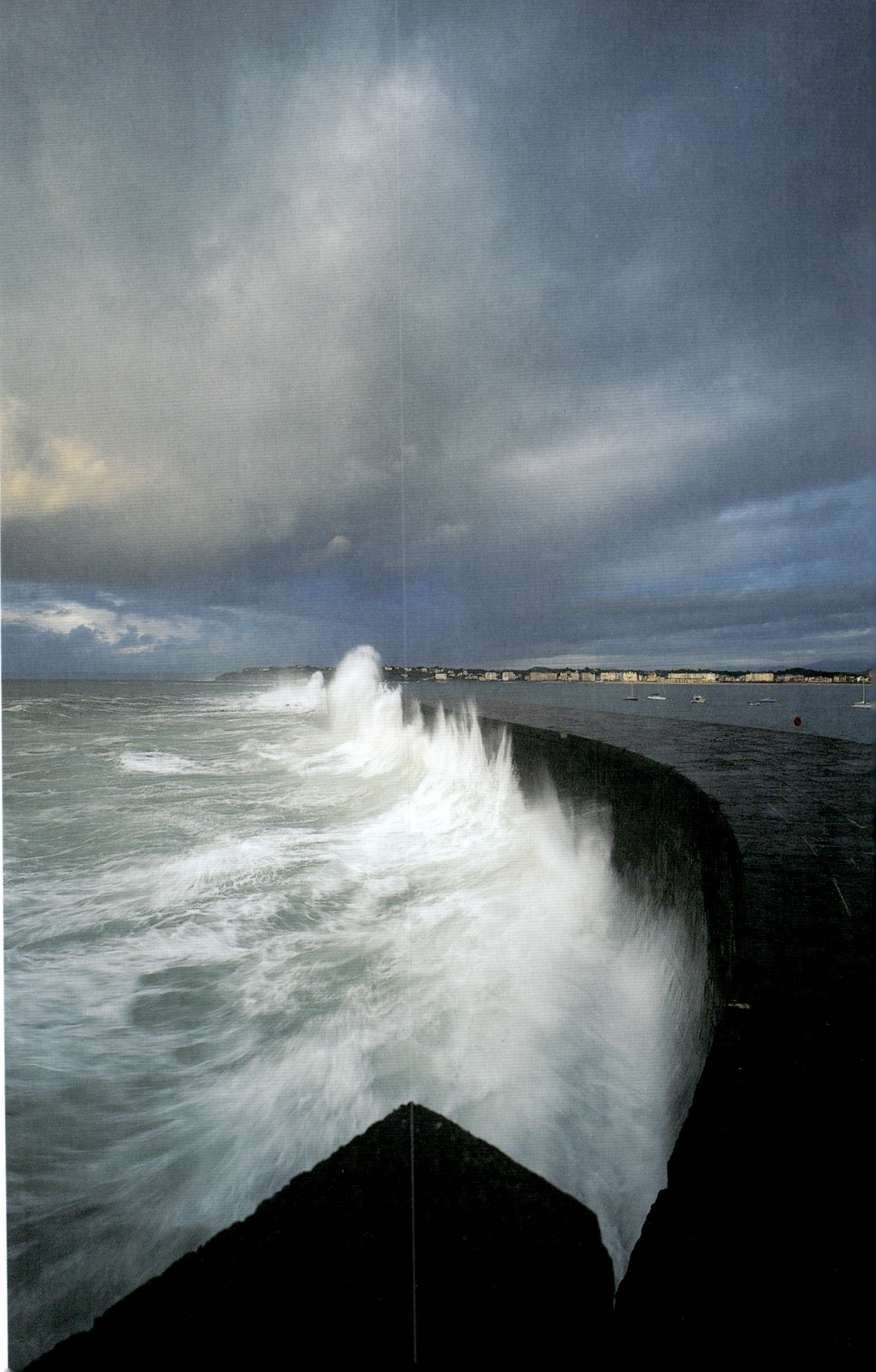

JANUARY 14

Your life is an island separated from all other islands and continents. Regardless of how many boats you send to other shores or how many ships arrive upon your shores.

Kahlil Gibran, from "Life"

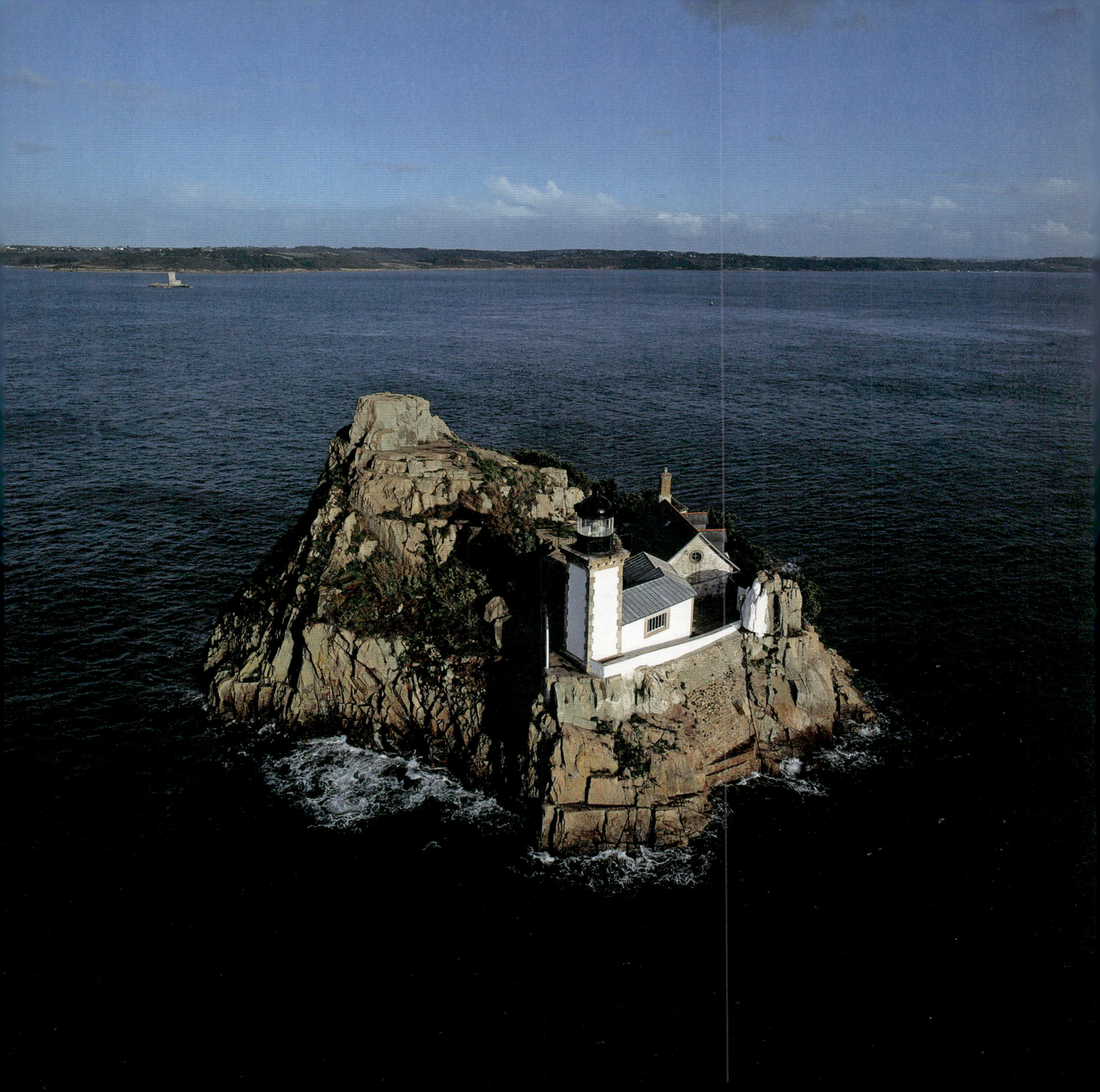

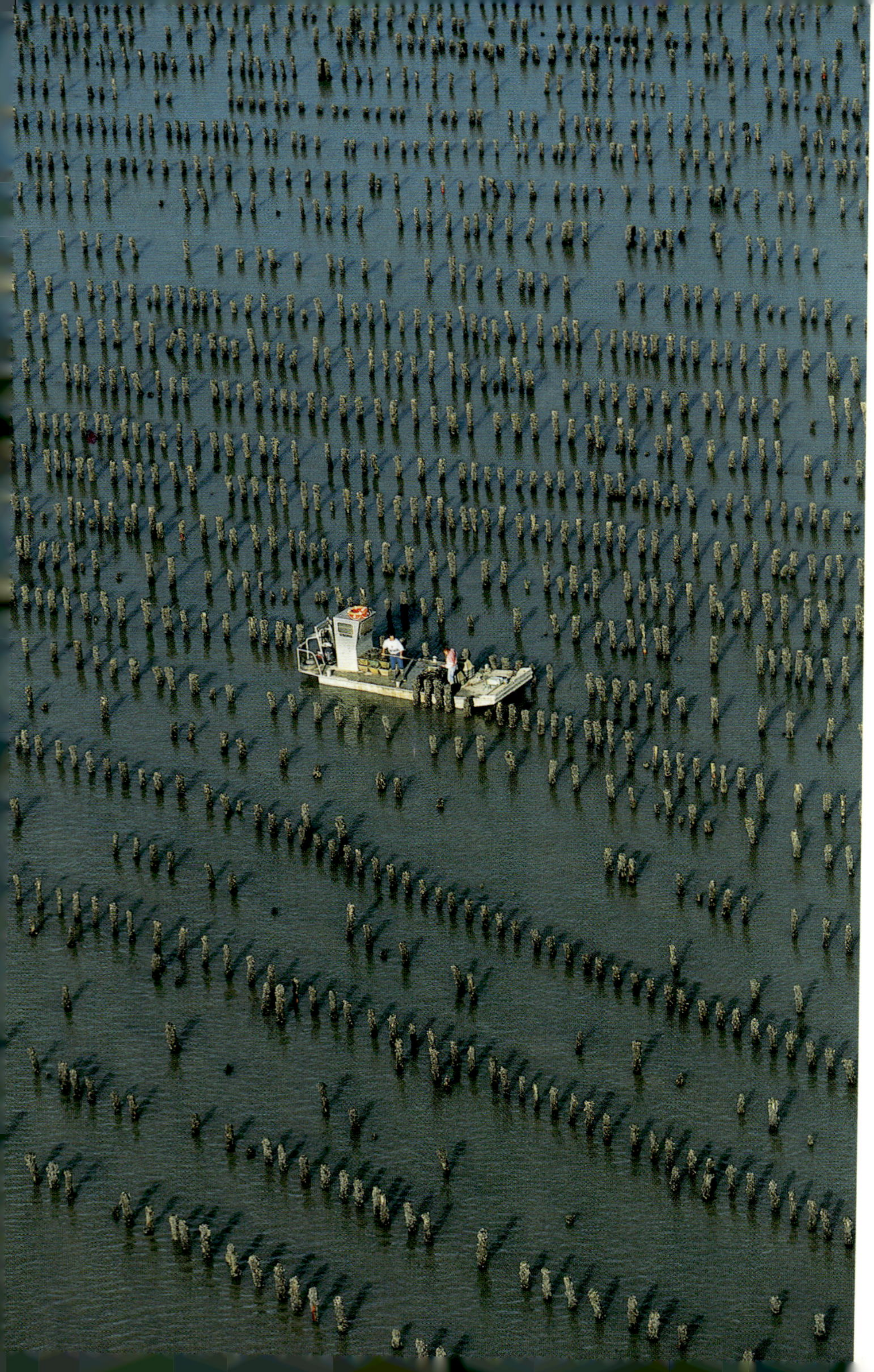

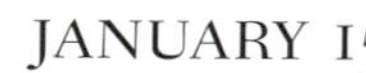

JANUARY 15

This sea, so luminous and deep,
how much I like to feel it,
there very close,
to hear its immense heartbeat!...
Because it is the free road from
here to everywhere...
the road familiar and known
since time immemorial.

Pierre Loti,
from *India (without the British)*, 1903

JANUARY 16

To have faith is to trust yourself to the water. When you swim you don't grab hold of the water, because if you do you will sink and drown. Instead you relax, and float.

Alan Watts

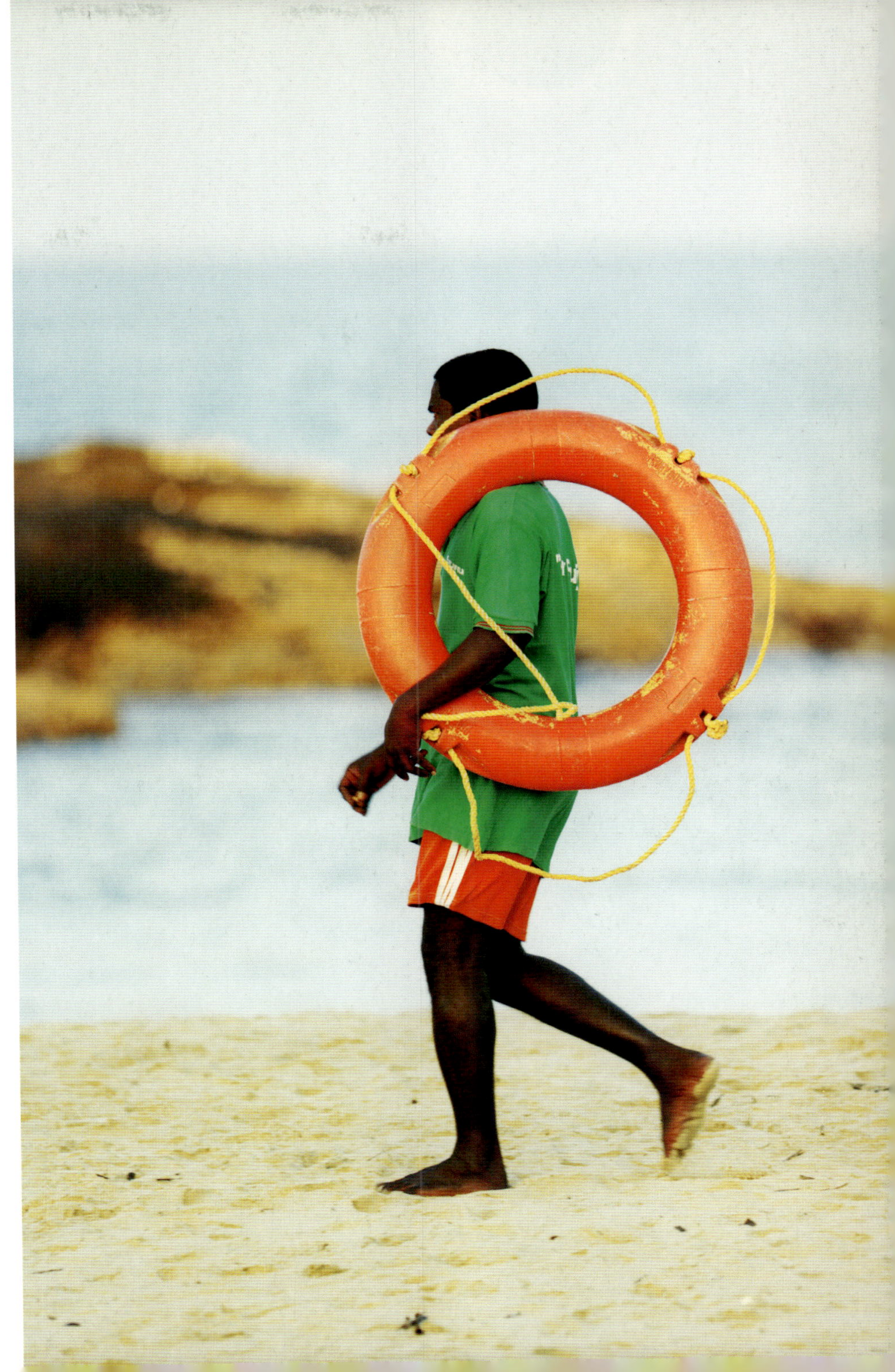

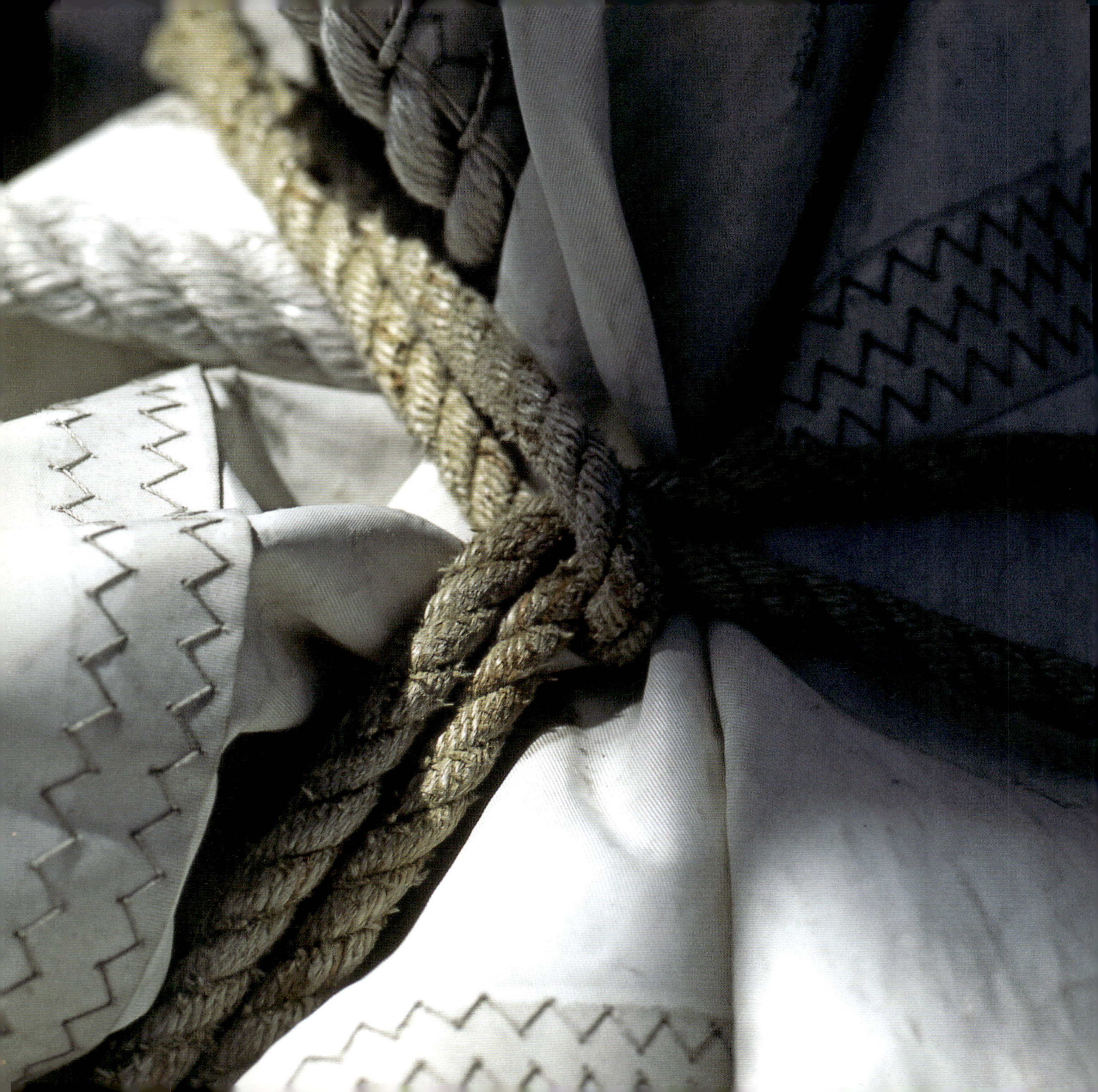

JANUARY 17

The greatest blunders, like the thickest ropes,
are often compounded of a multitude of strands.
Take the rope apart,
separate it into the small threads that compose it,
and you can break them one by one.

Victor Hugo, from *Les Misérables,* 1862

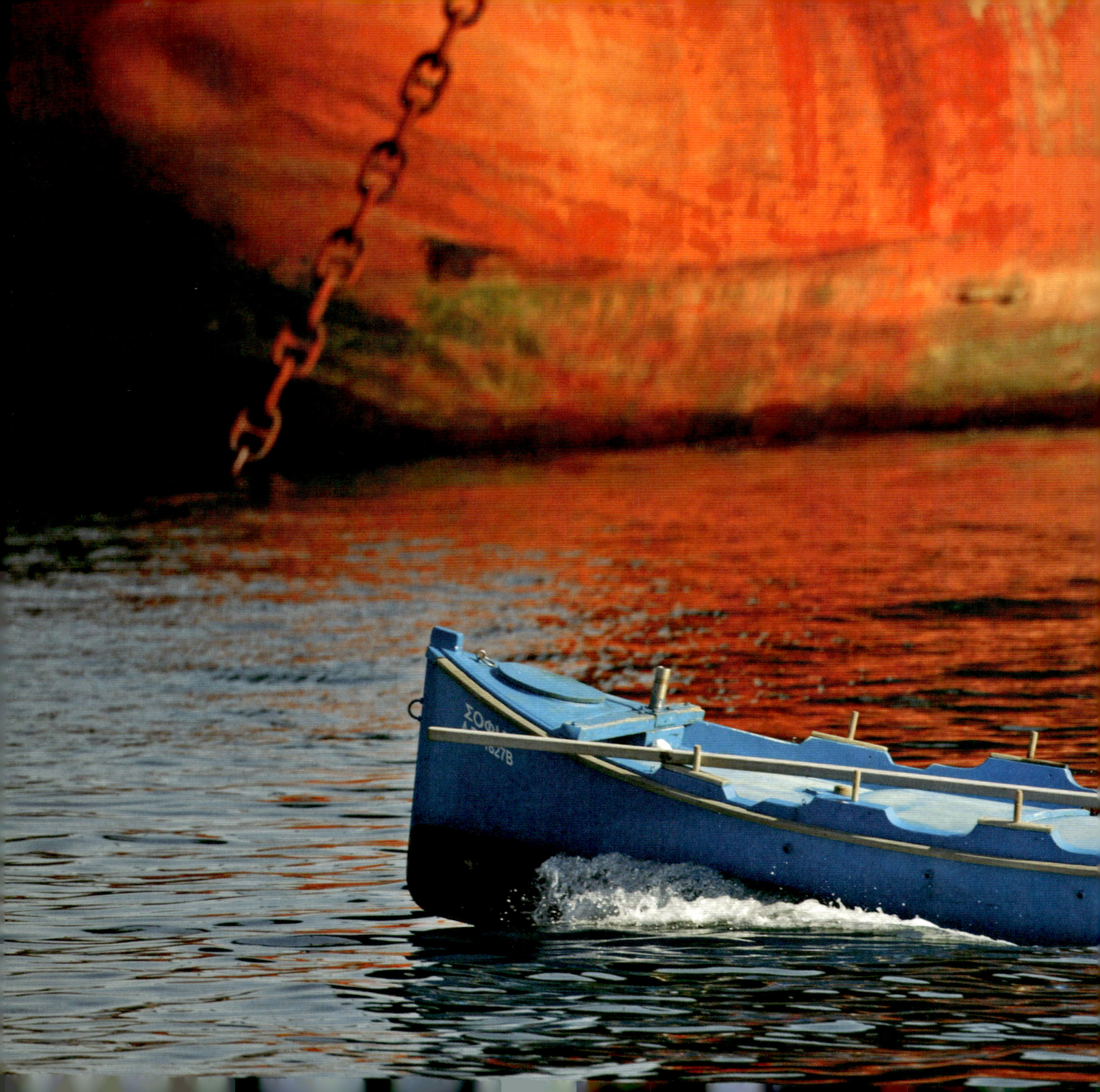

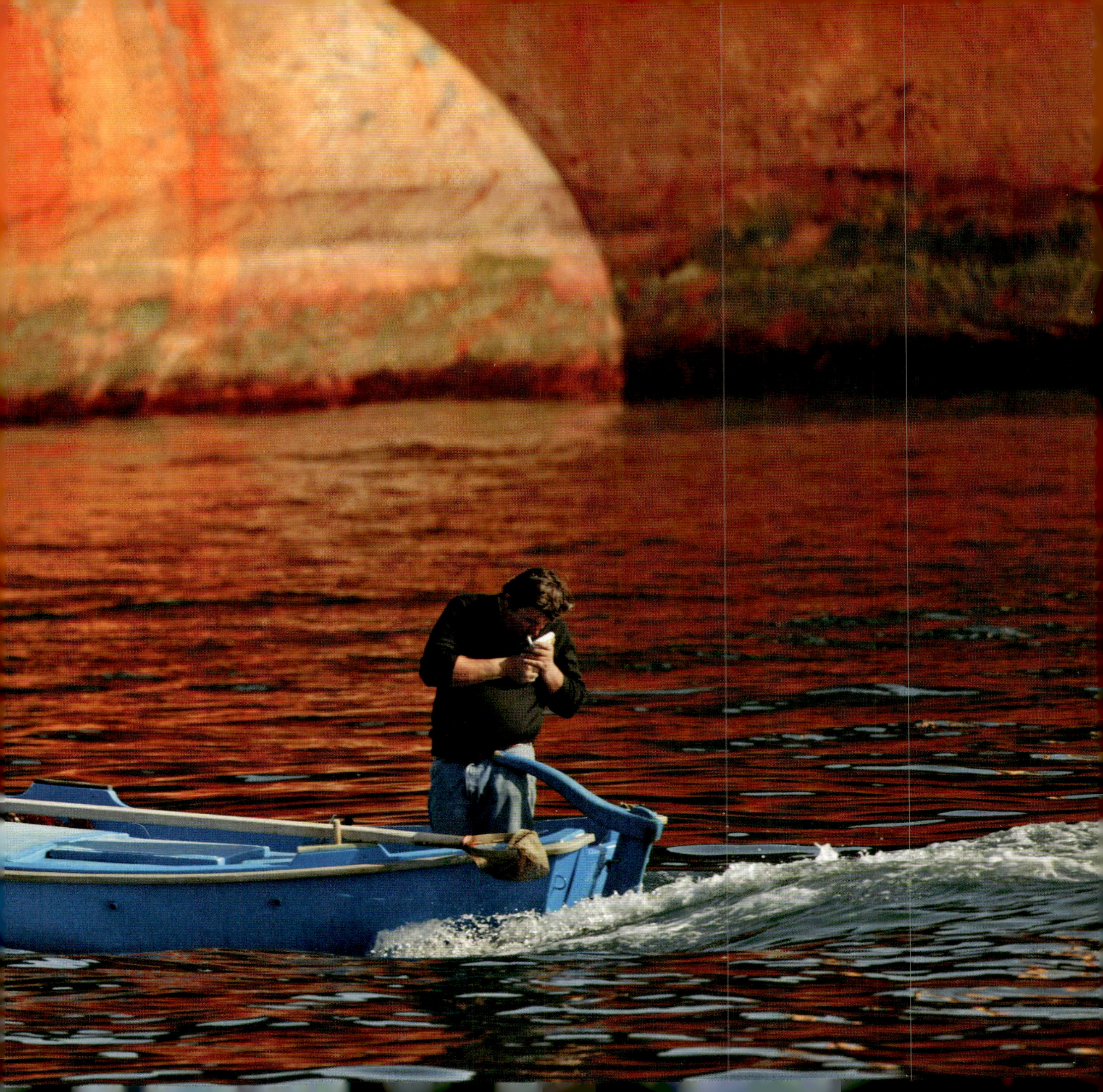

JANUARY 18

If you want to build a ship, don't drum up people to collect wood and don't assign them tasks and work, but rather teach them to long for the endless immensity of the sea.

Antoine de Saint-Exupéry

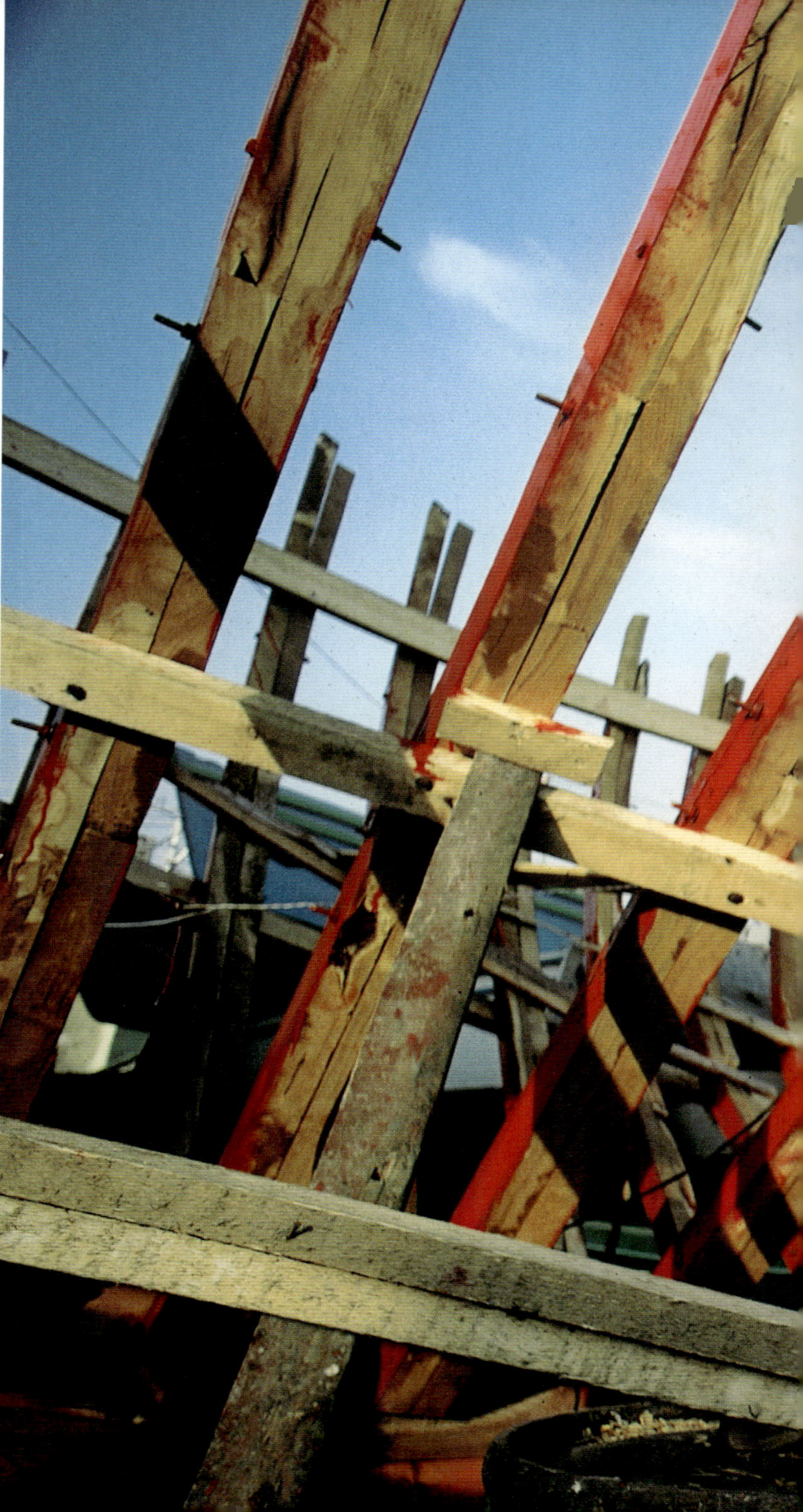

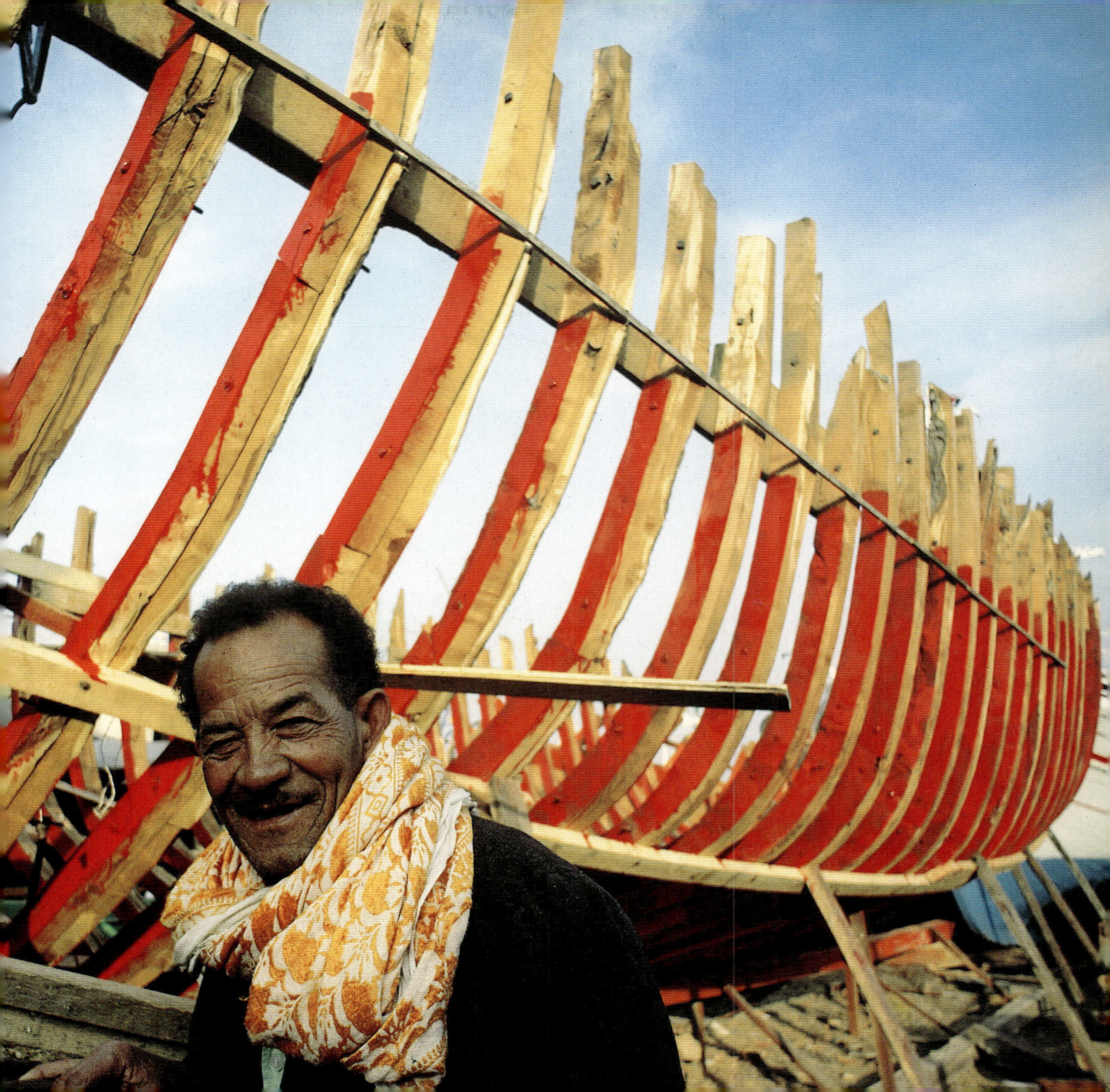

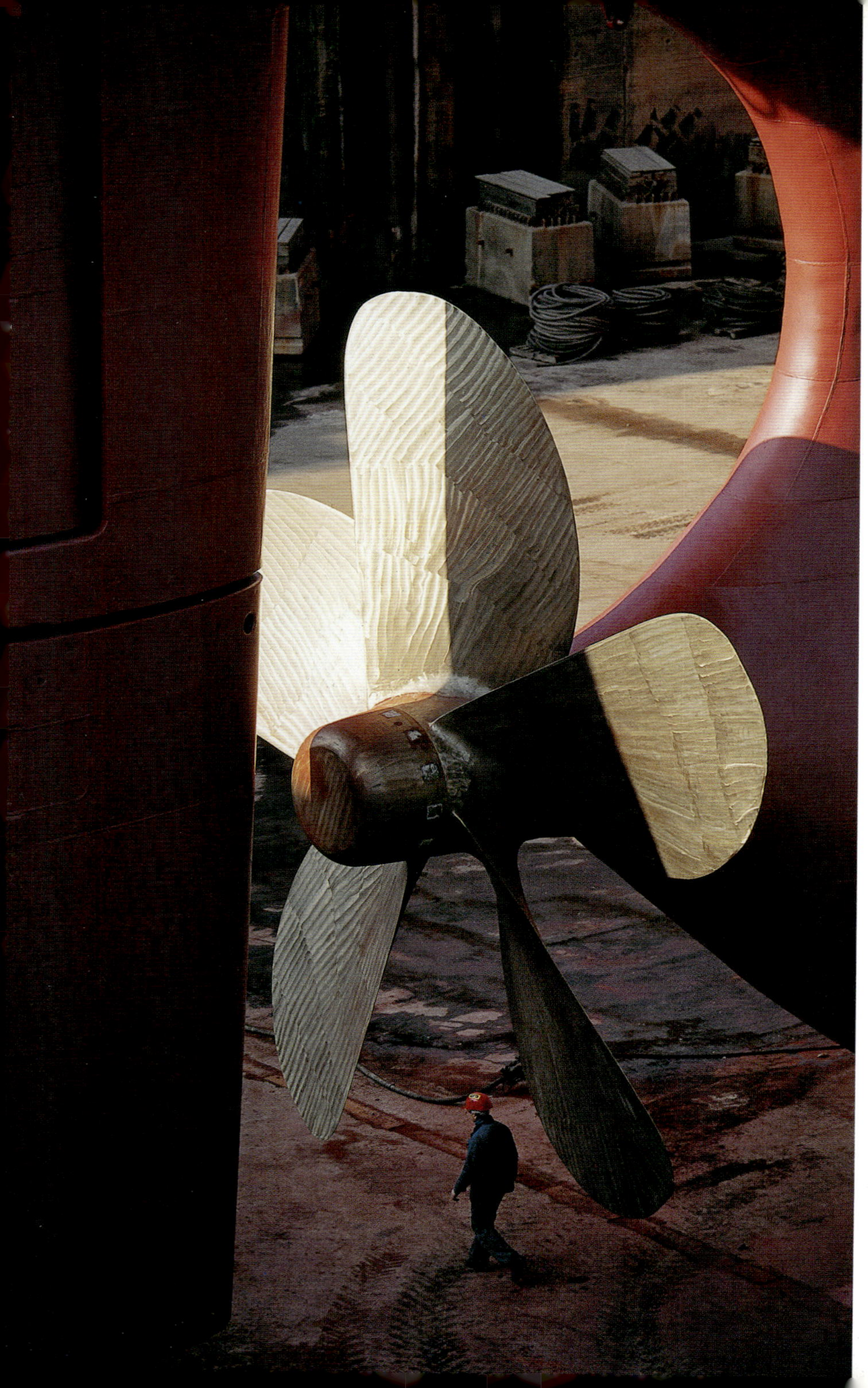

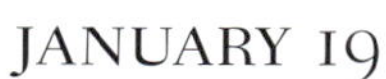

JANUARY 19

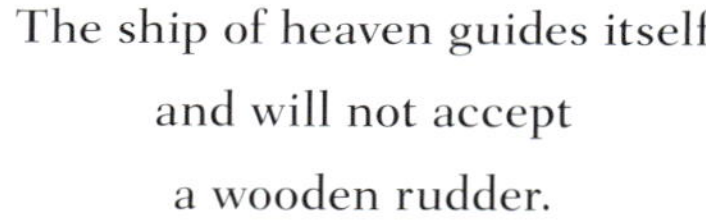

The ship of heaven guides itself
and will not accept
a wooden rudder.

Ralph Waldo Emerson,
from "The Sovereignty of Ethics," 1878

JANUARY 20

The sea howled, as if it'd had the voice of those ancient reefs animated by pagan mythology.

Jules Verne,
from *The Children of Captain Grant*,
1867–68

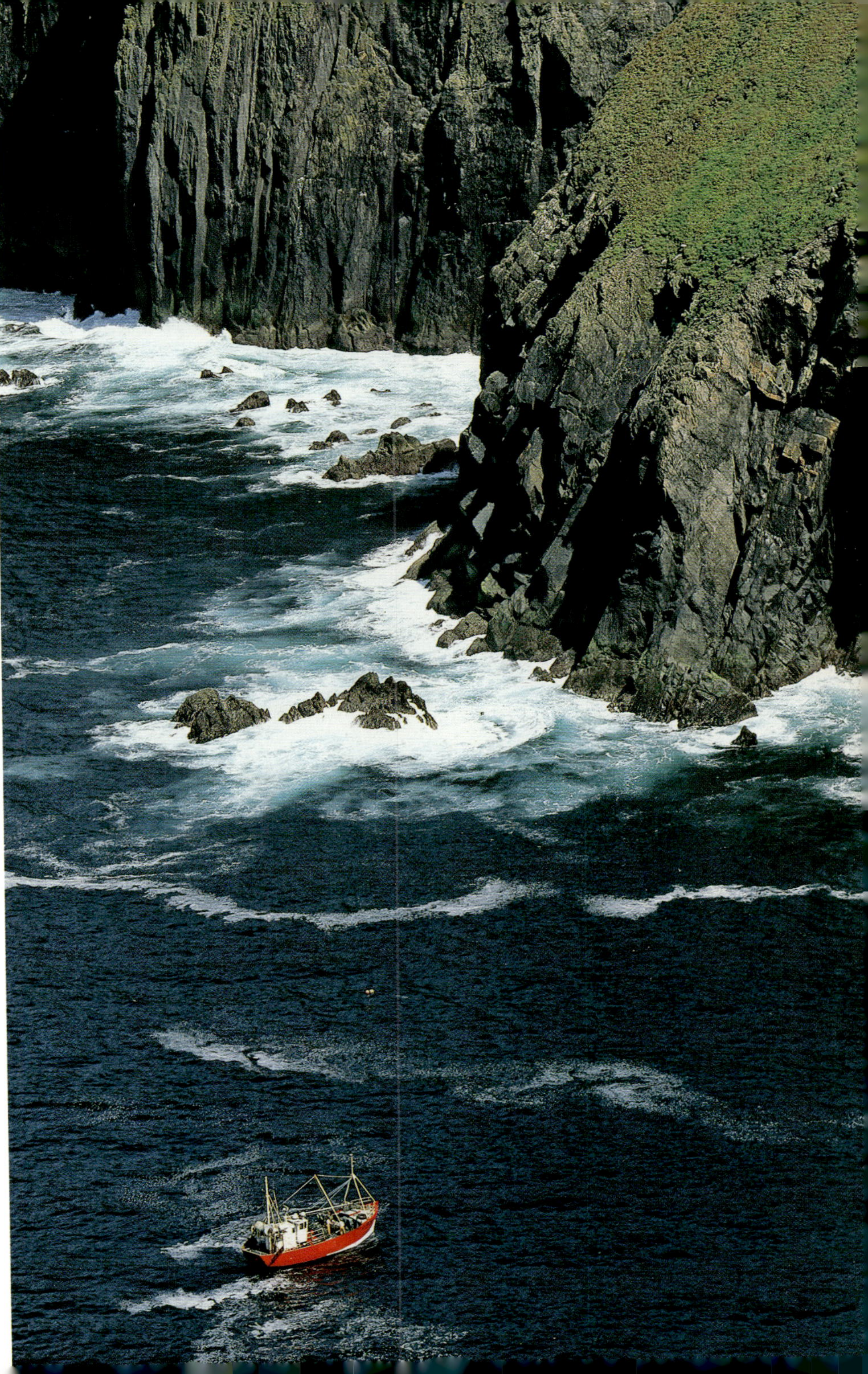

JANUARY 21

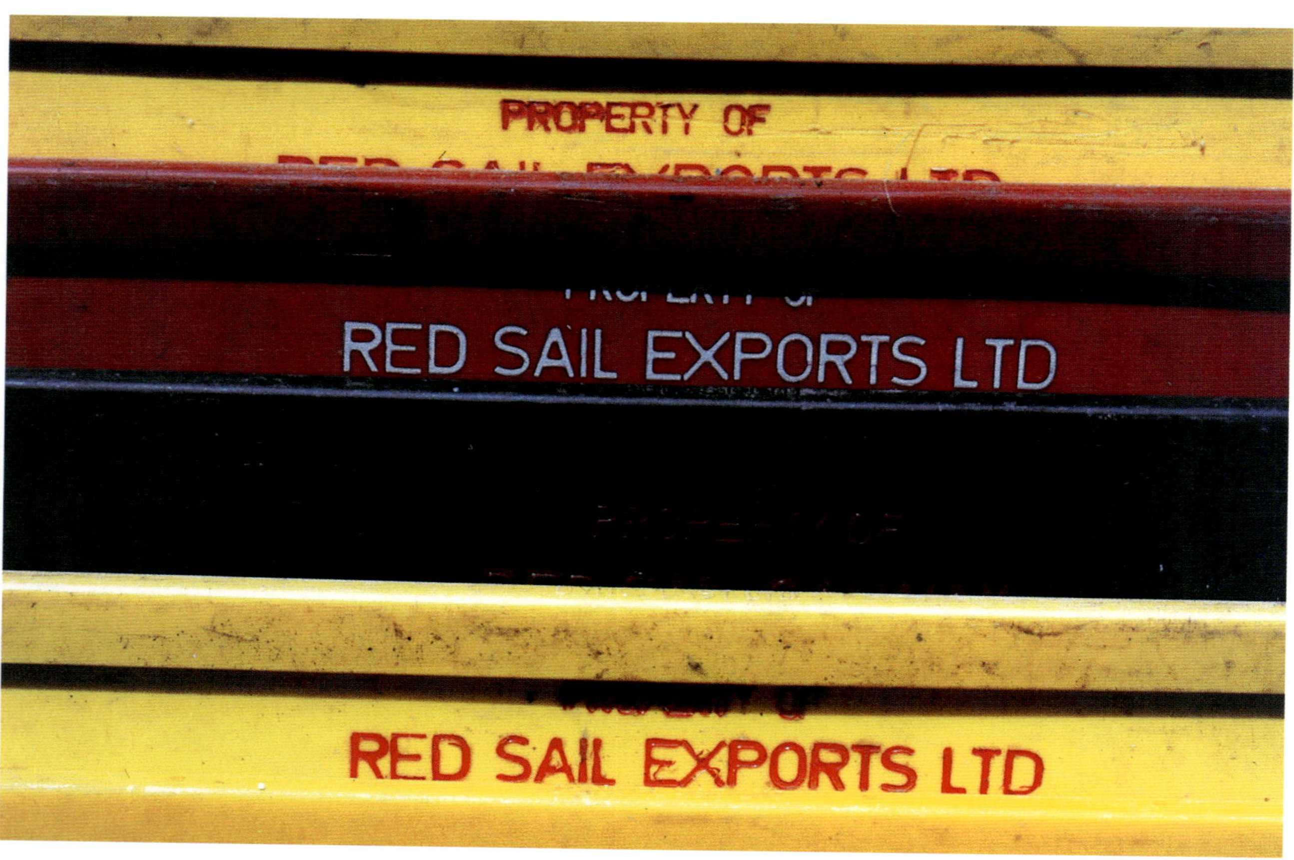

Anythin' for a quiet life, as the man said wen he took the sitivation at the lighthouse.

Charles Dickens, from *The Pickwick Papers,* 1837

JANUARY 22

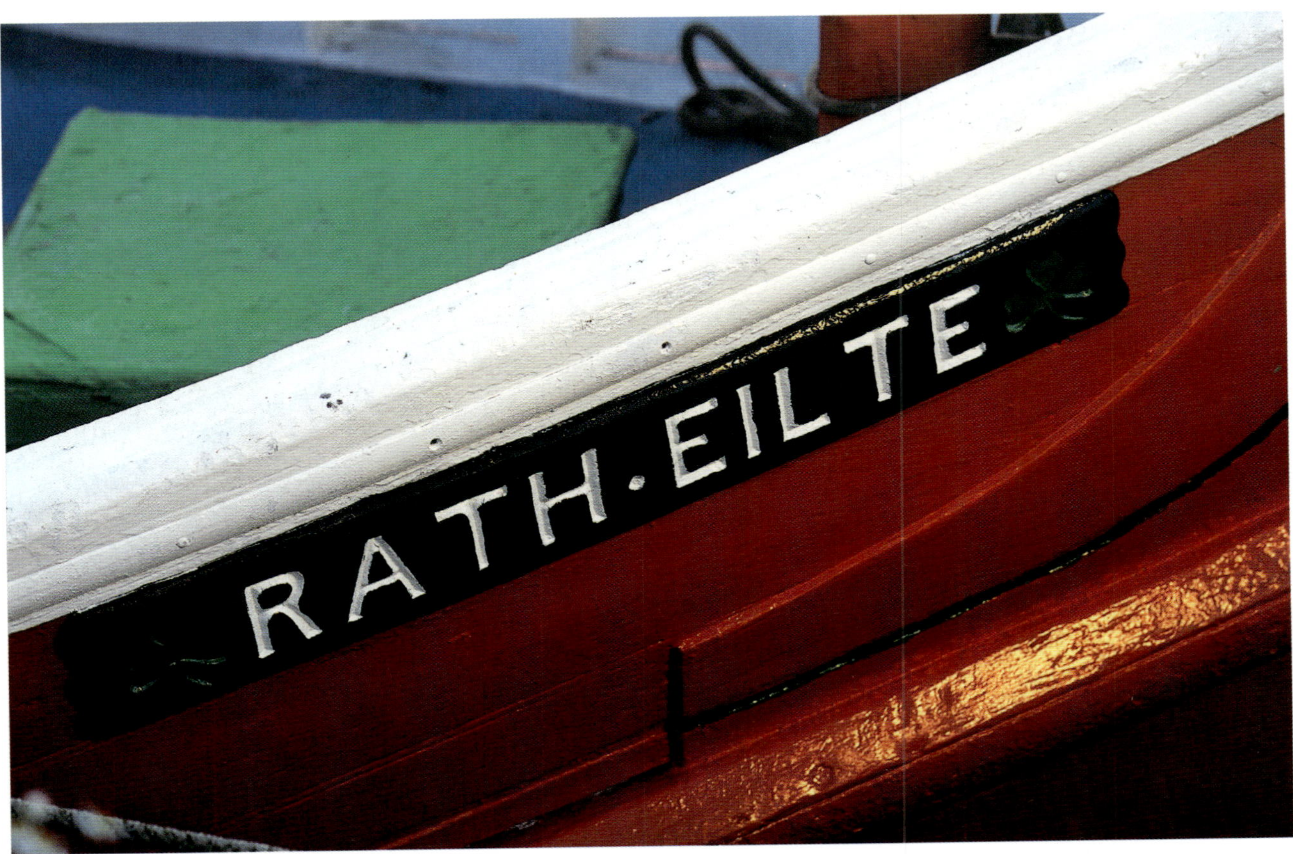

The sea speaks a language polite people never repeat. It is a colossal scavenger slang and has no respect.

Carl Sandburg, from "Two Nocturnes"

JANUARY 23

It is pleasurable, when winds disturb the waves of a great sea, to gaze out from land upon the great trials of another.

Lucretius

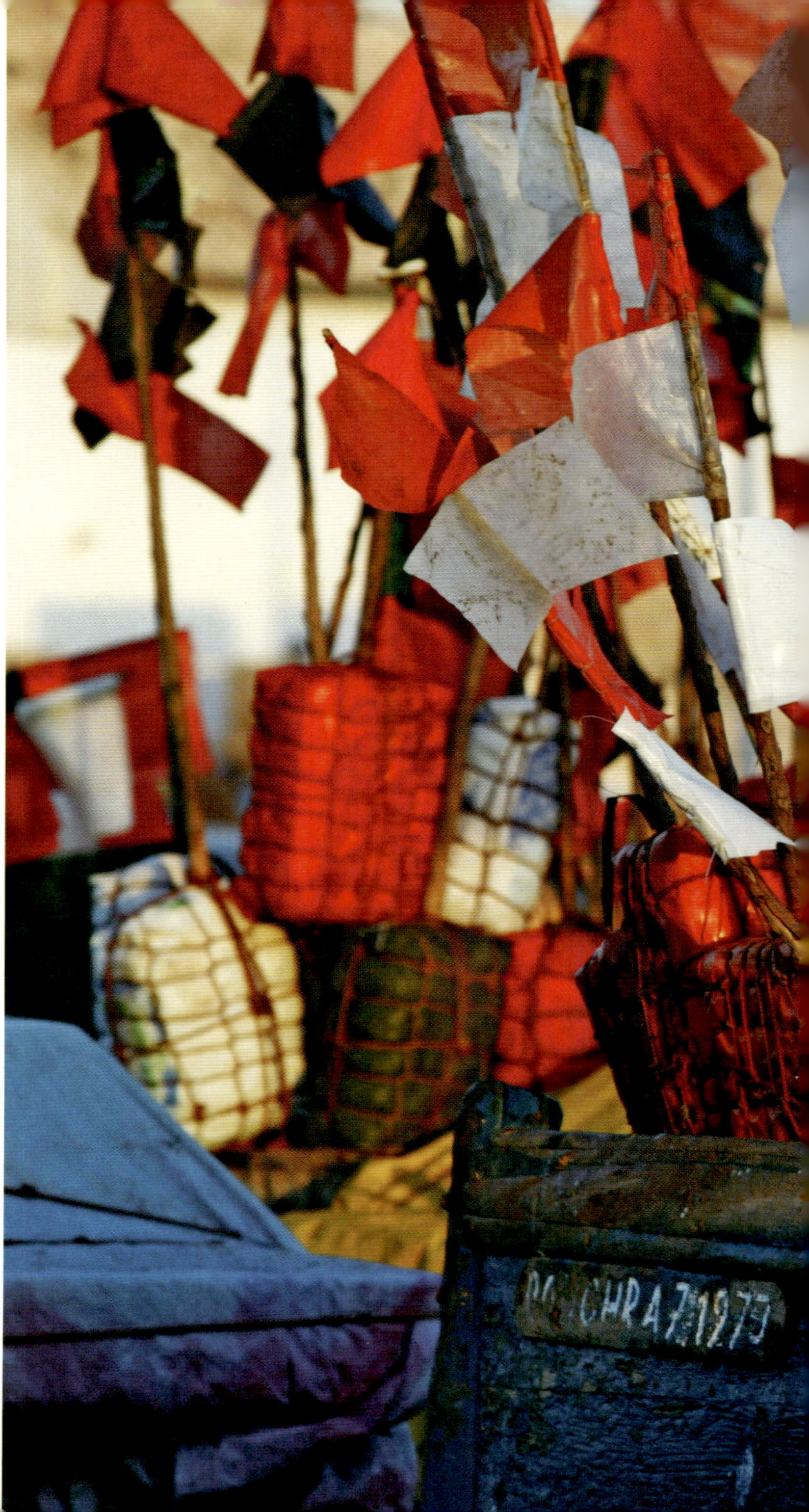

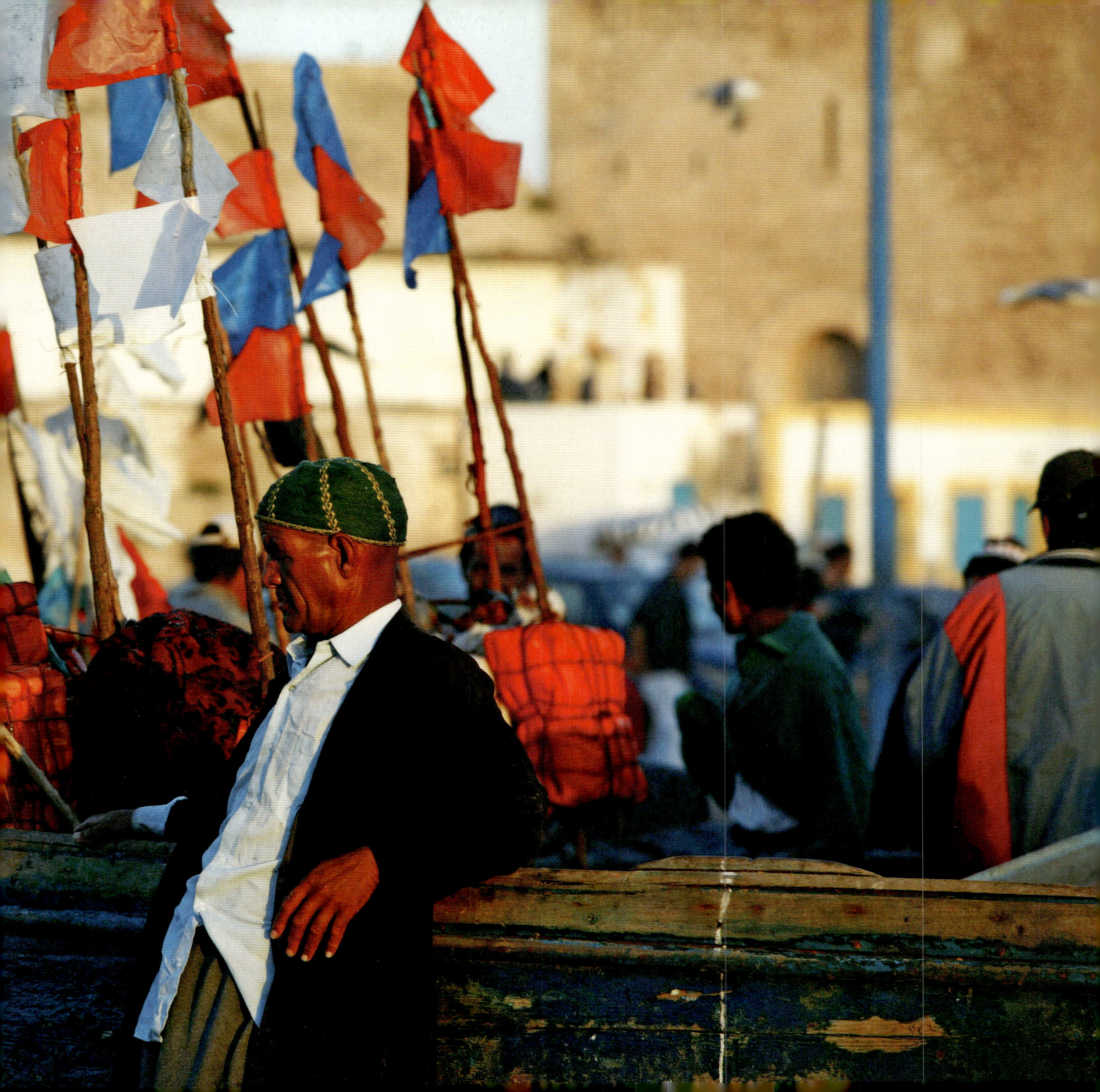

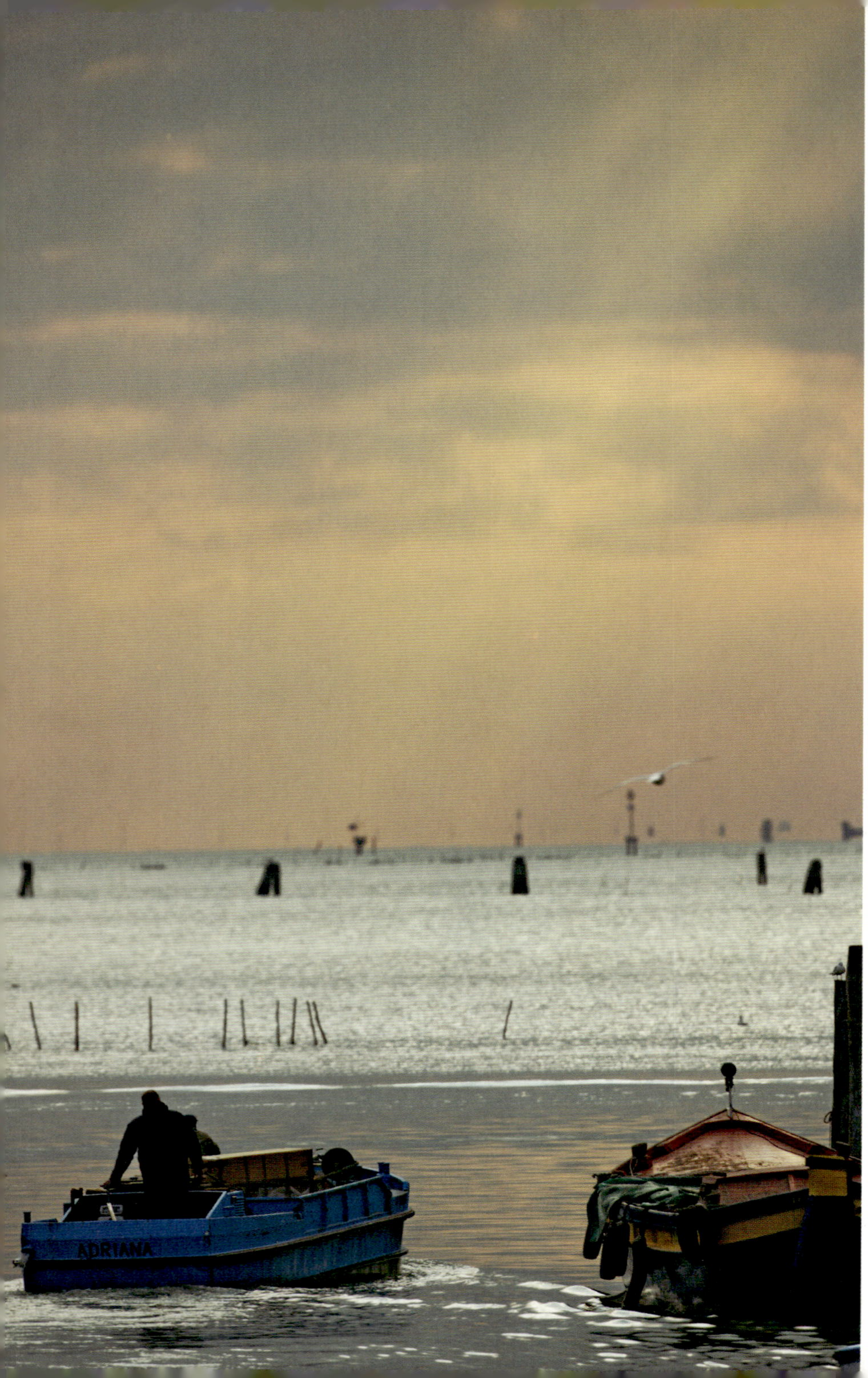

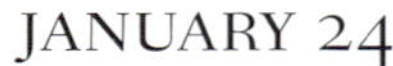

JANUARY 24

Fortune brings in some
boats that are not steered.

William Shakespeare,
from *Cymbeline*, Act IV, Scene 3

JANUARY 25

Happy is he, who like Ulysses
Has made a good voyage.

Joachim du Bellay,
from "Regrets," 1558

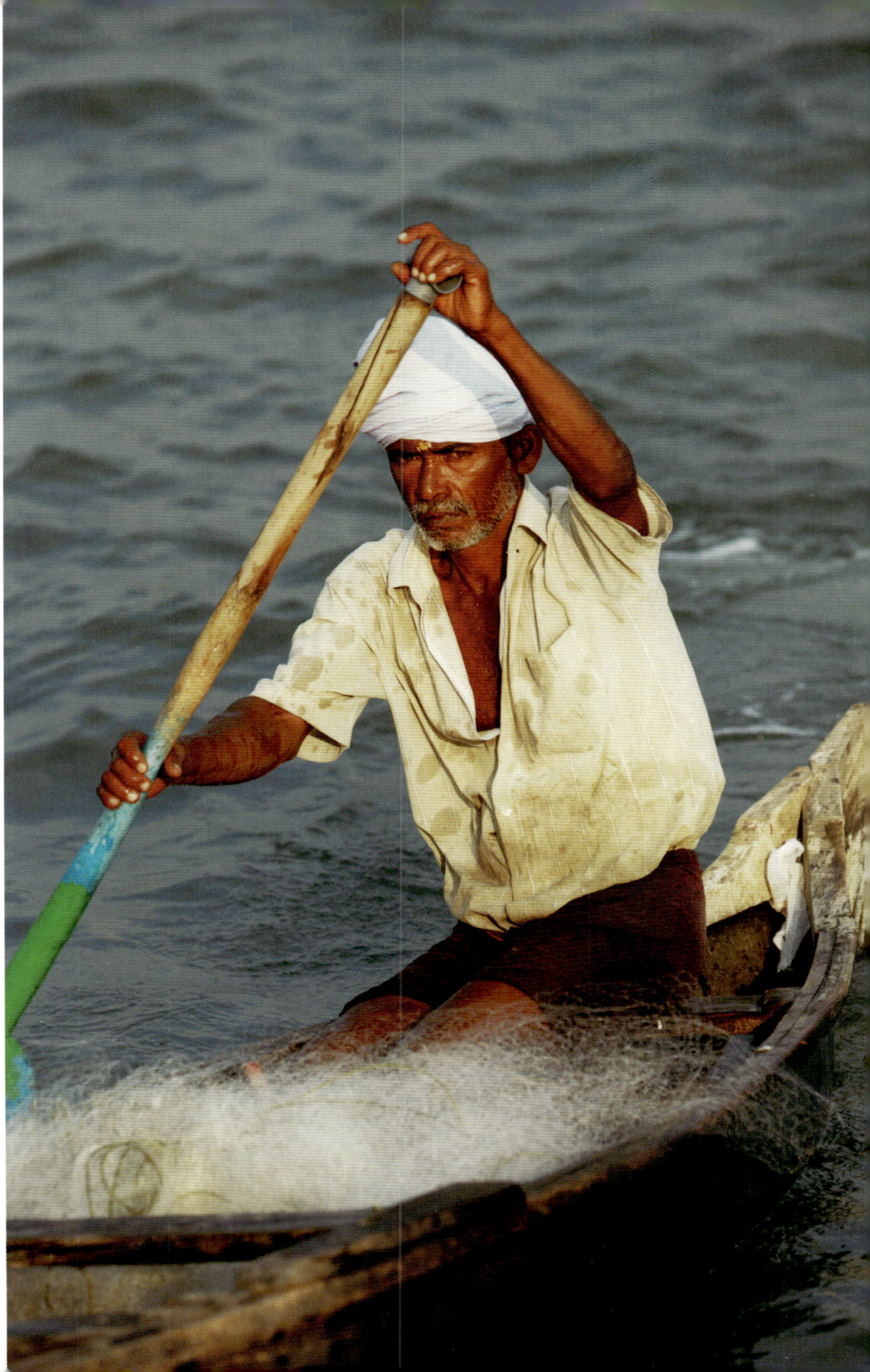

JANUARY 26

Men in a ship are always looking up,
and men ashore are usually looking down.

John Masefield,
from "Sea-Fever," 1902

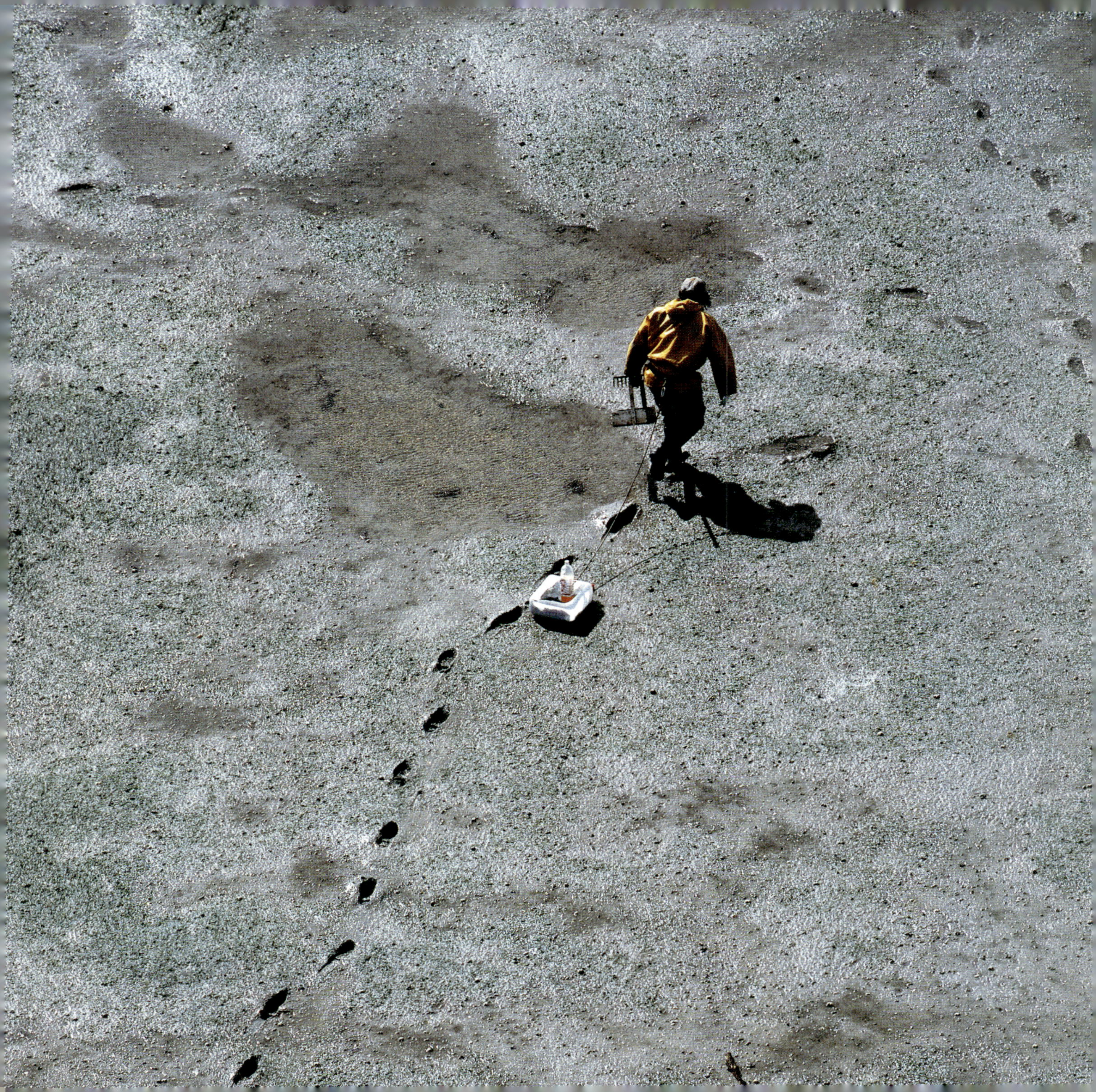

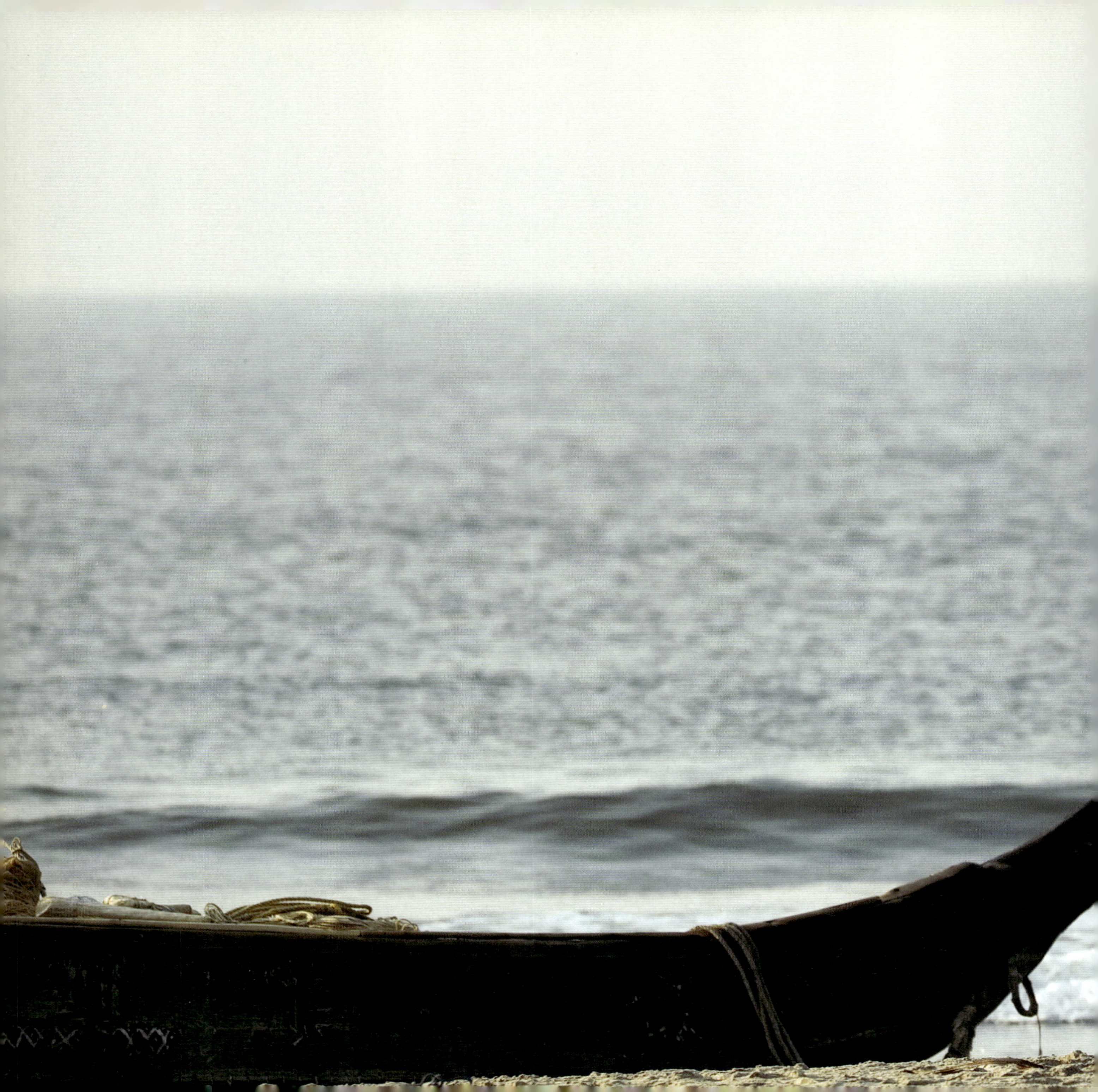

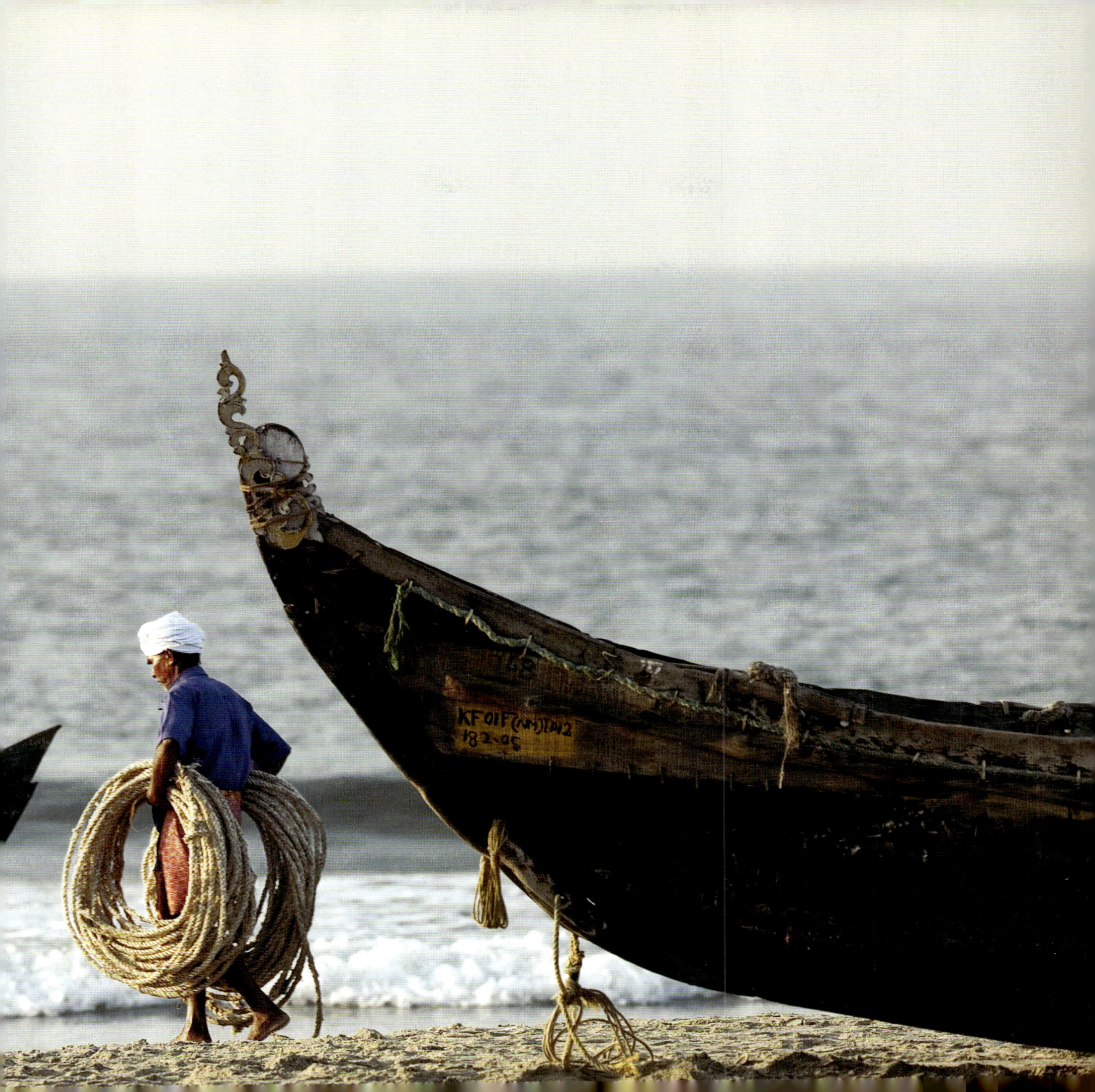

JANUARY 27

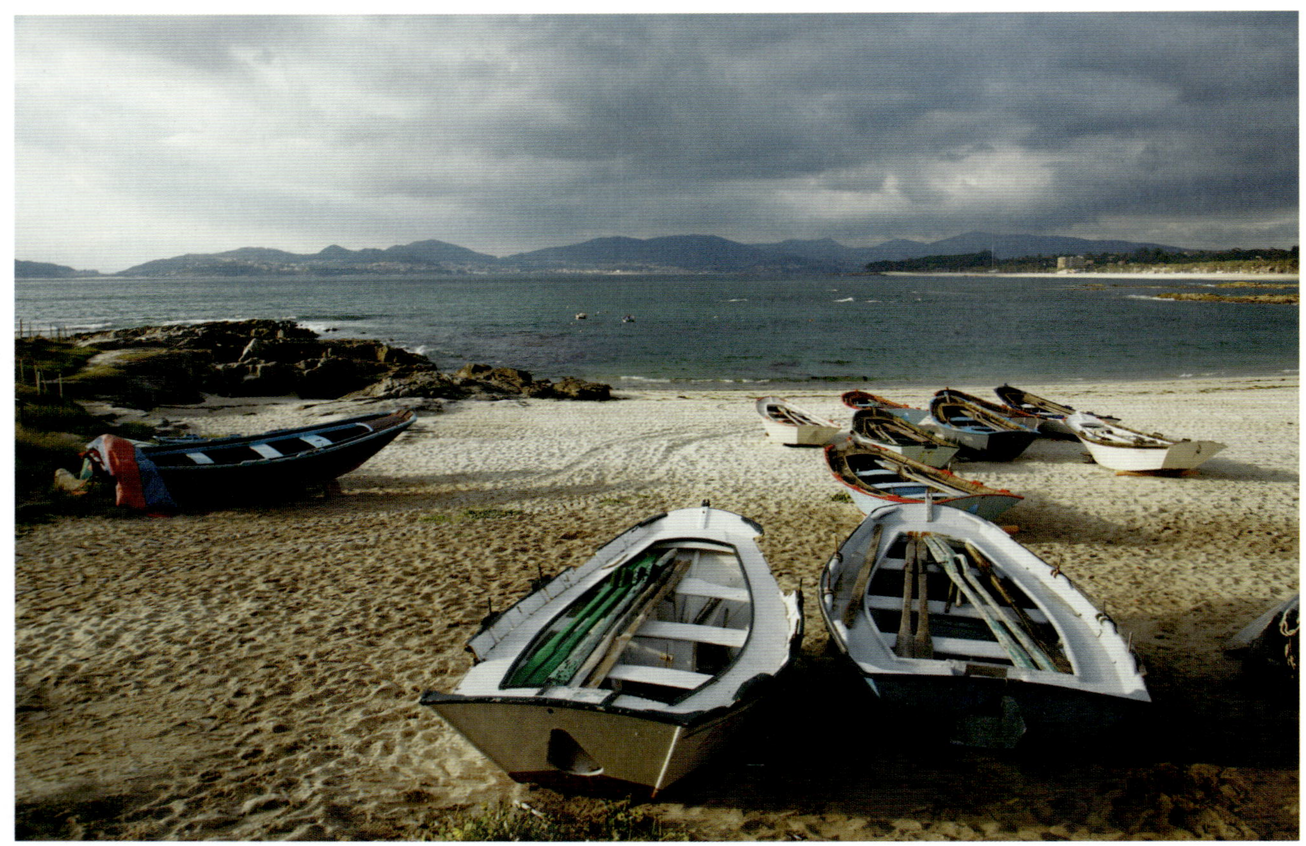

We set the sail; God makes the wind.

English proverb

JANUARY 28

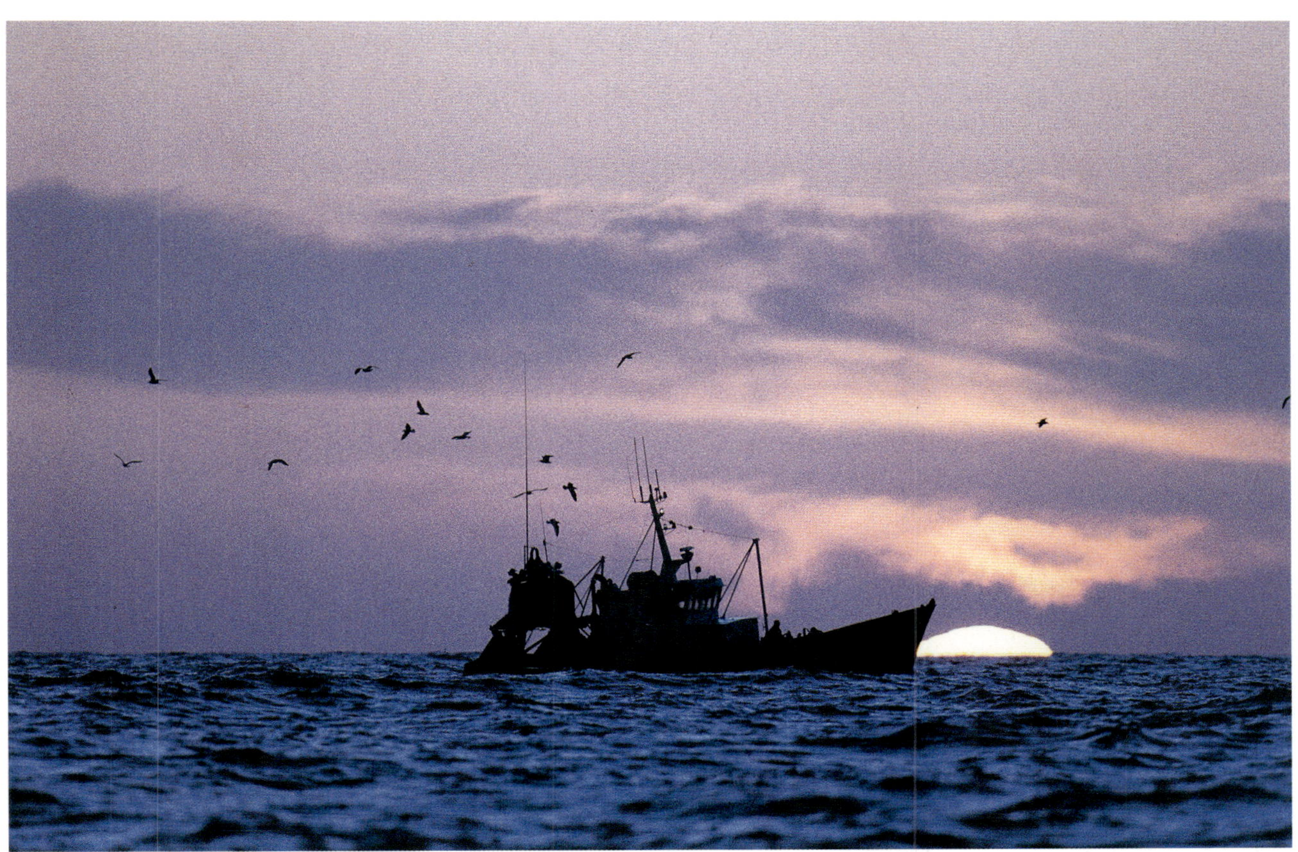

There is nothing more enticing, disenchanting, and enslaving than the life at sea.

Joseph Conrad, from *Lord Jim,* 1900

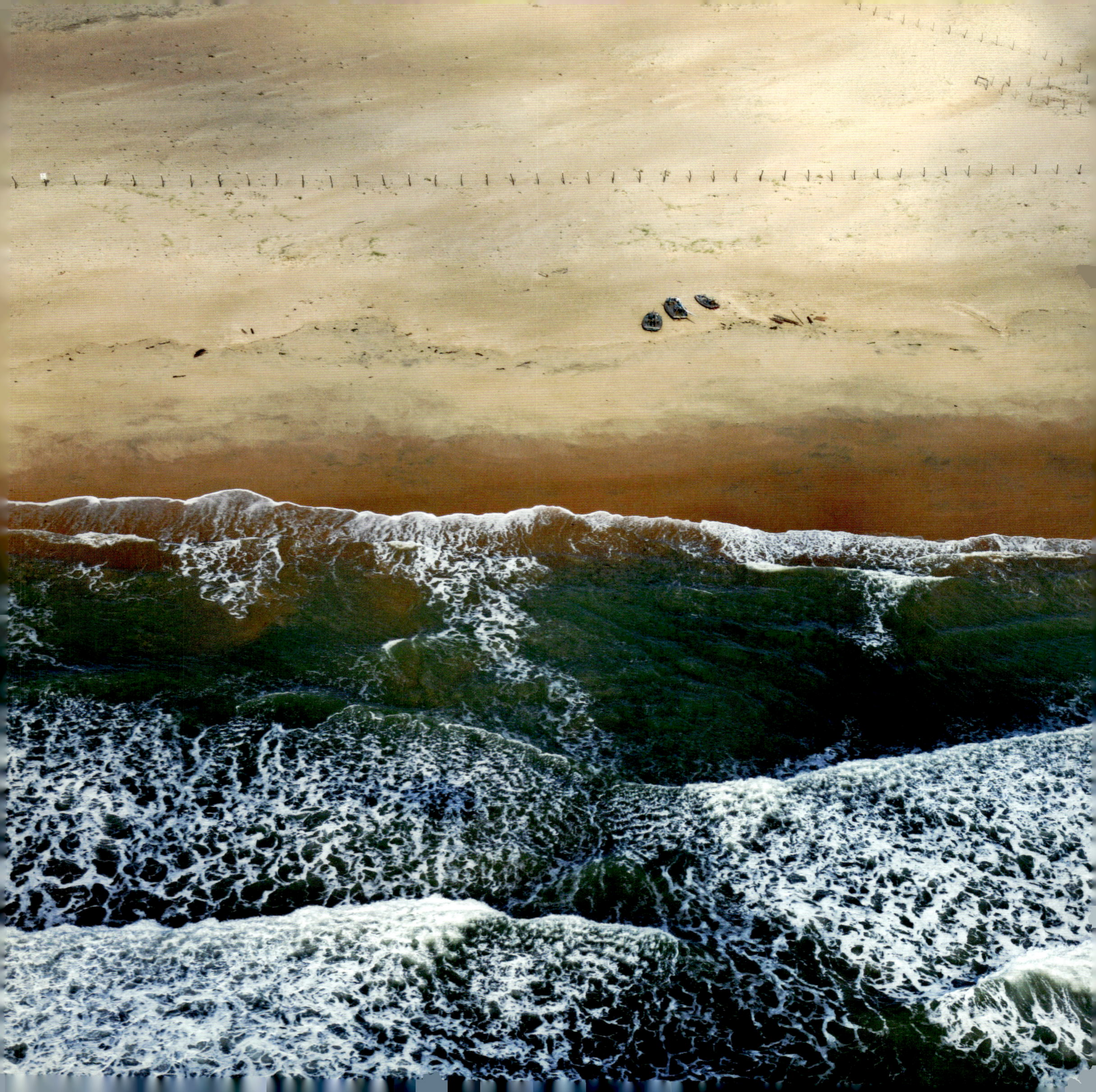

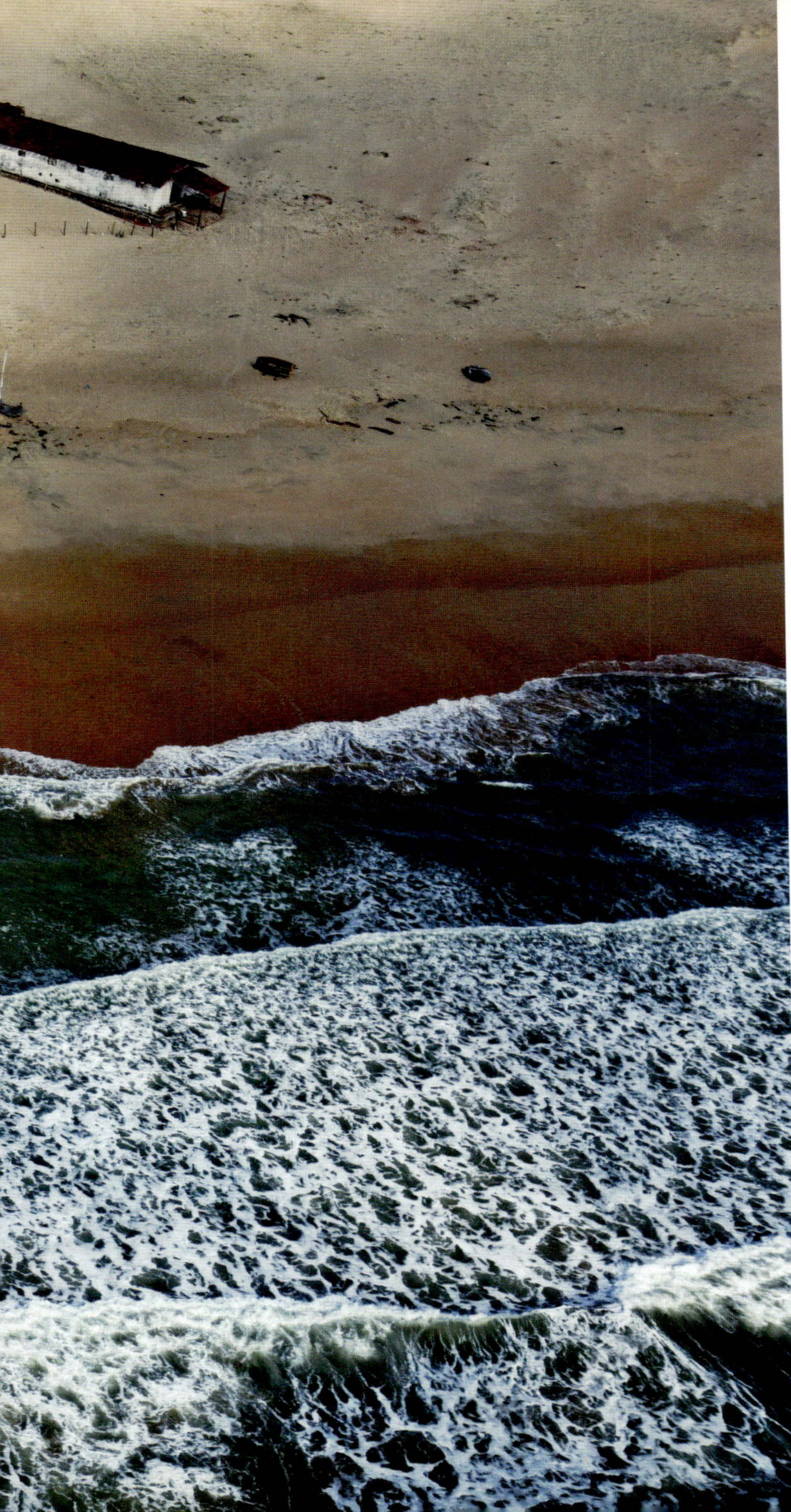

JANUARY 29

Like an eagle caged I pine
On this dull unchanging shore:
Oh give me the flashing brine,
The spray and the tempest's roar!

Epes Sargent,
from "A Life on the Ocean Wave," 1838

JANUARY 30

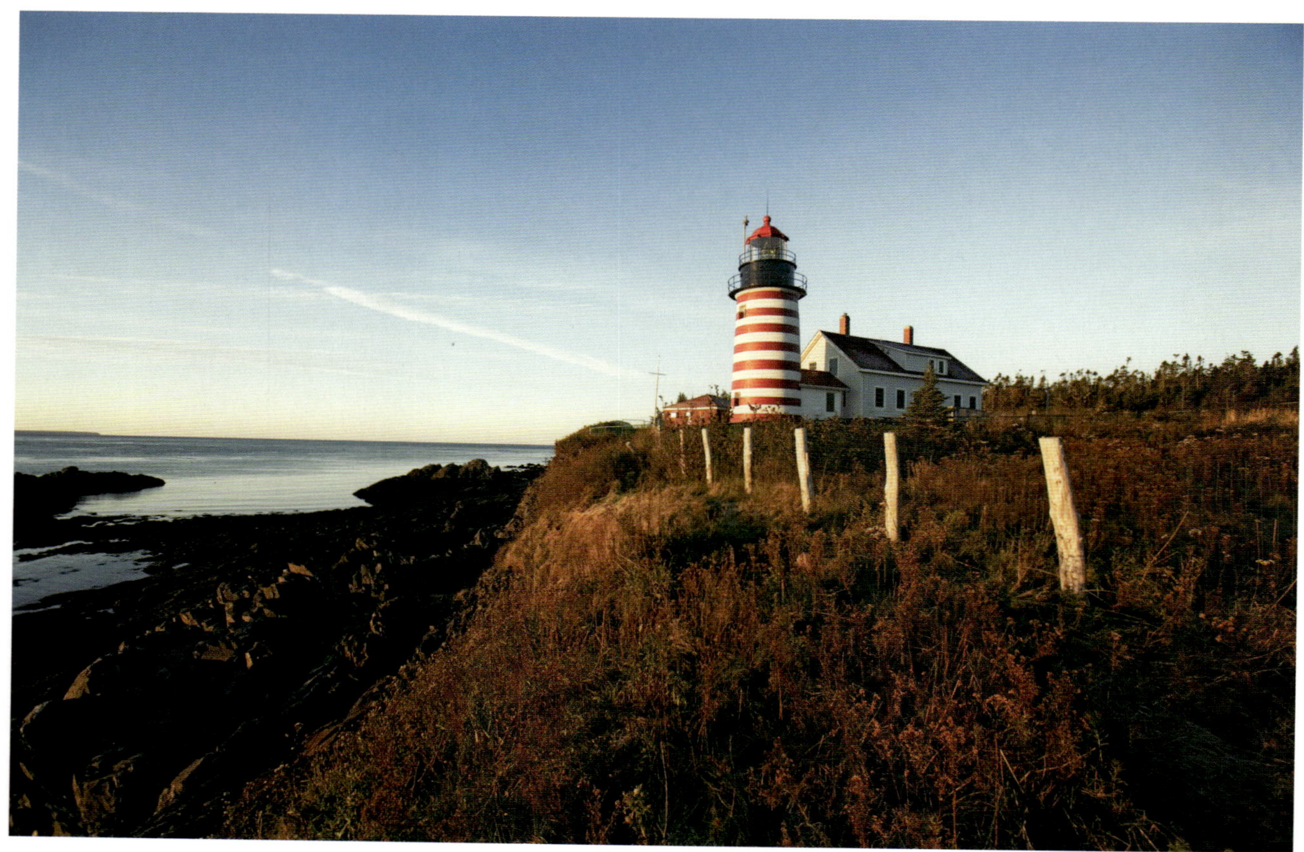

He that at sea prayes for more winde, as well
Under the poles may begge cold, heat in hell.

John Donne, from "The Calme," 1633

JANUARY 31

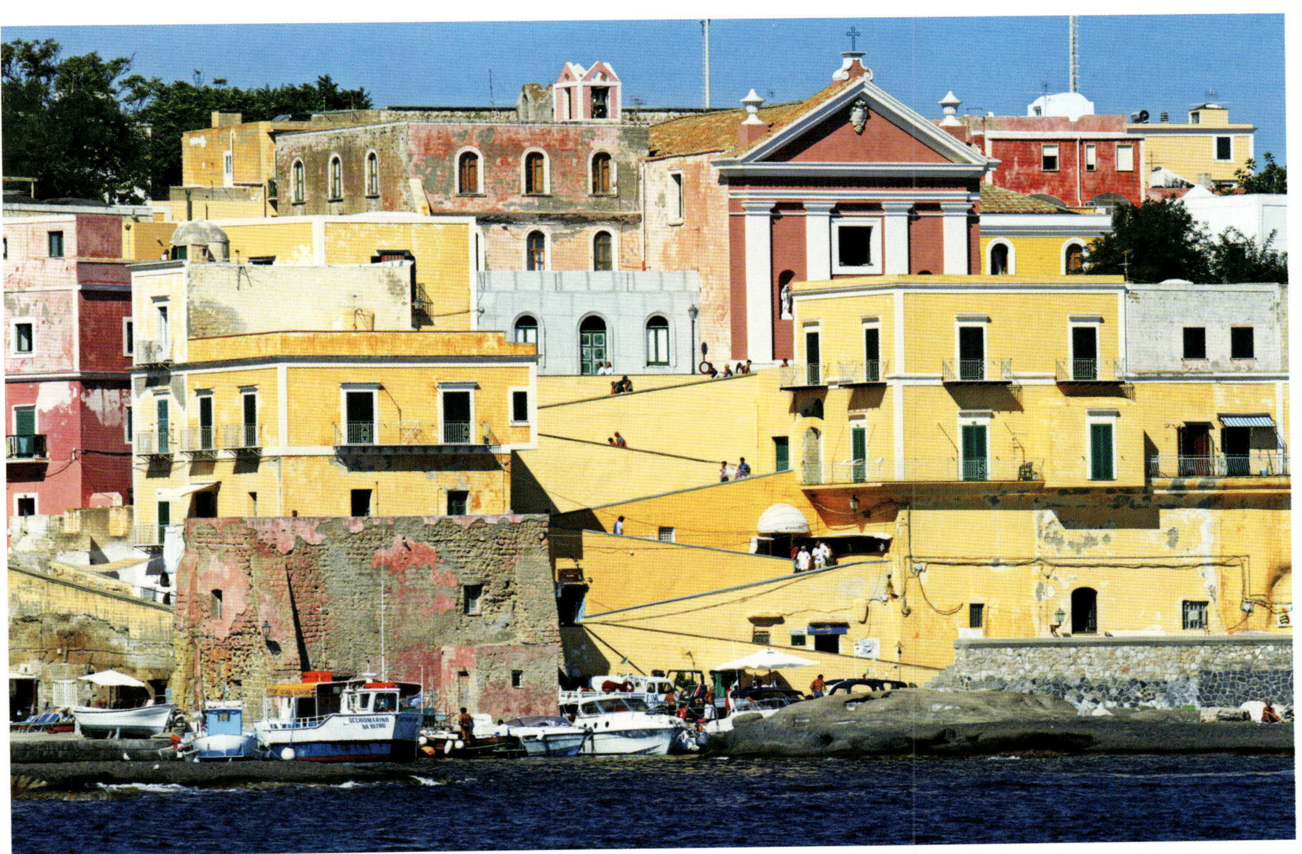

The primordial sea indefatigably repeats the same words and casts up
the same astonished beings on the same seashore.

Albert Camus

FEBRUARY 1

The breaking of a wave cannot explain the whole sea.

Vladimir Nabokov

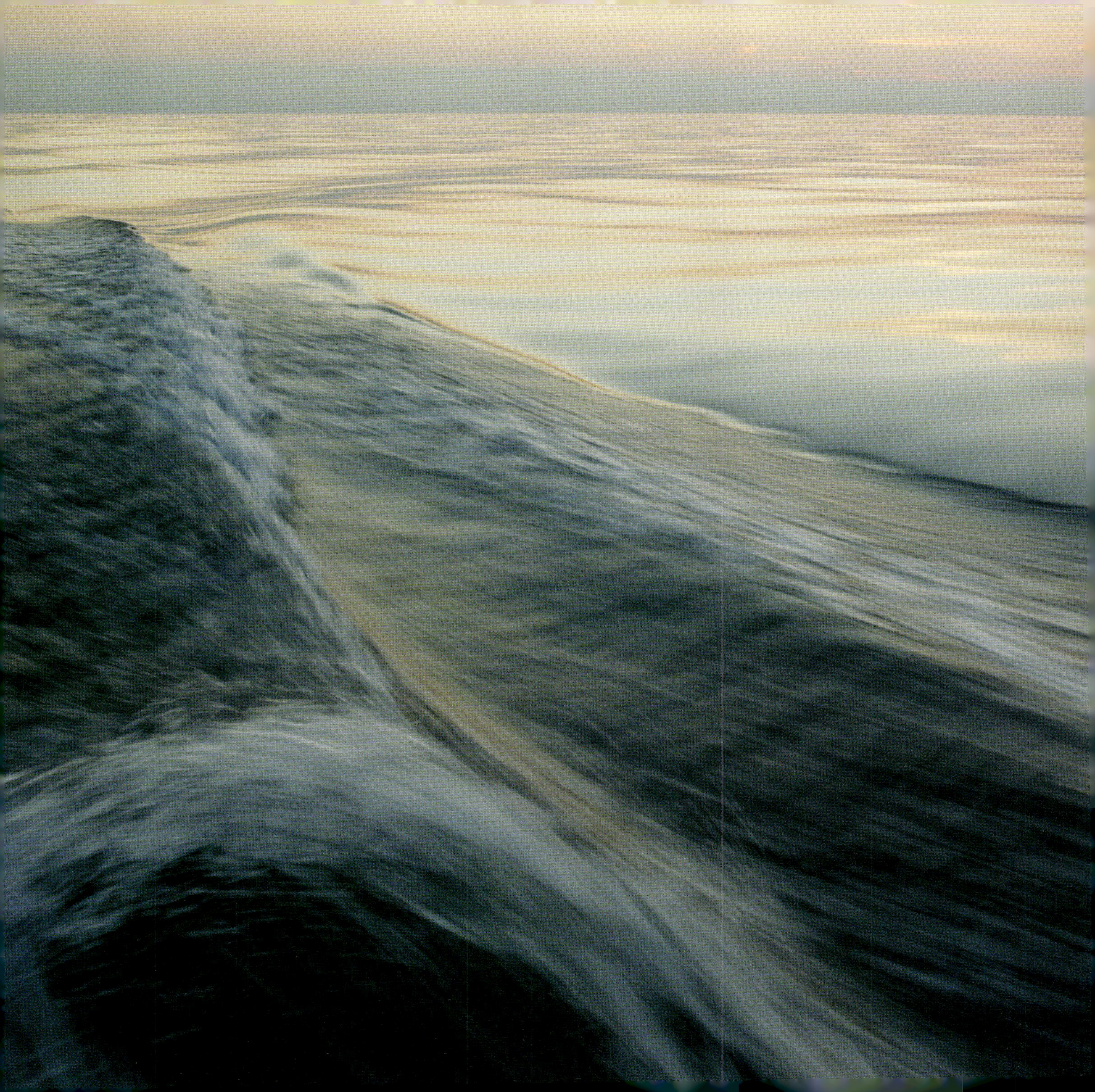

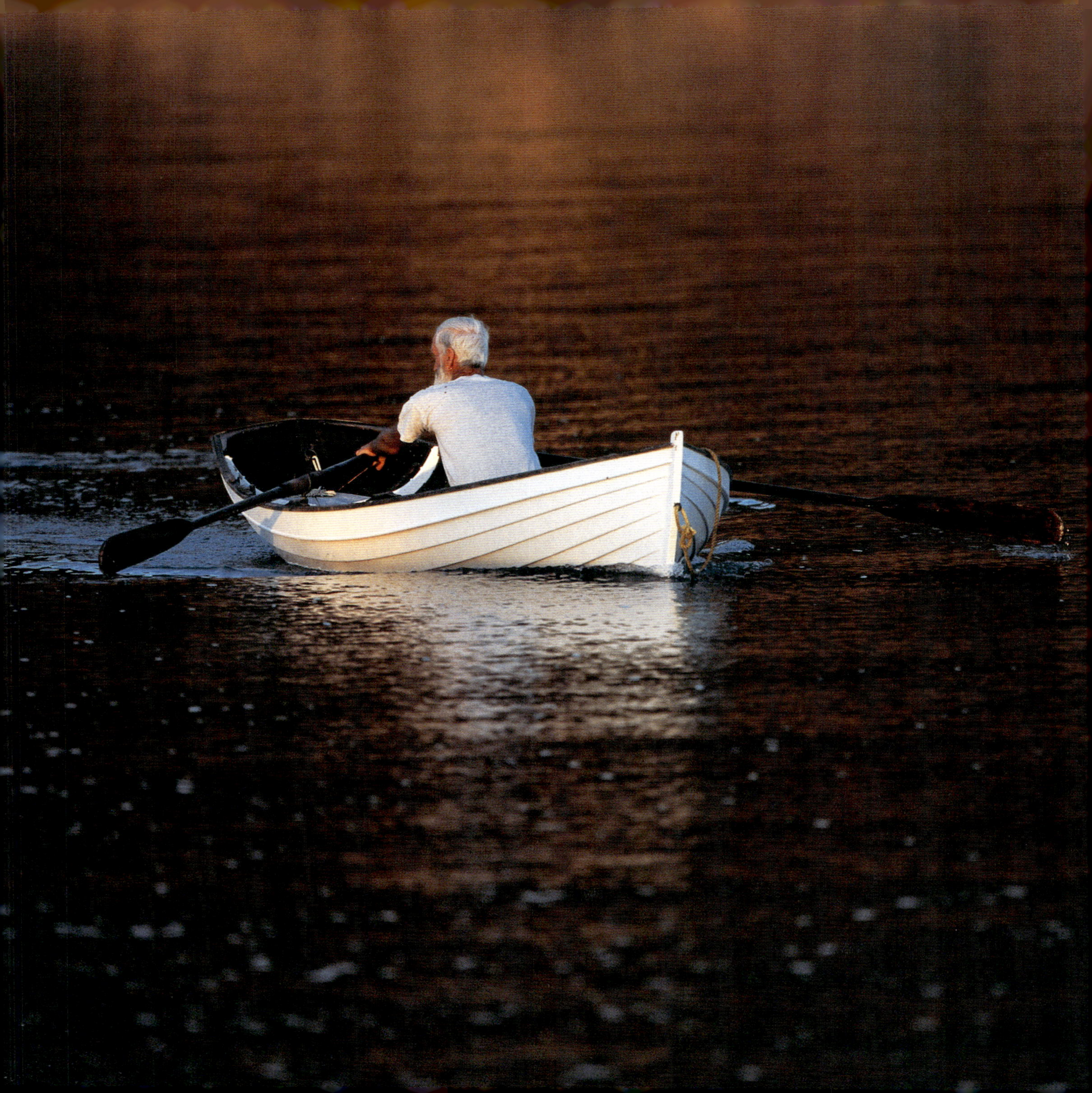

FEBRUARY 2

There never was a great man yet who spent all his life inland.

Herman Melville, from *White-Jacket,* 1850

FEBRUARY 3

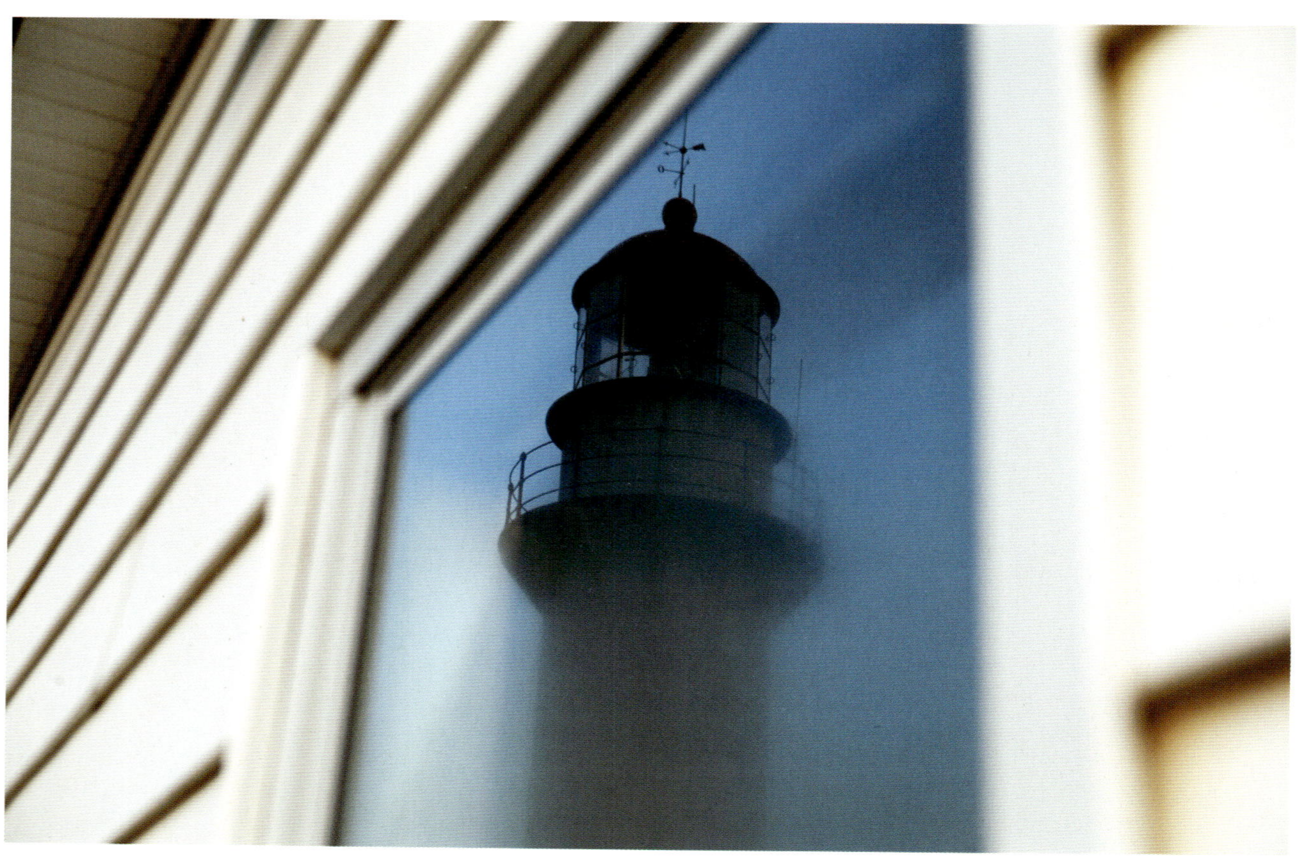

Inside my empty bottle I was constructing a lighthouse while all the others were making ships.

Charles Simic

FEBRUARY 4

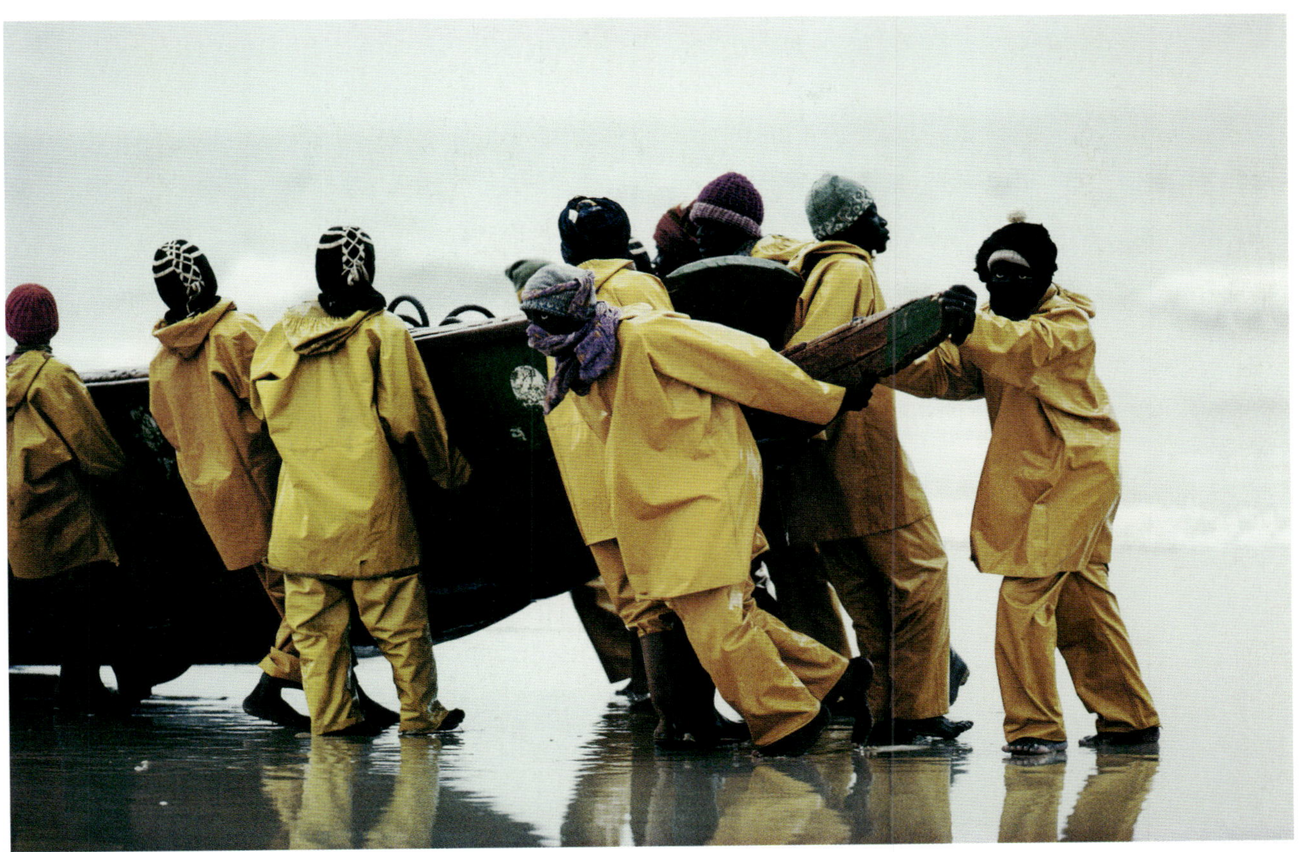

It isn't that life ashore is distasteful to me. But life at sea is better.

Sir Francis Drake

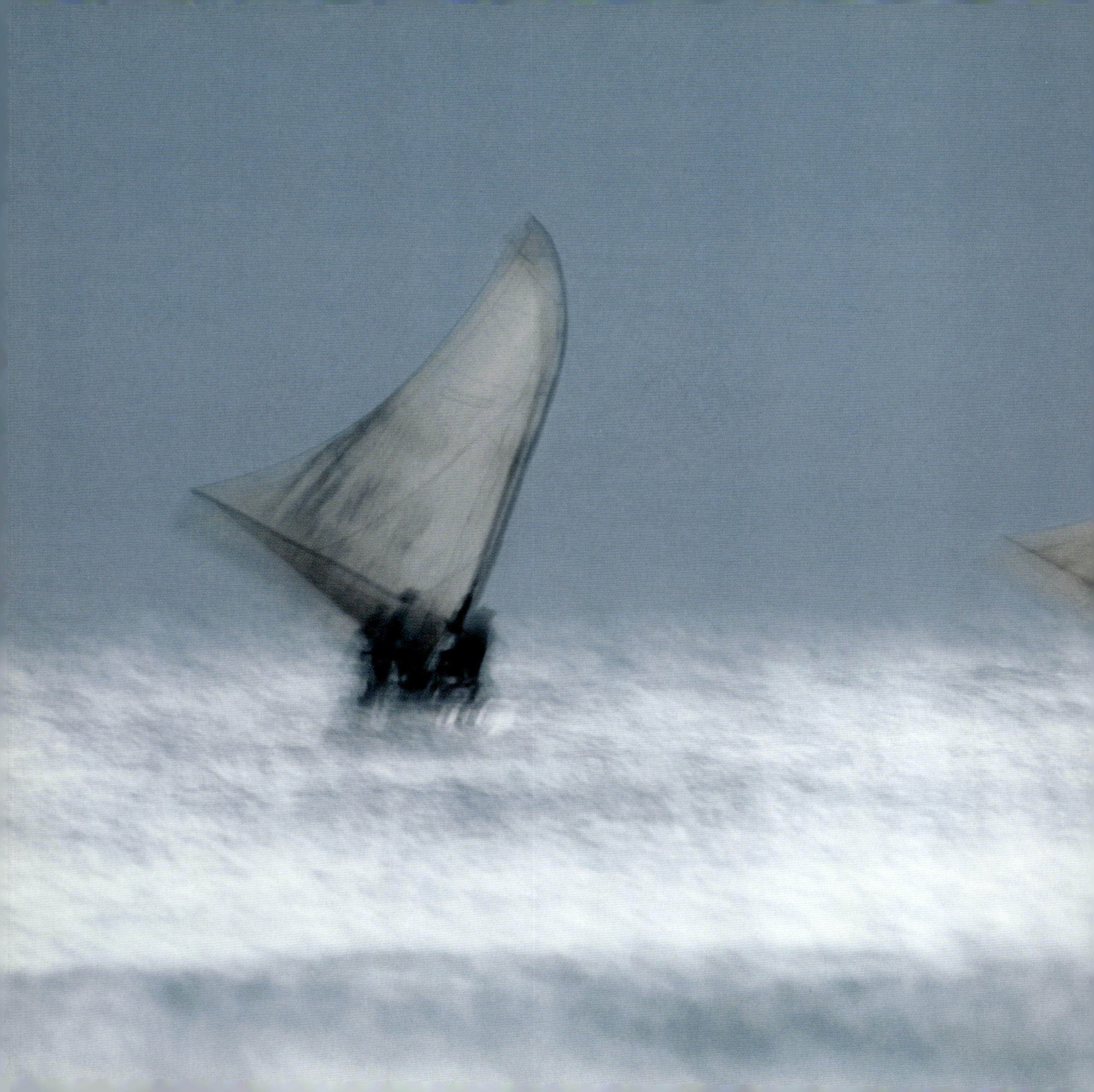

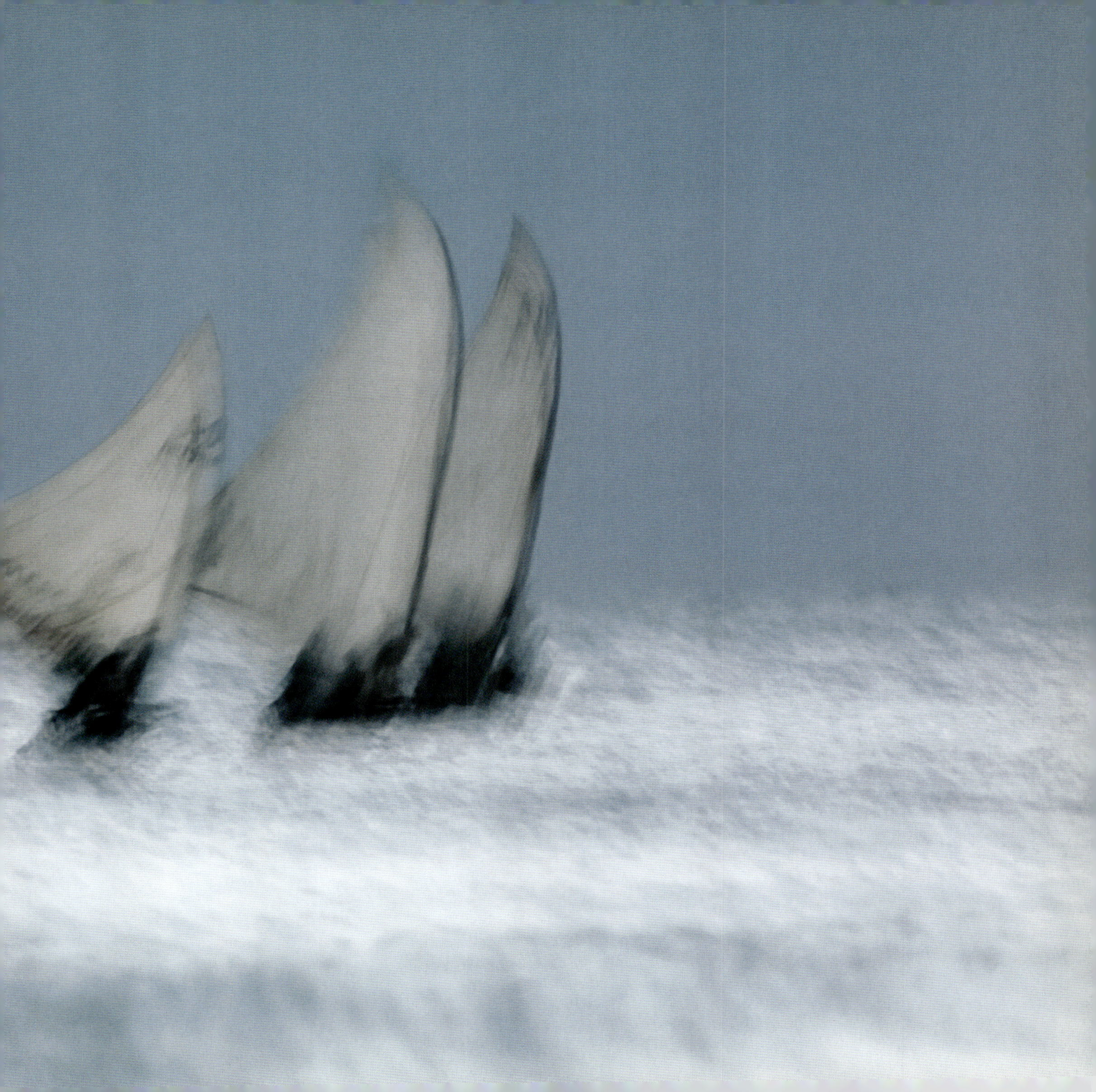

FEBRUARY 5

For me, my craft is sailing on,
Through mists to-day, clear seas anon.
Whate'er the final harbor be
'T is good to sail upon the sea!

John Kendrick Bangs,
from "The Voyage," 1887

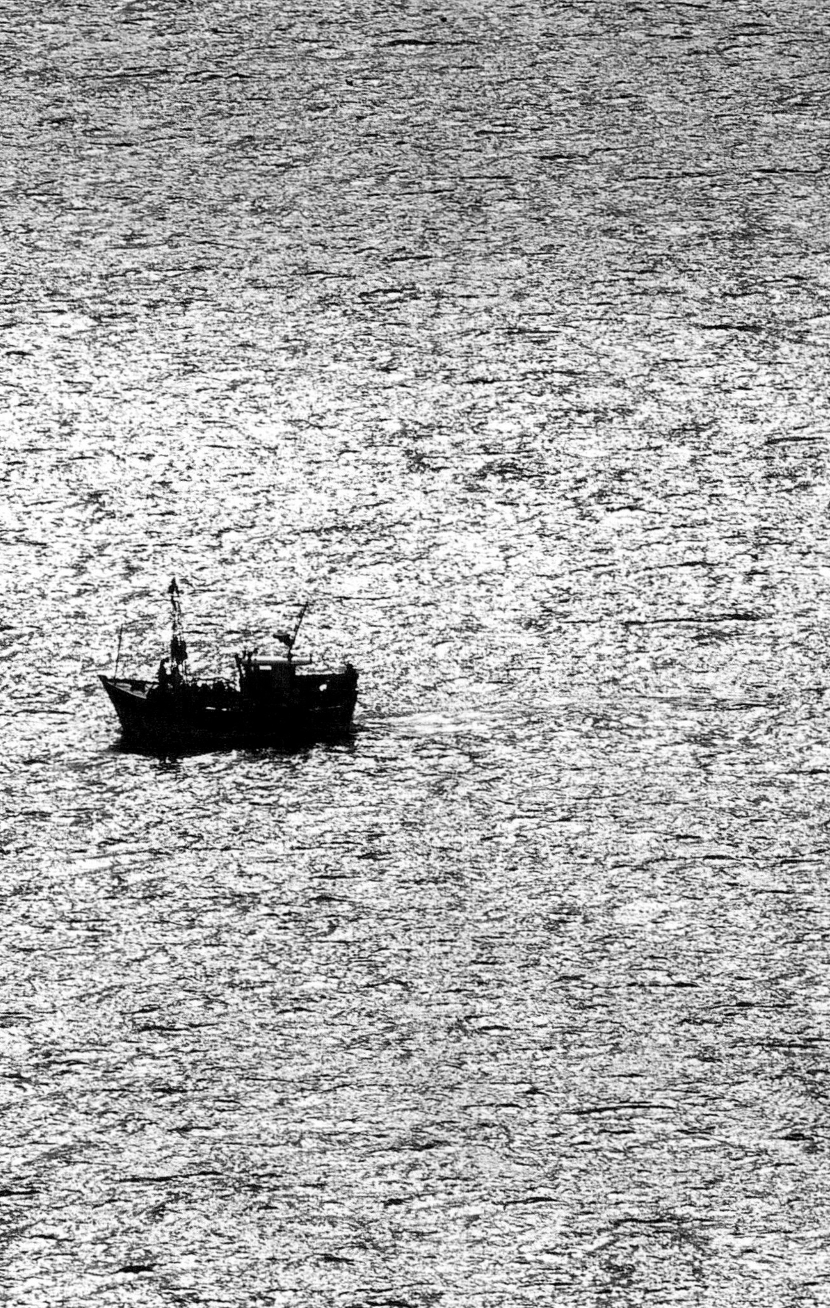

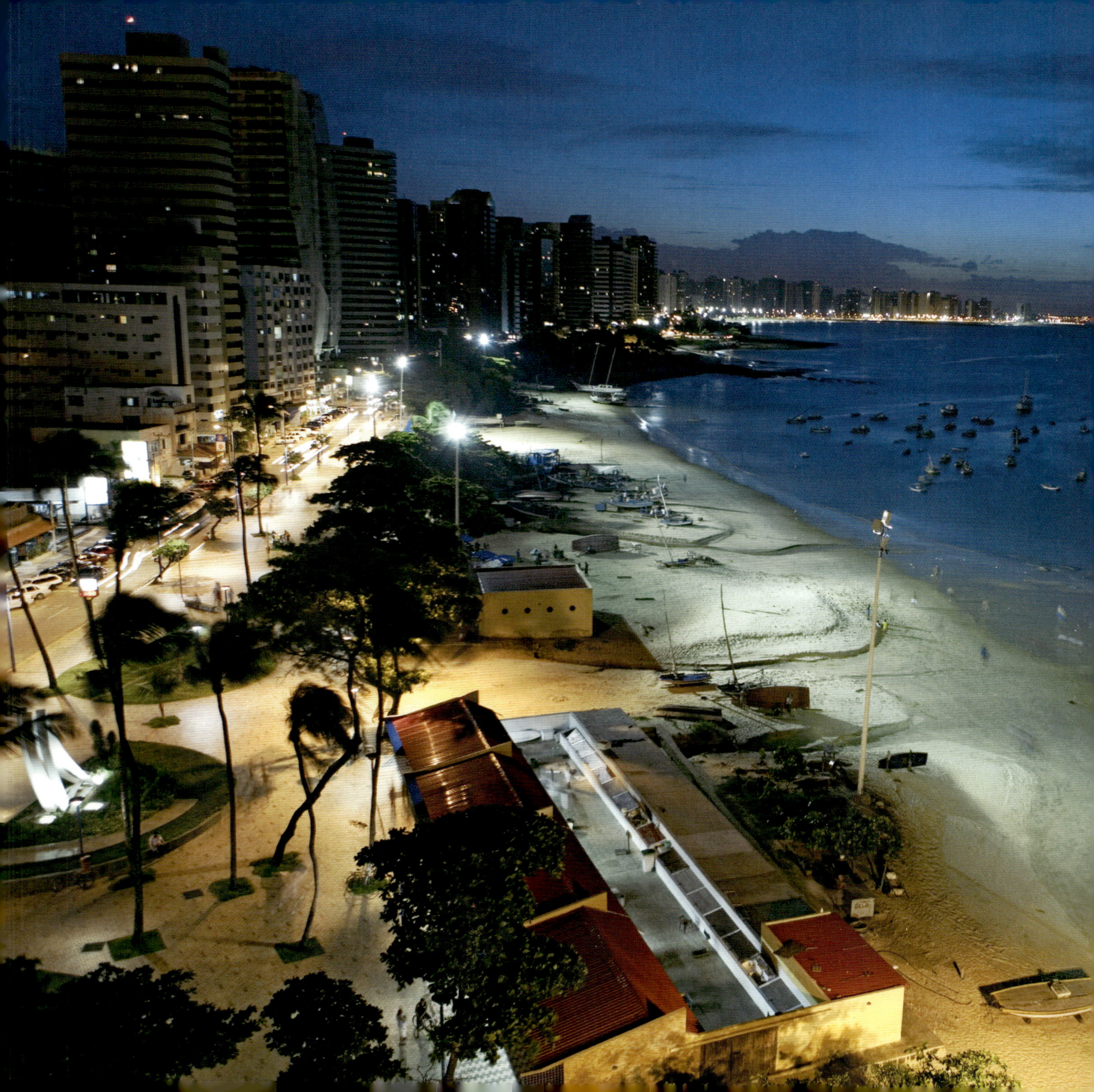

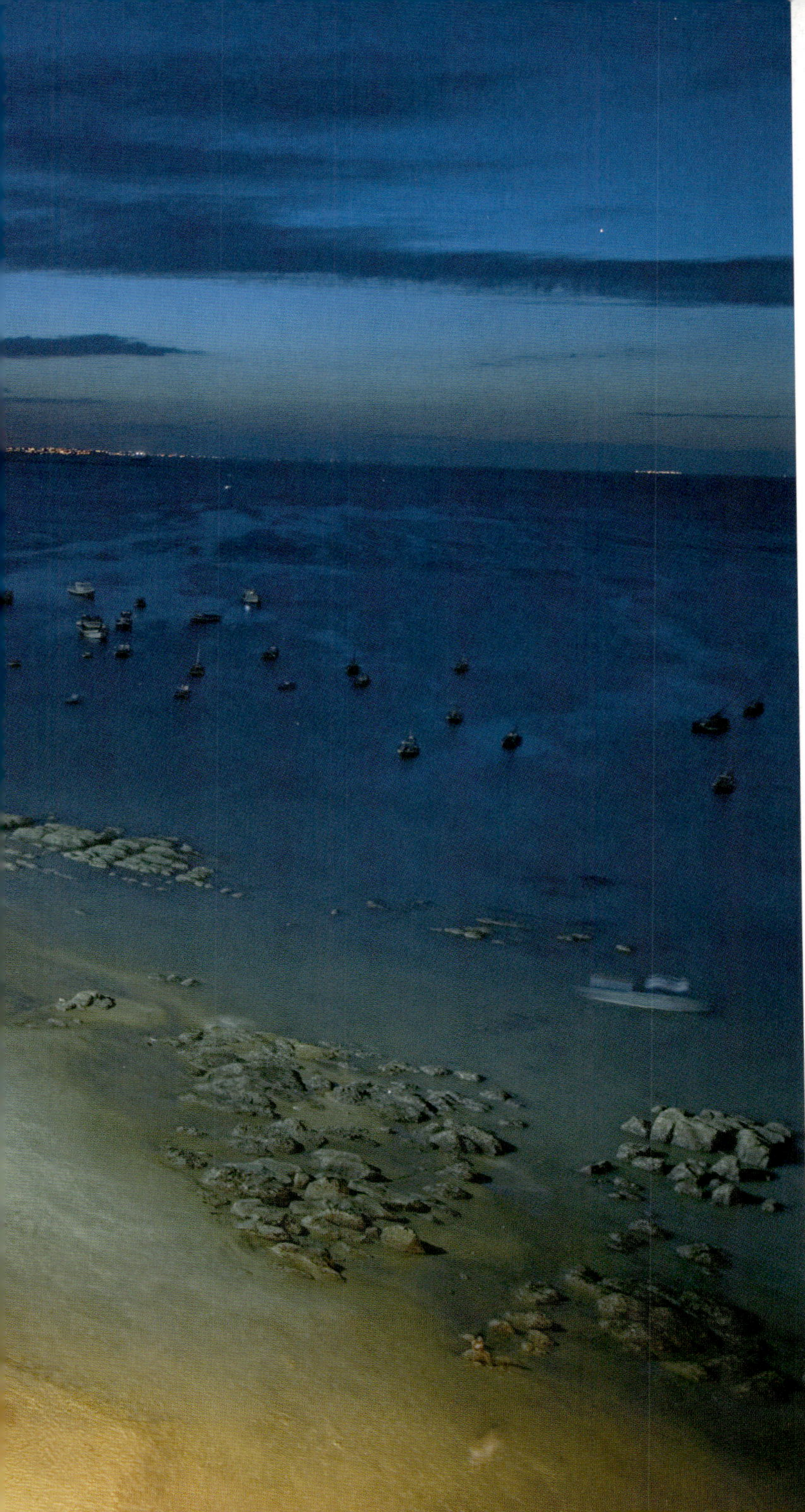

FEBRUARY 6

Still bent to make some port he knows not where,
still standing for some false impossible shore.

Matthew Arnold, "A Summer Night," 1852

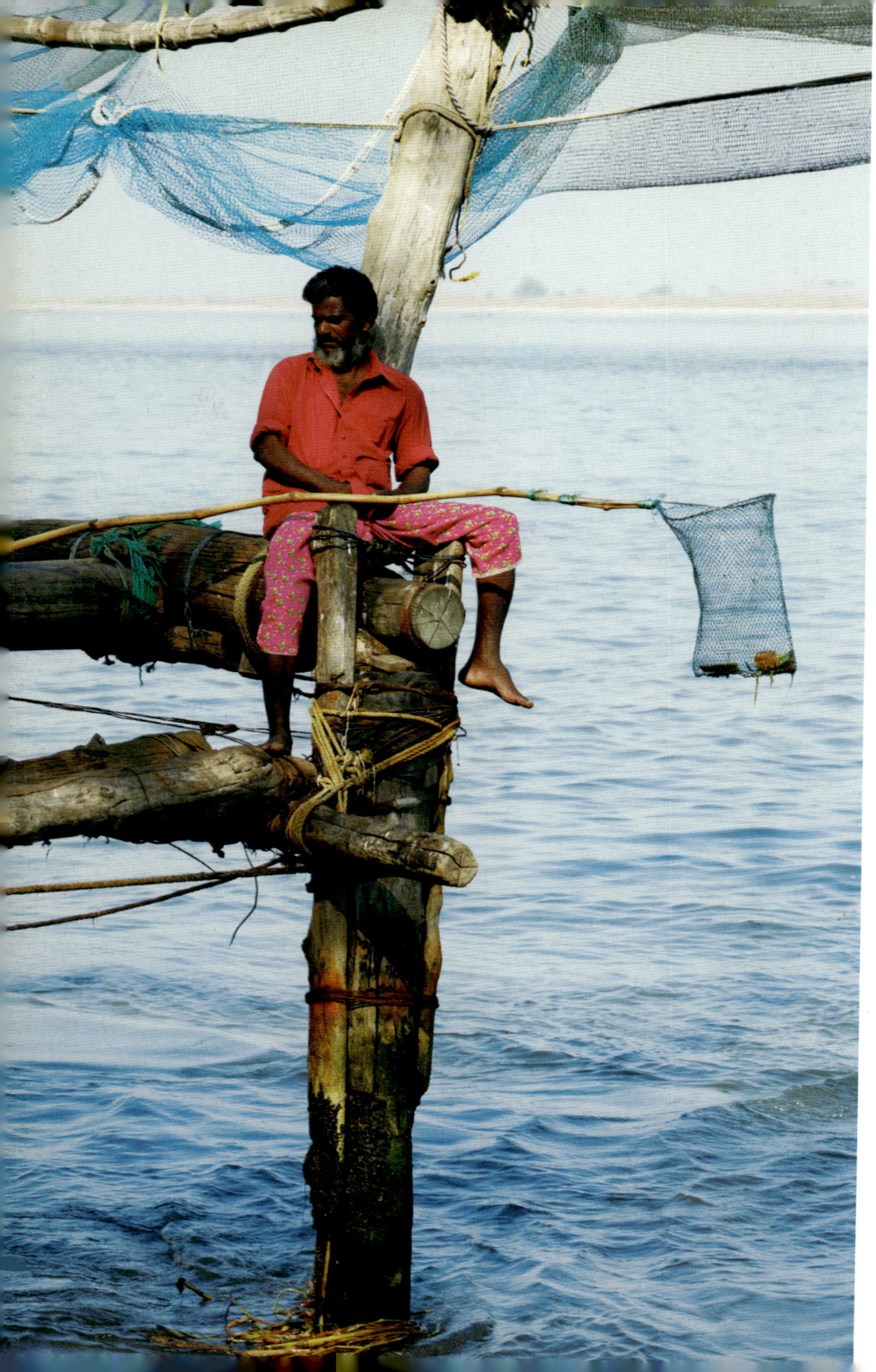

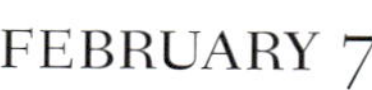

FEBRUARY 7

The gods do not deduct
from man's alloted span
the hours spent fishing.

Chinese proverb

FEBRUARY 8

We should not moor a ship with one anchor, or our life with one hope.

Epictetus,
from *Dissertations*

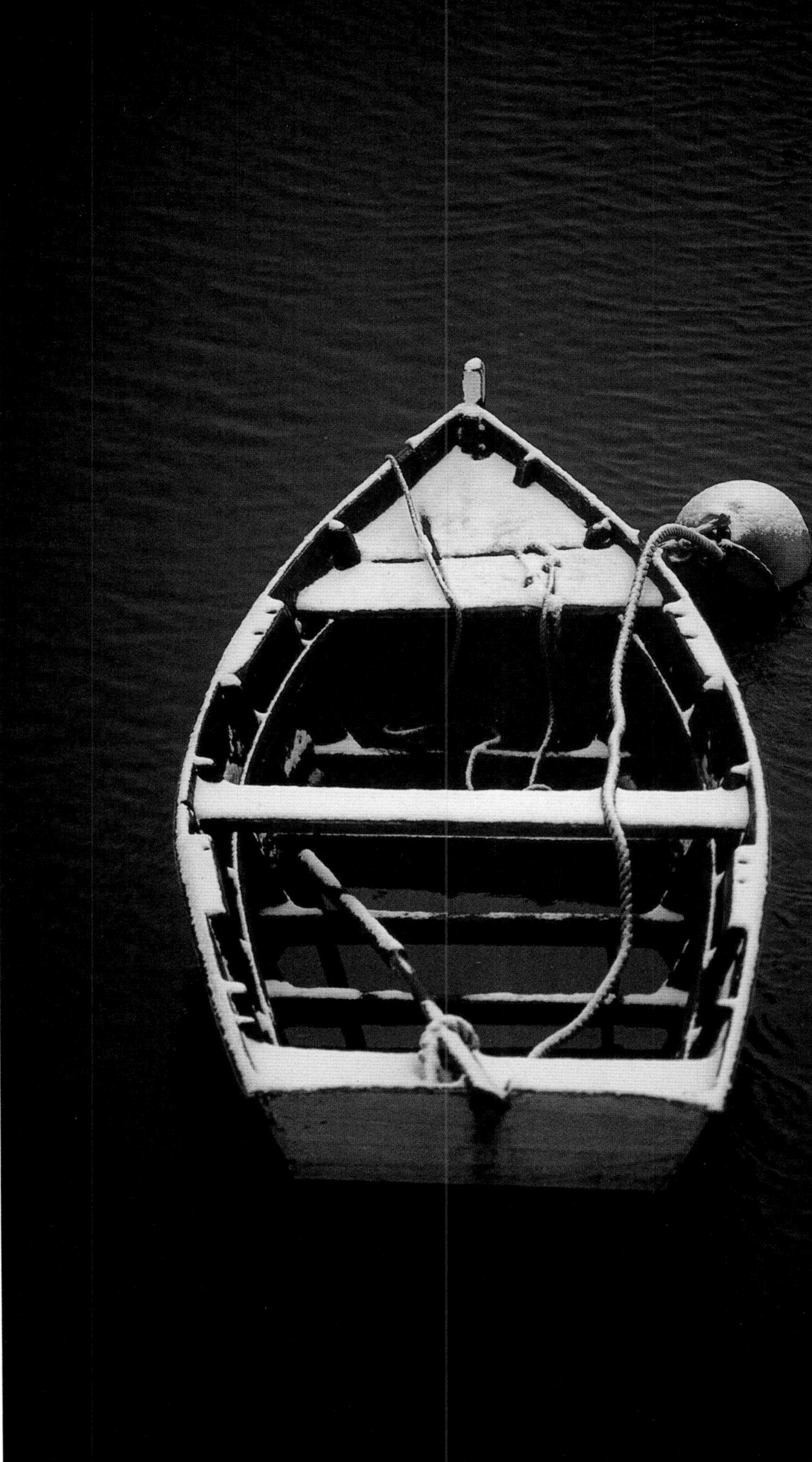

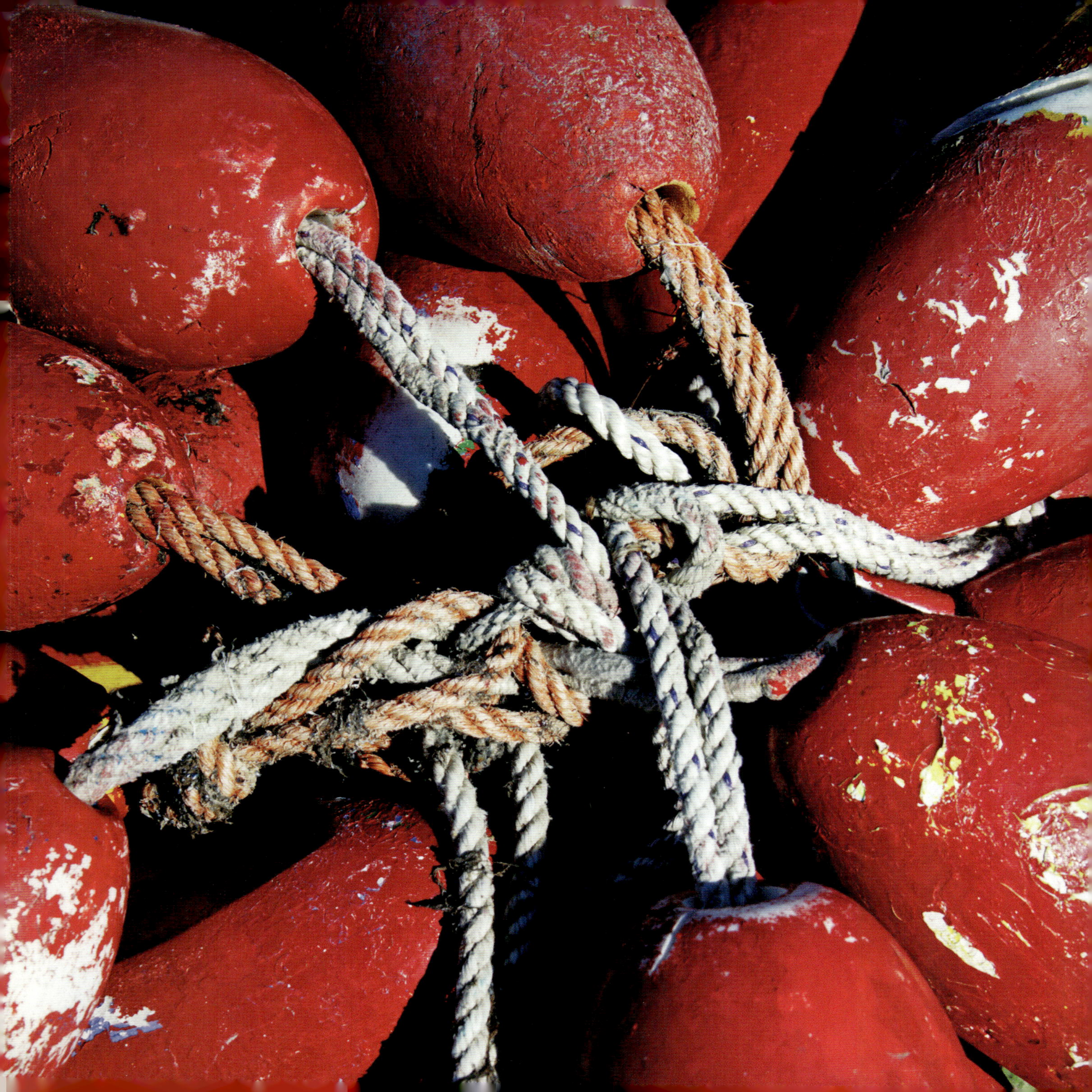

FEBRUARY 9

Men go abroad to wonder at the heights of mountains,
at the huge waves of the sea, at the long courses of the rivers,
at the vast compass of the ocean, at the circular motions of the stars;
and they pass by themselves without wondering.

St. Augustine, from *City of God,* 413–426

FEBRUARY 10

The swiftest harts have posted you by land,
And winds of all the corners kiss'd your sails,
To make your vessel nimble.

William Shakespeare,
from *Cymbeline,* Act II, Scene 4

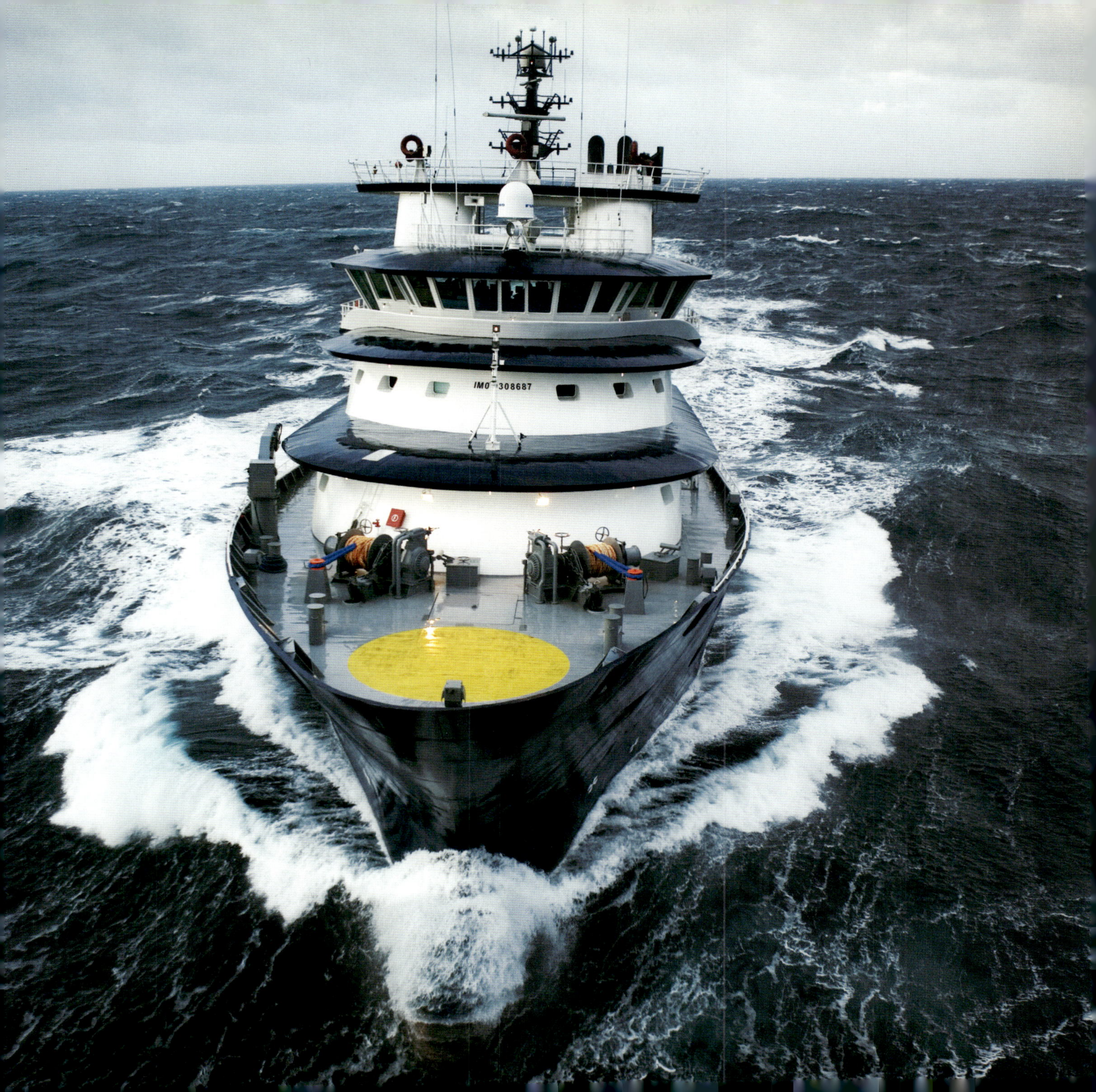
IMO 308687

FEBRUARY 11

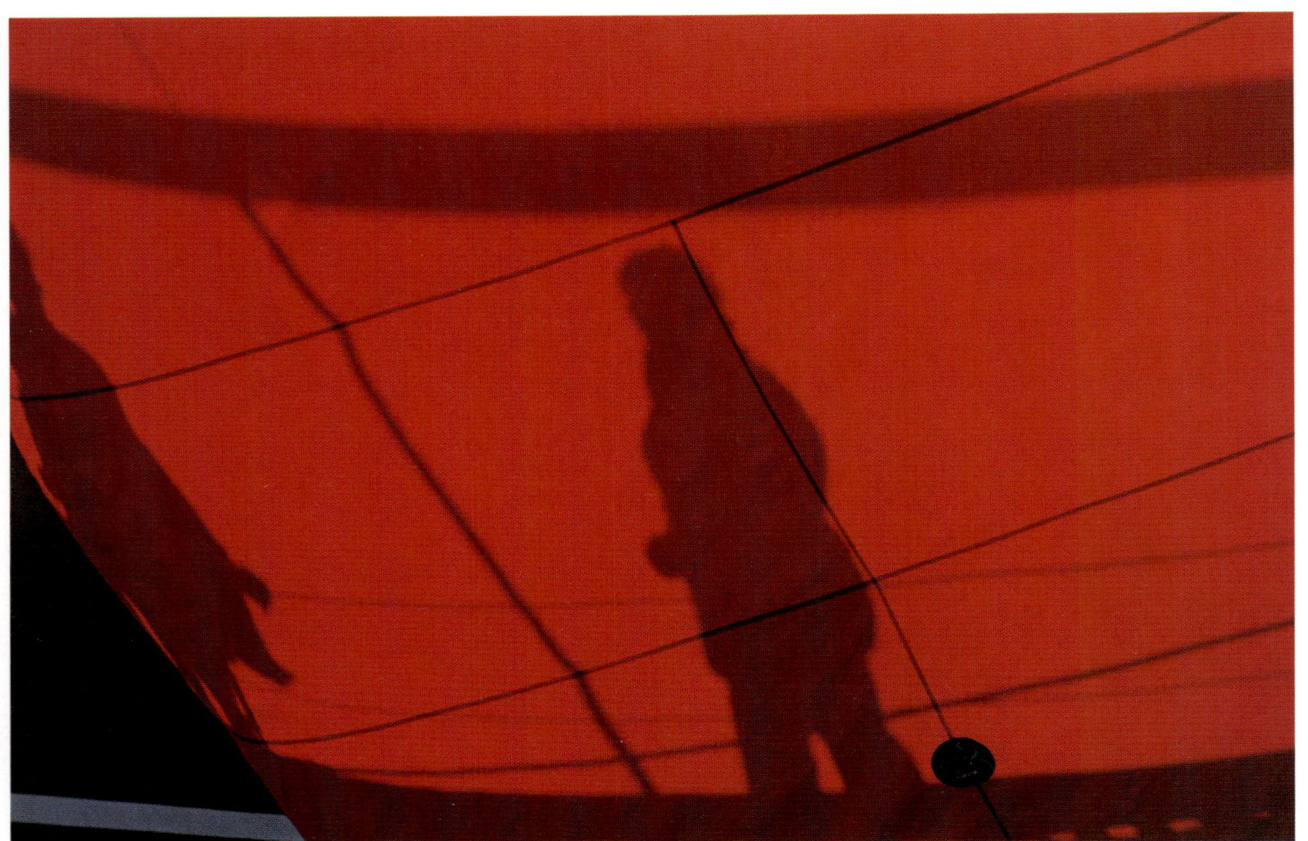

Make not your sail too big for your ballast.

English proverb

FEBRUARY 12

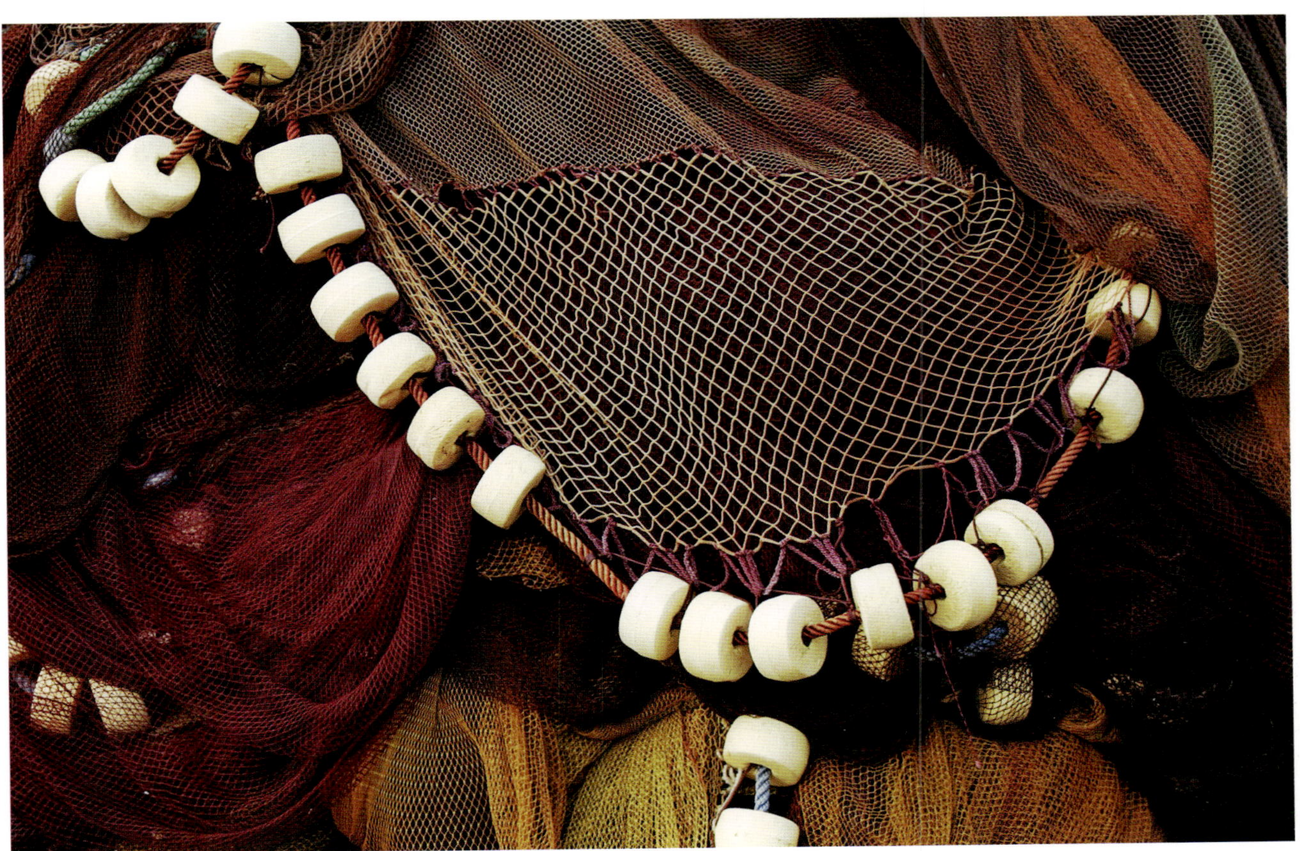

The fishermen know that the sea is dangerous and the storm terrible, but they have never found these dangers sufficient reason for remaining ashore.

Vincent van Gogh

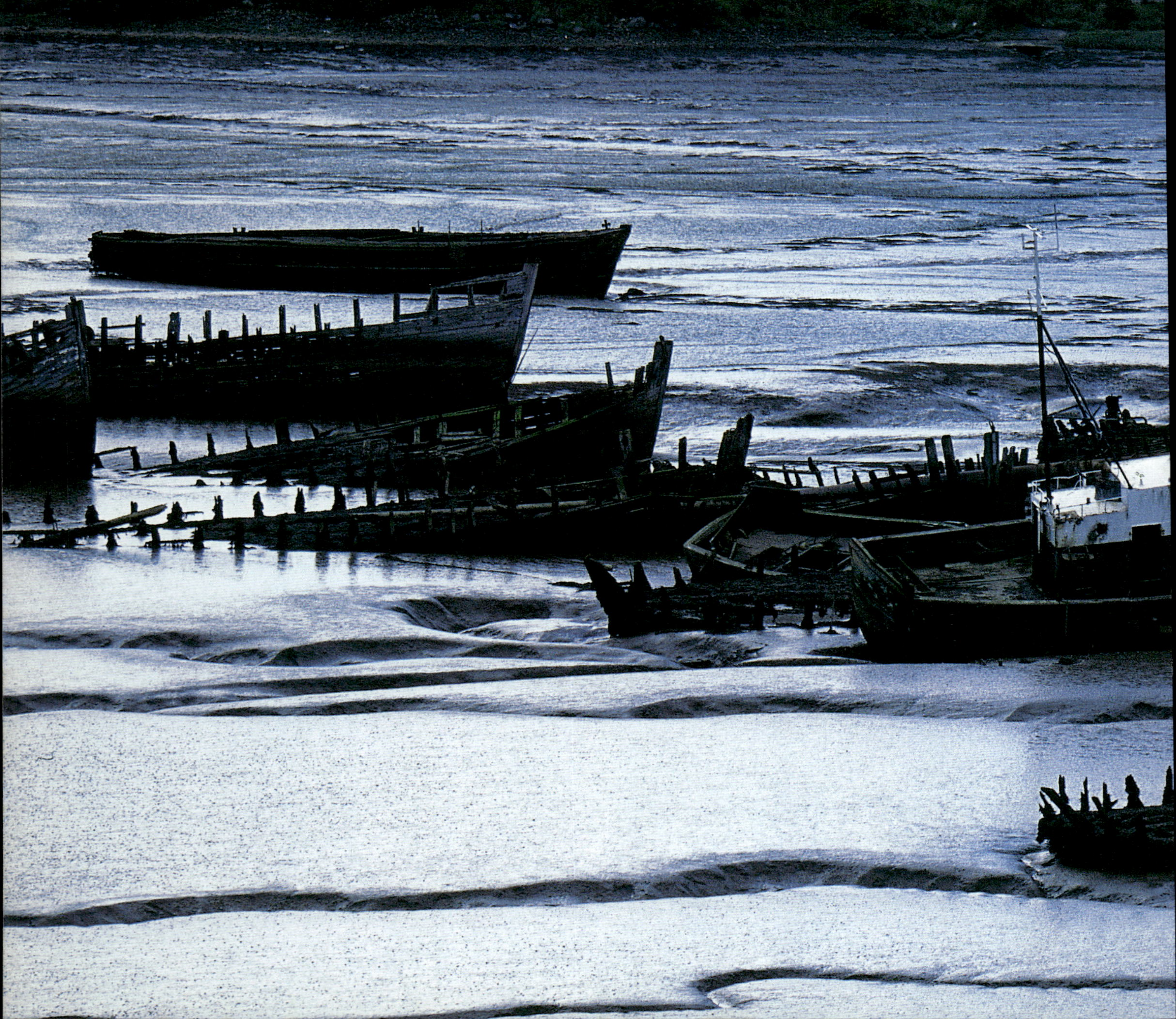

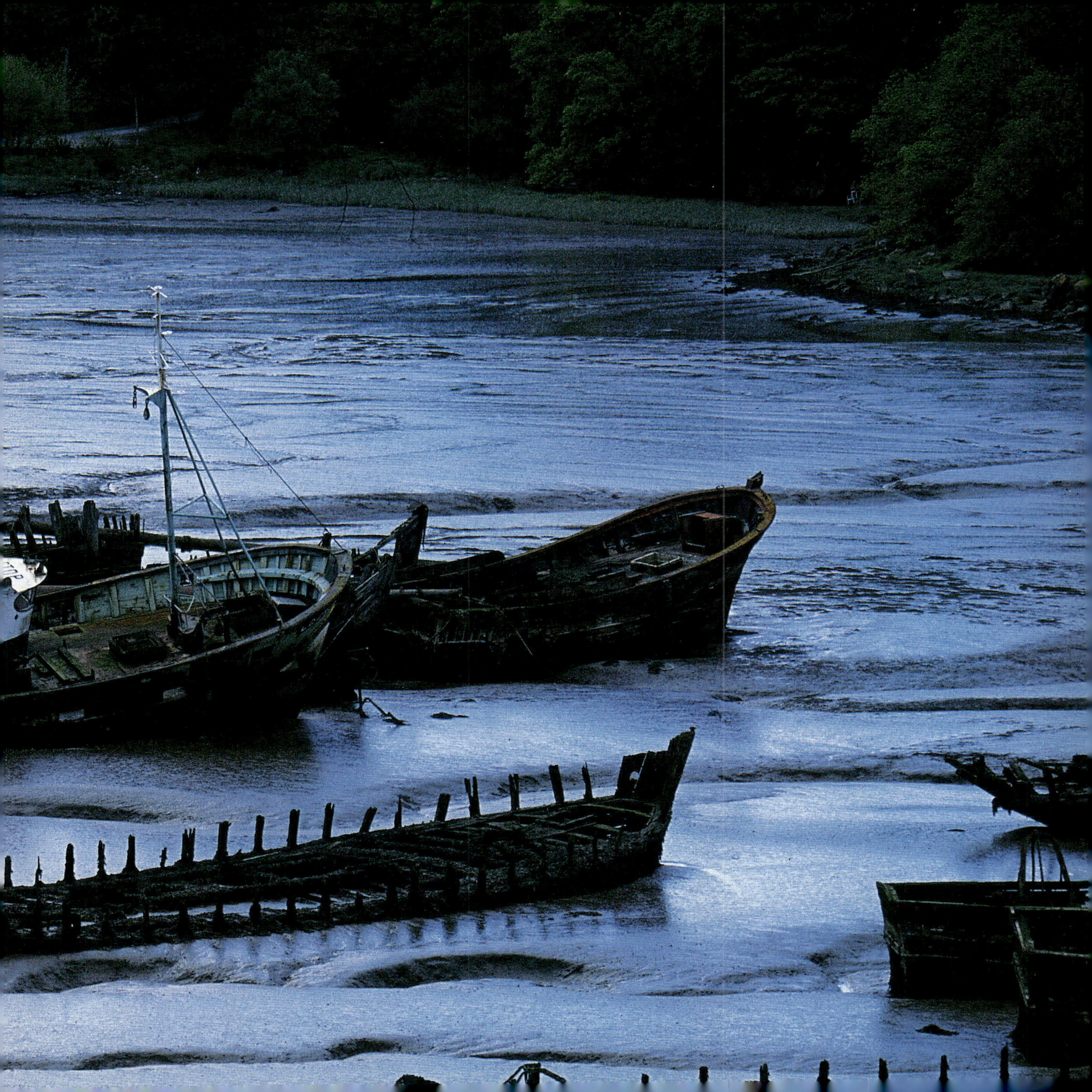

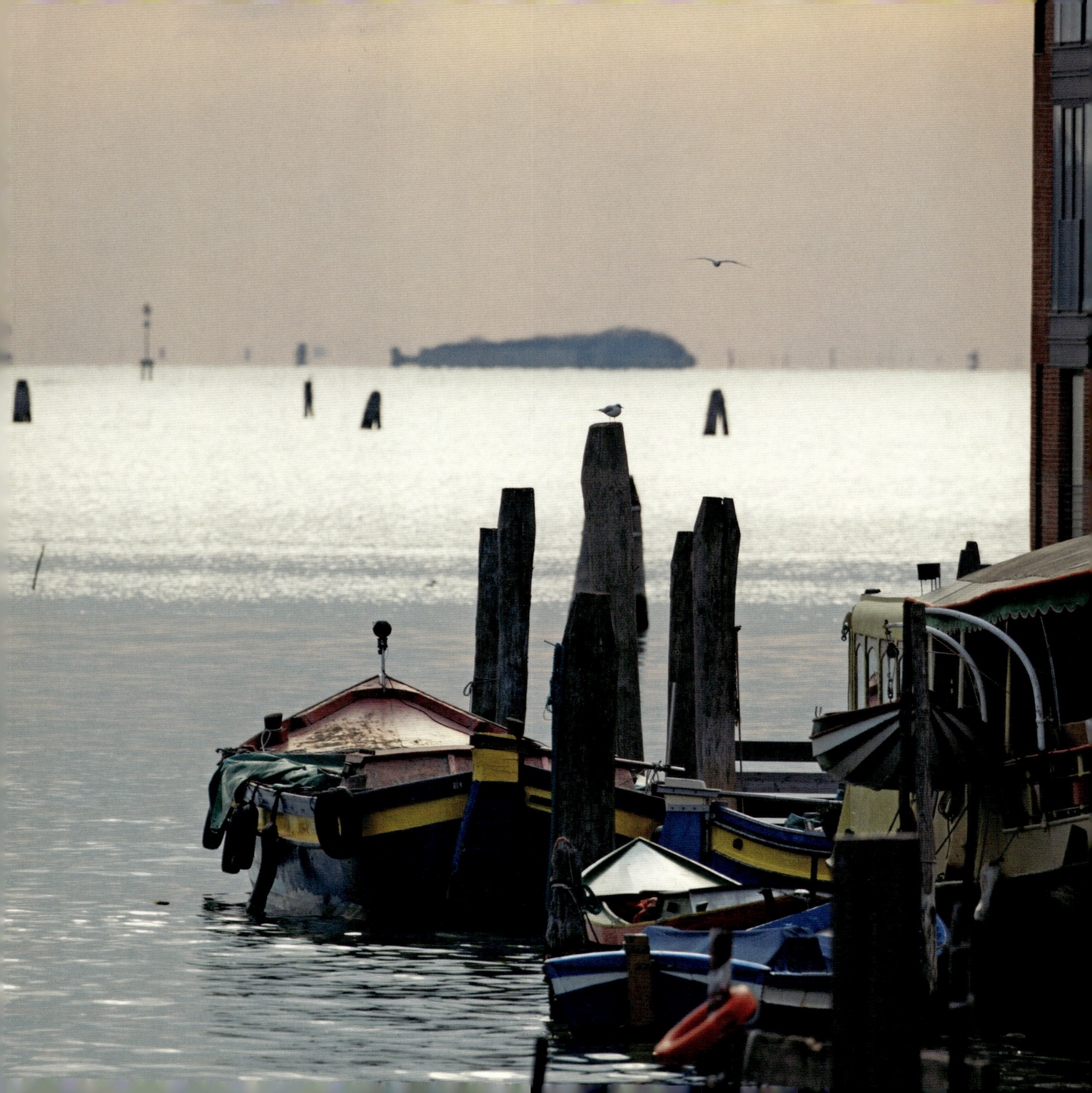

FEBRUARY 13

White sail upon the ocean verge,
Just crimsoned by the setting sun,
Thou hast thy port beyond the surge,
Thy happy homeward course to run
And winged hope, with heart of fire,
To gain the bliss of thy desire.

William Winter, "Arthur"

FEBRUARY 14

Great are the sea, and the heaven;
Yet greater is my heart.

Heinrich Heine, from "The Sea Hath Its Pearls"

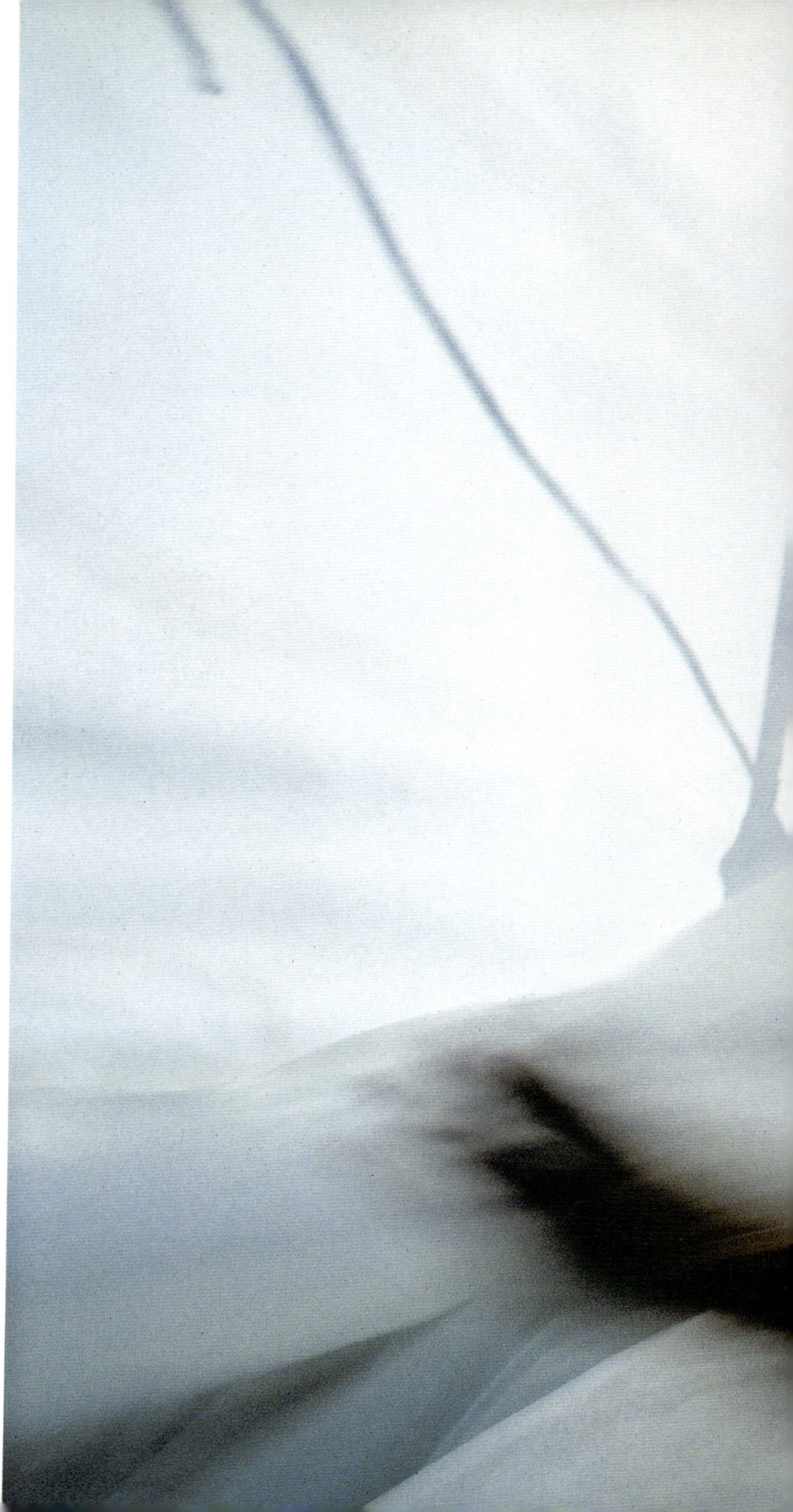

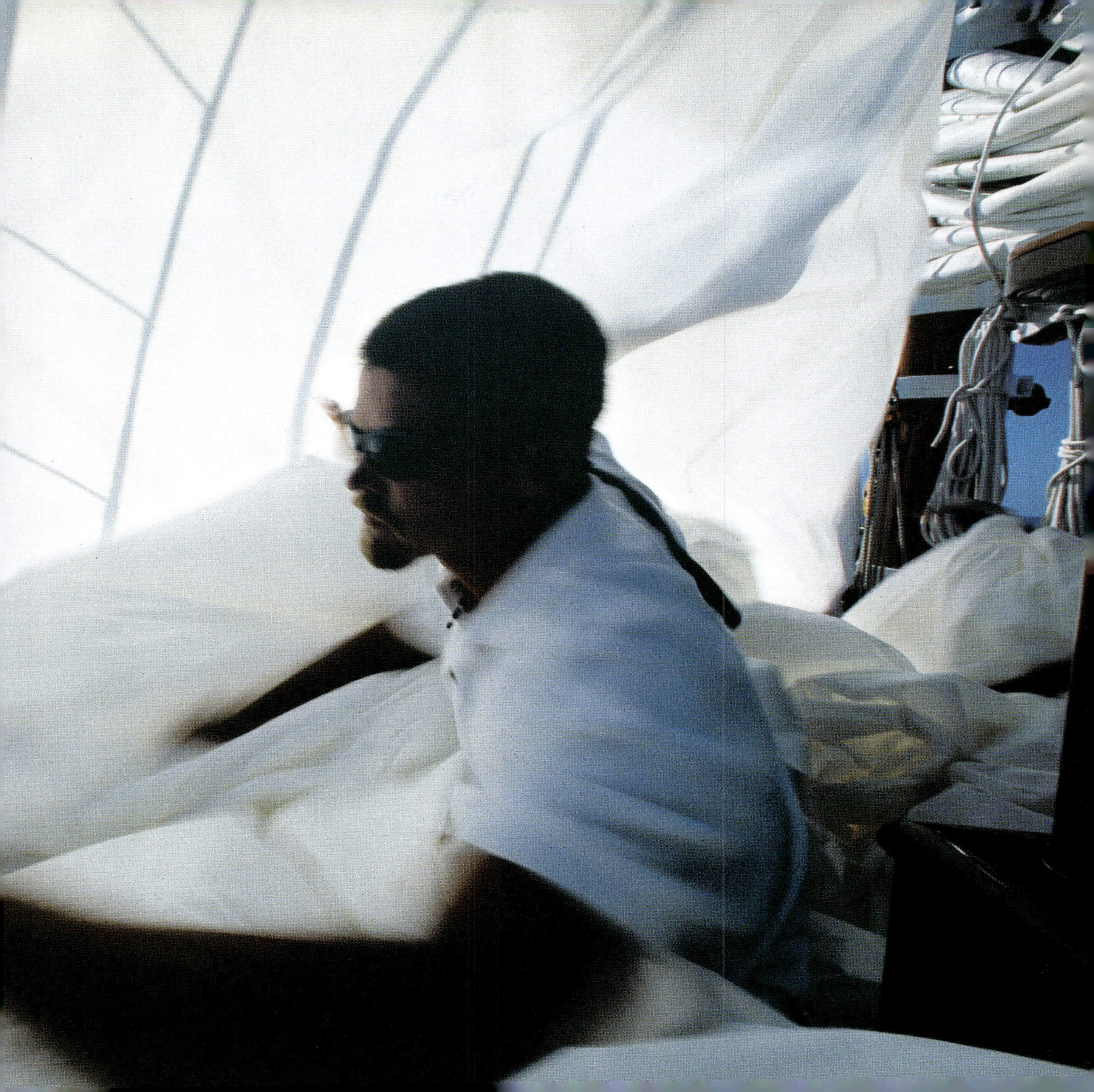

FEBRUARY 15

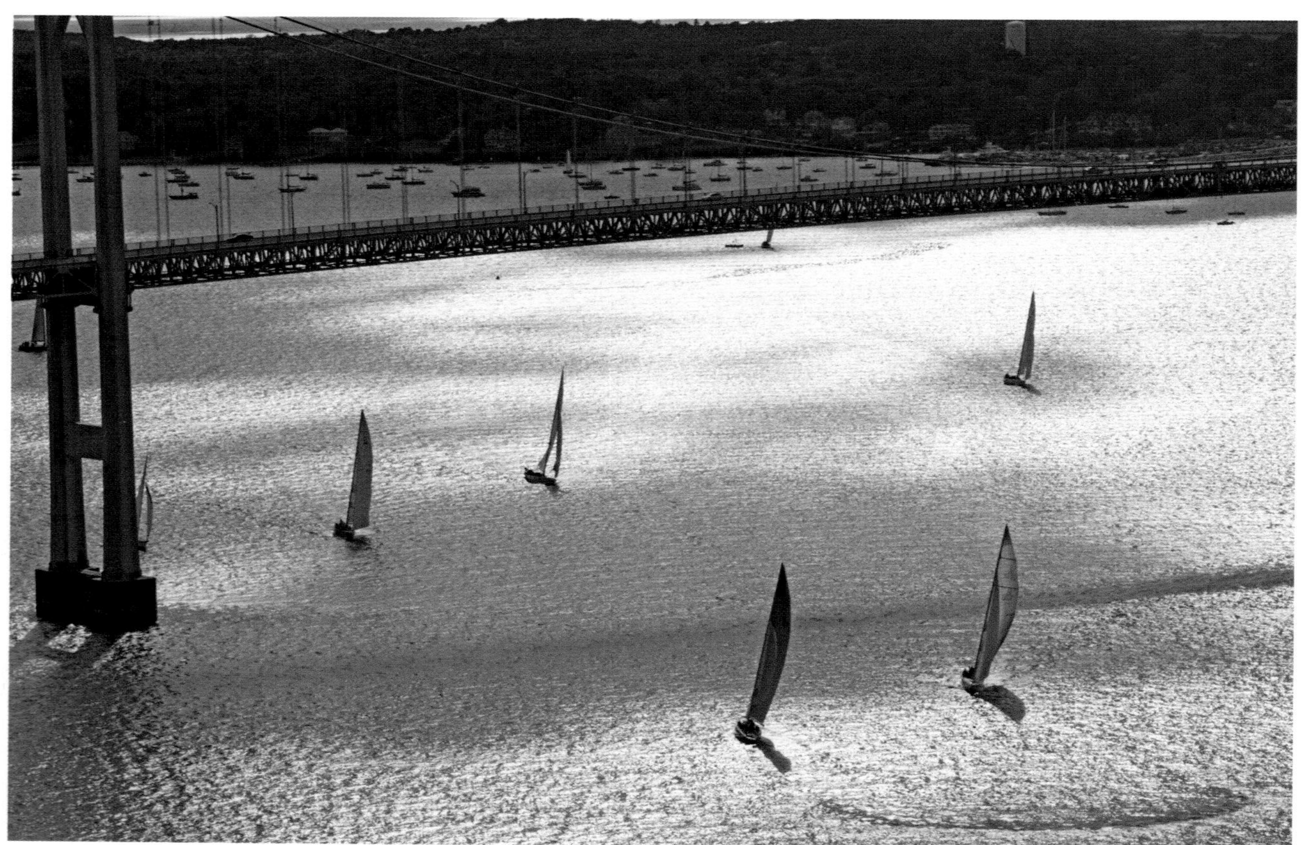

The sea is the same as it has been since before men ever went on it in boats.

Ernest Hemingway

FEBRUARY 16

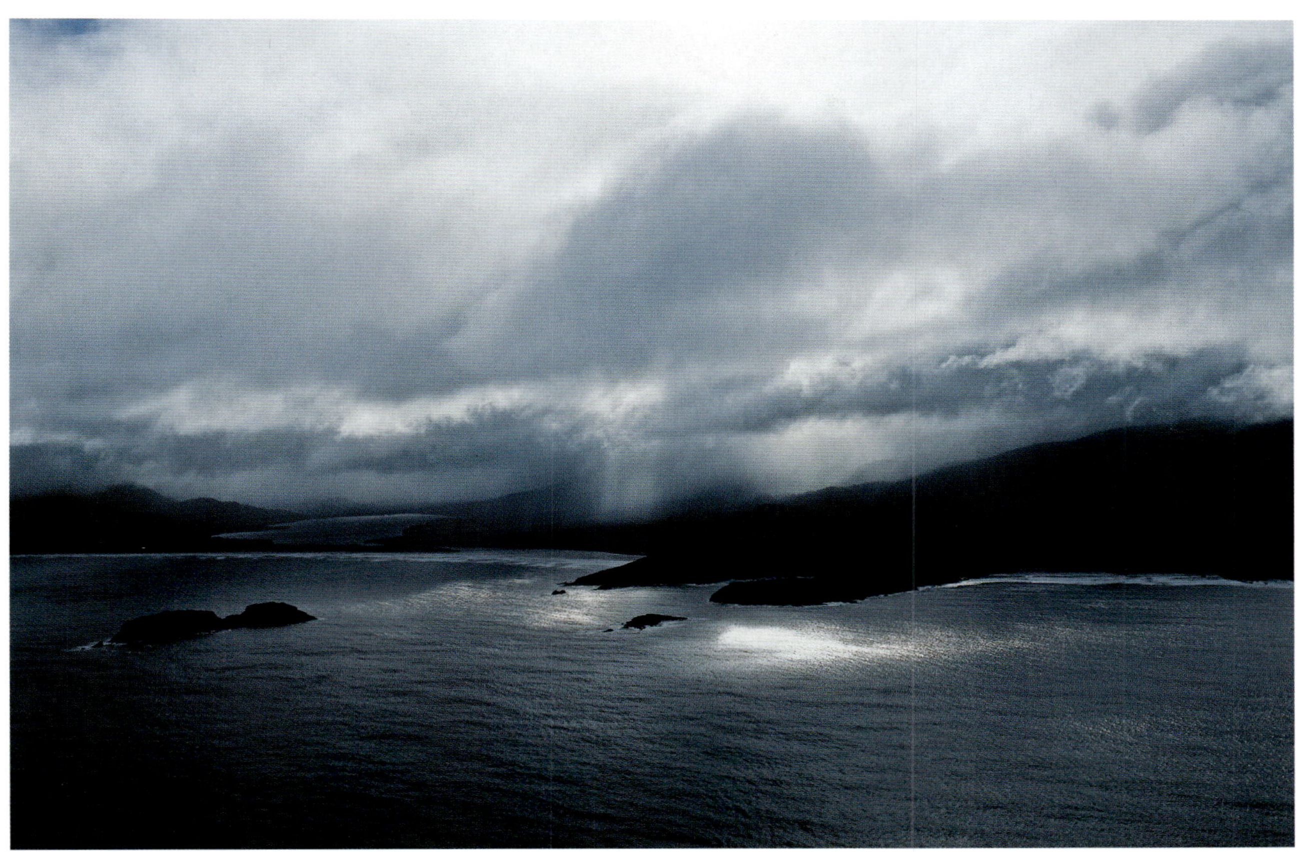

Any fool can carry on, but a wise man knows how to shorten sail in time.

Joseph Conrad, from *The Mirror of the Sea,* 1906

FEBRUARY 17

Since I grew tired of the chase
And search, I learned to find;
And since the wind blows in my face,
I sail with every wind.

Friedrich Nietzsche

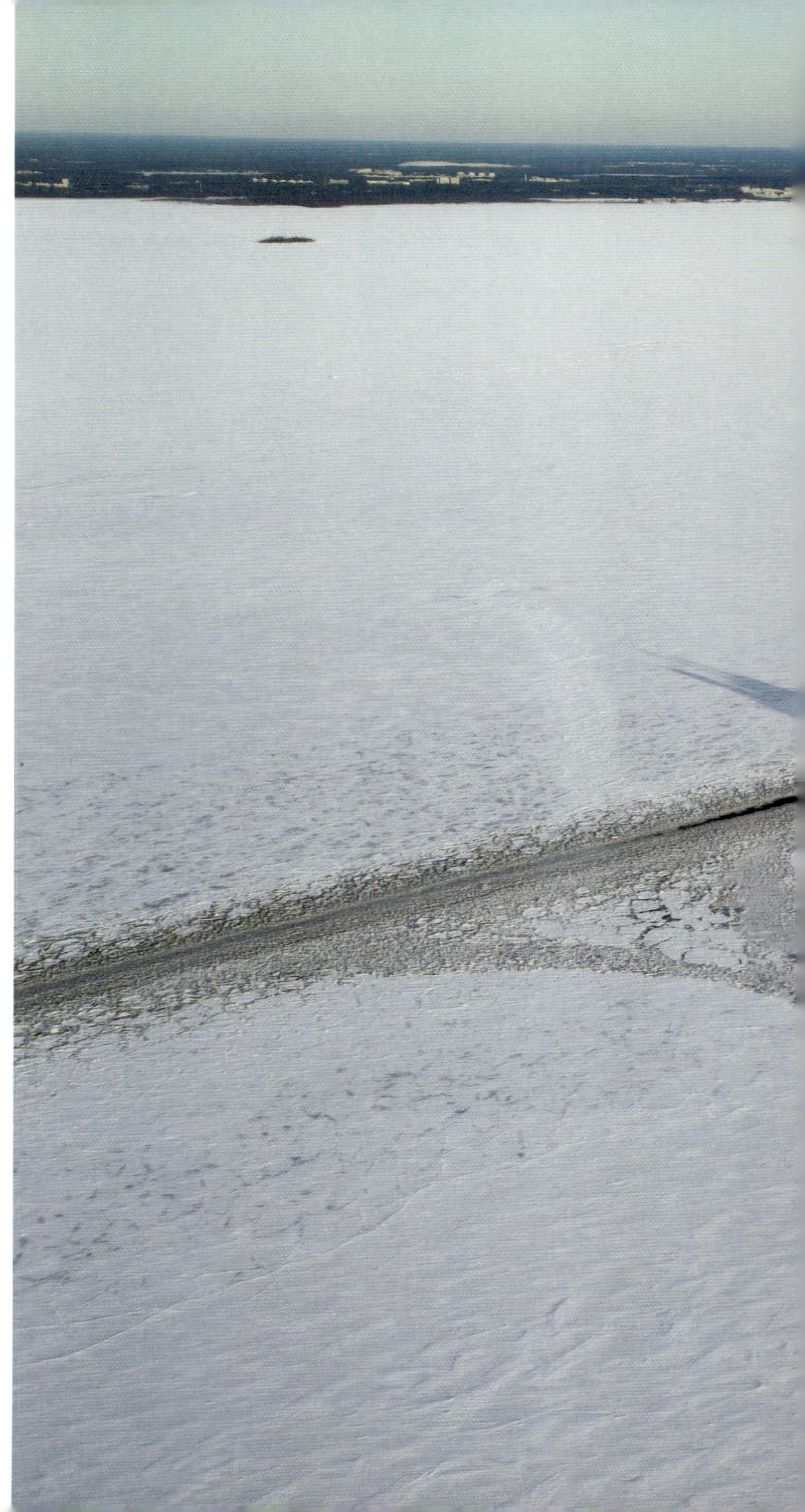

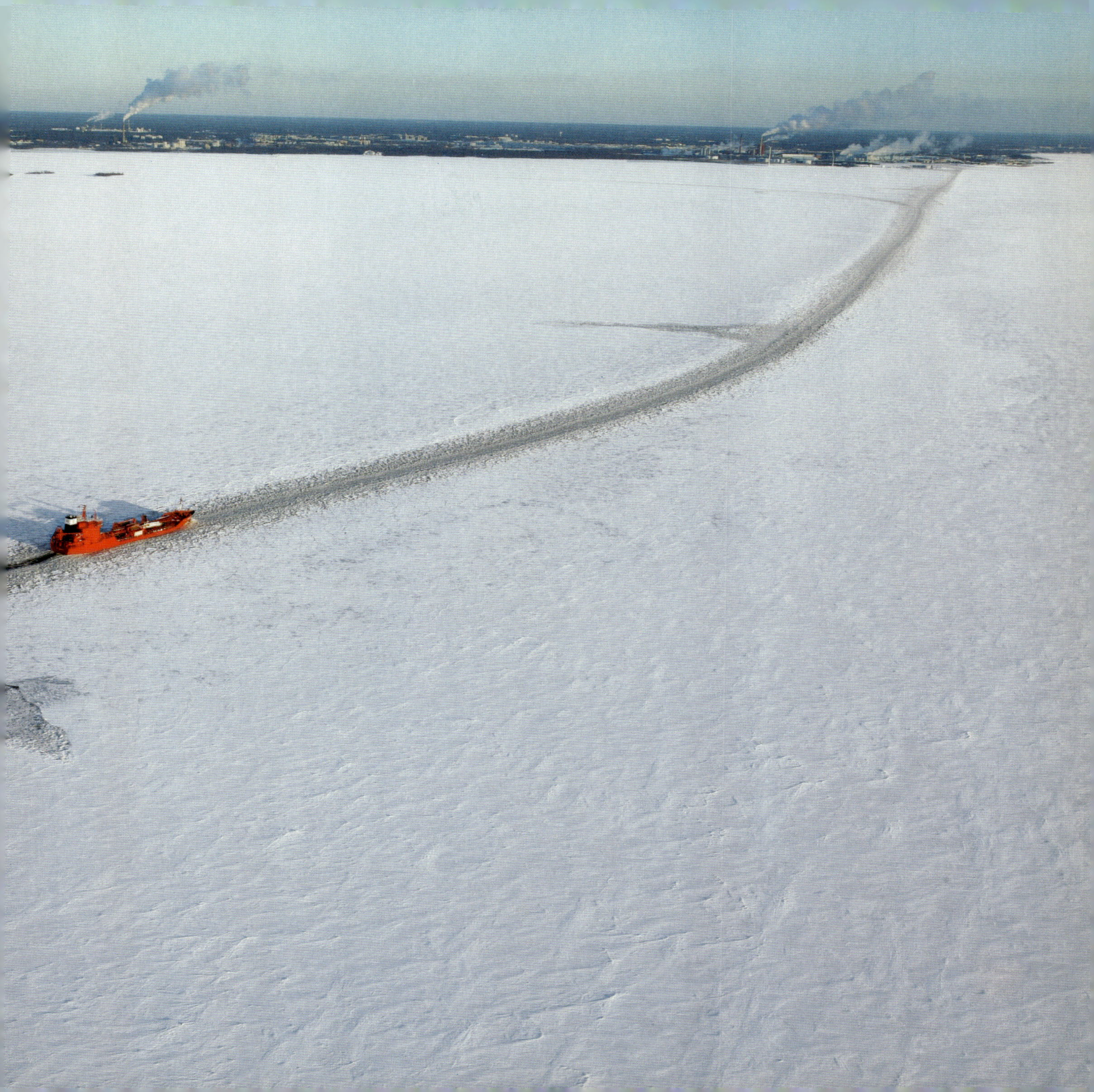

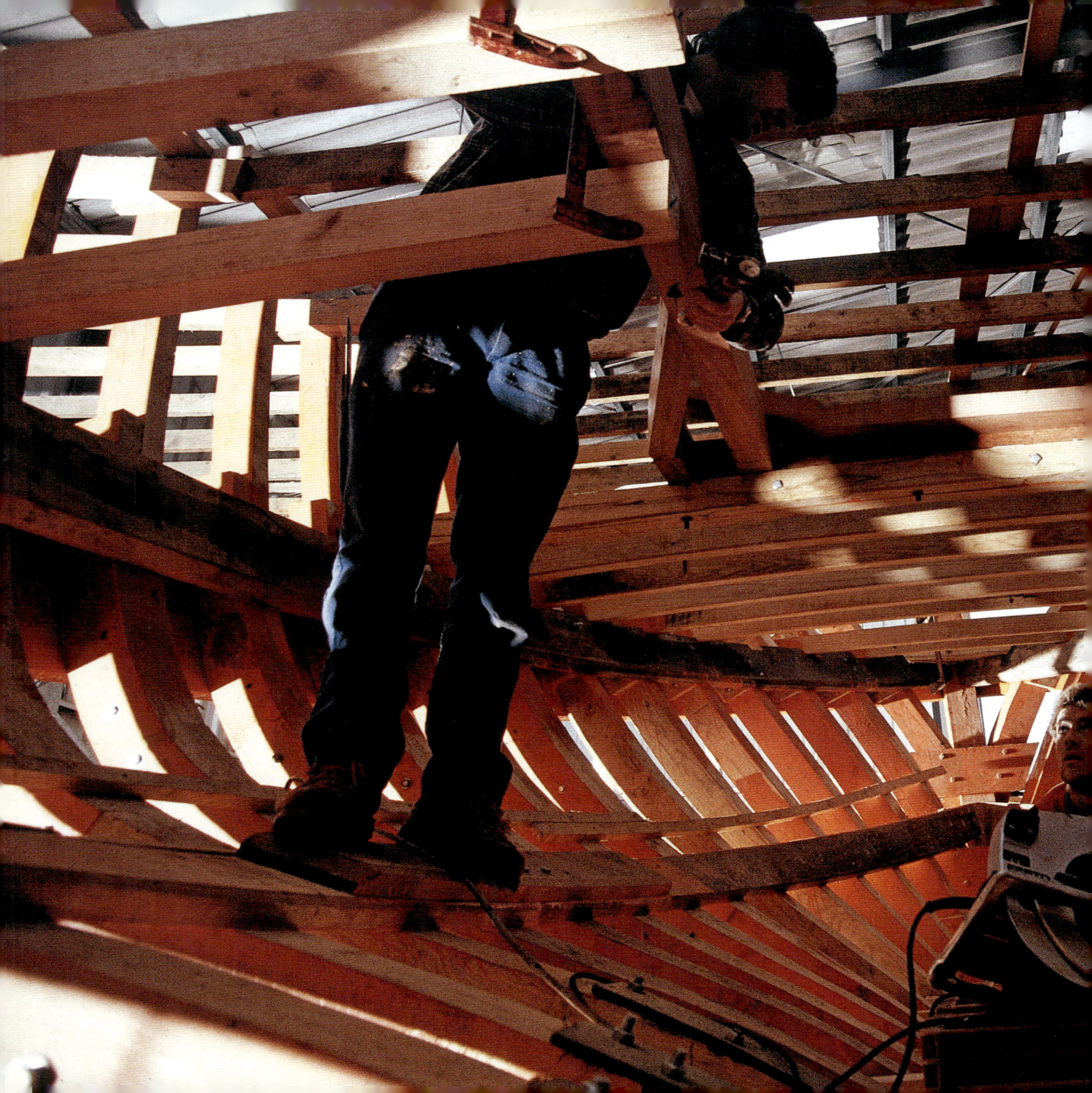

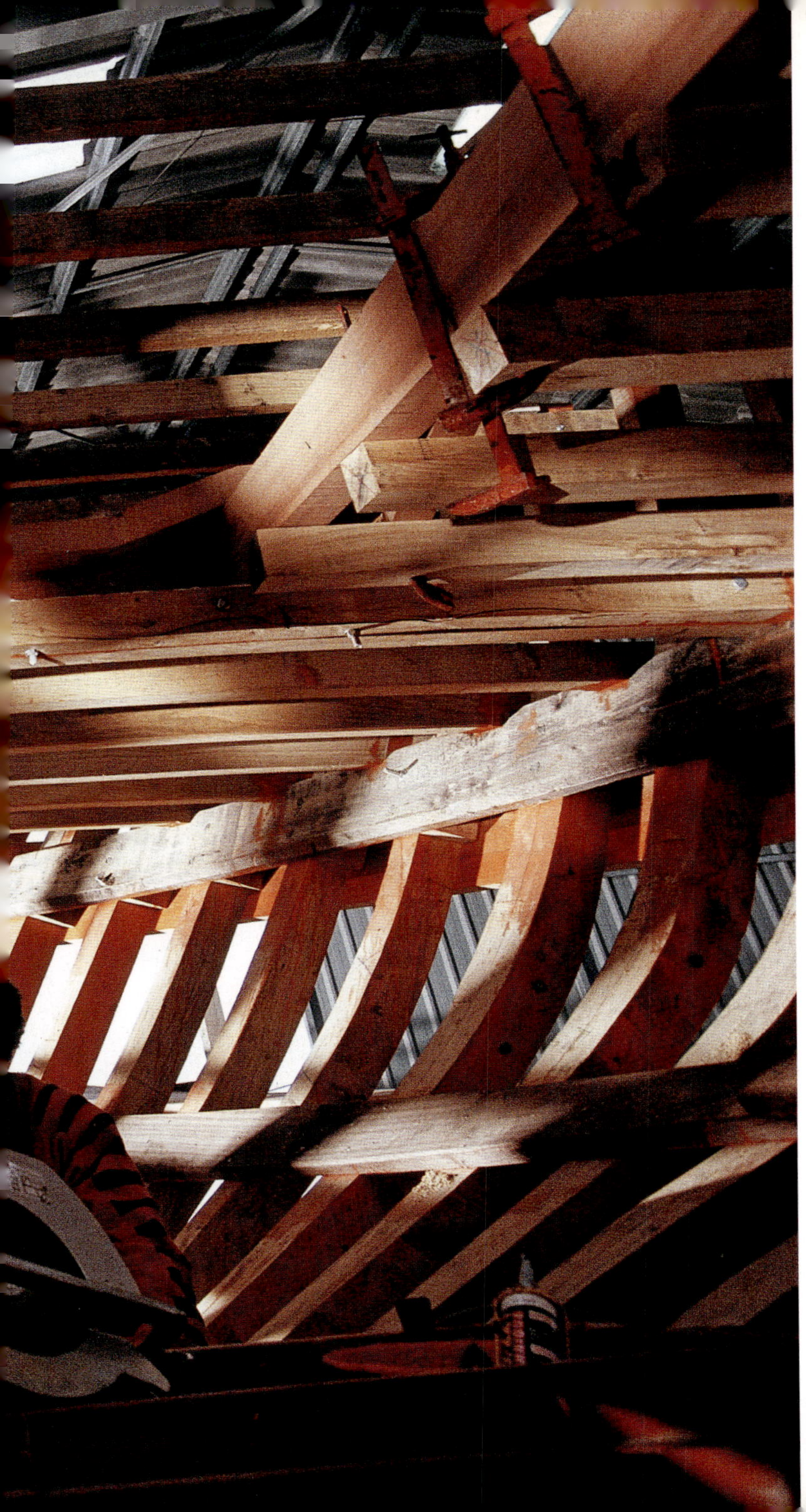

FEBRUARY 18

Light boats sail swift, though
greater hulks draw deep.

William Shakespeare,
from *Troilus and Cressida,* Act II, Scene 3

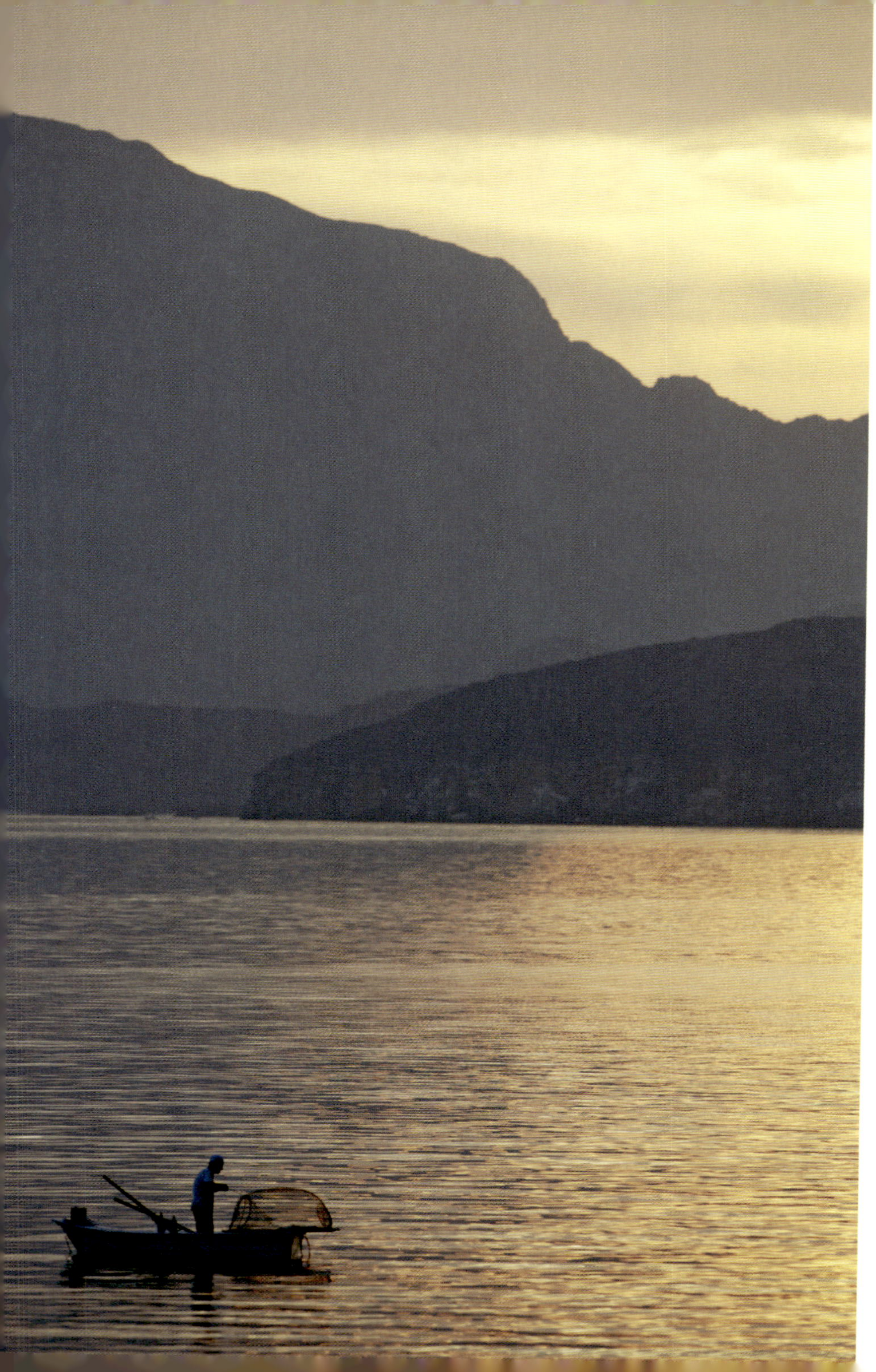

FEBRUARY 19

Anyone can hold the helm
when the sea is calm.

Publilius Syrus

FEBRUARY 20

Our crooked anchors
from the prow we cast.

Virgil, from *The Aeneid*

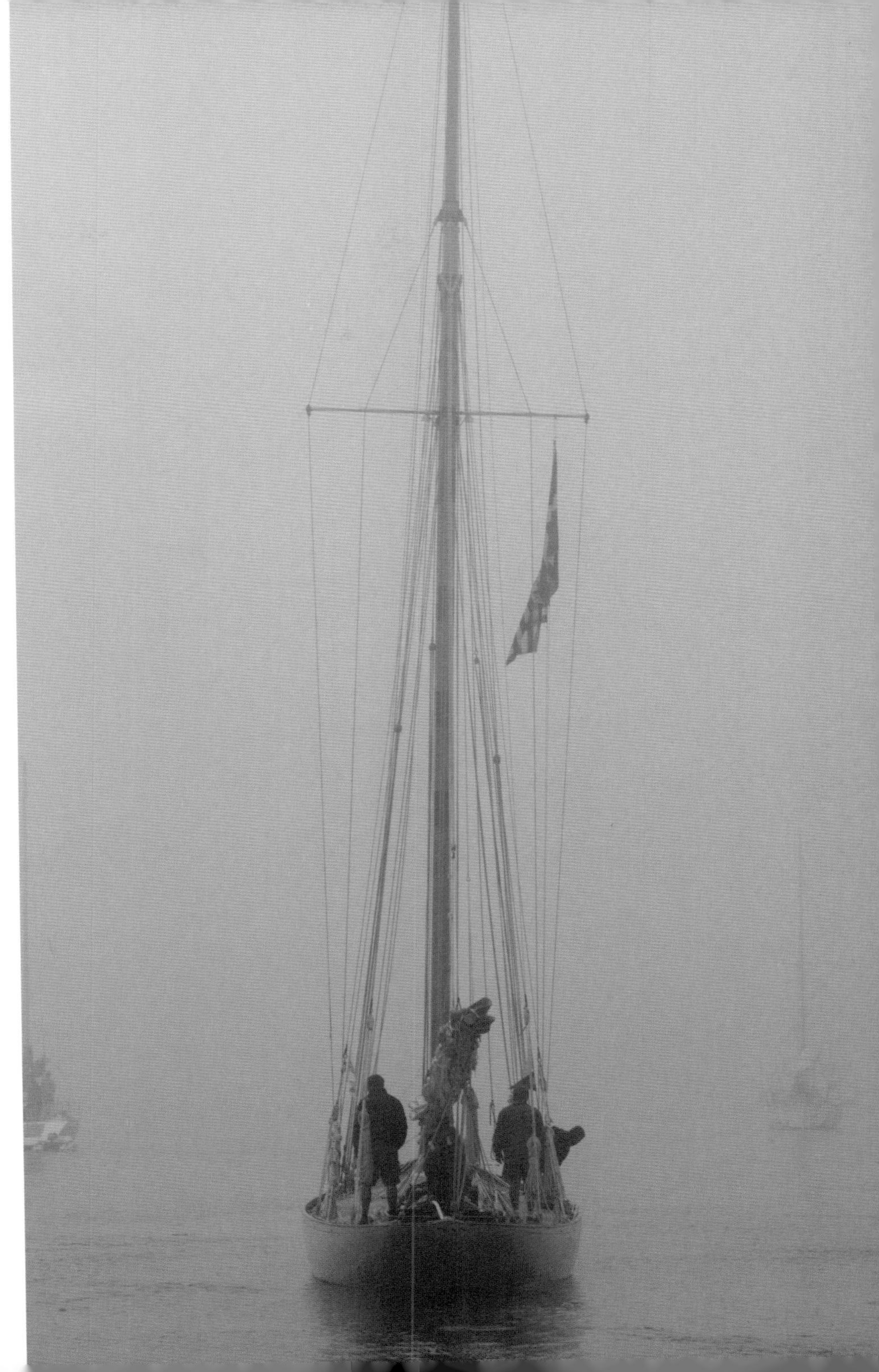

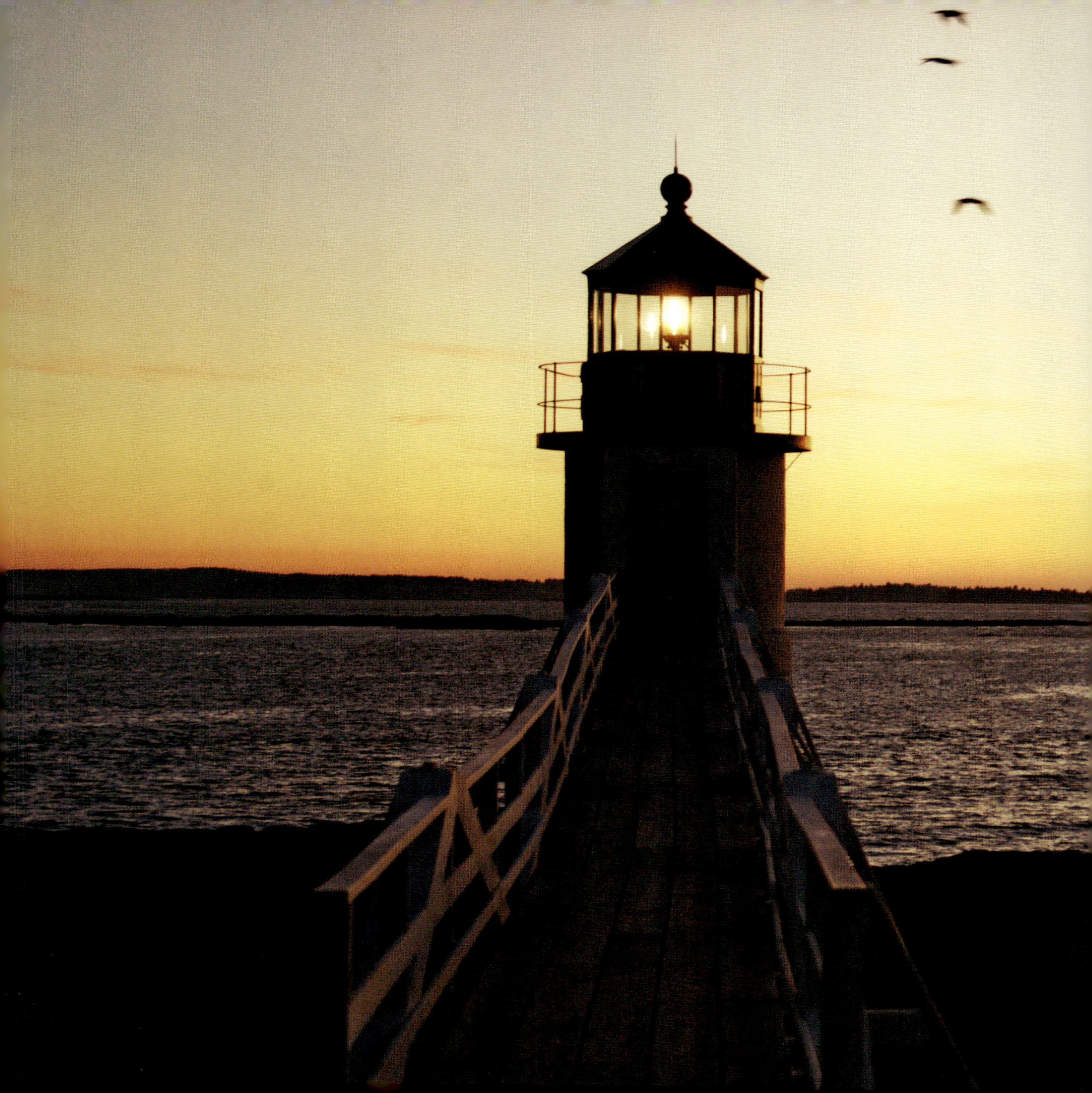

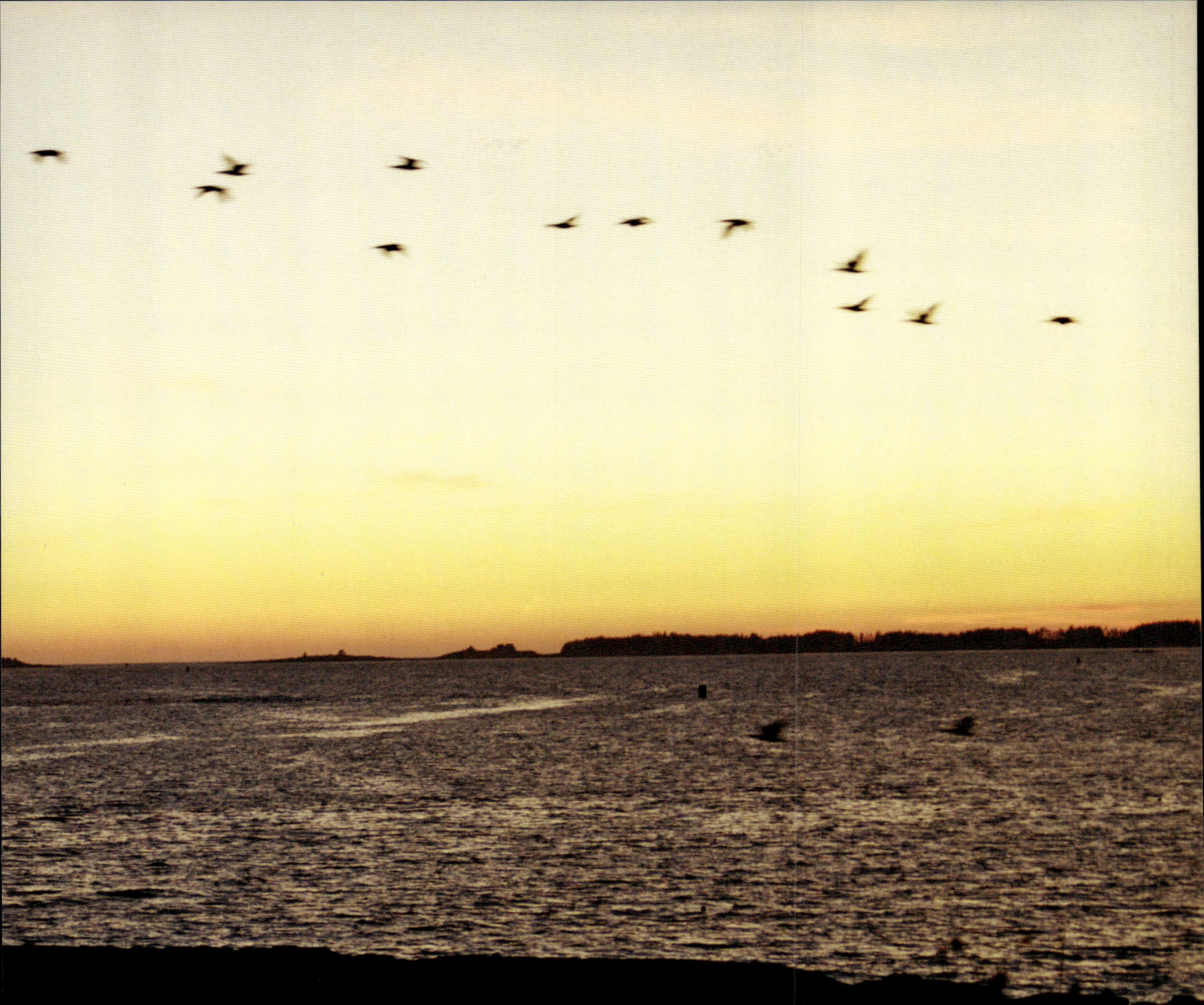

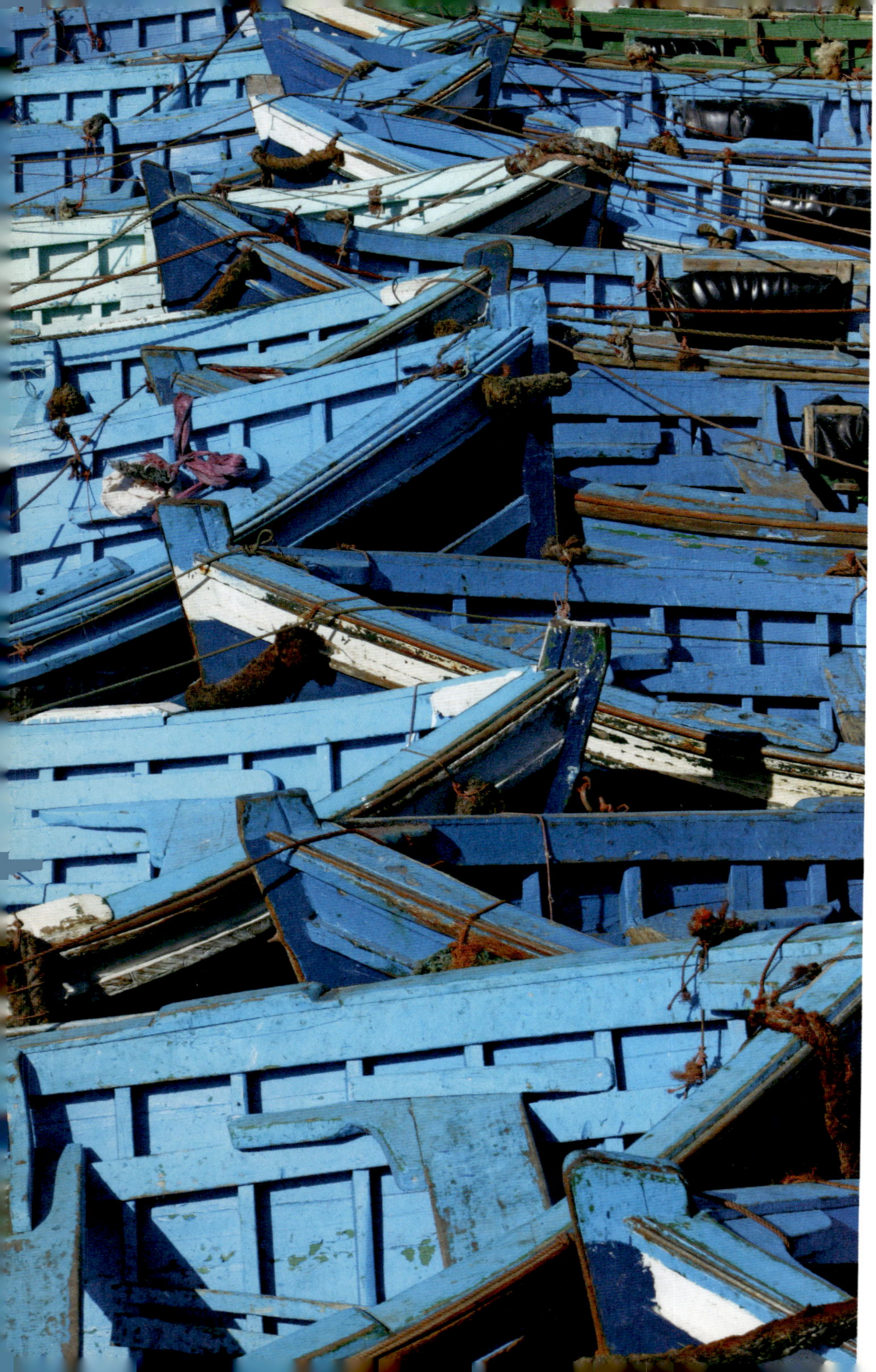

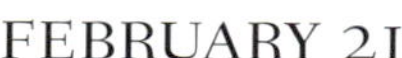

FEBRUARY 21

Red skies at night,
sailors delight.
Red skies at morning,
sailors take warning.

Traditional wisdom

FEBRUARY 22

When your money's gone
It's the same old song,
Get up Jack! John sit down!

From "Jolly Roving Tar,"
a traditional chantey

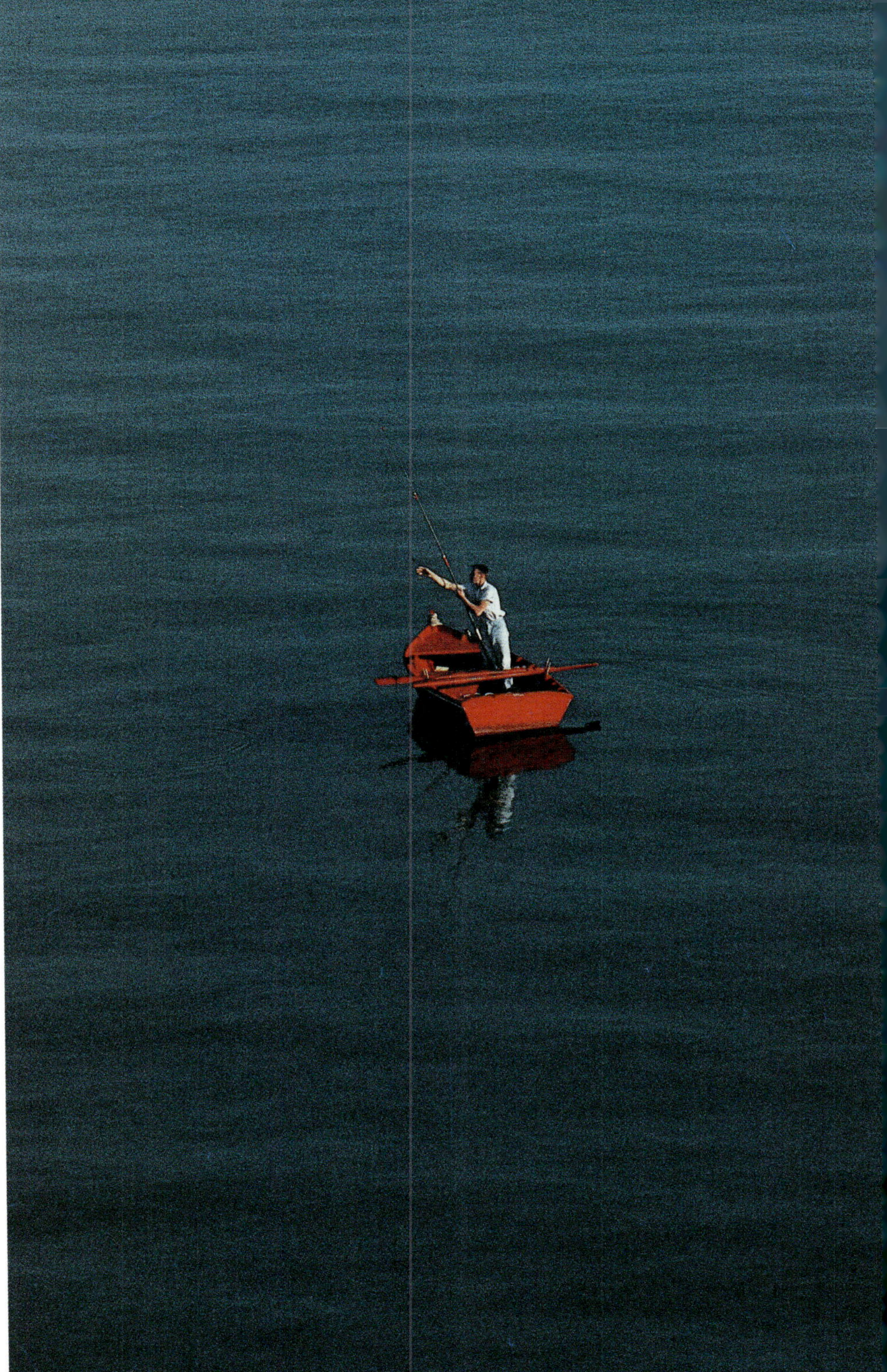

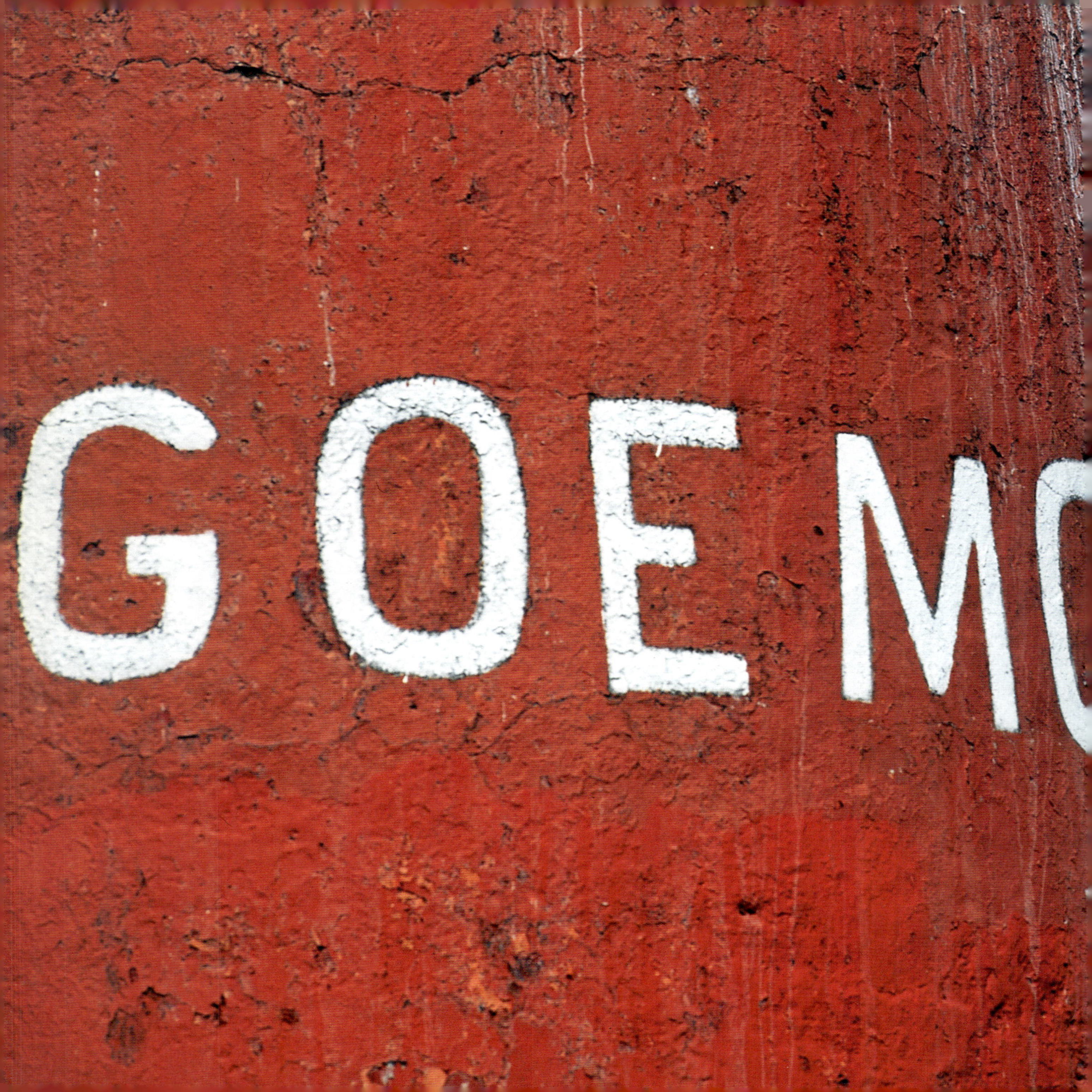
GOEM

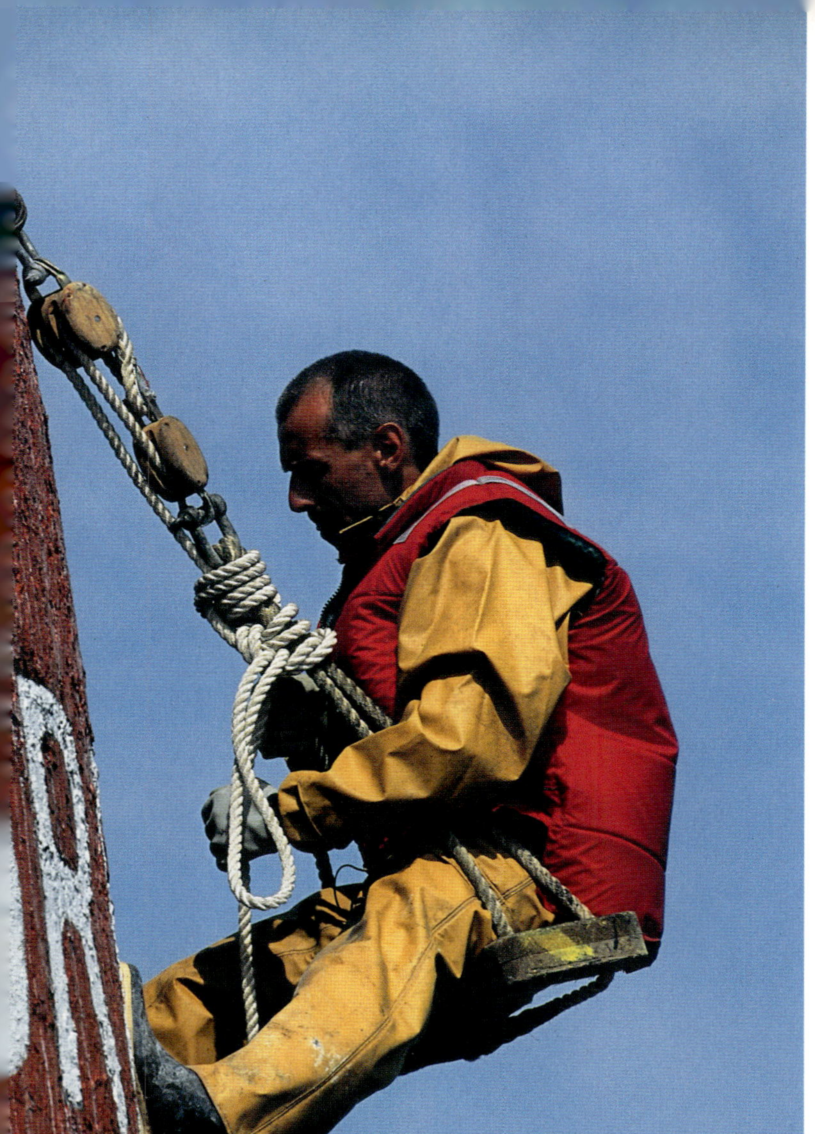

FEBRUARY 23

If a man is to be obsessed by something,
I suppose a boat is as good as anything,
perhaps a bit better than most.

E. B. White

FEBRUARY 24

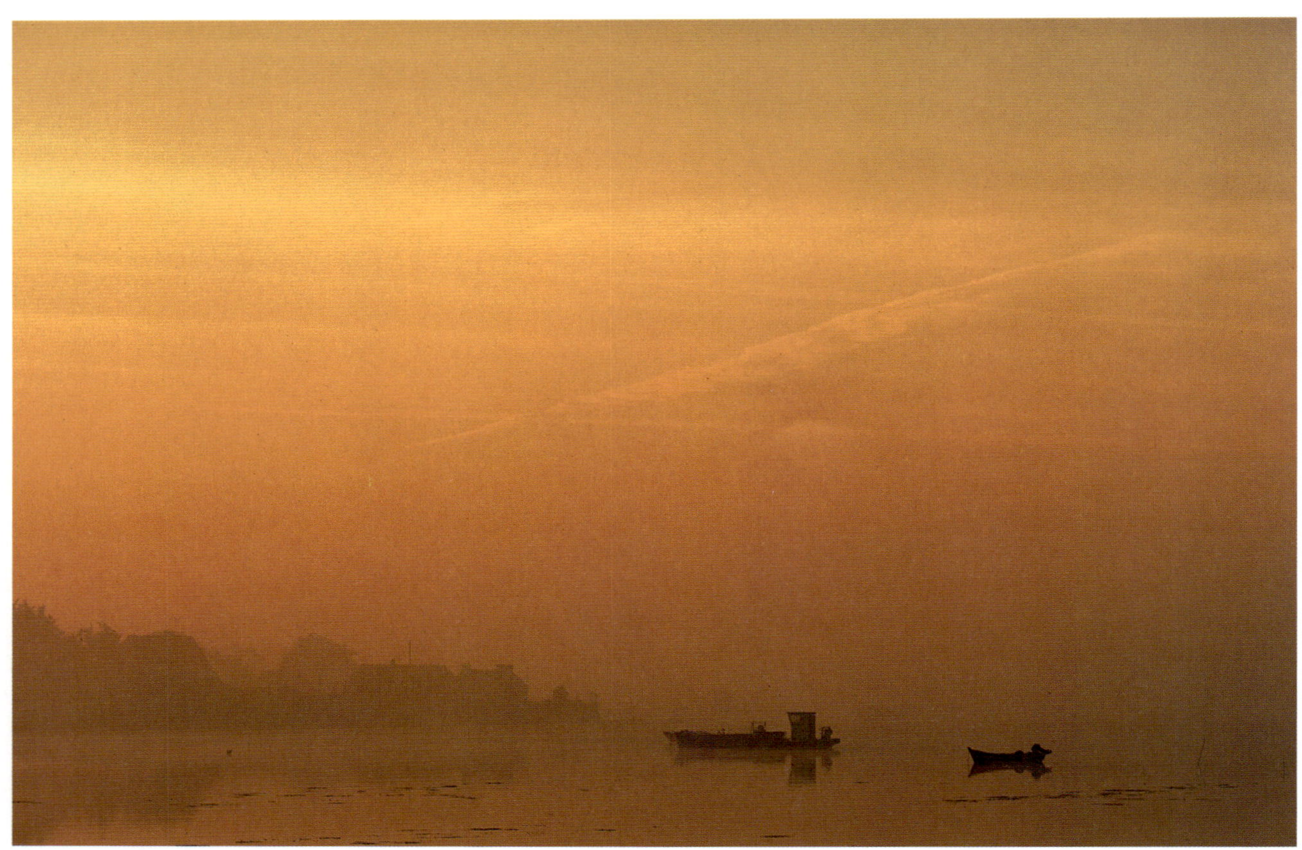

On life's vast ocean diversely we sail,
Reason the card, but passion is the gale.

Alexander Pope, from "Essay on Man," Epistle II, 1734

FEBRUARY 25

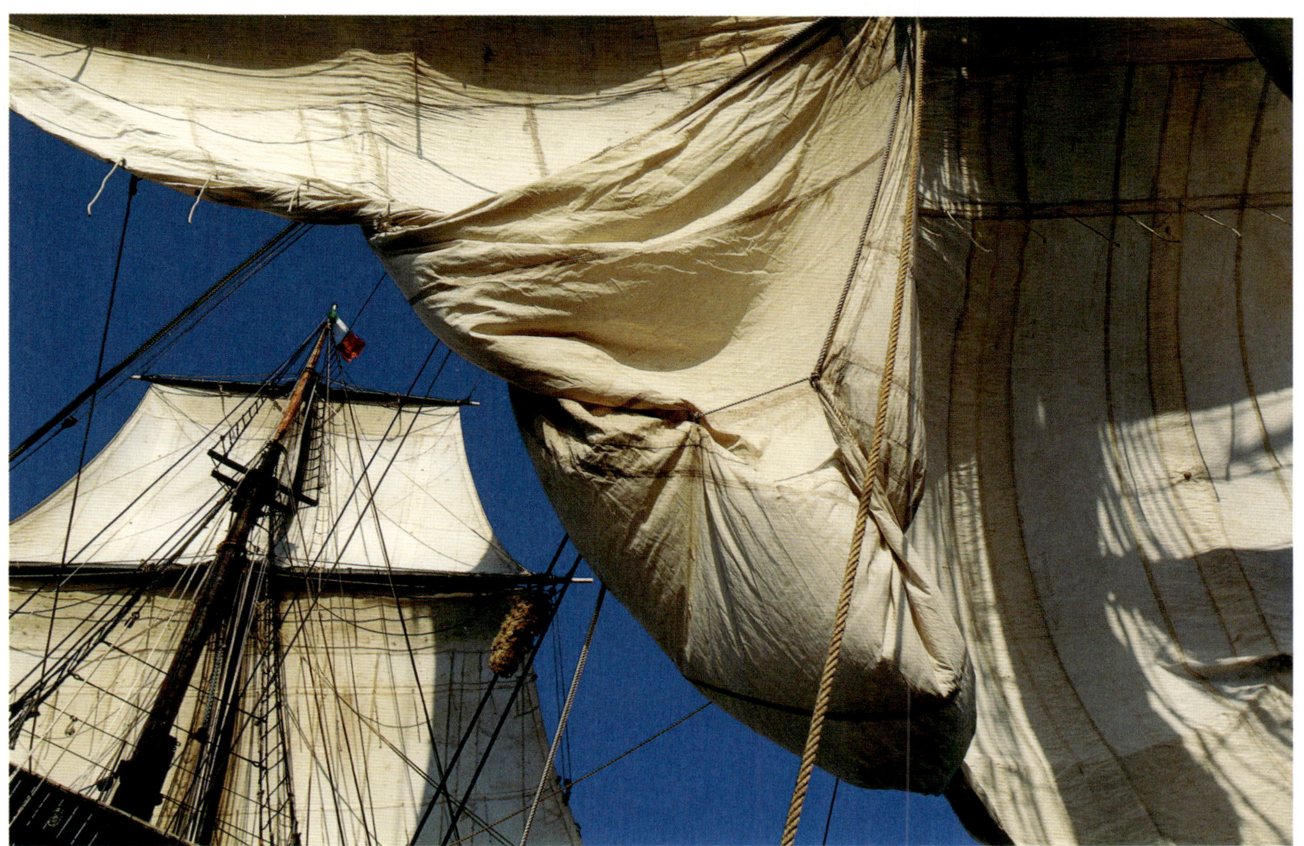

There is, one knows not what sweet mystery about this sea,
whose gently awful stirrings seem to speak of some hidden soul beneath.

Herman Melville, from *Moby-Dick,* 1851

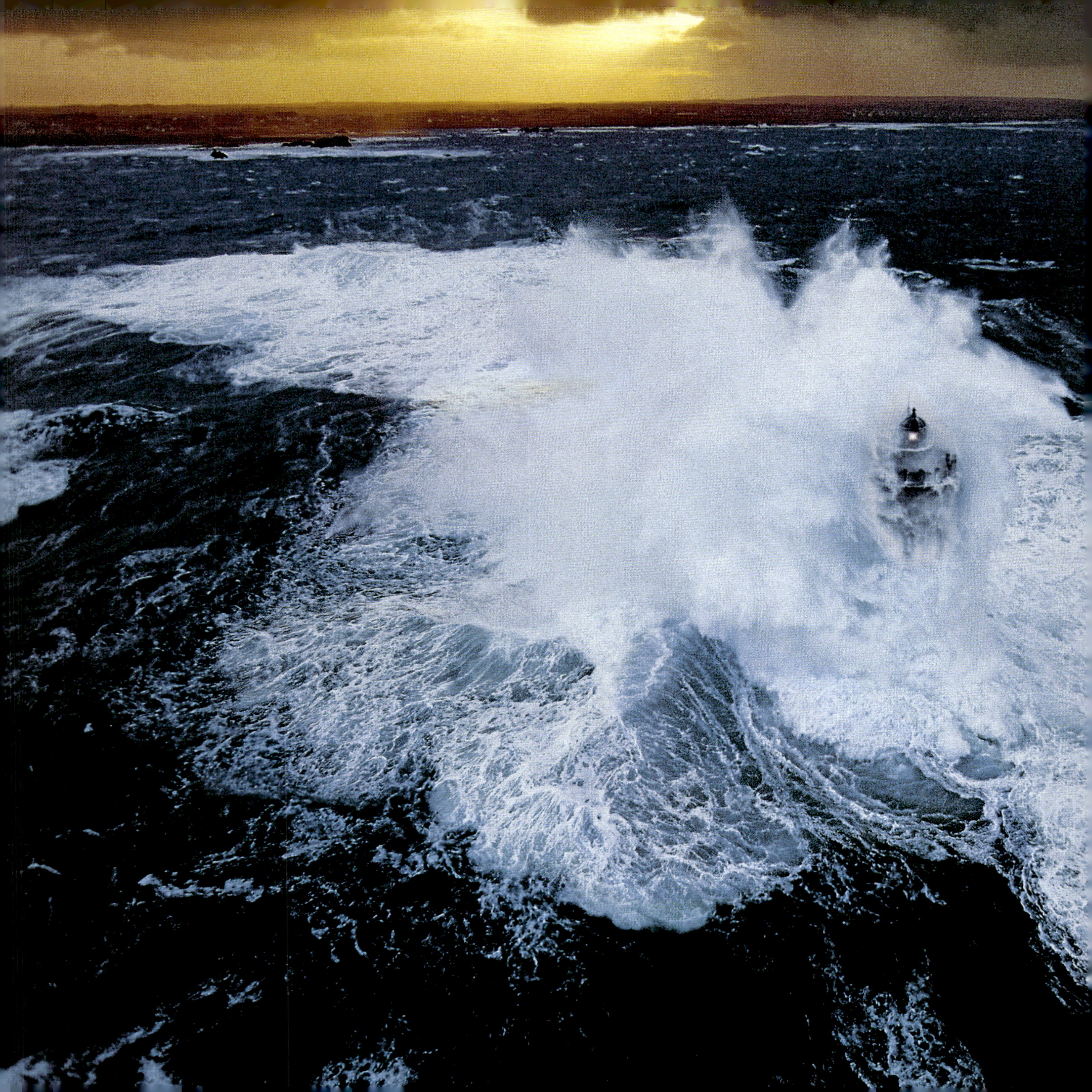

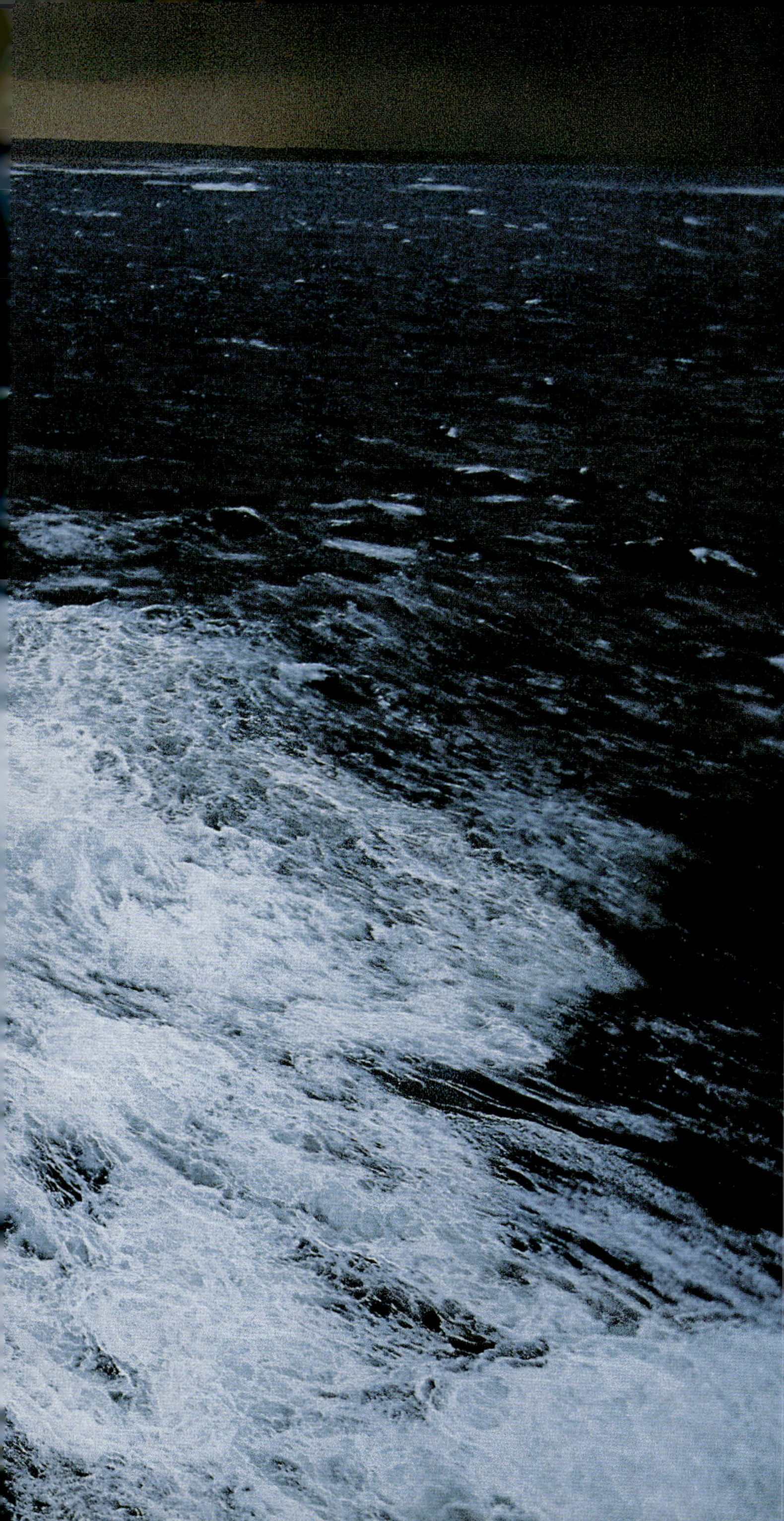

FEBRUARY 26

Meanwhile upon the watery plain there rises
A mountain billow with a mighty crest
Of foam, that shoreward rolls, and, as it breaks,
Before our eyes vomits a furious monster.

Jean Racine, from *Phaedra,*
Act V, Scene 4, 1677

FEBRUARY 27

If rightly made, a boat would be a sort
of amphibious animal, a creature of two
elements, related by one half its structure to
some swift and shapely fish, and by the other
to some strong-winged and graceful bird.

Henry David Thoreau,
from *A Week on the Concord and Merrimack Rivers,*
1849

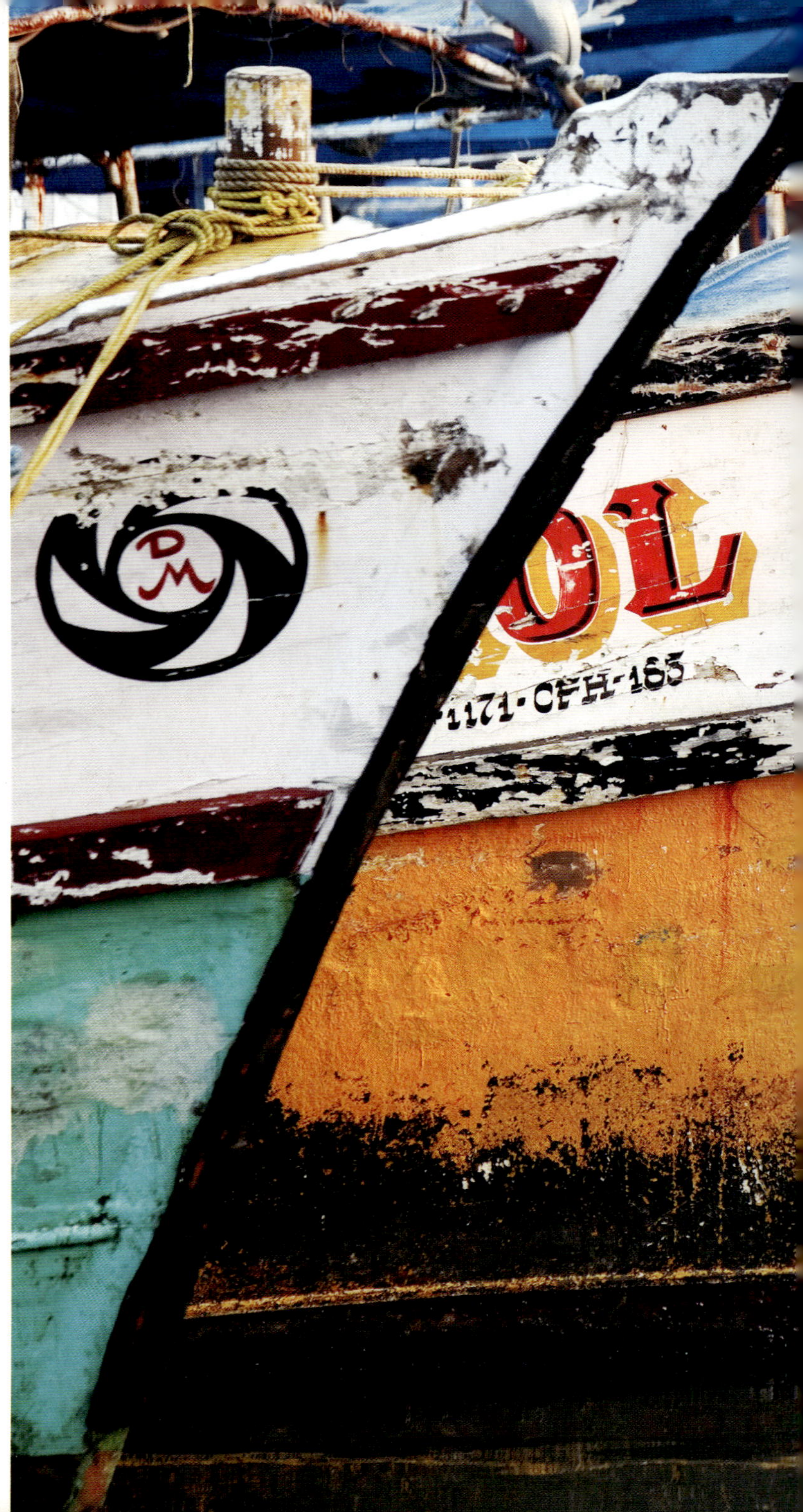

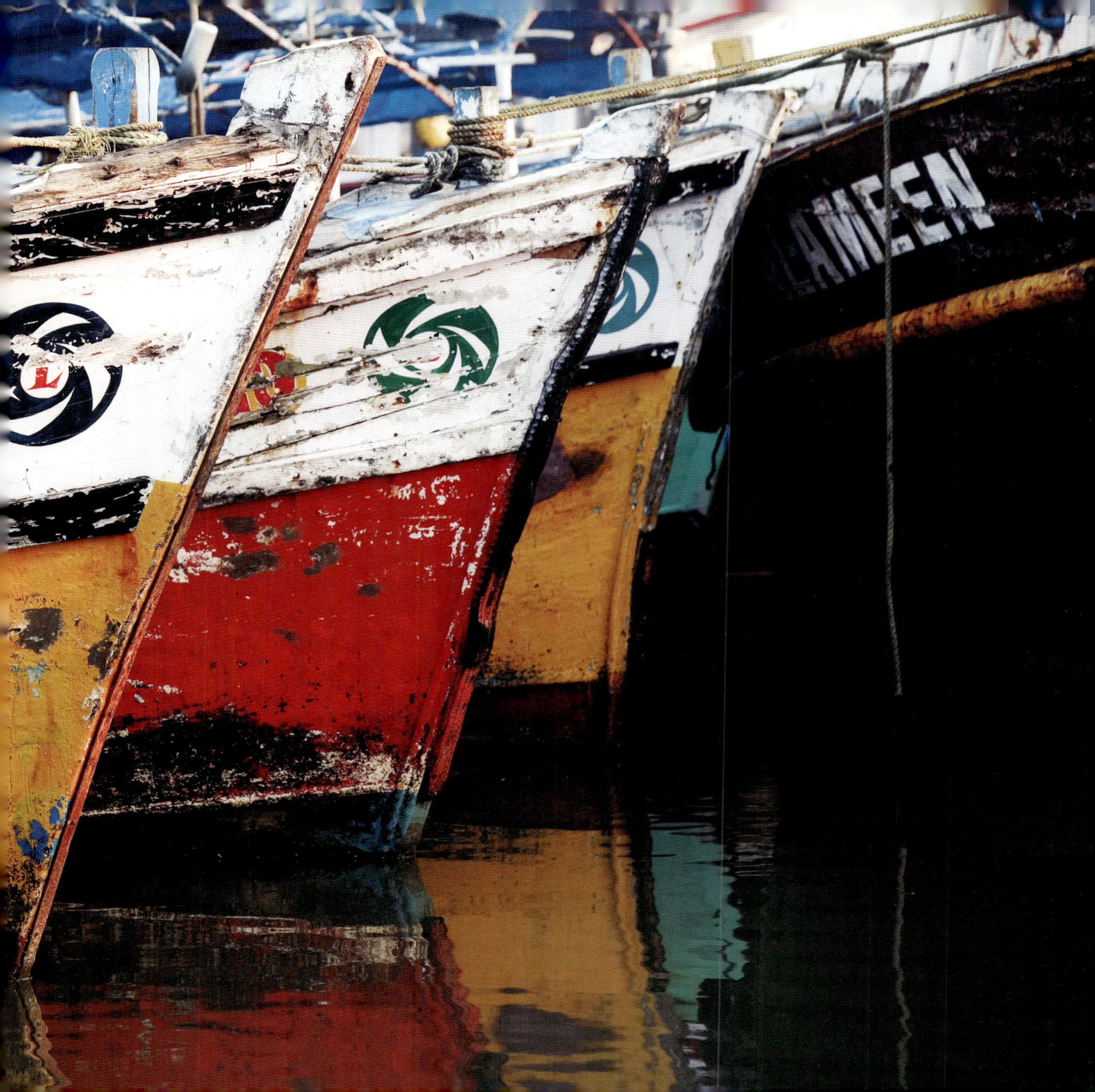
AMEEN

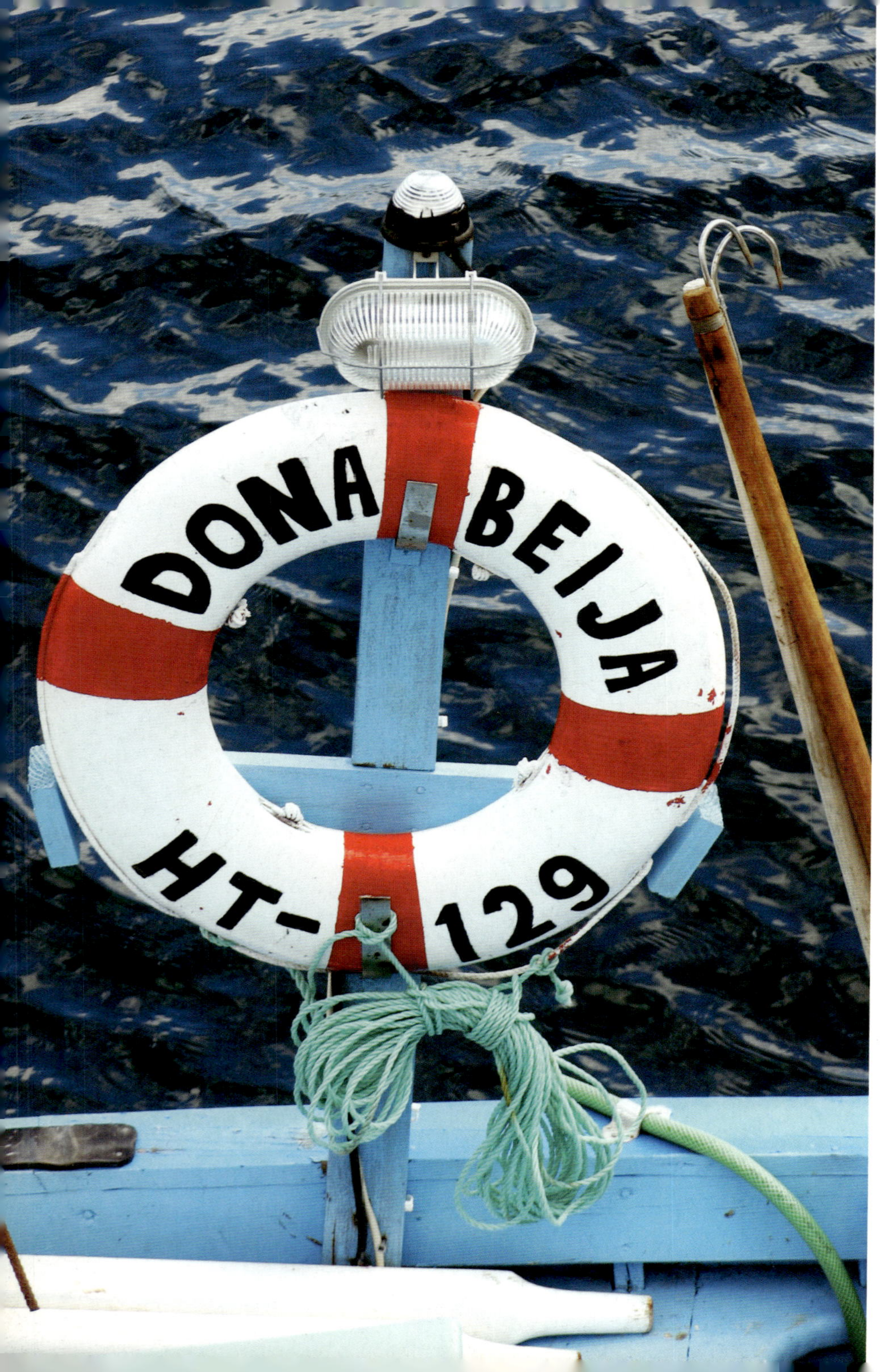

FEBRUARY 28

We would not take a sea voyage
for the sole pleasure of seeing
without hope of ever telling.

Blaise Pascal

MARCH 1

They change their climate,
not their soul,
who rush across the sea.

Horace

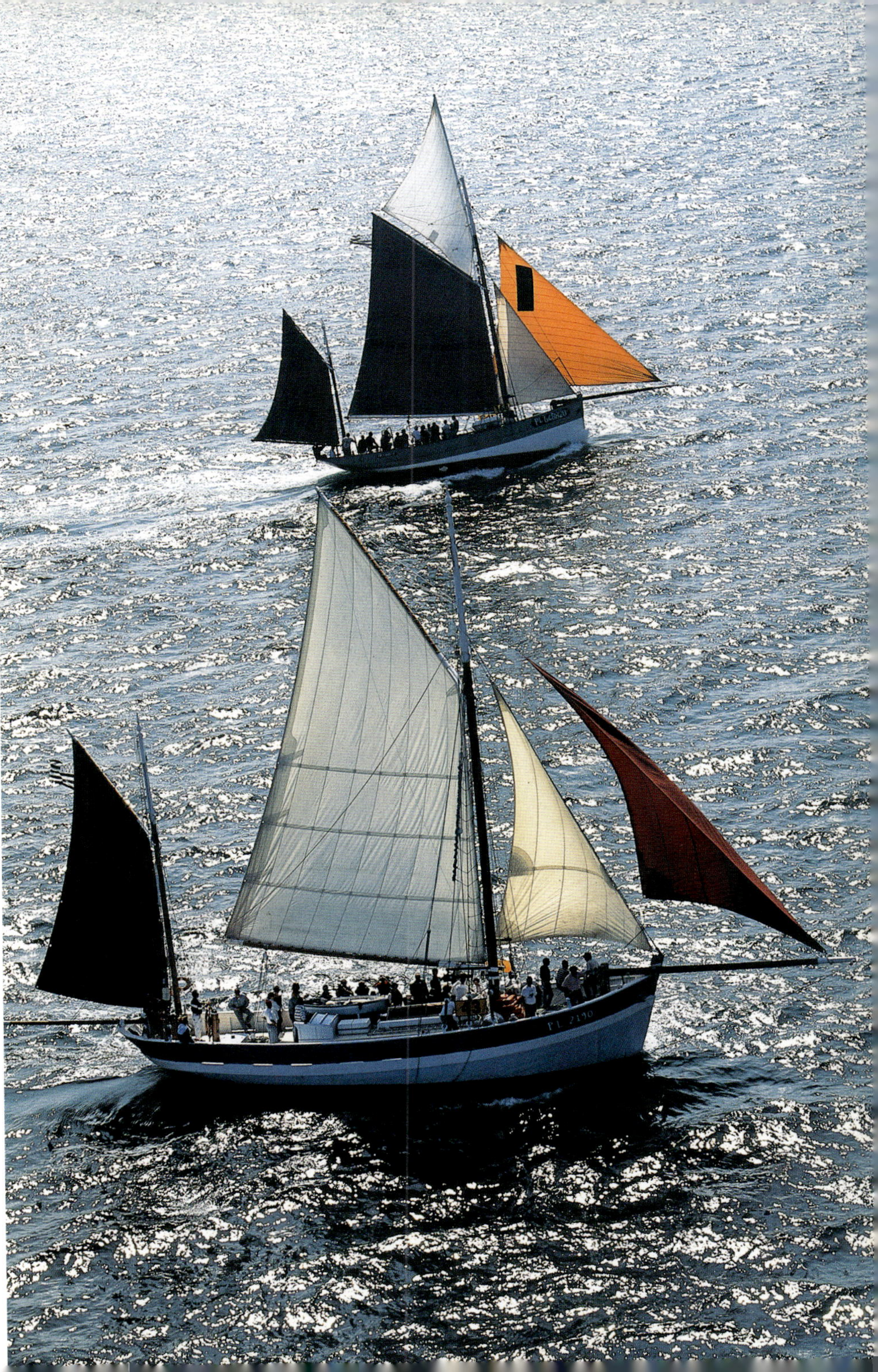

MARCH 2

Today I will let the old boat stand
Where the sweep of the harbor tide comes in
To the pulse of a far, deep-steady sway.
And I will rest and dream and sit on the deck
Watching the world go by.

Carl Sandburg,
from "Waiting," *Chicago Poems,* 1916

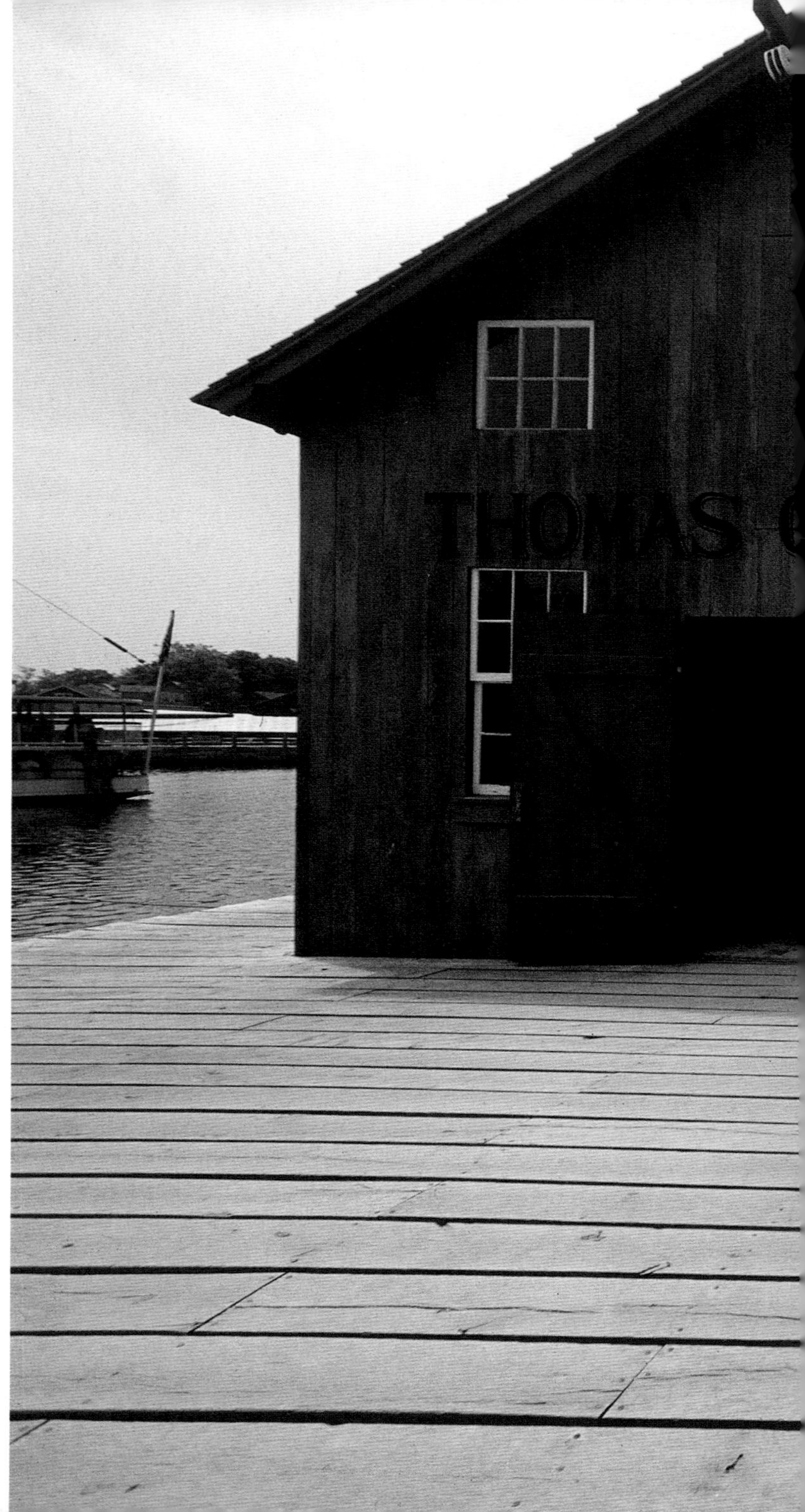

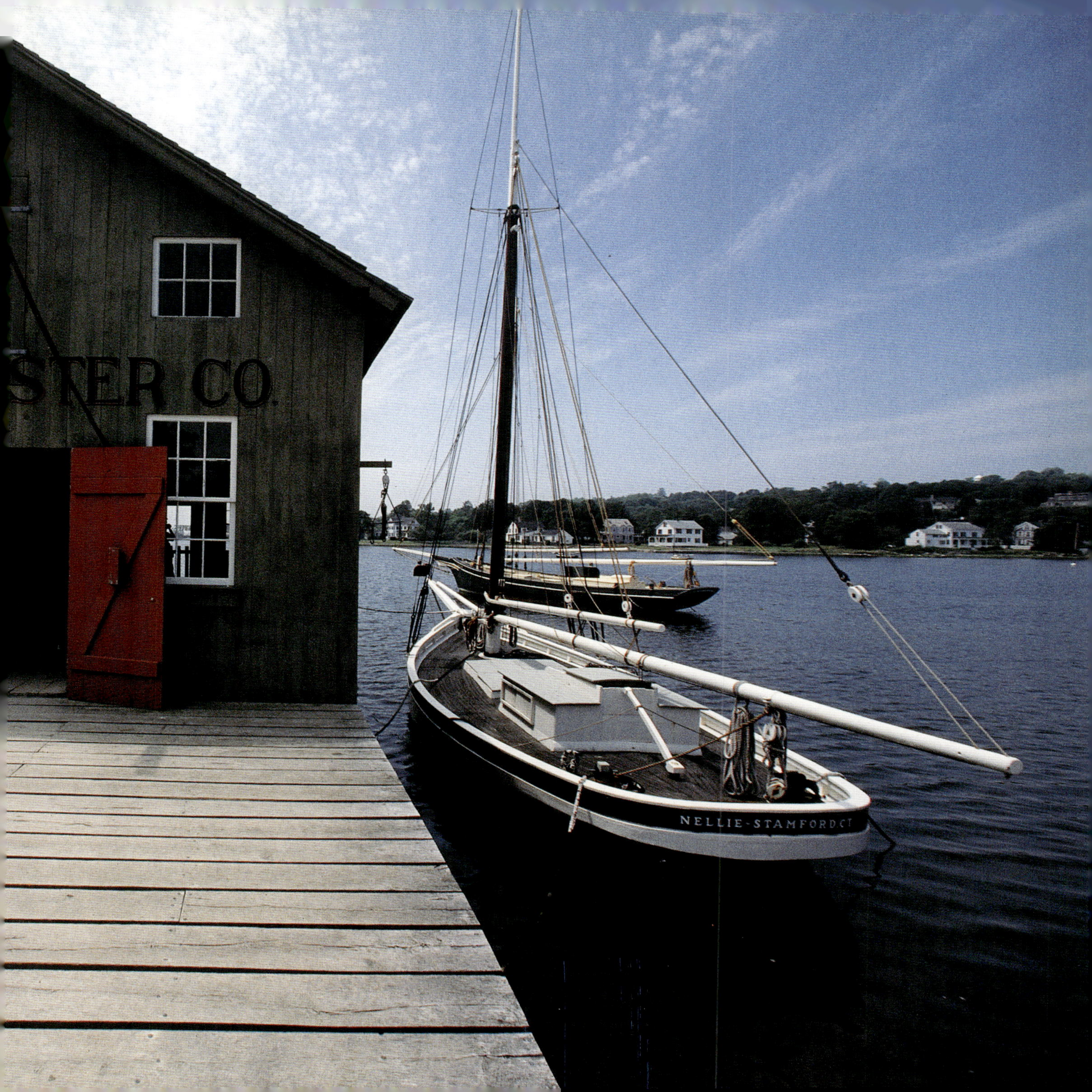
STER CO.
NELLIE-STAMFORD.CT

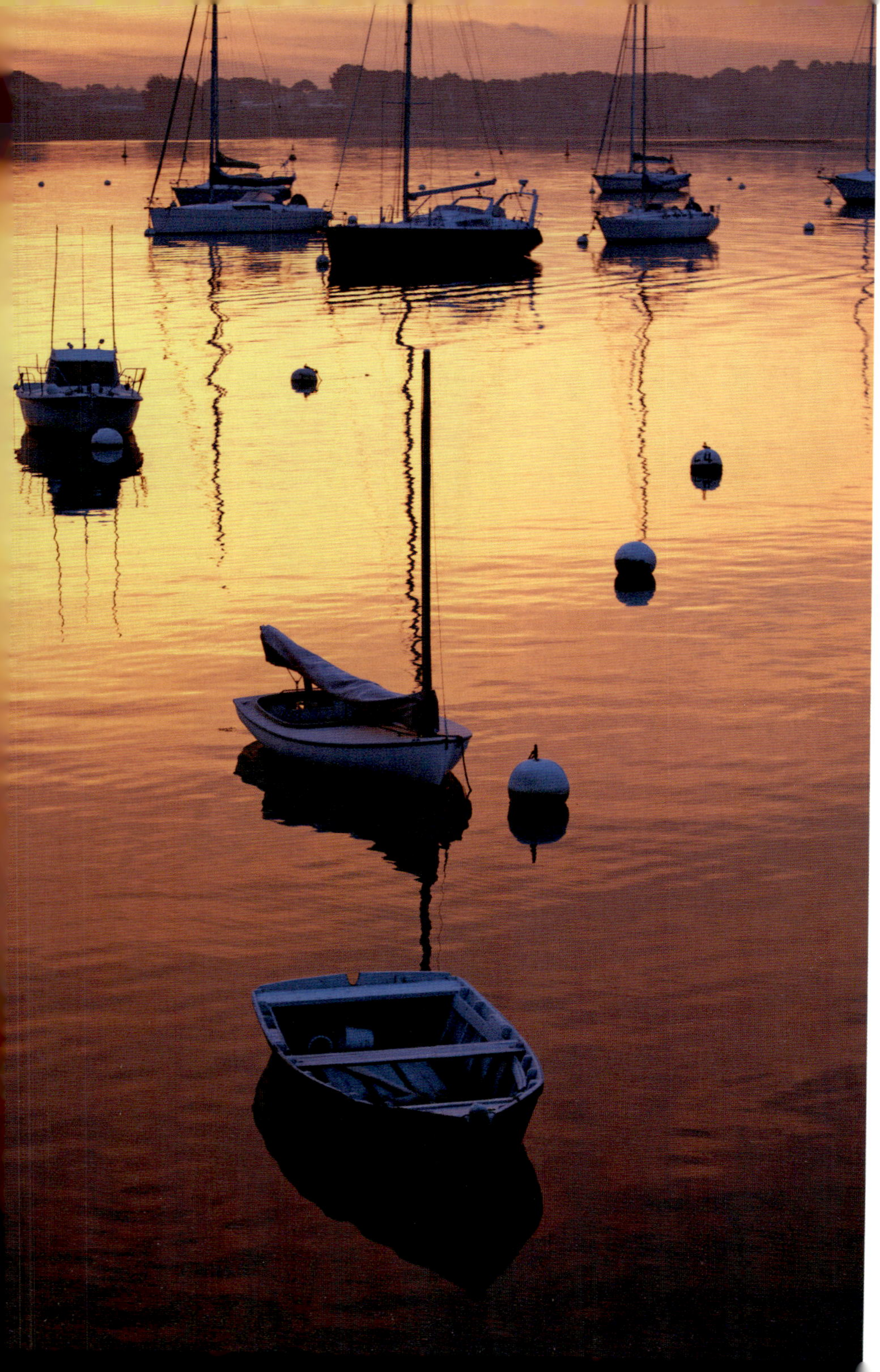

MARCH 3

You can't load a small boat with heavy cargo.

Chinese proverb

MARCH 4

Time and tide wait for no man.
A pompous and self-satisfied
proverb, and was true for a
billion years; but in our day of
electric wires and water-ballast
we turn it around: Man waits
not for time nor tide.

Mark Twain

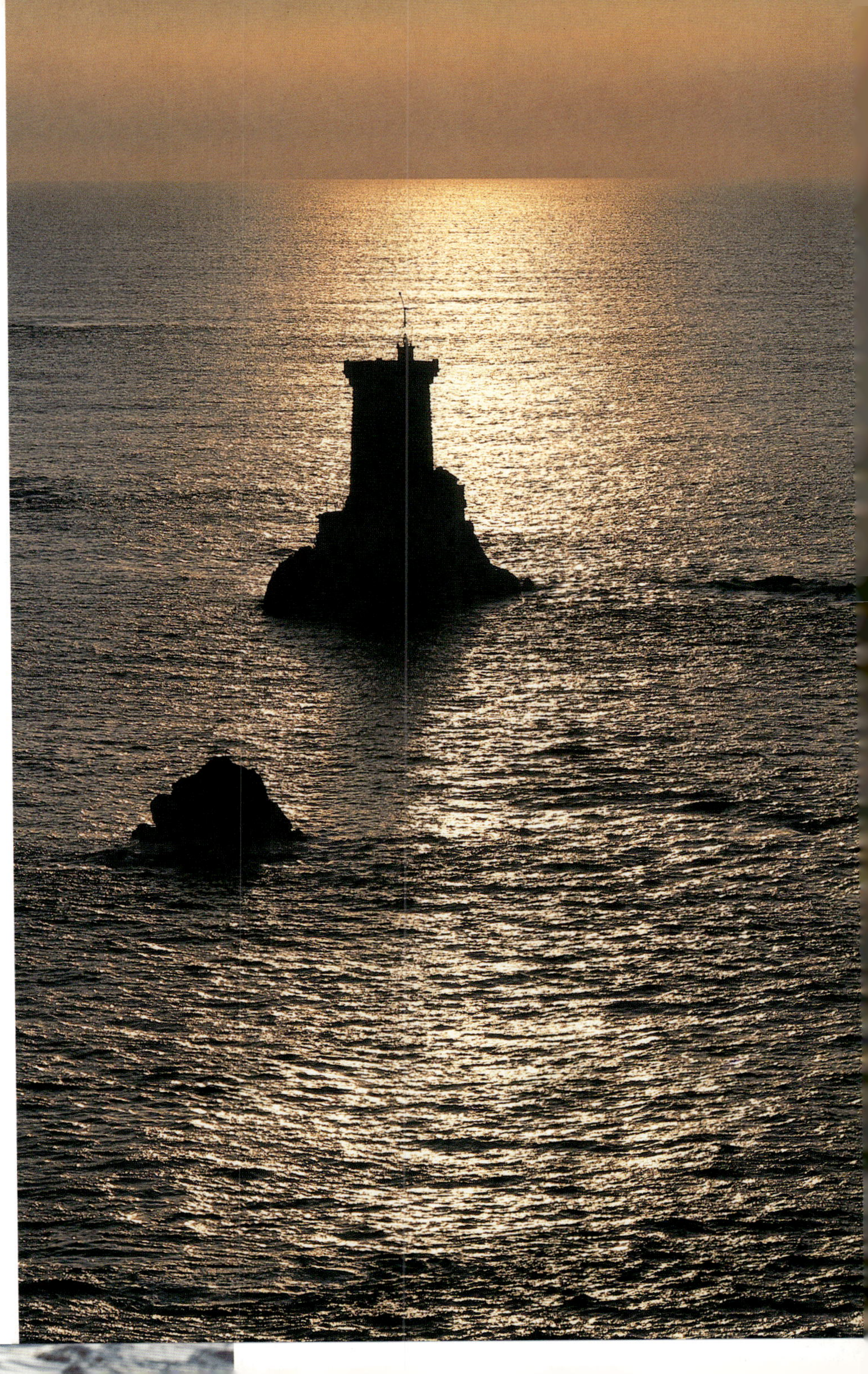

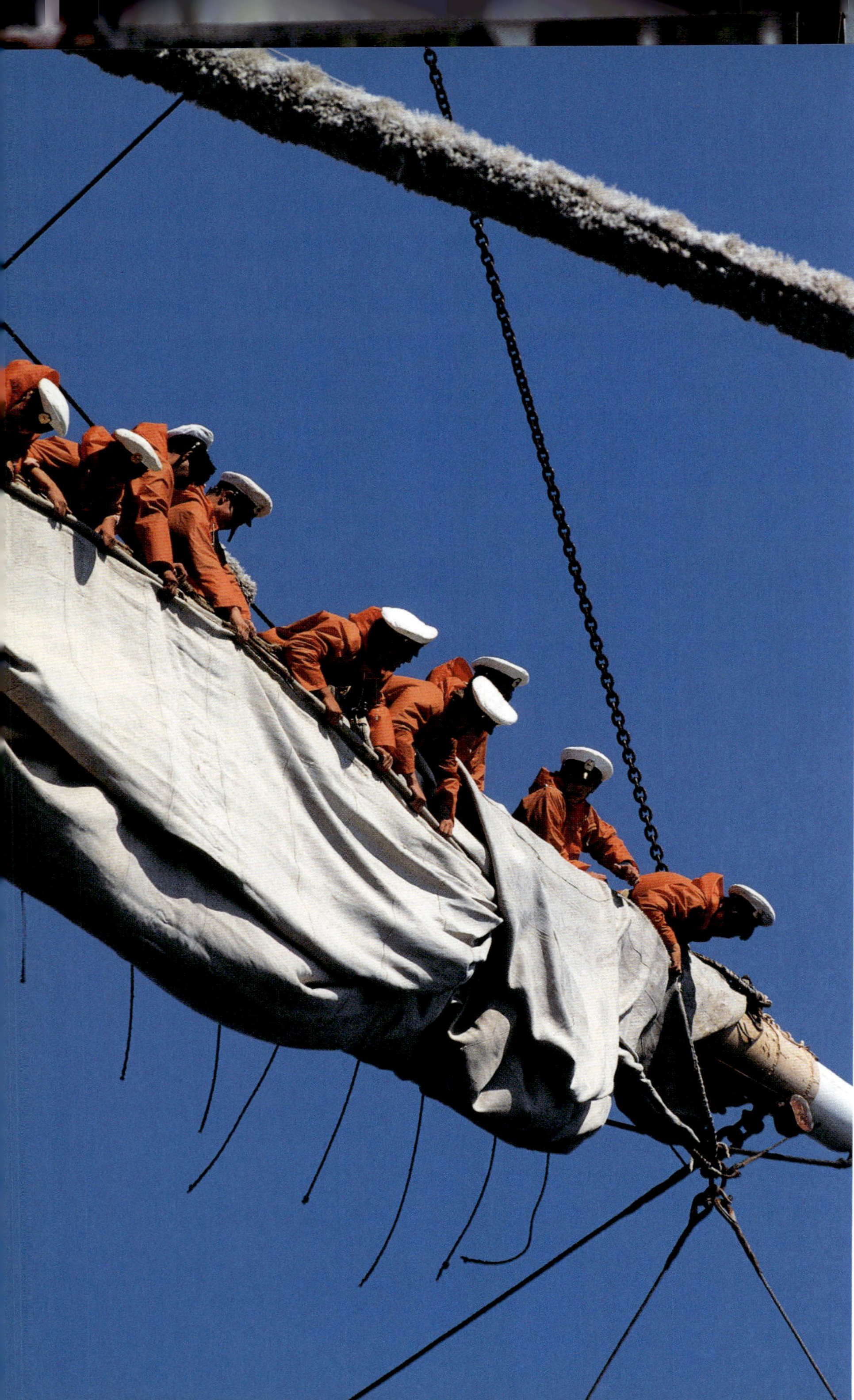

MARCH 6

There is nothing—
absolutely nothing—
half so much worth doing as
simply messing about in boats.

Kenneth Grahame,
from *The Wind in the Willows,* 1908

MARCH 7

The shipwrecked sailor
even fears calm water.

Ovid,
from *"To Atticus, His Constant Grief,"*
Epistulae Ex Ponto (Book II)

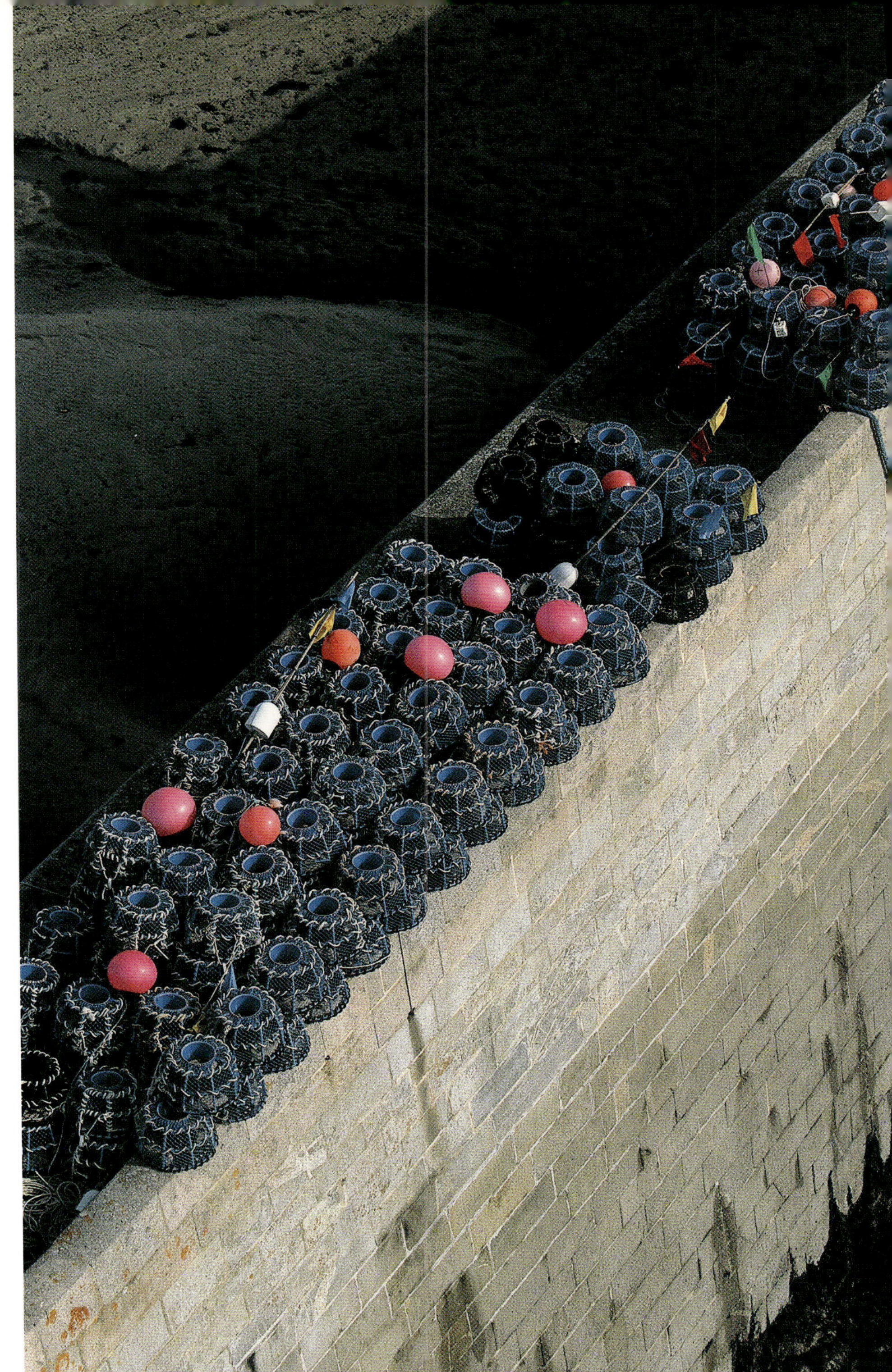

MARCH 8

I once knew a writer who, after saying beautiful things about the sea, passed through a Pacific hurricane, and he became a changed man.

Joshua Slocum,
from *Sailing Alone Around the World*, 1900

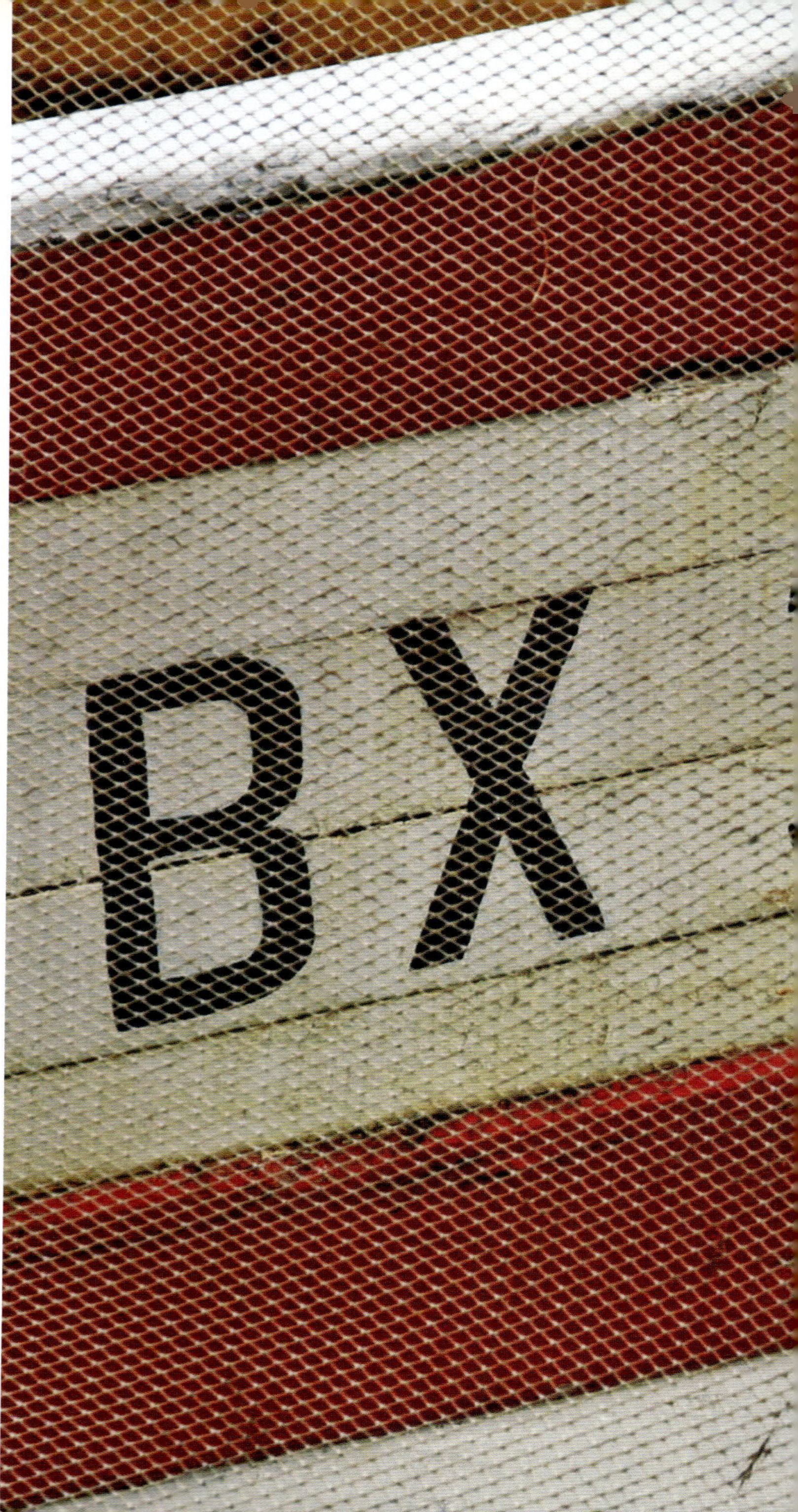

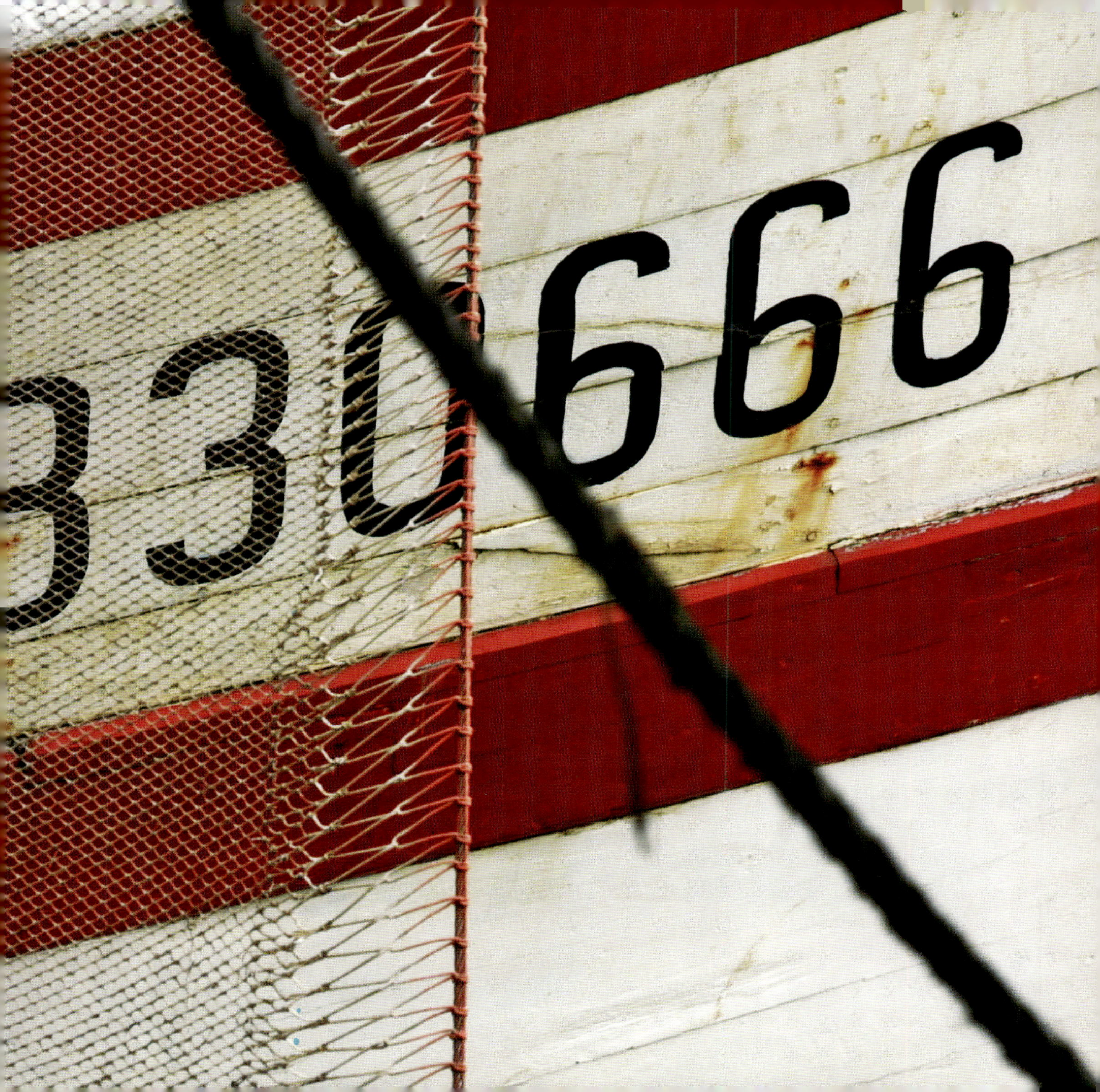
330666

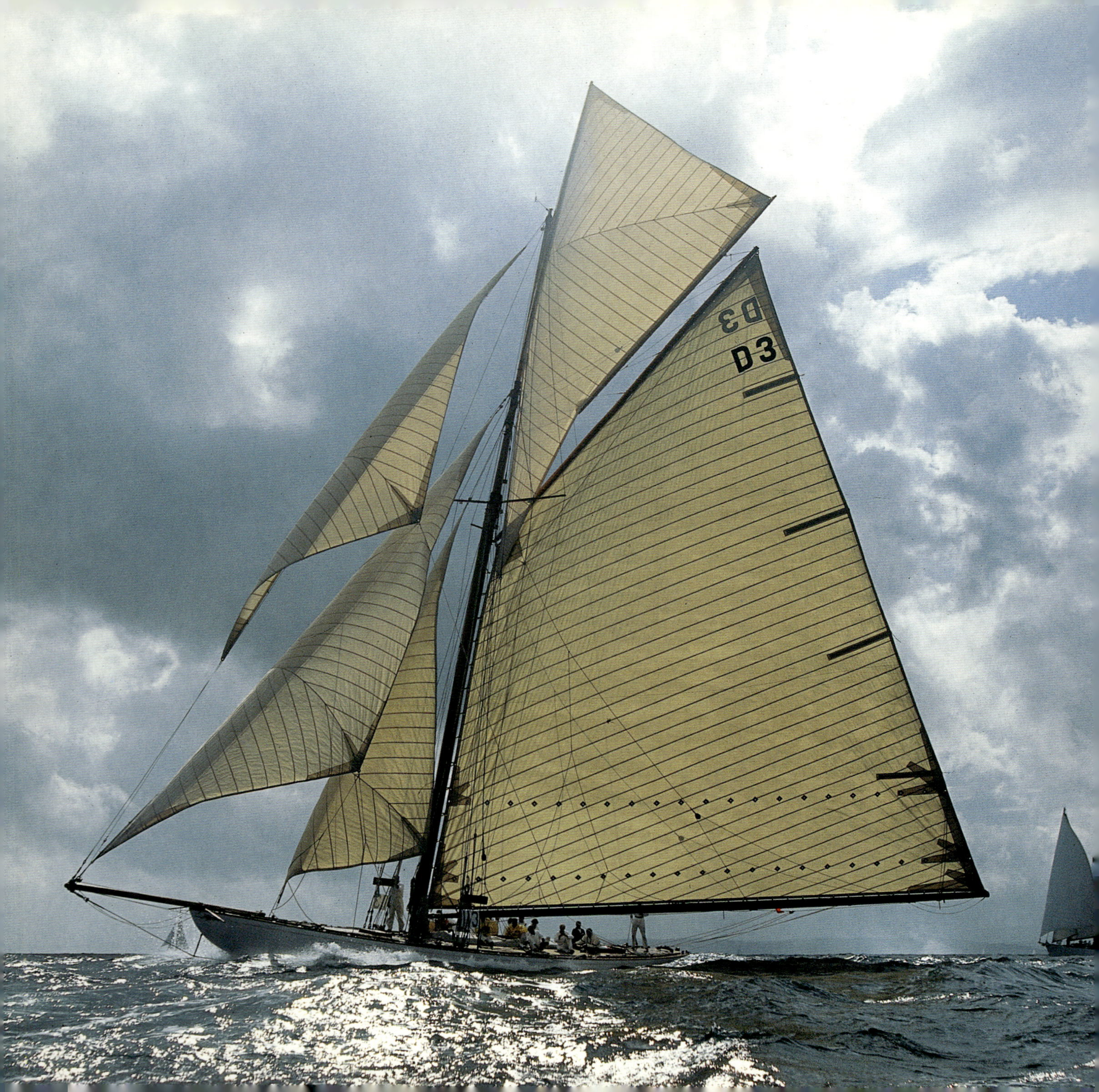
D3

MARCH 9

Twenty years from now you will be more disappointed by the things that you didn't do than by the ones you did do. So throw off the bowlines. Sail away from the safe harbor. Catch the trade winds in your sails. Explore. Dream. Discover.

Mark Twain

MARCH 10

When men come to like a sea-life,
they are not fit to live on land.

Samuel Johnson

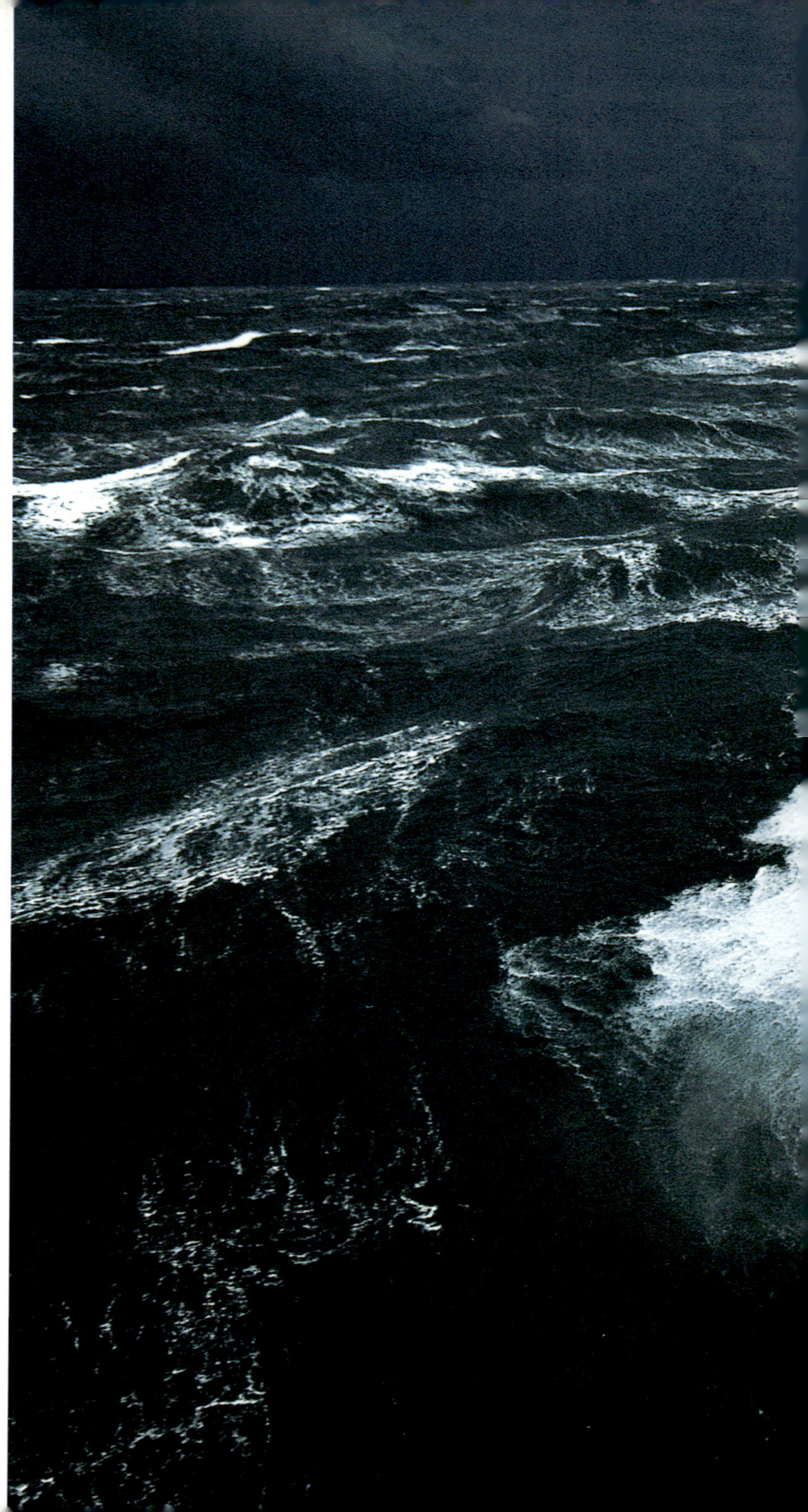

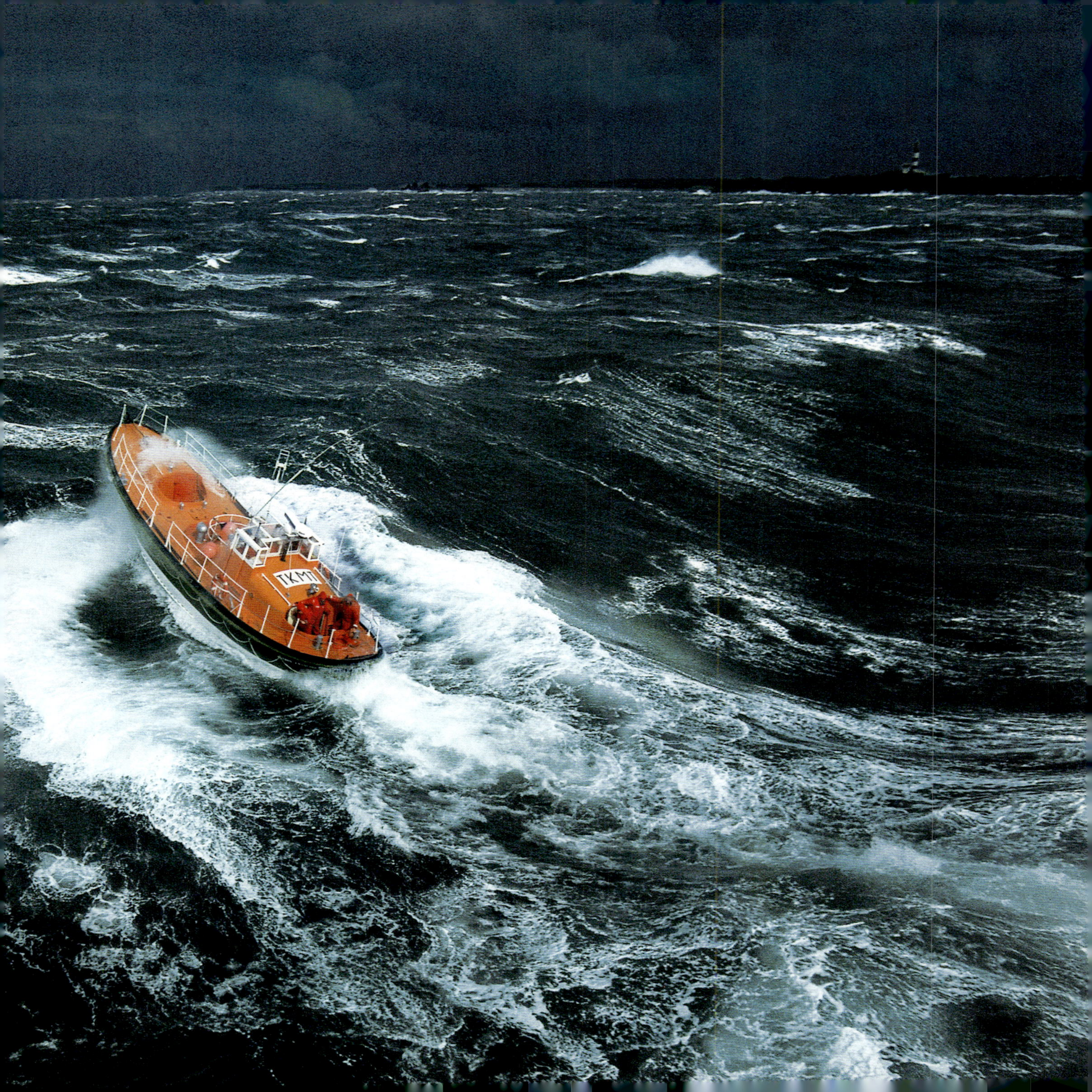

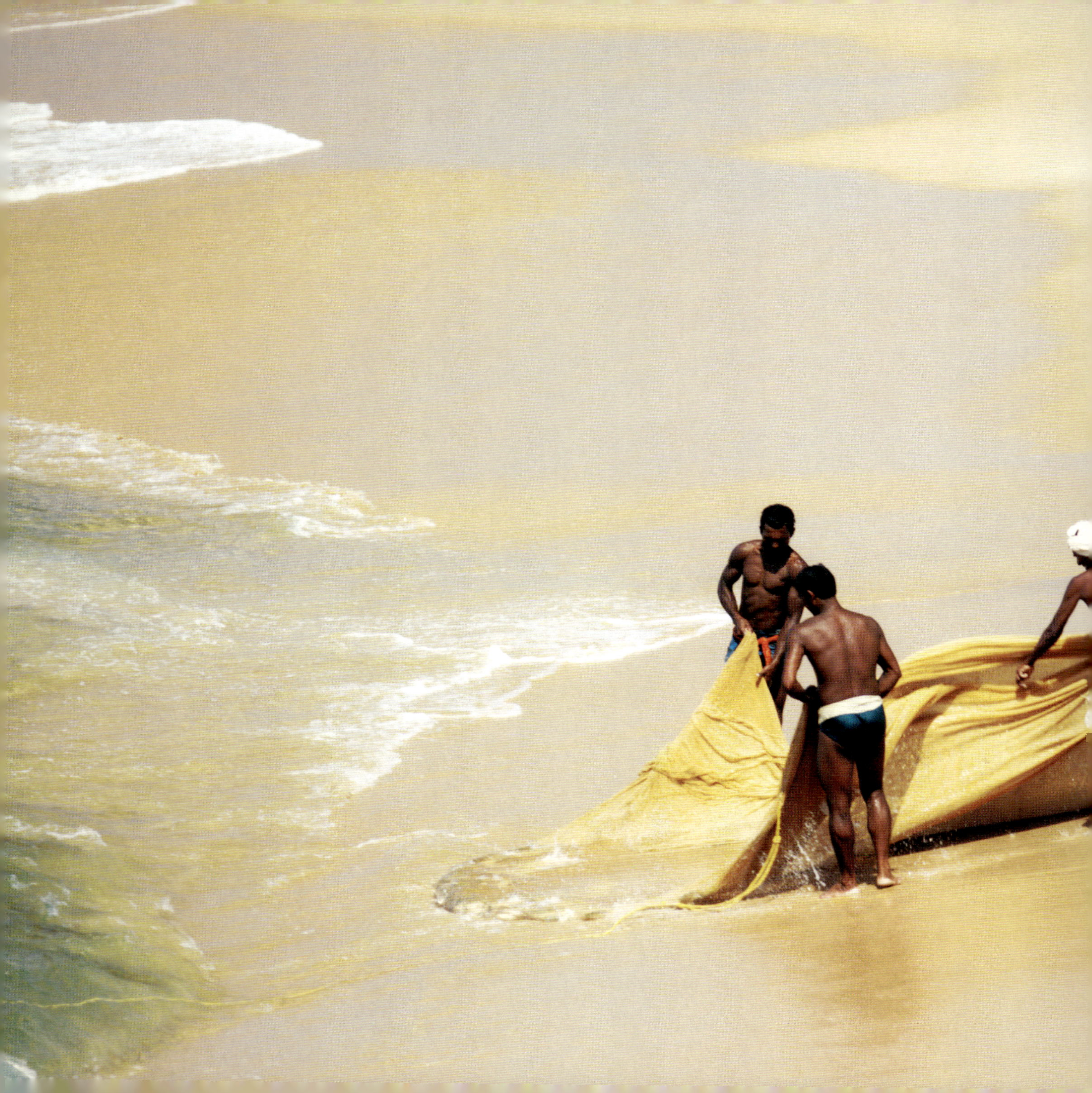

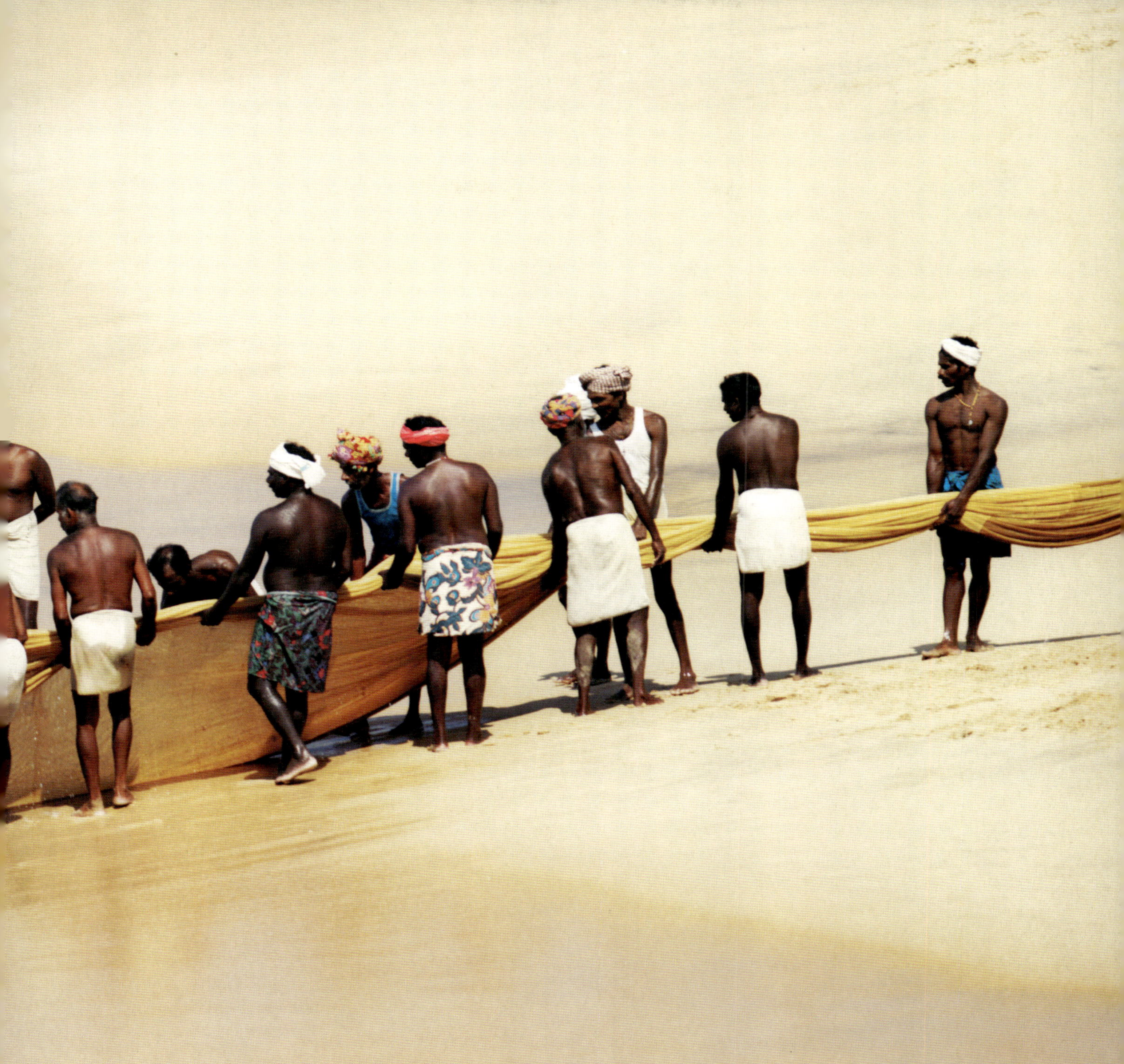

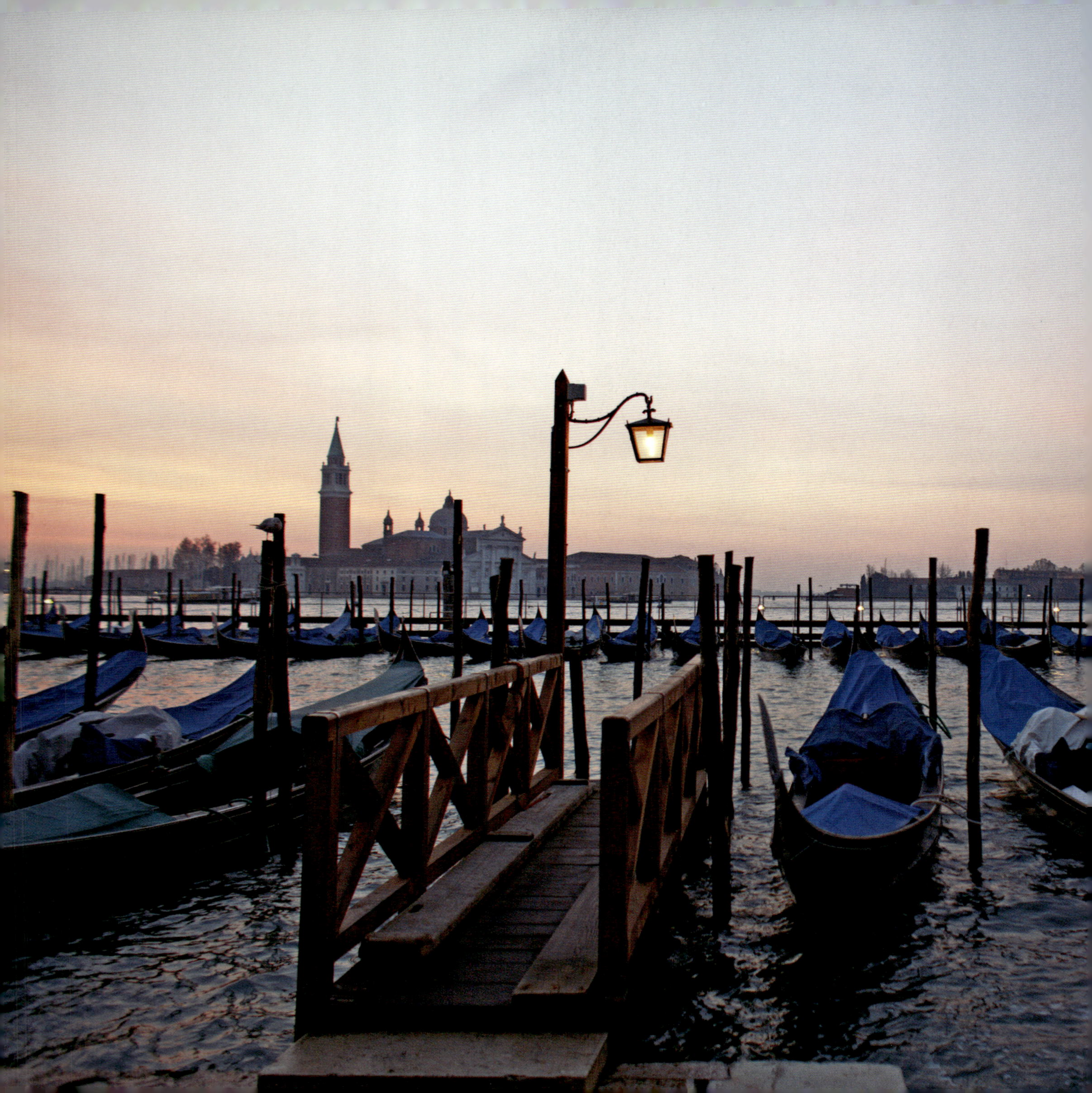

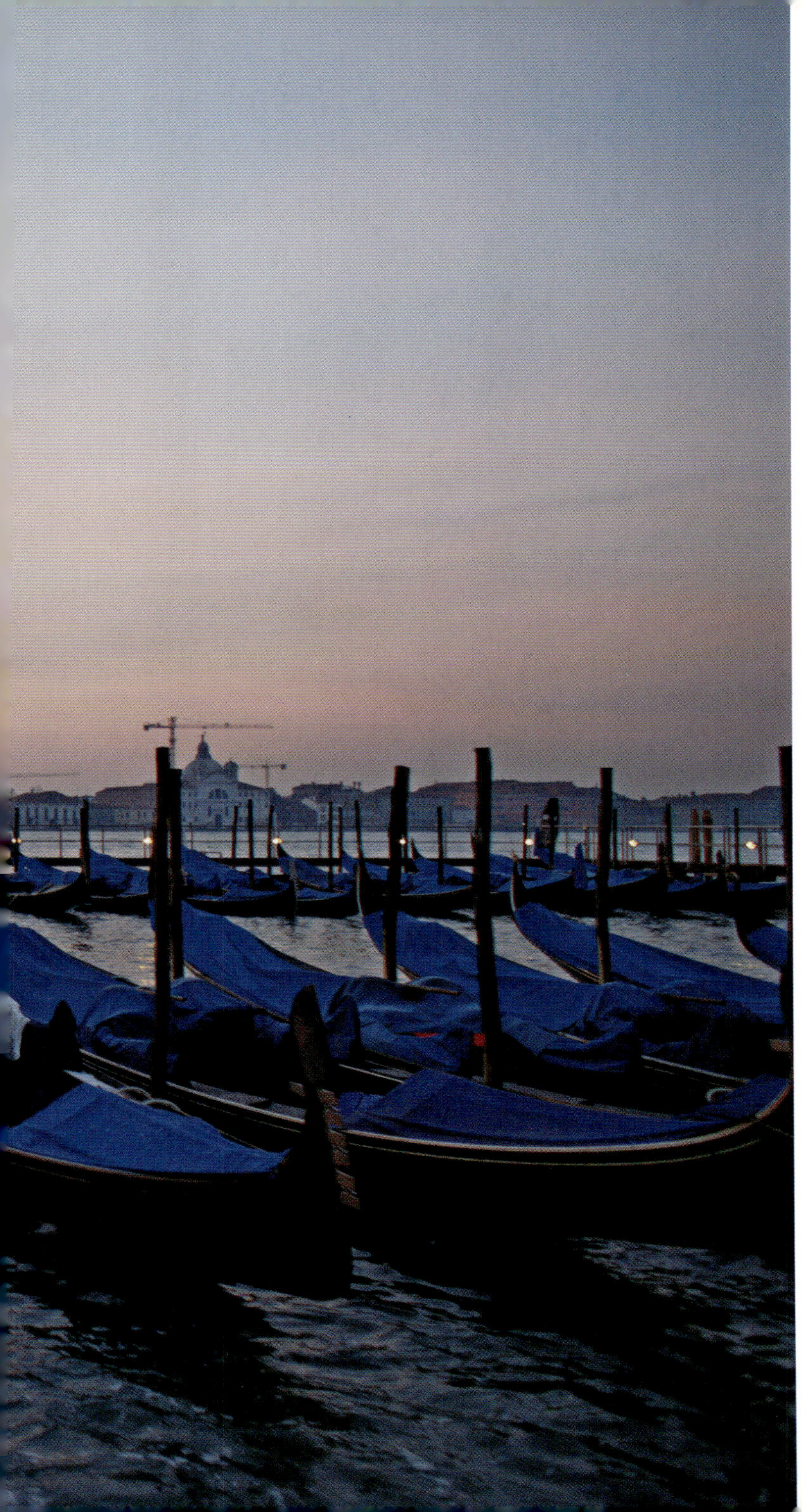

MARCH 11

A ship is safe in harbor,
but that's not what ships are for.

William Greenough Thayer Shedd

MARCH 12

The desire to build a house is the tired wish of a man content thenceforward with a single anchorage. The desire to build a boat is the desire of youth, unwilling yet to accept the idea of a final resting place.

Arthur Ransome,
from *Racundra's First Cruise,* 1923

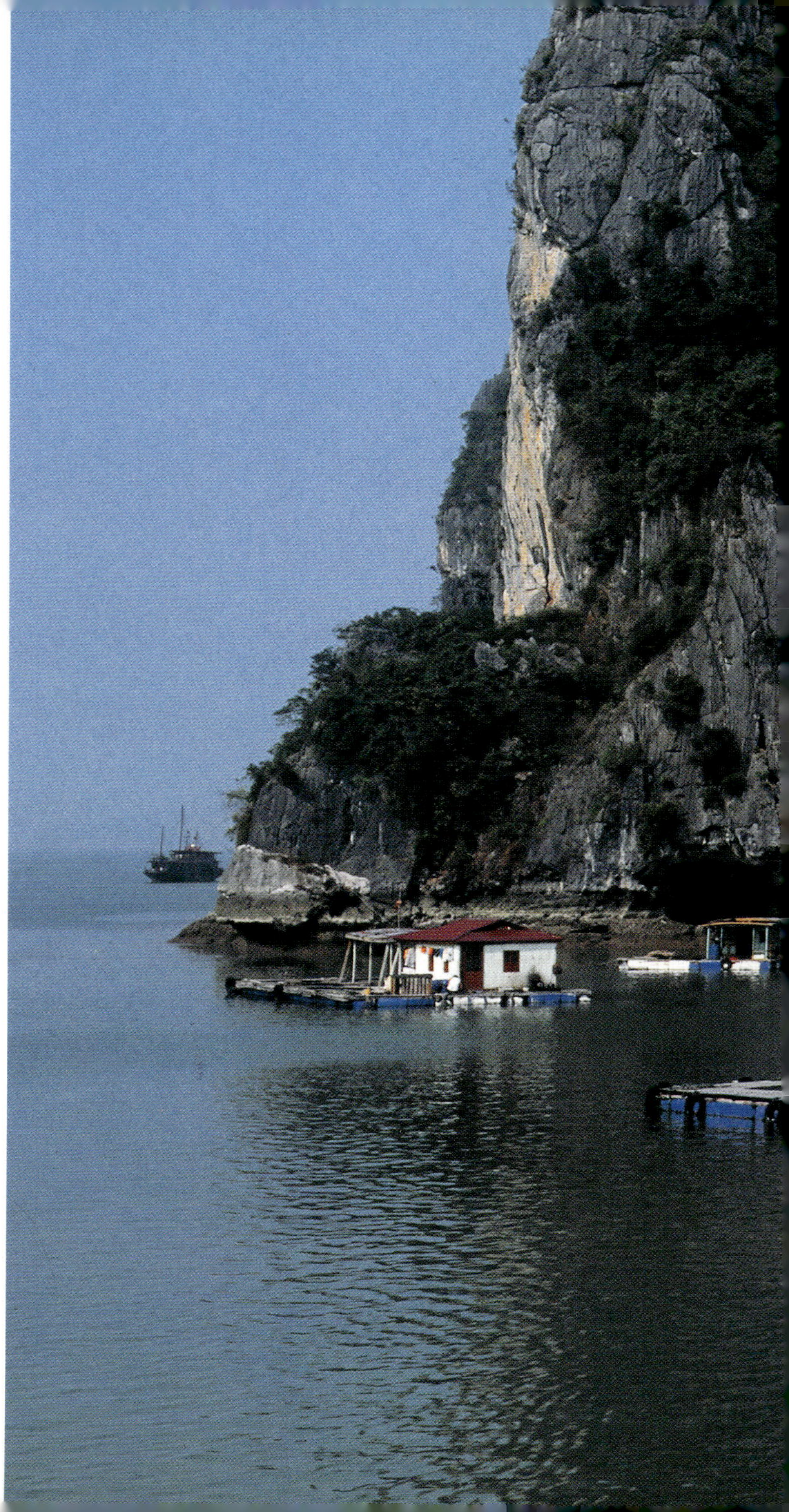

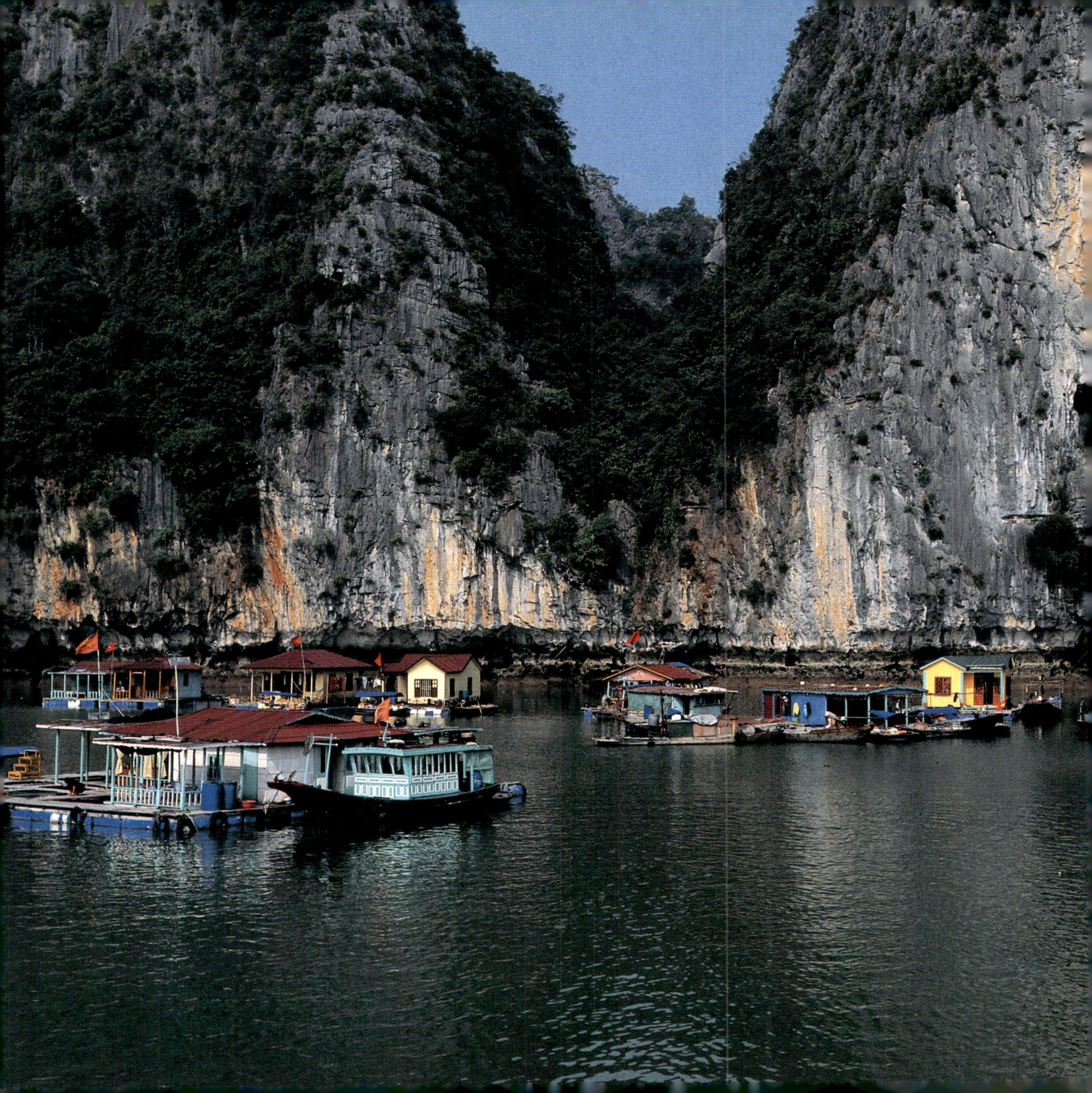

MARCH 13

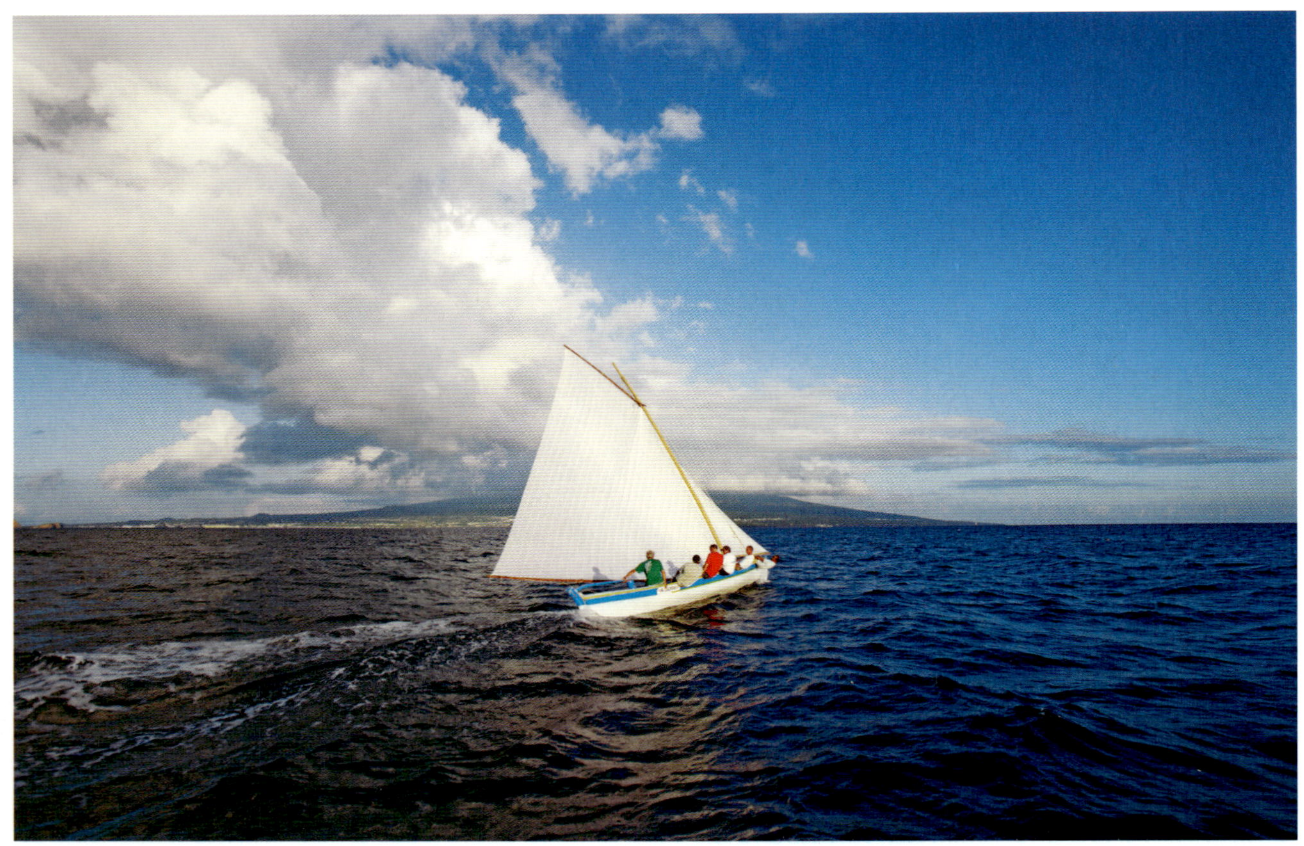

When asked, "What news from the sea?" the fish replied,
"I have a lot to say, but my mouth is full of water."

Armenian proverb

MARCH 14

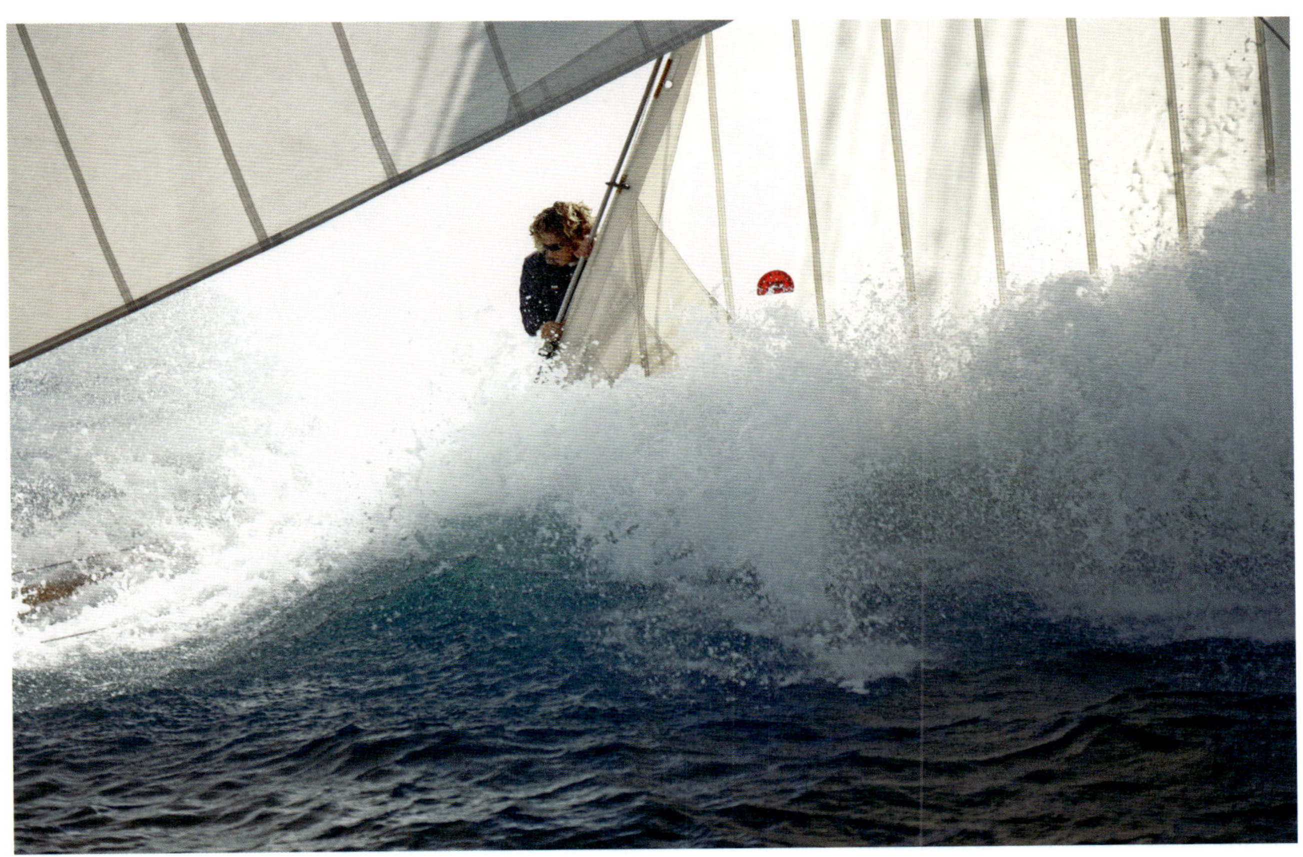

It was with a happy heart that the good Odysseus spread his sail to catch the wind and used his seamanship to keep his boat straight with the steering-oar.

Homer

MARCH 15

Build me straight, O worthy Master!
Staunch and strong, a goodly vessel,
That shall laugh at disaster,
And with wave and whirlwind wrestle!

Henry Wadsworth Longfellow,
from "The Building of the Ship," *The Seaside and the Fireside,* 1850

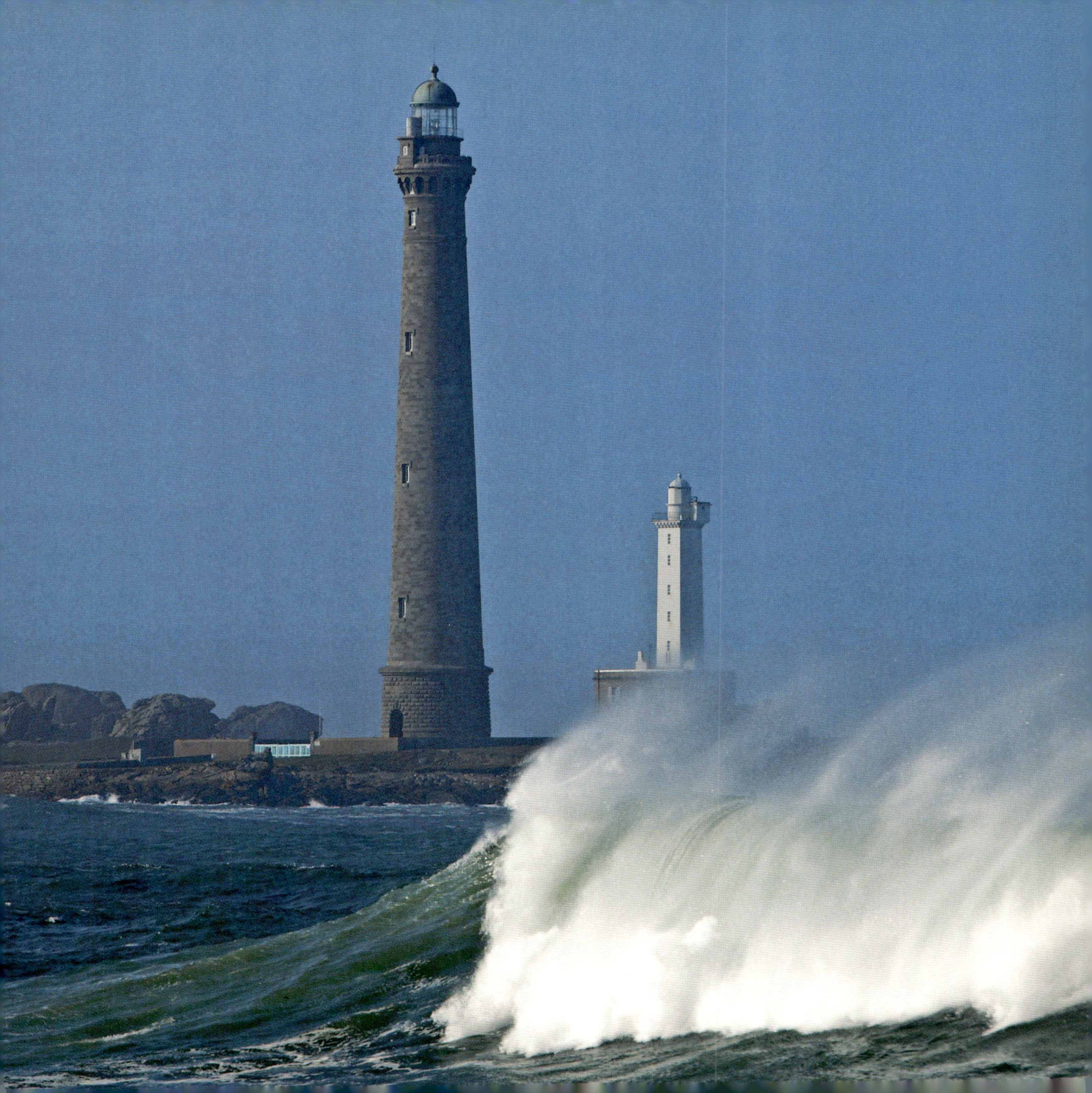

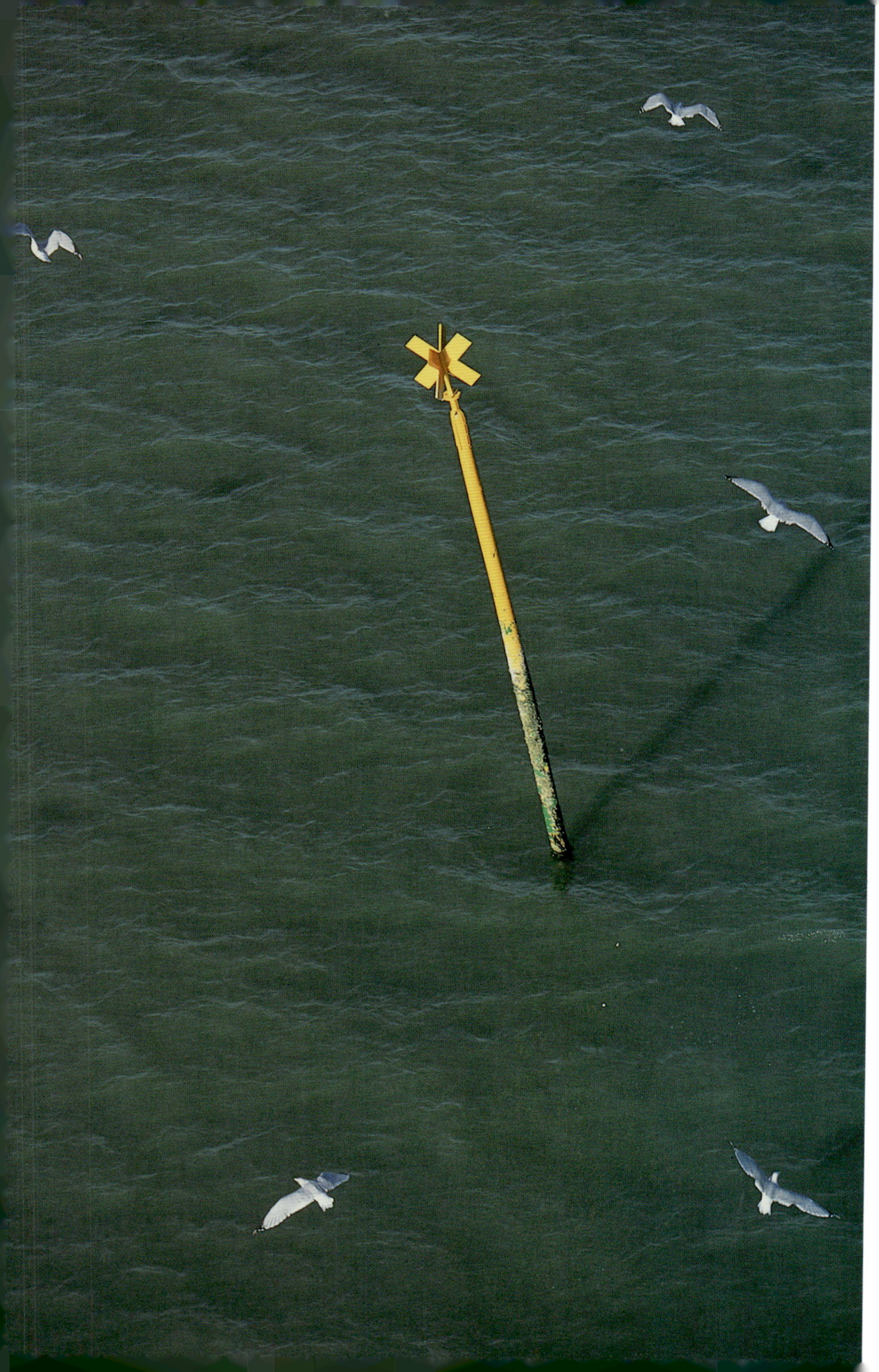

MARCH 16

Memory is a net;
one finds it full of fish when he
takes it from the brook;
but a dozen miles of water have
run through it without sticking.

Oliver Wendell Holmes,
from *The Autocrat at the Breakfast Table,* 1858

MARCH 17

I've never seen the point of the sea, except where it meets the land. The shore has a point. The sea has none.

Alan Bennett

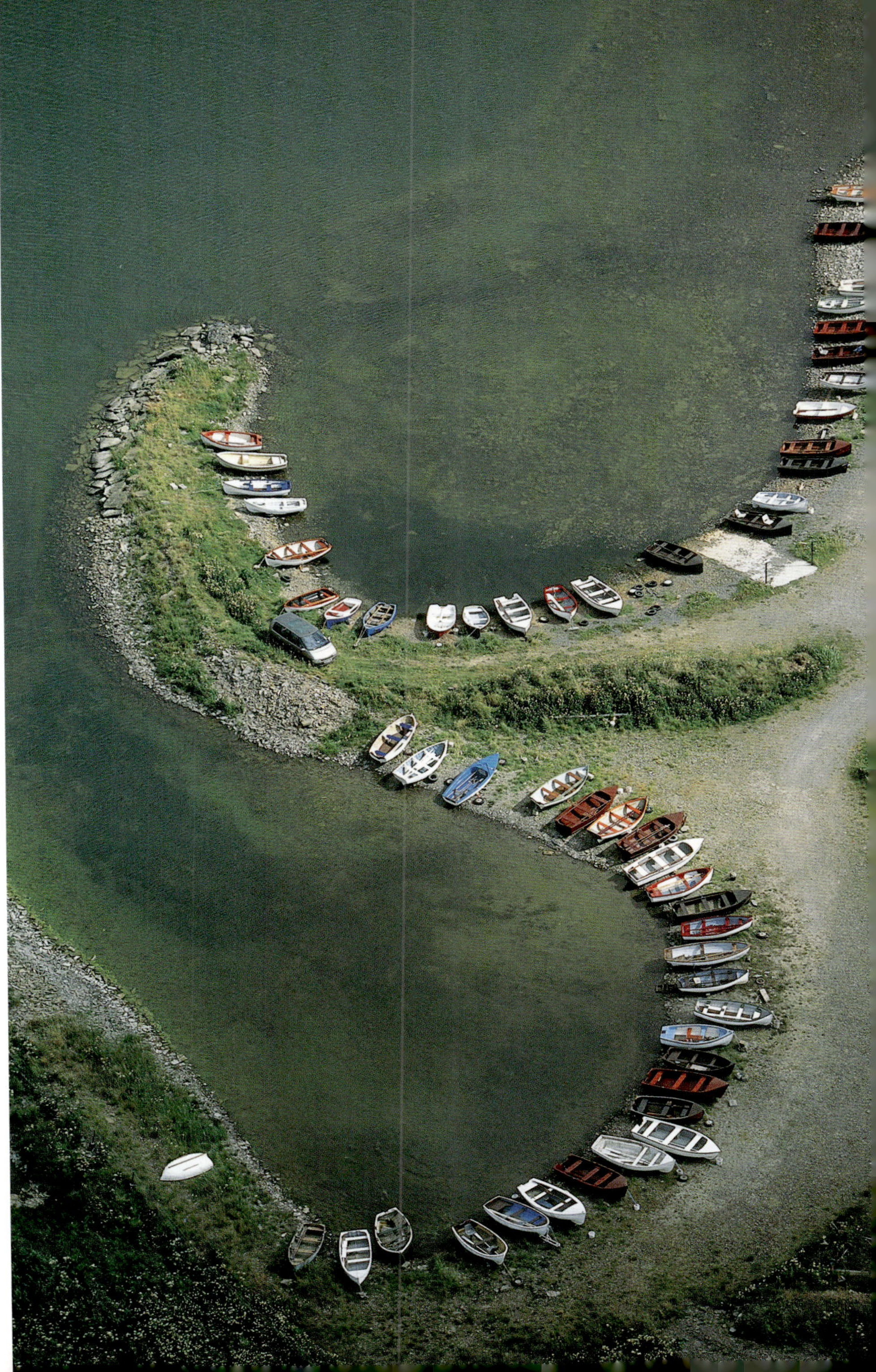

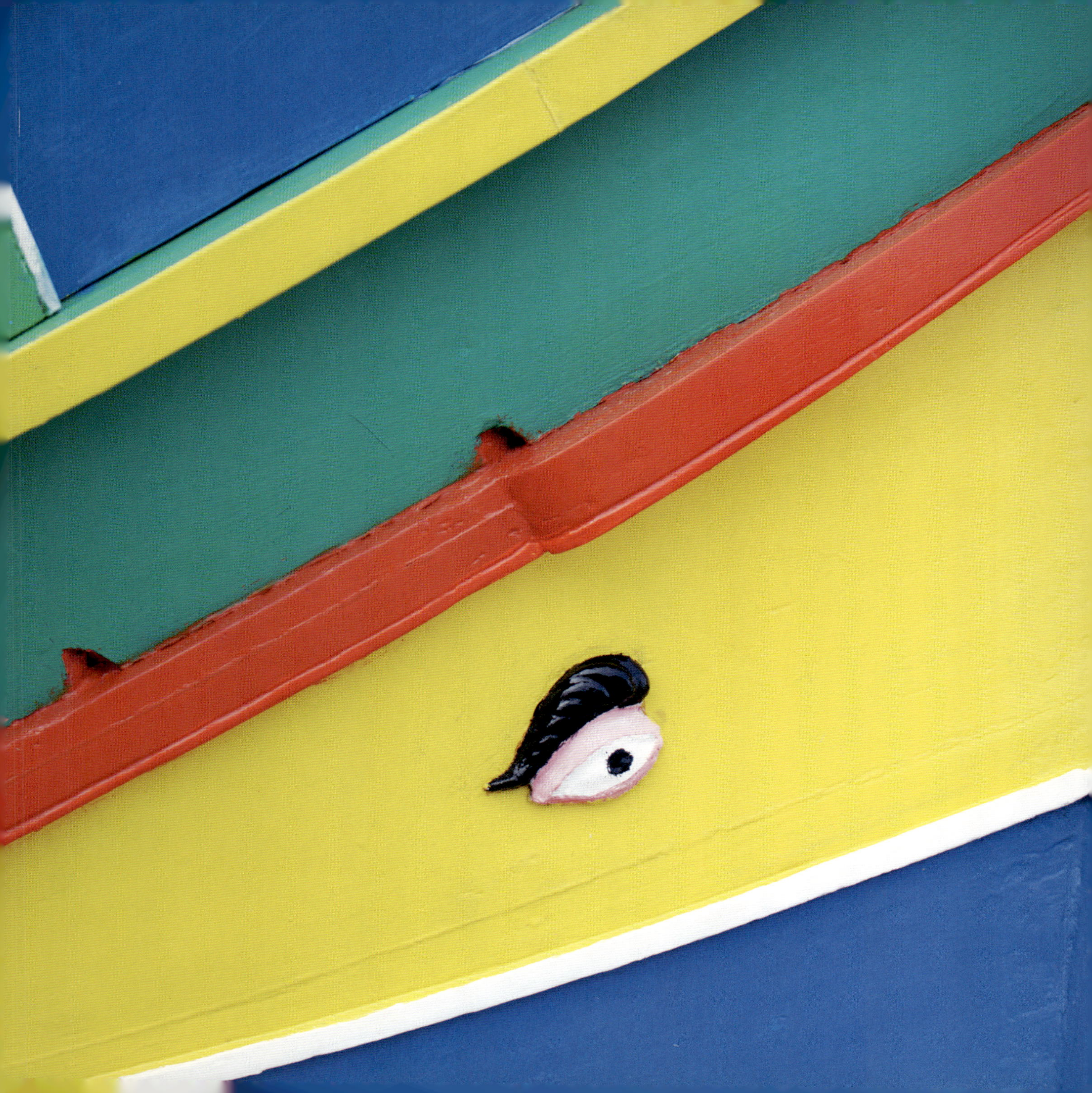

MARCH 18

On the land they know a child they have named Today.
On the sea they know three children they have named:
Yesterday, Today, To-morrow.

Carl Sandburg,
from "North Atlantic," *Smoke and Steel,* 1920

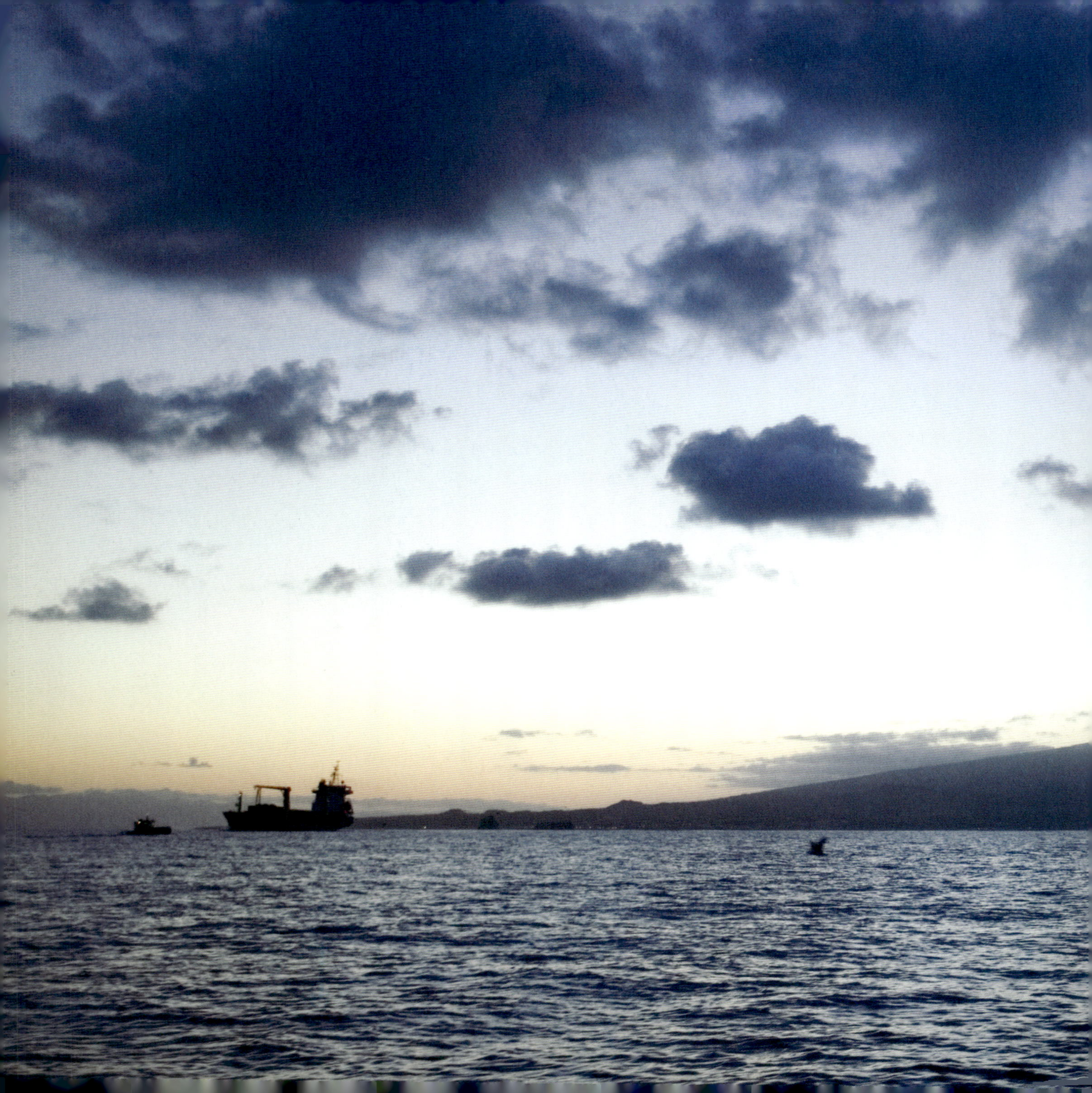

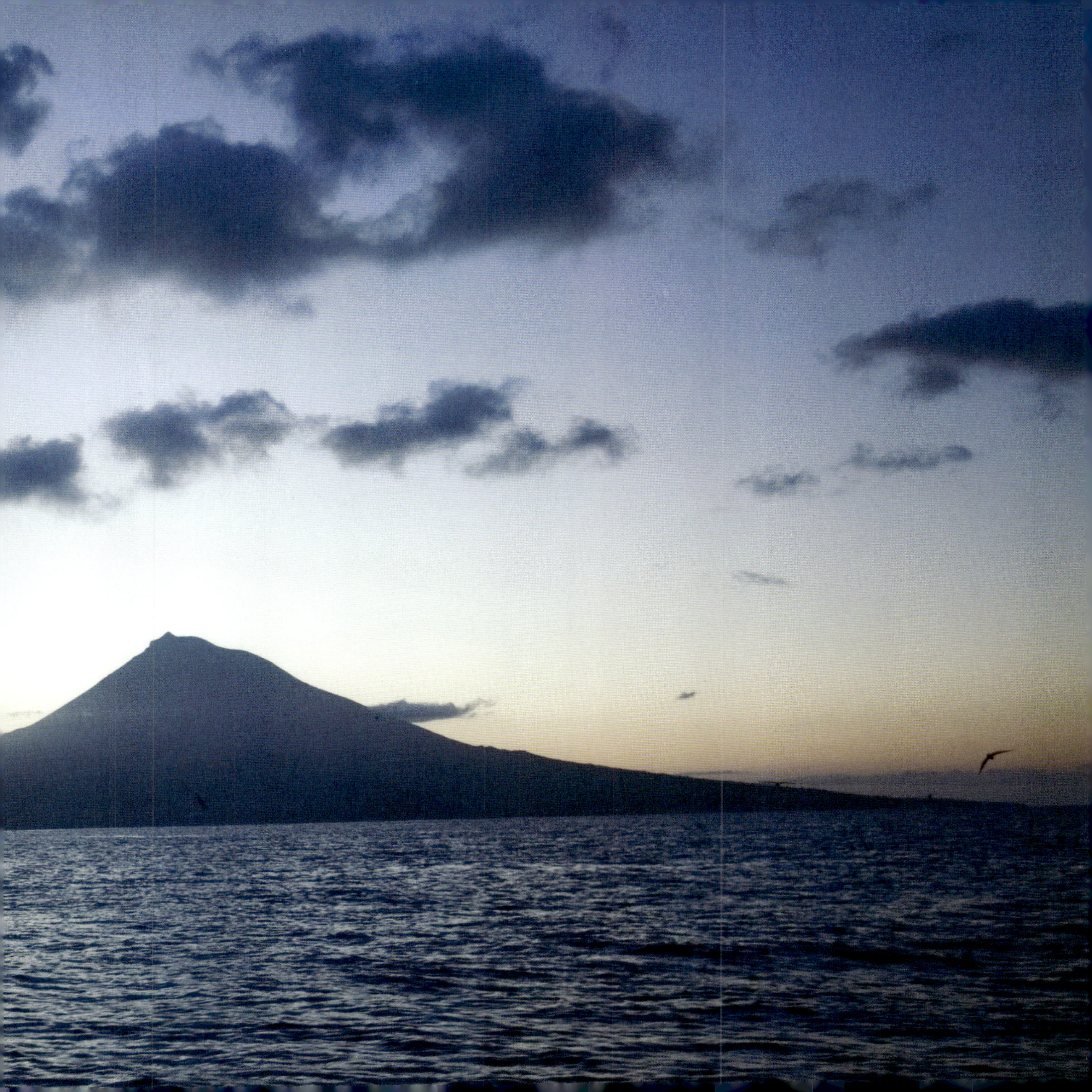

MARCH 19

Thus prepared, thy shorten'd sail
Shall, whene'er the winds increase,
Seizing each propitious gale,
Waft thee to the port of Peace.

Lord Melcombe,
from "Shorten Sail," 1919

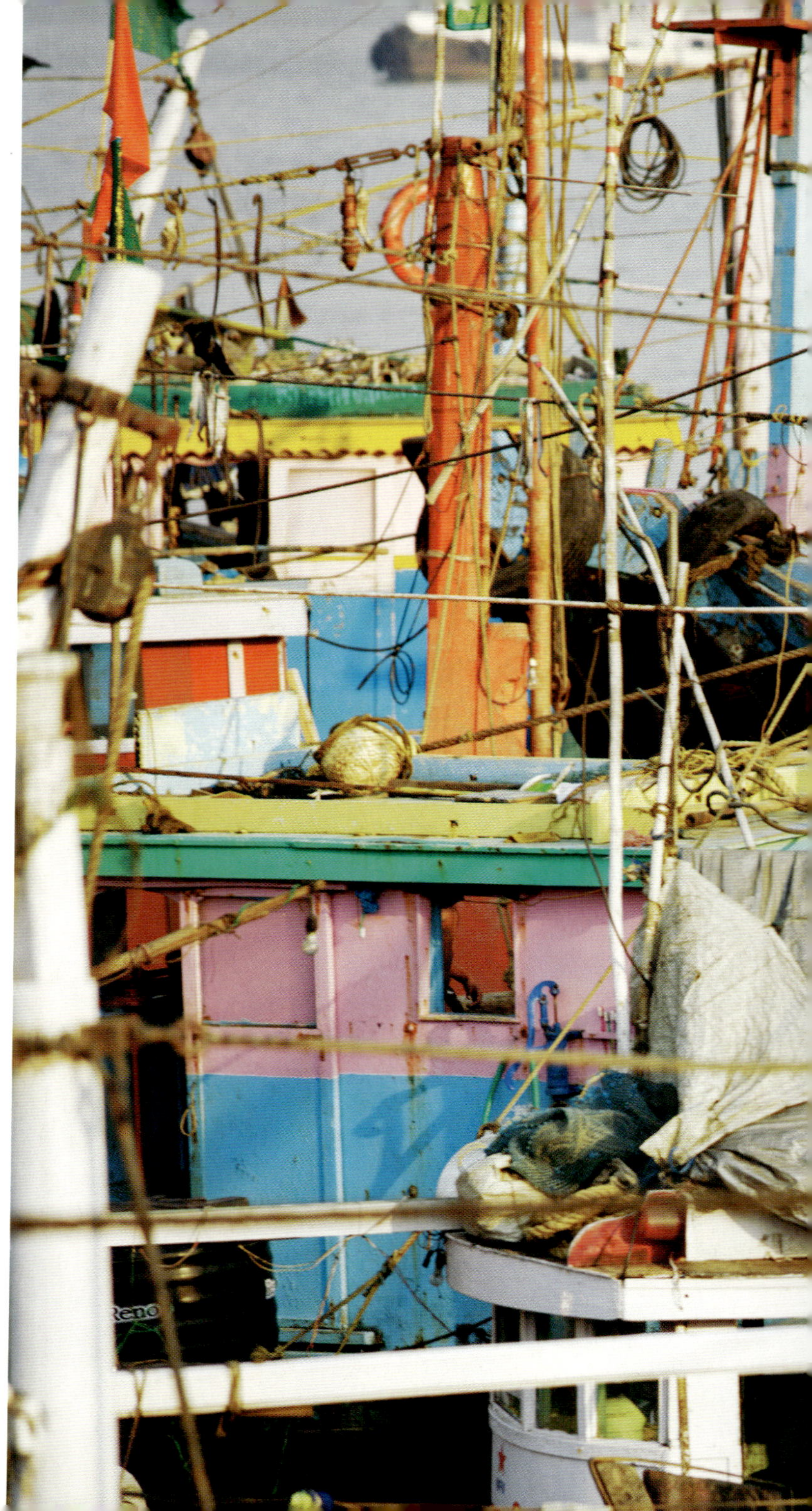

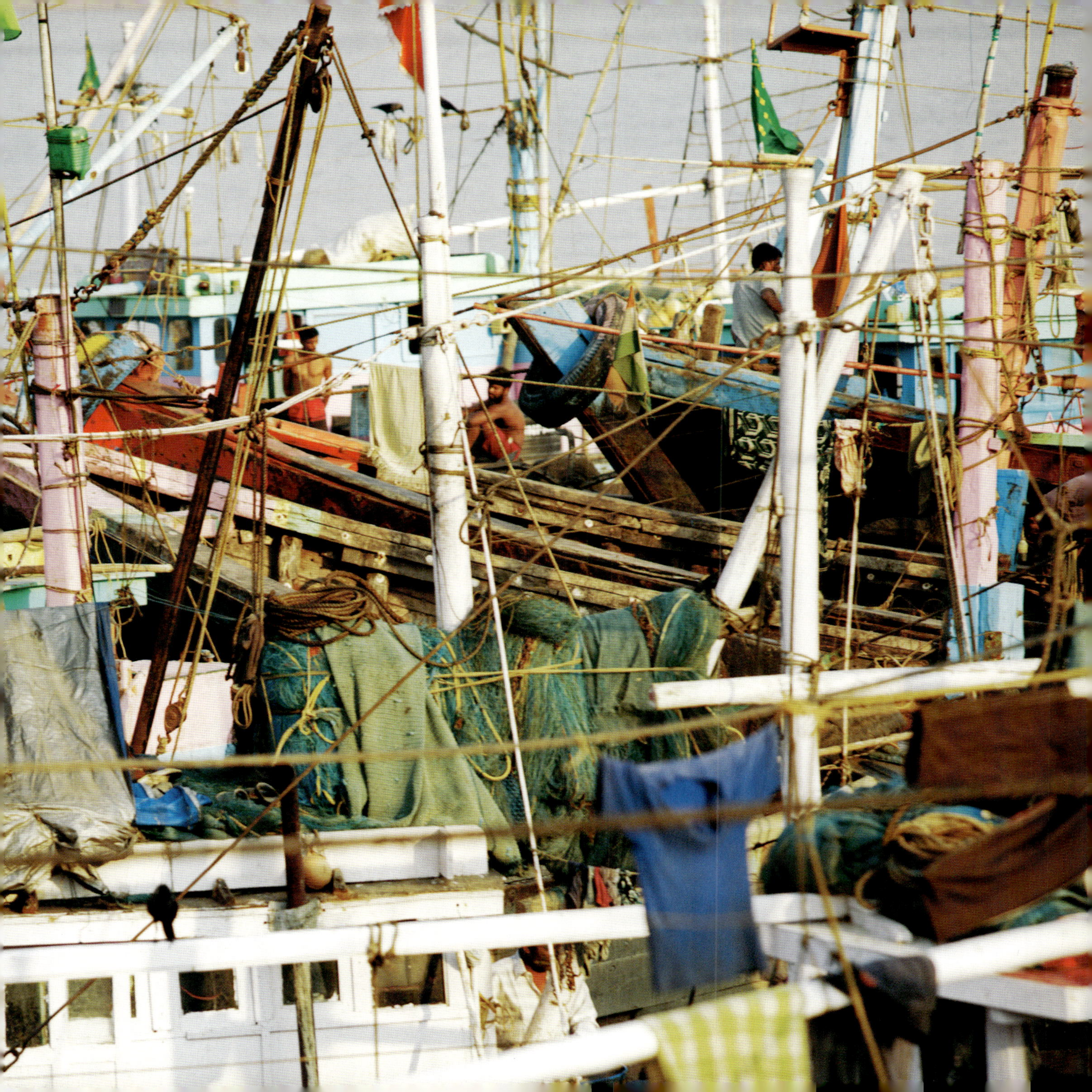

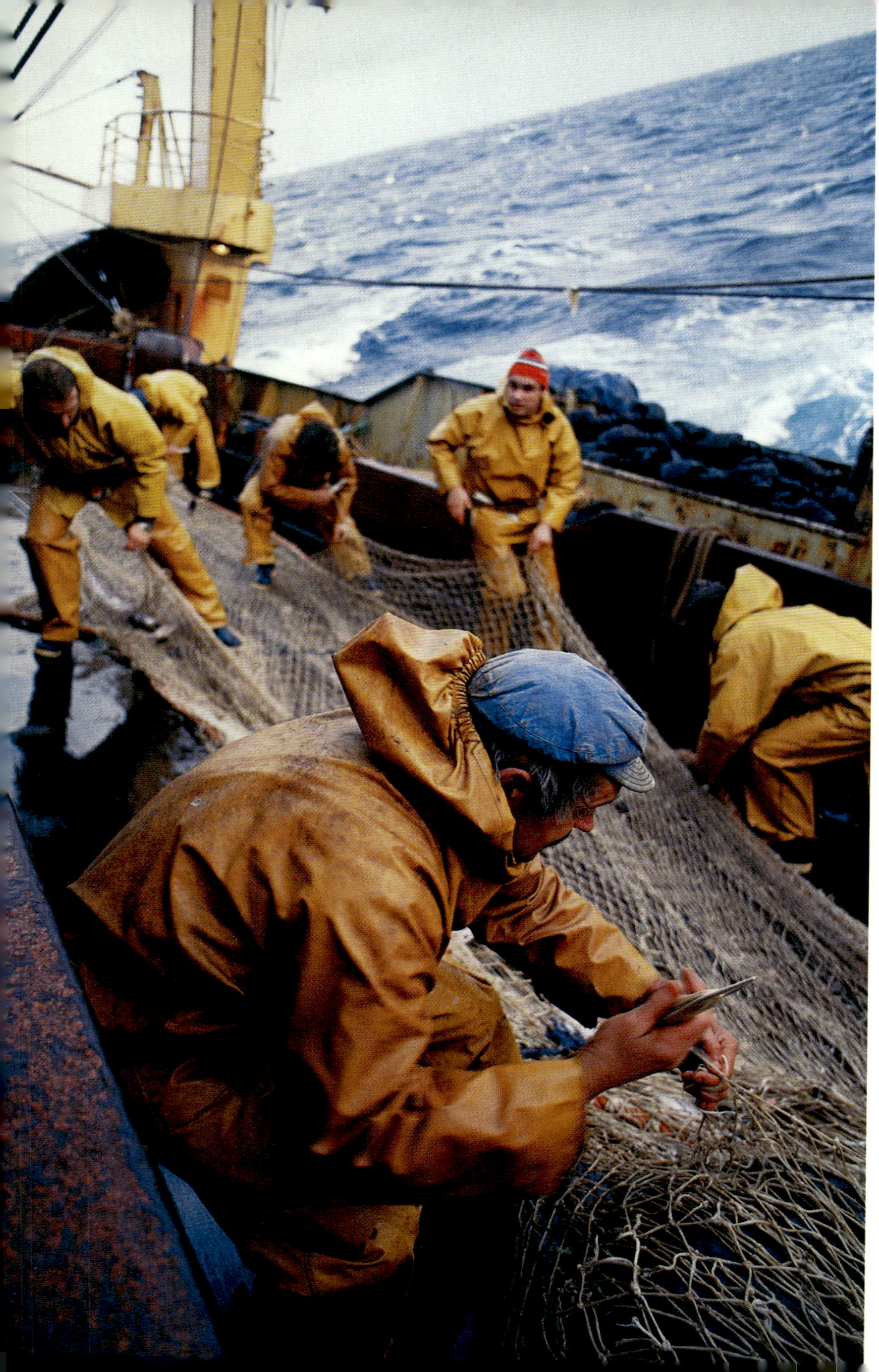

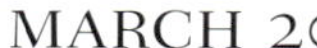

MARCH 20

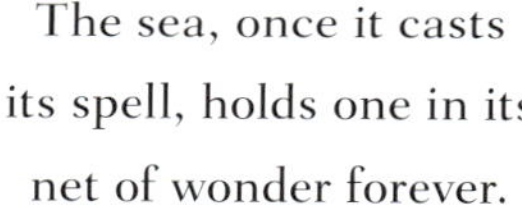

The sea, once it casts
its spell, holds one in its
net of wonder forever.

Jacques-Yves Cousteau

MARCH 21

He that will not sail till all dangers are over must never put to sea.

Thomas Fuller

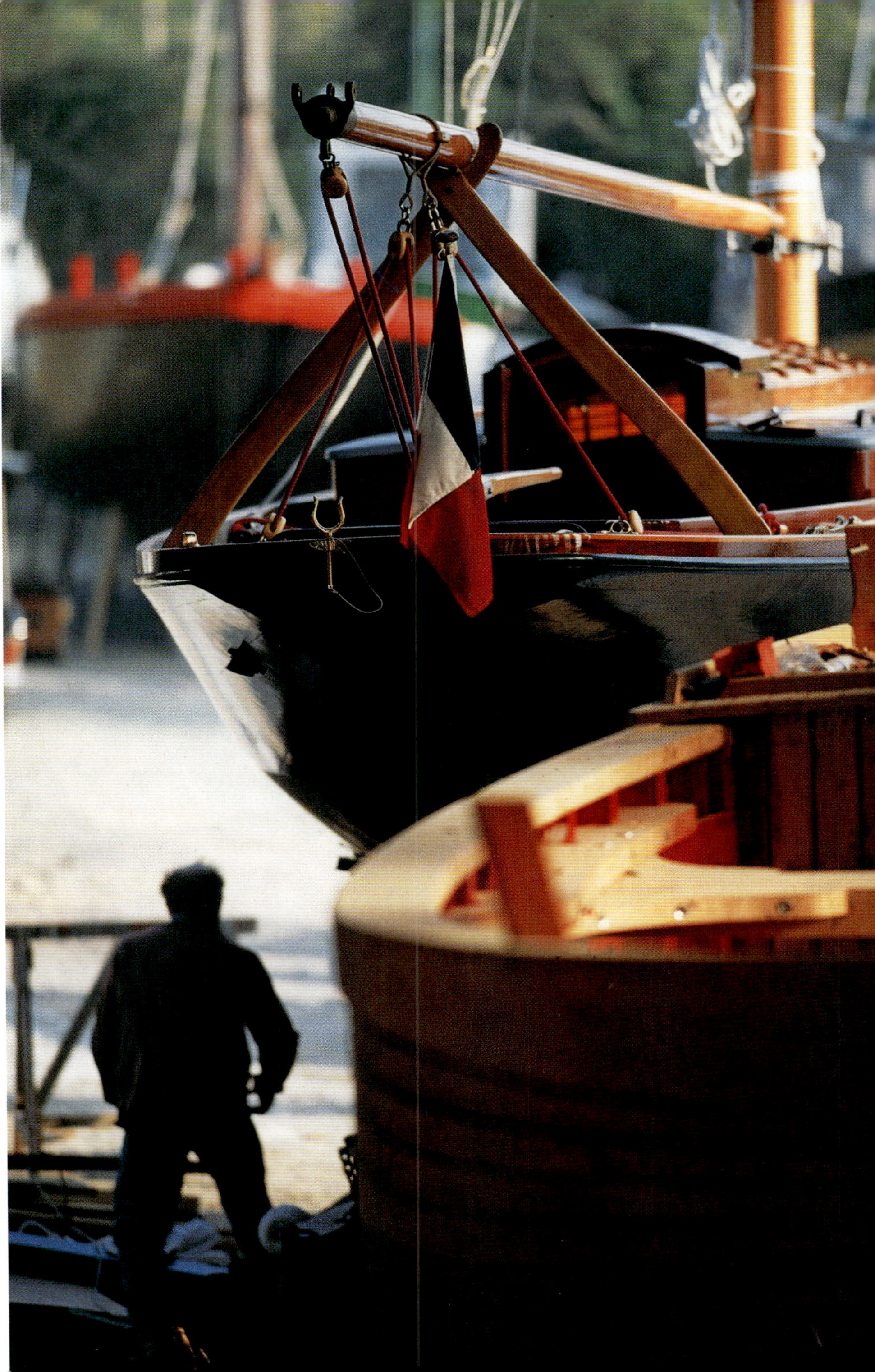

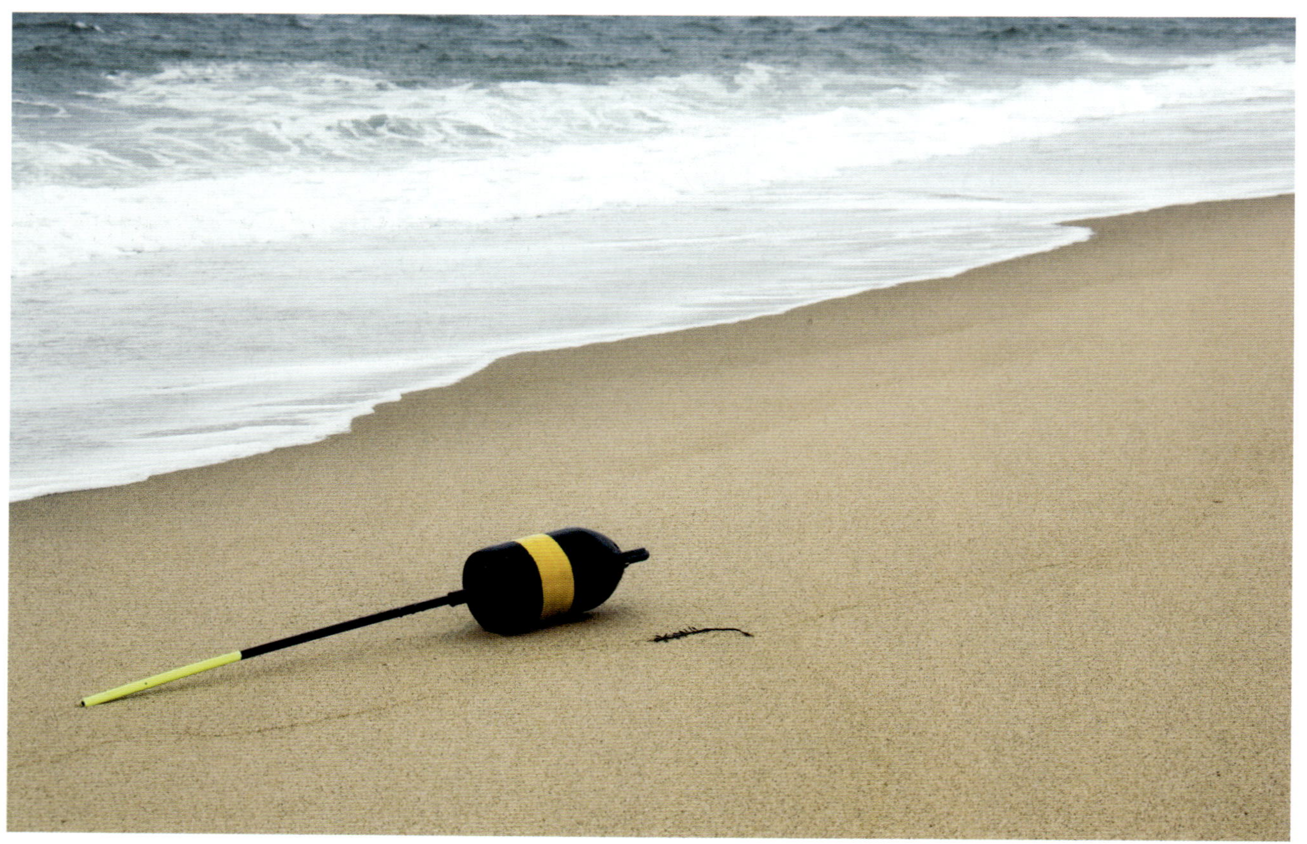

Though near shore, you're still in the ocean.

Malawian proverb

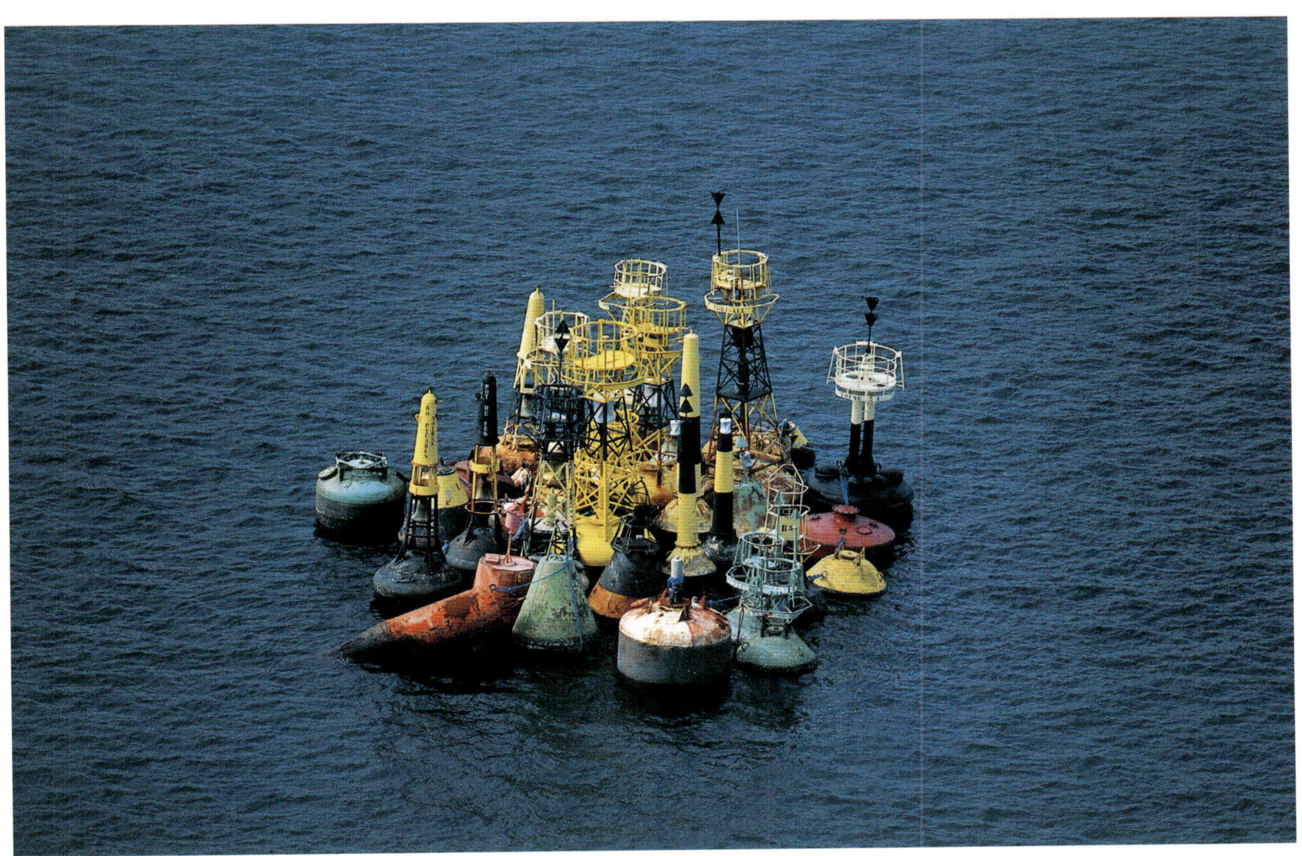

Man marks the earth with ruin—his control stops with the shore.

Lord Byron, from "Childe Harold's Pilgrimage," 1818

MARCH 24

To young men contemplating a voyage I'd say go.

Joshua Slocum,
from *Sailing Alone Around the World,* 1900

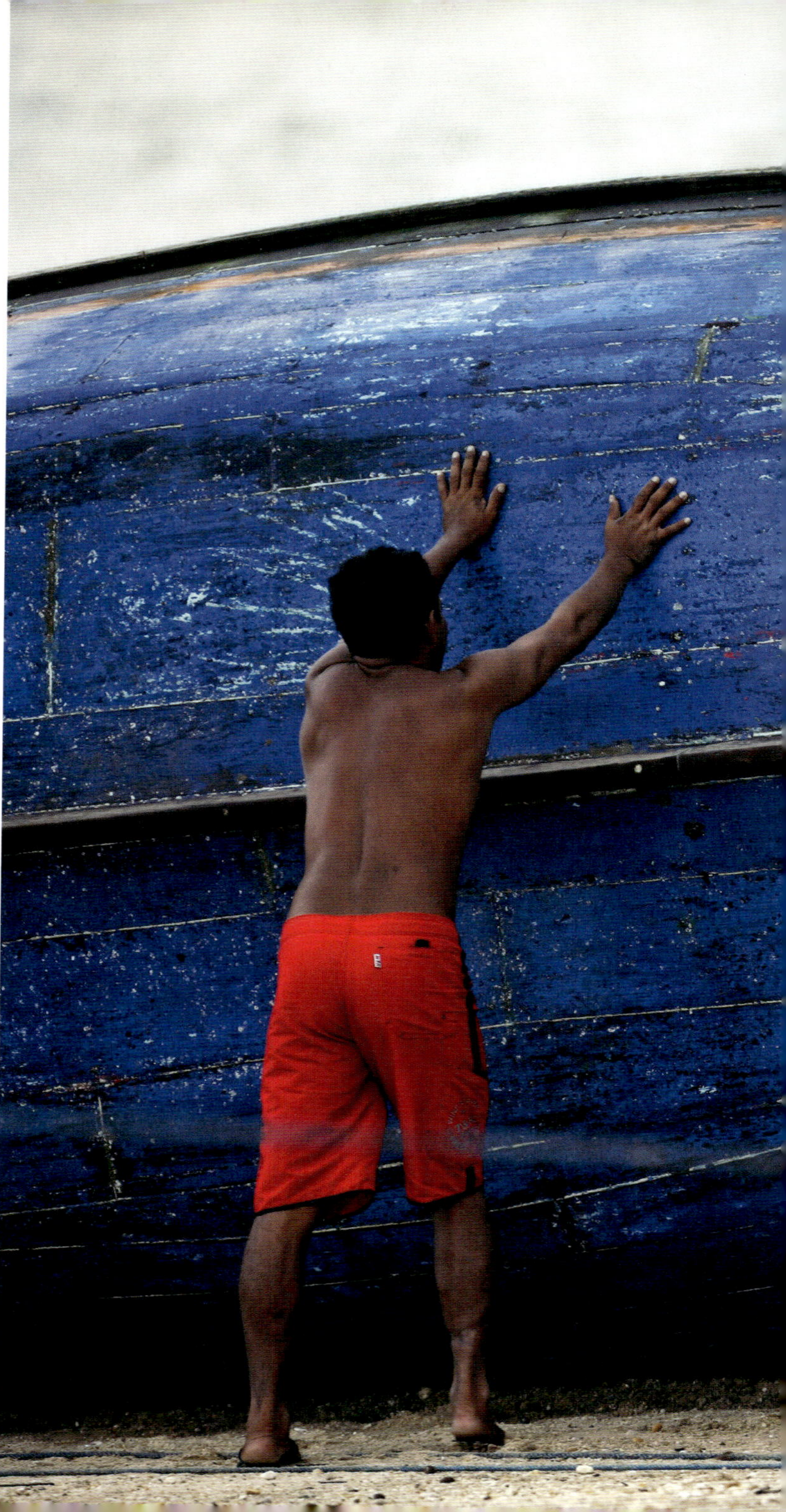

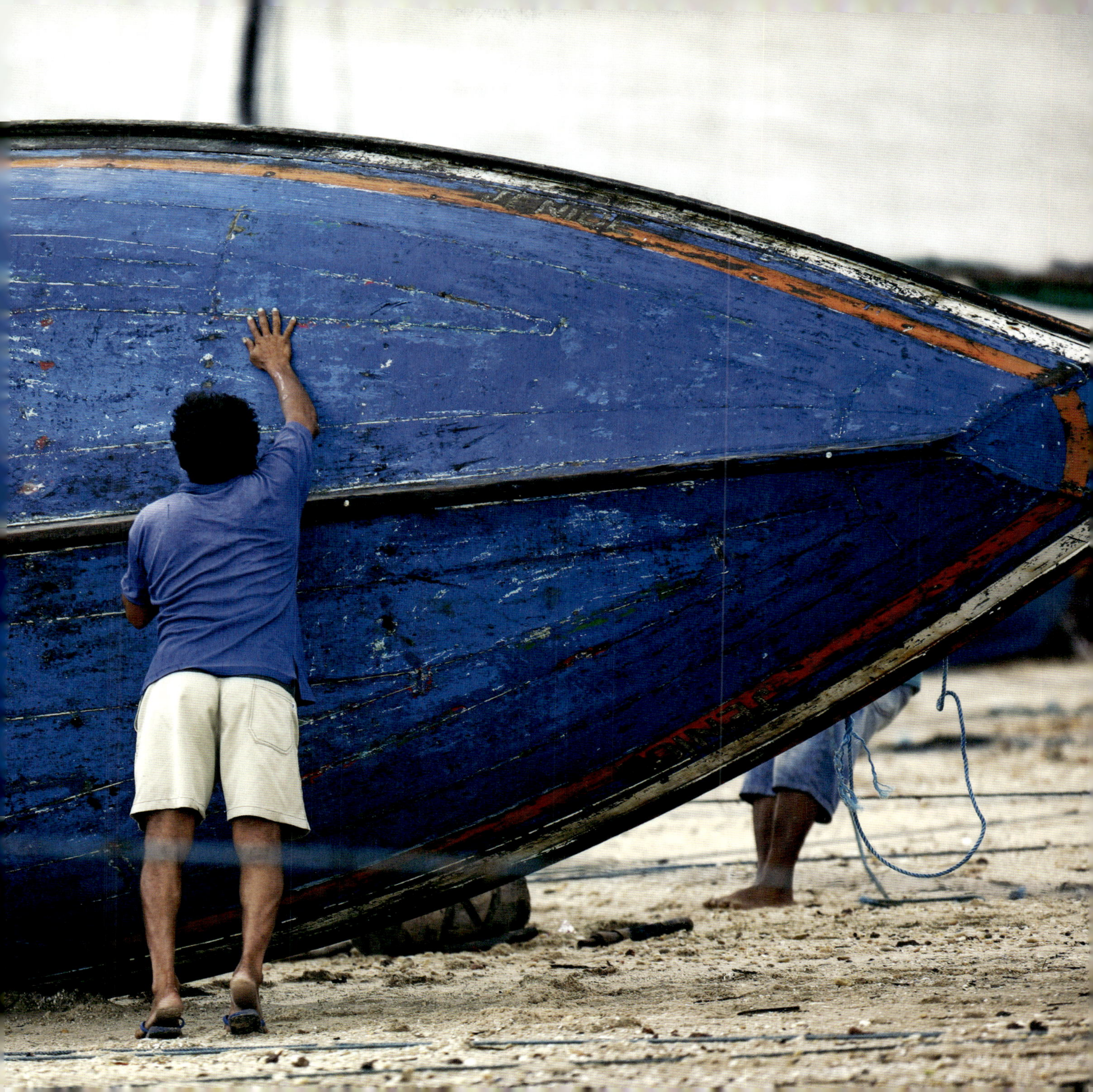

MARCH 25

The true peace of God begins
at any point a thousand miles
from the nearest land.

Joseph Conrad,
from *The Nigger of the Narcissus,* 1914

MARCH 26

The boisterous sea of liberty
is never without a wave.

Thomas Jefferson,
from a letter to Richard Rush, 1820

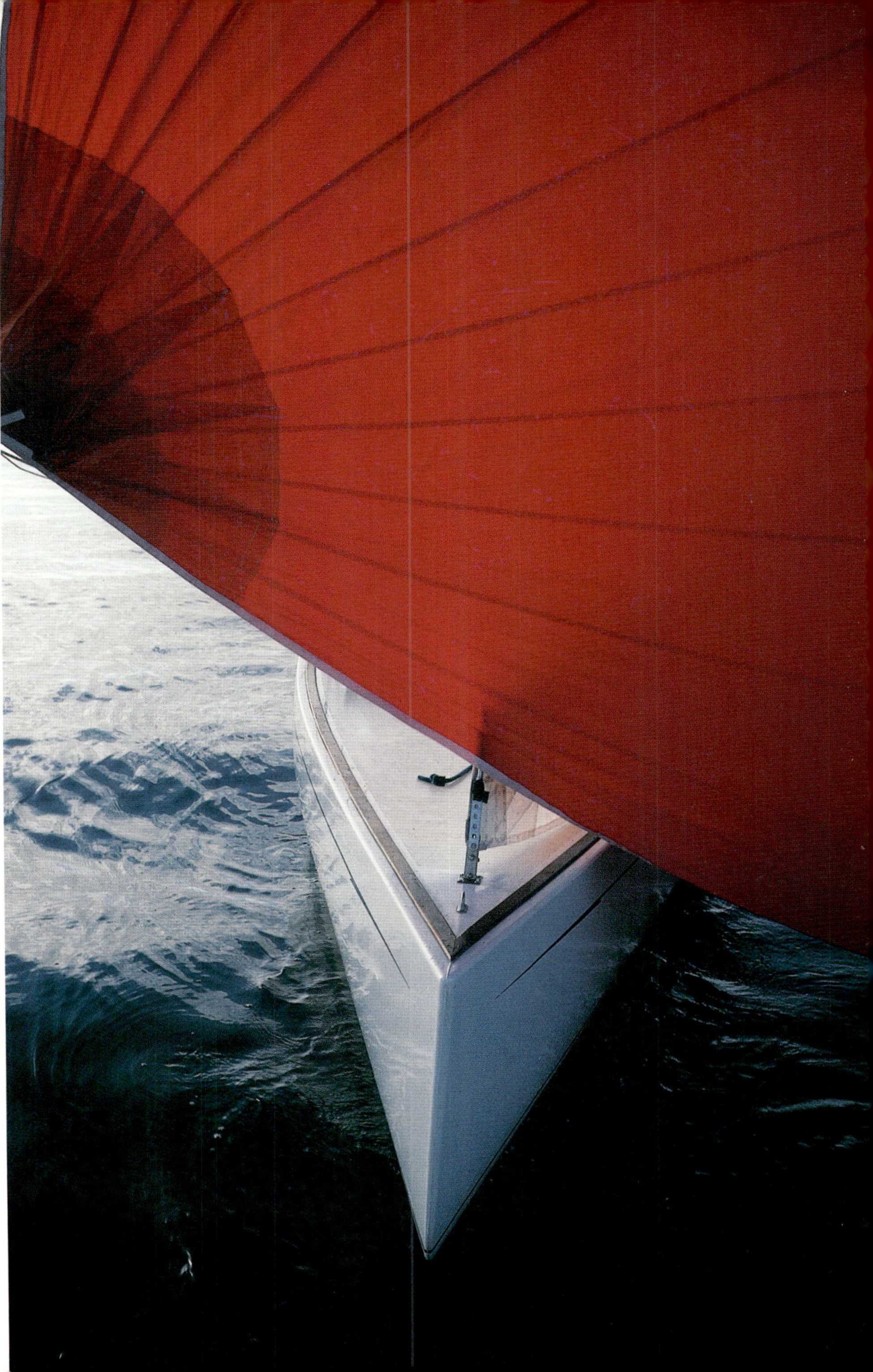

MARCH 27

The sailor out of water is, indeed, as wretched an animal as a fish out of water; for though the former hath, in common with amphibious animals, the bare power of existing on land, yet if he be kept there any time he never fails to become a nuisance.

Henry Fielding, from *The Journal of a Voyage to Lisbon,* 1755

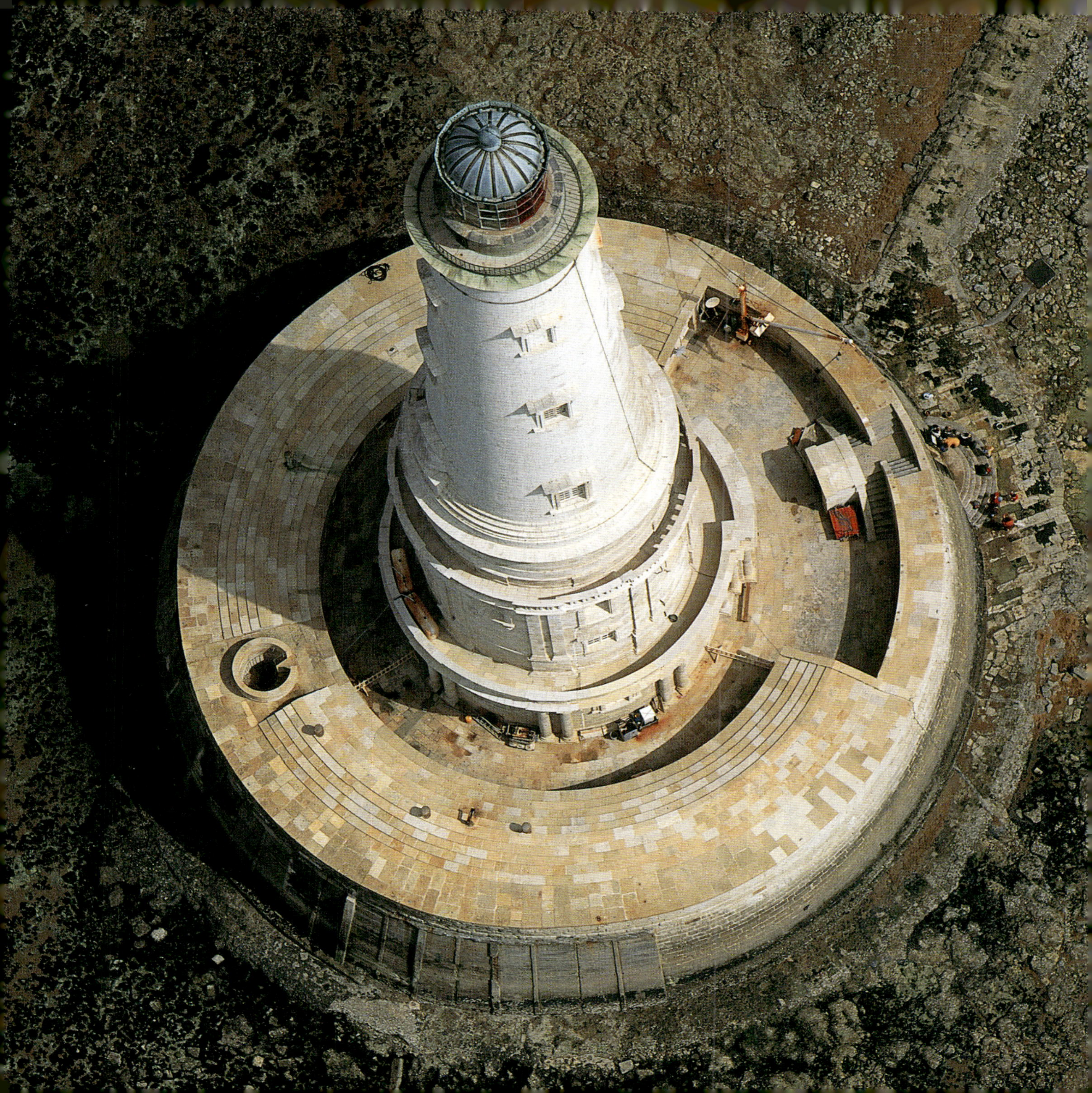

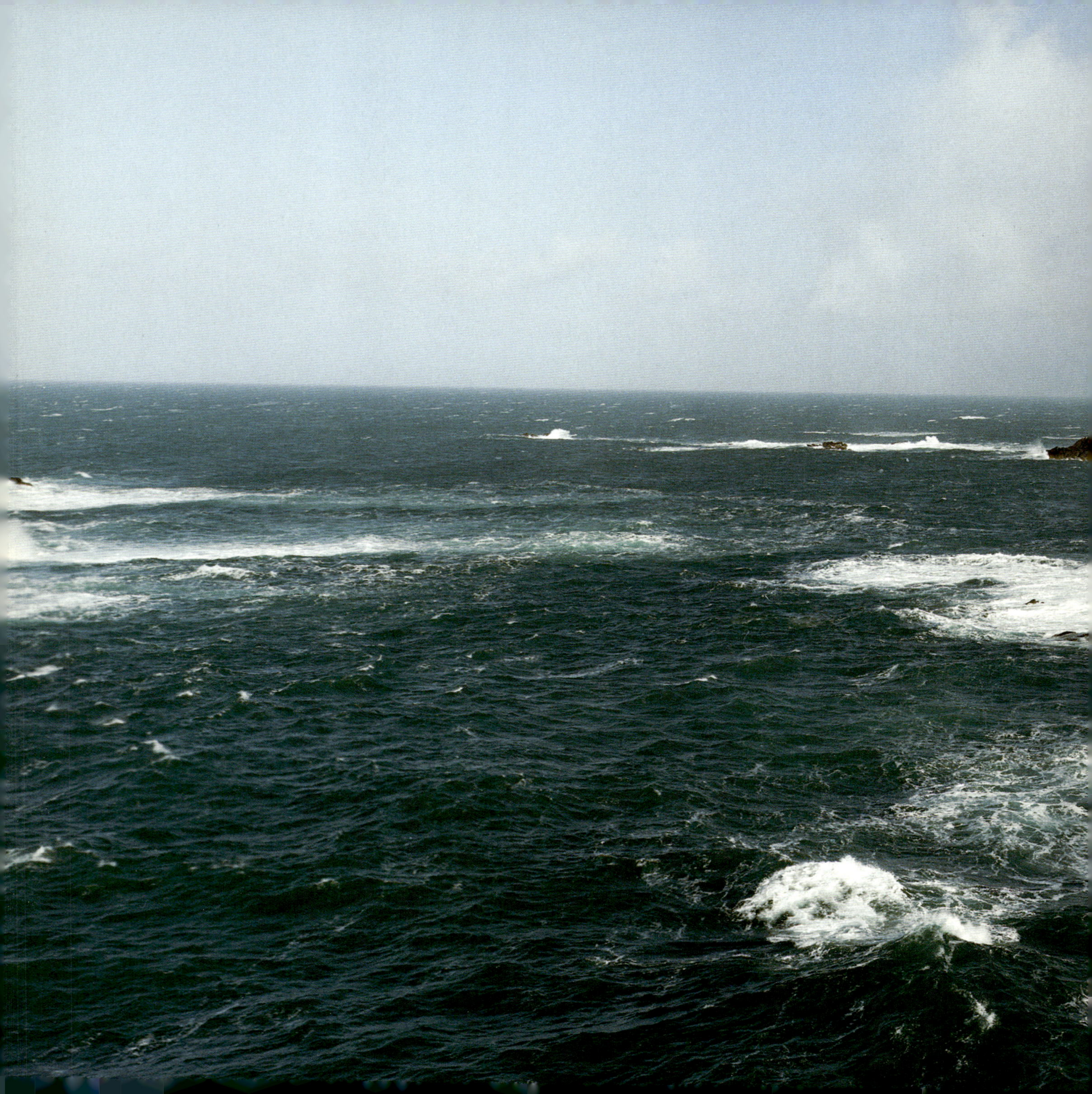

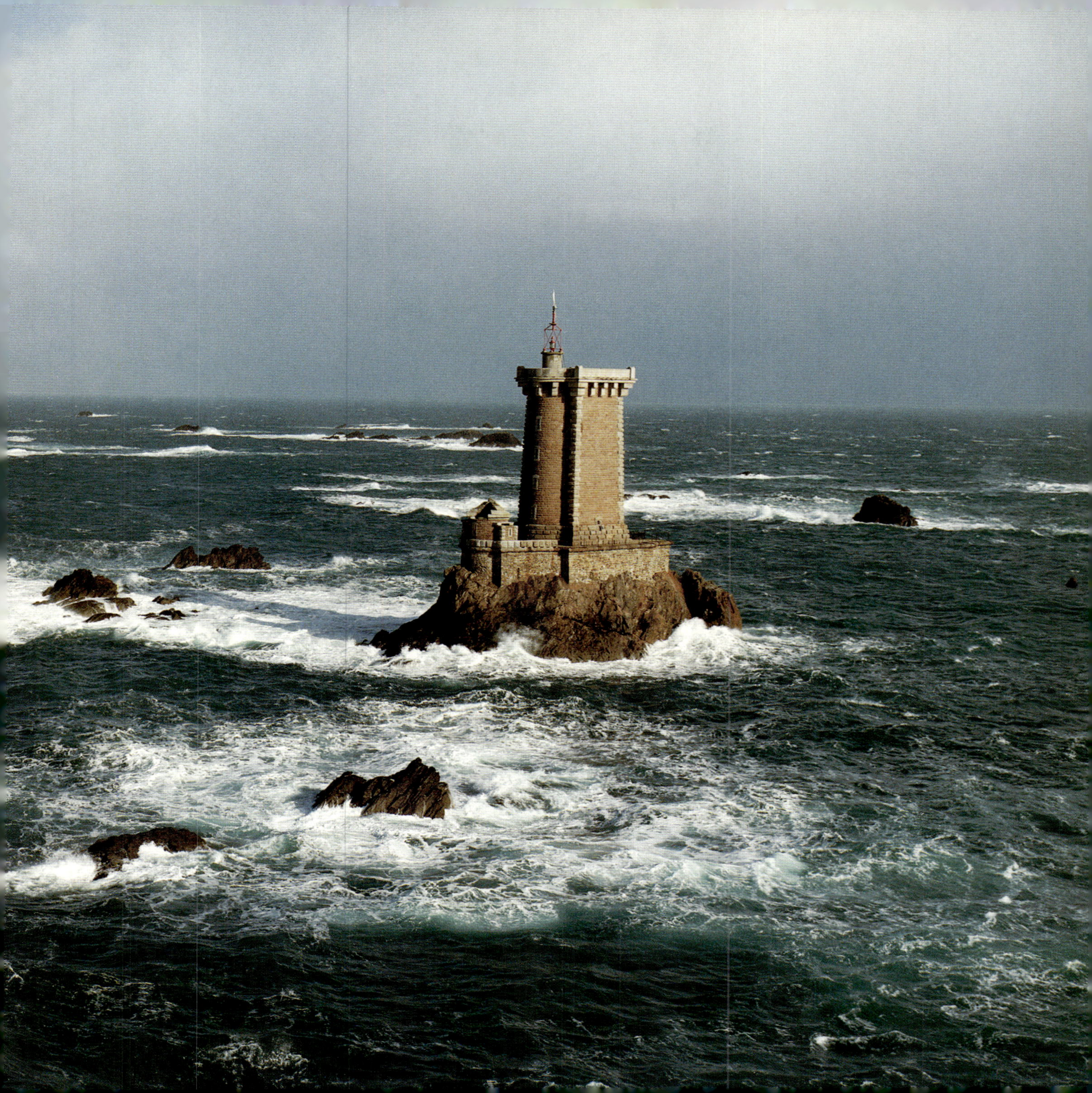

MARCH 28

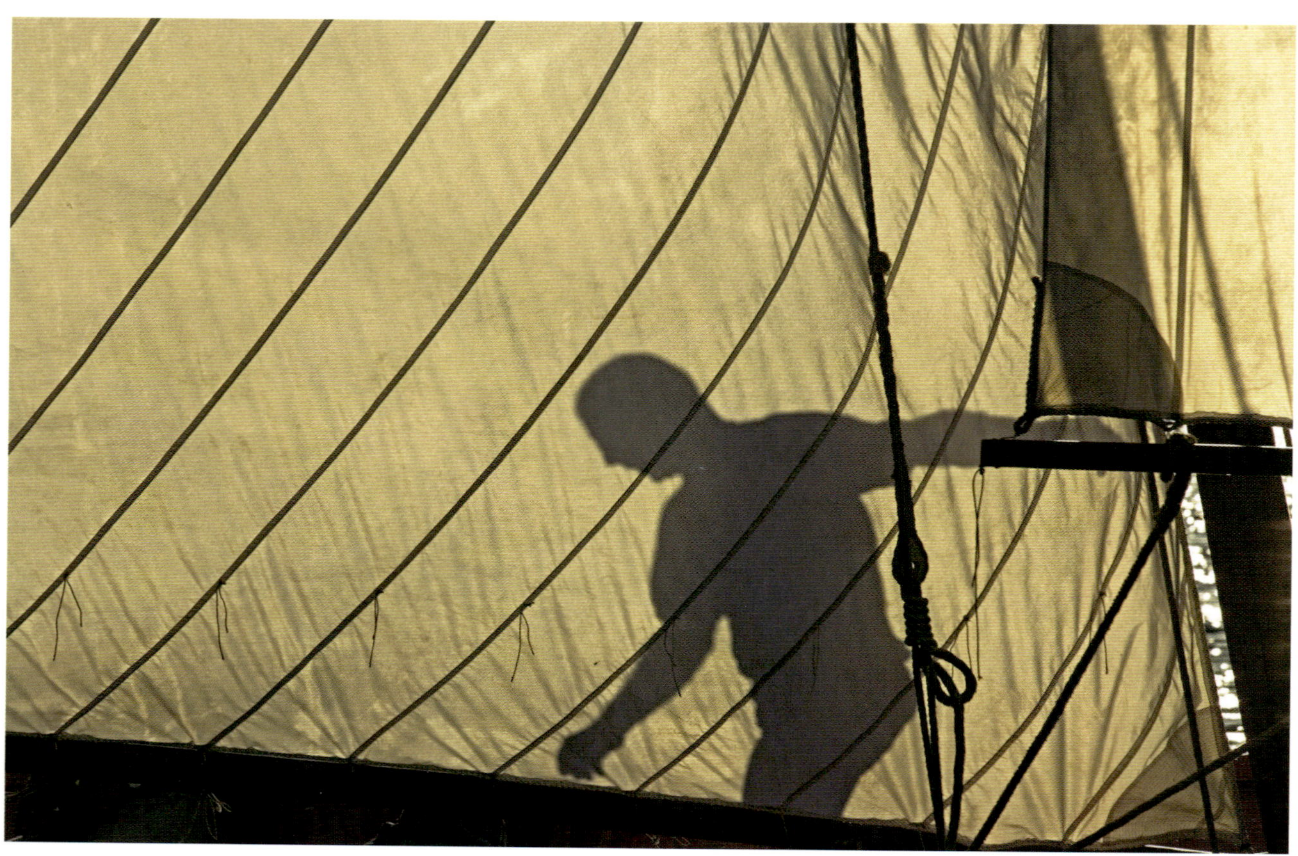

To sail is necessary.

Roman Consul Gnaeus Pompeius Magnus

MARCH 29

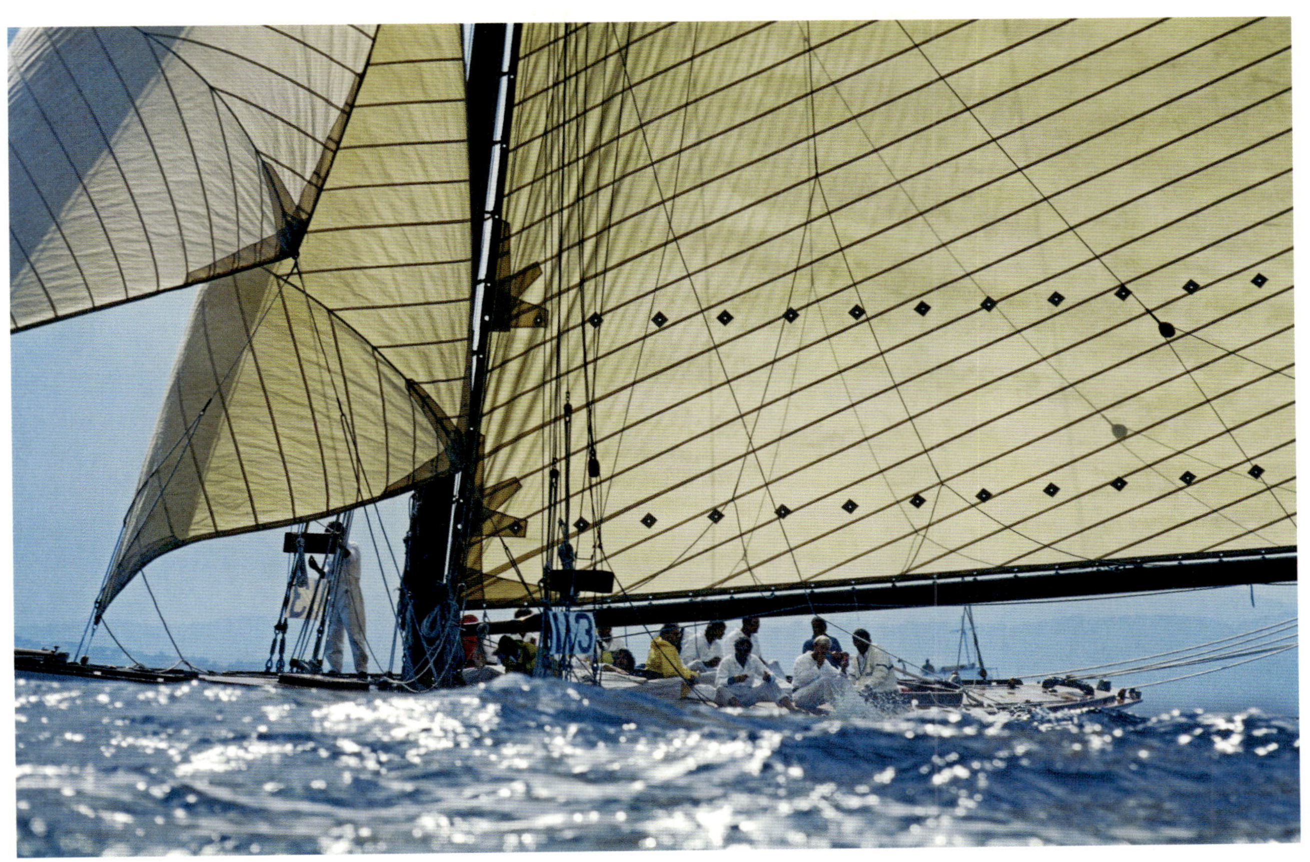

I cannot not sail.

E. B. White

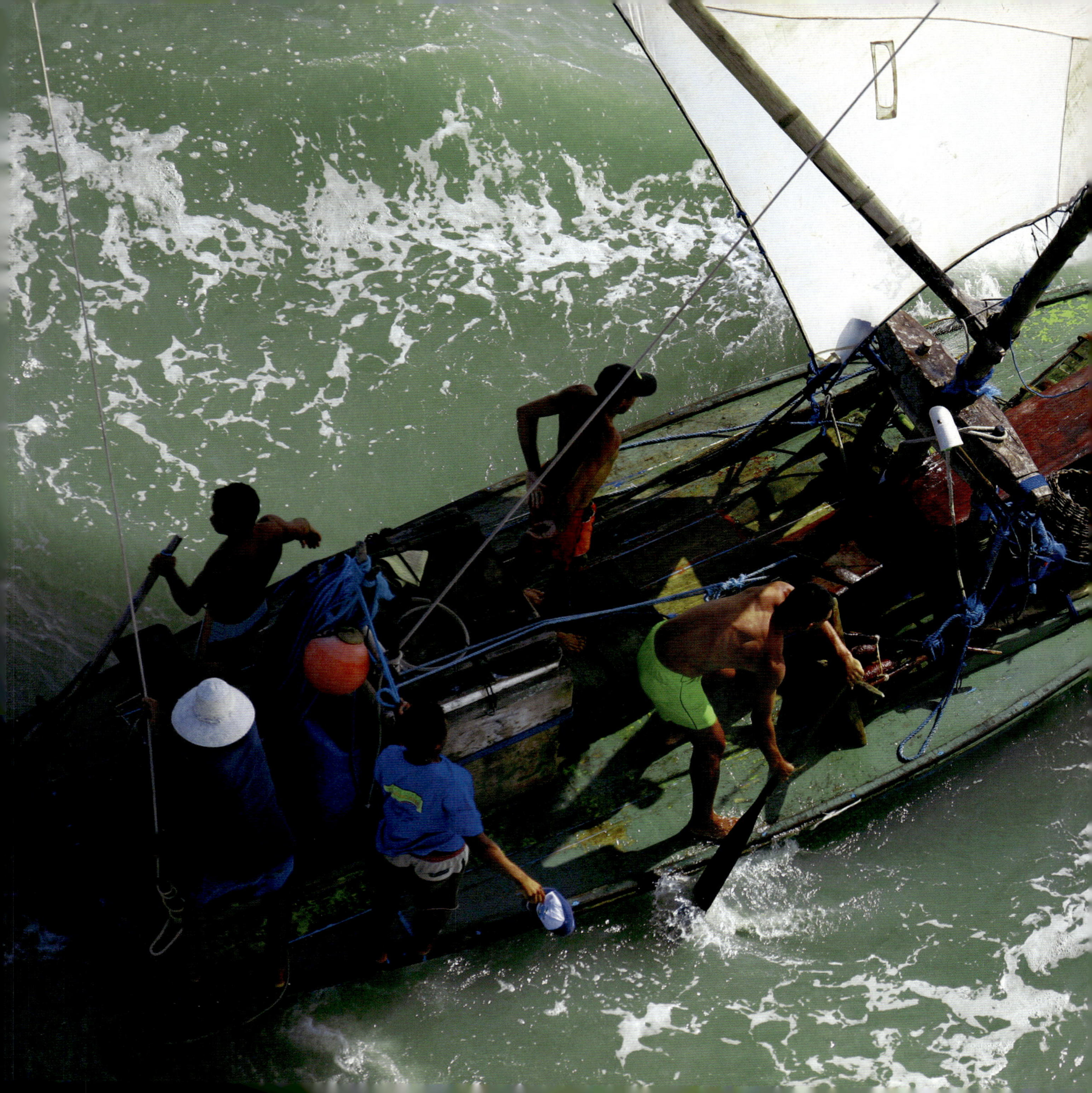

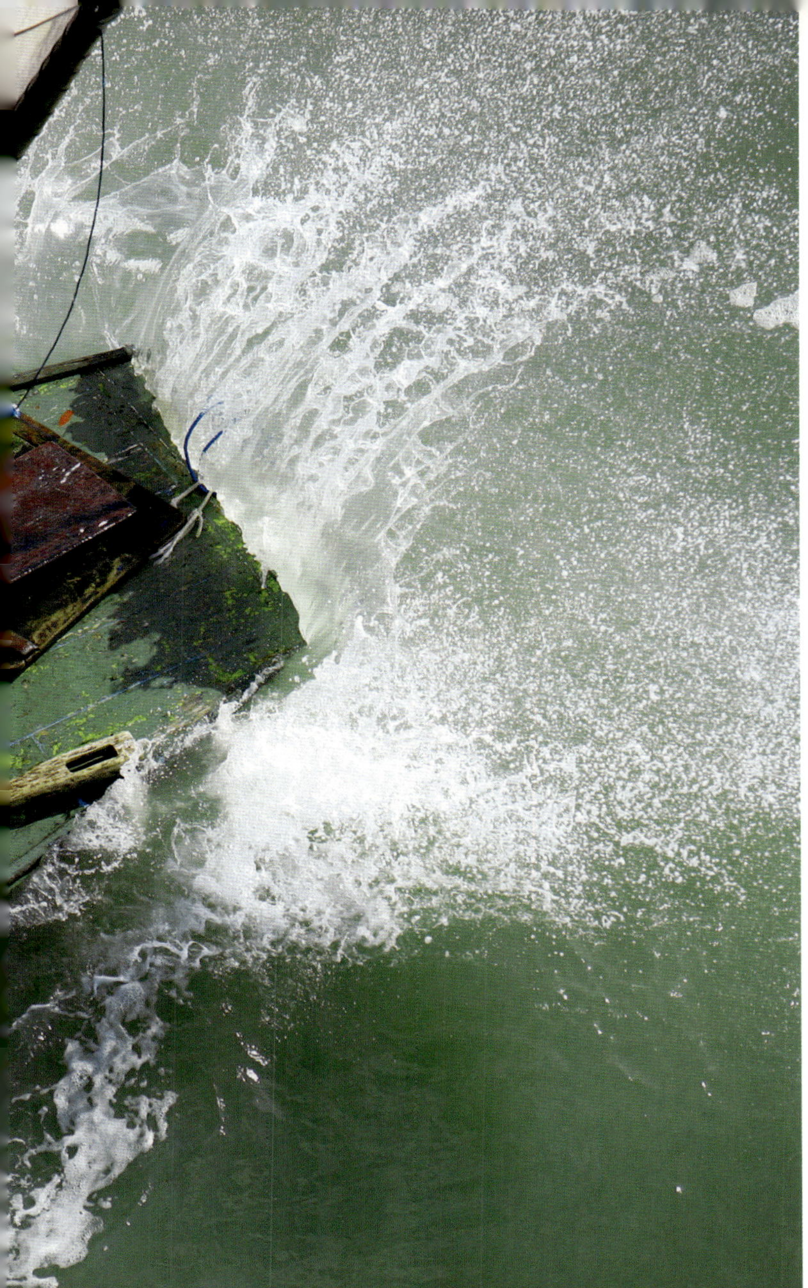

MARCH 30

Where is your ancient courage? You were used
To say extremity was the trier of spirits;
That common chances common men could bear;
That when the sea was calm all boats alike
Show'd mastership in floating.

William Shakespeare,
from *Coriolanus,* Act IV, Scene 4

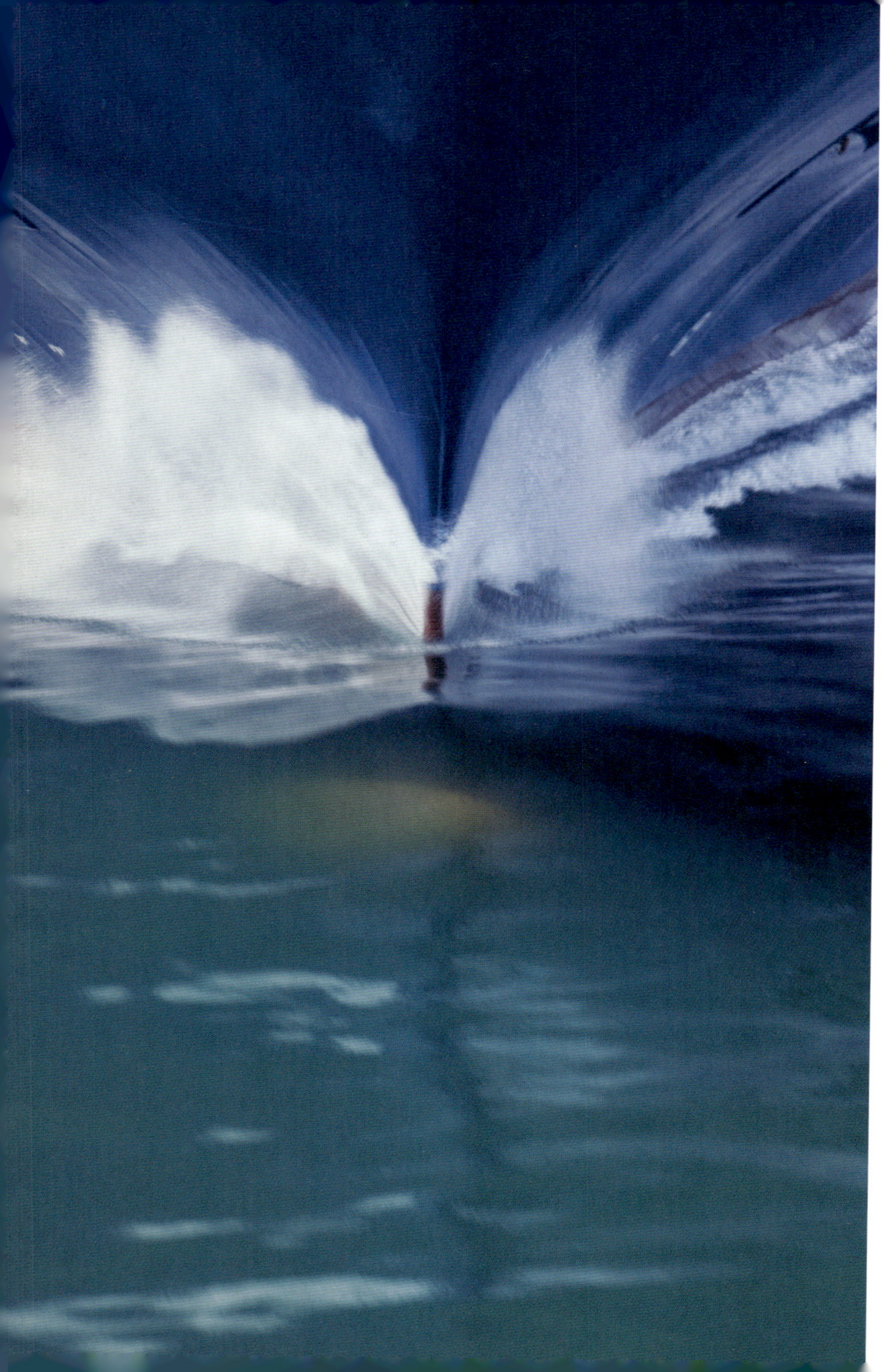

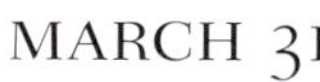

MARCH 31

Don't build a new ship
out of old wood.

Chinese proverb

APRIL 1

Under a spring mist
ice and water forget their
old differences.

Teitoku

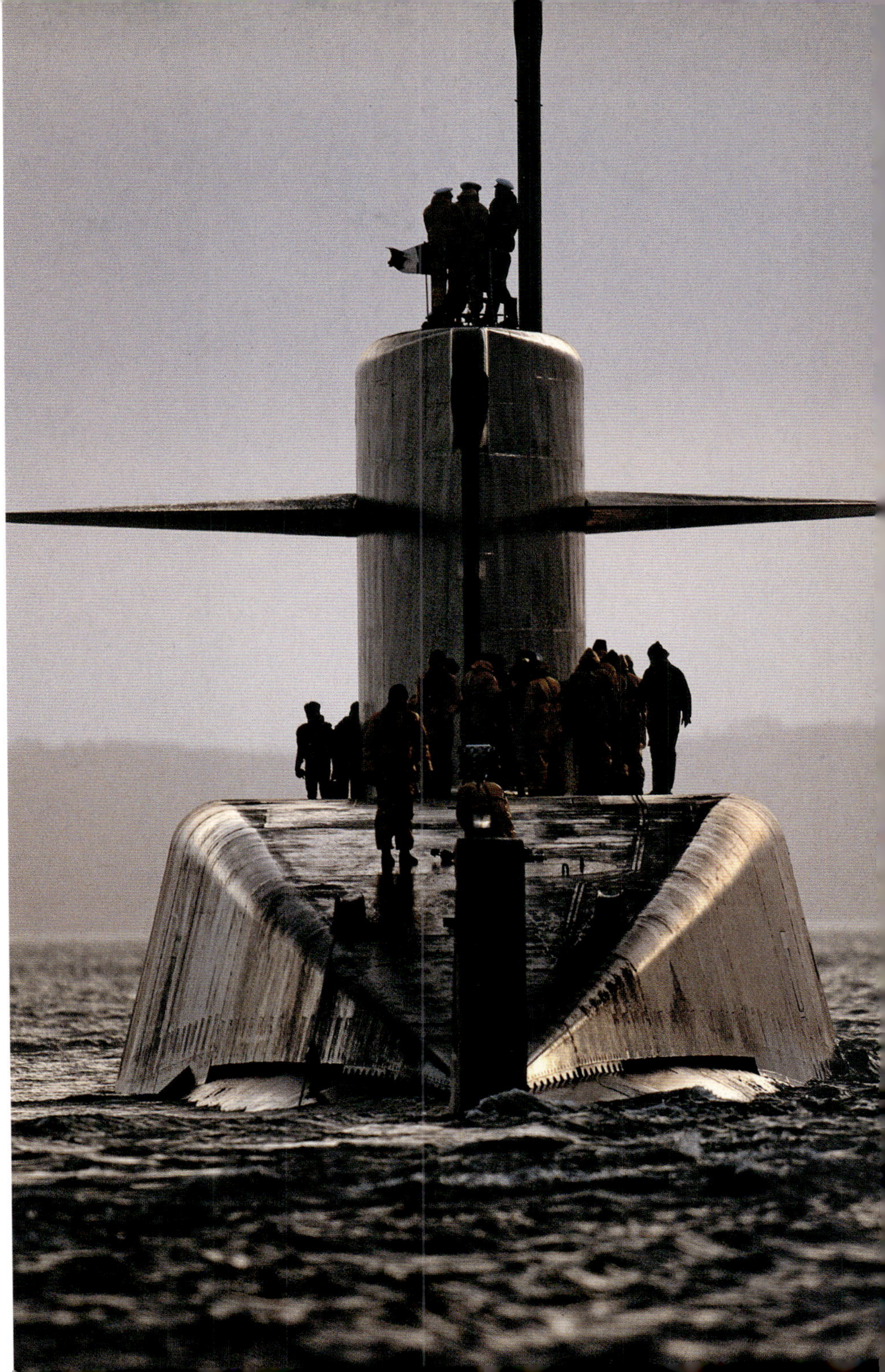

APRIL 2

Yes, faith is a goodly anchor;
When skies are sweet as a psalm,
At the bows it lolls so stalwart,
In its bluff, broad-shouldered calm.

James Russell Lowell,
from "After the Burial," 1868

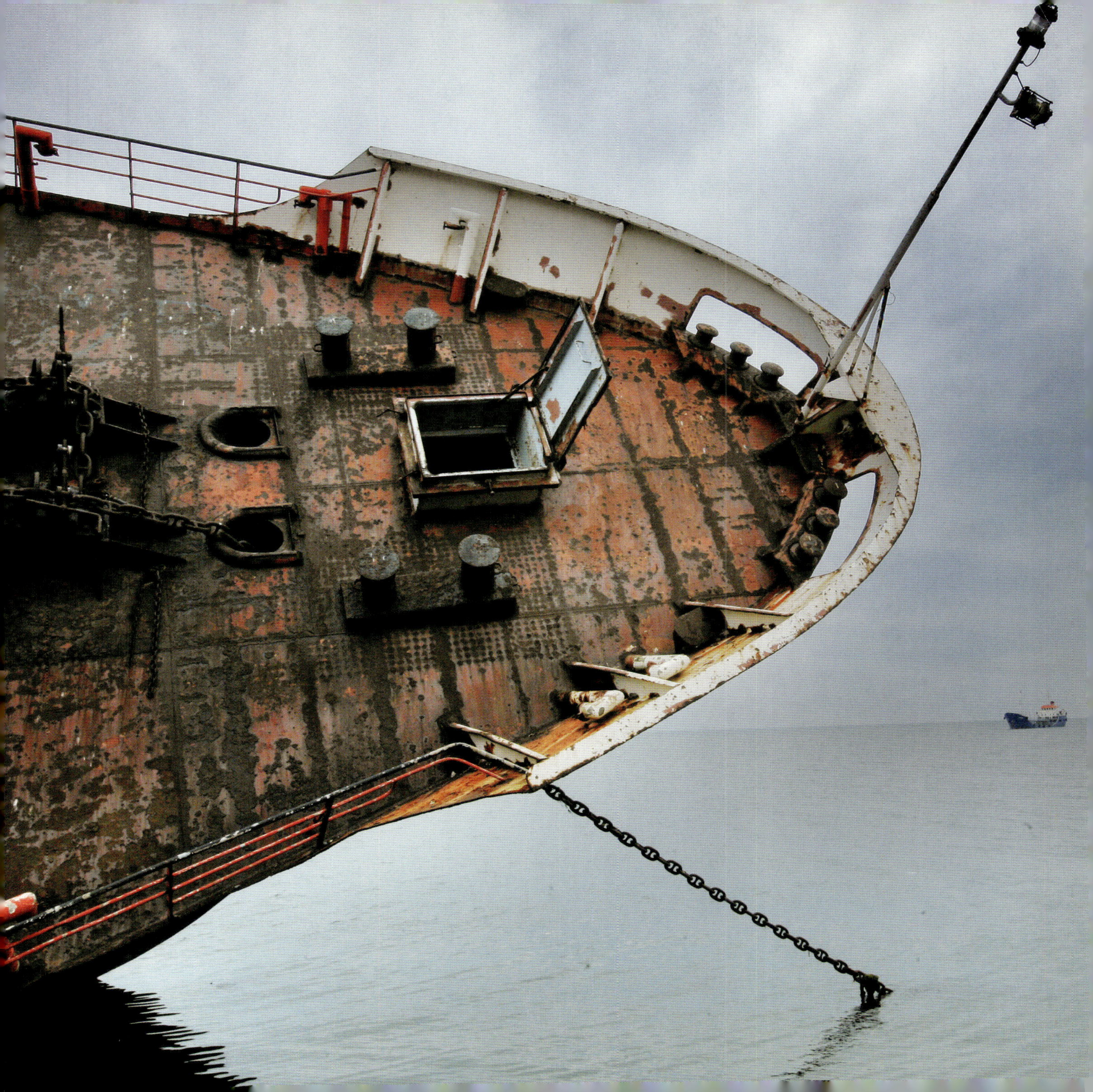

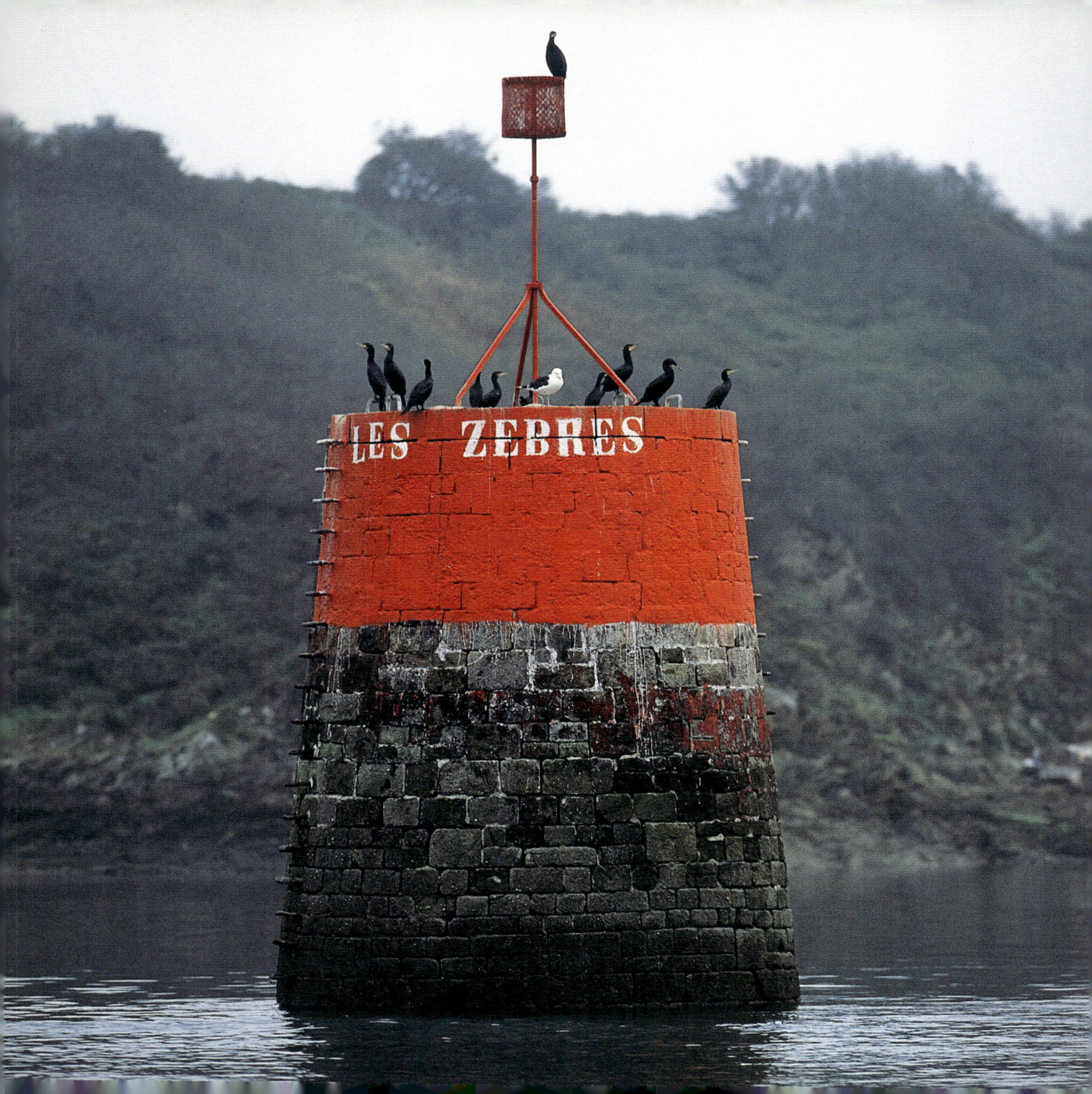
LES ZEBRES

APRIL 3

One cannot look at the sea without wishing for the wings of a swallow.

Sir Richard Burton

APRIL 4

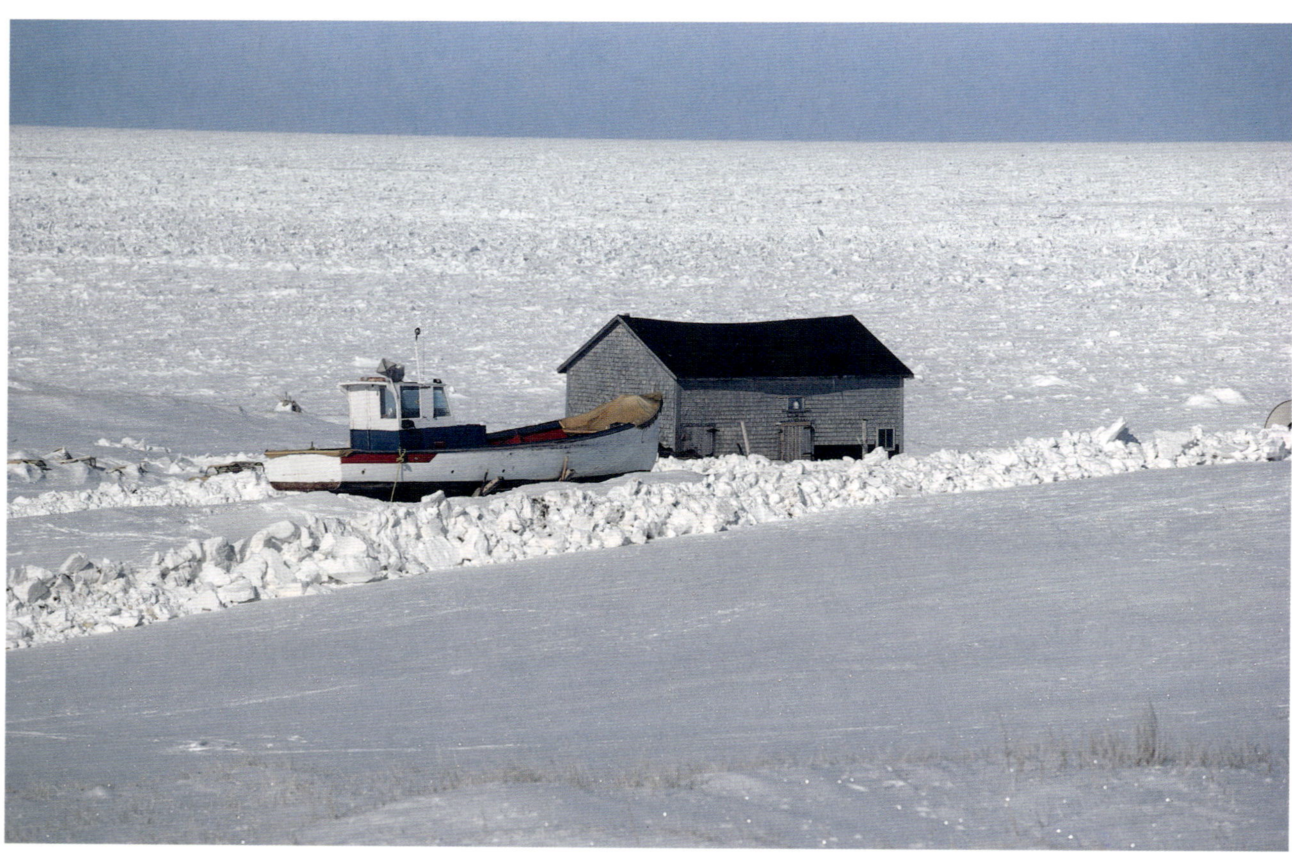

The sea drowns out humanity and time; it has no sympathy with either, for it belongs to eternity.

Oliver Wendell Holmes, from *The Autocrat at the Breakfast Table,* 1858

APRIL 5

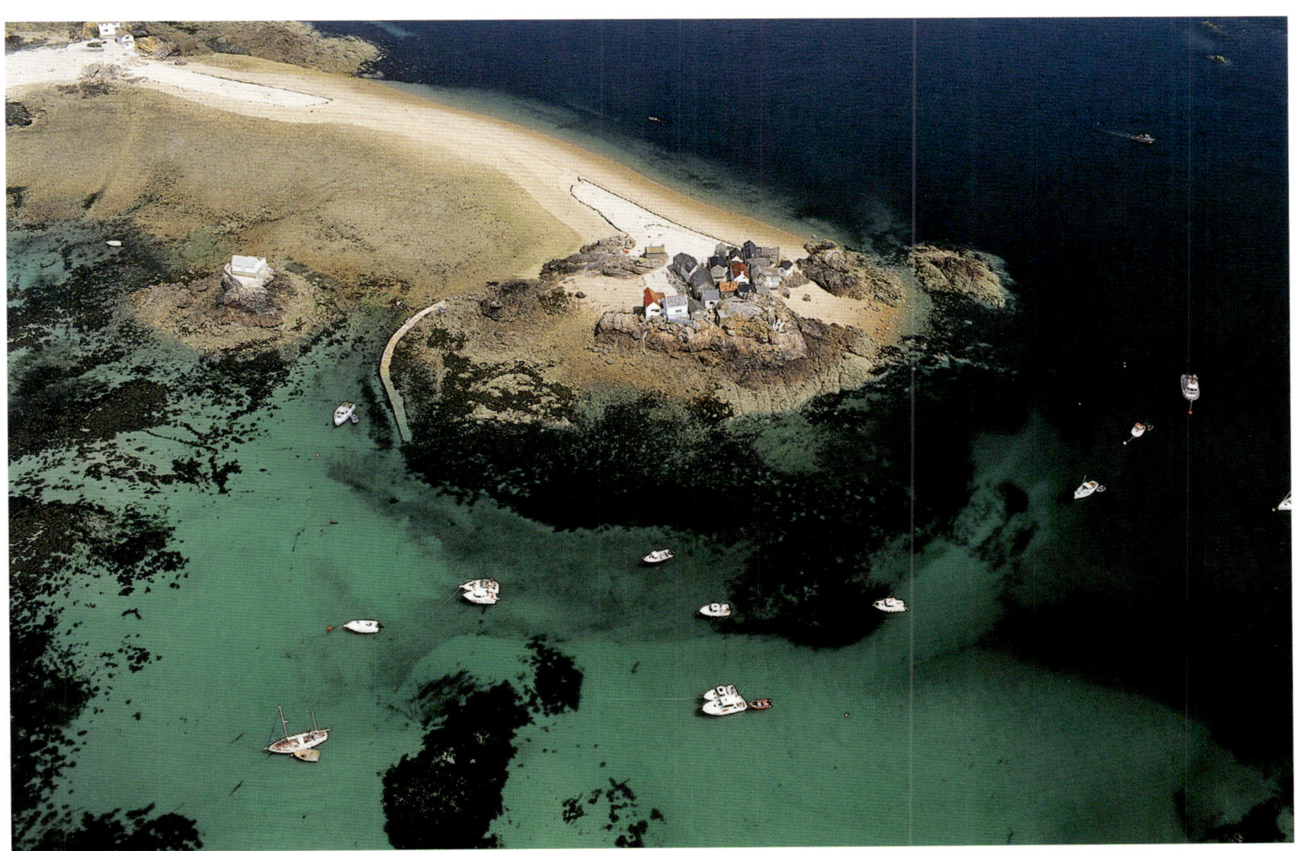

The mind is like an iceberg; it floats with one-seventh of its bulk above water.

Sigmund Freud

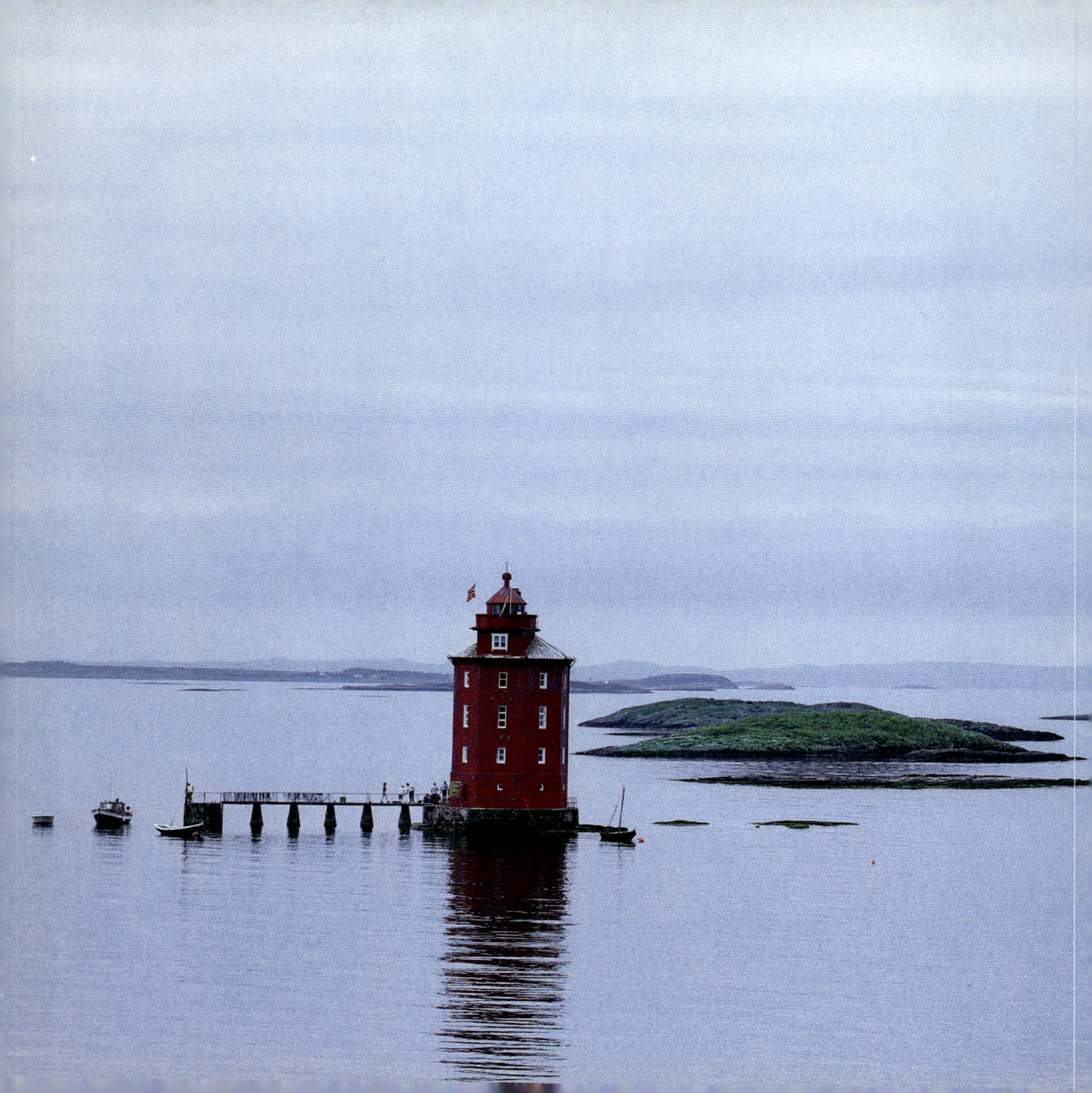

APRIL 6

From bourn to bourn, region to region.
By you being pardon'd, we commit no crime
To use one language in each several clime.

William Shakespeare,
from *Pericles, Prince of Tyre,* Act IV, Scene 4

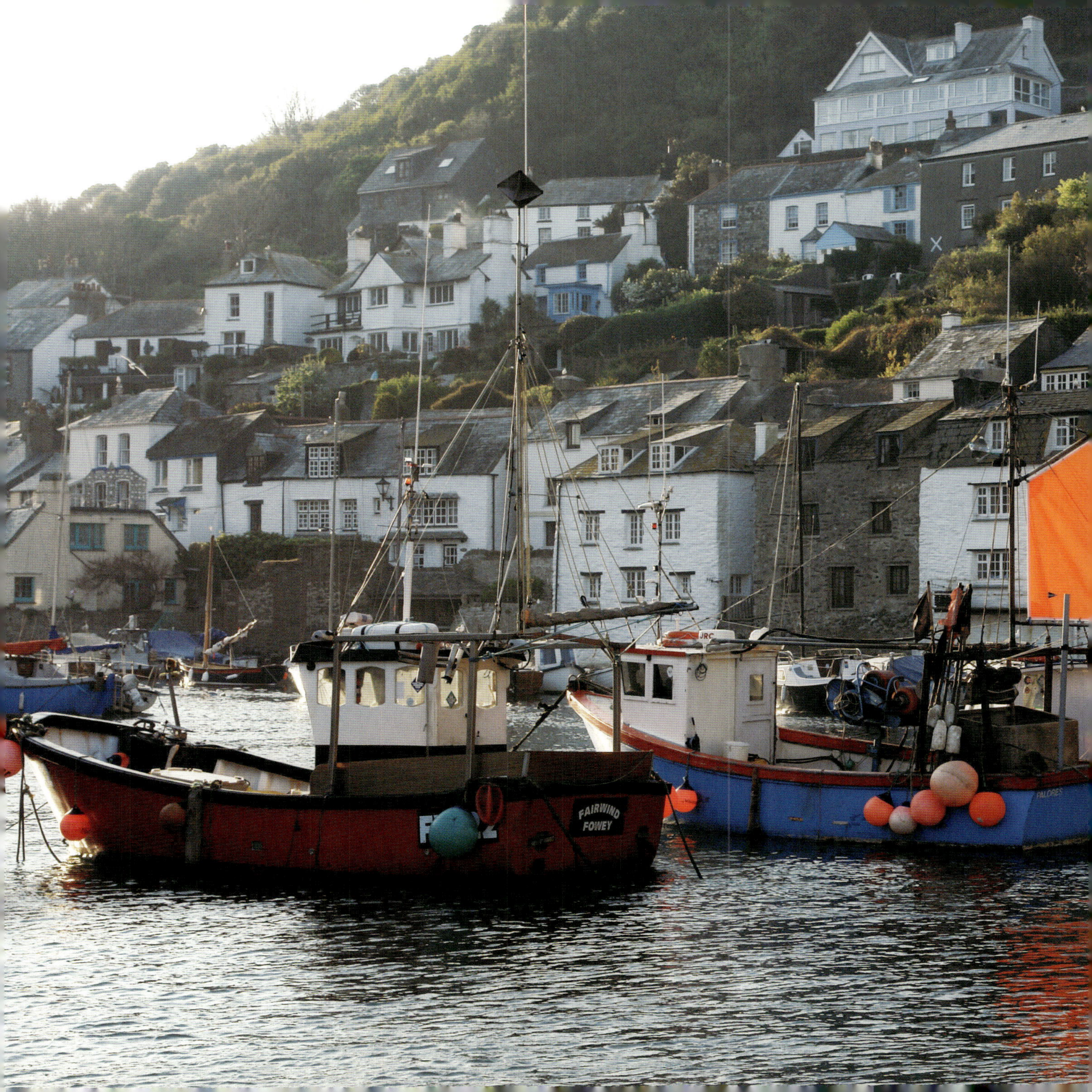
FAIRWIND
FOWEY

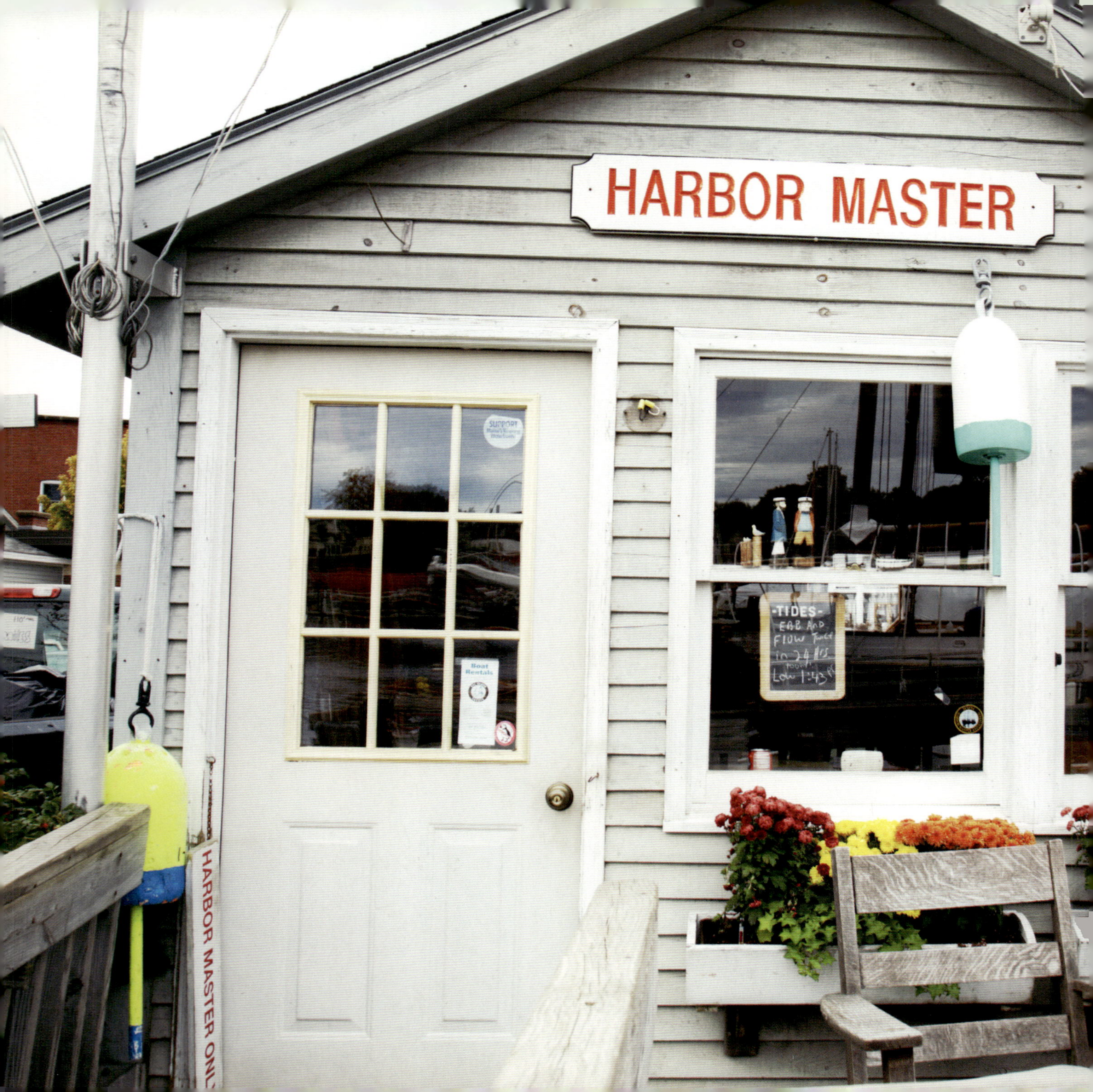
HARBOR MASTER
SUPPORT
Boat Rentals
-TIDES-
HARBOR MASTER

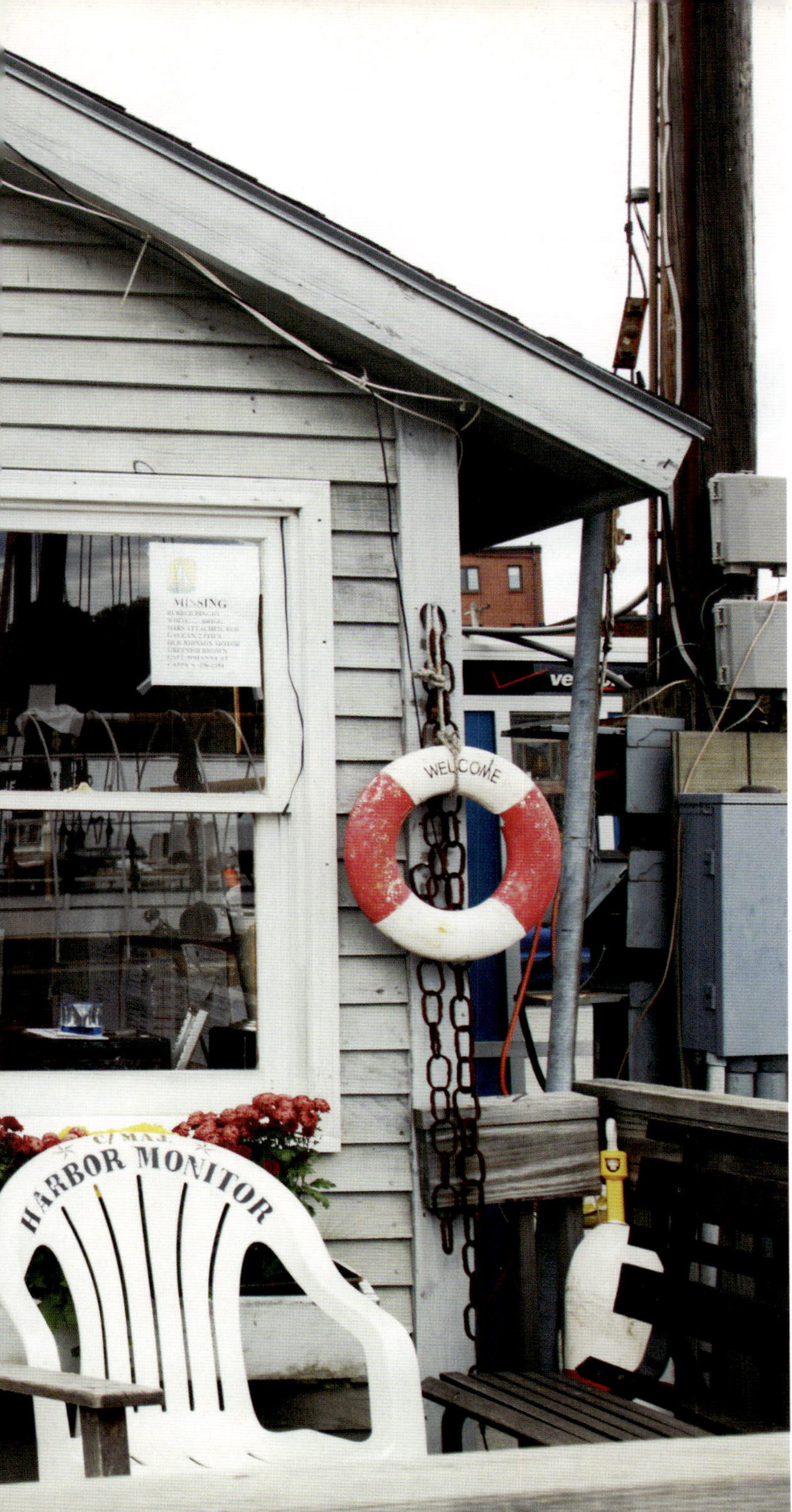

APRIL 7

To multiply the Harbors
does not reduce the Sea.

Emily Dickinson,
from her letters, 1873

APRIL 8

Fish of the ocean, fish of iron.

Arab proverb

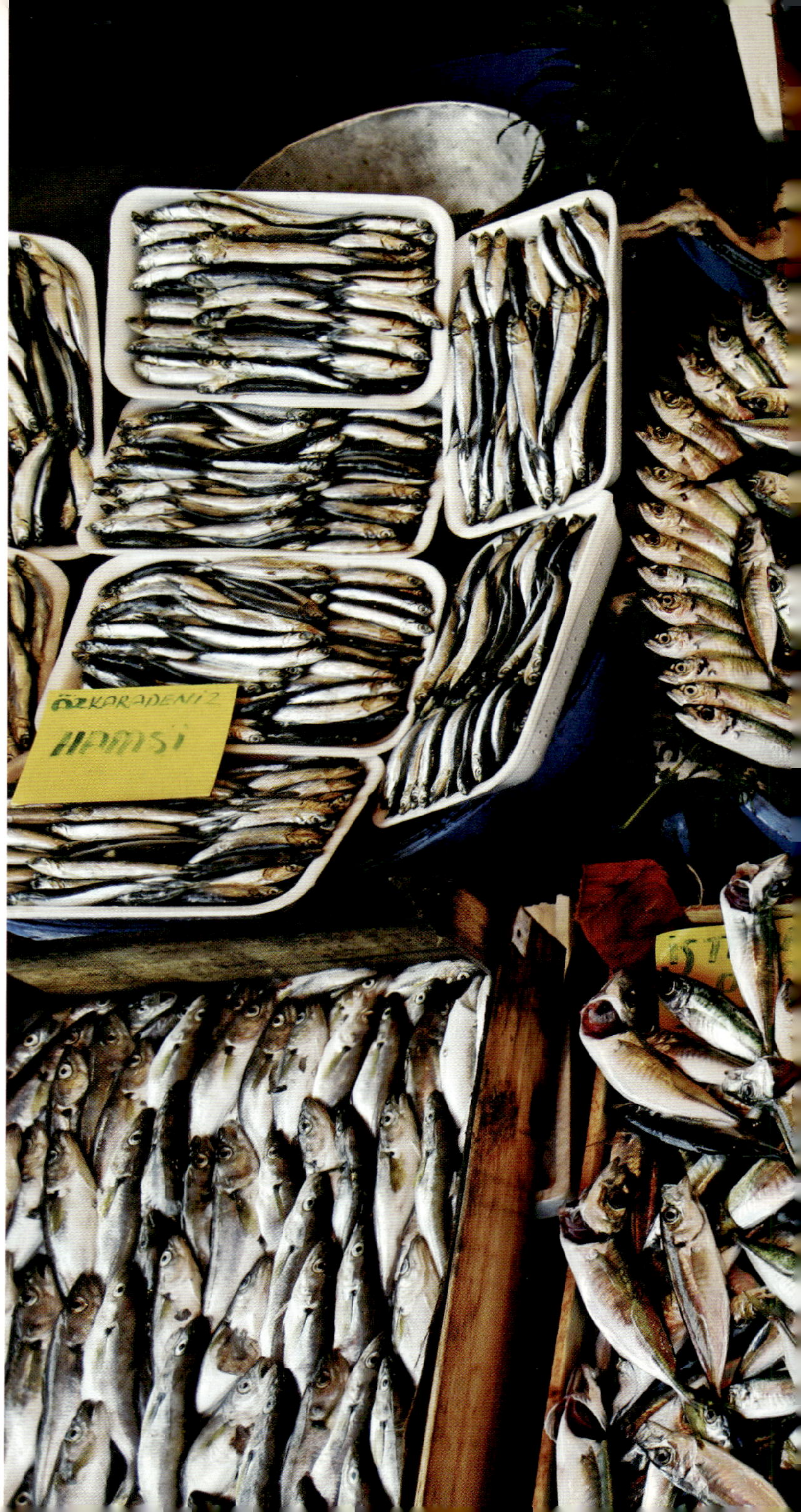

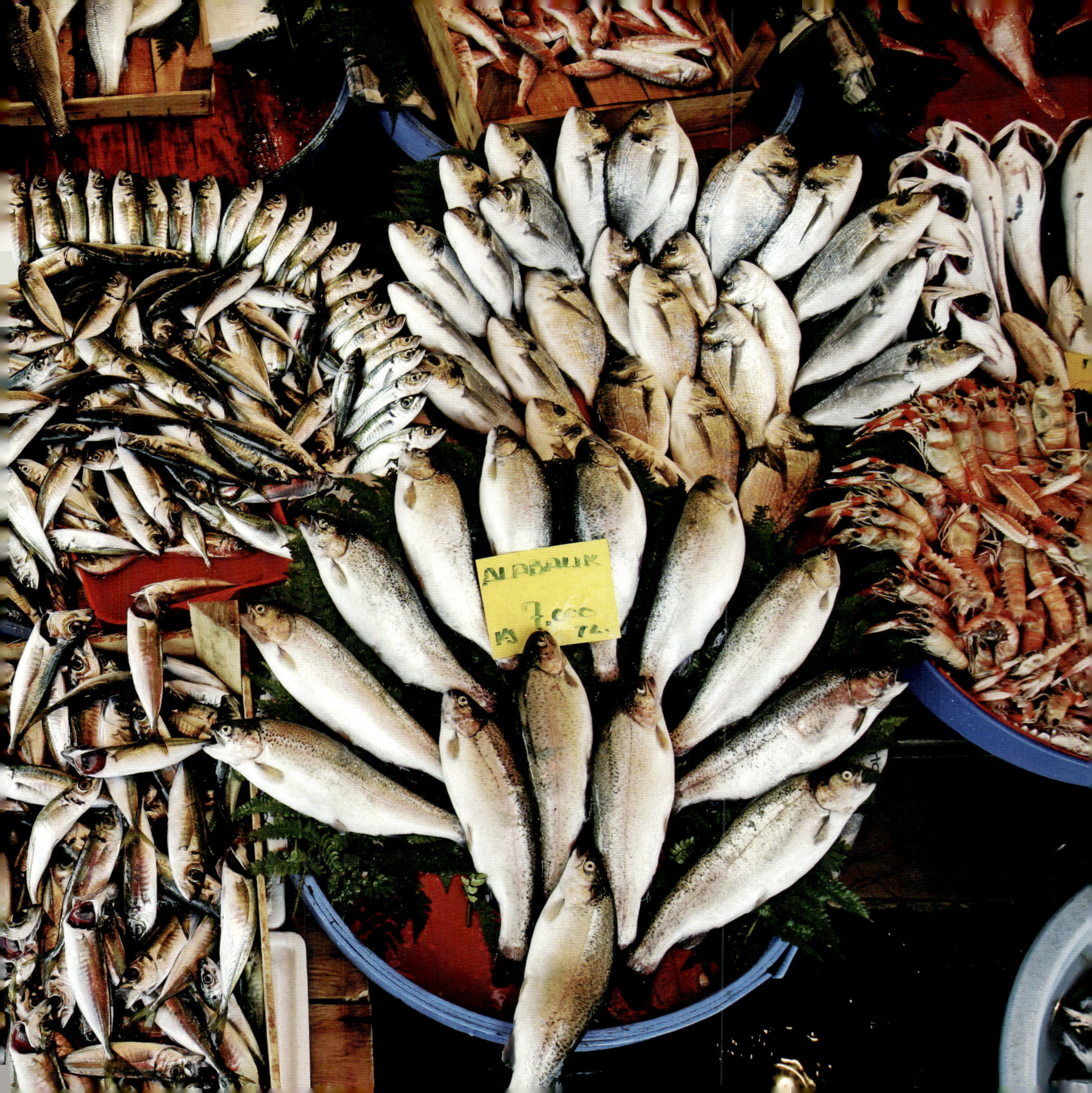
ALABALIK
7.000
TL.

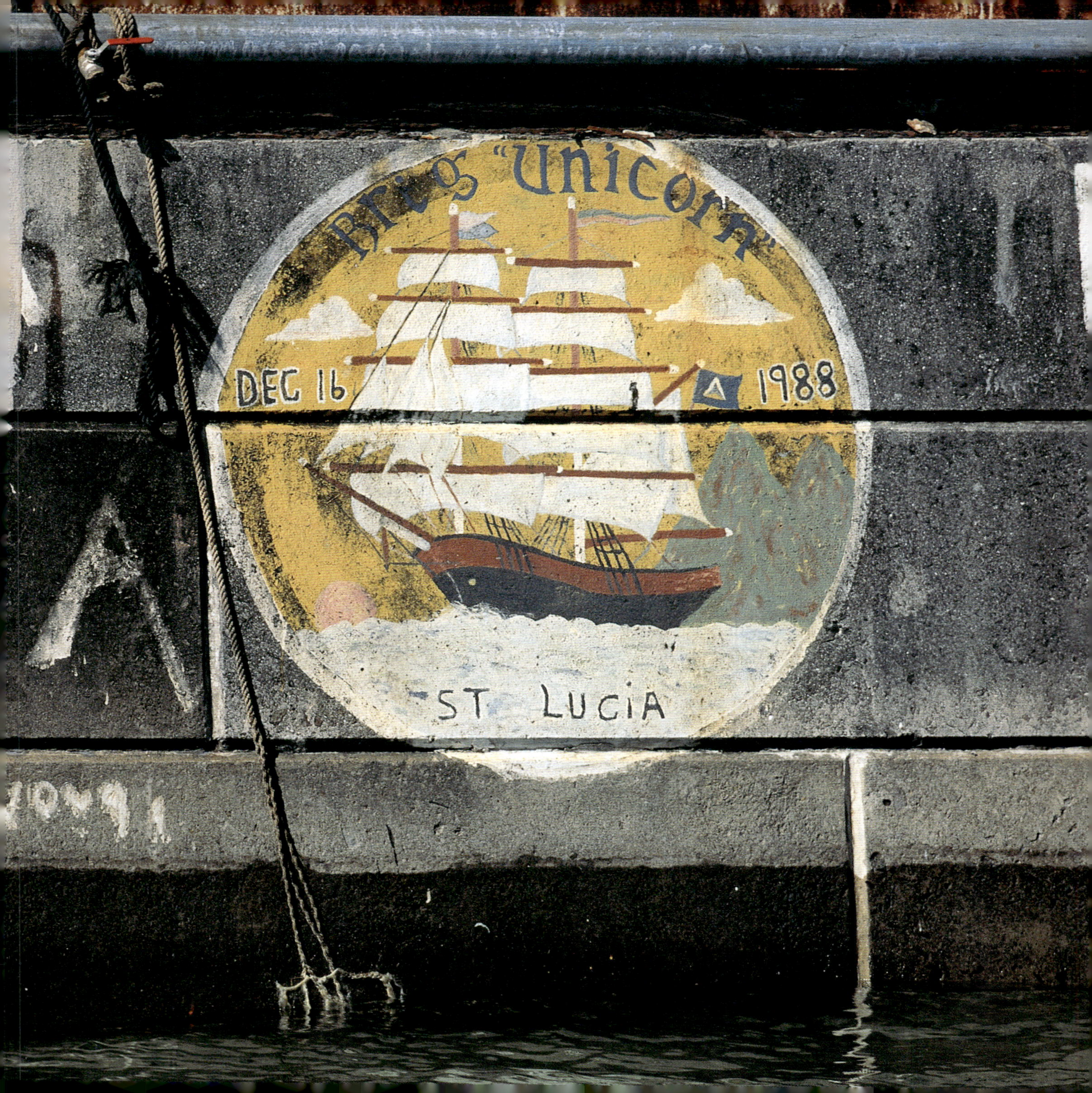
Brig "Unicorn"
DEC 16
1988
ST LUCIA

APRIL 9

Anon the master commandeth fast
To his ship-men in all the haste,
To dresse them soon about the mast
Their takeling to make.

Fifteenth-century English chantey

APRIL 10

This was charming, no doubt: but they shortly found out
That the Captain they trusted so well
Had only one notion for crossing the ocean,
And that was to tingle his bell.

Lewis Carroll,
from "The Hunting of the Snark," 1874

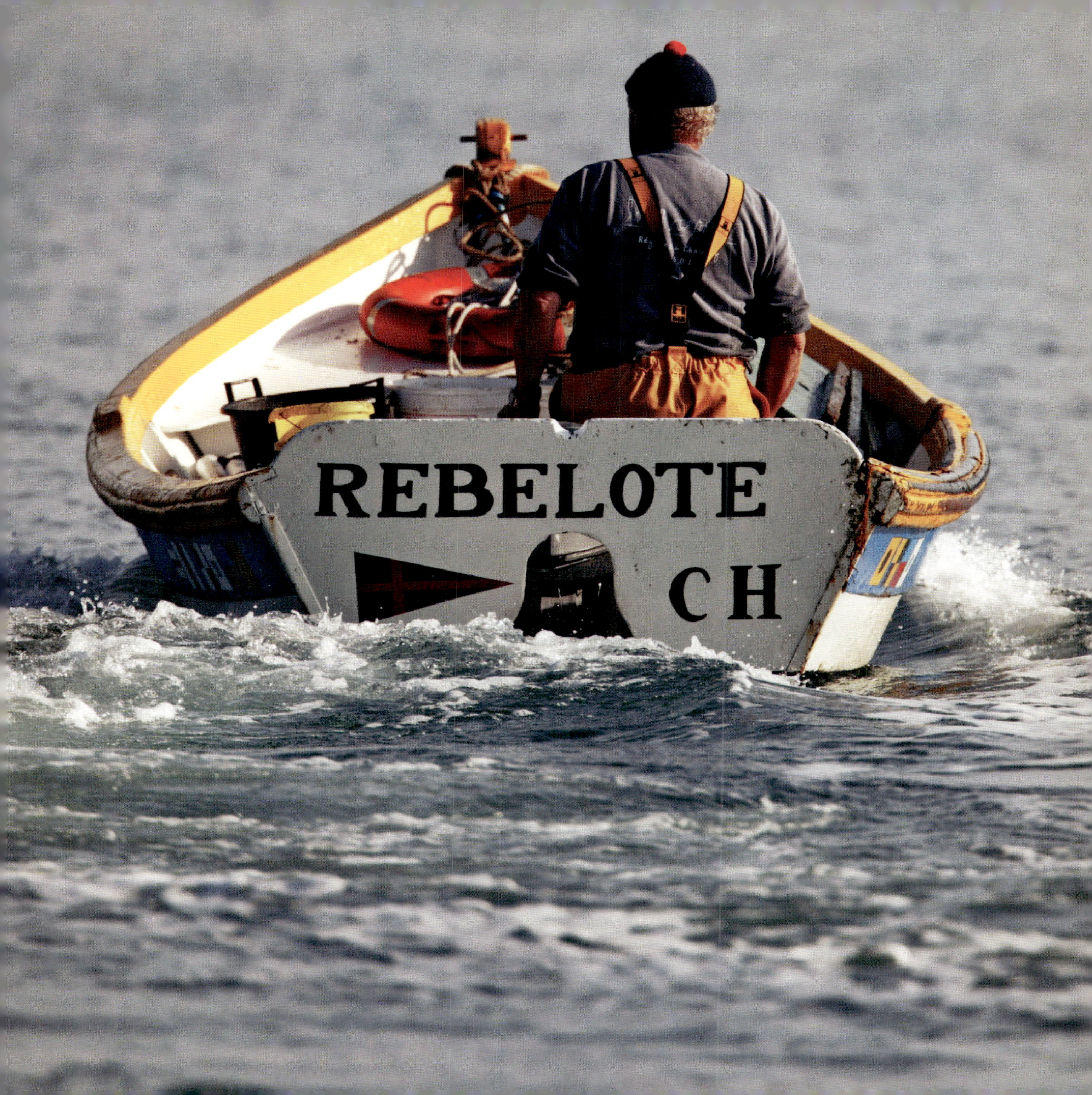
REBELOTE
CH

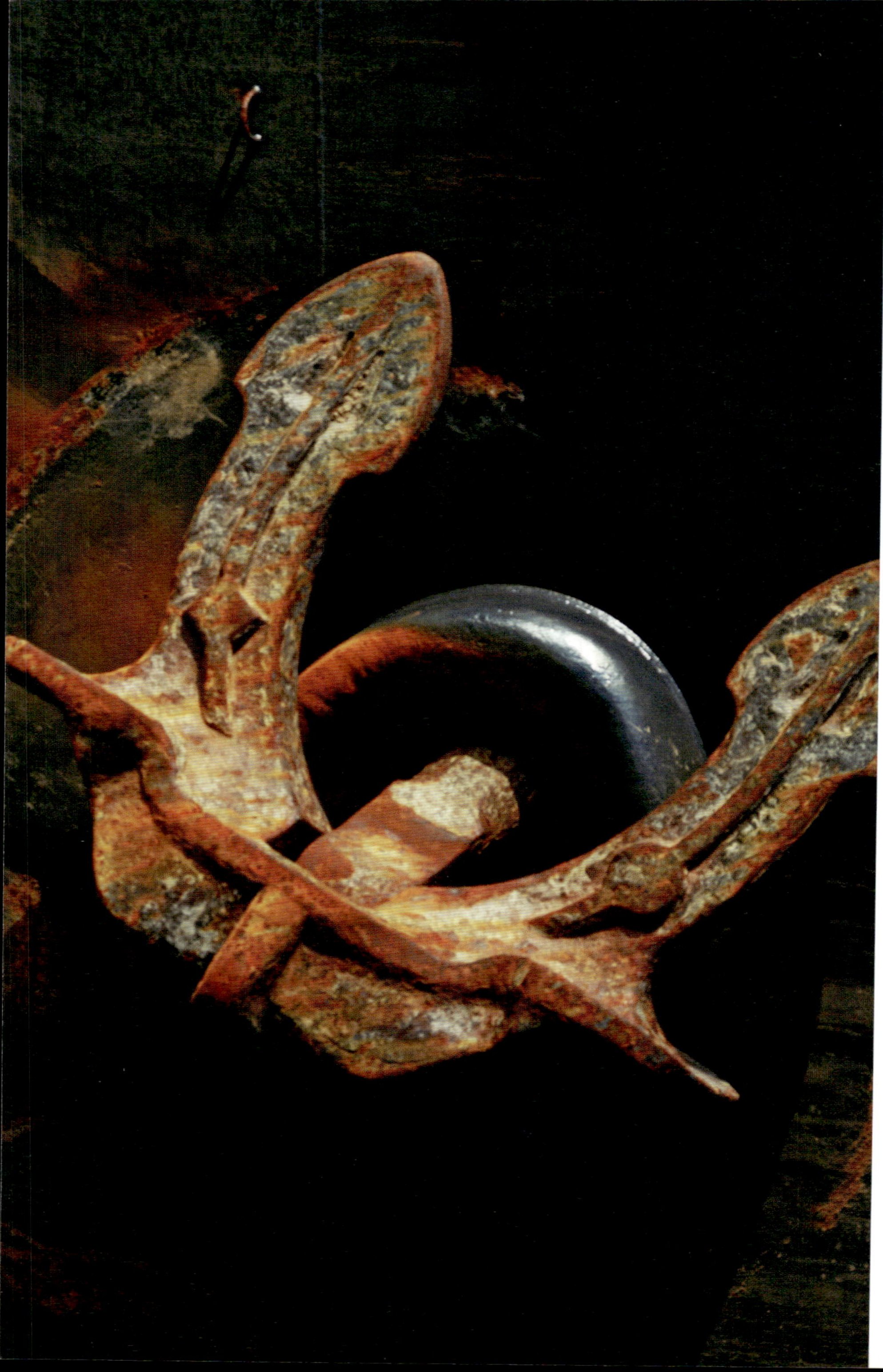

APRIL 11

If the highest aim of a captain
were to preserve his ship,
he would keep it in port forever.

St. Thomas Aquinas

APRIL 12

A ship is a bit of terra firma
cut off from the main; it is a state
in itself; and the captain
is its king.

Herman Melville,
from *White-Jacket,* 1850

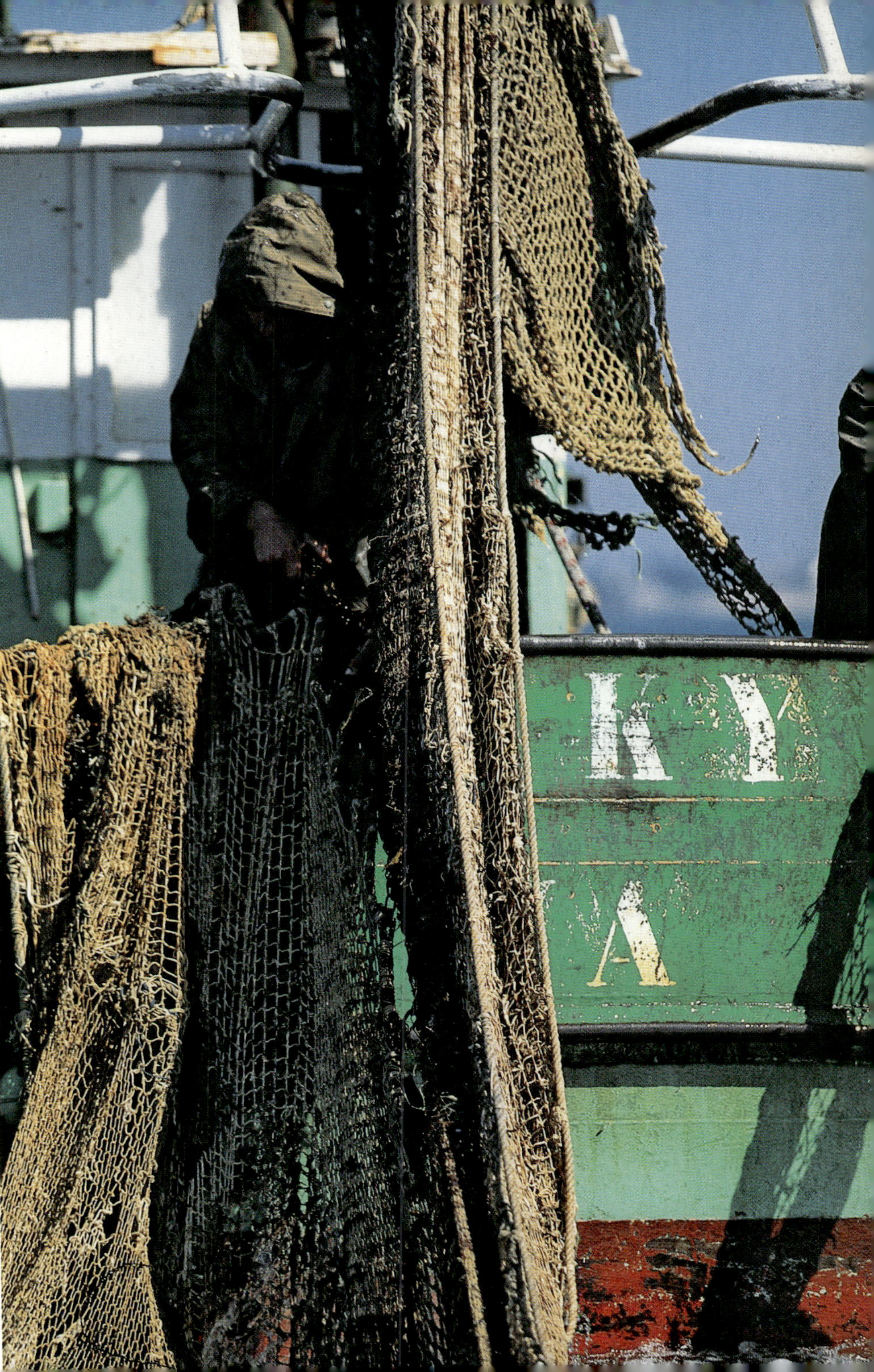

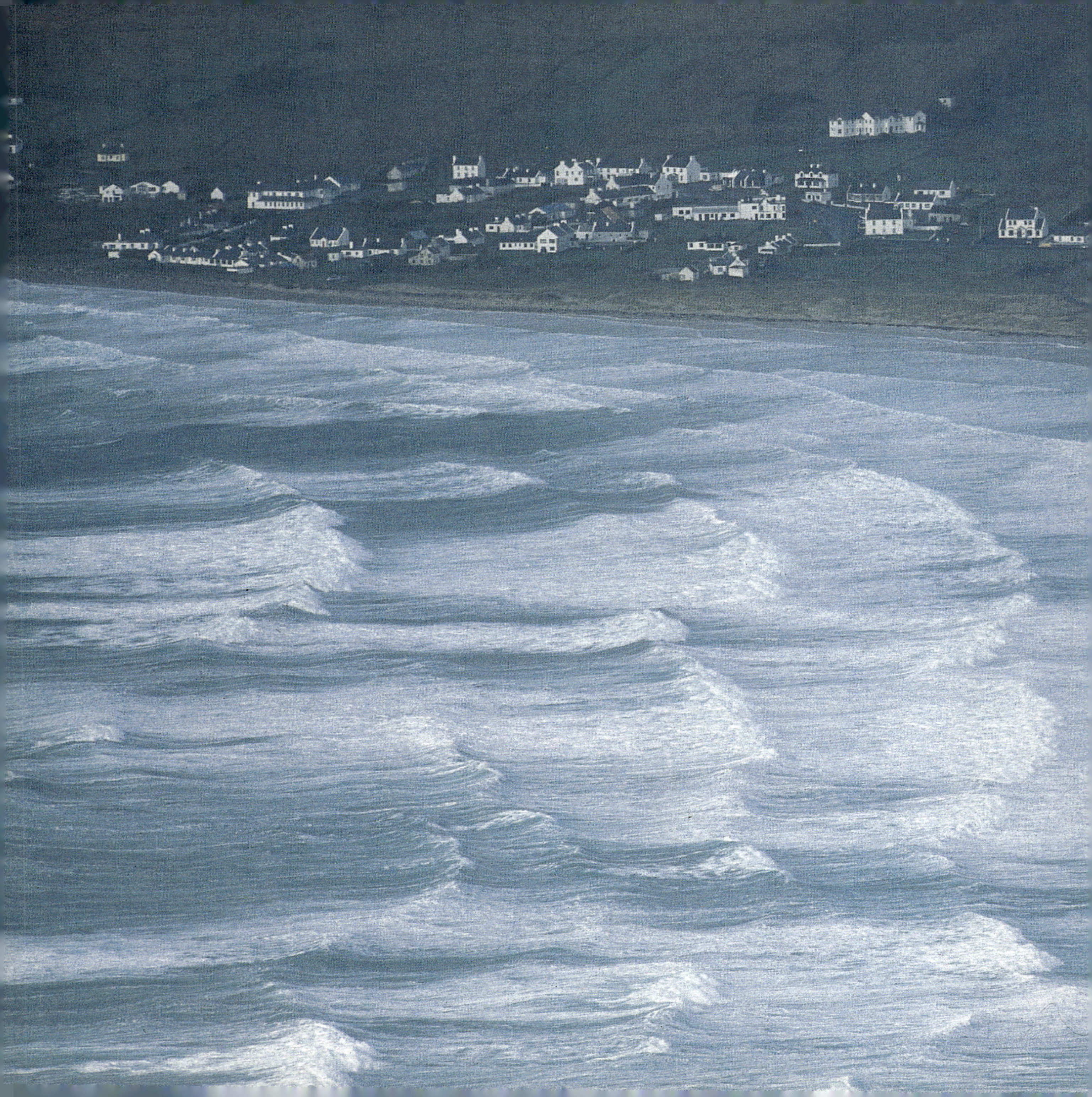

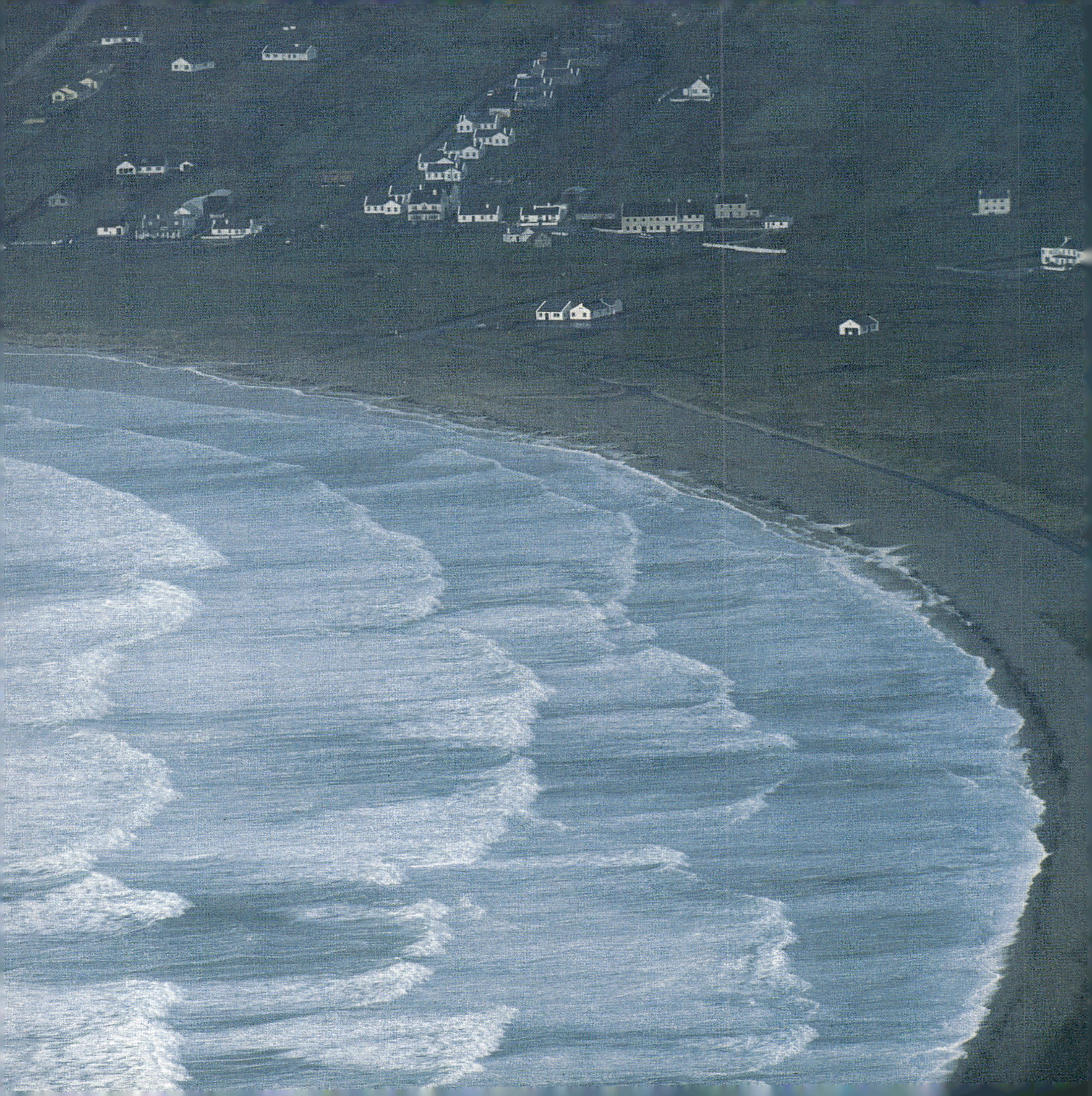

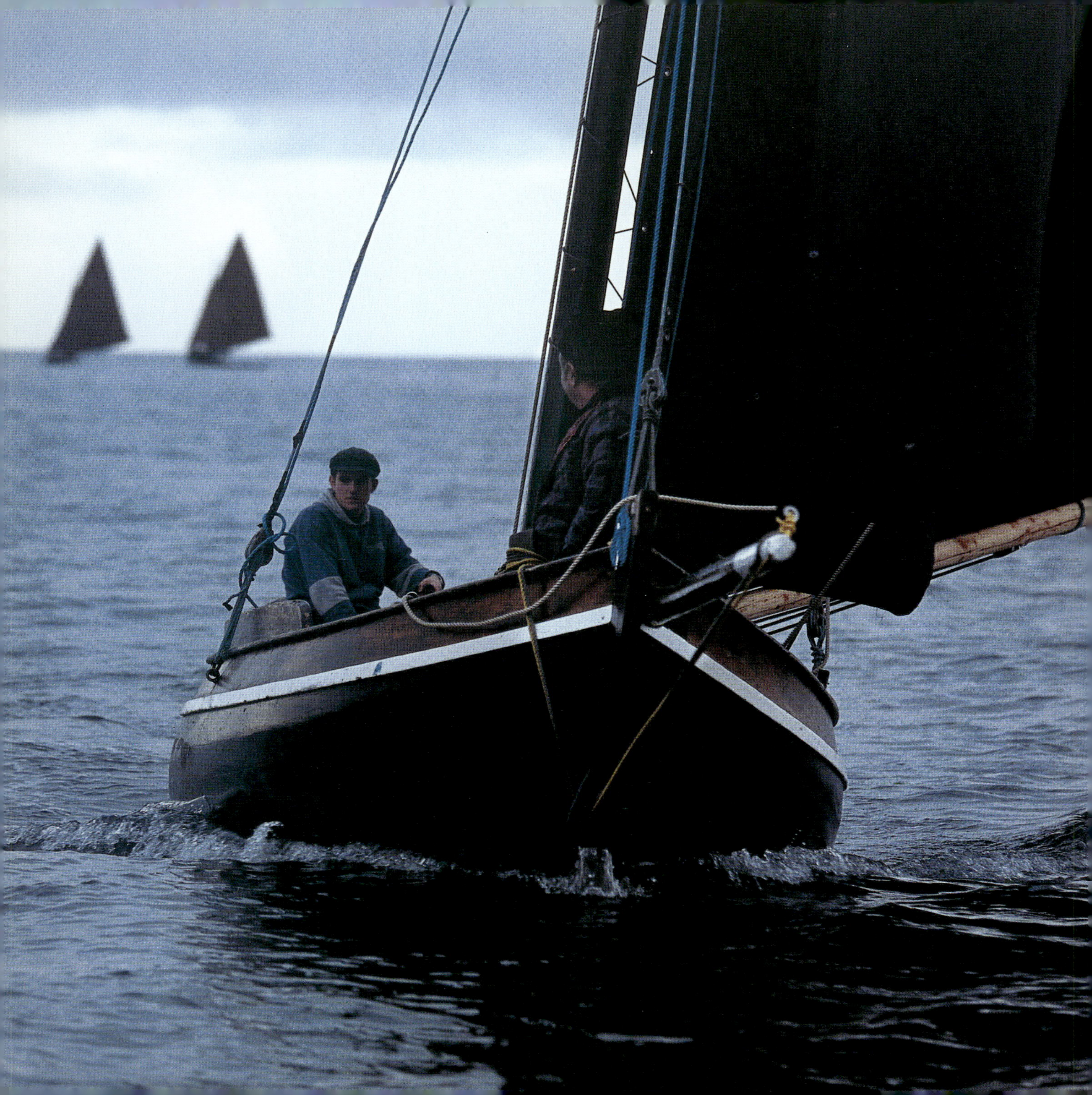

APRIL 13

Every day brings a ship,
Every ship brings a word;
Well for those who have no fear,
Looking seaward well assured
That the word the vessel brings
Is the word they wish to hear.

Ralph Waldo Emerson, from *English Traits,* 1856

APRIL 14

Vessels large may venture more,
But little boats should keep near shore.

Benjamin Franklin,
from "Poor Richard's Almanack," 1757

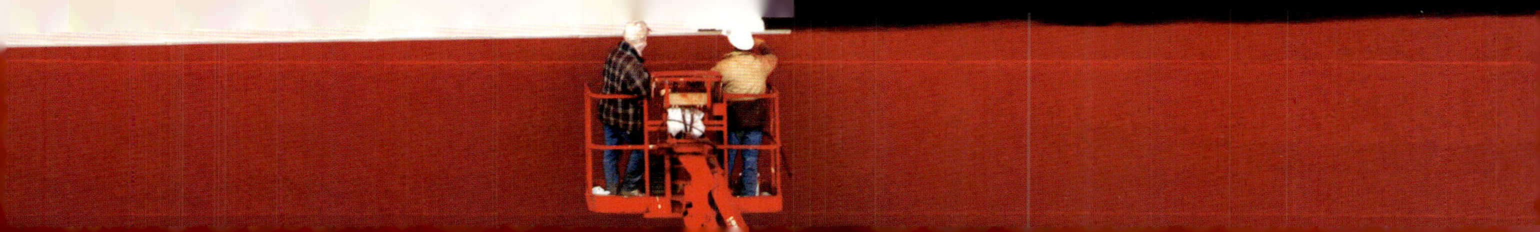

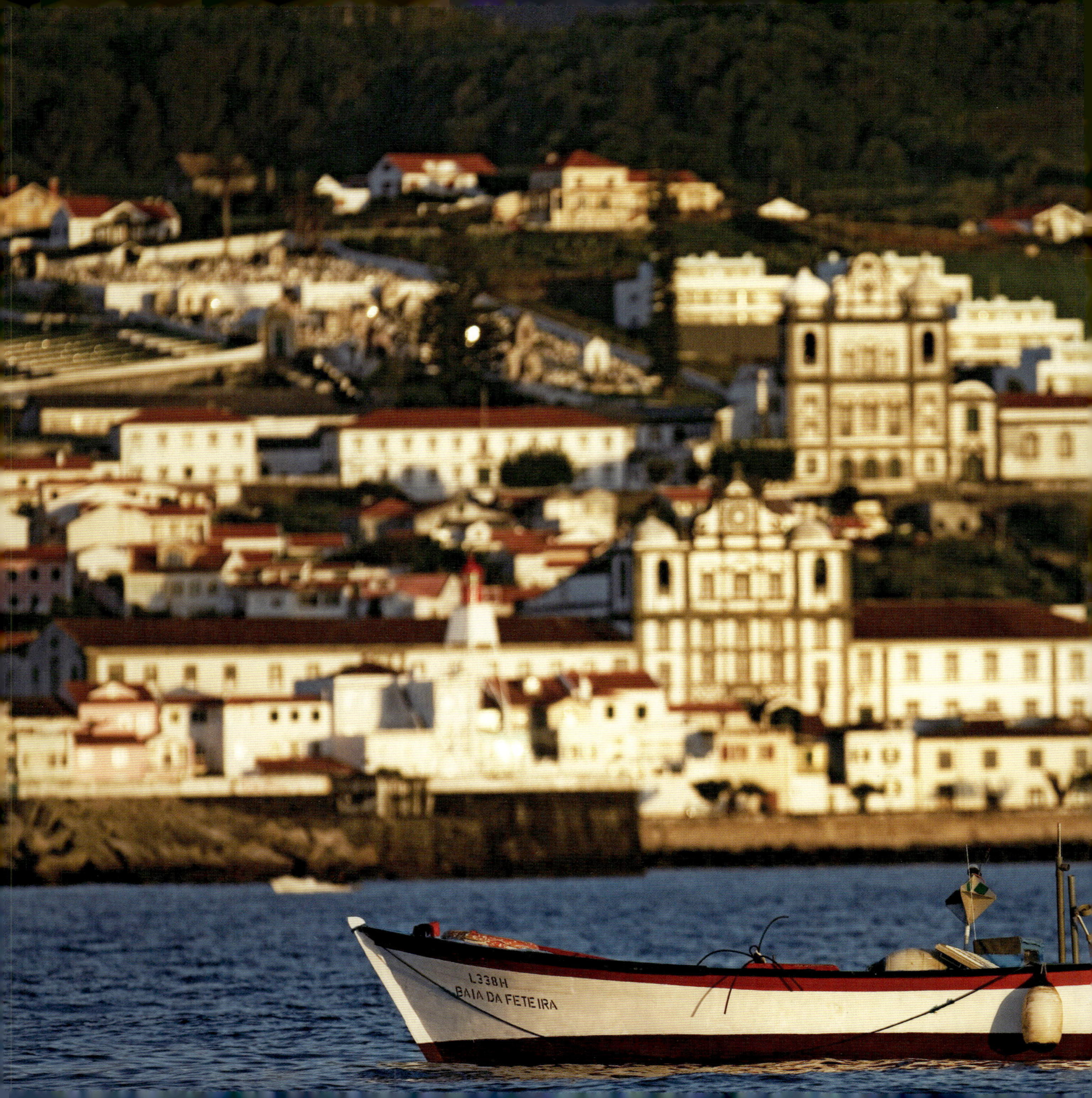
L338H
BAIA DA FETEIRA

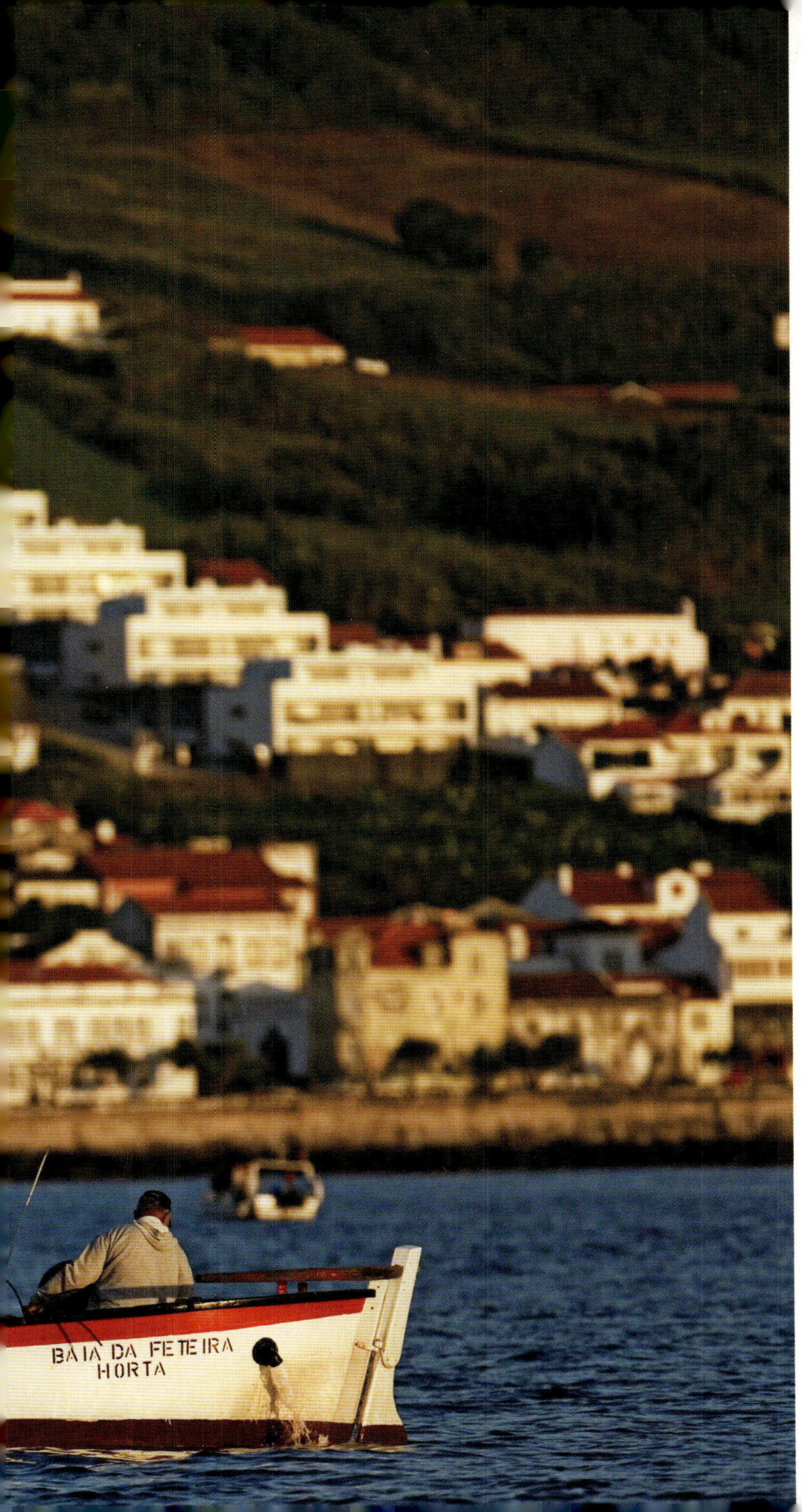

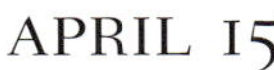

APRIL 15

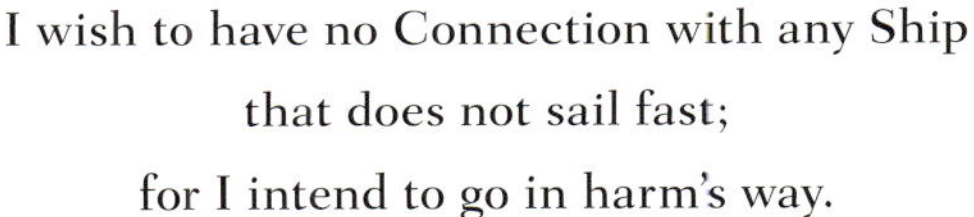

I wish to have no Connection with any Ship
that does not sail fast;
for I intend to go in harm's way.

John Paul Jones,
from a letter to M. LeRay de Chaumont, 1778

APRIL 16

The morning breaks; the steeds in their stalls
Stamp and neigh, as the hostler calls;
The day returns, but nevermore
Returns the traveler to the shore,
And the tide rises, the tide falls.

Henry Wadsworth Longfellow,
from "The Tide Rises, the Tide Falls," *Ultima Thule,* 1880

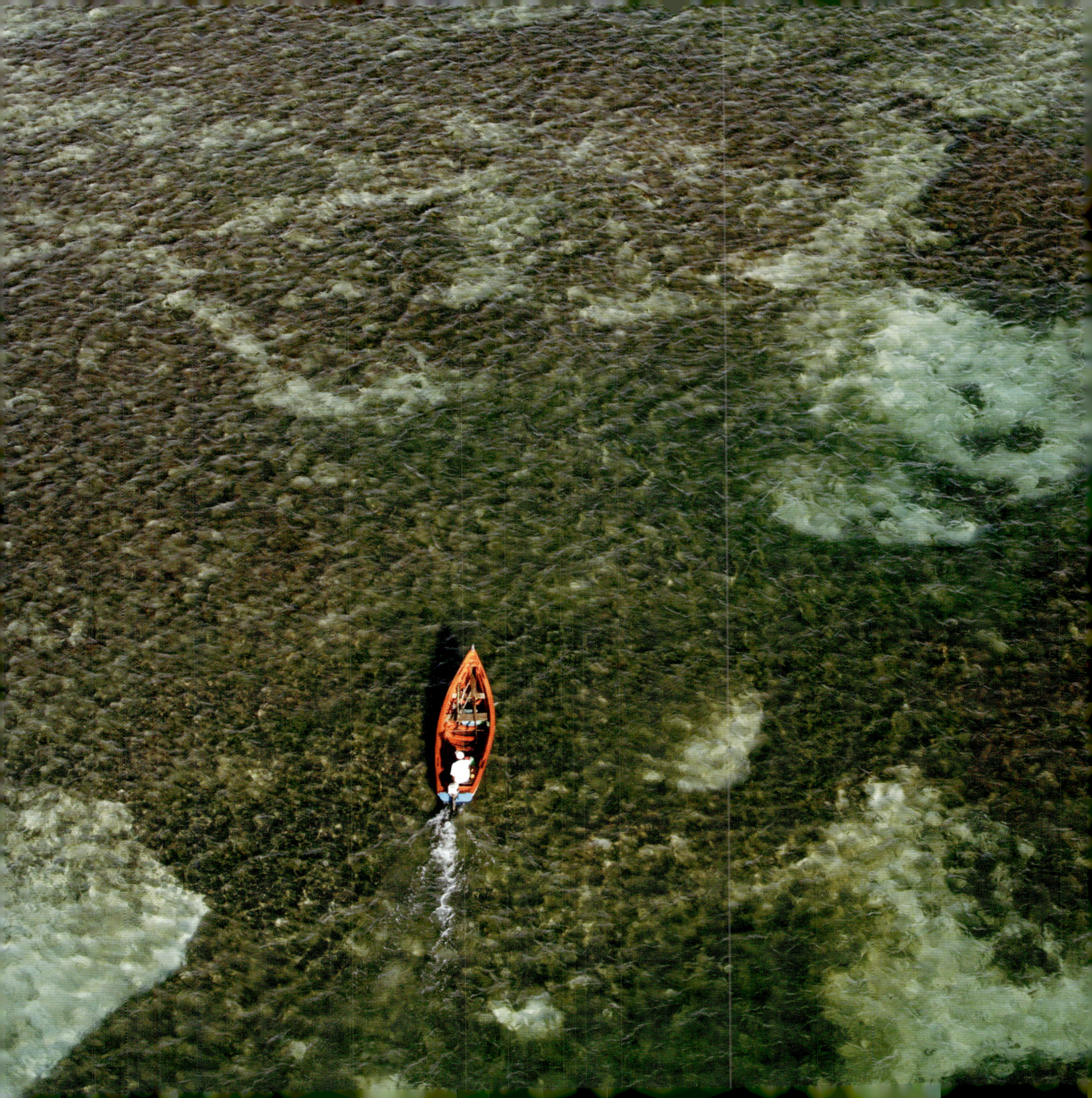

APRIL 17

I have the feel of the oar in my hand, the vision of a scorching blue sea in my eyes. And I see a bay, a wide bay, smooth as glass and polished like ice, shimmering in the dark. A red light burns far off upon the gloom of the land, and the night is soft and warm.

Joseph Conrad,
from "Youth," 1902

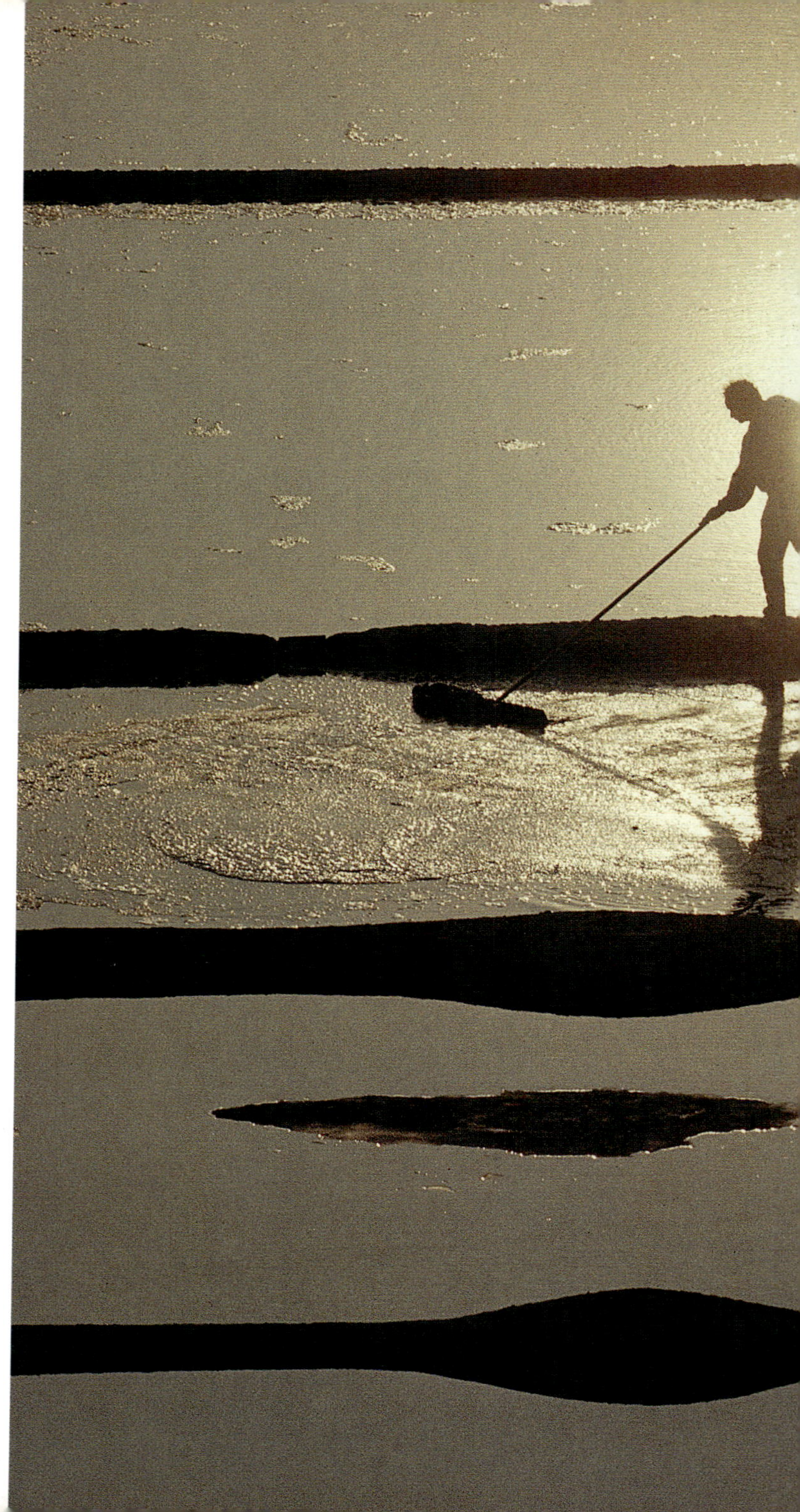

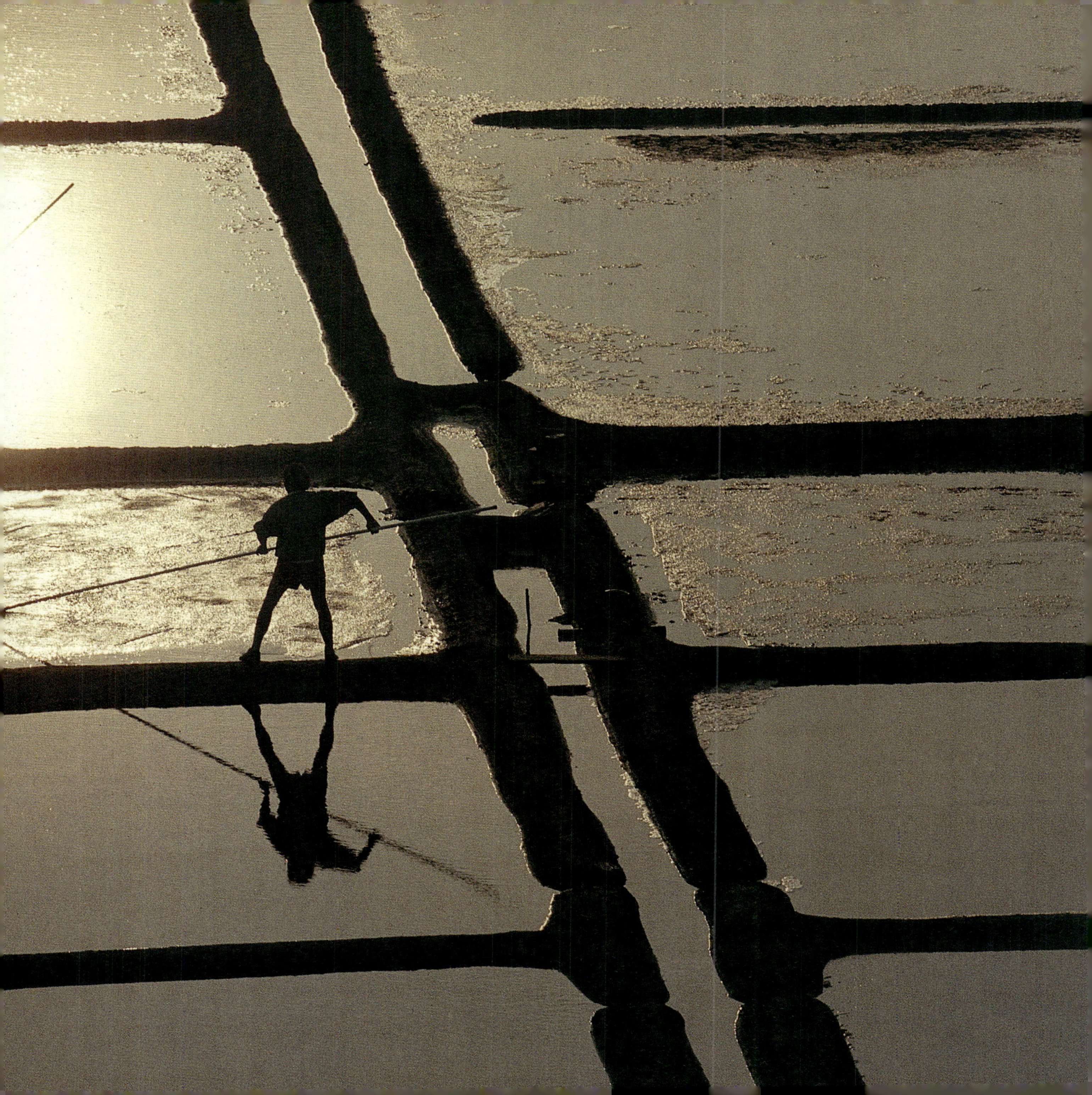

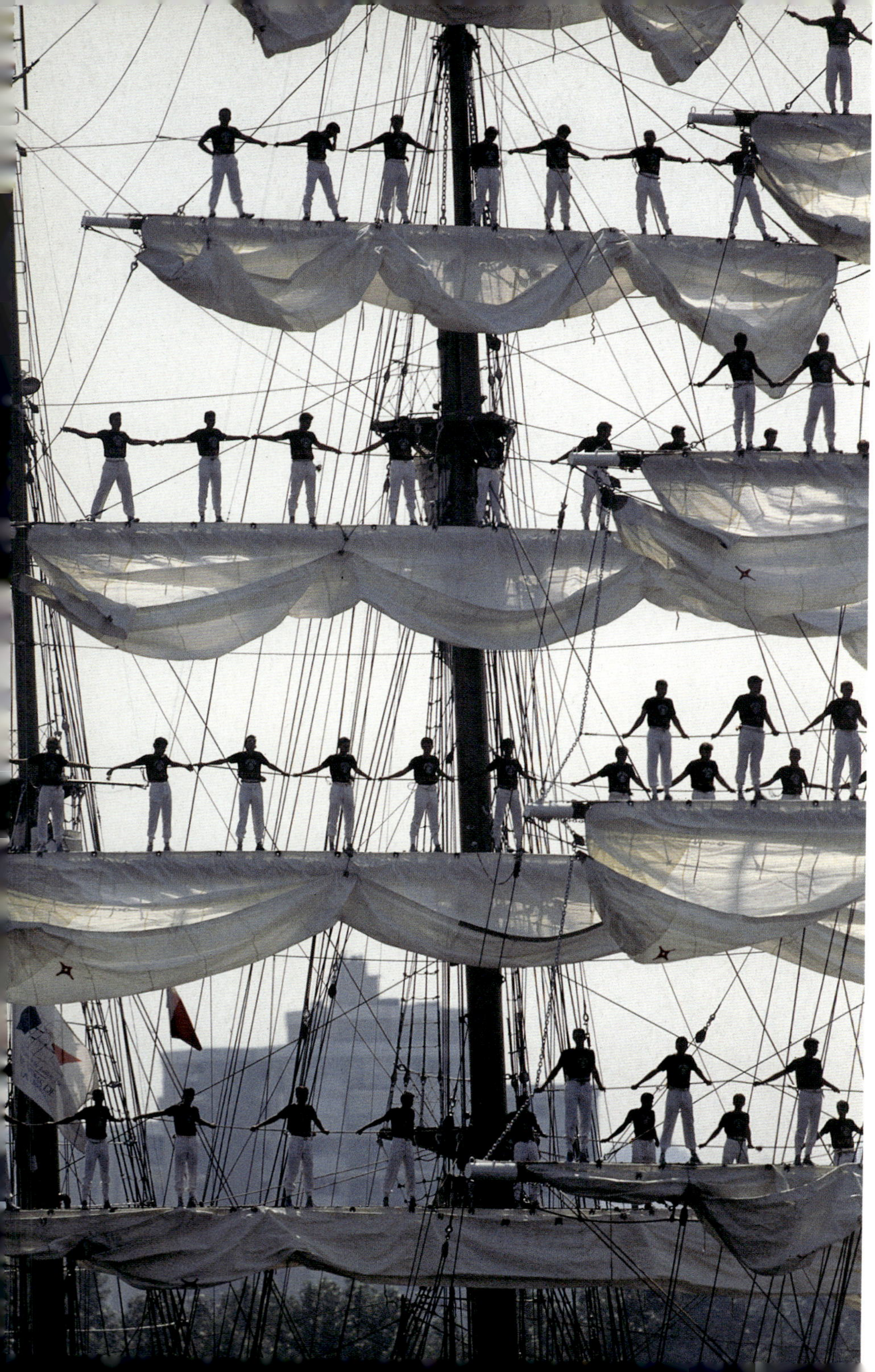

APRIL 18

O Captain! My Captain!
our fearful trip is done;
The ship has weather'd every
rack, the prize we sought is won;
The port is near, the bells I hear,
the people all exulting.

Walt Whitman,
"O Captain! My Captain!"
from *Leaves of Grass*, 1900

APRIL 19

To the Ocean now I fly,
And those happy climes that ly
Where day never shuts his eye,
Up in the broad fields of the sky.

John Milton,
from *Comus: A Masque Presented at Ludlow Castle*, 1634

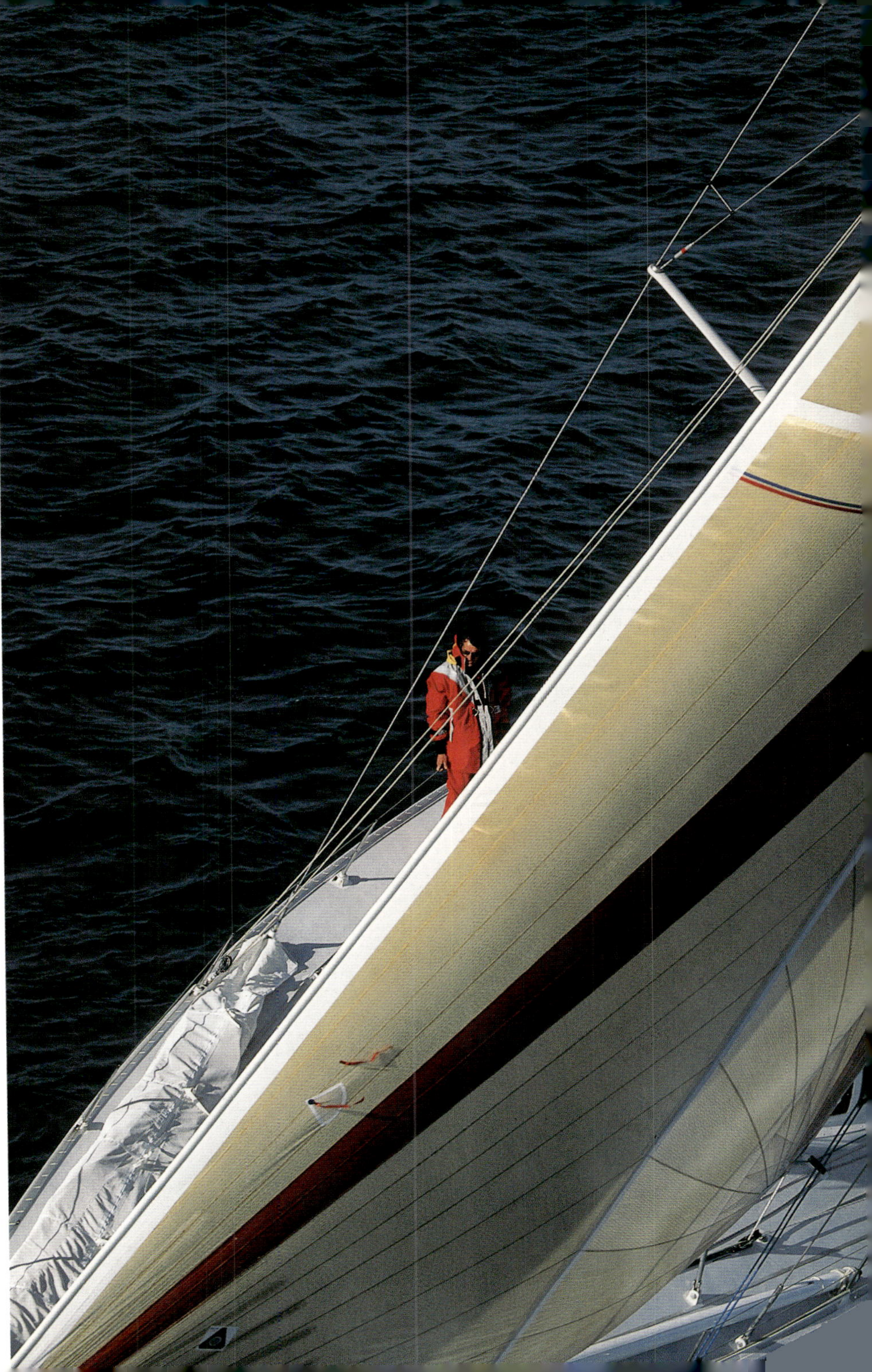

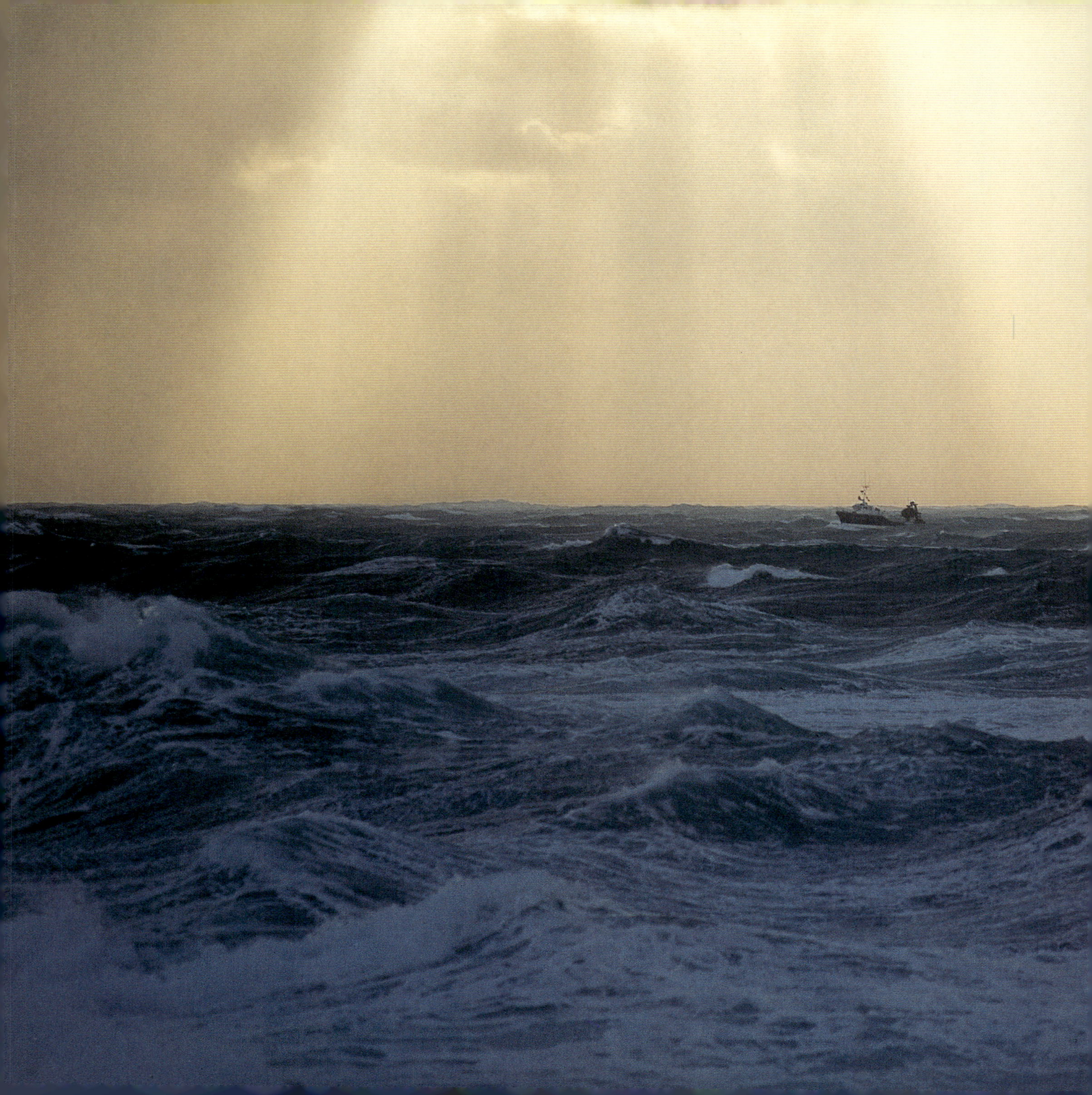

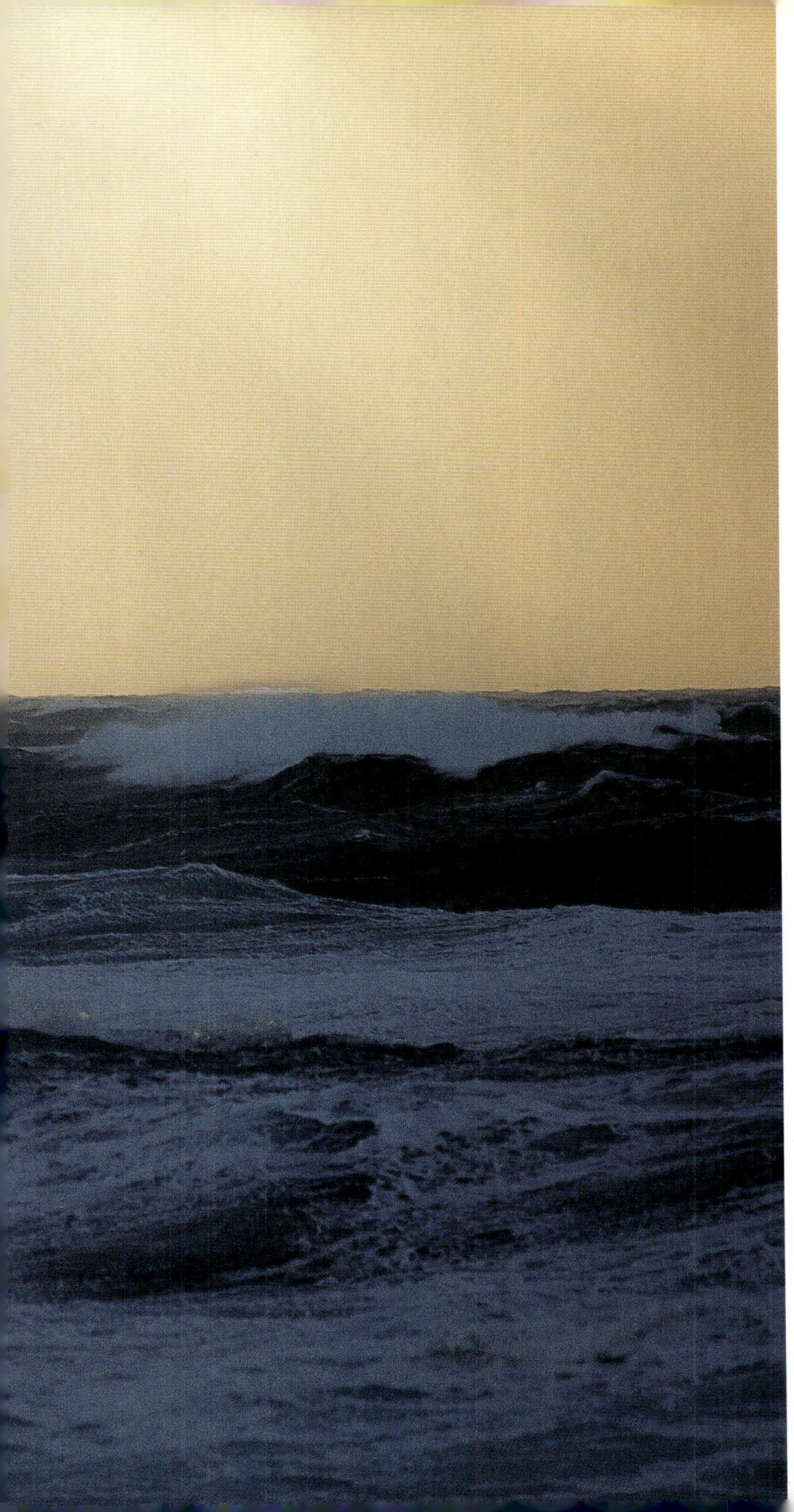

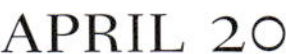

APRIL 20

On board ship there are many sources of joy of which the land knows nothing. You may flirt and dance at sixty; and if you are awkward in the turn of a valse, you may put it down to the motion of the ship. You need wear no gloves, and may drink your soda-and-brandy without being ashamed of it.

Anthony Trollope,
from *John Caldigate,* 1879

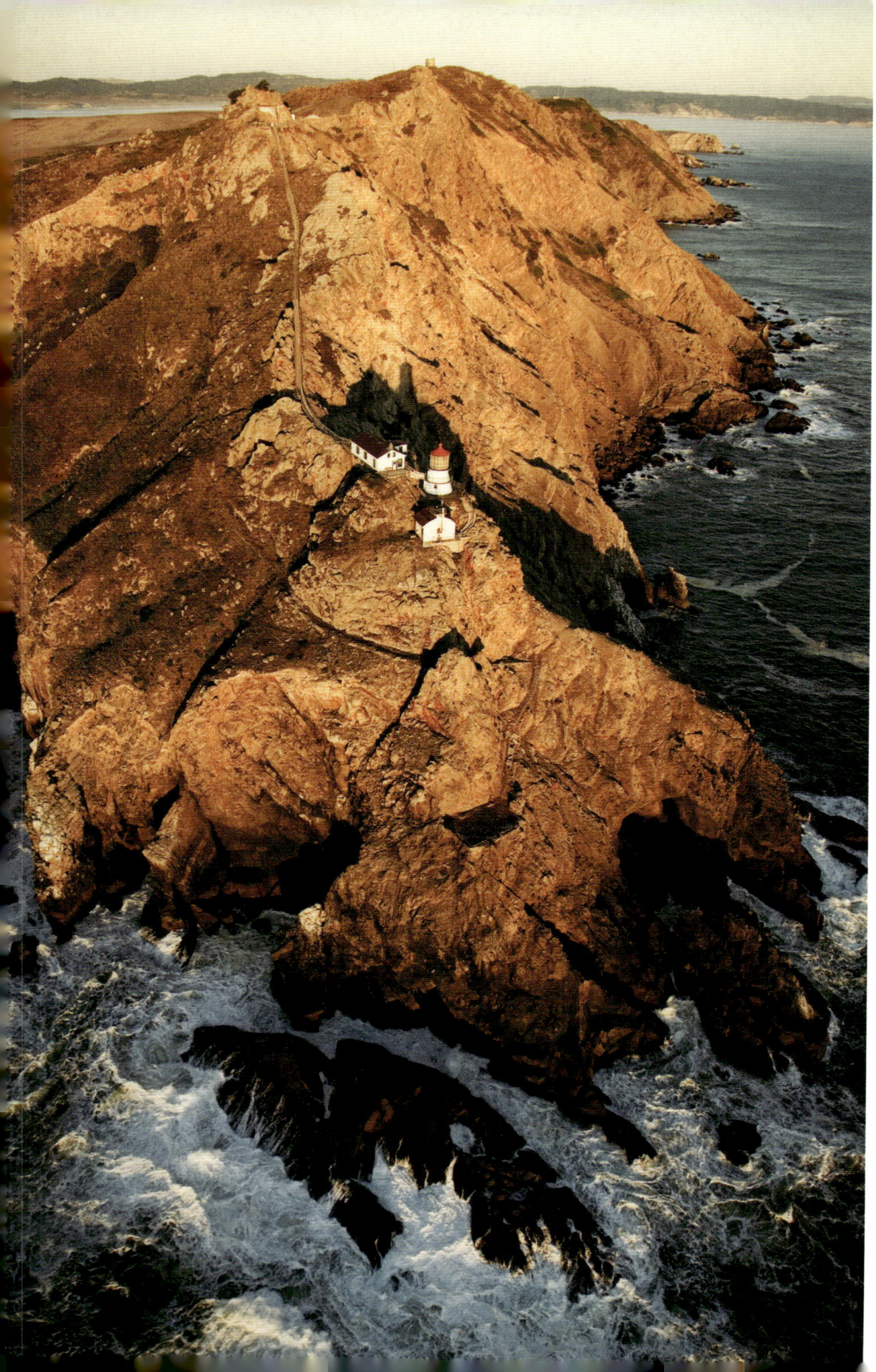

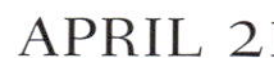

This lighthouse was the
cynosure of all eyes.

Henry David Thoreau

APRIL 22

Don't sail out farther
than you can row back.

Danish proverb

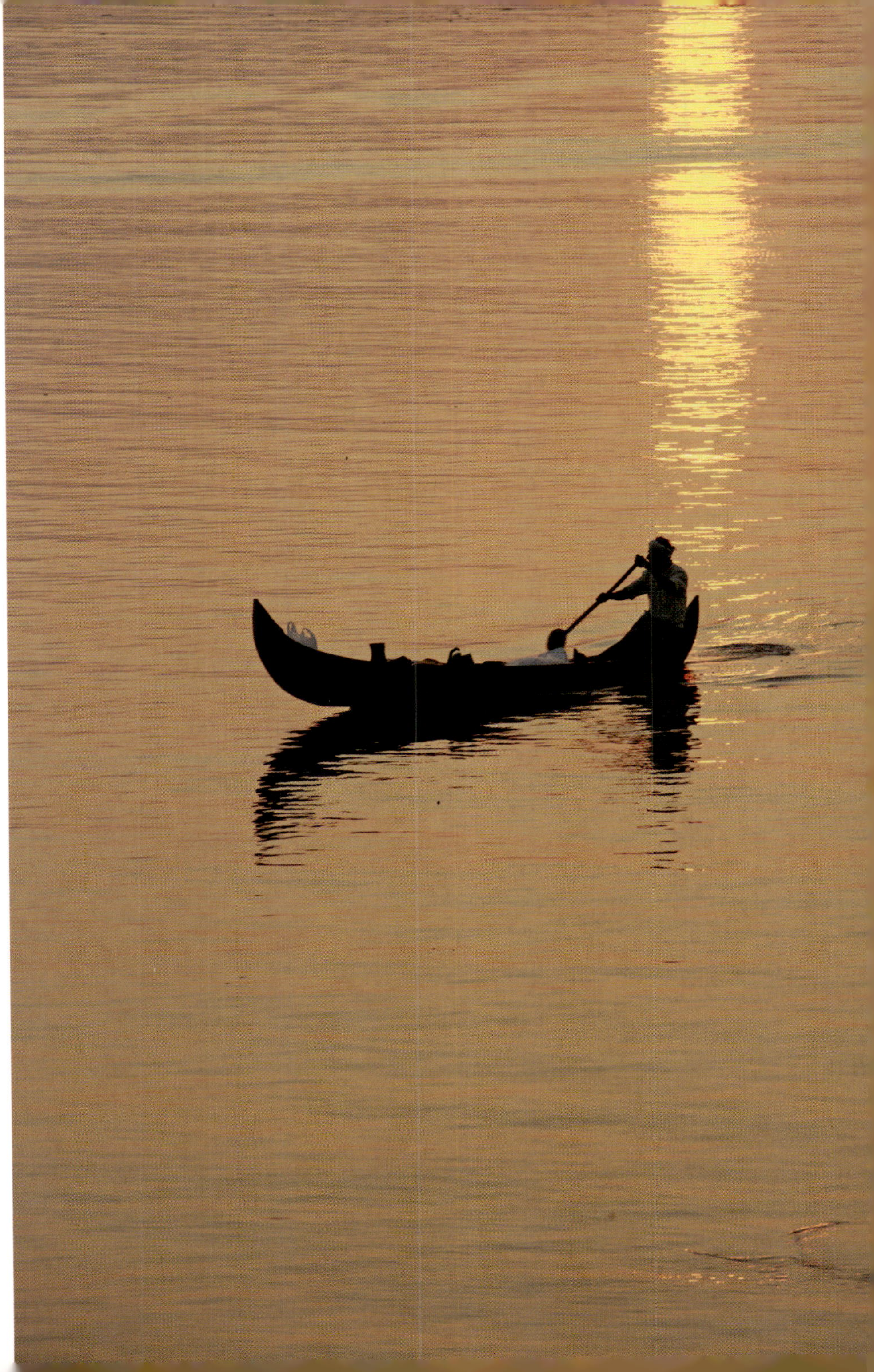

APRIL 23

Blue sheets of water, left and right,
Spread between quays of rose and green,
To the world's end and out of sight,
And still expanded, though unseen.

Charles Baudelaire,
from "Parisian Dream," *Les Fleurs du mal,* 1861

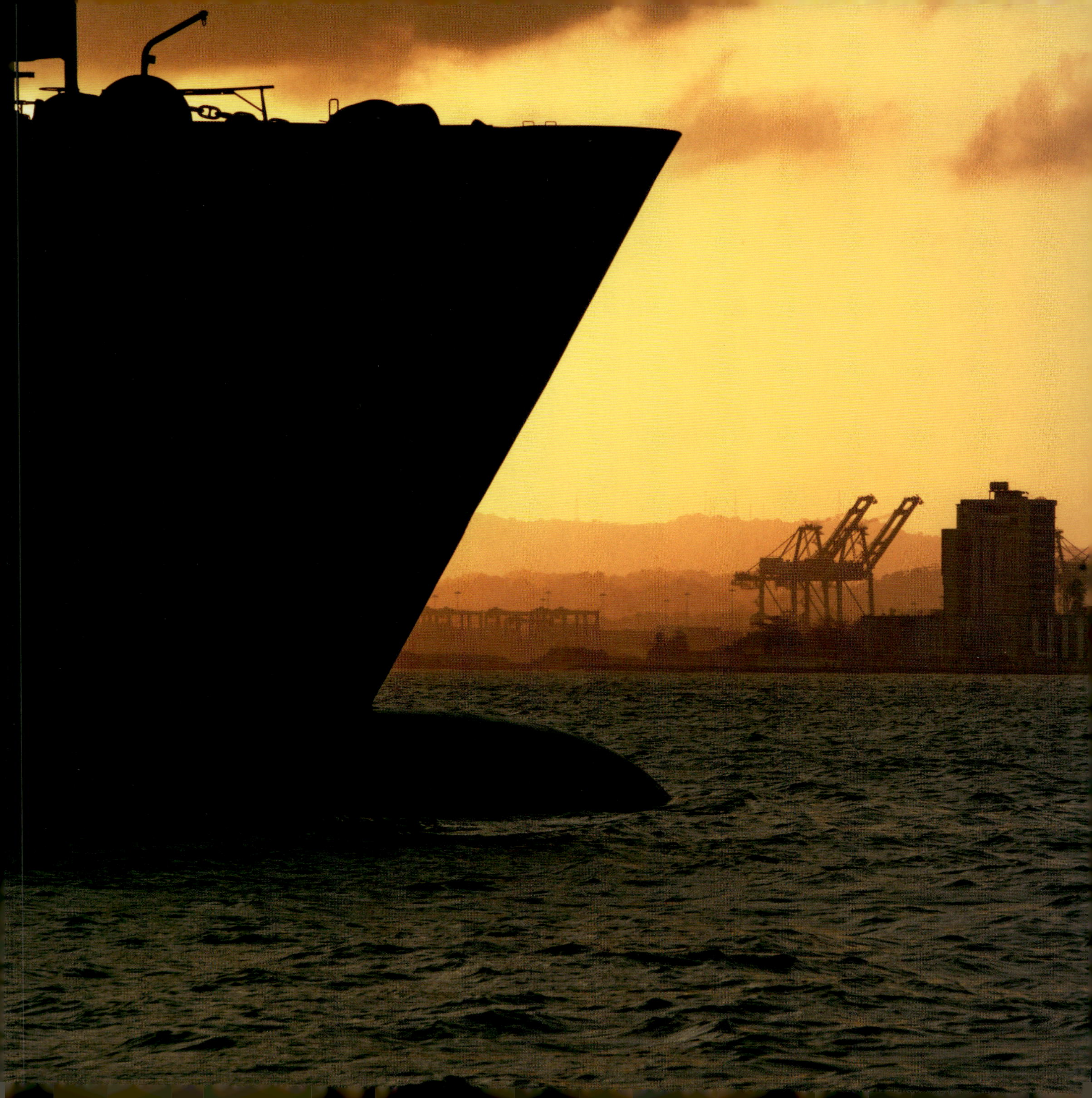

APRIL 24

Admire a small ship, but put your freight in a large one.

Hesiod, from "Works and Days"

APRIL 25

The human heart is like a ship on a stormy sea driven about by winds blowing from all four corners of heaven.

Martin Luther,
from the preface to his translation
of the Psalms, 1534

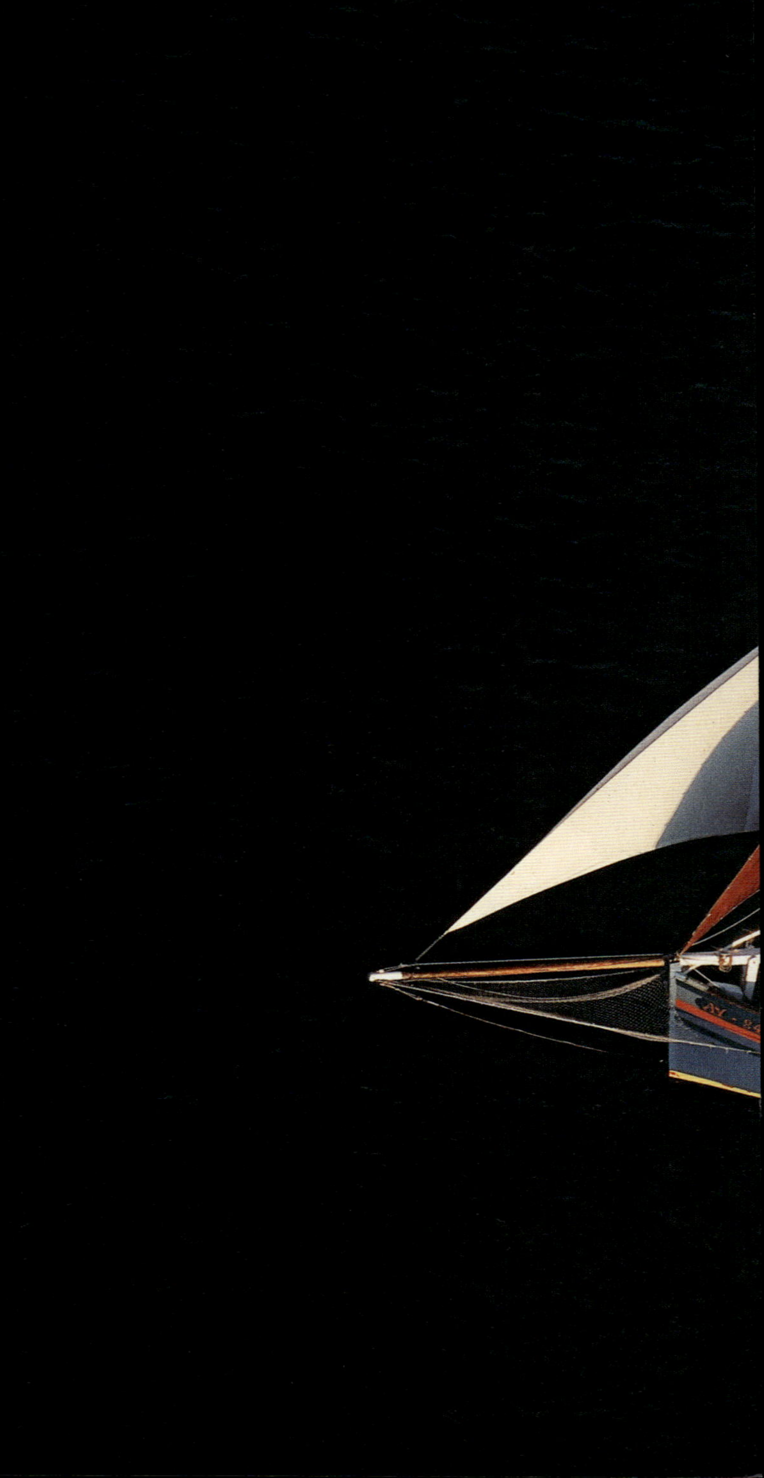

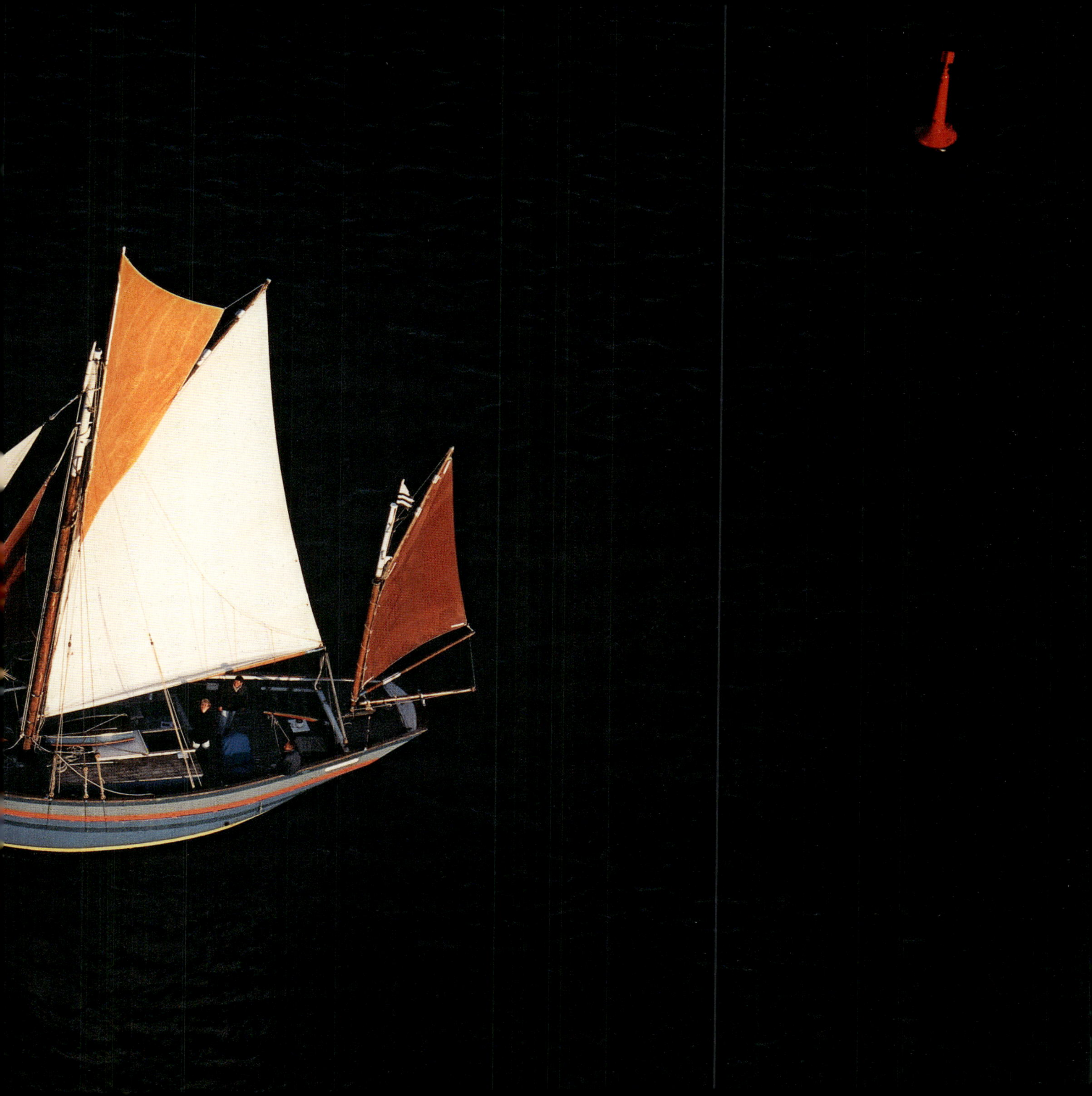

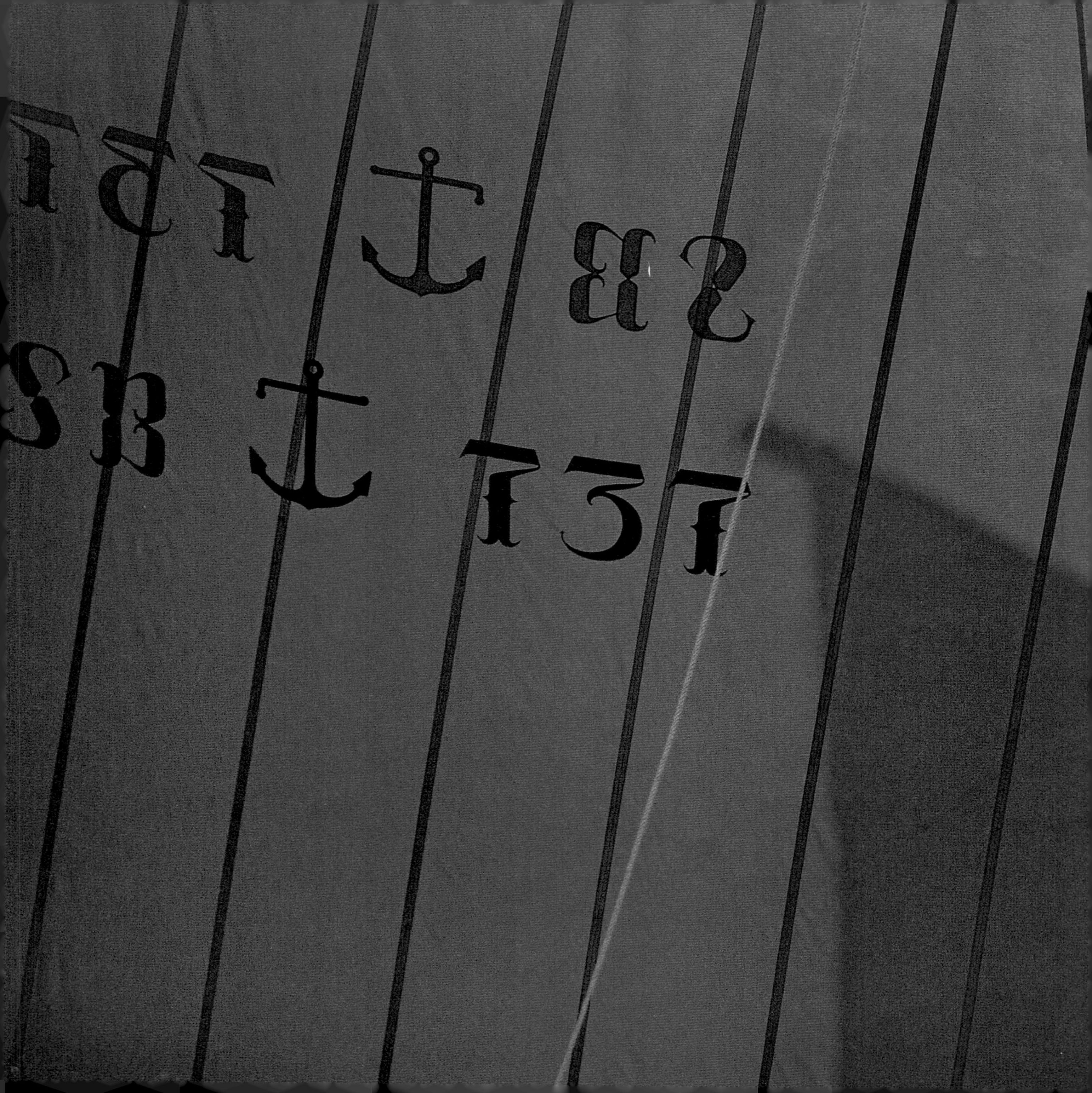

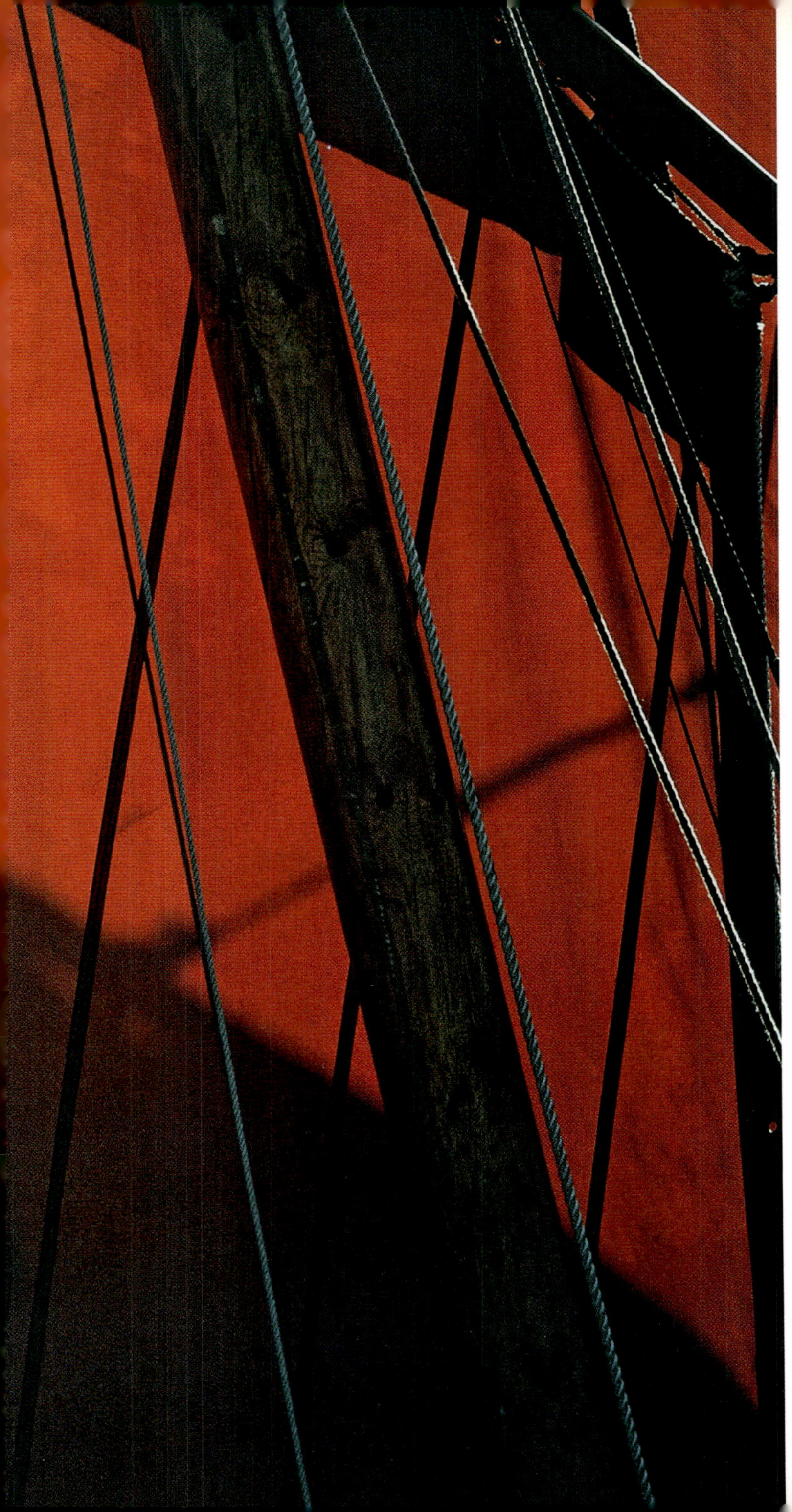

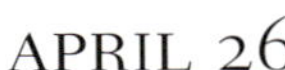

APRIL 26

In spite of rock and tempest's roar,
In spite of false lights on the shore,
Sail on, nor fear to breast the sea!
Our hearts, our hopes, are all with thee,
Our hearts, our hopes, our prayers, our tears,
Our faith triumphant o'er our fears,
Are all with thee—are all with thee!

Henry Wadsworth Longfellow,
from "The Building of the Ship,"
The Seaside and the Fireside, 1850

APRIL 27

Every ship is a romantic object,
except that we sail in.

Ralph Waldo Emerson,
from "Experience," *Essays: Second Series,* 1844

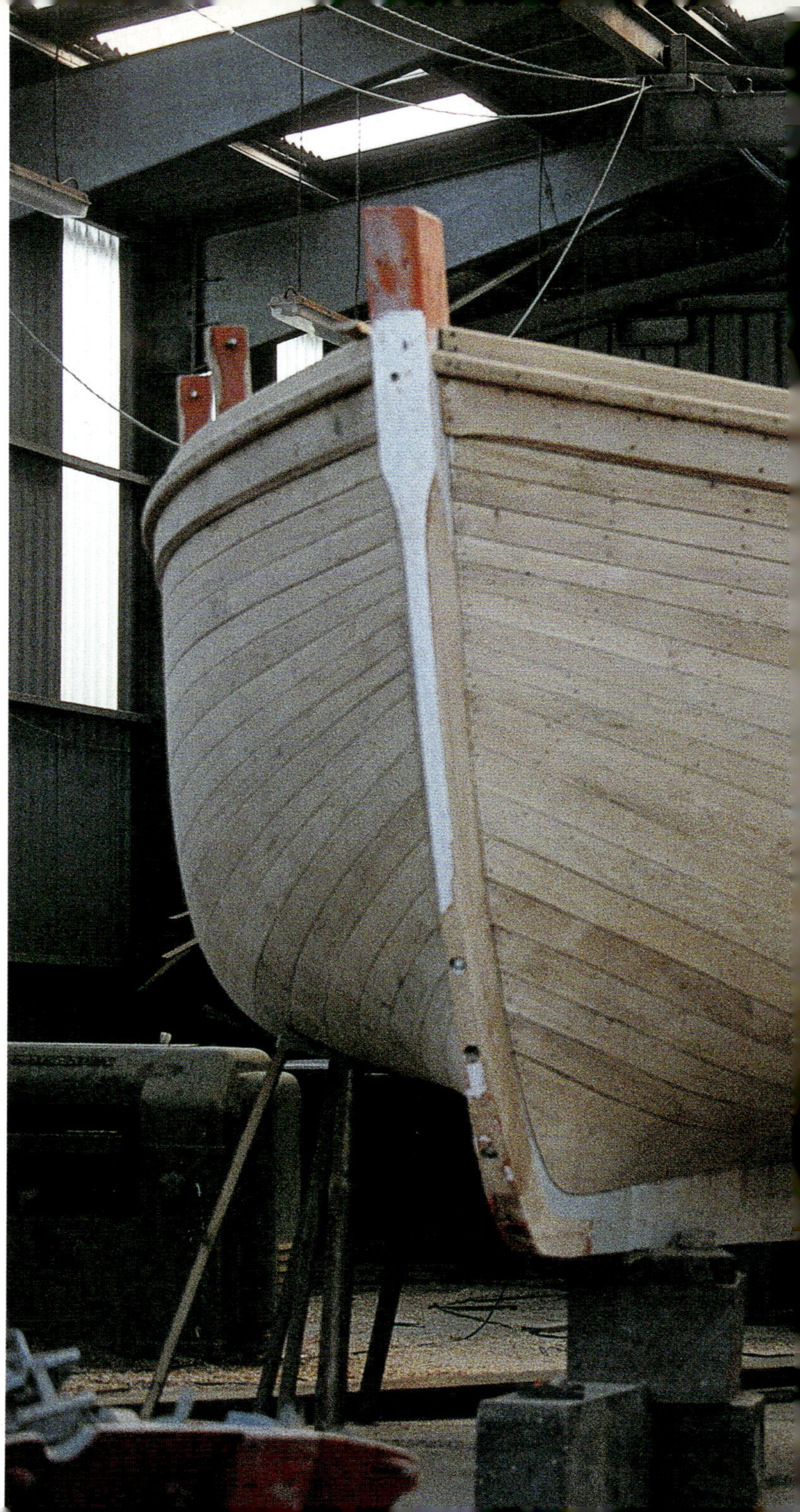

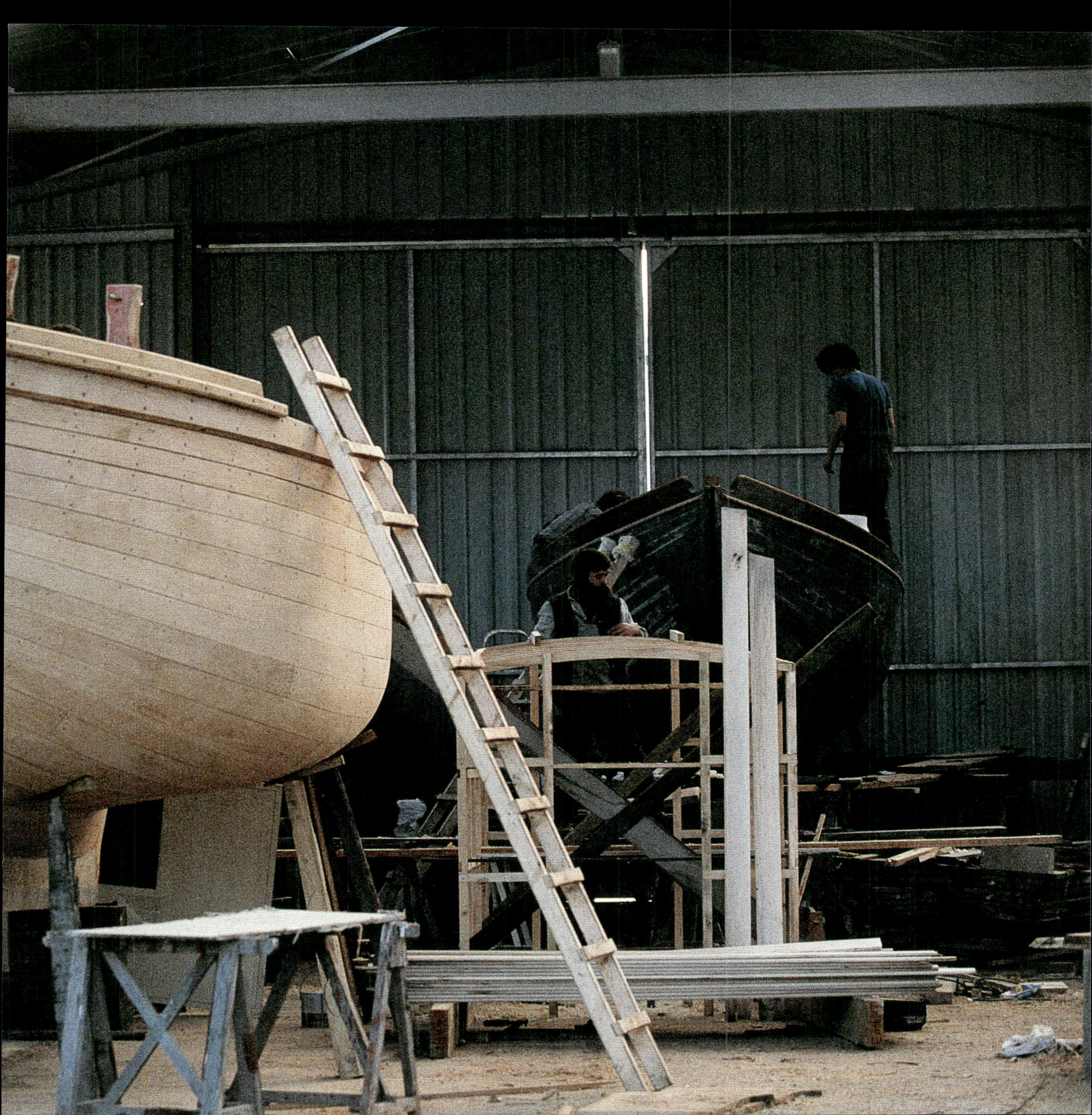

APRIL 28

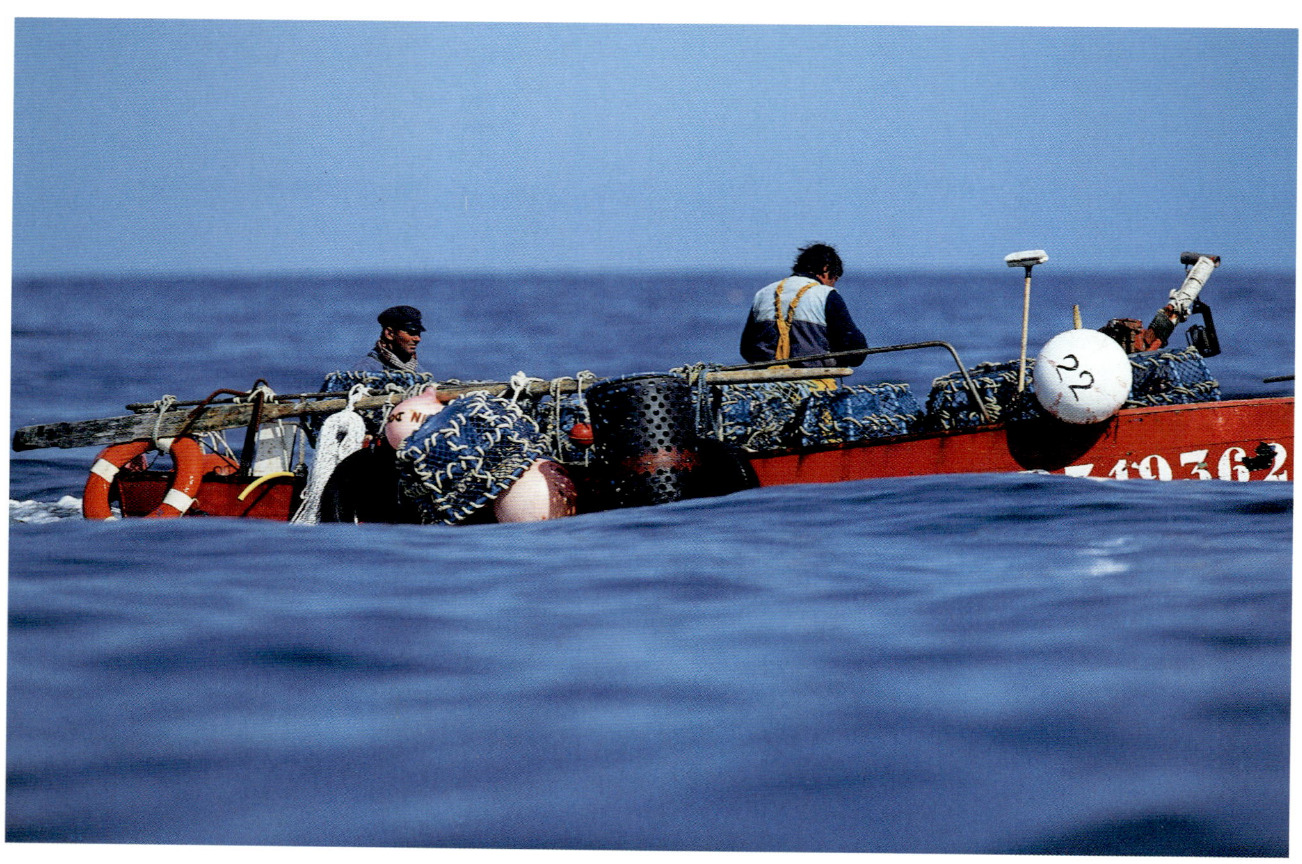

The pessimist complains about the wind;
the optimist expects it to change; the realist adjusts the sails.

William Arthur Ward

APRIL 29

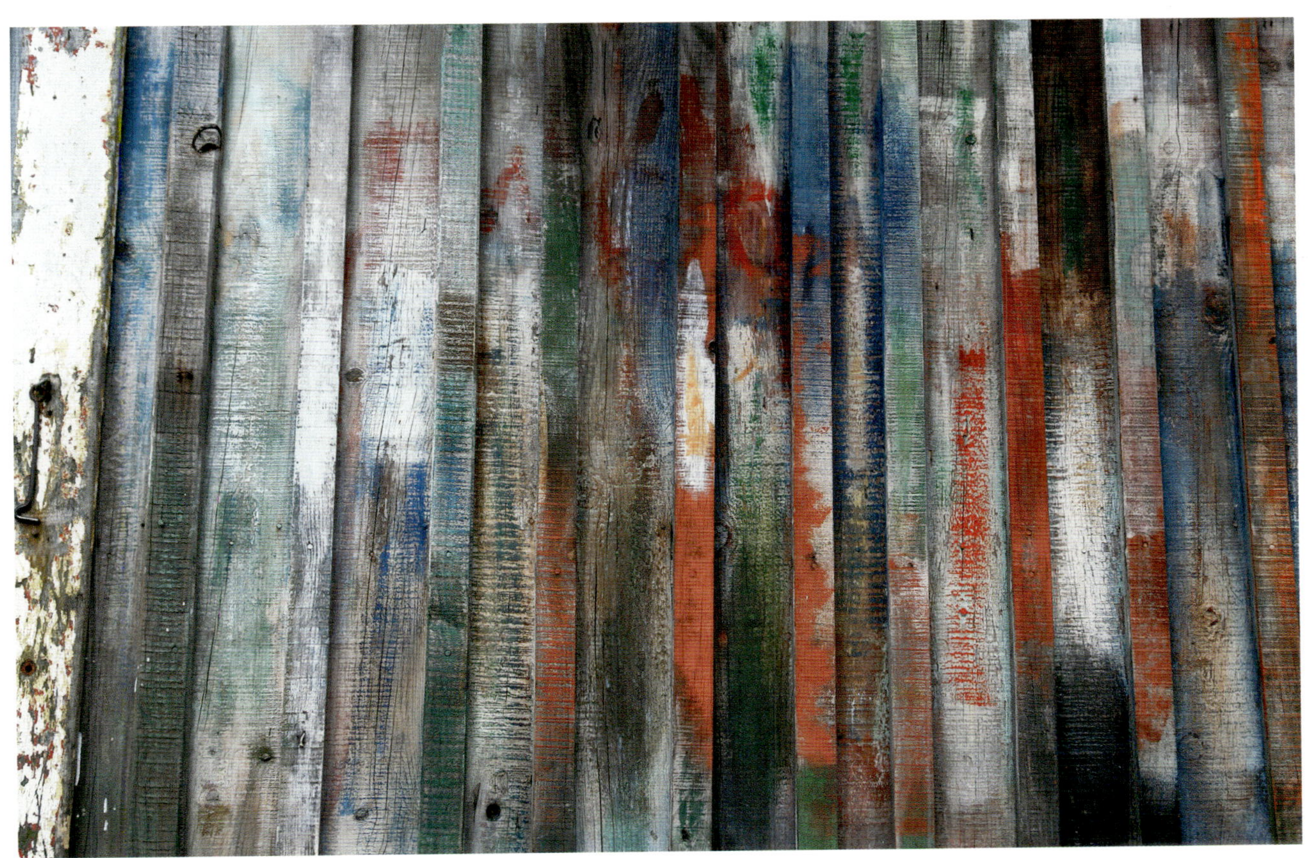

A tempest has burst upon us; but what doth it concern me?
I have left nothing undone that was mine to do.

Epictetus

APRIL 30

But let the ruffian Boreas once enrage
The gentle Thetis, and anon behold
The strong-ribb'd bark through liquid mountains cut,
Bounding between the two moist elements.

William Shakespeare,
from *Troilus and Cressida,* Act I, Scene 3

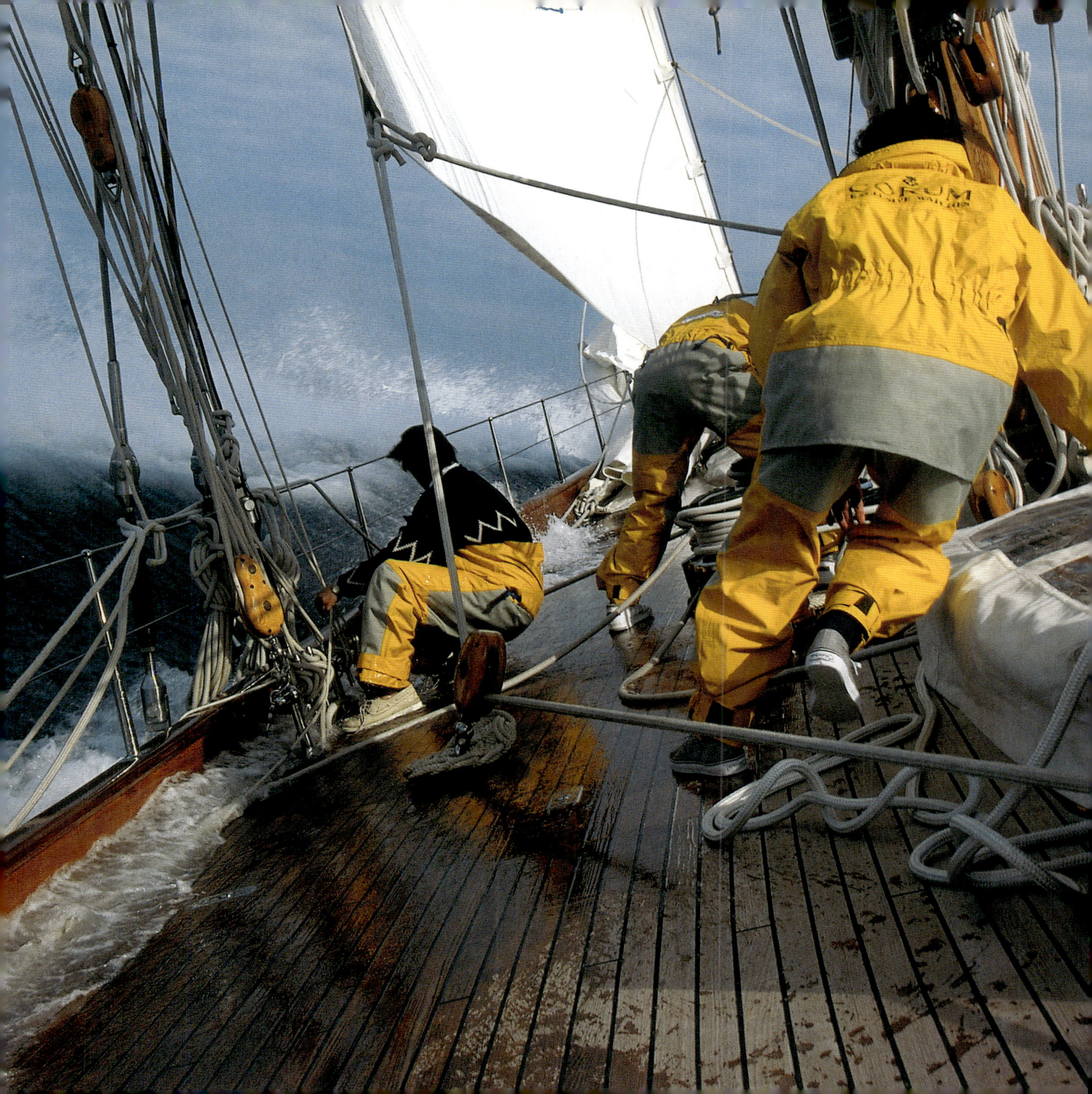
CORUM

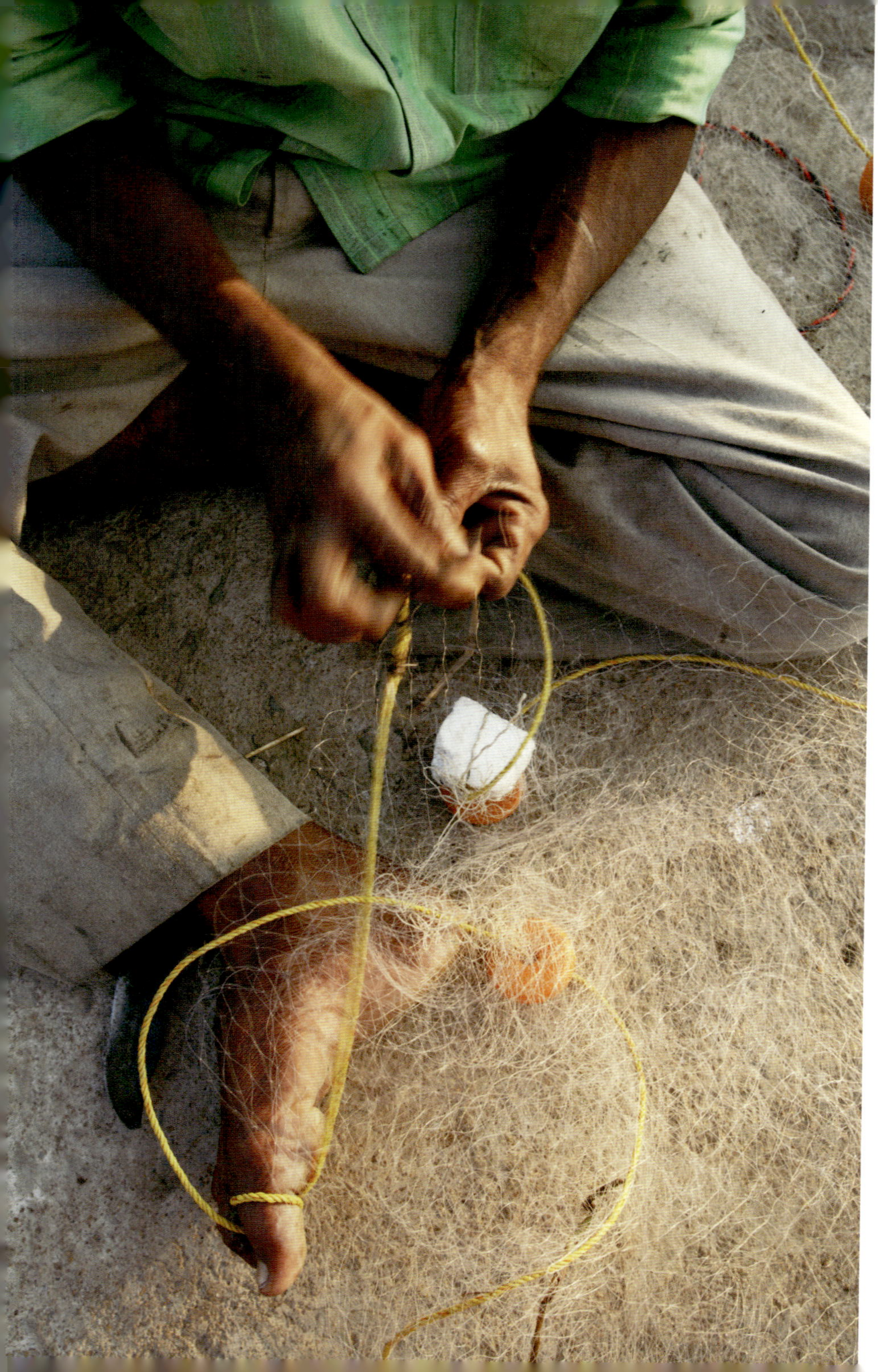

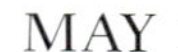

MAY 1

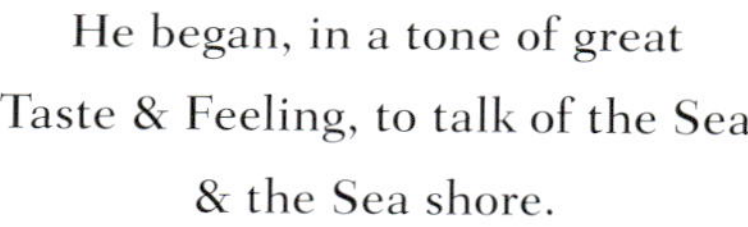

He began, in a tone of great
Taste & Feeling, to talk of the Sea
& the Sea shore.

Jane Austen, from *Sanditon,* 1817

MAY 2

Do they ask me what pleasure
I find on the sea?
—Why, absence from land is a
pleasure to me.

Philip Freneau

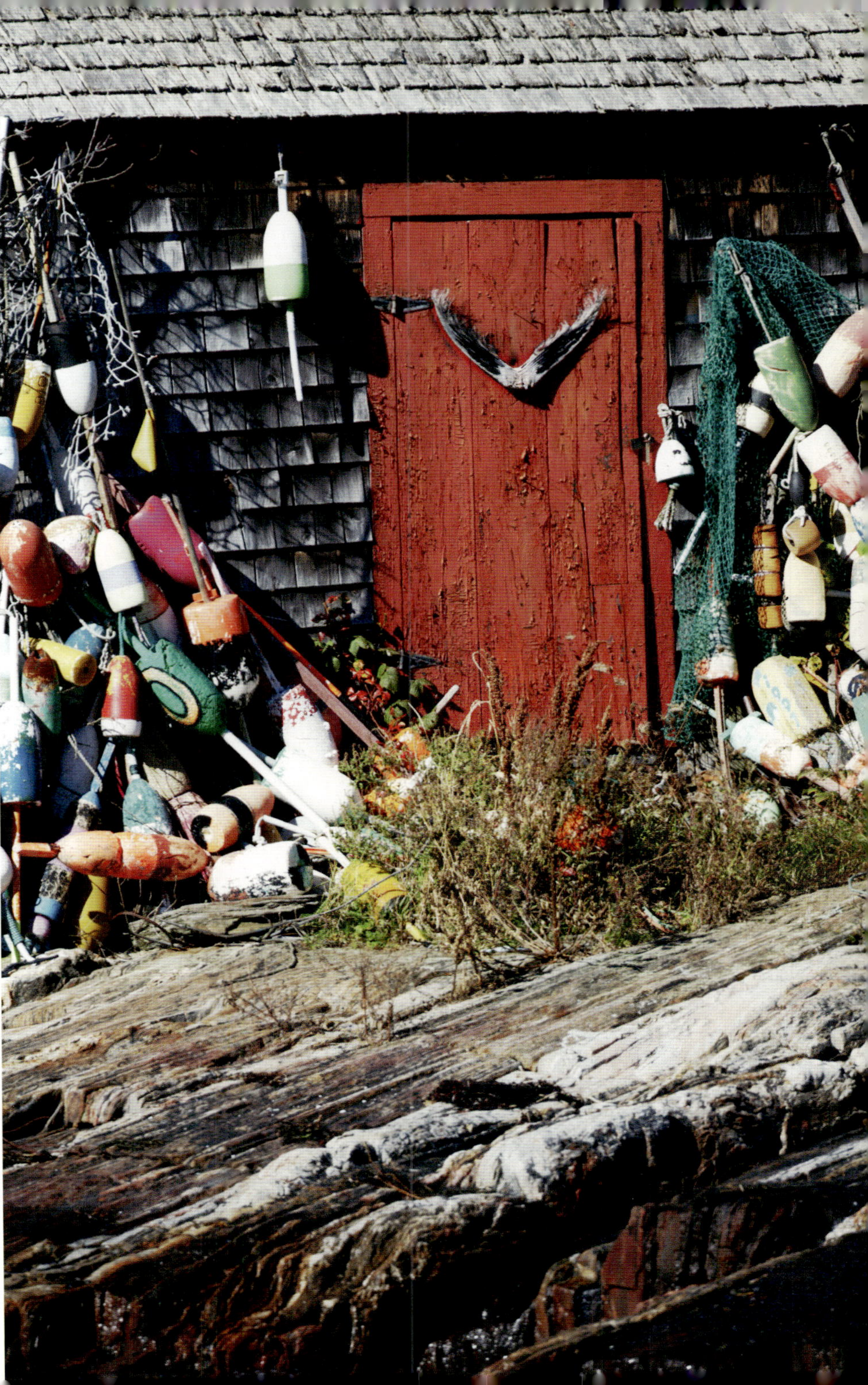

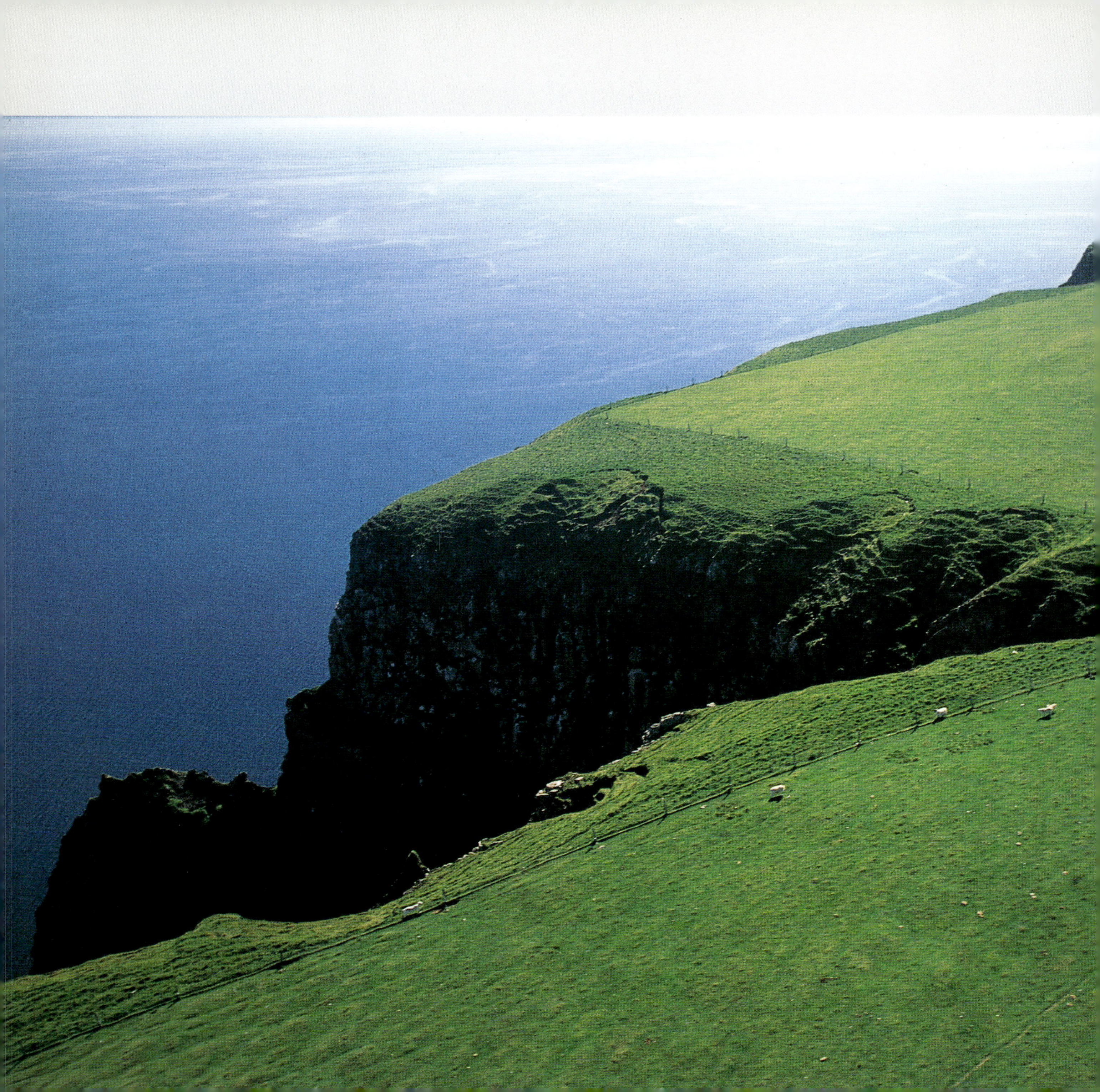

MAY 3

As this appalling ocean surrounds the verdant land, so in the soul of man there lies one insular Tahiti, full of peace and joy, but encompassed by all the horror of the half known life. God keep thee! Push not off from that isle, thou canst never return!

Herman Melville, from *Moby-Dick,* 1851

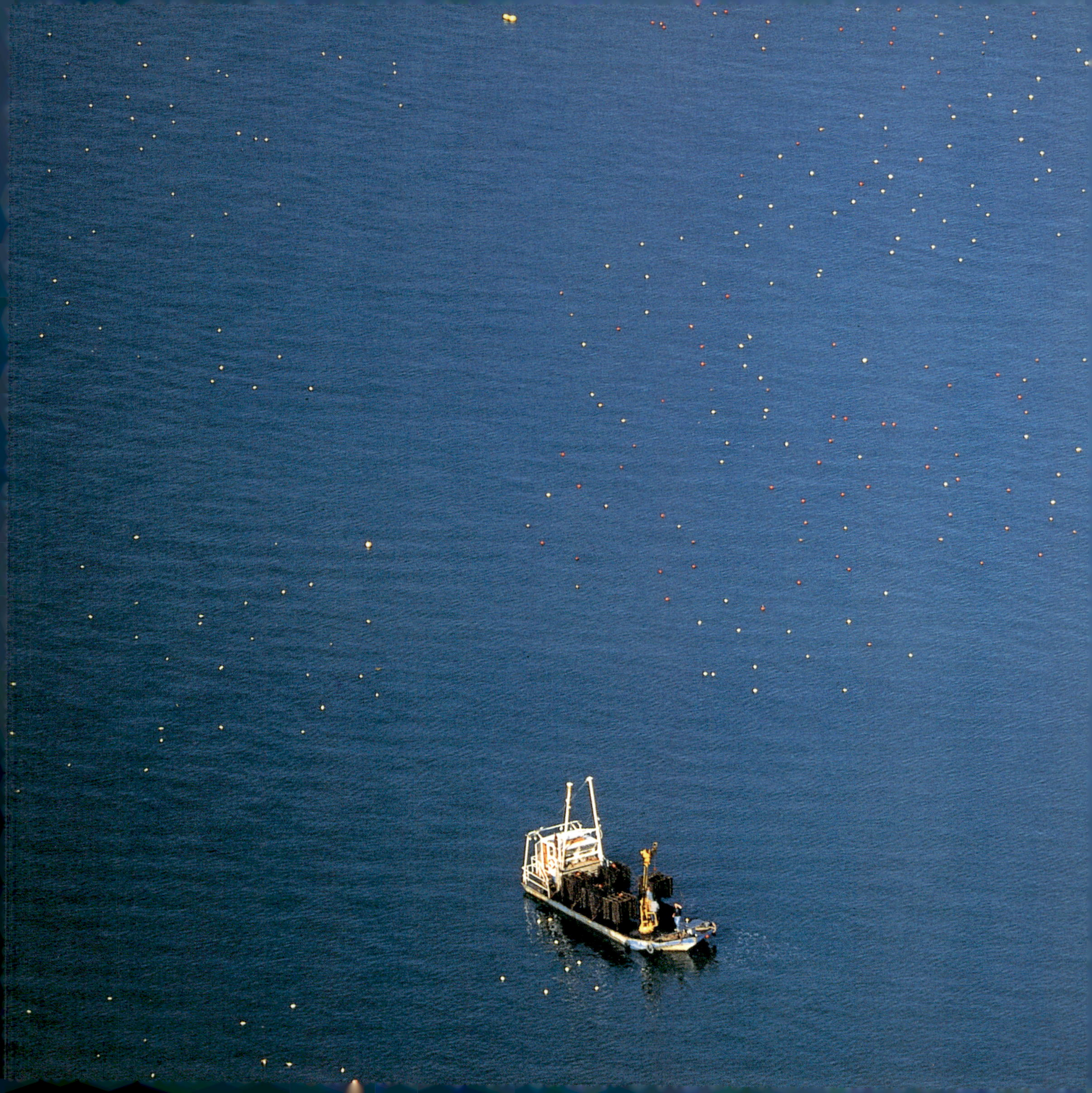

MAY 4

Water can do without fishes,
fishes cannot do without water.

Chinese proverb

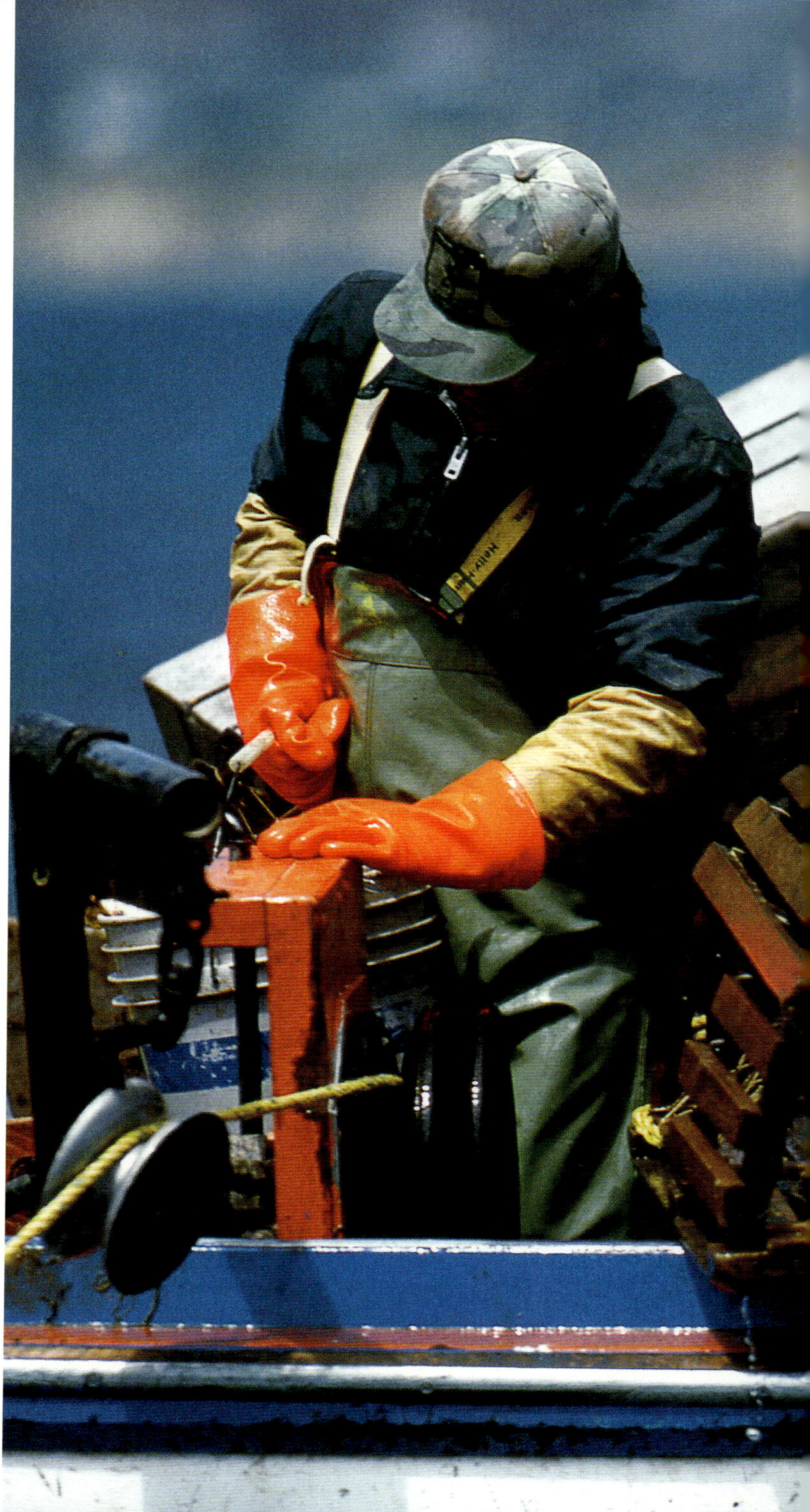

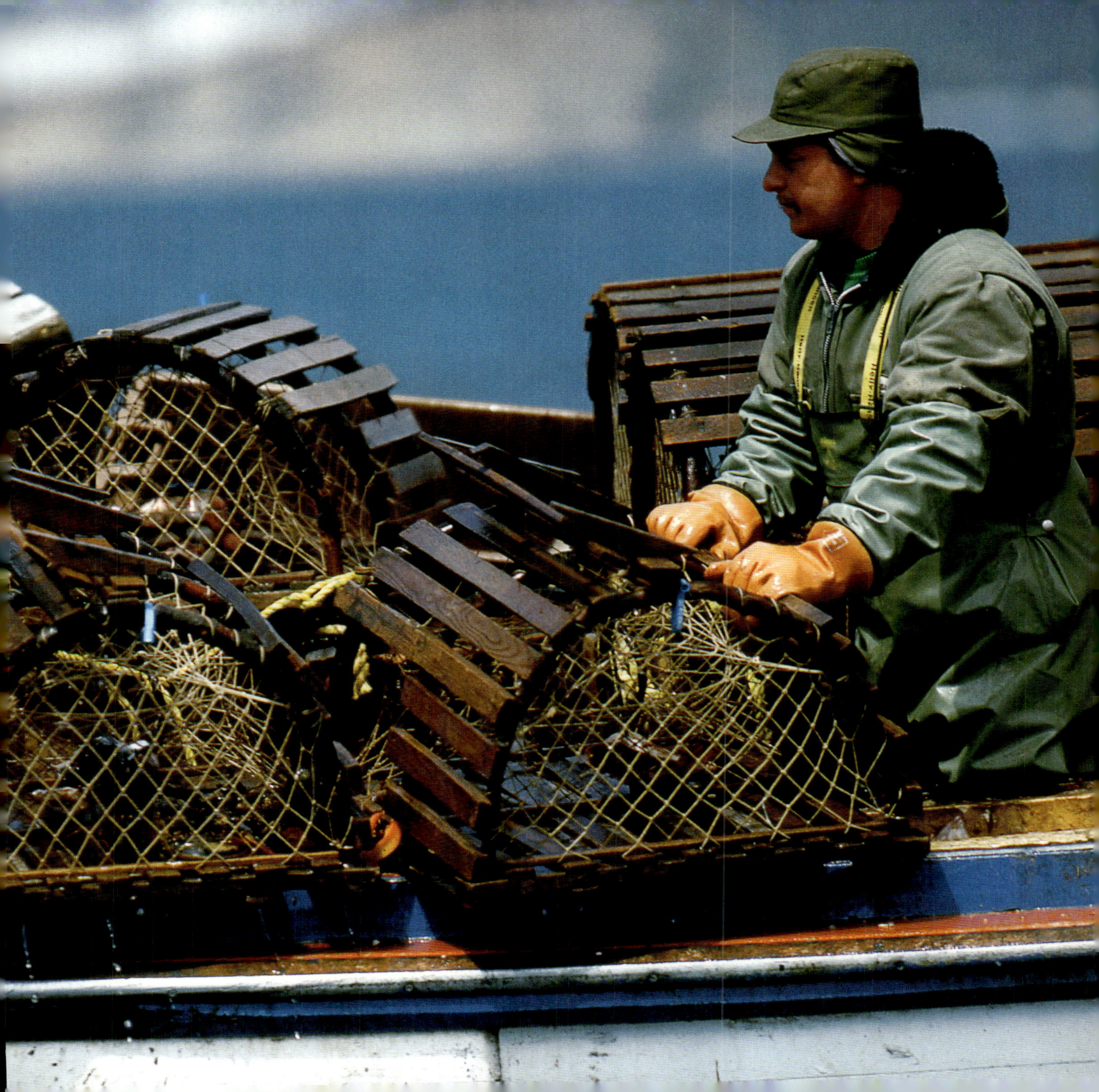

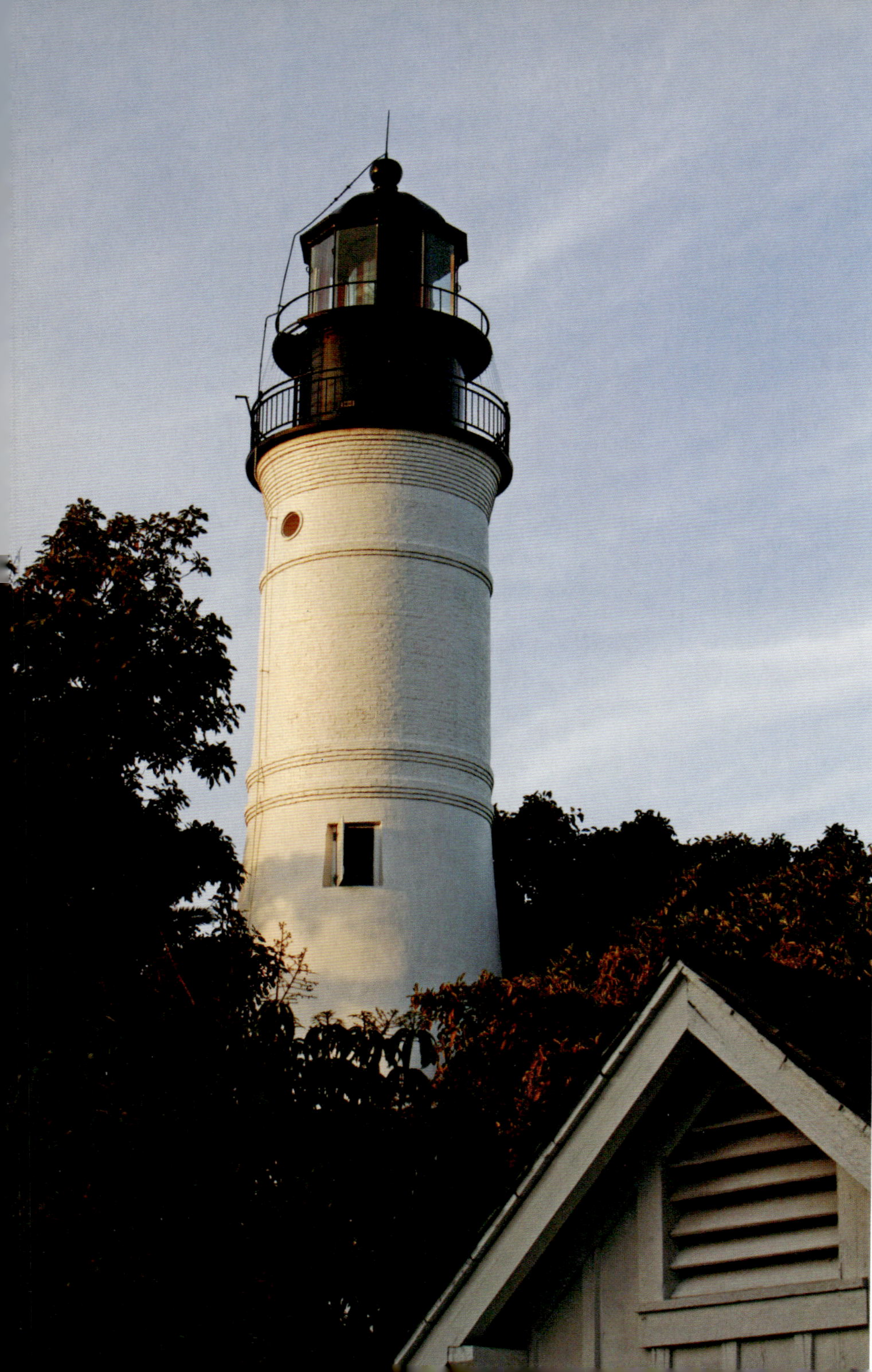

MAY 5

Surely the lighthouse-keeper
has a responsible, if an easy,
office. When his lamp goes out,
he goes out; or, at most, only
one such accident is pardoned.

Henry David Thoreau,
from *Cape Cod,* 1865

MAY 6

Neither nation nor art has
partitioned the sea into empires.
The ocean and its treasures are
the common property of all men.

John Adams

MAY 7

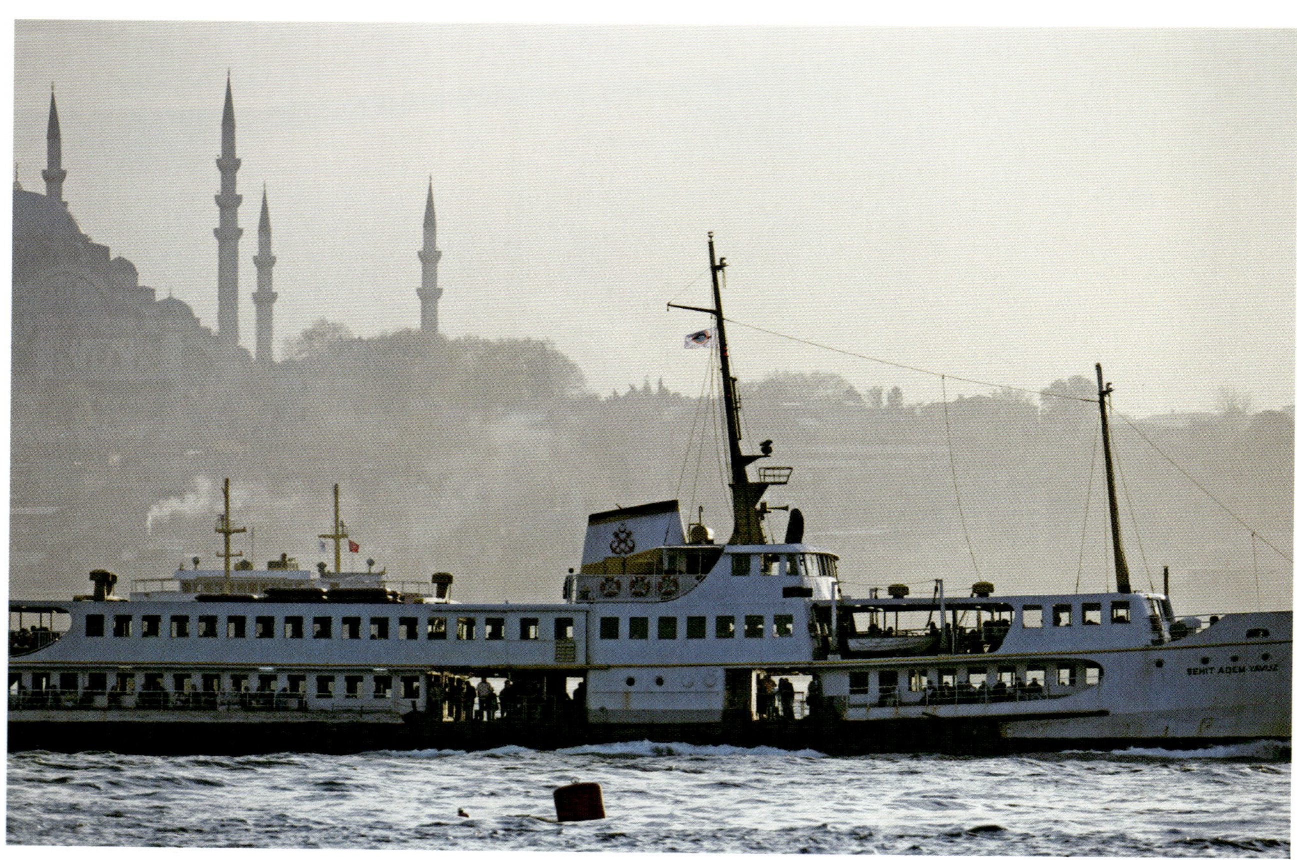

The surface of the water is beautiful, but it is no good to sleep on.

Ghanaian proverb

MAY 8

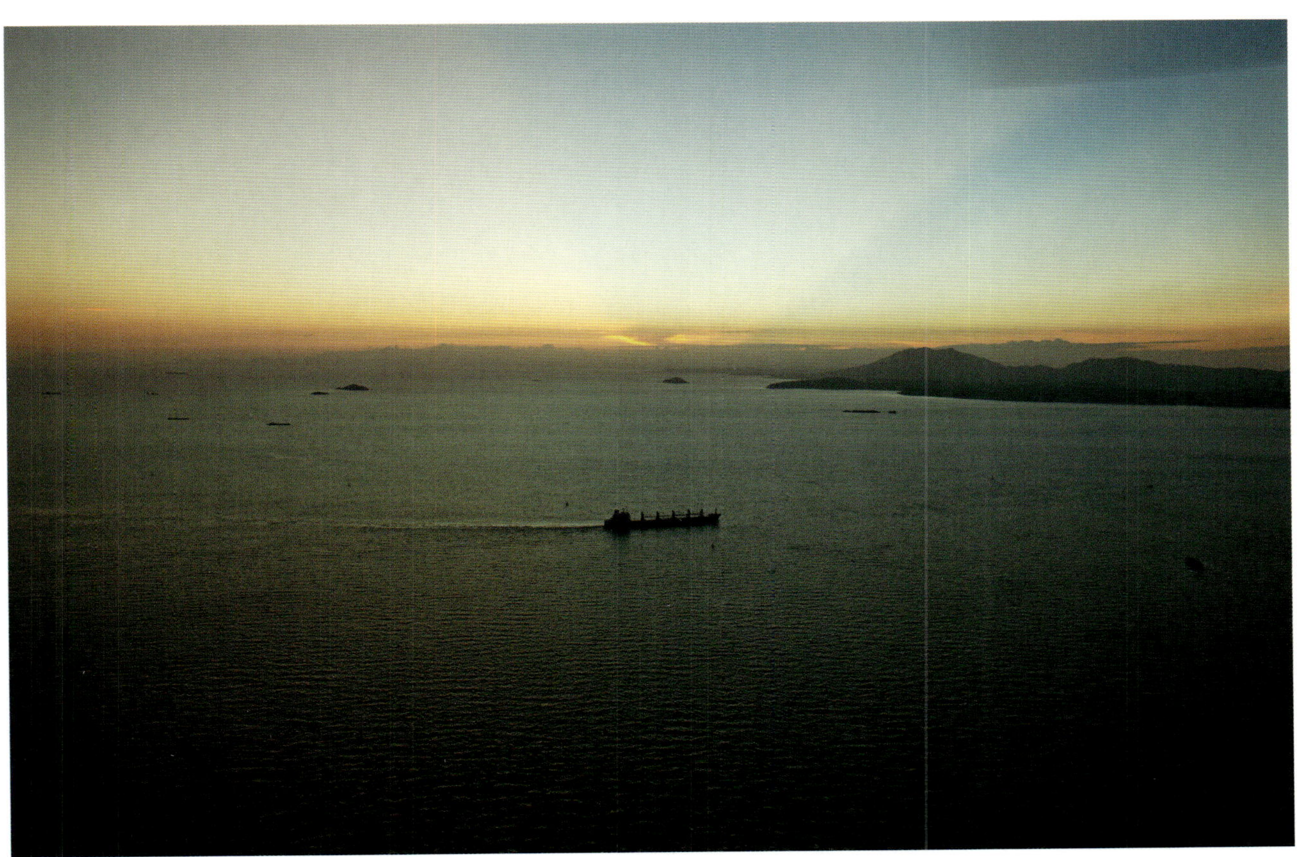

The days pass happily with me wherever my ship sails.

Joshua Slocum, from *Sailing Alone Around the World,* 1900

MAY 9

A life on the ocean wave!
A home on the rolling deep,
Where the scattered waters rave,
And the winds their revels keep!

Epes Sargent,
from "A Life on the Ocean Wave"

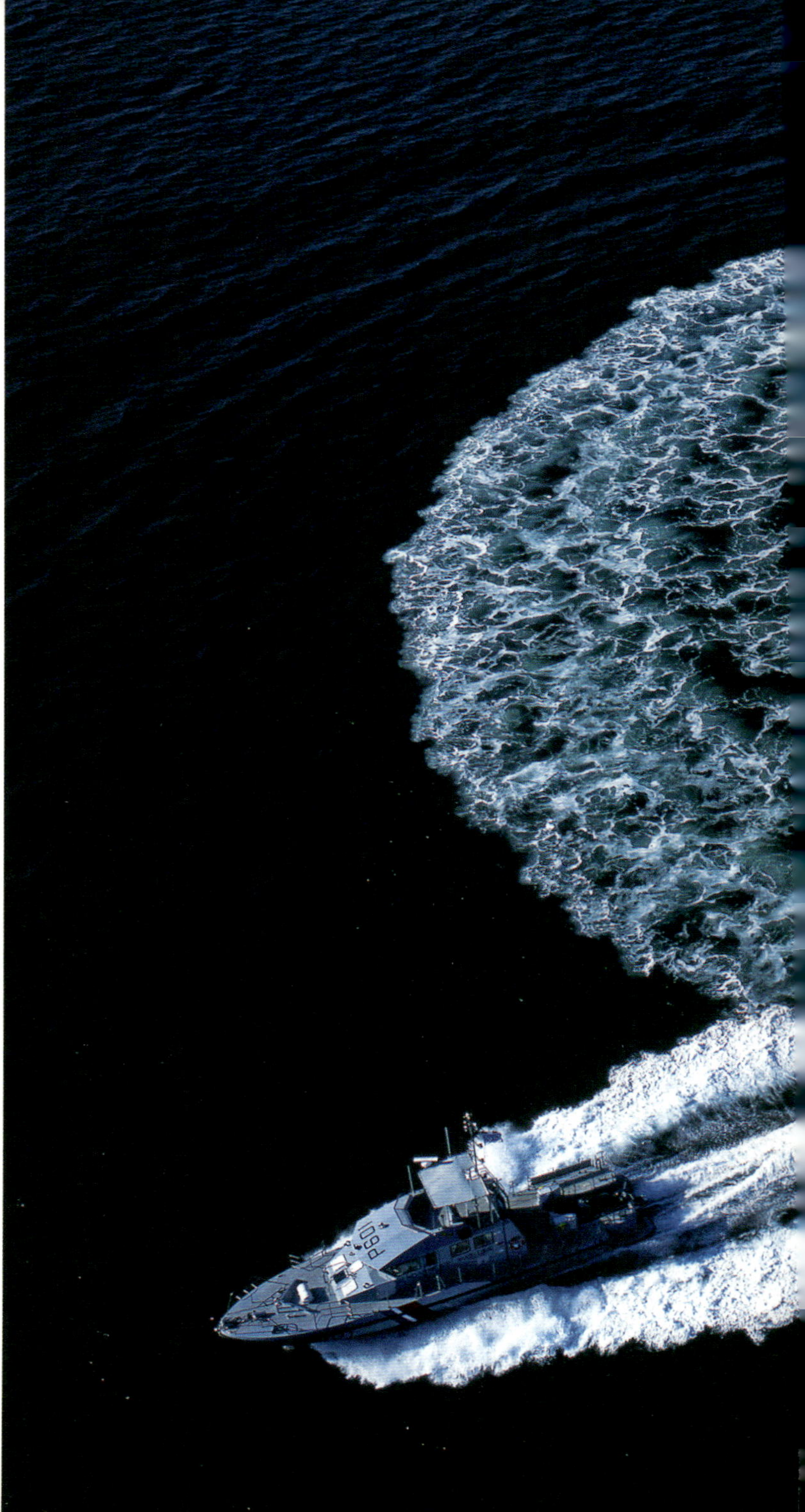

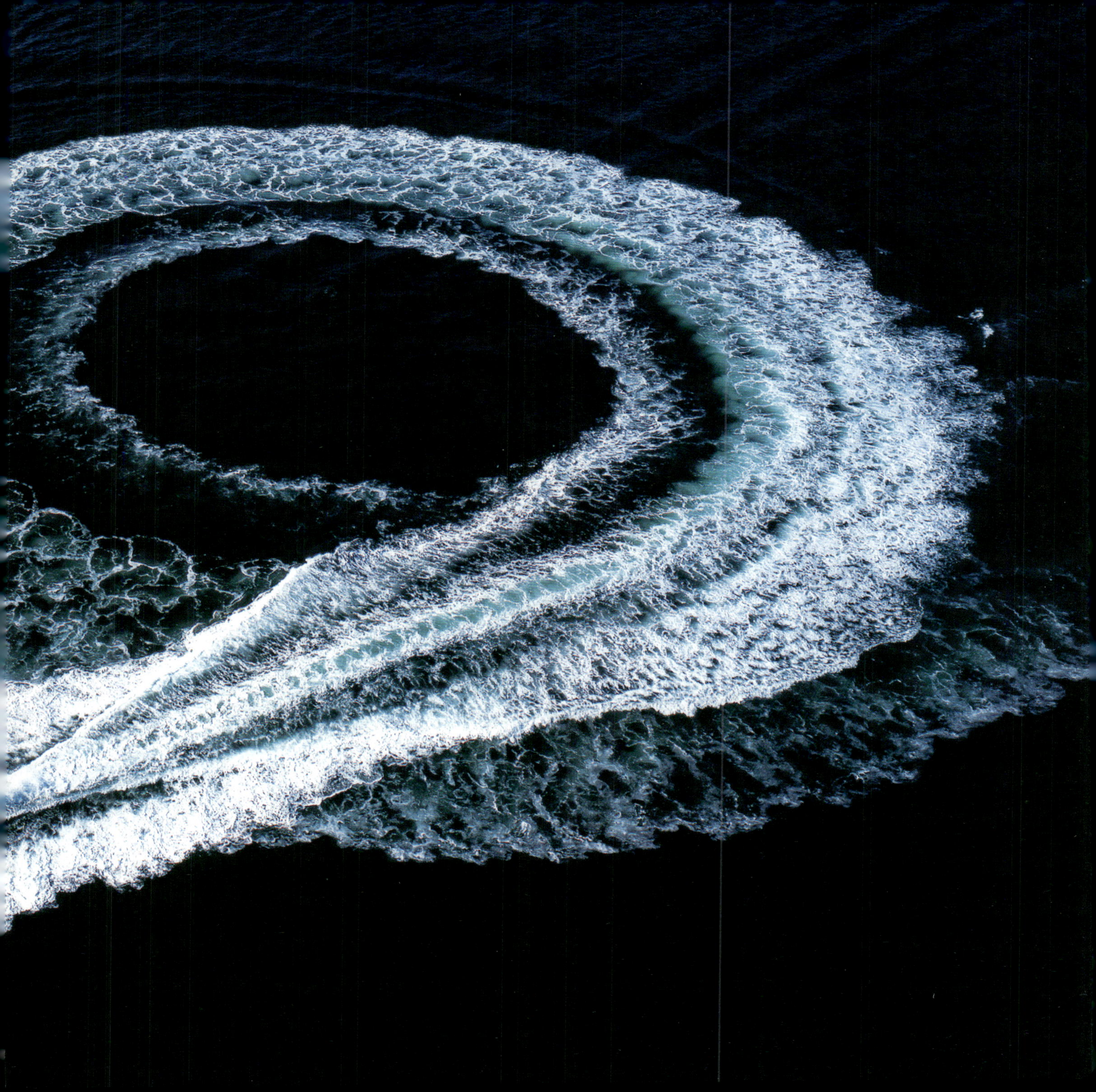

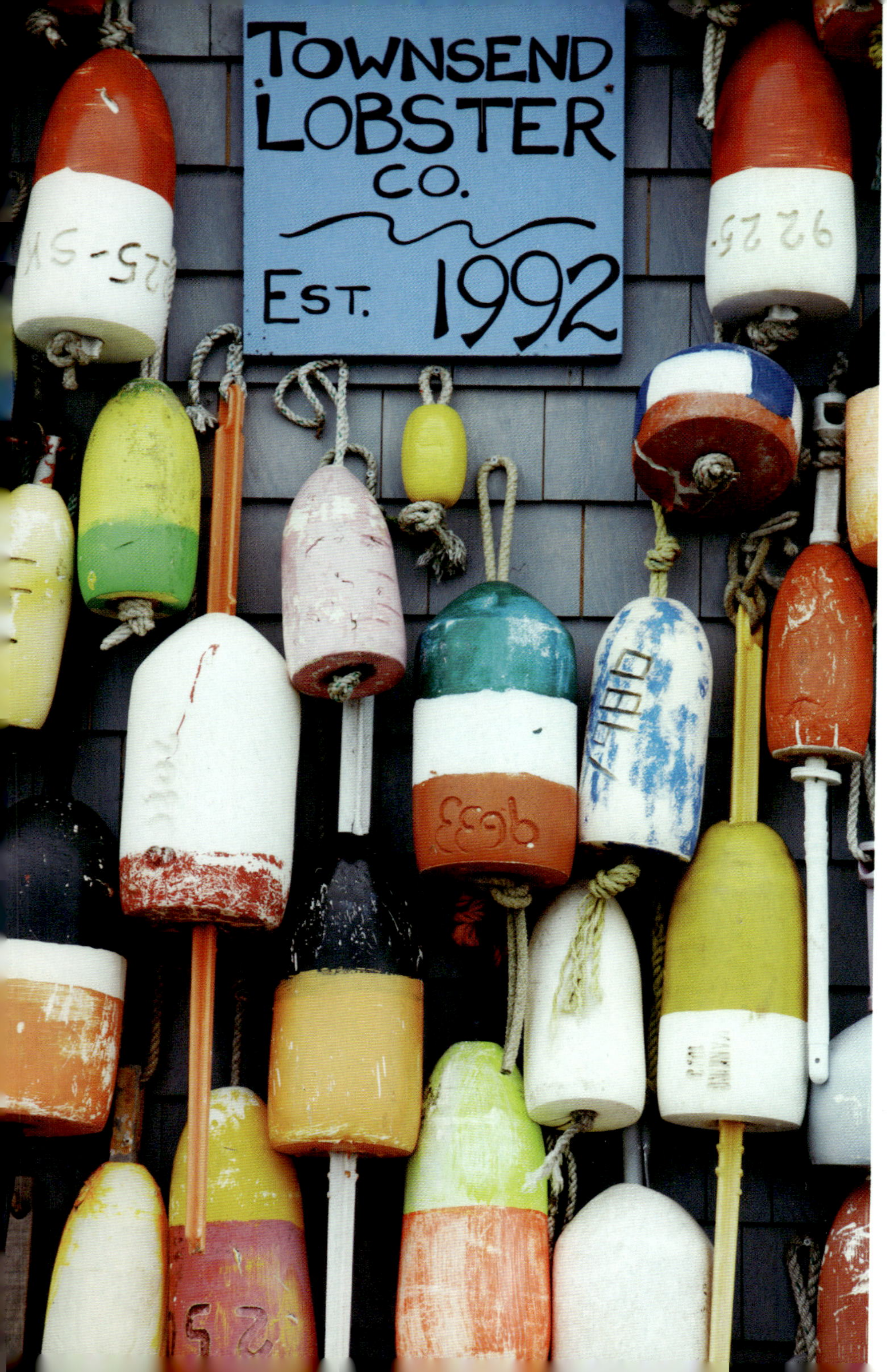

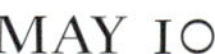

MAY 10

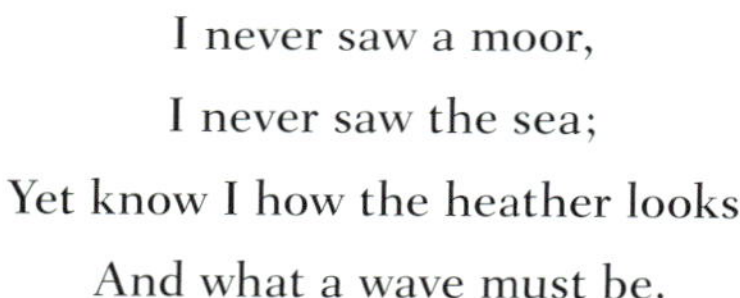

I never saw a moor,
I never saw the sea;
Yet know I how the heather looks,
And what a wave must be.

Emily Dickinson,
from "I never saw a moor,"
Time and Eternity, 1890

MAY 11

Ports are no good—ships rot,
men go to the devil.

Joseph Conrad,
from *The Mirror of the Sea,* 1906

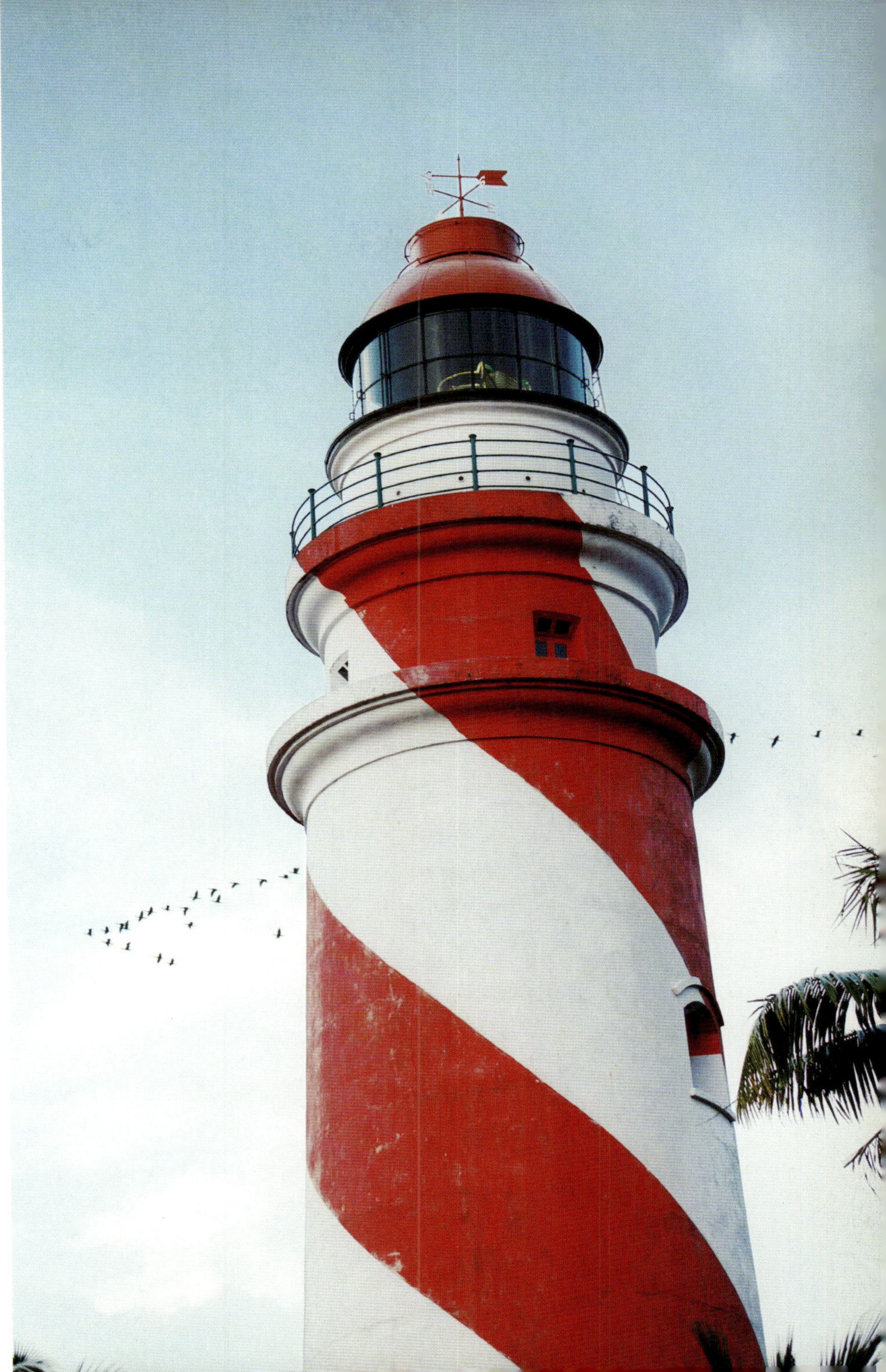

MAY 12

The world's a ship on its voyage out, and not a voyage complete.

Herman Melville, from *Moby-Dick,* 1851

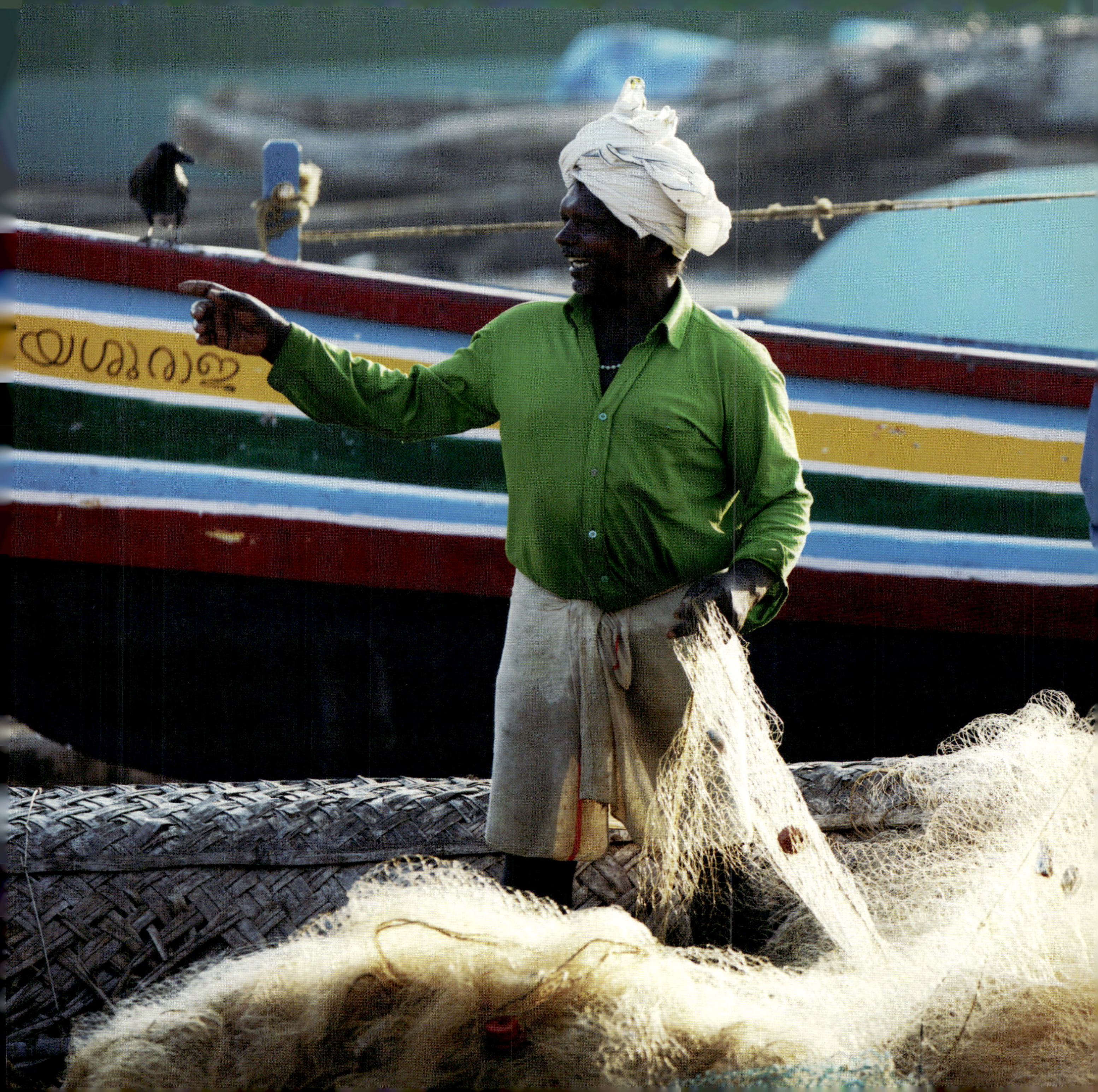
യശുരാജ

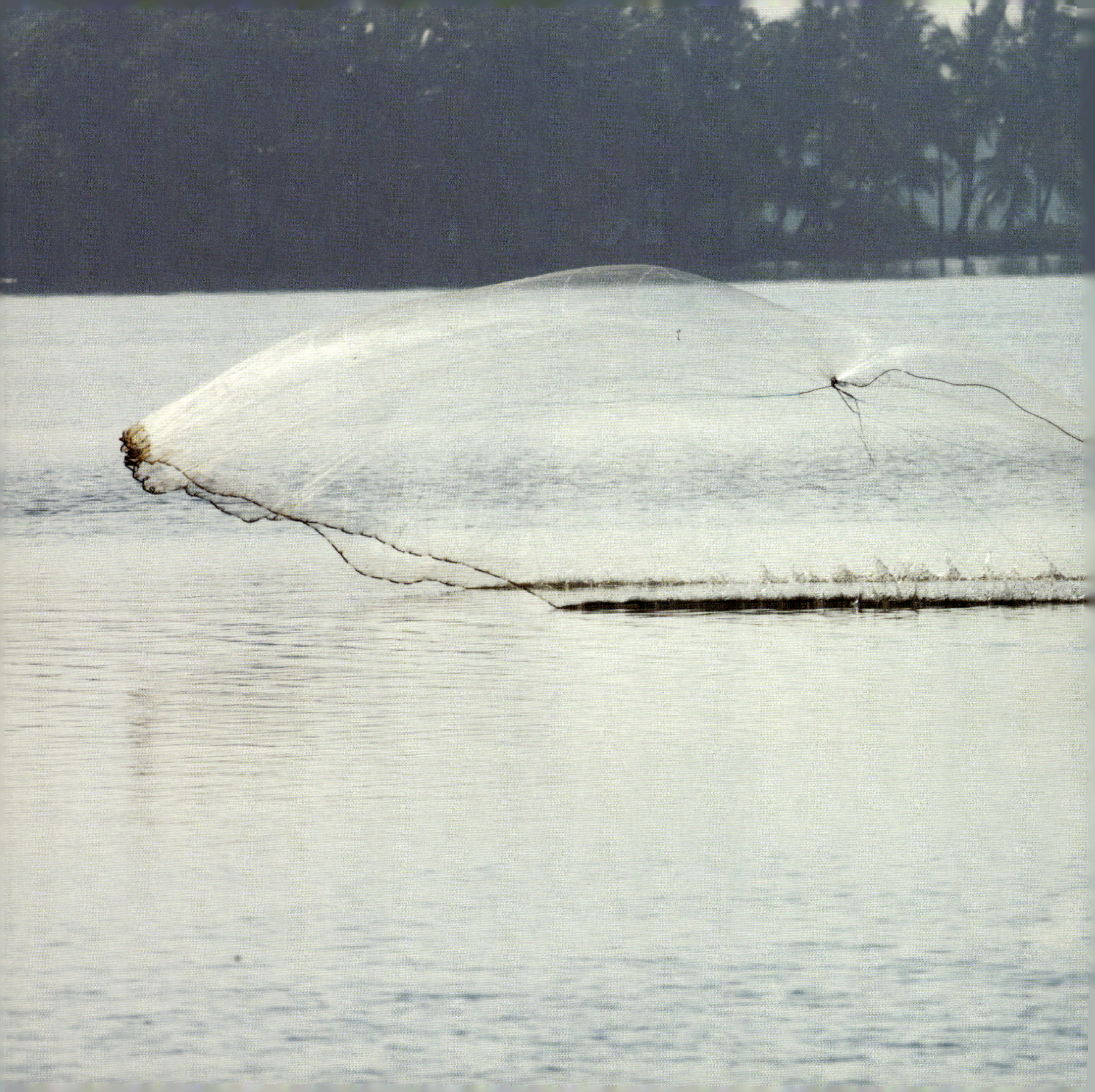

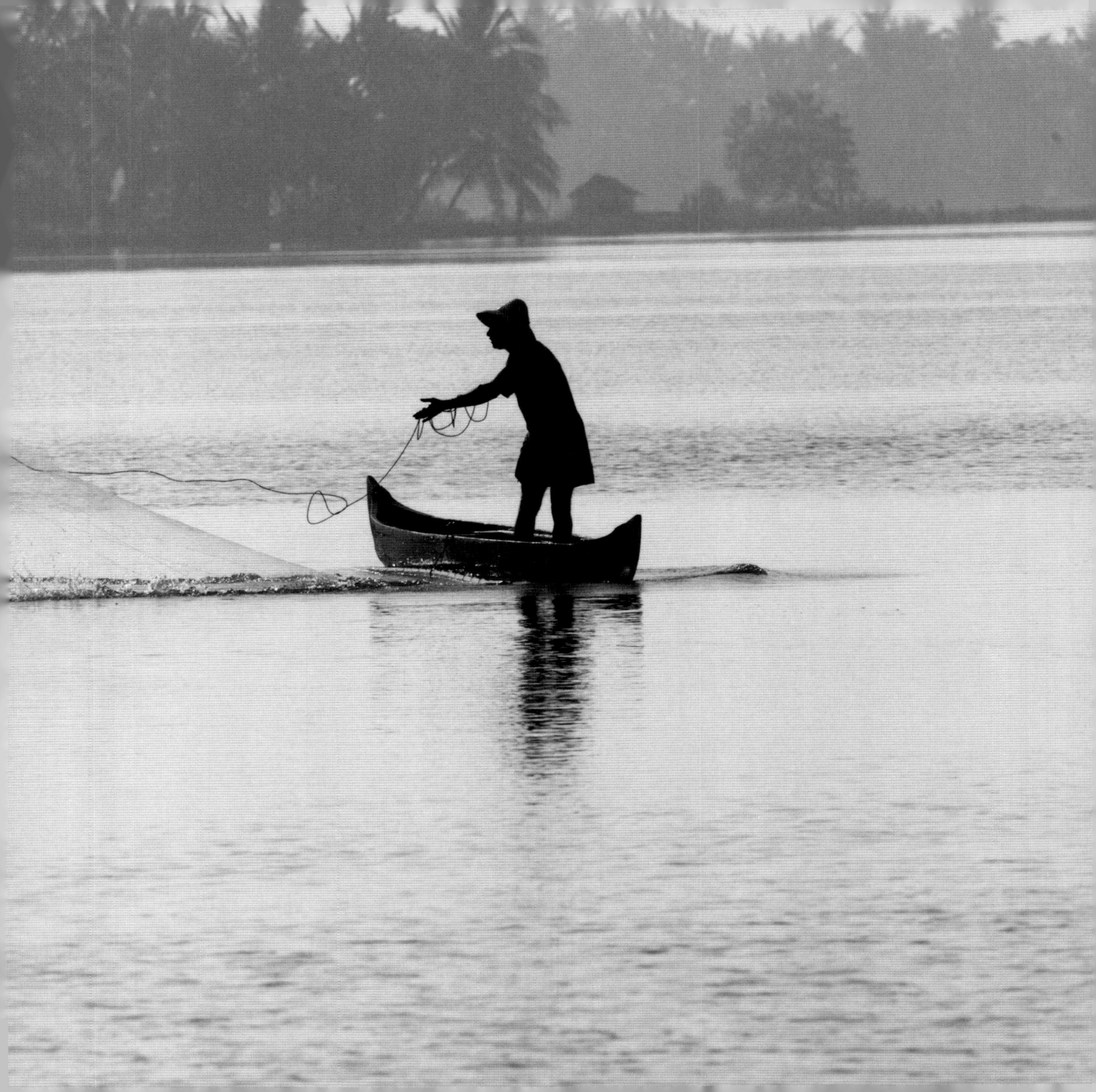

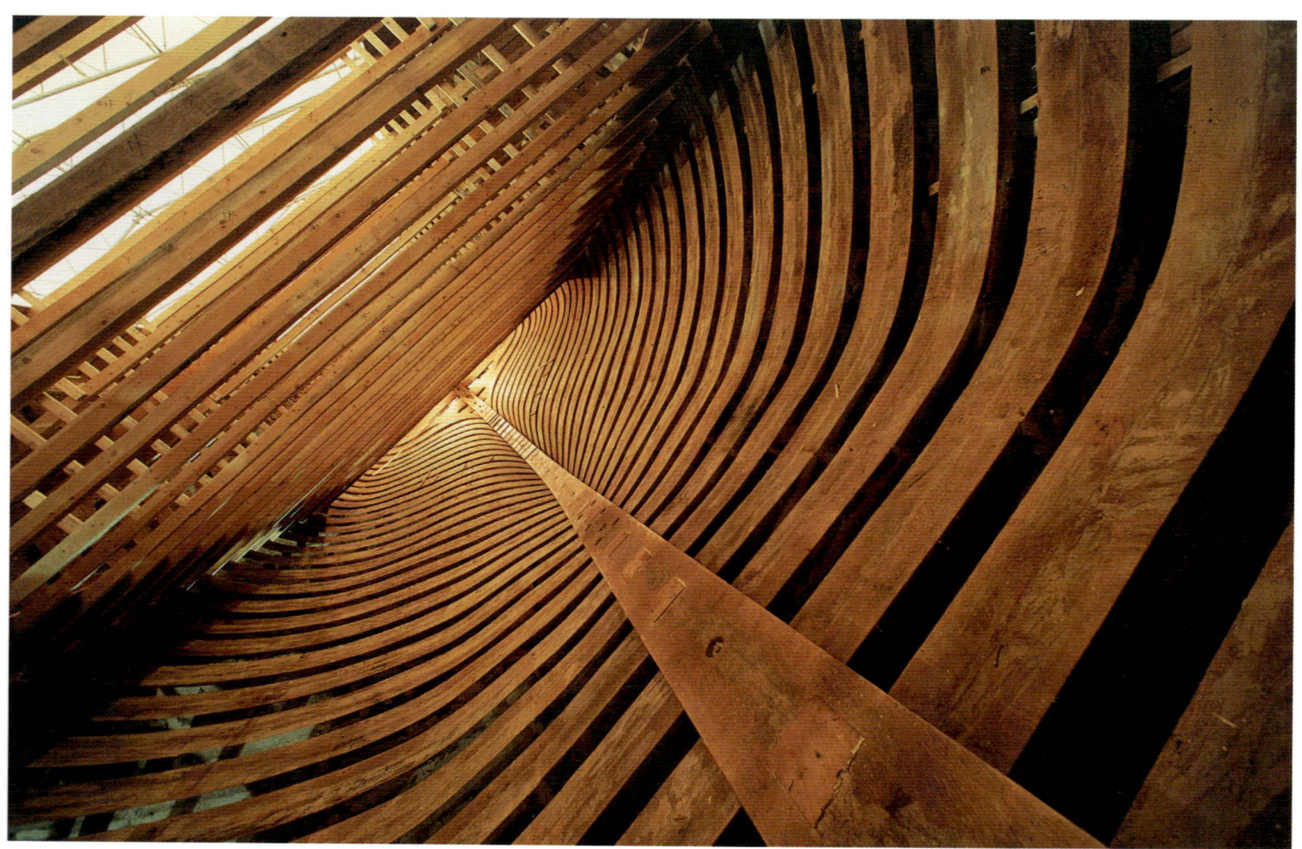

There is but a plank between a sailor and eternity.

Thomas Gibbons

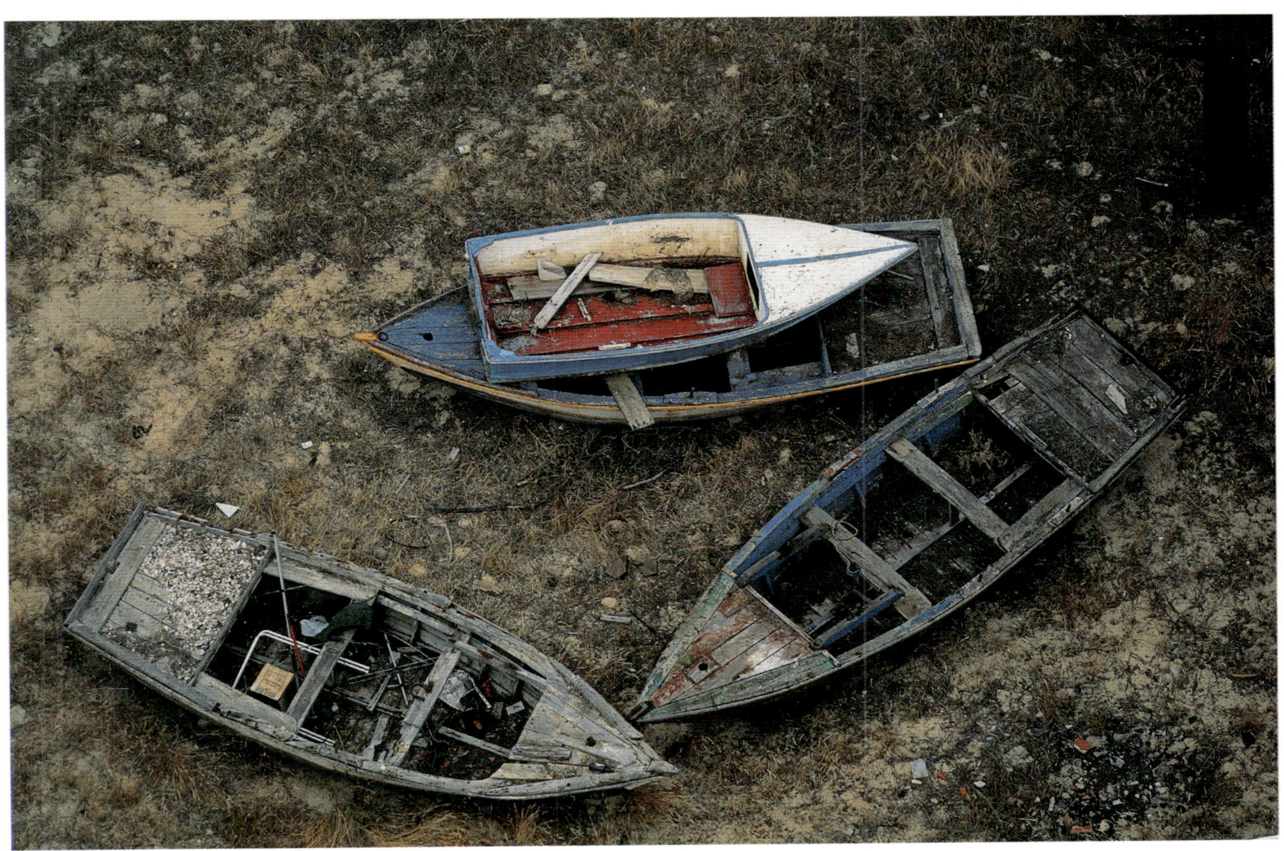

The sea becomes the shore, the shore becomes the sea.

Indonesian proverb

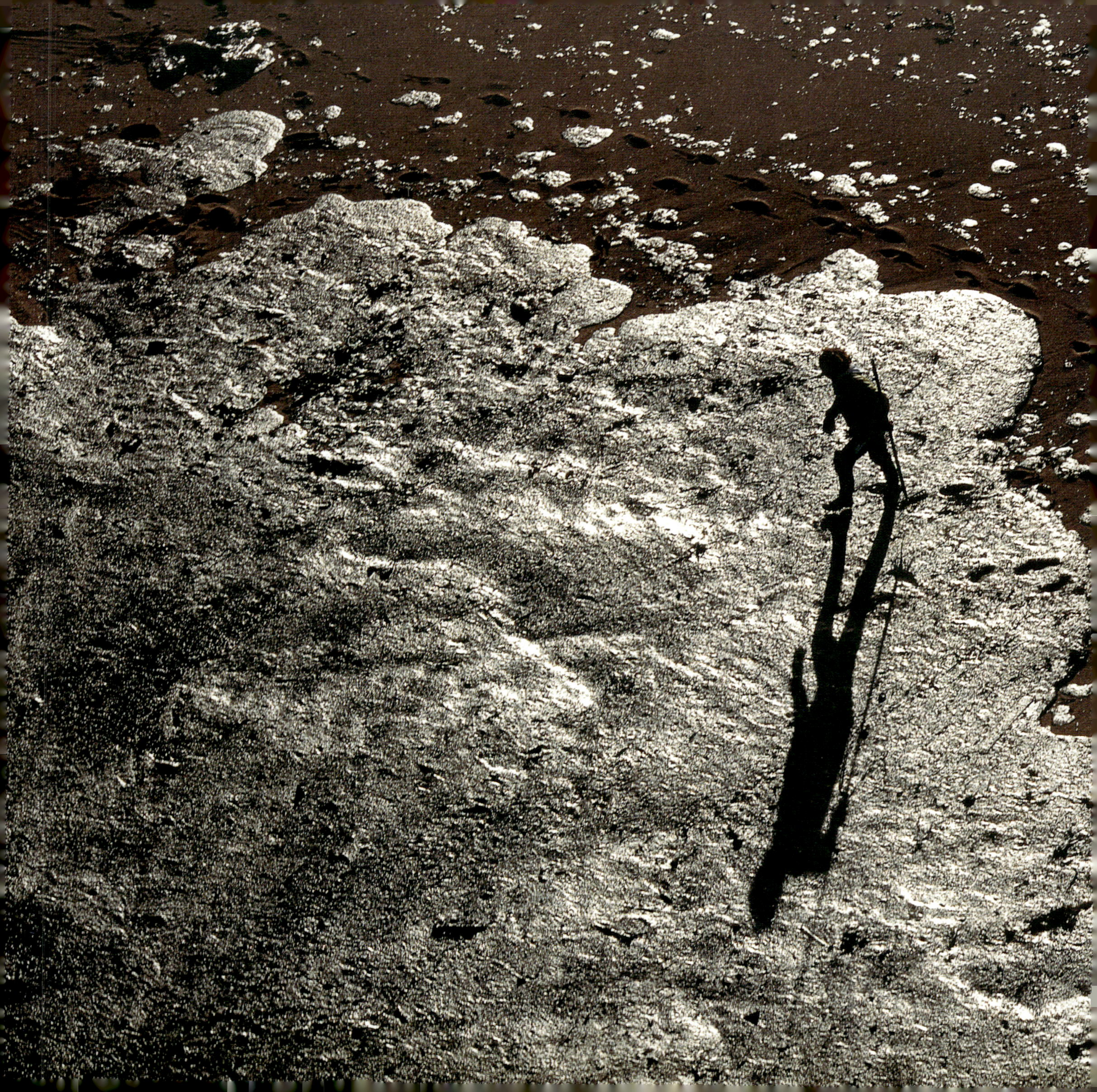

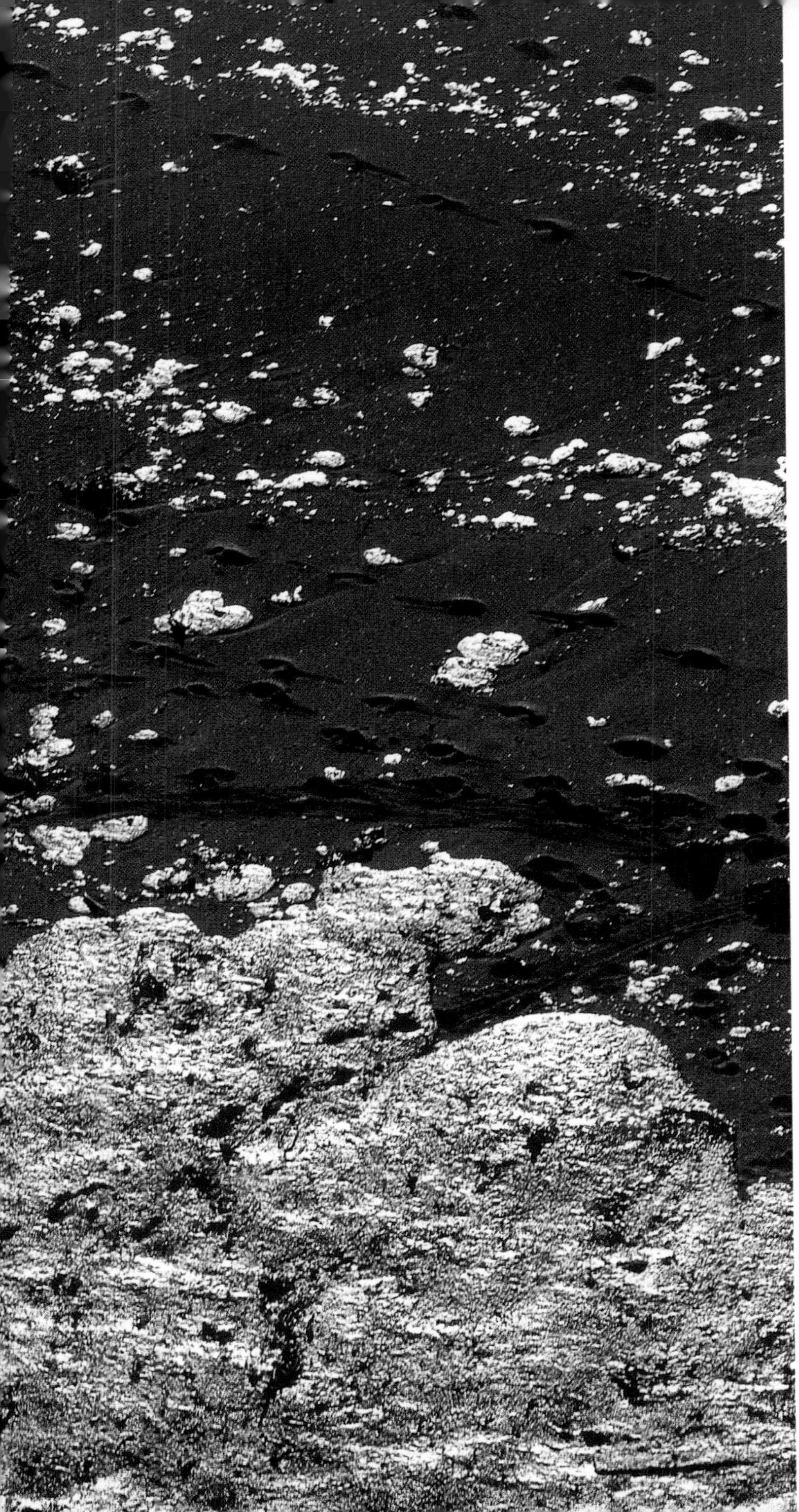

MAY 15

You can't complain about the sea if you suffer shipwreck for the second time.

Icelandic proverb

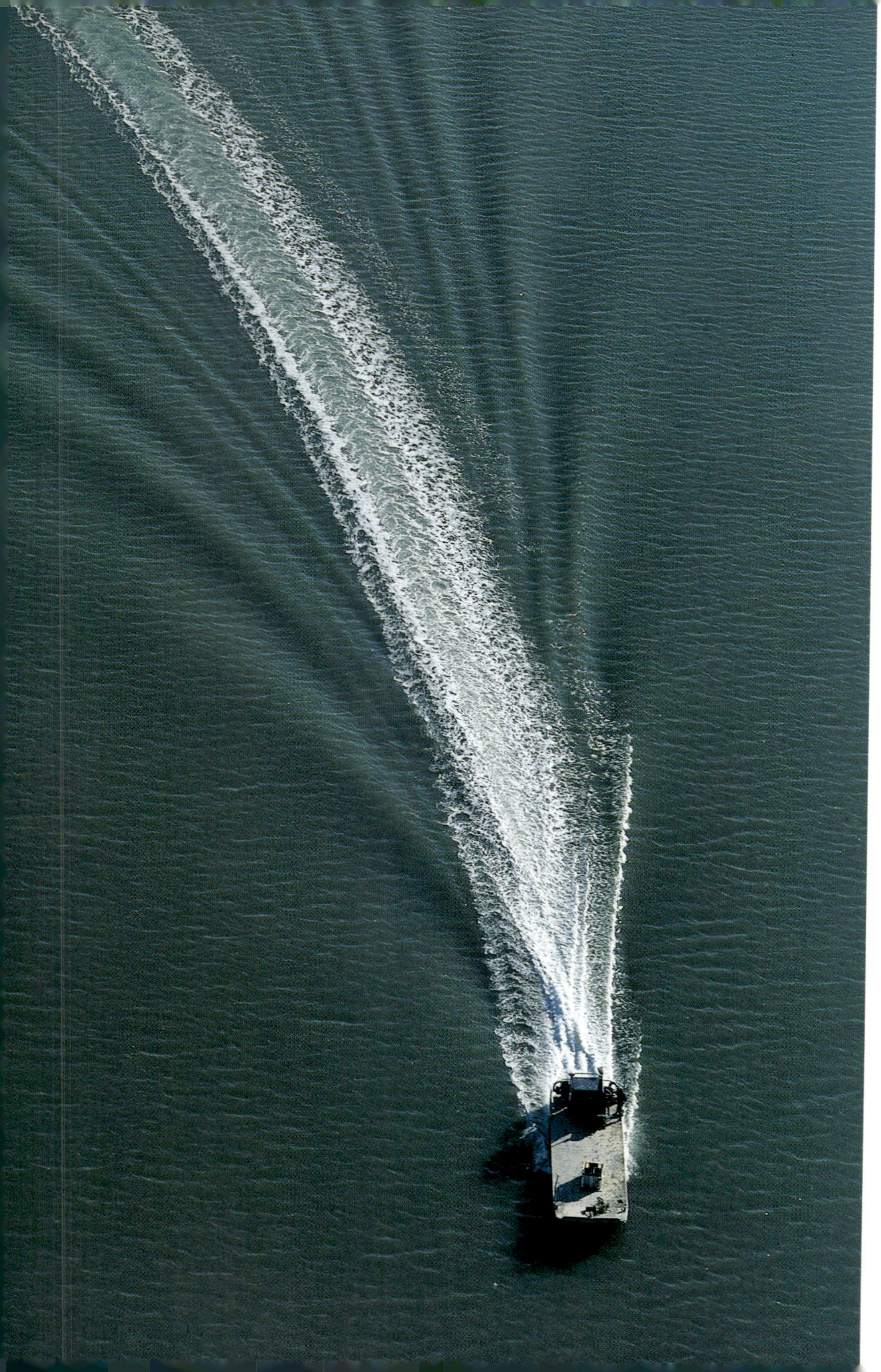

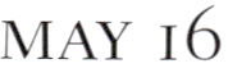

MAY 16

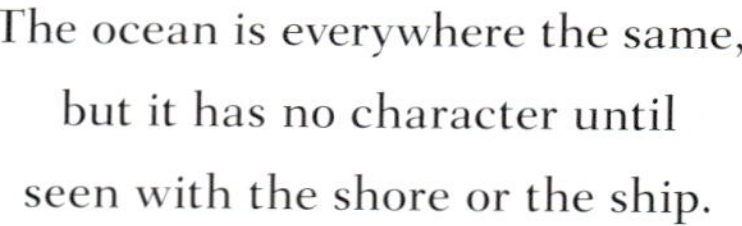

The ocean is everywhere the same,
but it has no character until
seen with the shore or the ship.

Ralph Waldo Emerson,
from "The Method of Nature,"
Nature, Addresses, and Lectures, 1849

MAY 17

There are more tears poured
on the ground than there
is water in the ocean.

Buddha

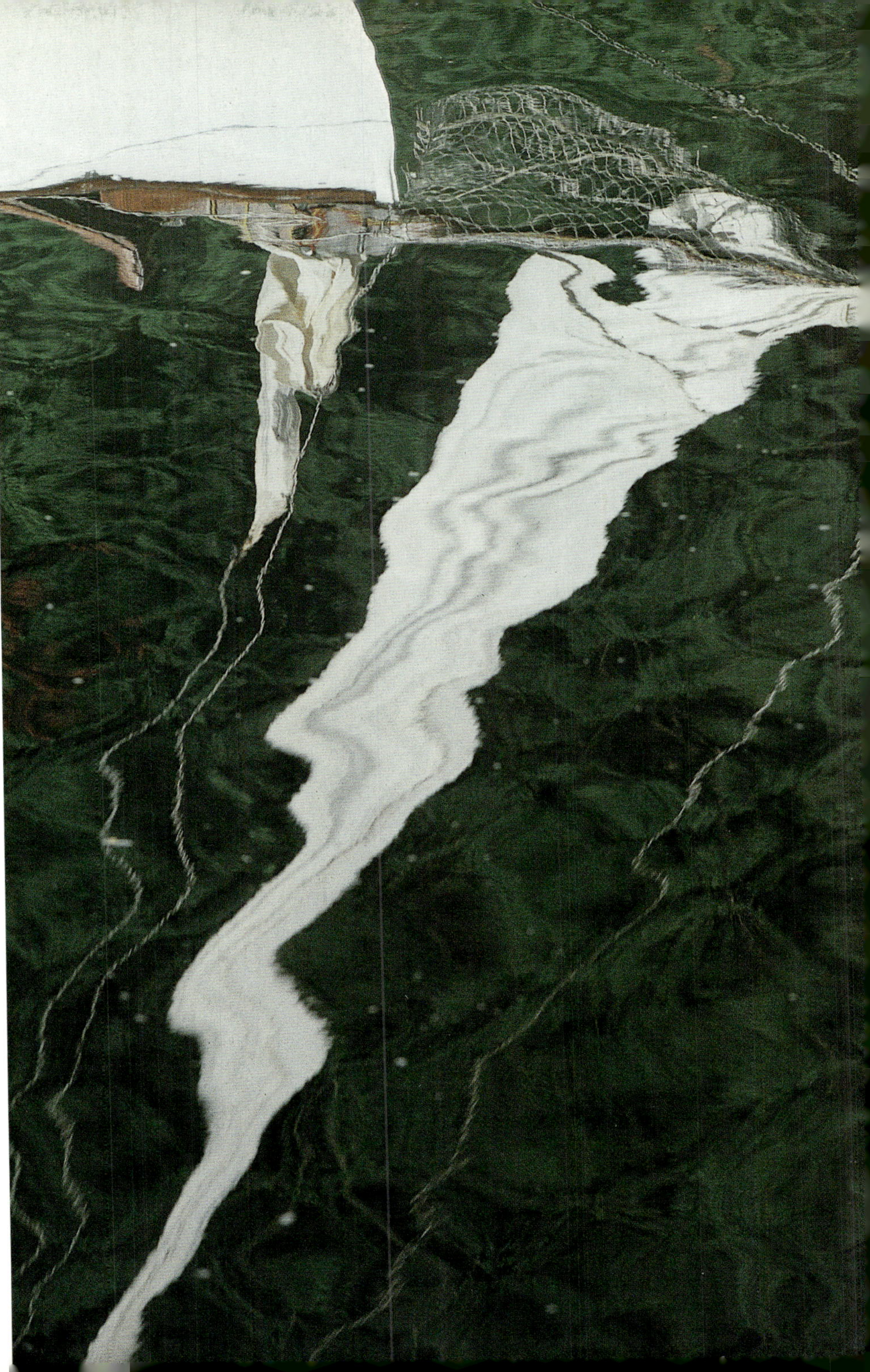

MAY 18

Ocean: A body of water occupying about two-thirds of a world made for man—who has no gills.

Ambrose Bierce, from *The Devil's Dictionary,* 1911

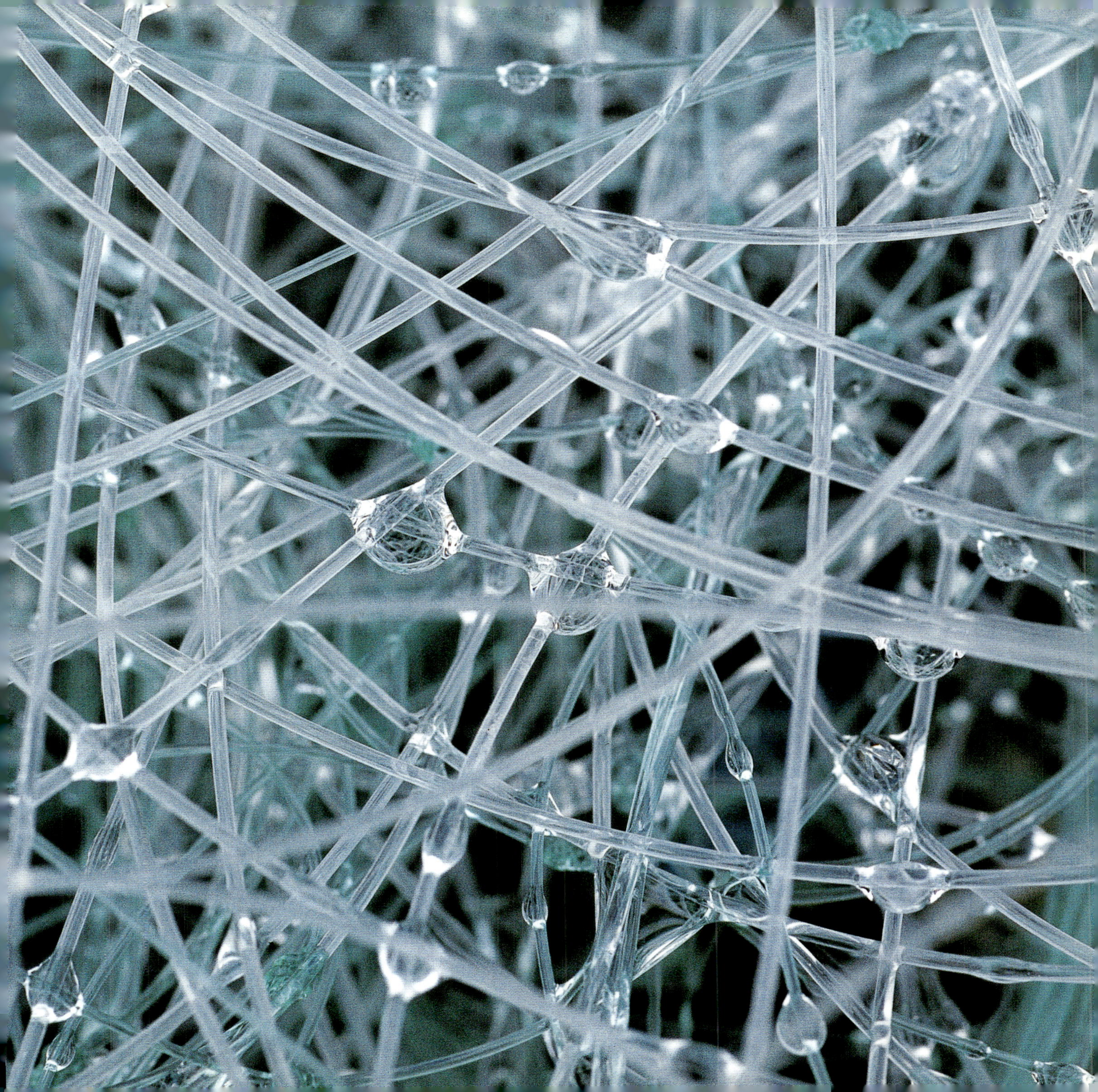

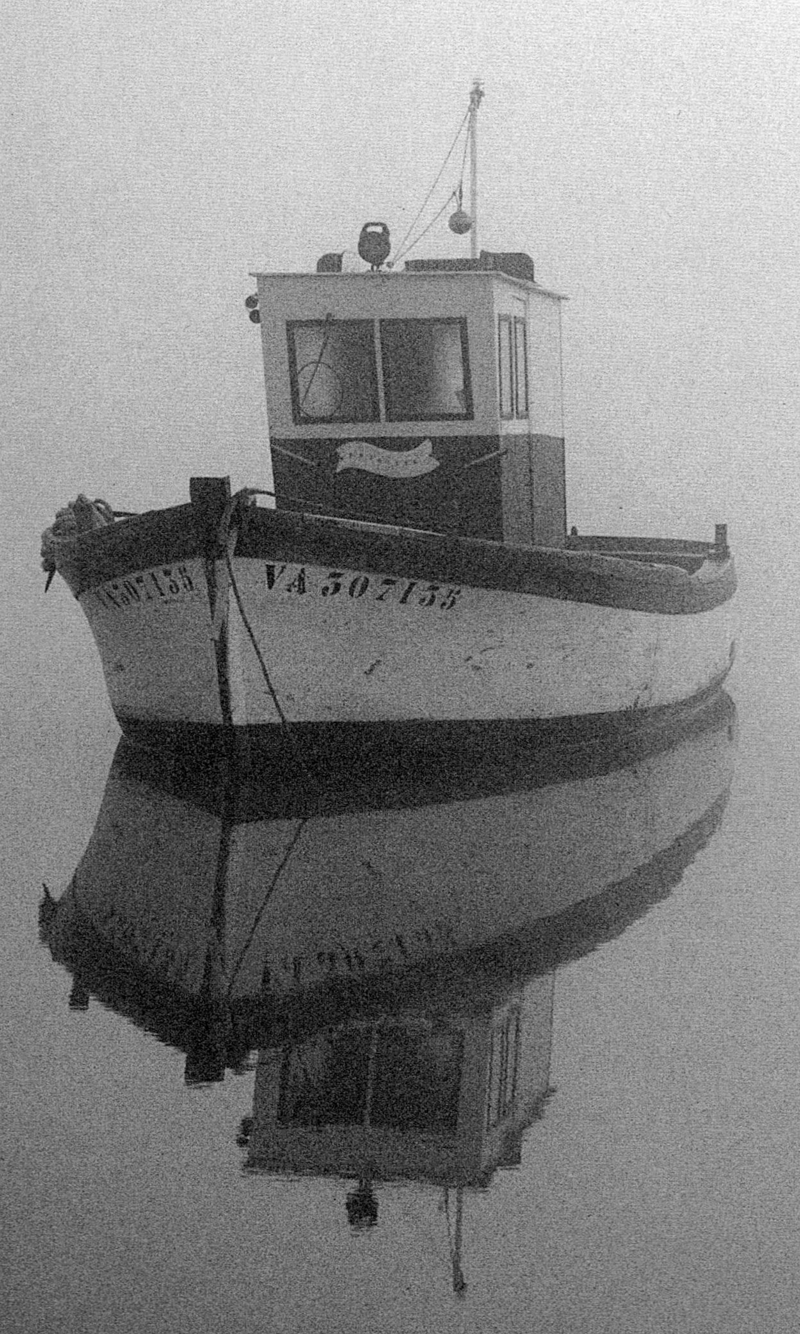
VA 307135

MAY 19

As I gaze upon the sea!
All the old romantic legends,
All my dreams, come back to me.

Henry Wadsworth Longfellow,
from "The Secret of the Sea," *The Seaside and the Fireside,* 1850

MAY 20

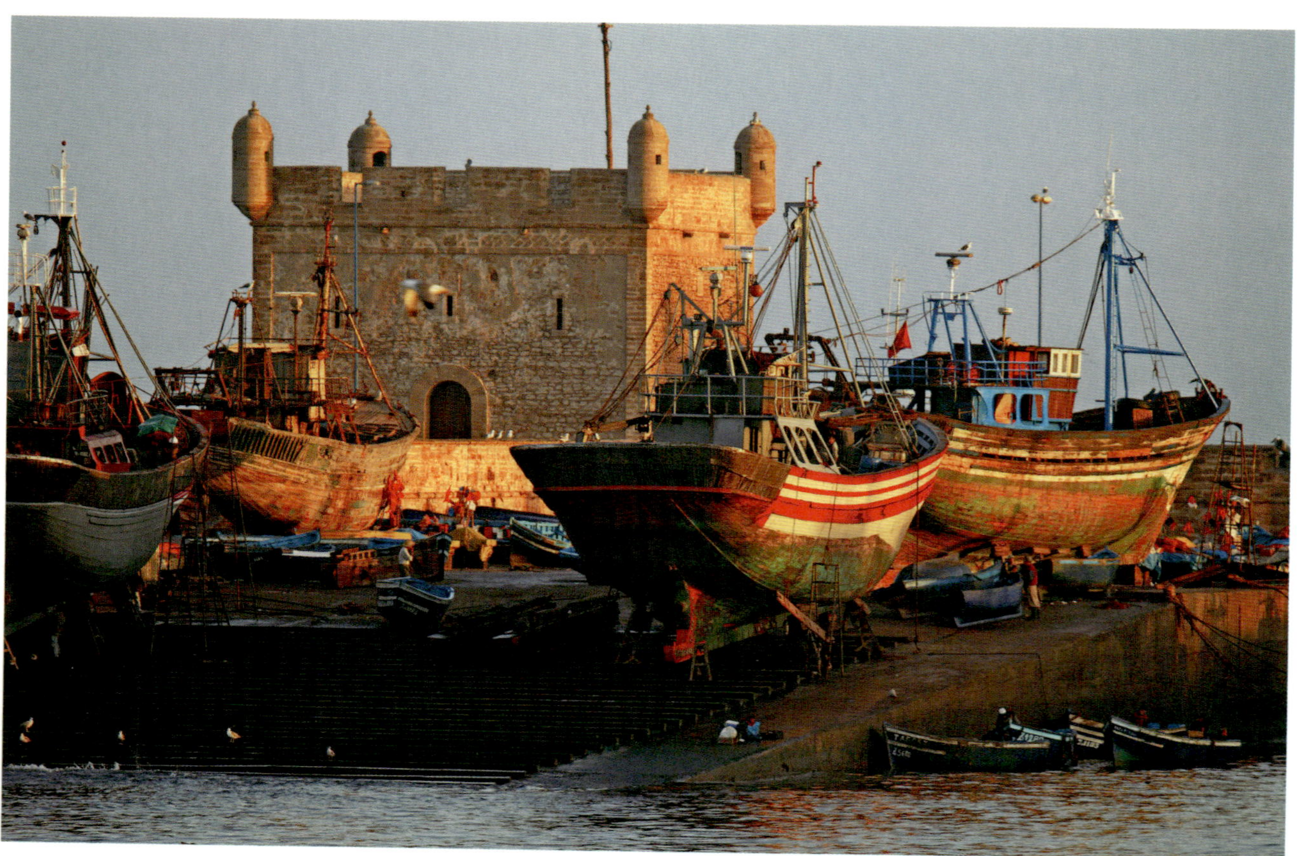

No foreign banished wight shall anchor in this port;
Our realm it brooks no stranger's force, let them elsewhere resort.

Elizabeth I

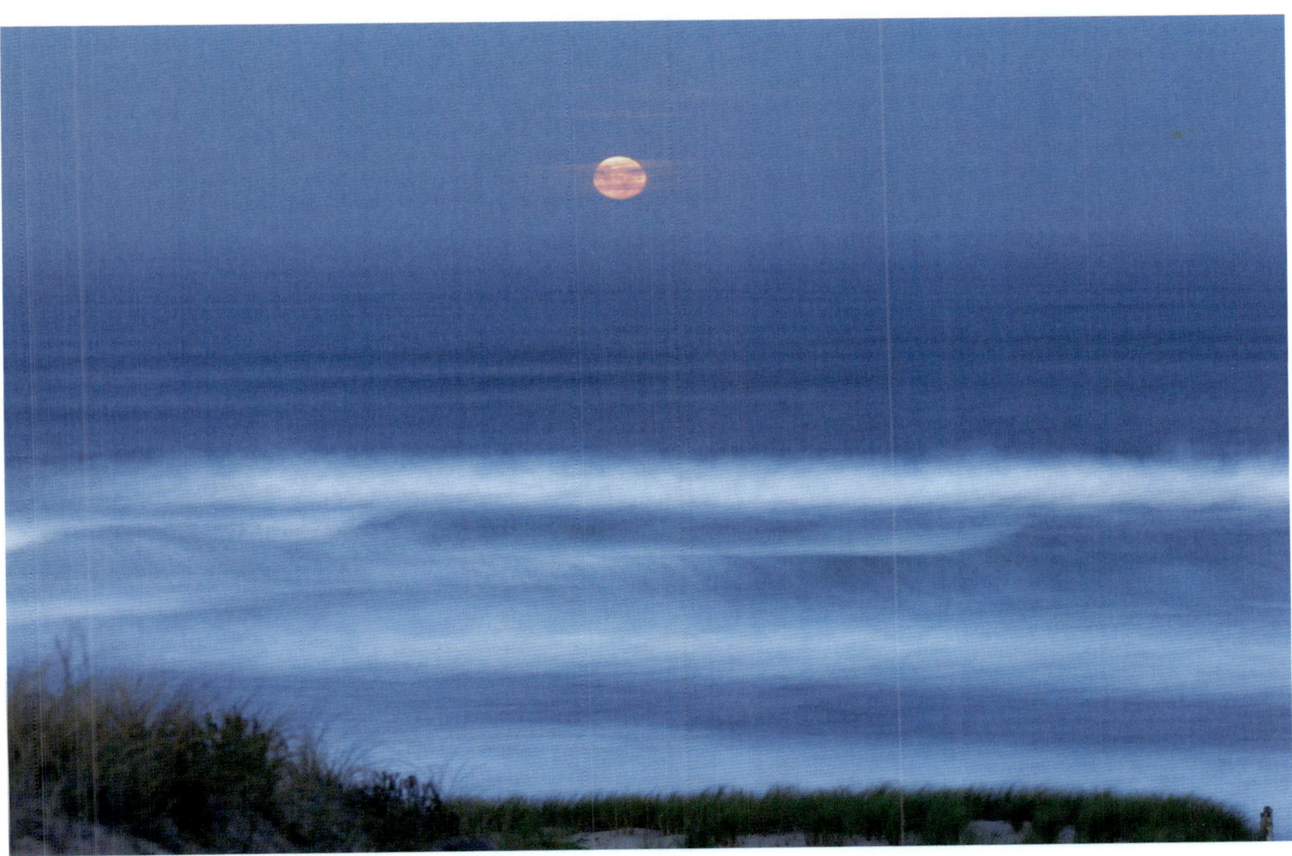

We may not arrive at our port within a calculable period, but we would preserve the true course.

Henry David Thoreau, from *Walden,* 1854

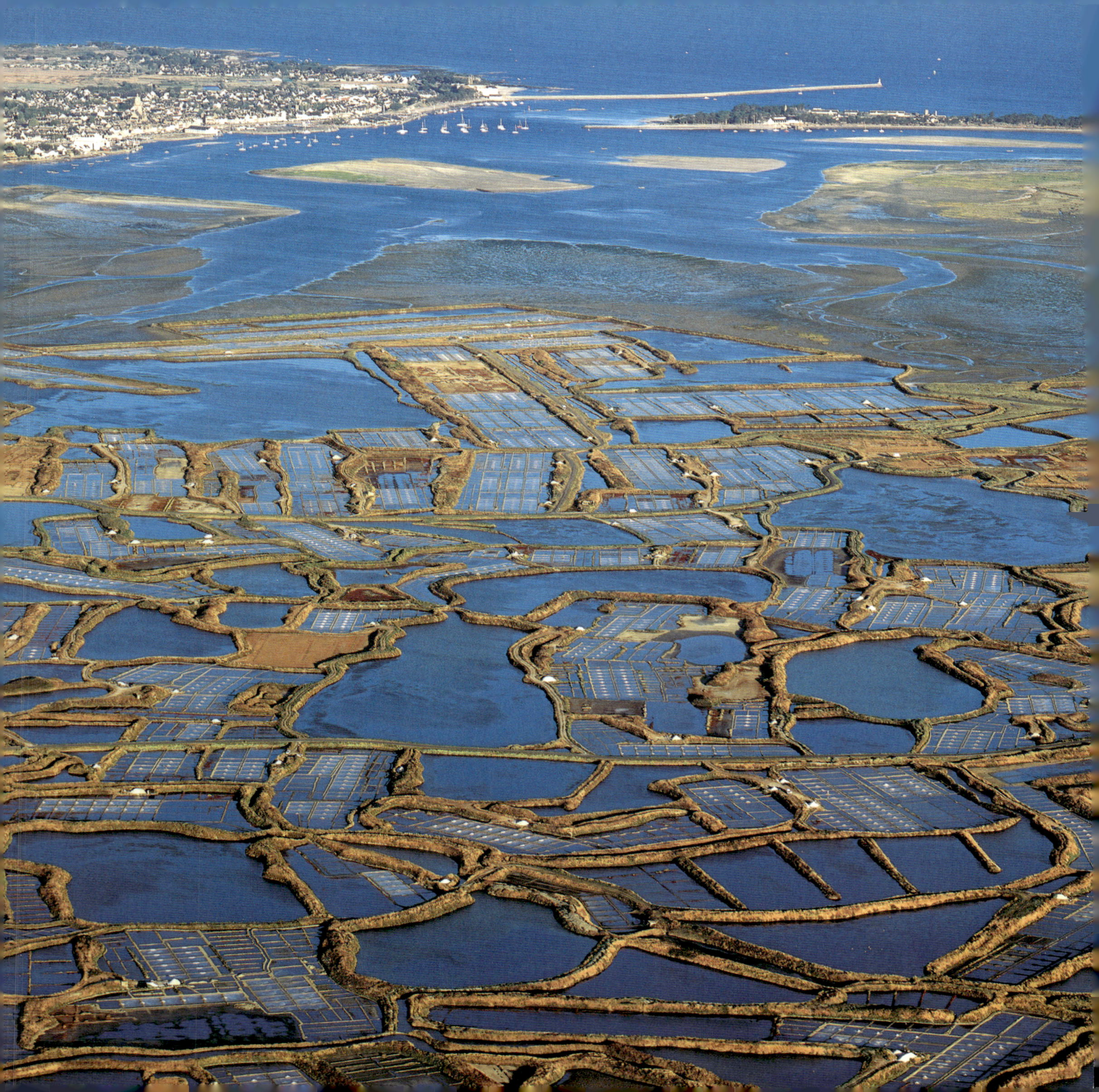

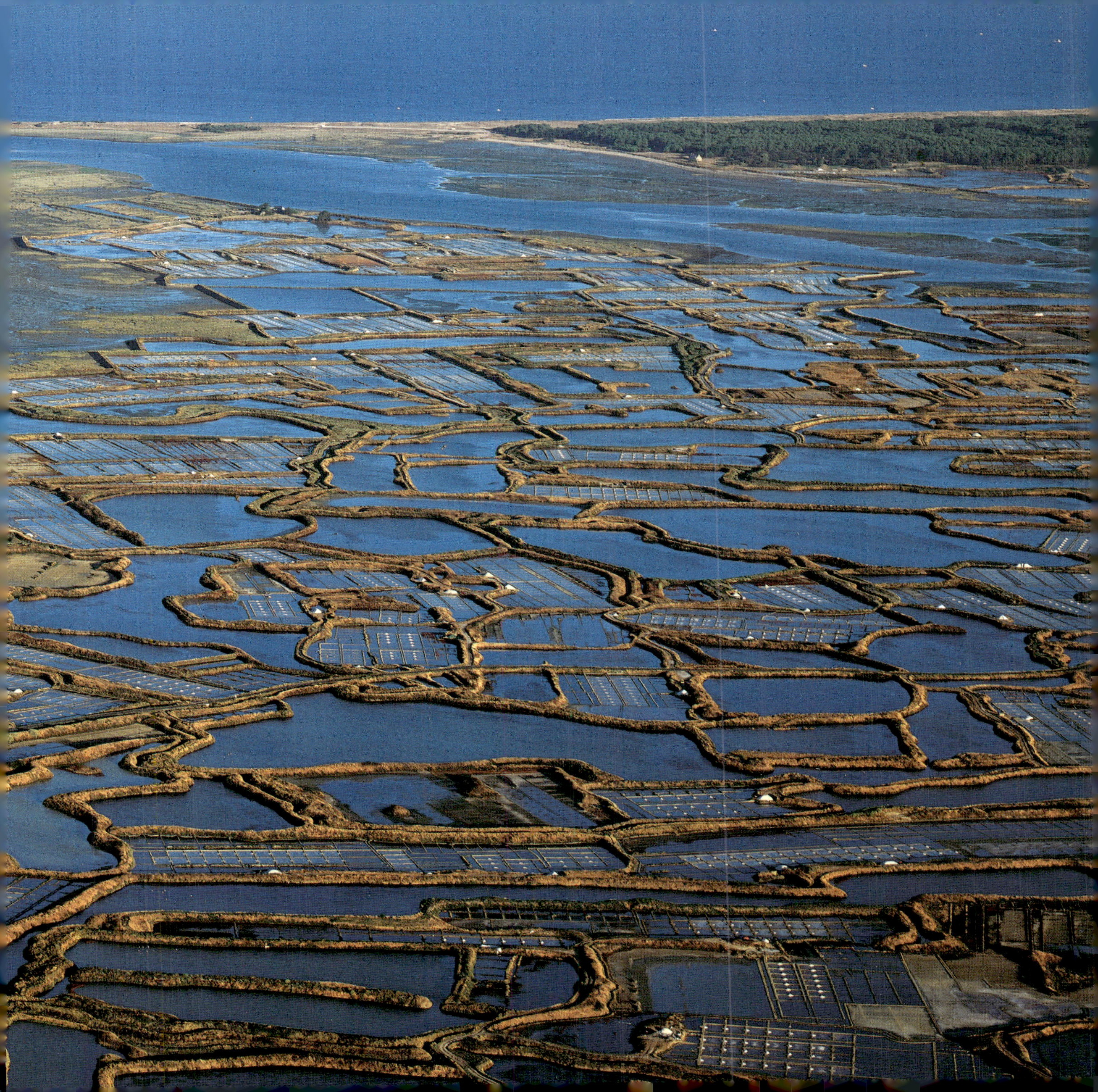

MAY 22

Wind whines and whines the shingle,
The crazy pierstakes groan,
A senile sea numbers each single
Slime silvered stone.

James Joyce, from "On the Beach at Fontana," 1914

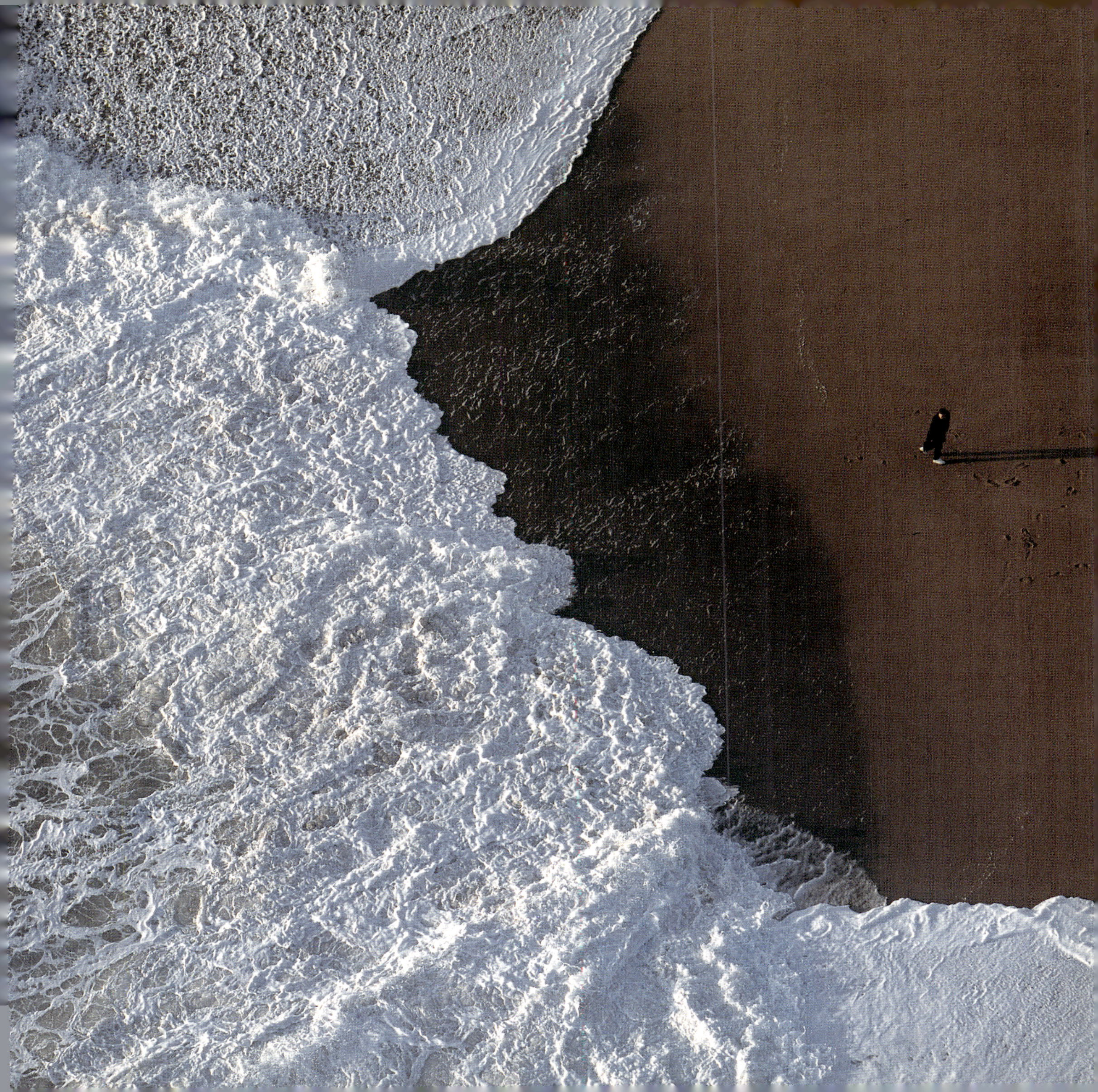

MAY 23

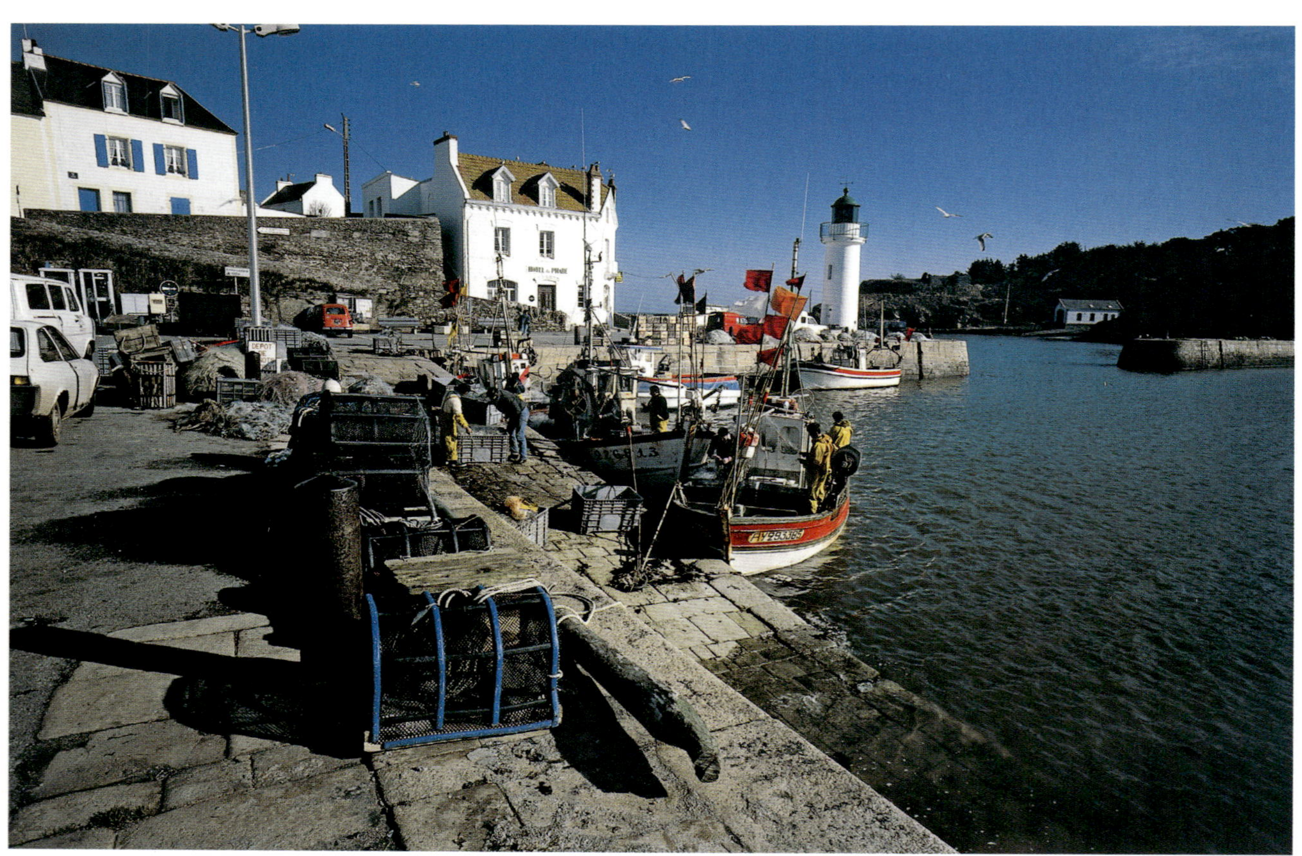

And the sea will grant each man new hope . . . his sleep brings dreams of home.

Christopher Columbus

MAY 24

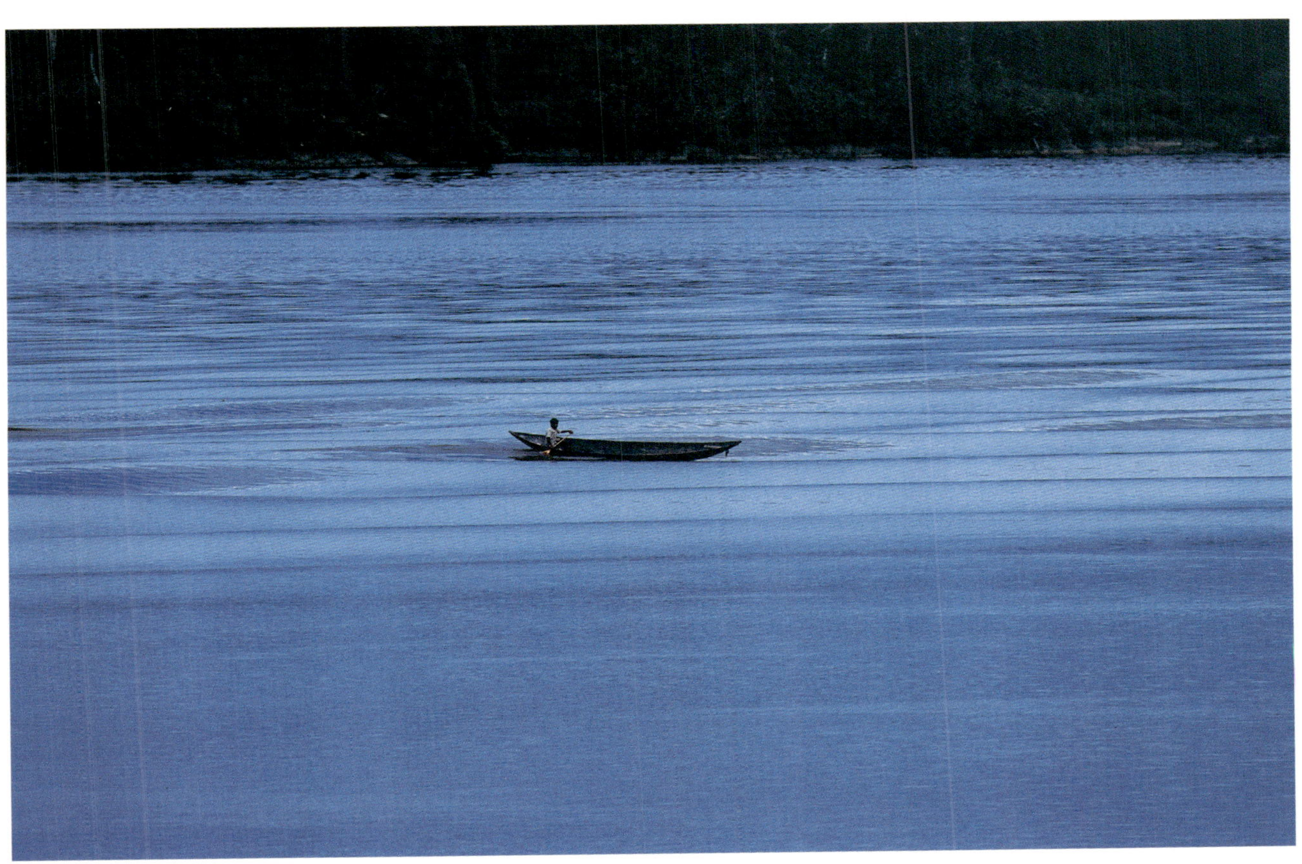

There are people who fish and those who just disturb the water.

Chinese proverb

MAY 25

Once you have fallen into the water,
you're not scared of water anymore.

Russian proverb

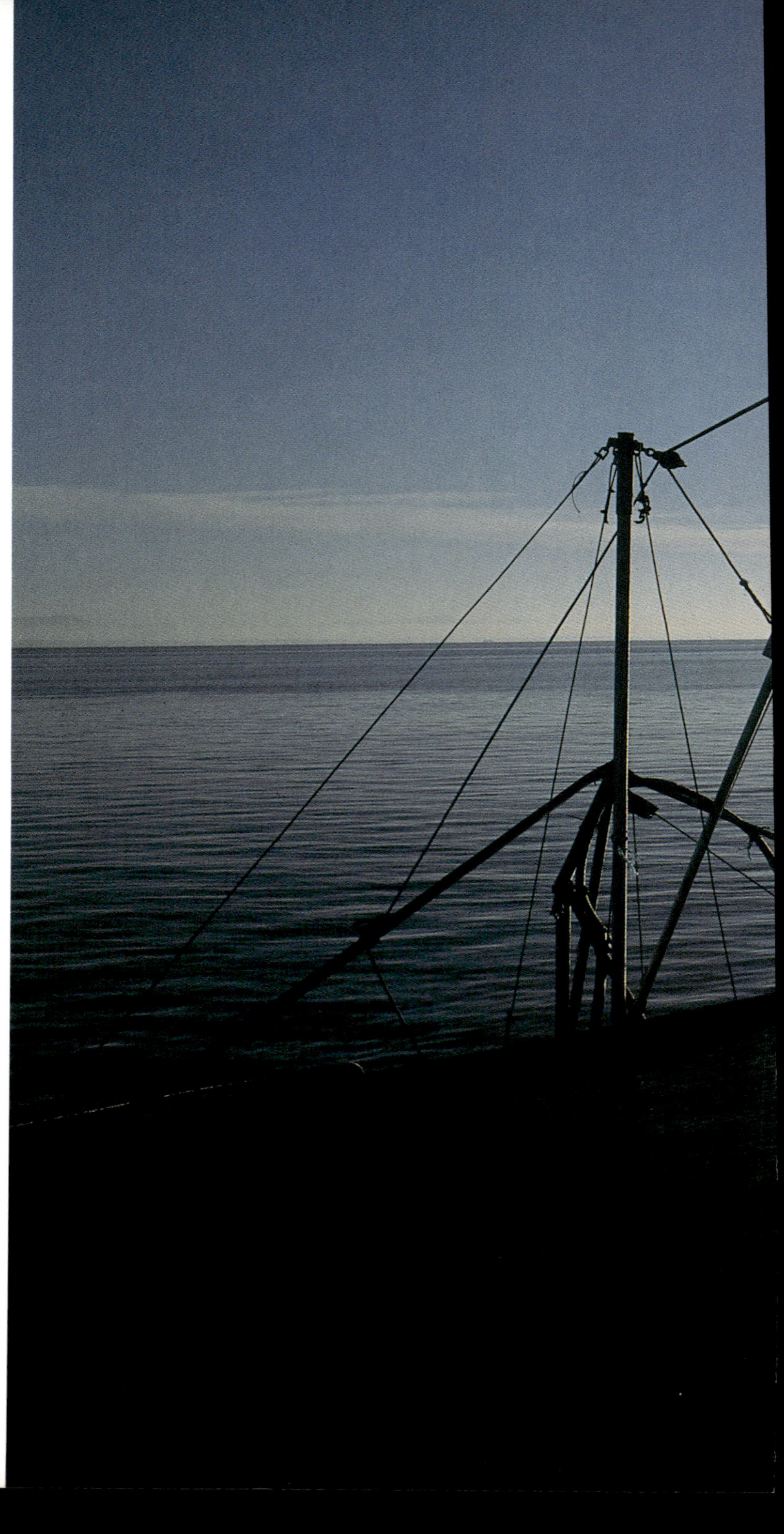

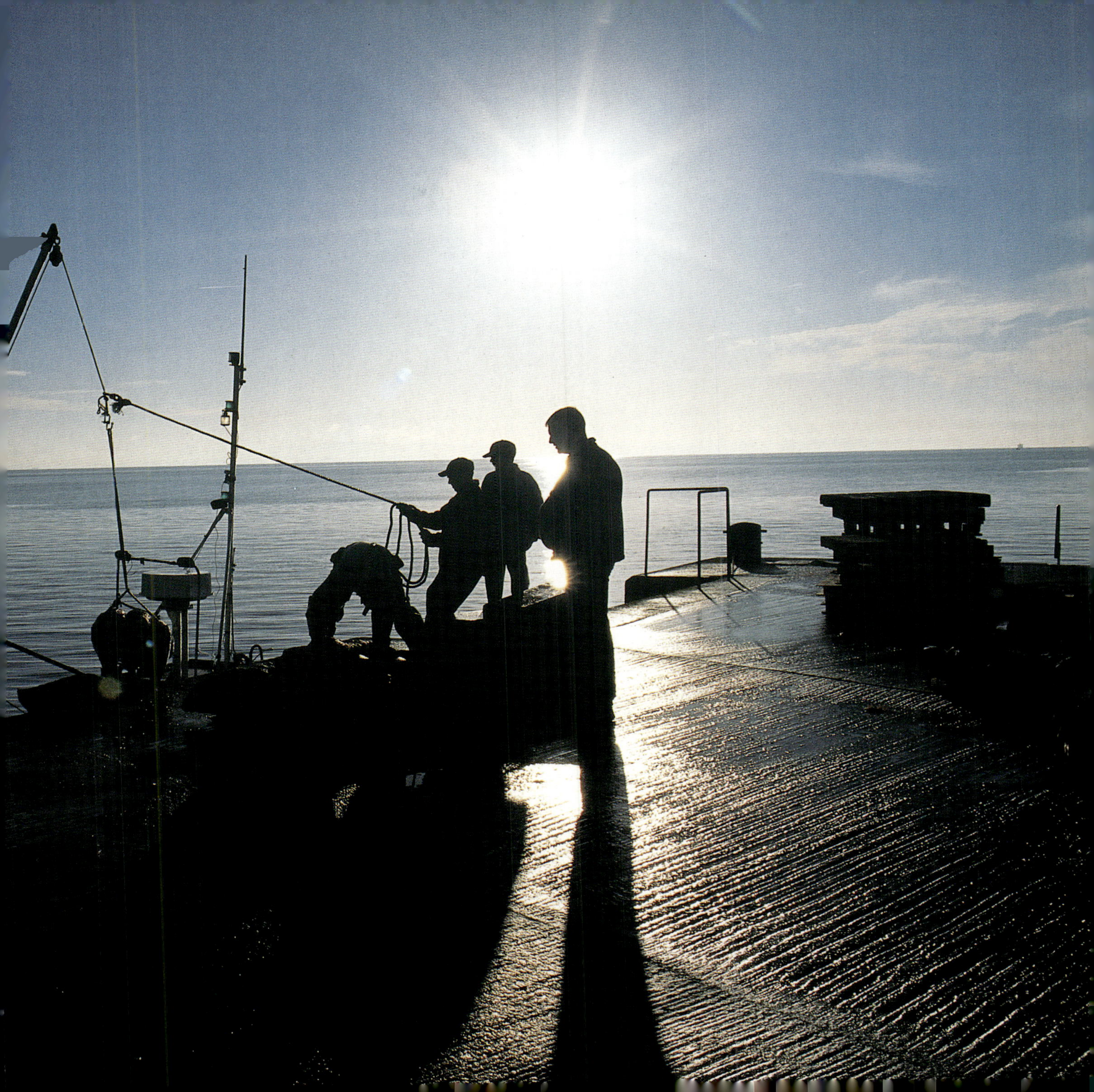

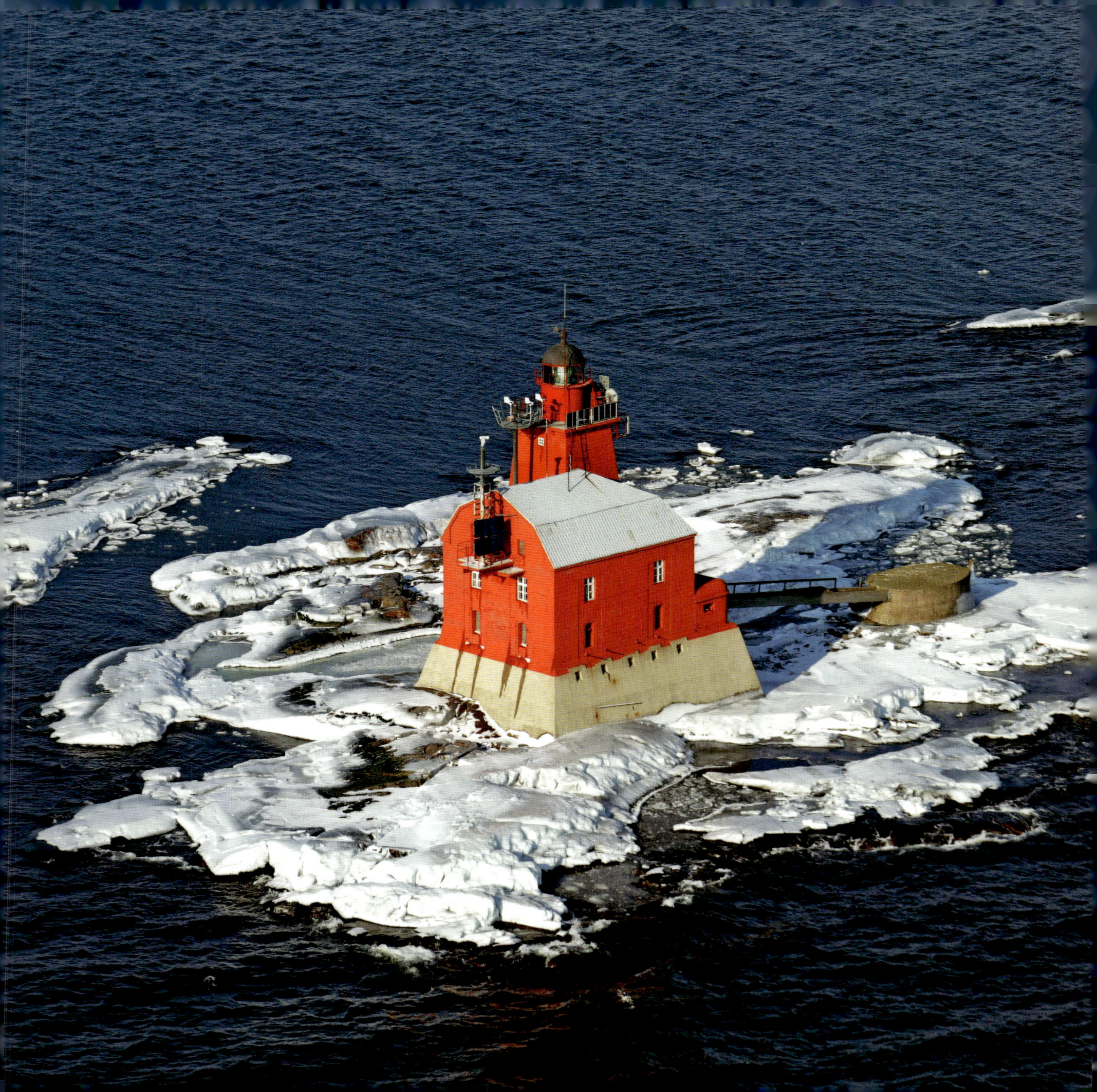

MAY 26

List how I, care wretched,
on ice-cold sea
Weathered the winter, wretched outcast
Deprived of my kinsmen;
Hung with hard ice-flakes,
where hail-scur flew
There I heard naught save the harsh sea
And ice-cold wave.

From "The Seafarer,"
tenth-century Anglo-Saxon poem

MAY 27

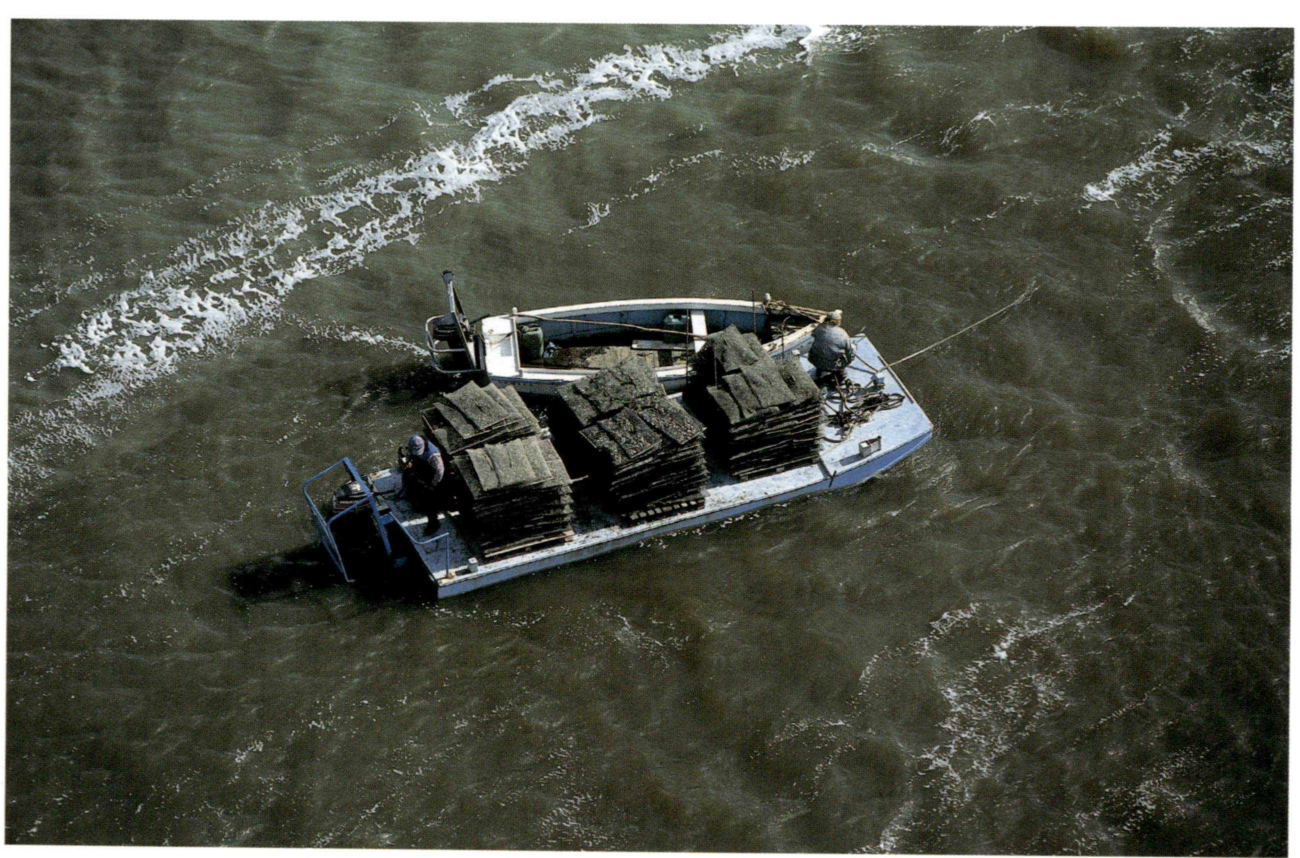

If you are in a boat, you are more afraid of fire than you are of water.

Japanese proverb

MAY 28

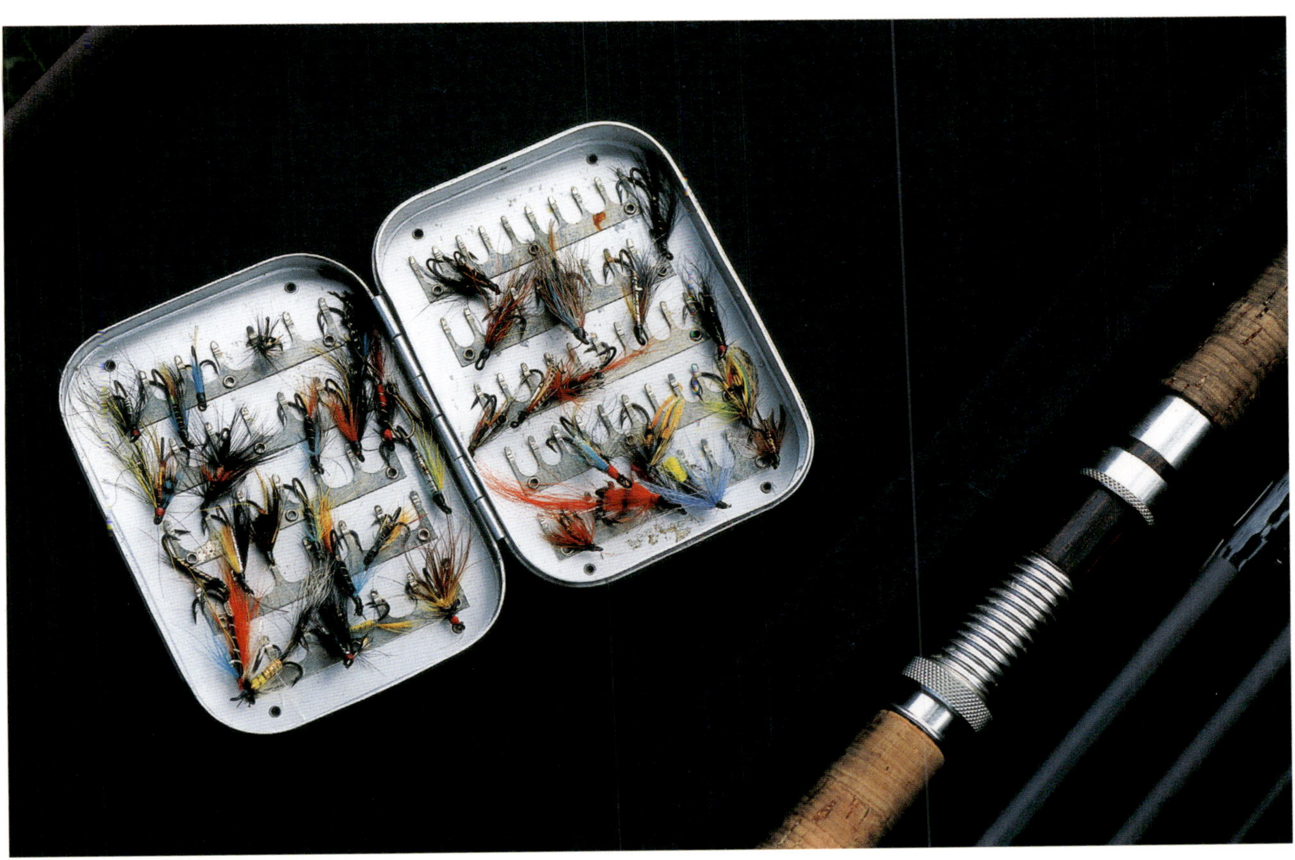

A man travels the world over in search of what he needs and returns home to find it.

George Moore

MAY 29

It is of great use to the sailor, to know the length of his line, though he cannot with it fathom all the depths of the ocean. It is well he knows, that it is long enough to reach the bottom, at such places as are necessary to direct his voyage, and caution him against running upon shoals that may ruin him.

John Locke,
from "An Essay Concerning Human Understanding," 1690

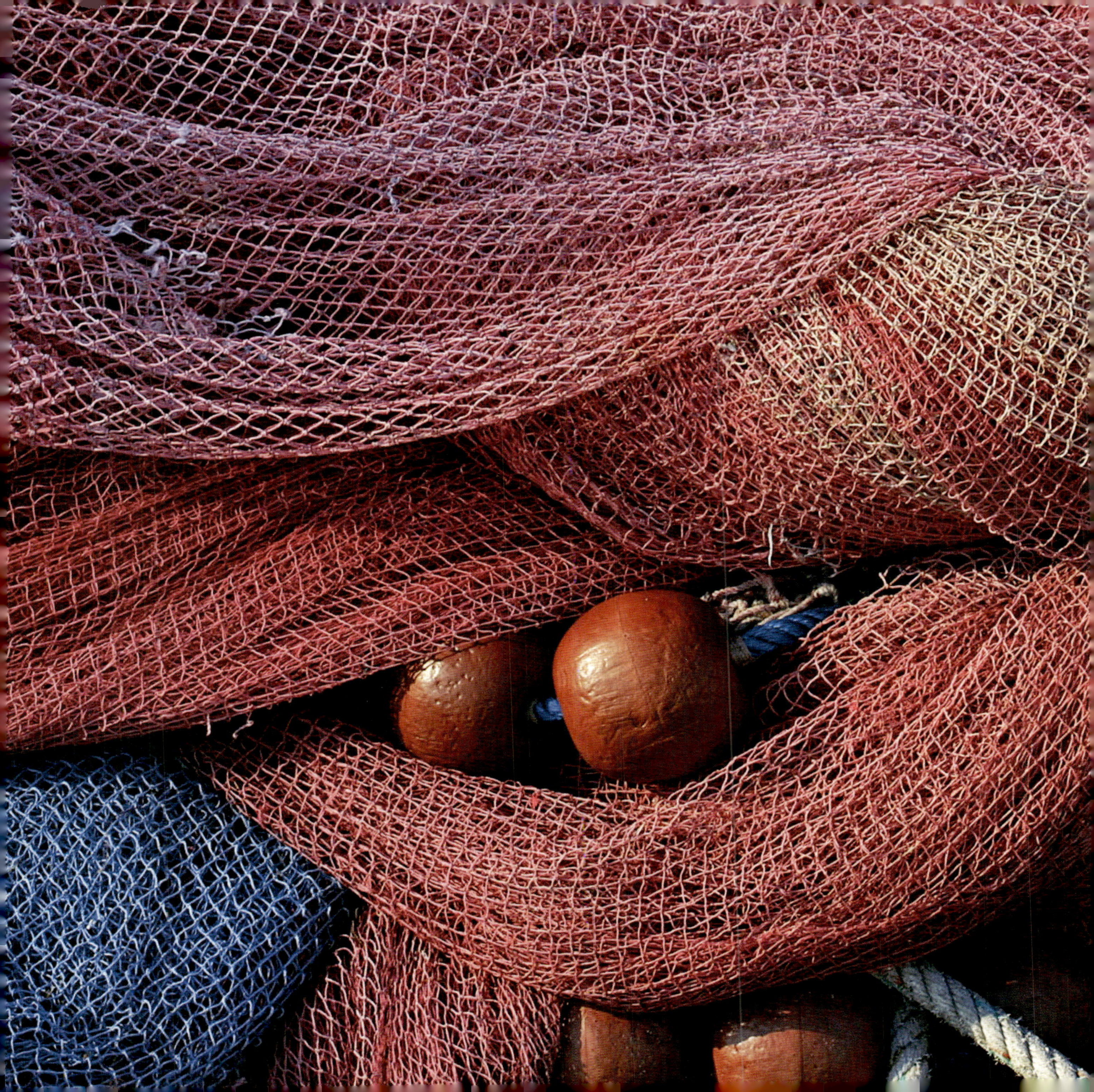

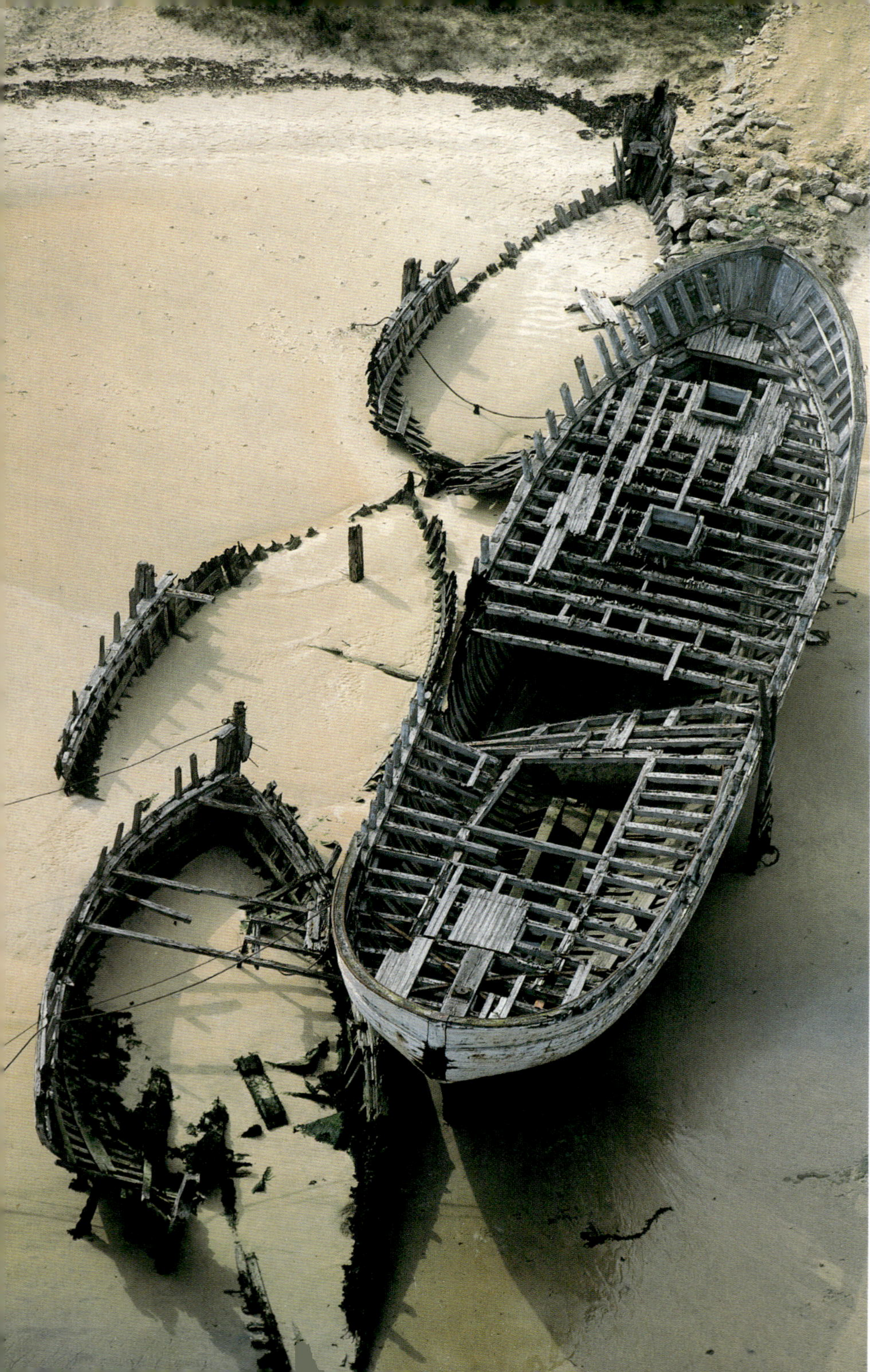

MAY 30

A life on the ocean wave,
A home on the rolling deep,
For the spark the nature gave
I have there the right to keep.

Ambrose Bierce,
from *The Devil's Dictionary,* 1911

MAY 31

When I must shipwrack, I would do it in a Sea, where mine impotencie might have some excuse; not in a sullen weedy lake, where I could not have so much as exercise for my swimming.

John Donne,
from a letter to Sir Henry Goodyear,
c. 1608

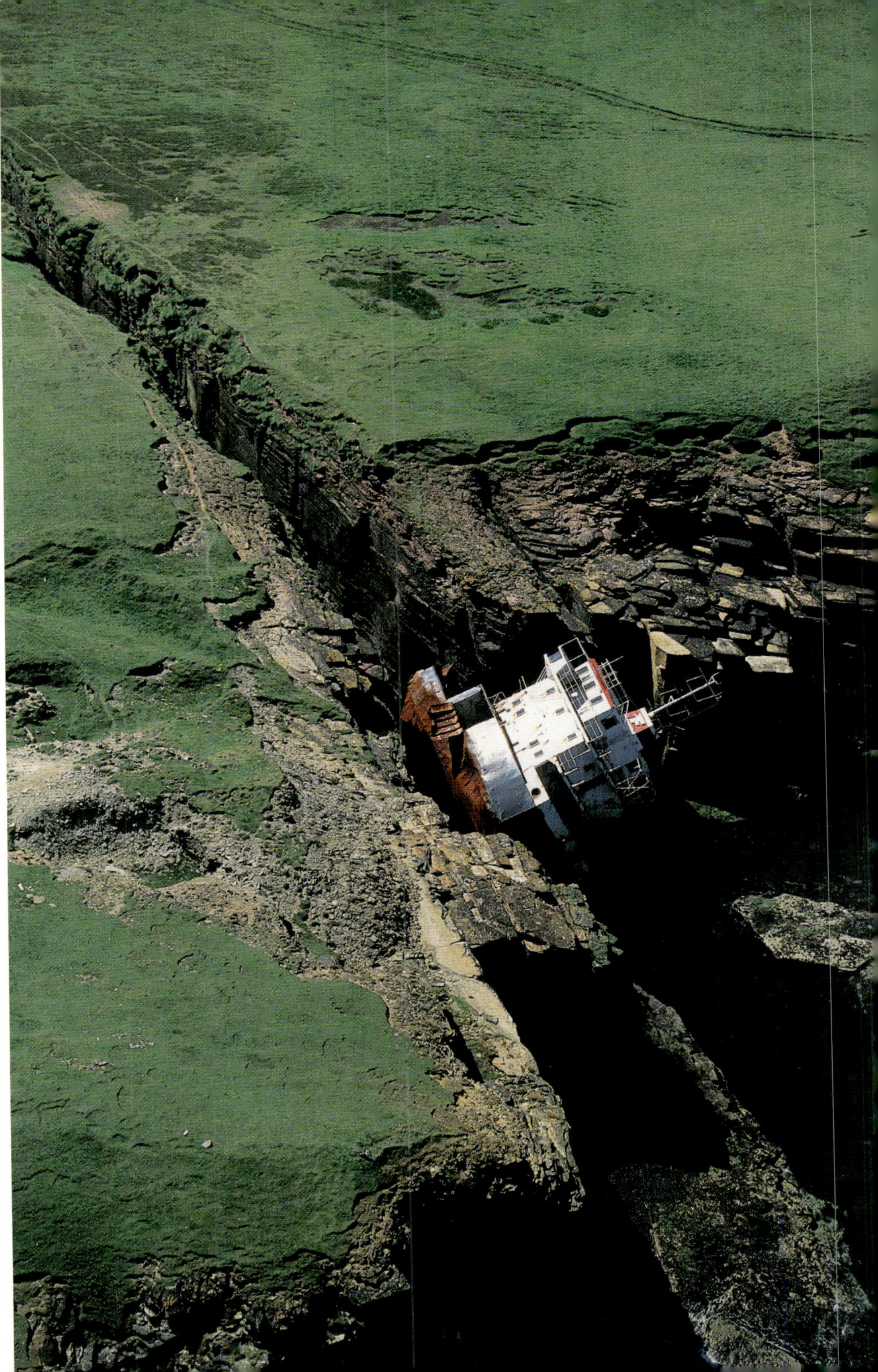

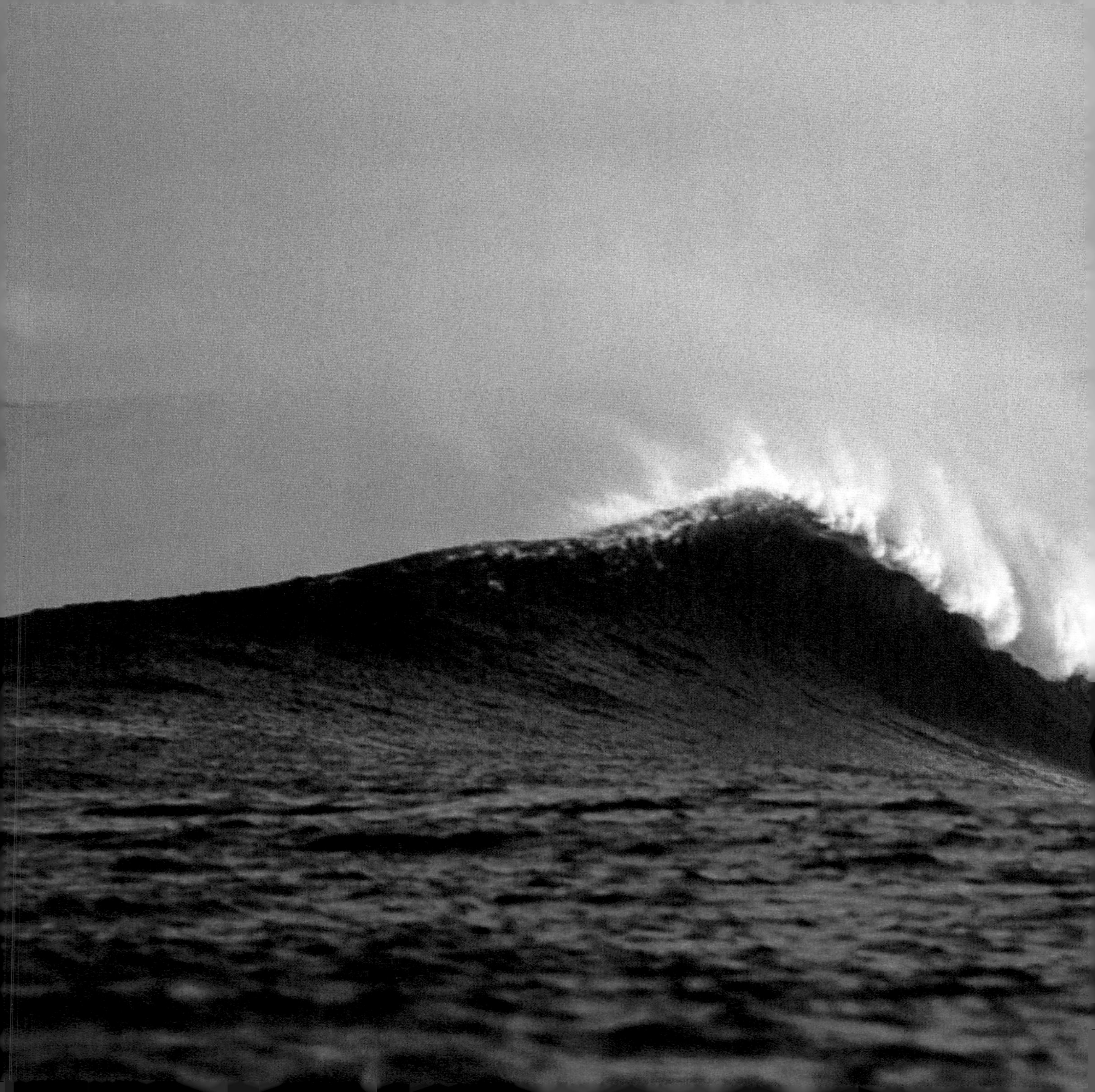

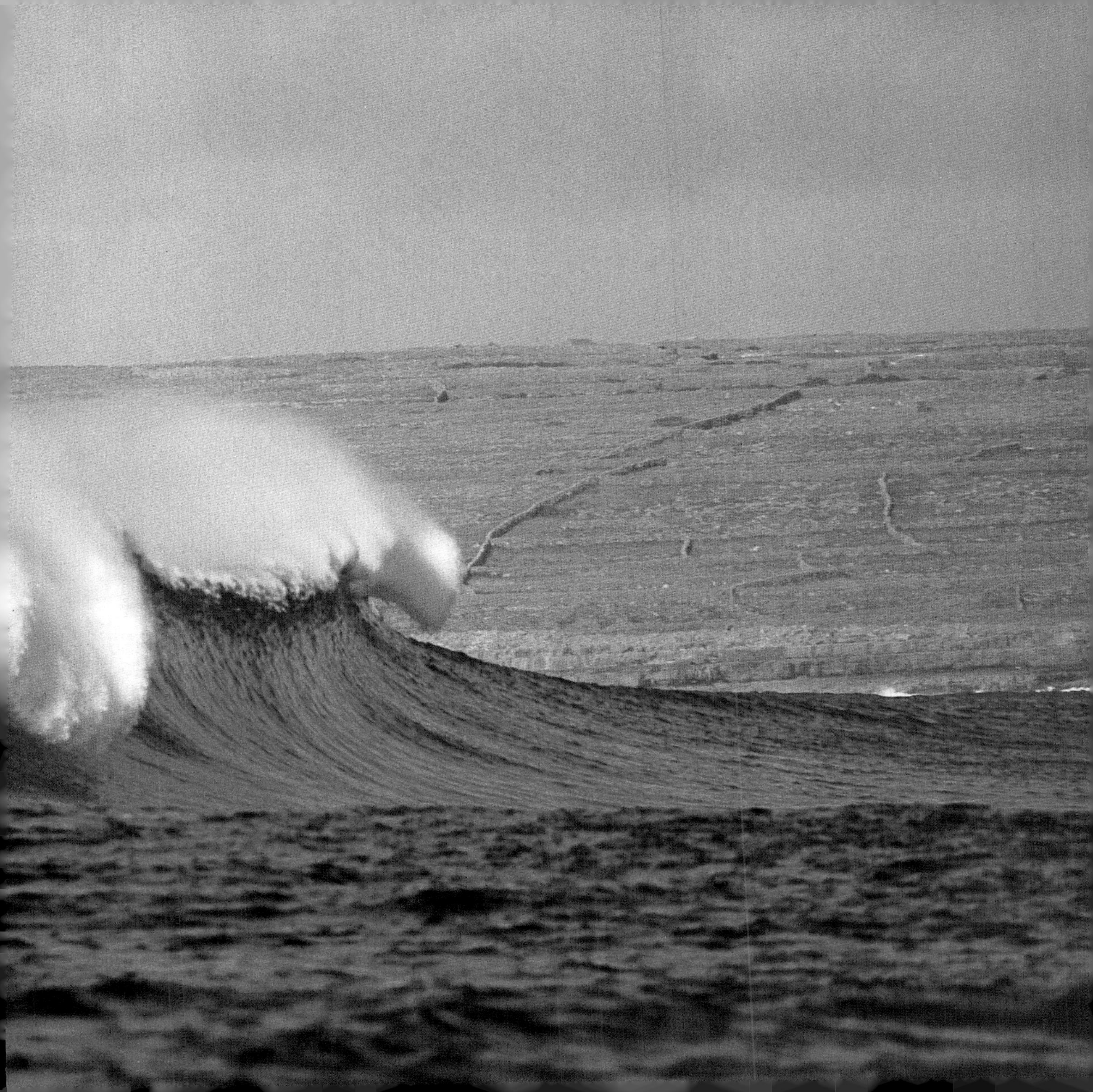

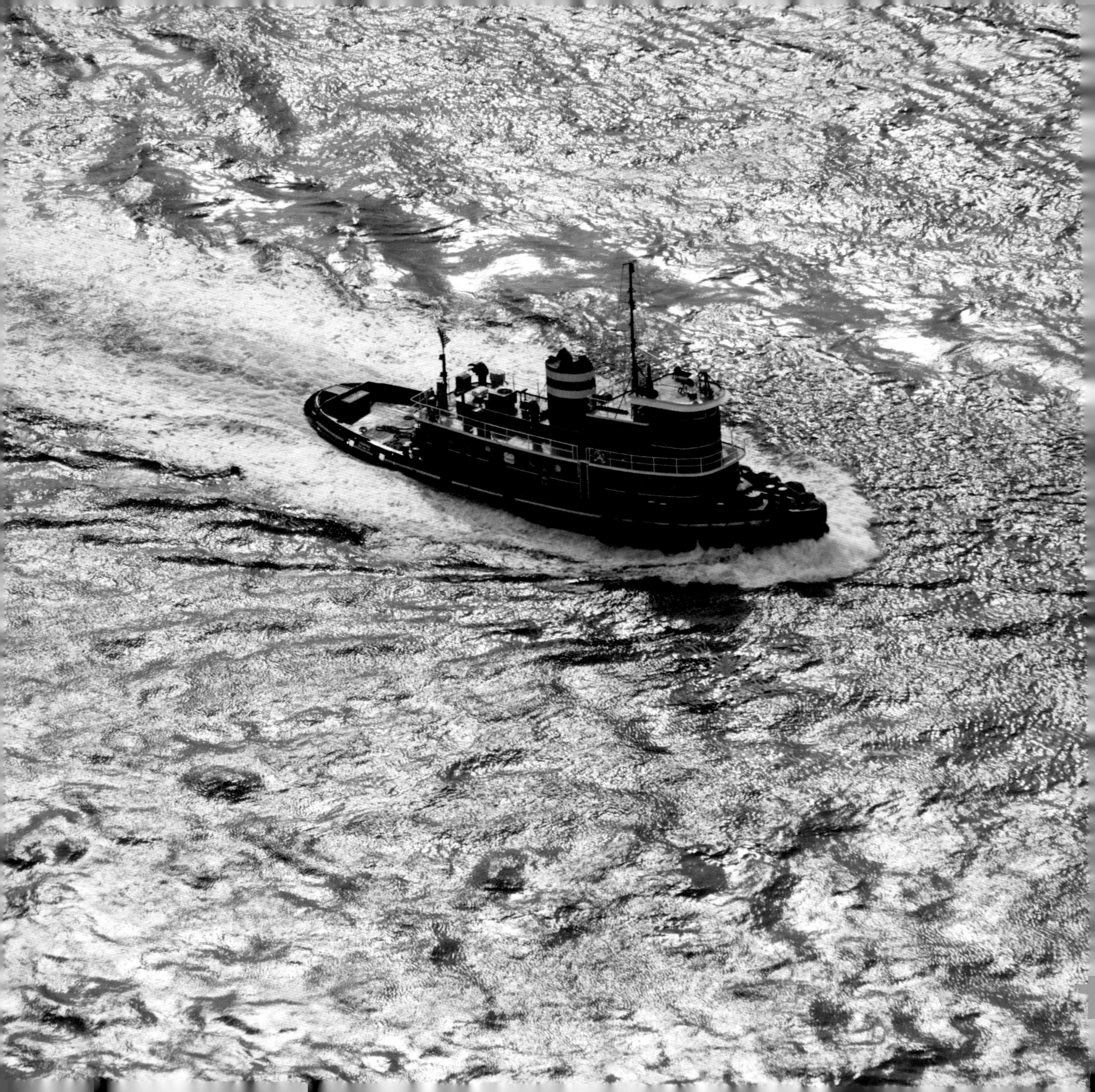

JUNE 1

Ebb, ocean of life, (the flow will return,)
Cease not your moaning you fierce old mother,
Endlessly cry for your castaways, but fear not, deny not me,
Rustle not up so hoarse and angry against my feet as I touch you or gather from you.
I mean tenderly by you and all,
I gather for myself and for this phantom looking down where we lead,
and following me and mine.

Walt Whitman,
from "As I Ebb'd with the Ocean of Life," *Leaves of Grass,* 1900

JUNE 2

As usual I finish the day before the sea, sumptuous this evening beneath the moon, which writes Arab symbols with phosphorescent streaks on the slow swells.

Albert Camus

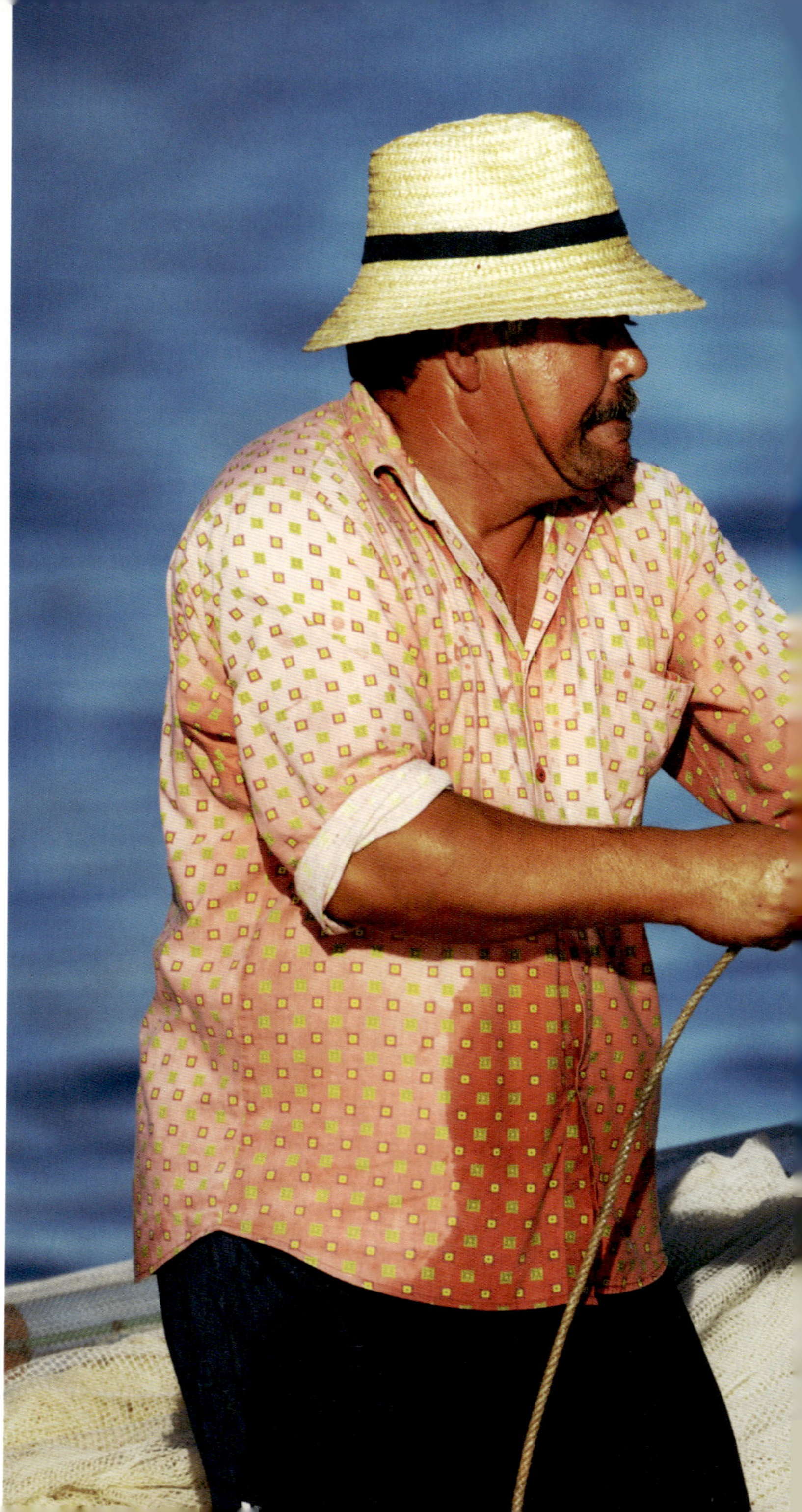

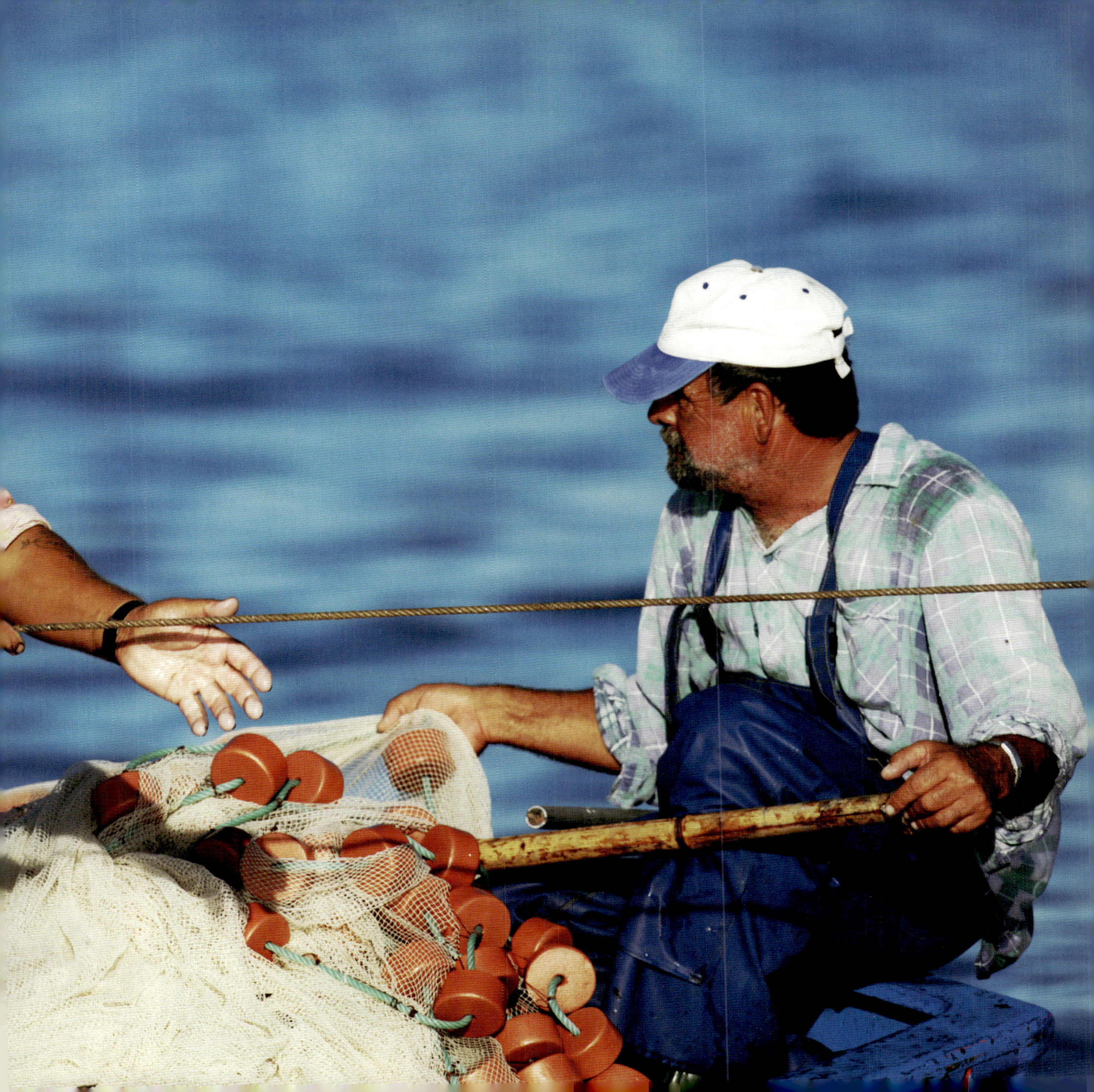

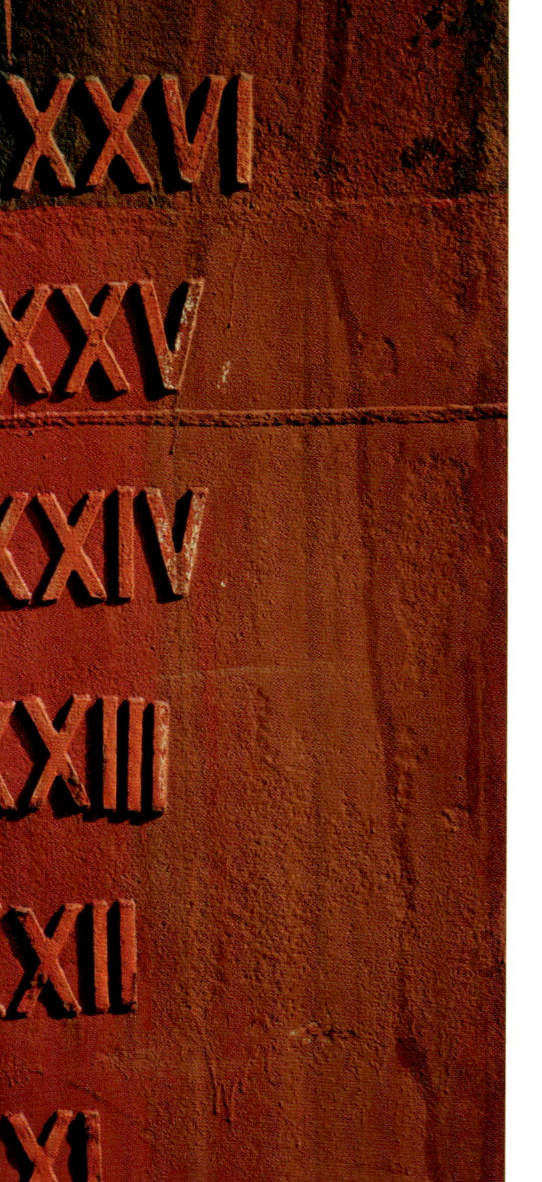

JUNE 3

Let me roll around the globe,
let me rock upon the sea:
let me race and pant out my
life with an eternal breeze
and an endless sea before.

Herman Melville,
from *Redburn*, 1849

JUNE 4

The sea! the sea! the open sea!
The blue, the fresh, the ever free!

Bryan W. Procter,
from "The Sea," c. 1837

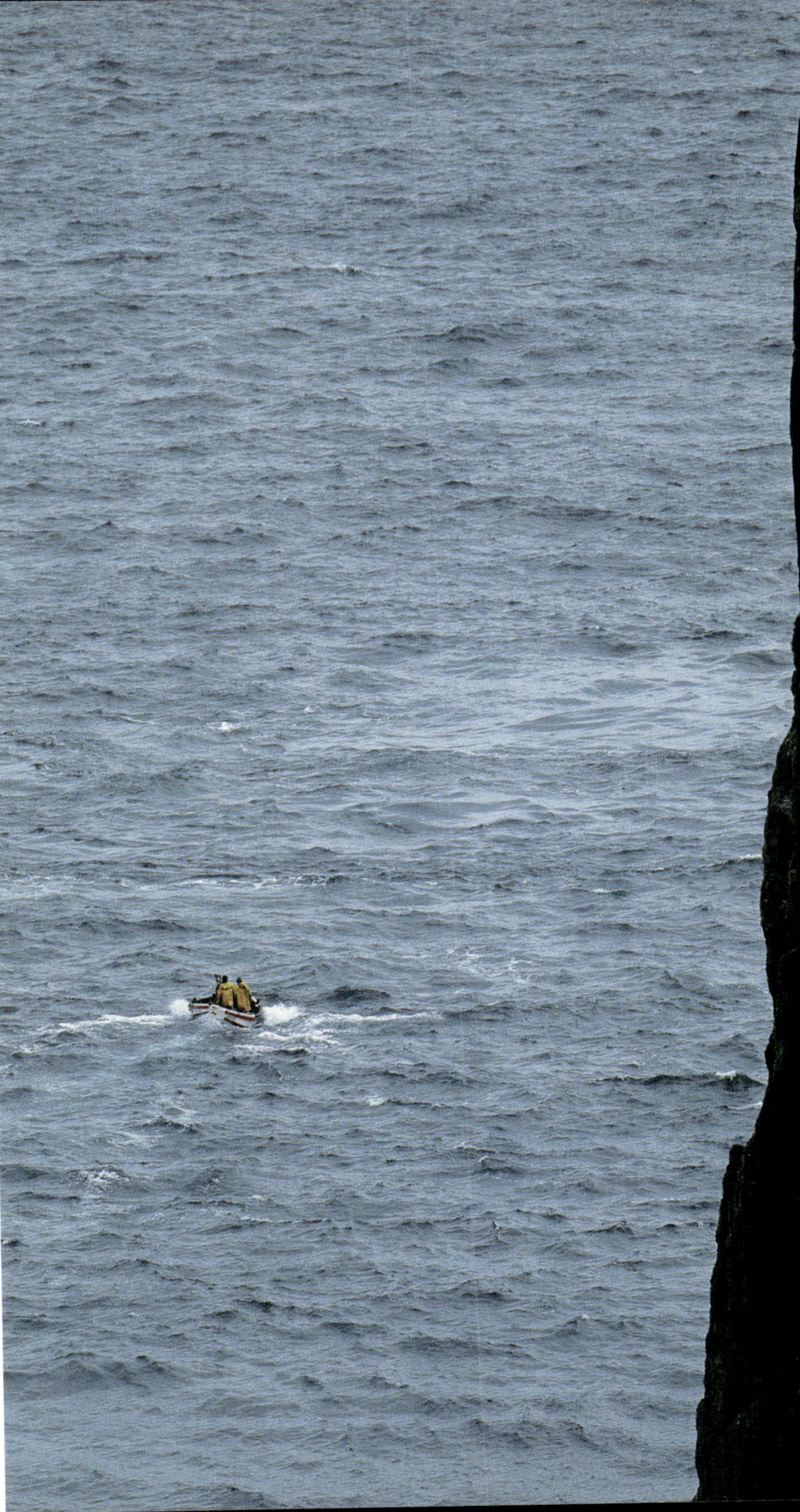

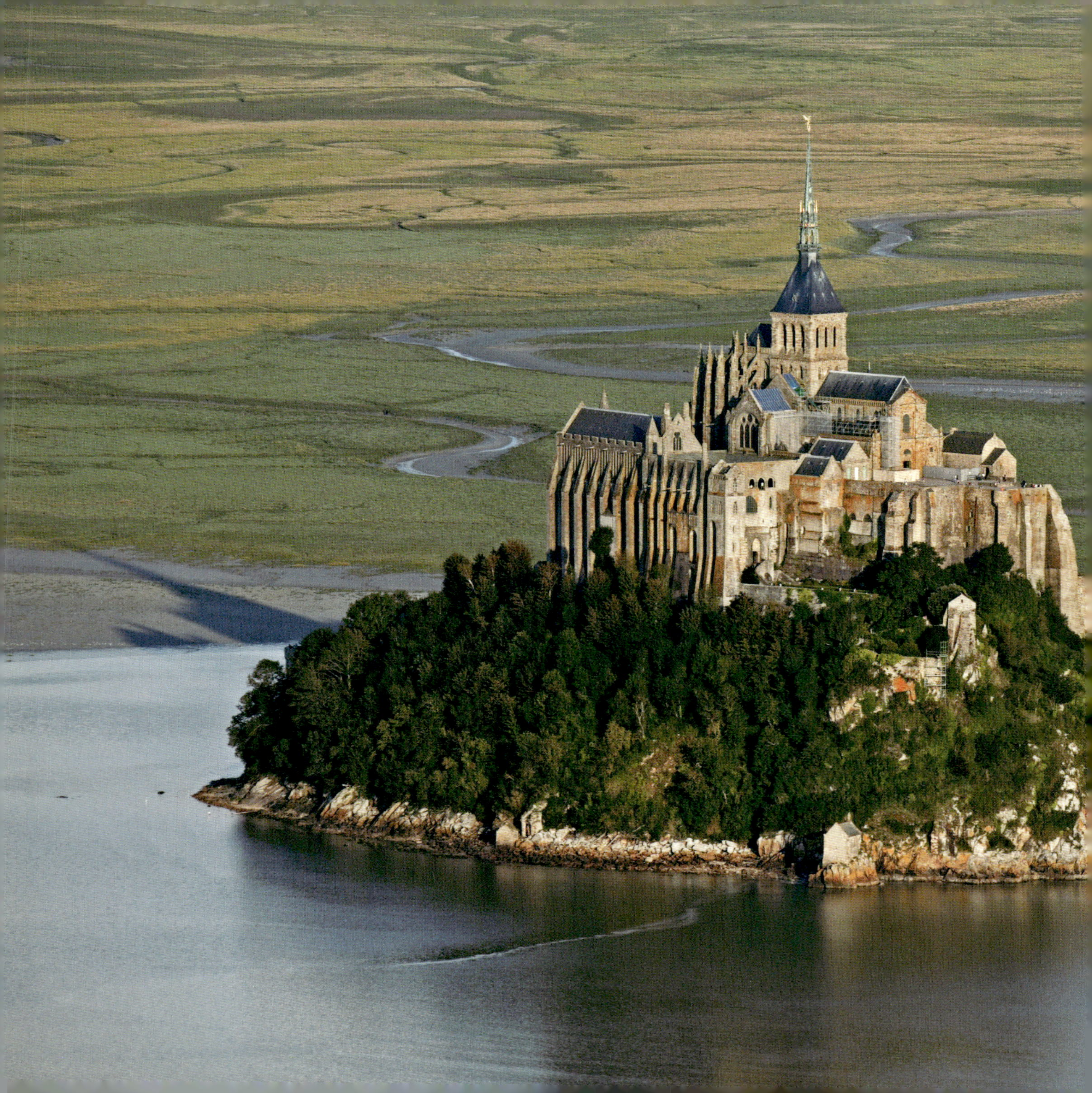

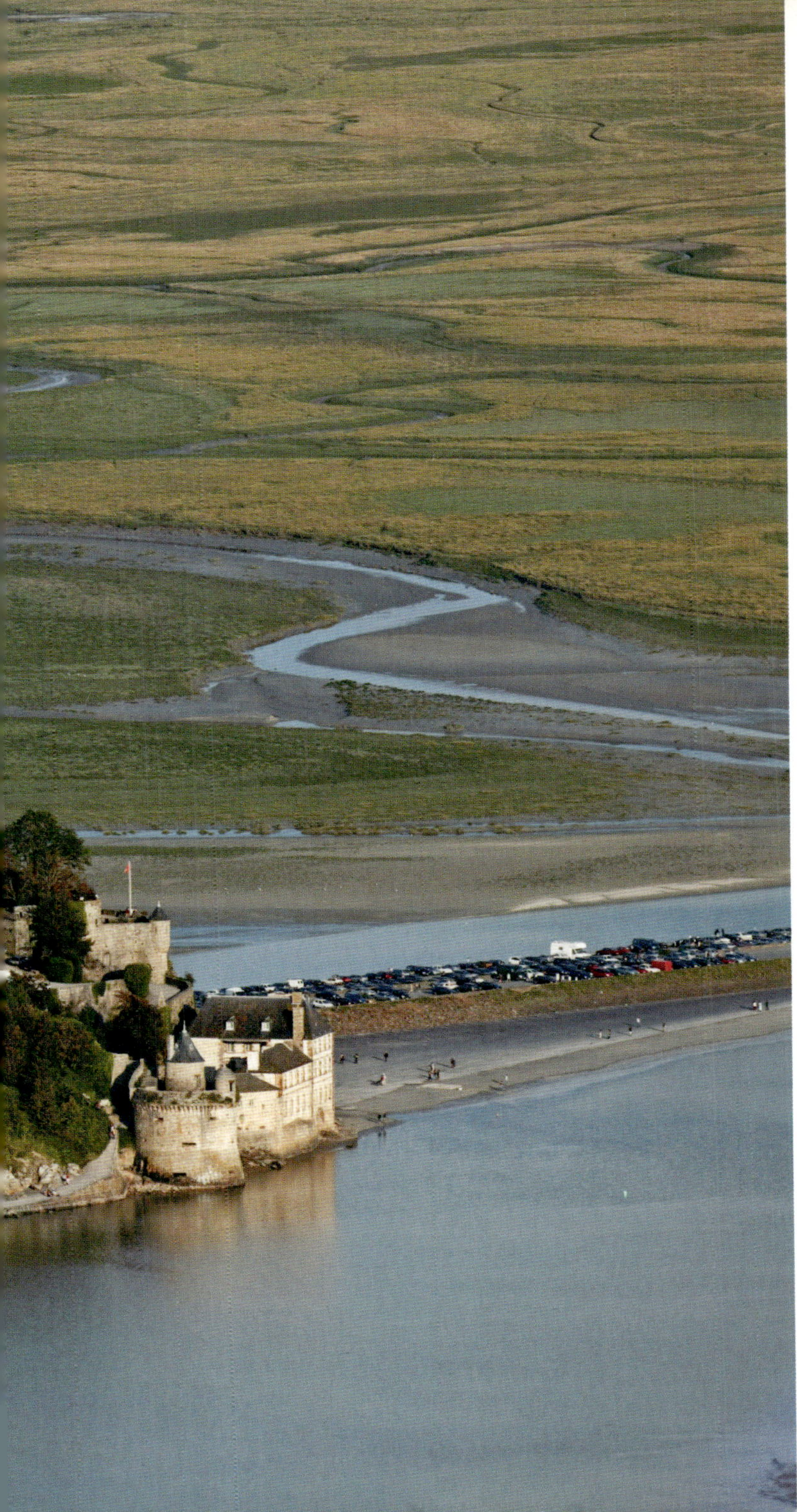

JUNE 5

Do not require a description of the countries towards which you sail. The description does not describe them to you, and tomorrow you arrive there, and know them by inhabiting them.

Ralph Waldo Emerson,
from "The Over-Soul," *Essays: First Series,* 1841

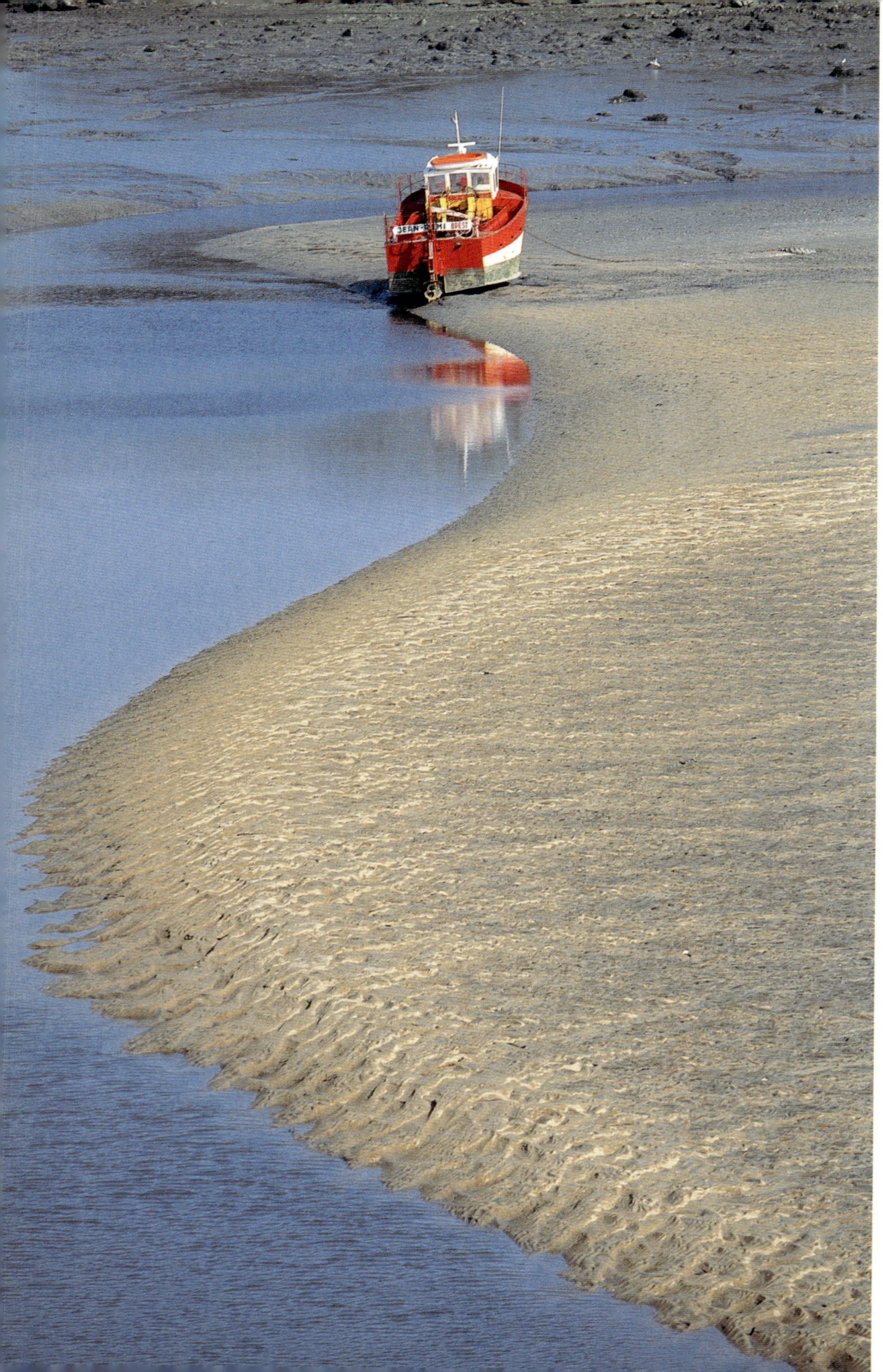

JUNE 6

There are more consequences
to a shipwreck than the
underwriters notice.

Henry David Thoreau,
from *Cape Cod*, 1865

JUNE 7

Each human being is a ship that must sail its own course, even if it go in company with another ship.

D. H. Lawrence,
from *Kangaroo,* 1923

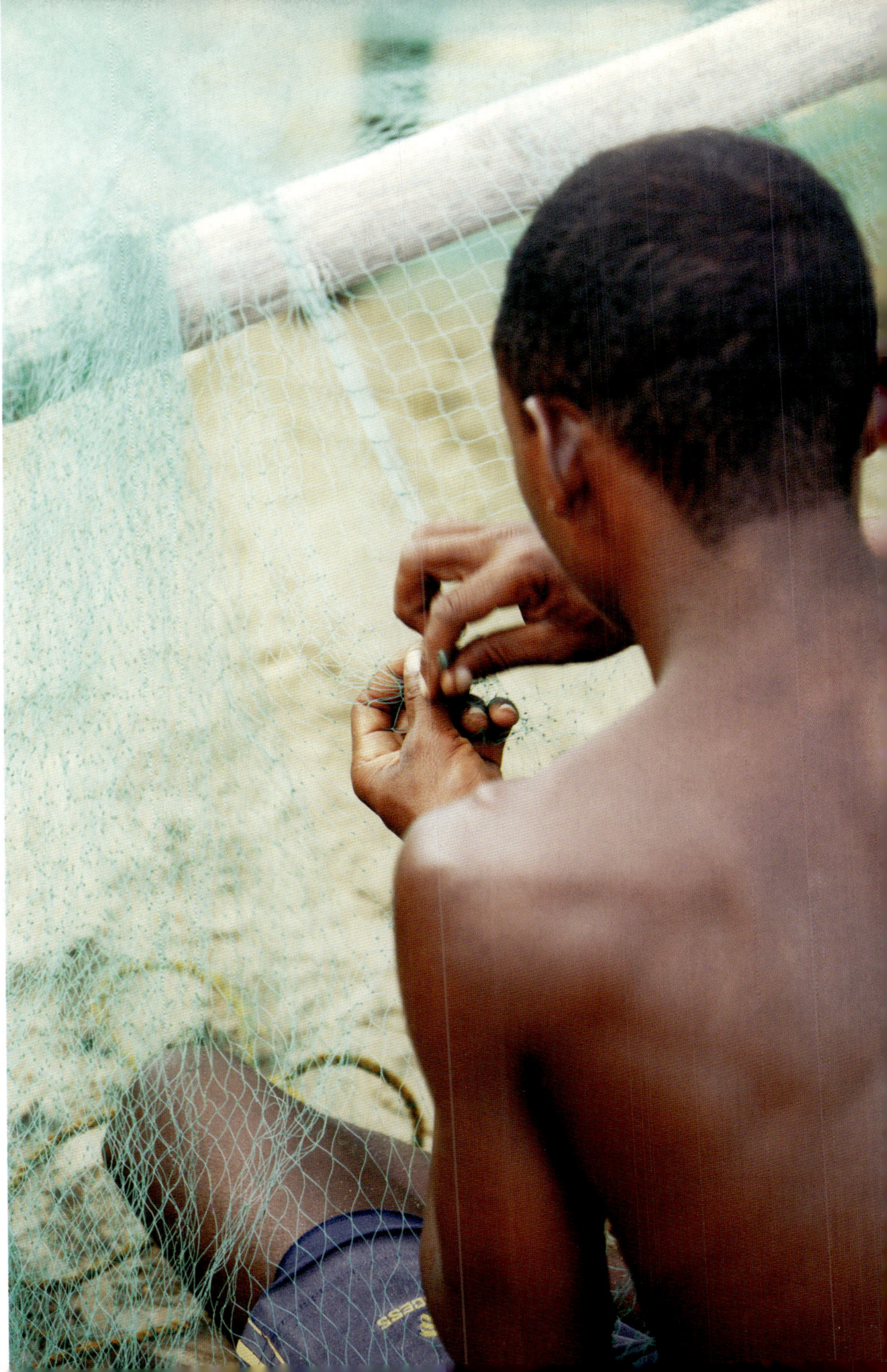

JUNE 8

The shouts of sailors double near the shores;
They stretch their canvas and they ply their oars.

Virgil, from *The Aeneid*

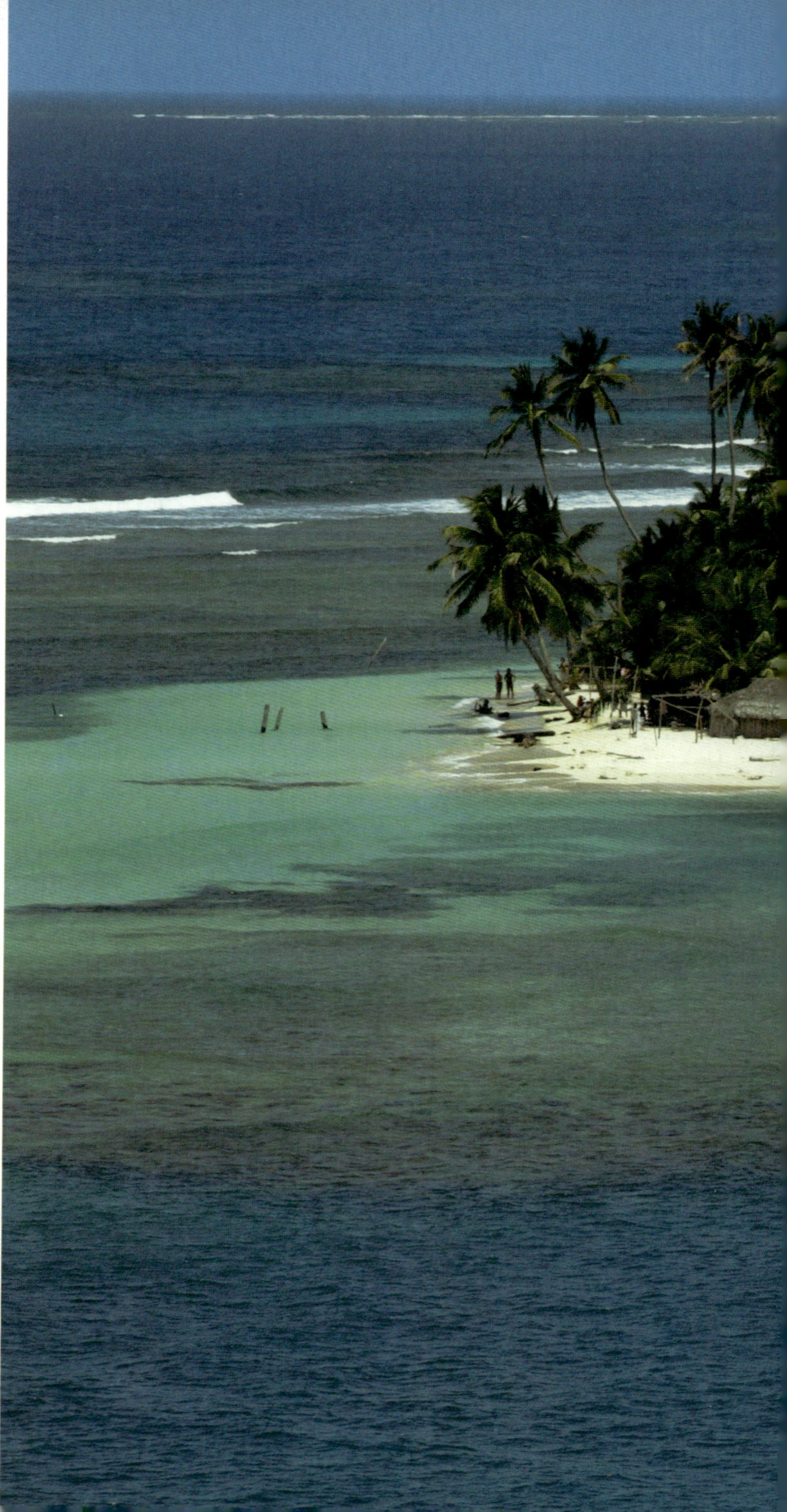

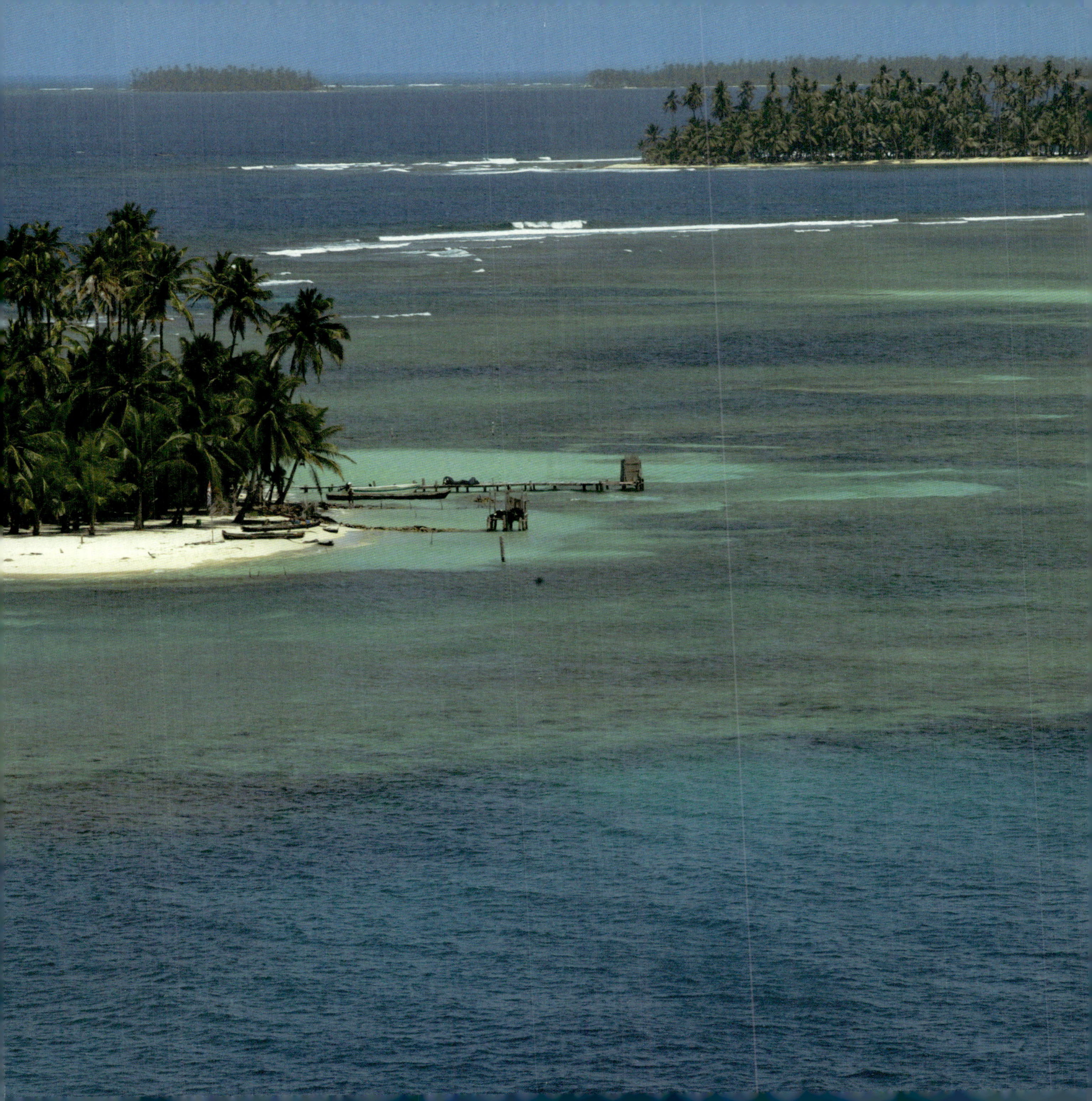

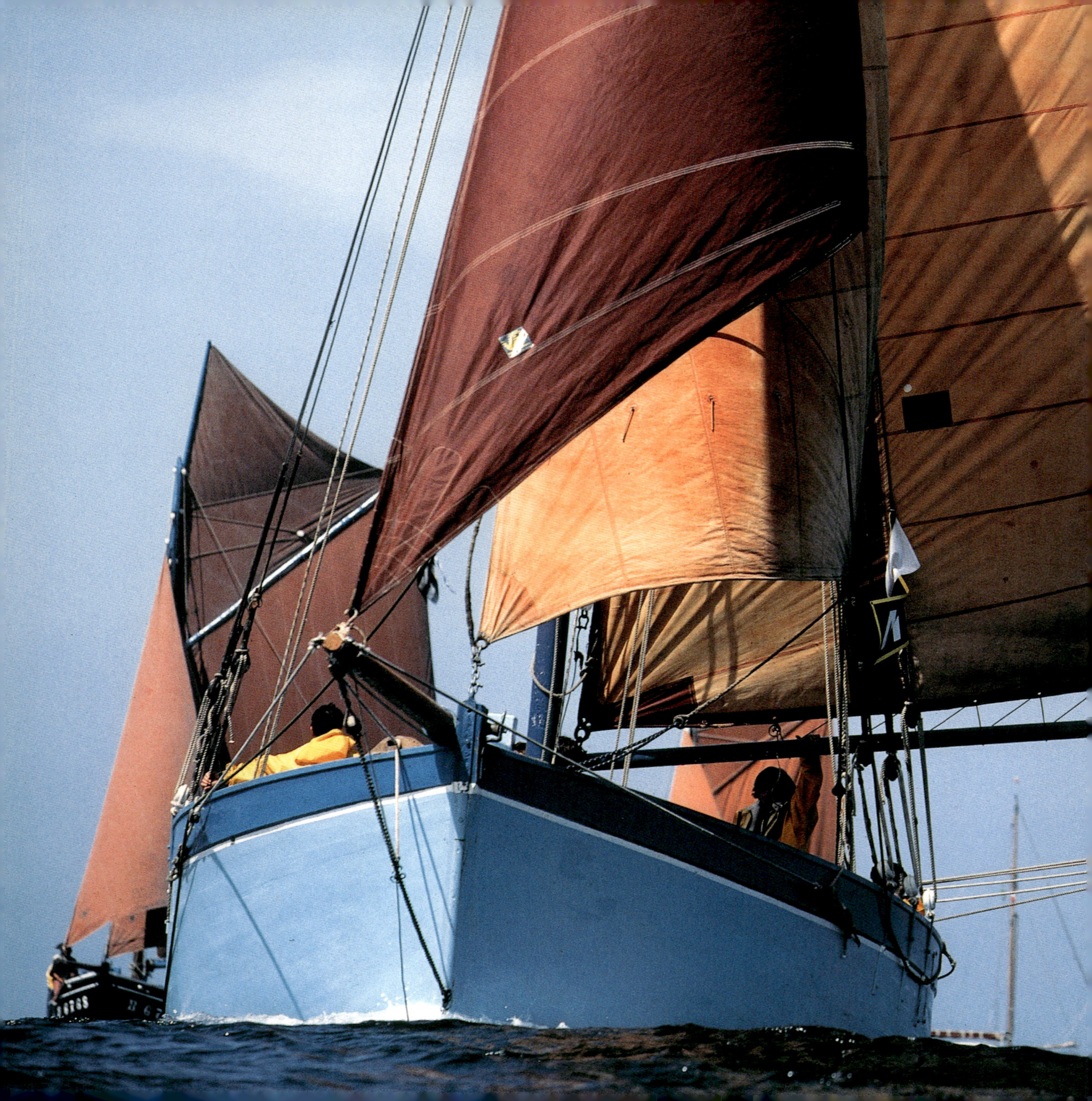

JUNE 9

When you go sweeping by in your full, flowing skirts,
You resemble a trim ship as it puts to sea
Under full sail and goes rolling
Lazily, to a slow and easy rhythm.

Charles Baudelaire,
from "The Beautiful Ship," *Les Fleurs du mal,* 1857

JUNE 10

But oars alone can ne'er prevail
To reach the distant coast;
The breath of heaven must swell the sail,
Or all the toil is lost.

Wiliam Cowper, from "Human Frailty," 1782

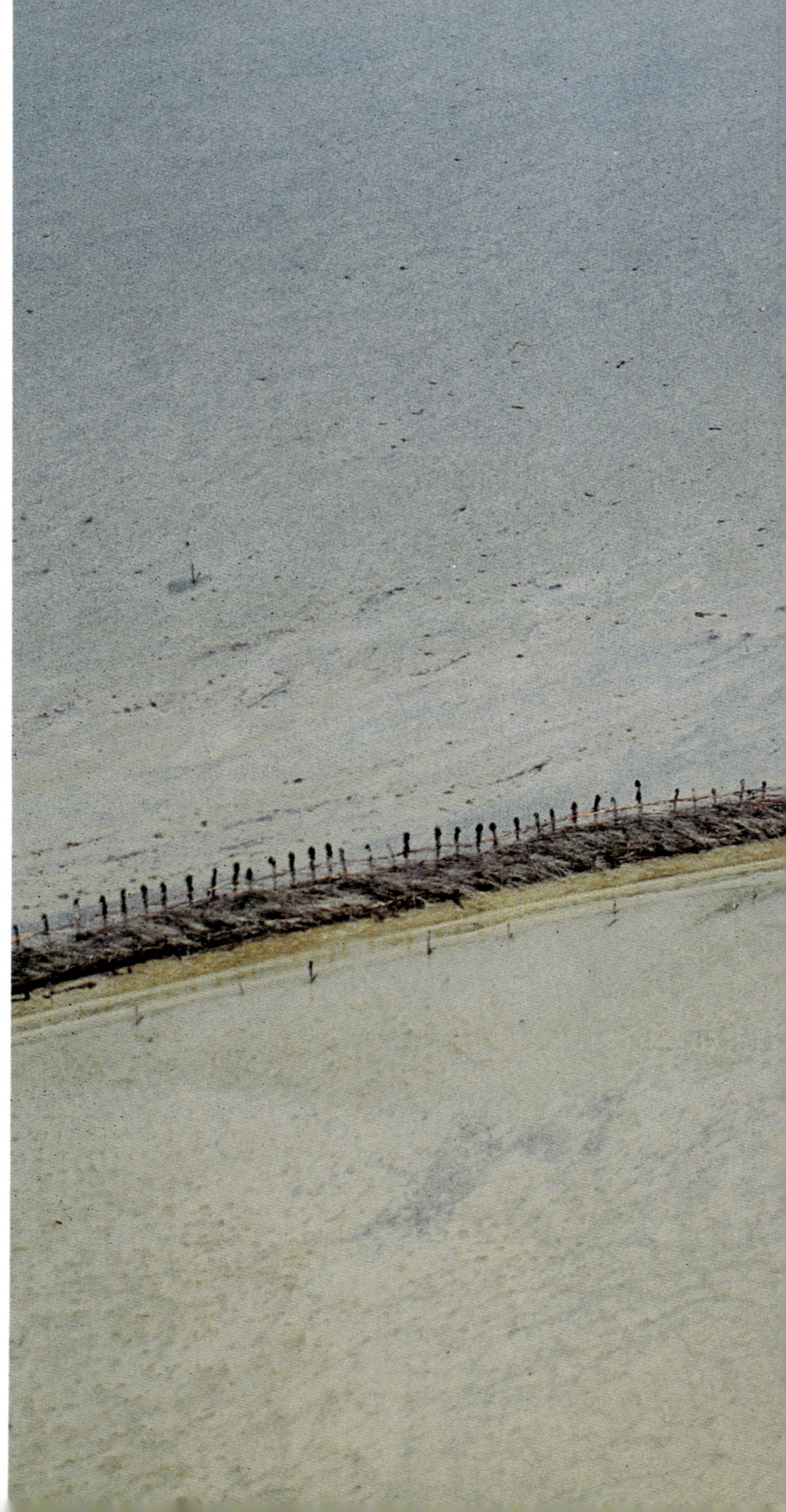

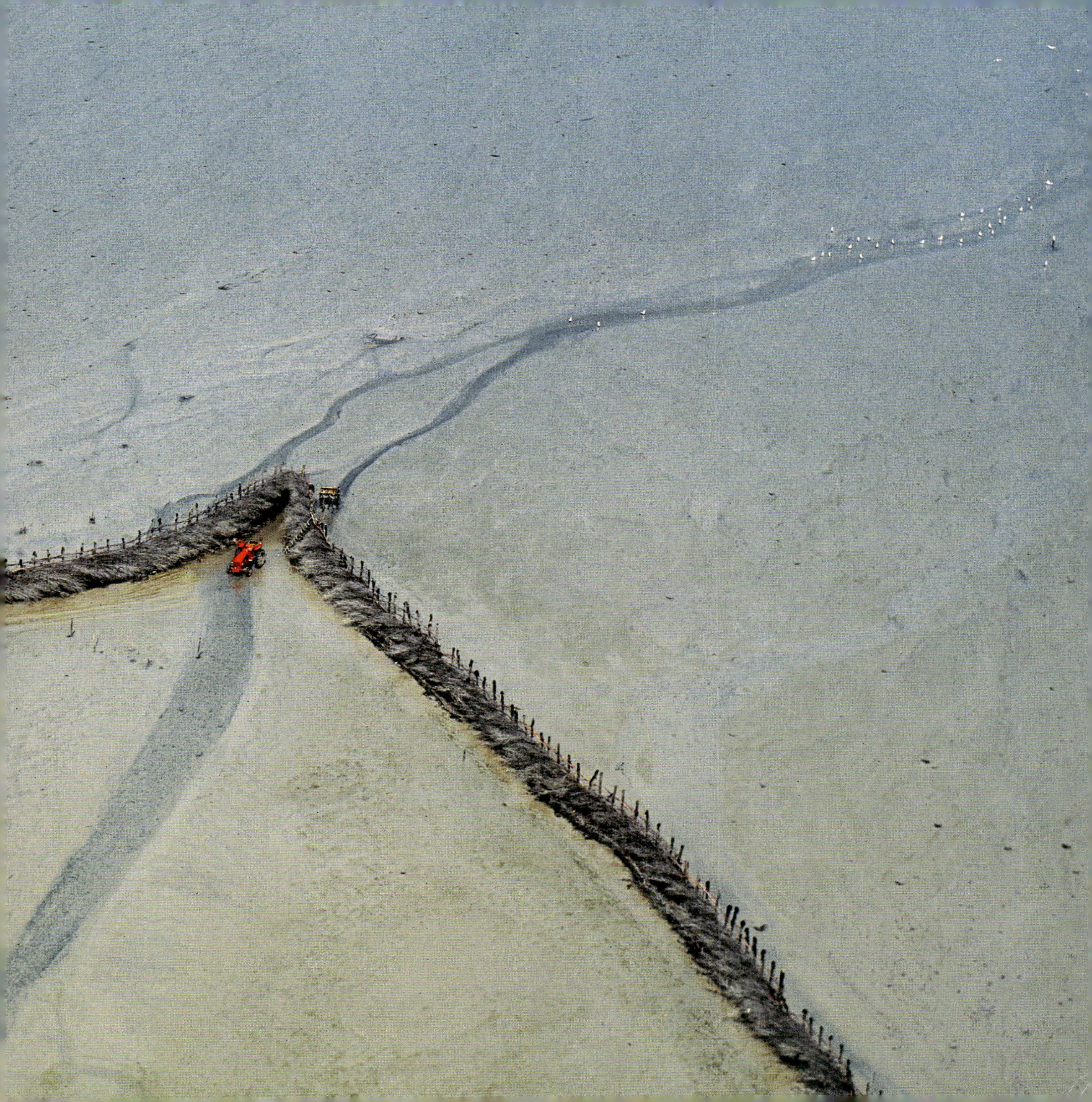

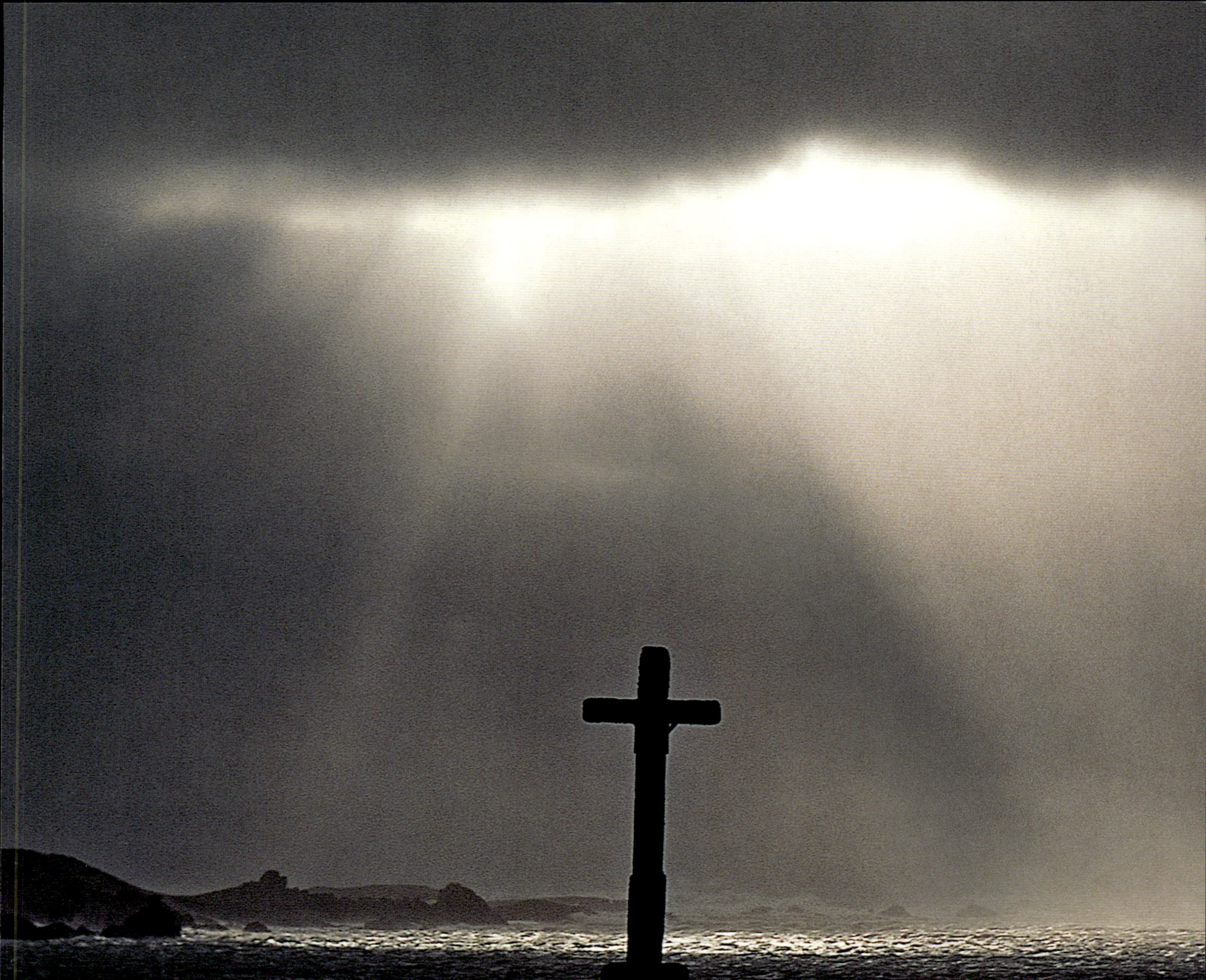

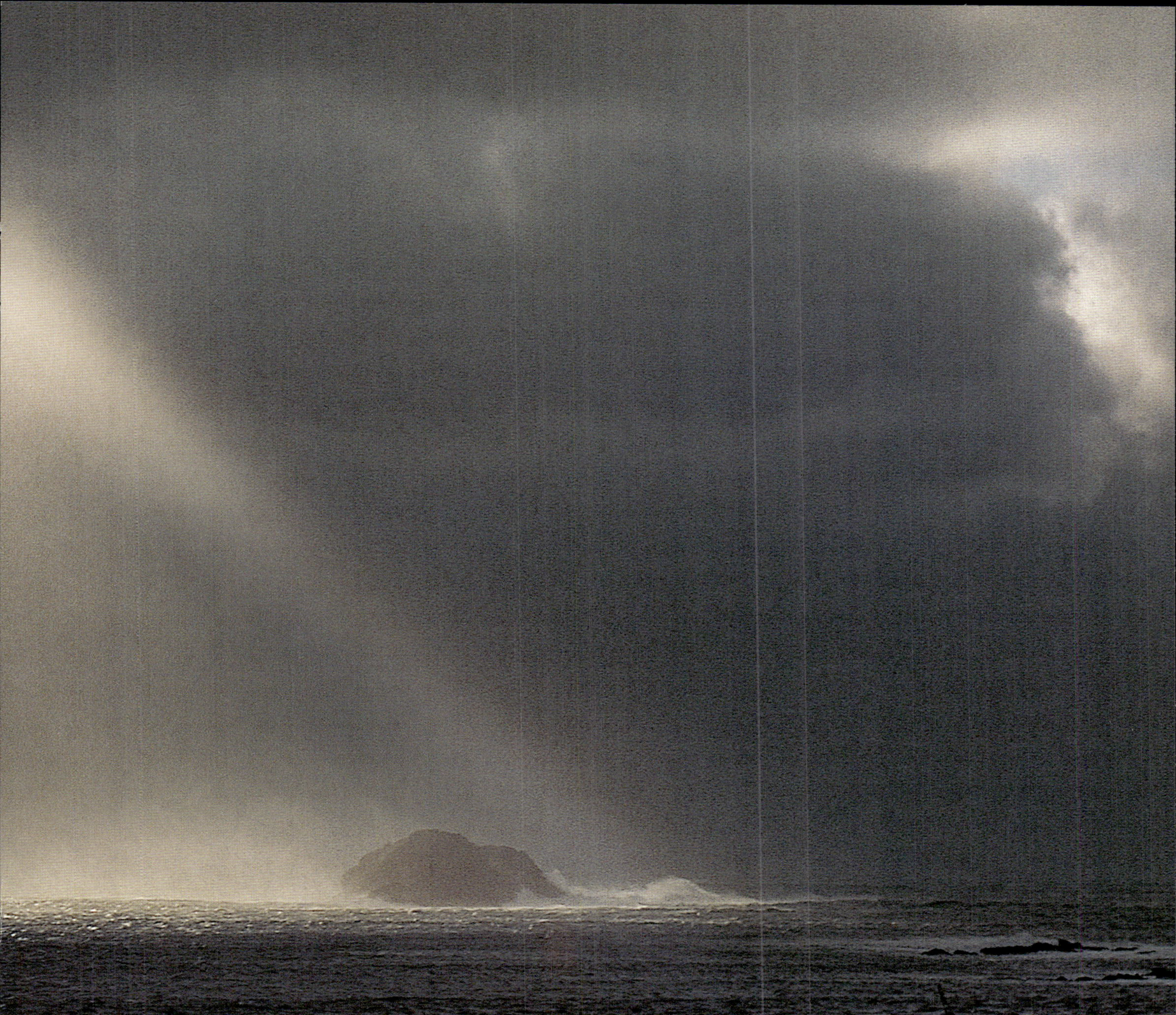

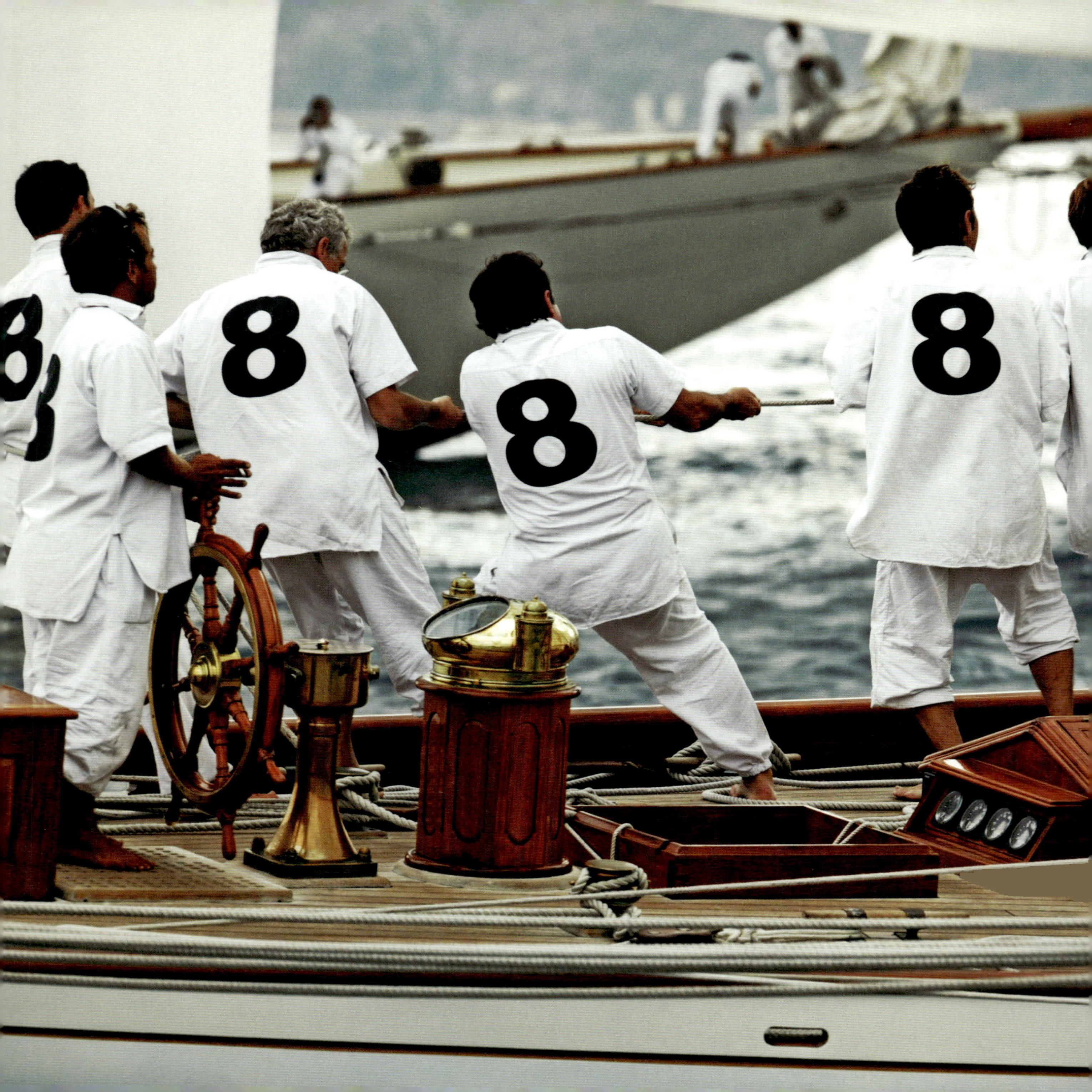
8
8
8
8

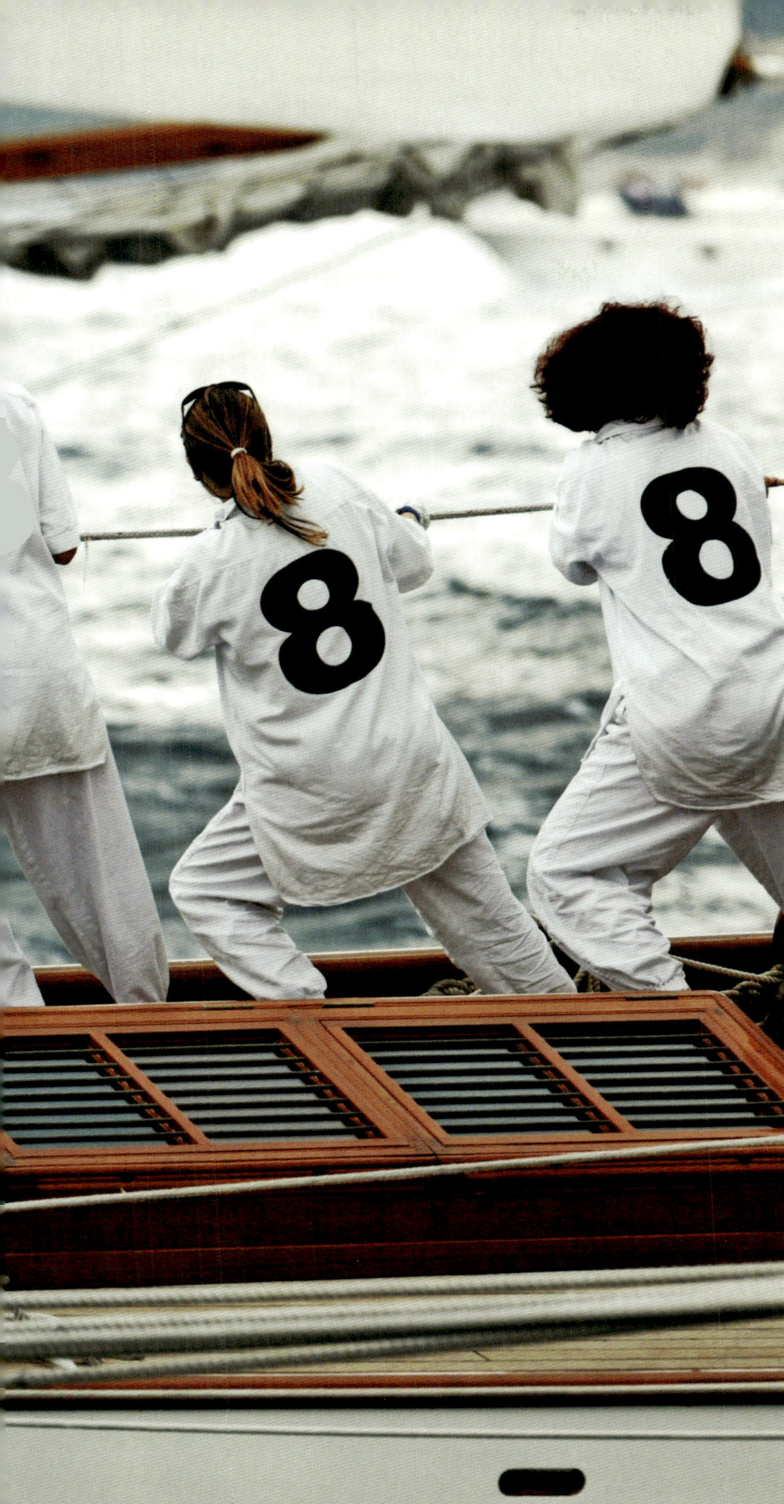

JUNE 11

A song is as necessary to sailors as the drum and fife to a soldier. They can't pull in time, or pull with a will, without it.

Richard Henry Dana Jr.,
from *Two Years Before the Mast,* 1840

JUNE 12

Give me a spirit that on this life's rough sea
Loves t' have his sails fill'd with a lusty wind,
Even till his sail-yards tremble, his masts crack,
And his rapt ship run on her side so low
That she drinks water, and her keel plows air.

George Chapman,
from *The Conspiracy and Tragedy of Charles, Duke of Byron,* 1608

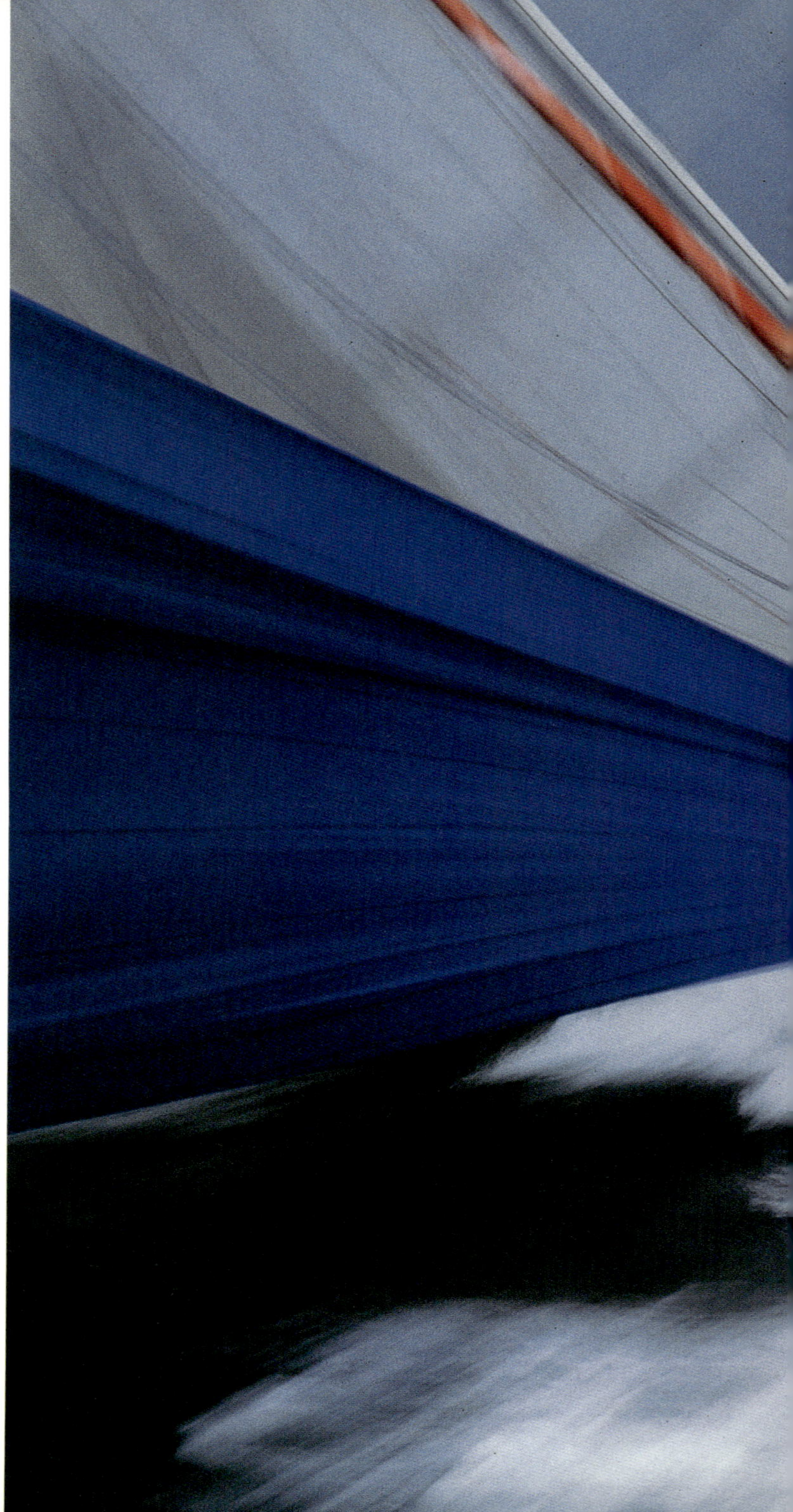

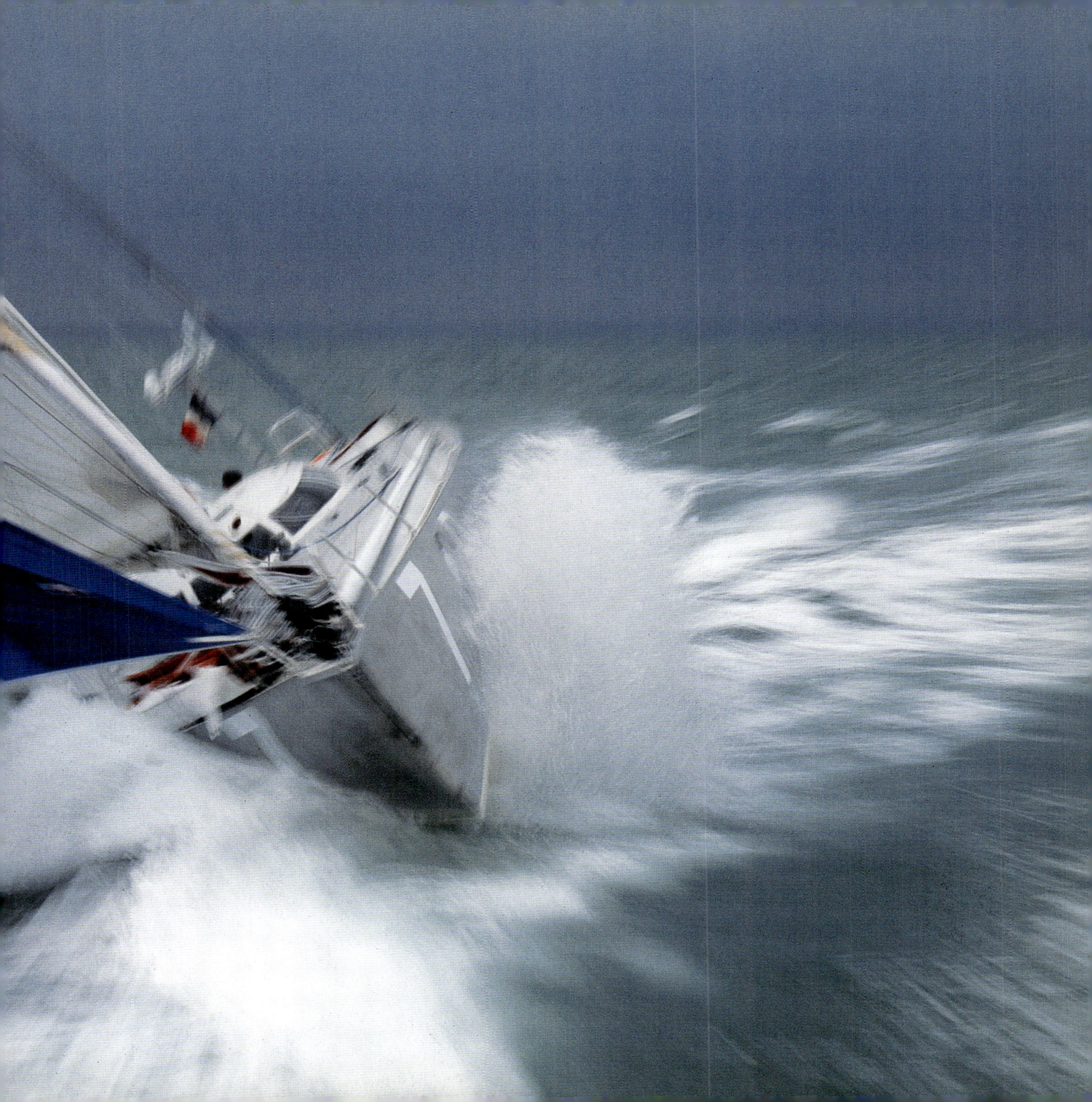

JUNE 13

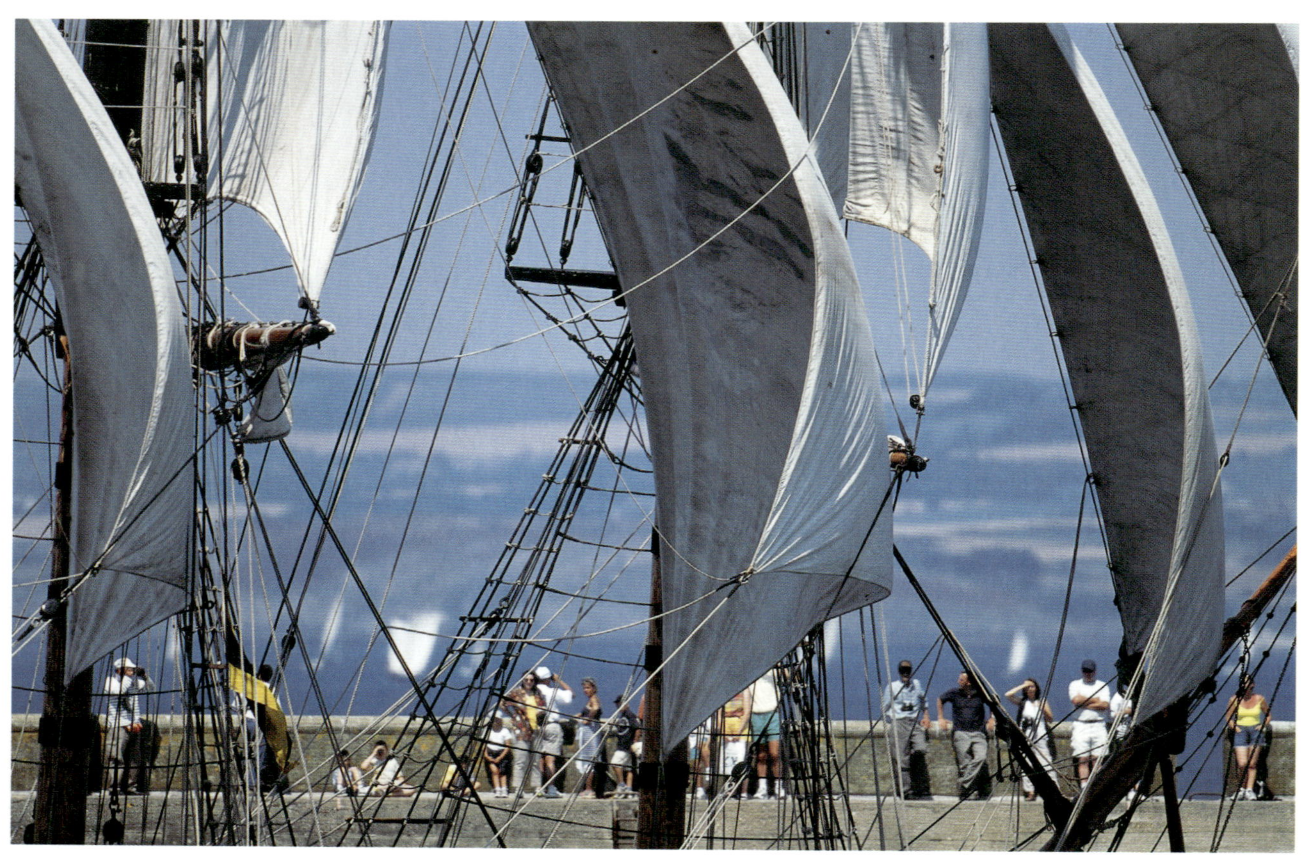

The wind sits in the shoulder of your sail,
And you are stay'd for.

William Shakespeare, from *Hamlet,* Act I, Scene 3

JUNE 14

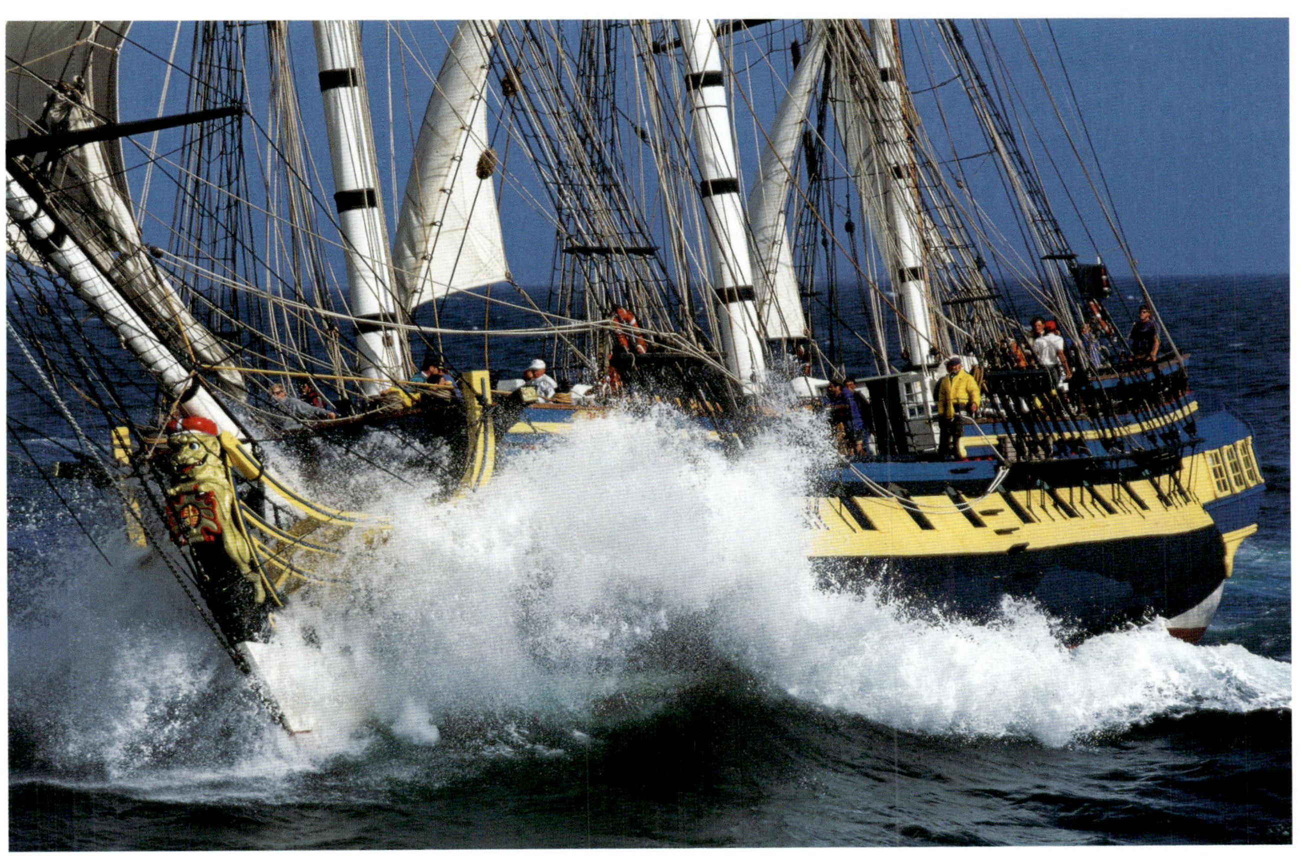

He who has suffer'd Ship-wrack feares to saile
Upon the Seas, though with a gentle gale.

Robert Herrick, from "Hesperides," 1648

JUNE 15

There is no harbor of peace from the changing waves of joy and despair.

Euripides

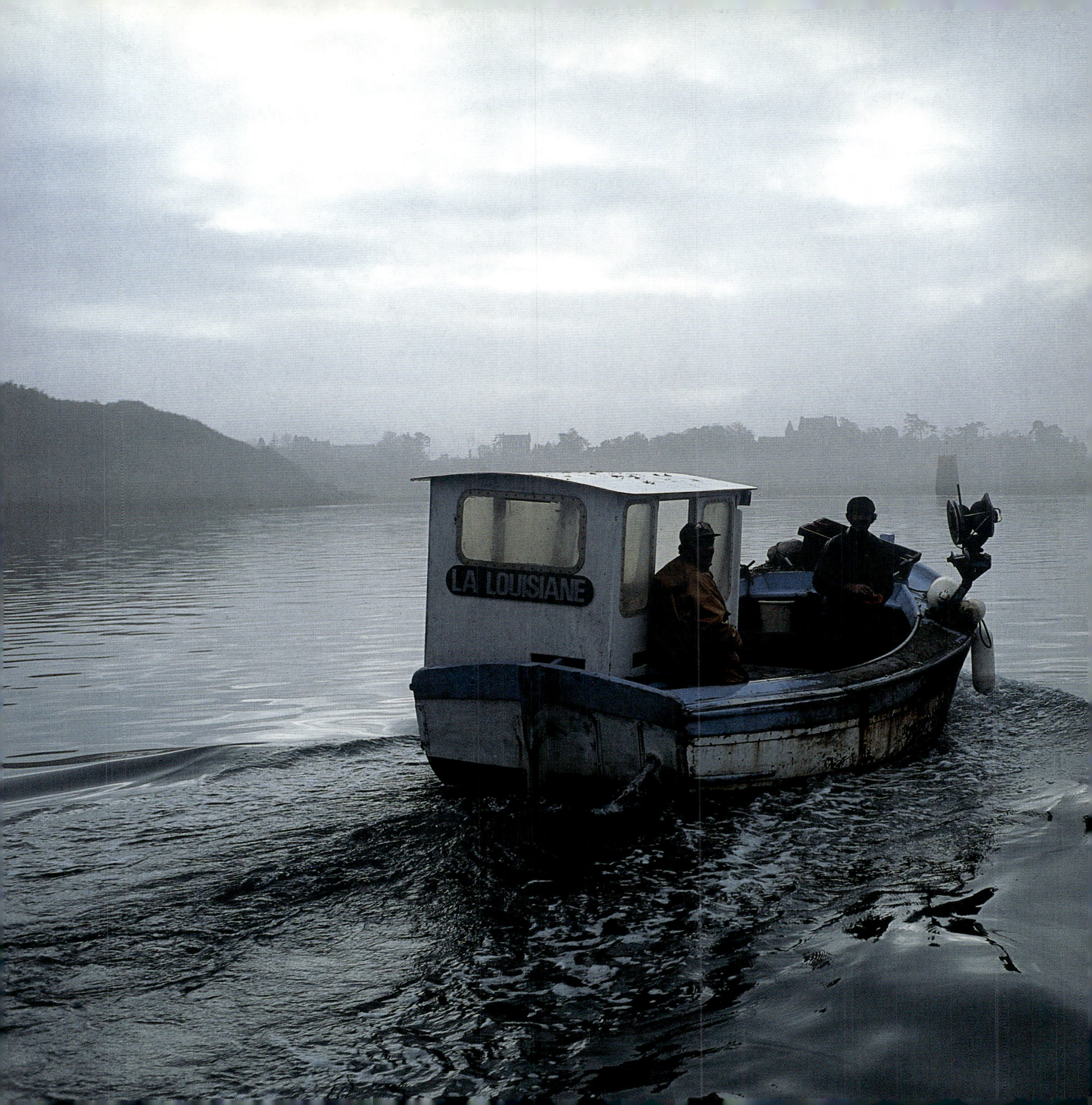
LA LOUISIANE

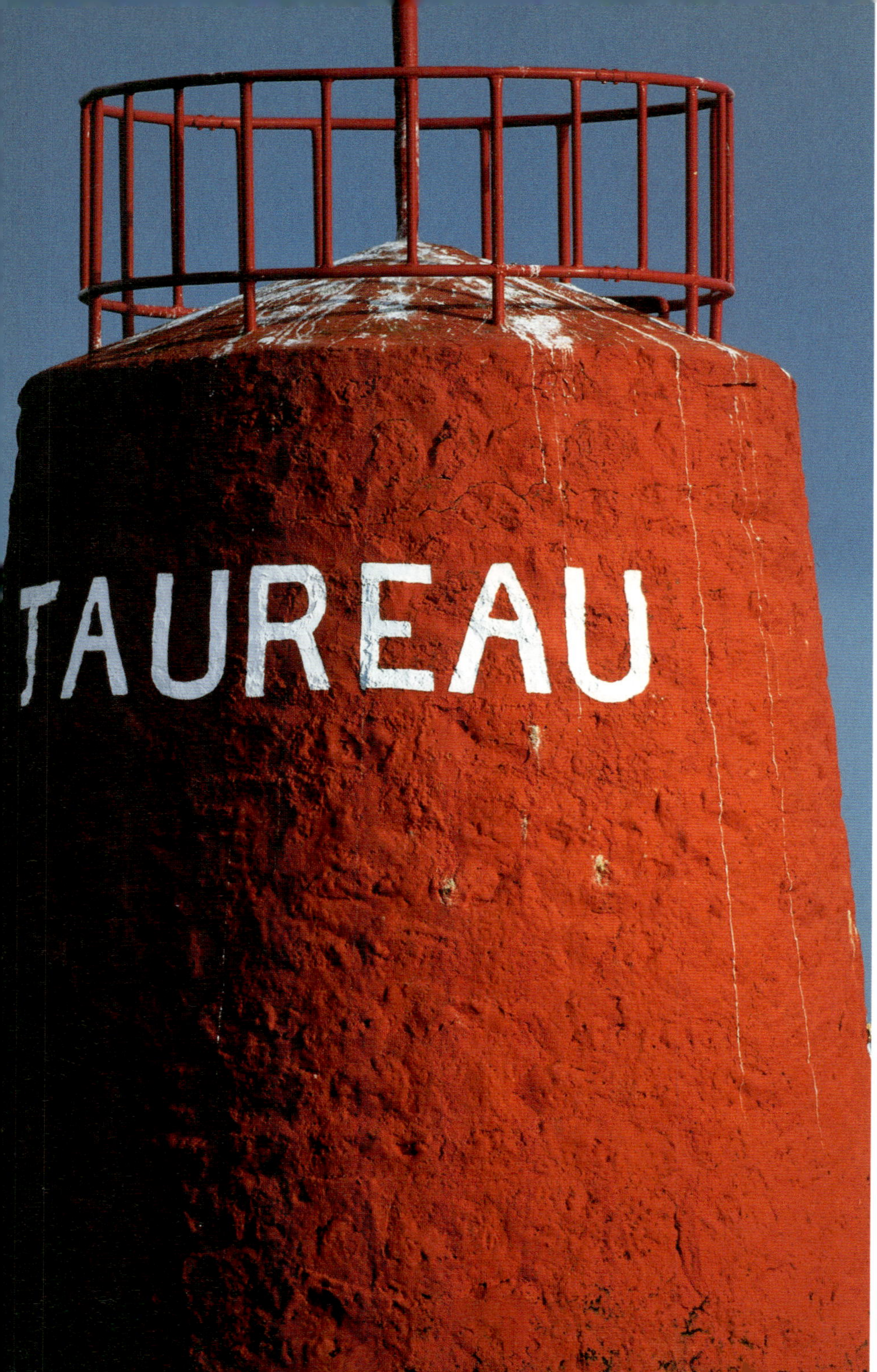

JUNE 16

The sea complains upon
a thousand shores.

Alexander Smith,
from *War Sonnets,* 1855

JUNE 17

Pray to God but continue
to row to the shore.

Russian proverb

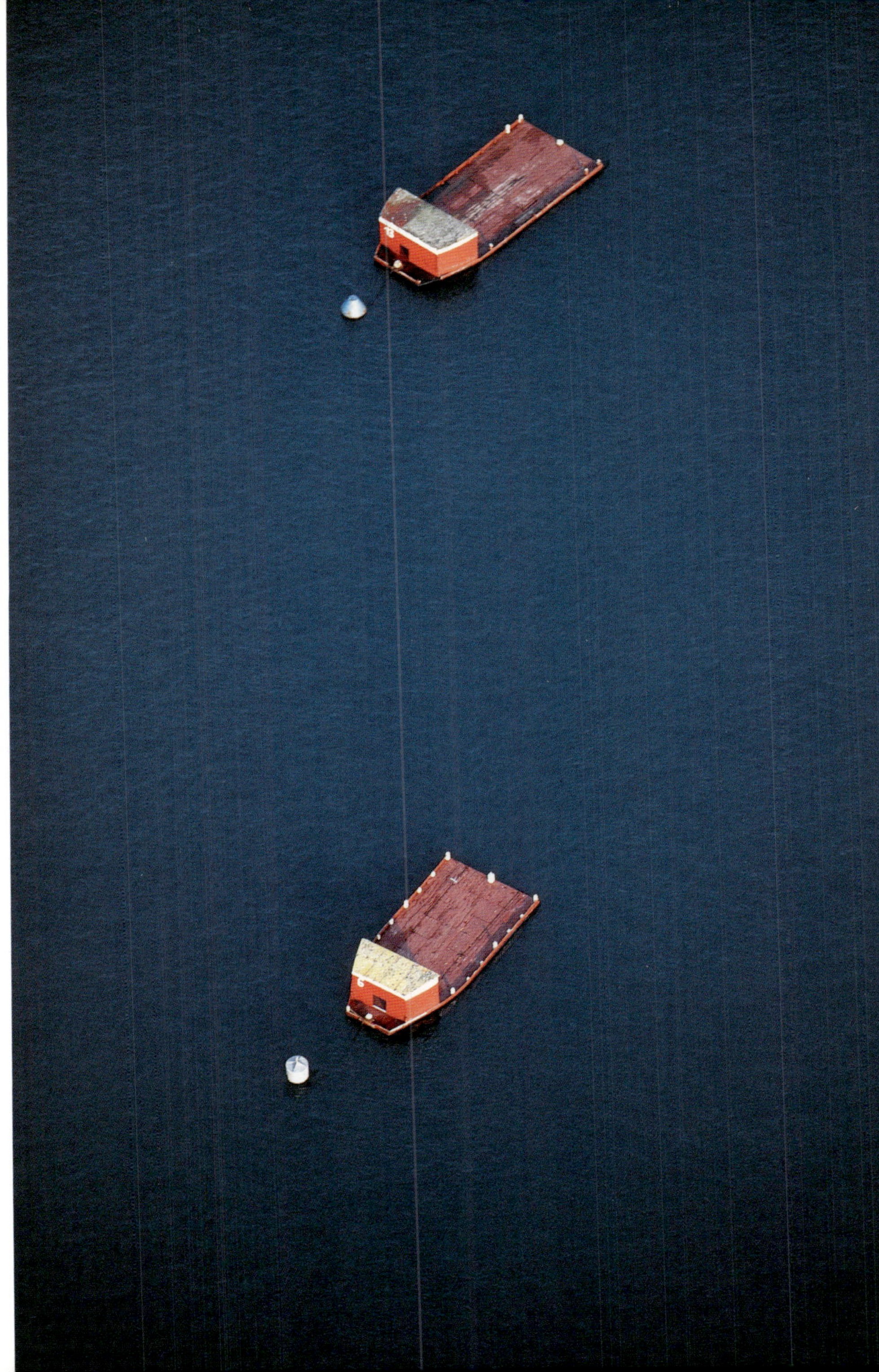

JUNE 18

The moral earth, too, is round! The moral earth, too, has its antipodes! The antipodes, too, have their right to exist! There is still another world to be discovered—and more than one! Set sail, you philosophers!

Friedrich Nietzsche,
from *The Gay Science,* 1882

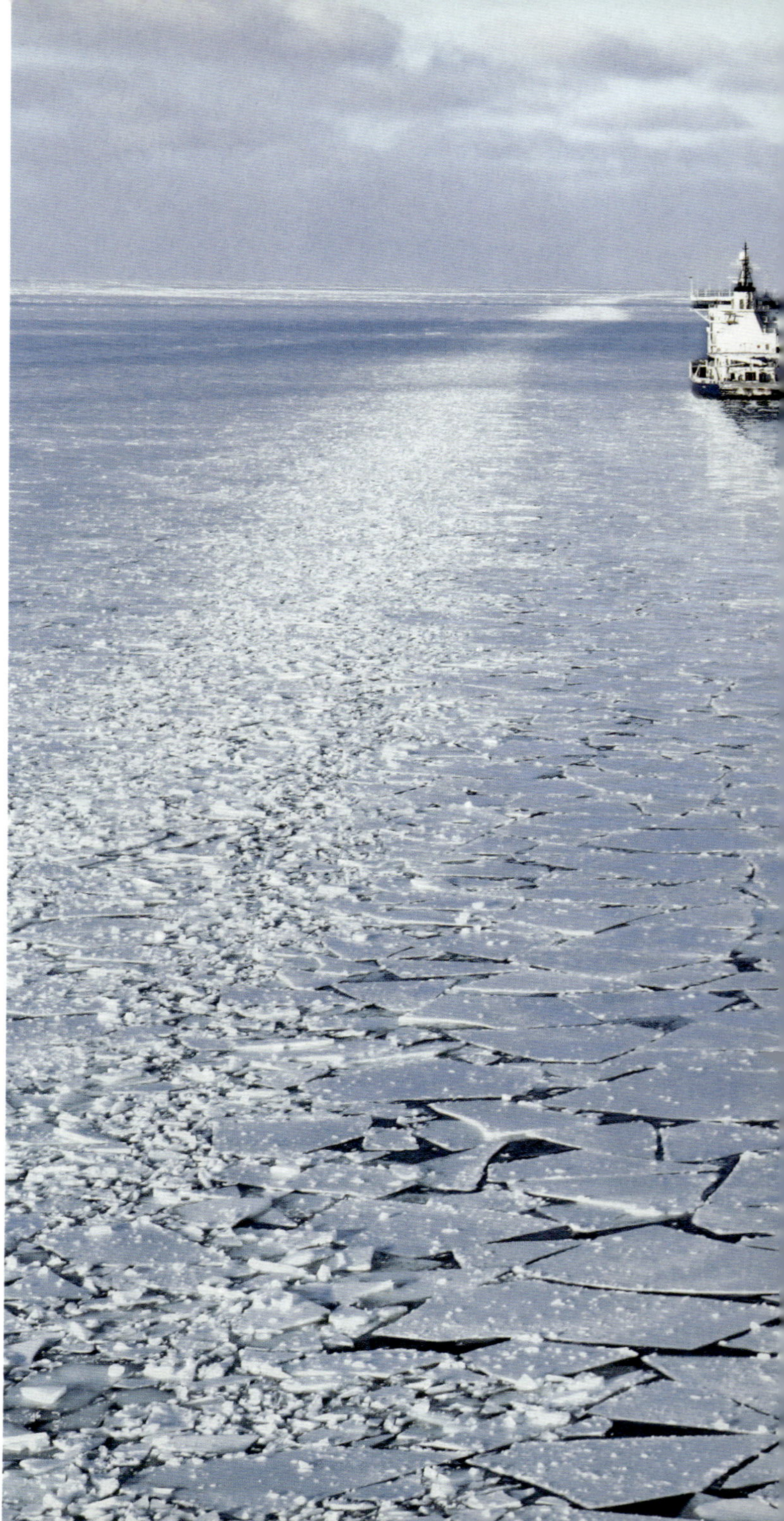

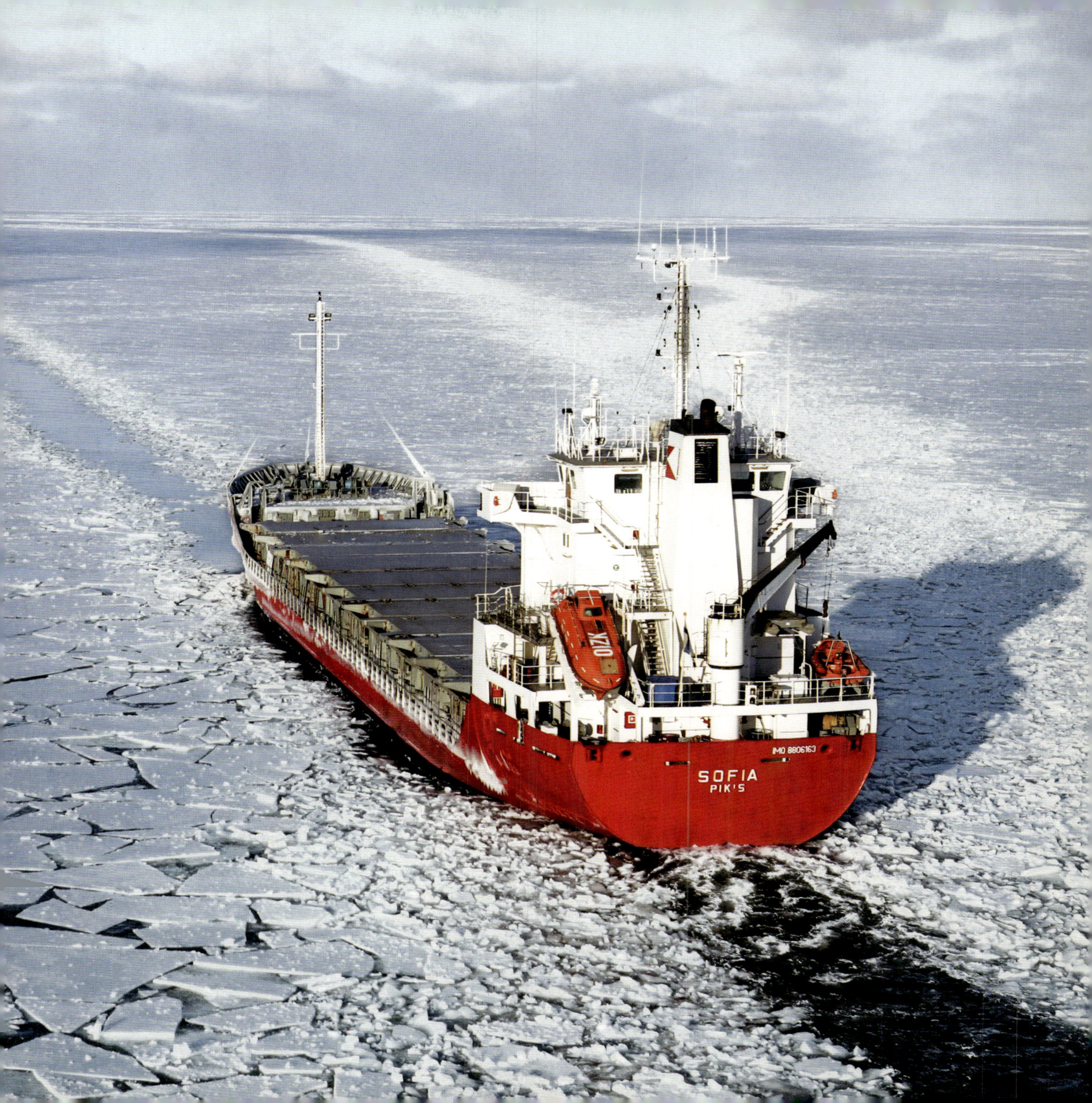
IMO 8806163
SOFIA
PIK'S

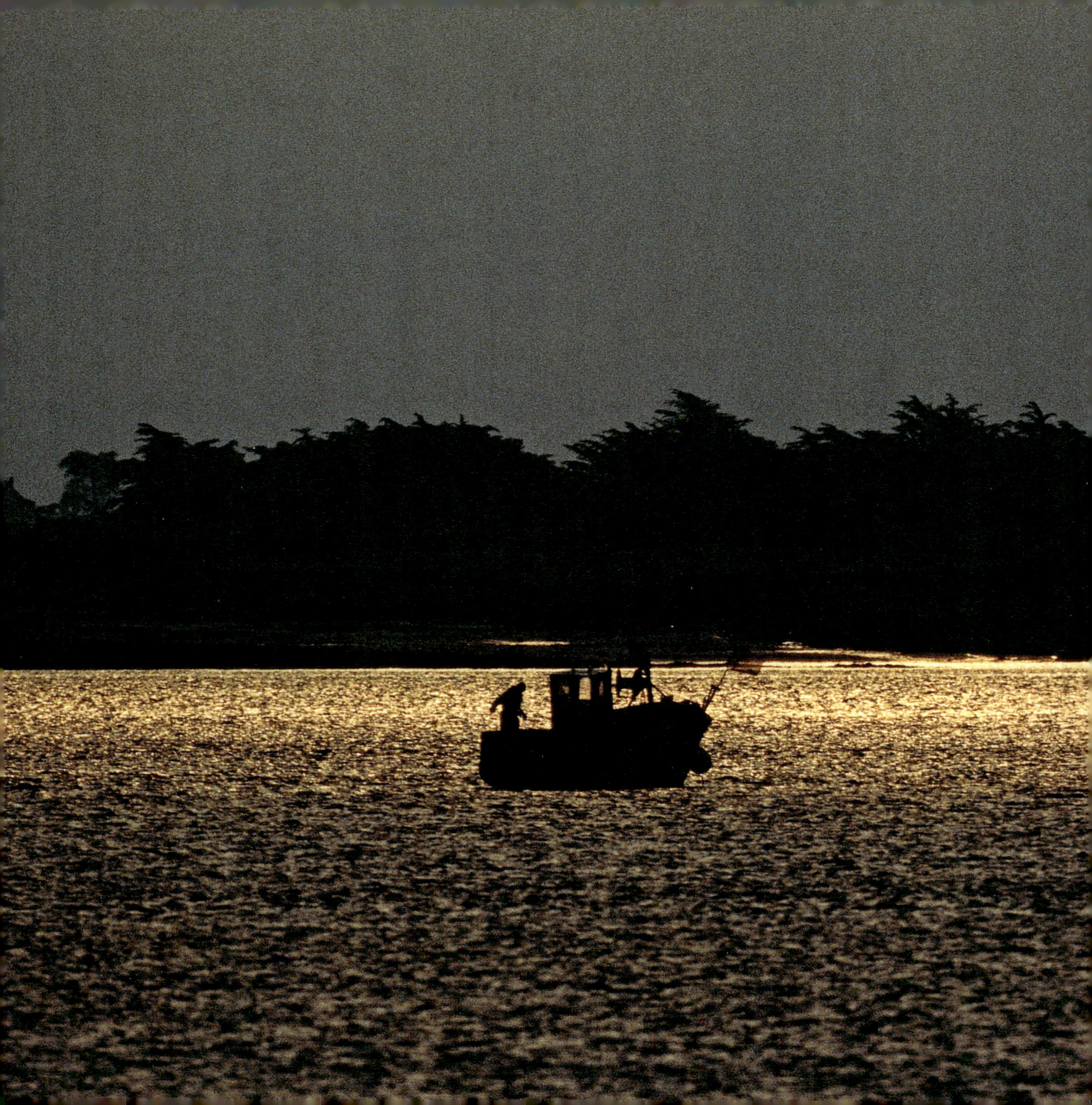

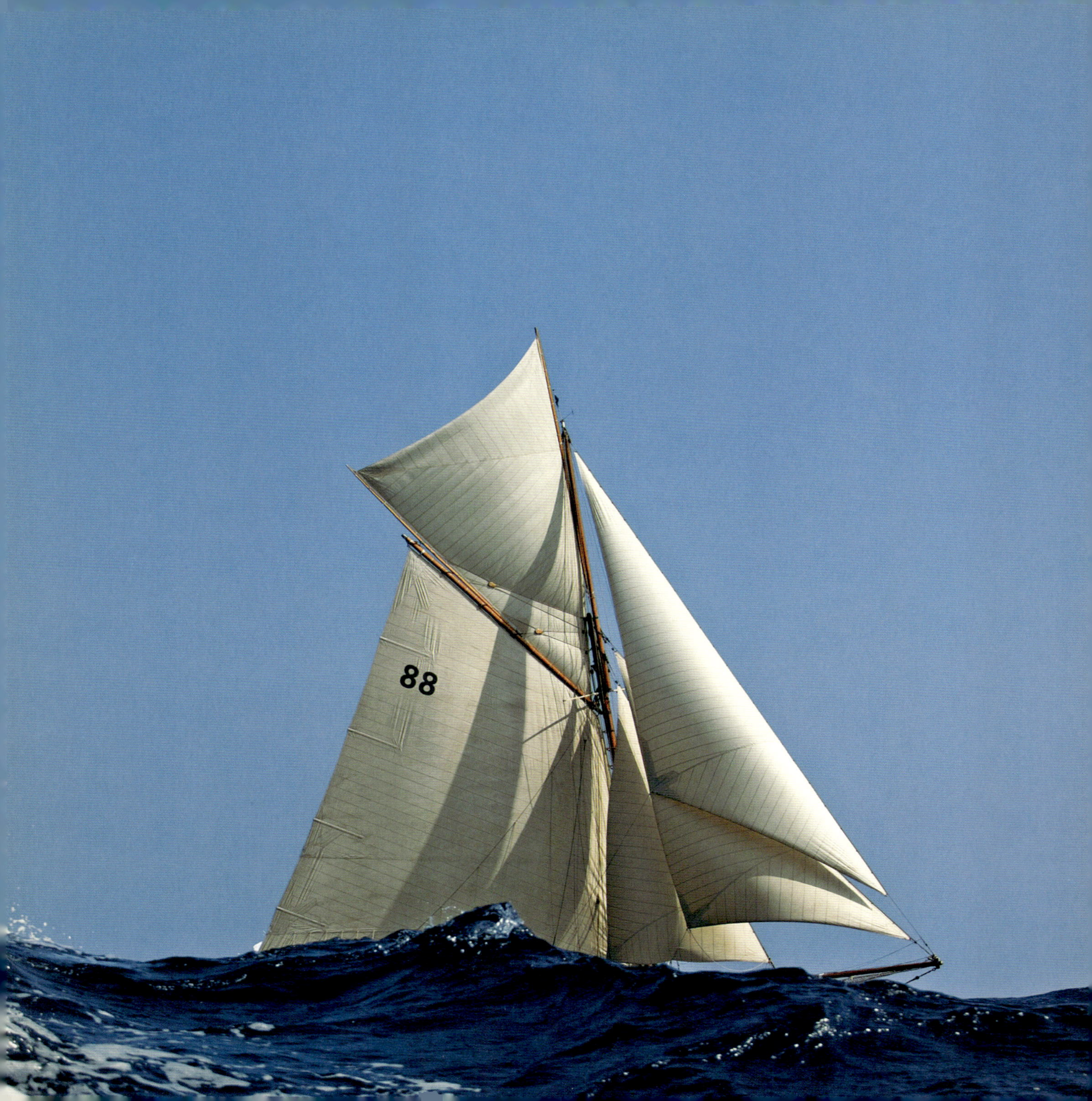
88

JUNE 19

Over the sea our galleys went,
With cleaving prows in order brave
To a speeding wind and a bounding wave—
A gallant armament.

Robert Browning,
from "The Wanderers"

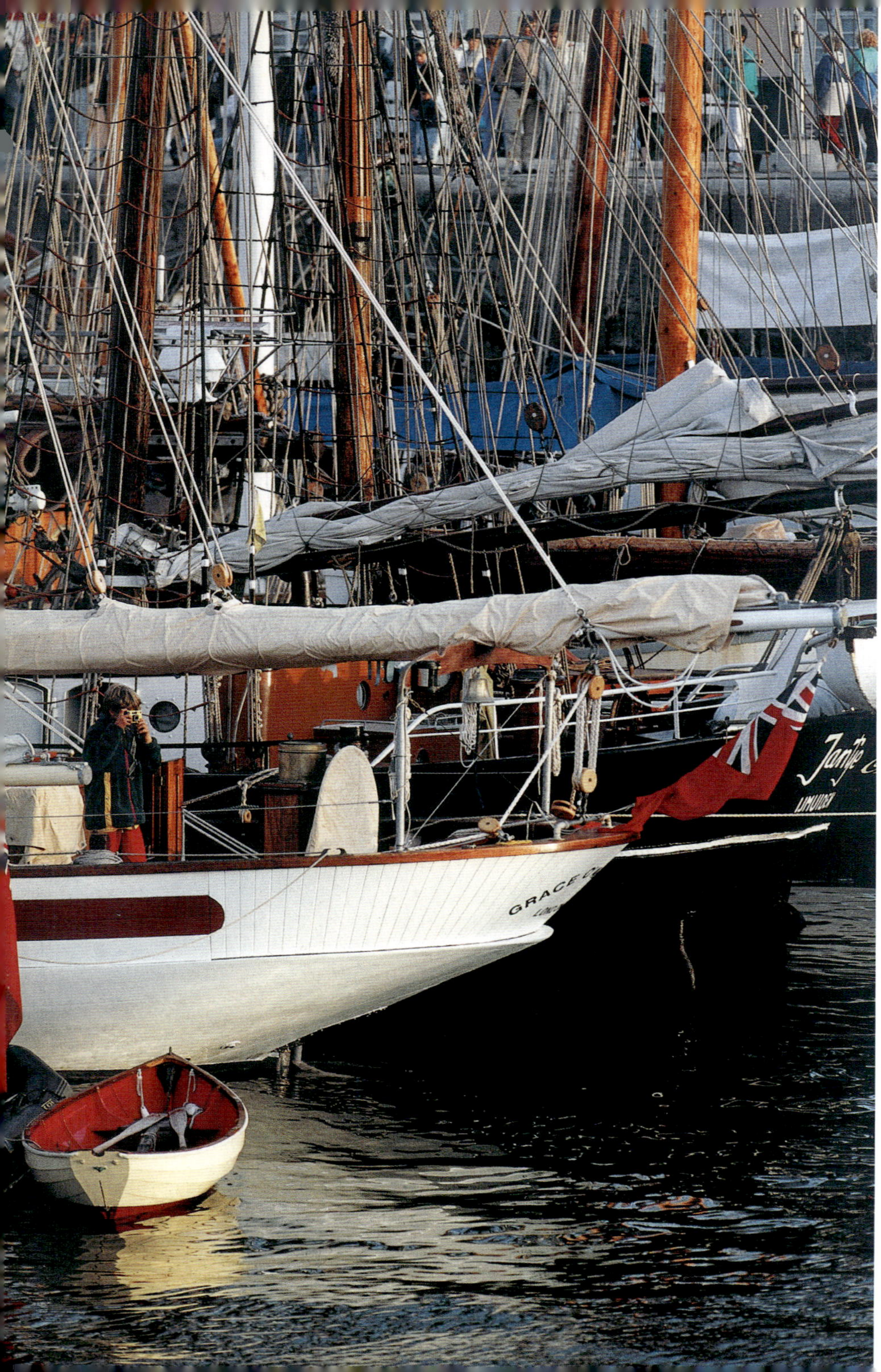

JUNE 20

The sea never buys fish.

Turkish proverb

JUNE 21

No matter how big the
sea may be, sometimes
two ships meet.

Chinese proverb

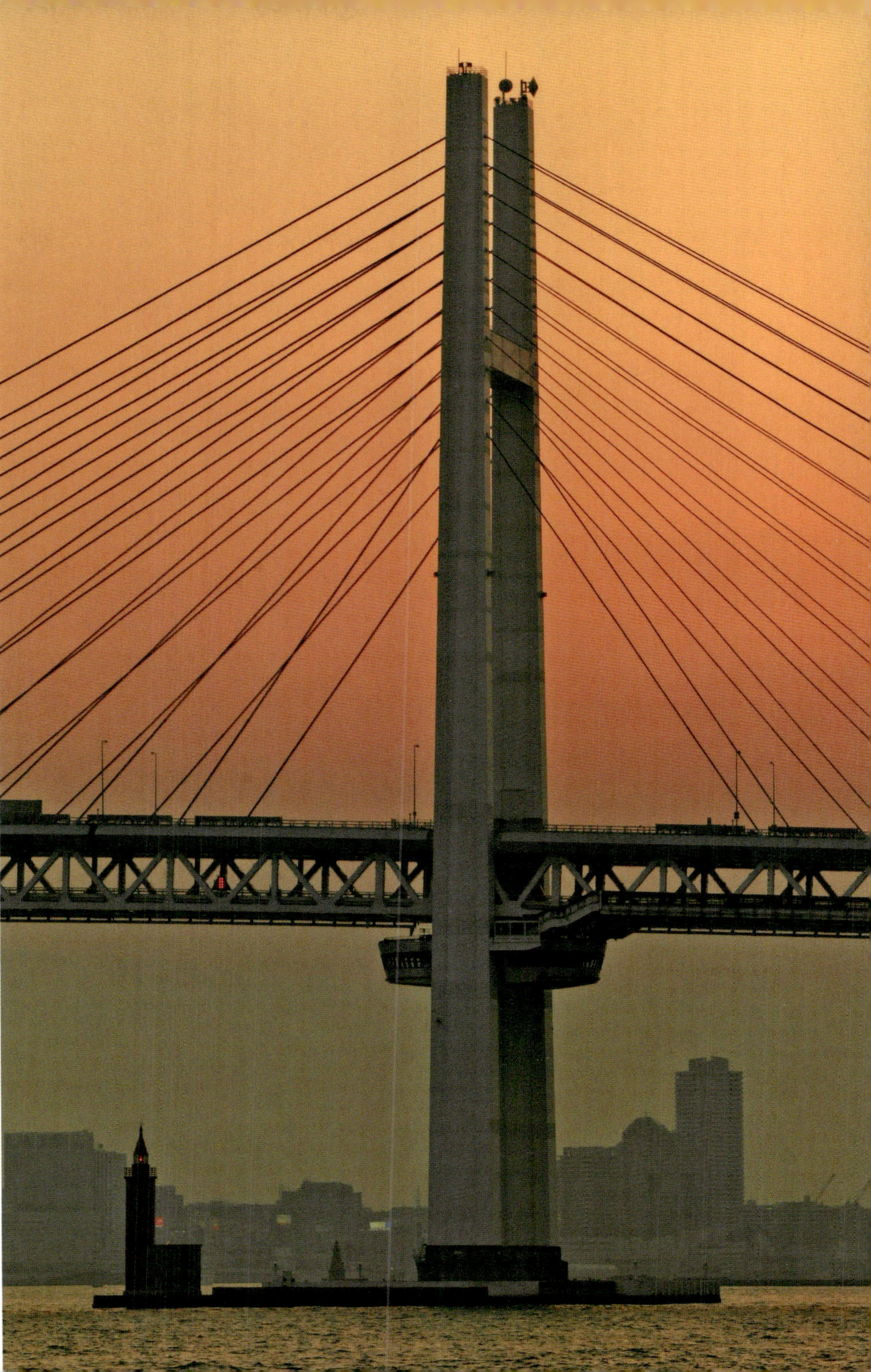

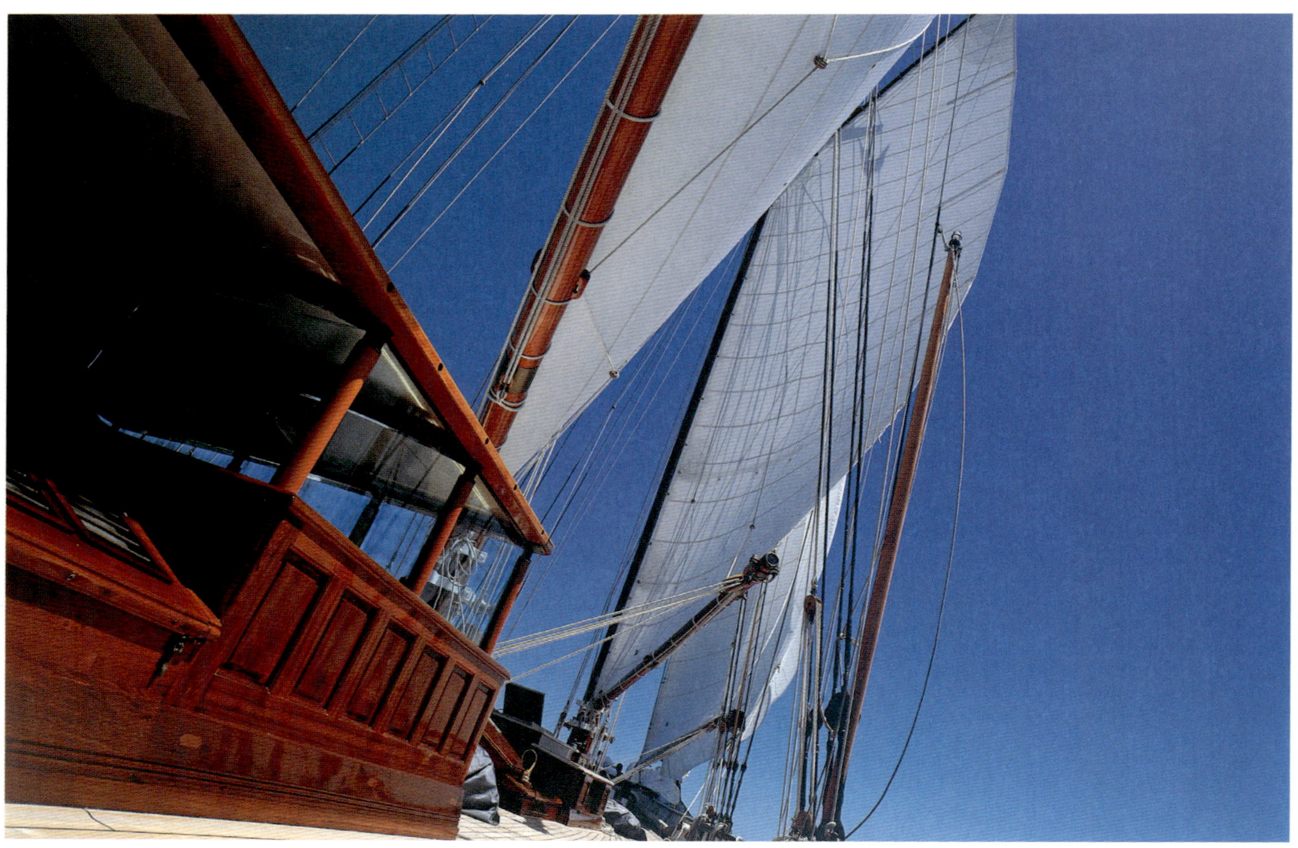

But where, after all, would be the poetry of the sea were there no wild waves?

Joshua Slocum, from *Sailing Alone Around the World,* 1900

JUNE 23

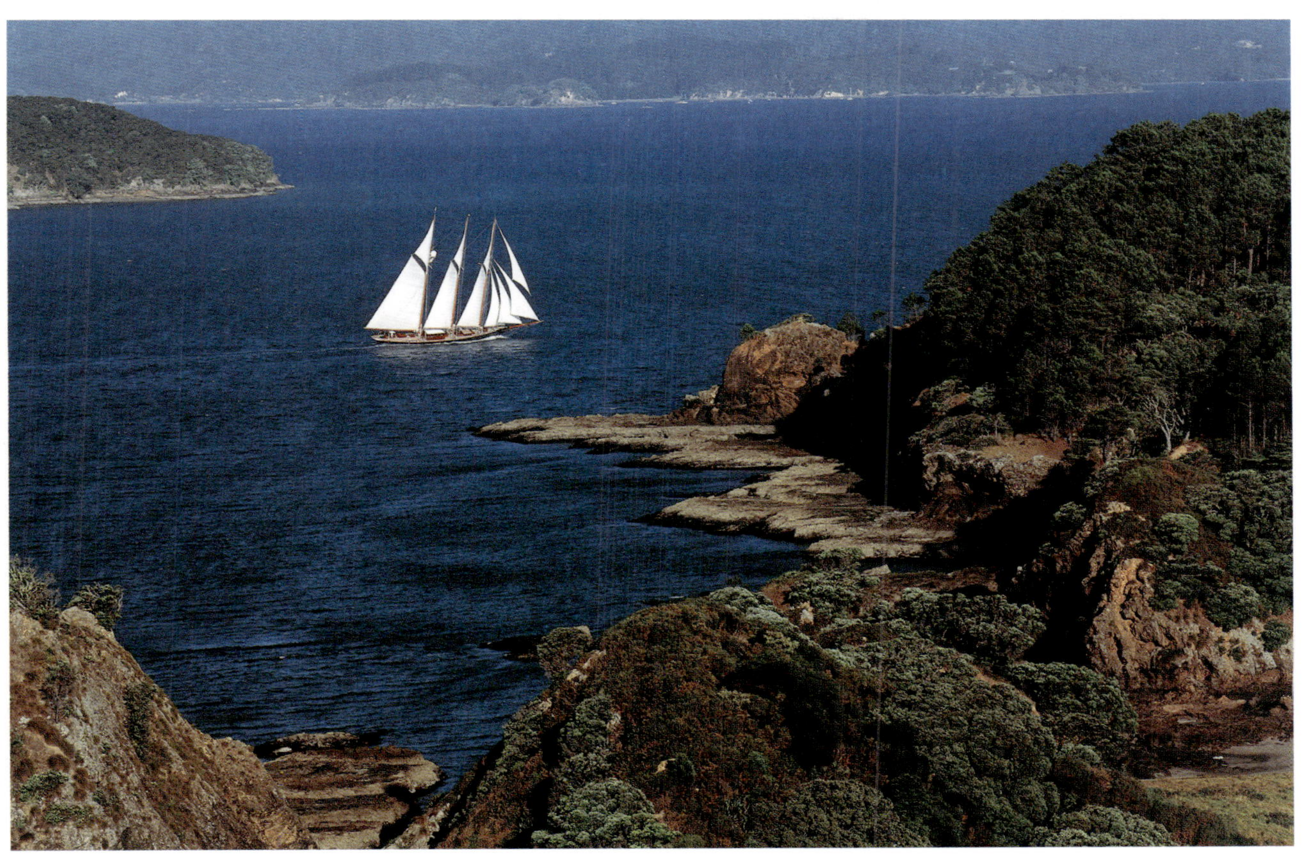

How the water sports and sings! (surely it is alive!)

Walt Whitman, from "Song at Sunset," *Leaves of Grass,* 1900

JUNE 24

It is far better not to know where one is, and realize that one does not know, than to be certain one is in a place where one is not.

Lieutenant Barral,
from *Digressions on the Navigation of Cape Horn,* 1827

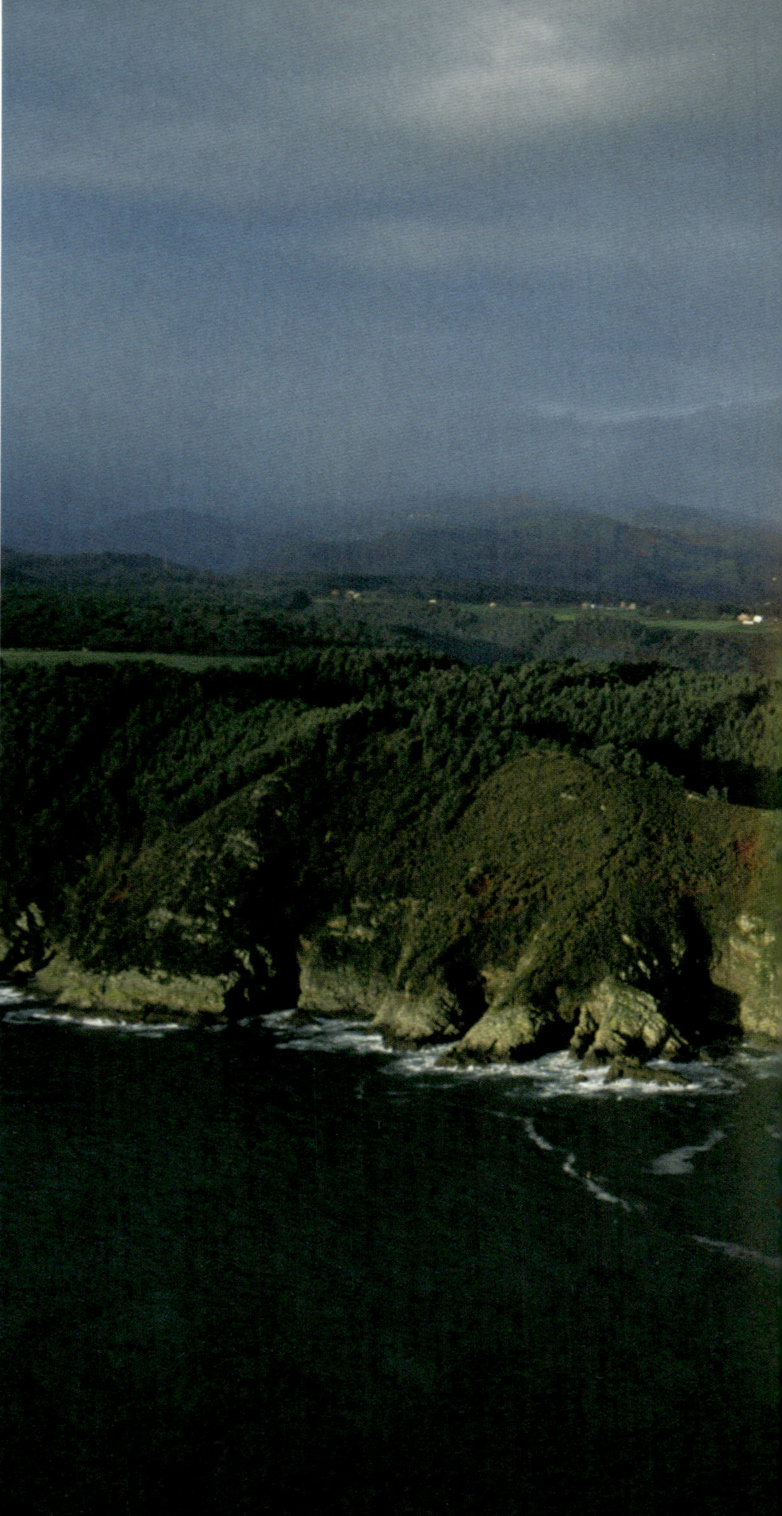

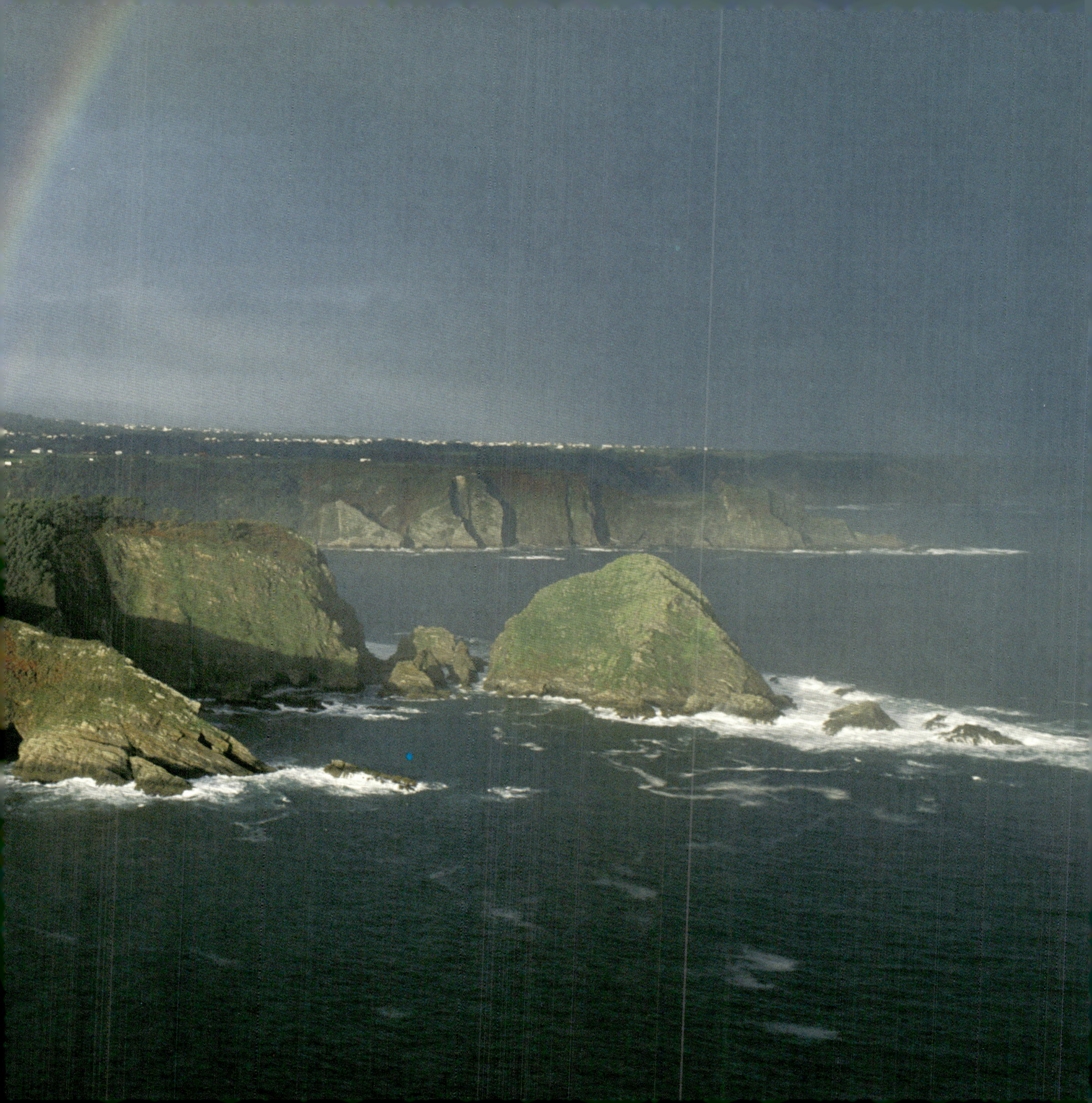

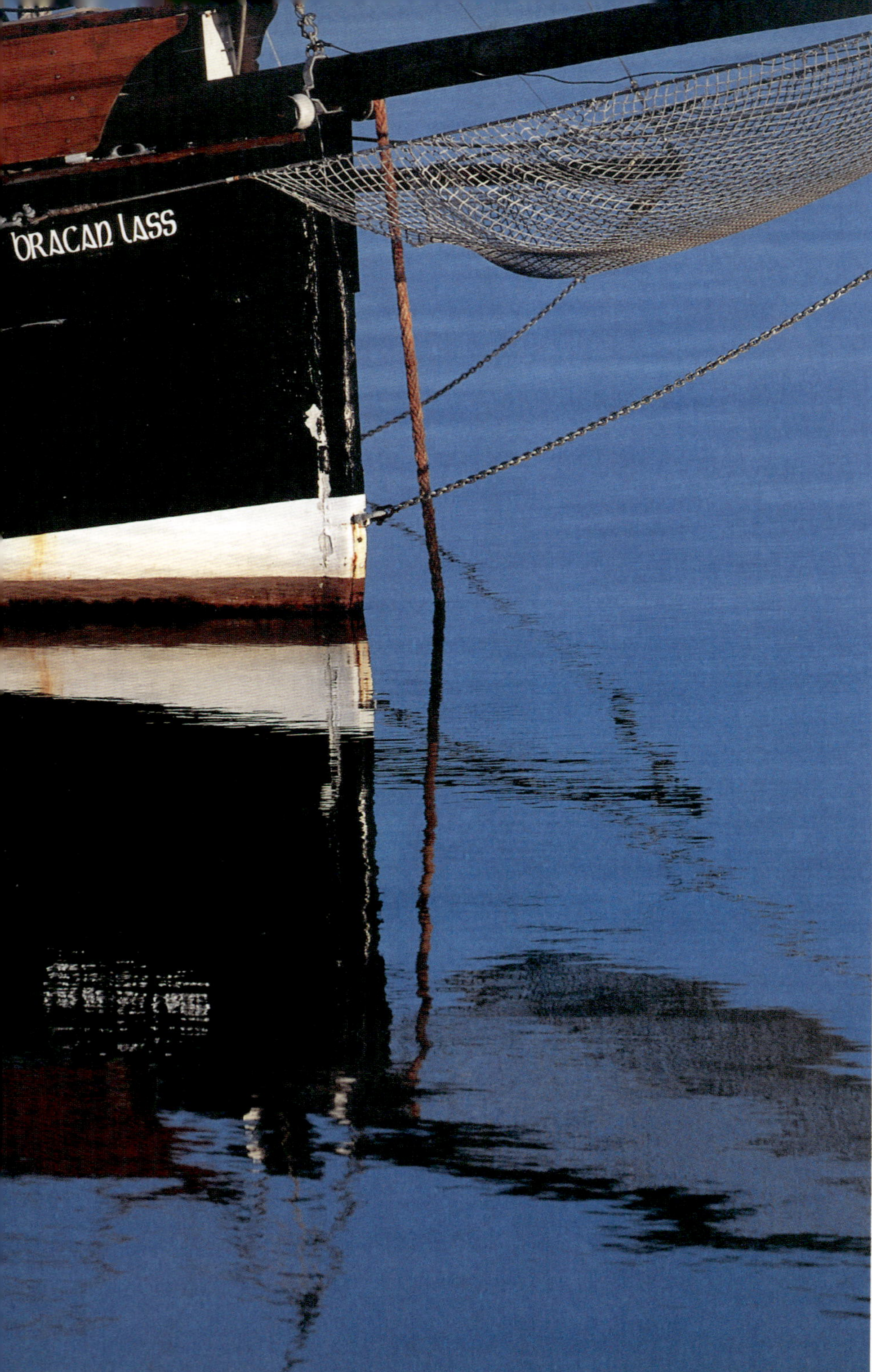

JUNE 25

Under heaven nothing is more
soft and yielding than water.
Yet for attacking the solid and
strong, nothing is better.
It has no equal.

Lao-Tzu

JUNE 26

The obstinacy of sailors
is not always regulated
by the importance of the
matter in dispute.

Richard Walter,
from *Anson's Voyage Around the World,*
1748

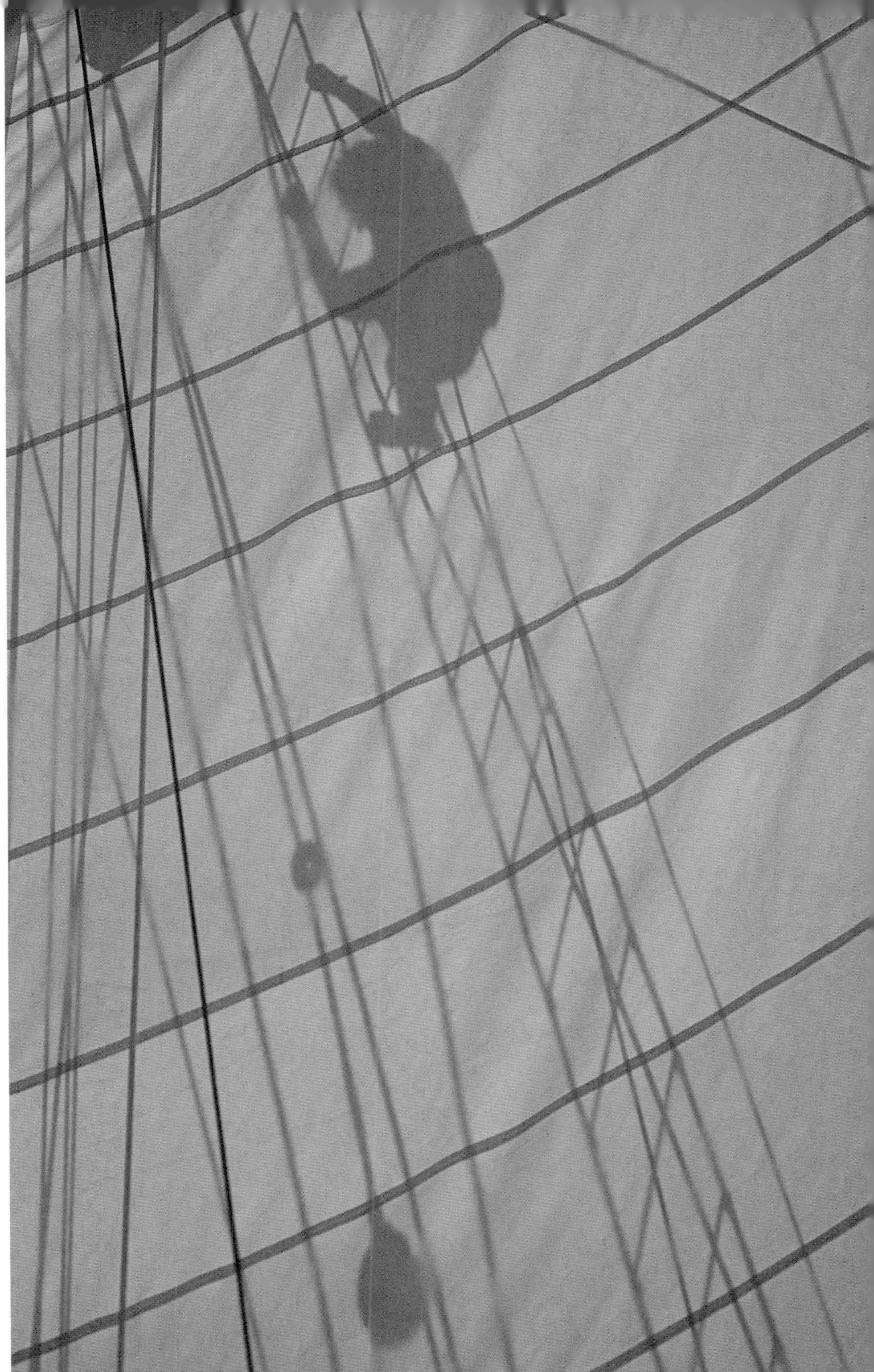

JUNE 27

And so by many winding nooks he strays
With willing sport, to the wild ocean.
Then let me go and hinder not my course:
I'll be as patient as a gentle stream
And make a pastime of each weary step,
Till the last step have brought me to my love.

William Shakespeare,
from *The Two Gentlemen of Verona,* Act II, Scene 7

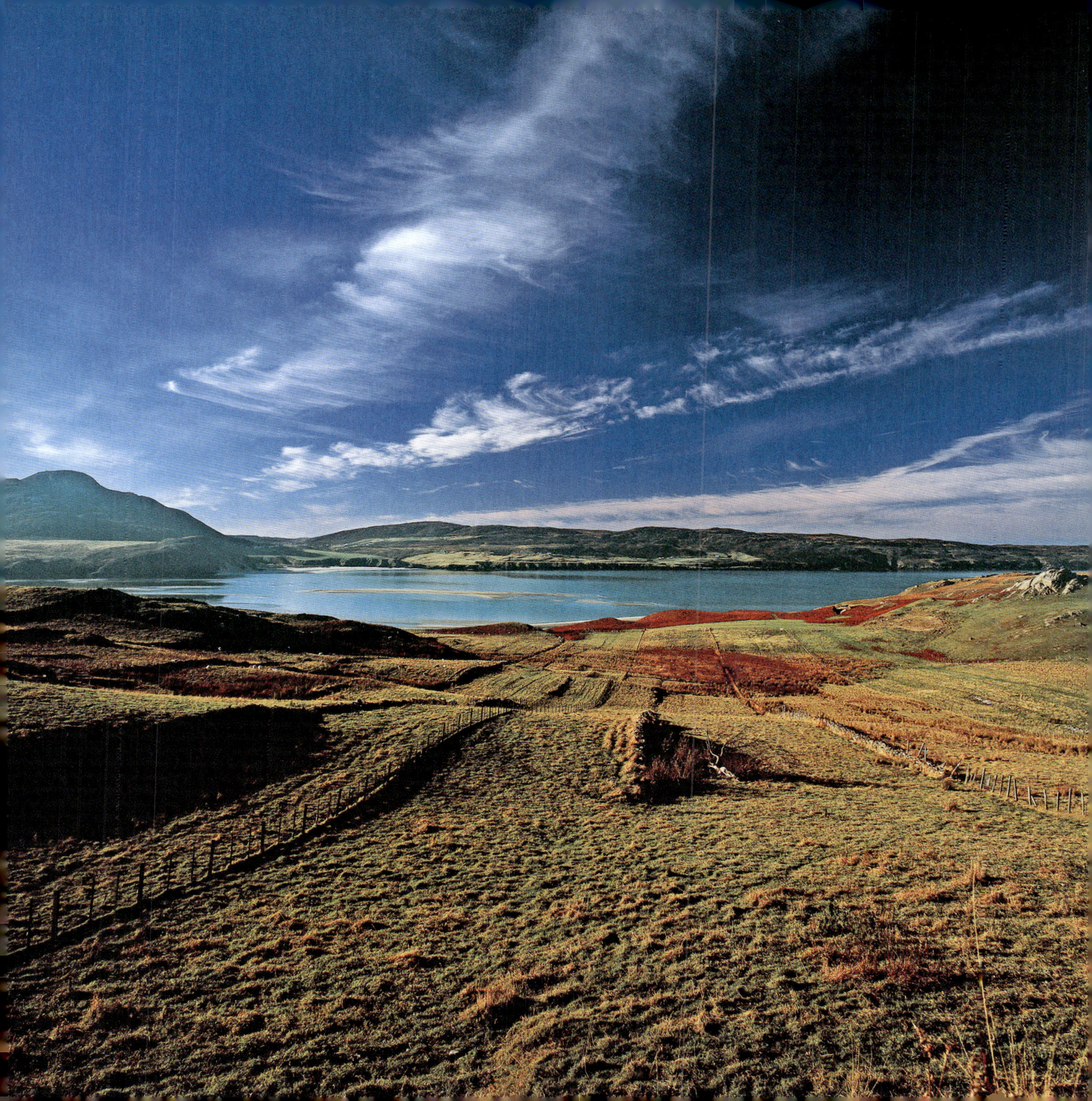

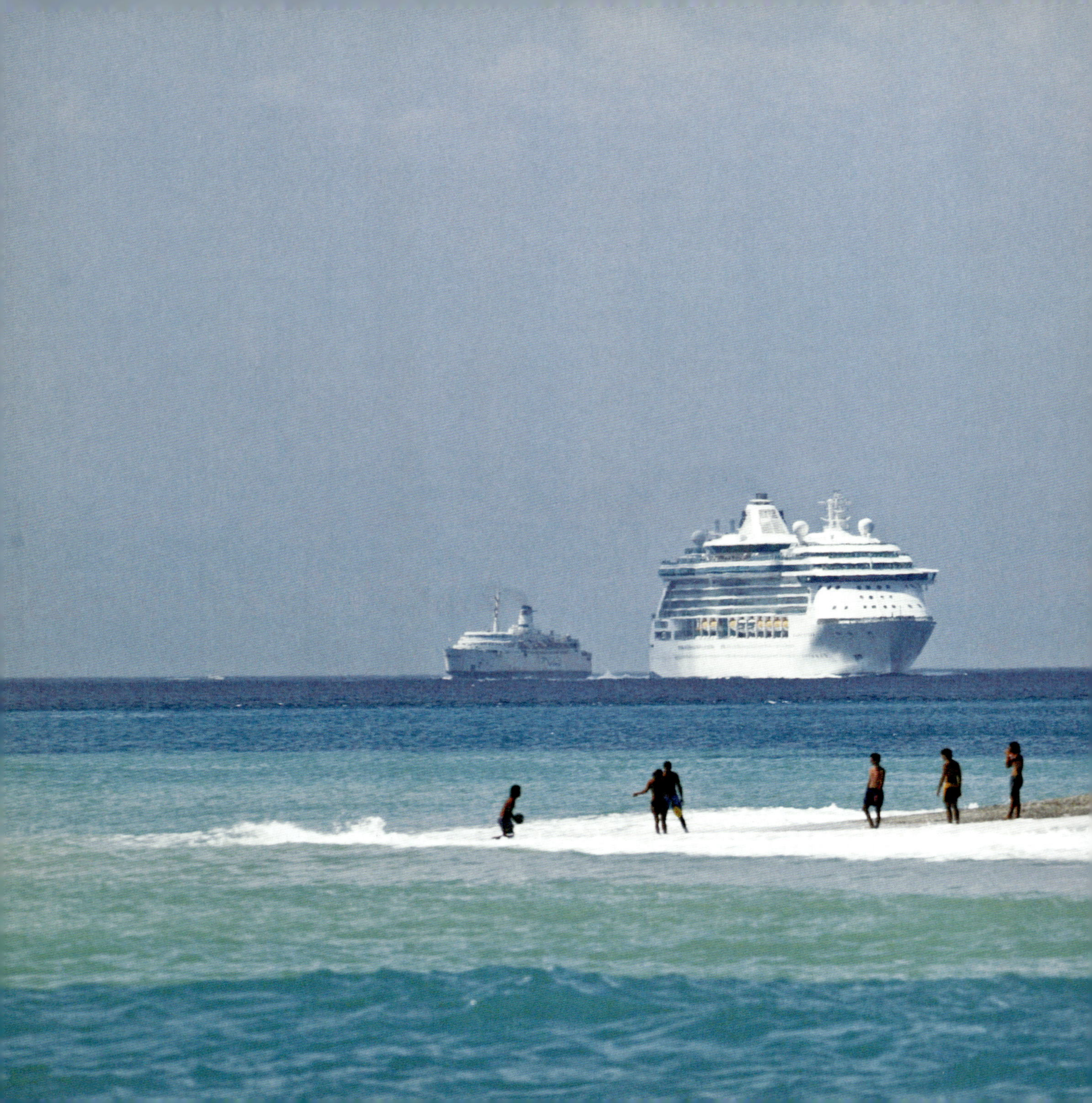

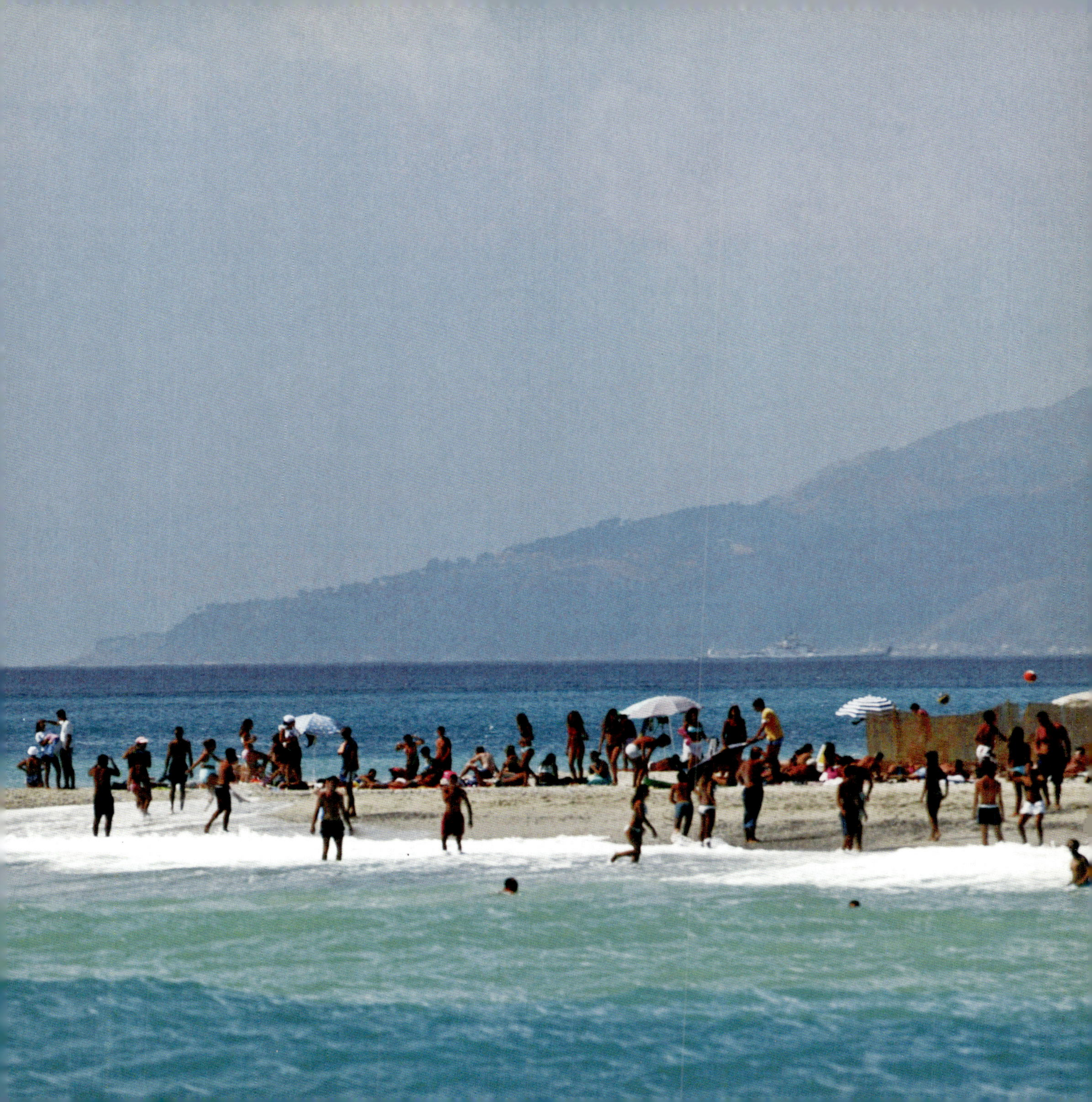

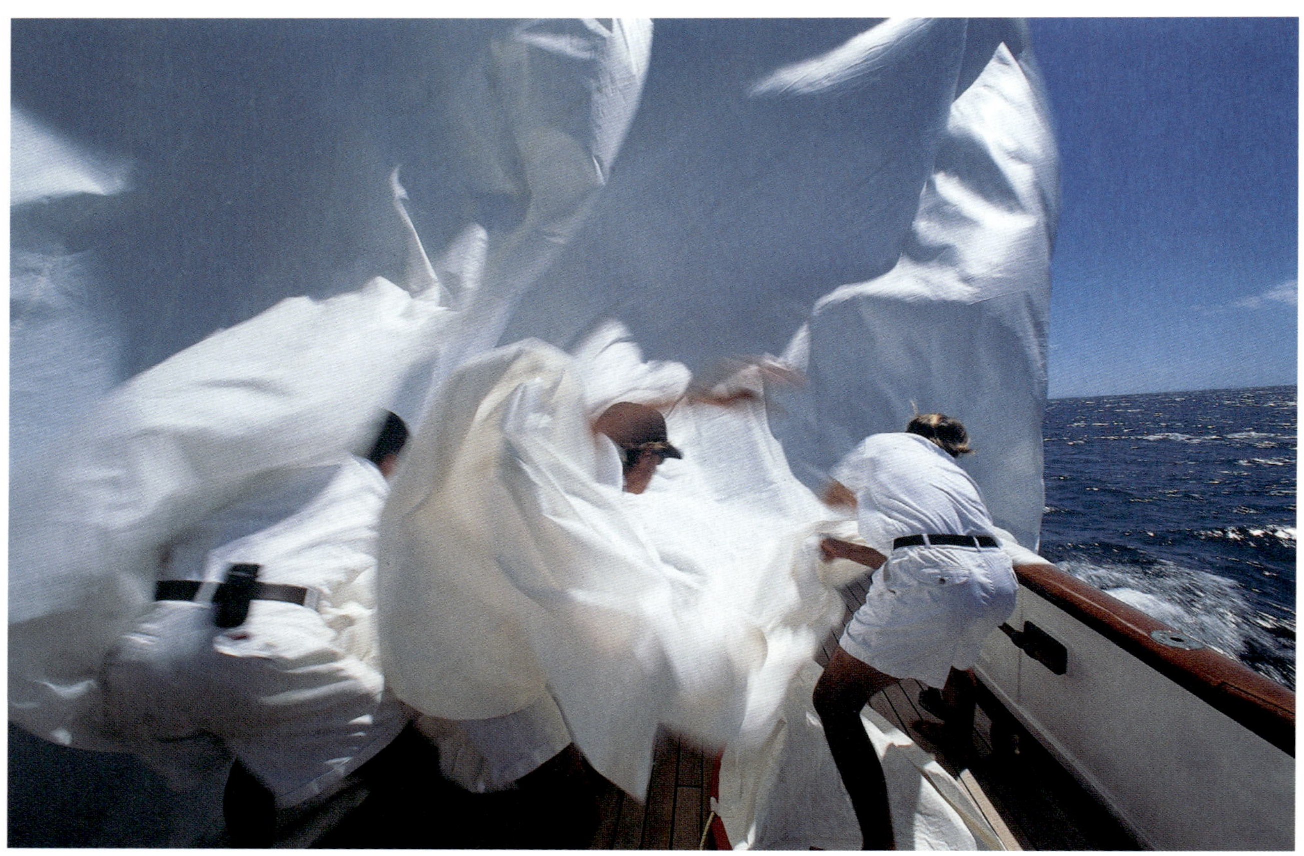

I have seen old ships sail like swans asleep.

James Elroy Flecker, from "The Old Ships," 1915

JUNE 29

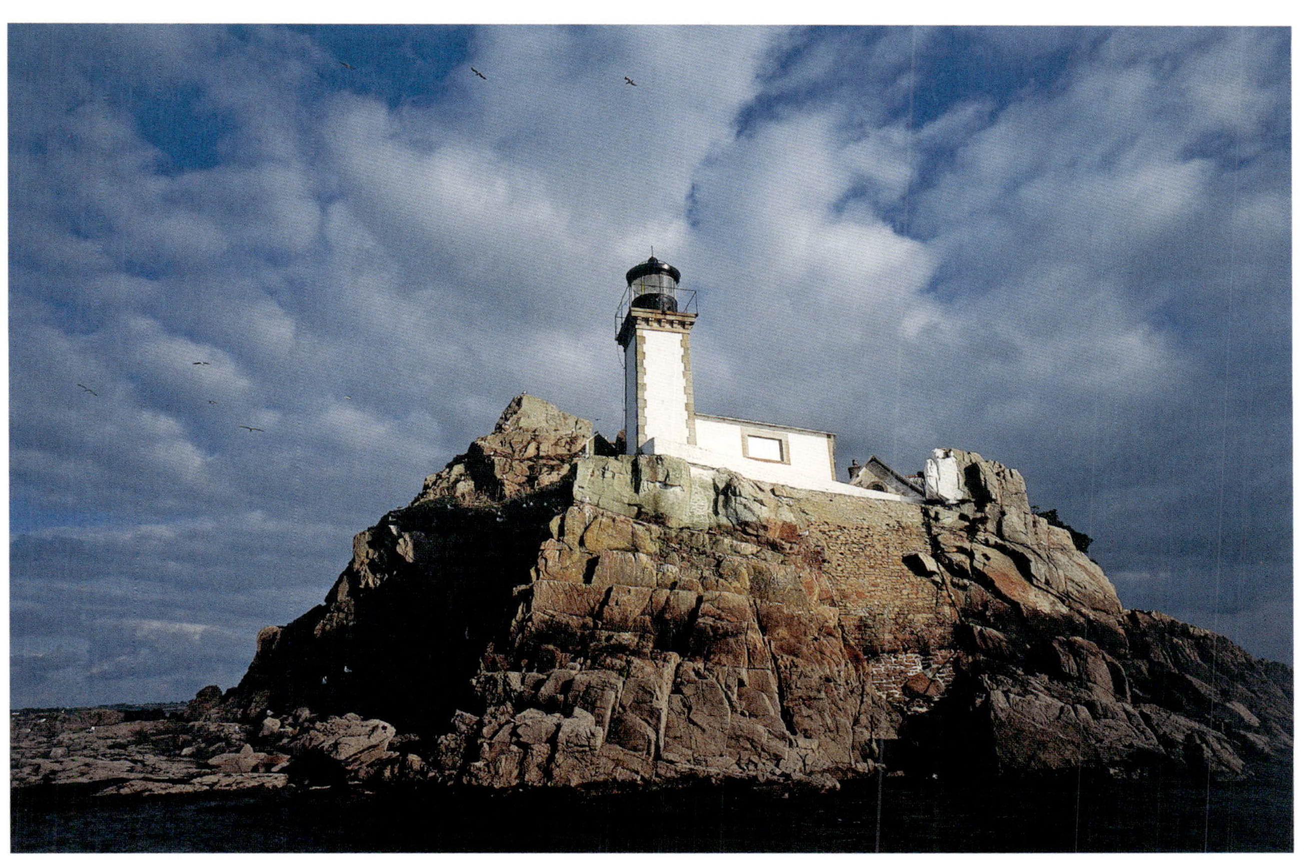

We are as near to Heaven by sea as by land.

Sir Humphrey Gilbert

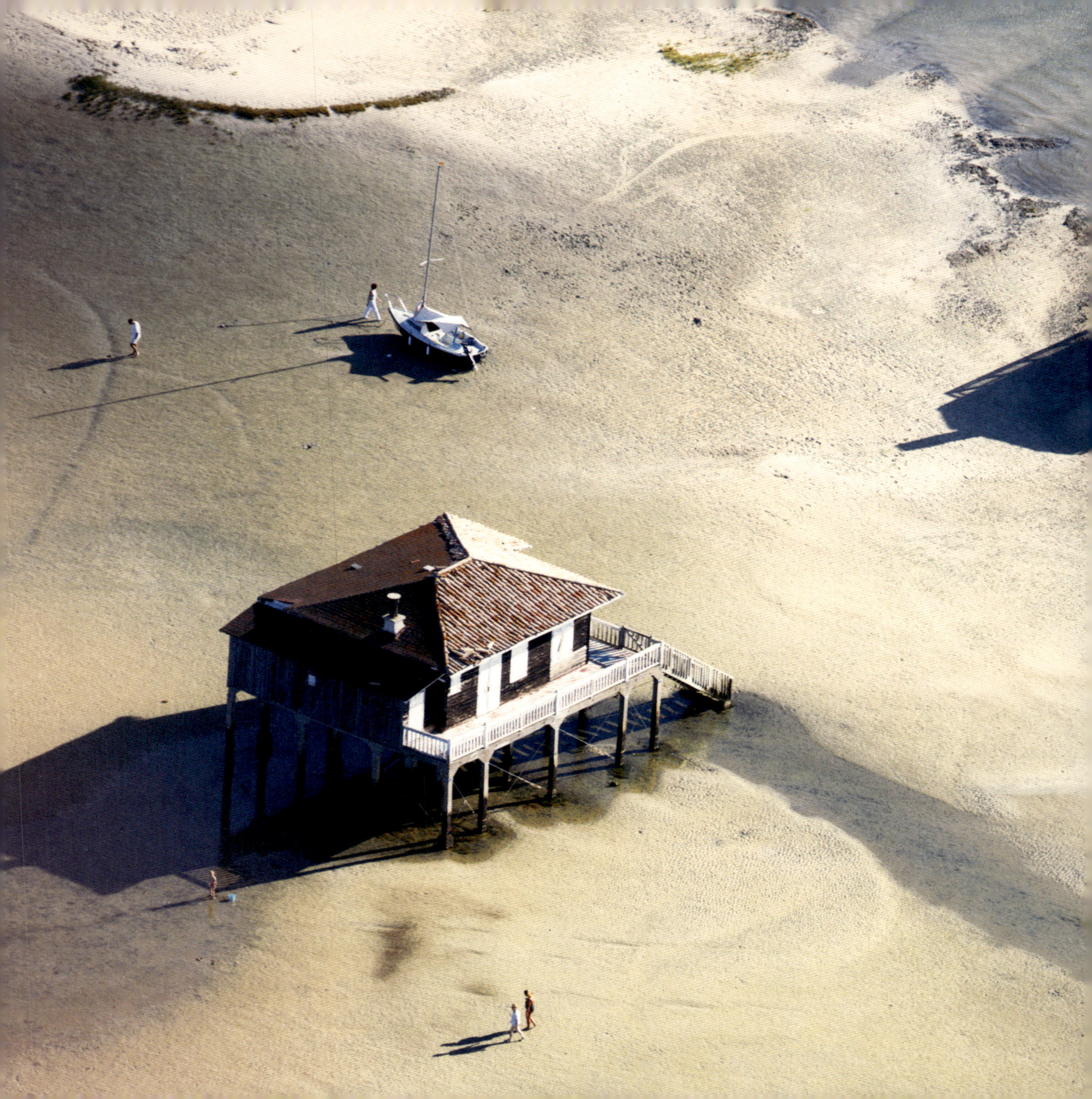

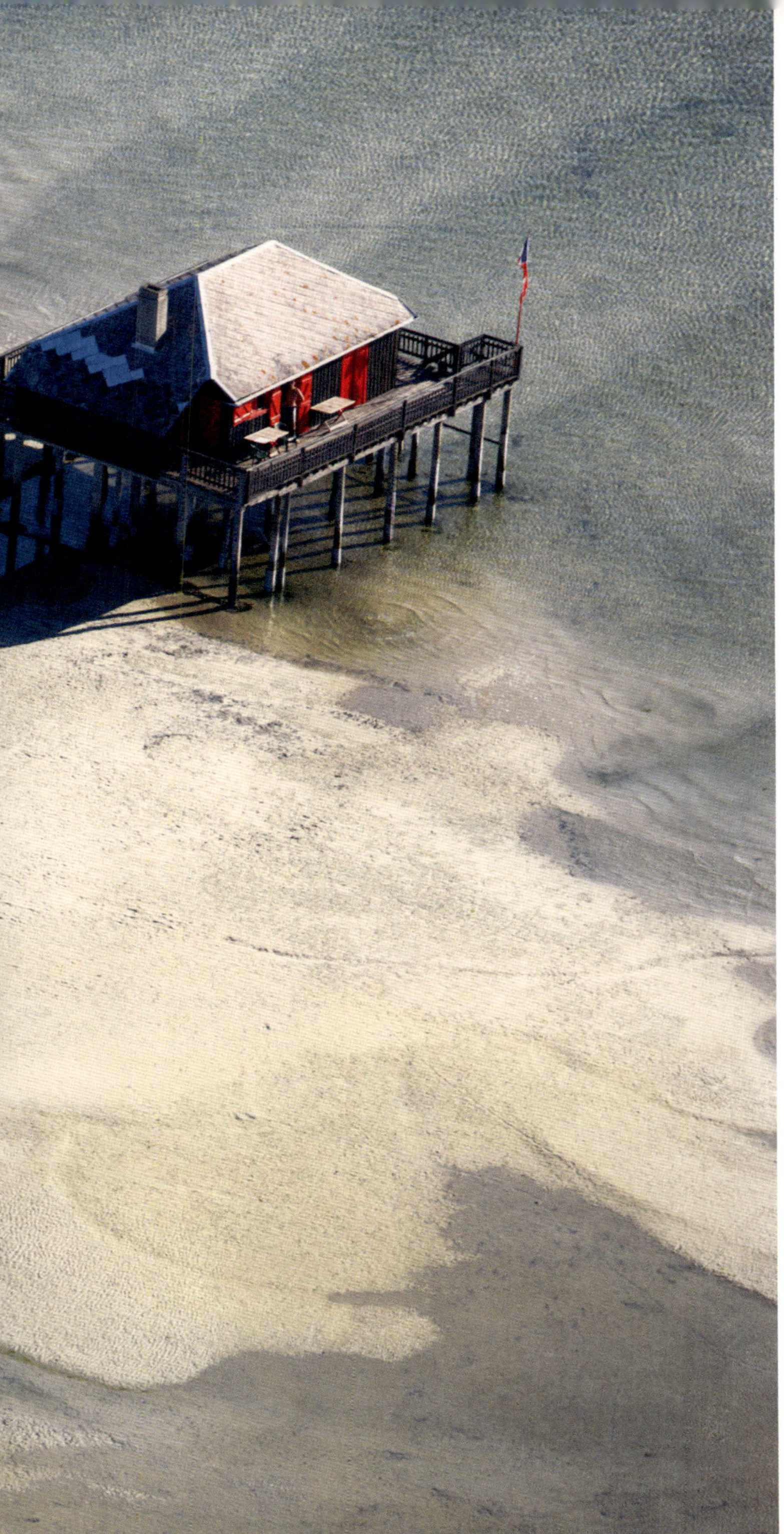

JUNE 30

I to the world am like a drop of water
That in the ocean seeks another drop.

William Shakespeare,
from *The Comedy of Errors,* Act I, Scene 2

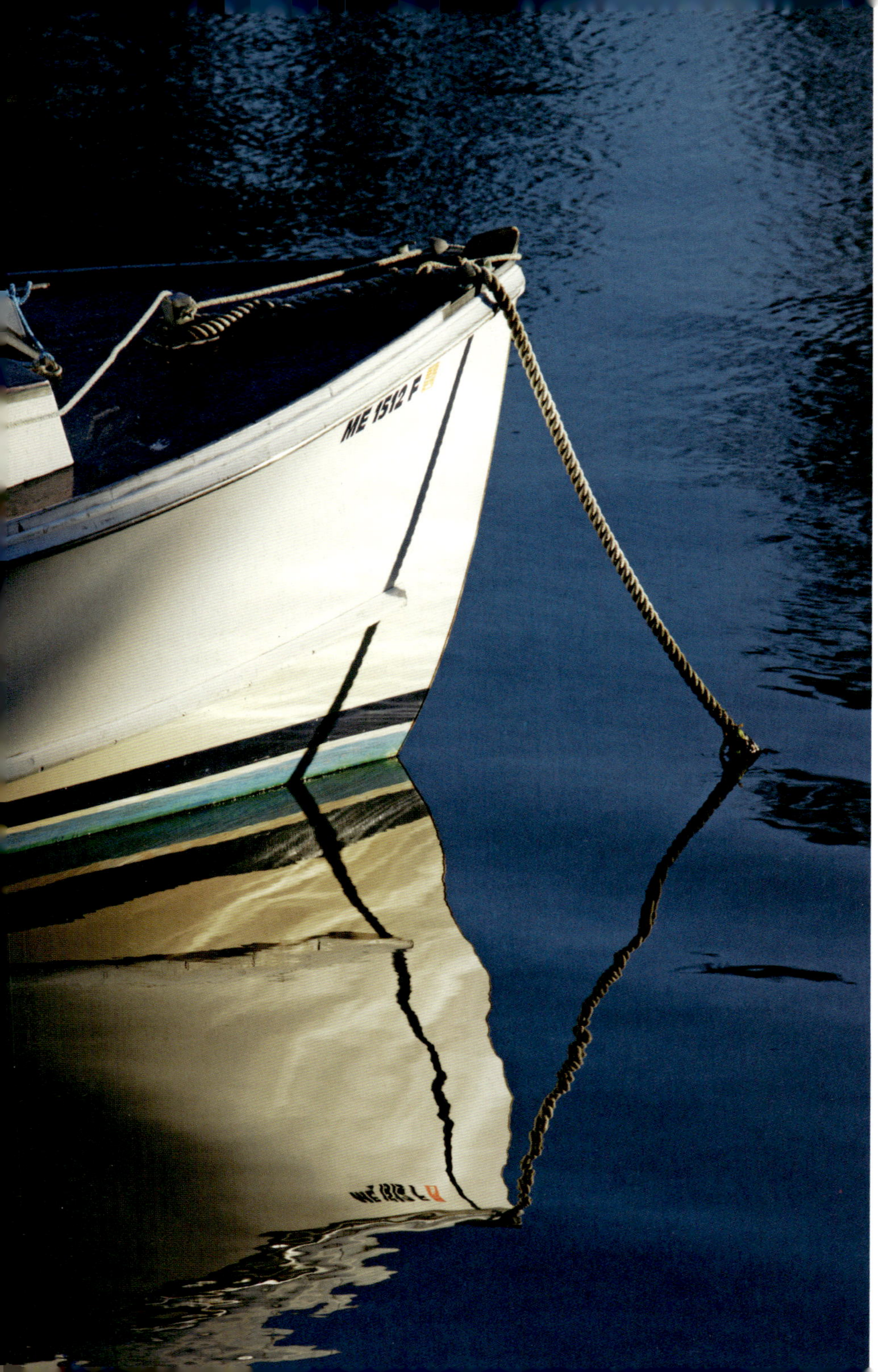

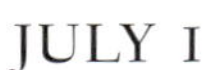

JULY 1

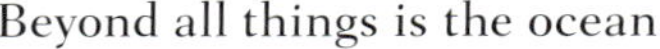

Beyond all things is the ocean.

Seneca

JULY 2

The boat sails by,
the shore remains.

Cambodian proverb

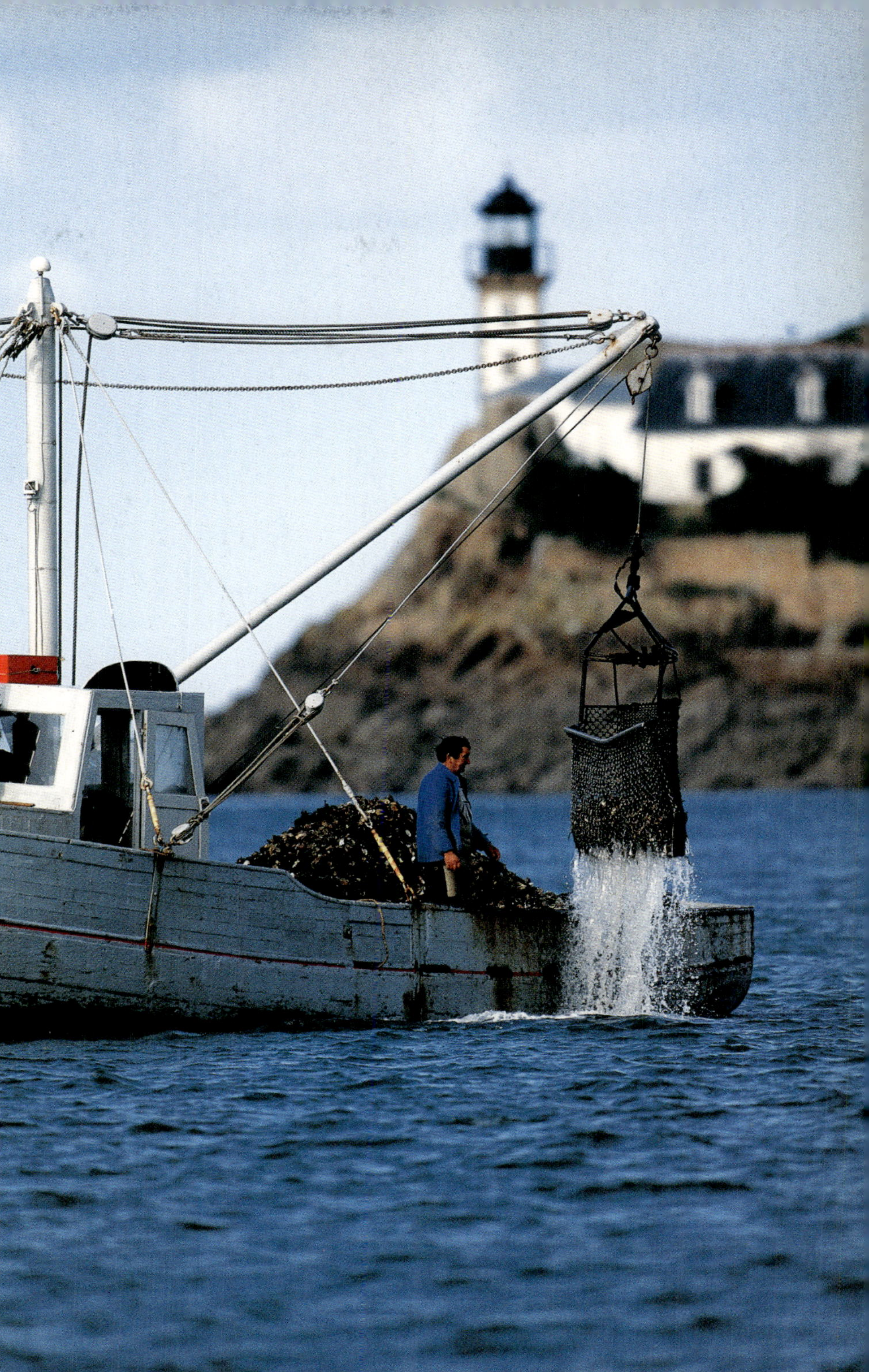

JULY 3

And biased by full sails, meridians reel,
Thy purpose—still one shore beyond desire!
The sea's green crying towers a-sway, beyond.

Hart Crane

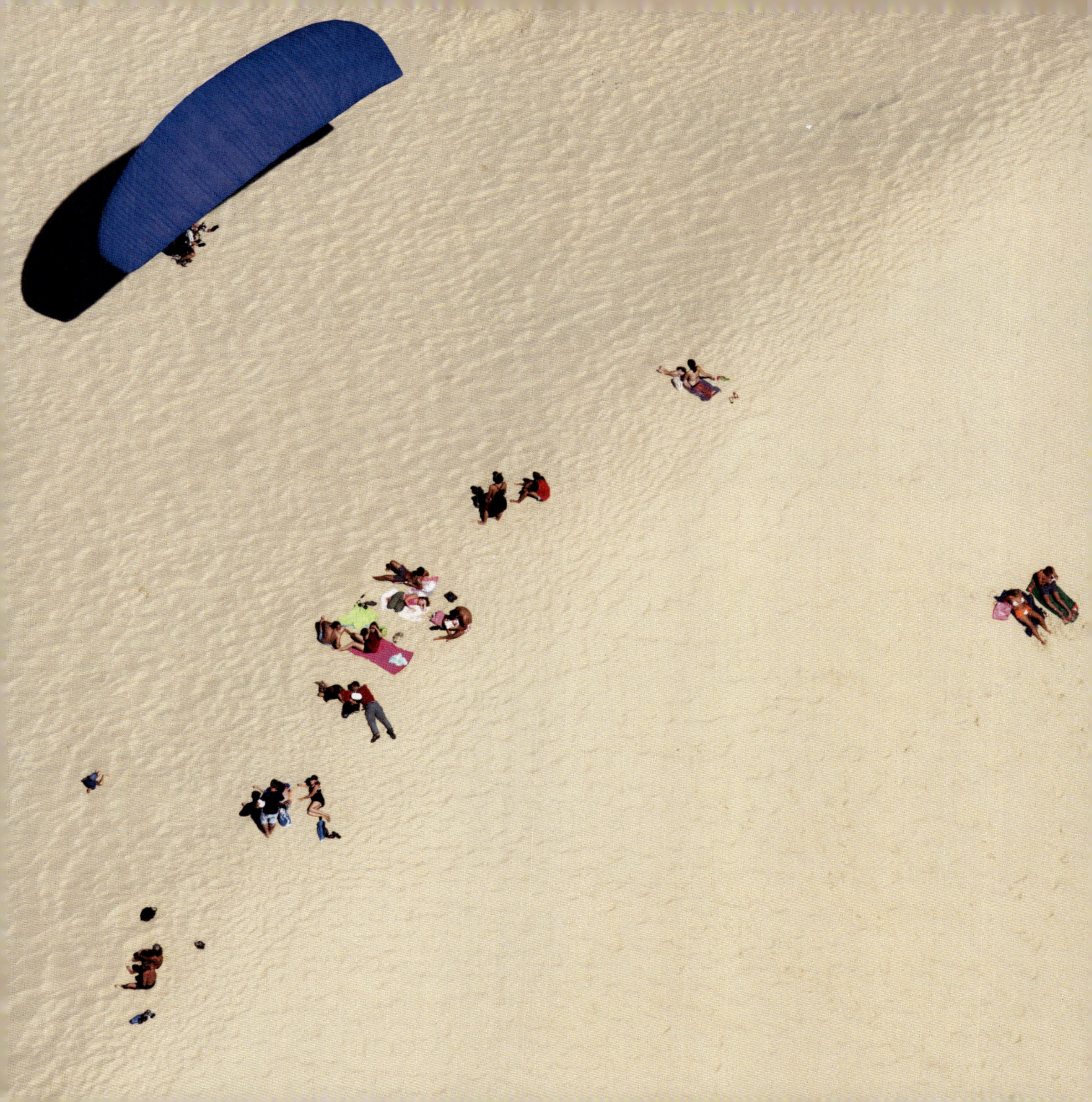

JULY 4

Behold at last,
Each tall and tapering mast,
Is swung into its place;
Shrouds and stays
Holding it firm and fast!

Henry Wadsworth Longfellow,
from "The Building of the Ship,"
The Seaside and the Fireside, 1850

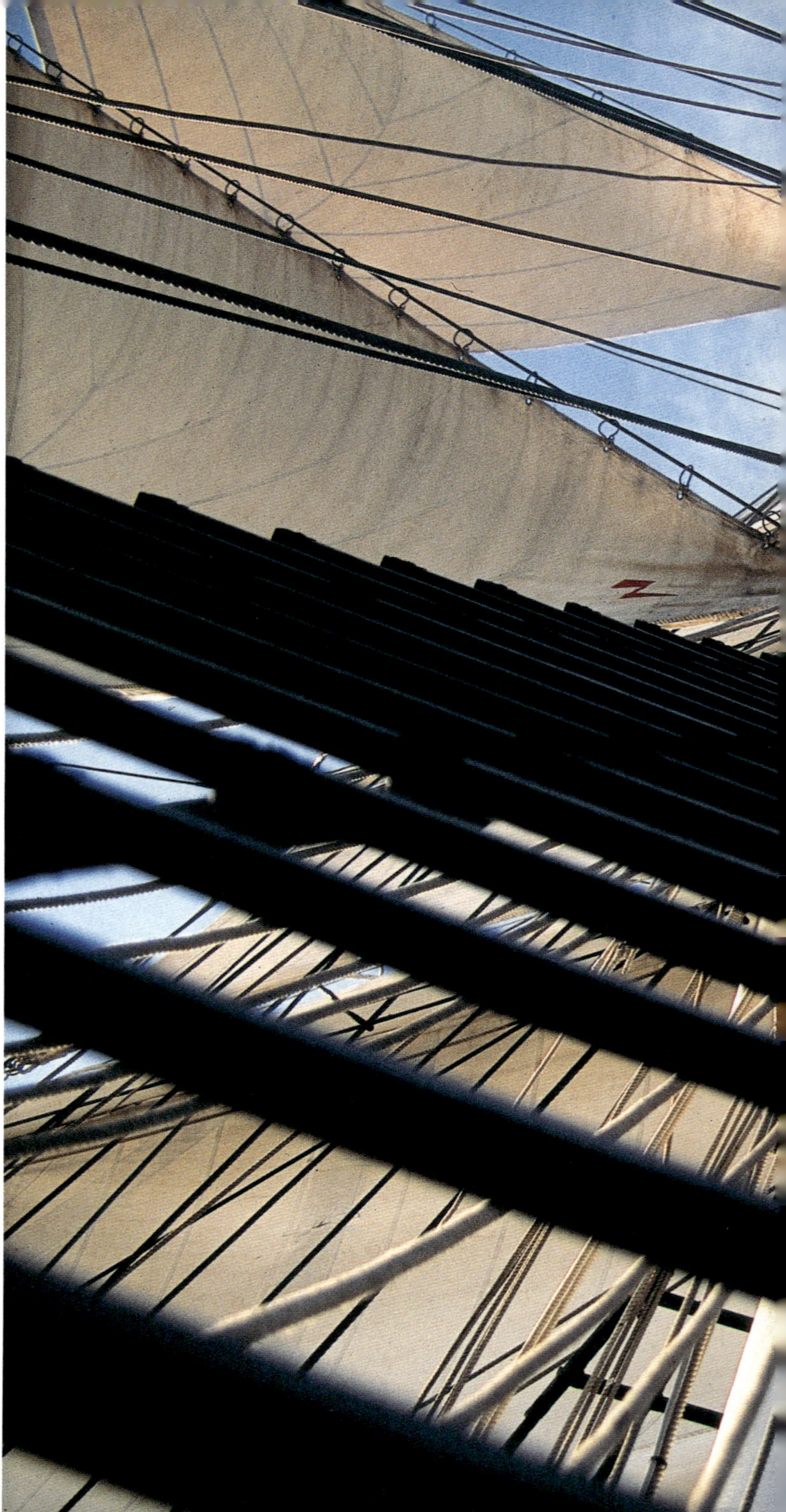

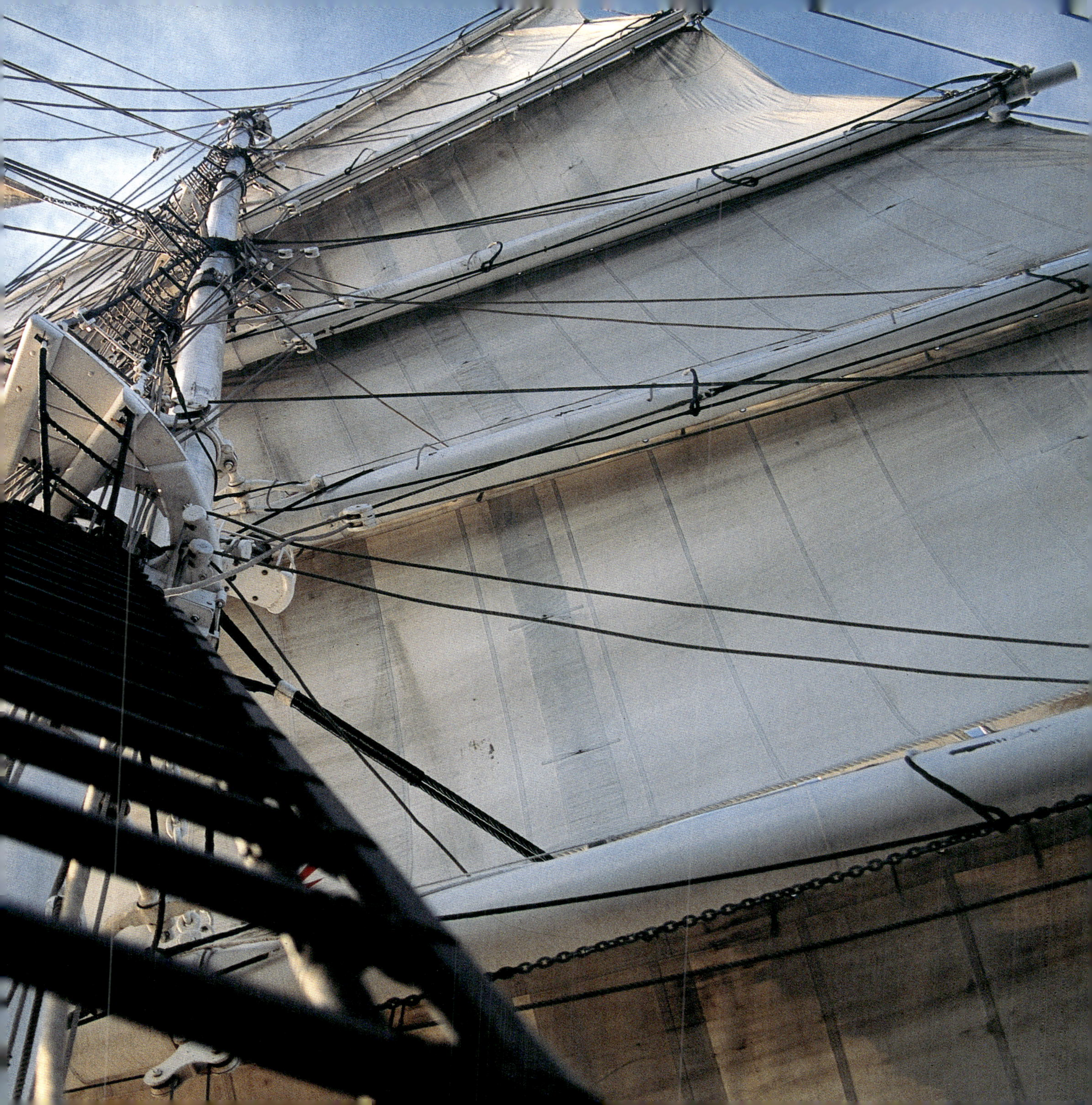

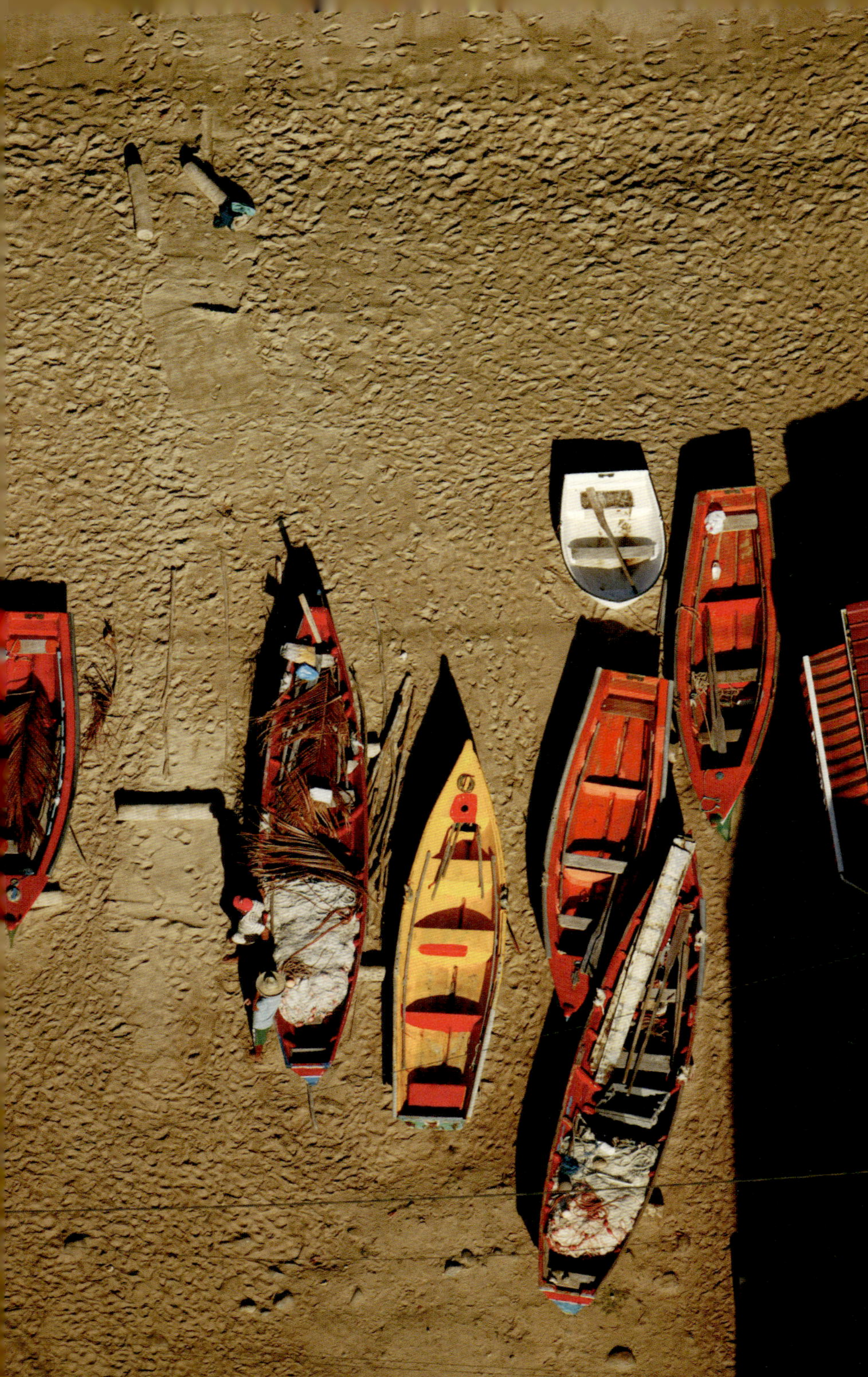

JULY 5

Water, water, everywhere,
Nor any drop to drink.

Samuel Taylor Coleridge,
from "The Rime of the Ancient Mariner," 1798

JULY 6

How happy is the sailor's life,
From coast to coast to roam;
In every port he finds a wife,
In every land a home.

Jonathan Swift
(as Isaac Bickerstaffe)

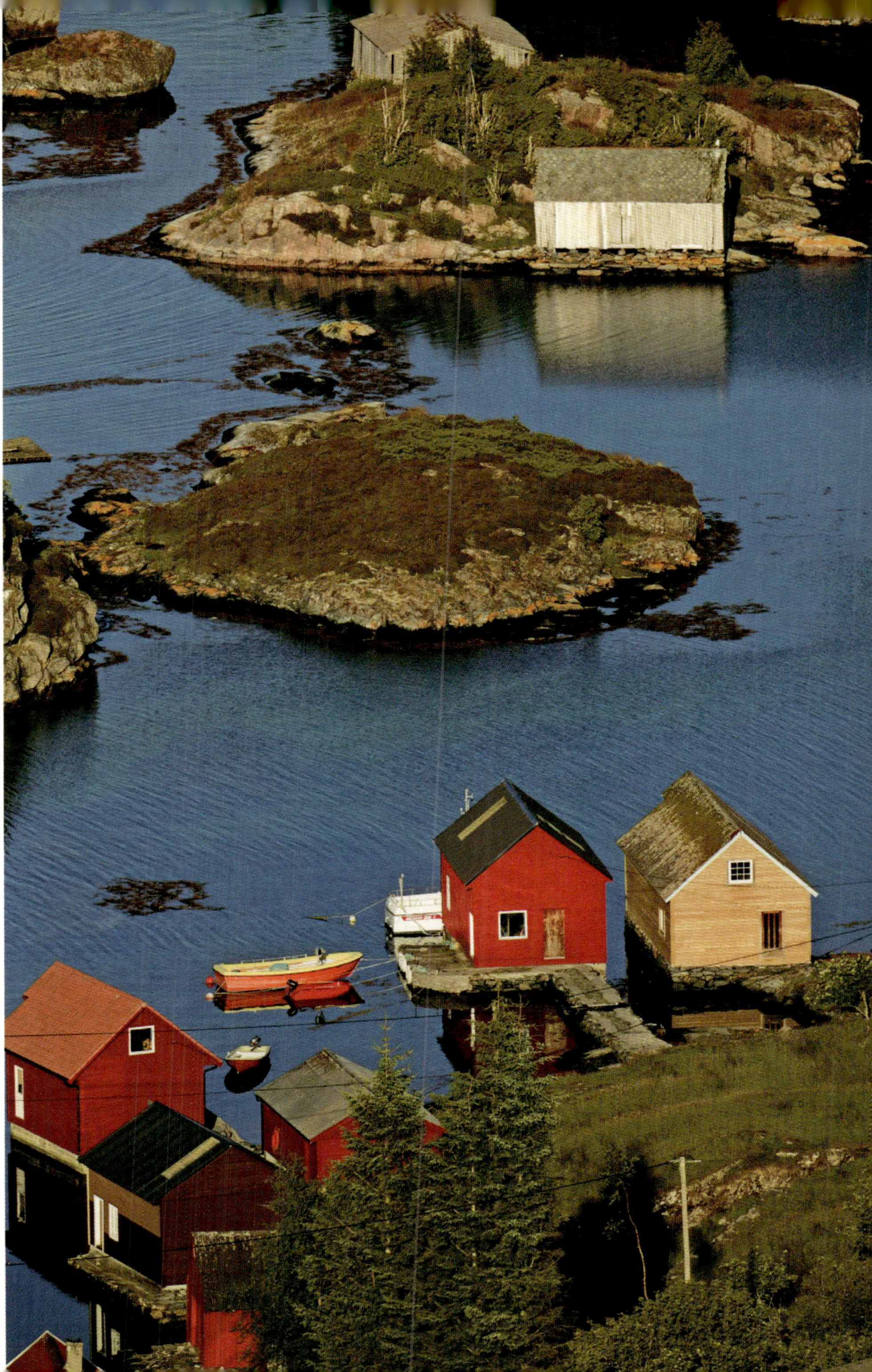

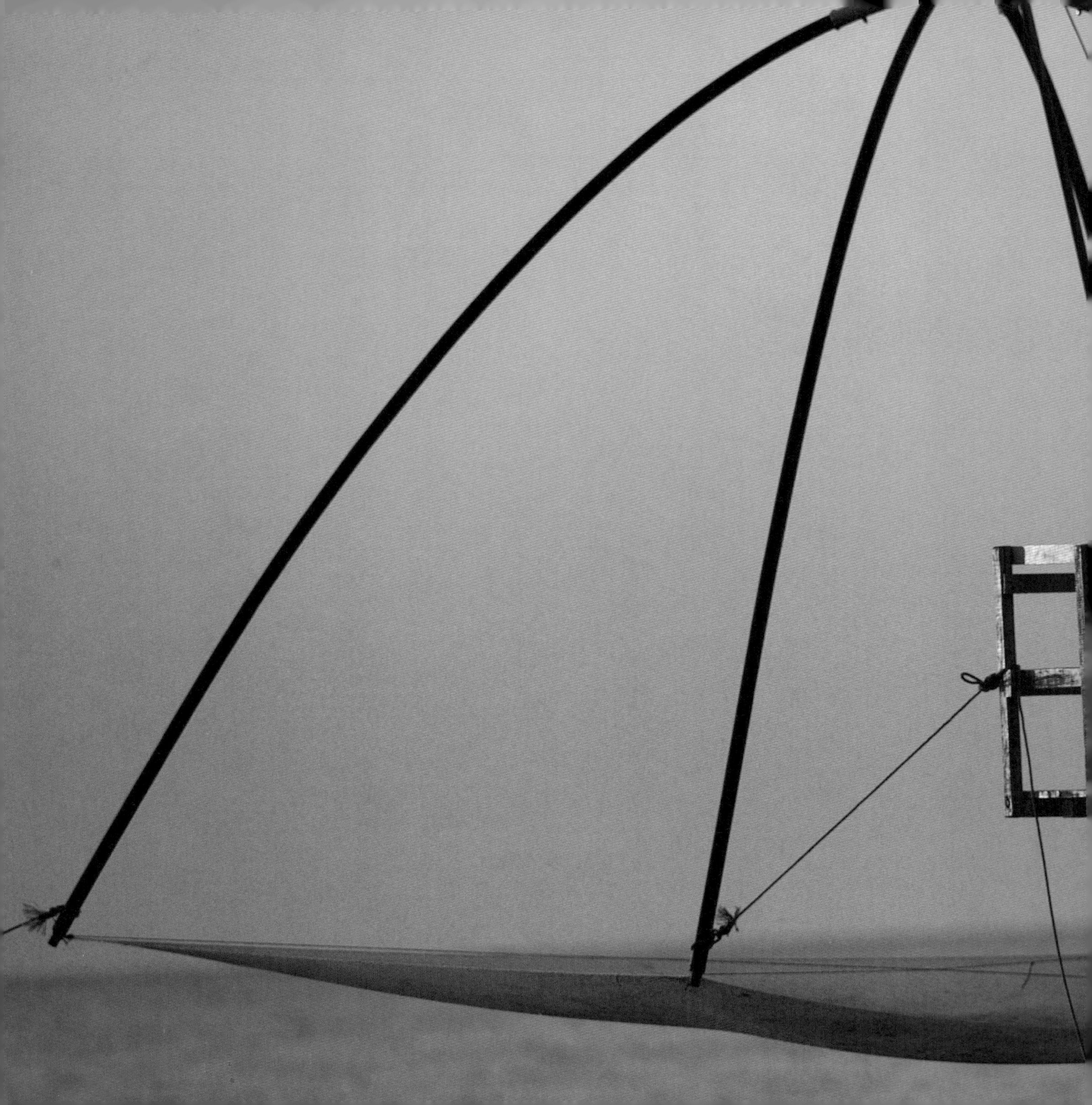

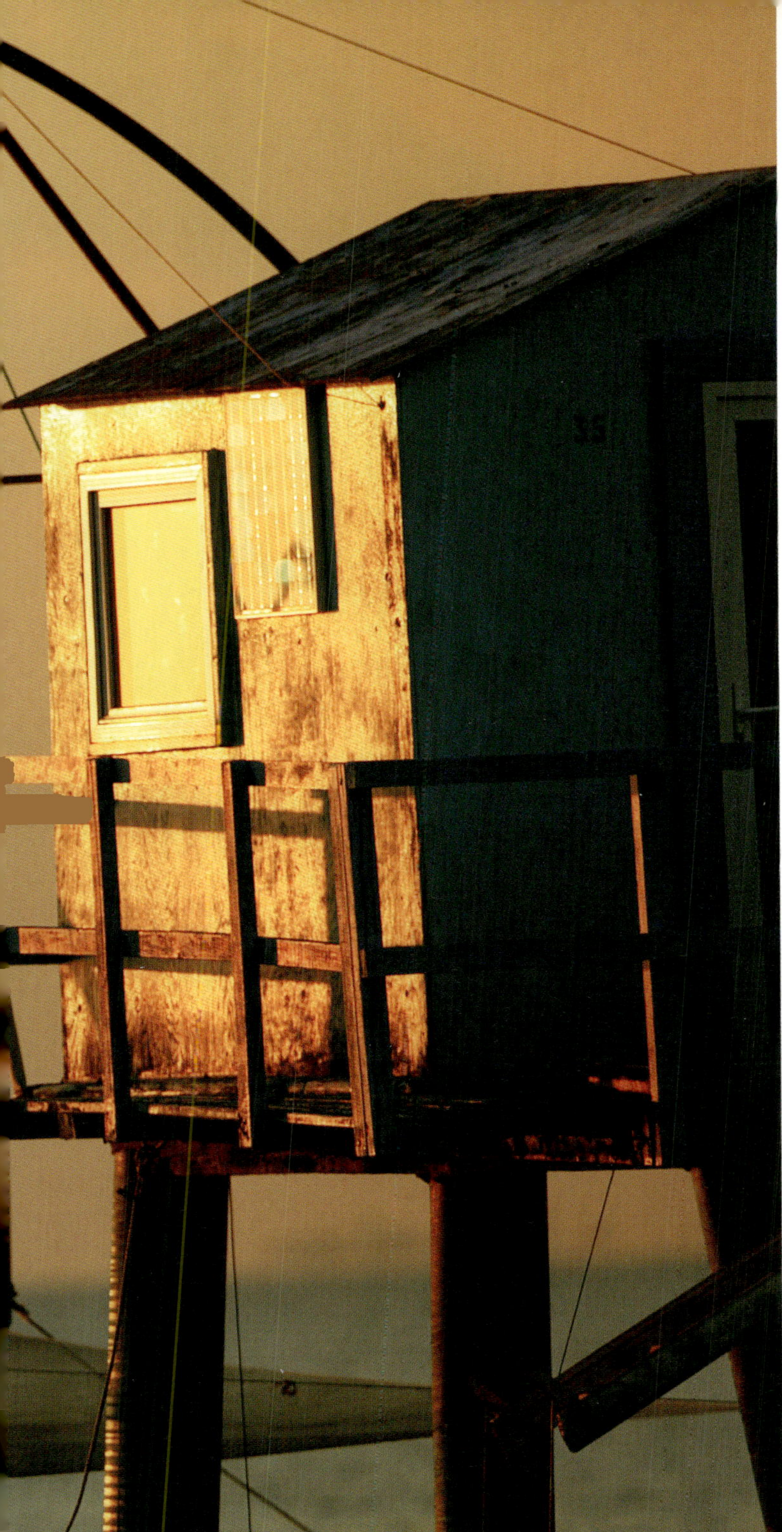

JULY 7

If I had my will I would live in a ship on the sea, and never come nearer to humanity than that!

Eleonora Duse

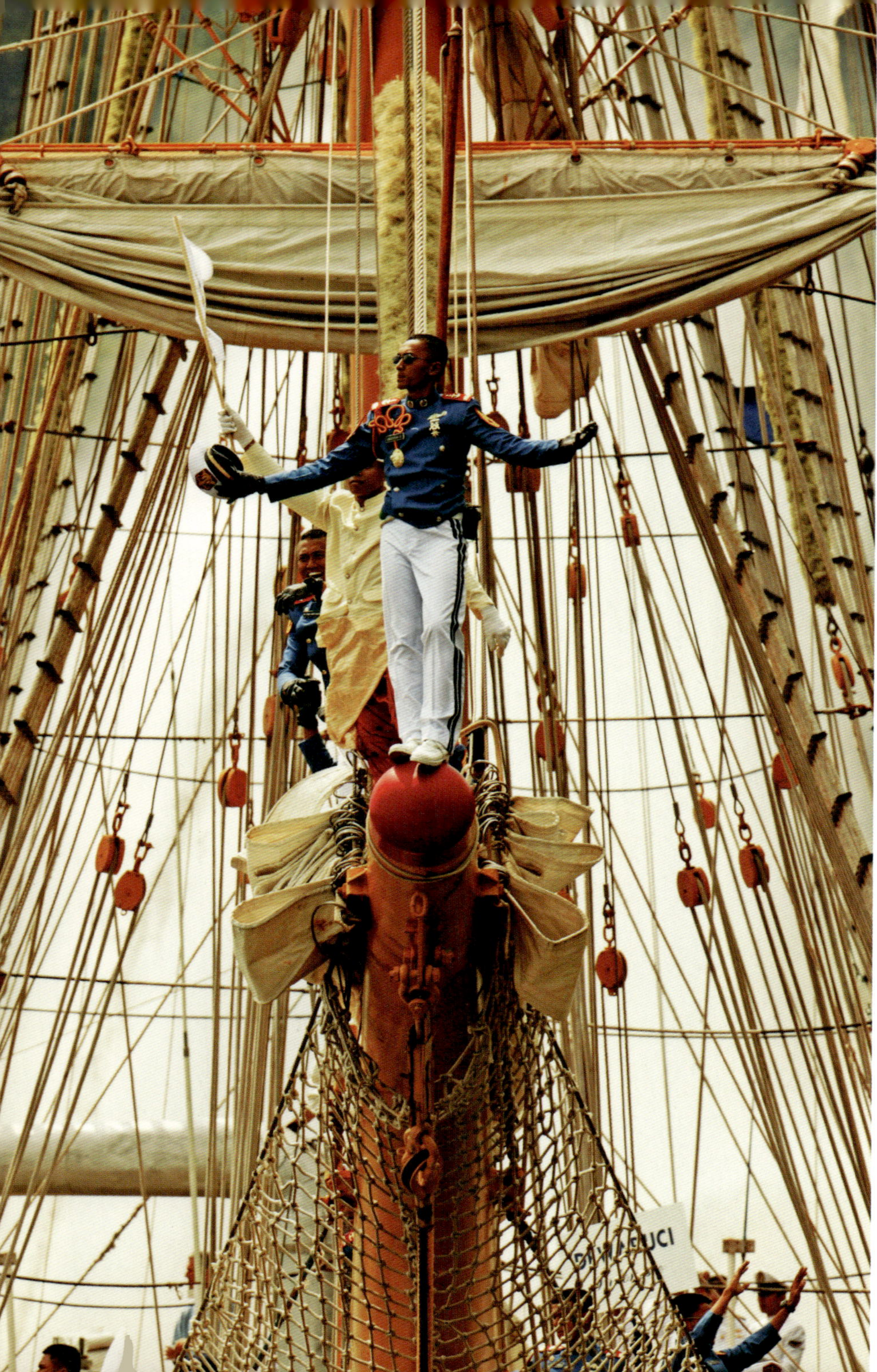

JULY 8

He that is embarked with the
devil must sail with him.

Danish proverb

JULY 9

Heave or sink it, leave or drink it,
we were masters of the sea!

Rudyard Kipling,
from "The Last Chantey," 1892

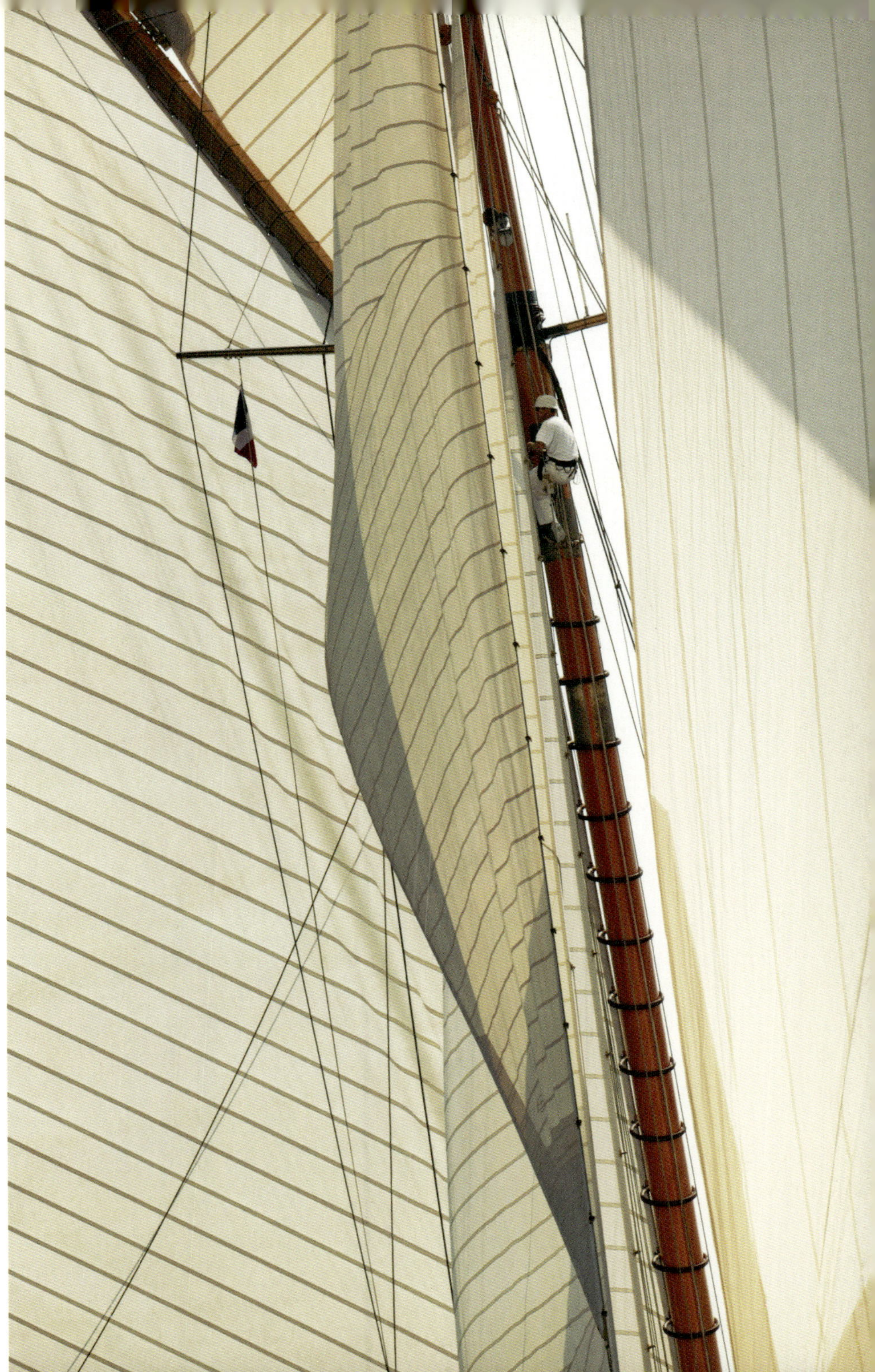

JULY 10

Merchant and pirate were for a long period one and the same person.

Friedrich Nietzsche

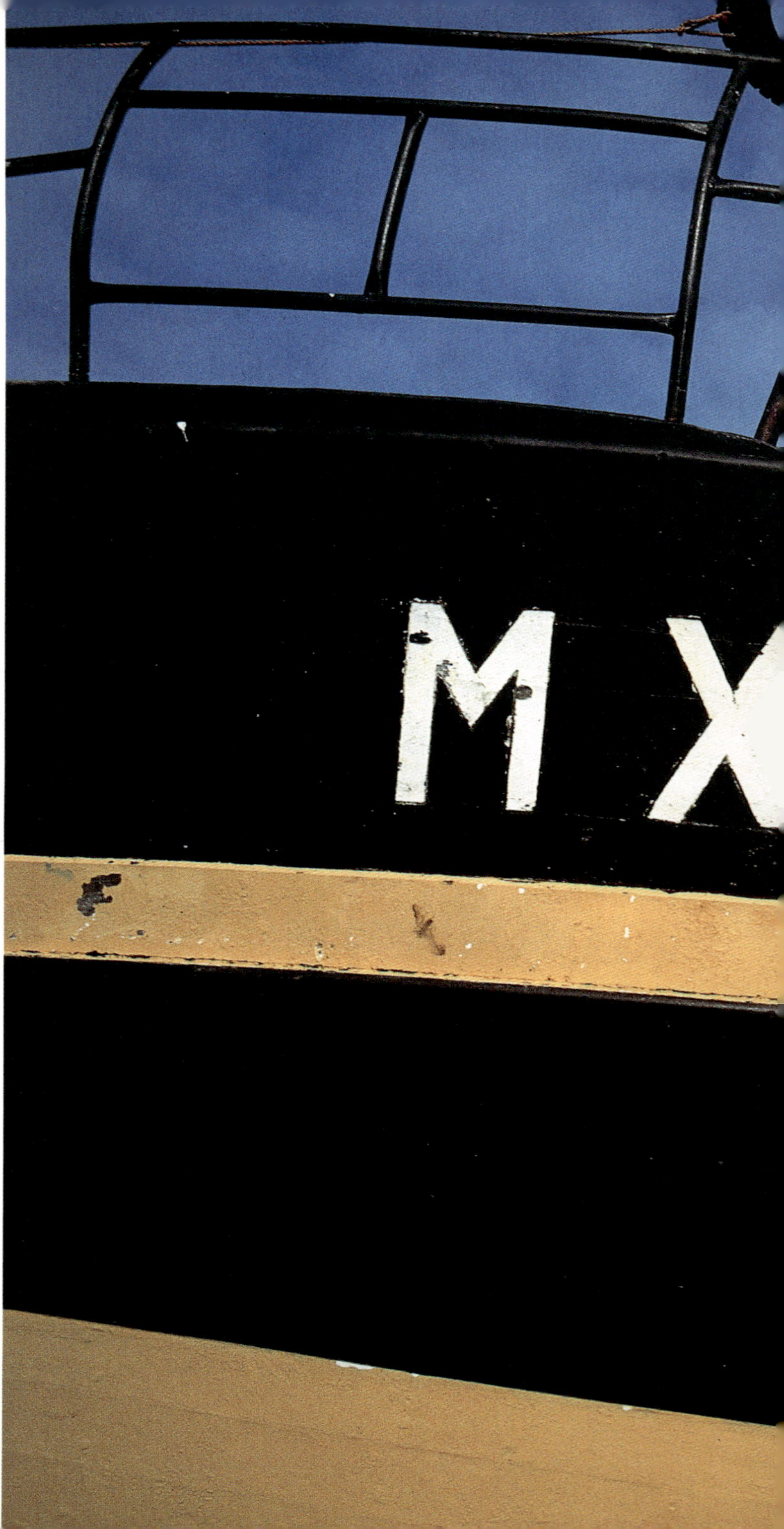

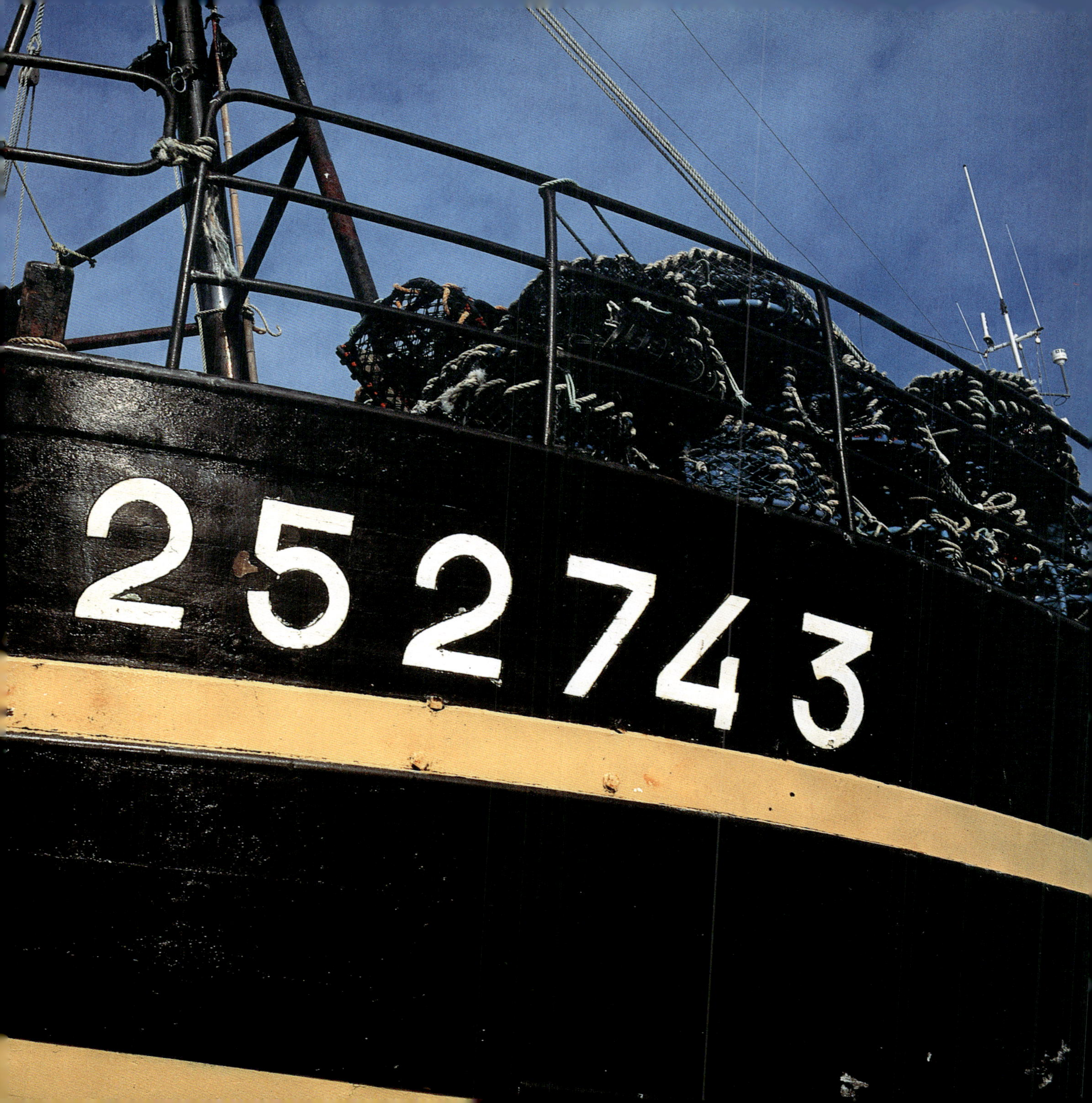

252743

JULY 11

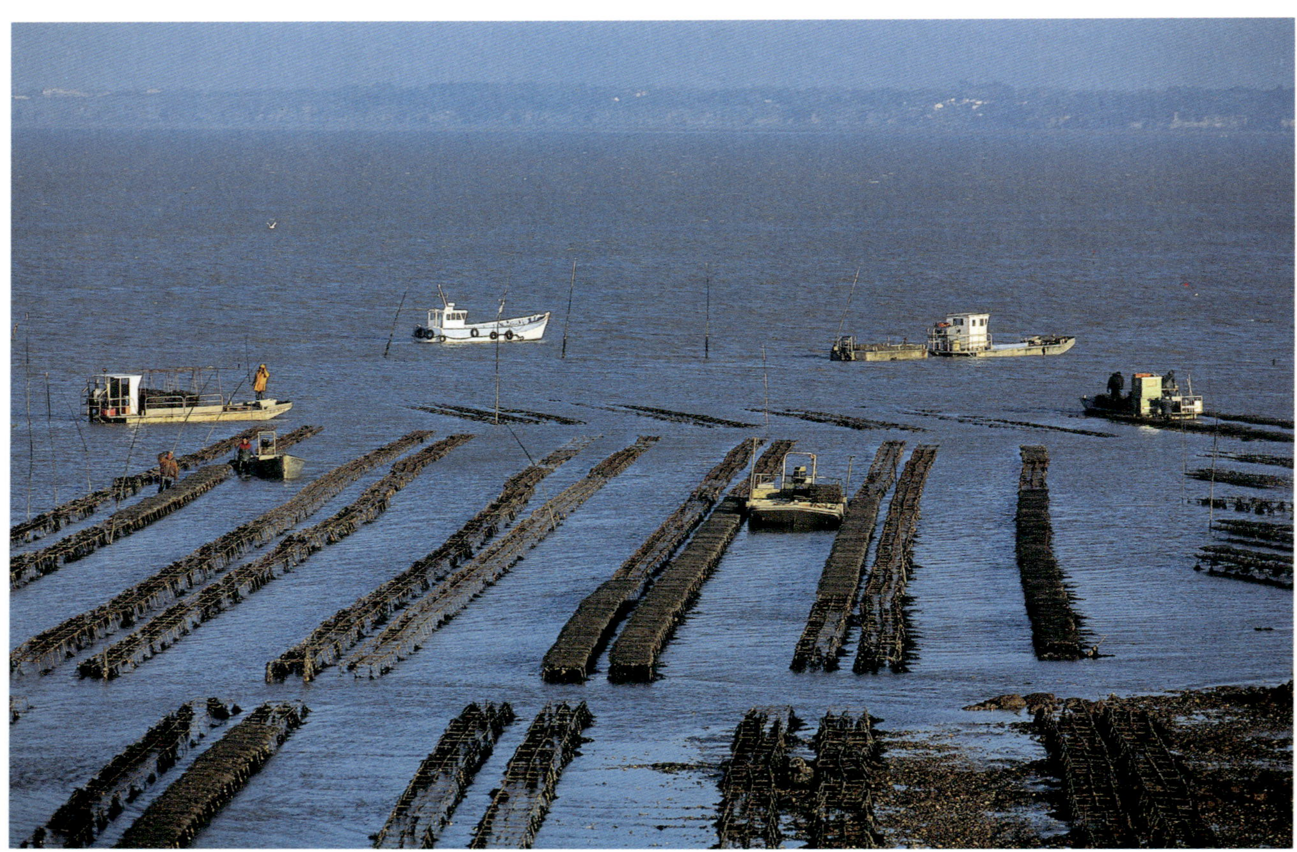

A man is no sailor if he cannot sleep when he turns-in, and turn out when he's called.

Richard Henry Dana Jr., from *Two Years Before the Mast,* 1840

JULY 12

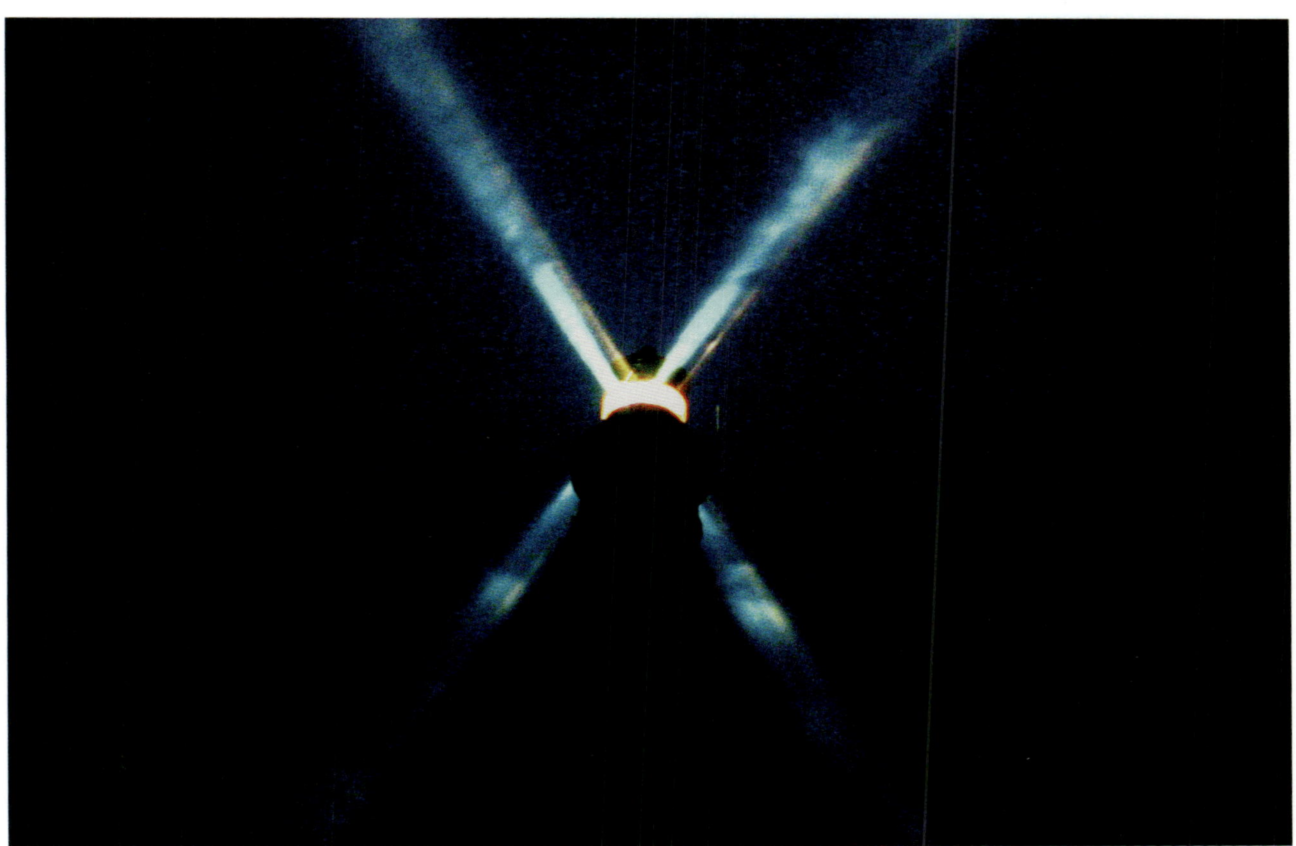

Strong winds, the bane of ships, are borne of the night.

Homer, from *The Odyssey*

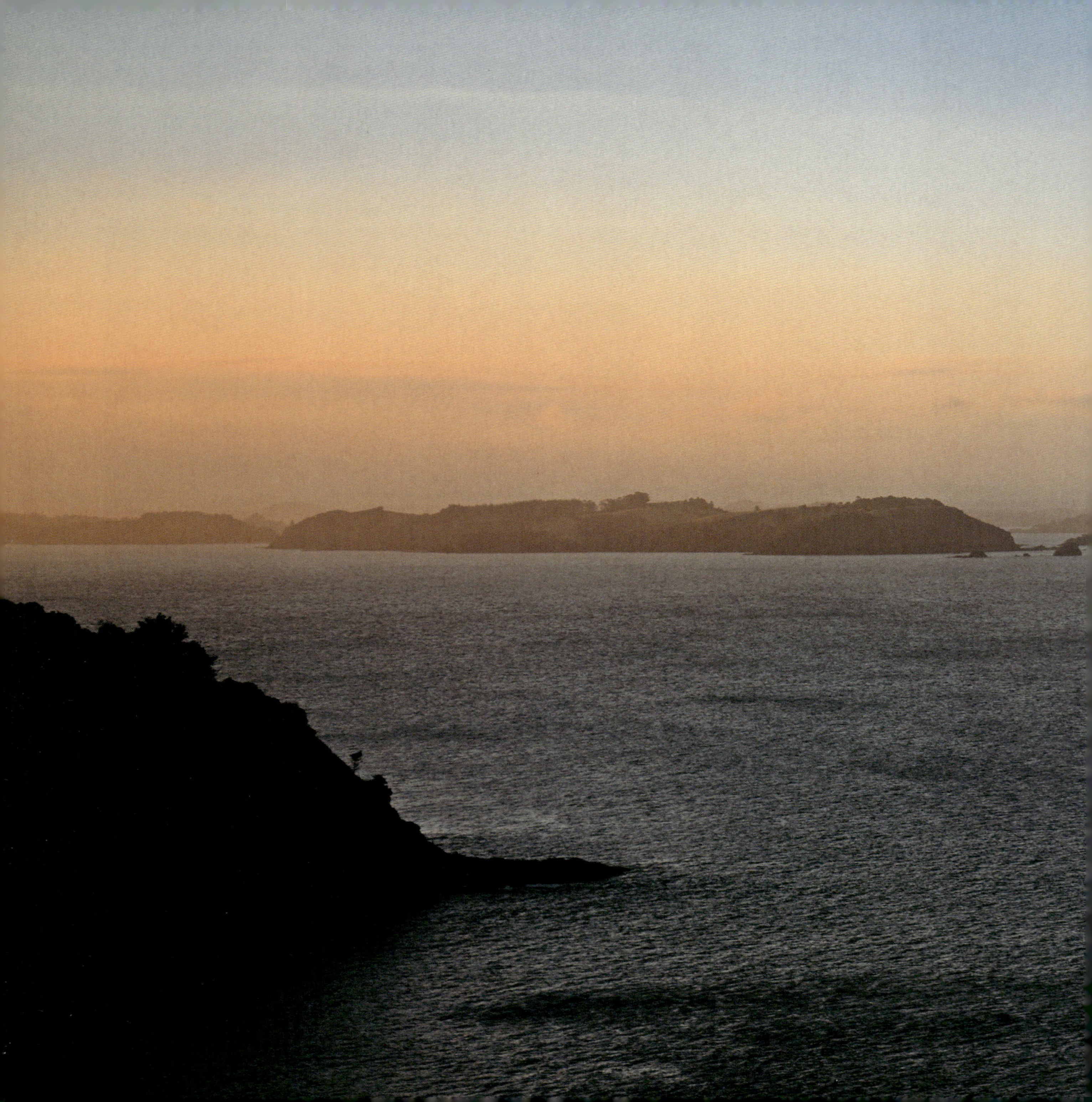

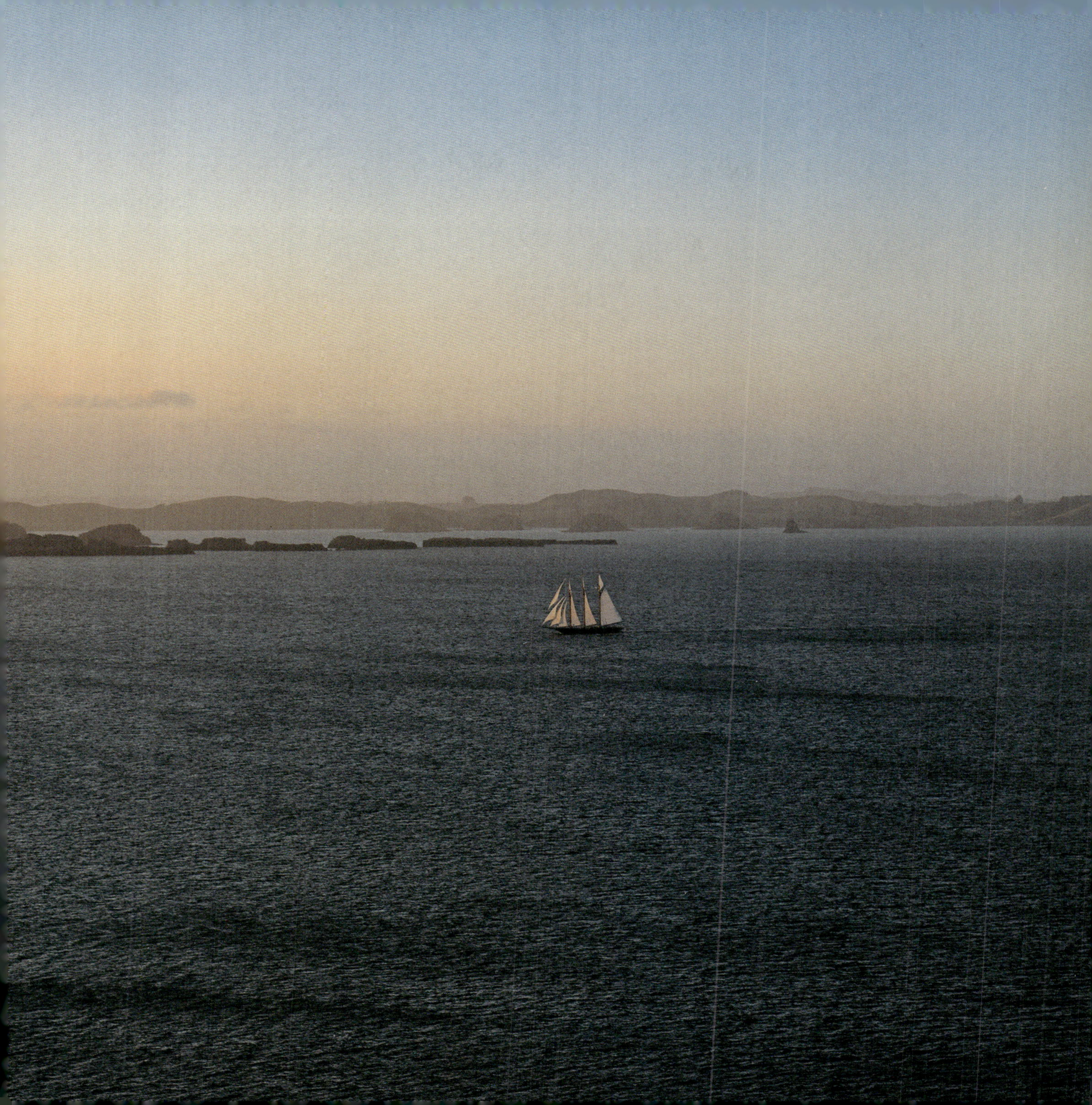

JULY 13

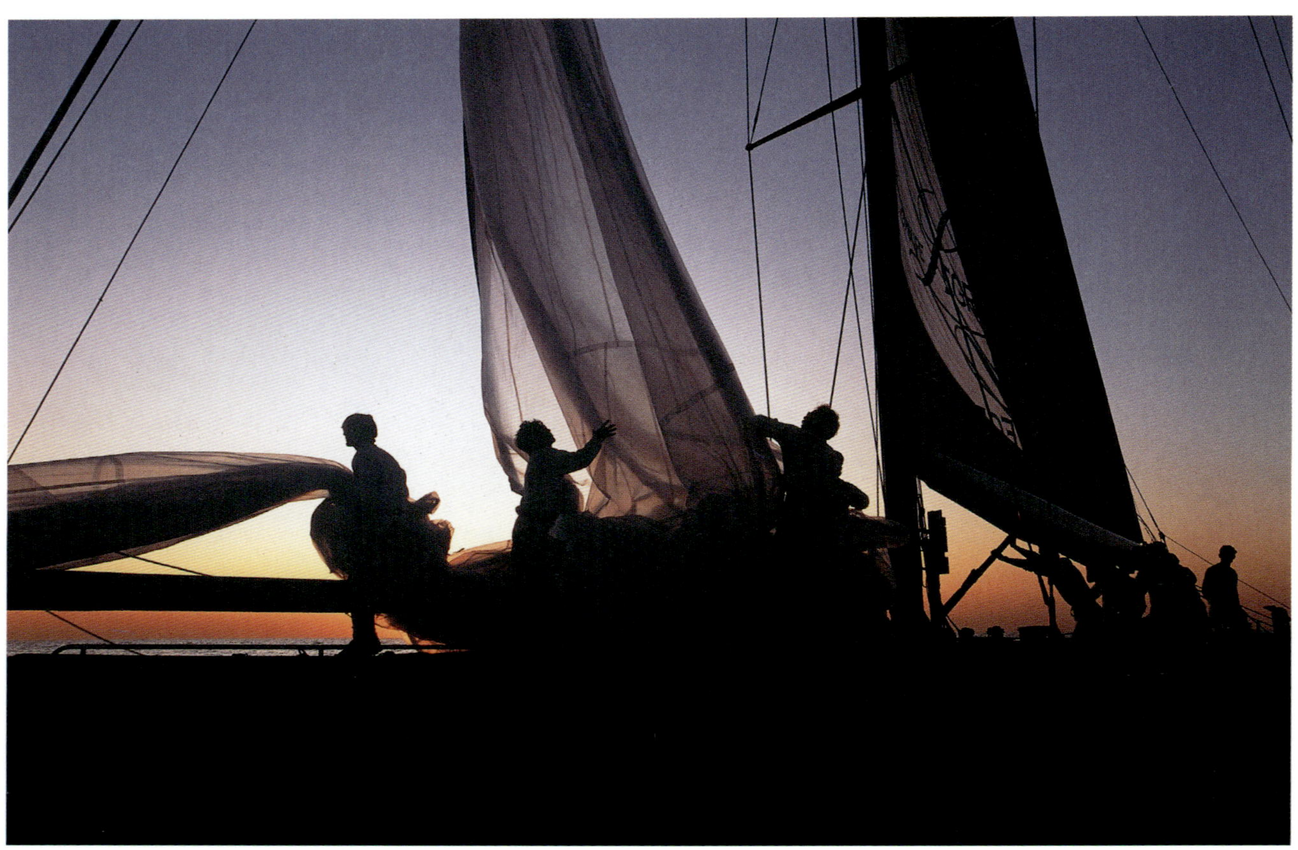

Oh, was there ever sailor free to choose
That didn't settle somewhere near the sea?

Rudyard Kipling, from "The Virginity," 1903

JULY 14

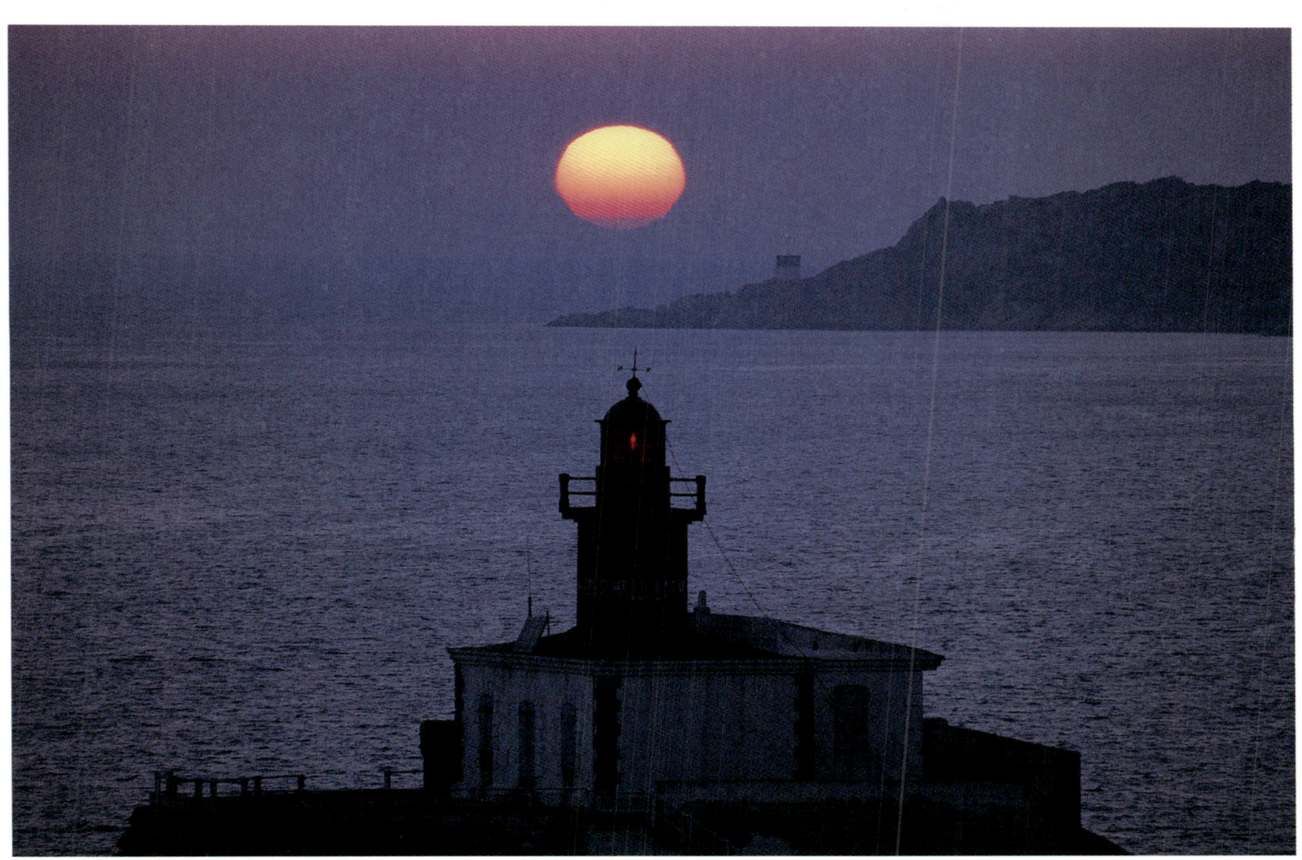

Sail how thou canst, have wind and tide thy friend.

William Shakespeare, *Henry VI,* Part III, Act V, Scene 1

JULY 15

If you look seaward, Traveller, you will see
a spectre rise and hear it sing, "Stop, here,
and eat my lotus flowers, here's where they're sold.

Charles Baudelaire,
from "The Voyage," *Les Fleurs du mal,* 1857

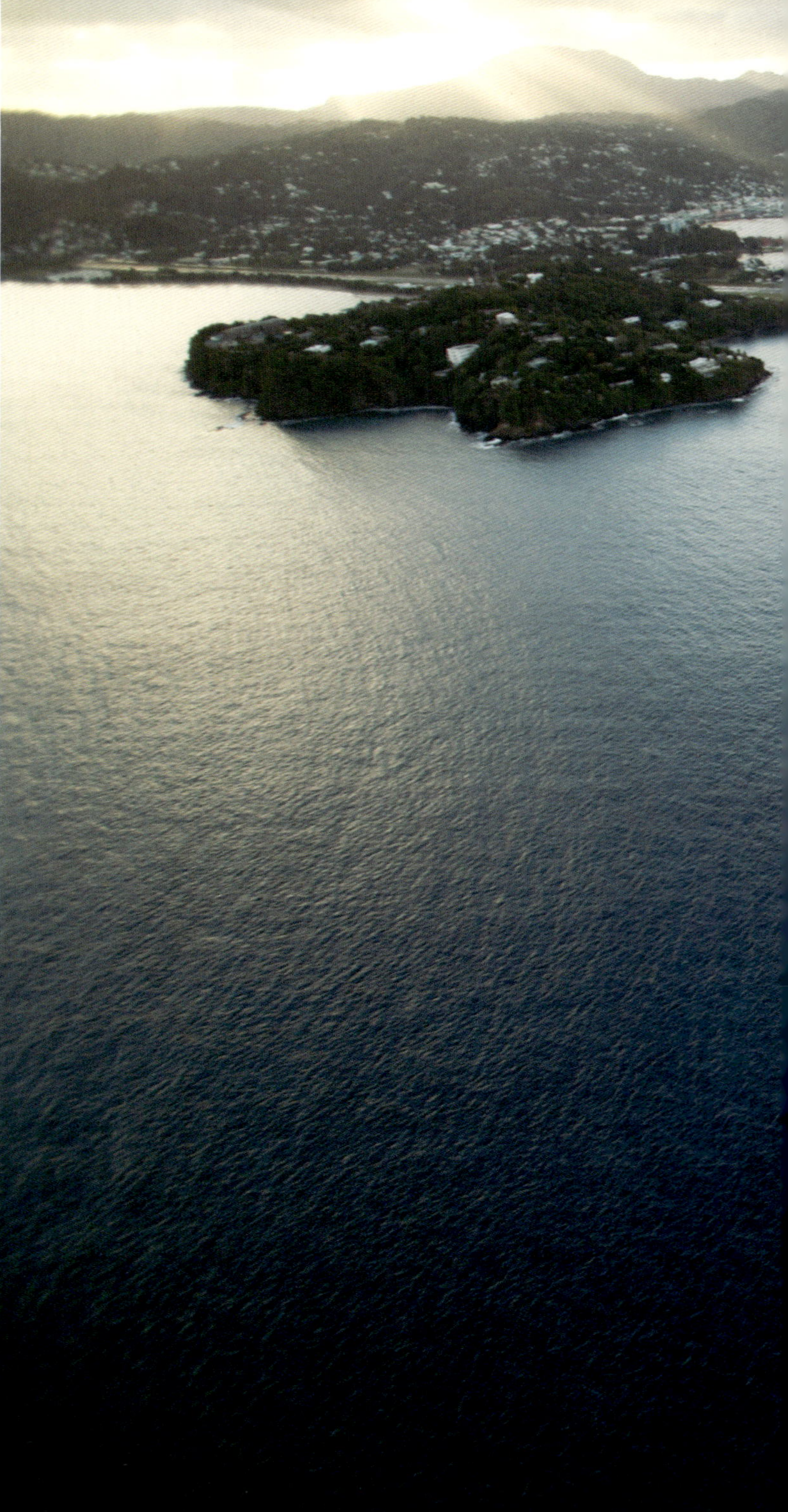

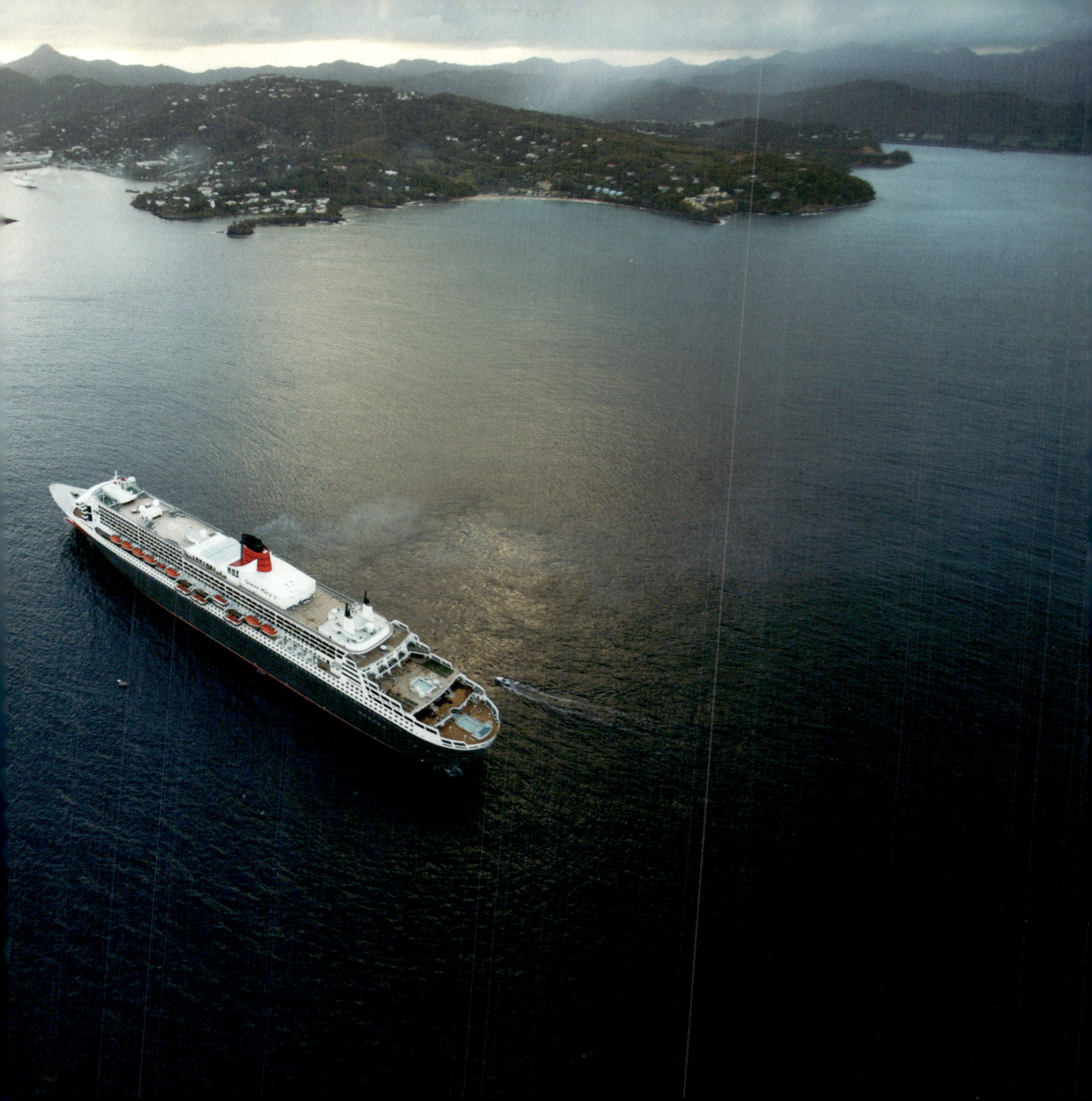

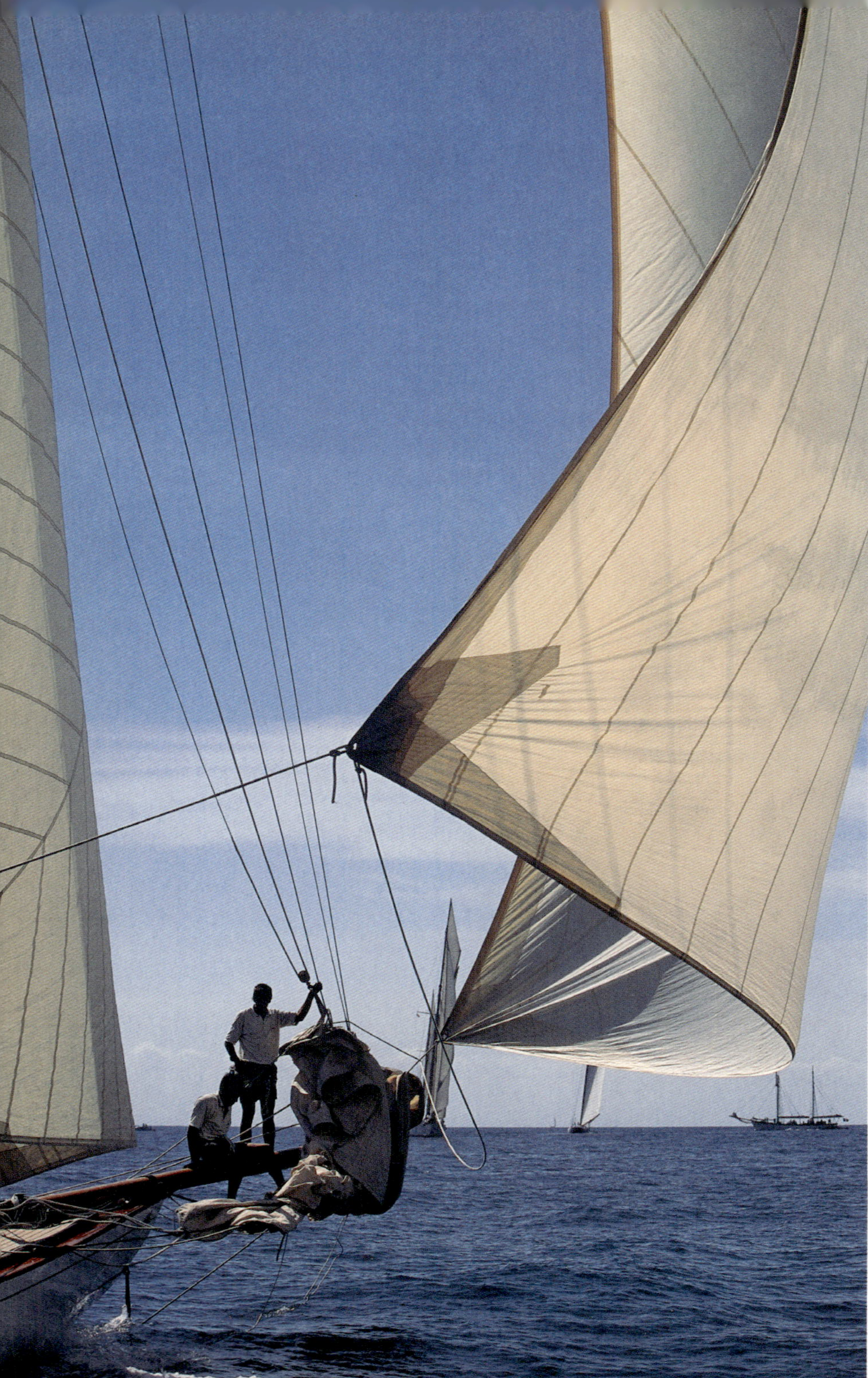

JULY 16

A knot is never "nearly right";
it is either exactly right or it is
hopelessly wrong, one or the
other; there is no in between.

Clifford Ashley,
from *The Ashley Book of Knots,* 1944

JULY 17

Smooth seas do not
make skillful sailors.

African proverb

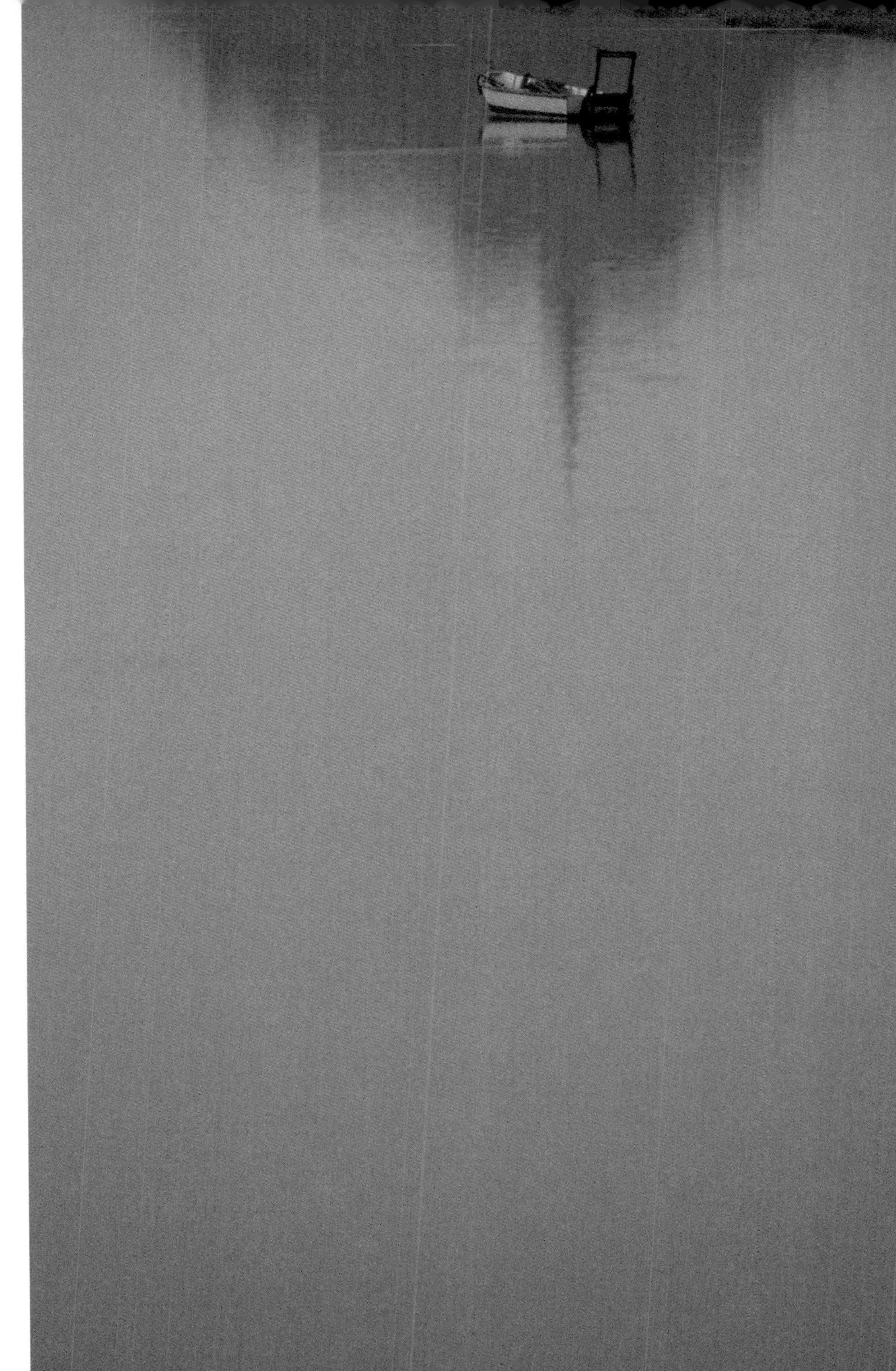

JULY 18

You have heard the beat of the off-shore wind
And the thresh of the deep-sea rain;
You have heard the song—how long! how long!
Pull out on the trail again.

Rudyard Kipling,
from "L'Envoi," 1892

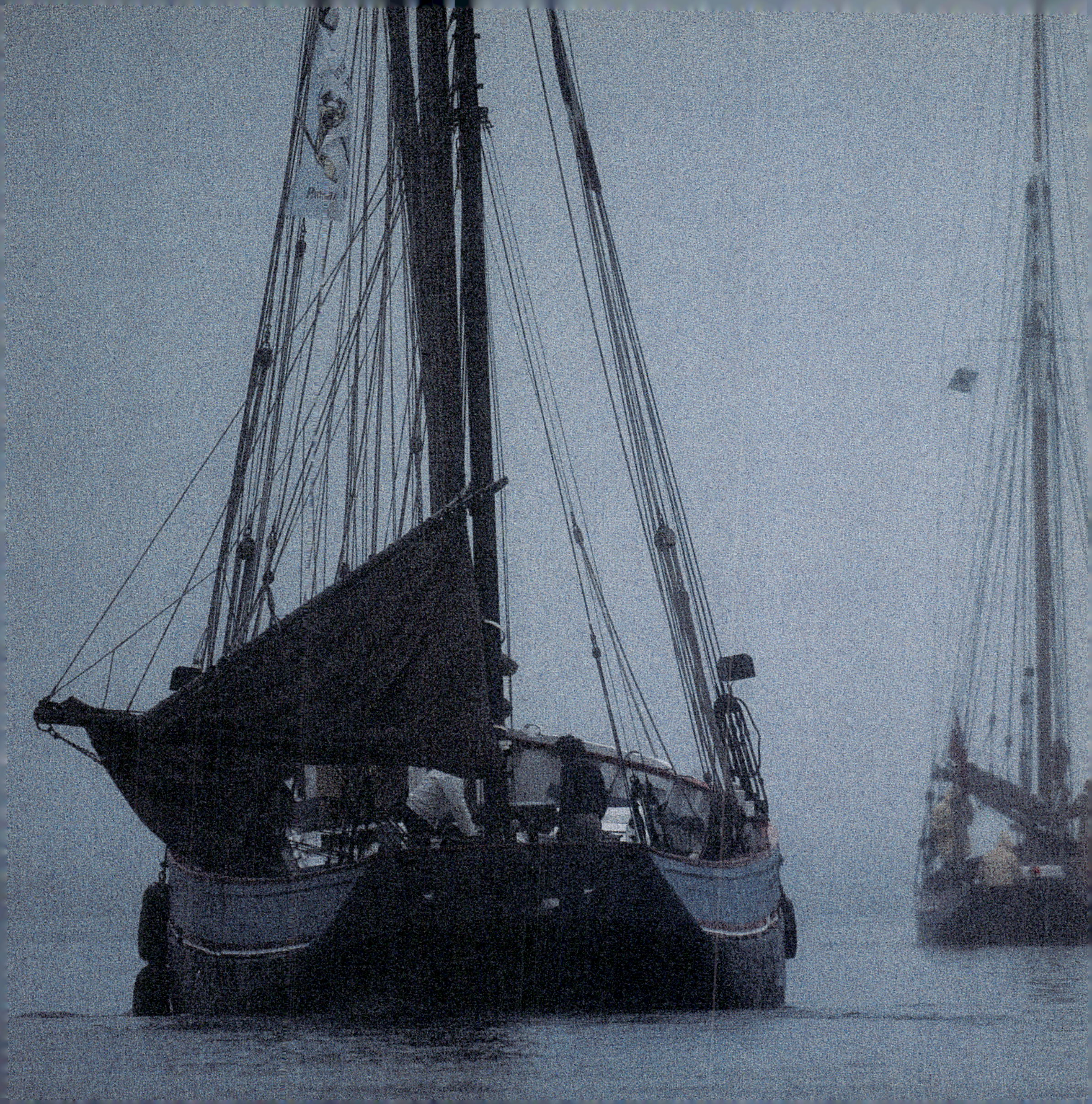

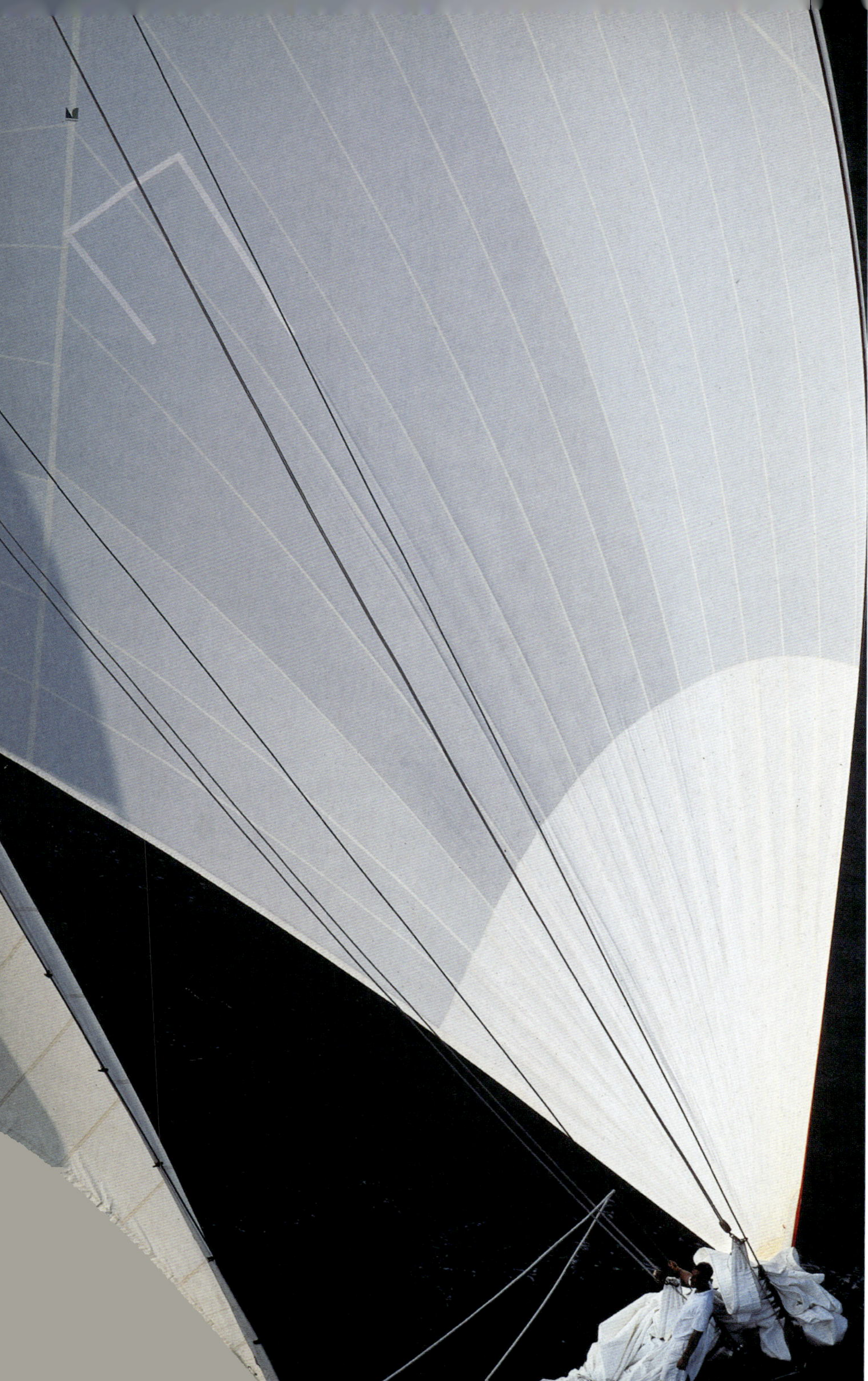

JULY 19

Navigation is essential; life is not.

Hanseatic proverb

JULY 20

Surely oak and threefold brass
surrounded his heart
who first trusted a frail vessel to
the merciless ocean.

Horace, from *Odes,* 23 BC

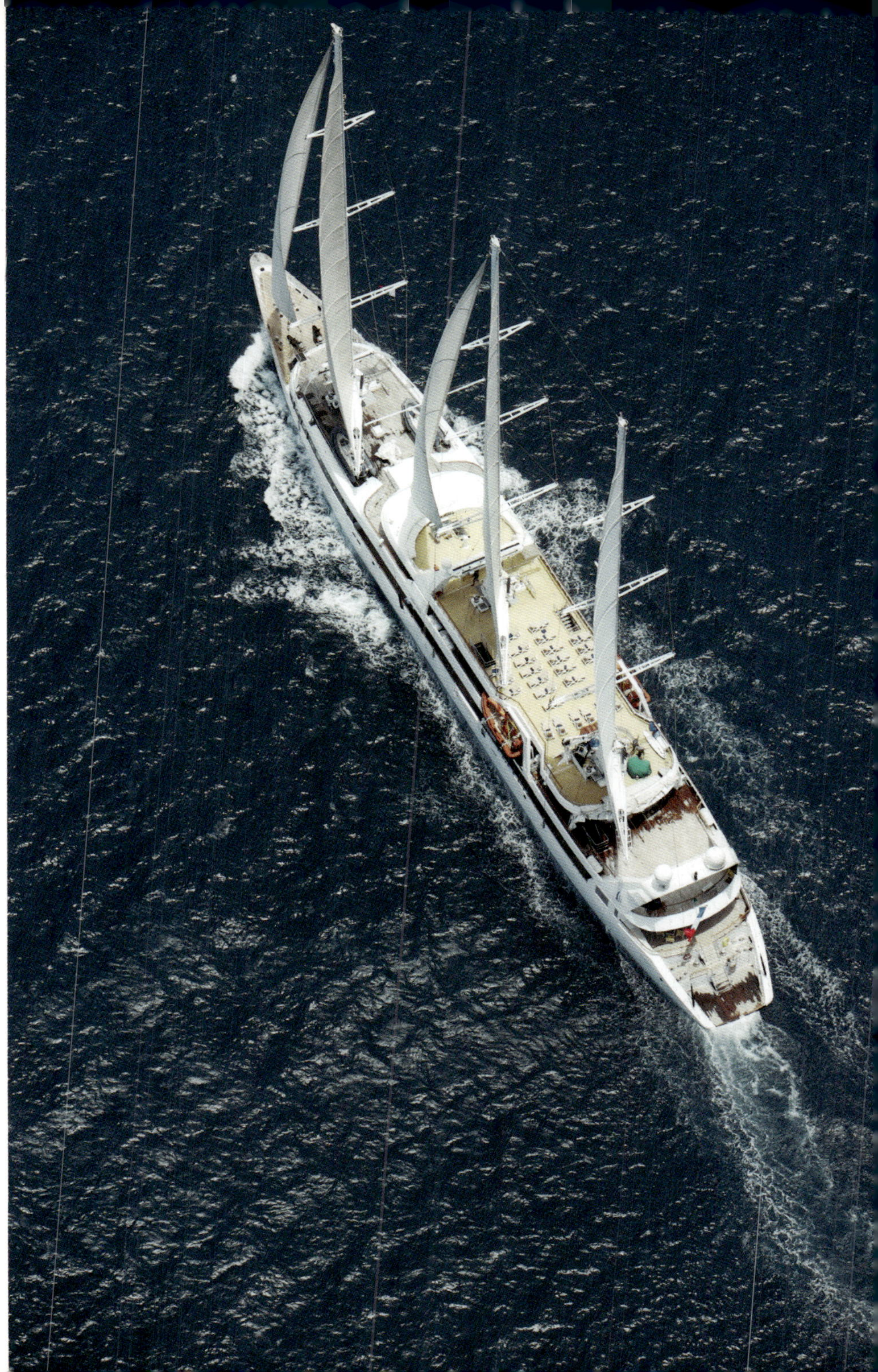

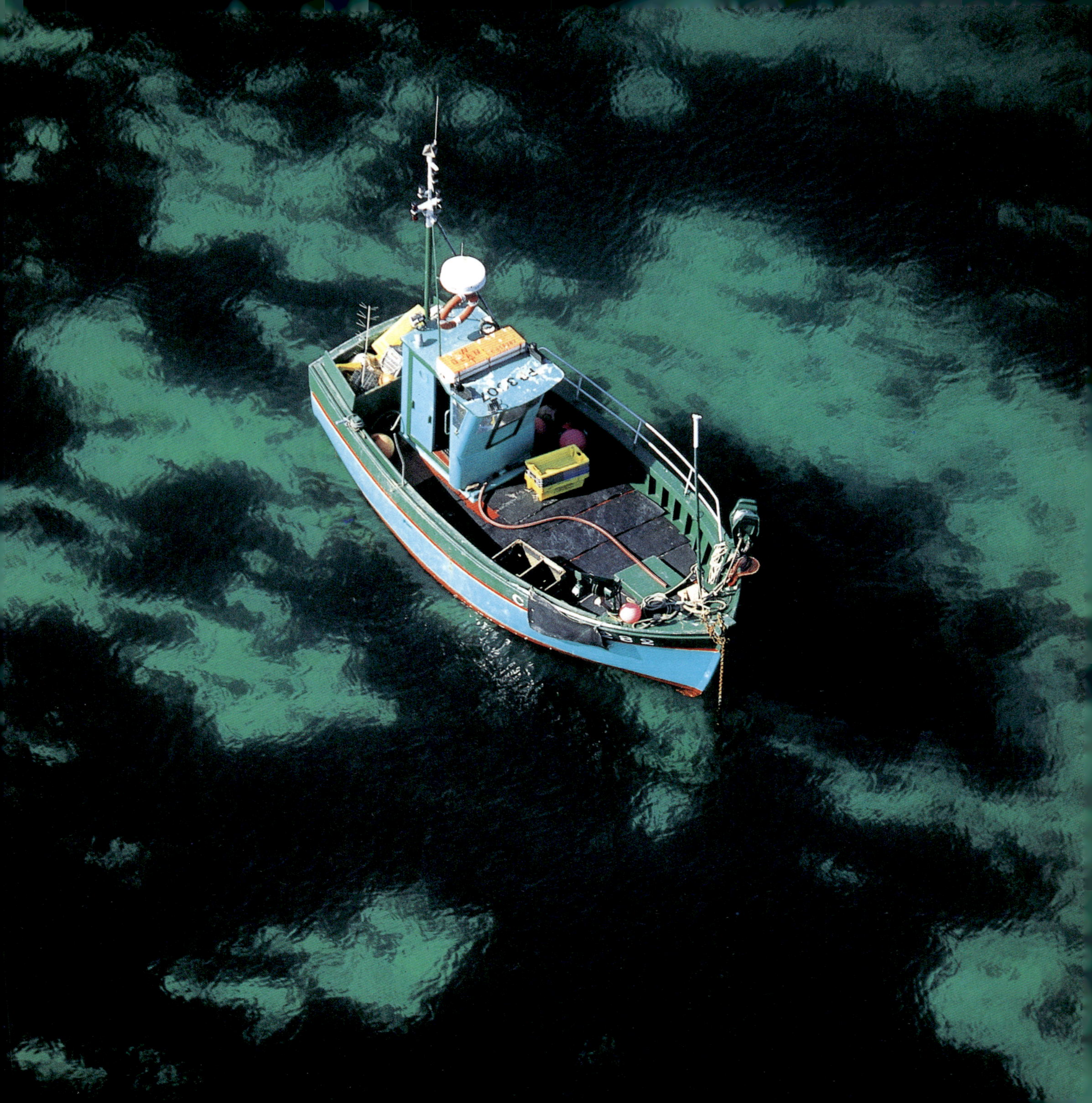

JULY 21

All the earth's full rivers cannot fill
The sea, that drinking, thirsteth still.

Christina Rossetti,
from "By the Sea," 1862

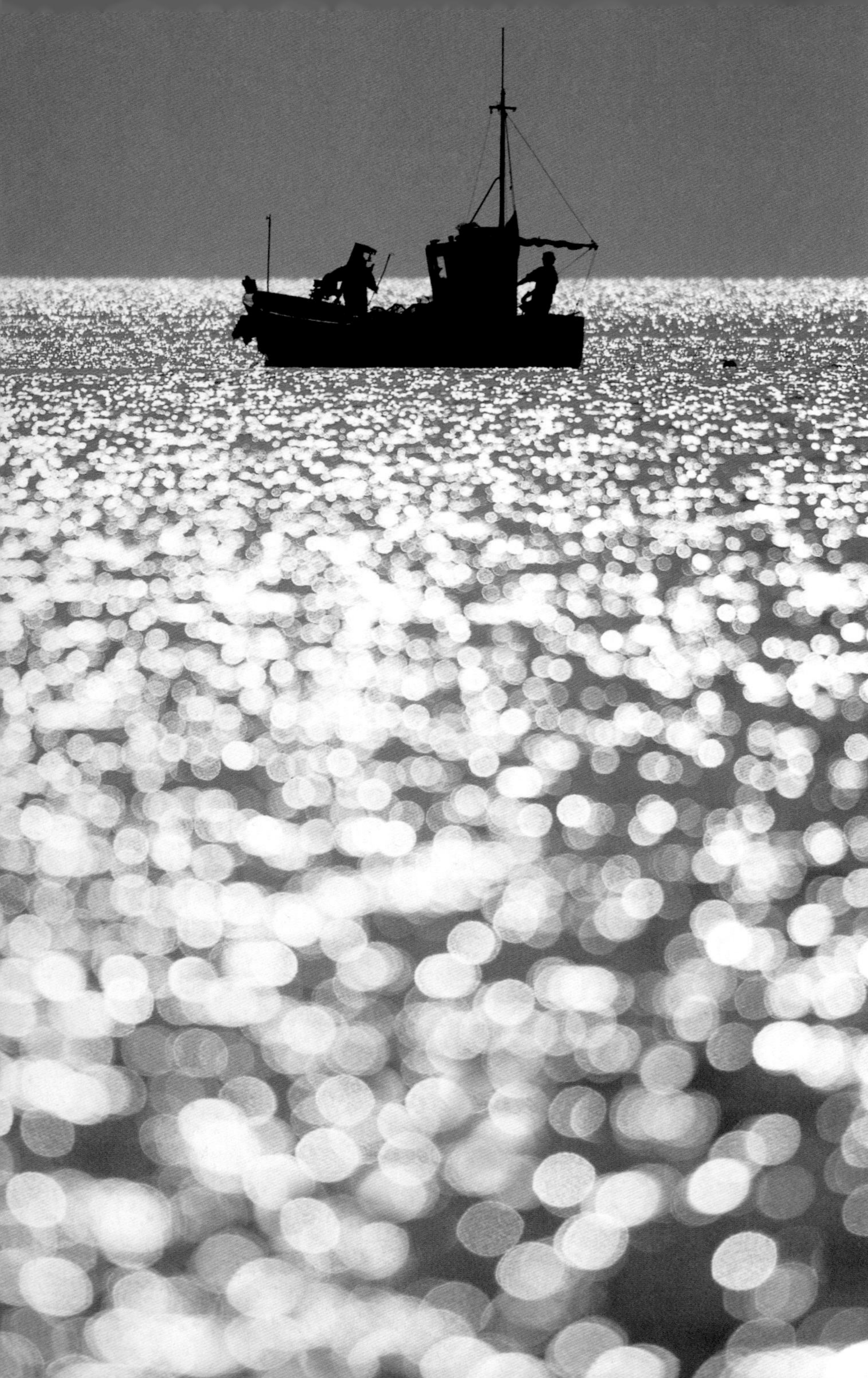

JULY 22

Each man makes his
own shipwreck.

Latin proverb

JULY 23

There are finer fish in the sea
than have ever been caught.

Irish proverb

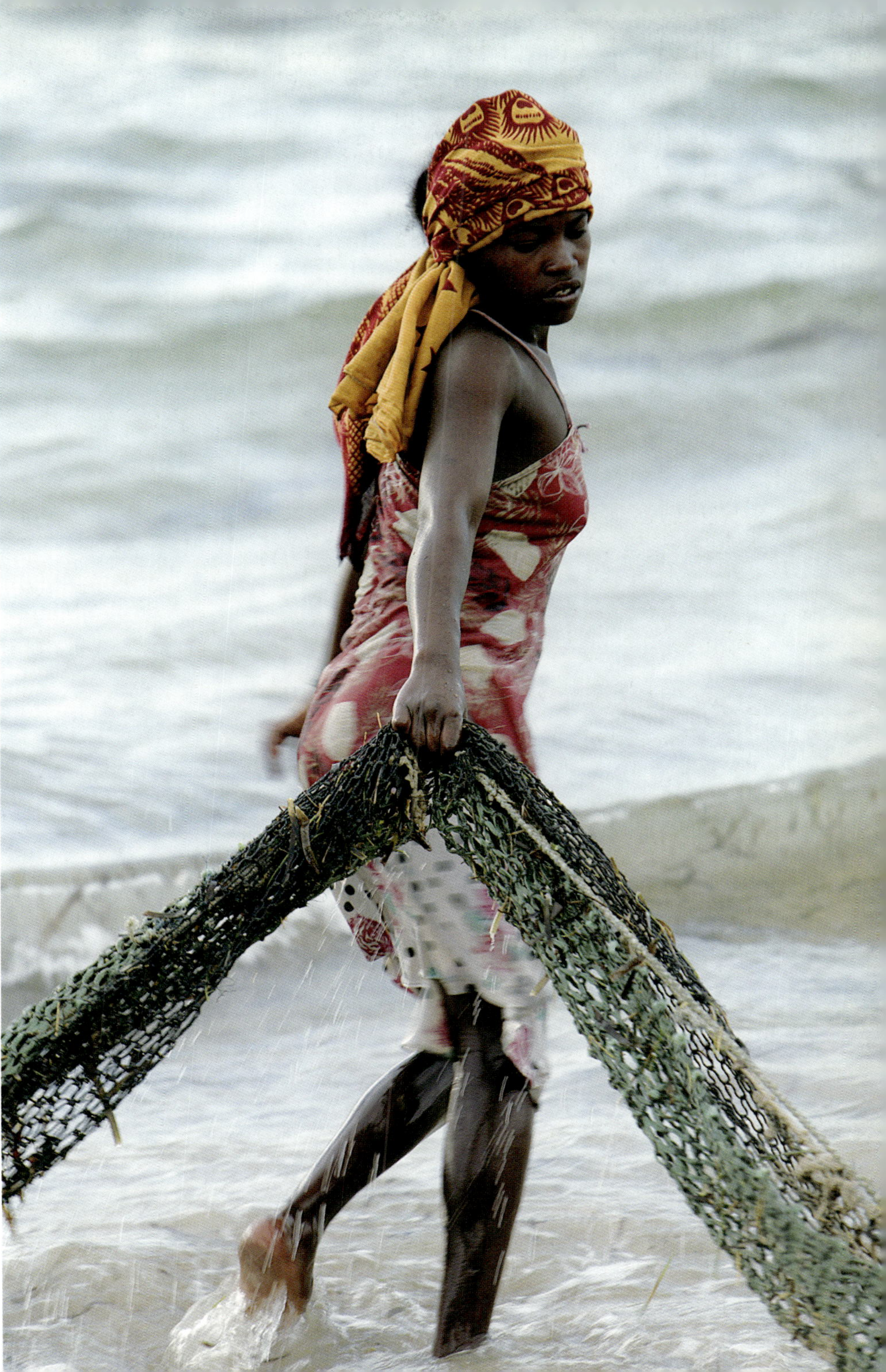

JULY 24

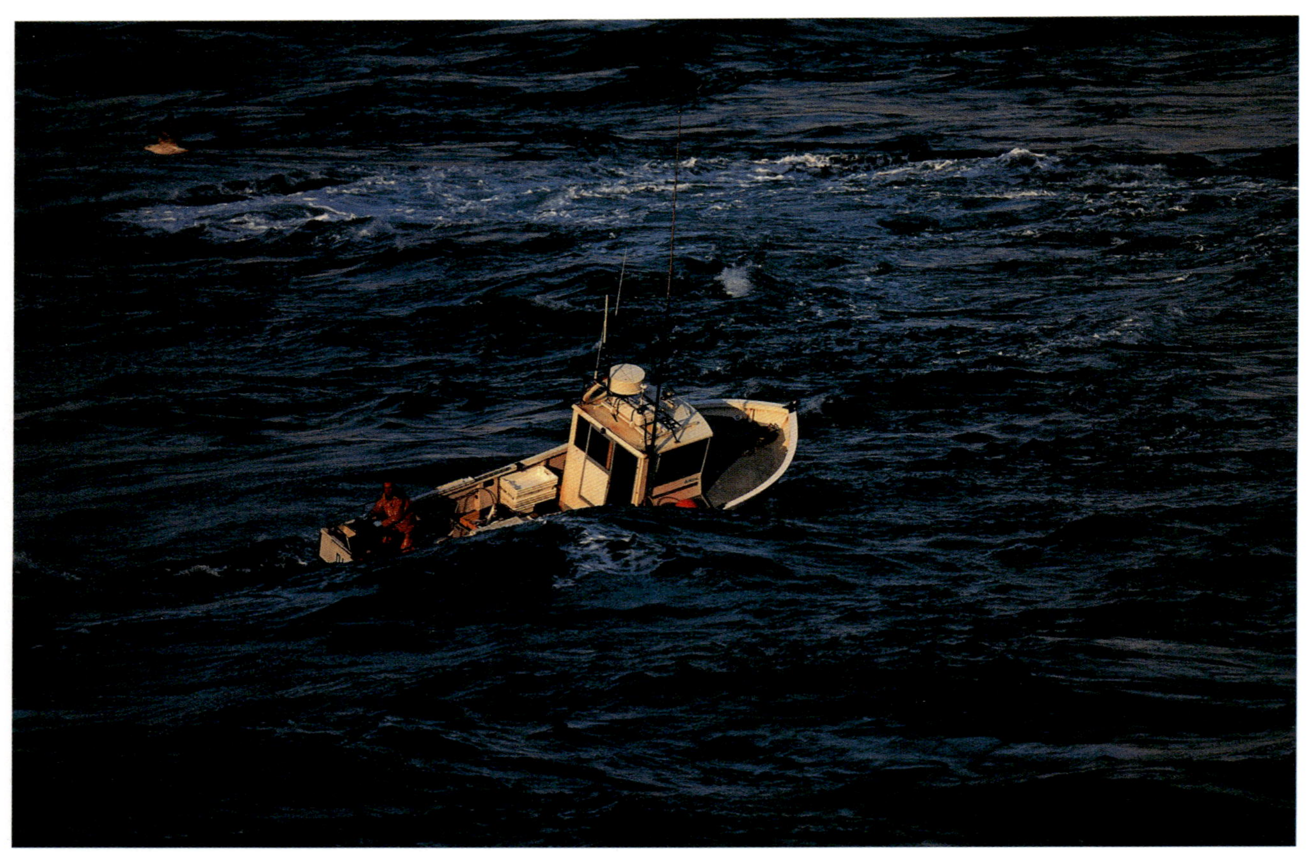

A ship which is about to sink makes her lamentations just like any other living thing.

James Fenimore Cooper, from *The Red Rover,* 1828

JULY 25

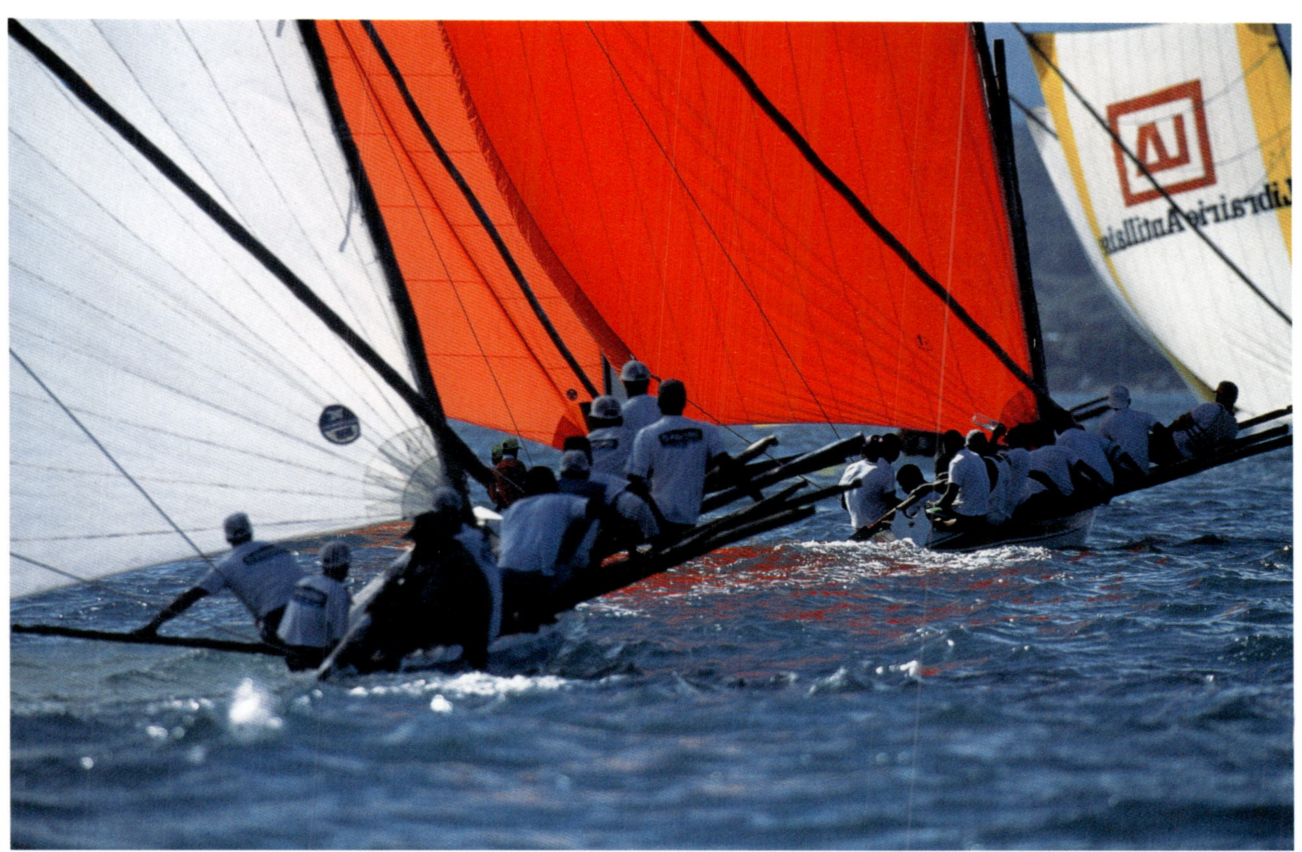

One leak will sink a ship: and one sin will destroy a sinner.

John Bunyan, from *Pilgrim's Progress,* 1684

JULY 26

The annals of this voracious beach! Who could write them, unless it were a shipwrecked sailor? How many who have seen it have seen it only in the midst of danger and distress, the last strip of earth which their mortal eyes beheld. Think of the amount of suffering which a single strand had witnessed!

Henry David Thoreau,
from *Cape Cod,* 1865

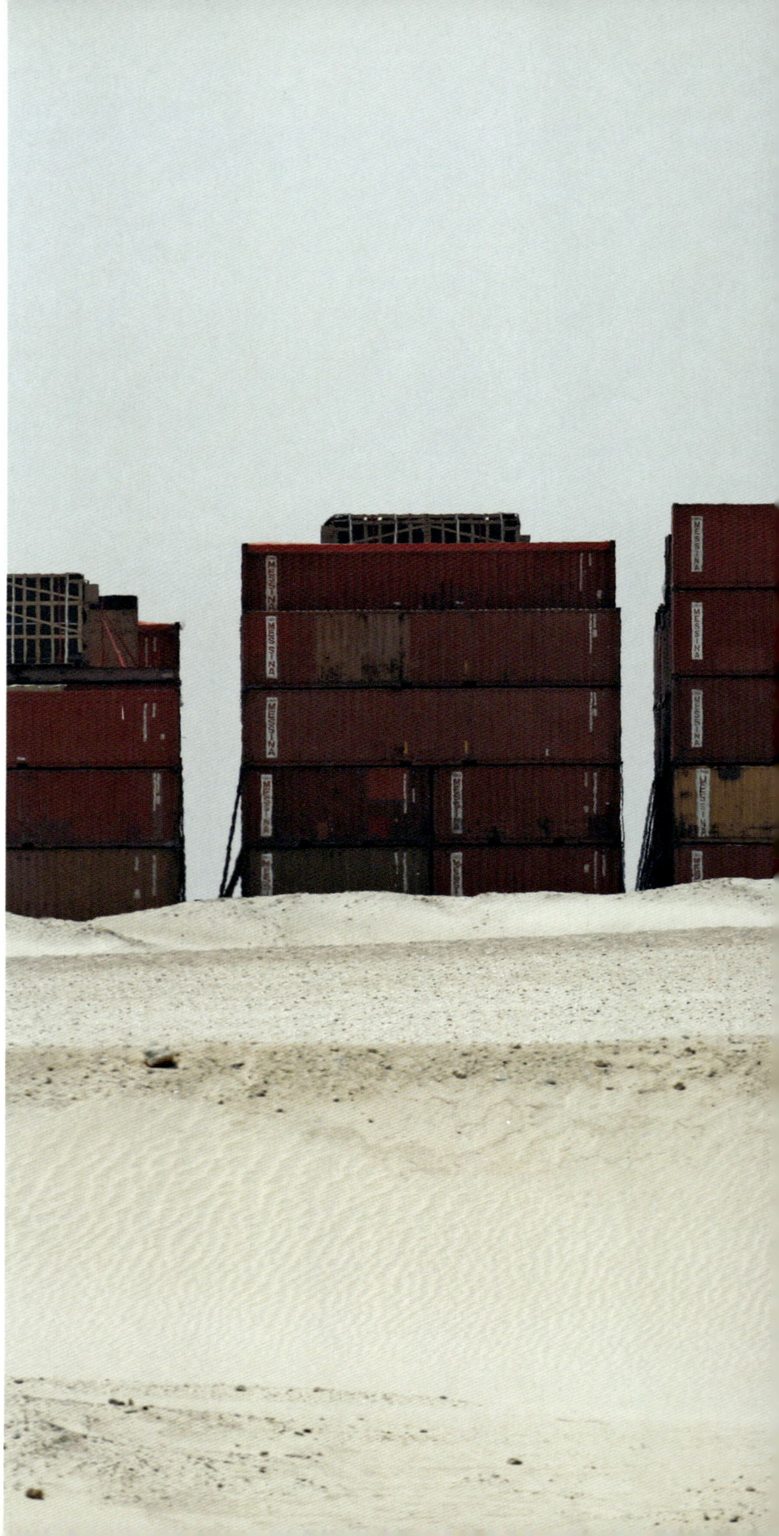

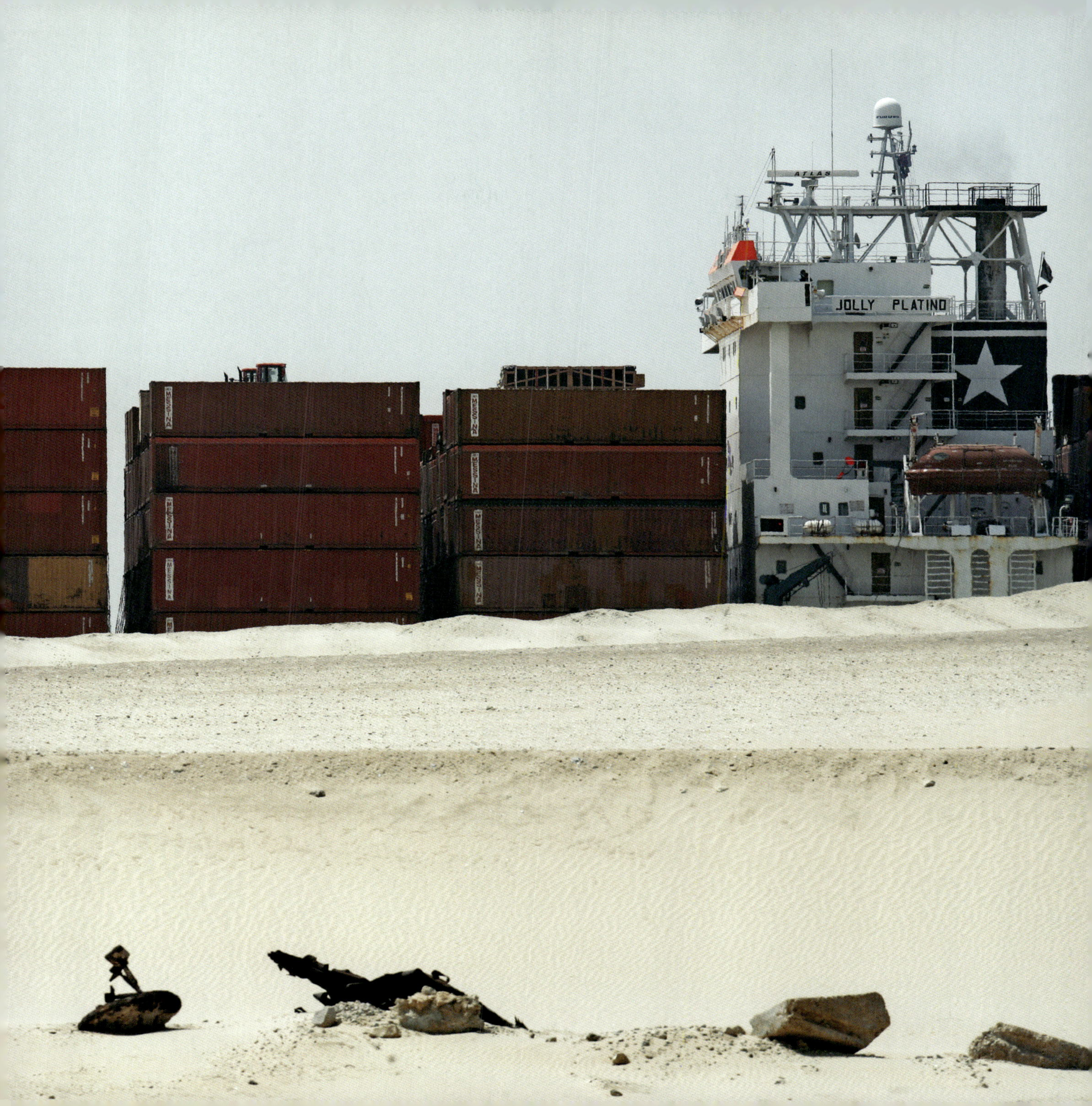
JOLLY PLATINO
MESSINA

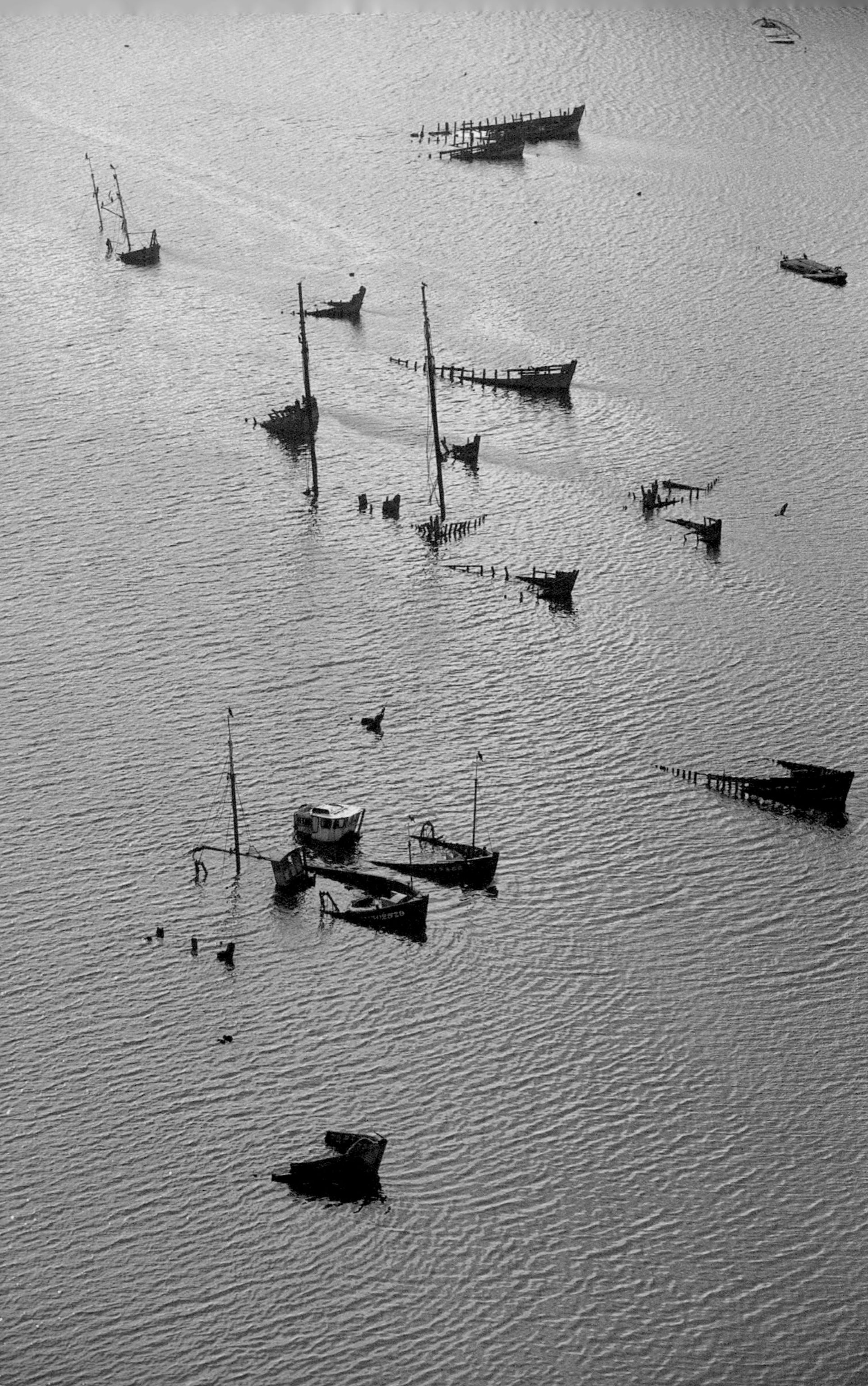

JULY 27

Don't buy a boat that
is under water.

Congolese proverb

JULY 28

Where water is the boss,
there must the land obey.

African proverb

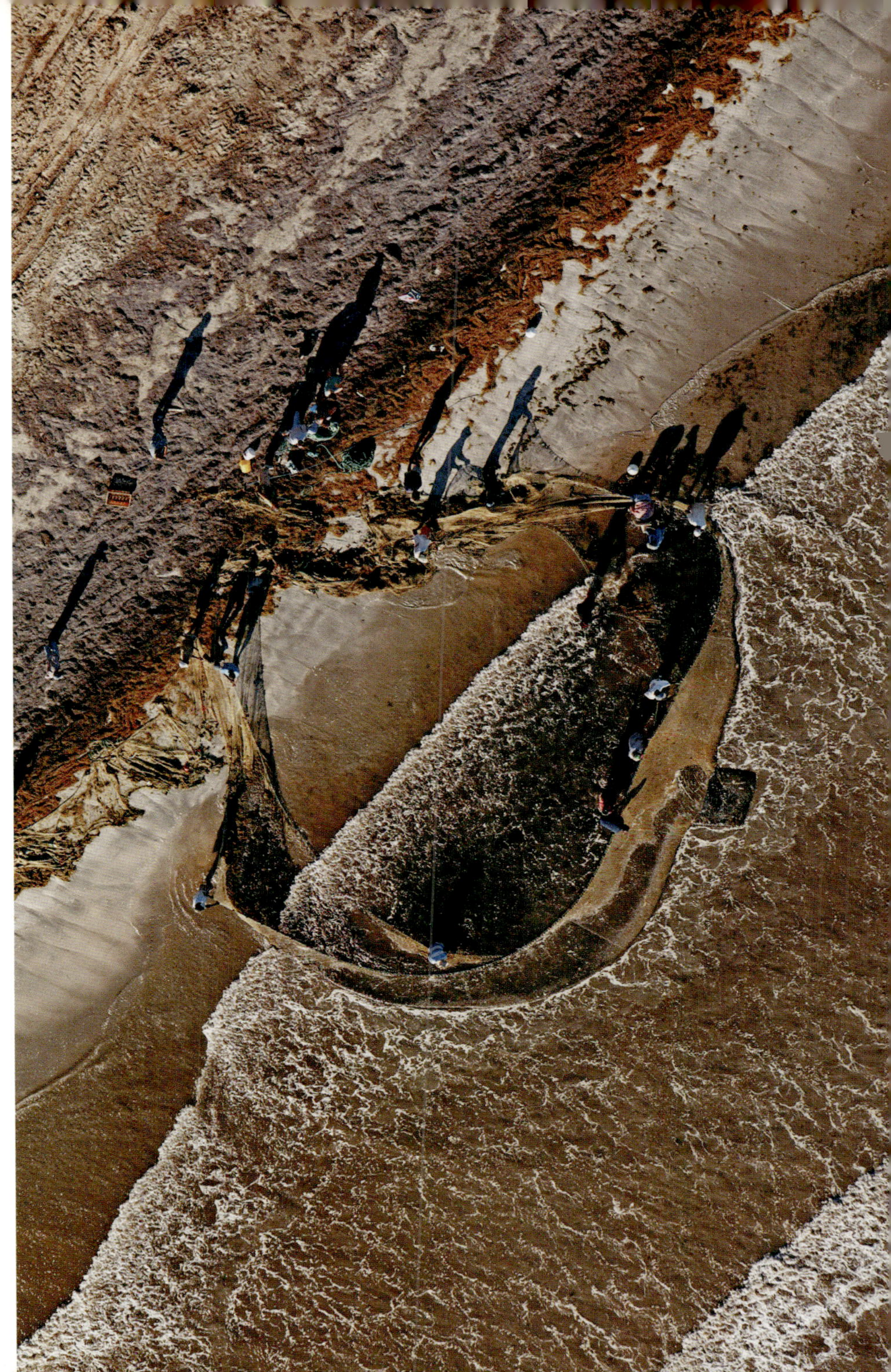

JULY 29

The flying sea-bird mocked the floating dulse:
"Poor wandering water-weed, where dost thou go,
Astray upon the ocean's restless pulse?"
It said: "I do not know."

Elisabeth (Cabazza) Pullen,
from "The Sea-Weed," 1900

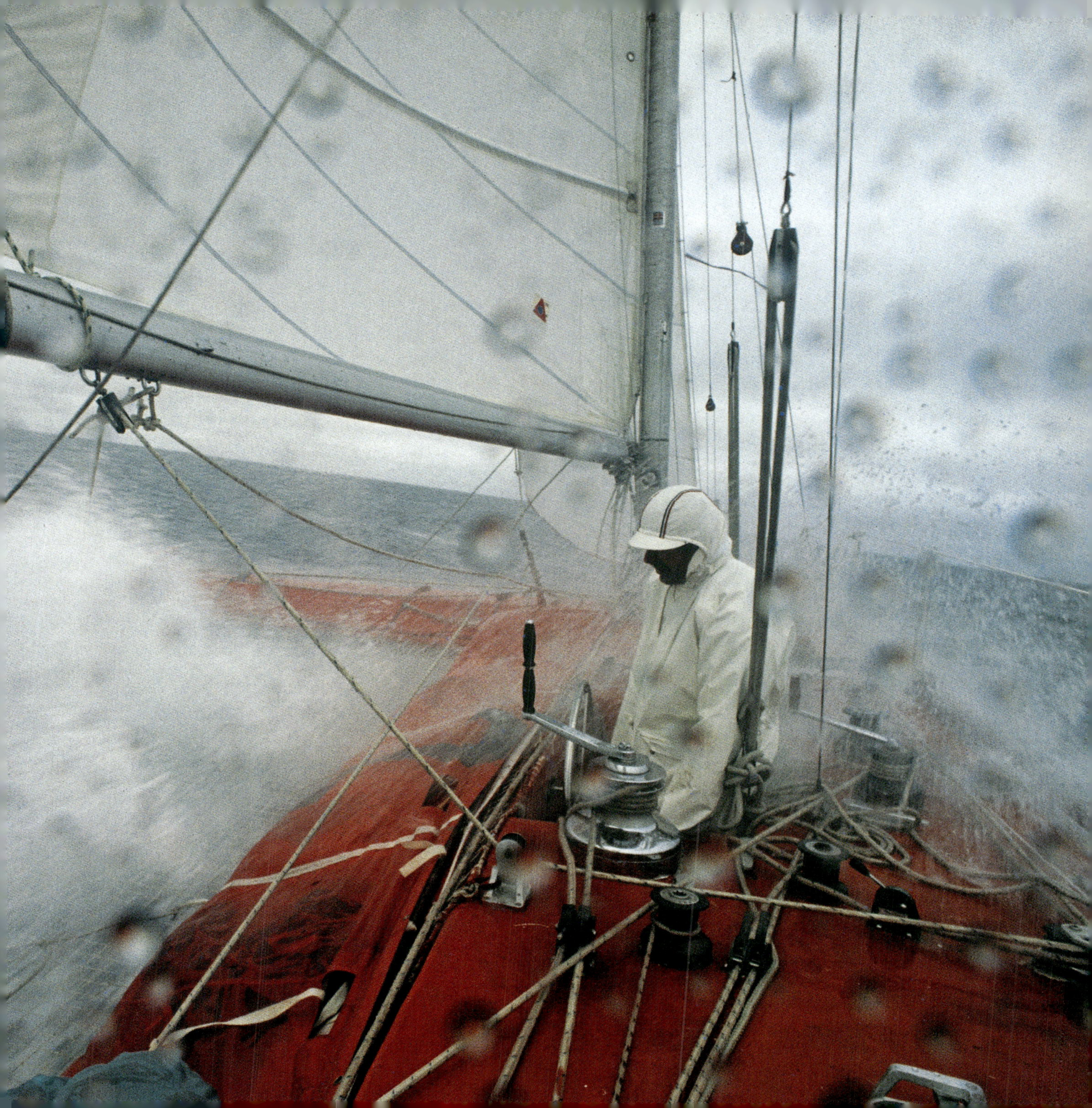

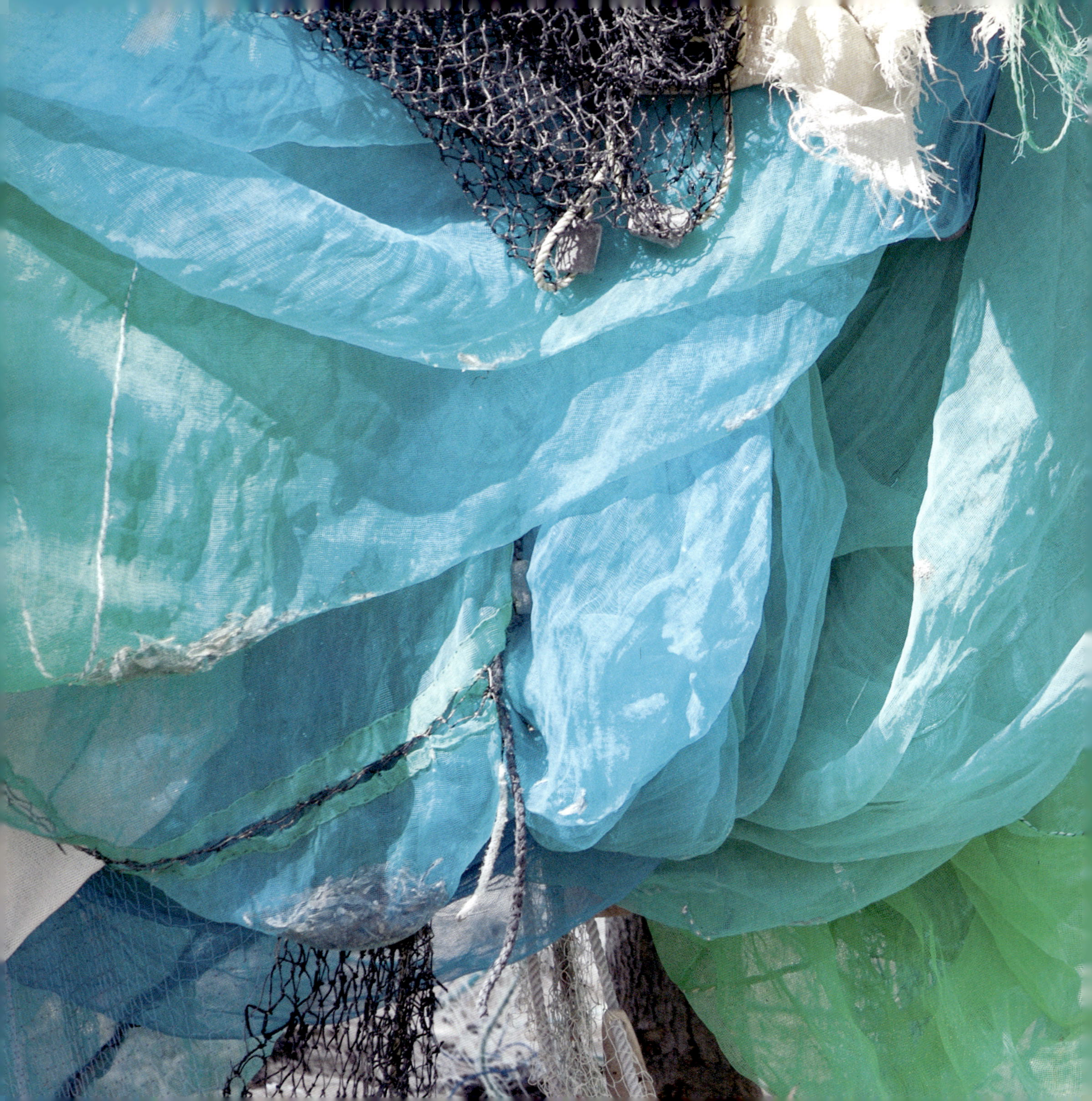

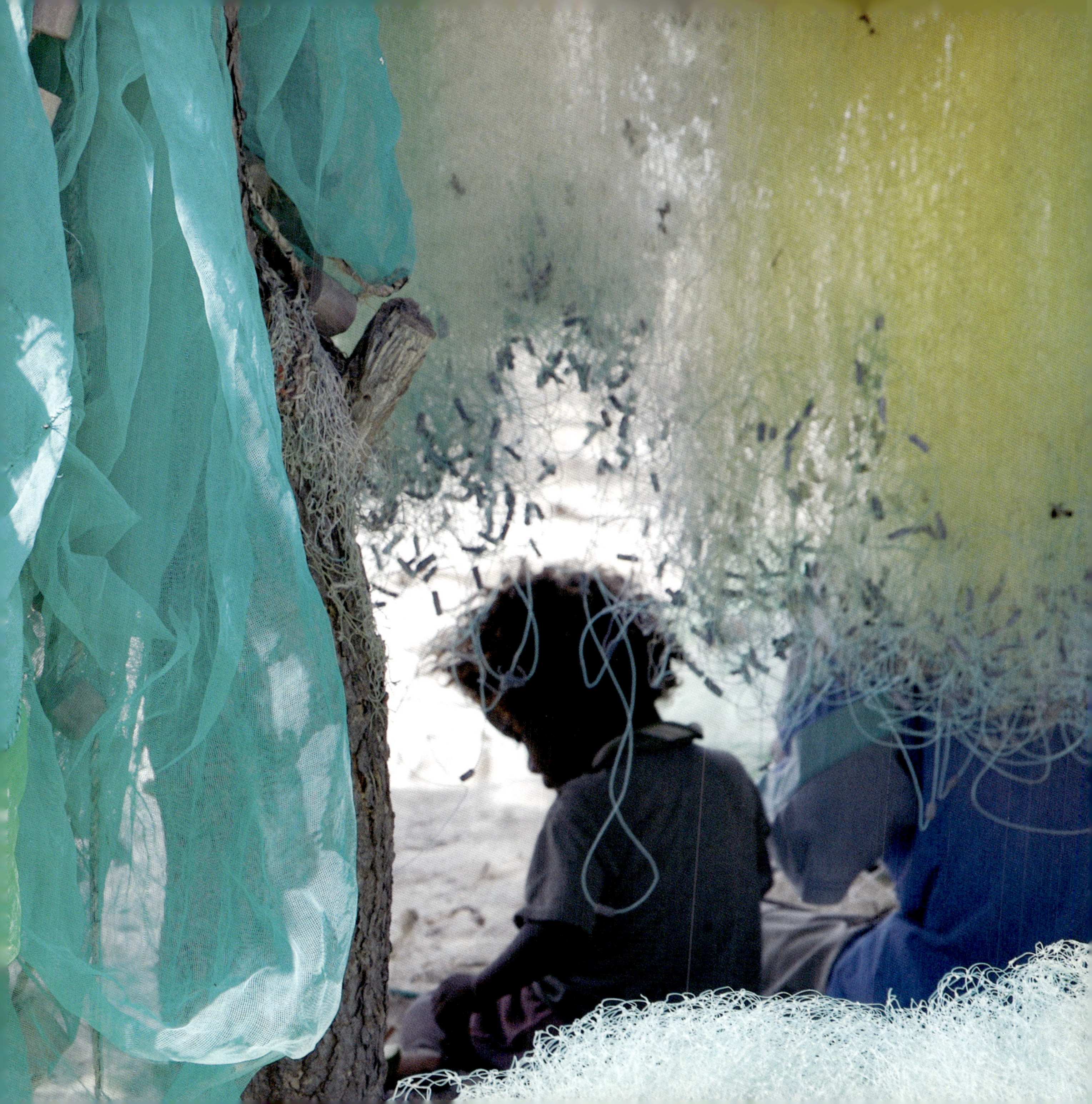

JULY 30

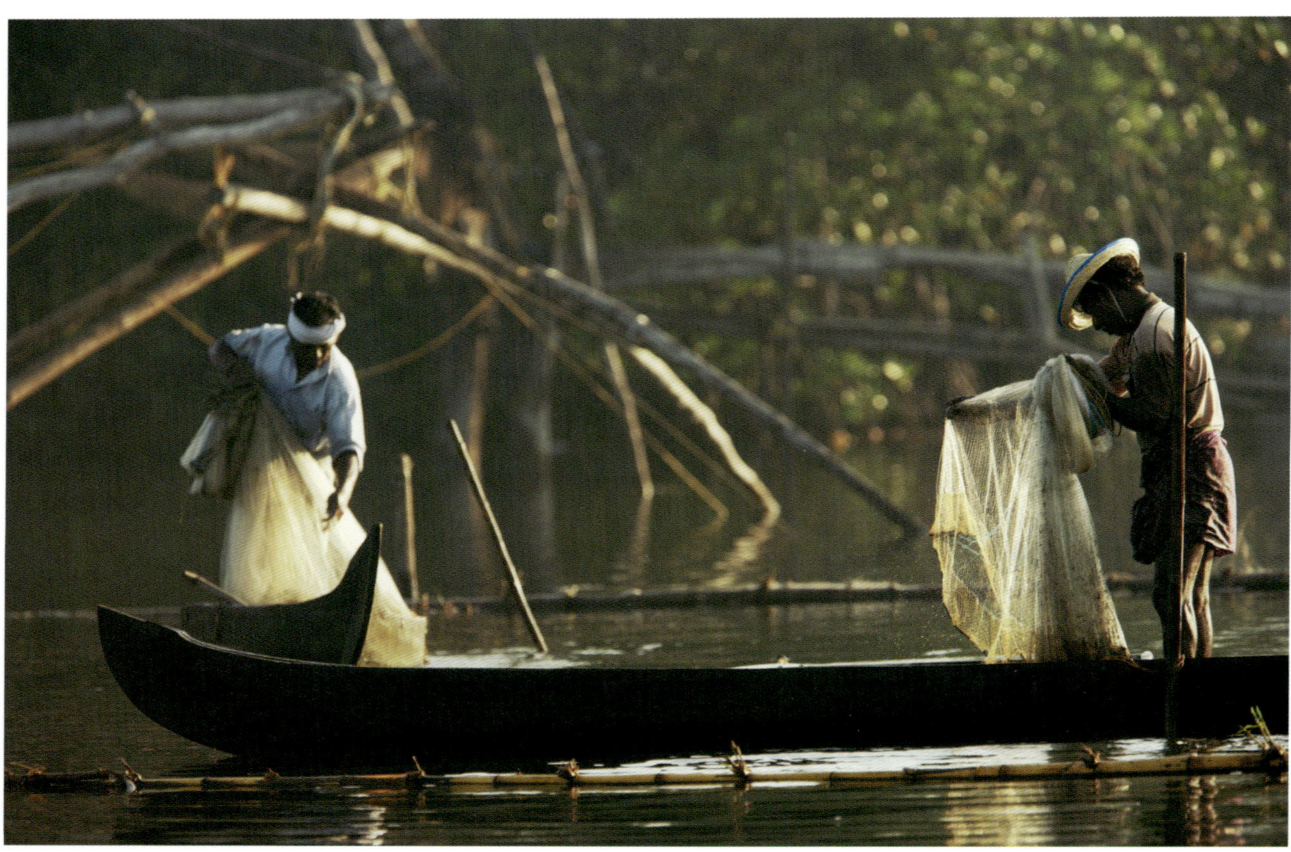

Many men go fishing all of their lives without knowing that it is not fish they are after.

Henry David Thoreau

JULY 31

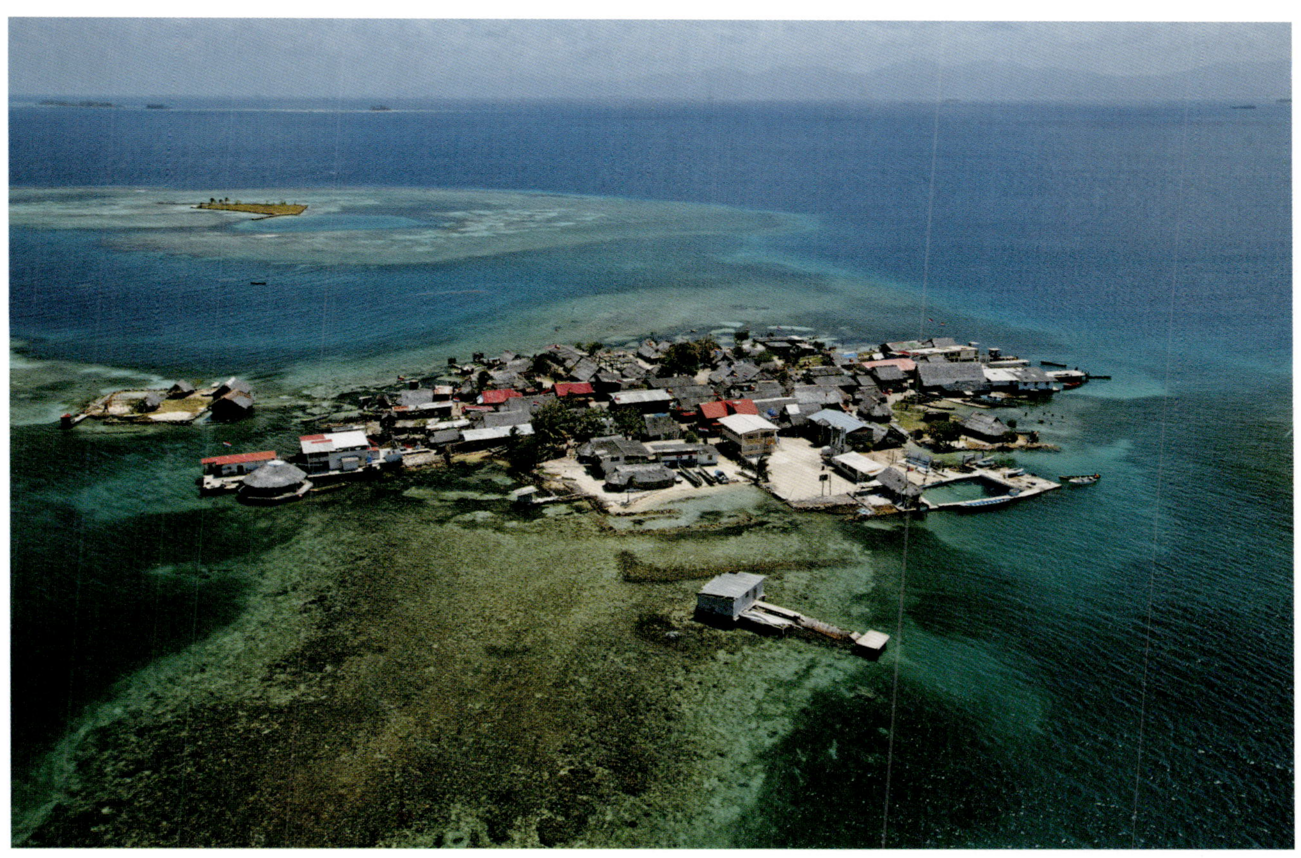

Those who sleep close to water find tranquility.

Hawaiian proverb

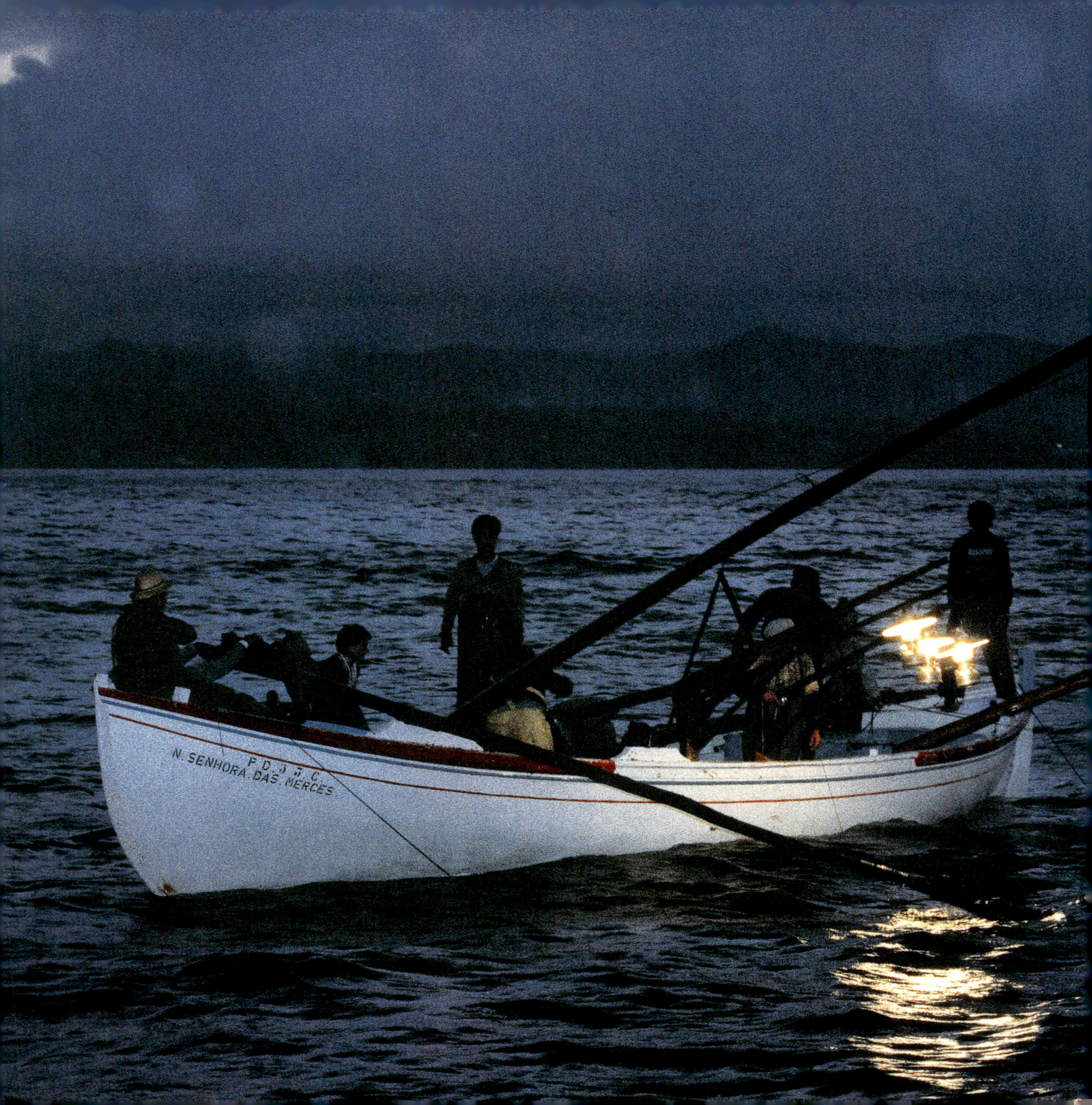
N. SENHORA. DAS. MERCES

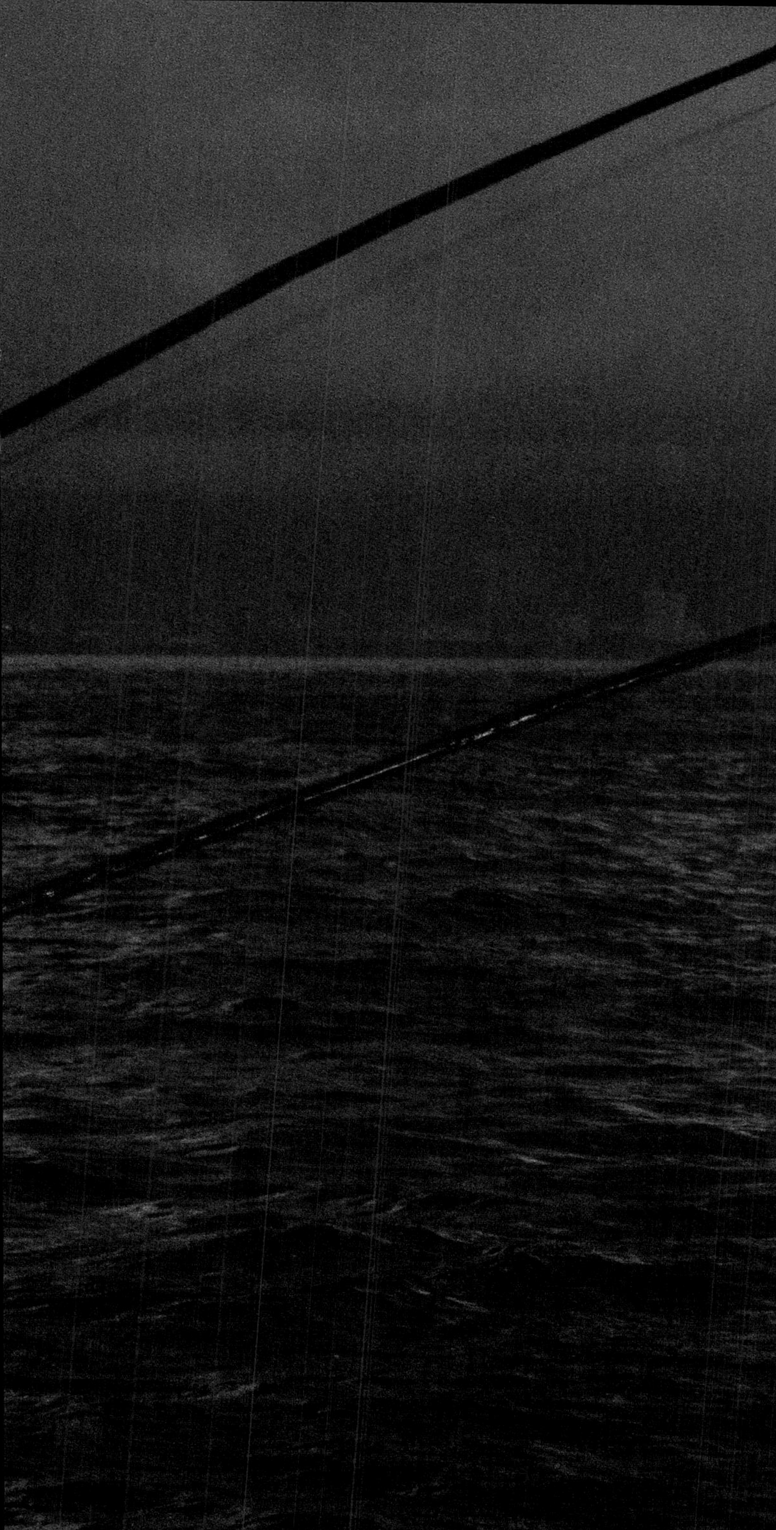

AUGUST 1

To most men experience is like the stern lights of a ship, which illumine only the track it has passed.

Samuel Taylor Coleridge,
from *Table Talk,* 1820

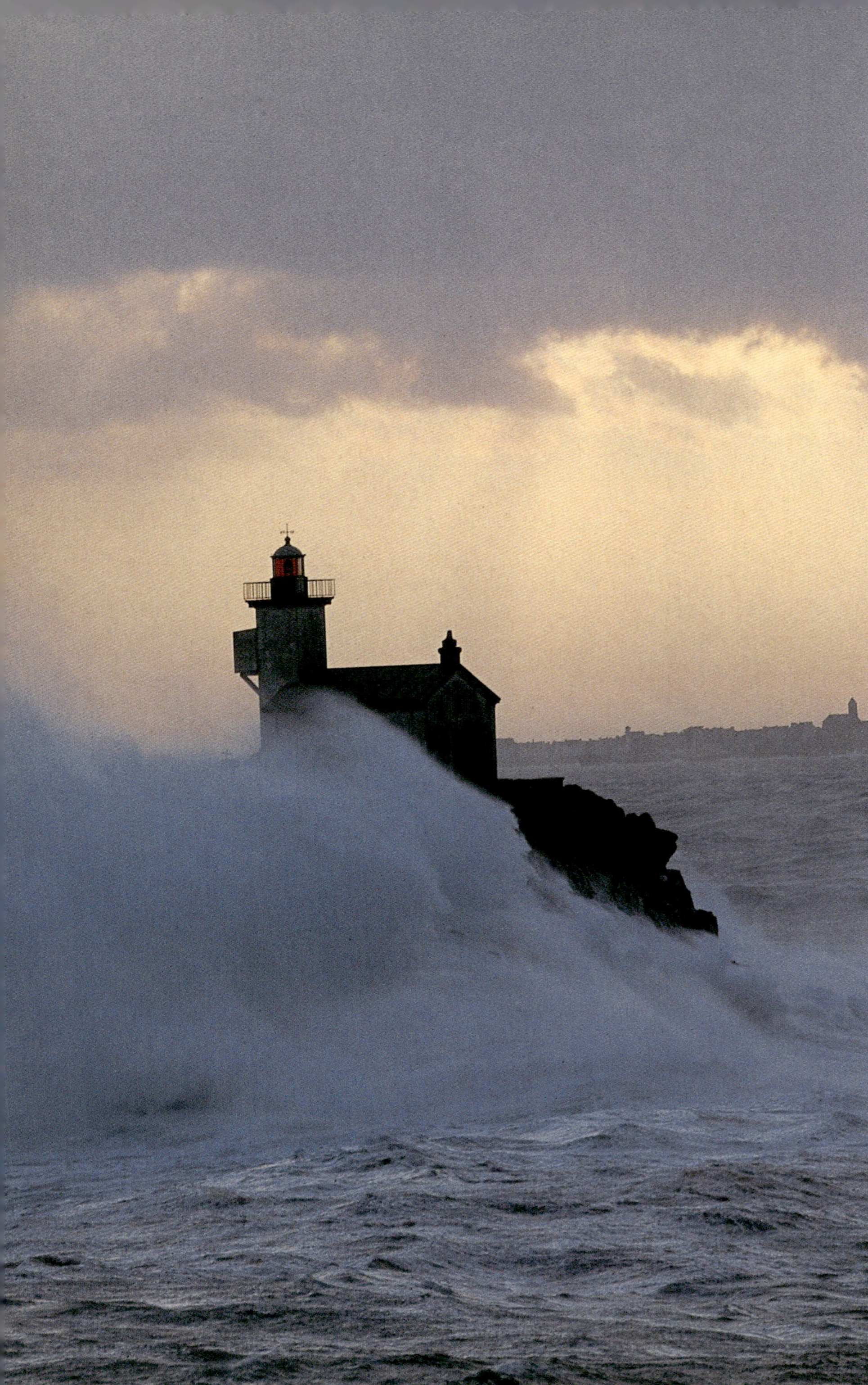

AUGUST 2

He who wants to go fishing must
not be afraid of the water.

Hungarian proverb

AUGUST 3

The seaman's story is of tempest.

Sextus Propertius,
from *Elegies*

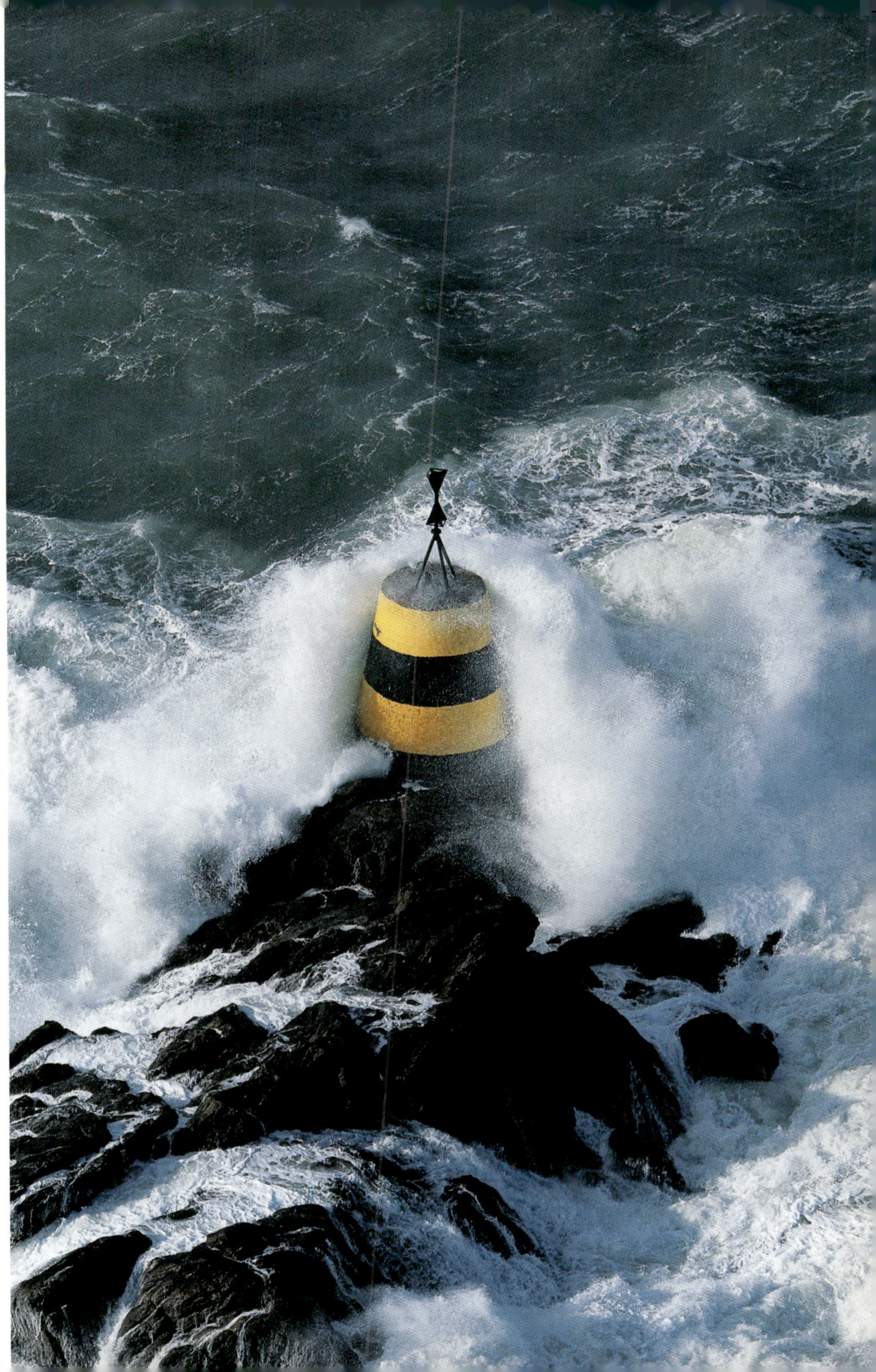

AUGUST 4

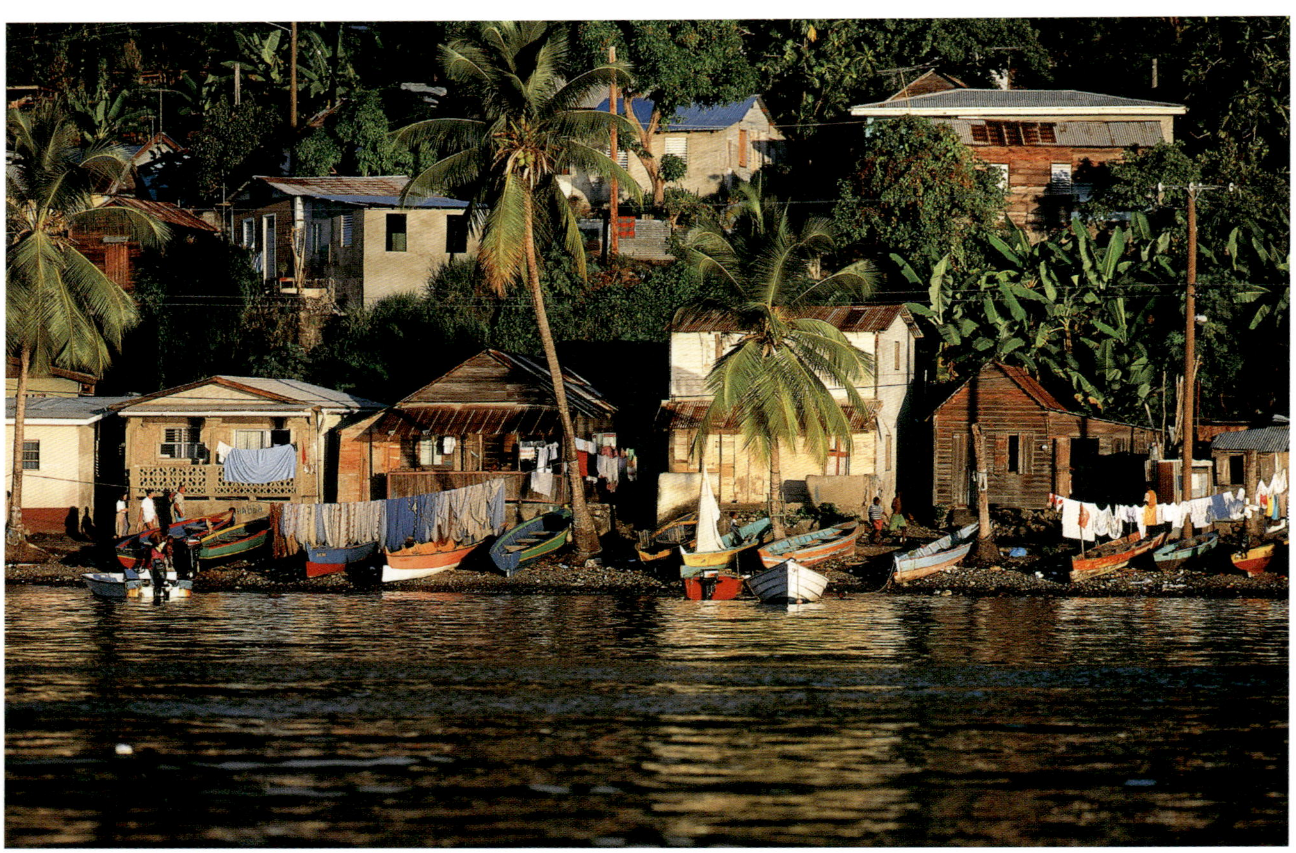

The boat is like a plow, drawn by a winged bull.

Henry David Thoreau, from *Journals,* 1858

AUGUST 5

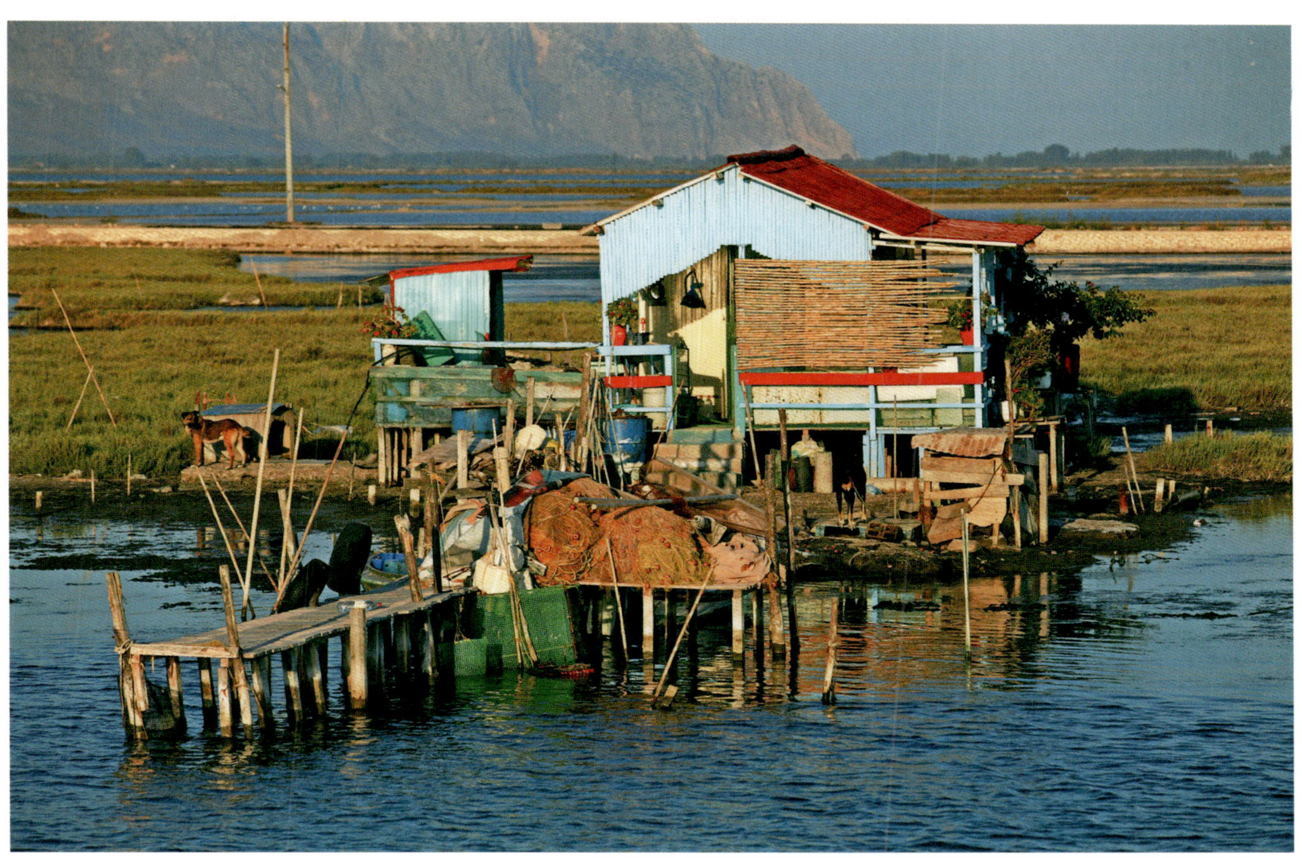

He who is not lucky, let him not go to sea.

Latin proverb

AUGUST 6

Consider the sea's listless chime:
Time's self it is, made audible—
The murmur of the earth's own shell.
Secret continuance sublime
Is the sea's end: our sight may pass
No furlong farther. Since time was,
This sound hath told the lapse of time

Dante Gabriel Rossetti,
from "The Sea-Limits"

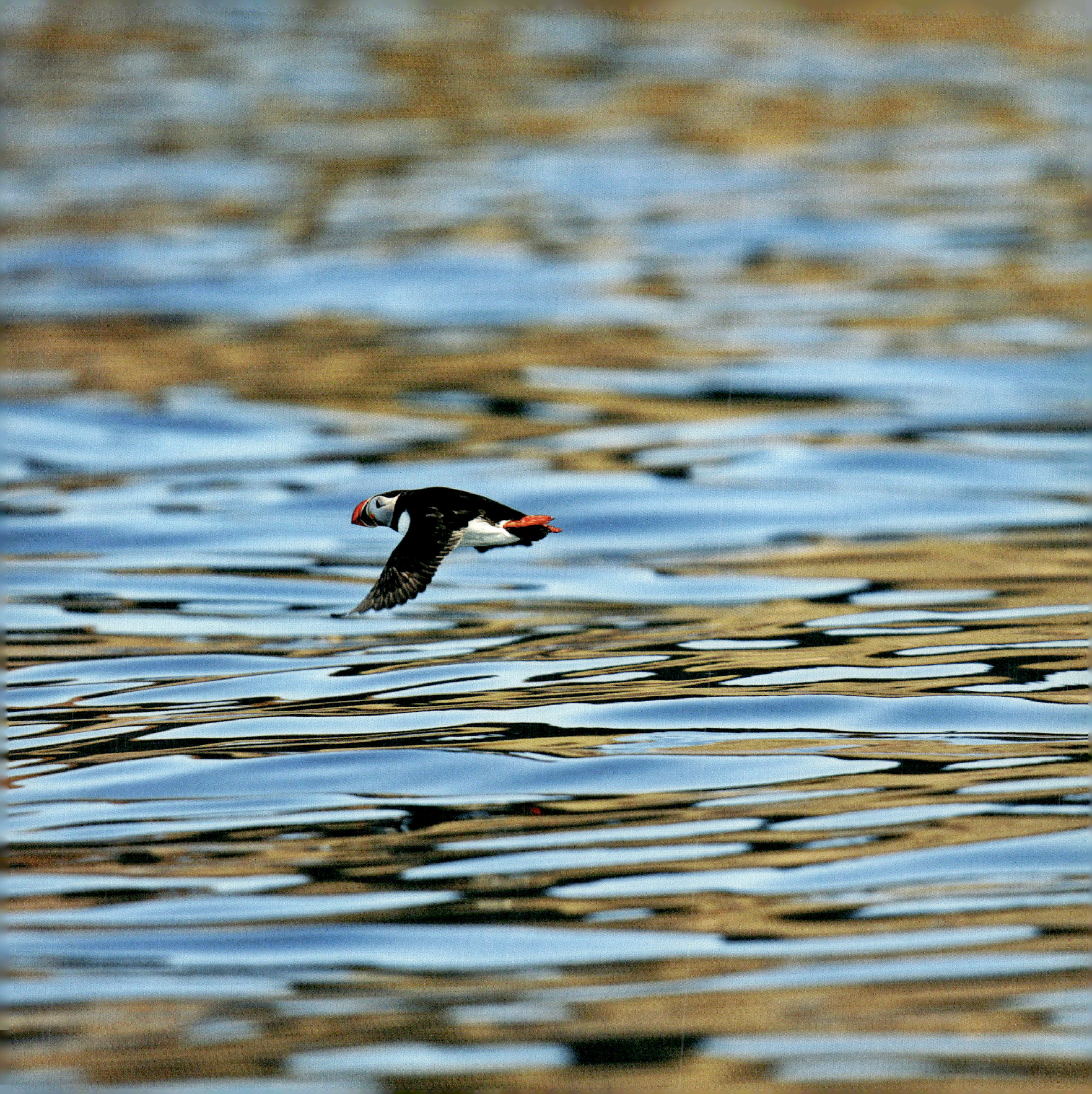

AUGUST 7

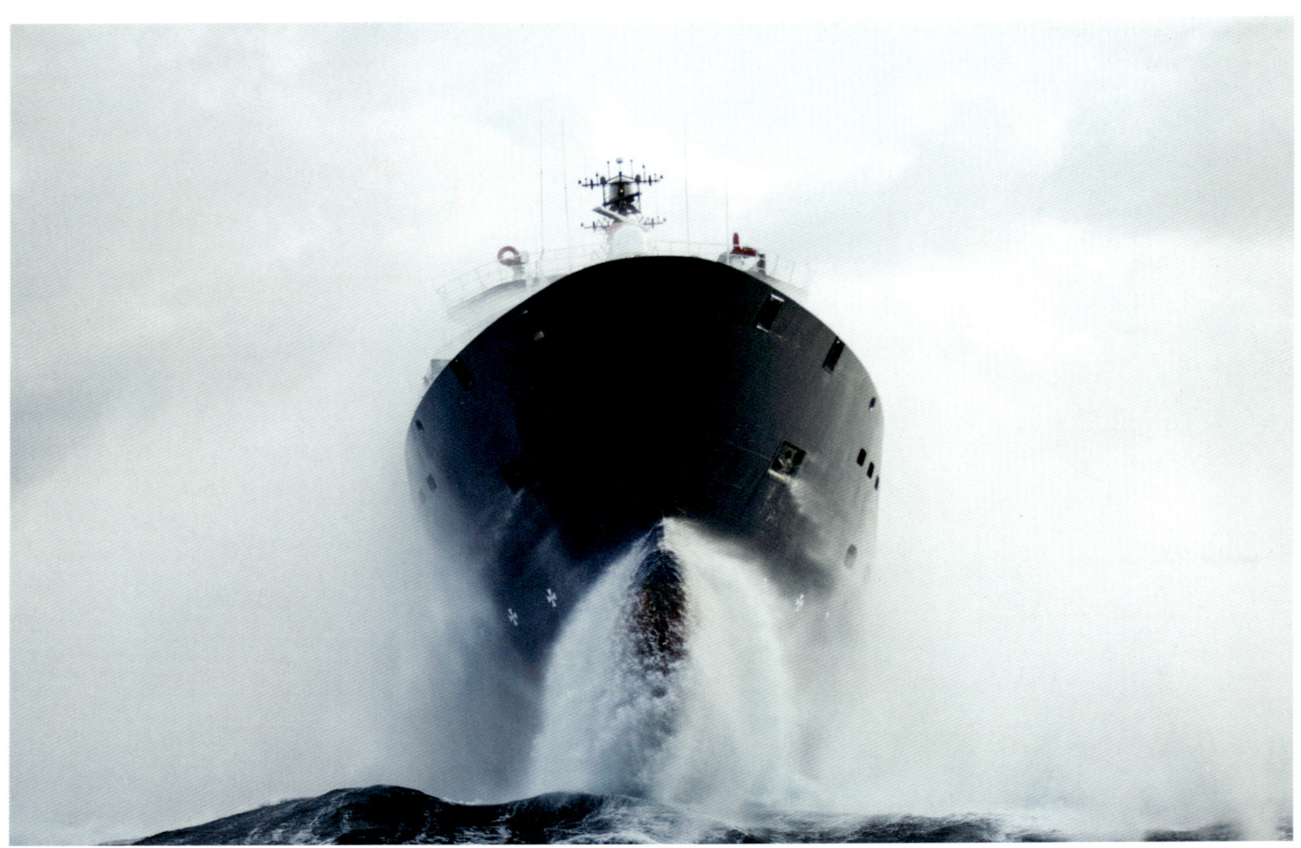

The sea has never been friendly to man. At most it has been the accomplice of human restlessness.

Joseph Conrad, from *The Mirror of the Sea,* 1906

AUGUST 8

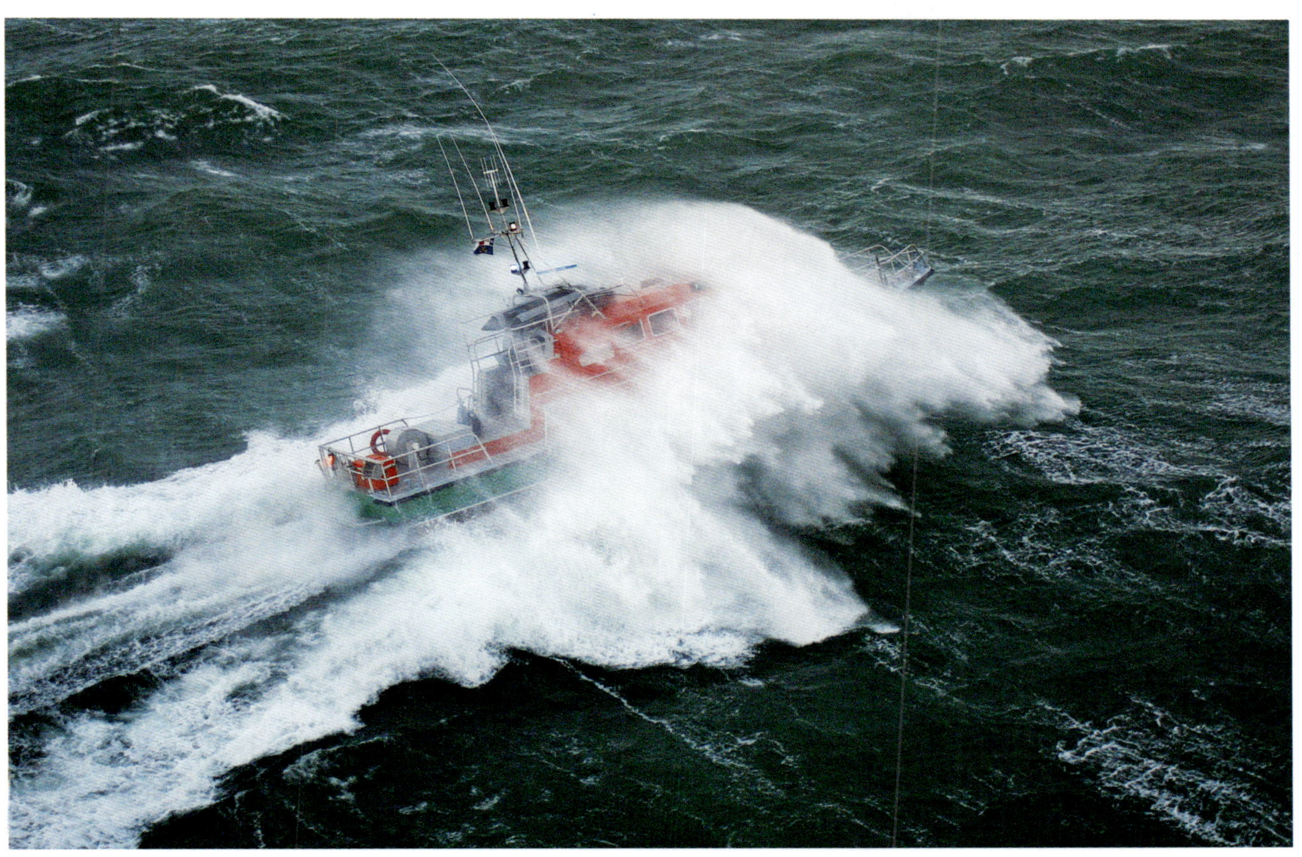

When from thy shore the tempest beat us back,
I stood upon the hatches in the storm.

William Shakespeare, *Henry VI,* Part II, Act III, Scene 2

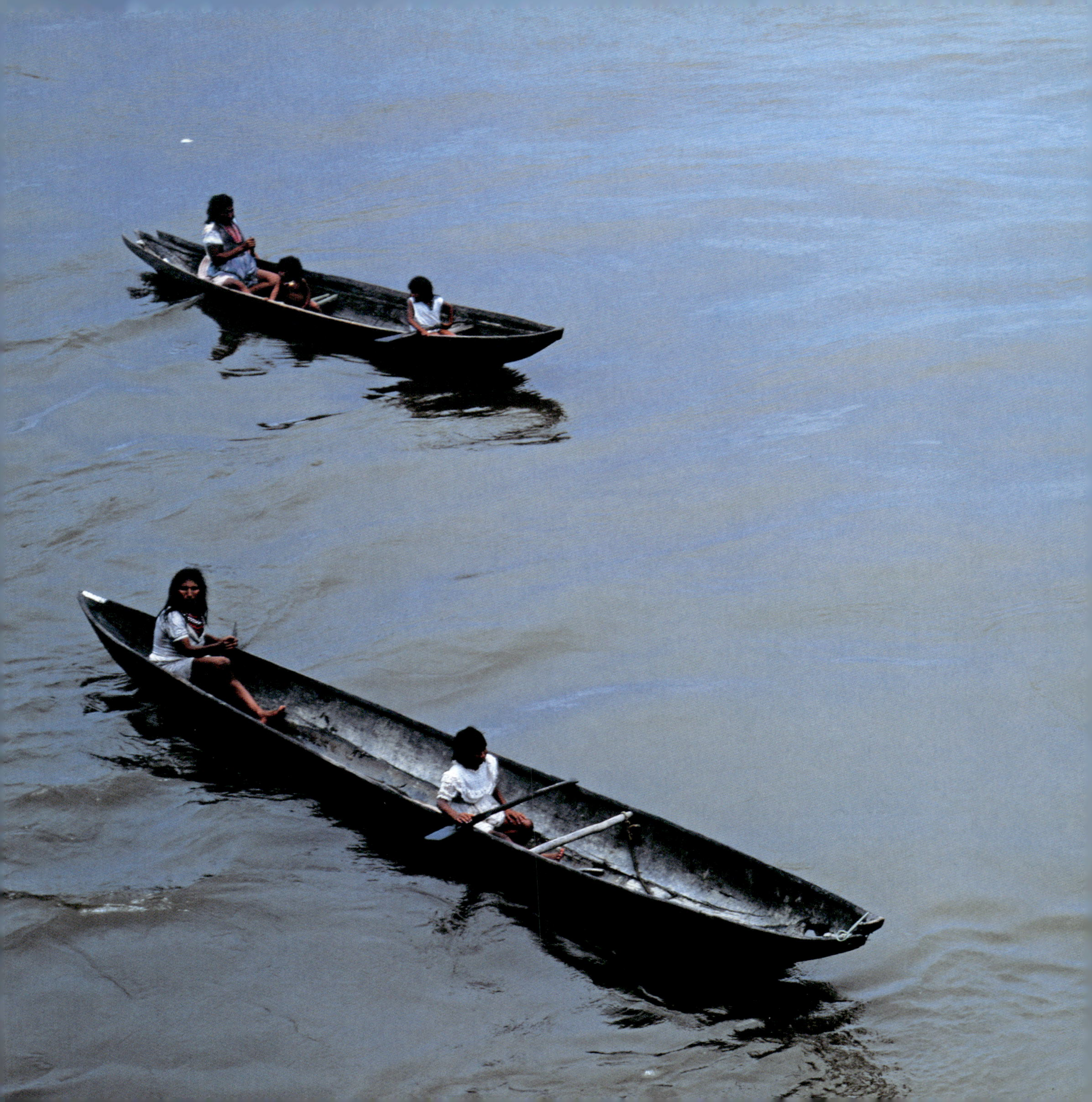

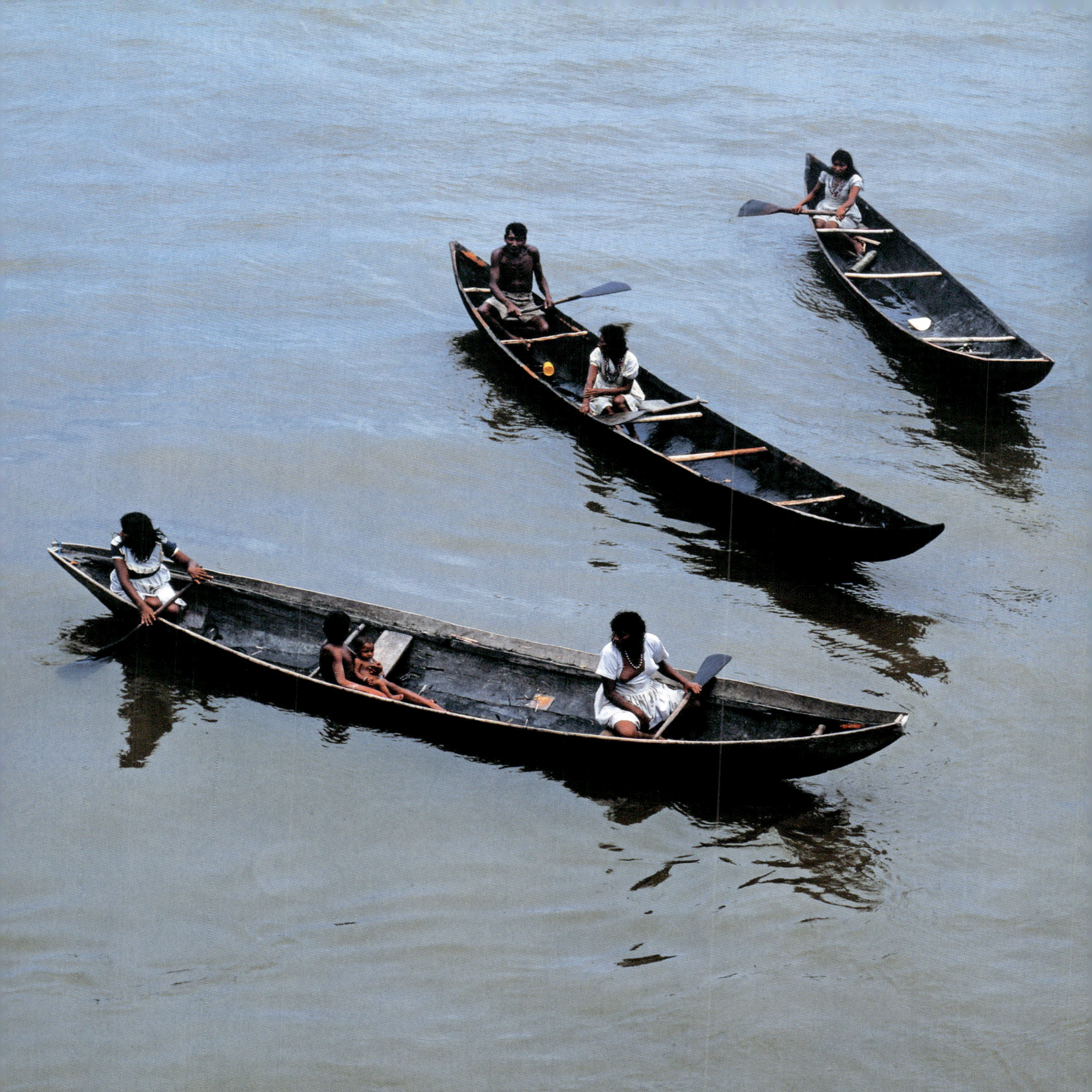

AUGUST 9

There be triple ways to take, of the eagle or the snake,
Or the way of a man with a maid;
But the sweetest way to me is a ship's upon the sea
In the heel of the North-East Trade.

Rudyard Kipling, from "L'Envoi," 1892

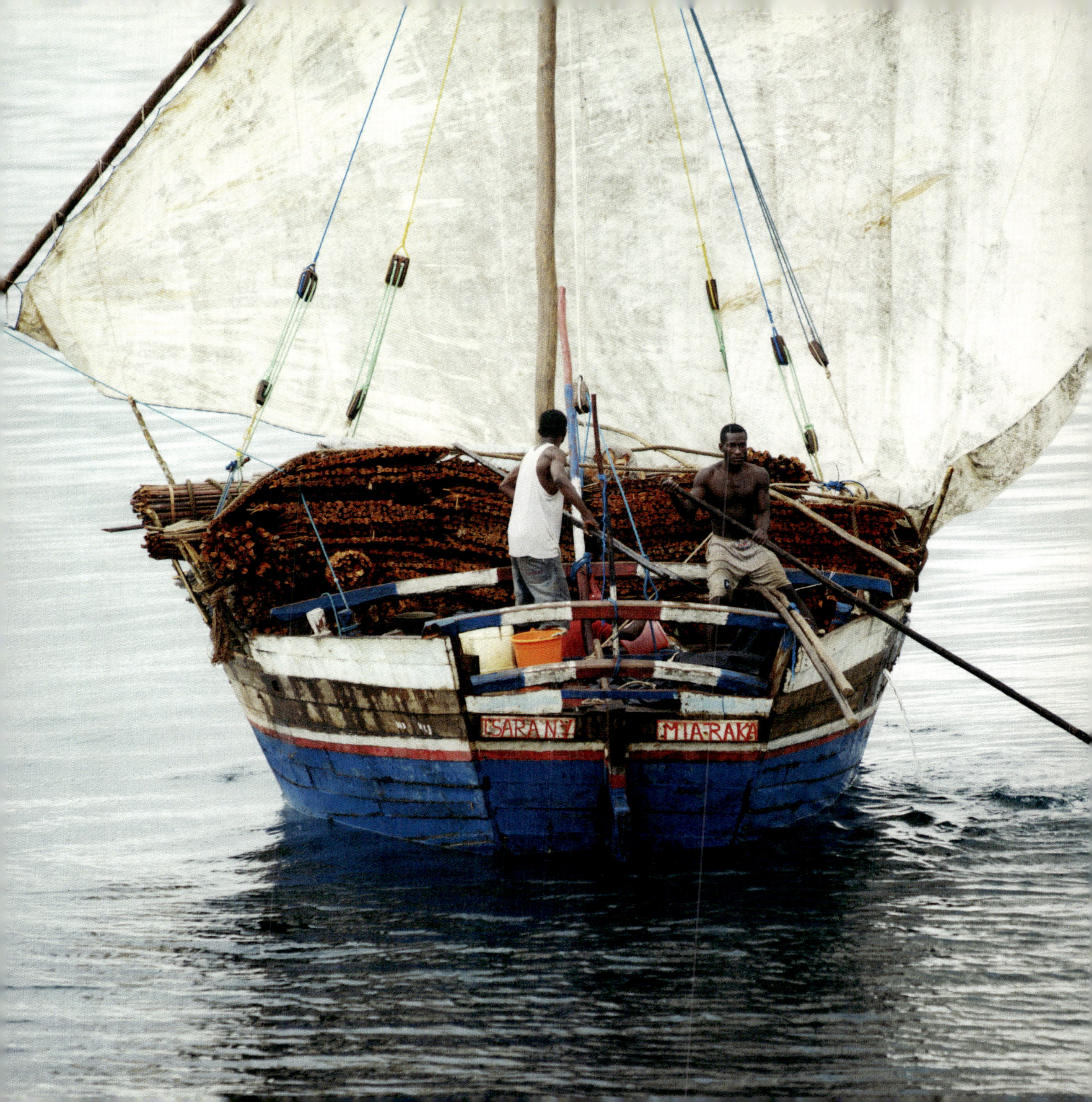
TSARA N.Y
MIA-RAKA

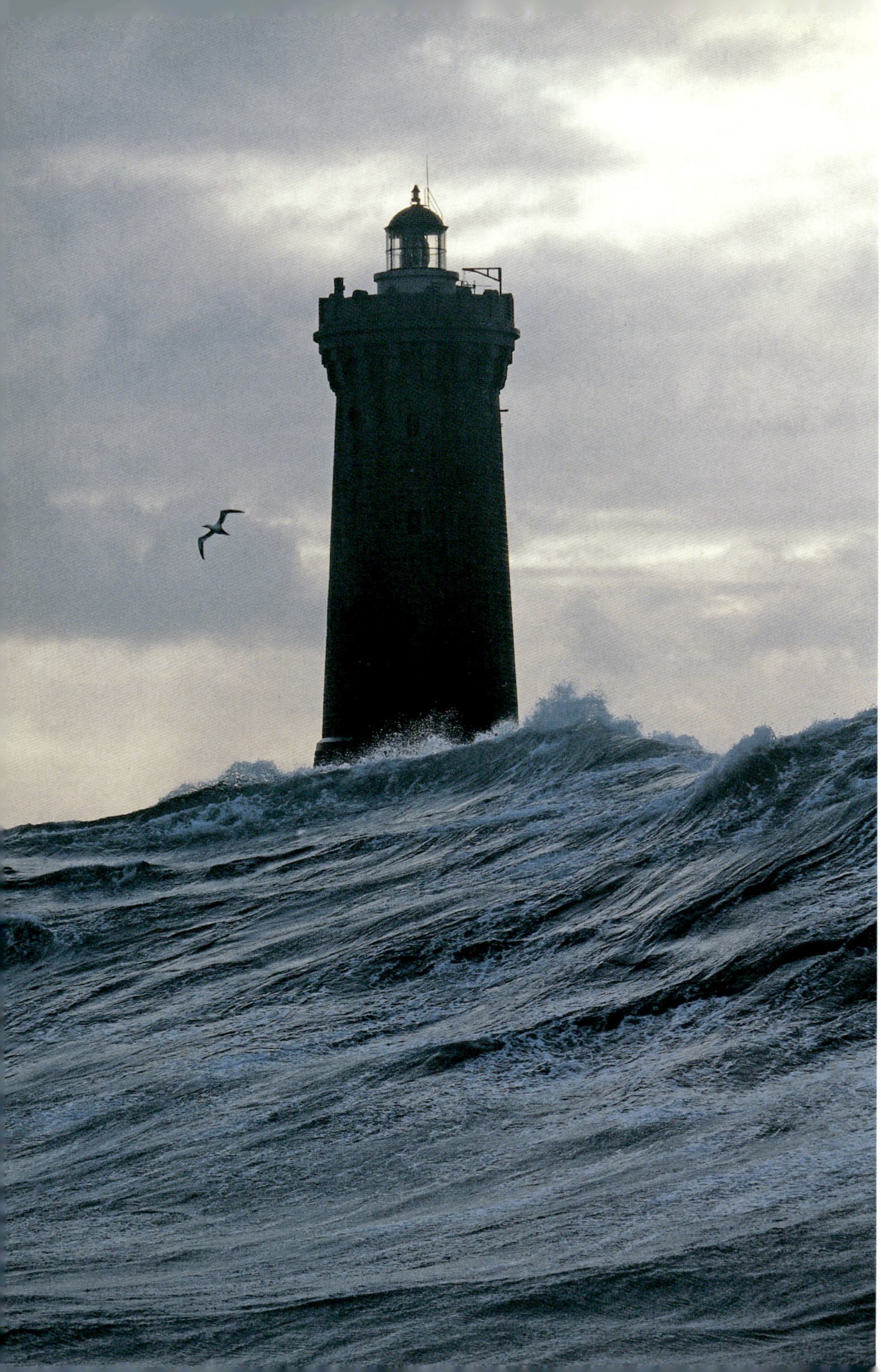

AUGUST 10

He who goes to sea for pleasure
would go to hell for a pastime.

Samuel Johnson

AUGUST 11

I hate storms, but calms
undermine my spirits.

Bernard Moitessier

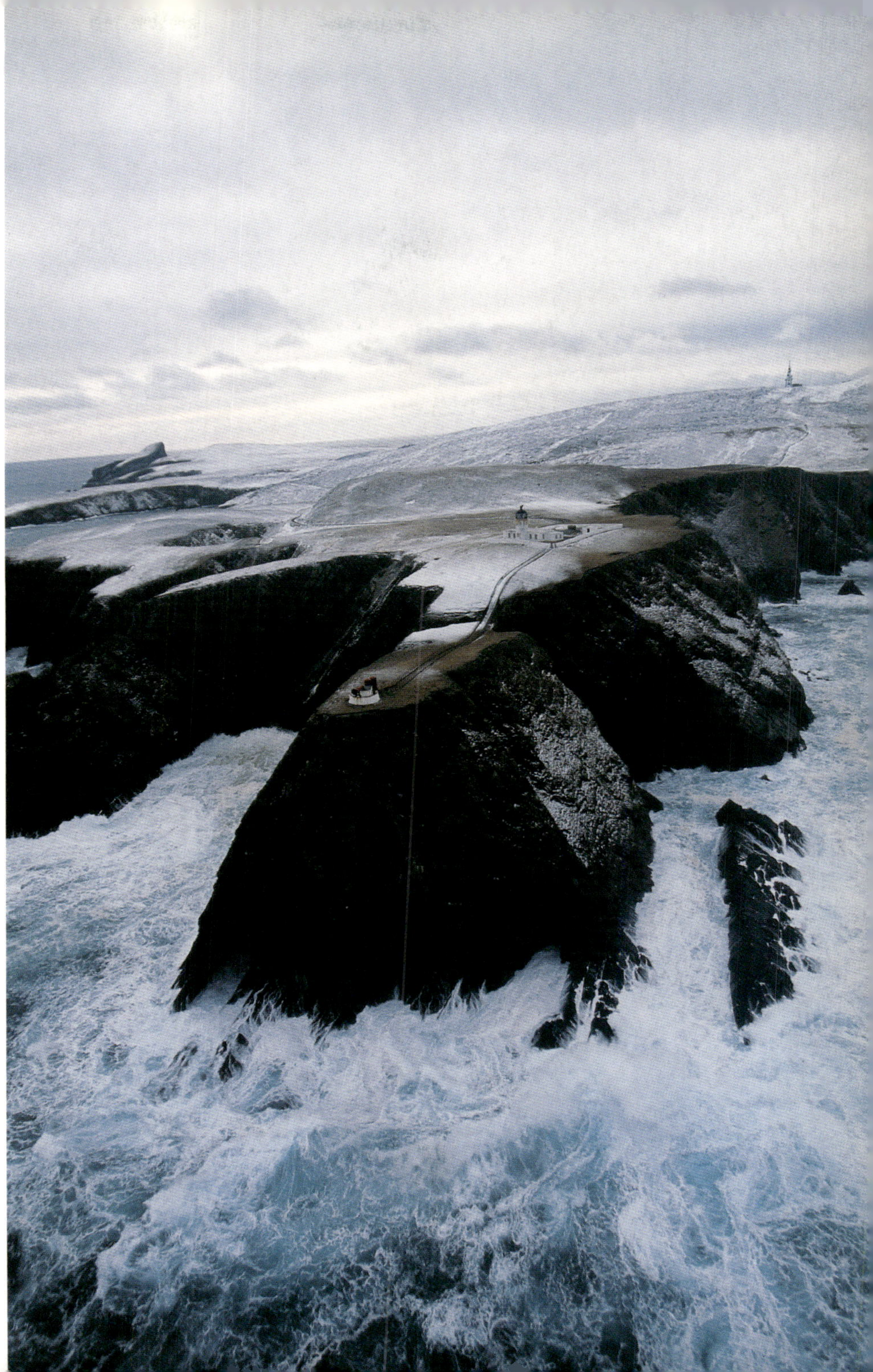

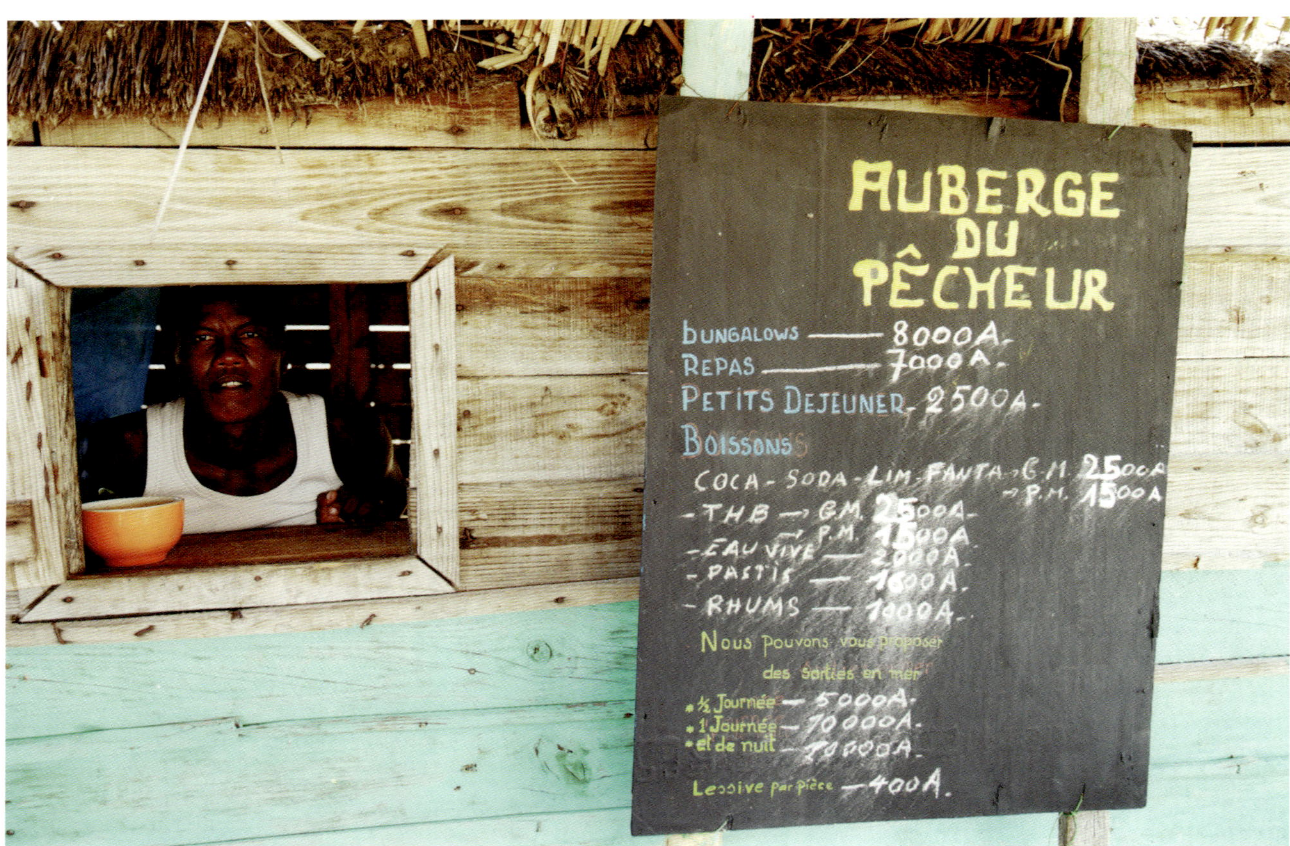

Under the best of conditions, a voyage is one of the severest tests to try a man.

Ralph Waldo Emerson, from *English Traits,* 1856

AUGUST 13

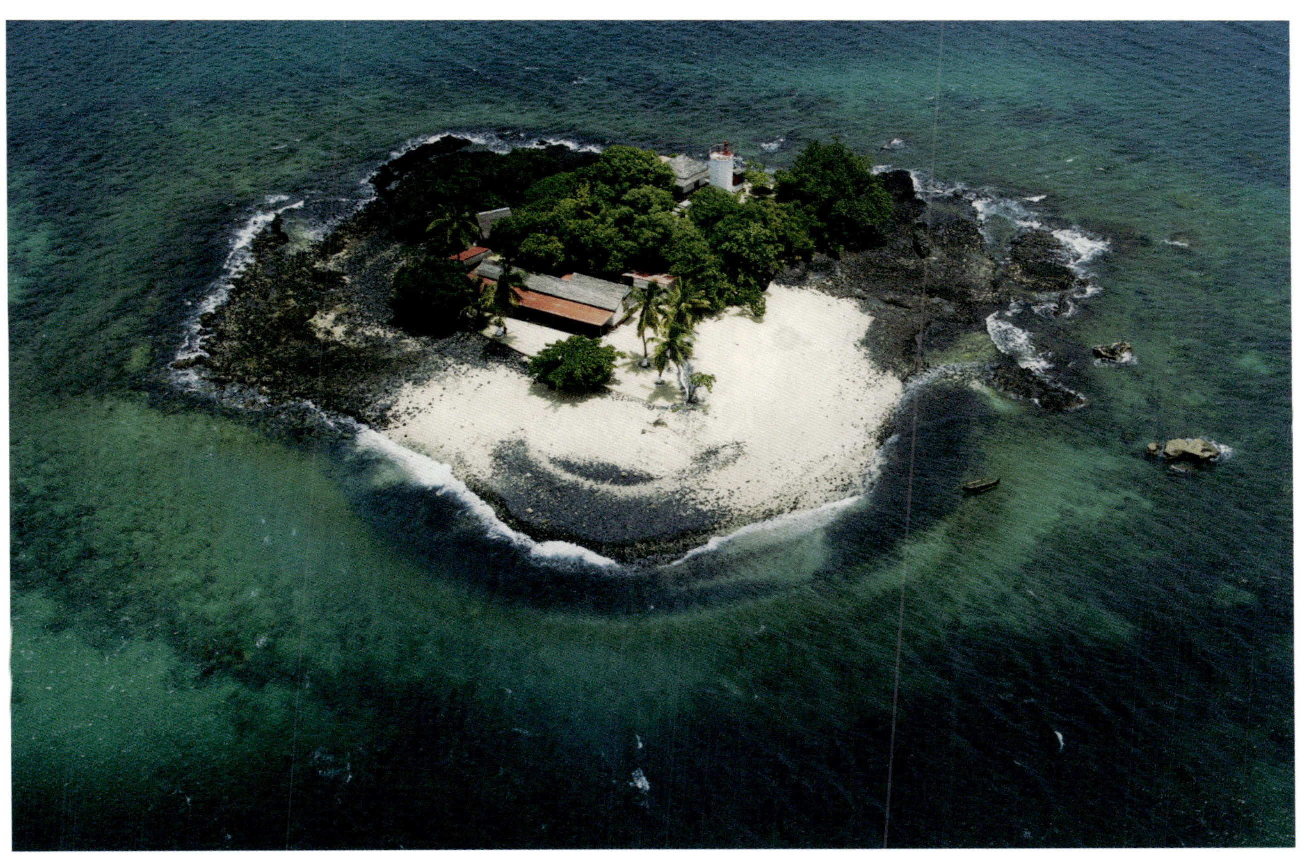

Nothing is so sweet as to return from sea and listen to the raindrops on the rooftops of home.

Sophocles

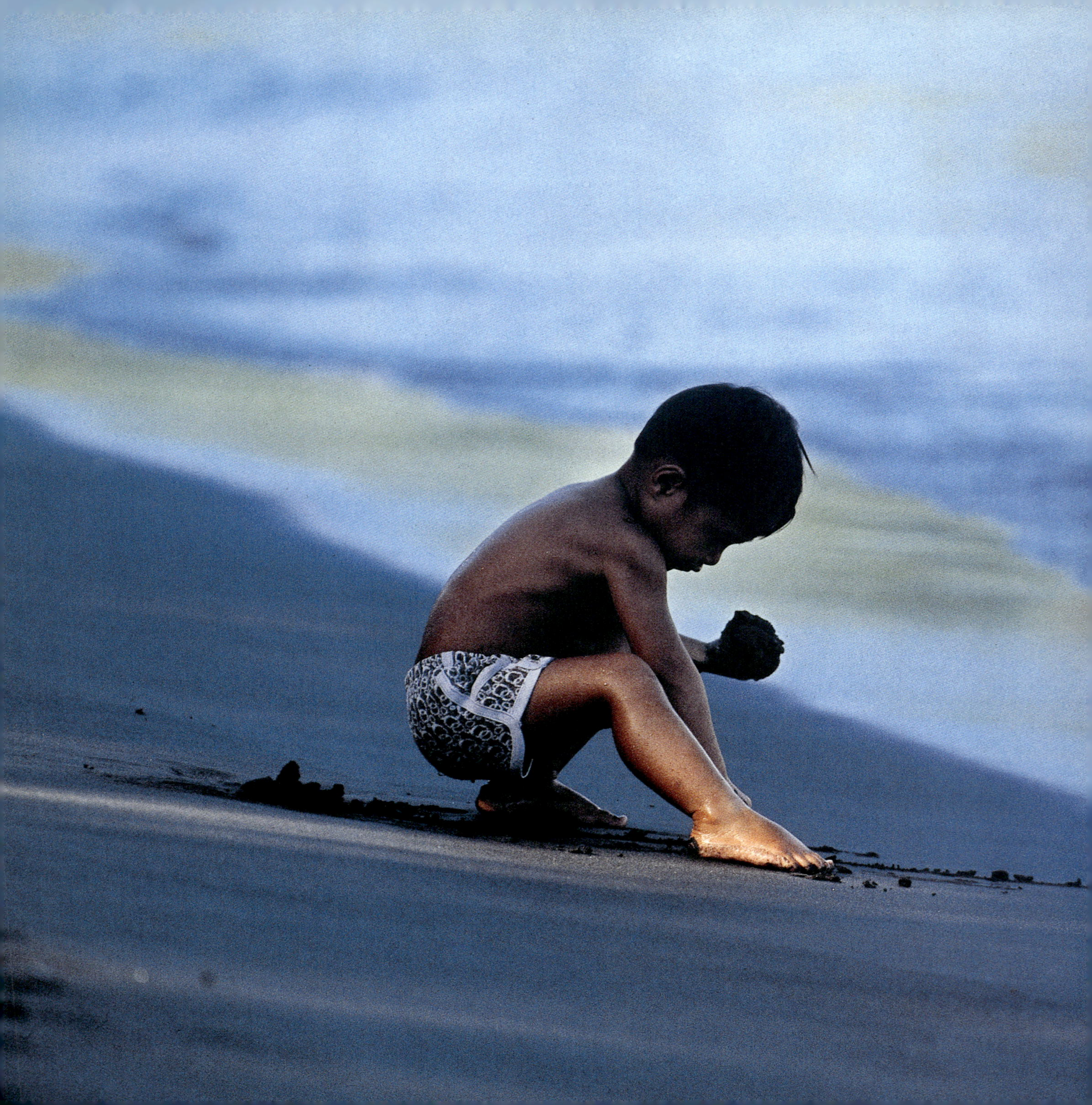

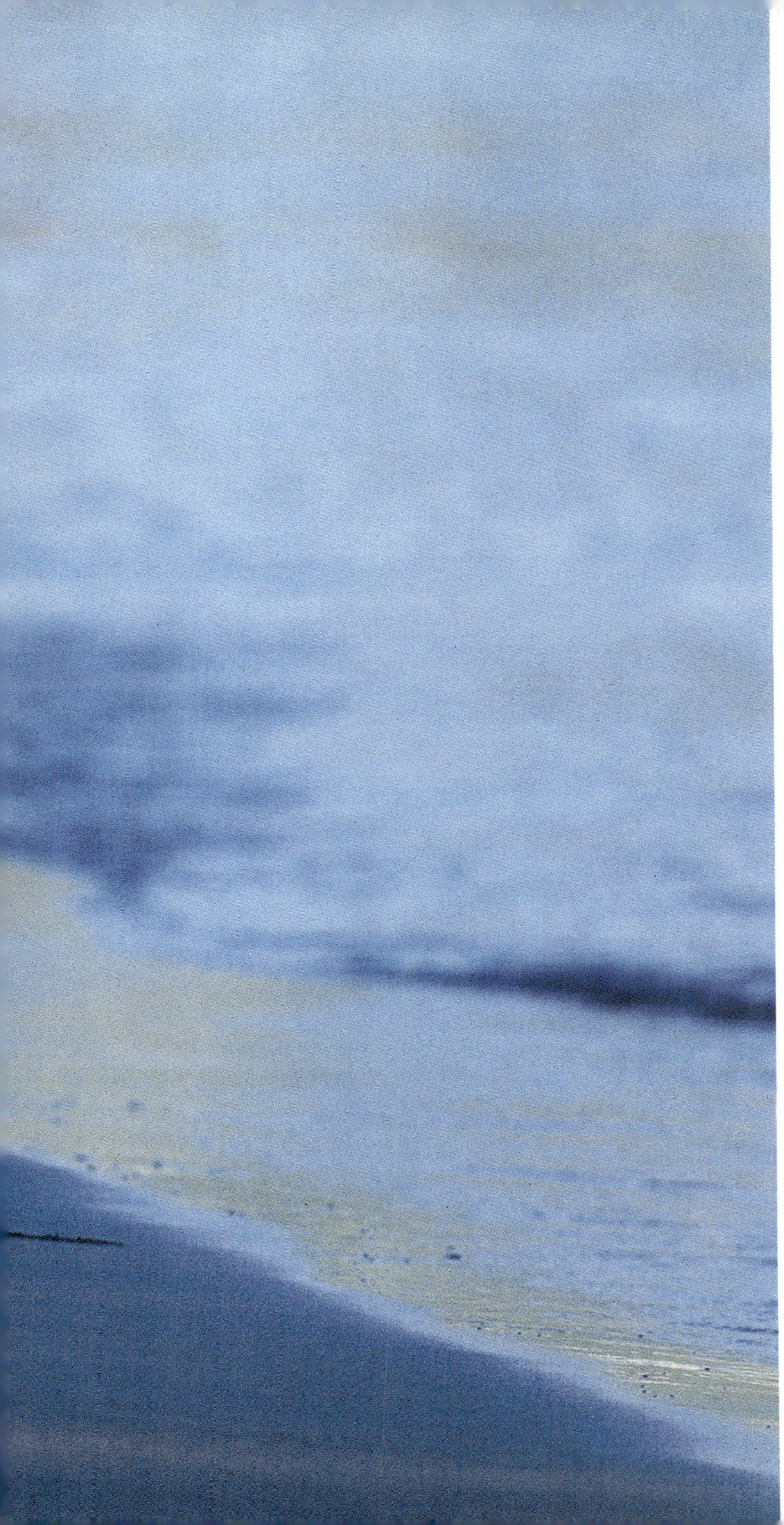

AUGUST 14

There are many advantages in sea-voyaging,
but security is not one of them.

Saadi, from *The Gulistan of Saadi,* 1258

AUGUST 15

The sea takes without asking.
The sea is a worker, a thief and a loafer.
Why does the sea let go so slow?
Or never let go at all?

Carl Sandburg,
from "North Atlantic," *Smoke and Steel*, 1920

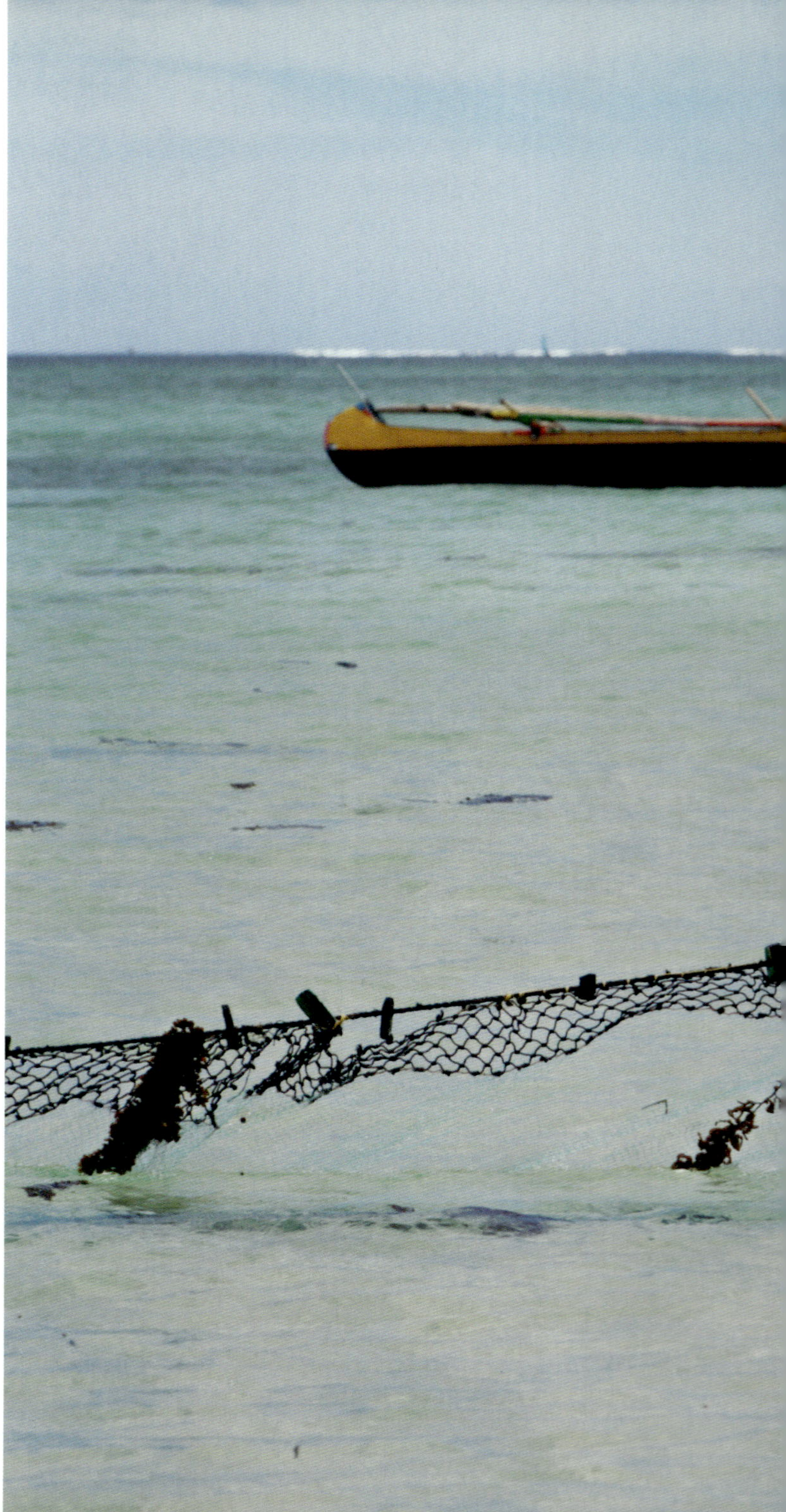

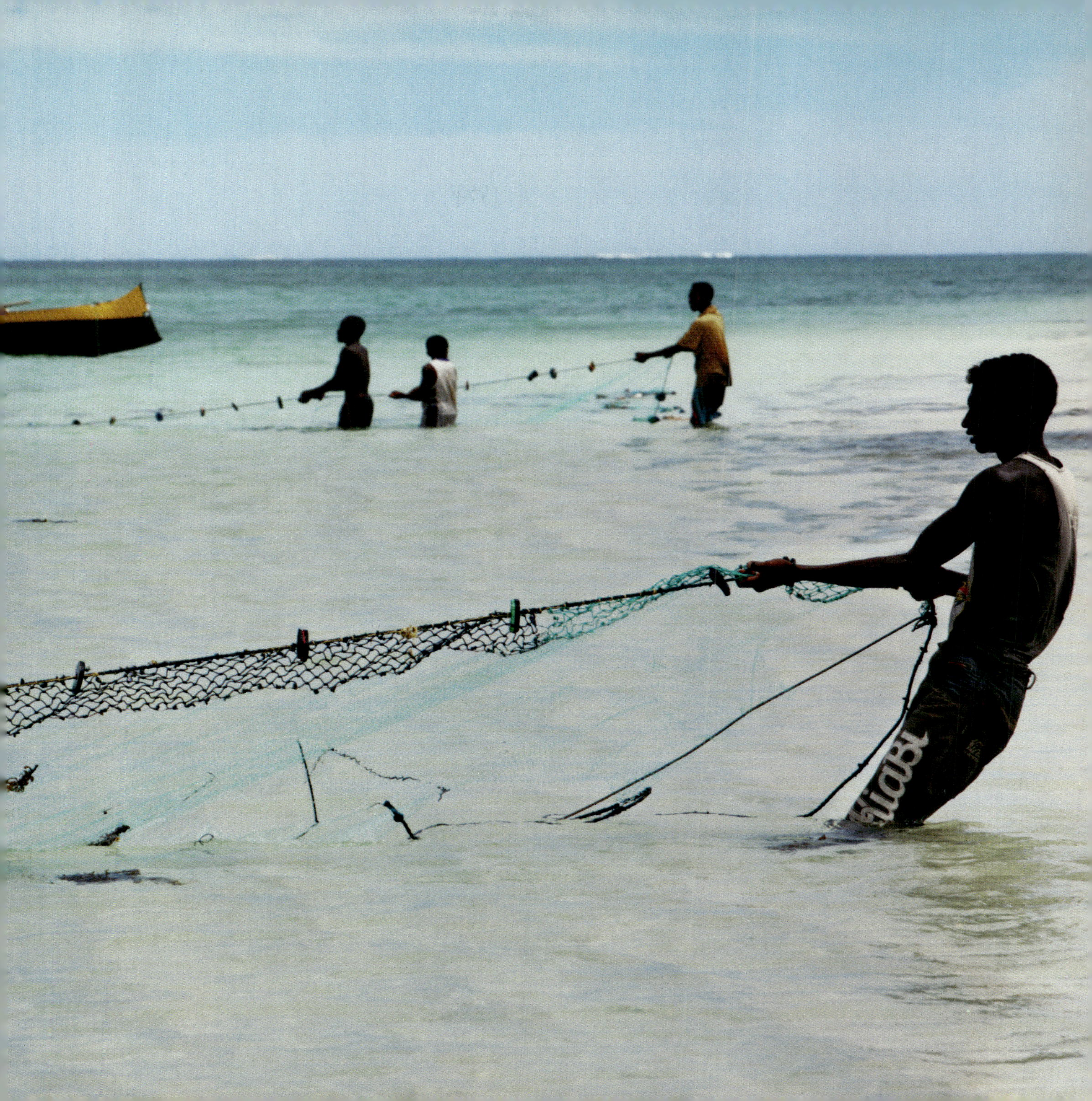

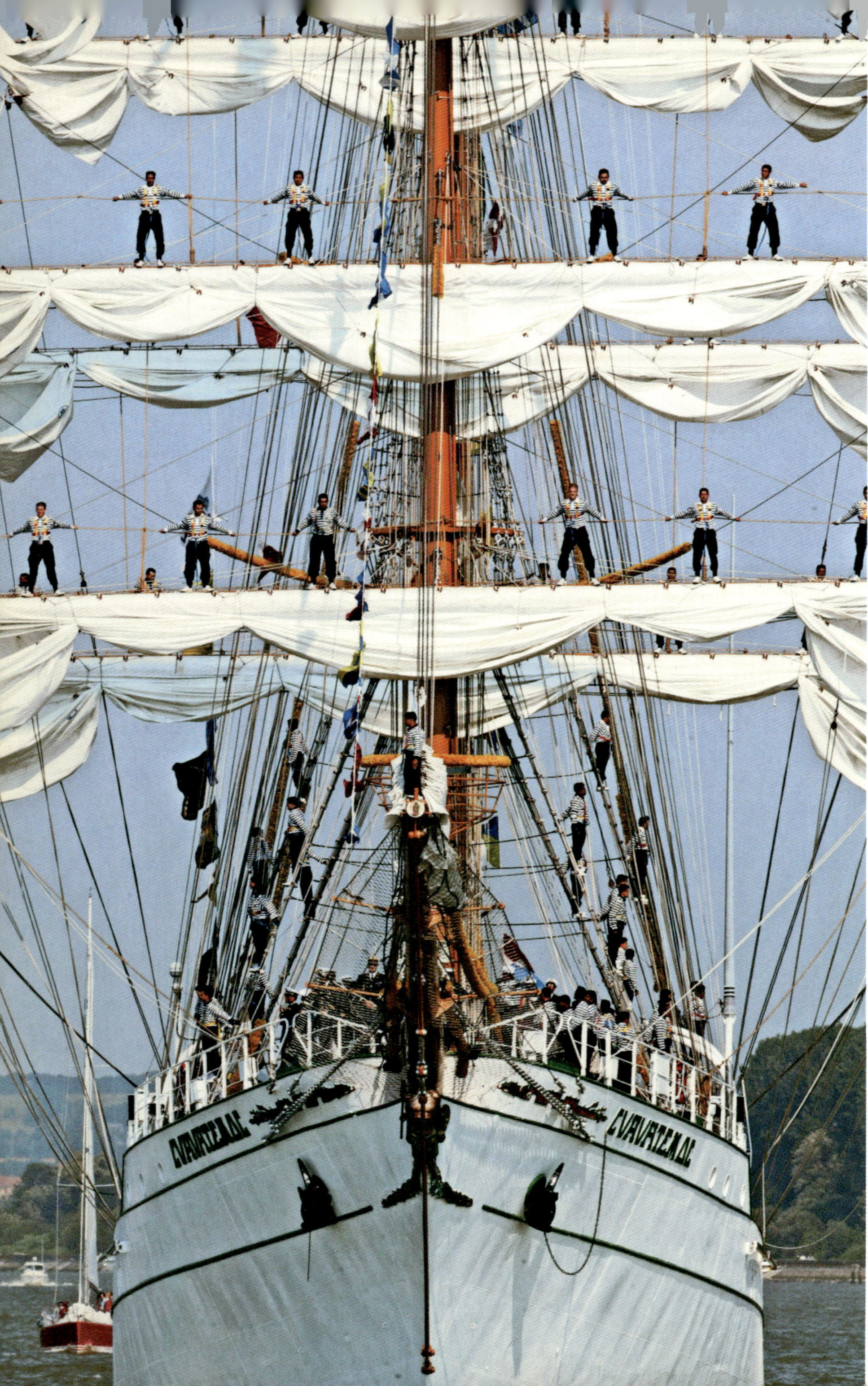

AUGUST 16

A ship is always referred to as "she" because it costs so much to keep her in paint and powder.

Admiral Chester Nimitz

AUGUST 17

We sail within a vast sphere,
ever drifting in uncertainty,
driven from end to end.

Blaise Pascal, from *Pensées*, 1670

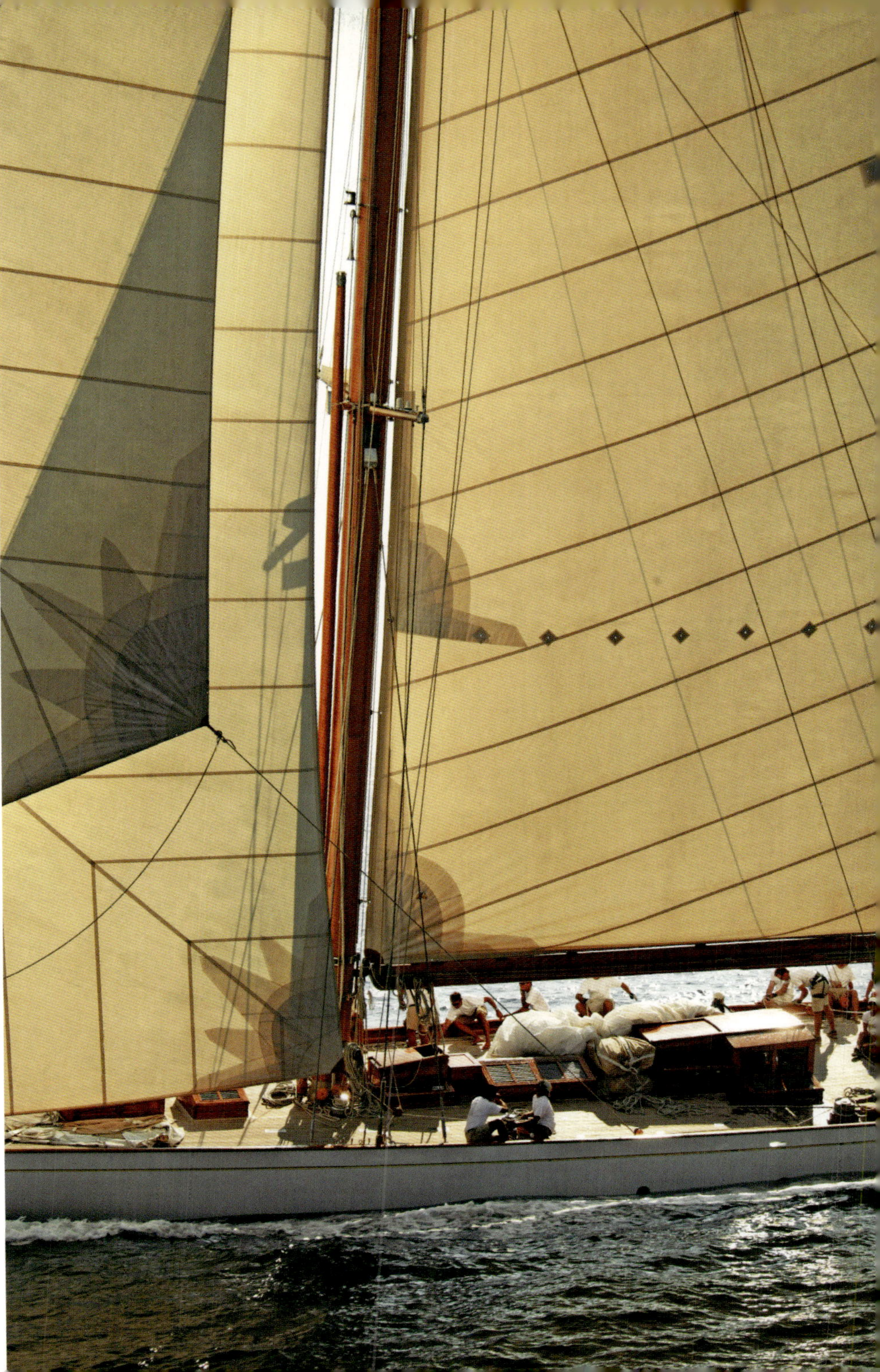

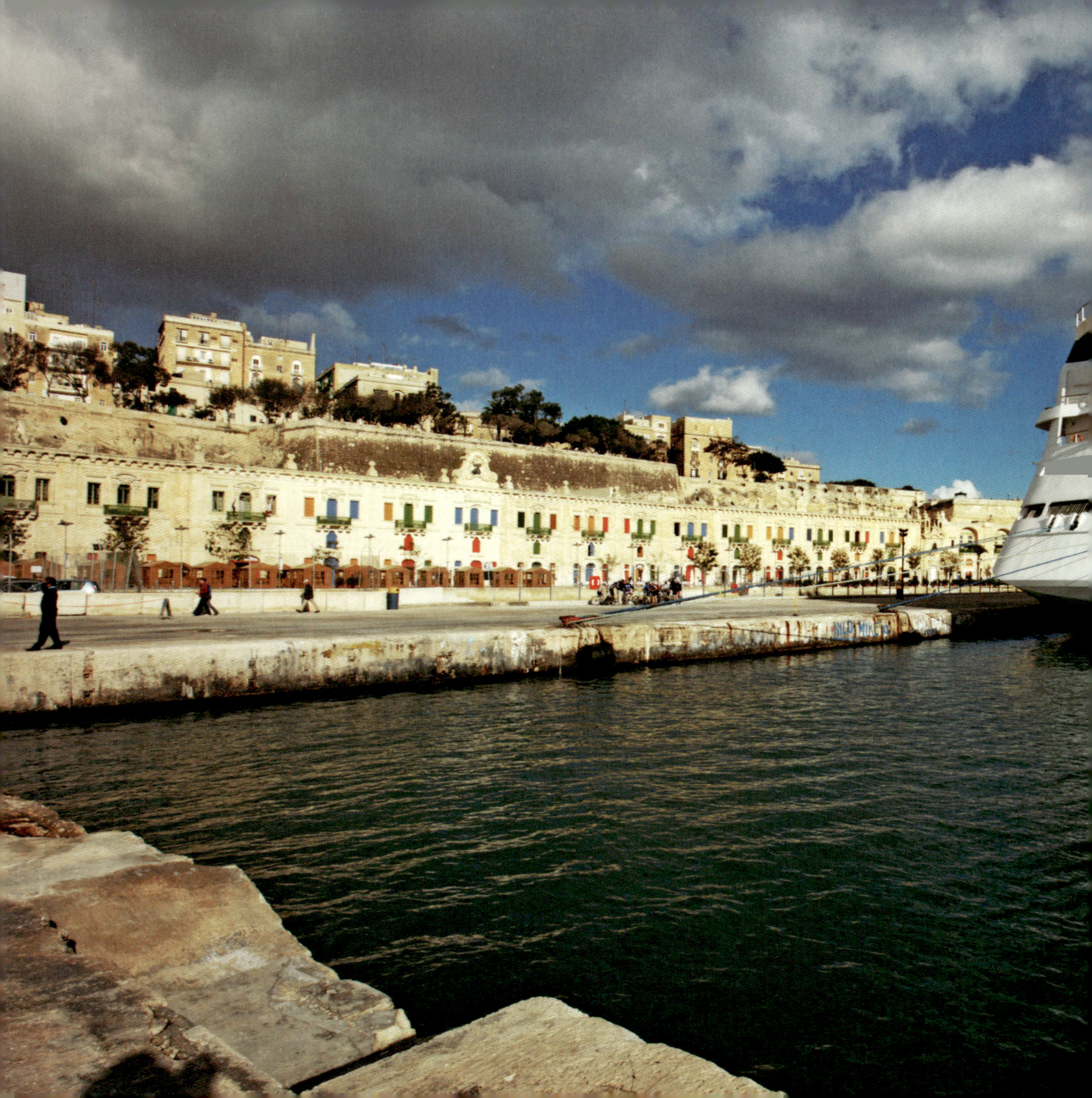

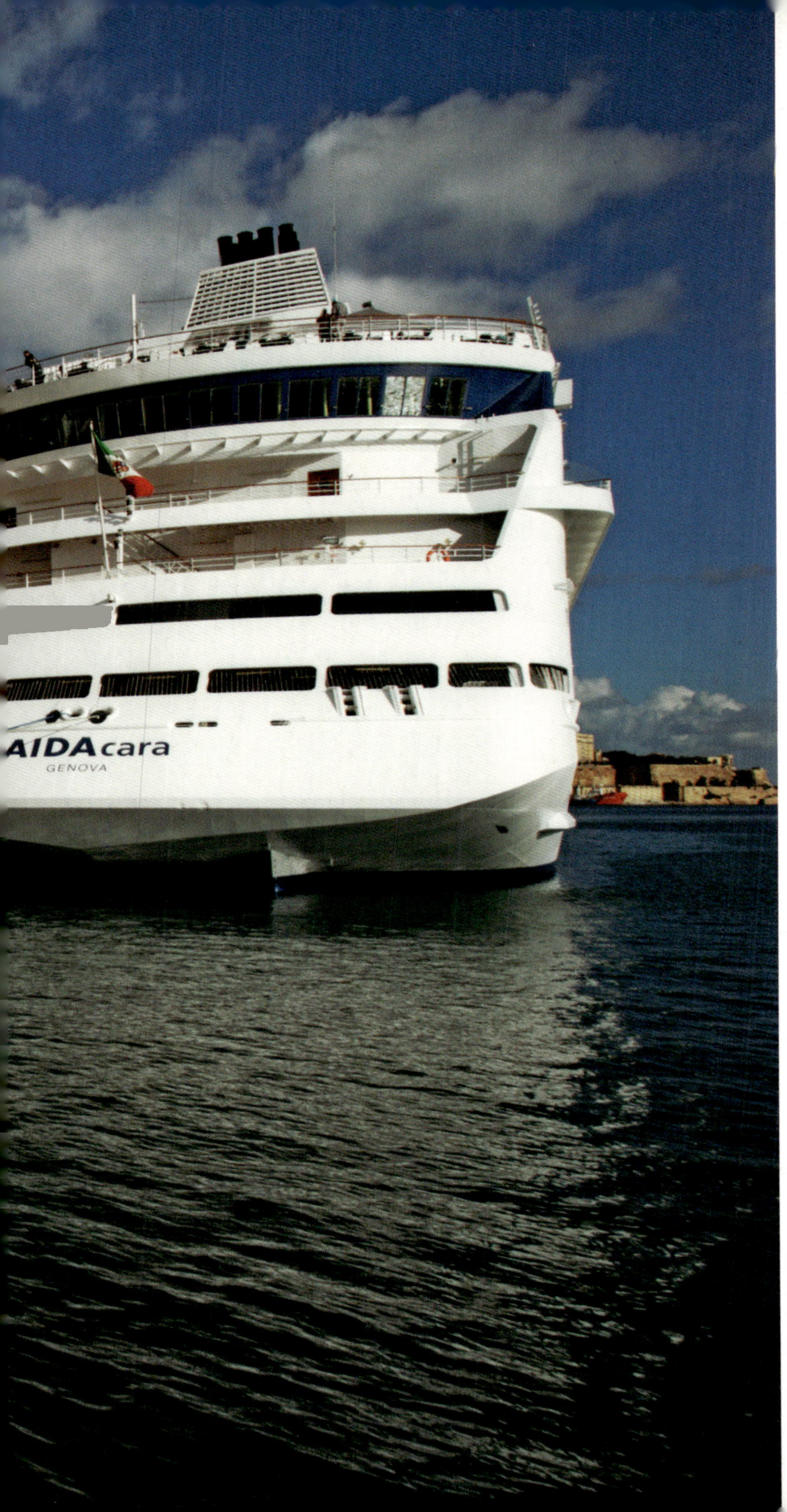

AUGUST 18

No man can swim ashore and
carry his baggage with him.

Latin proverb

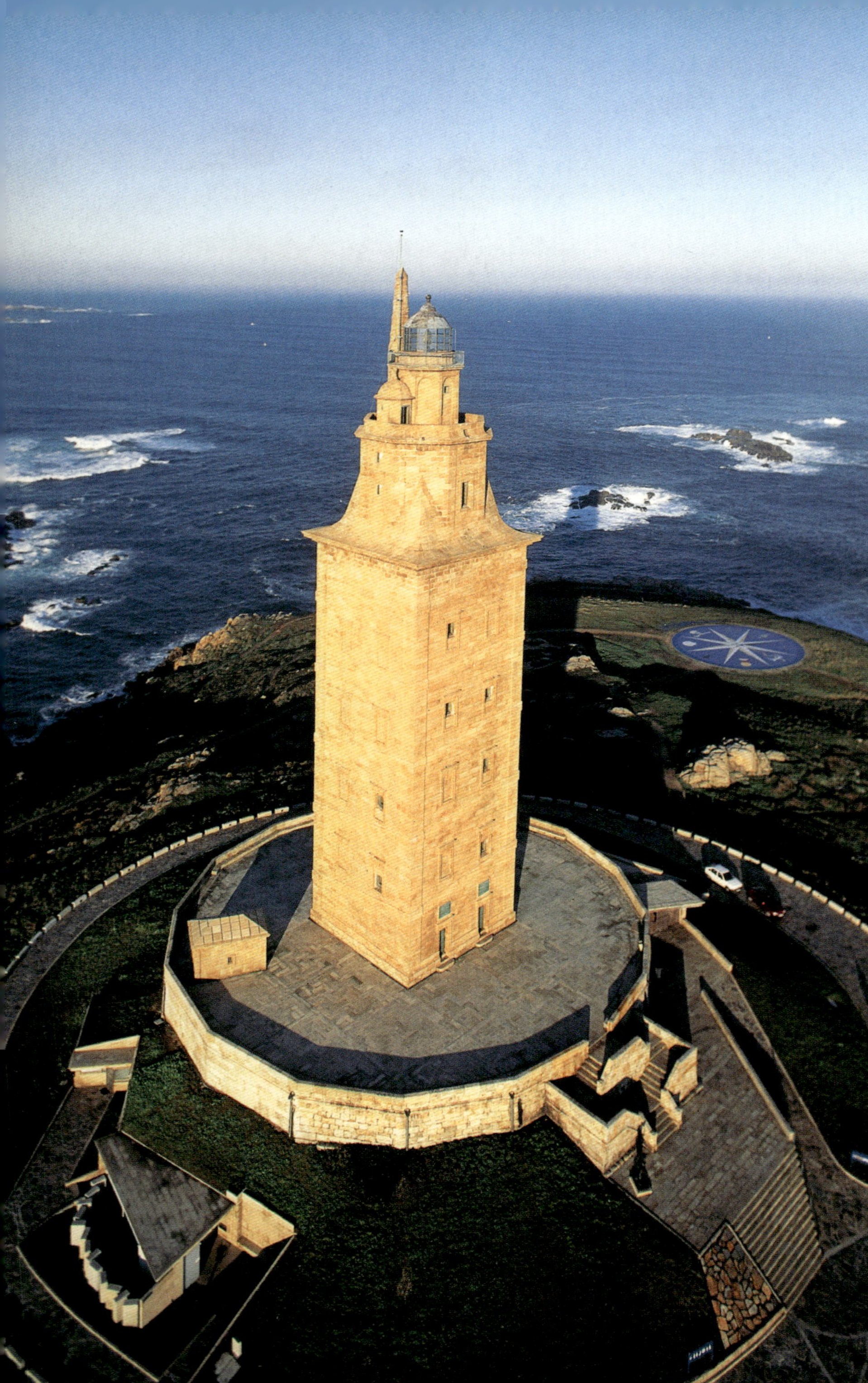

AUGUST 19

There are three types of people.
Those who are alive,
those who are dead, and
those who are at sea.

Anacharsis

AUGUST 20

I joined the Navy to see the world;

And what did we see?

We saw the sea.

Irving Berlin, from *Follow the Fleet*, 1936

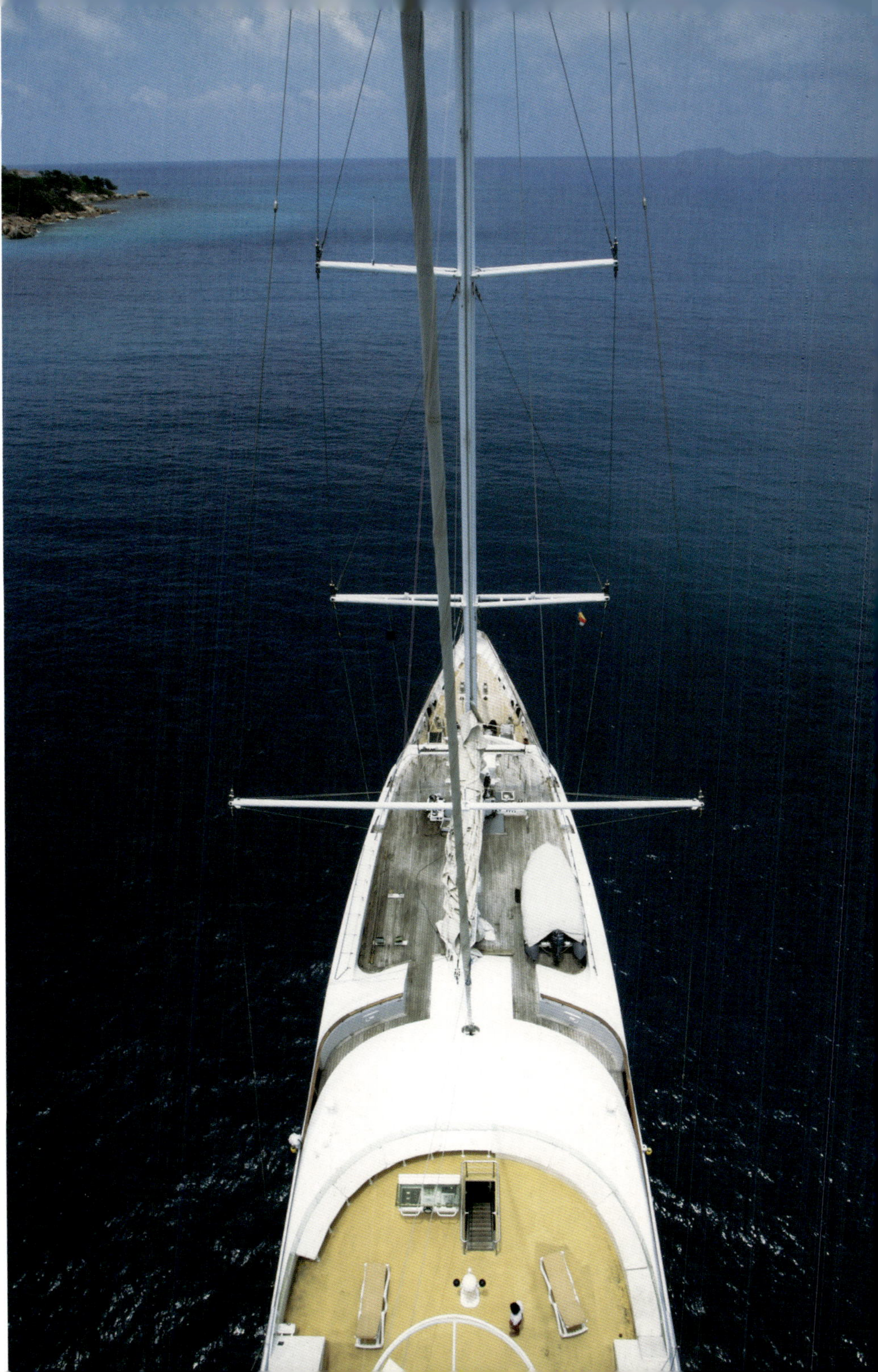

AUGUST 21

The sea's vast depths lie open to the fish;
Wherever the breezes blow the bird may fly;
So to the brave man every land's a home.

Ovid, from "Fasti"

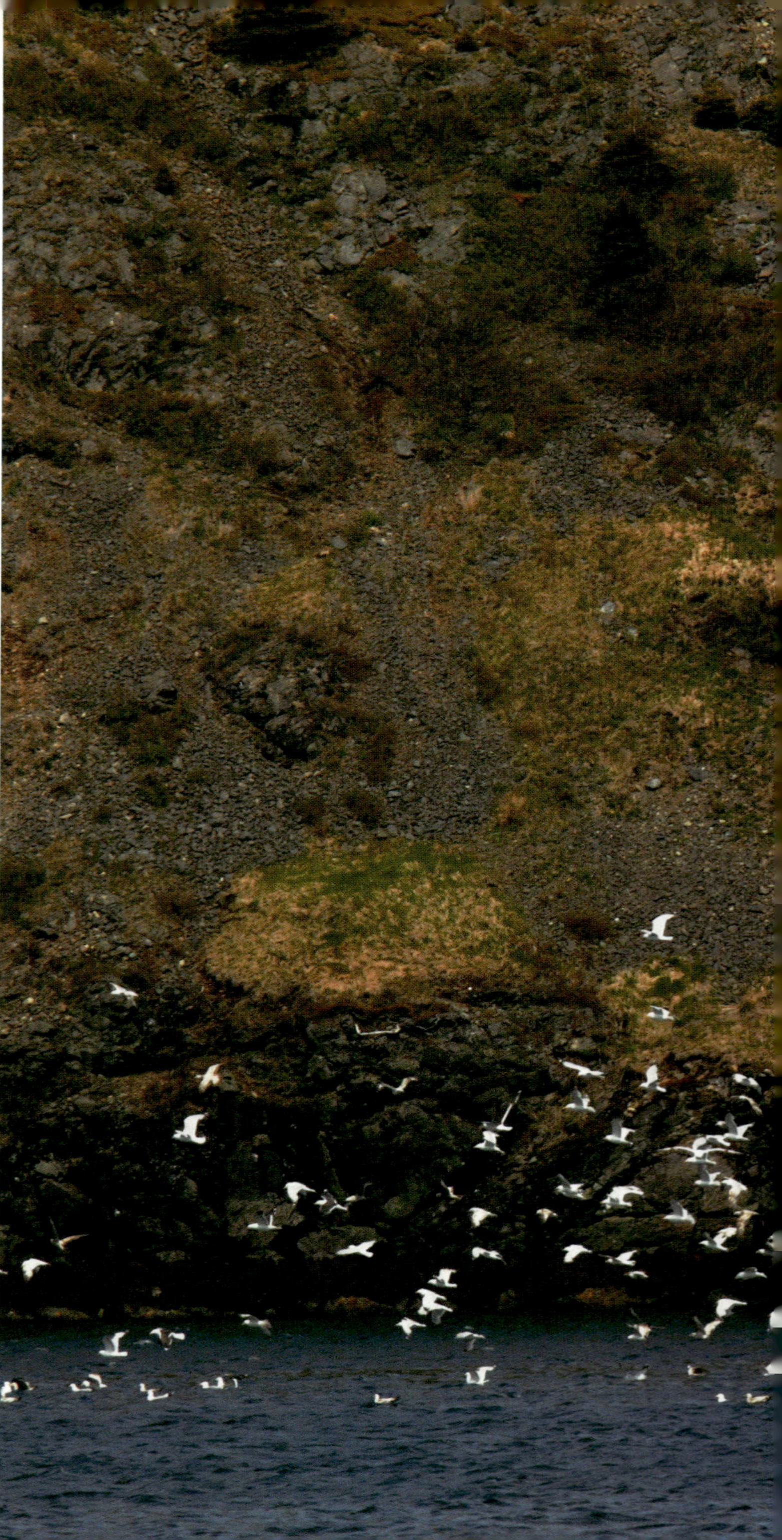

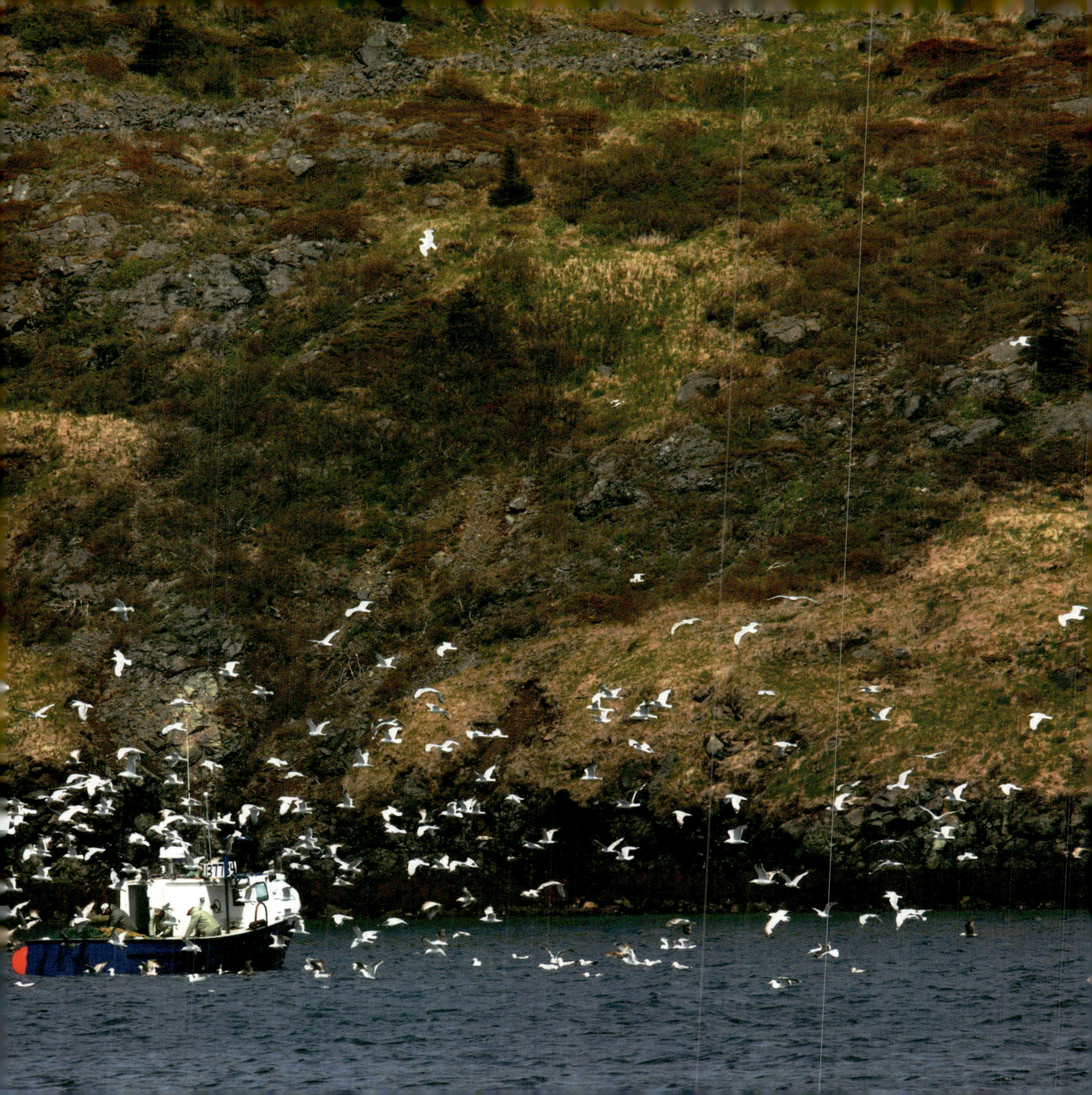

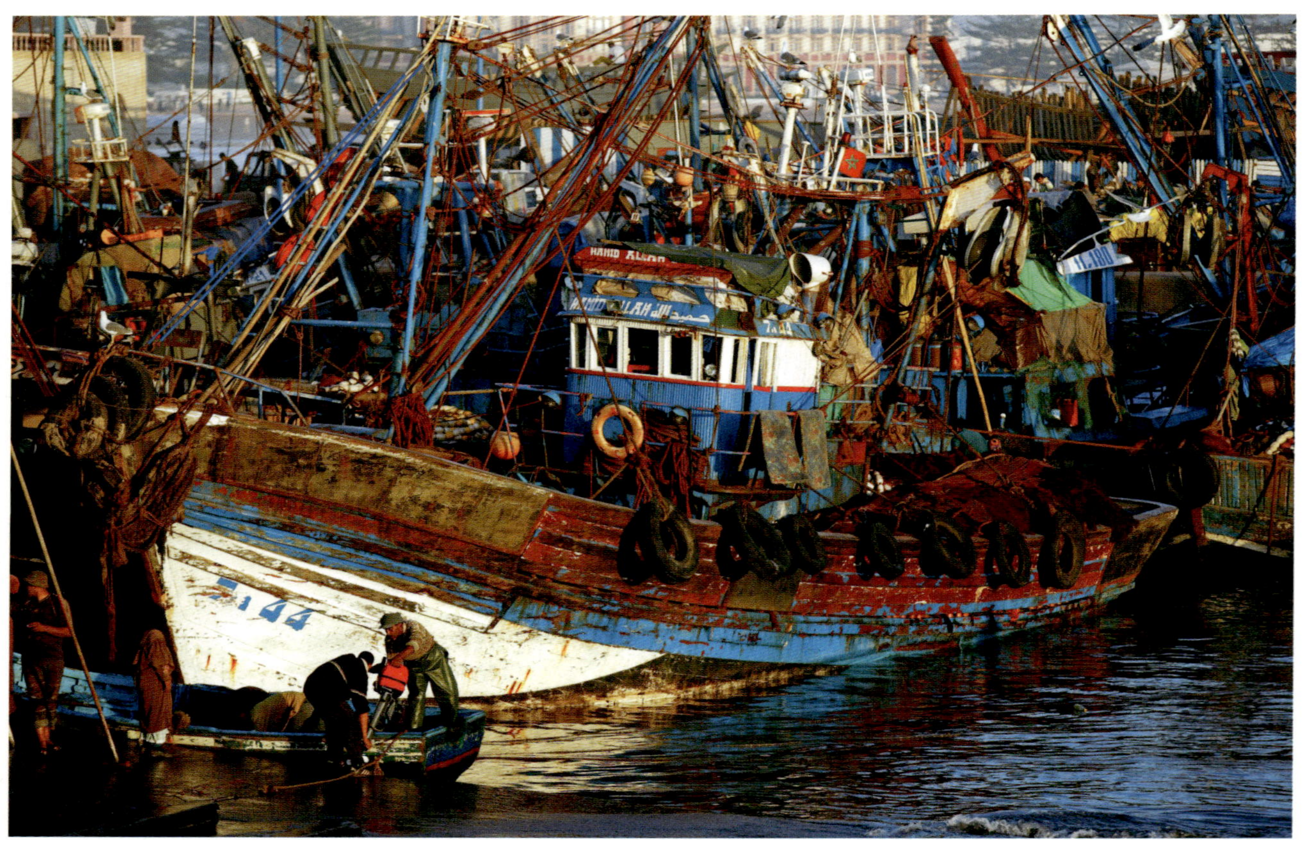

Sea, I am like you, filled with broken voices,
And my ships, singing, give a name to the years.

Guillaume Apollinaire, from "The Sirens," *The Bestiary,* 1911

AUGUST 23

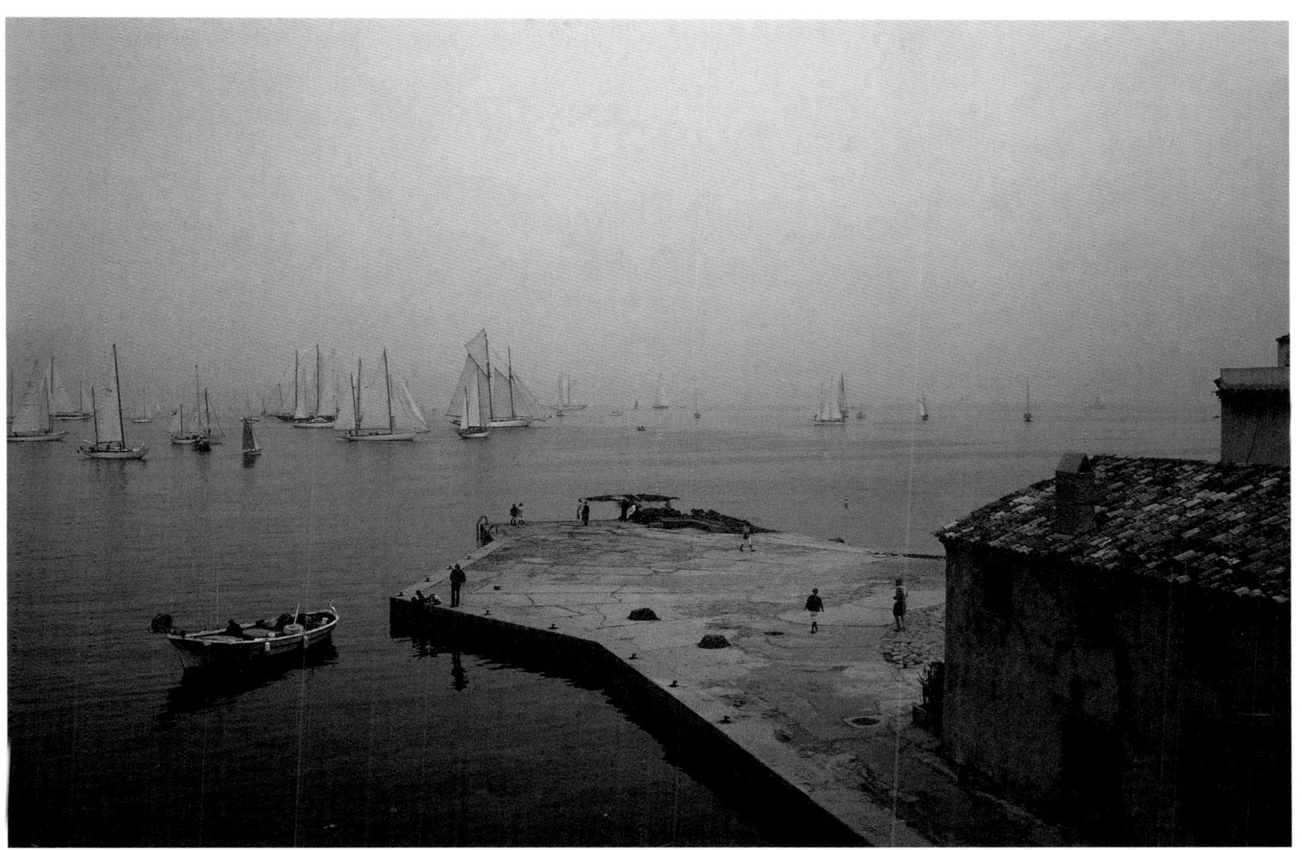

Roll on, thou deep and dark blue Ocean,—roll!
Ten thousand fleets sweep over thee in vain.

Lord Byron, from "Childe Harold's Pilgrimage," 1818

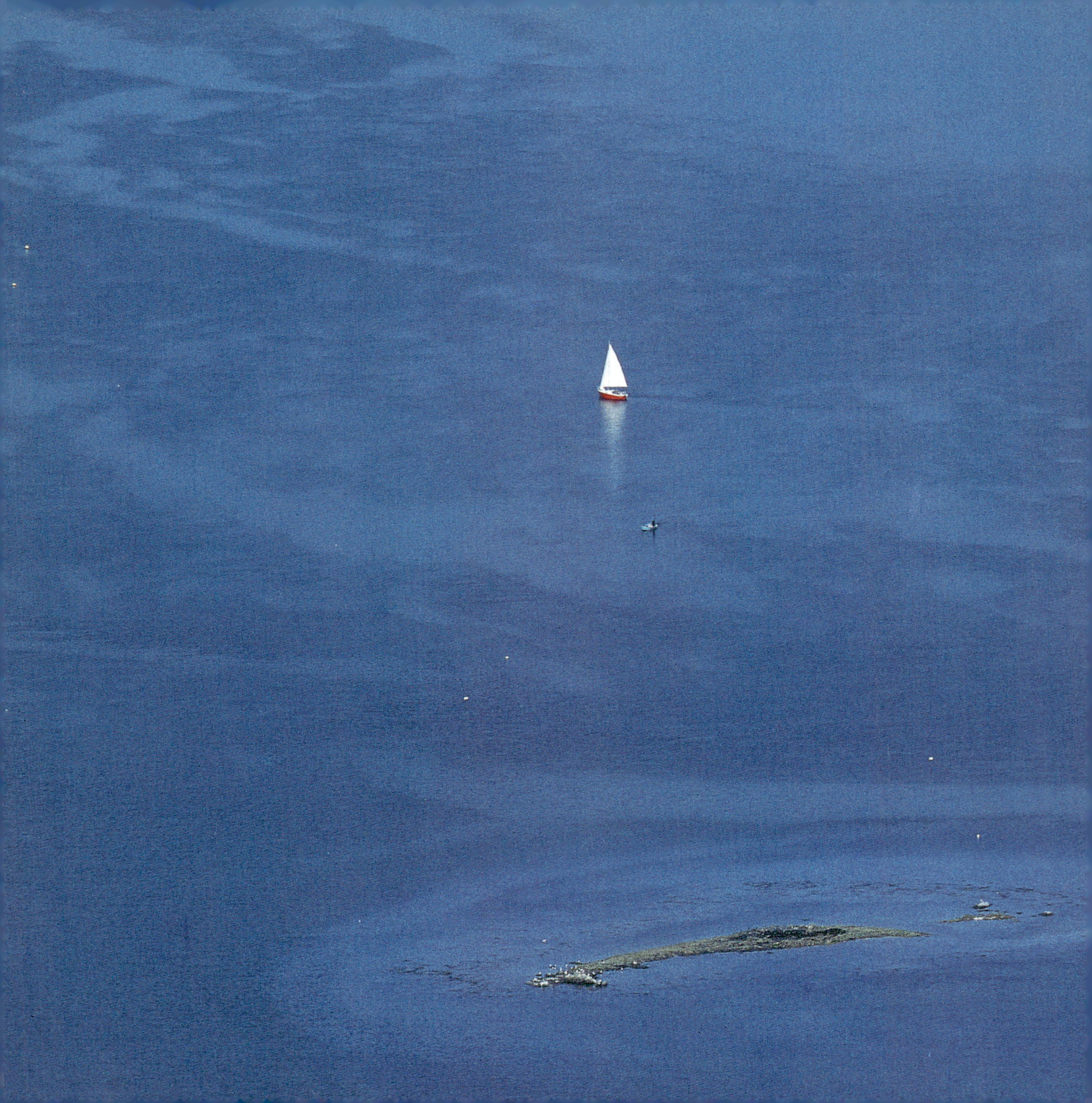

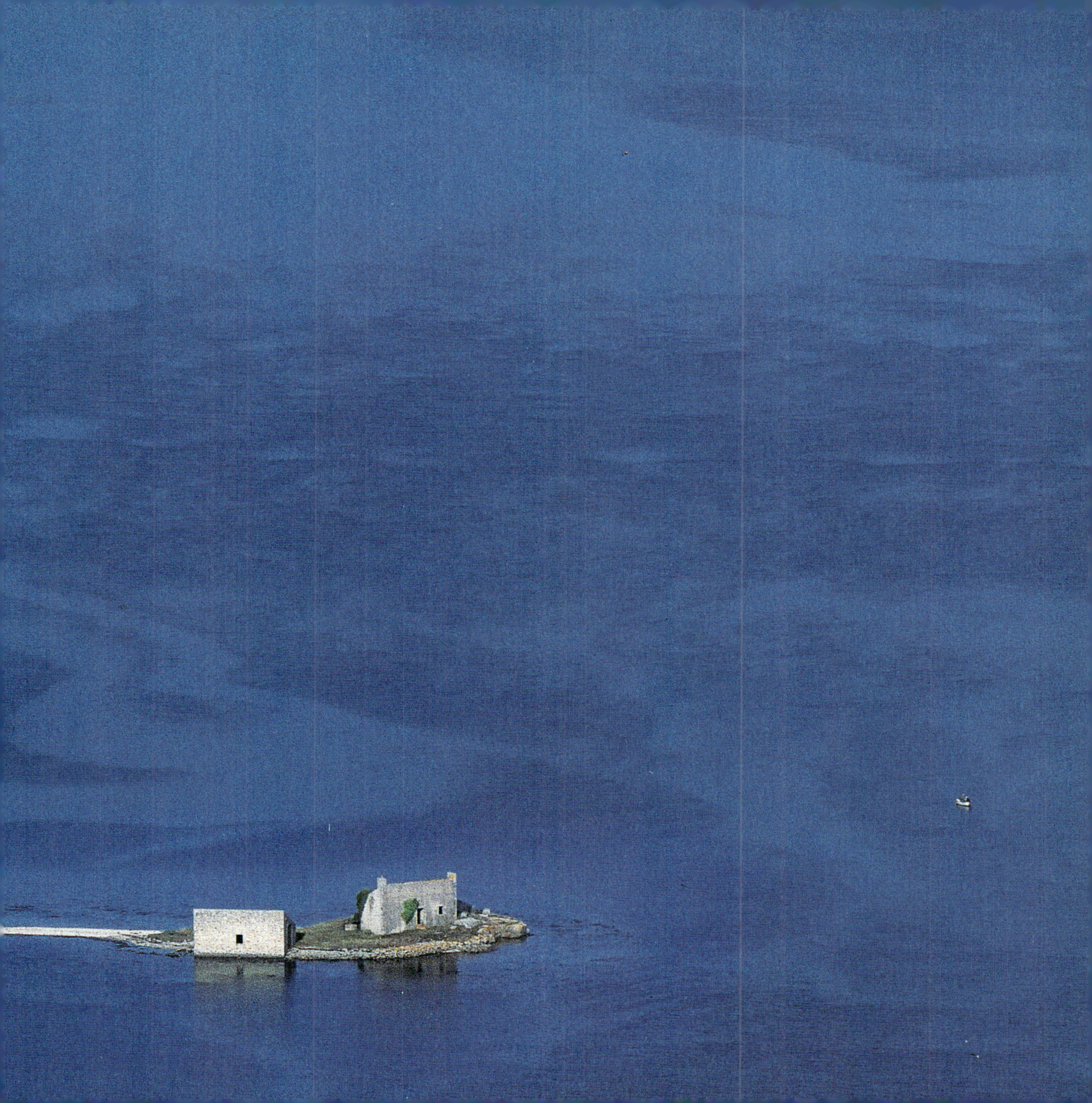

AUGUST 24

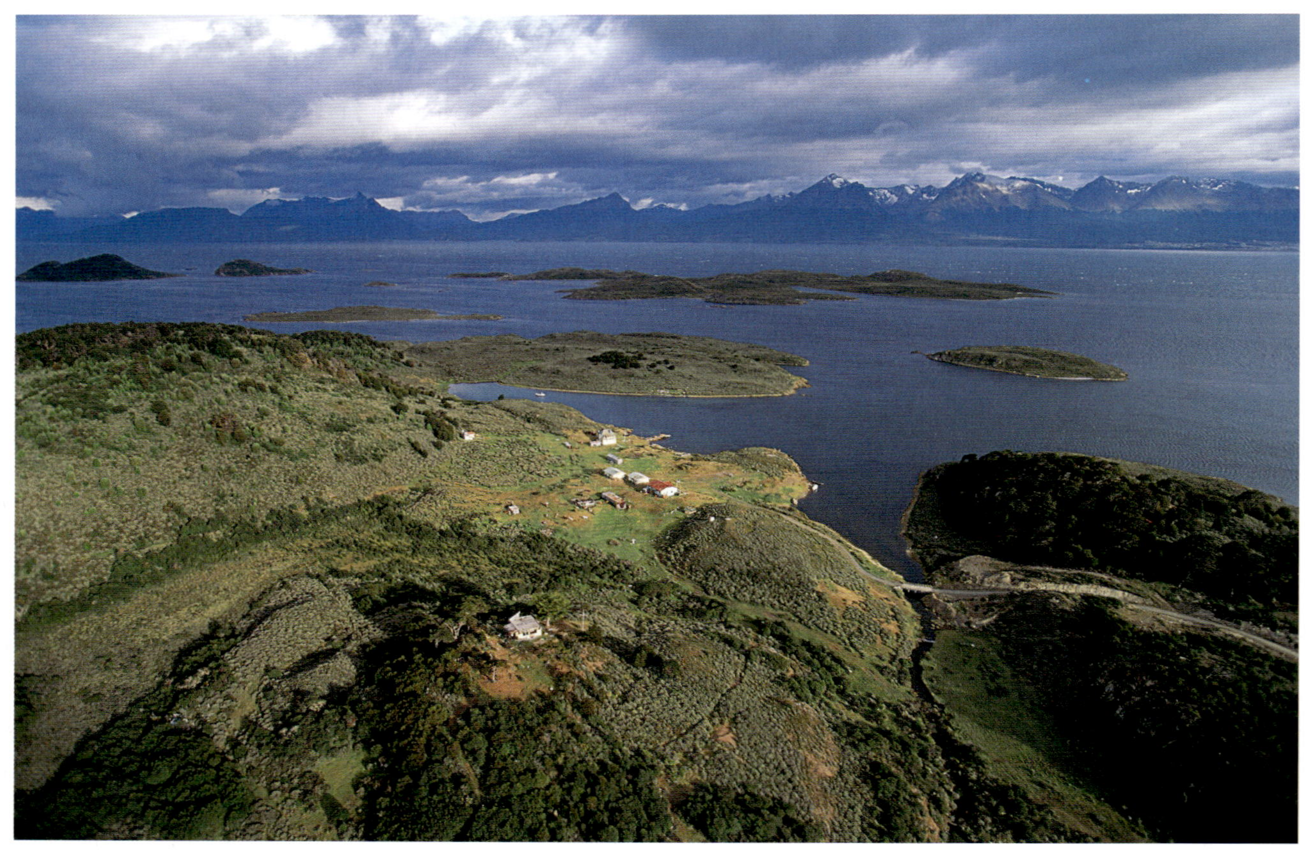

The bleat, the bark, bellow, and roar
Are waves that beat on Heaven's shore

William Blake, from "Auguries of Innocence"

AUGUST 25

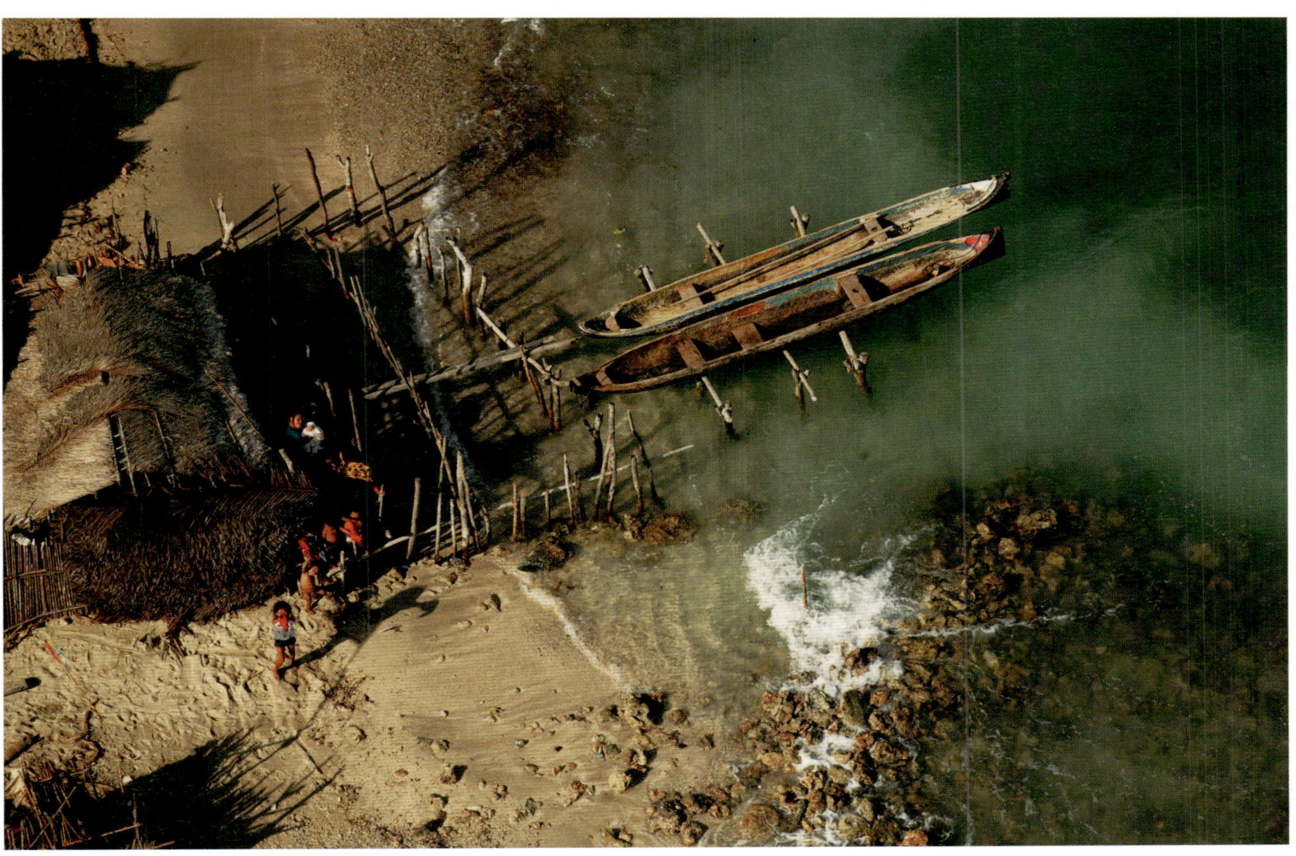

Most of us, I suppose, are a little nervous of the sea.
No matter what its smiles may be, we doubt its friendship.

H. M. Tomlinson, from *The Sea and the Jungle,* 1913

AUGUST 26

We greatly prefer the sea to all our relations.

Jane Austen,
in a letter to her sister Cassandra, 1801

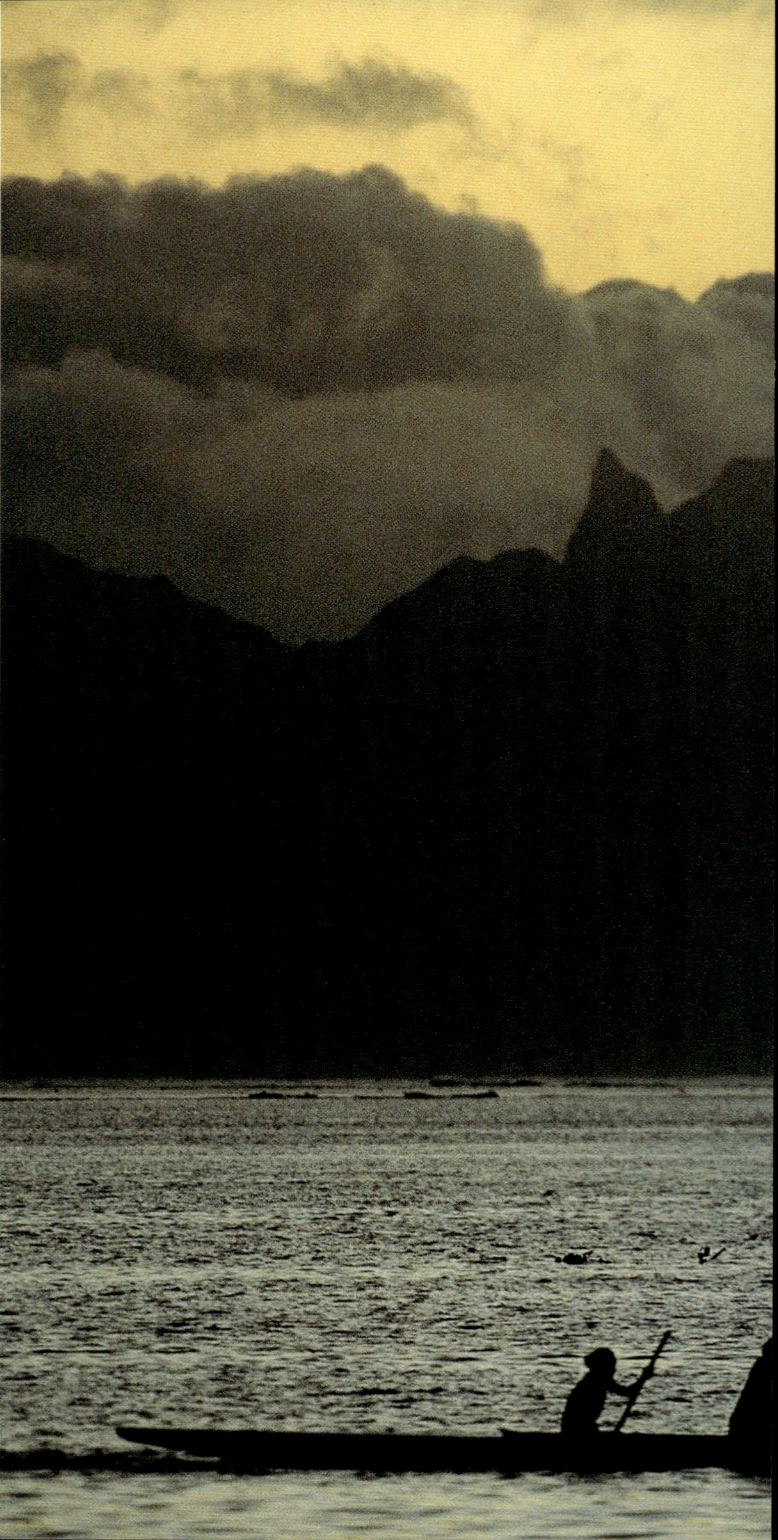

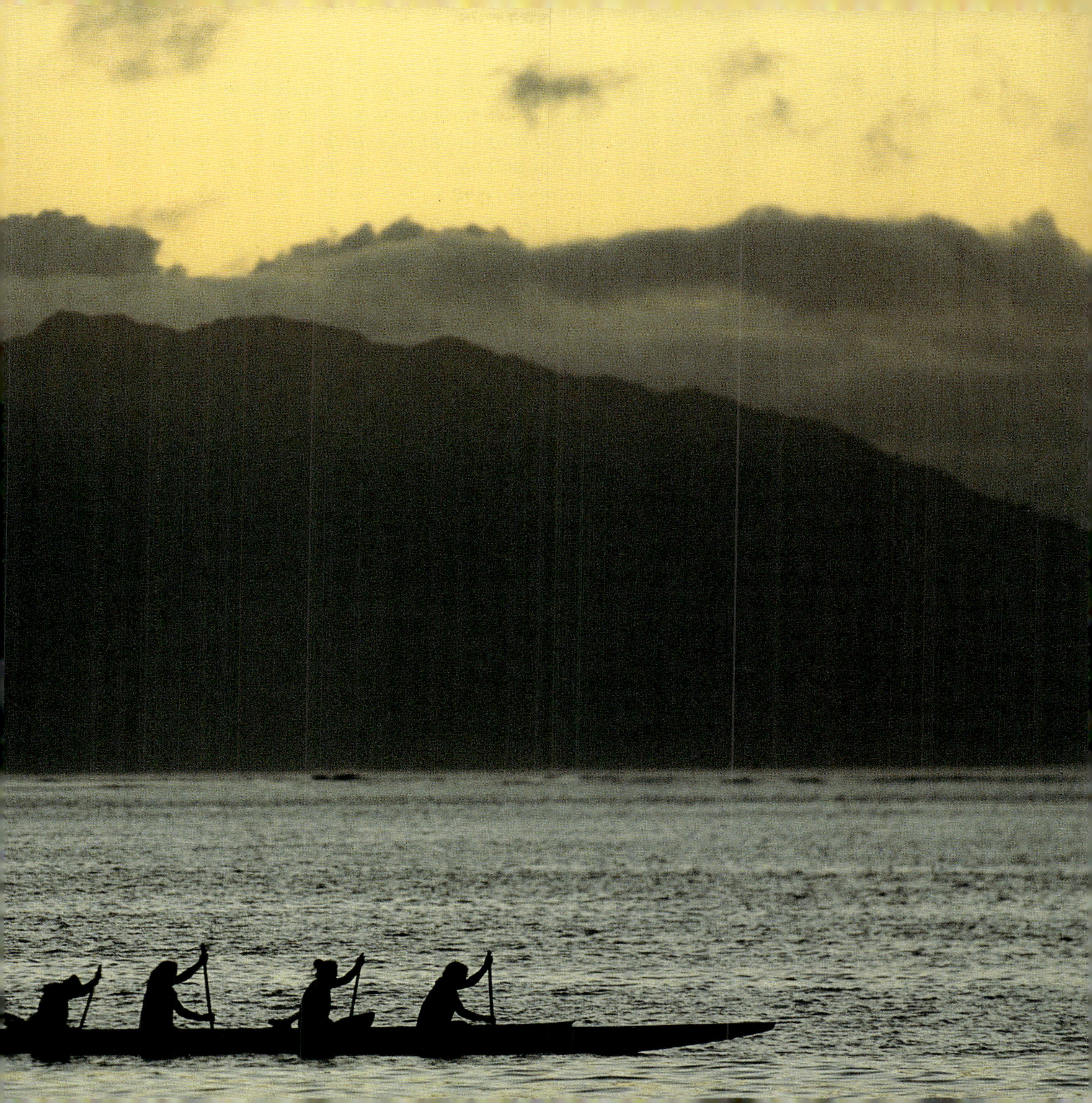

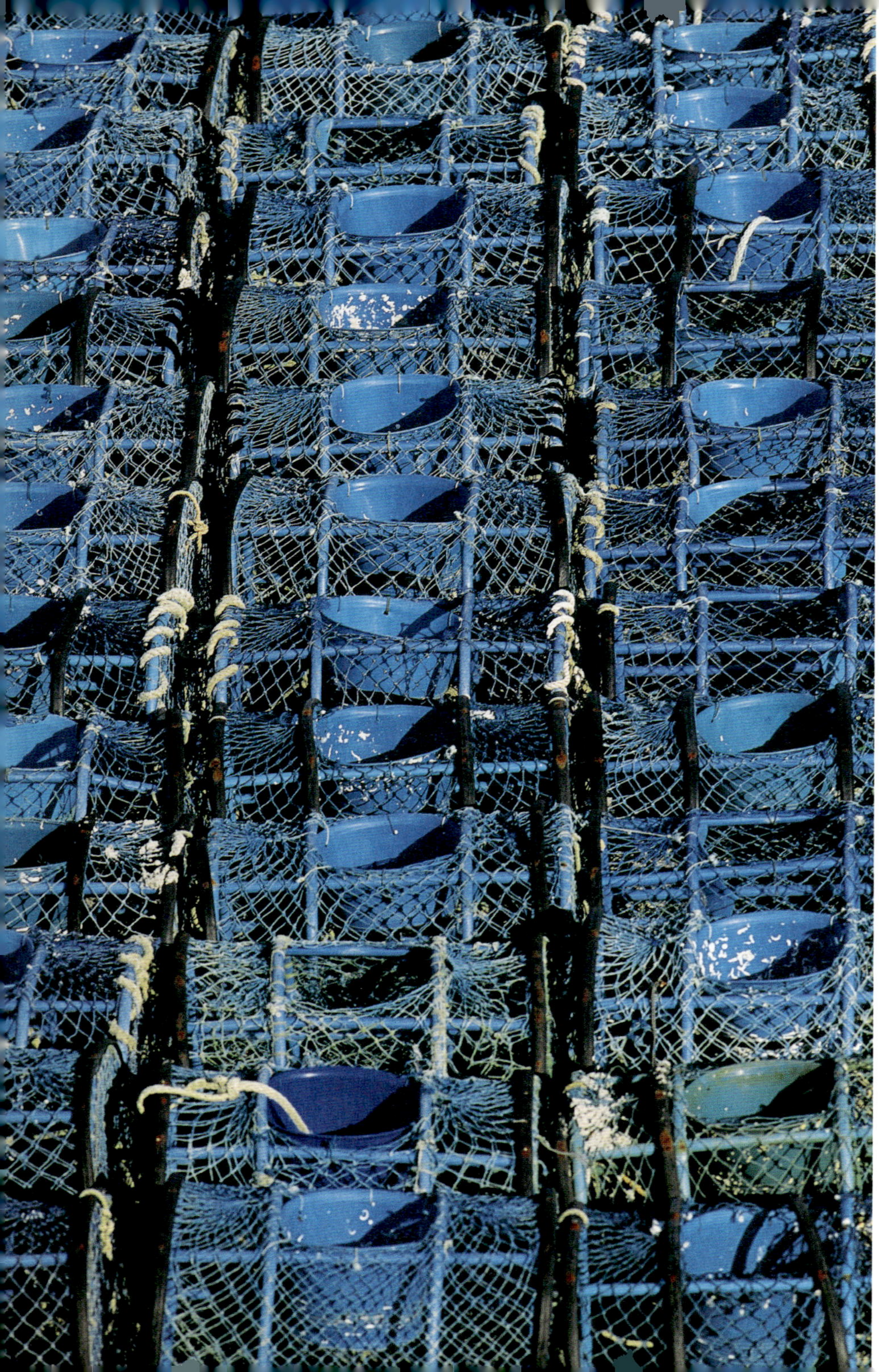

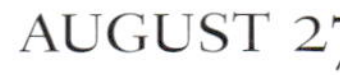

AUGUST 27

If the seawater were hotter
we could catch boiled fish.

French proverb

AUGUST 28

All you that would be seamen
must bear a valiant heart.

Martyn Parker

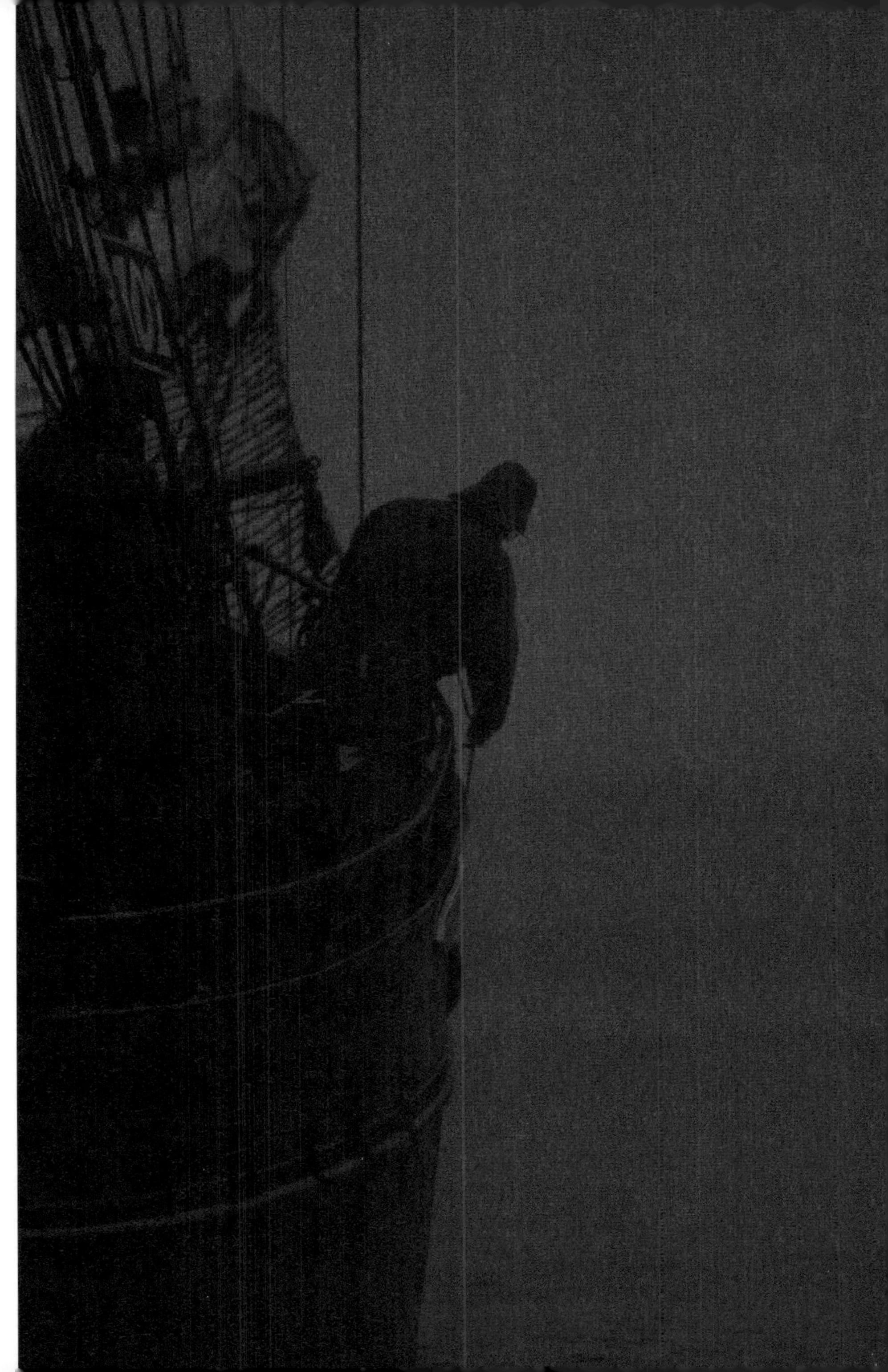

AUGUST 29

We sang together on the wide sea,
Like men at peace on a peaceful shore;
Each sail was loosed to the wind so free,
Each helm made sure by the twilight star.

Robert Browning, from "The Wanderers"

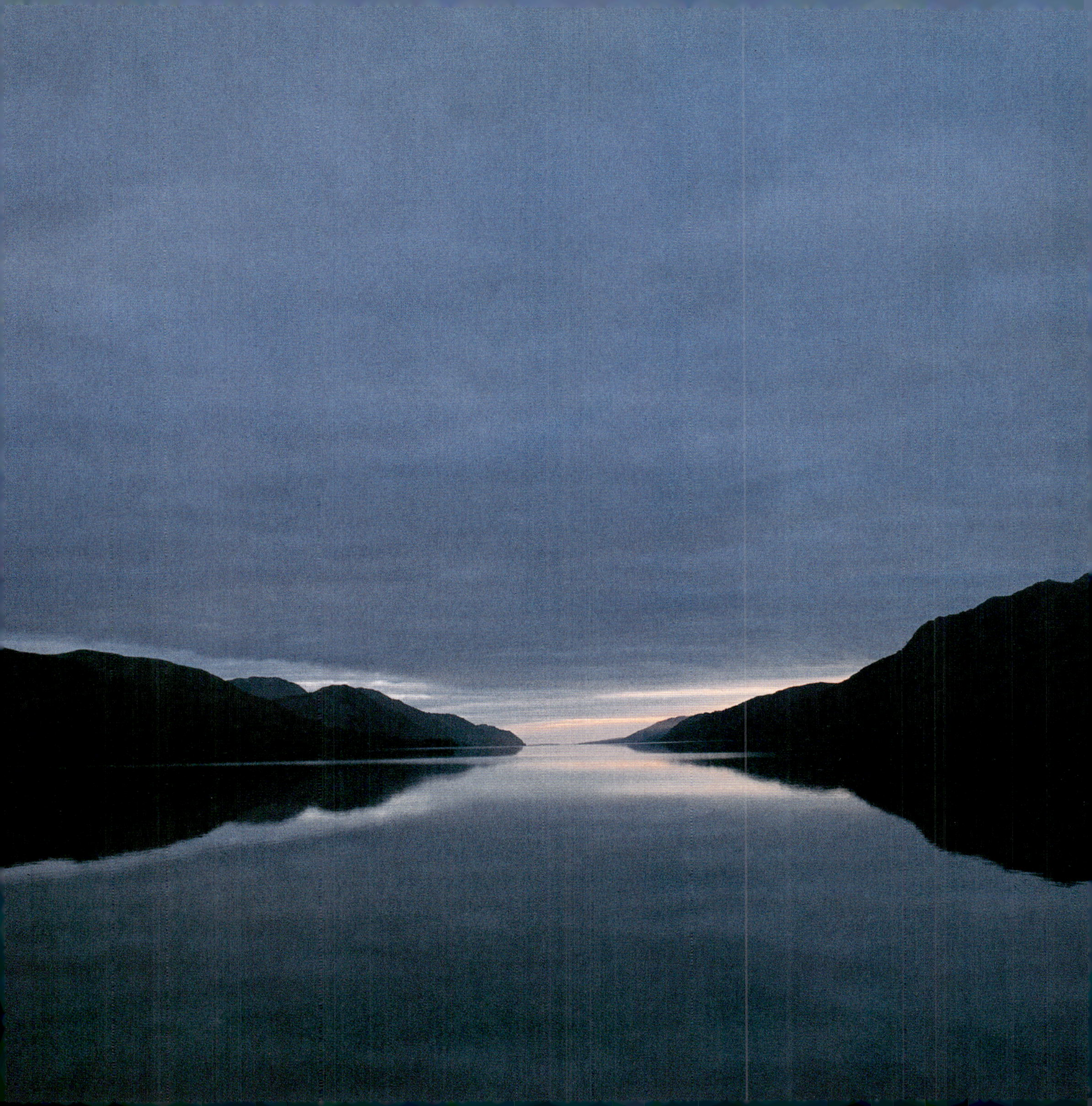

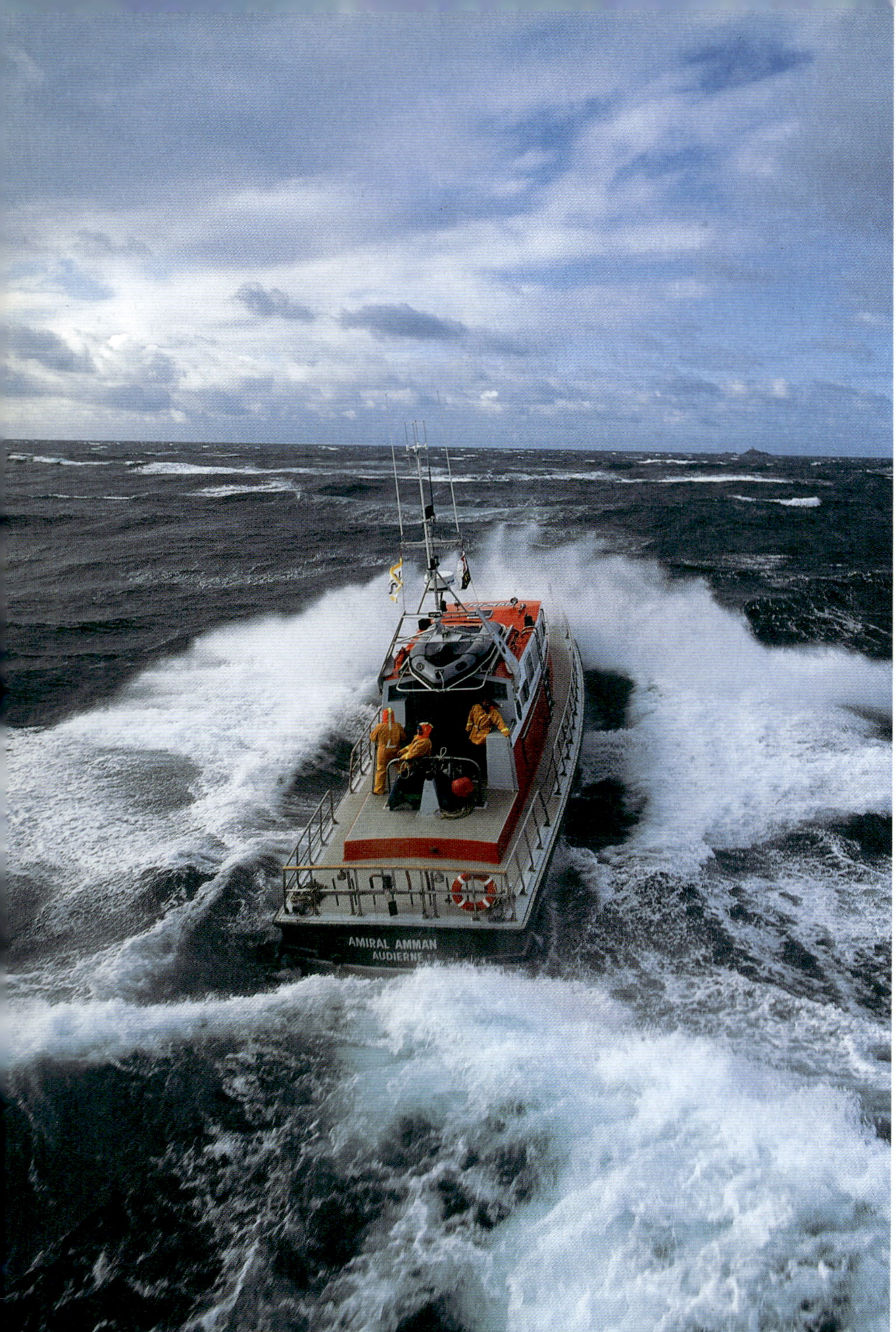

AUGUST 30

One does not discover new lands
without consenting to lose sight
of the shore for a very long time.

André Gide

AUGUST 31

Half a mile out, where is the reef, the white-headed combers thrust suddenly skyward out of the placid turquoise-blue and come rolling in to shore. One after another they come, a mile long, with smoking crests, the white battalions of the infinite army of the sea.

Jack London,
from *The Cruise of the Snark*, 1913

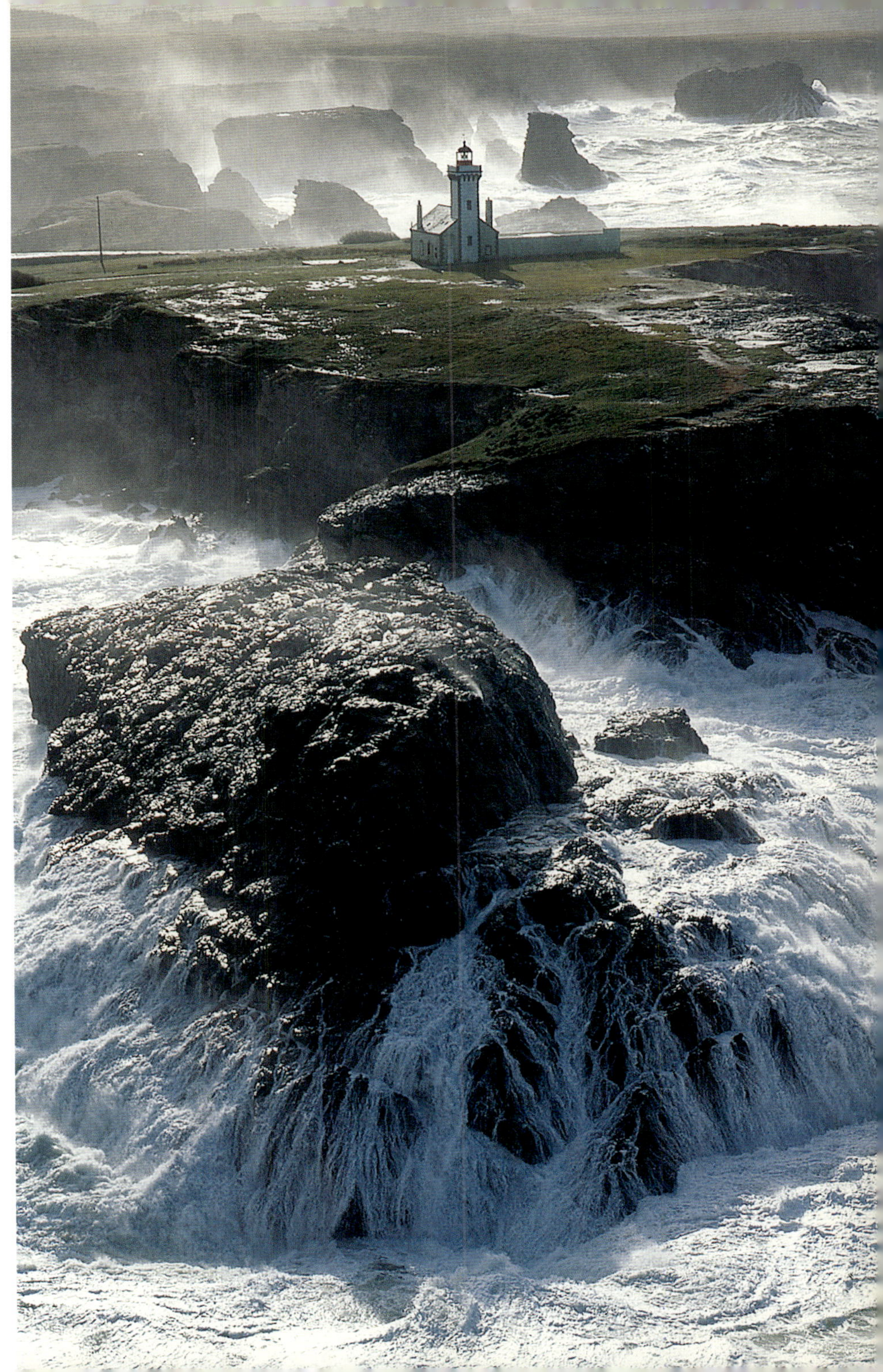

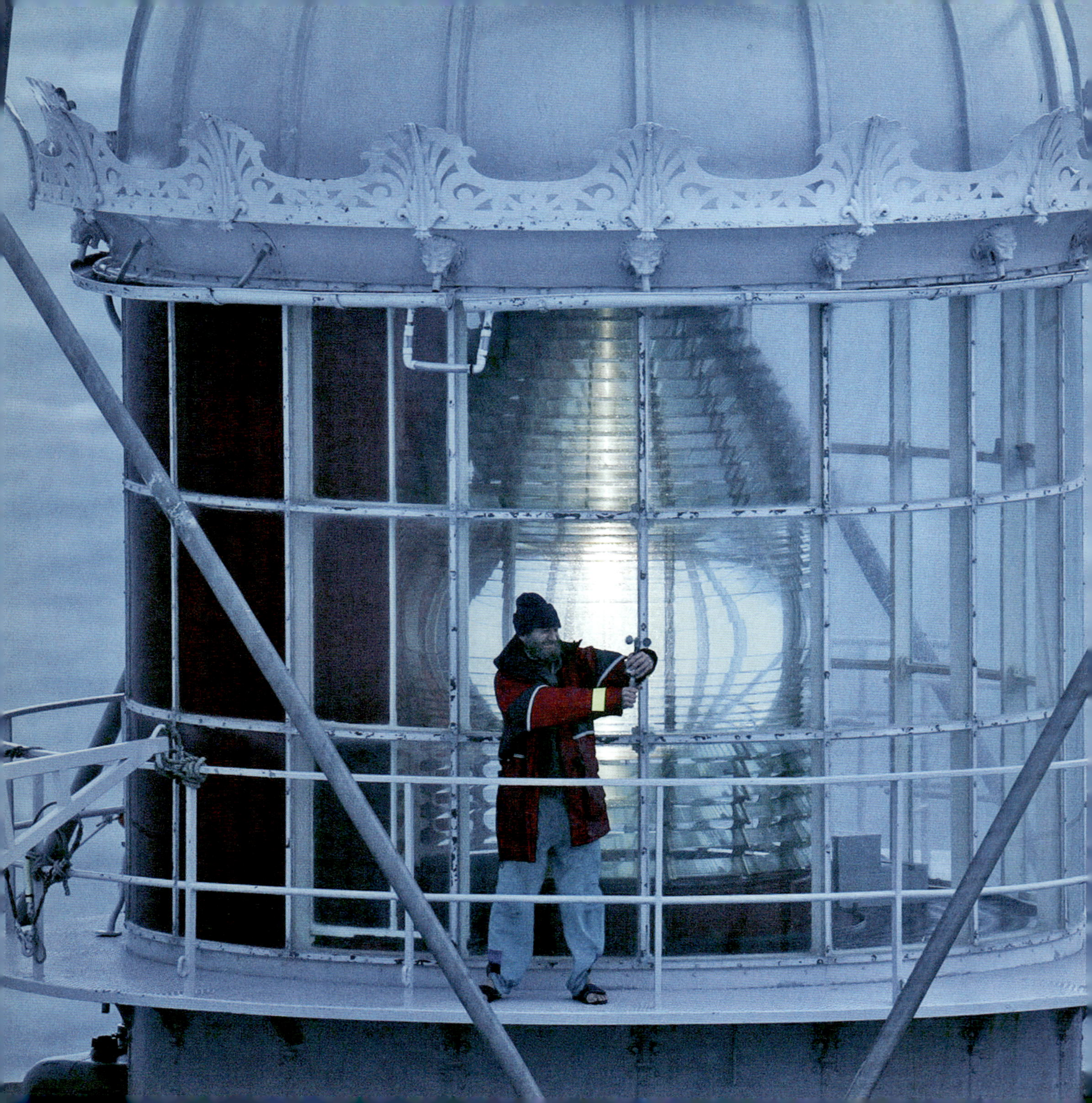

SEPTEMBER 1

A singular disadvantage of the sea lies in the fact
that after successfully surmounting one wave, you discover
that there is another behind it just as important
and just as nervously anxious to do something
effective in the way of swamping boats.

Stephen Crane,
from *The Open Boat,* 1898

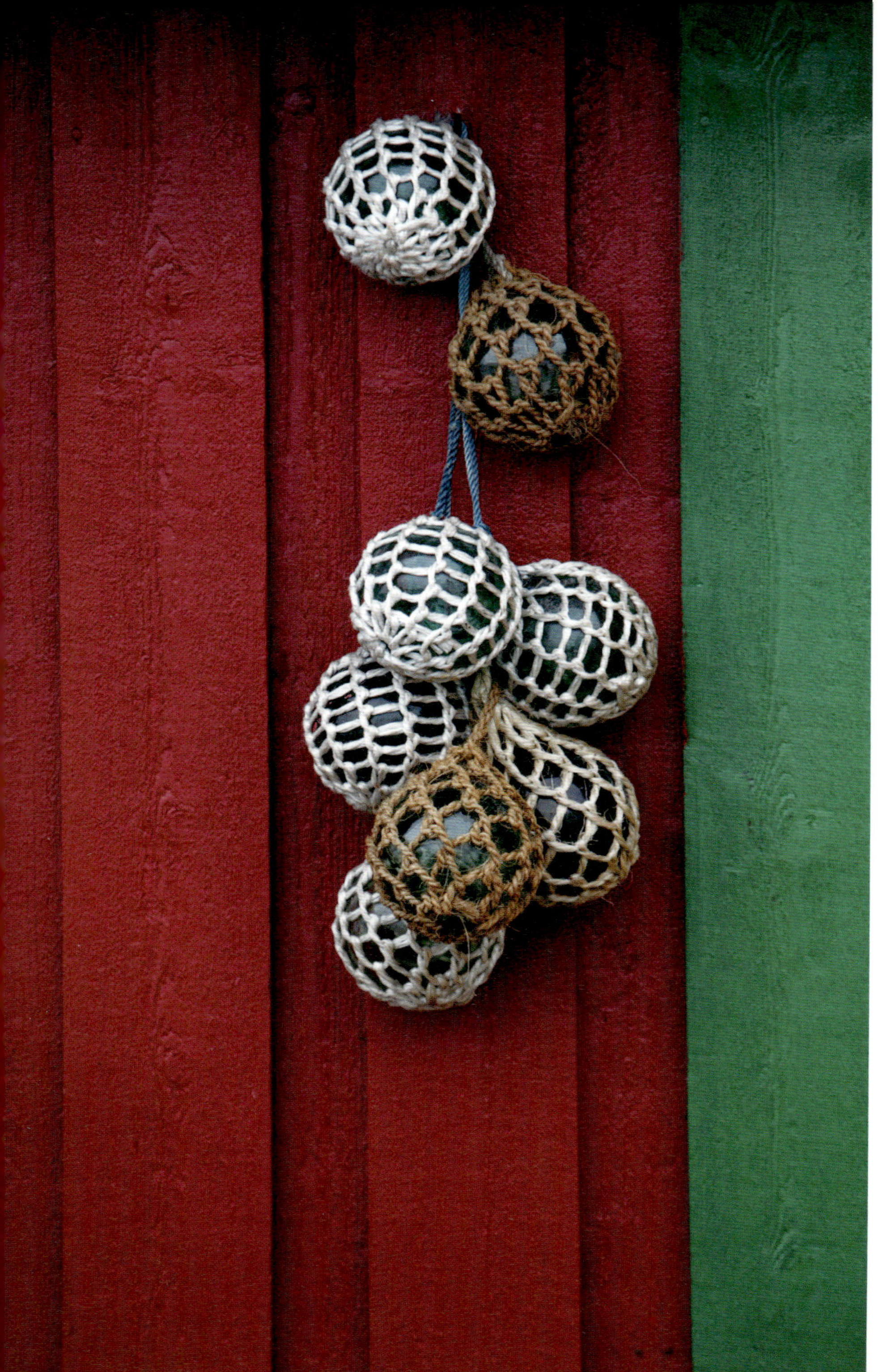

SEPTEMBER 2

He who doesn't enter the sea will never be drowned by the sea.

Cuban proverb

SEPTEMBER 3

An anchor is a forged piece of iron, admirably adapted to its end. . . . To its perfection its size bears witness, for there is no other appliance so small for the great work it has to do.

Joseph Conrad,
from *The Mirror of the Sea*, 1906

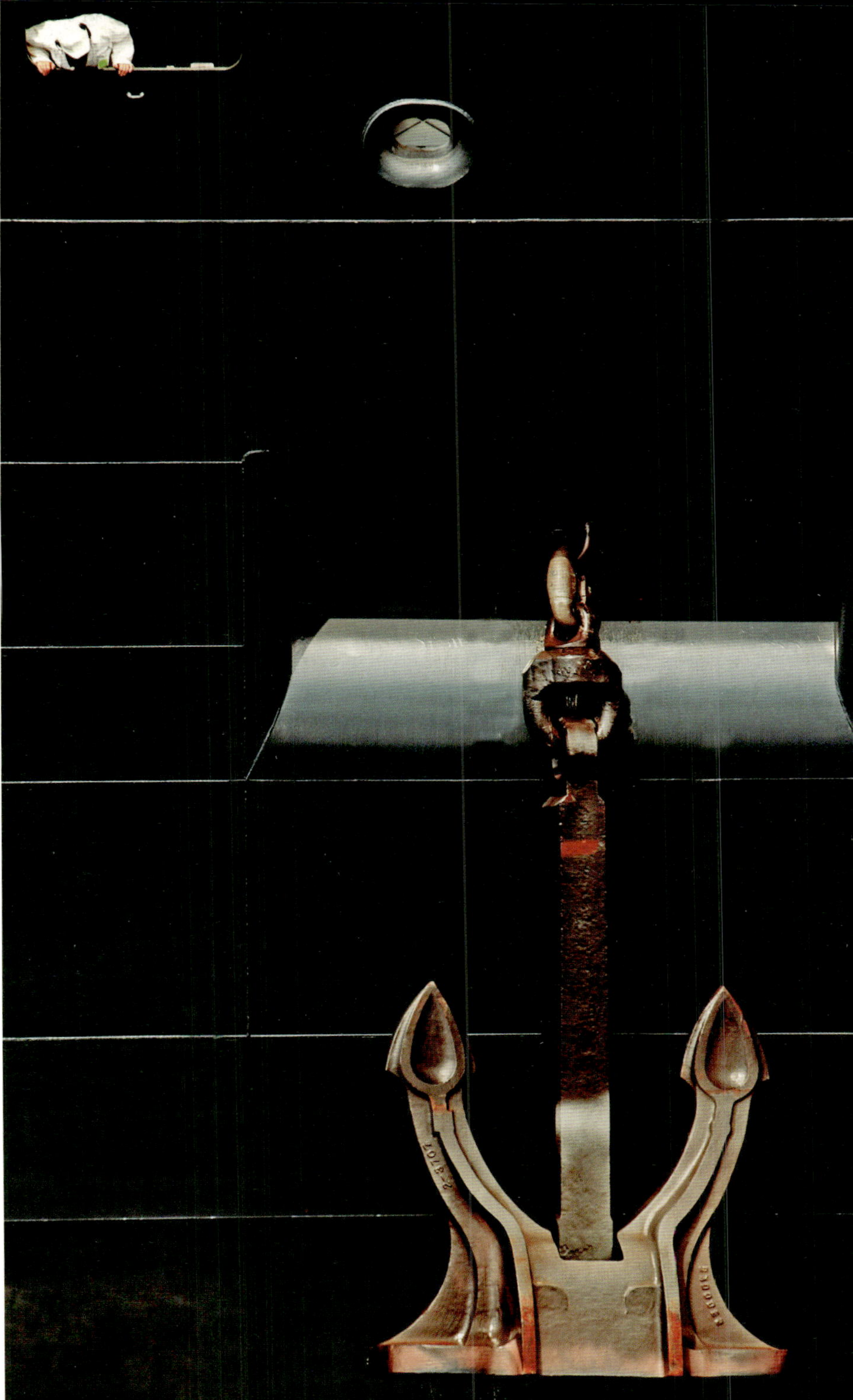

SEPTEMBER 4

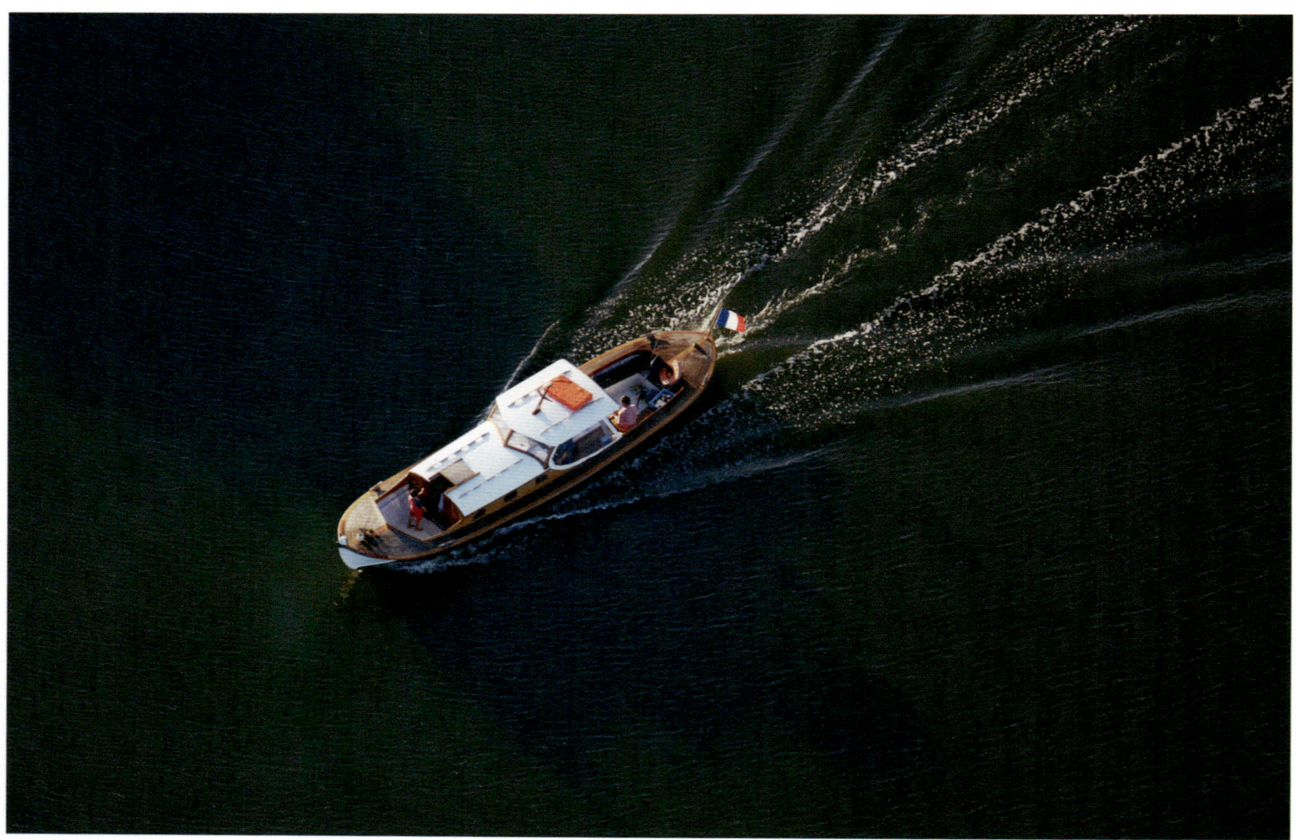

A boat is the nearest approach to a floating, moving, safe bit of land a man can make.

T. C. Lethbridge

SEPTEMBER 5

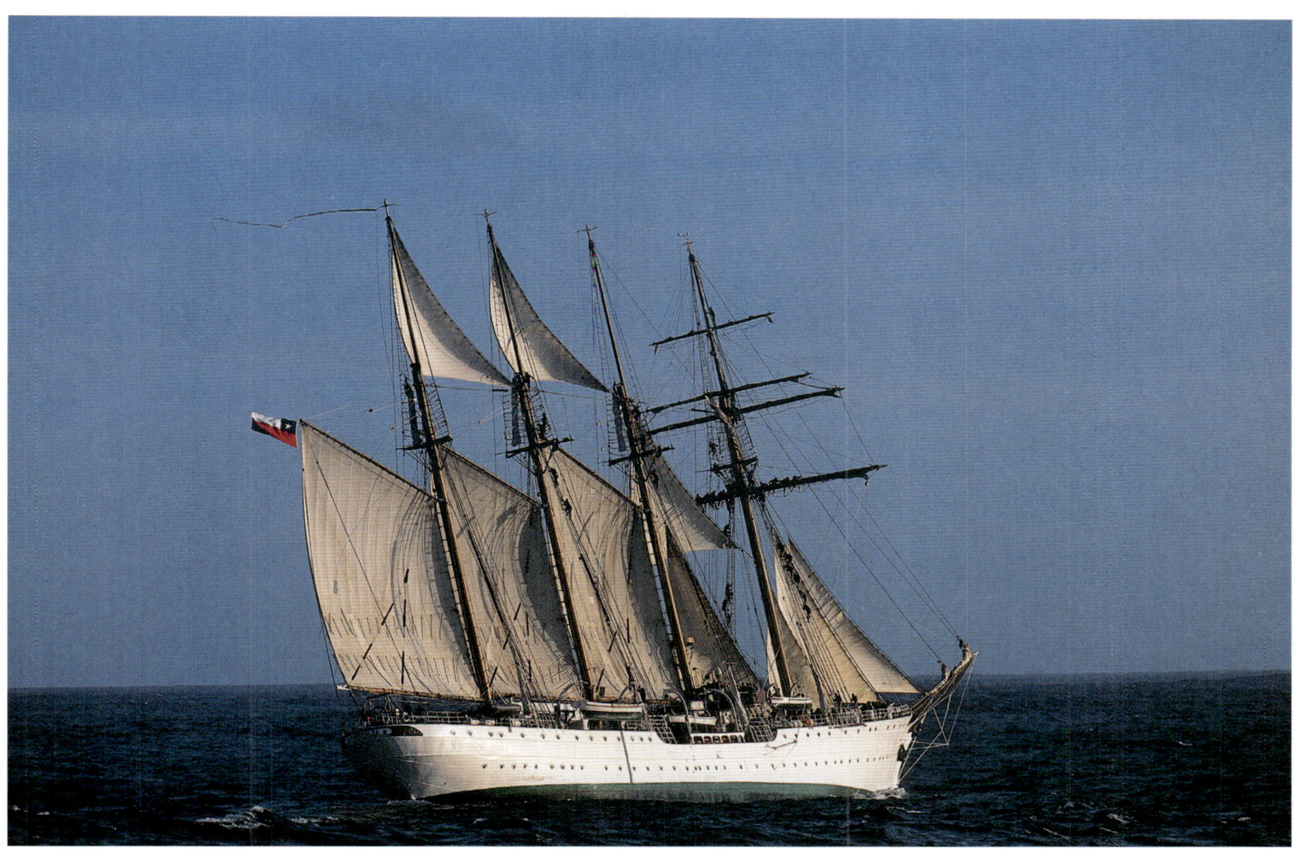

He might begin the Day of Judgement, but he would probably find himself in the dock long before it was over.

Samuel Butler, from his notebooks, 1912

SEPTEMBER 6

My heart like a bird was fluttering joyously
And soaring freely around the rigging;
Beneath a cloudless sky the ship was rolling
Like an angel drunken with the radiant sun.

Charles Baudelaire,
from "A Voyage to Cythera," *Les Fleurs du mal,* 1857

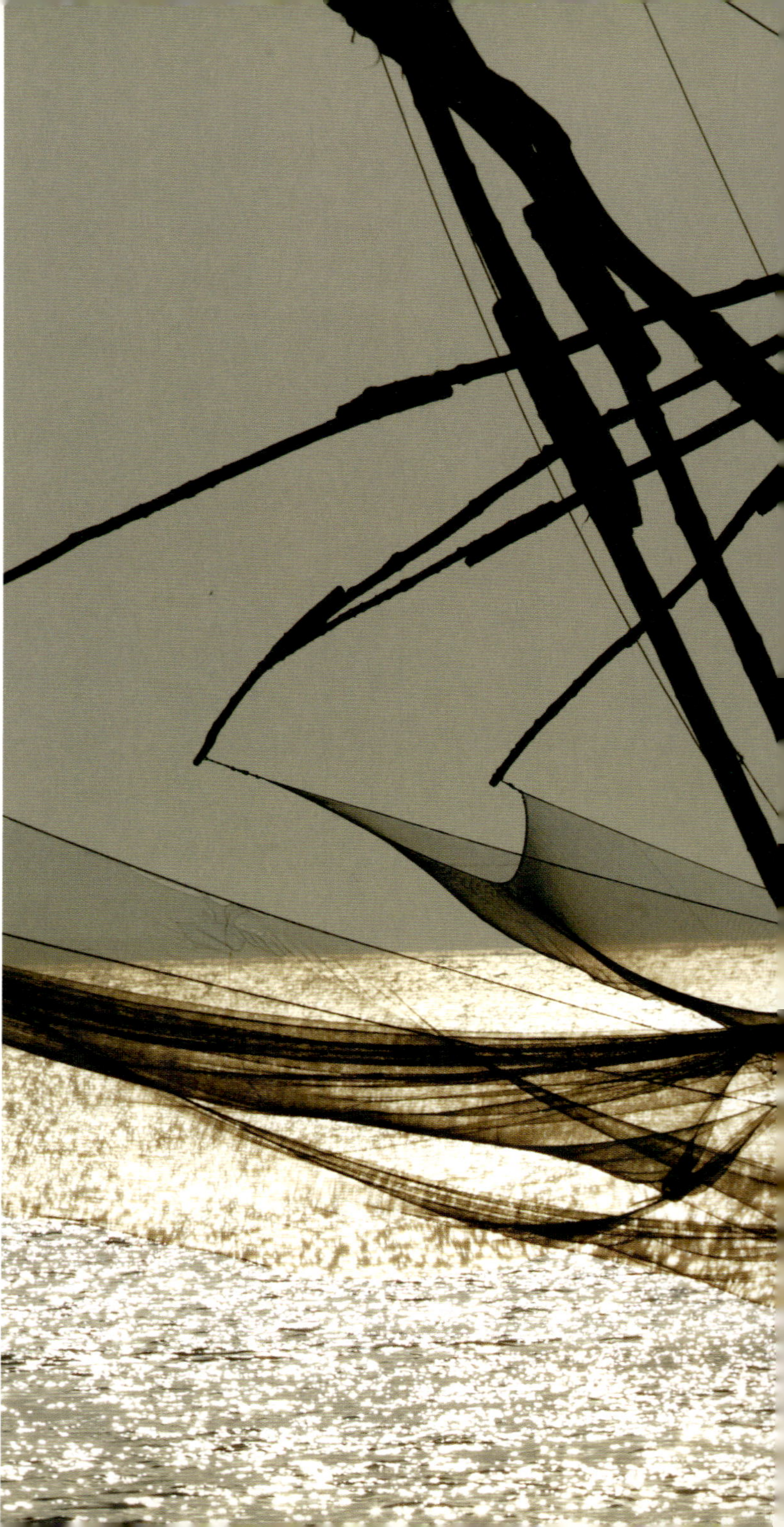

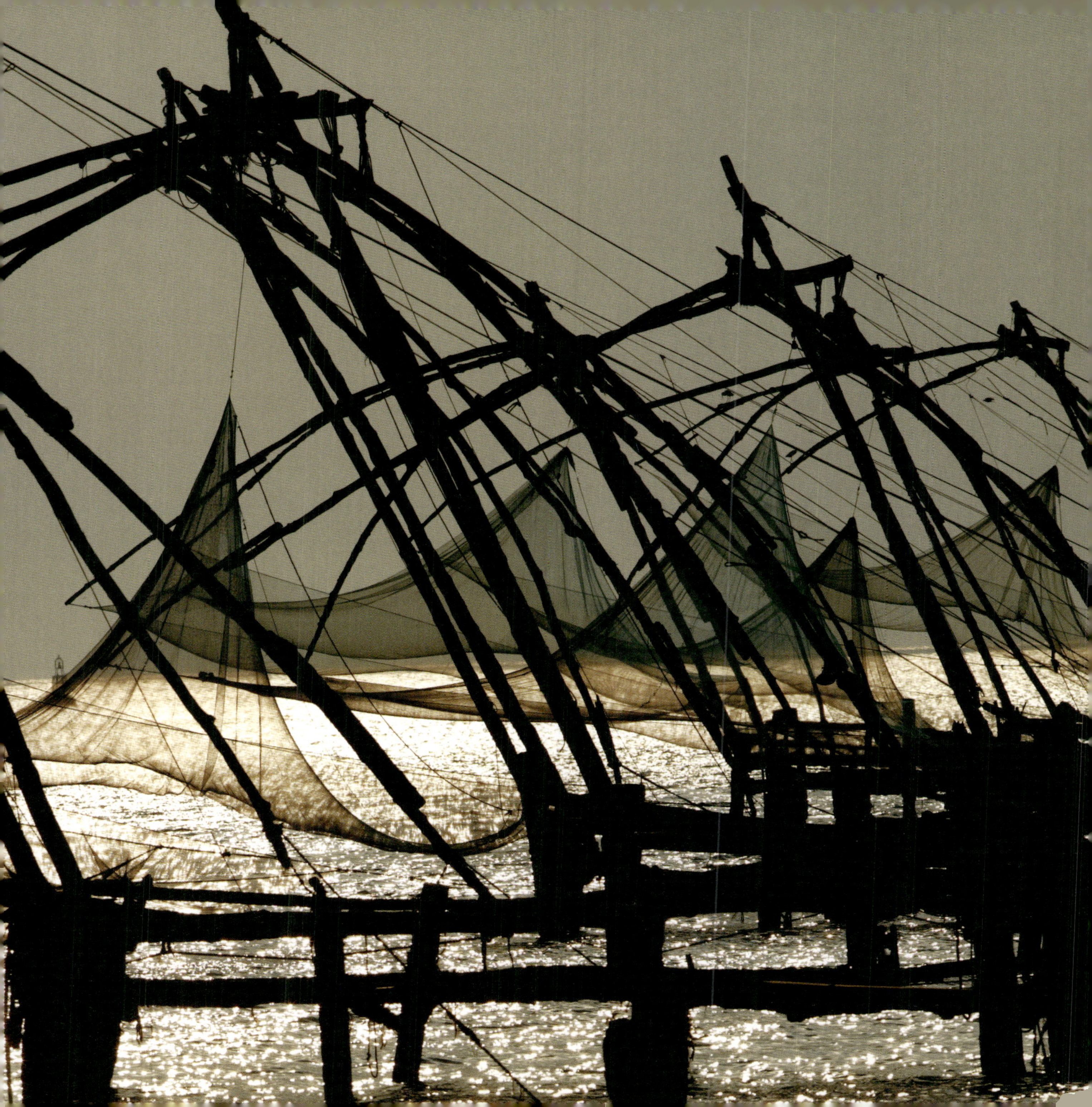

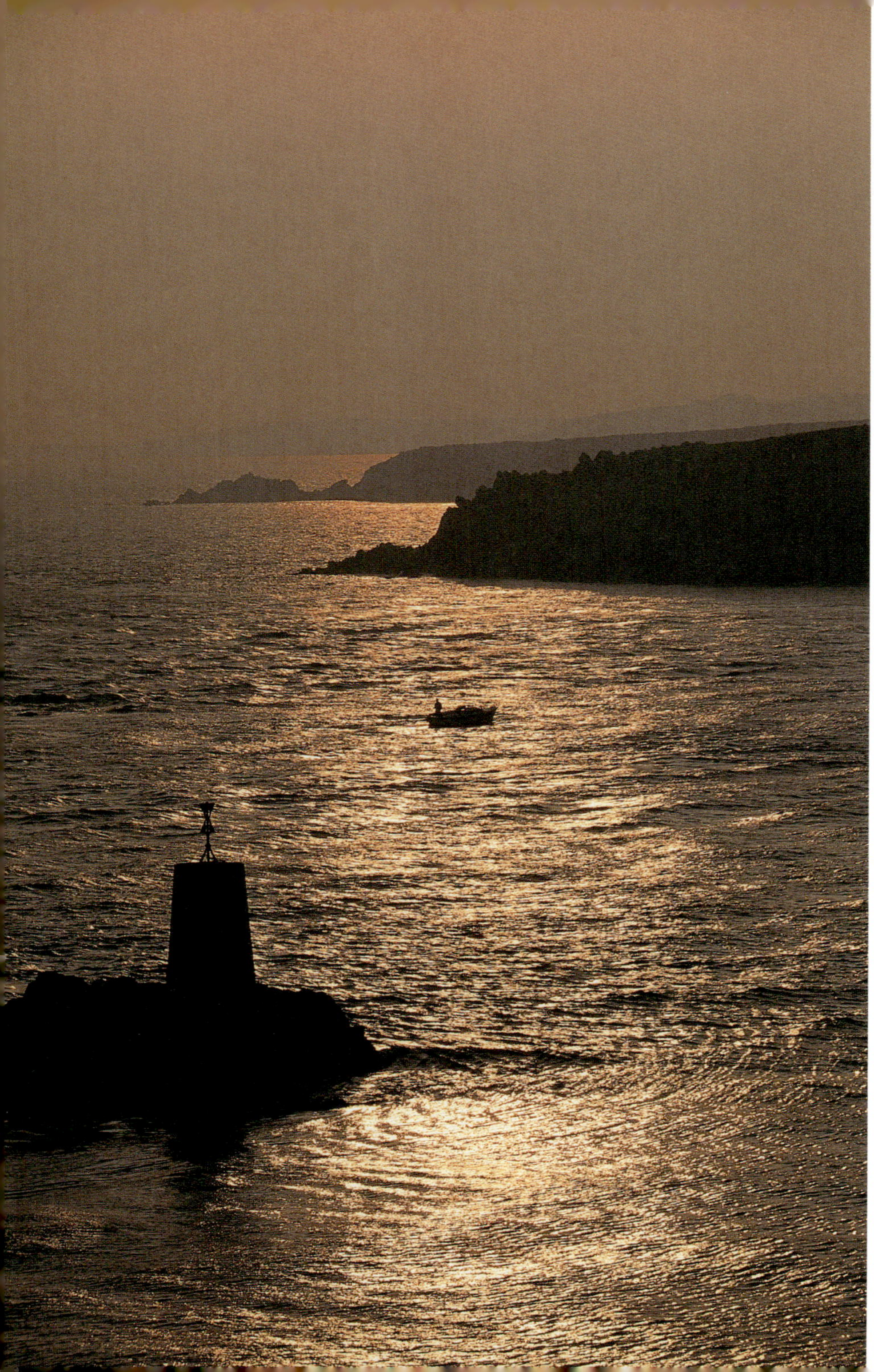

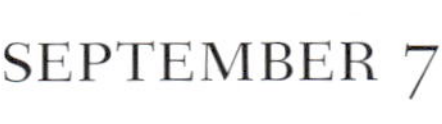

SEPTEMBER 7

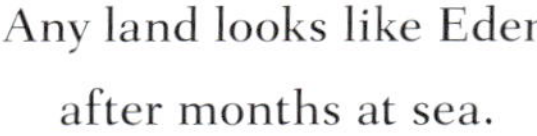

Any land looks like Eden
after months at sea.

Robert Hughes

SEPTEMBER 8

Be like a headland of rock
on which the waves break
incessantly; but it stands fast
and around it the seething
of the waters sink to rest.

Marcus Aurelius

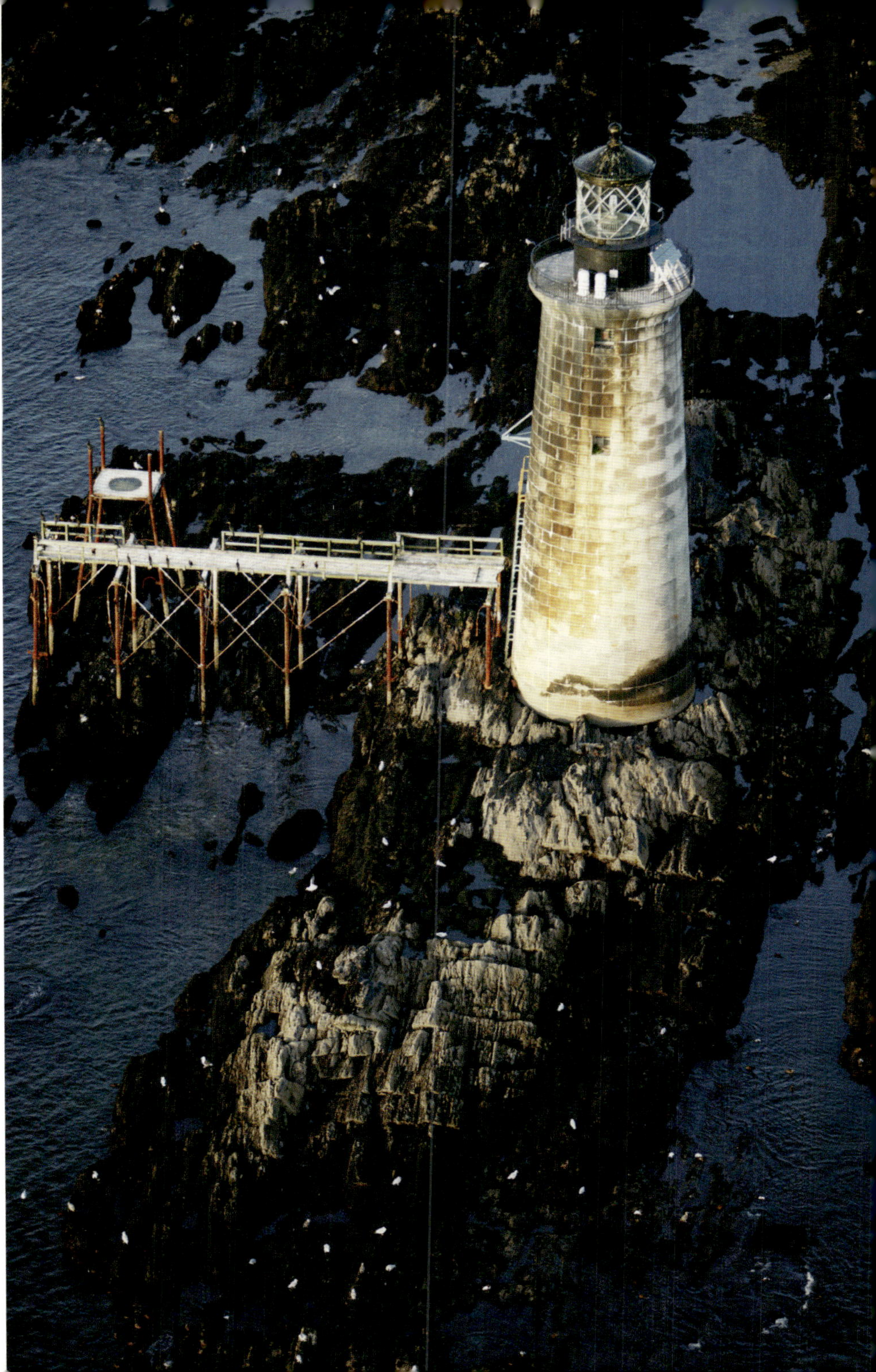

SEPTEMBER 9

Those who want to row on the ocean of human knowledge do not get far,
and the storm drives those out of their course who set sail.

Franz Grillparzer, from *Notebooks and Diaries,* 1819

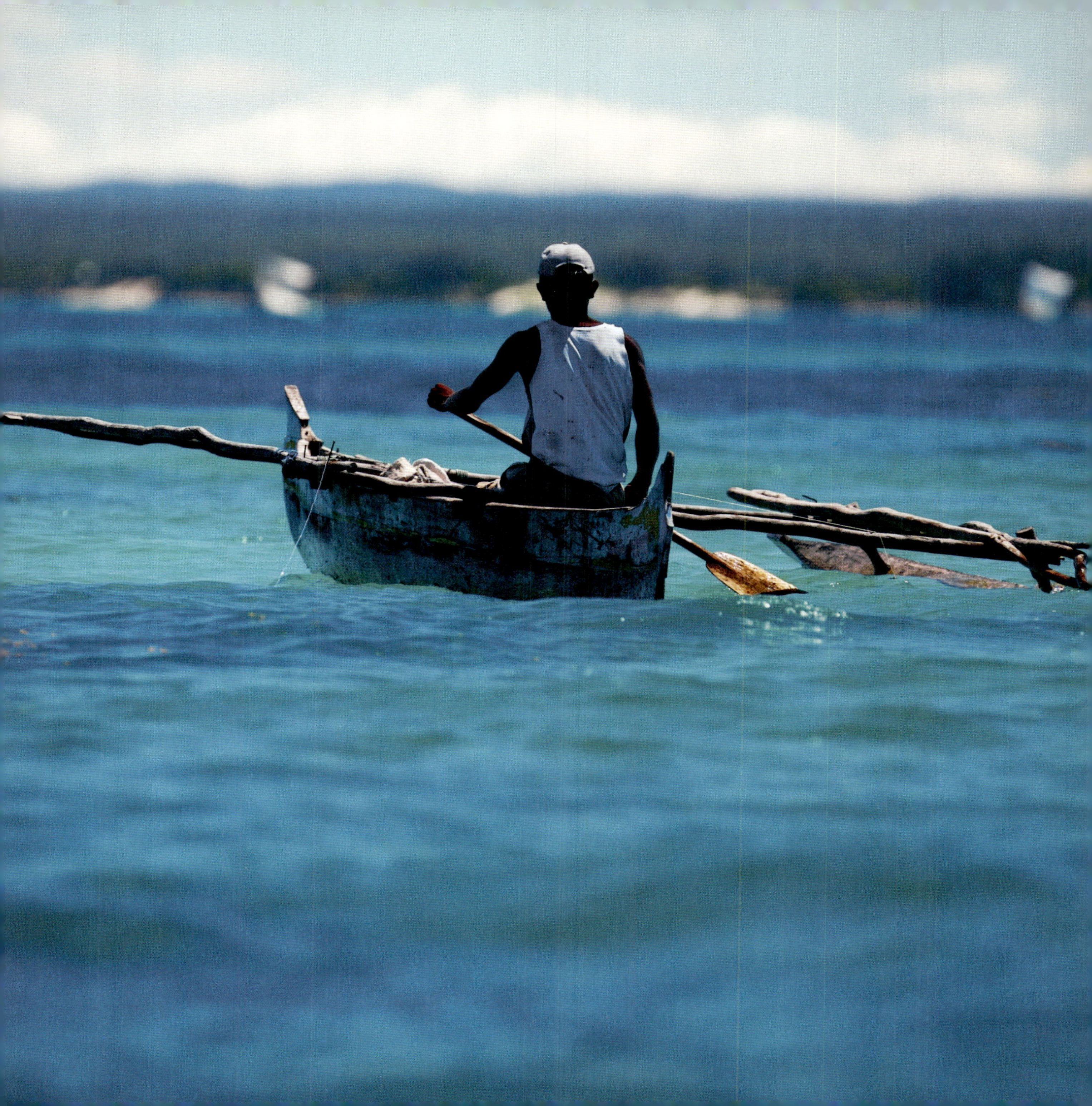

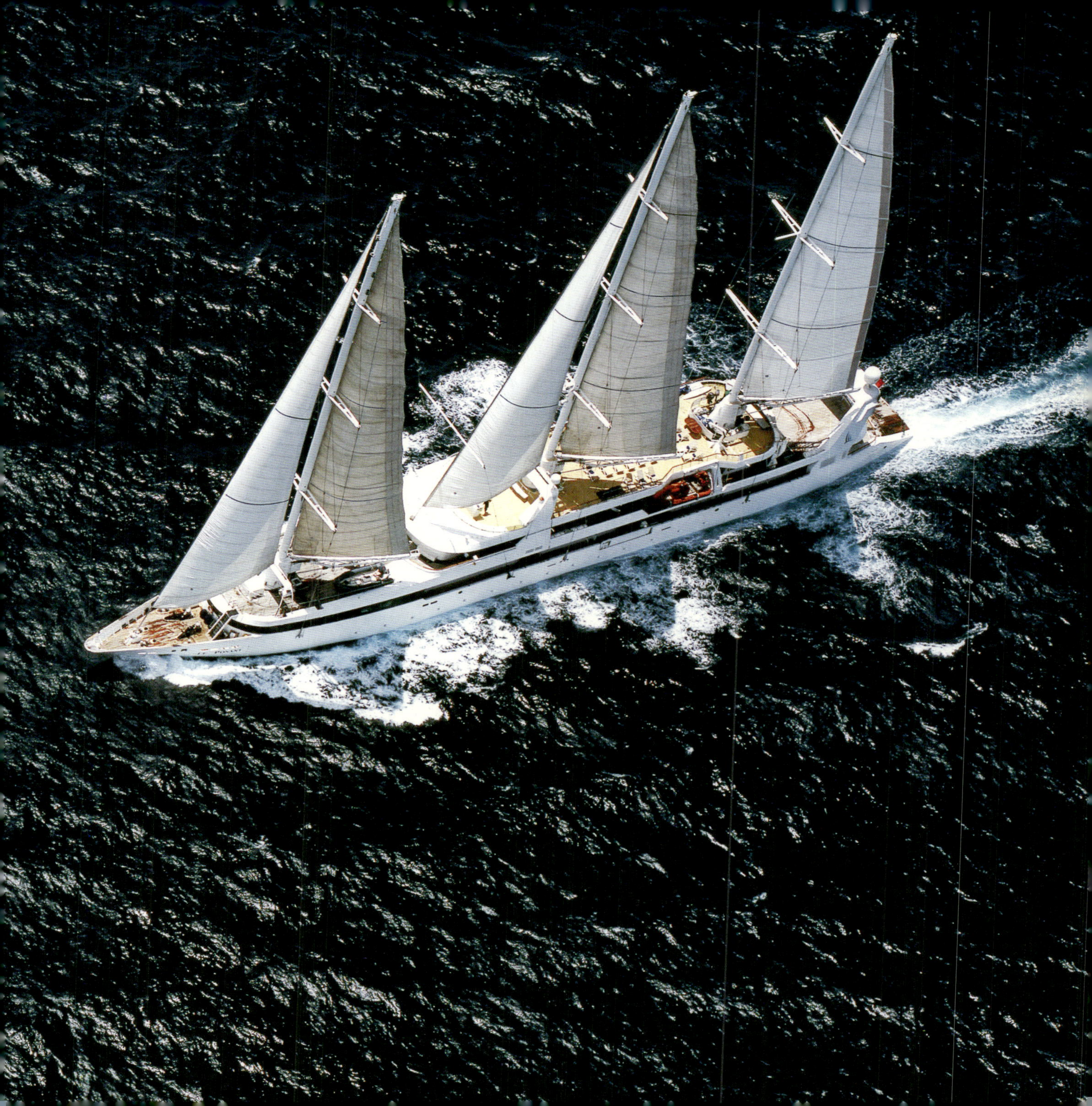

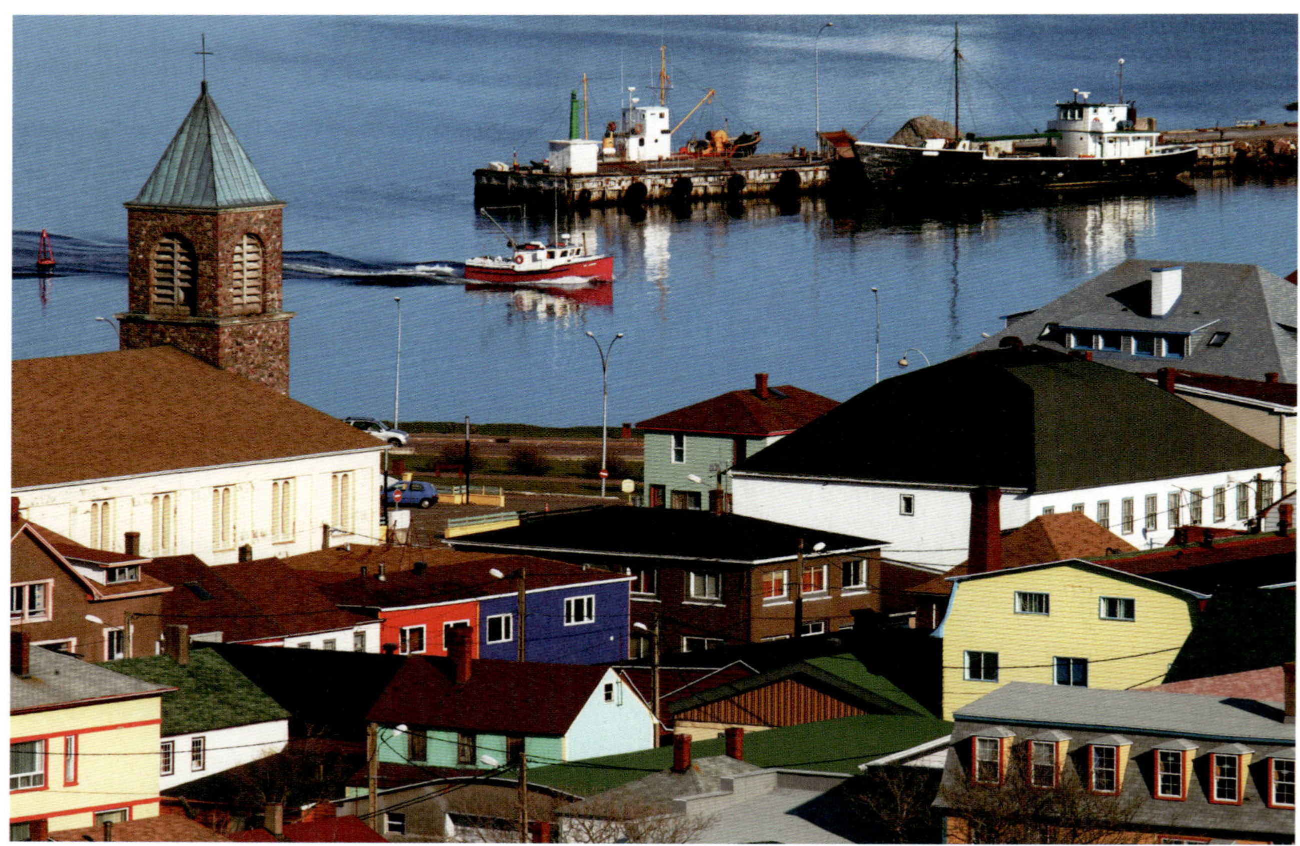

Our fathers water'd with their tears
This sea of time whereon we sail.

Matthew Arnold, from "Stanzas from the Grand Chartreuse," 1855

SEPTEMBER 11

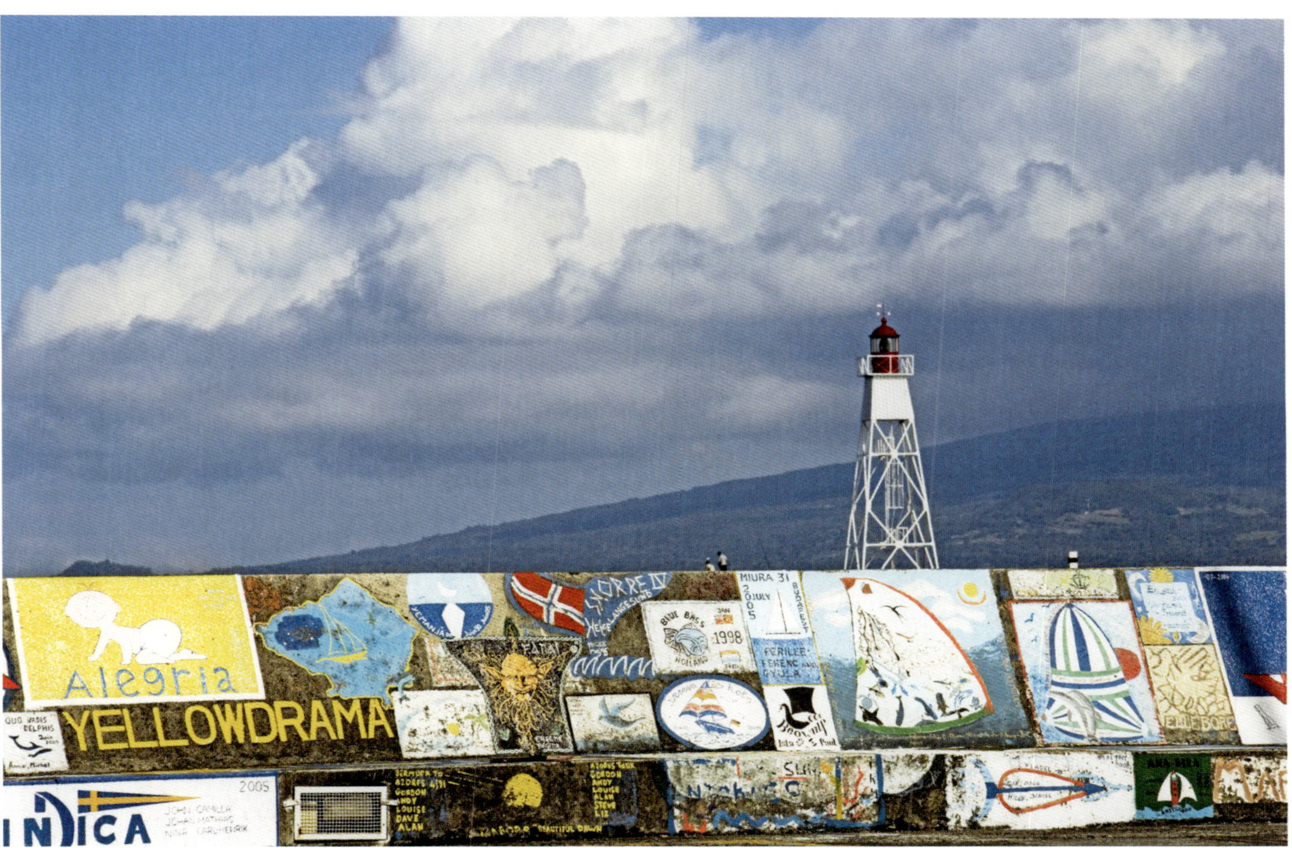

Now when the raging storms no longer reign, but southern gales invite us to the main,
we launch our vessels, with a prosp'rous wind, and leave the cities and the shores behind.

Virgil, from *The Aeneid*

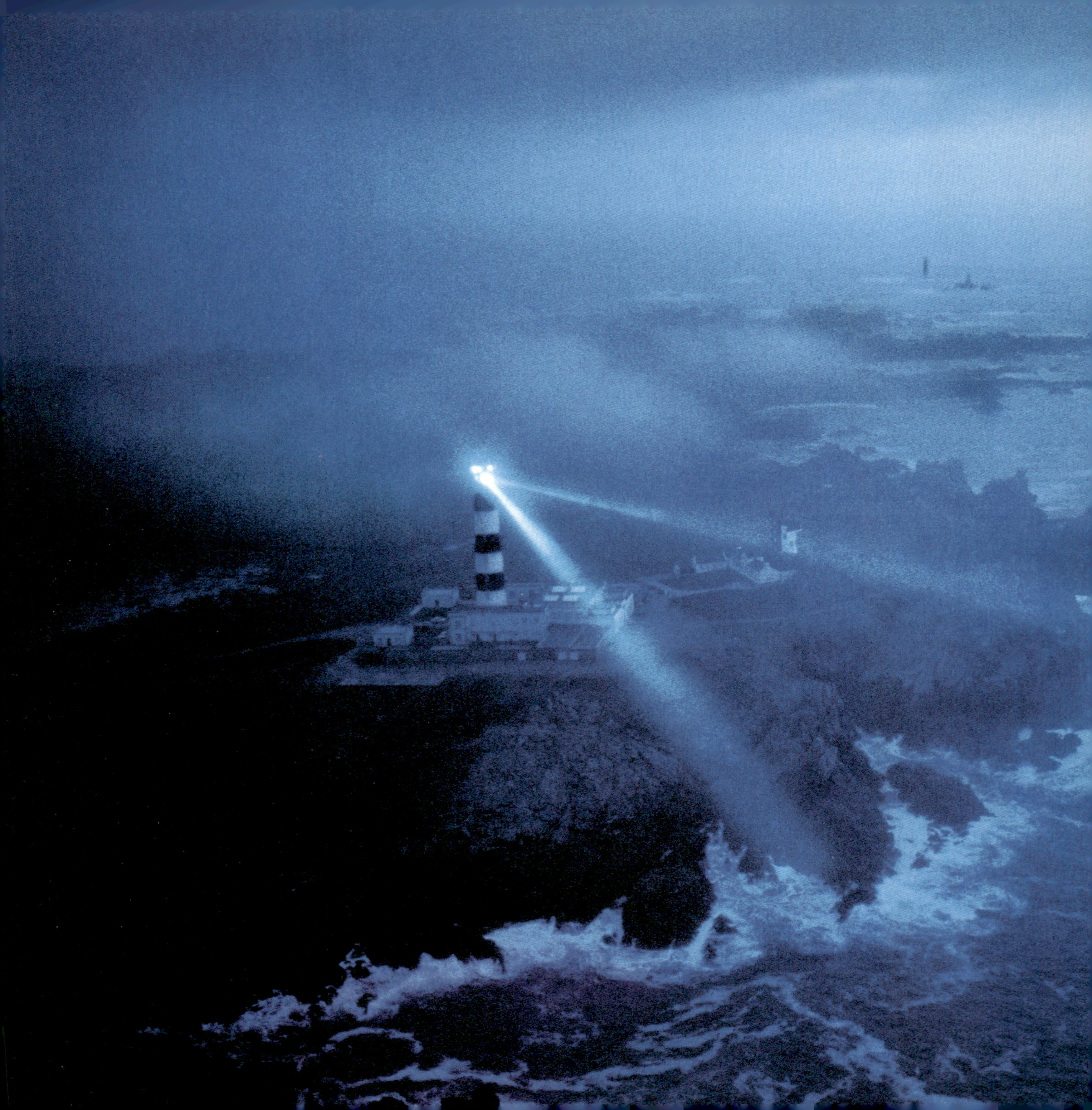

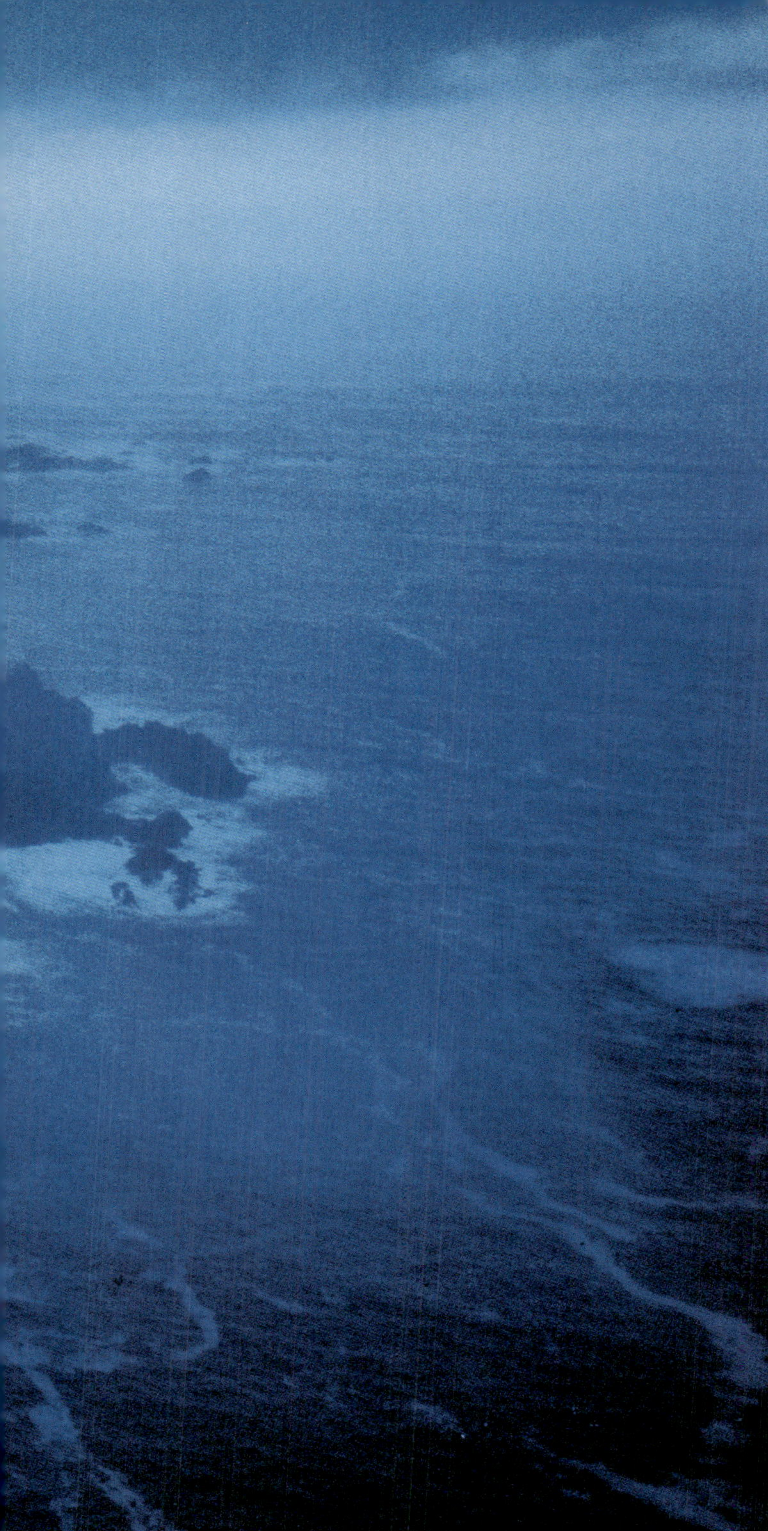

SEPTEMBER 12

I must go down to the seas again,
to the lonely sea and the sky,
And all I ask is a tall ship and a star to sail her by.

John Masefield,
from "Sea Fever," *Saltwater Ballads*, 1902

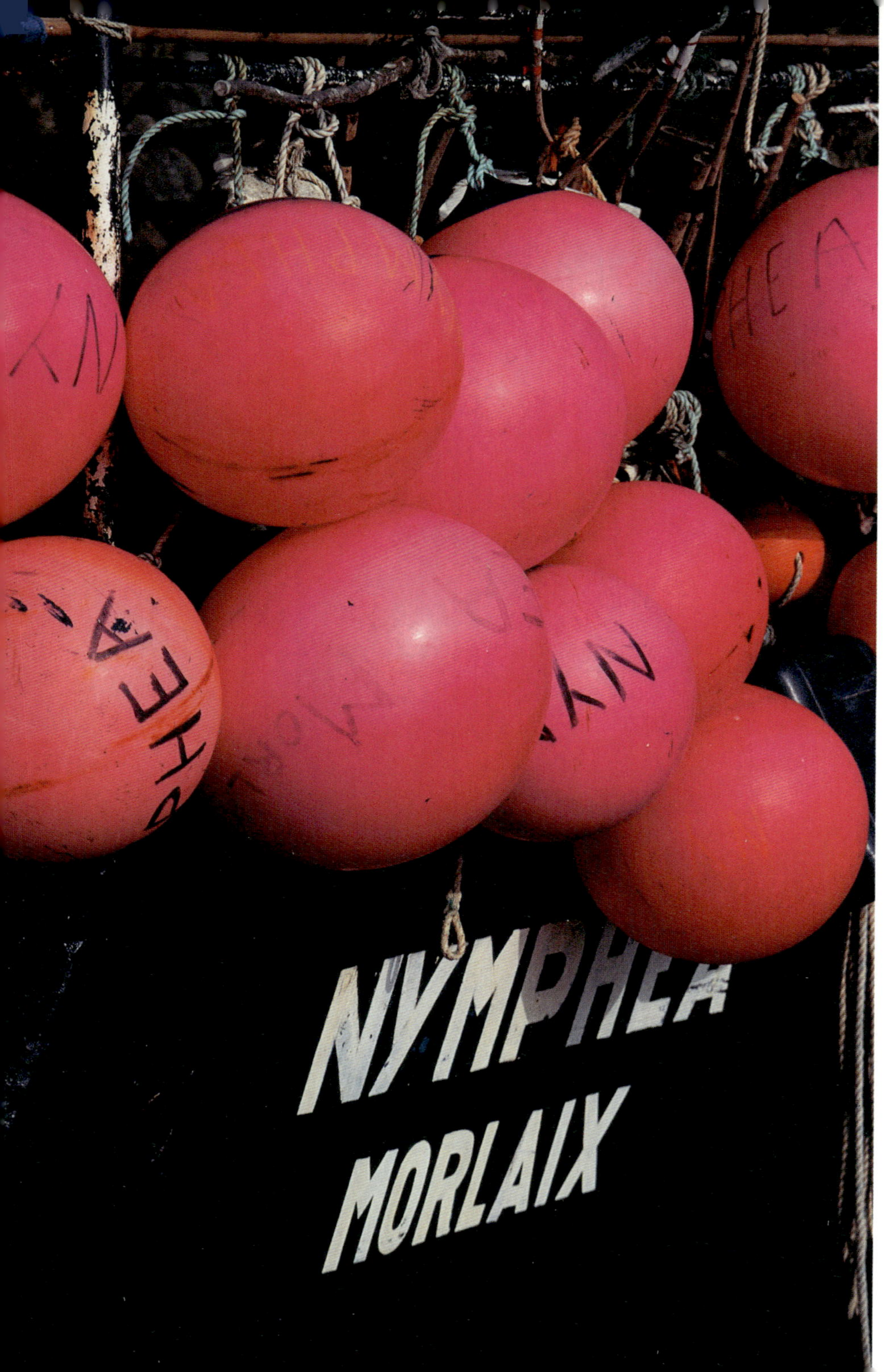

SEPTEMBER 13

And he was lost among the waves,
His ship rolled helpless in the sea,
The fourth month of his voyage
He shouted grievously
"Beloved, do not think of me."

Alun Lewis,
from "The First Month of His Absence"

SEPTEMBER 14

All the water in the sea doesn't
even reach the knees of the
man who fears not death.

Indian proverb

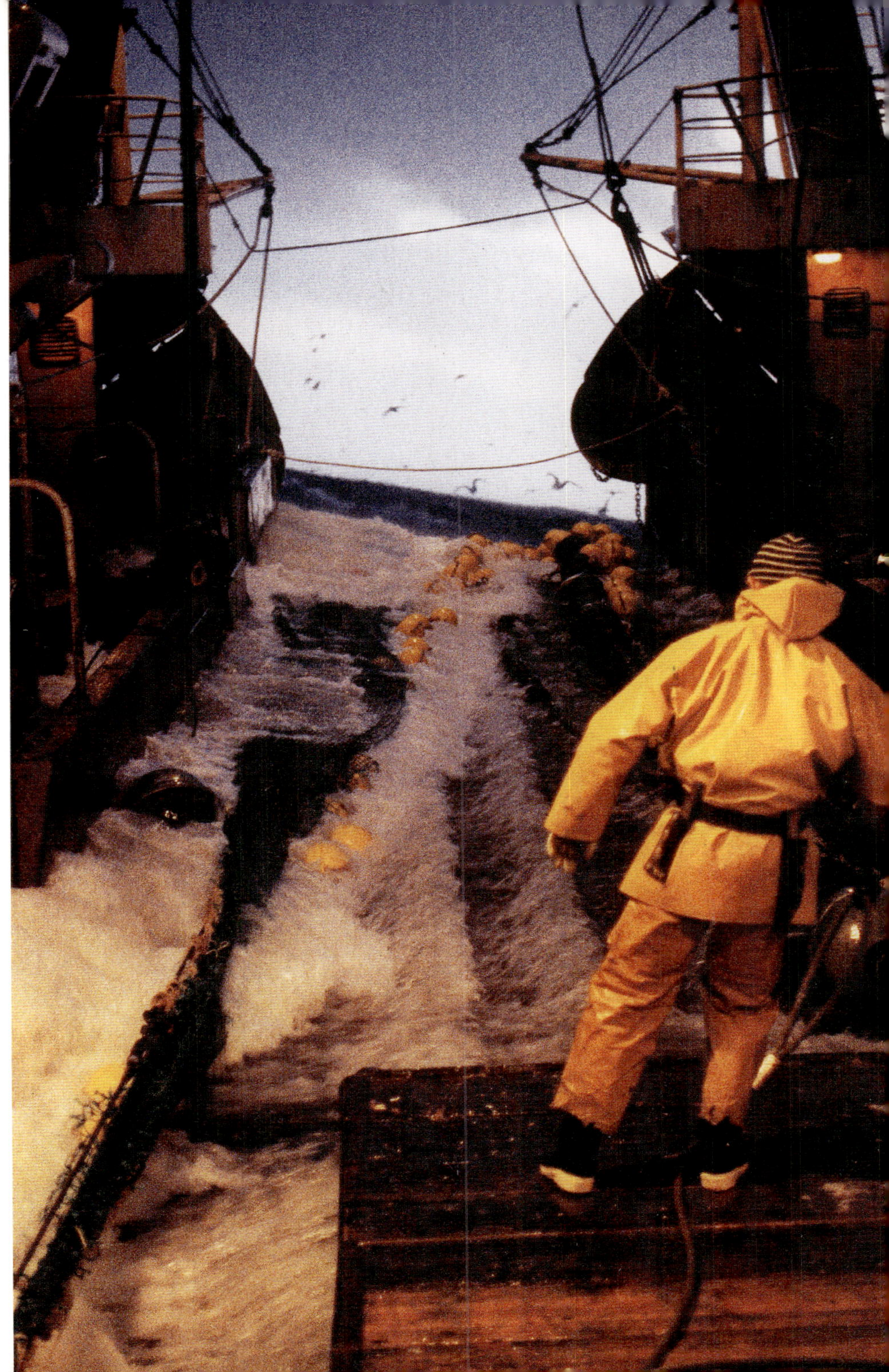

SEPTEMBER 15

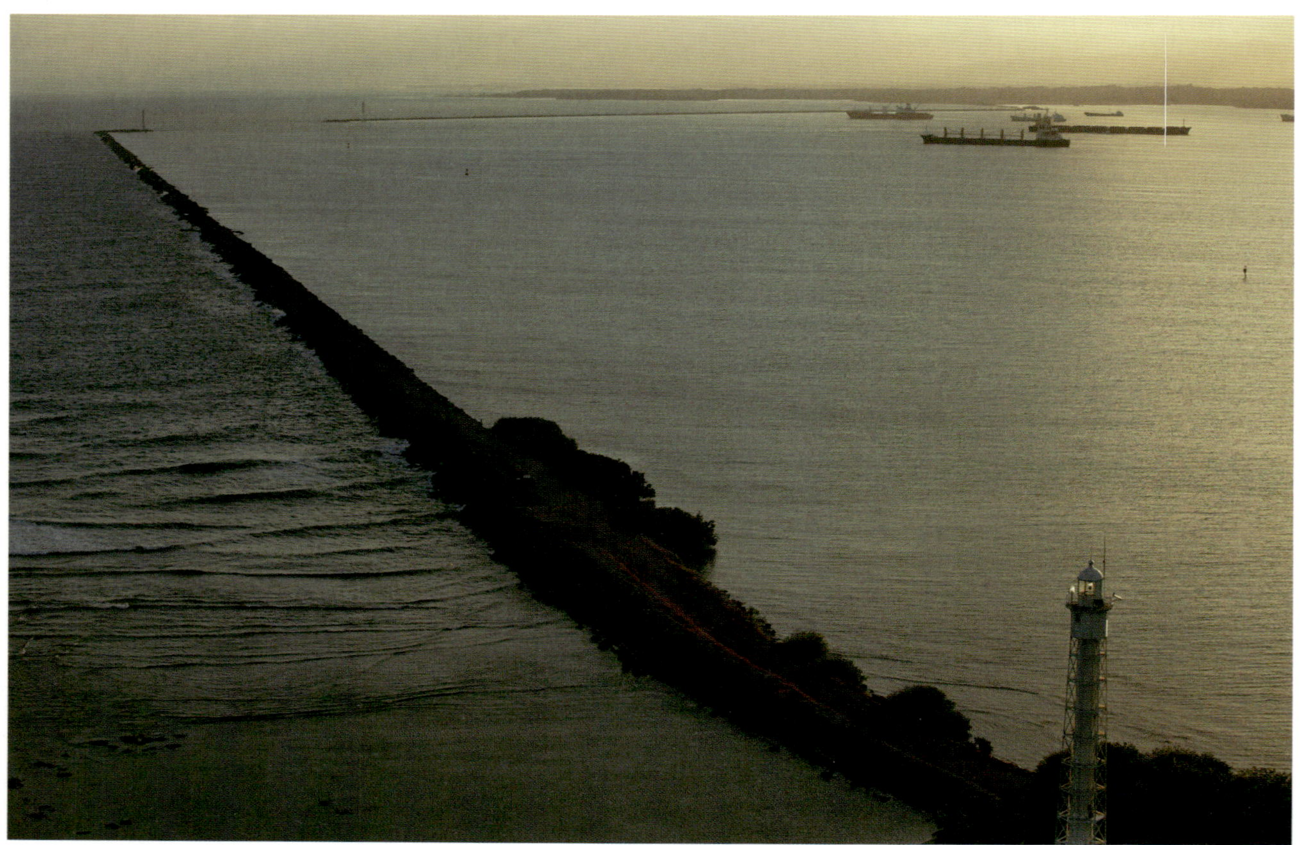

The waves forever rolling to the land are too far traveling and untamable to be familiar.

Henry David Thoreau, from *Cape Cod,* 1865

SEPTEMBER 16

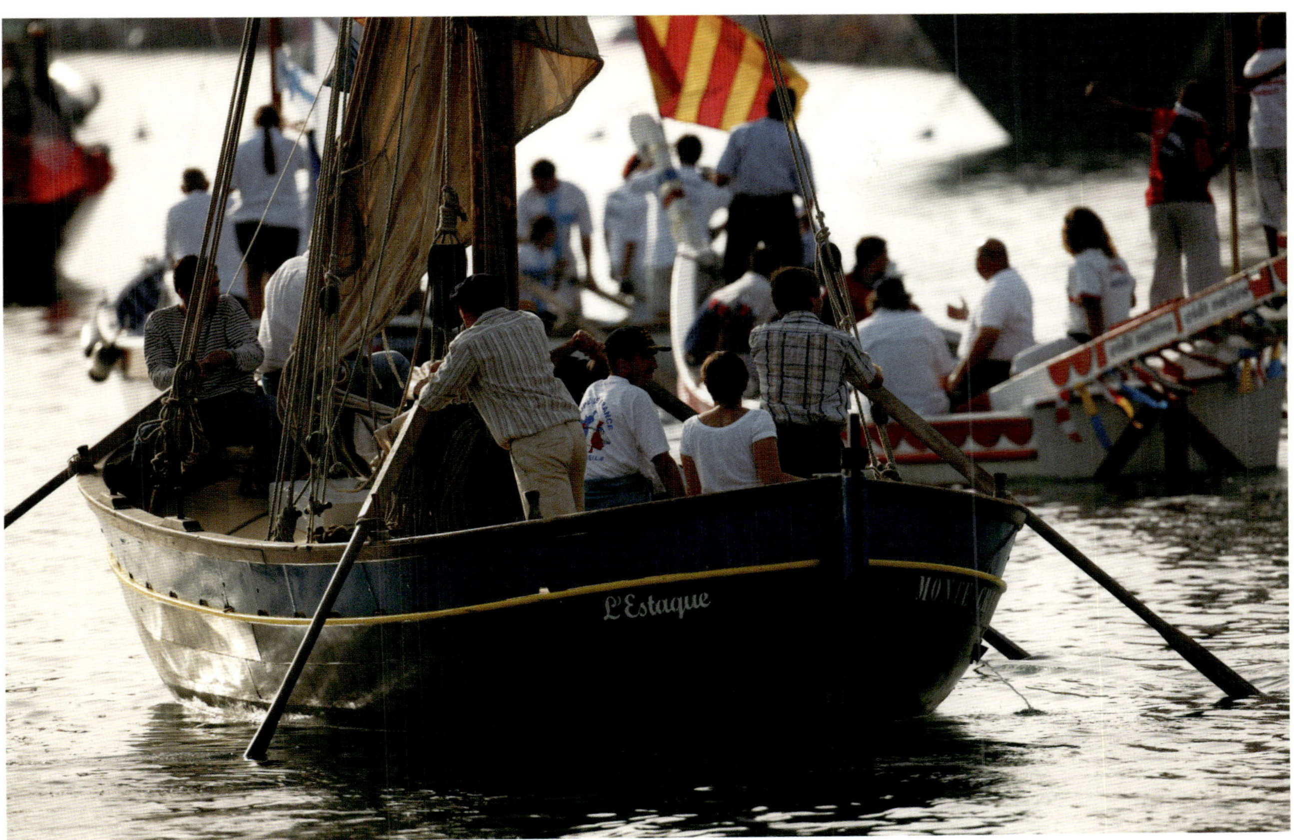

The wind breaketh my heart; that should carry me hence now stays me here.

Sir Walter Raleigh

SEPTEMBER 17

When life's last sun goes feebly down
And death comes to our door,
When all the world's a dream to us,
We'll go to sea no more.

Scottish chantey

SEPTEMBER 18

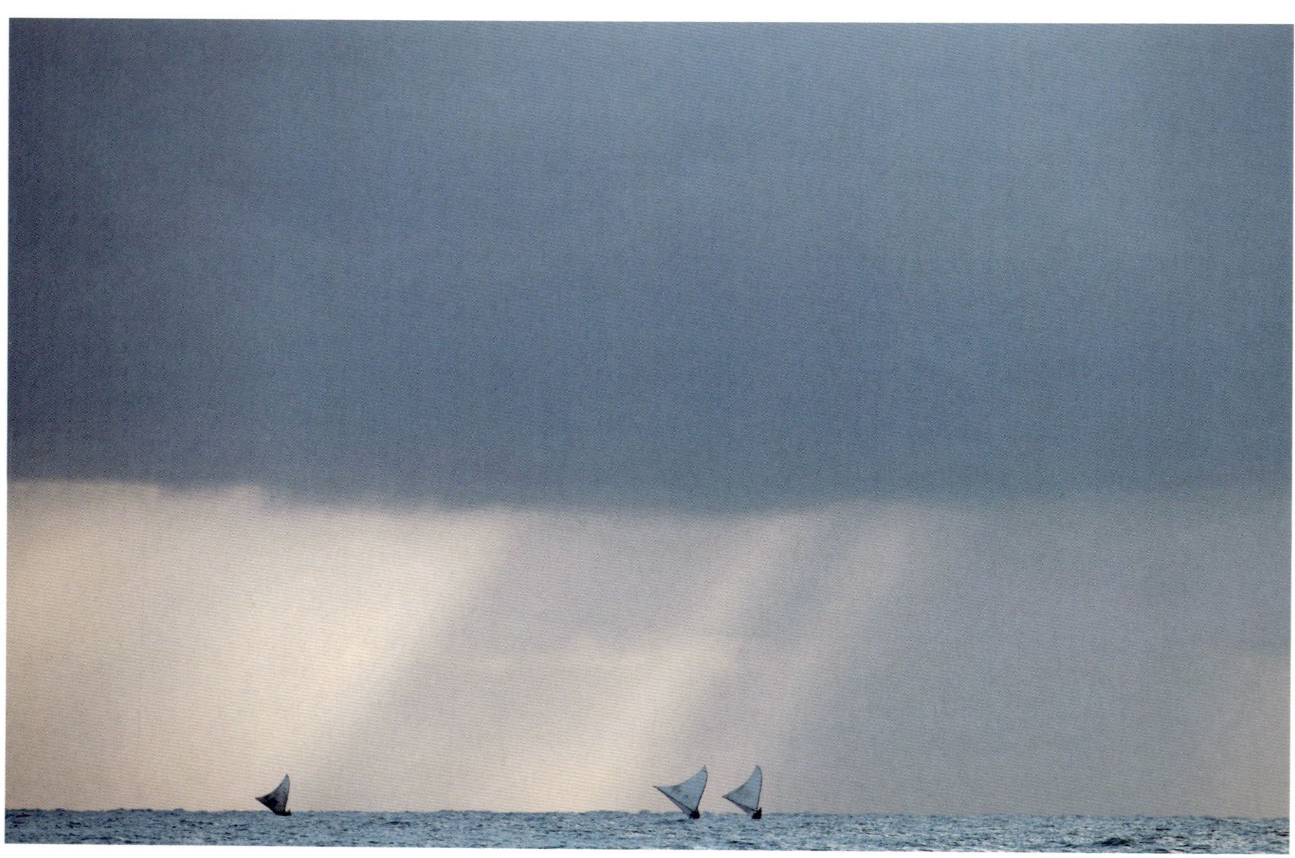

Although thy soul sail leagues and leagues beyond—
Still leagues beyond those leagues, there is more sea.

Dante Gabriel Rossetti, from "Sonnet," *The House of Life,* 1870

SEPTEMBER 19

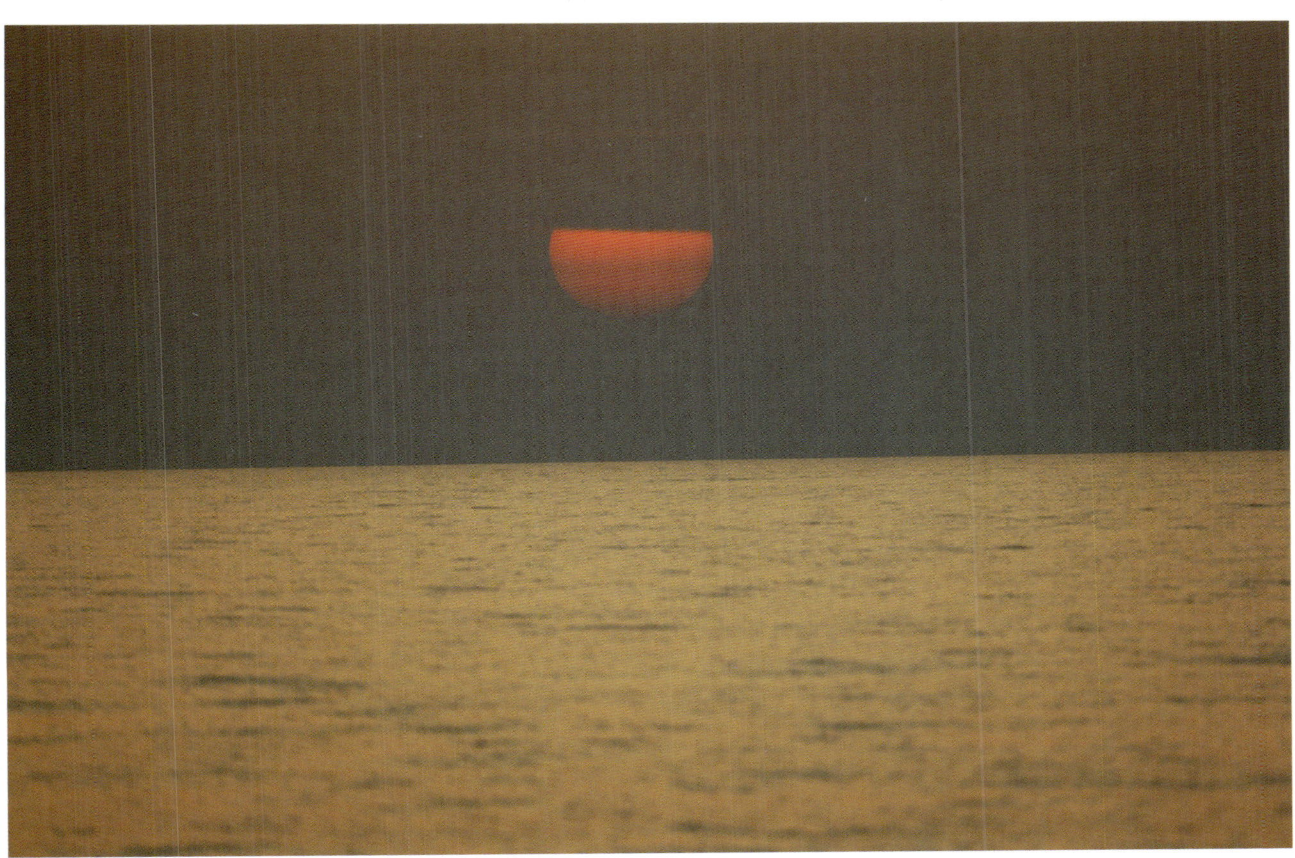

No one can know the pleasure of sailing free over the great oceans save those who have had the experience.

Joshua Slocum, from *Sailing Alone Around the World,* 1900

SEPTEMBER 20

Now was the hour that wakens fond desire
In men at sea, and melts their thoughtful heart
Who in the morn have bid sweet friends farewell,
And pilgrim newly on his road with love
Thrills, if he hears the vesper bell from far,
That seems to mourn for the expiring day.

Dante Aleghieri, from *Purgatorio*

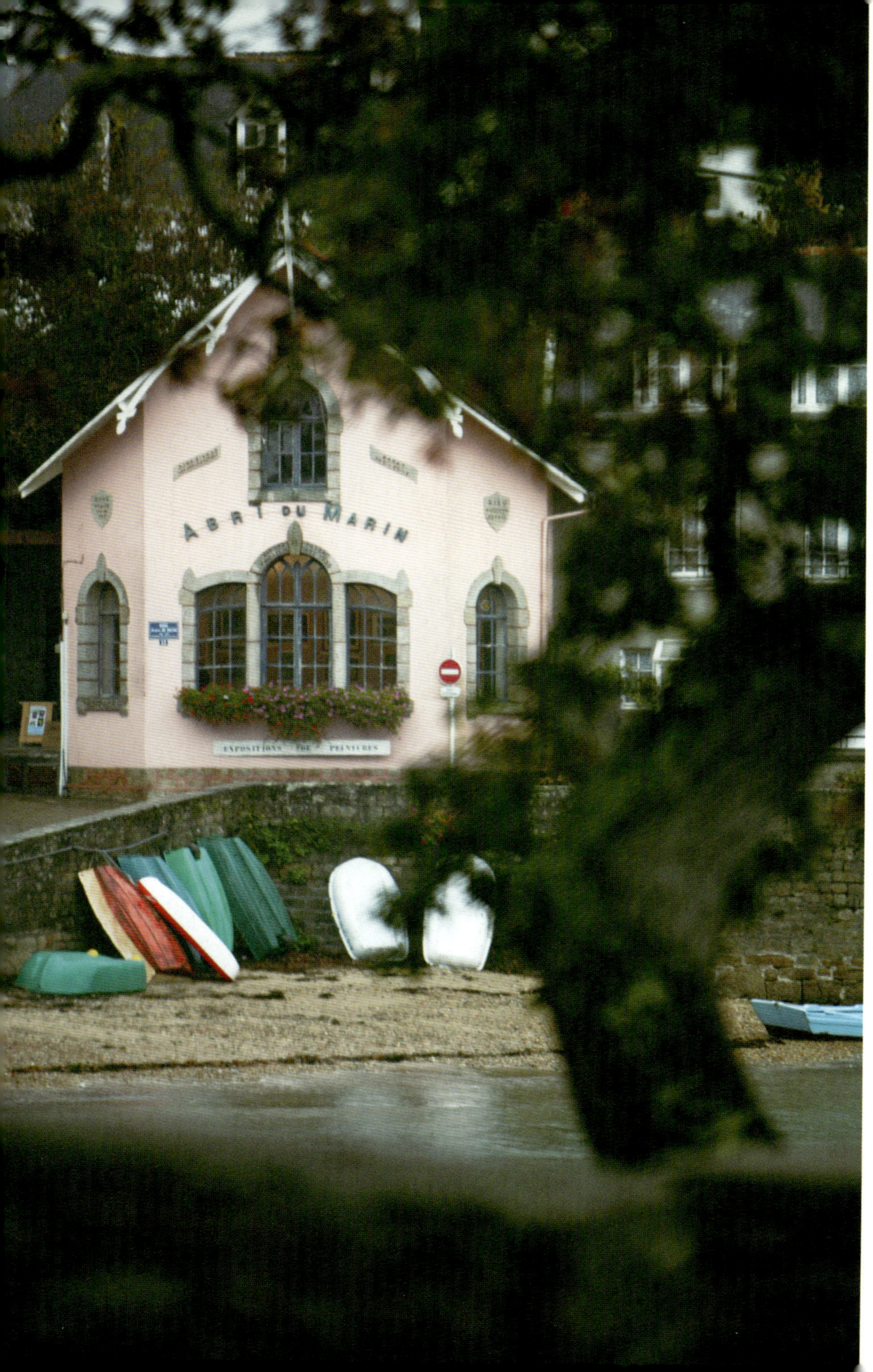

SEPTEMBER 21

Everything can be found
at sea according to the
spirit of your quest.

Joseph Conrad,
from *A Personal Record,* 1912

SEPTEMBER 22

The sea washed away
all mortal evils.

Euripides,
from *Iphigenia in Tauris*

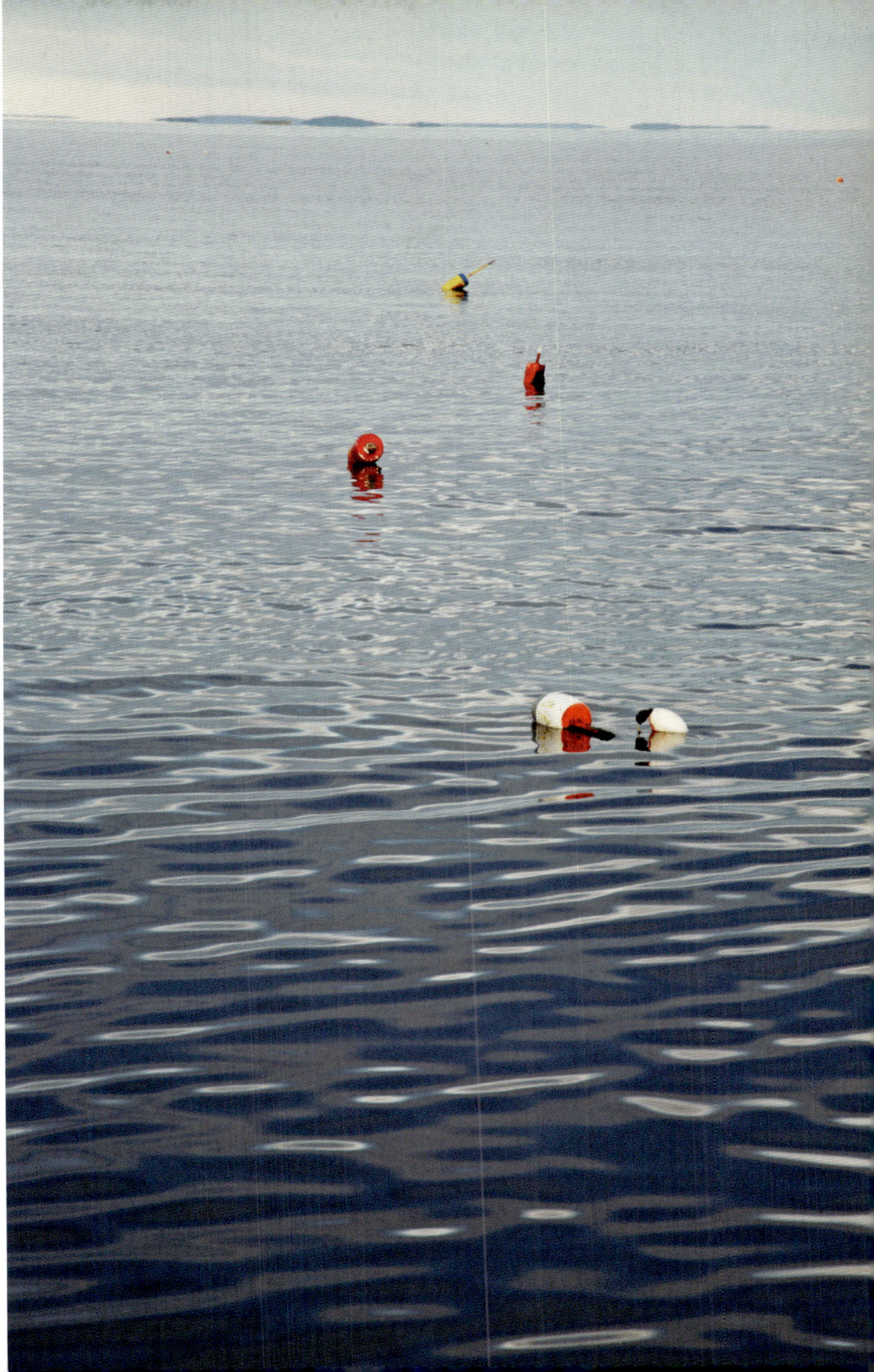

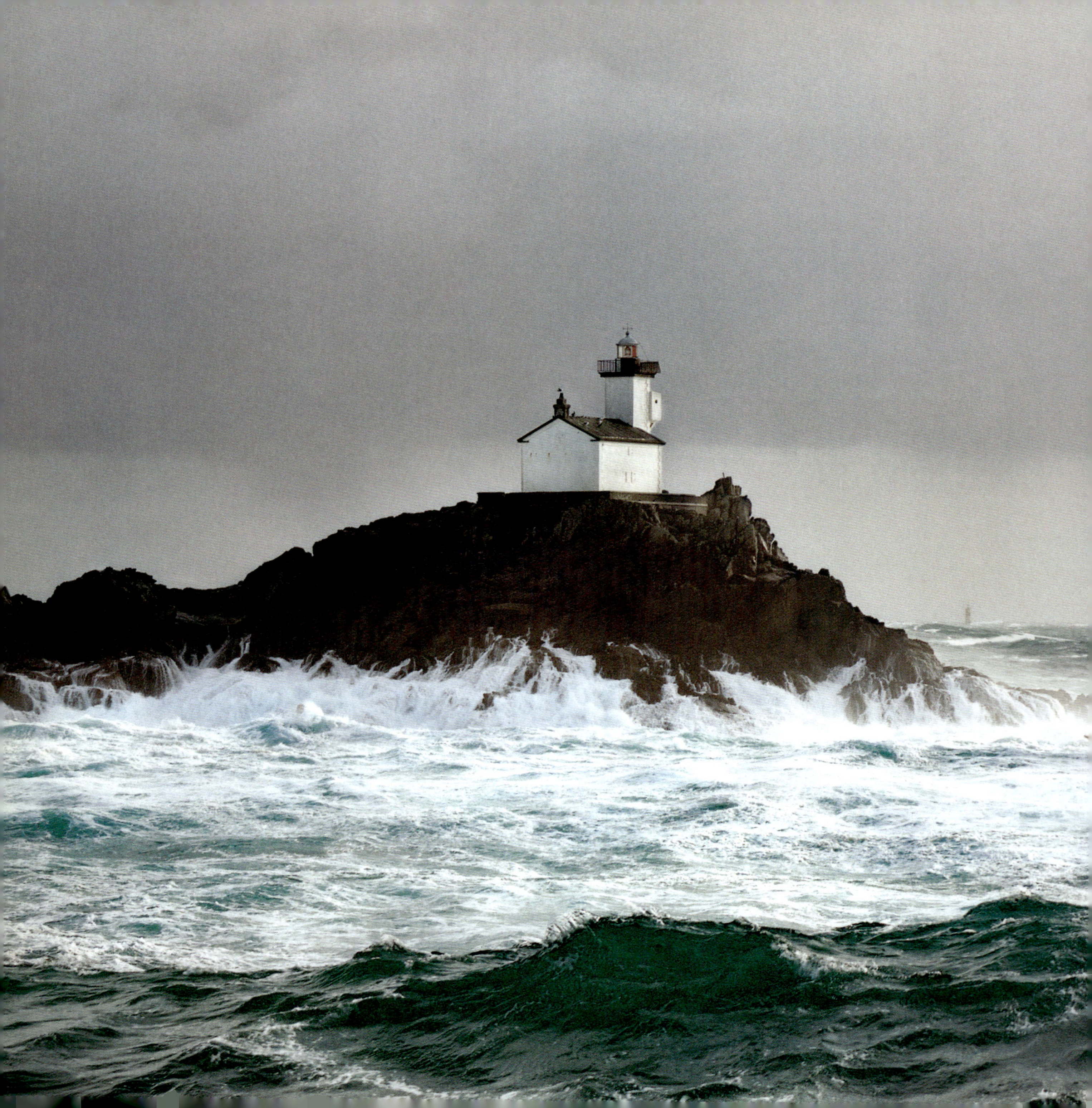

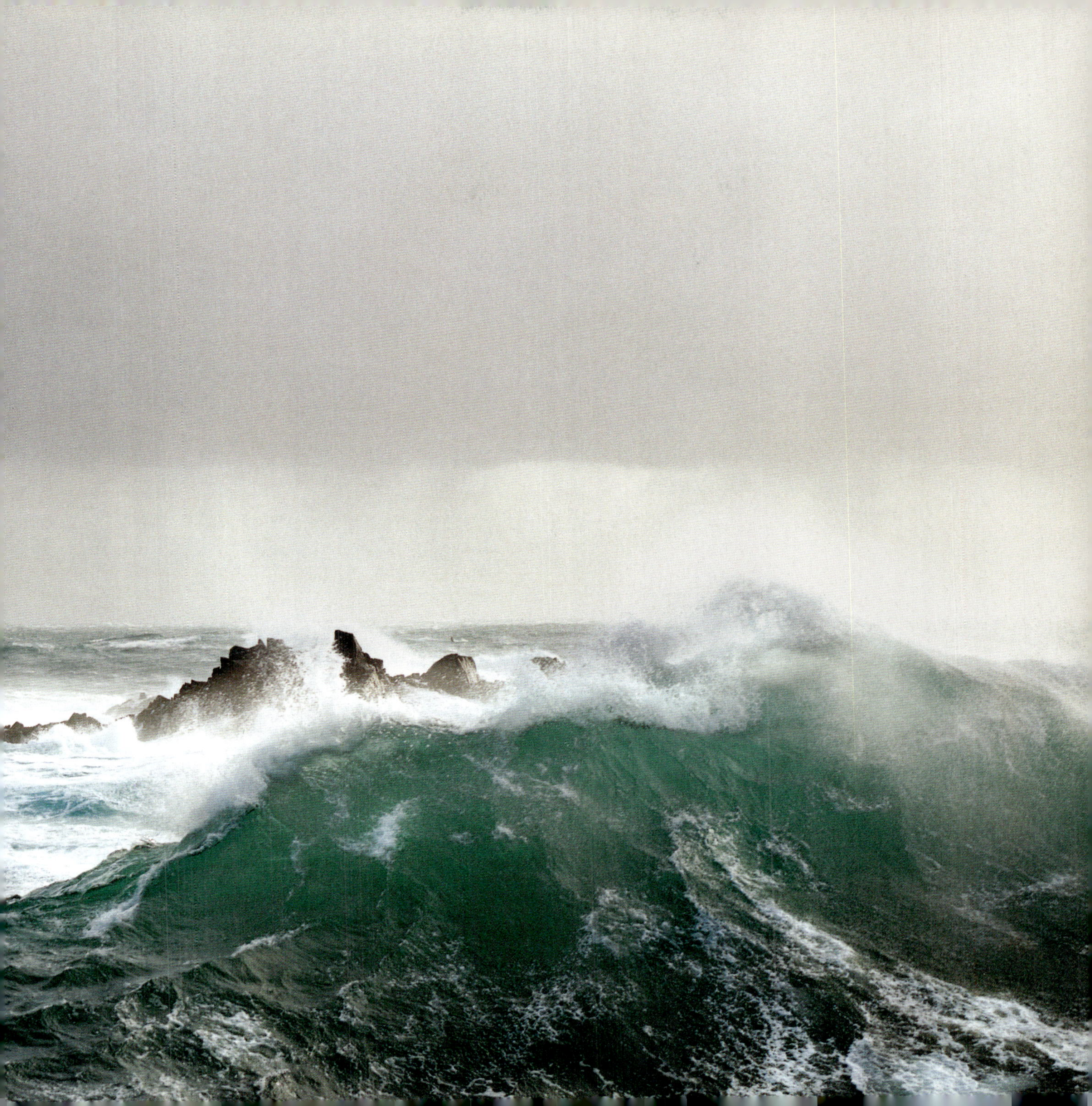

SEPTEMBER 23

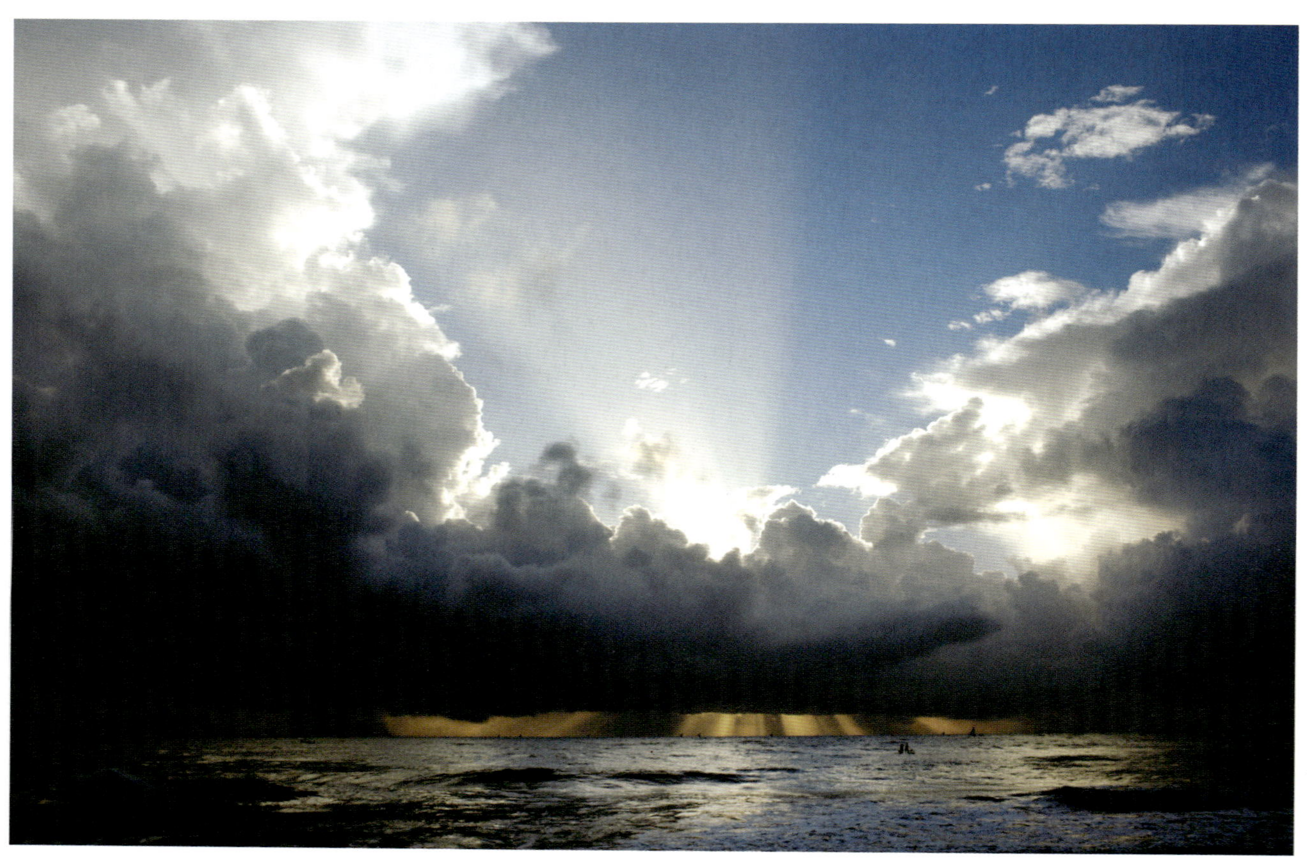

Seamen learn to get to know each other during a storm.

Corsican proverb

SEPTEMBER 24

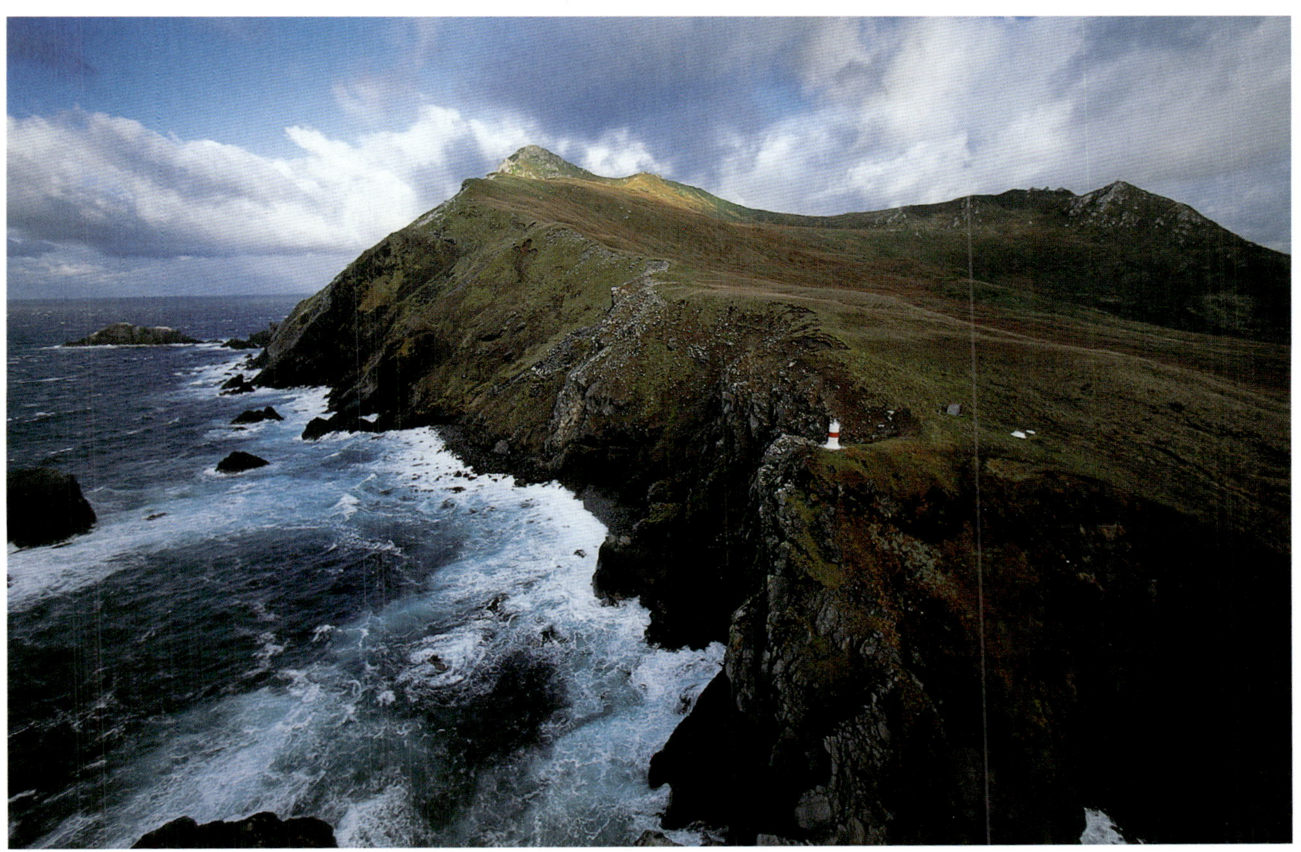

I see the waves upon the shore
Like light dissolved in star-showers thrown.

Percy Bysshe Shelley, from "Stanzas Written in Dejection, Near Naples," 1824

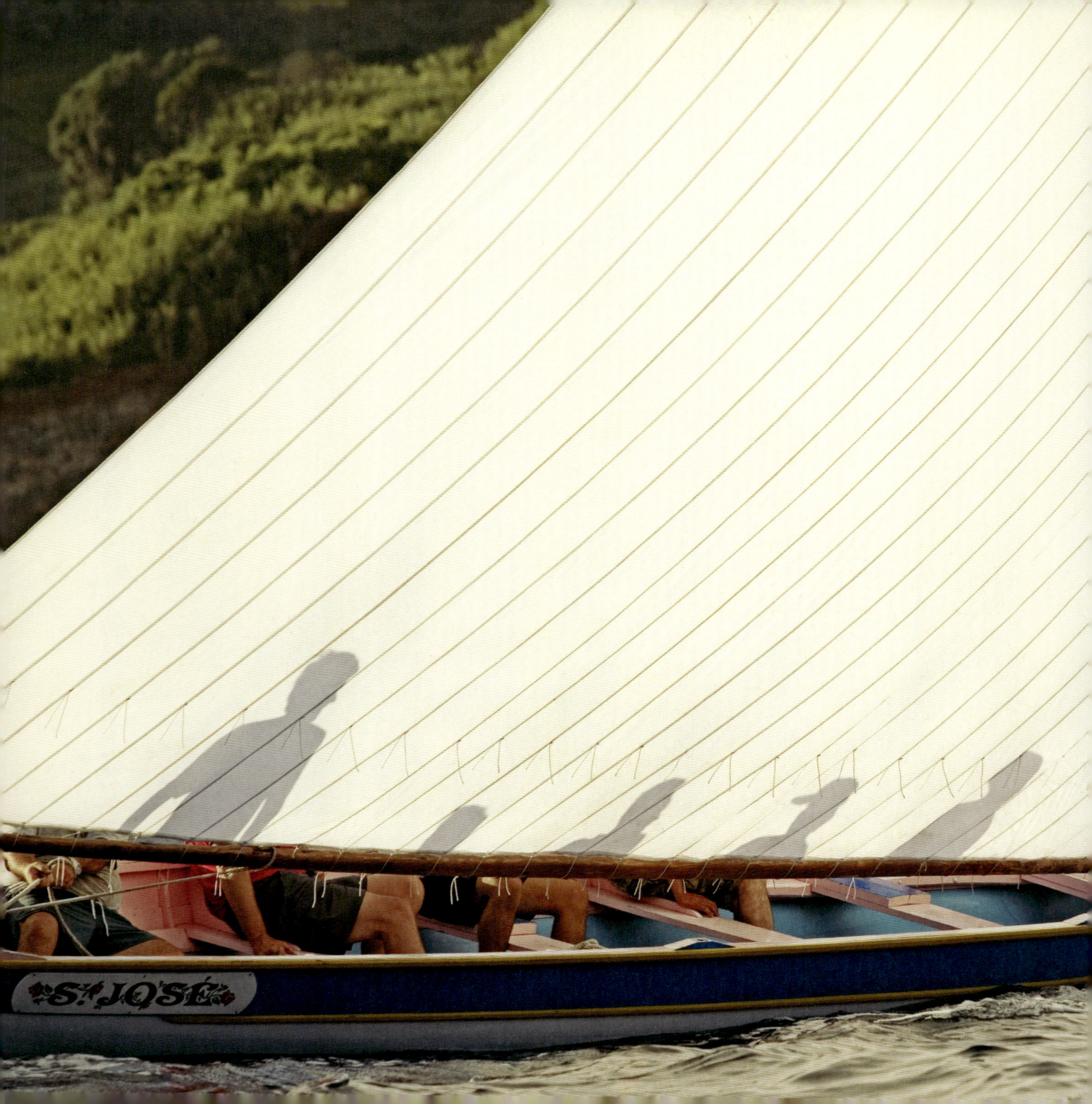
S. JOSÉ

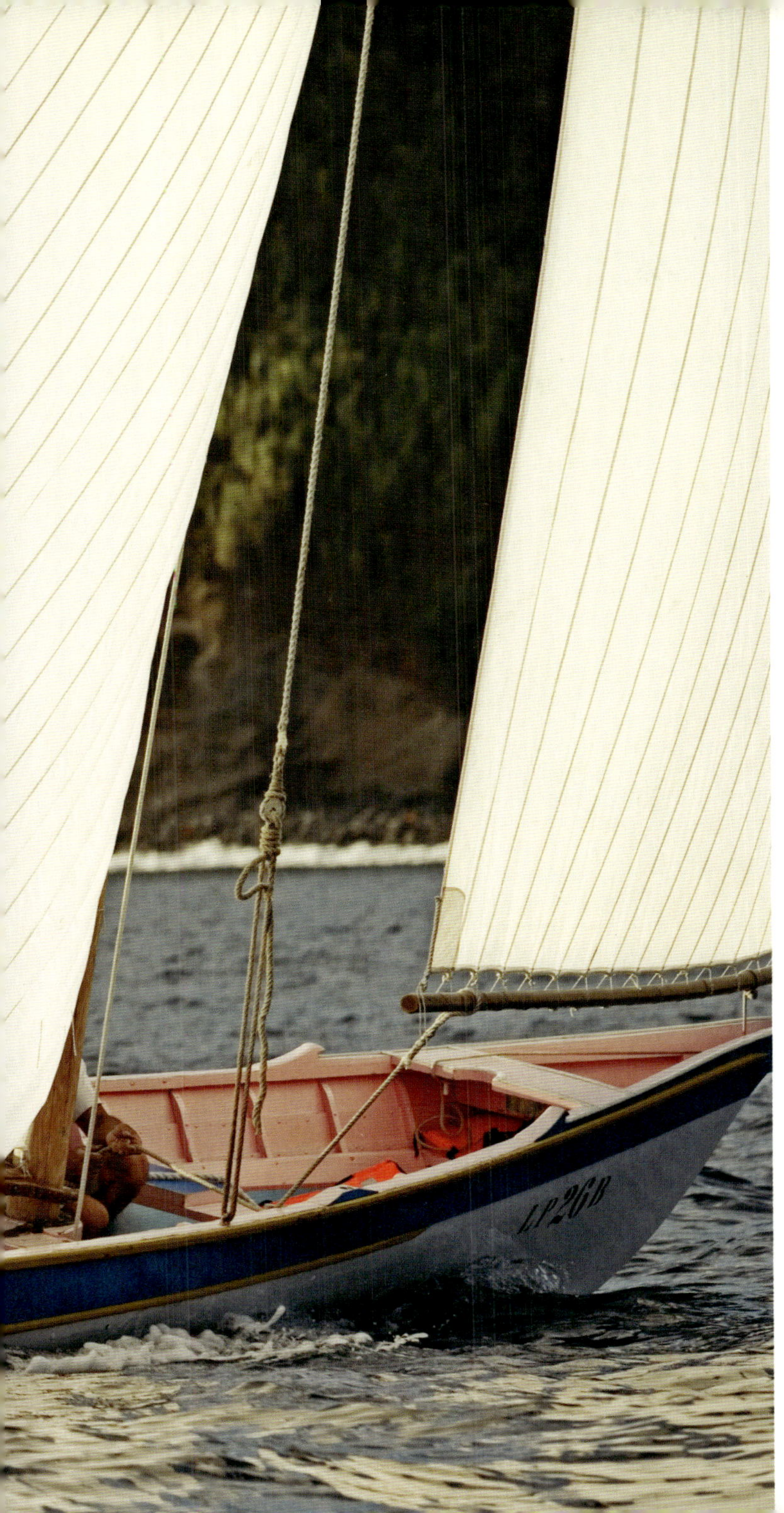

SEPTEMBER 25

I am kin of the changer.
I am a son of the sea
and the sea's wife, the wind.

Carl Sandburg,
from "North Atlantic," *Smoke and Steel,* 1920

SEPTEMBER 26

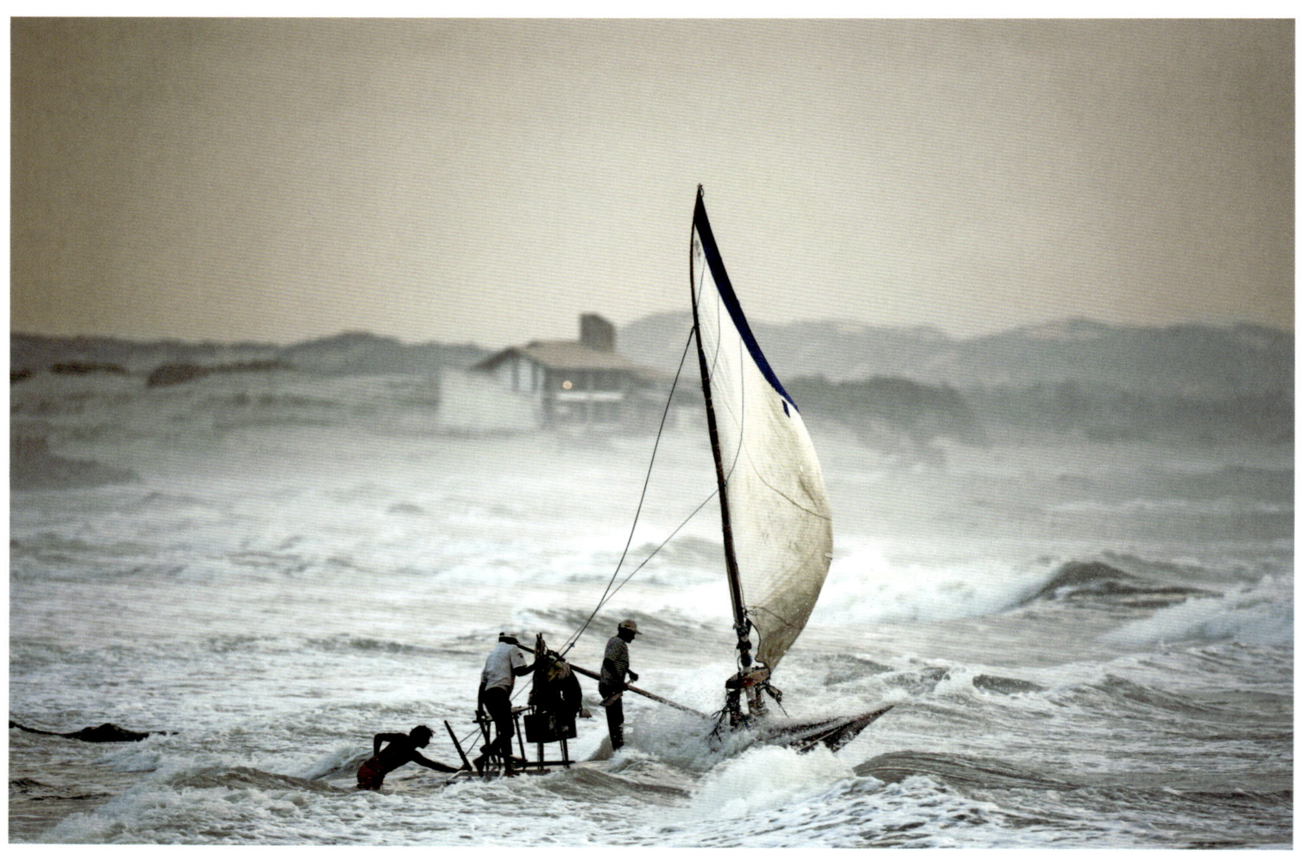

Sea gull, sea gull sit on the sand
It's never good weather when you're on the land.

English proverb

SEPTEMBER 27

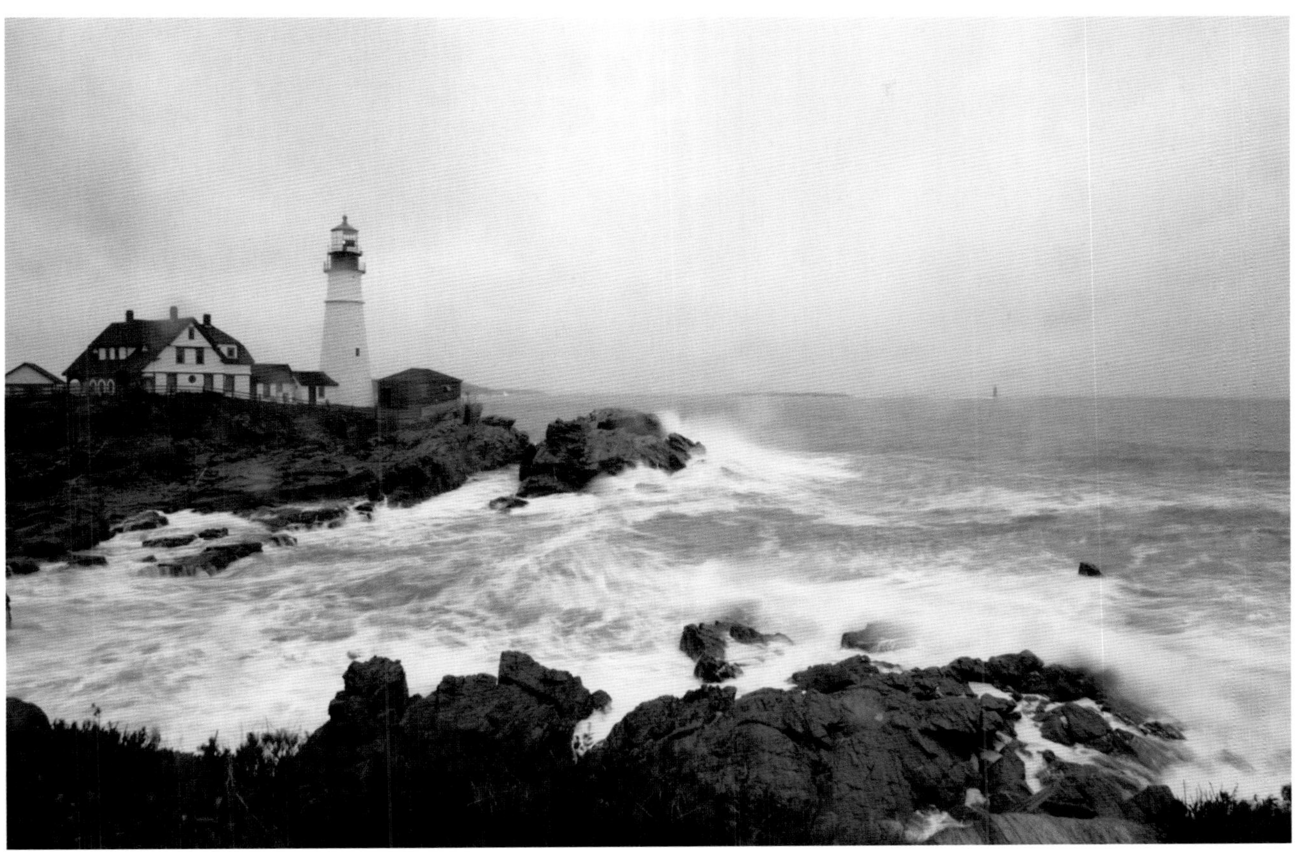

Not a twinkling star or beacon's light
Abates the perils of a stormy night.

William Wordsworth, from "To the Moon," 1835

SEPTEMBER 28

Of all fabricks a ship is the most excellent, requiring more art in building, rigging, sayling, trimming, defending, and moaring.

Captain John Smith,
from *Advertisements,* 1631

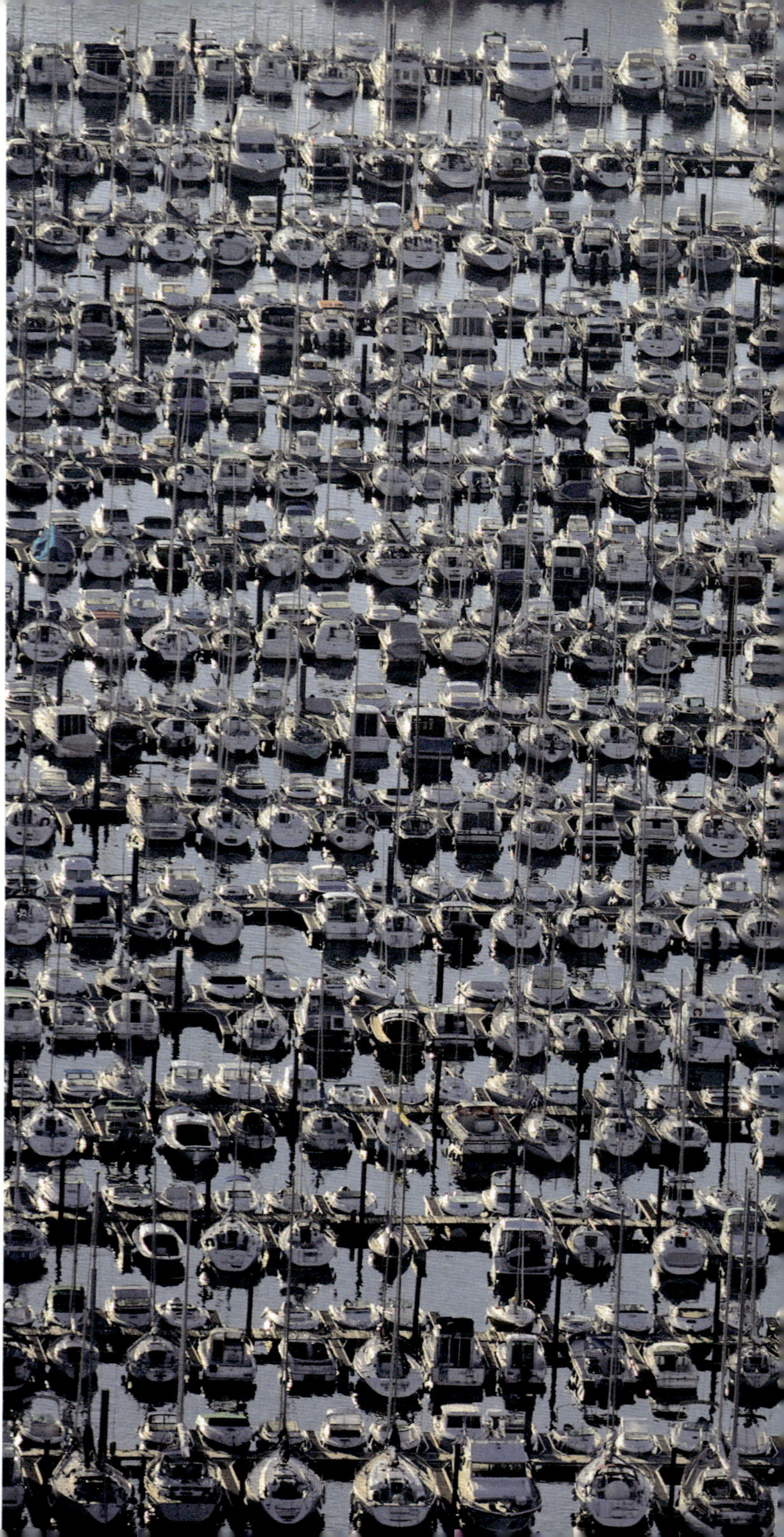

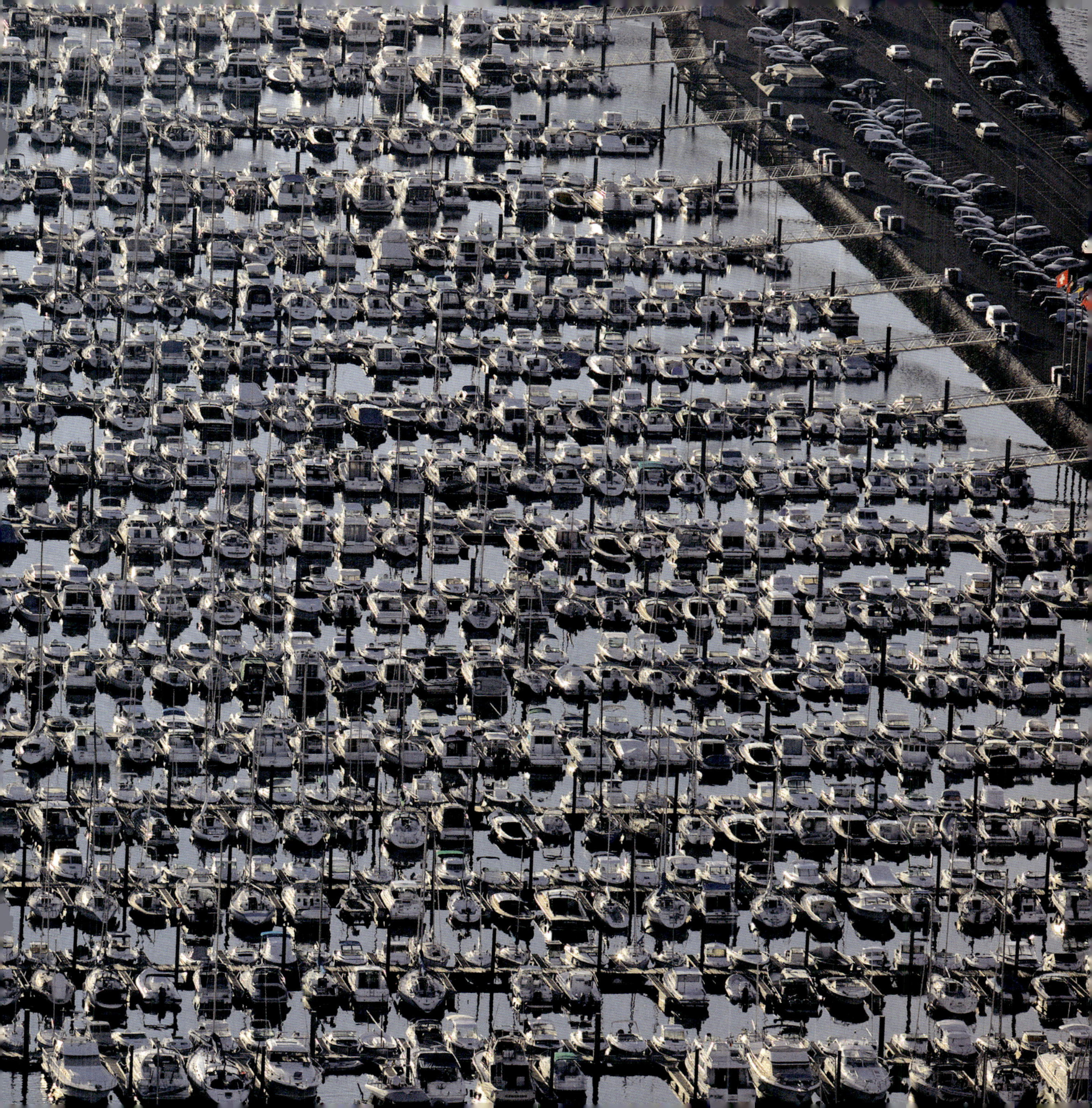

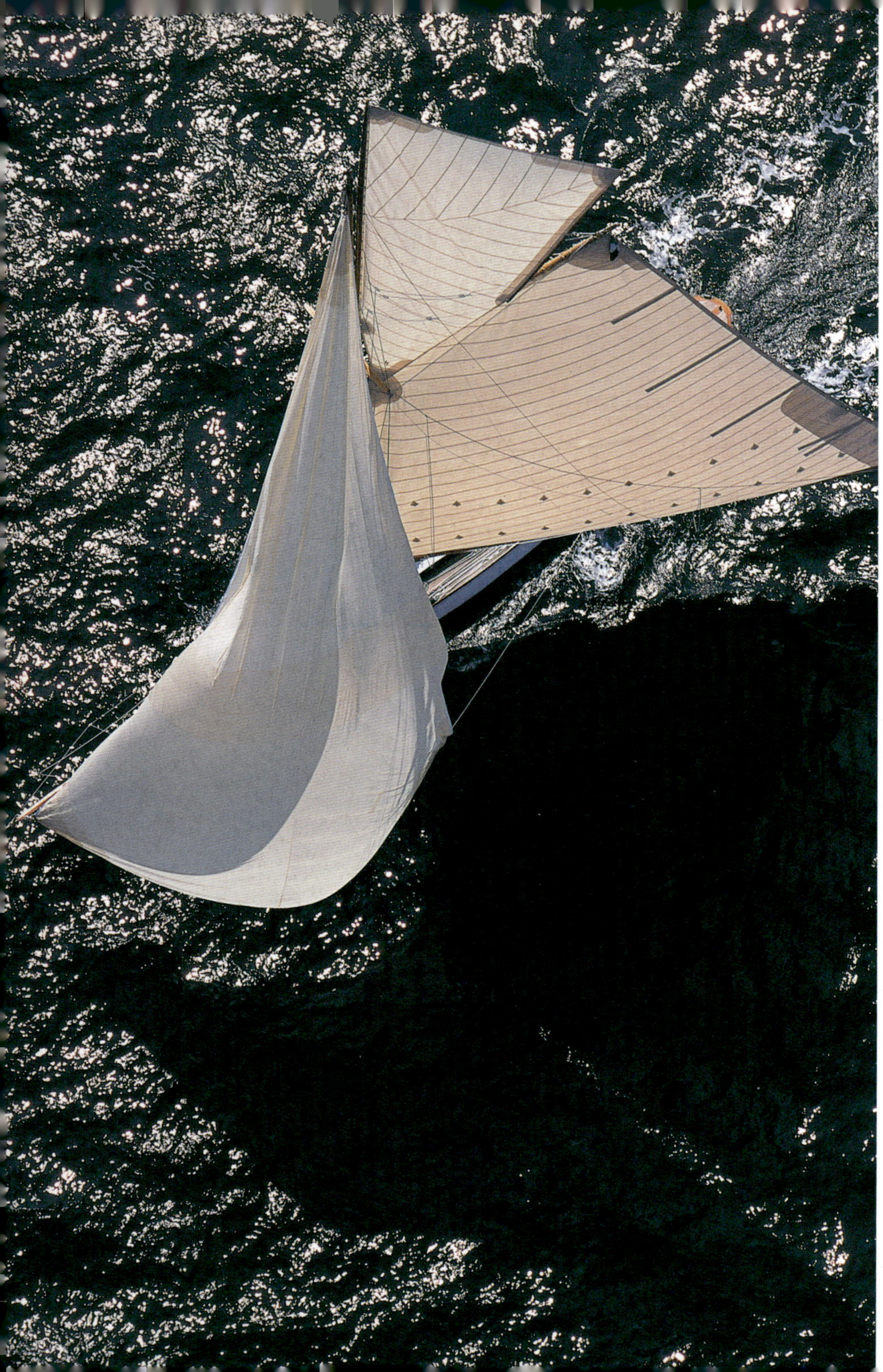

SEPTEMBER 29

If one does not know to which port one is sailing, no wind is favorable.

Seneca

SEPTEMBER 30

Twas them days a ship was part of the sea, and a man was part of the ship, and the sea joined all together and made it one.

Eugene O'Neill,
from *The Hairy Ape,* 1922

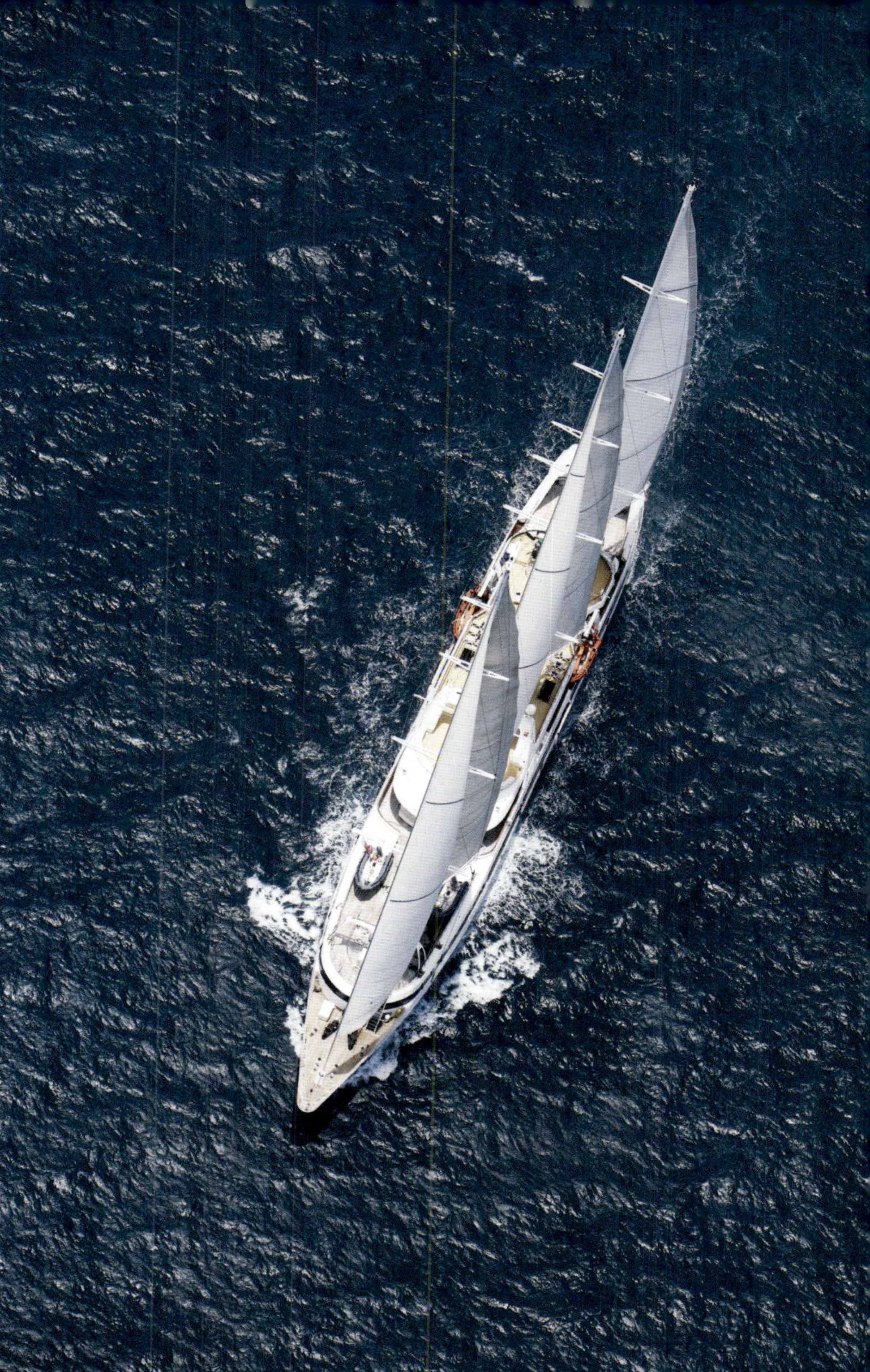

OCTOBER 1

And you who love no pomps of fog or glamour,
Who fear no shocks,
Brave foam and lightning, hurricane and clamour—
Exiles: the rocks!

Victor Hugo,
from "Ocean's Song," *Chastisements,* 1853

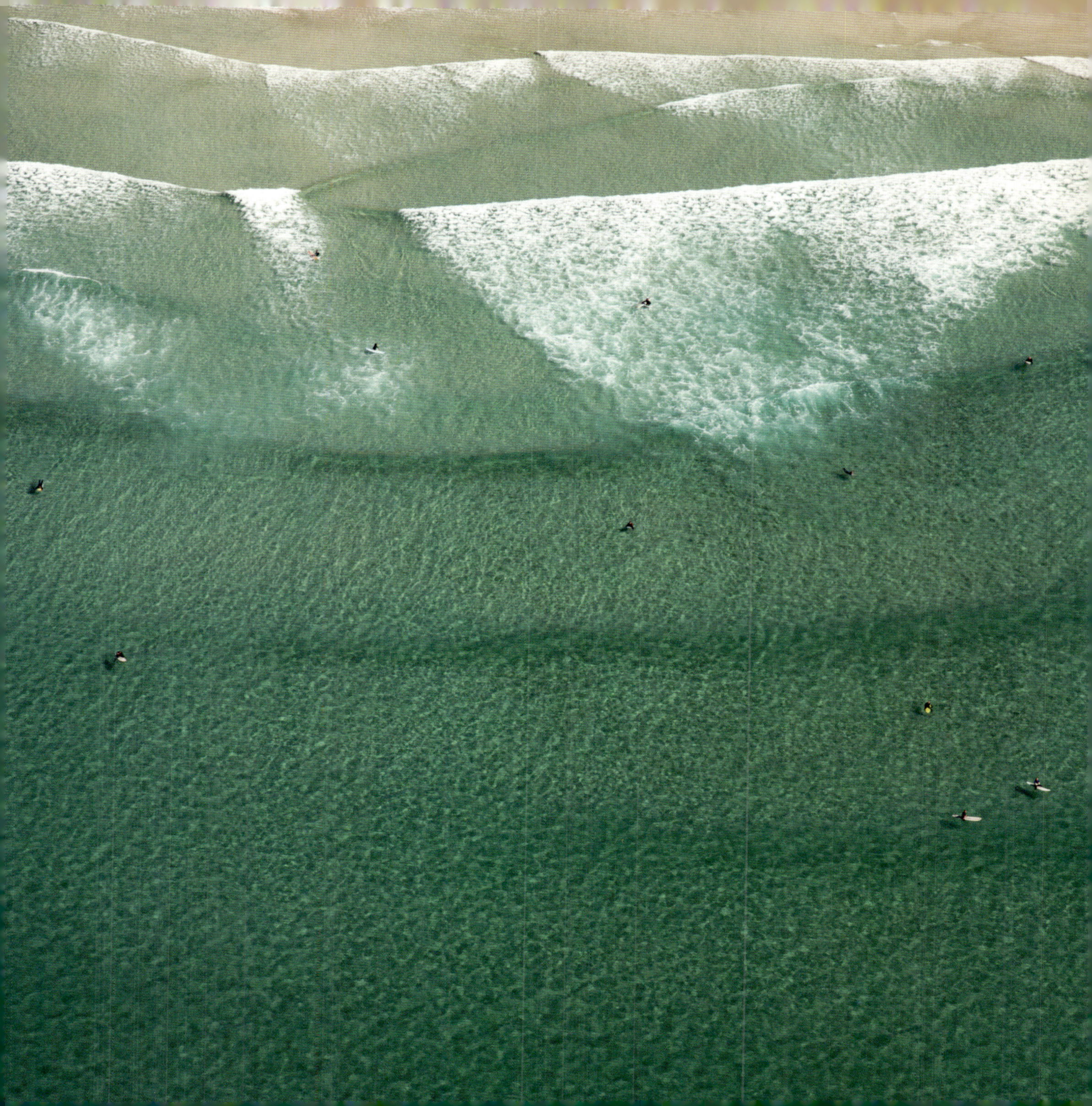

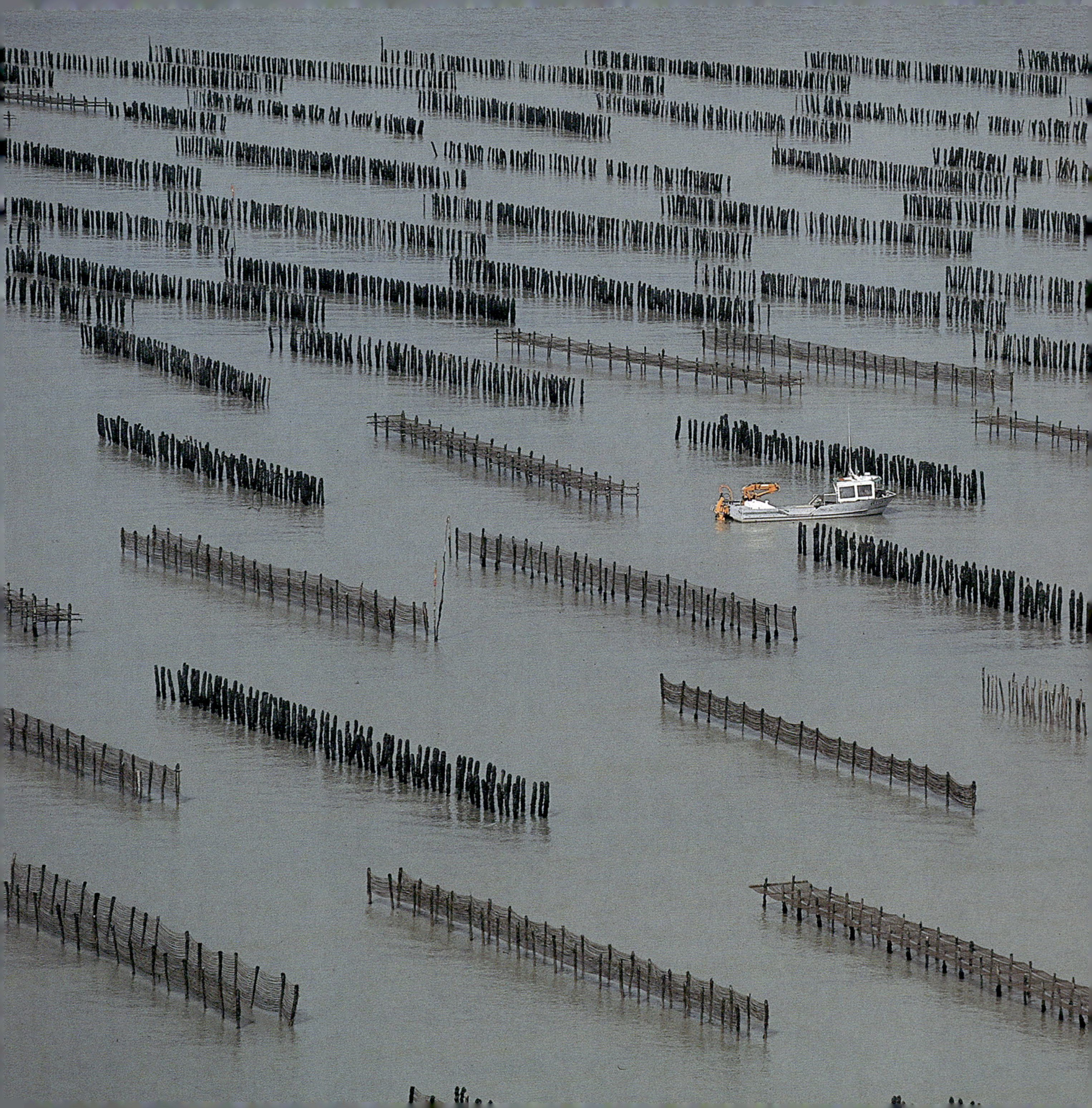

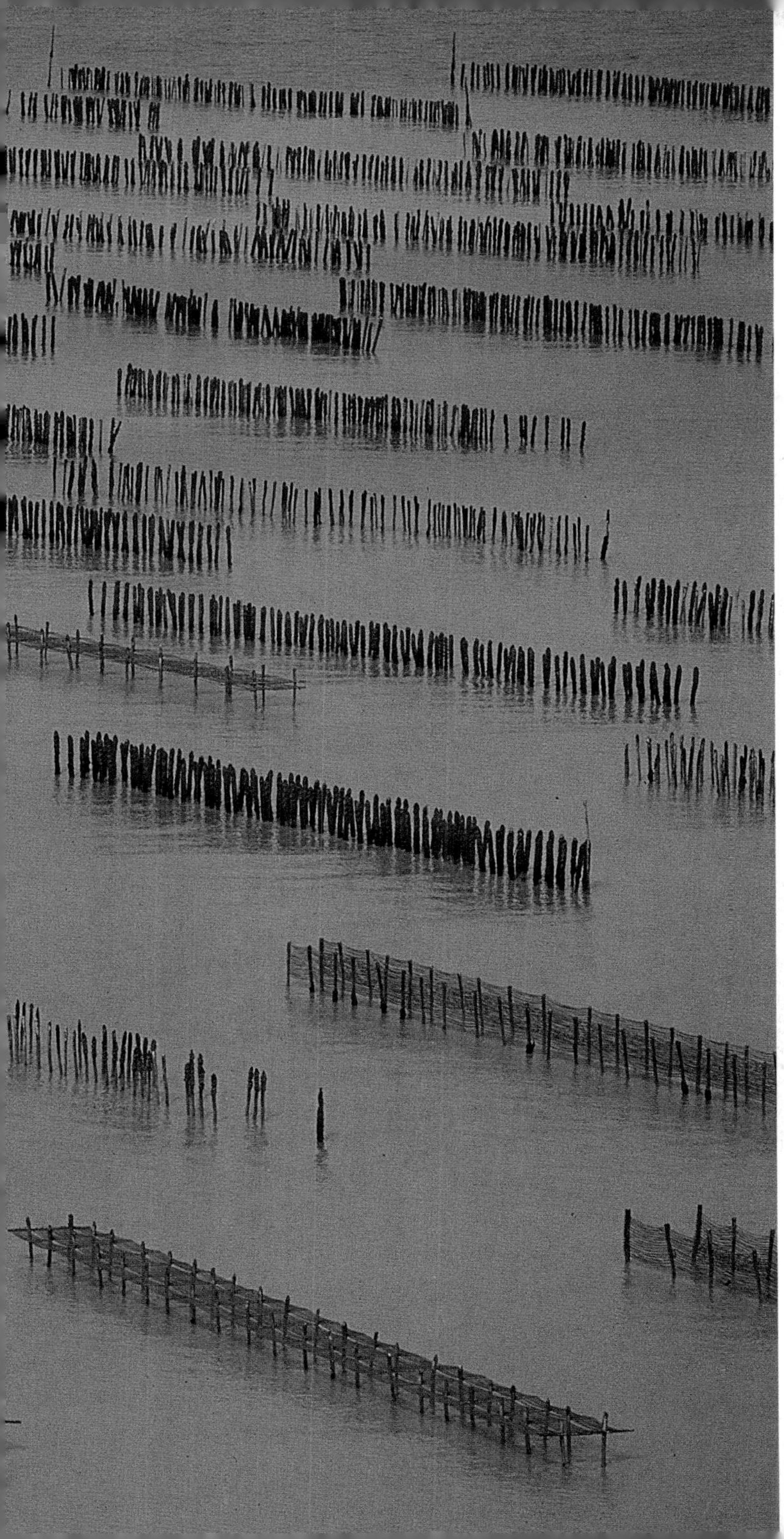

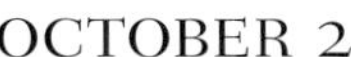

OCTOBER 2

The ocean is a wilderness reaching round the globe, wilder than a Bengal jungle, and fuller of monsters, washing the very wharves of our cities and the gardens of our sea-side residences. Serpents, bears, hyenas, tigers rapidly vanish as civilization advances, but the most populous and civilized city cannot scare a shark far from its wharves.

Henry David Thoreau,
from *Cape Cod,* 1906

OCTOBER 3

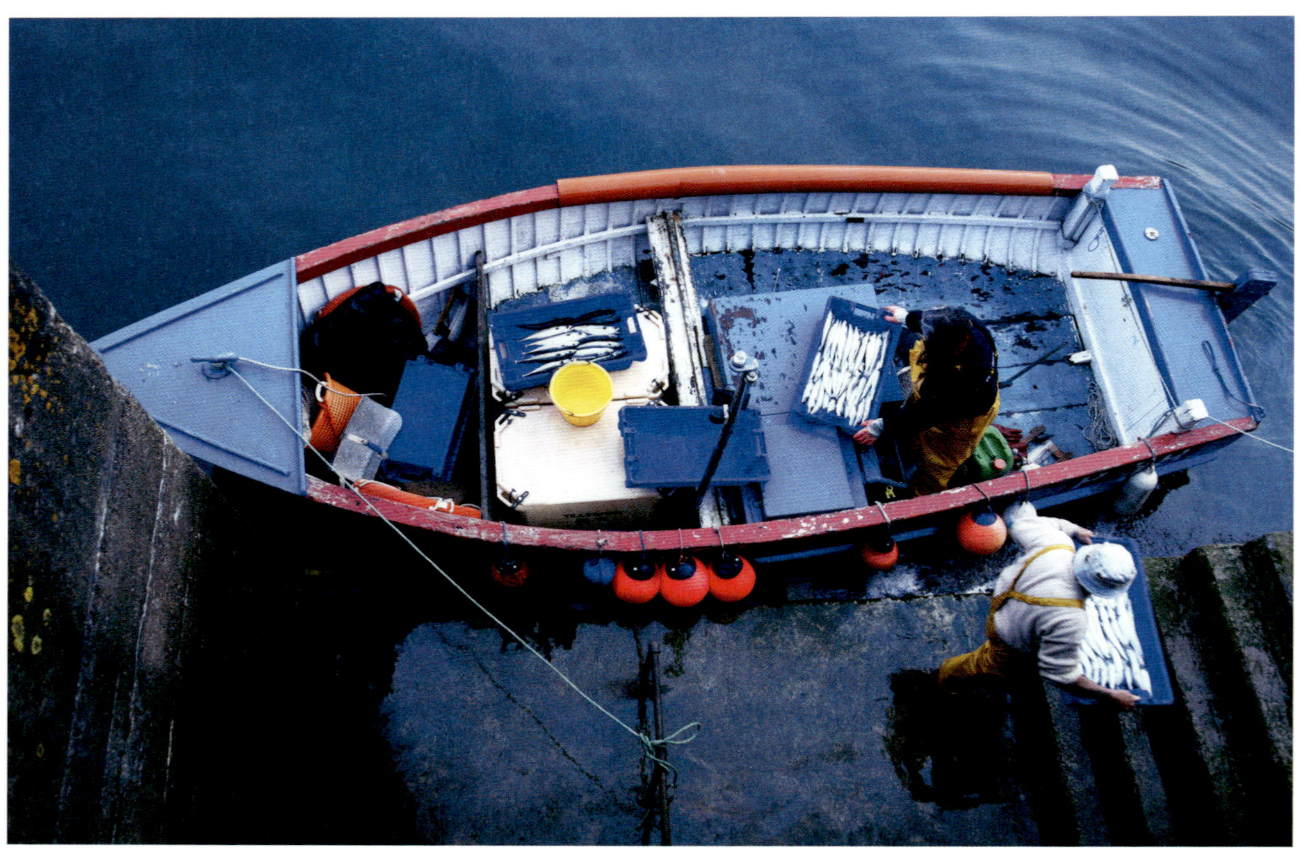

If you cannot catch a fish, do not blame the sea.

Greek proverb

OCTOBER 4

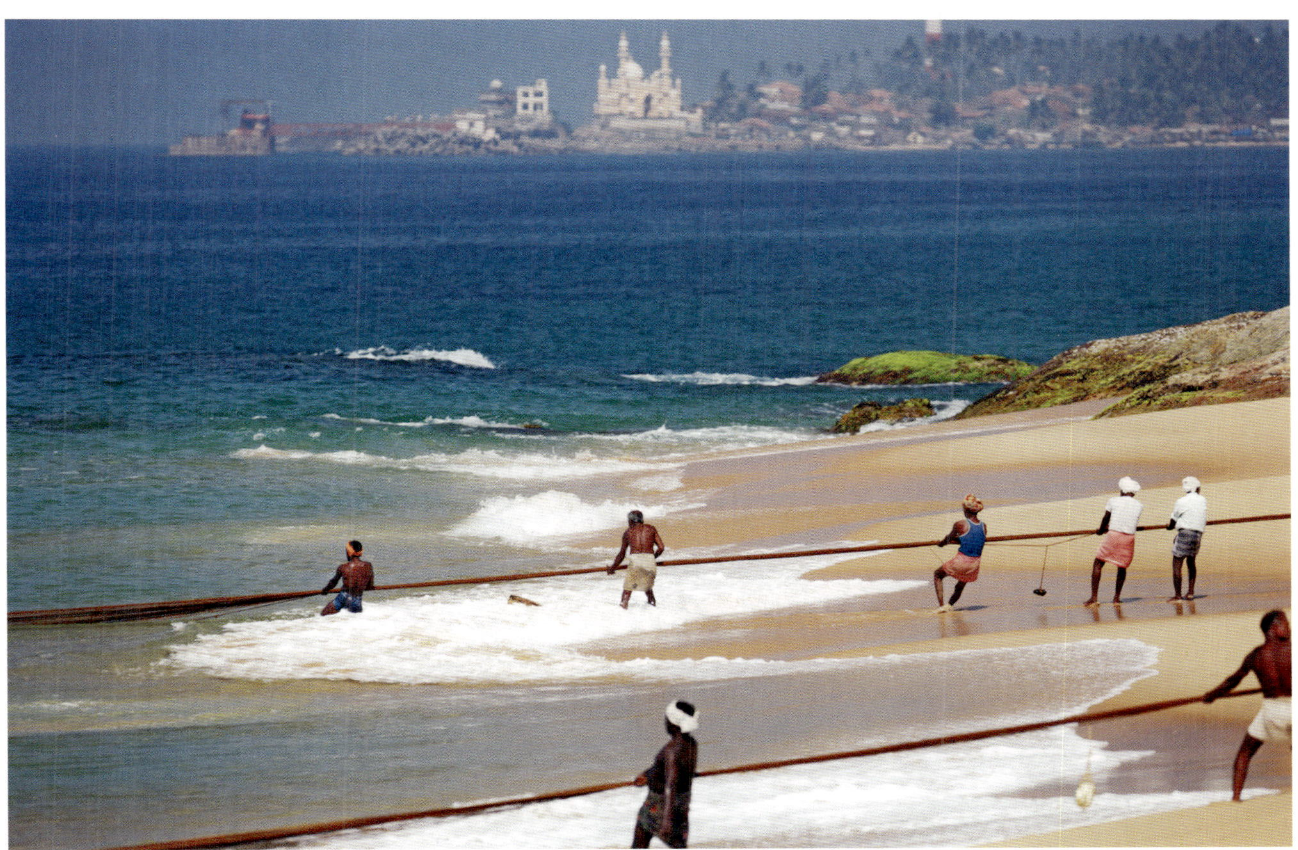

The voice of the sea speaks to the soul. The touch of the sea is sensuous,
enfolding the body in its soft, close embrace.

Kate Chopin, from *The Awakening,* 1899

OCTOBER 5

There isn't no call to go talking of pushing and pulling. Boats are quite tricky enough for those that sit still without looking further for the cause of trouble.

J. R. R. Tolkien,
from *The Fellowship of the Ring*, 1954

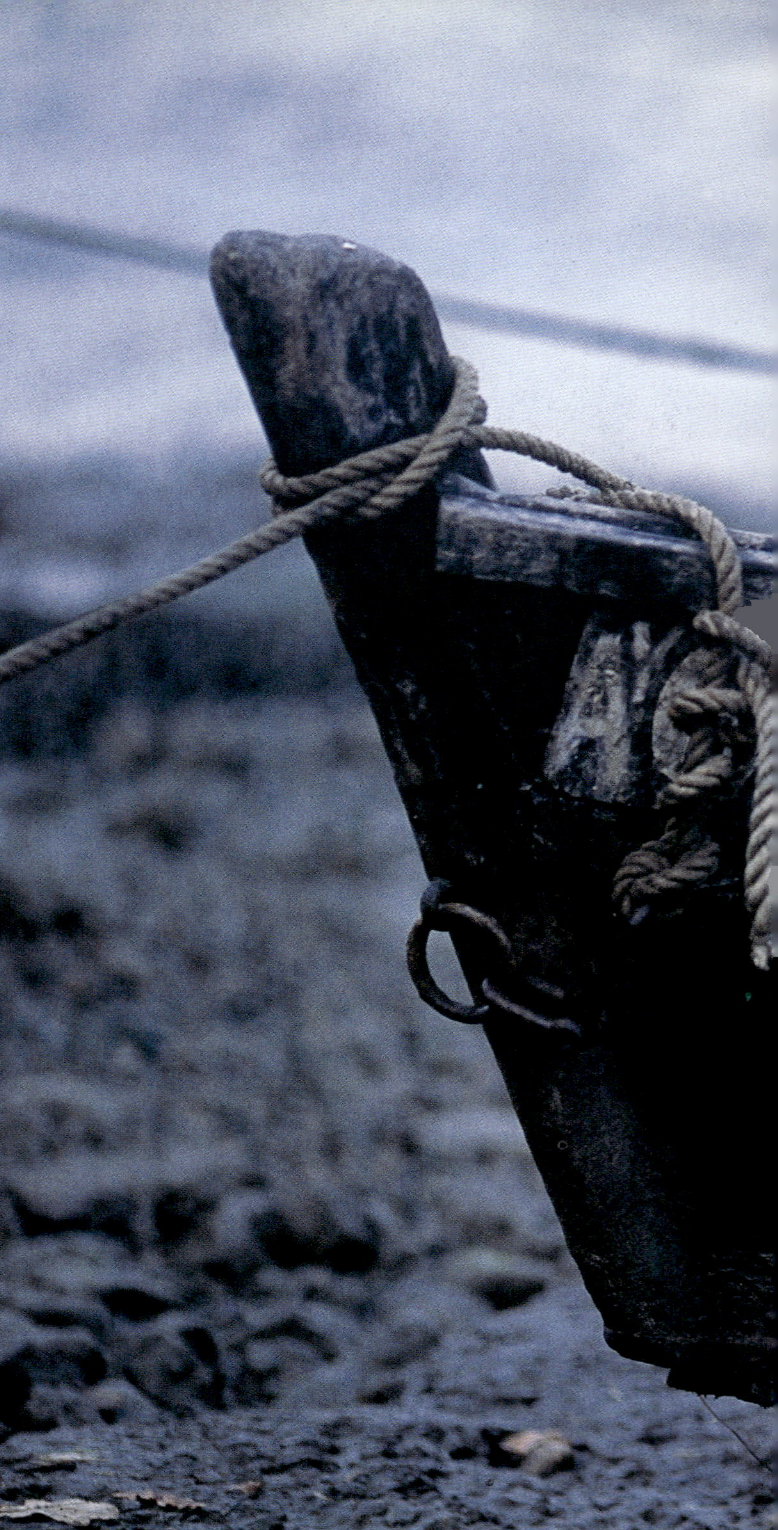

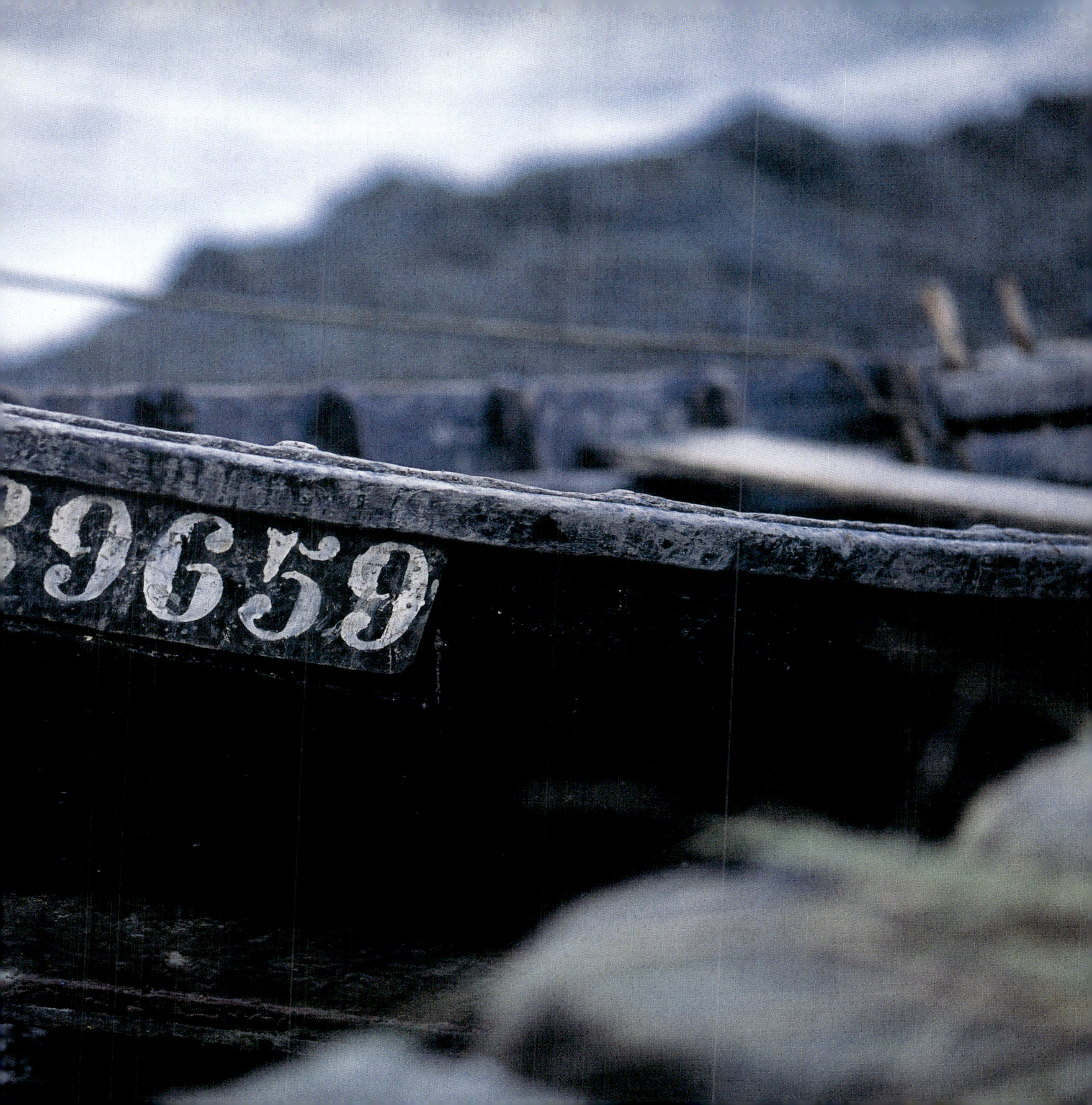
39659

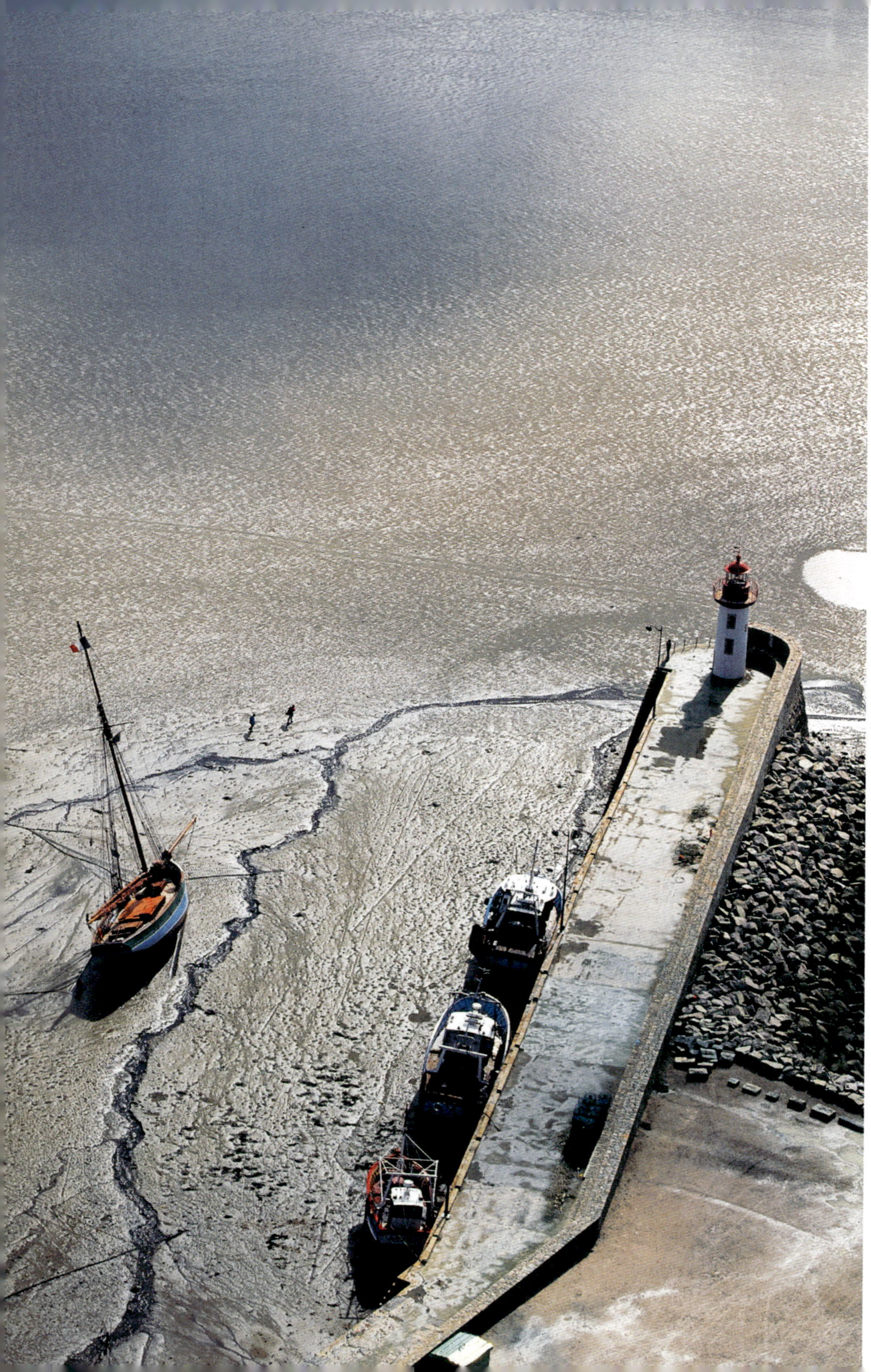

OCTOBER 6

They are ill discoverers that
think there is no land when
they see nothing but sea.

Francis Bacon, from "Of Travel," 1625

OCTOBER 7

Only the guy who isn't rowing
has time to rock the boat.

Jean-Paul Sartre

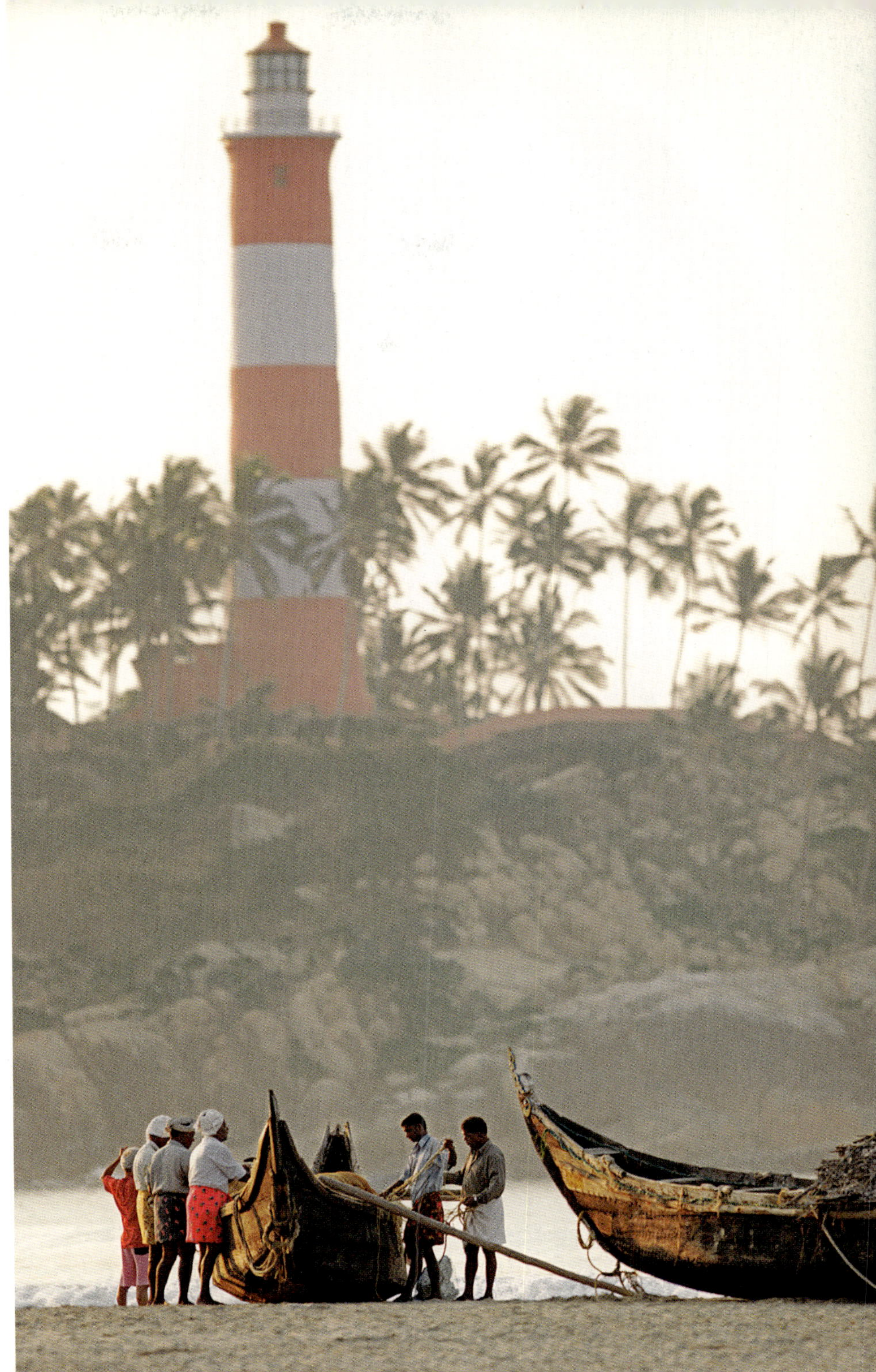

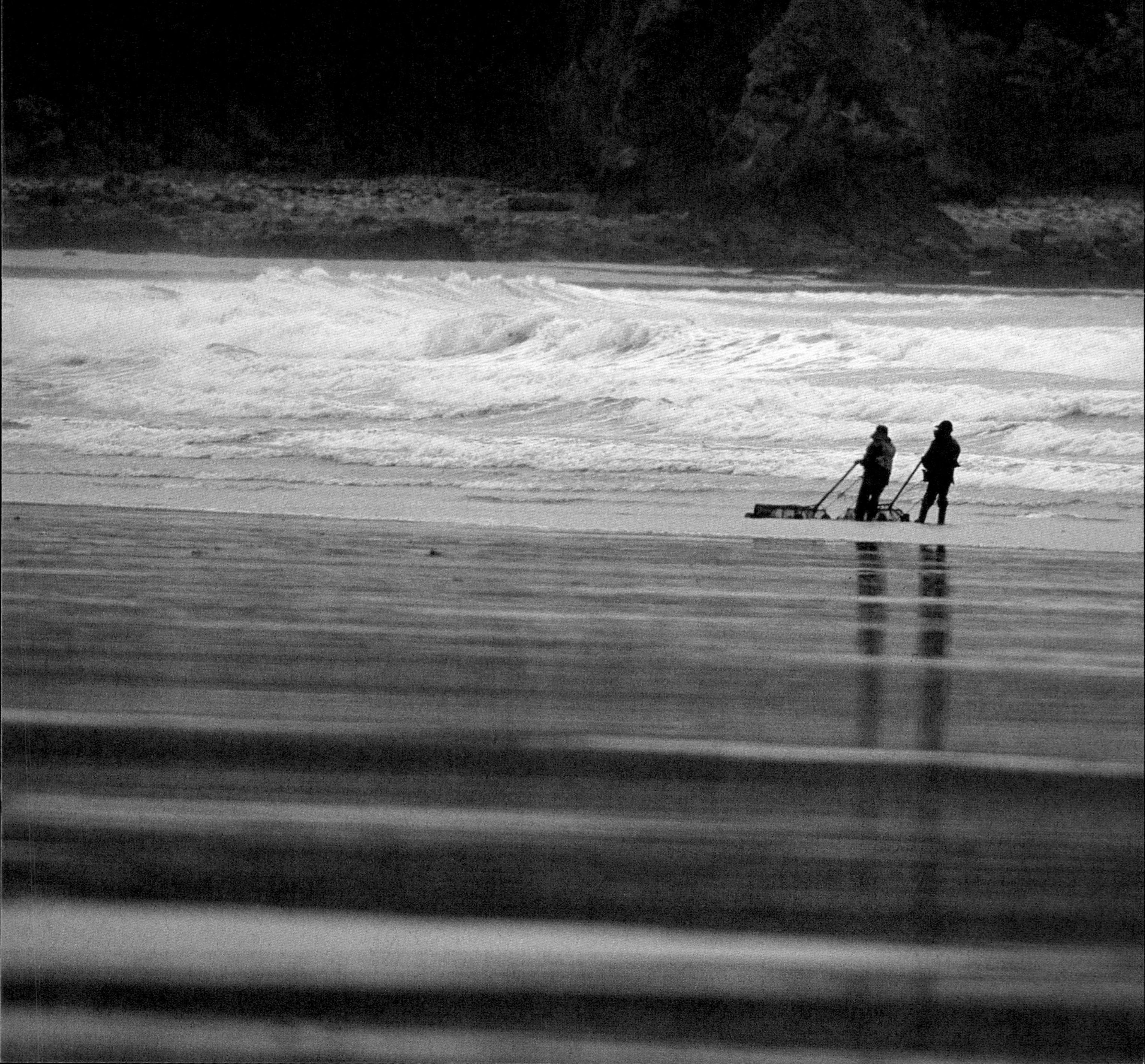

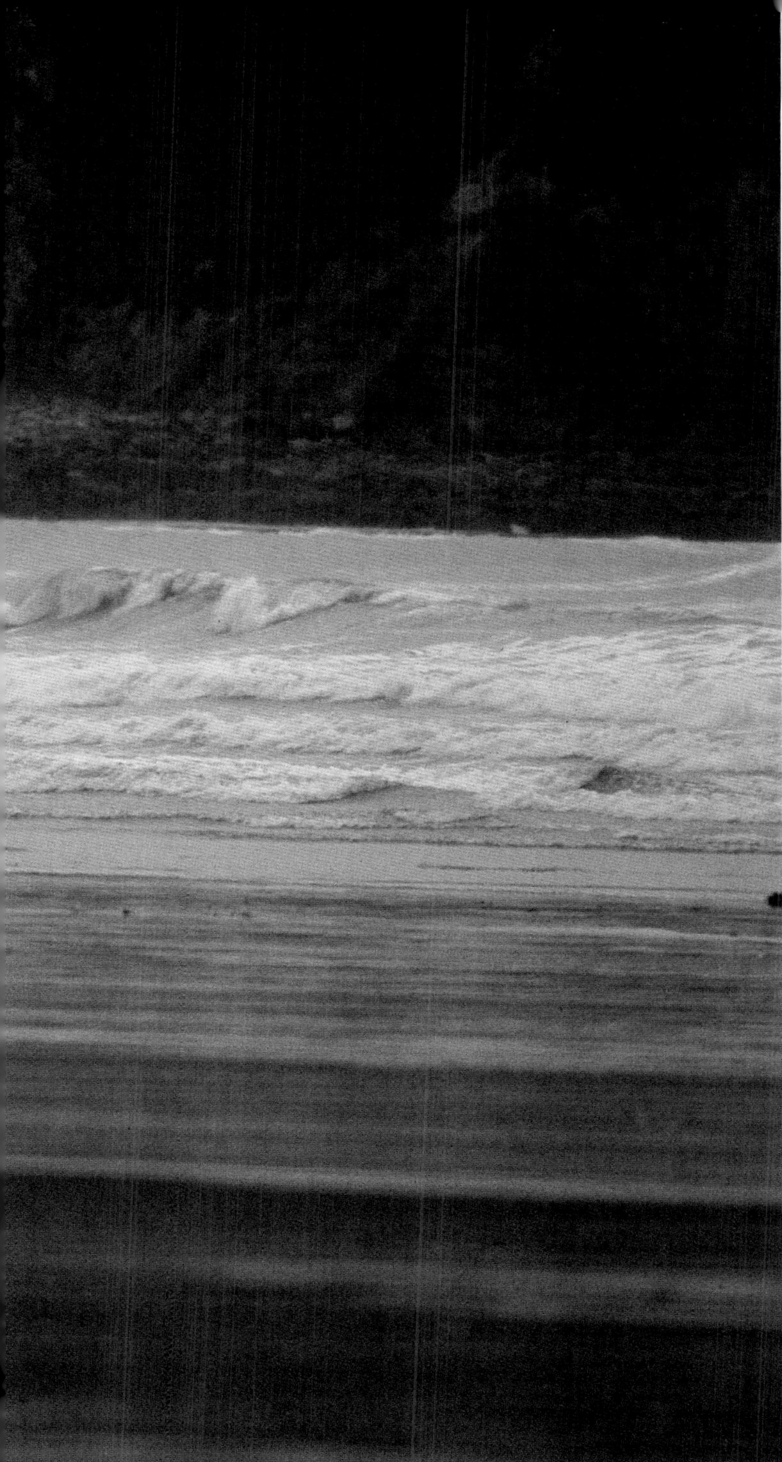

OCTOBER 8

I stand amid the roar
Of a surf-tormented shore,
And I hold within my hand
Grains of the golden sand—
How few! yet how they creep
Through my fingers to the deep,
While I weep—while I weep!

Edgar Allan Poe,
from "A Dream Within a Dream," 1849

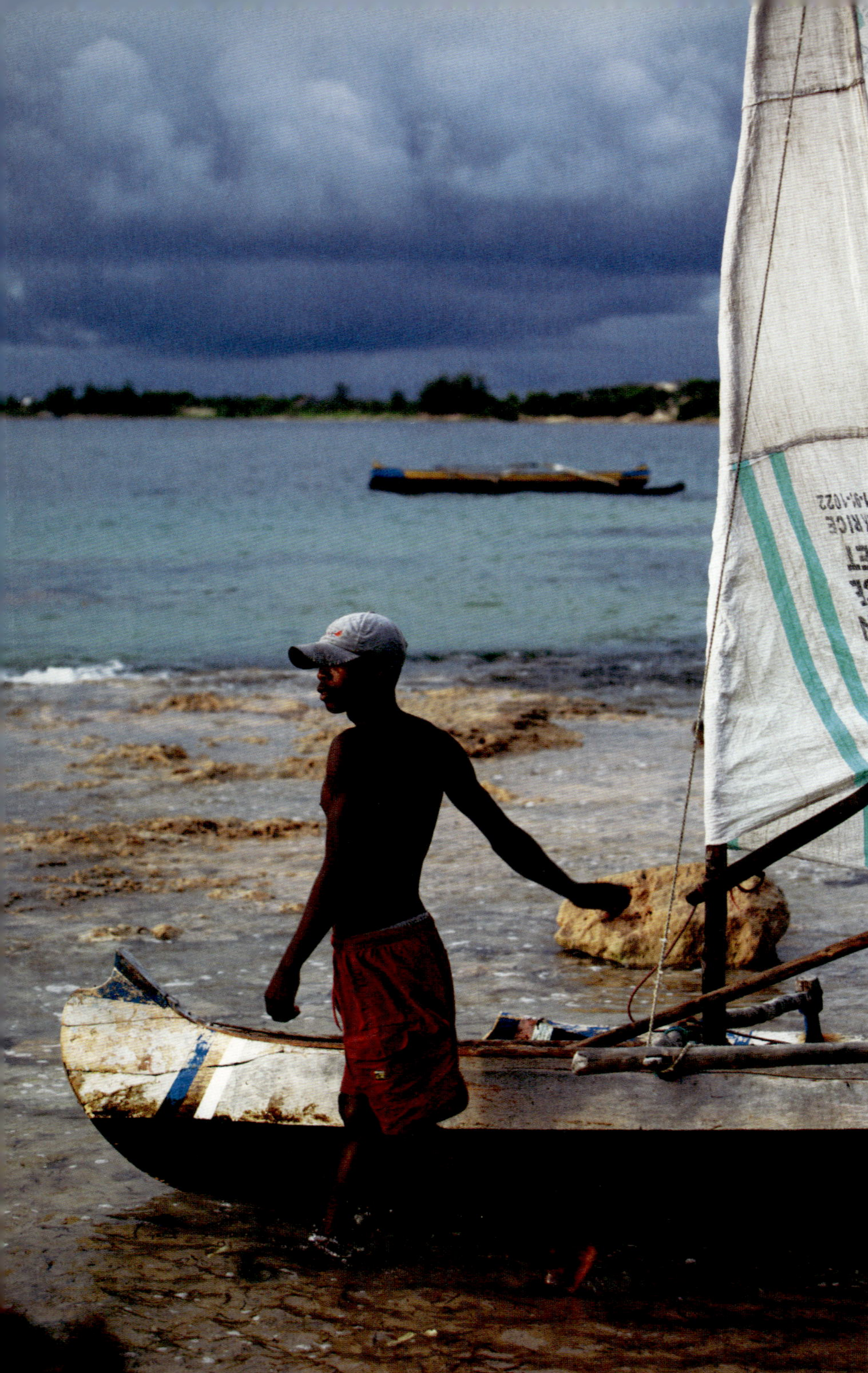

OCTOBER 9

The maister of shippes in Navigation... ought to be such a one as can governe himselfe, for else it is not possible for him to governe his company well.

William Bourne,
from *A Regiment for the Sea,* 1577

OCTOBER 10

Wide sea, that one continuous
murmur breeds along the
pebbled shore of memory!

John Keats,
from *Book of Endymion,* 1818

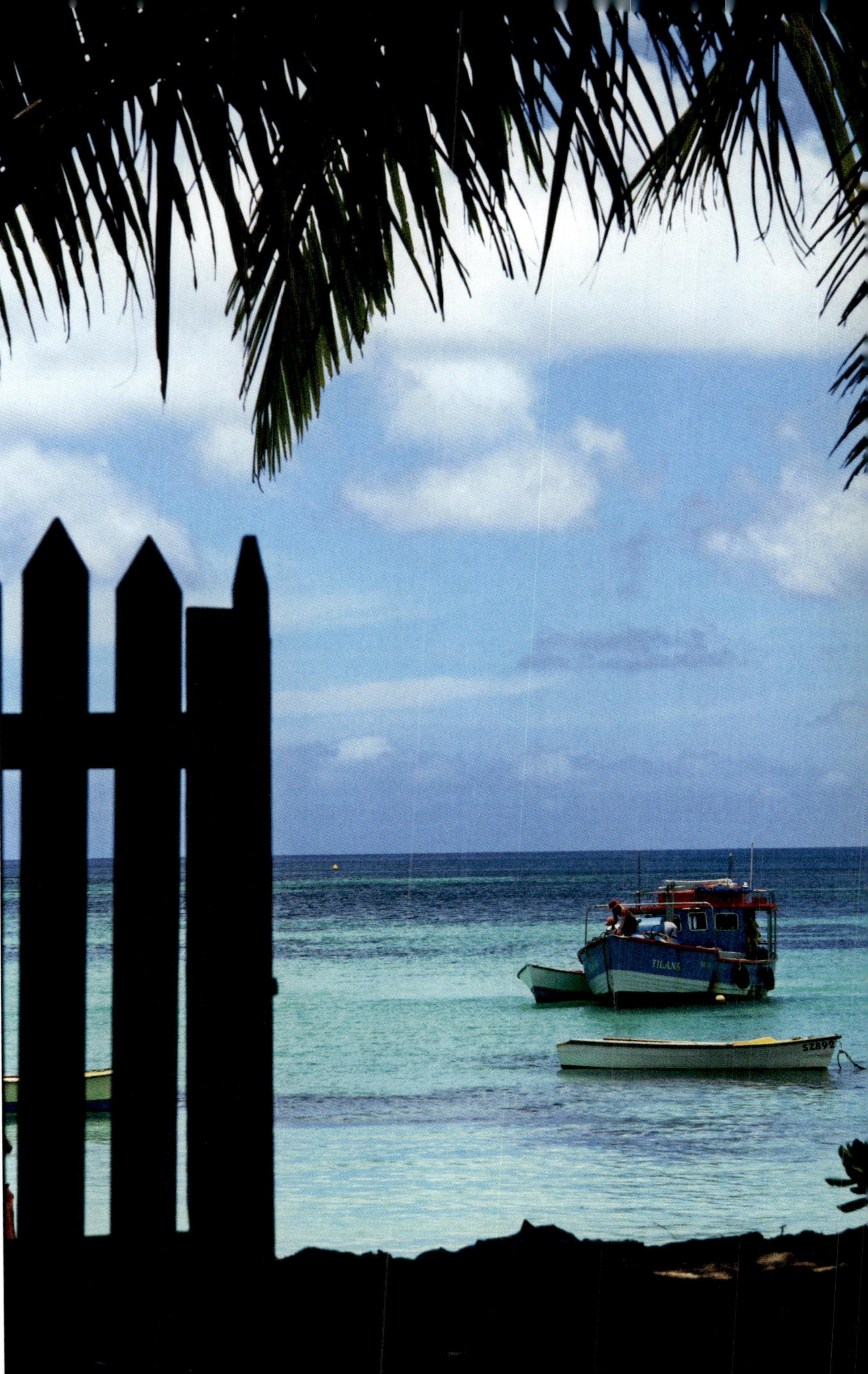

OCTOBER 11

There is really something strangely cheering
to the spirits in the meeting of a ship at
sea, containing a society of creatures
of the same species and in the same
circumstances with ourselves, after we had
been long separated and excommunicated
as it were from the rest of mankind.

Benjamin Franklin, 1726

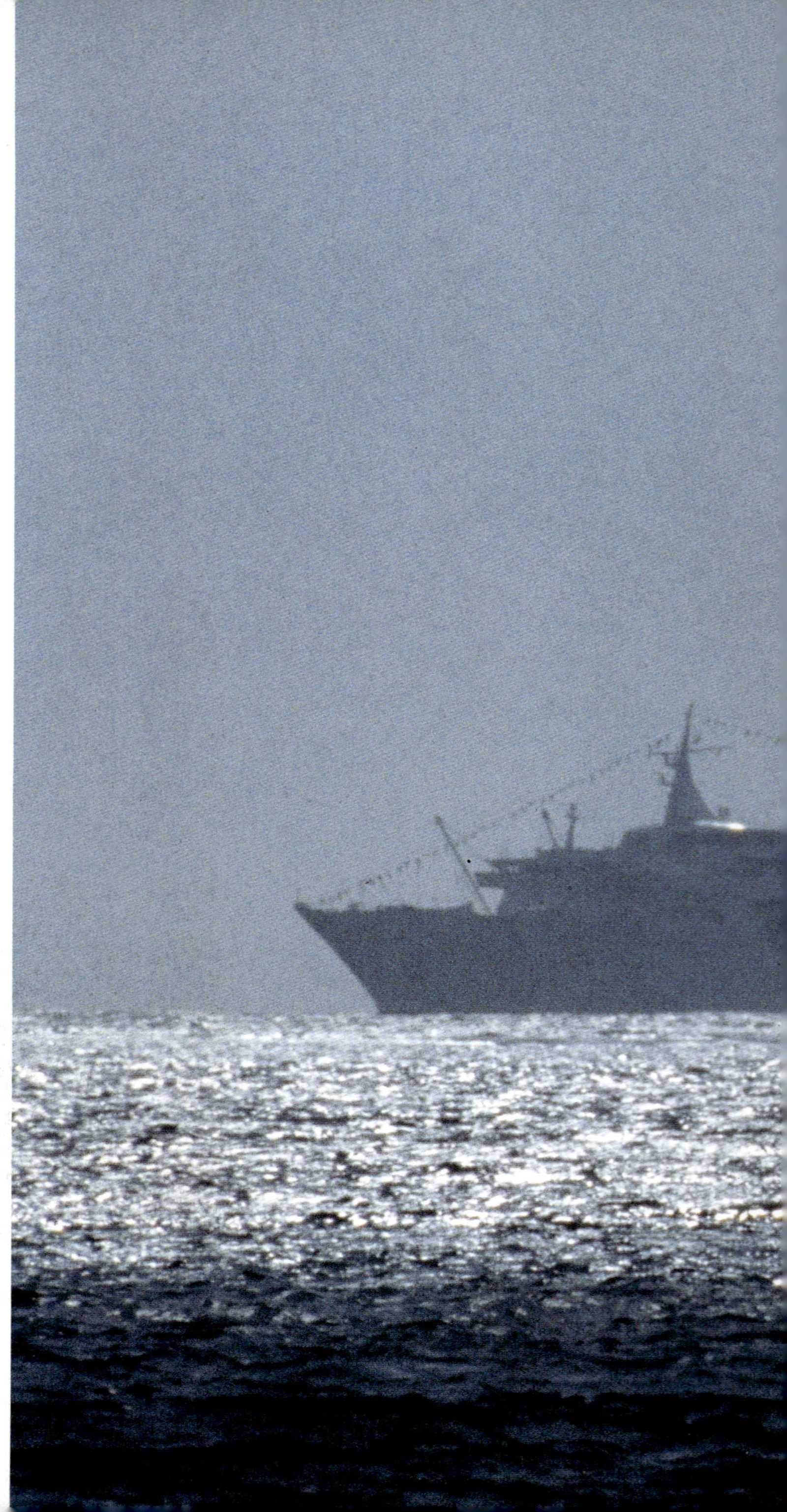

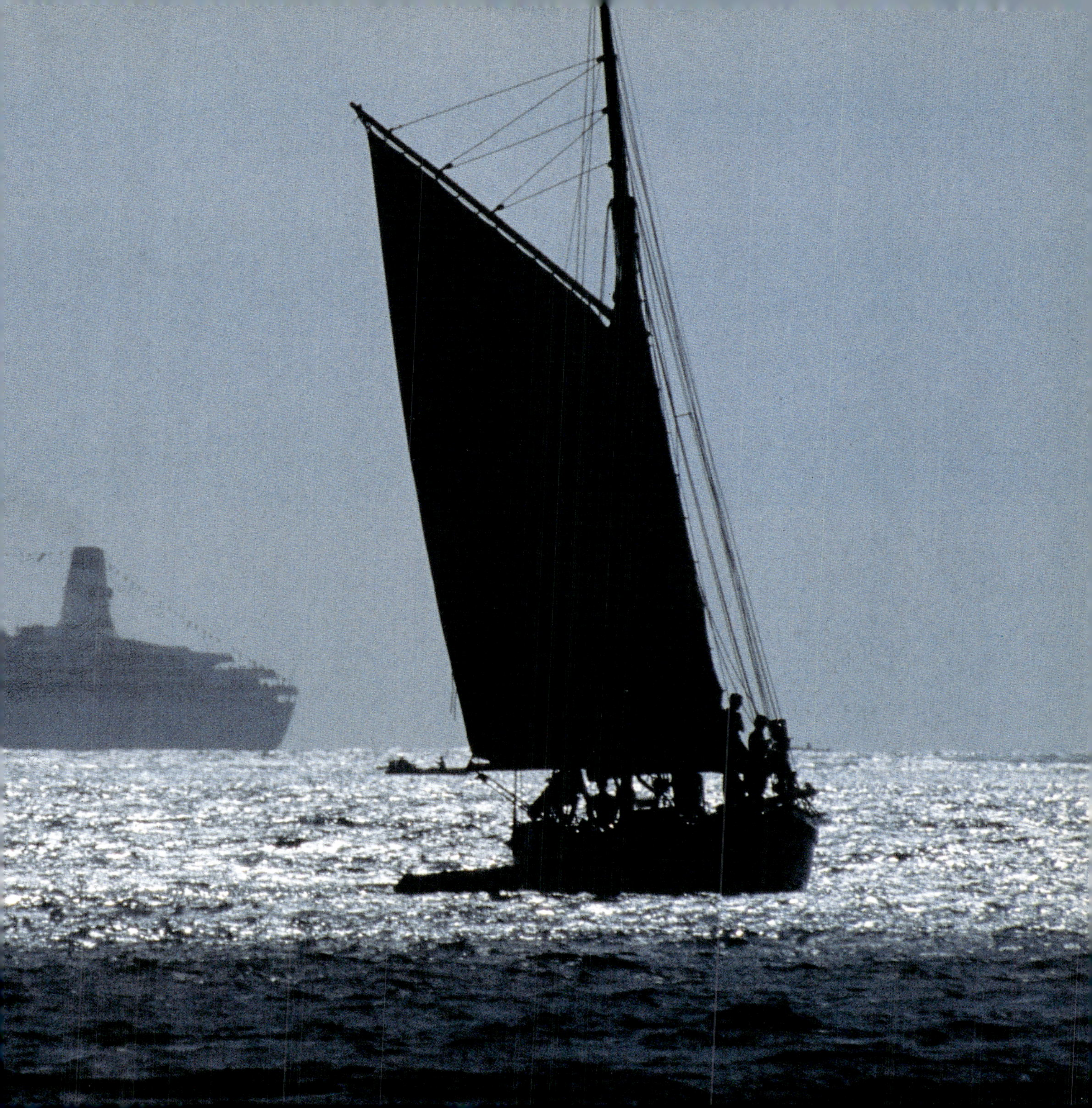

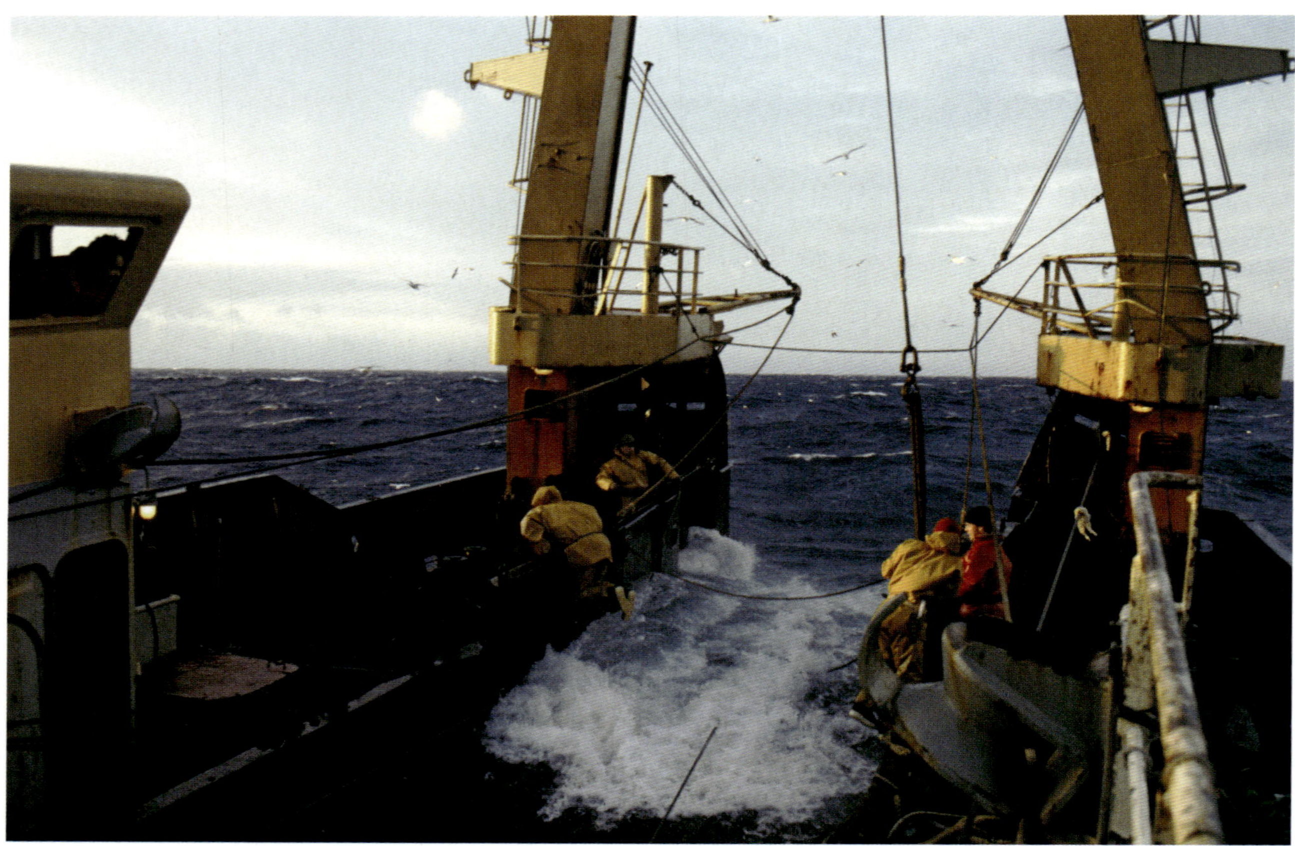

There is not so helpless and pitiable an object in the world as a landsman beginning a sailor's life.

Richard Henry Dana Jr., from *Two Years Before the Mast,* 1834

OCTOBER 13

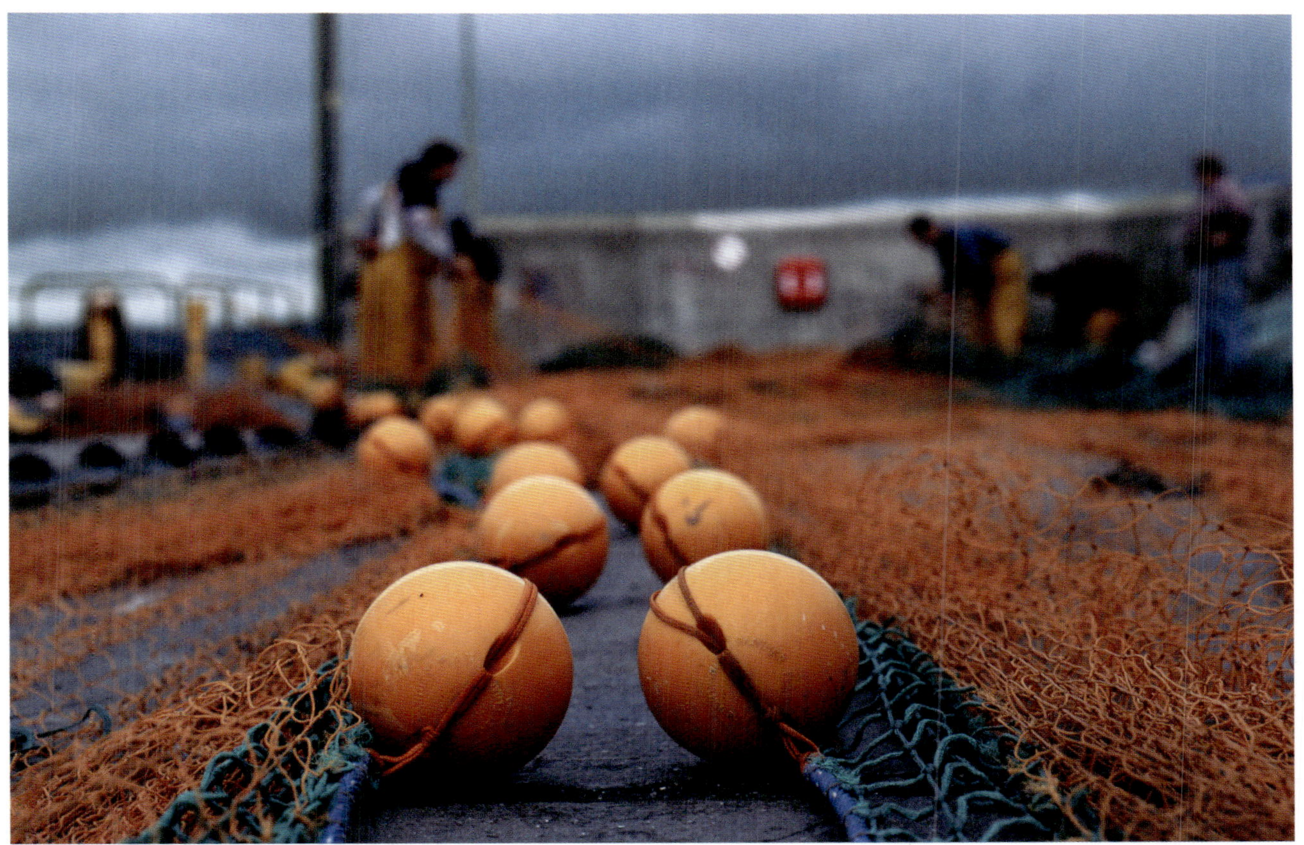

The cure for anything is saltwater—sweat, tears, or the sea.

ஐ

Isak Dinesen

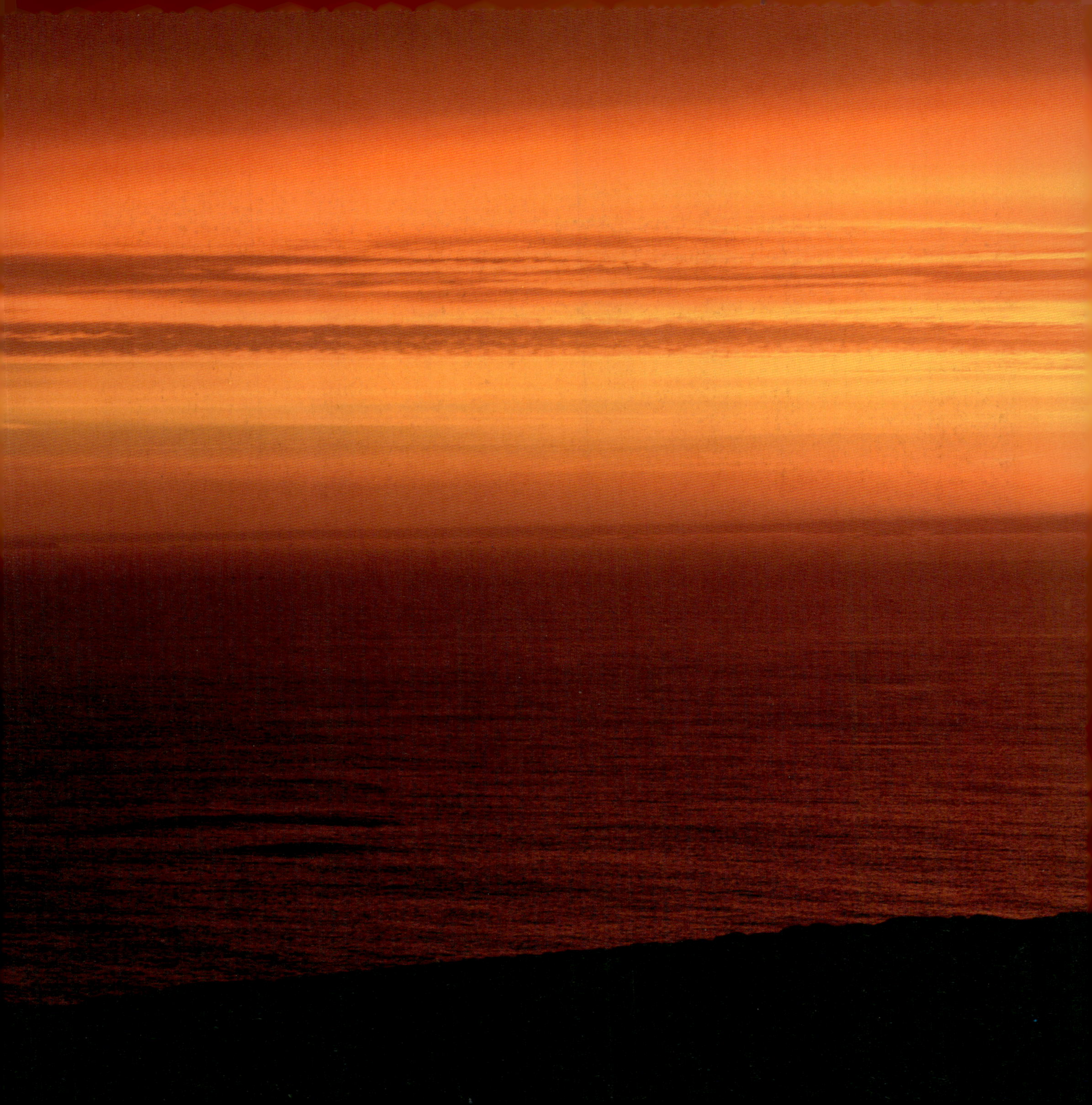

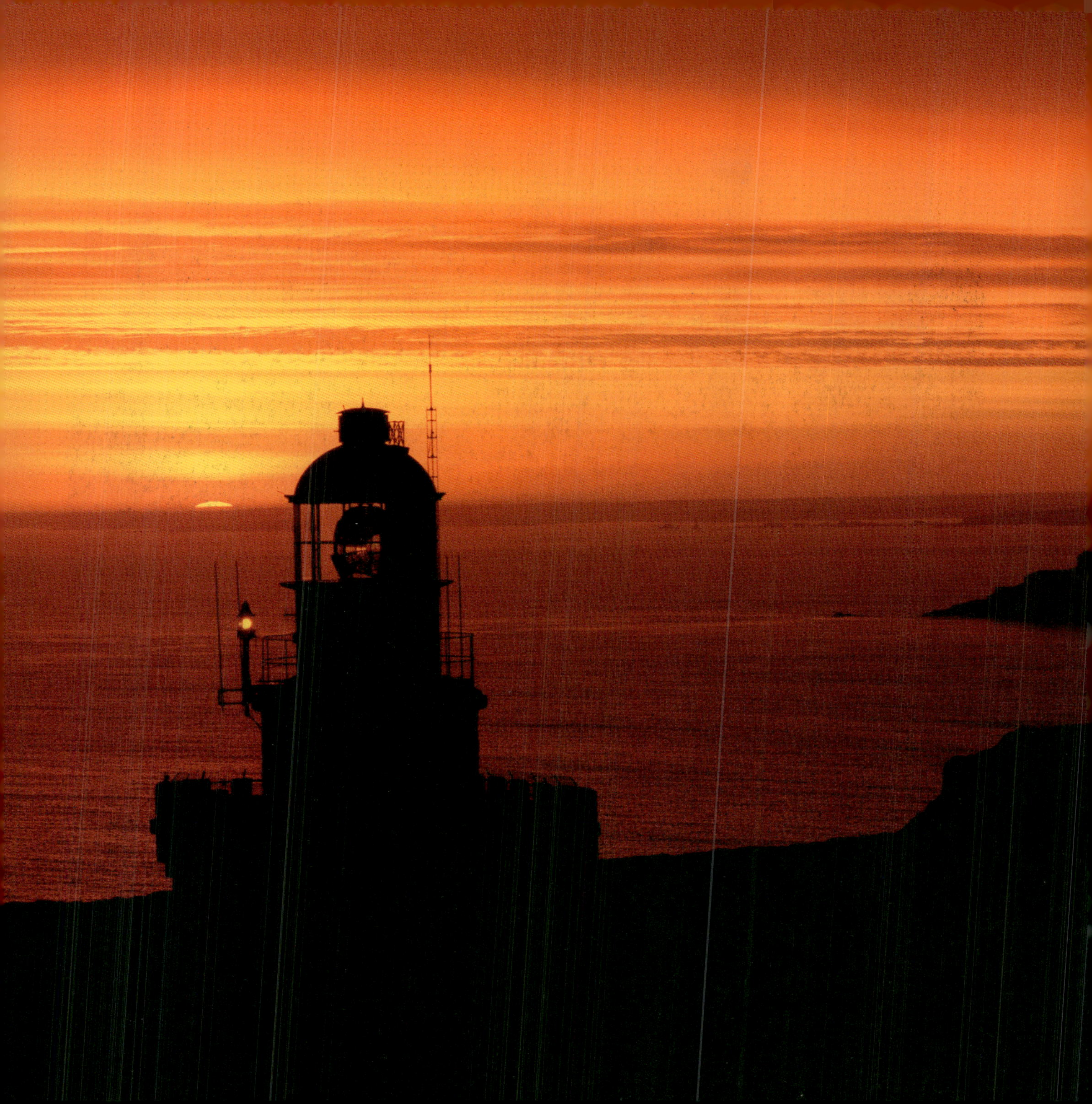

OCTOBER 14

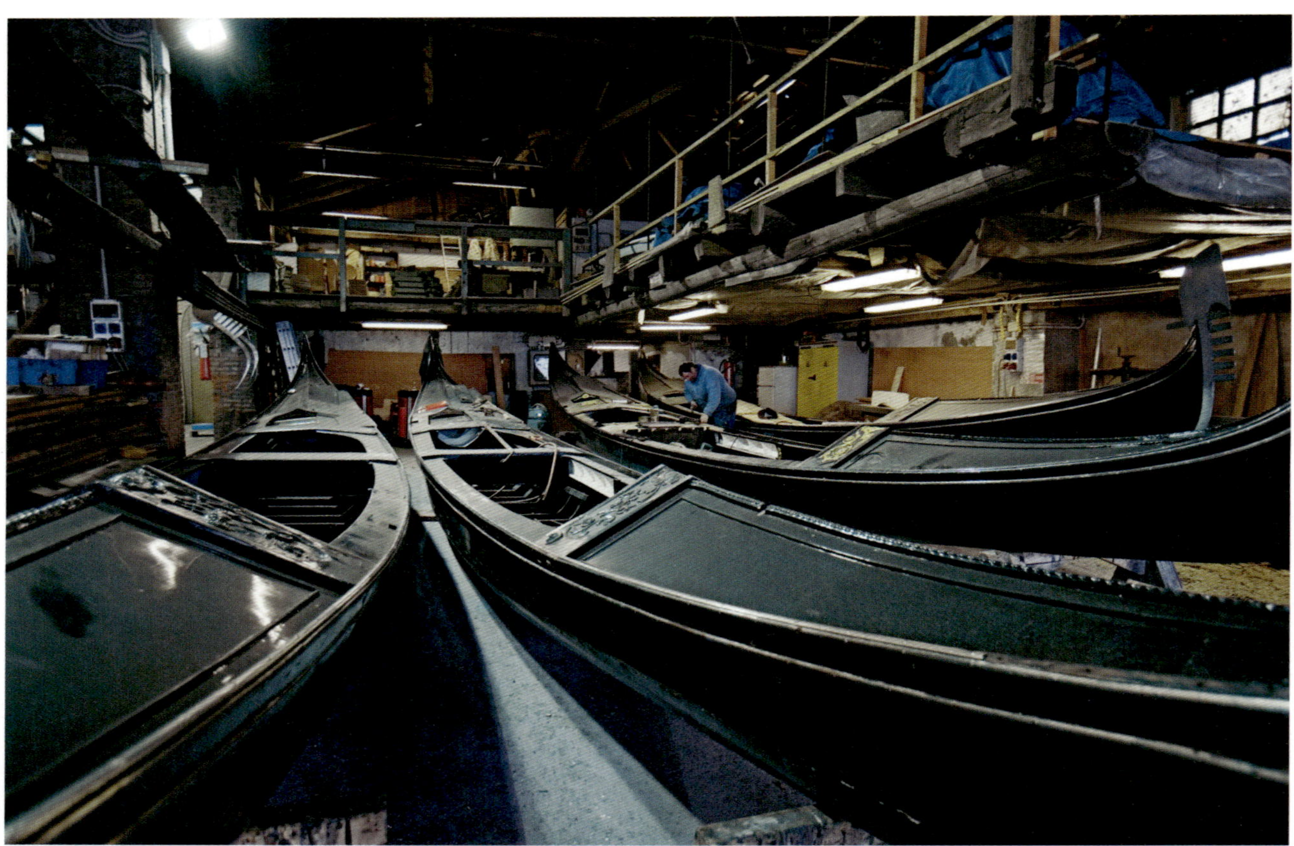

The humblest craft that floats makes its appeal
to a seaman by the faithfulness of her life.

Joseph Conrad, from *The Mirror of the Sea,* 1906

OCTOBER 15

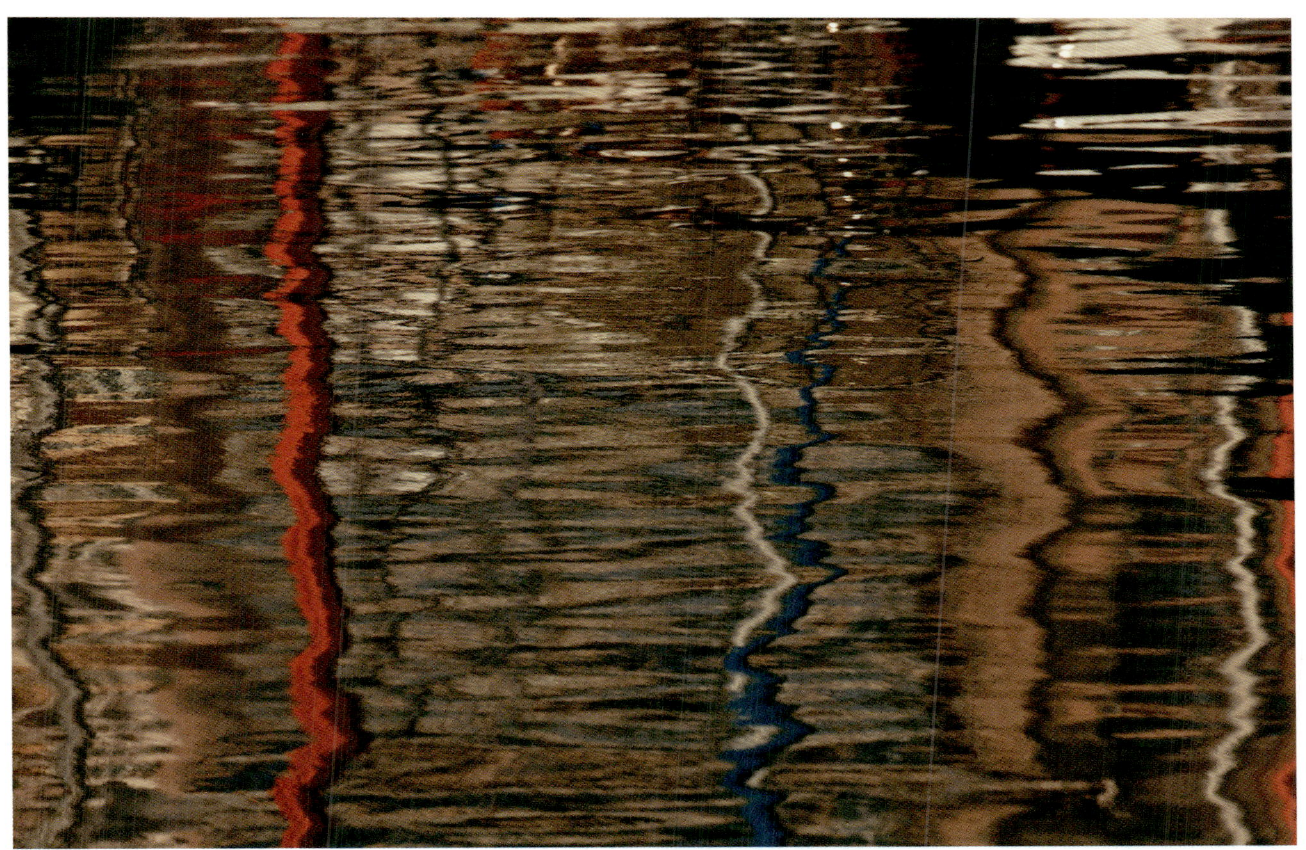

Learning is like rowing upstream; not to advance is to drop back.

Chinese proverb

OCTOBER 16

Ideals are like stars: you will not succeed
in touching them with your hands,
but like the seafaring man on the ocean
desert of waters, you choose them as
your guides, and following them,
you reach your destiny.

Carl Schurz

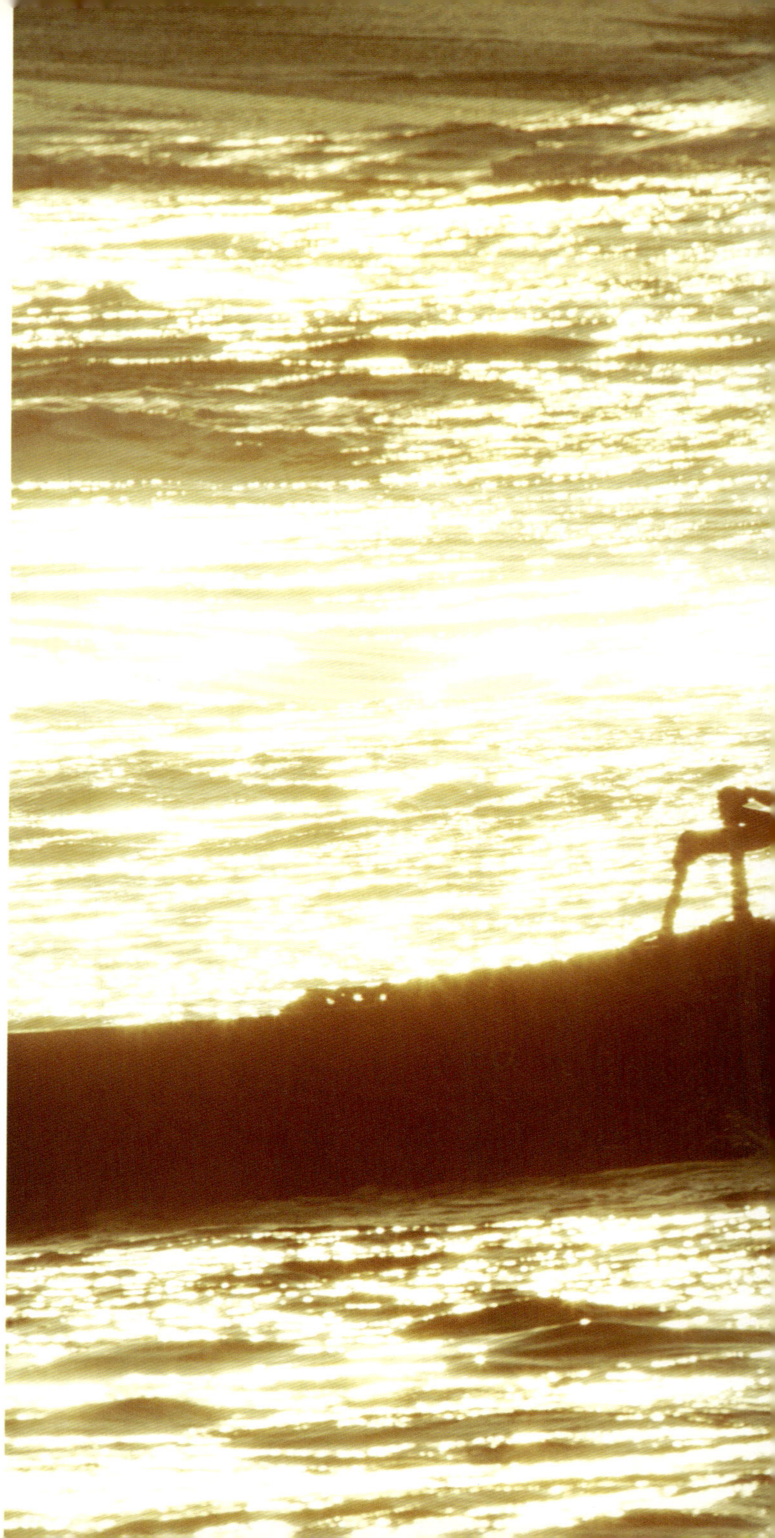

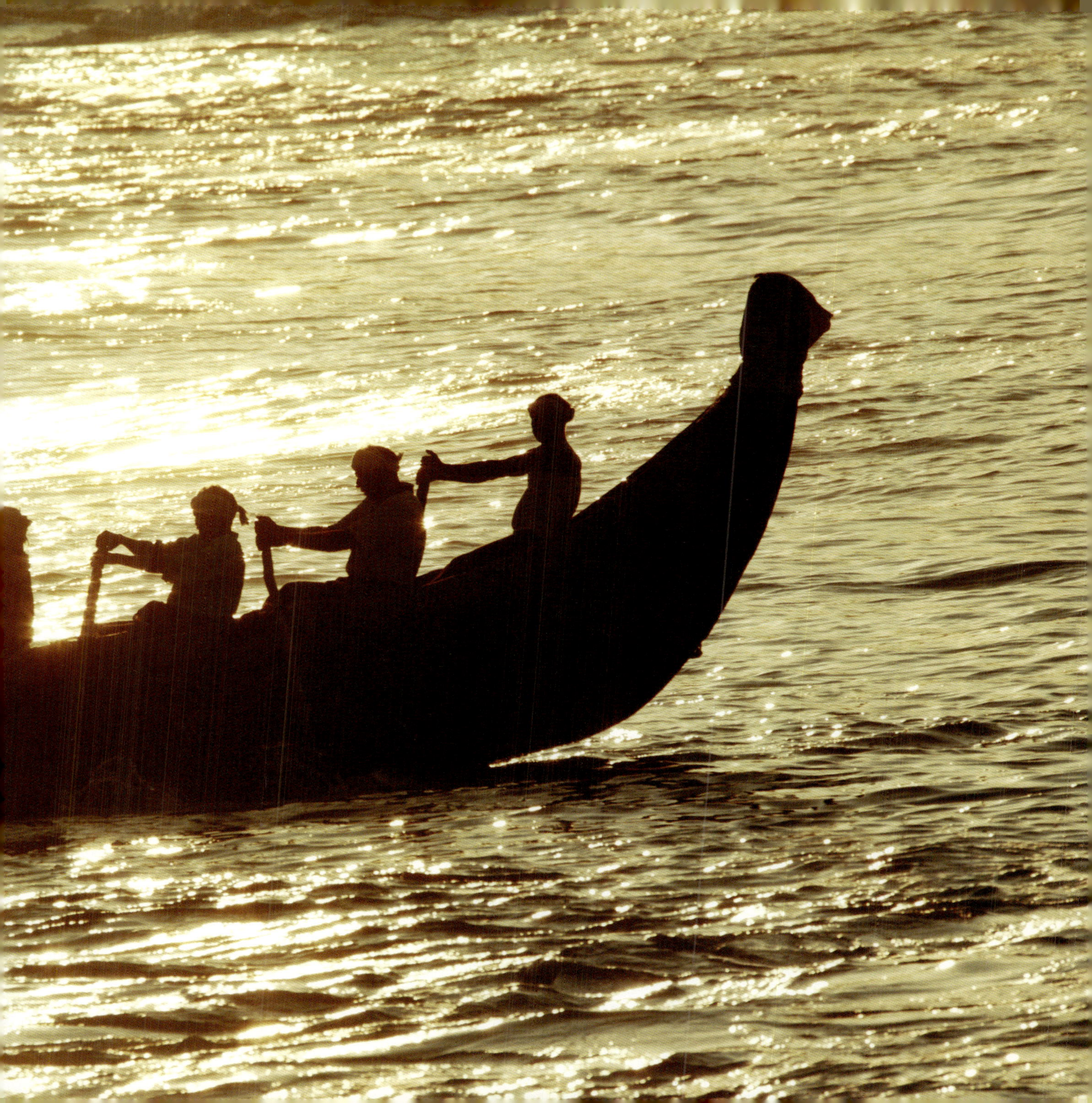

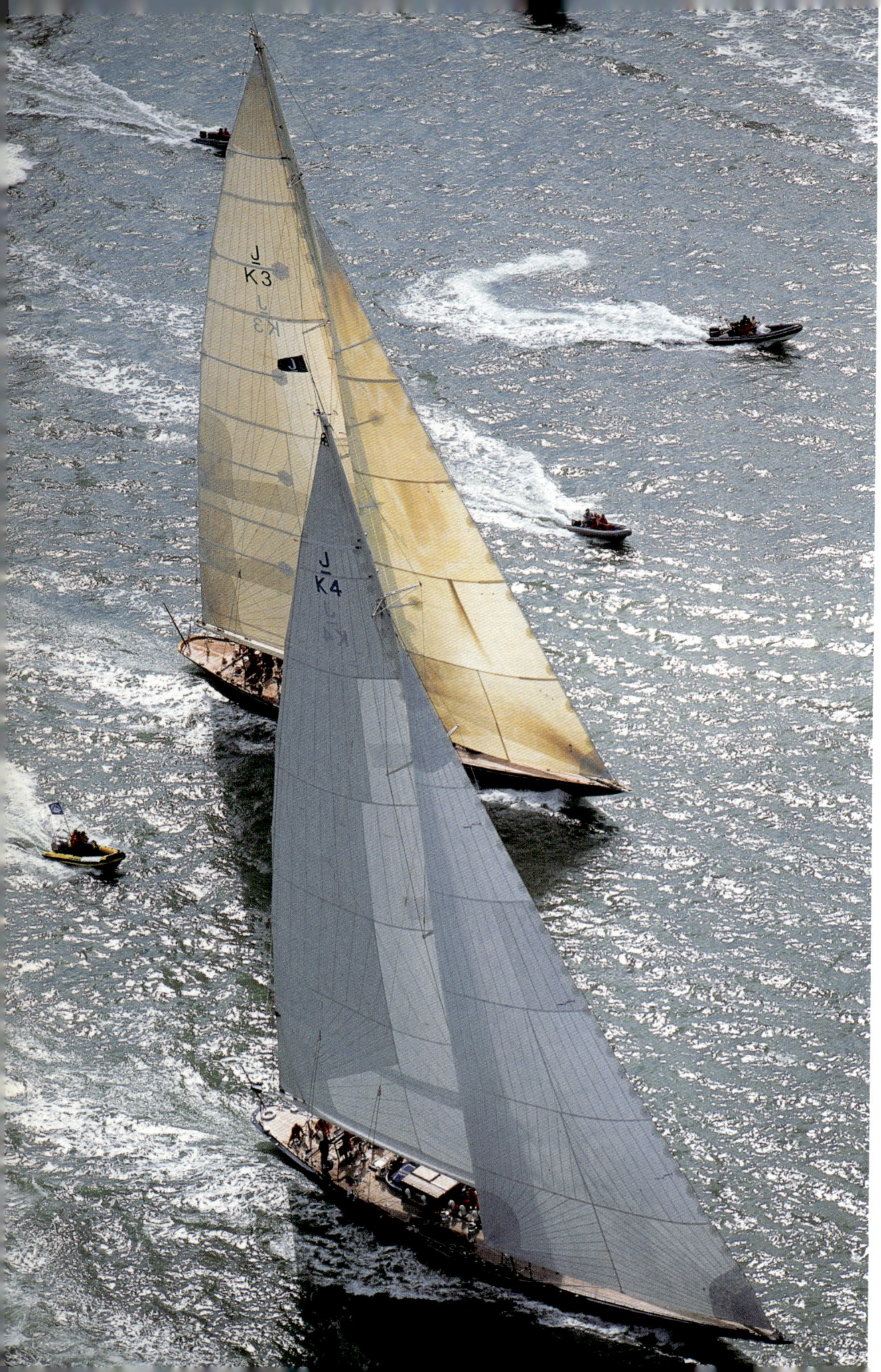

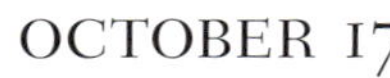

OCTOBER 17

The ships are crack sailing craft
and their skippers the most
experienced there are; they drive
the vessels like racehorses on
an unswerving course that goes
straight as a die.

Caligula

OCTOBER 18

Exultation is the going
Of an inland soul to sea.

Emily Dickinson,
from "Exultation is the going,"
Time and Eternity, 1890

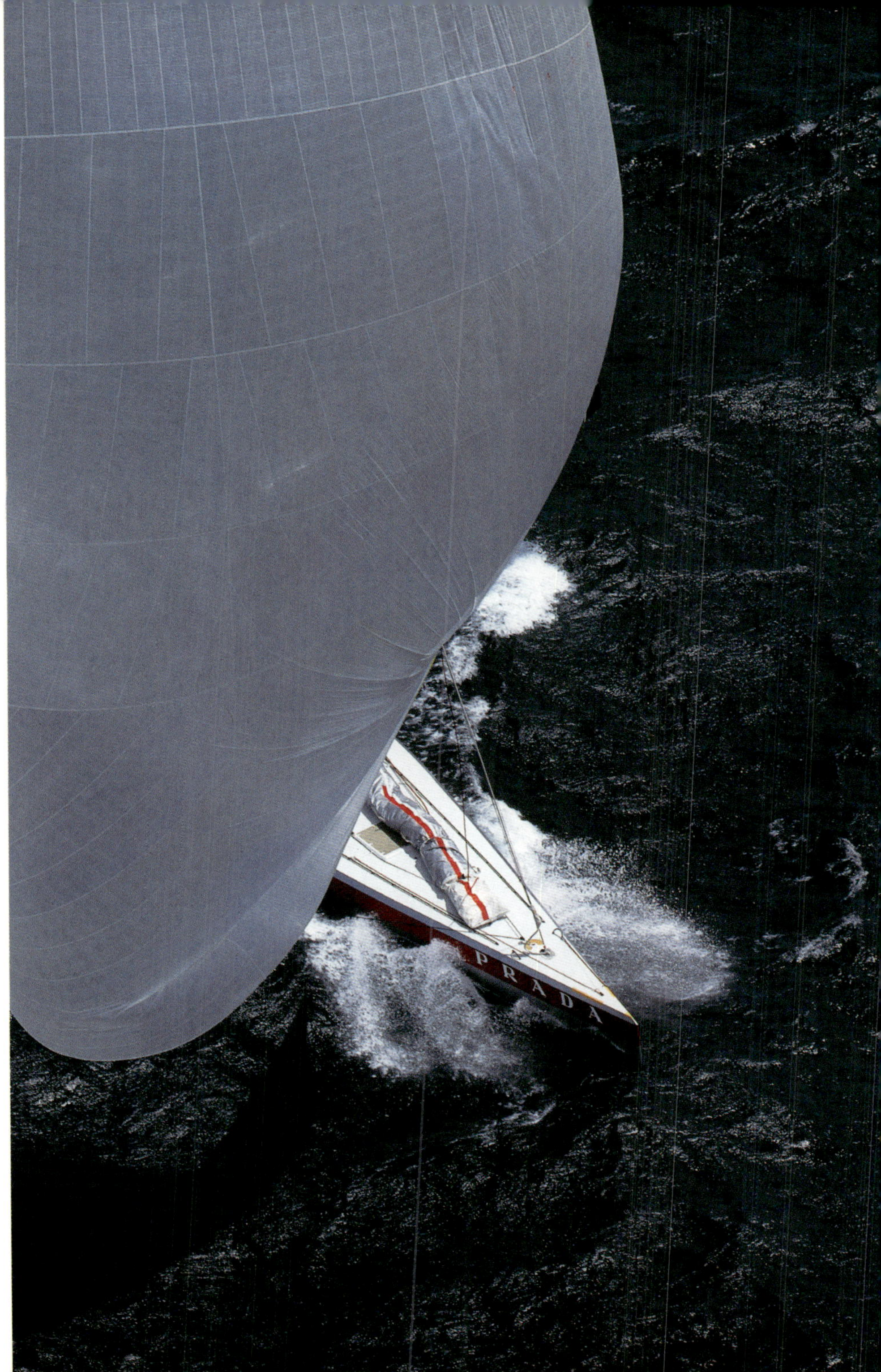

OCTOBER 19

I have seen tempests, when the scolding winds
Have riv'd the knotty oaks; and I have seen
The ambitious ocean swell and rage and foam,
To be exalted with the threat'ning clouds:
But never till to-night, never till now,
Did I go through a tempest dropping fire.
Either there is a civil strife in heaven,
Or else the world, too saucy with the gods,
Incenses them to send destruction.

William Shakespeare, *Julius Caesar,* Act I, Scene 3

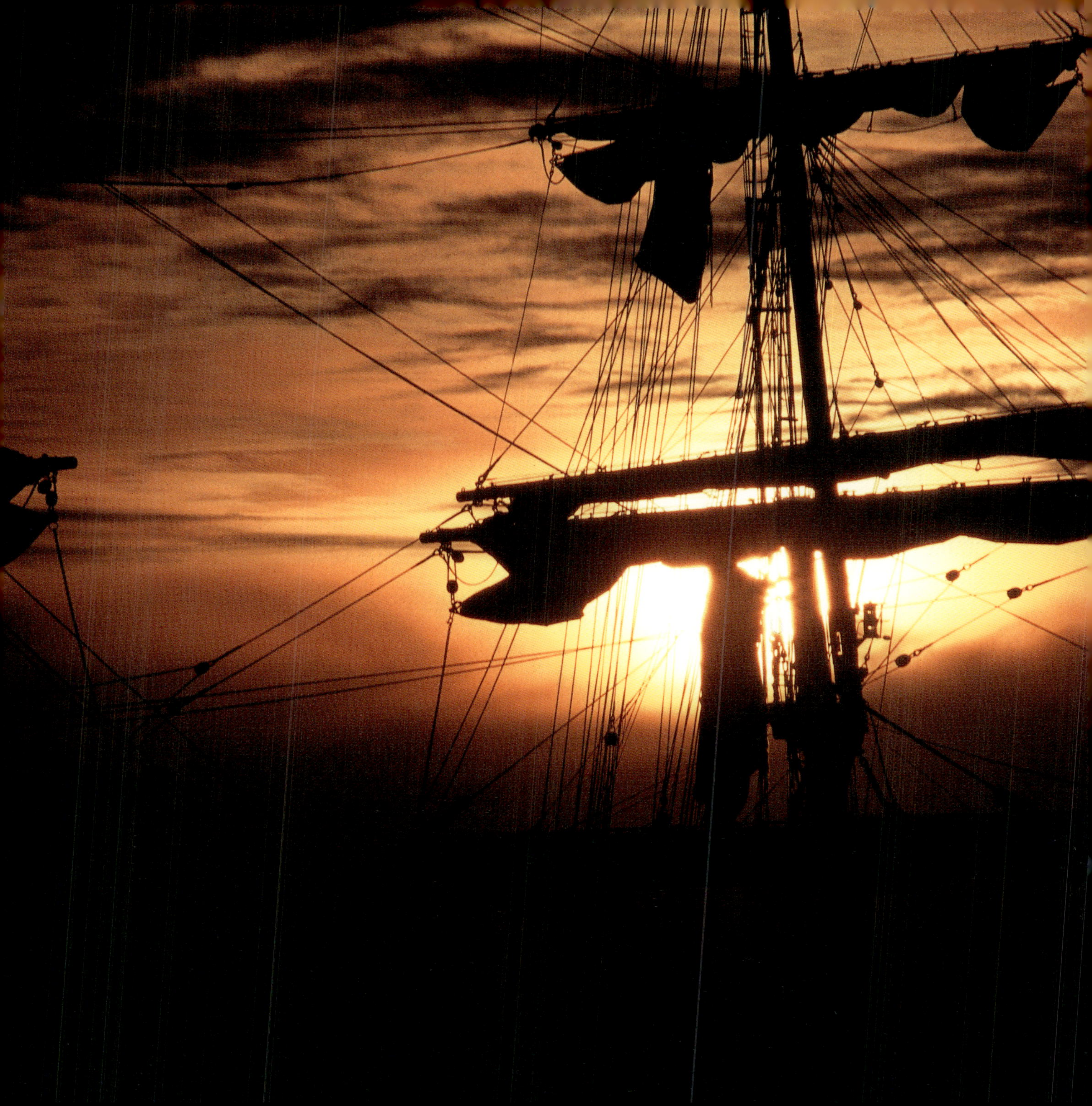

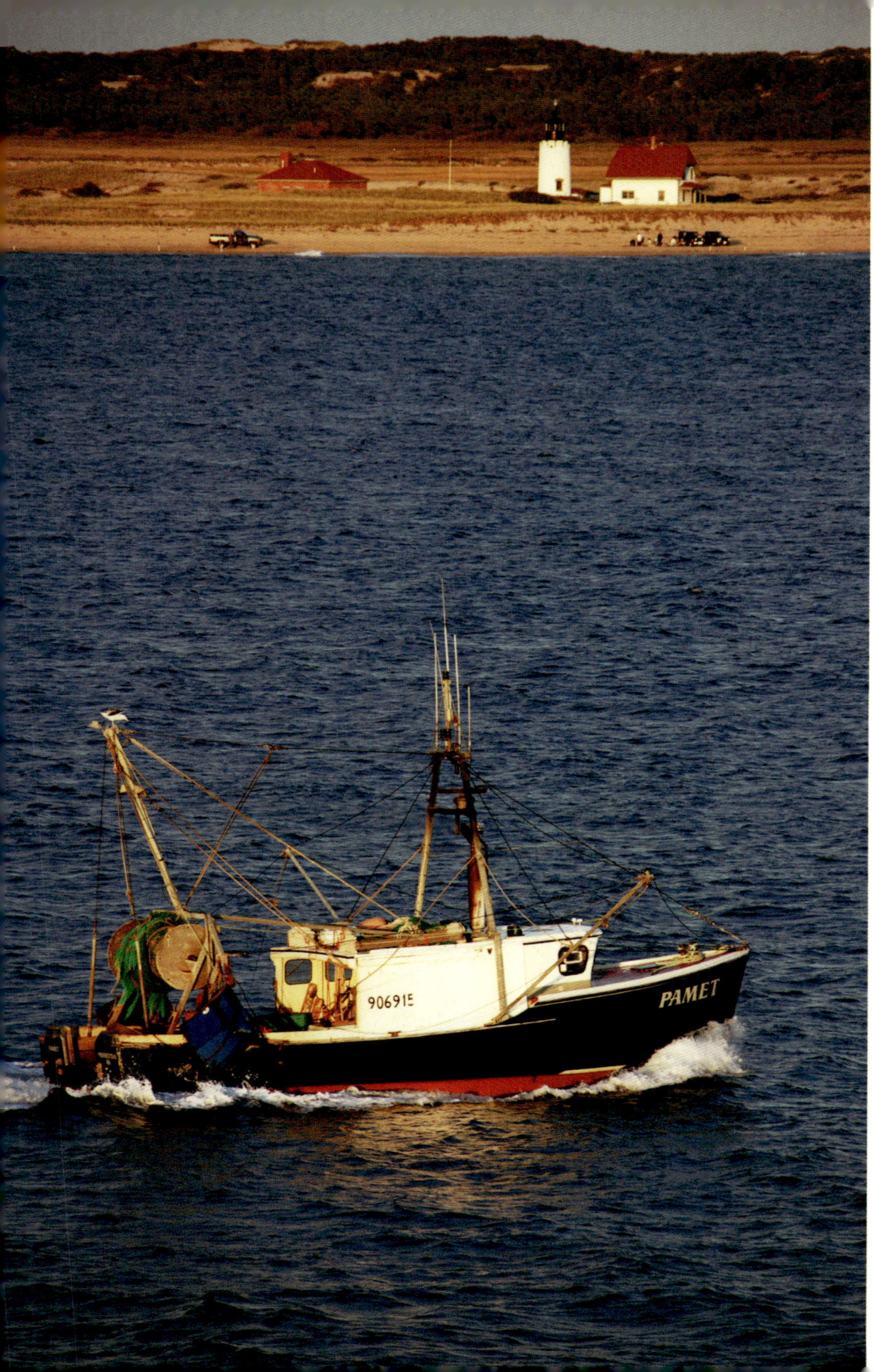

OCTOBER 20

May the holes in your net be
no larger than the fish in it.

Irish proverb

OCTOBER 21

They attack the one man with their hate and their shower of weapons. But he is like some rock which stretches into the vast sea and which, exposed to the fury of the winds and beaten against by the waves, endures all the violence.

Virgil, from *The Aeneid*

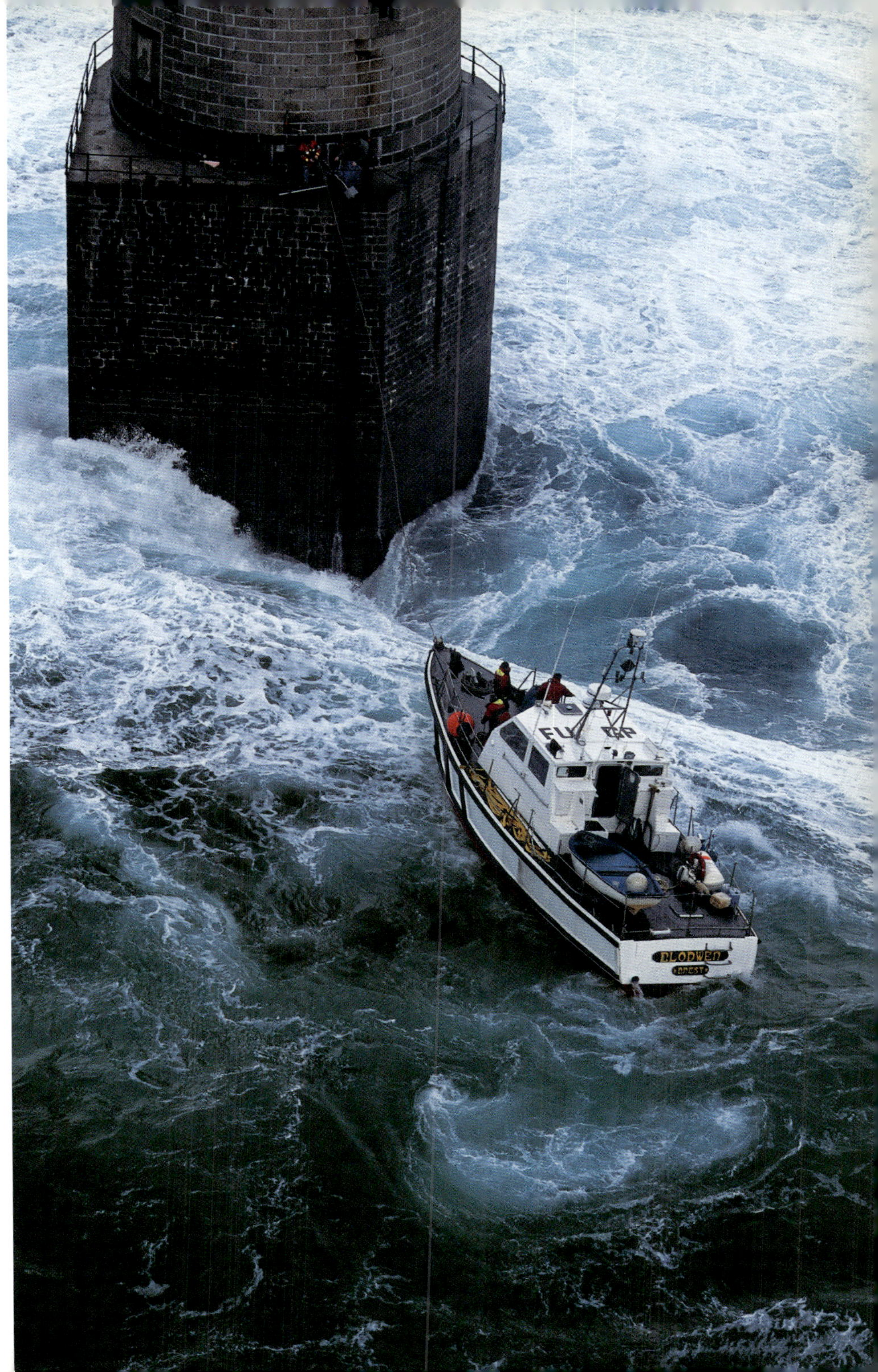

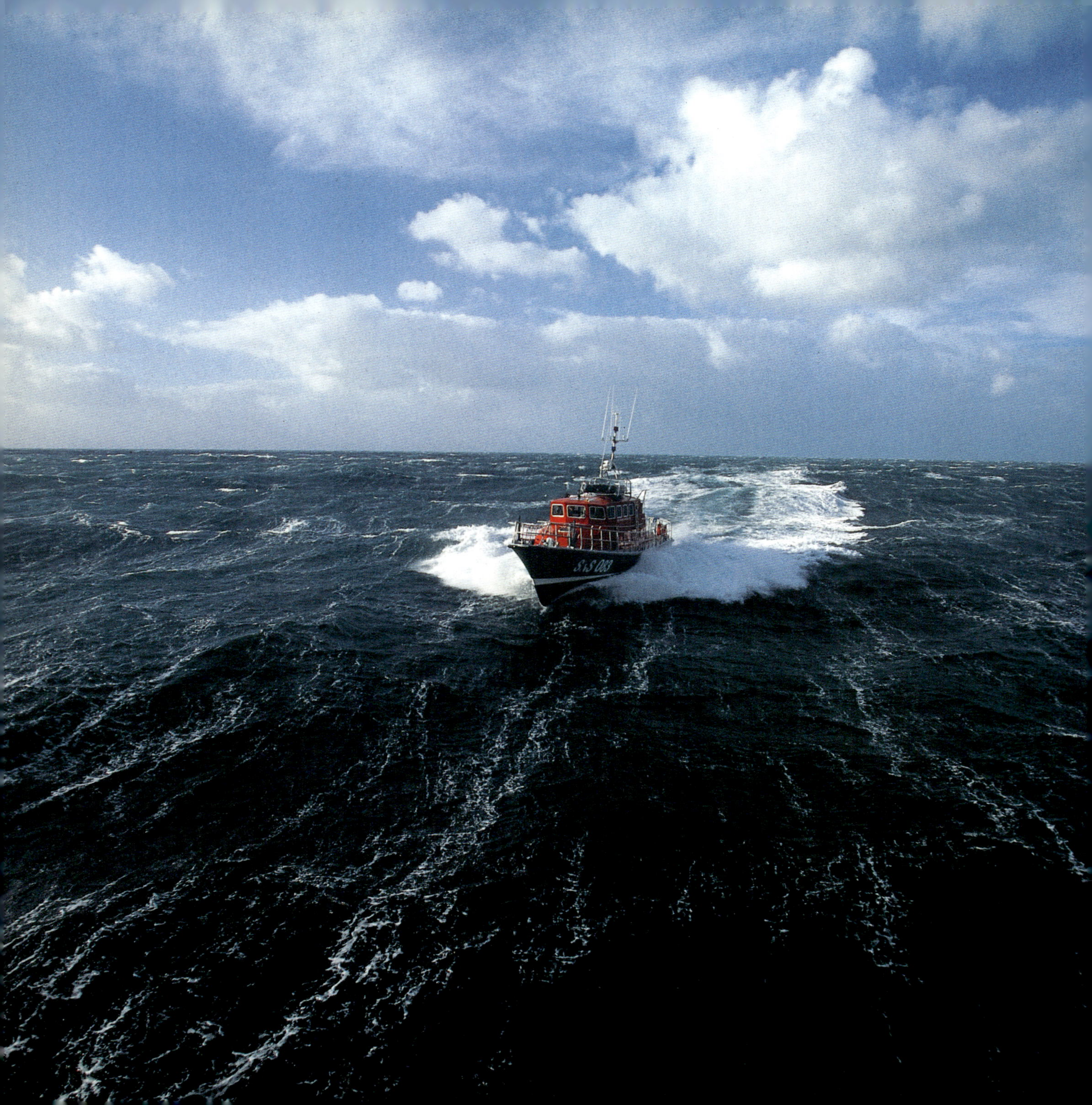

OCTOBER 22

The occasion that moved me to take such a voyage in hand,
was only a curiosity of mind, a desire of novelties,
and a longing to learn out the bounds of the Ocean.

Lucian of Samothrace

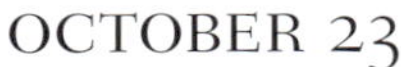

OCTOBER 23

O Lord, have mercy,
Thy sea is so large
And my ship is so small.

Breton fisherman's prayer

OCTOBER 24

When the sandpiper and the clam grapple, it is the fisherman that profits.

Chinese proverb

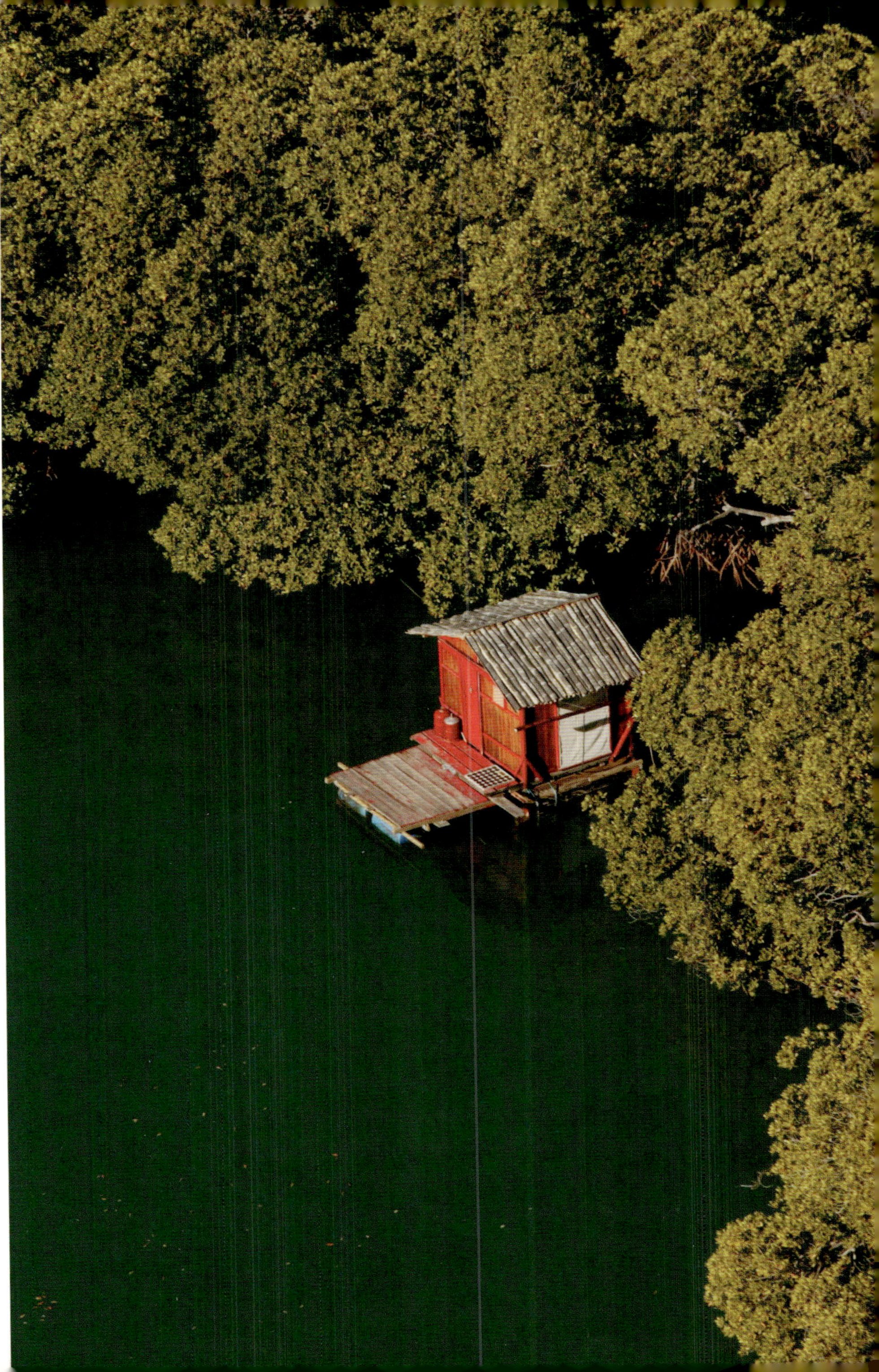

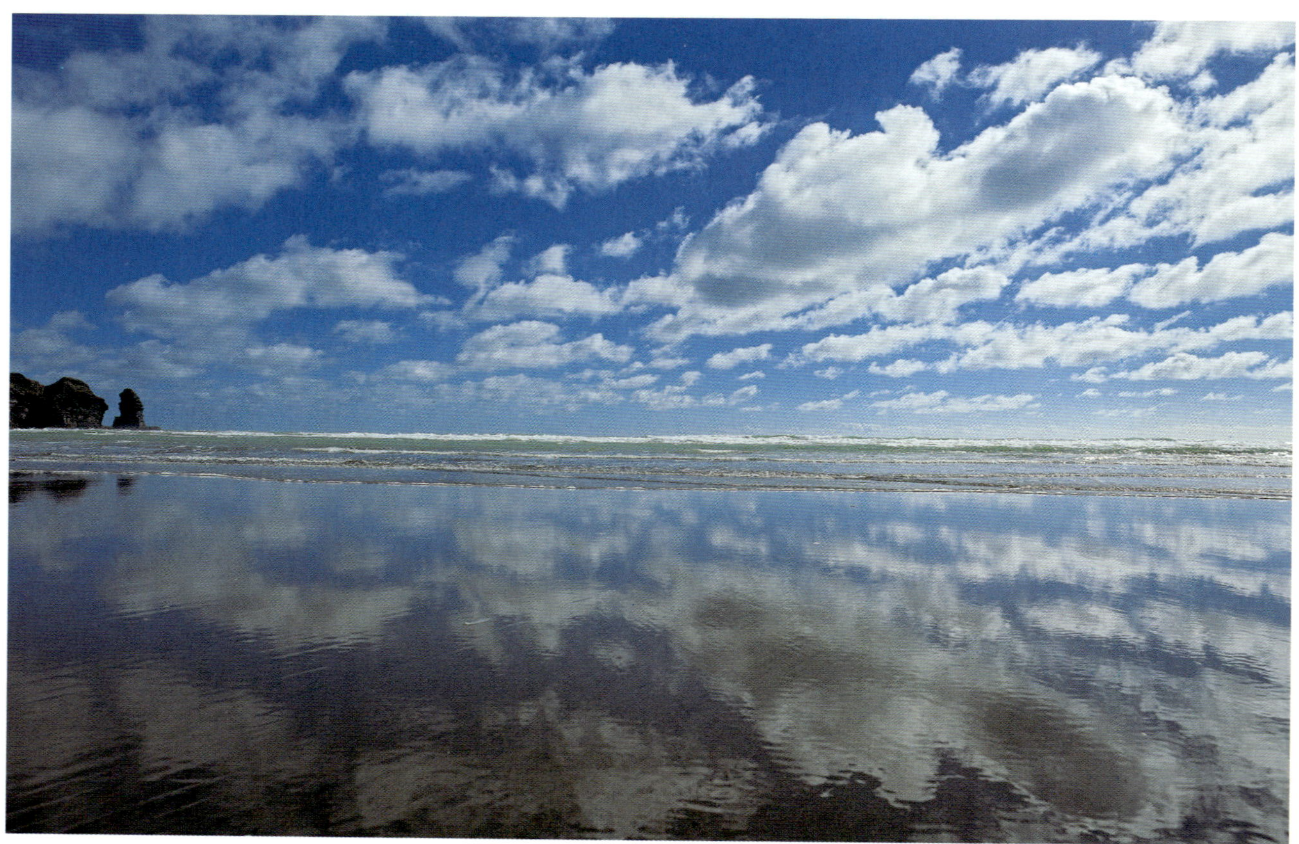

The wonders of the sea are as marvelous as the glories of the heavens; and they proclaim, in songs divine, that they too are the work of holy fingers.

Matthew Fontaine Maury, from *The Physical Geography of the Sea,* 1855

OCTOBER 26

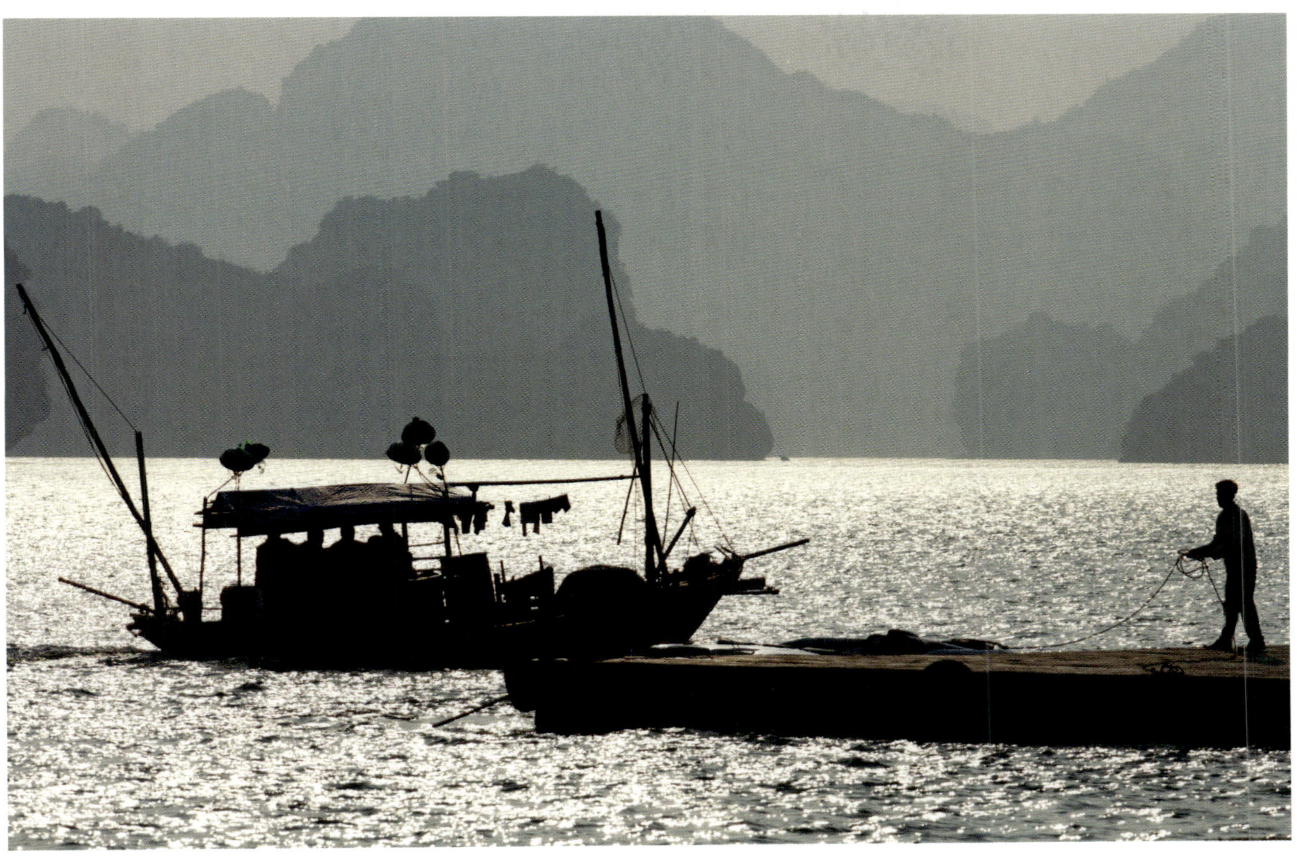

The ocean is an object of no small terror.

Edmund Burke, from "On the Sublime and Beautiful," 1757

OCTOBER 27

There's a magic in the distance,
where the sea-line meets the sky.

Alfred Noyes,
from "Forty Singing Seamen," 1930

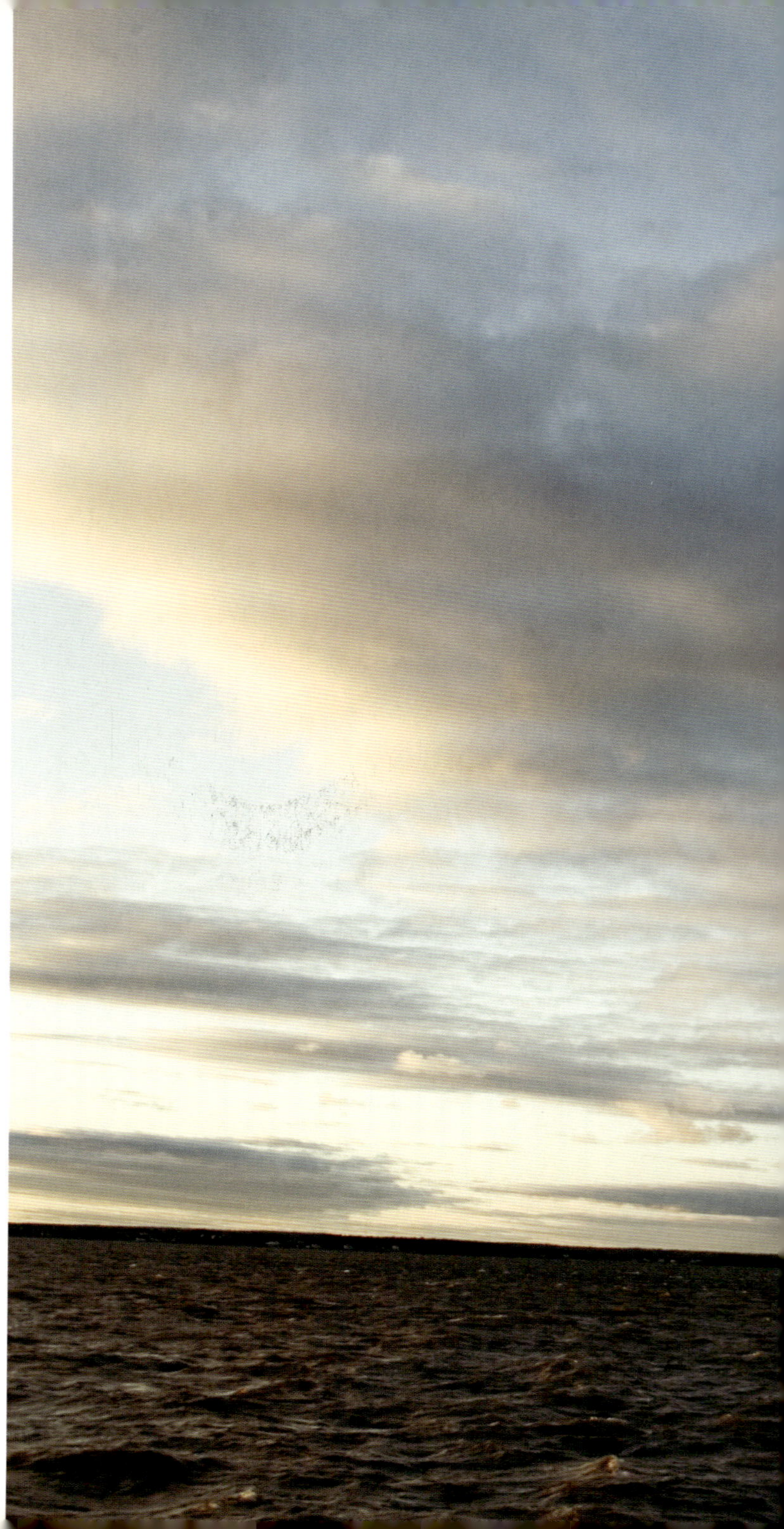

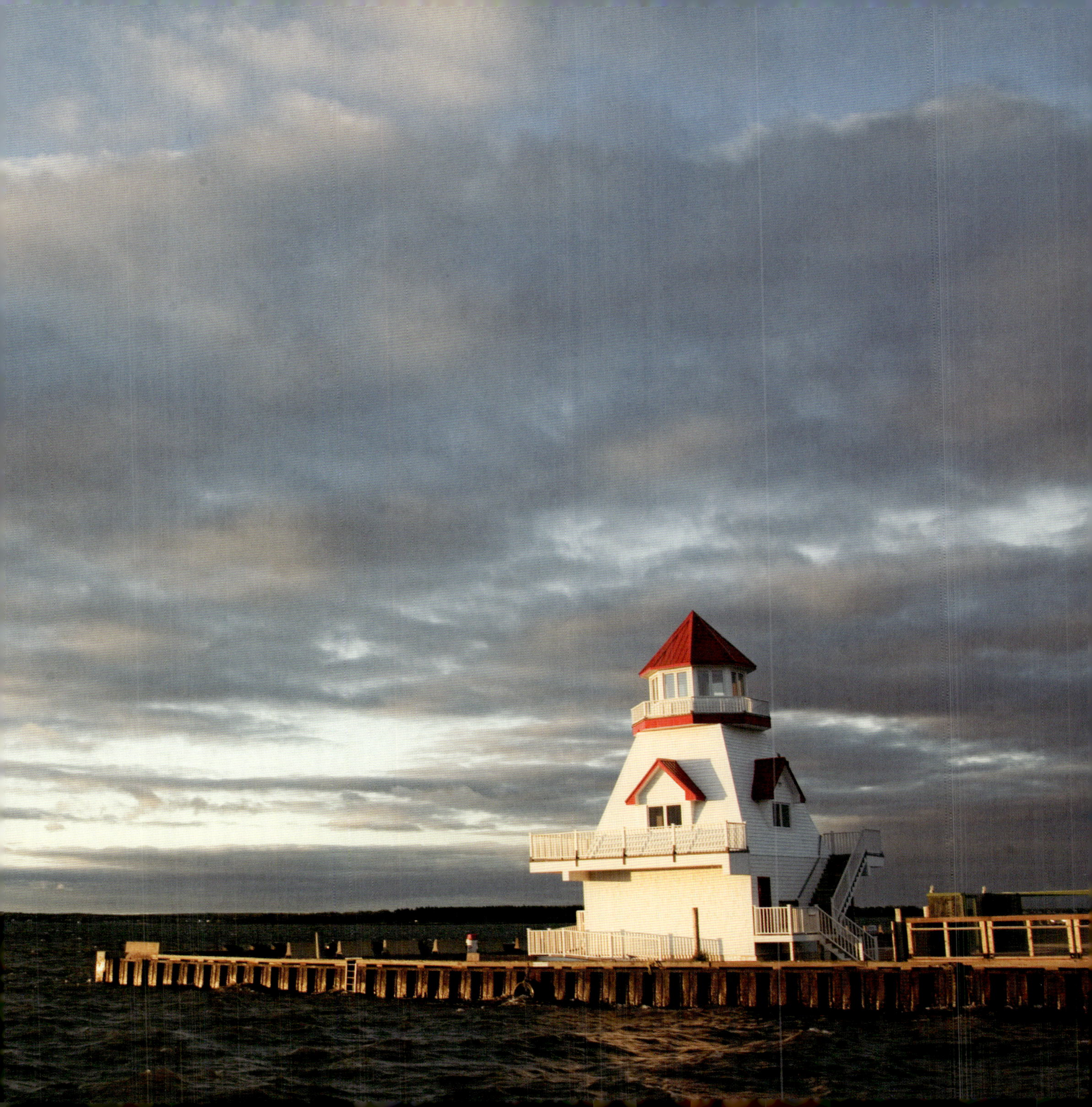

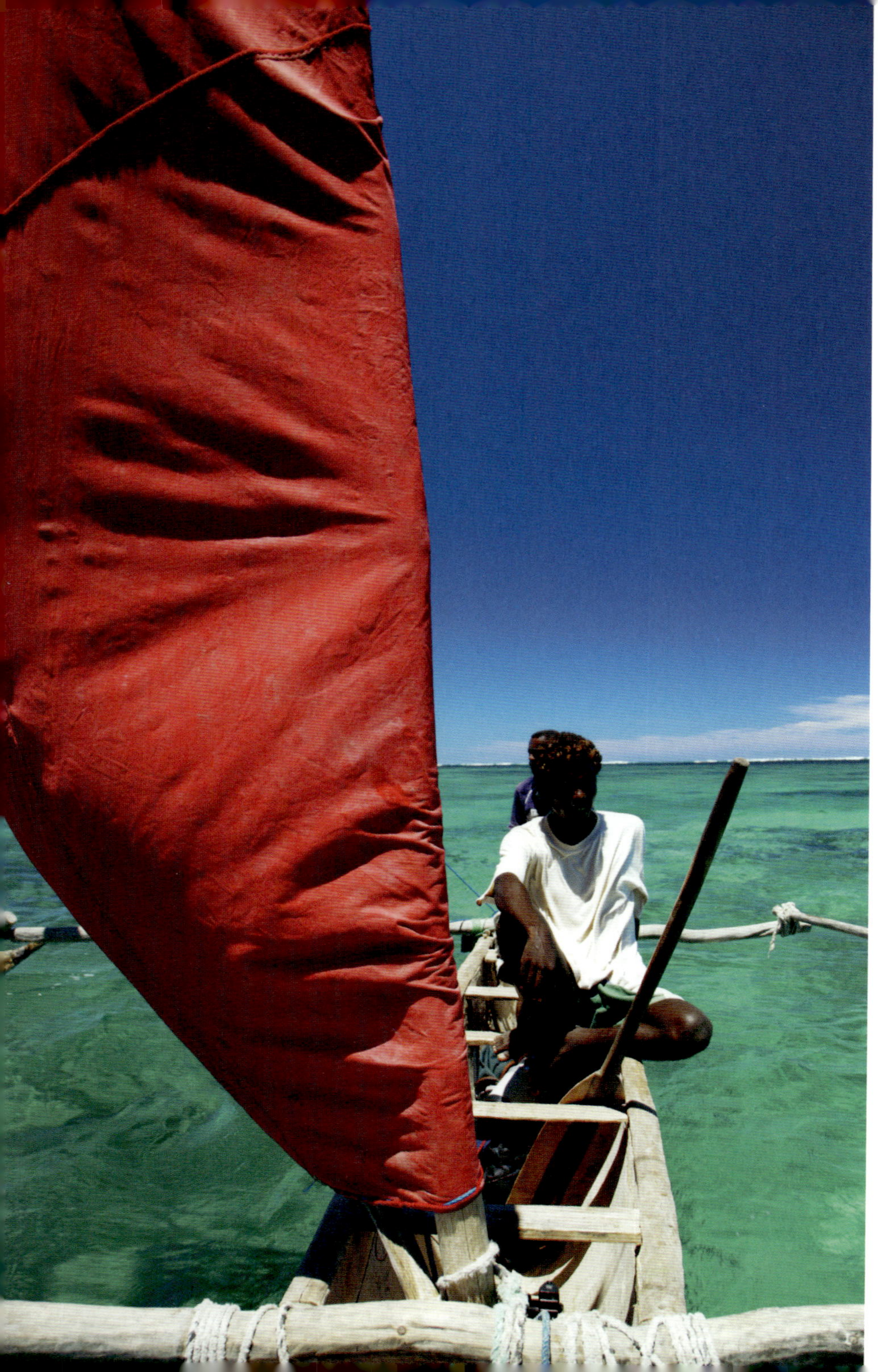

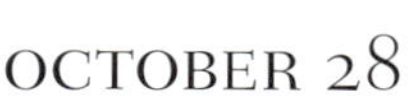

OCTOBER 28

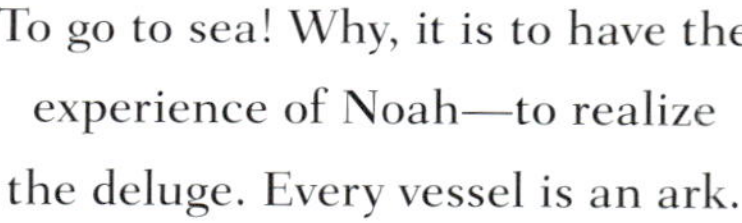

To go to sea! Why, it is to have the experience of Noah—to realize the deluge. Every vessel is an ark.

Henry David Thoreau,
from *Cape Cod,* 1865

OCTOBER 29

Up anchor! Up anchor!
Set sail and away!
The ventures of dreamland
Are thine for a day

Silas Weir Mitchell,
from "Dream-land," 1891

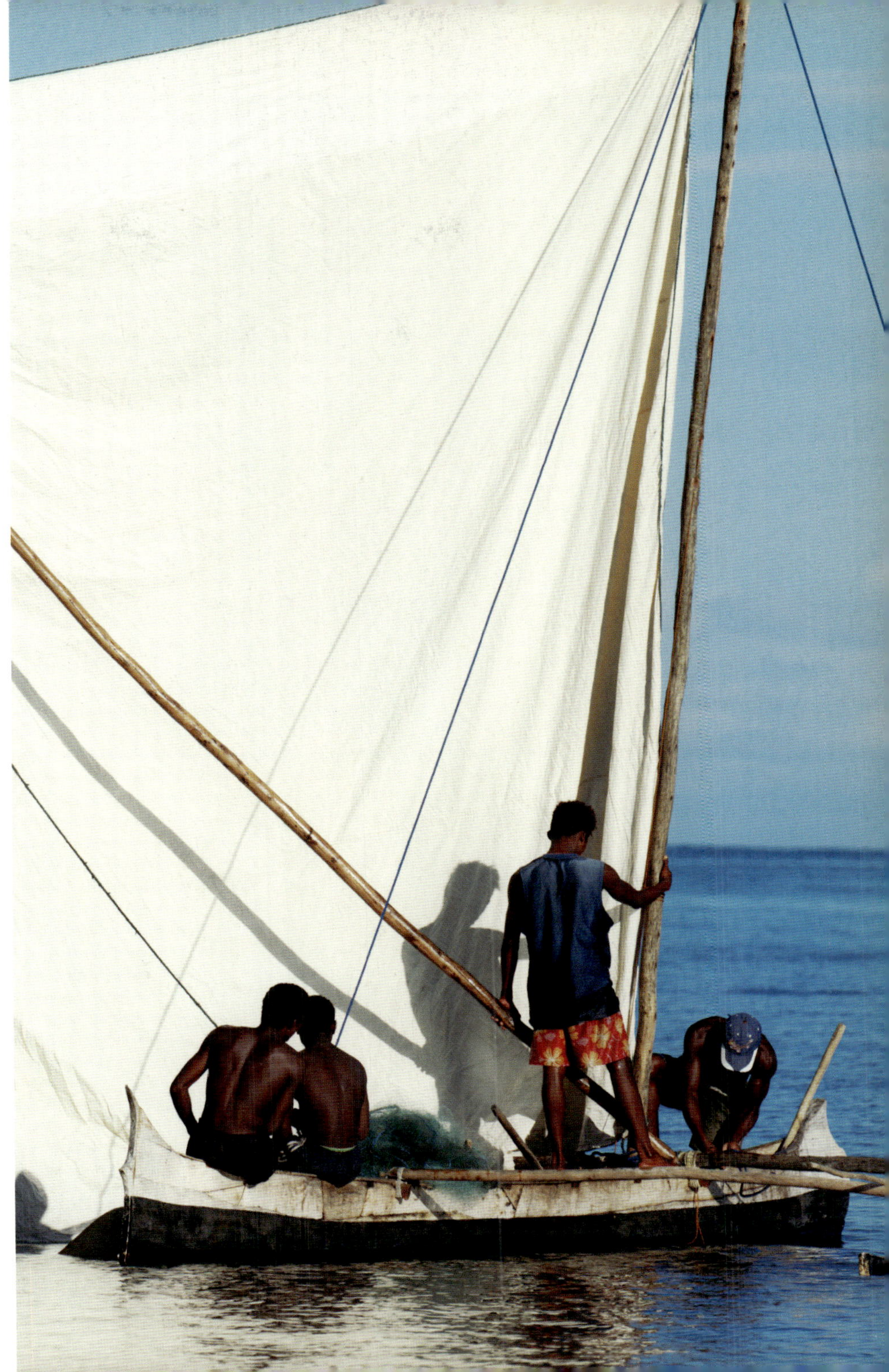

OCTOBER 30

Fish die belly upward, and rise to the surface.
It's their way of falling.

André Gide

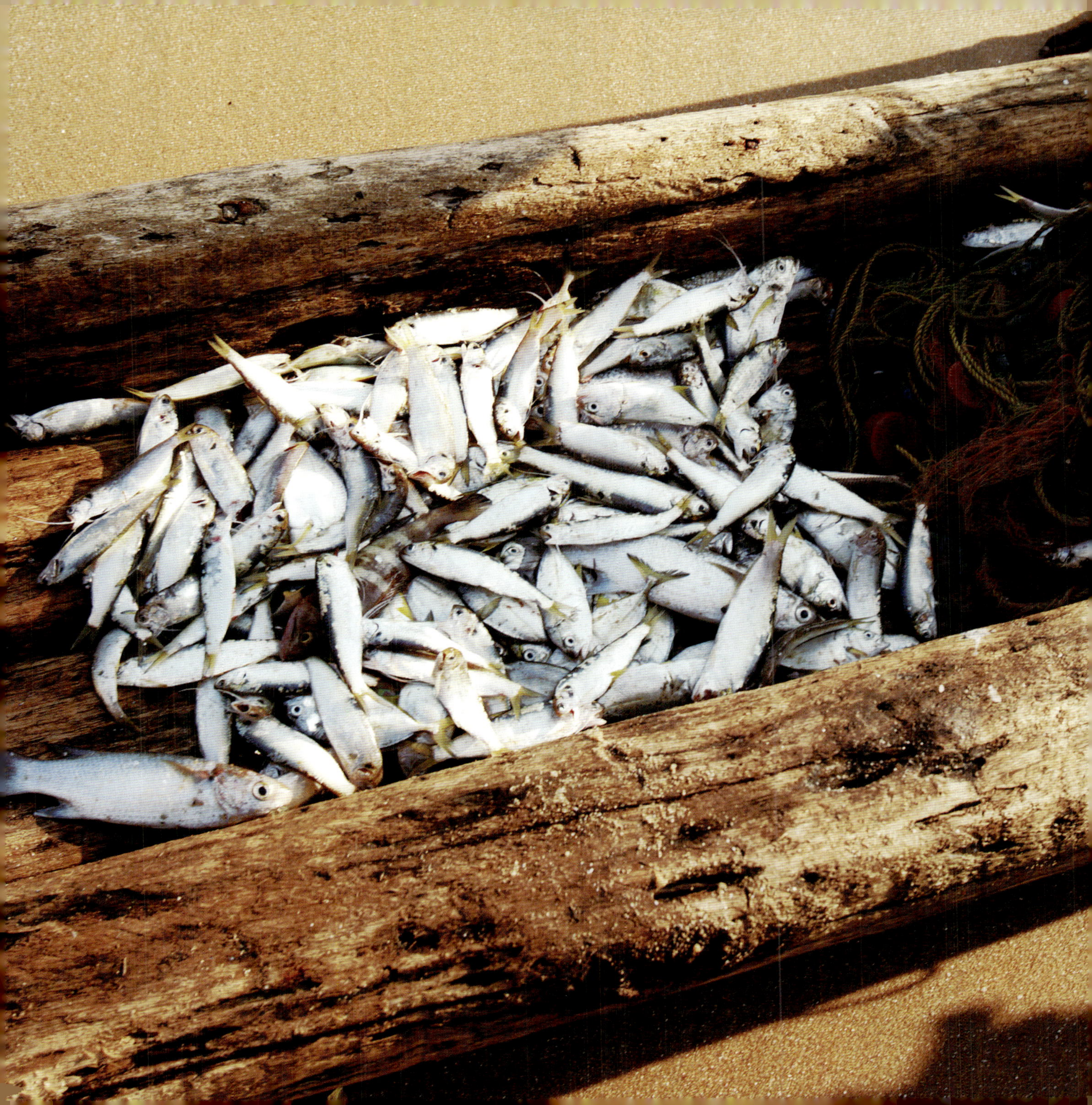

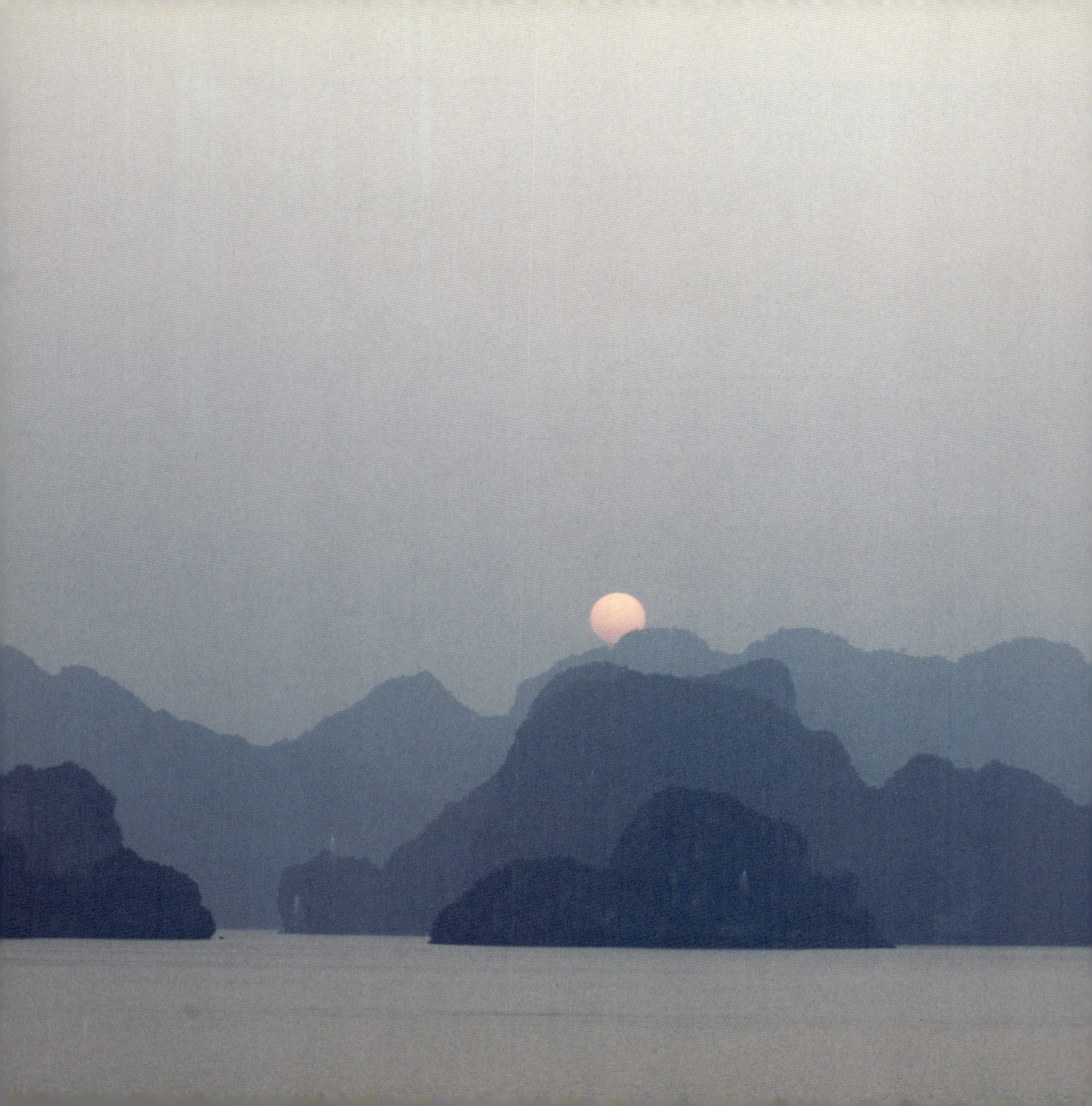

OCTOBER 31

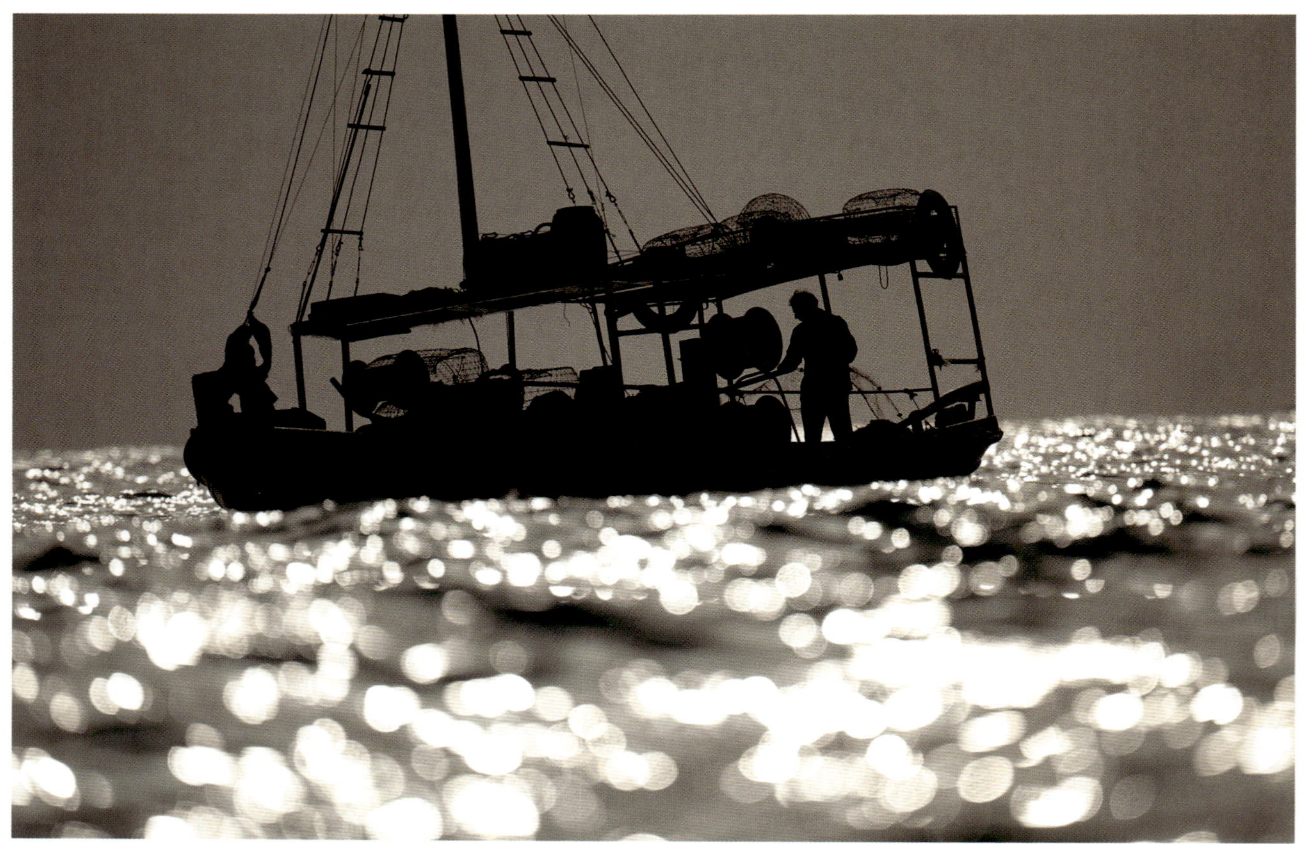

I will go back to the great sweet mother,
Mother and lover of men, the sea.

Algernon Chalres Swinburne, from "The Triumph of Time," 1866

NOVEMBER 1

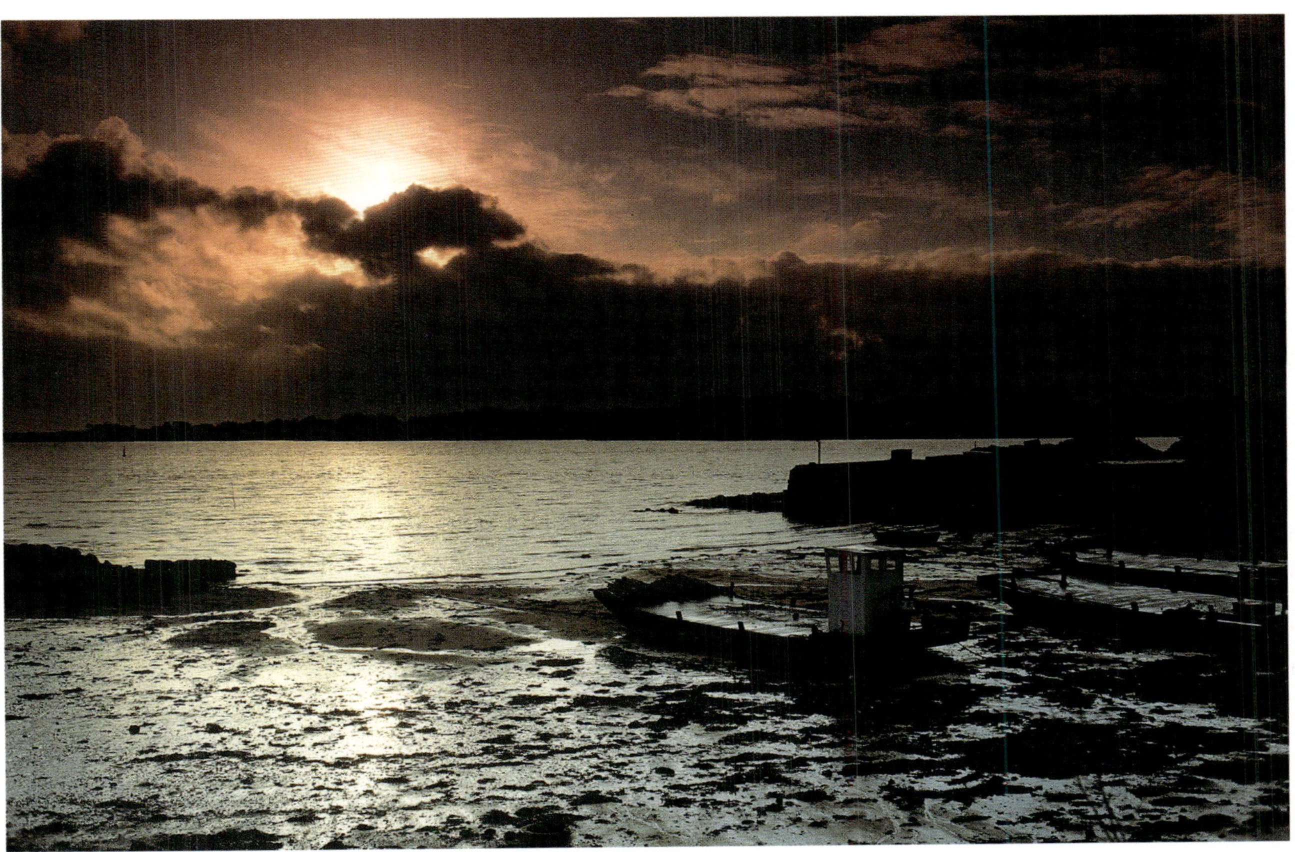

The sea never changes and its works, for all the talk of men, are wrapped in mystery.

Joseph Conrad, from *Falk*, 1903

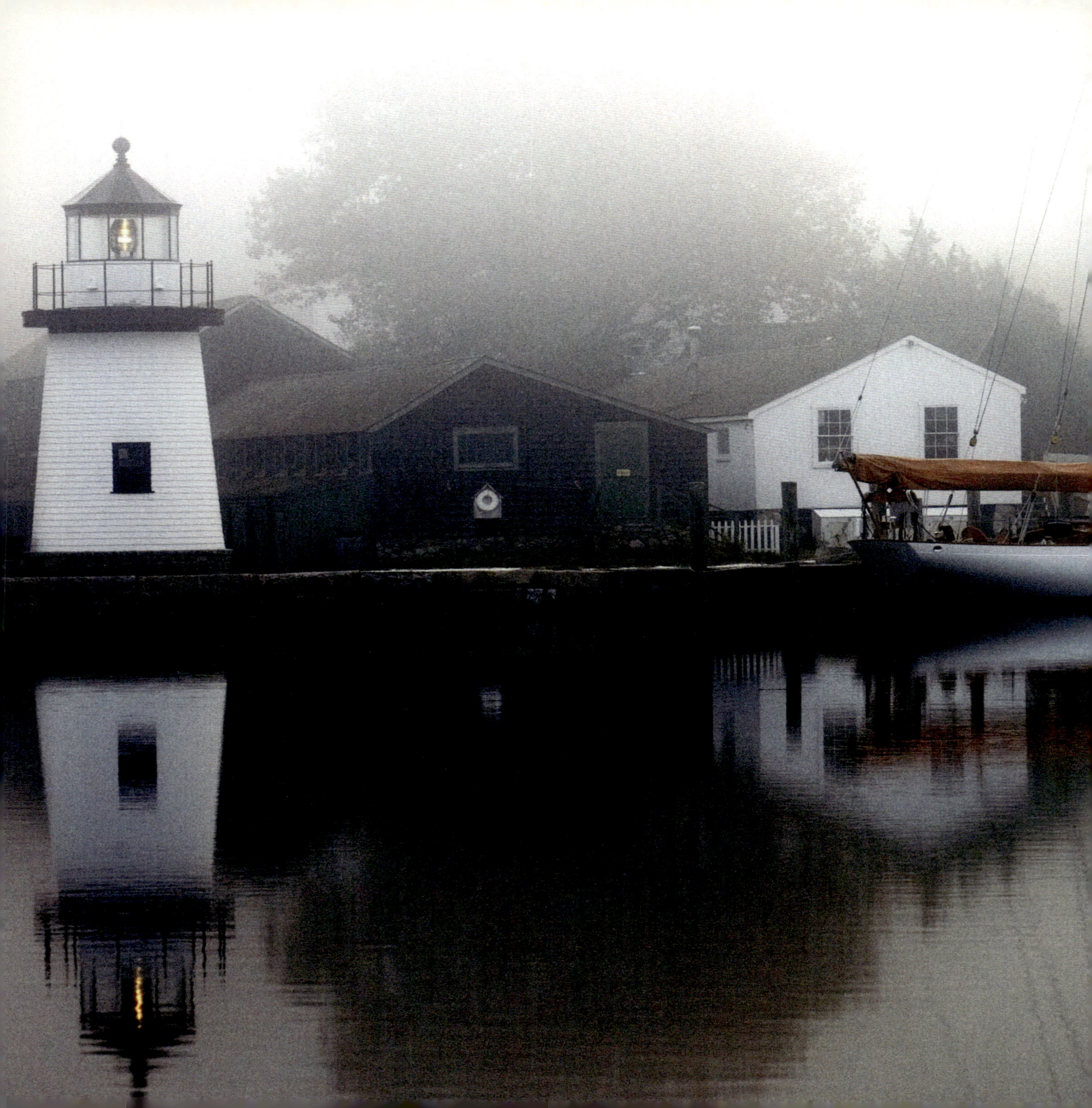

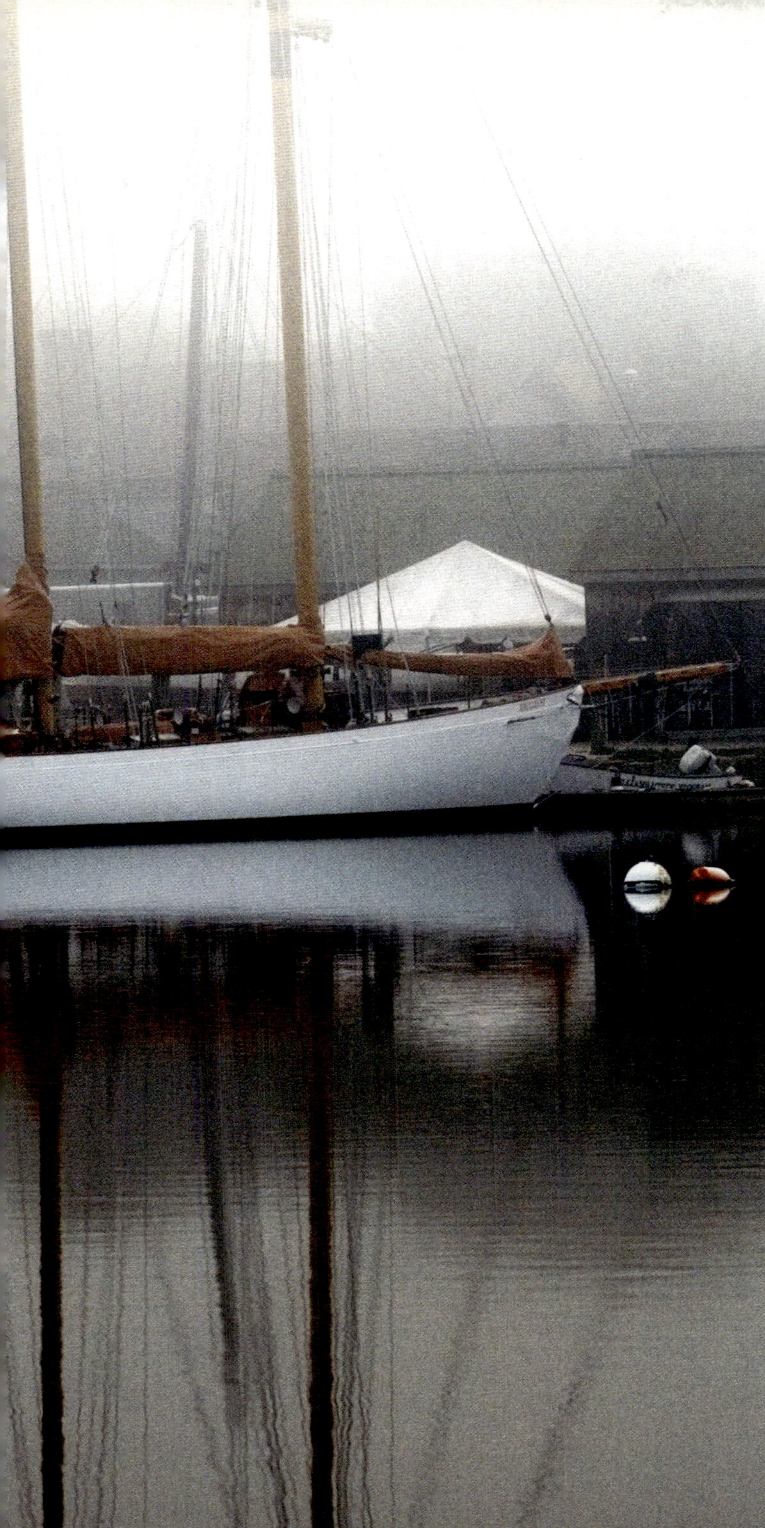

NOVEMBER 2

The whispering waves were half asleep,
The clouds were gone to play,
And on the bosom of the deep
The smile of Heaven lay.

Percy Bysshe Shelley,
from "To Jane: The Recollection," 1822

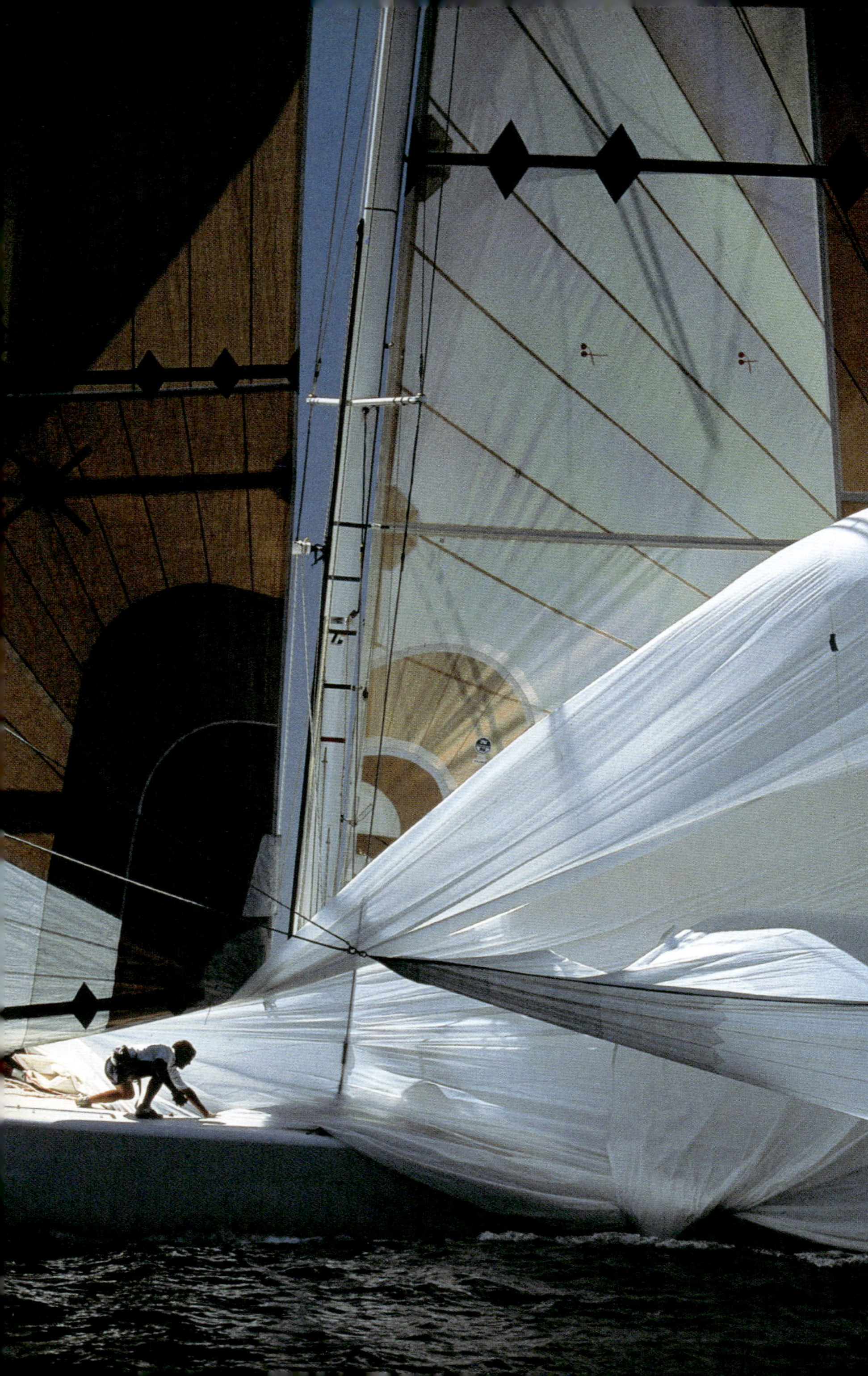

NOVEMBER 3

For one thing, I was no longer alone; a man is never alone with the wind—and the boat made three.

Hilaire Belloc, from *First and Last,* 1911

NOVEMBER 4

One foot cannot stand
on two boats.

Chinese proverb

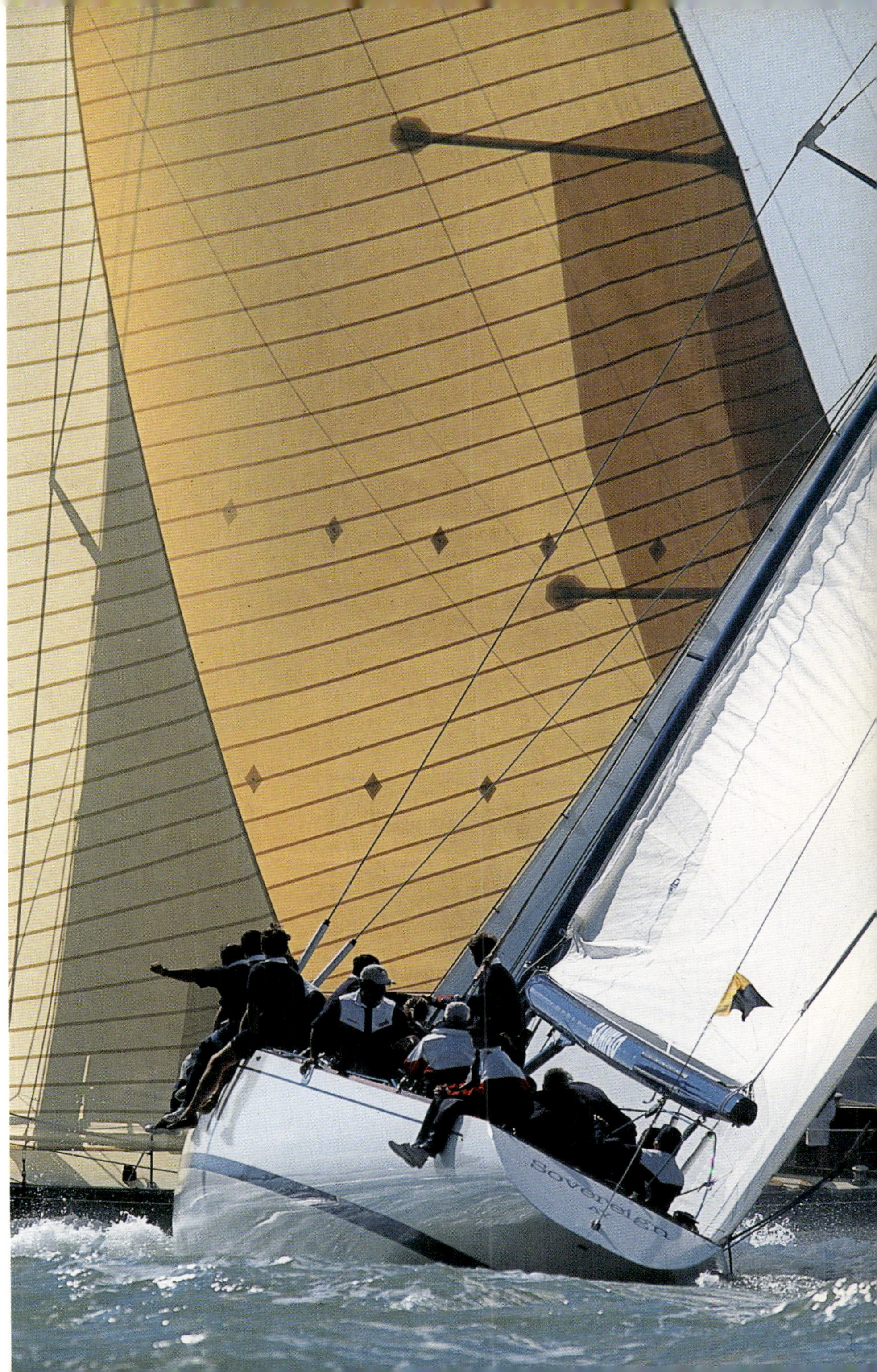

NOVEMBER 5

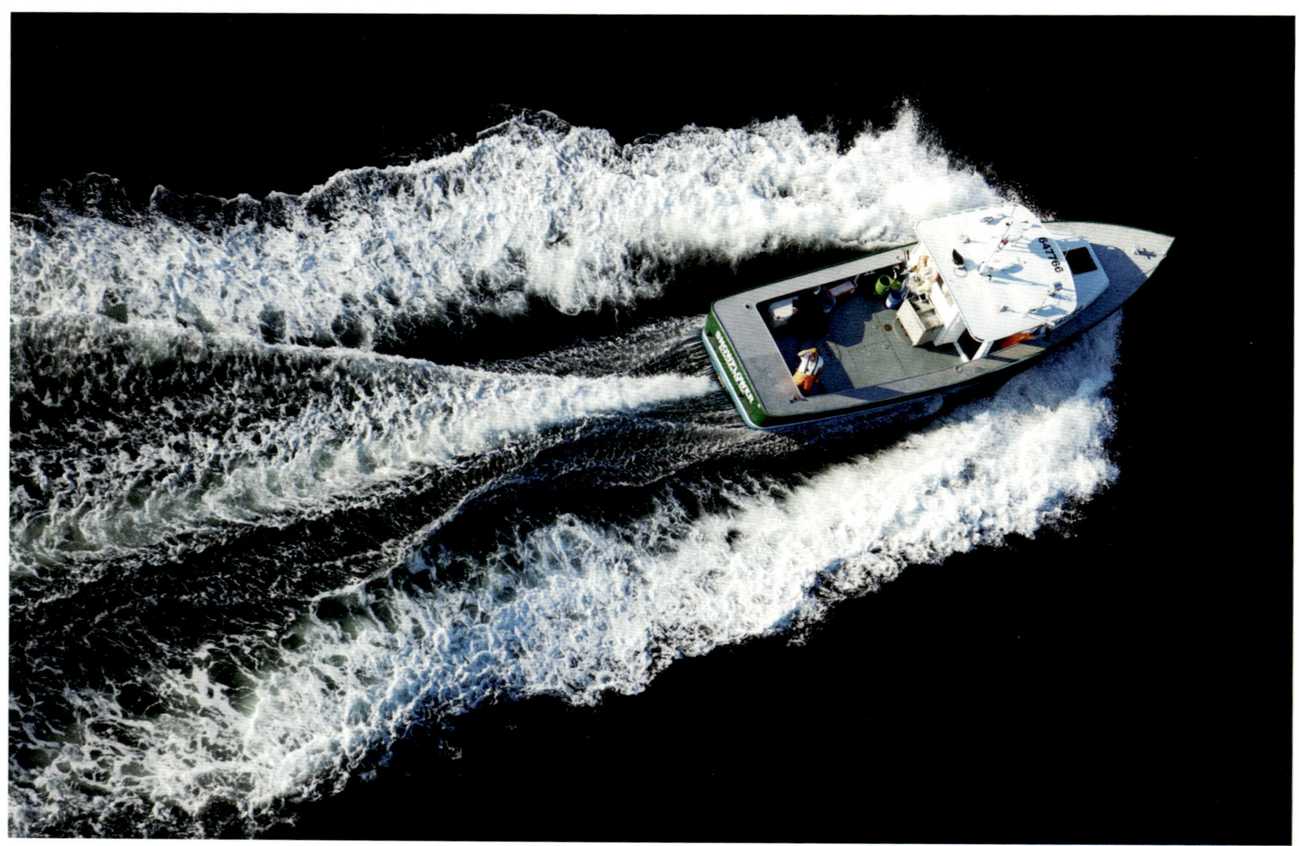

You must not lose faith in humanity. Humanity is an ocean;
if a few drops of the ocean are dirty, the ocean does not become dirty.

Mahatma Gandhi

NOVEMBER 6

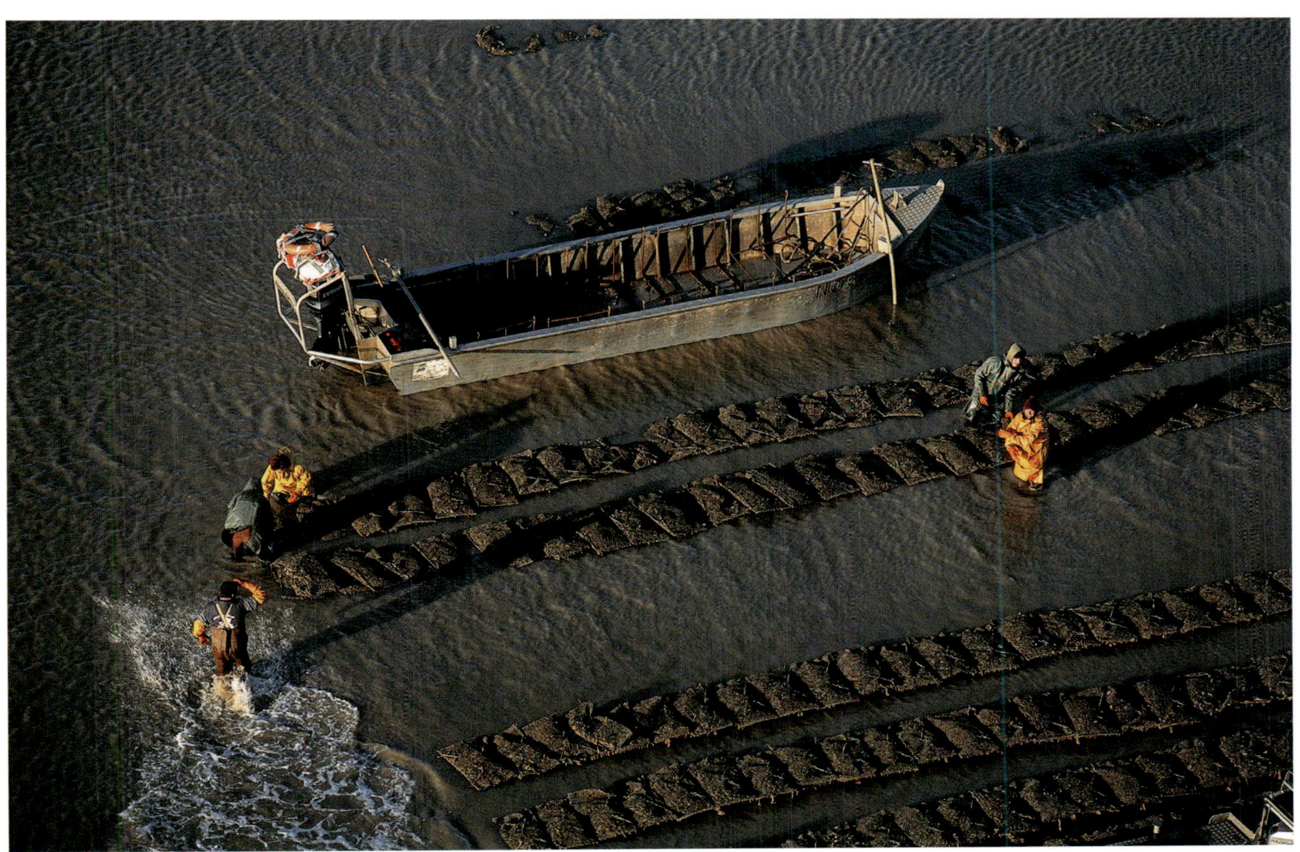

The north wind and a beautiful whore will never wake you up in the morning.

French proverb

NOVEMBER 7

As the bird trims her to the gale,
I trim myself to the storm of time,
I man the rudder, reef the sail,
Obey the voice at eve obeyed in prime:
"Lowly faithful, banish fear,
Right onward drive unharmed;
The port, well worth the cruise, is near,
And every wave is charmed."

Ralph Waldo Emerson, from "Terminus," 1866

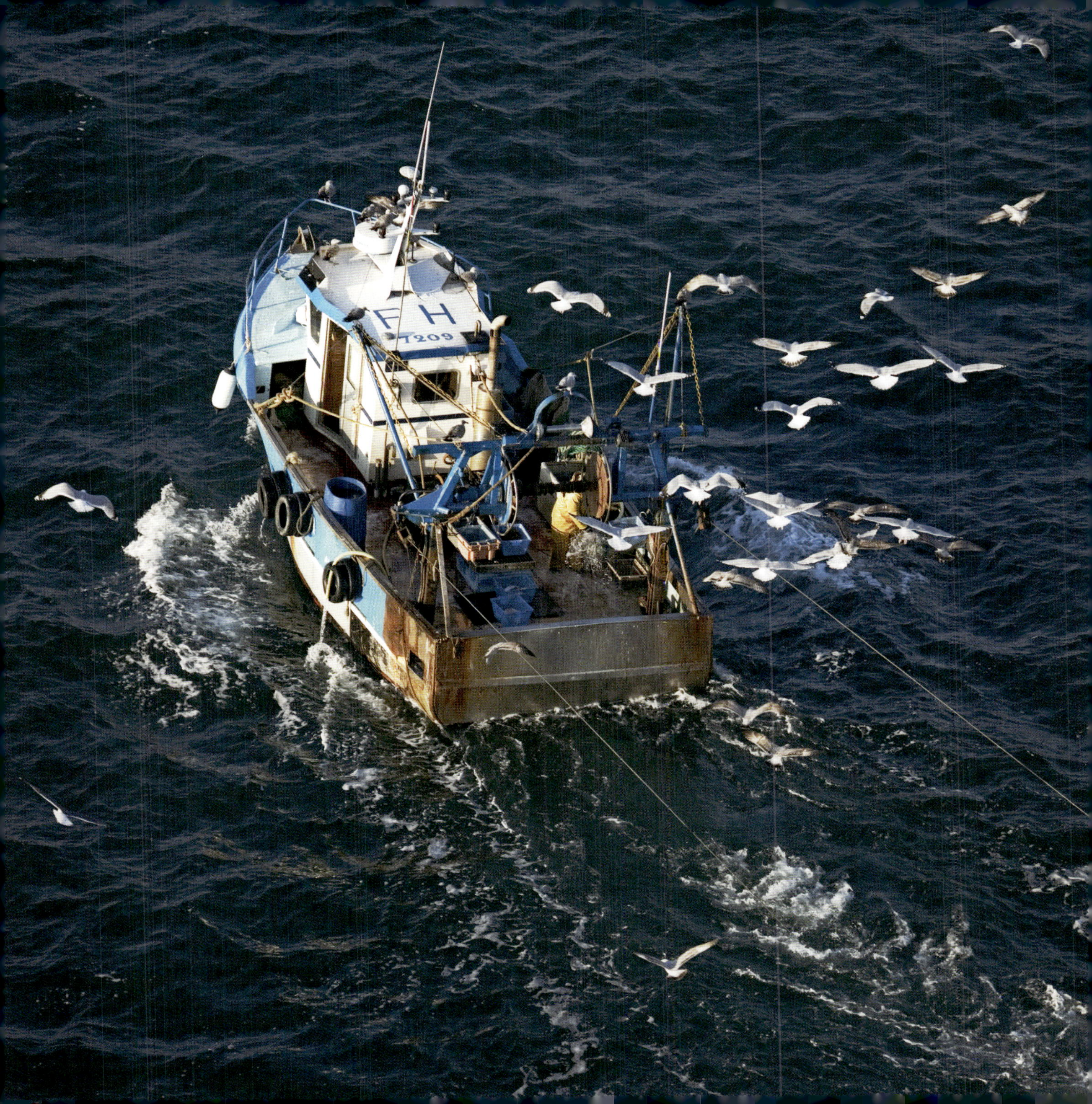
FH

NOVEMBER 8

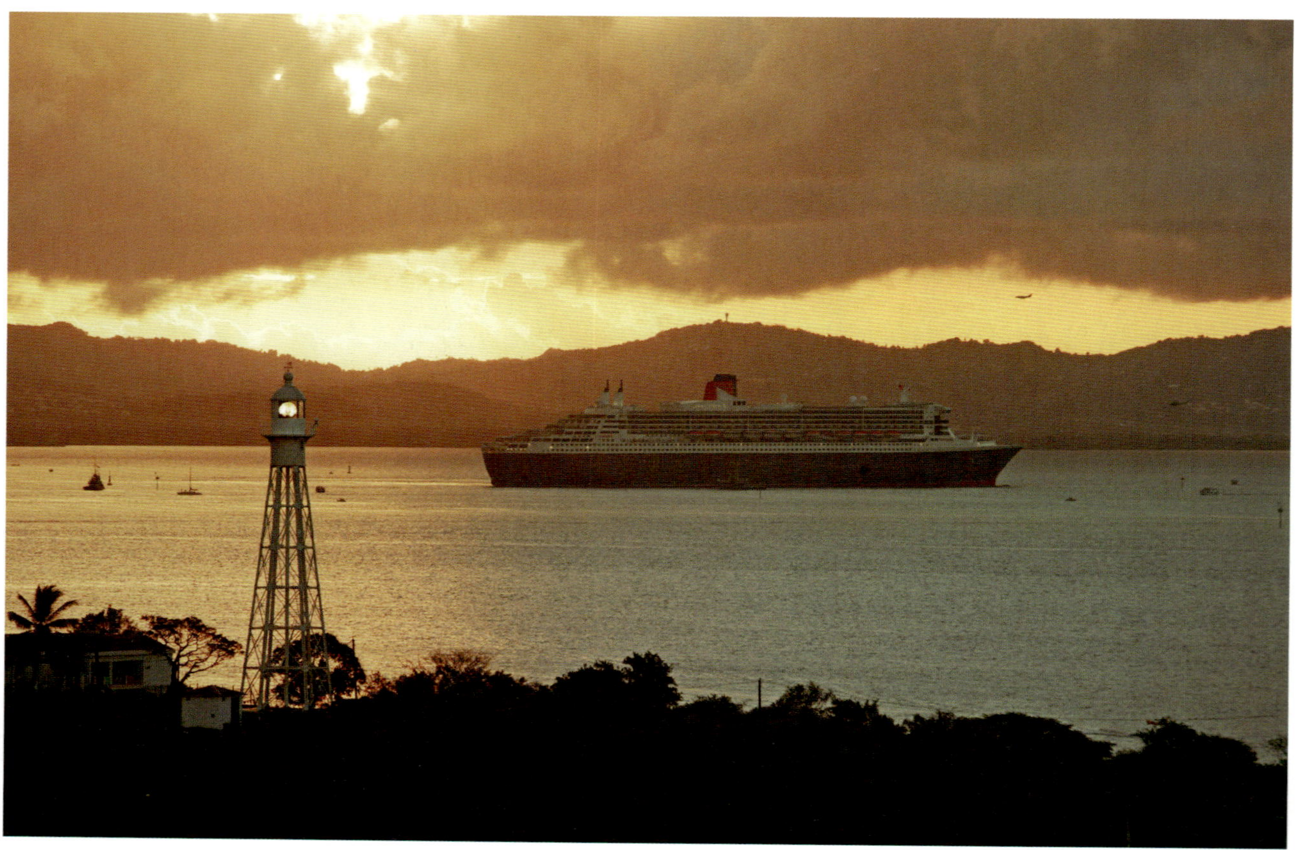

But now come, let us launch a sable ship into the boundless sea.

Homer, from *The Iliad*

NOVEMBER 9

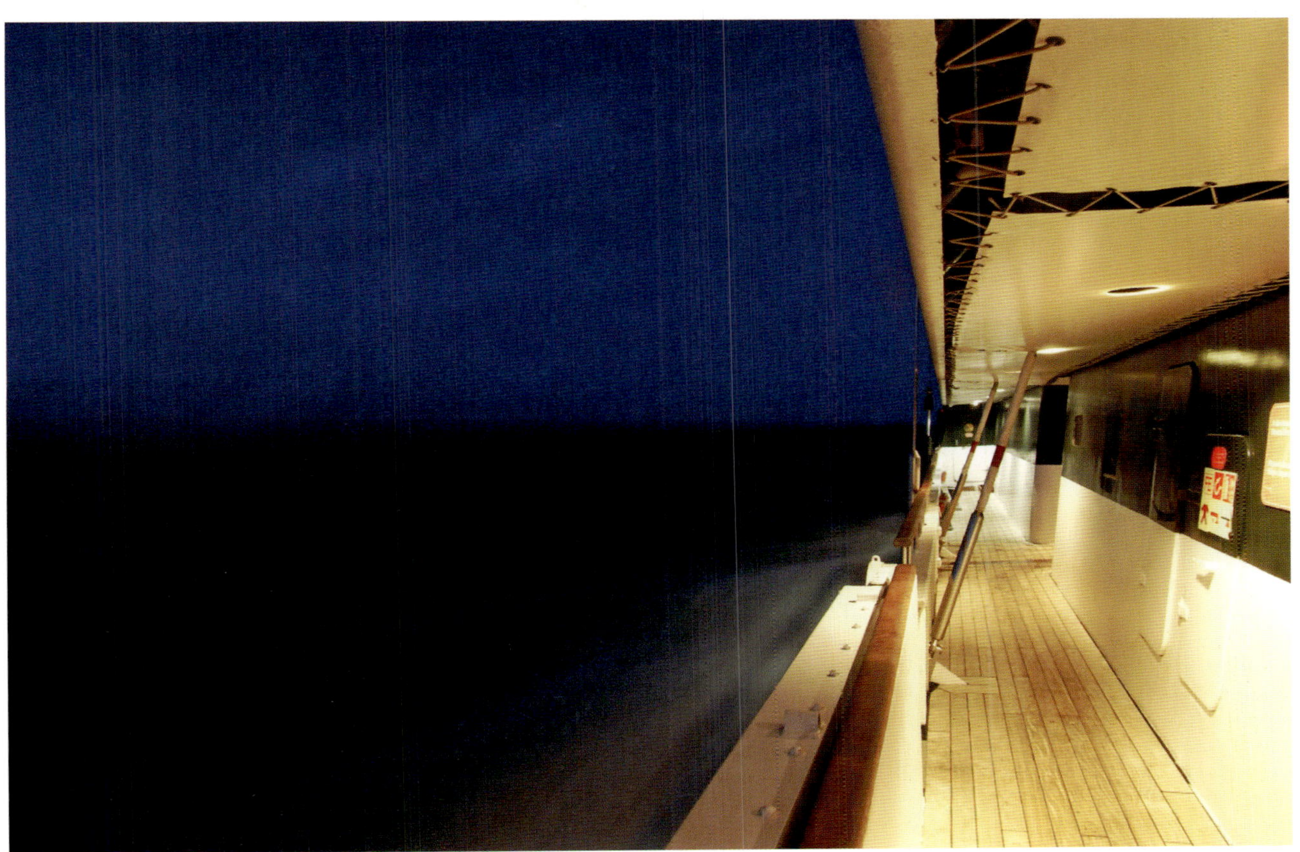

Not to have control over the senses is like sailing in a rudderless ship, bound to break to pieces on coming in contact with the very first rock.

Mahatma Gandhi

NOVEMBER 10

Full fathom five thy father lies;
Of his bones are coral made;
Those are pearls that were his eyes:
Nothing of him that doth fade
But doth suffer a sea-change
Into something rich and strange.

William Shakespeare, from *The Tempest,* Act I, Scene 2

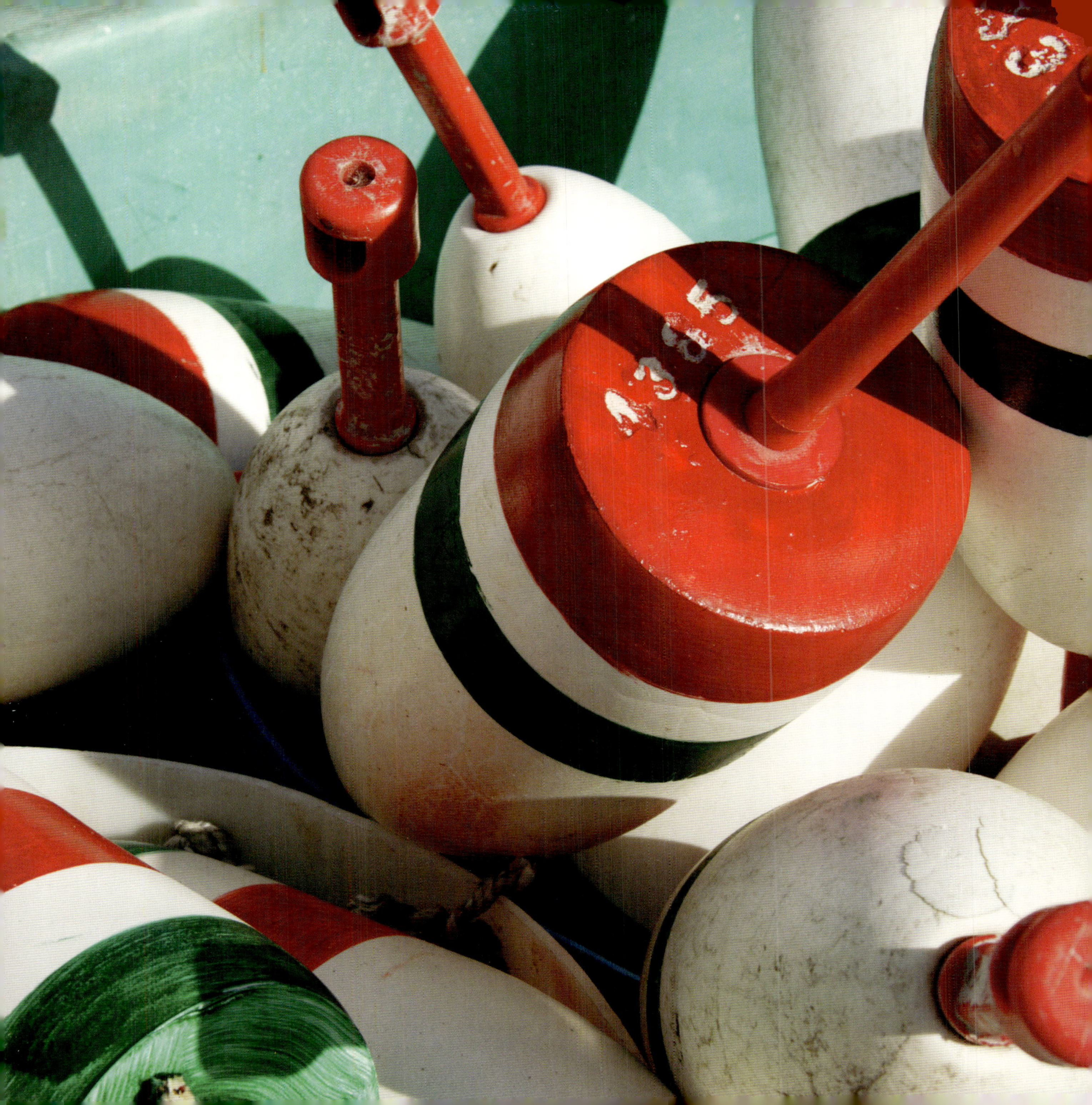

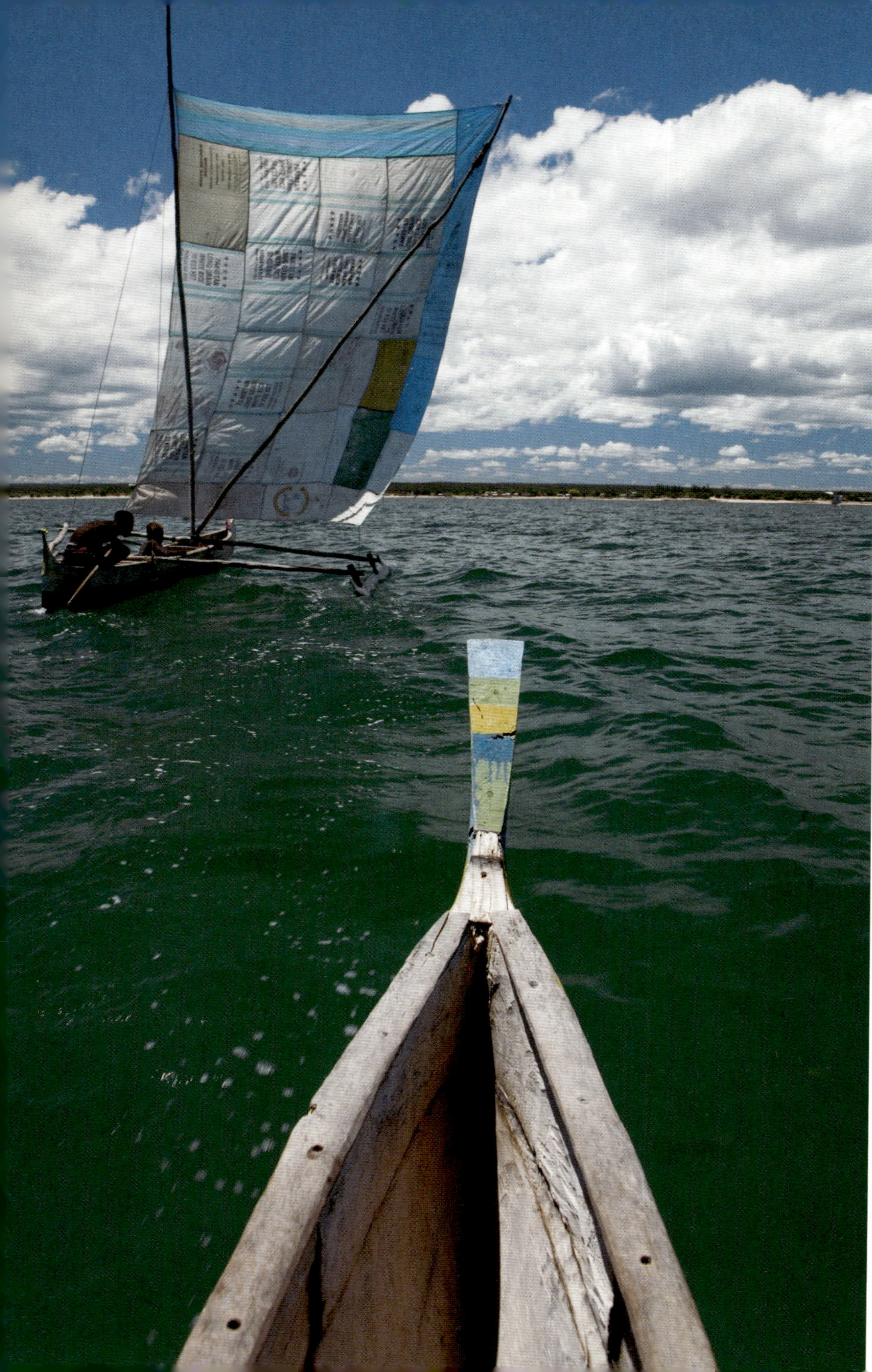

NOVEMBER 11

Mackerel skies and mares' tails,
soon will be time to shorten sails.

Traditional wisdom

NOVEMBER 12

The storm made bliss of my
sea-borne awakenings.
Lighter than a cork, I danced
on the waves
Which men call eternal rollers
of victims,
For ten nights, without once
missing the foolish eye of the
harbor lights!

Arthur Rimbaud,
from "The Drunken Boat," 1871

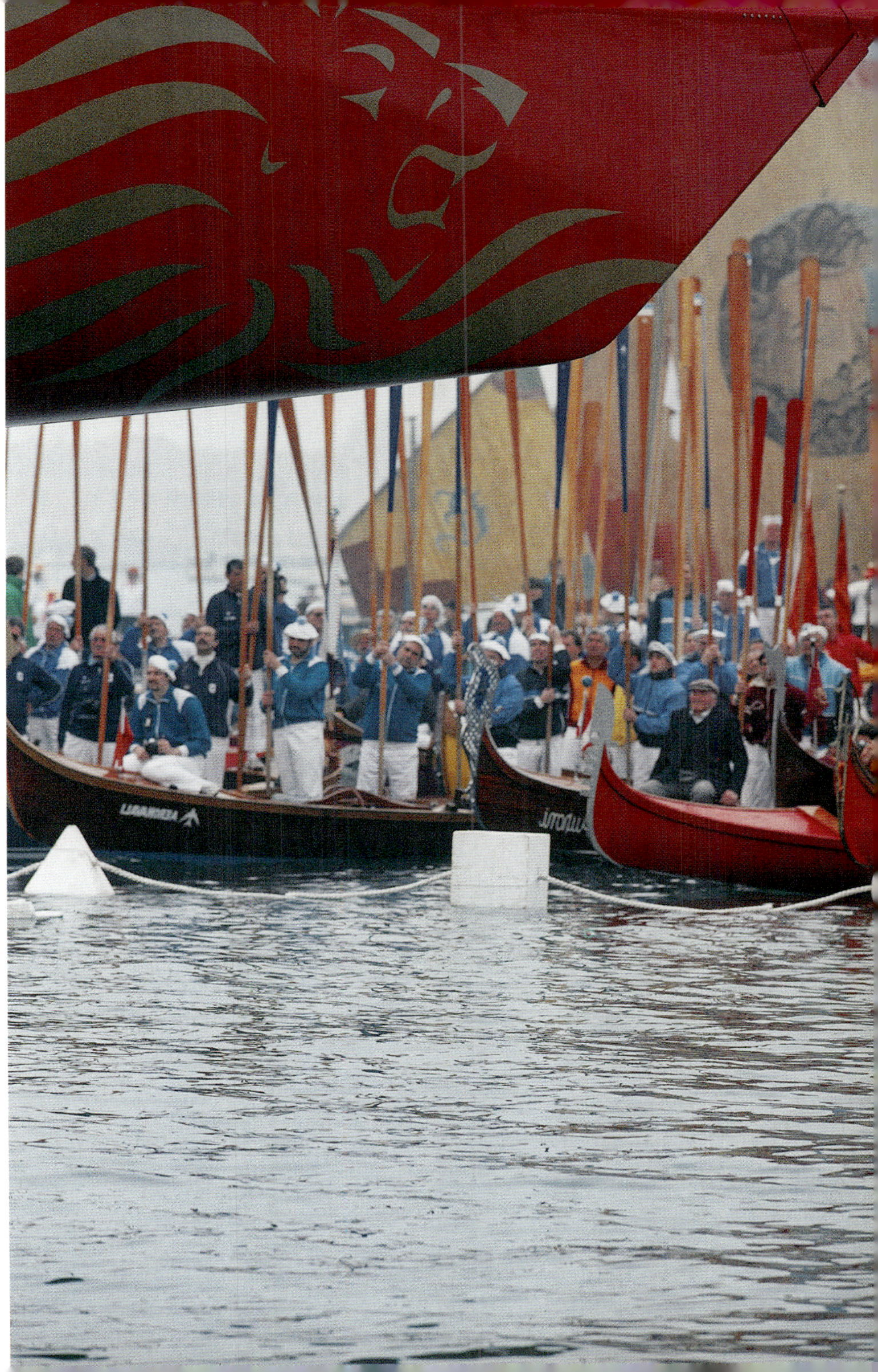

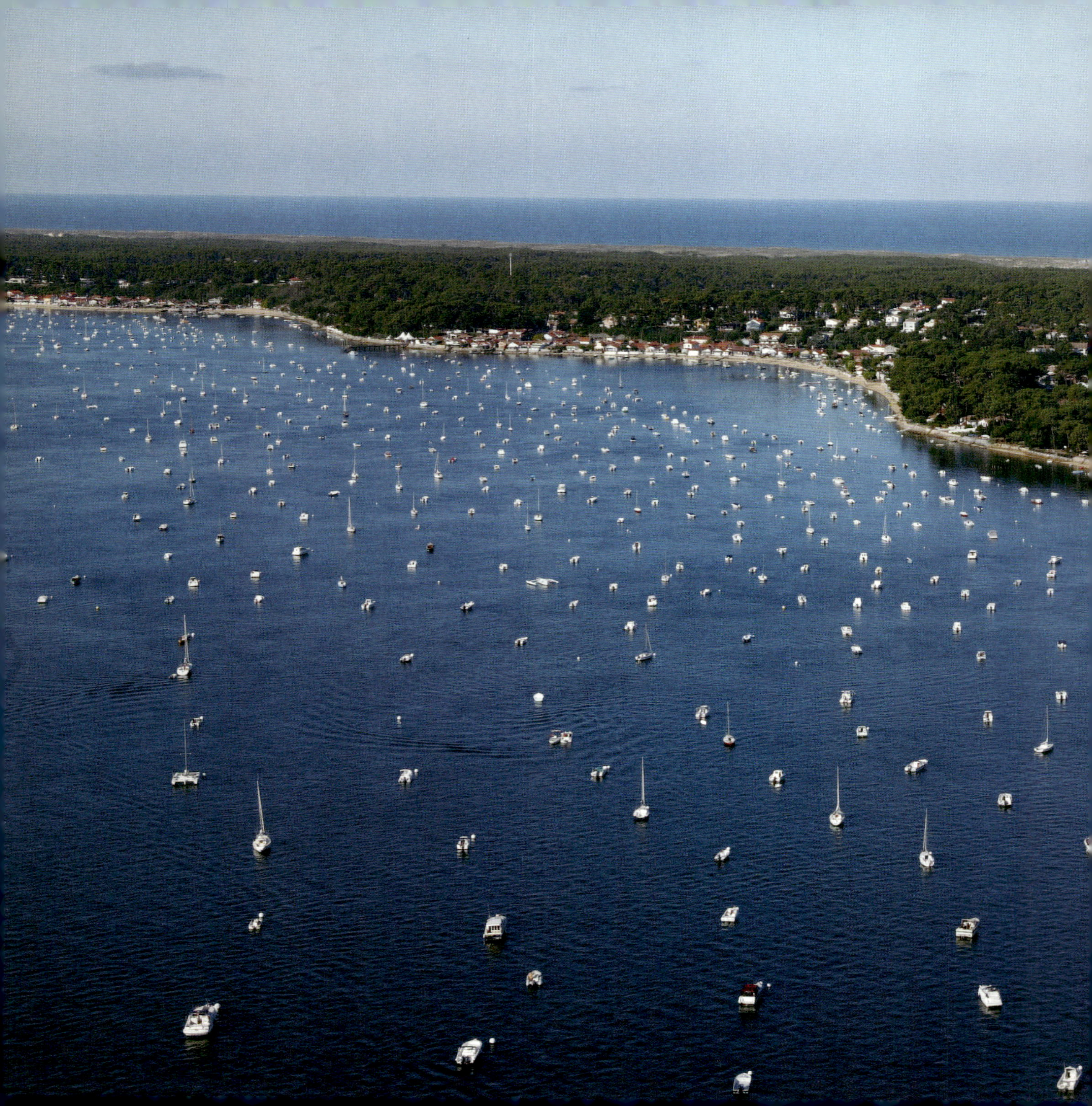

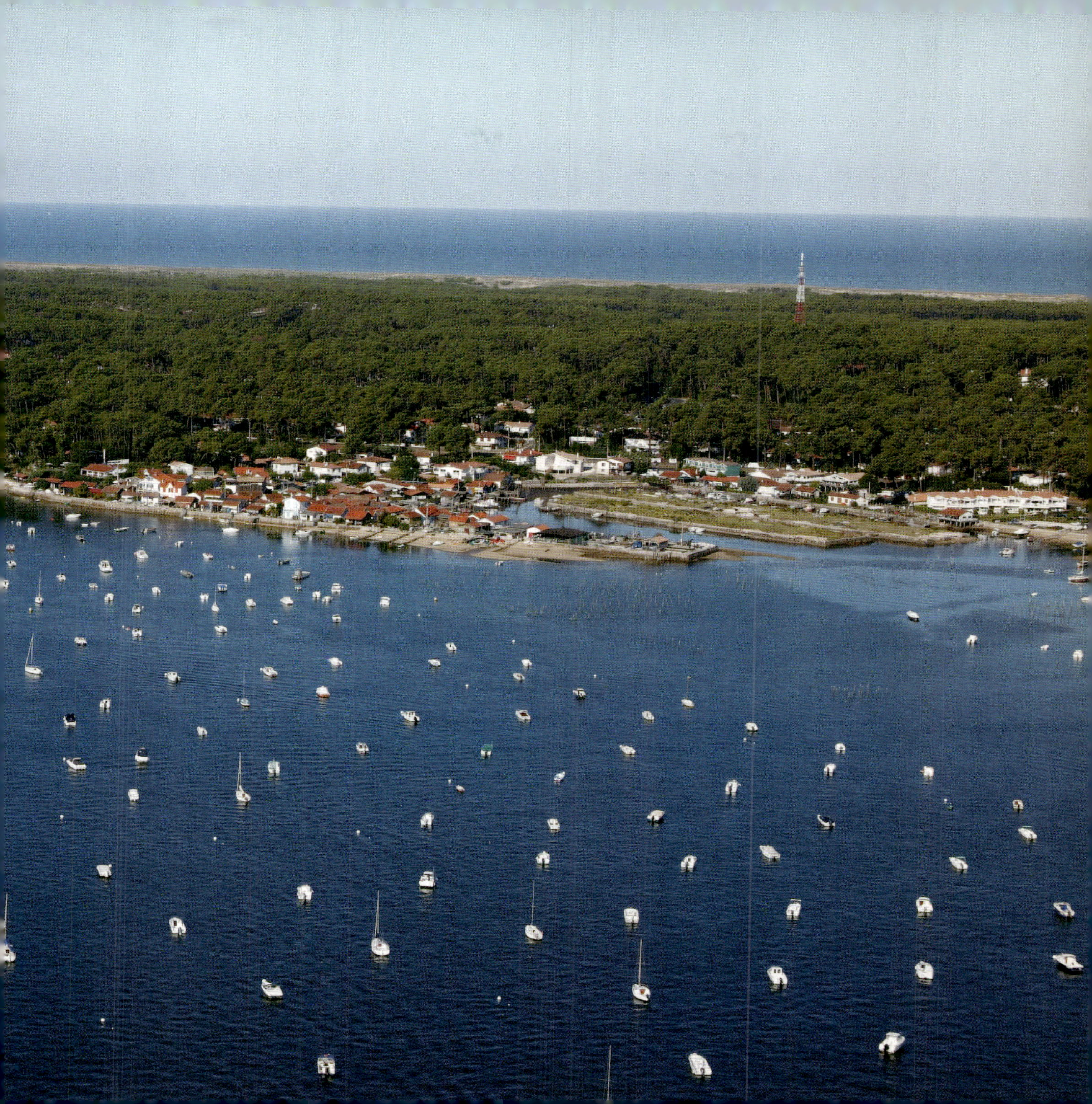

NOVEMBER 13

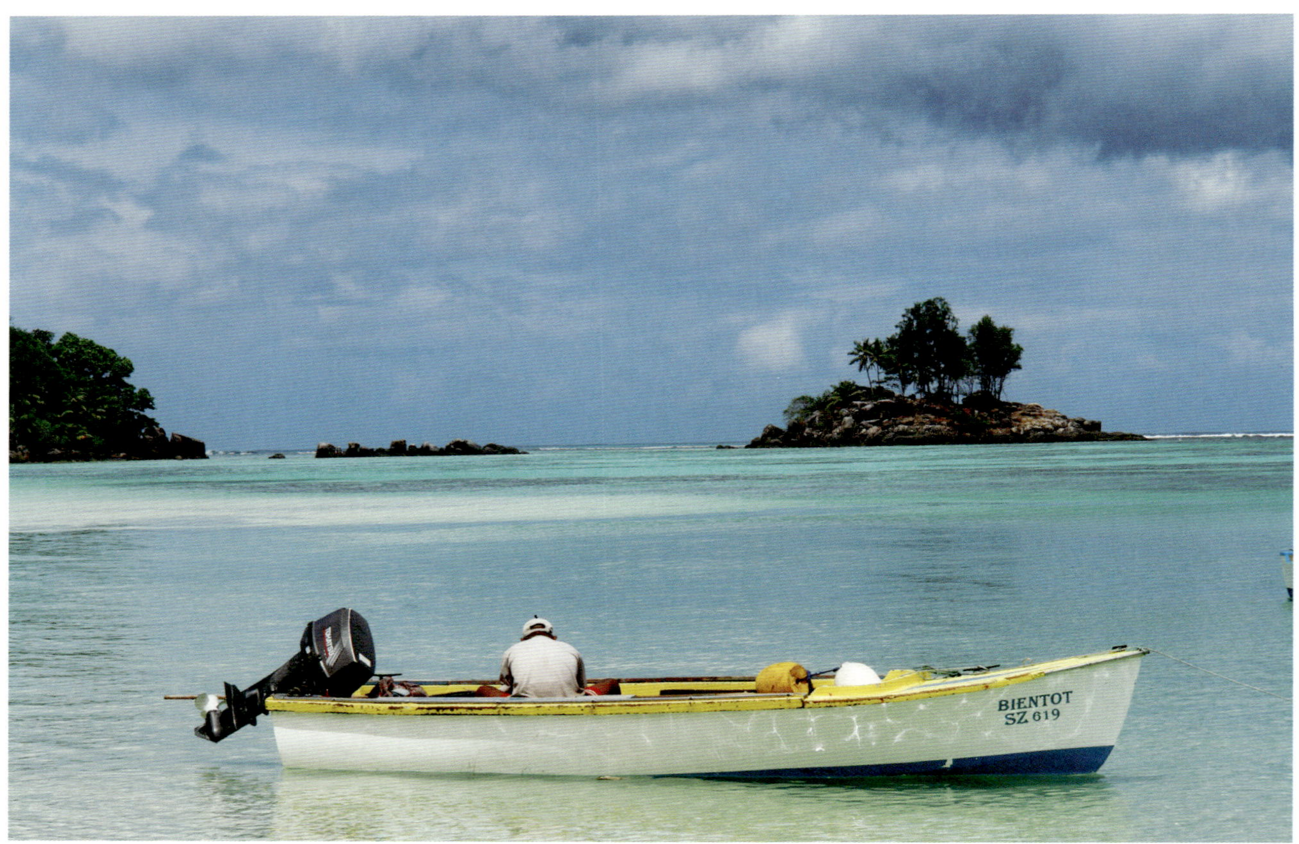

We all like to see people sea-sick when we are not ourselves.

Mark Twain, from *Innocents Abroad,* 1869

NOVEMBER 14

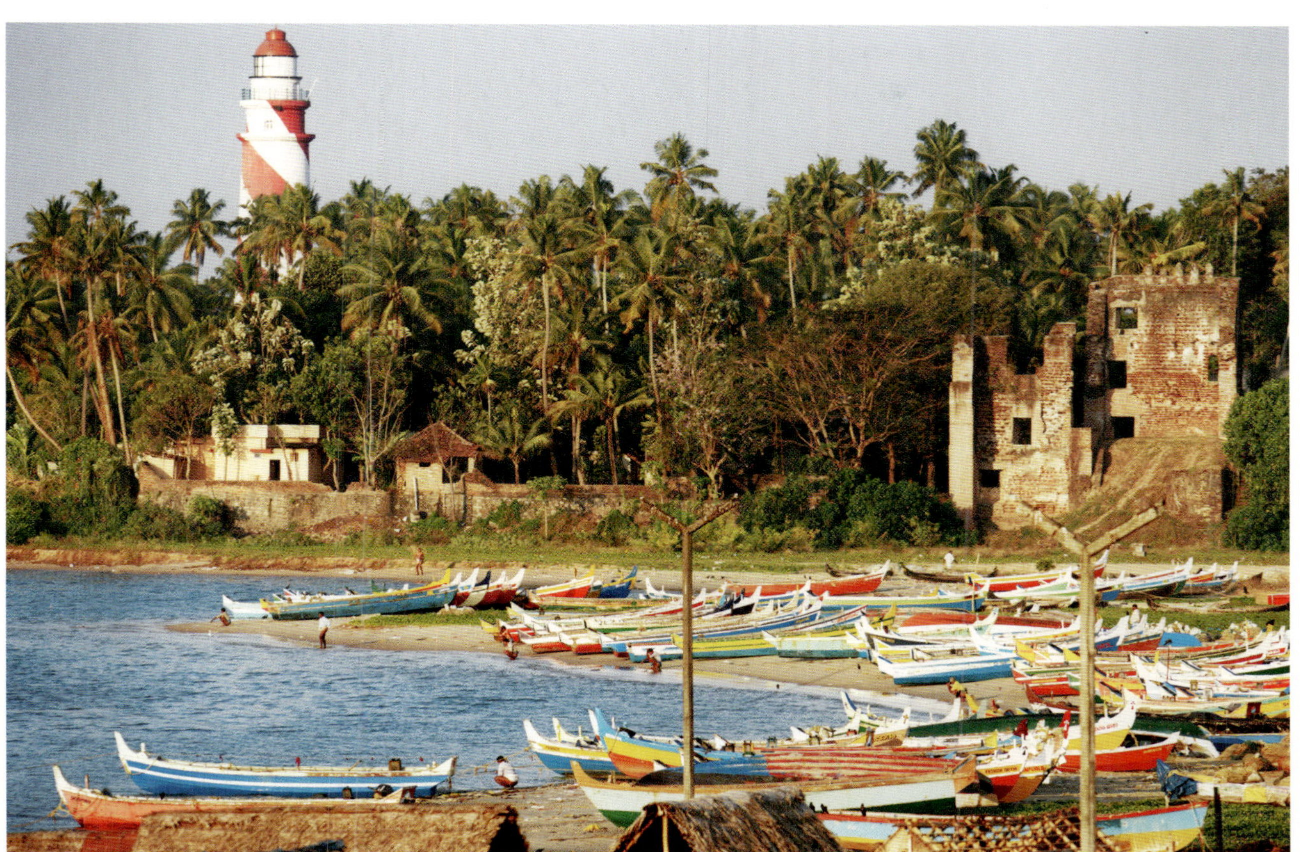

Ships are to little purpose without skillful Sea Men.

Richard Hakluyt, from *Voyages,* 1589

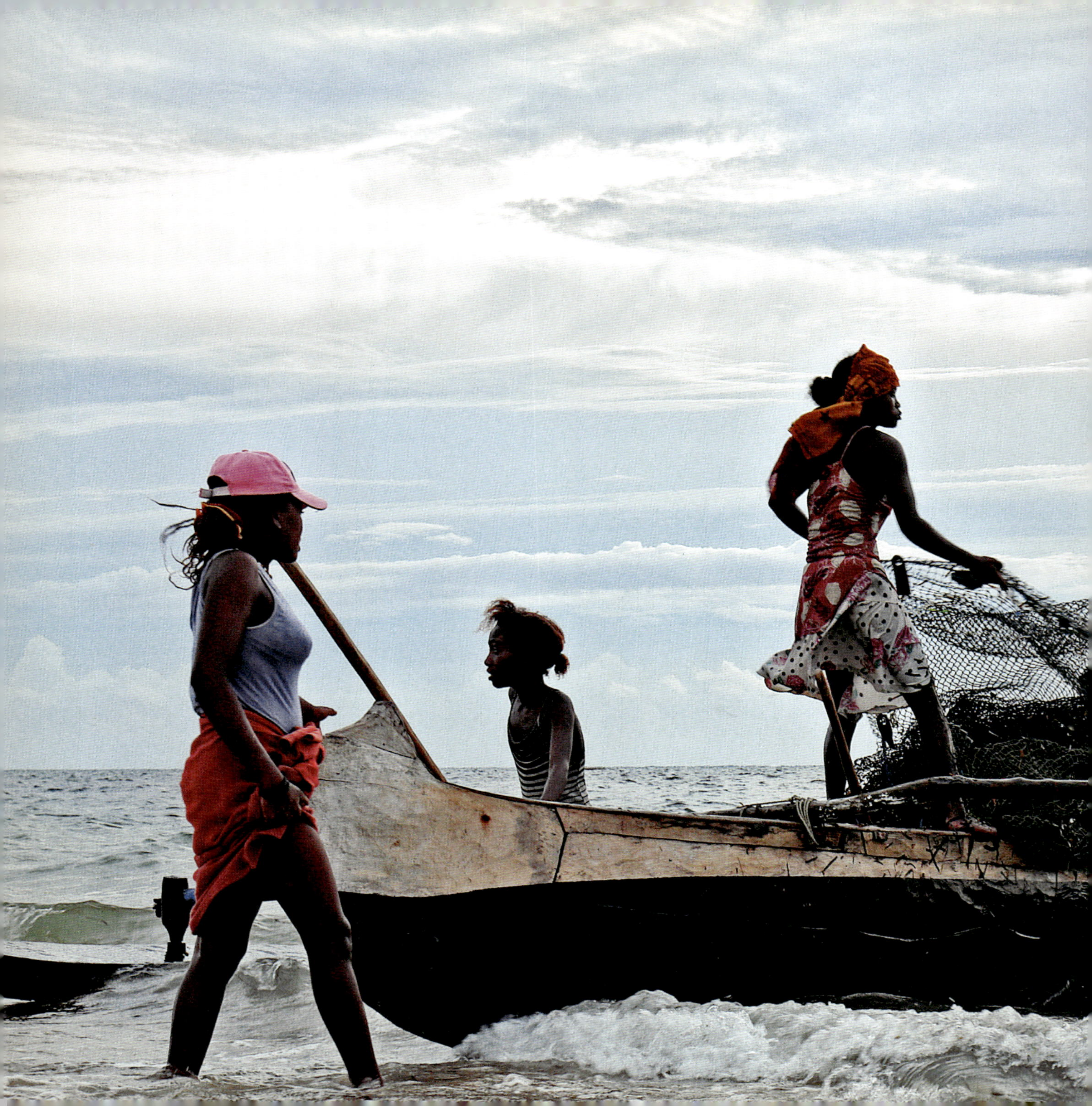

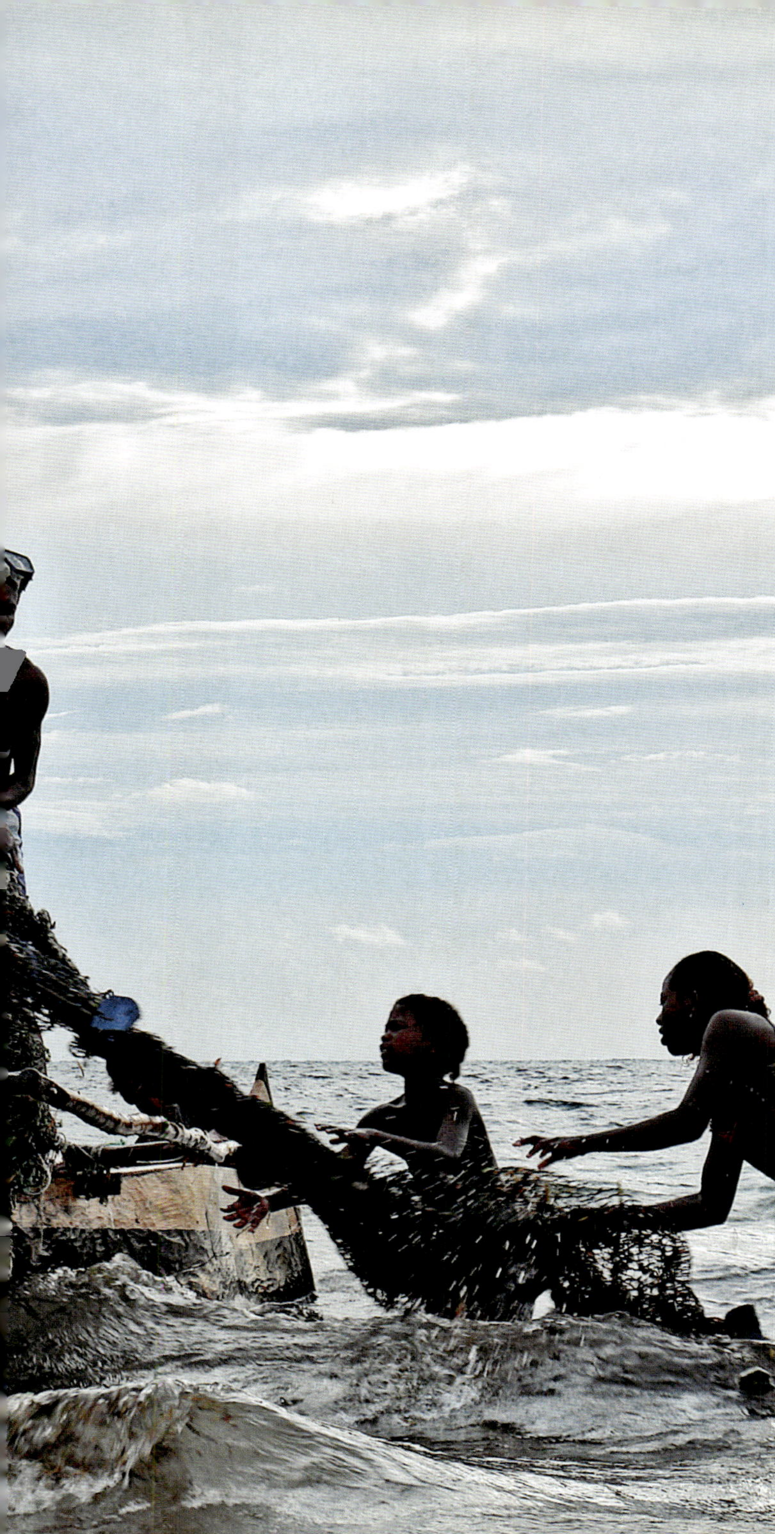

NOVEMBER 15

Once more upon the waters! Yet once more!
And the waves bound beneath me as a steed
That knows his rider.

Lord Byron,
from "Childe Harold's Pilgrimage," 1818

NOVEMBER 16

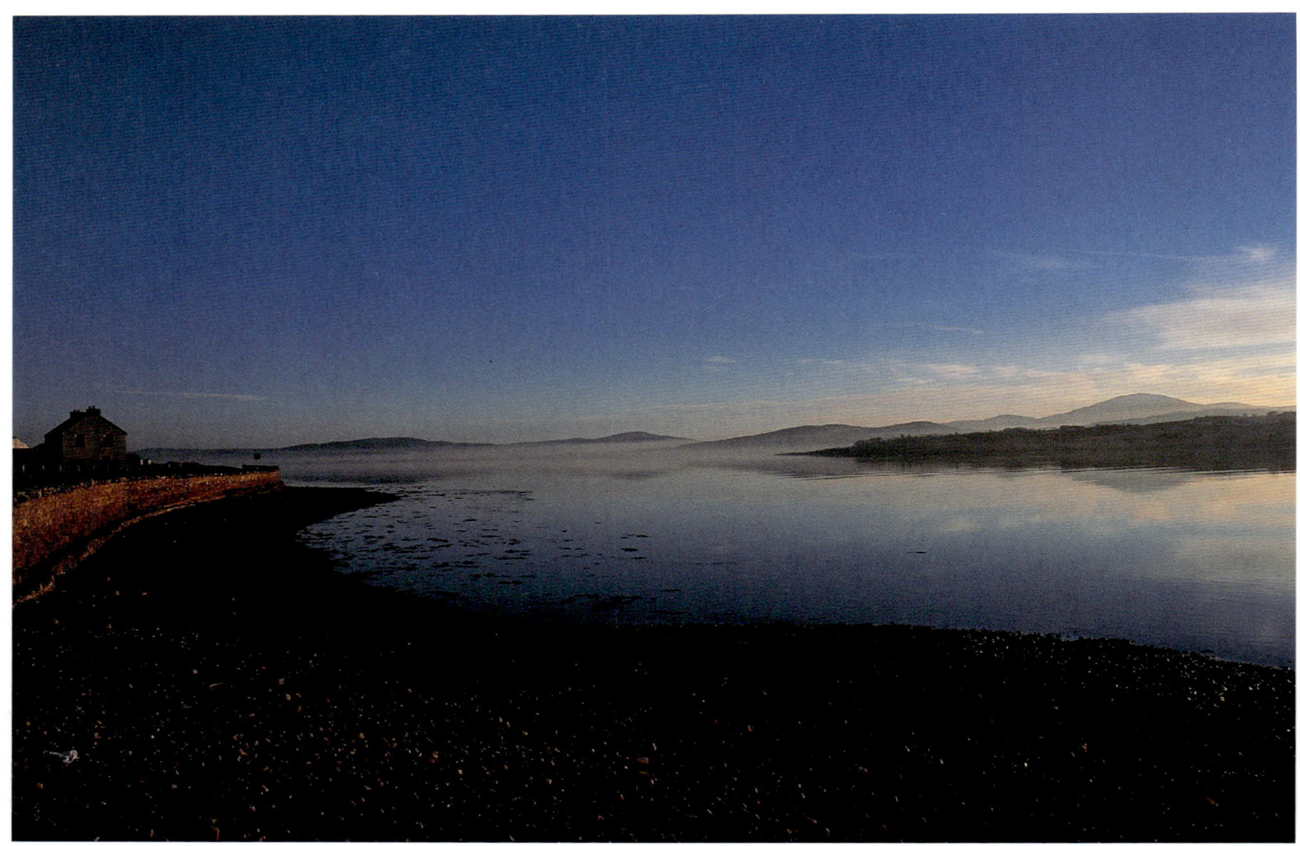

The earth and ocean seem
To sleep in one another's arms, and dream.

Percy Bysshe Shelley, from "Epipsychidion," 1821

NOVEMBER 17

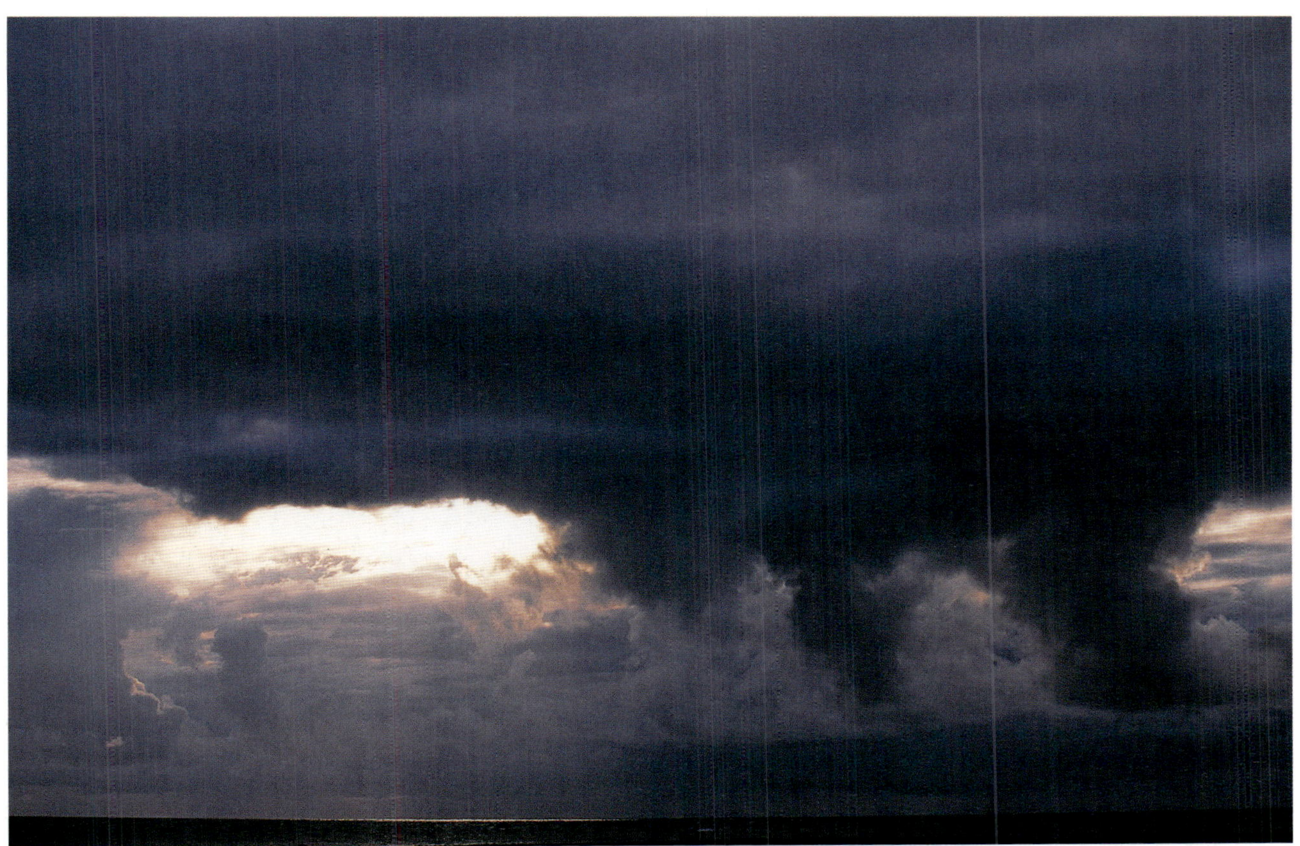

The gentleness of heaven broods o'er the Sea.

William Wordsworth, from "It Is a Beauteous Evening, Calm and Free," 1802

NOVEMBER 18

The restless ocean may at any moment cast up a whale or a wrecked vessel at your feet. All the reporters in the world, the most rapid stenographers, could not report the news it brings.

Henry David Thoreau,
from *Cape Cod,* 1865

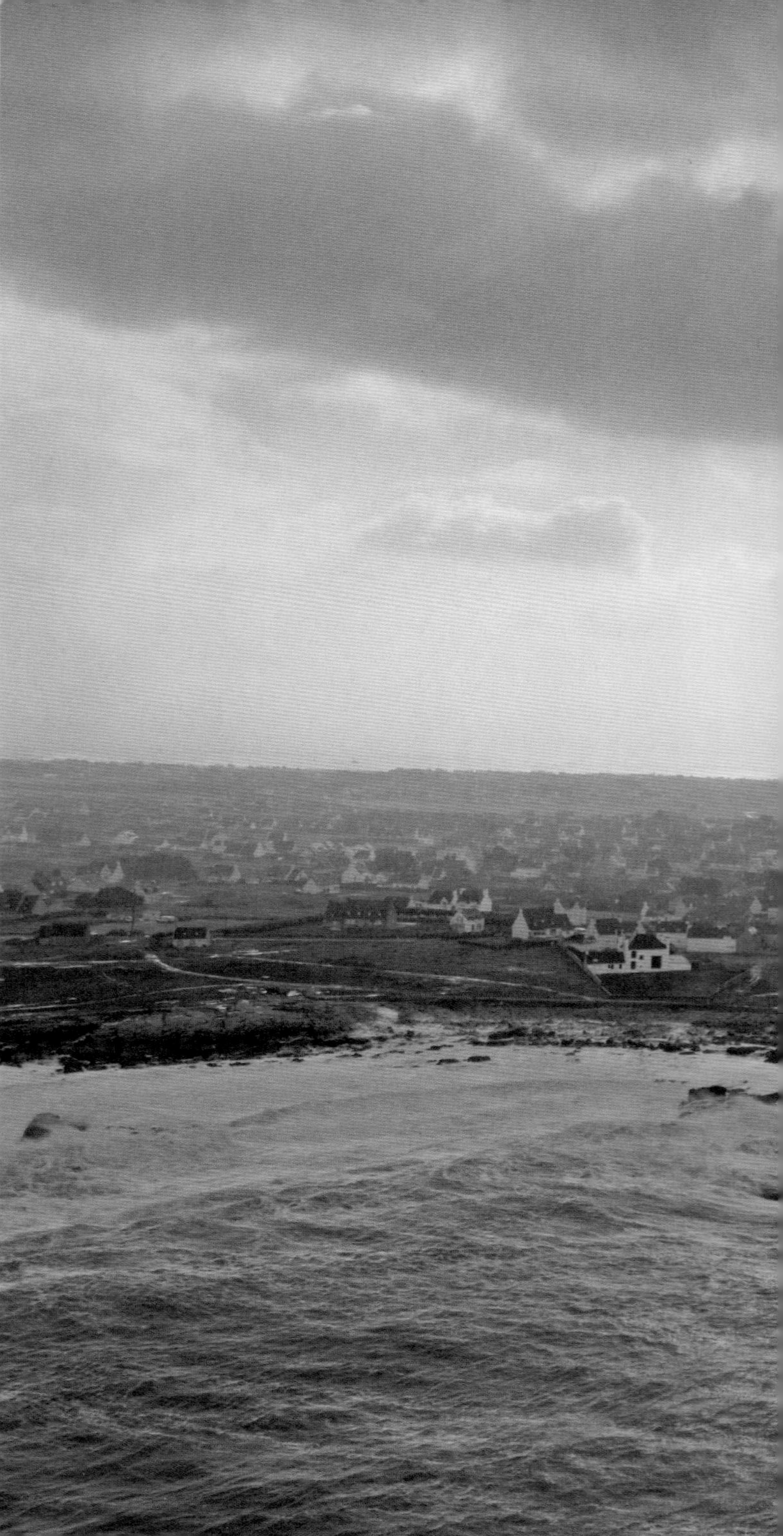

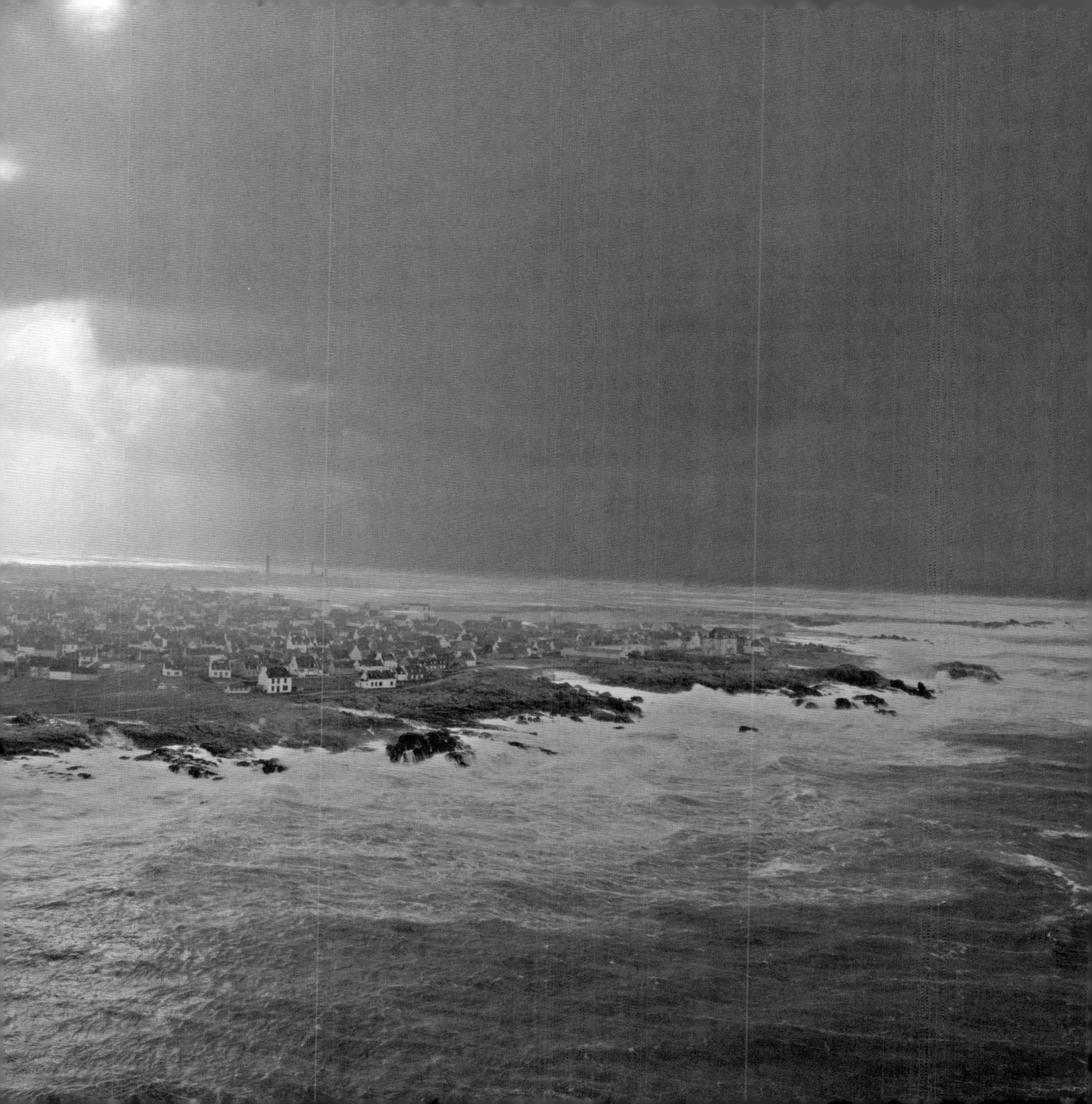

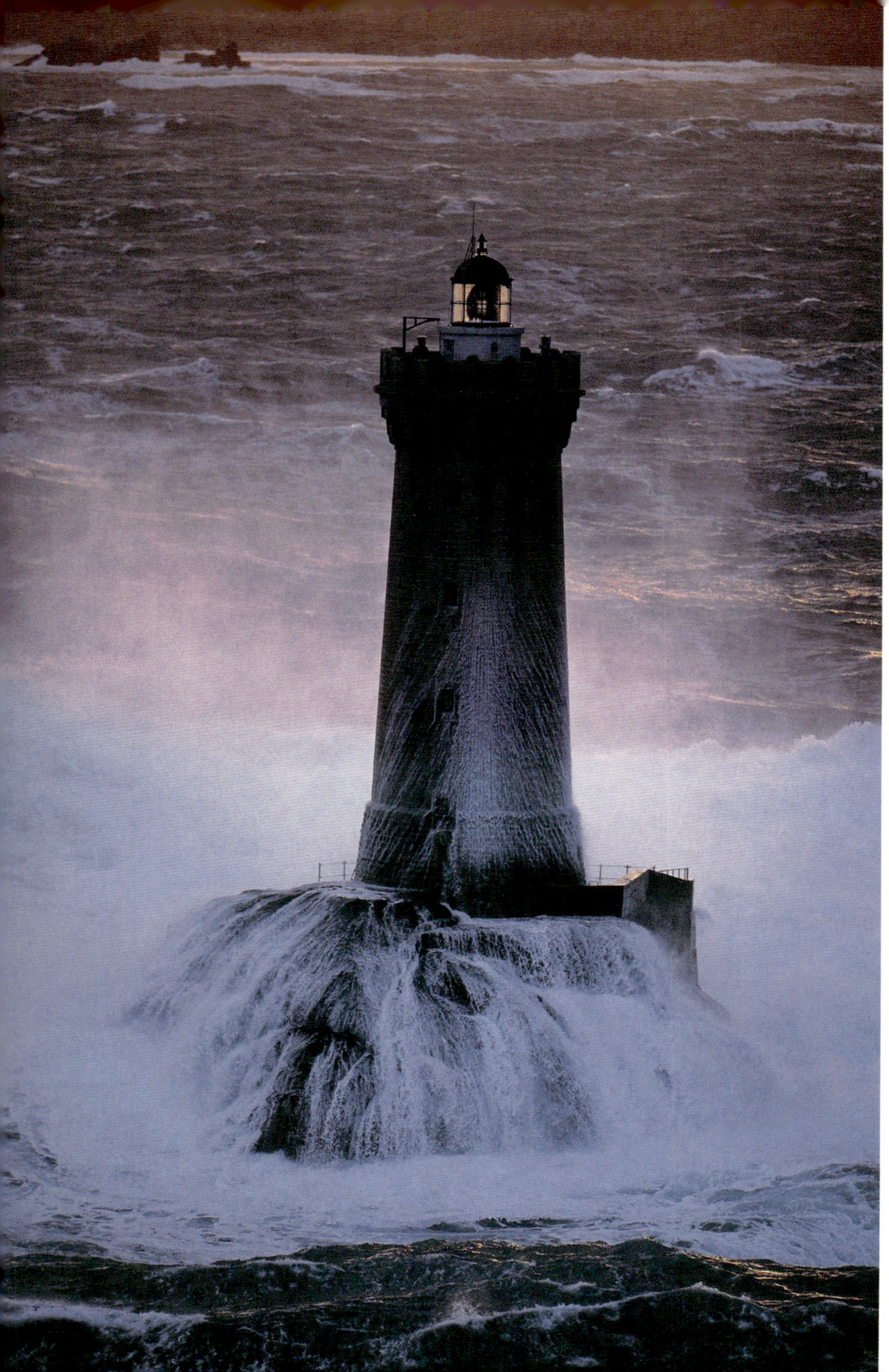

NOVEMBER 19

The waves which dash upon the shore are, one by one, broken, but the ocean conquers nevertheless.

Lord Byron,
from "Childe Harold's Pilgrimage," 1818

NOVEMBER 20

When beholding the tranquil beauty and brilliancy of the ocean's skin, one forgets the tiger heart that pants beneath it; and would not willingly remember that this velvet paw but conceals a remorseless fang.

Herman Melville,
from *Moby-Dick,* 1851

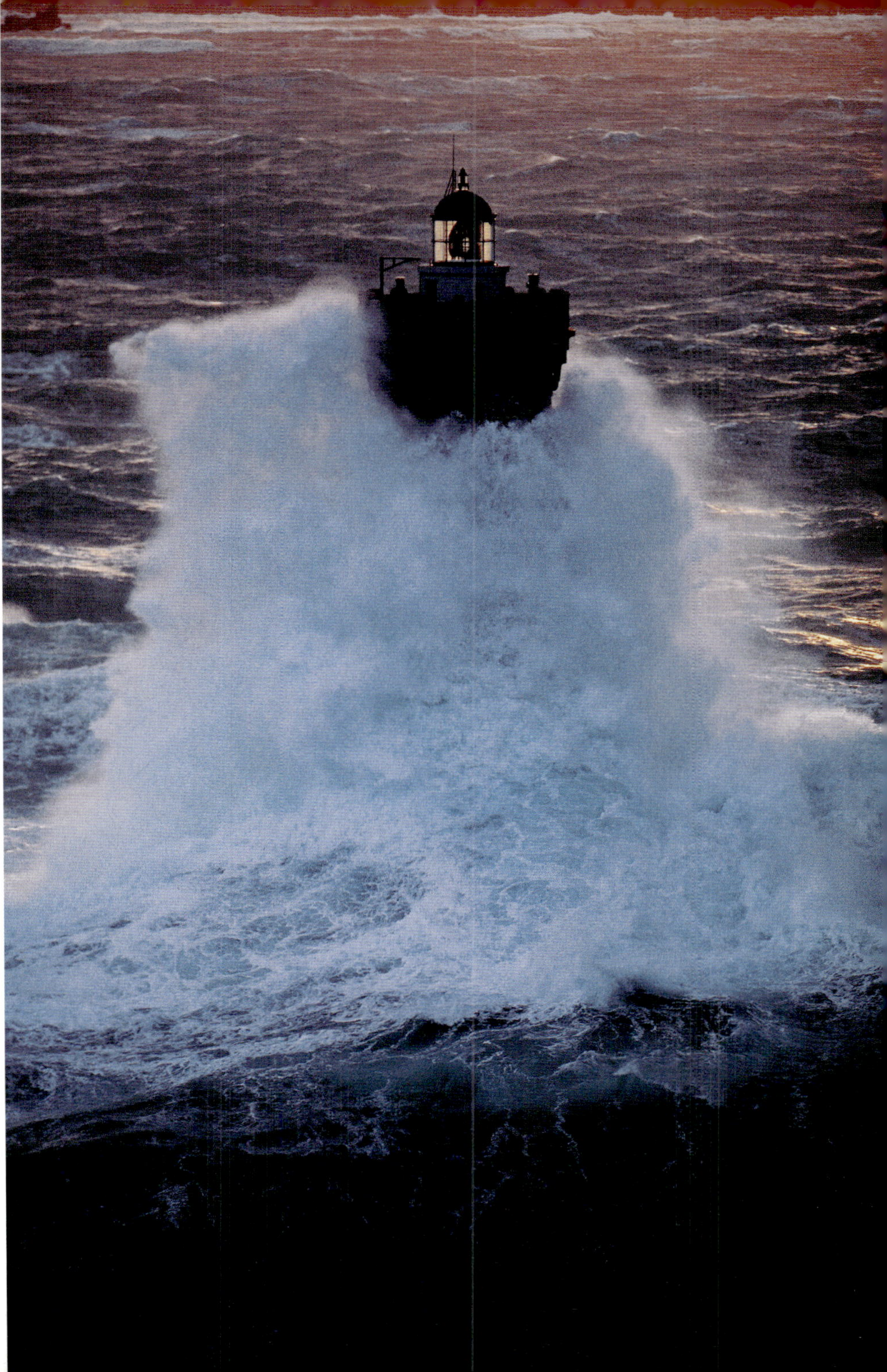

NOVEMBER 21

The ship was cheered, the harbor cleared
Merrily did we drop,
Below the kirk, below the hill,
Below the lighthouse top.

Samuel Taylor Coleridge,
from "Rime of the Ancient Mariner," 1798

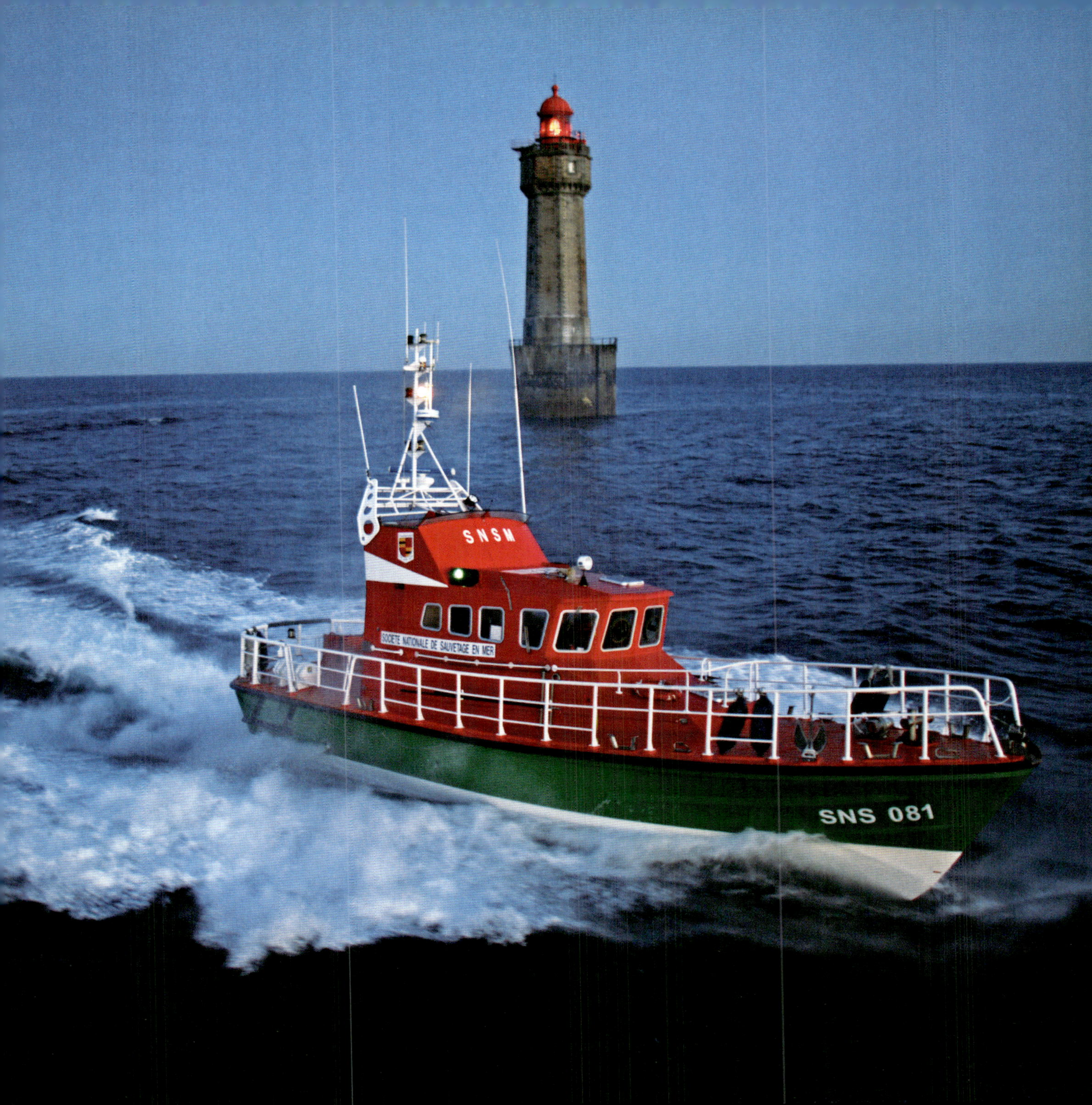
SNSM
SOCIETE NATIONALE DE SAUVETAGE EN MER
SNS 081

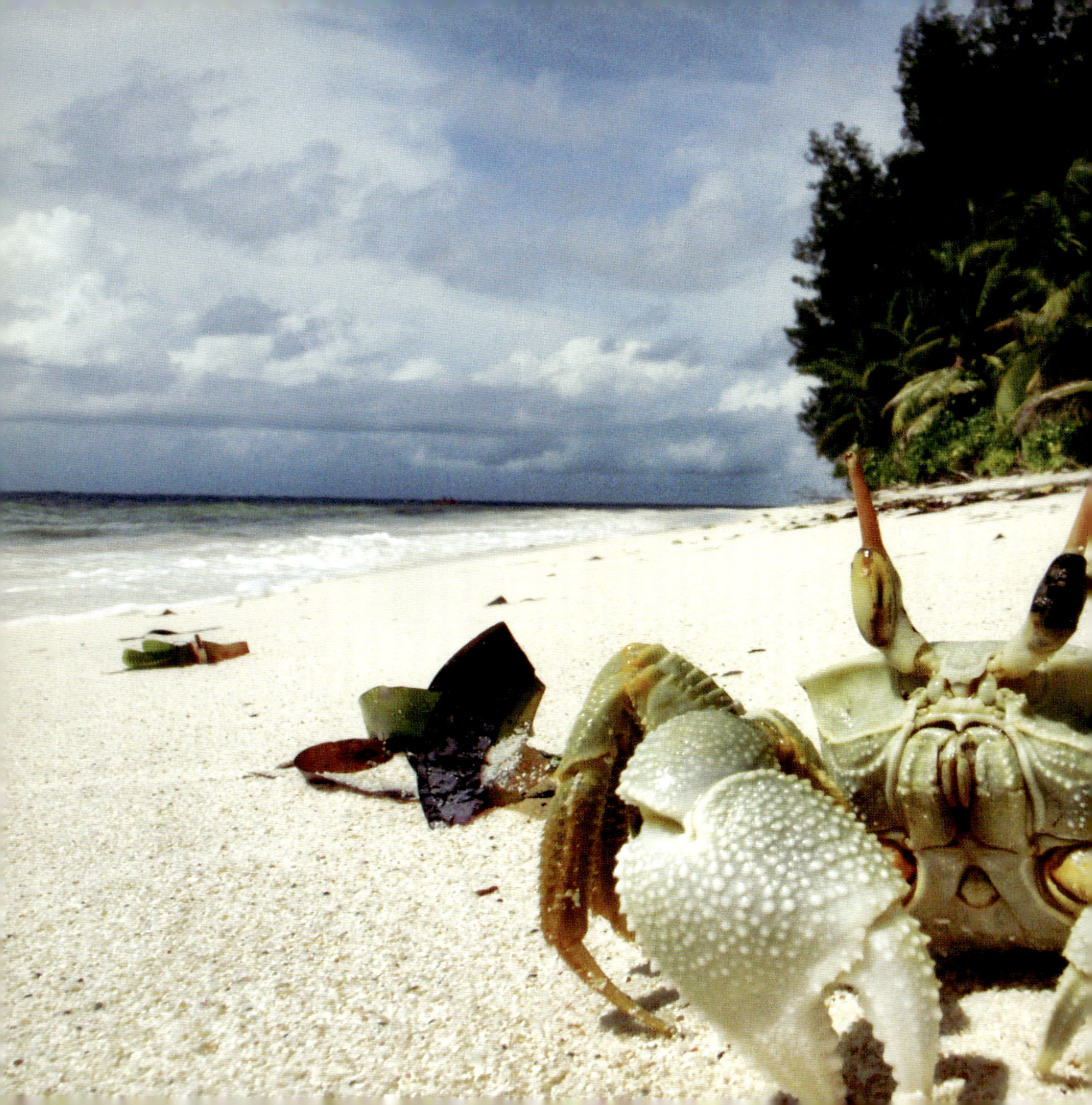

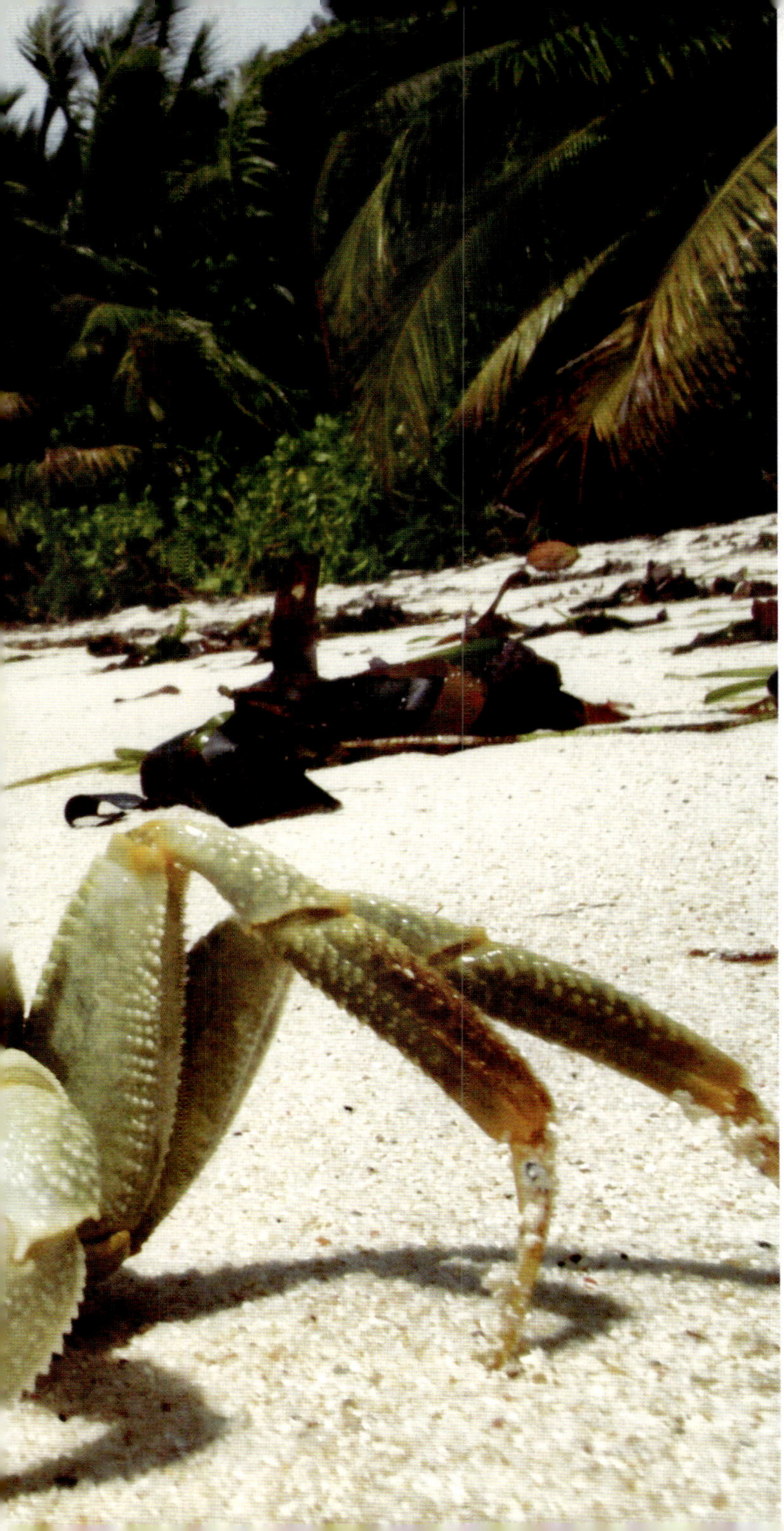

NOVEMBER 22

I should have been a pair of ragged claws
Scuttling across the floors of silent seas.

T. S. Eliot,
from "The Love Song of J. Alfred Prufrock," 1915

NOVEMBER 23

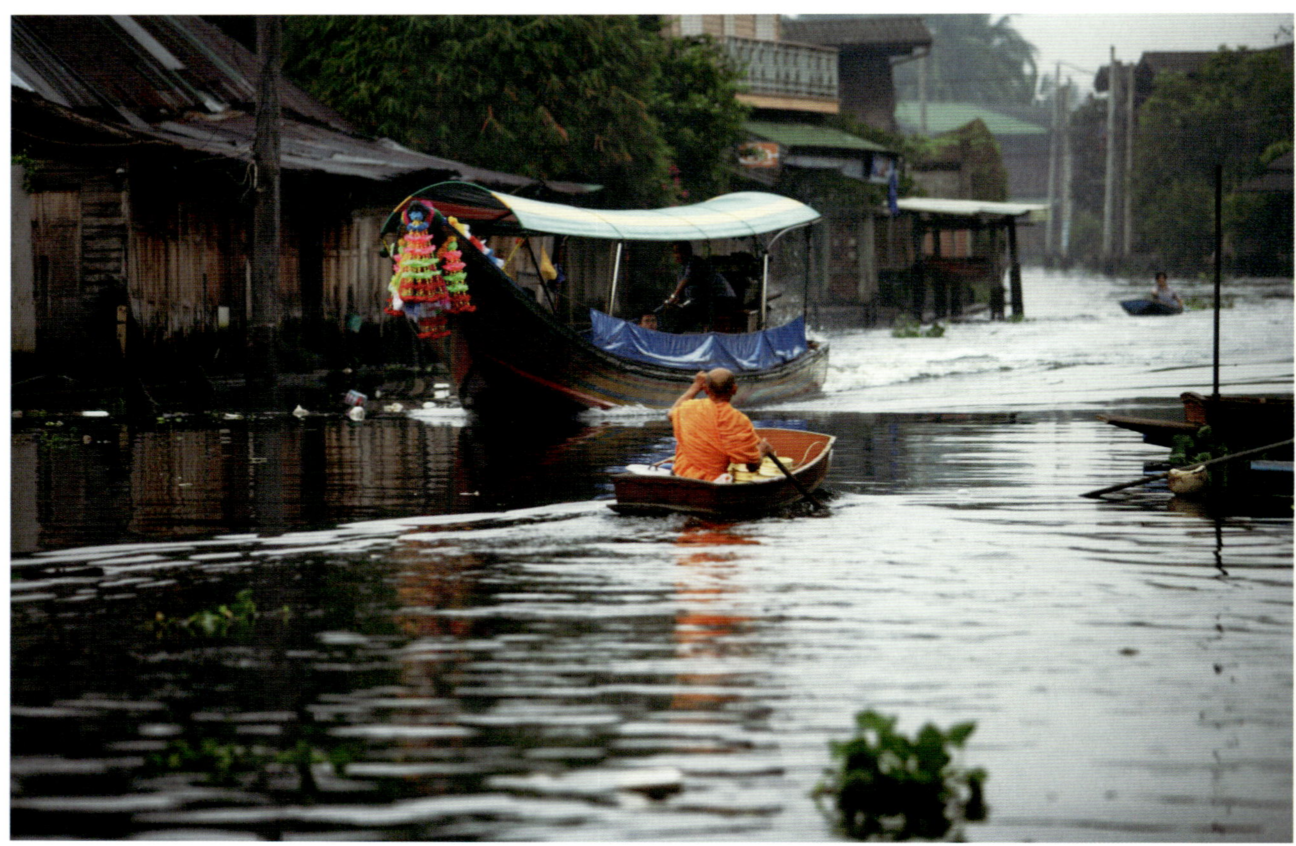

Nodding the head does not row the boat.

Irish proverb

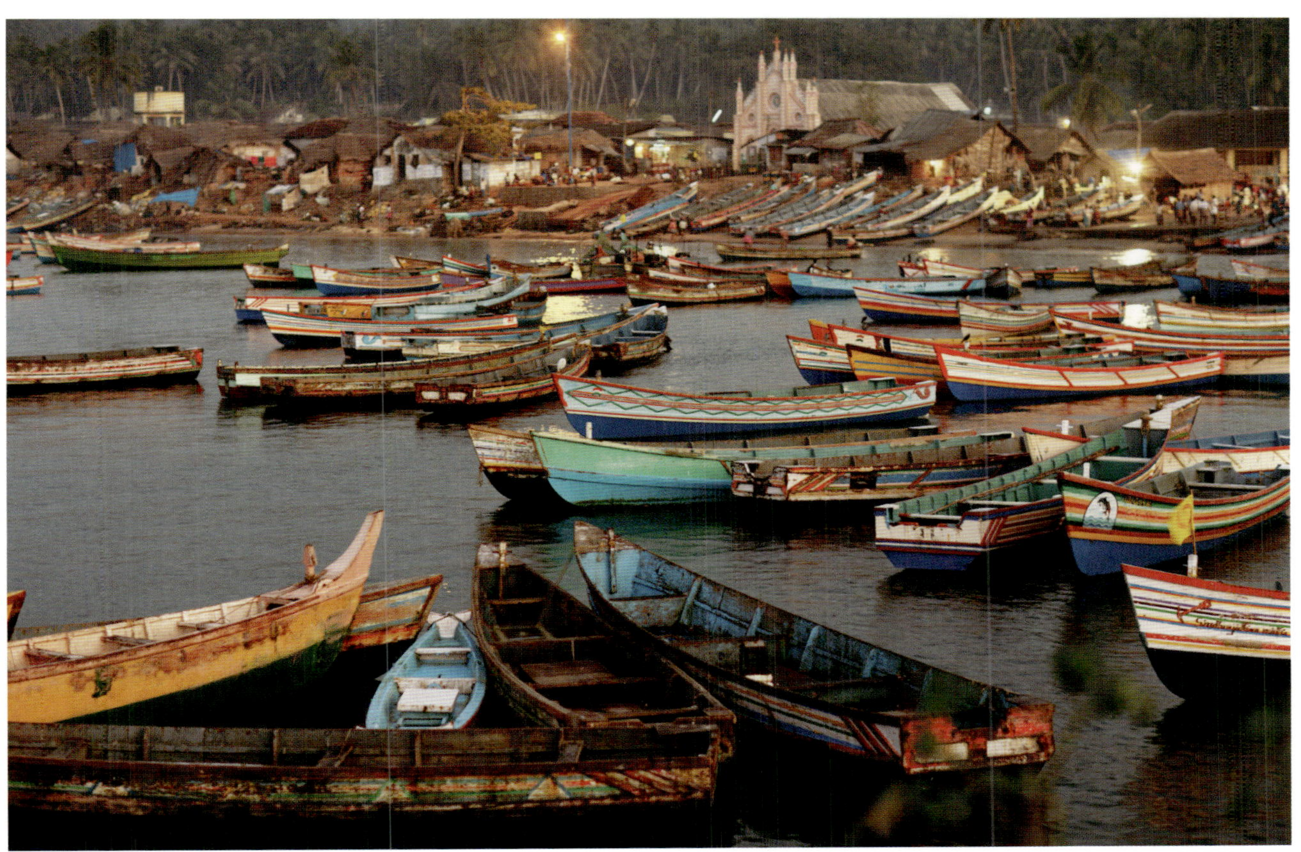

Home is the sailor, home from the sea.

Robert Louis Stevenson, from "Requiem," 1887

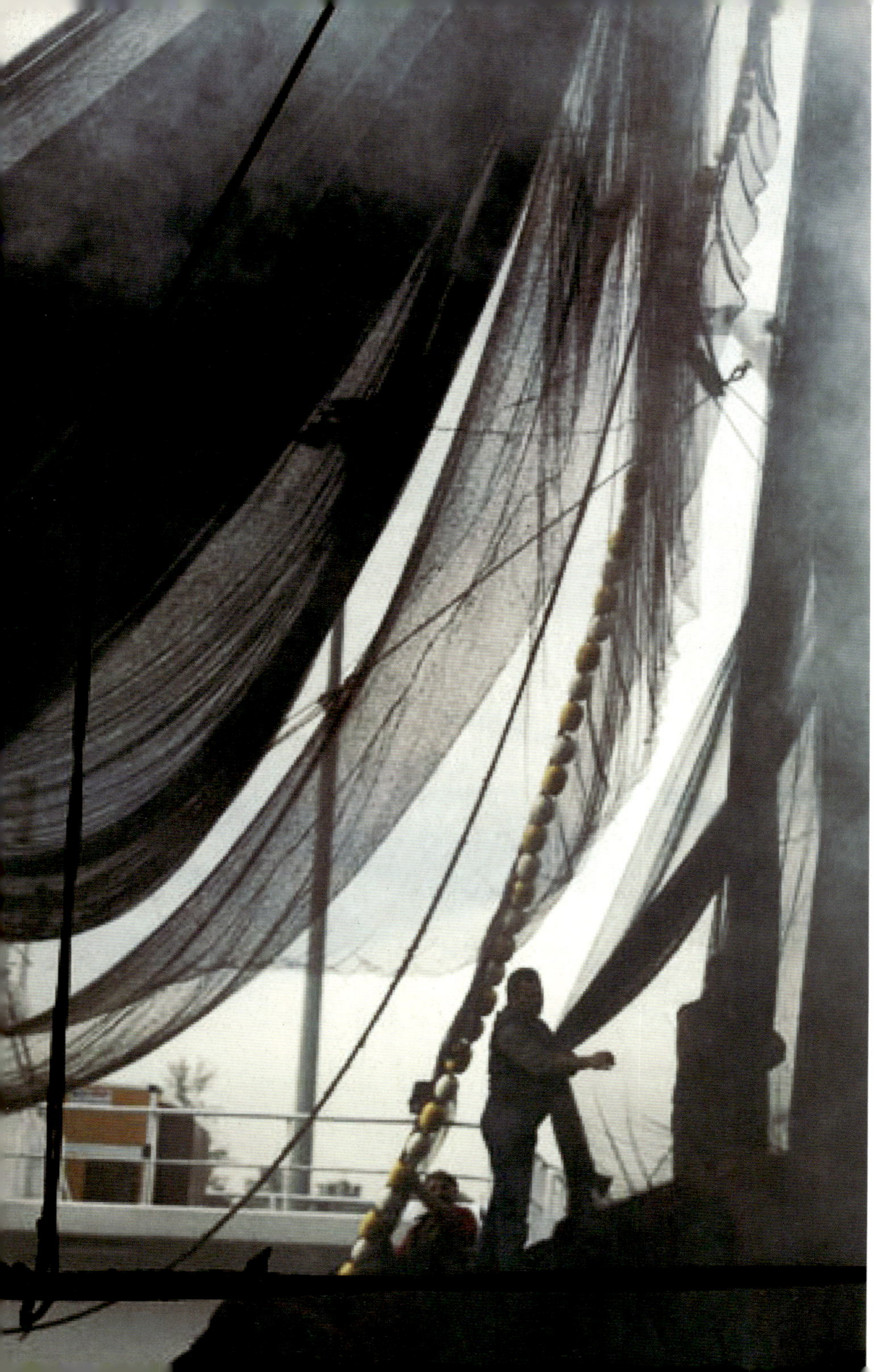

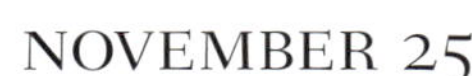

NOVEMBER 25

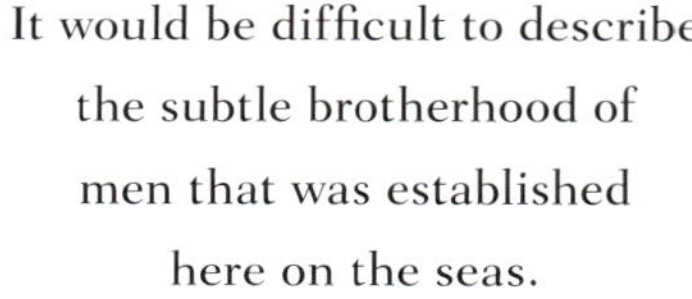

It would be difficult to describe
the subtle brotherhood of
men that was established
here on the seas.

Stephen Crane,
from "The Open Boat," 1897

NOVEMBER 26

Instead of tying,
Seamen always say,
"Make Fast!"

Captain John Smith,
from *A Sea Grammar,* 1627

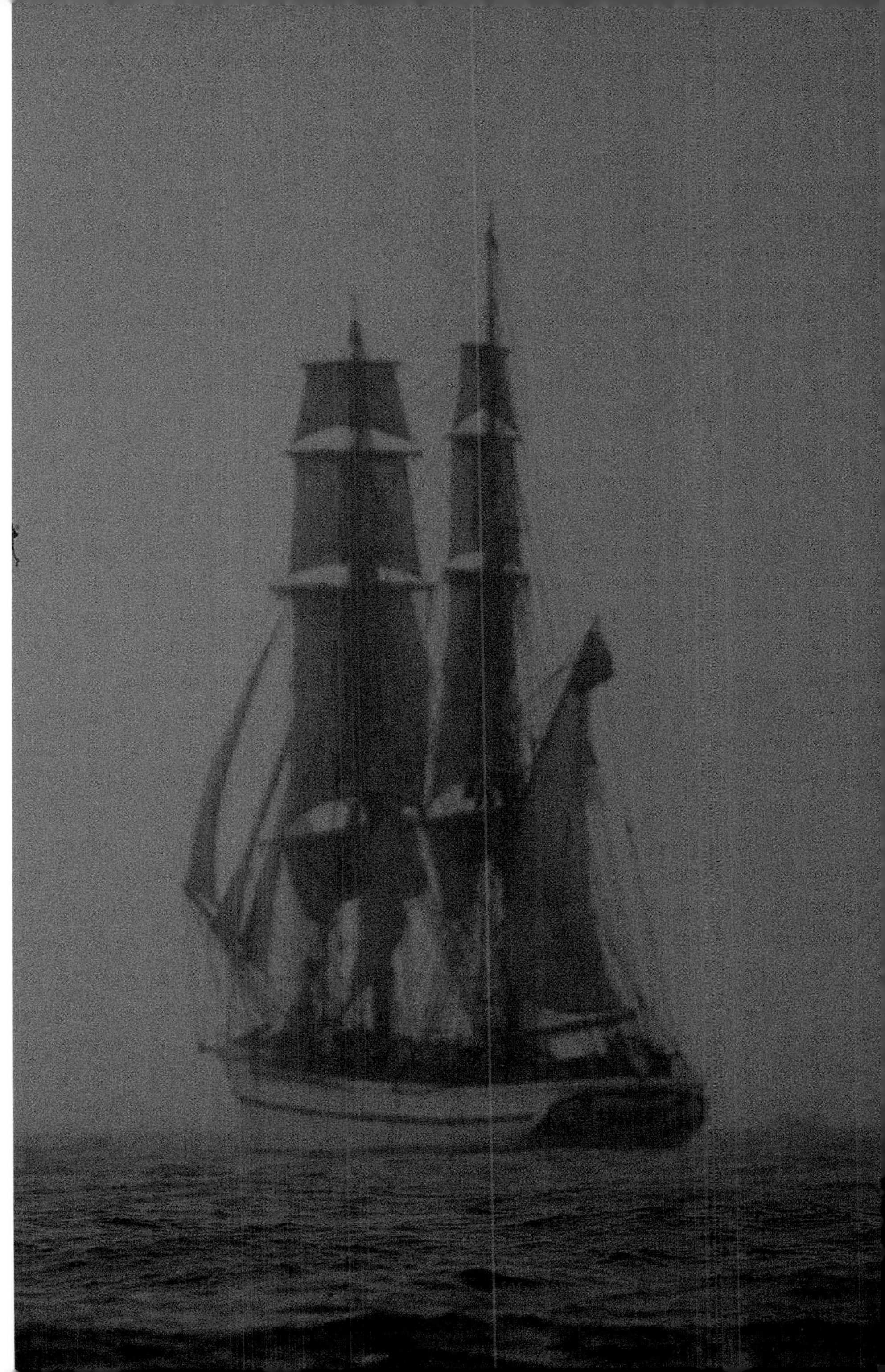

NOVEMBER 27

Cease, rude Boreas, blustering railer!
List, ye landsmen all, to me;
Messmates, hear a brother sailor
Sing the dangers of the sea.

George A. Stevens,
from *The Storm,* 1772

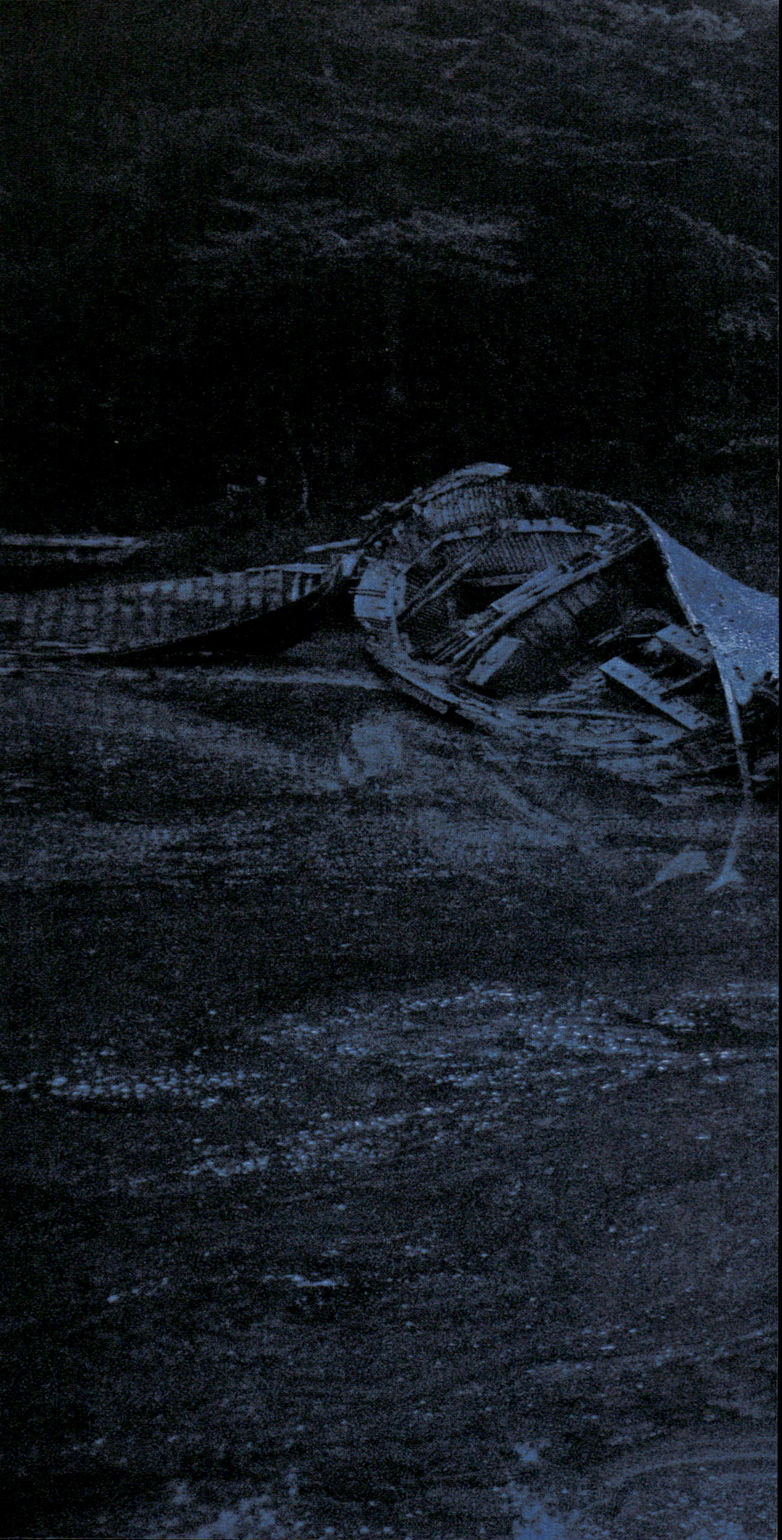

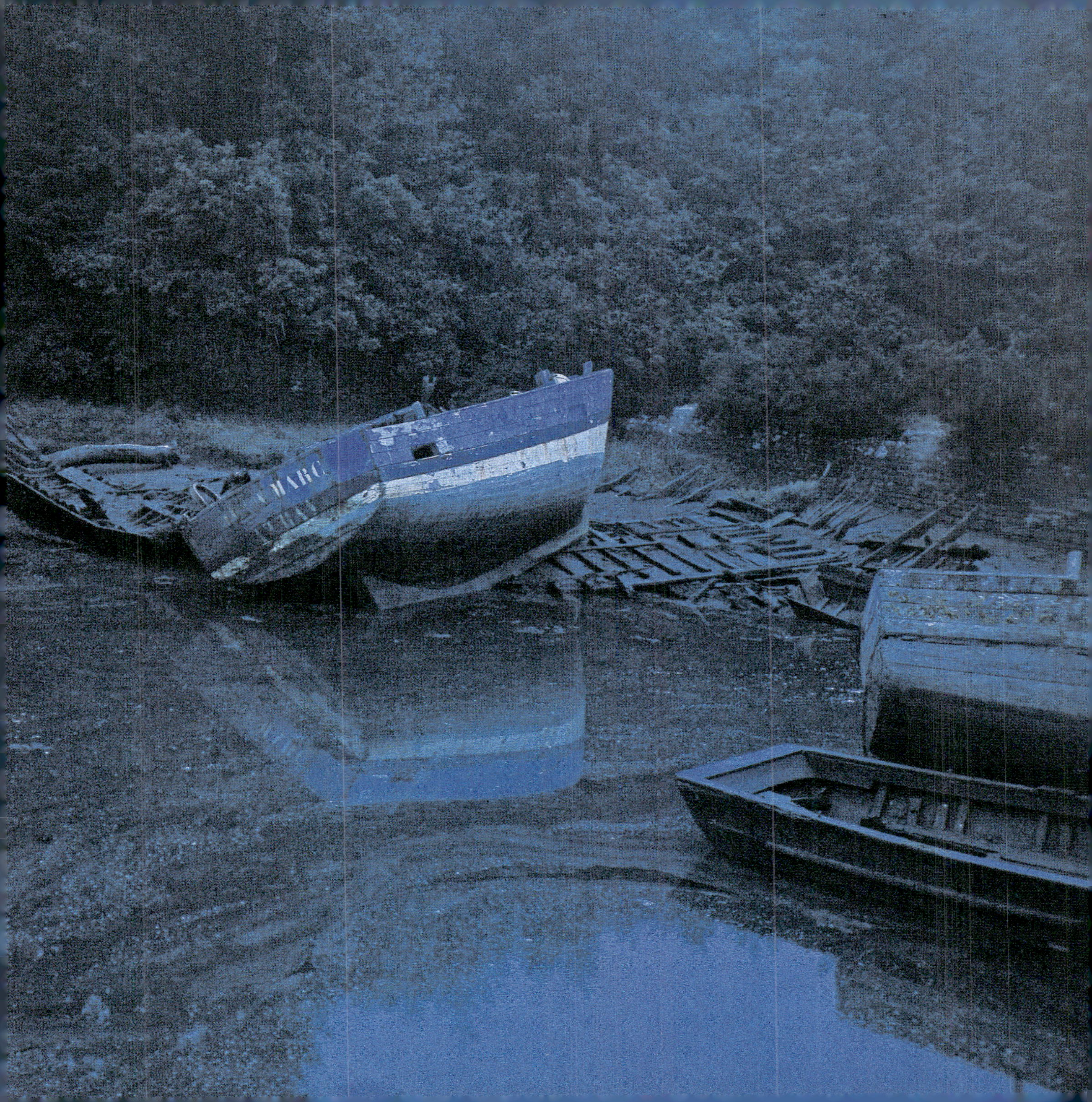
MARC

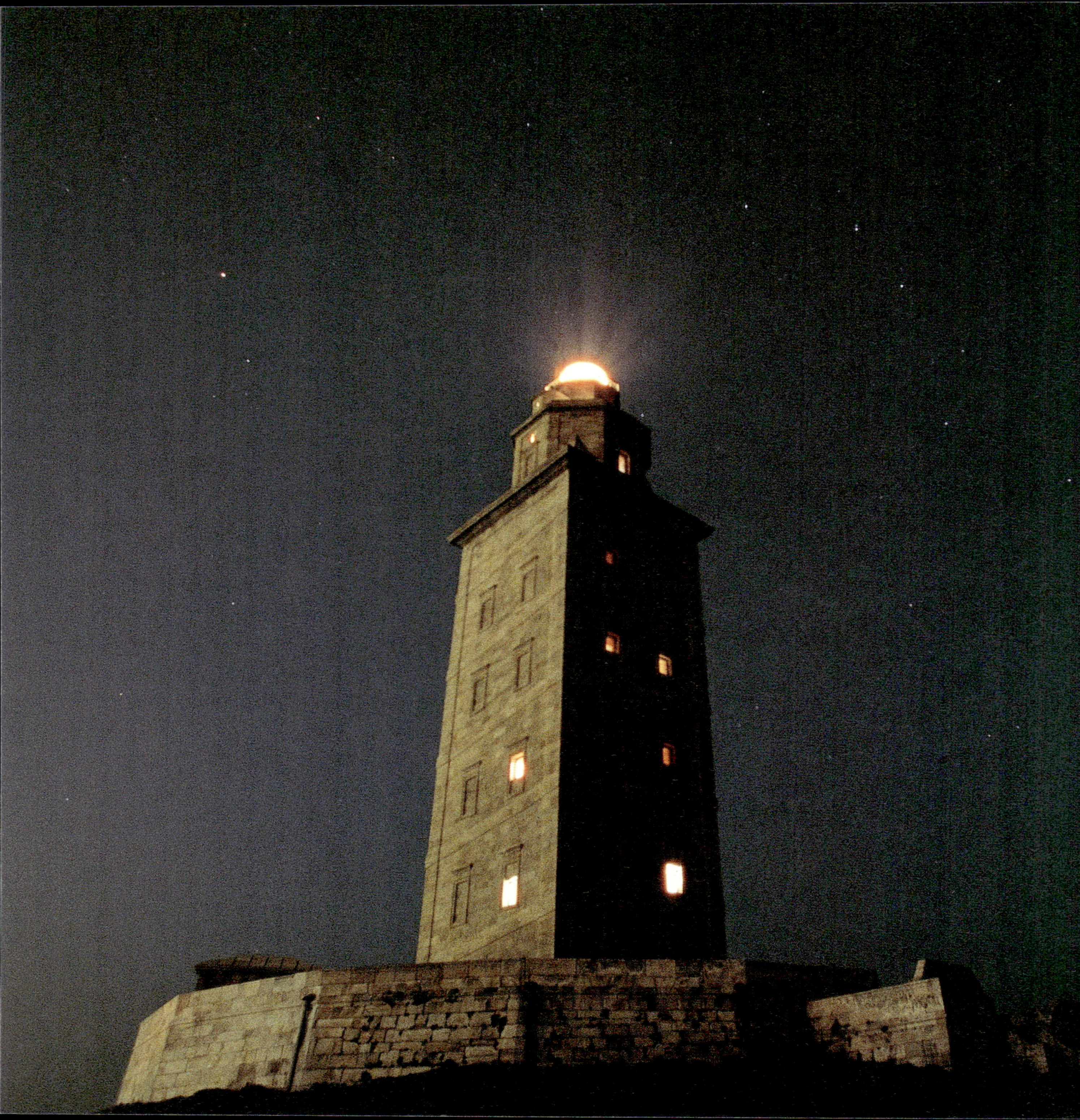

NOVEMBER 28

A compass can go wrong, the start never.

English proverb

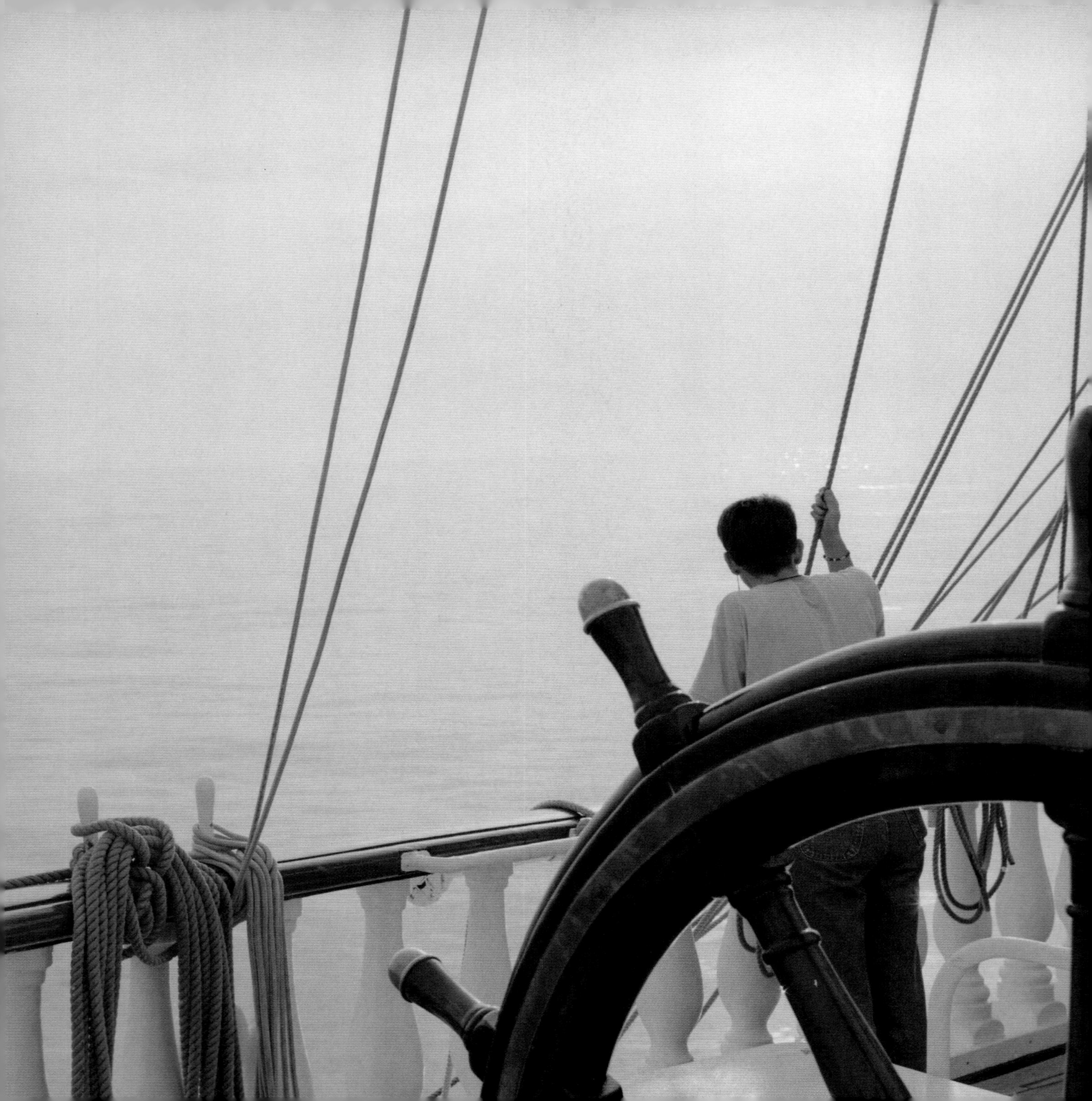

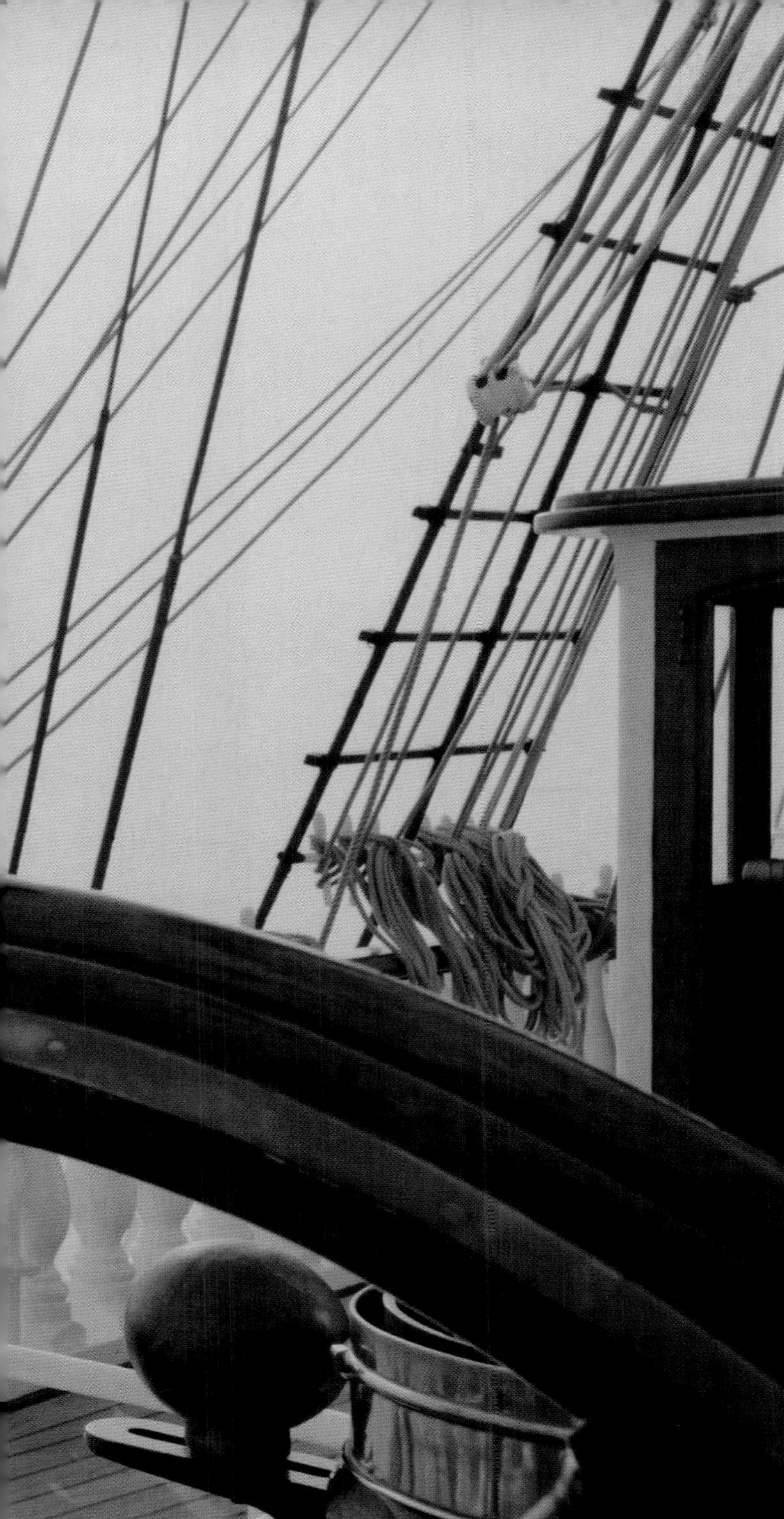

NOVEMBER 29

The mariner of old said to Neptune in a great tempest, "O God! thou mayest save me if thou wilt, and if thou wilt thou mayest destroy me; but whether or no, I will steer my rudder true."

Montaigne,
from *Of Glory*

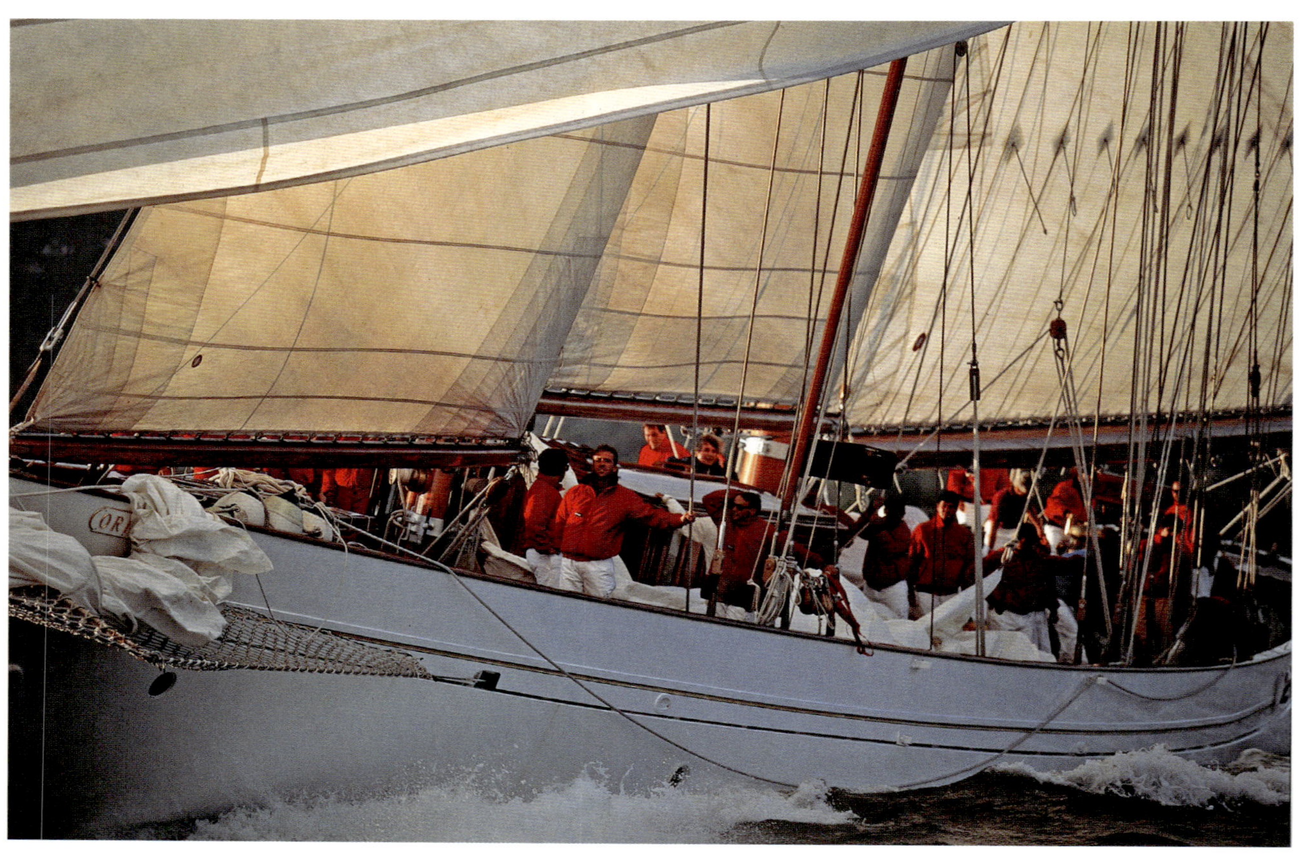

She starts—she moves—she seems to feel
The thrill of life along her keel.

Henry Wadsworth Longfellow, from "The Building of the Ship," *The Seaside and the Fireside,* 1849

DECEMBER 1

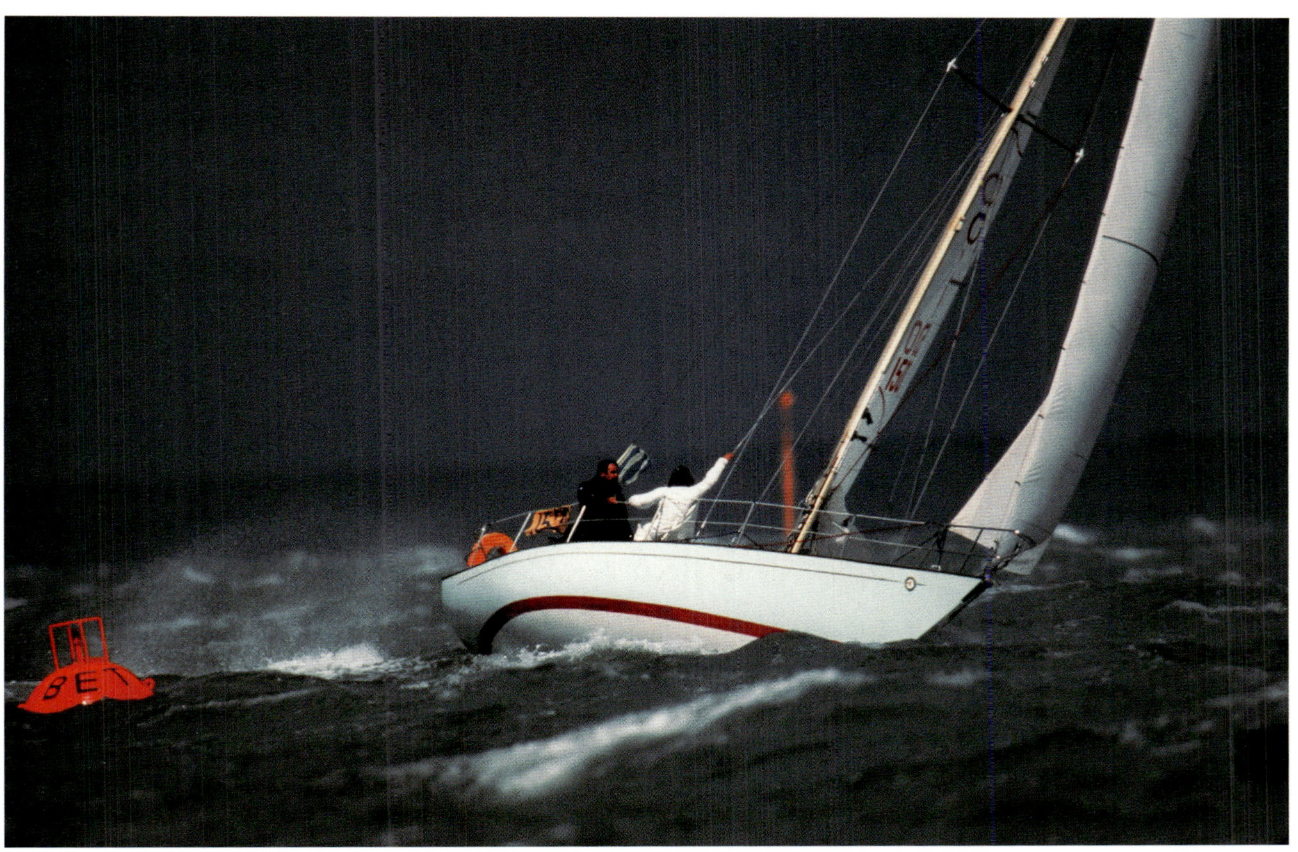

For who are so free as the sons of waves?

David Garrick, "Heart of Oak," 1759

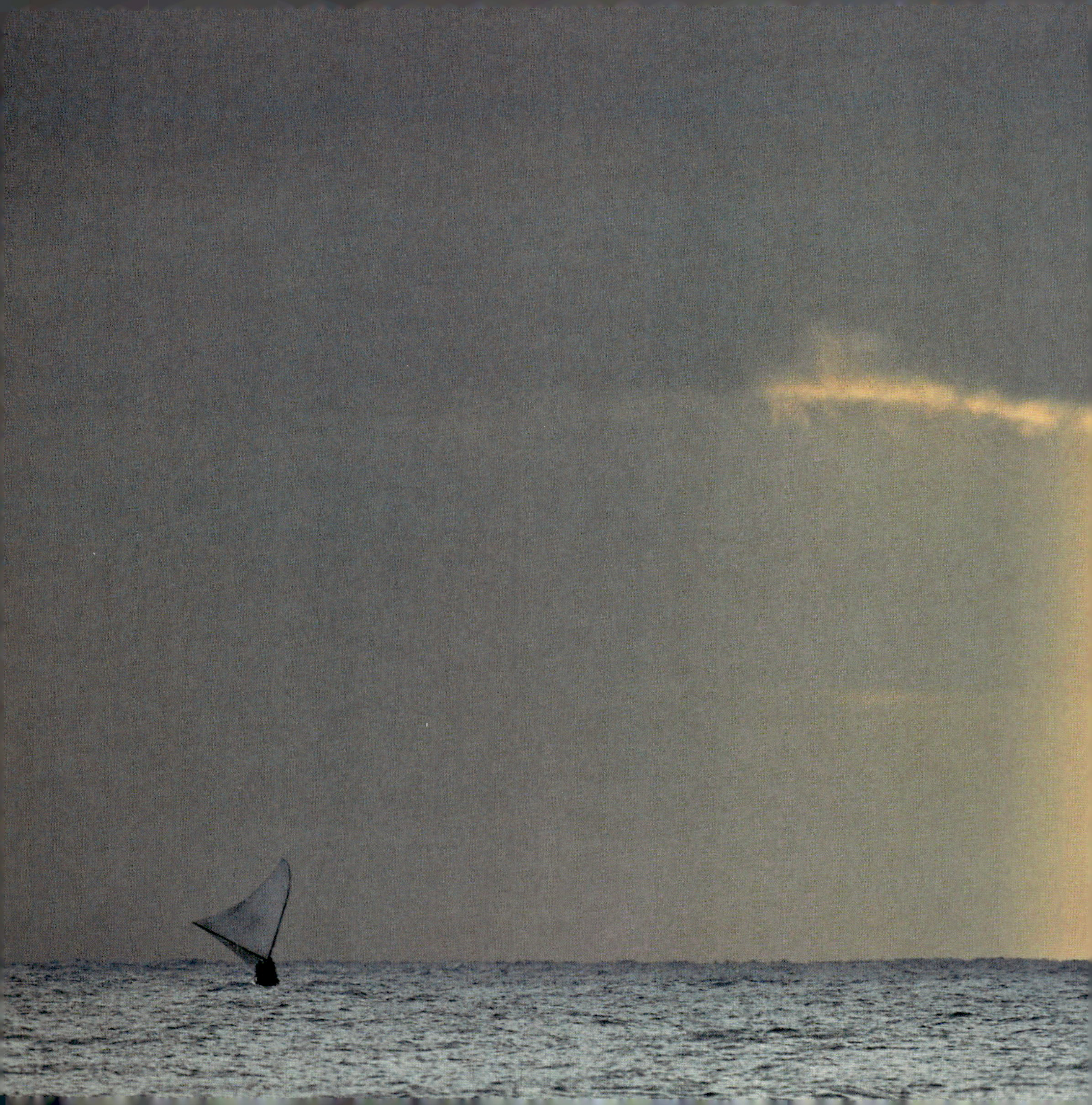

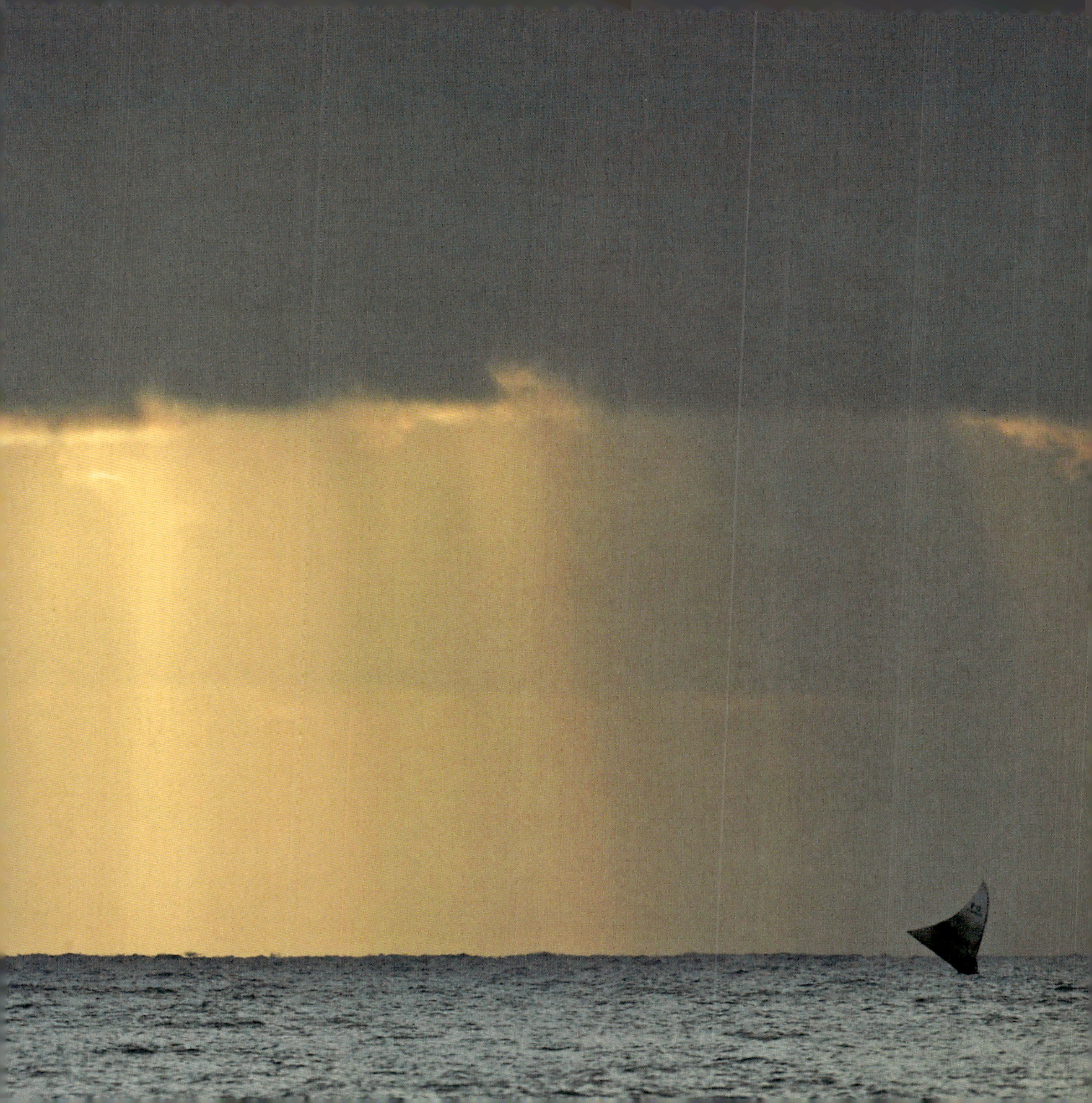

DECEMBER 2

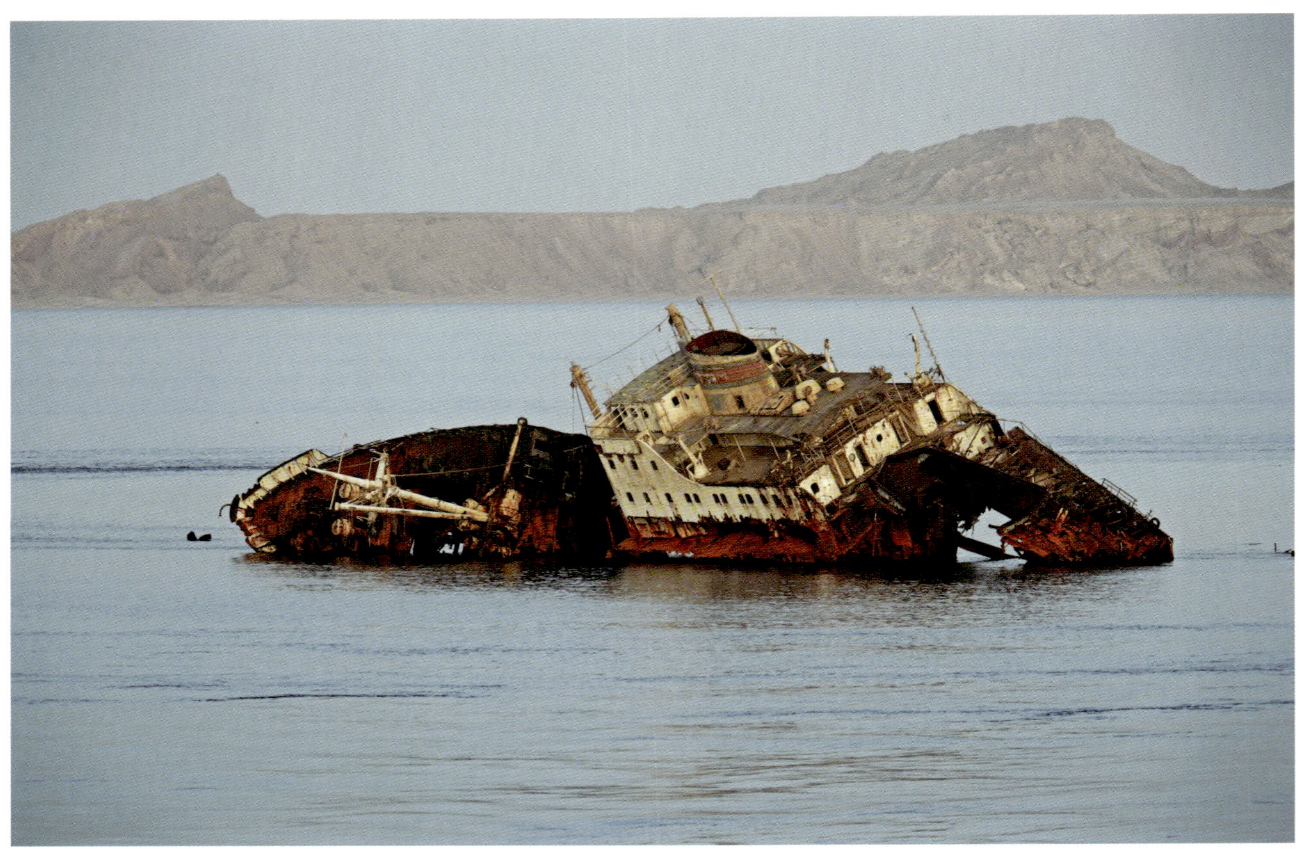

After the ship has sunk, everyone knows how she might have been saved.

Italian proverb

DECEMBER 3

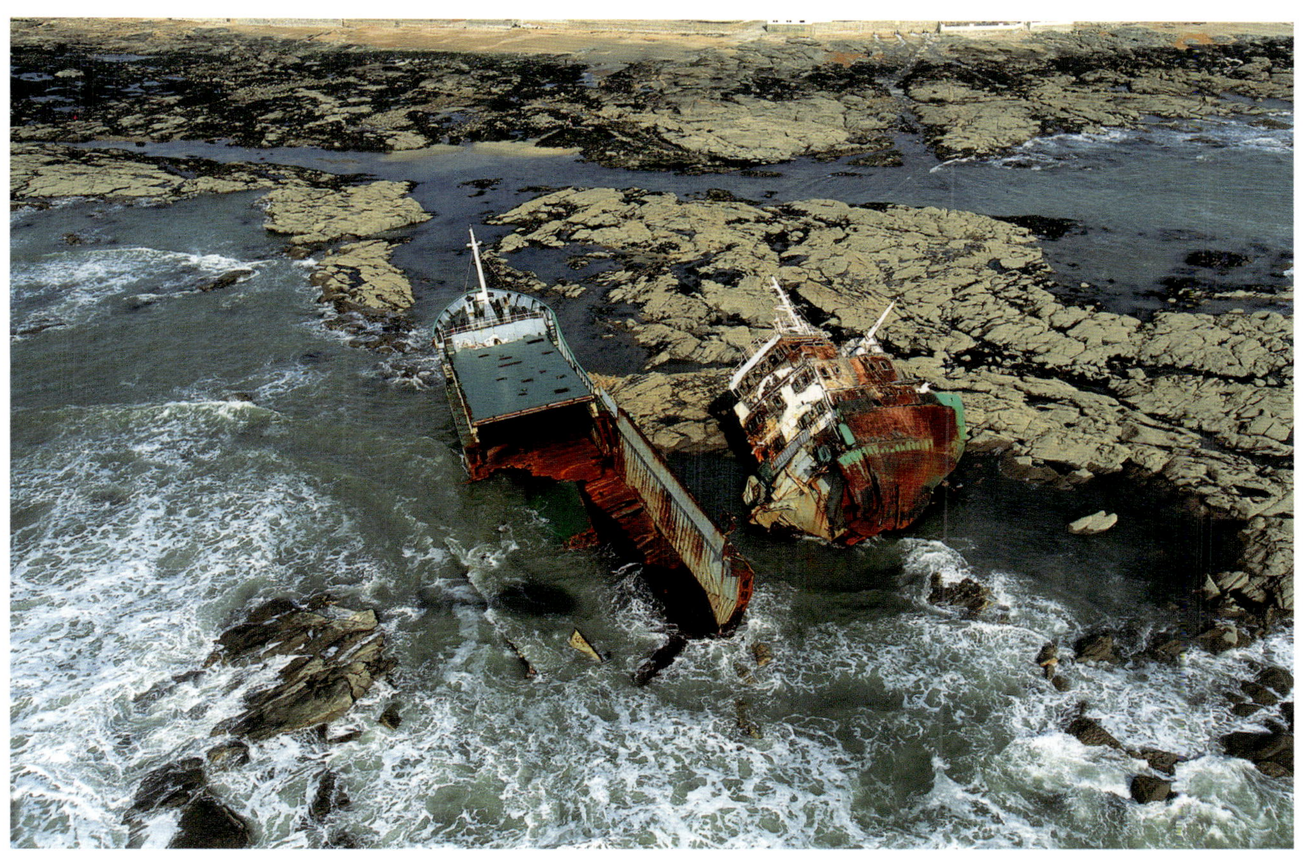

I have seen the hungry ocean gain
Advantage on the kingdom of the shore.

William Shakespeare, from Sonnet LXIV

DECEMBER 4

Singing blow ye winds in the morning,
Blow ye winds high ho!
Clear away your running gear,
And blow me bully boys, blow!

English chantey,
"Blow Ye Winds"

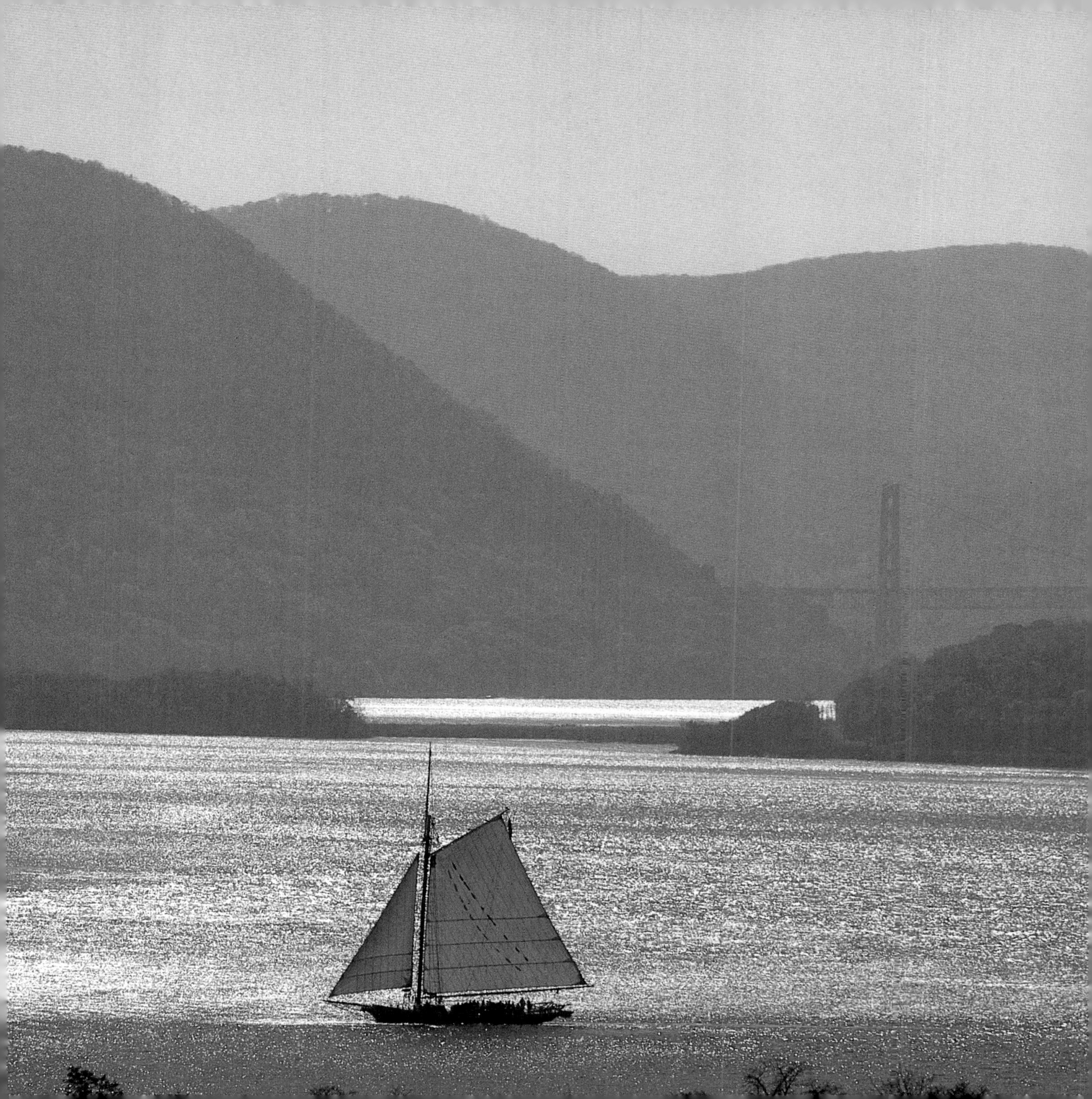

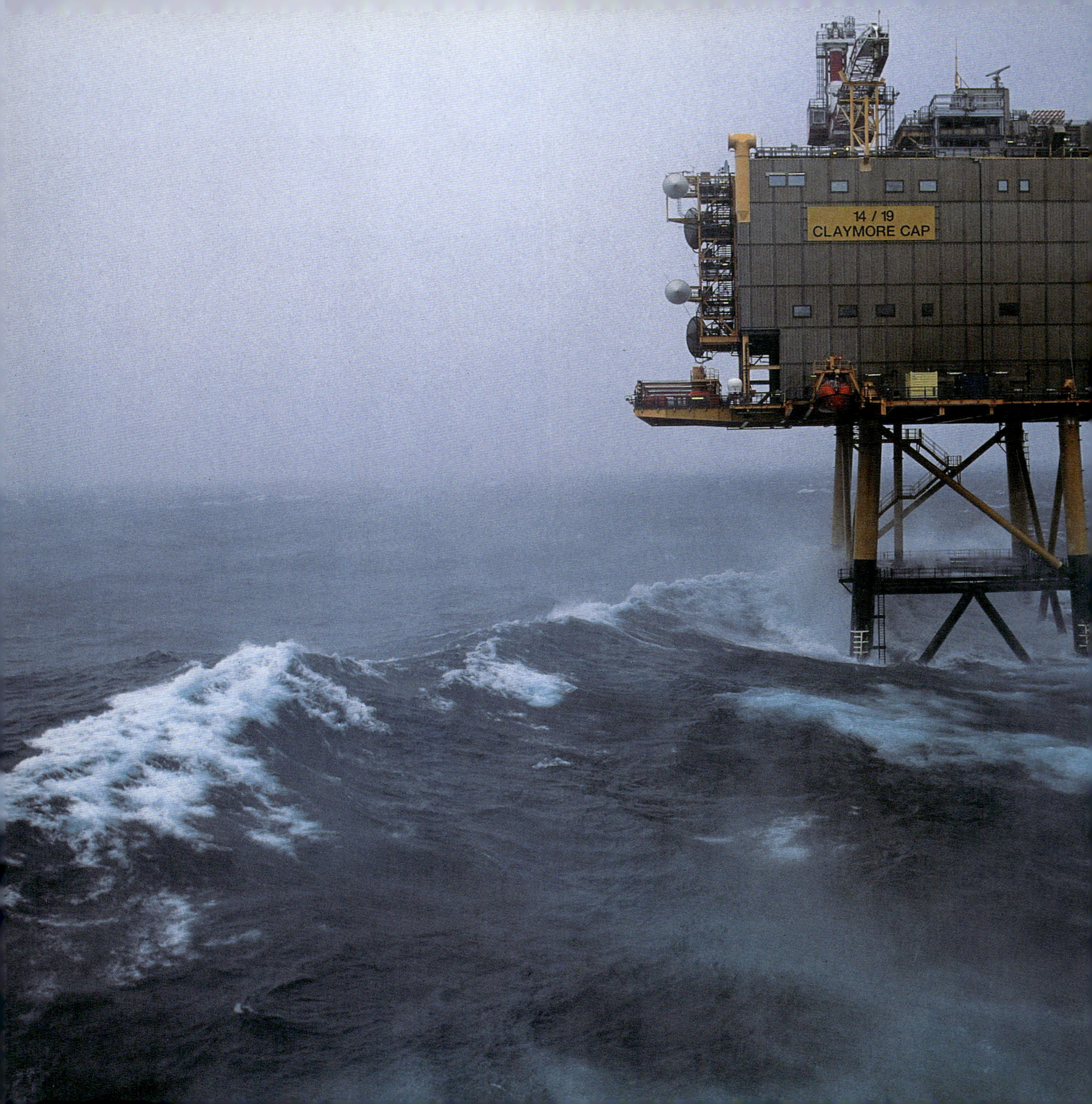
14 / 19
CLAYMORE CAP

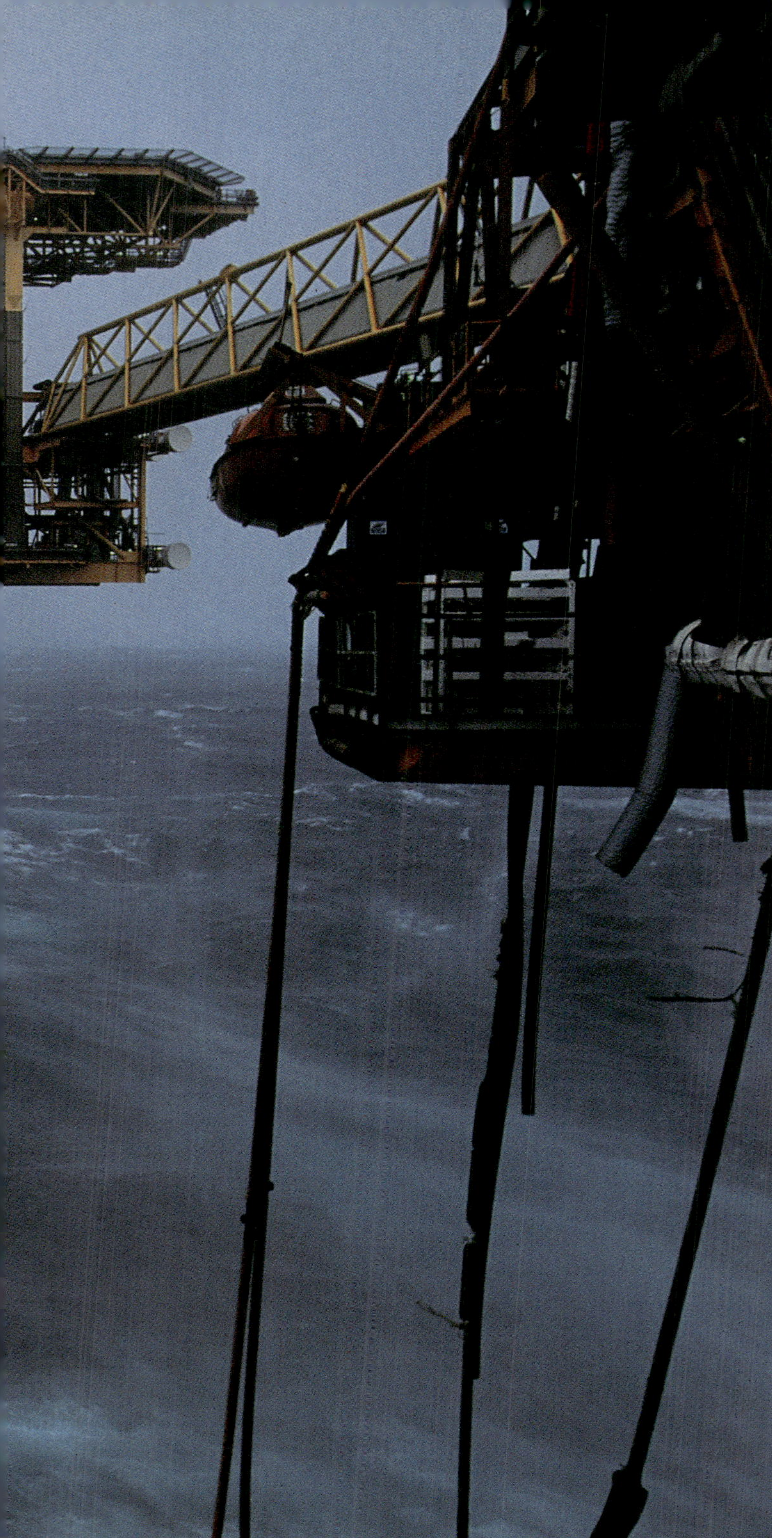

DECEMBER 5

Impenetrable and heartless, the sea
has given nothing of itself to the
suitors for its precarious favors.

Joseph Conrad,
from *The Mirror of the Sea*, 1906

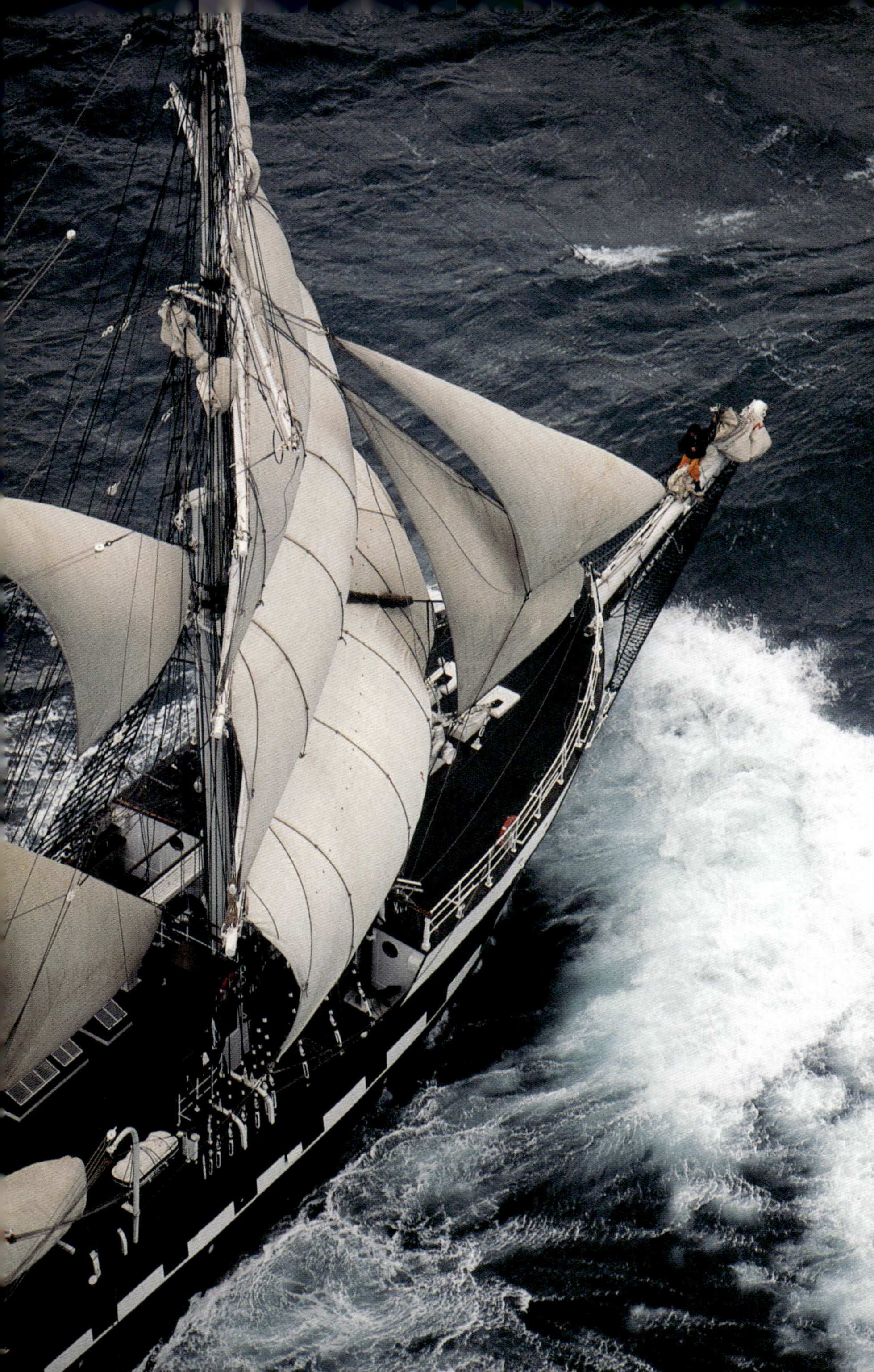

DECEMBER 6

The wonder is always new that
any sane man can be a sailor.

Ralph Waldo Emerson,
from *English Traits,* 1856

DECEMBER 7

The sea is the great disturber.
Nothing human can endure for
long unchanged in its presence.

Filson Young

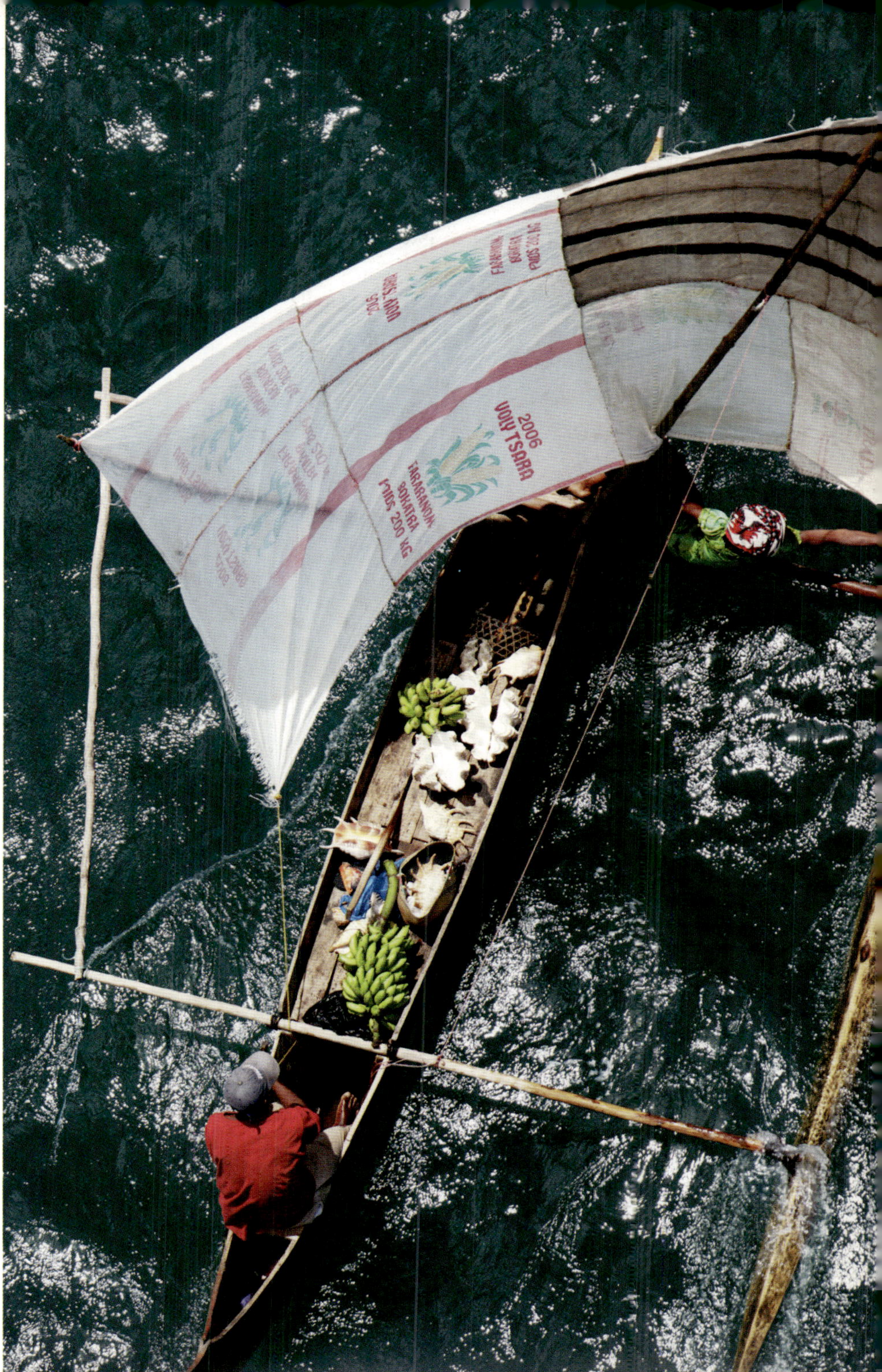

DECEMBER 8

The love that is given to ships is profoundly
different from the love men feel for
every other work of their hands.

Joseph Conrad,
from *The Mirror of the Sea,* 1906

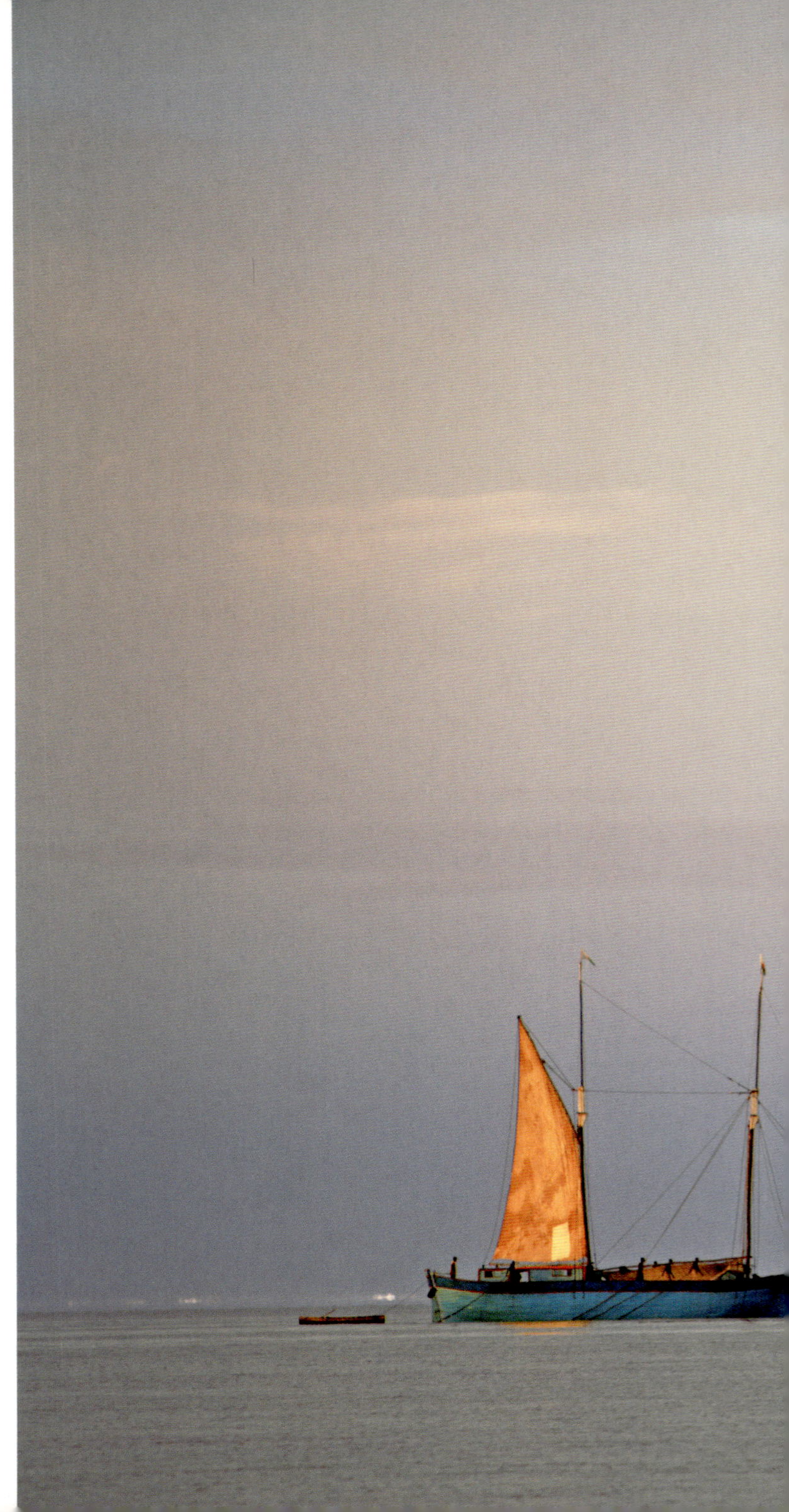

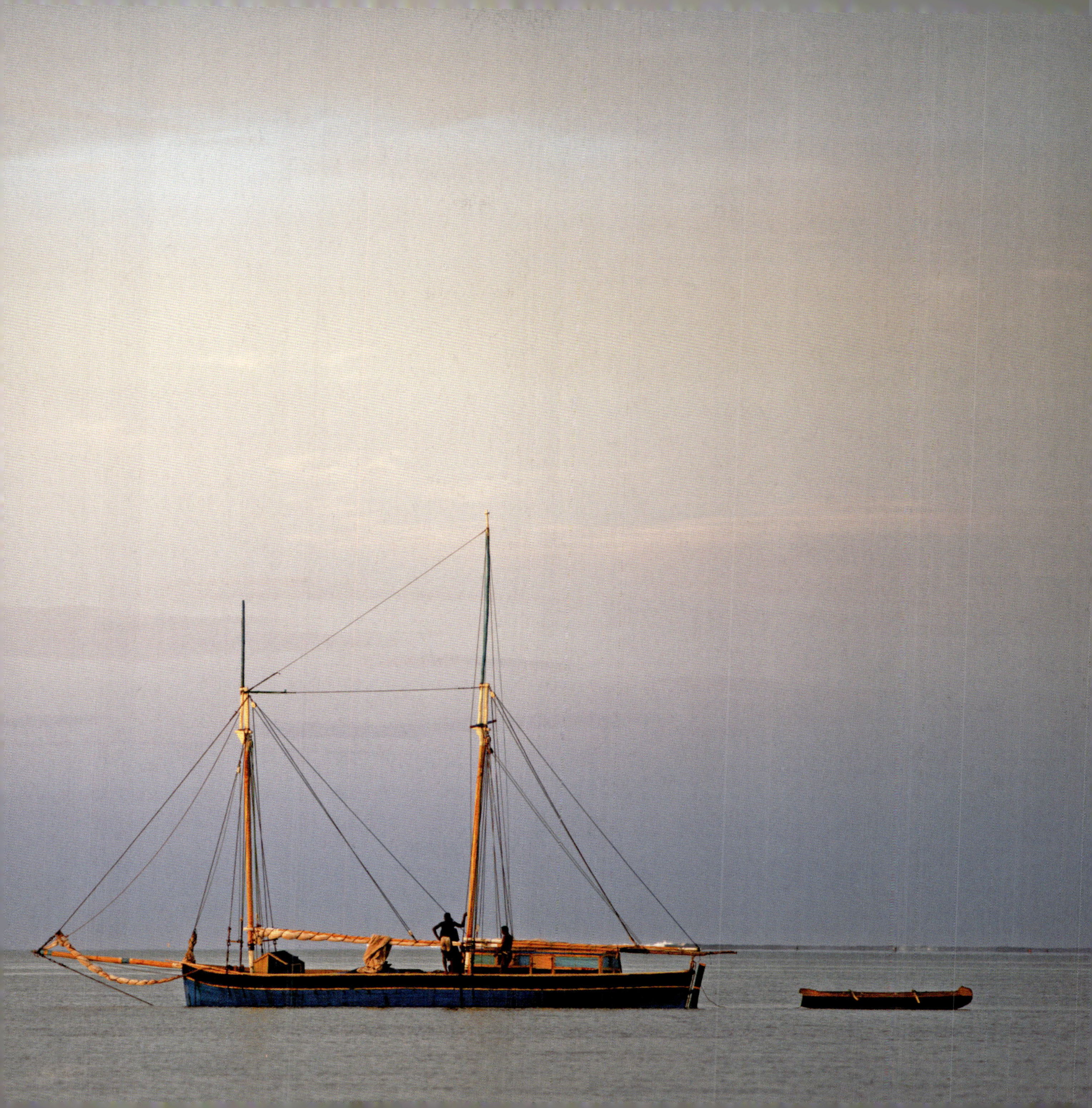

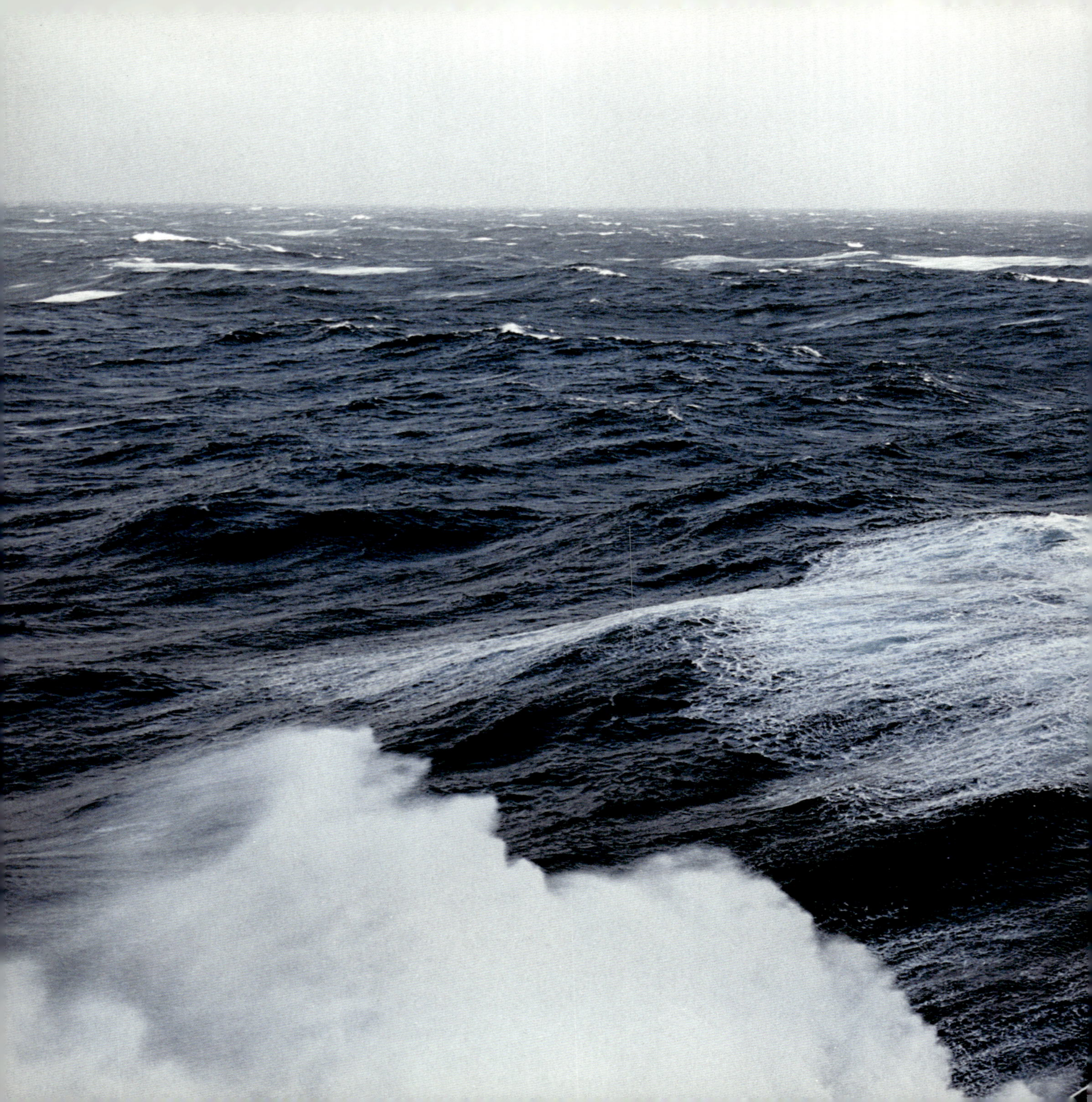

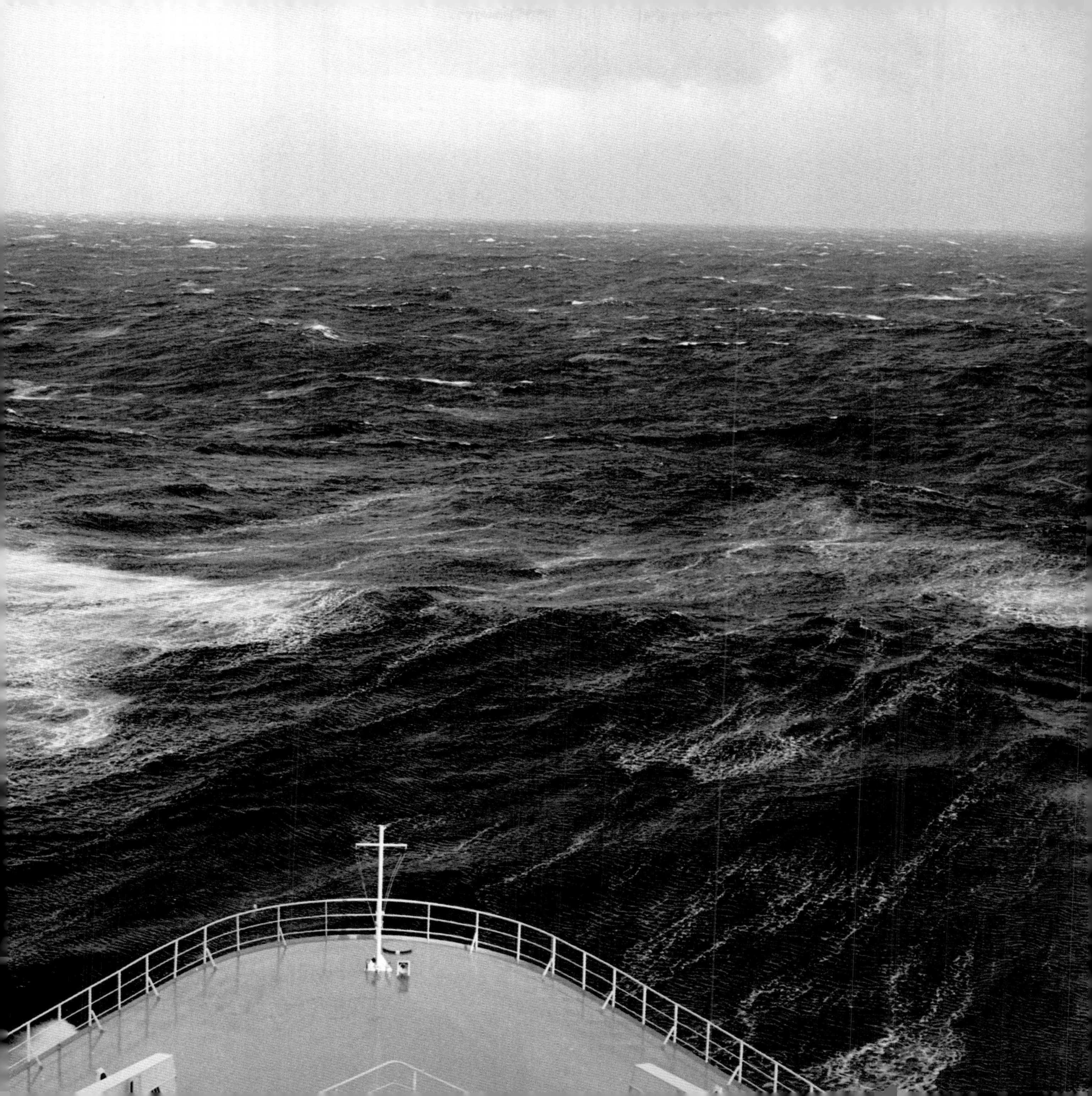

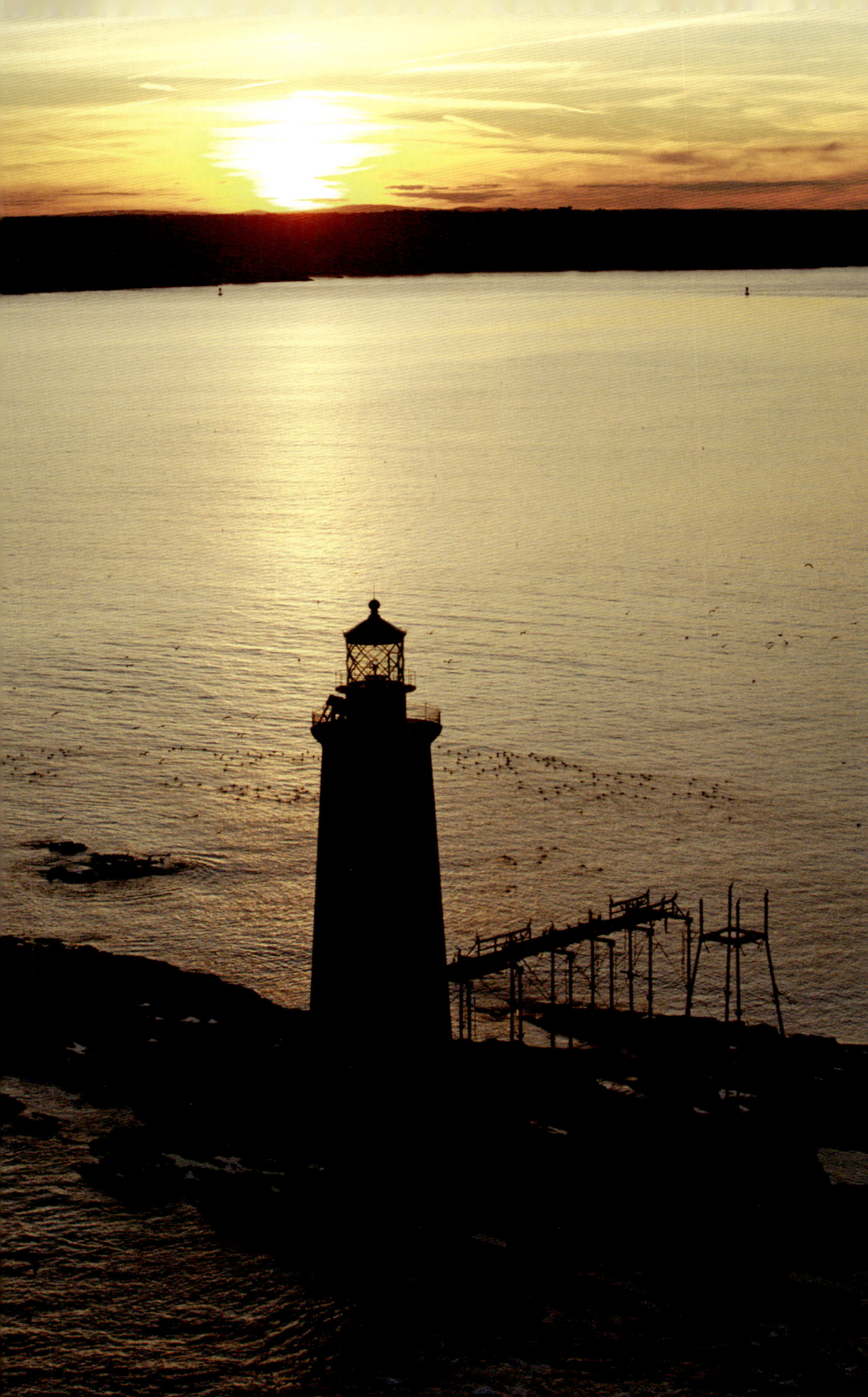

DECEMBER 9

How little do the landsmen know
Of what we sailors feel,
When the waves do mount and
winds do blow!
But we have hearts of steel!

From *The Sailor's Resolution*,
eighteenth century

DECEMBER 10

Nothing will compare with the early breaking of day upon the wide ocean.

Richard Henry Dana Jr.,
from *Two Years Before the Mast,* 1840

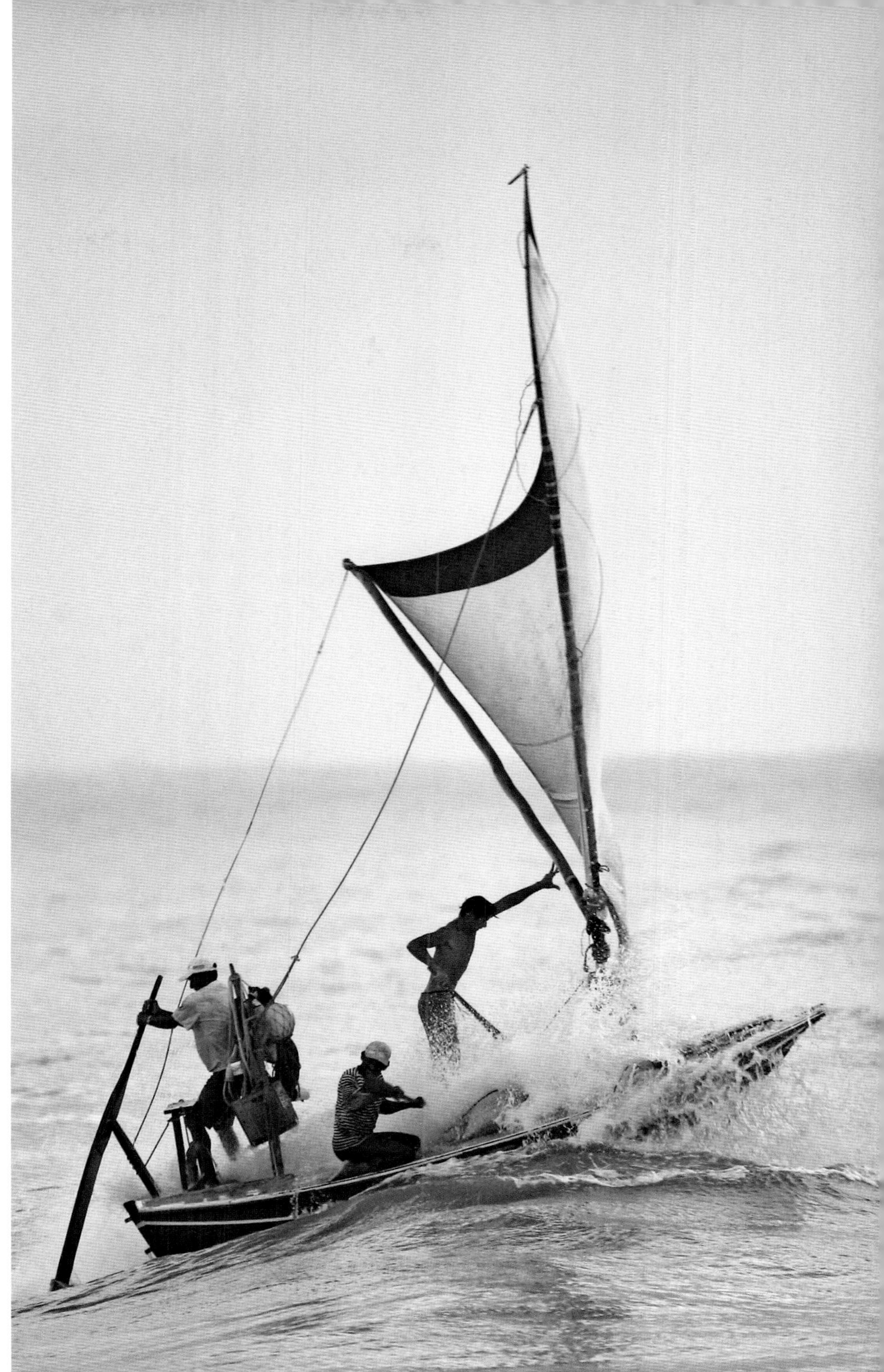

DECEMBER 11

The shine of sunlight on the violet sea,
the roar of cities when the sun goes down;
these stir our hearts with restless energy.

Charles Baudelaire,
from "The Voyage," *Les Fleurs du mal,* 1857

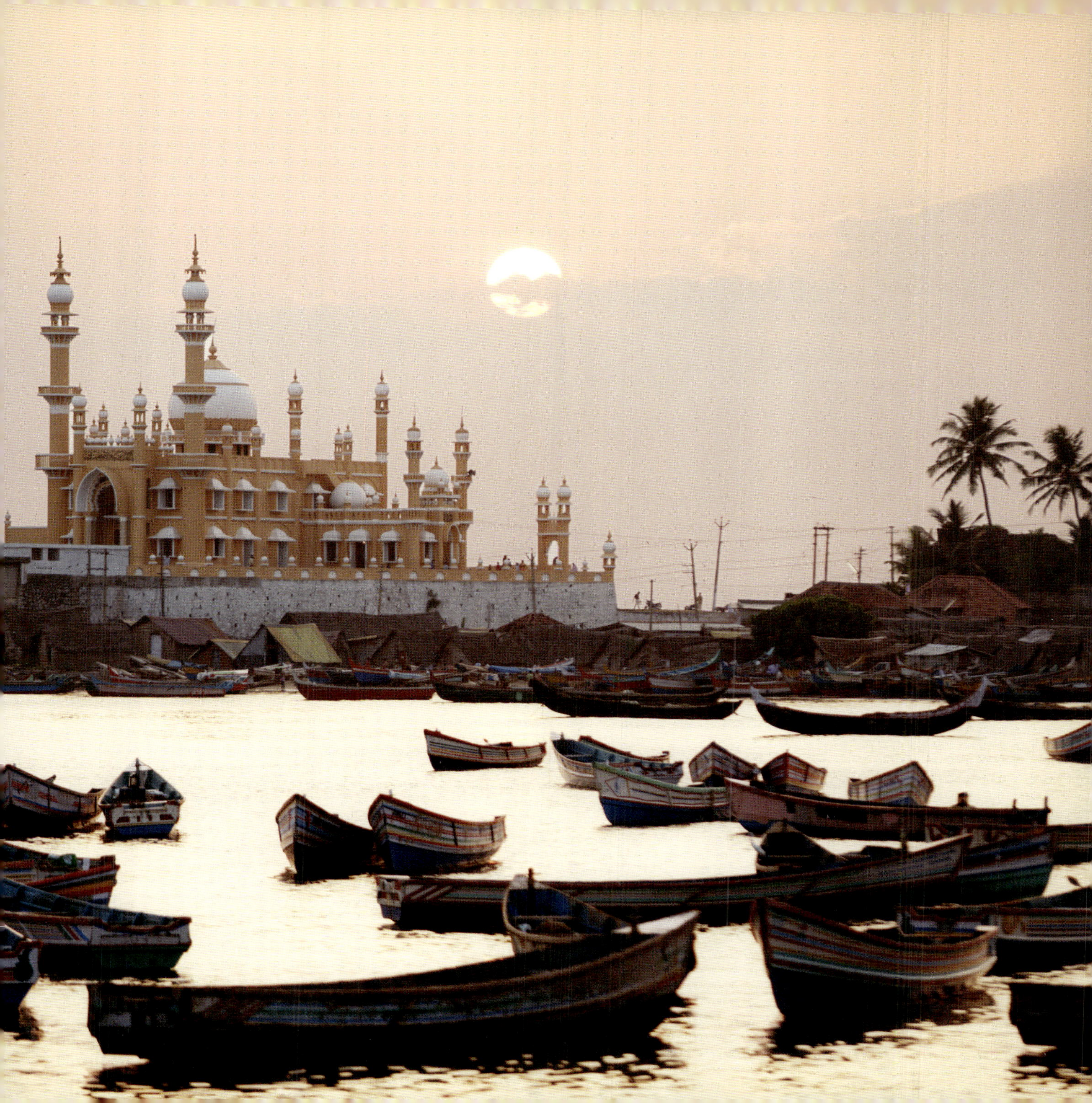

DECEMBER 12

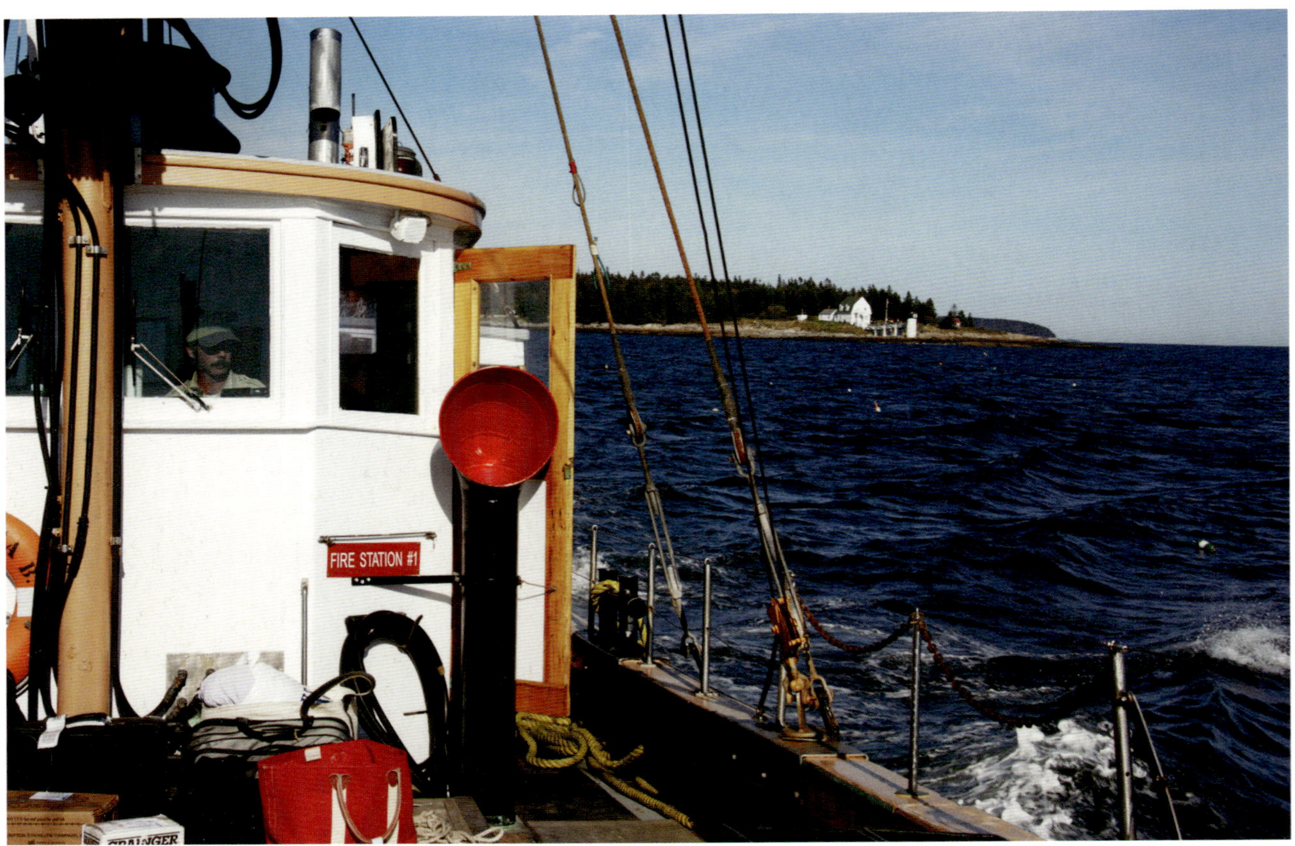

The water that a ship sails on is the same water that swallows it up.

Chinese proverb

DECEMBER 13

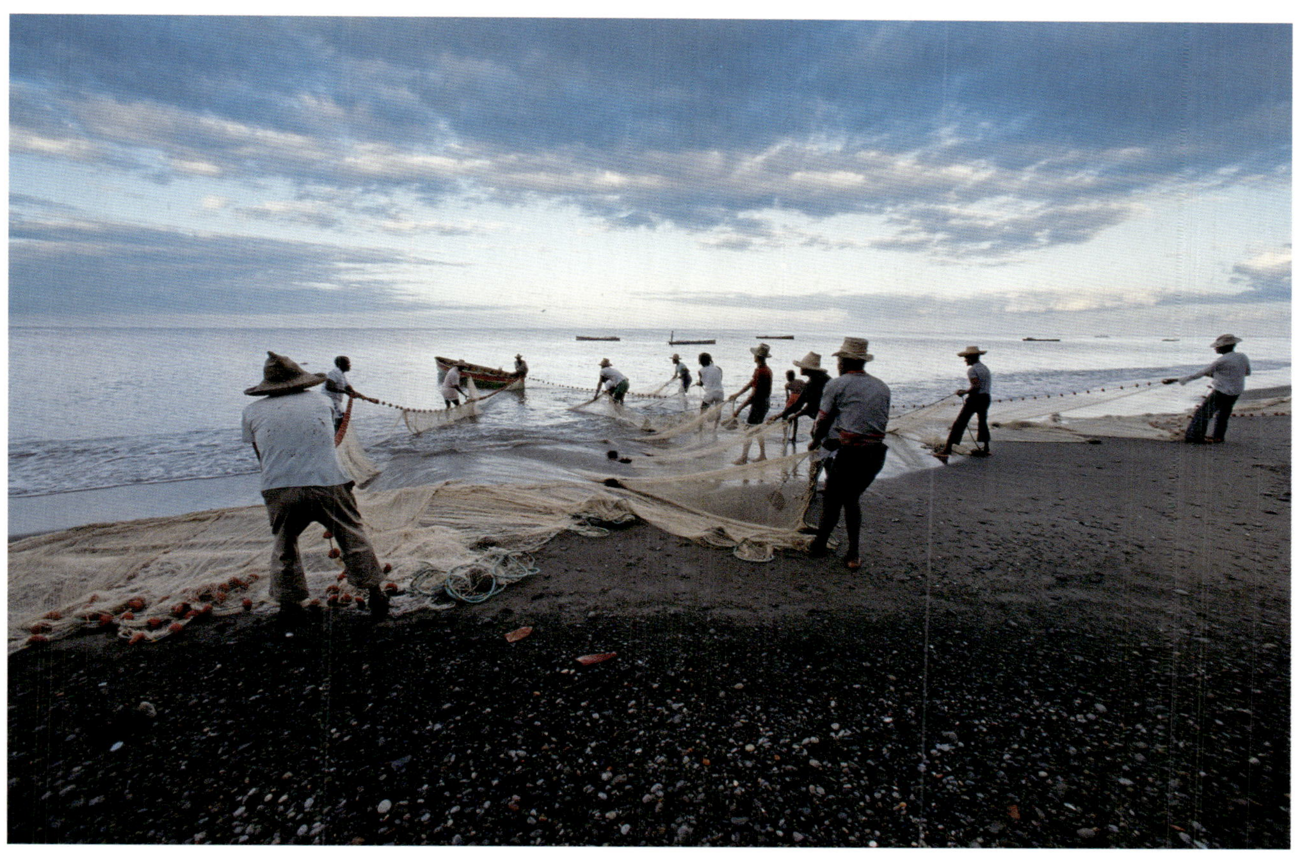

The sea language is not soon learned, much less understood.

Sir William Monson, from *Naval Tracts,* 1682

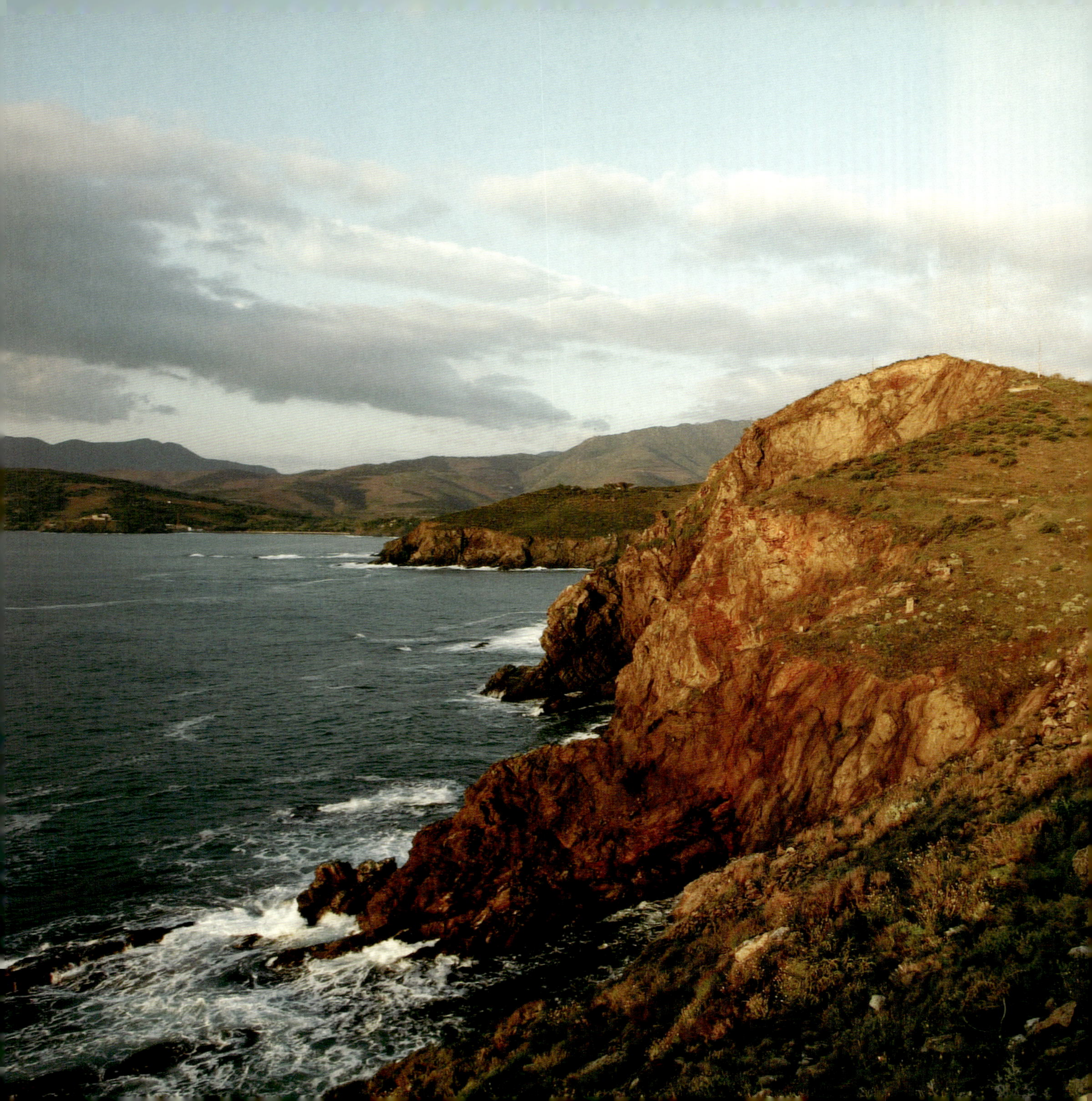

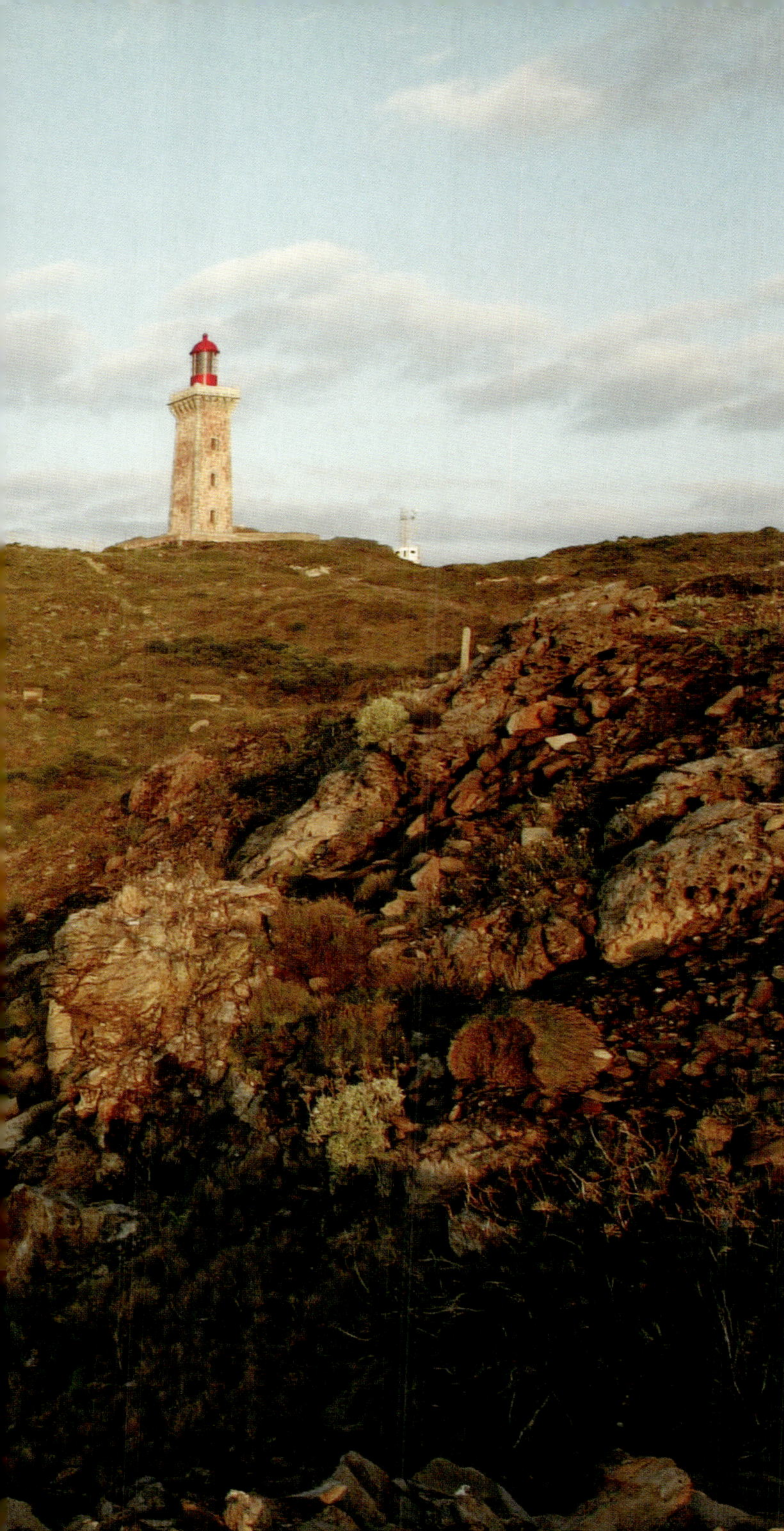

DECEMBER 14

Who won't be ruled by the rudder
must be ruled by the rock.

English proverb

DECEMBER 15

Now, little ship, look out! Beside you is the ocean: to be sure, it does not always roar... But hours will come when you realize that it is infinite and that there is nothing more awesome than infinity.

Friedrich Nietzsche,
from *The Gay Science,* 1882

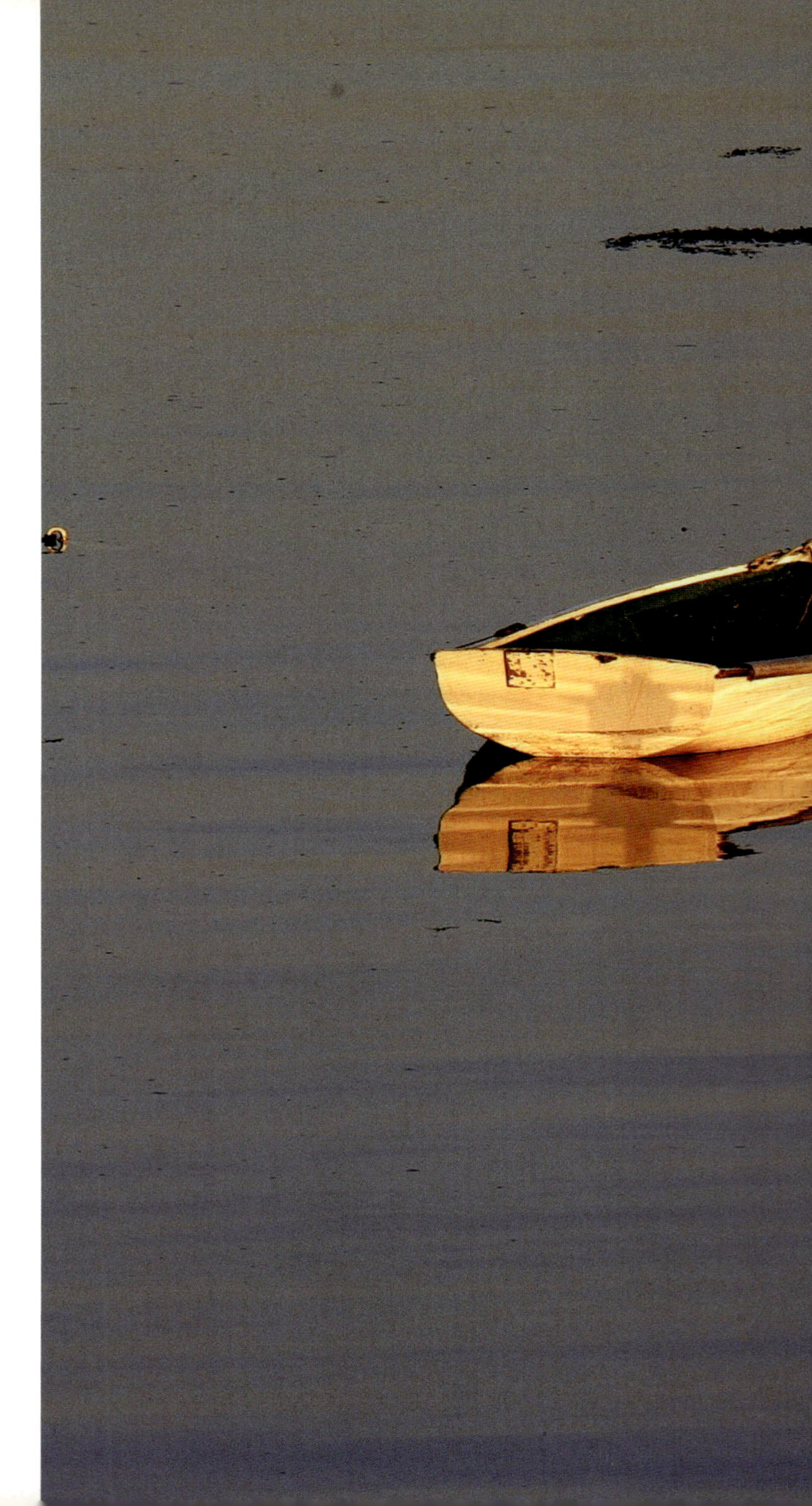

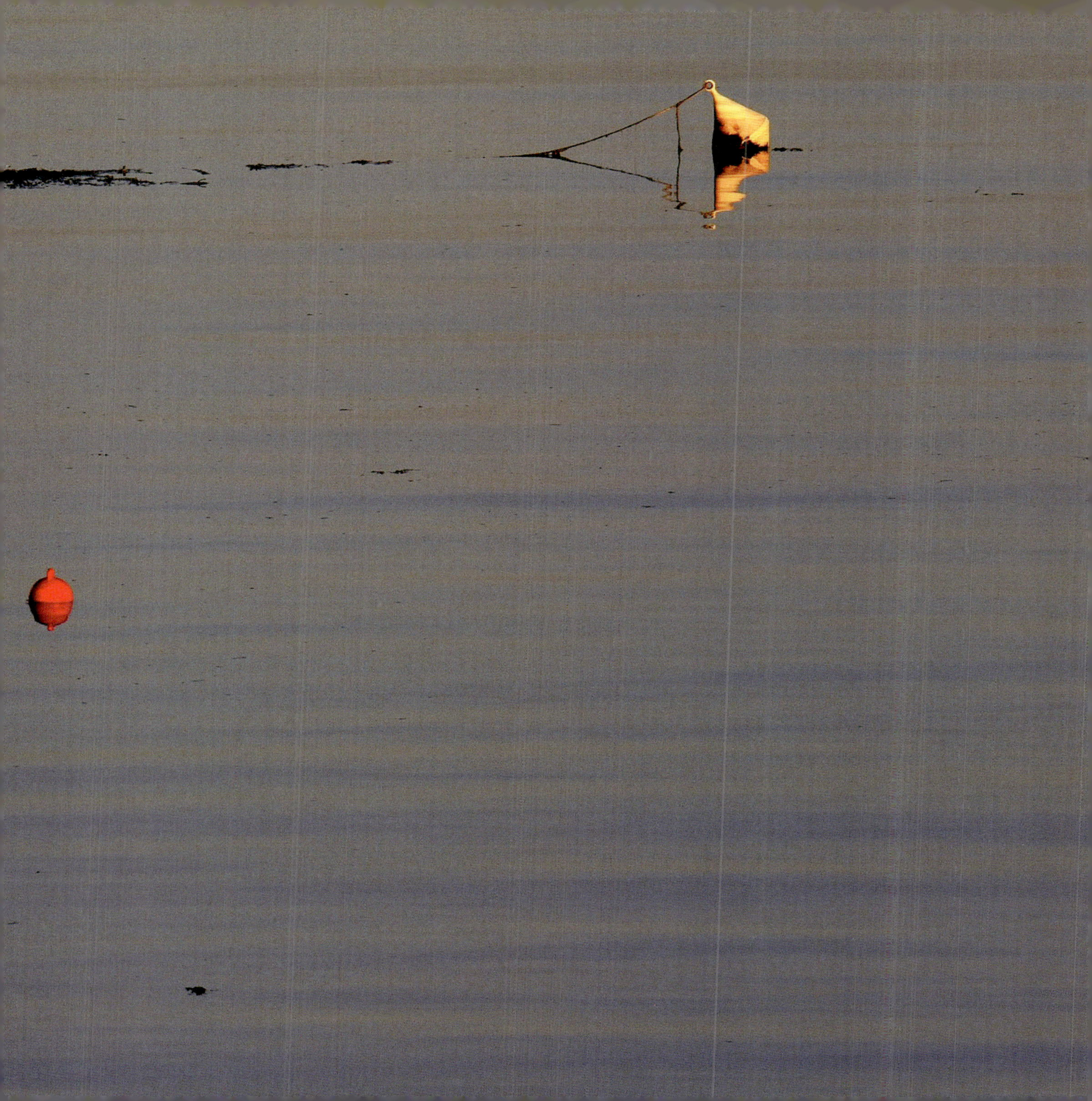

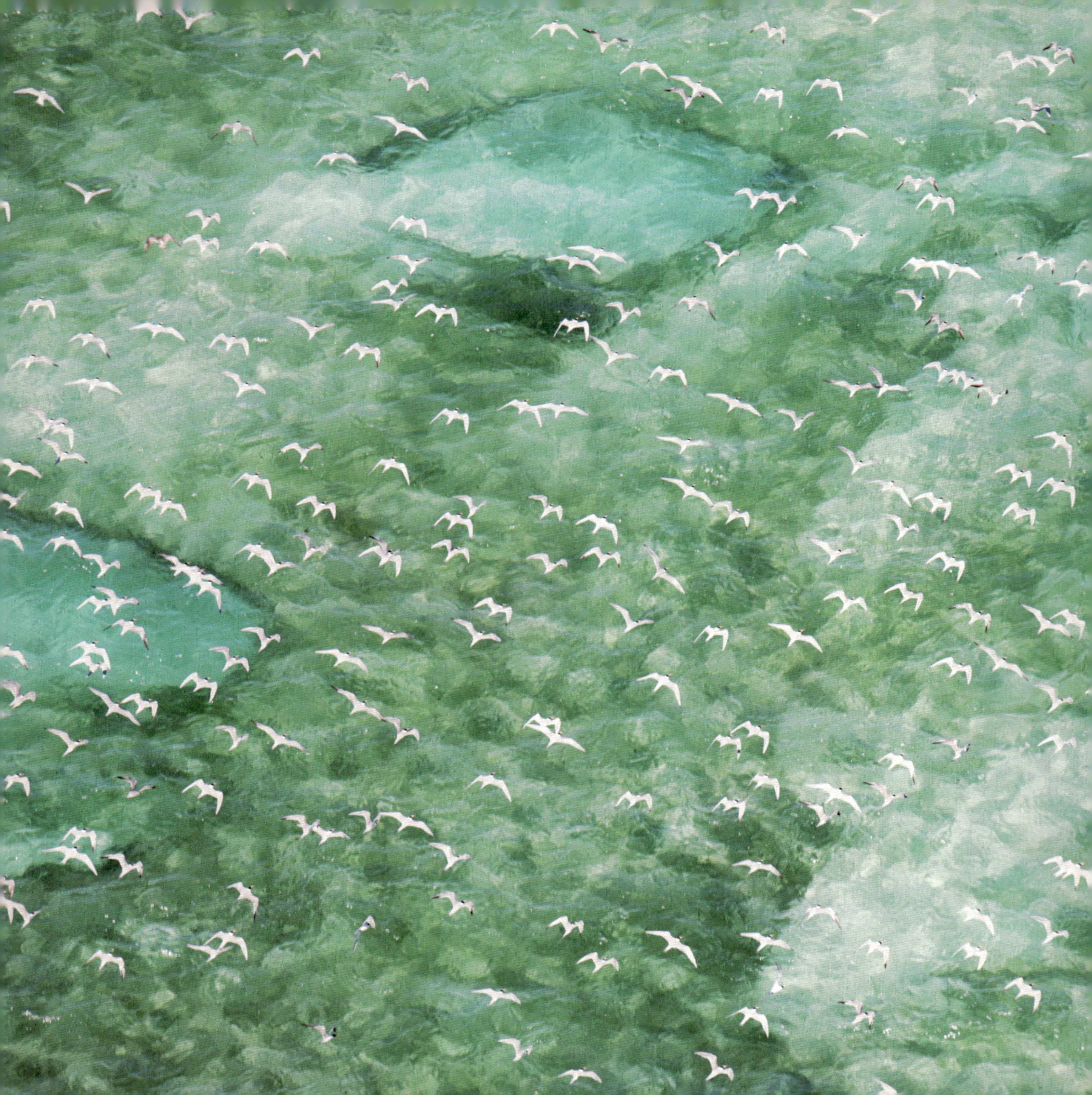

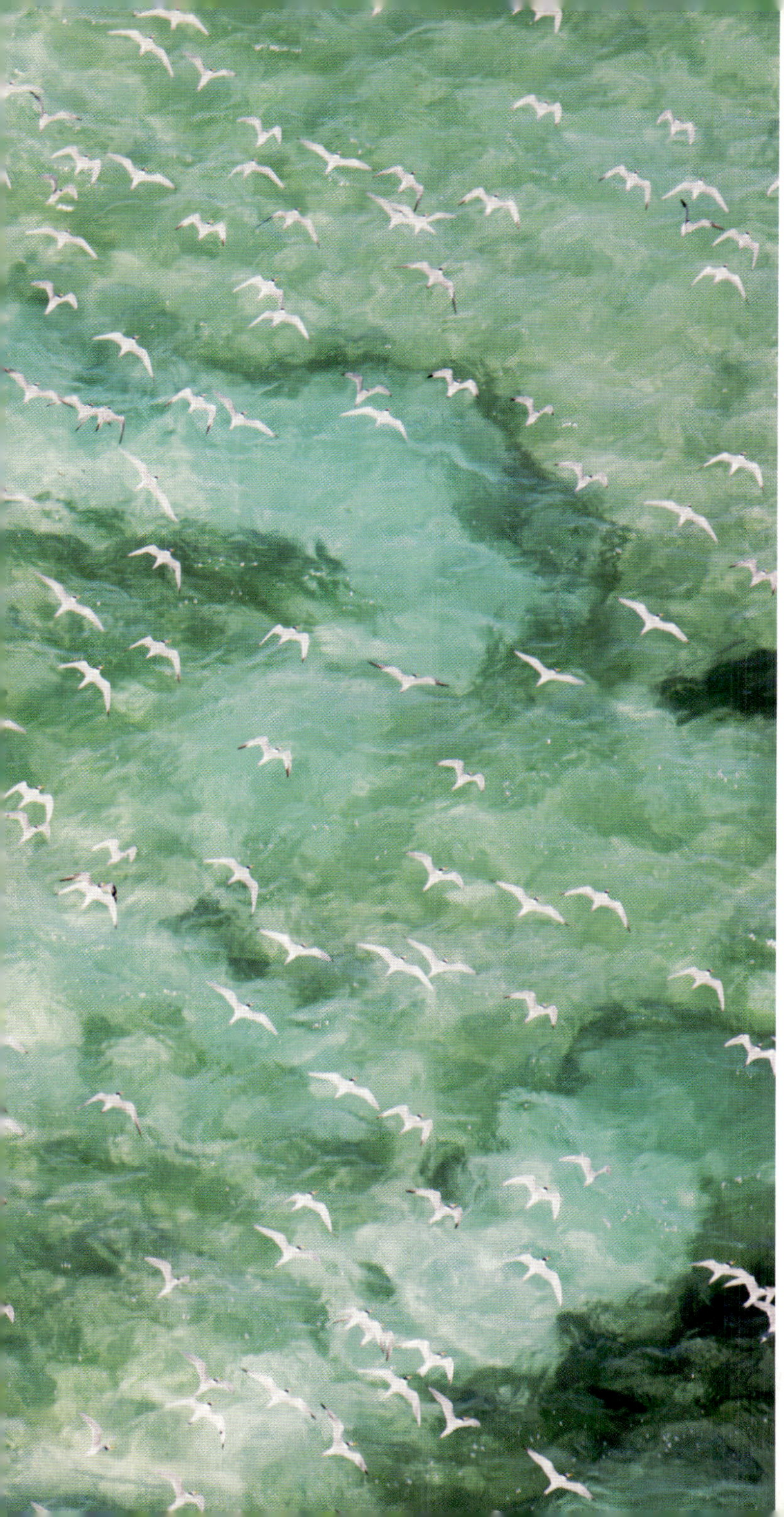

DECEMBER 16

On and on,
O white brother!
Thunder does not daunt thee!
How thou movest!
By thine impulse—
With no wing!
Fairest thing
The wide sea shows me!
On and on
O white brother!
Art thou gone!

Padraic Colum,
from "The Sea Bird to the Wave," 1914

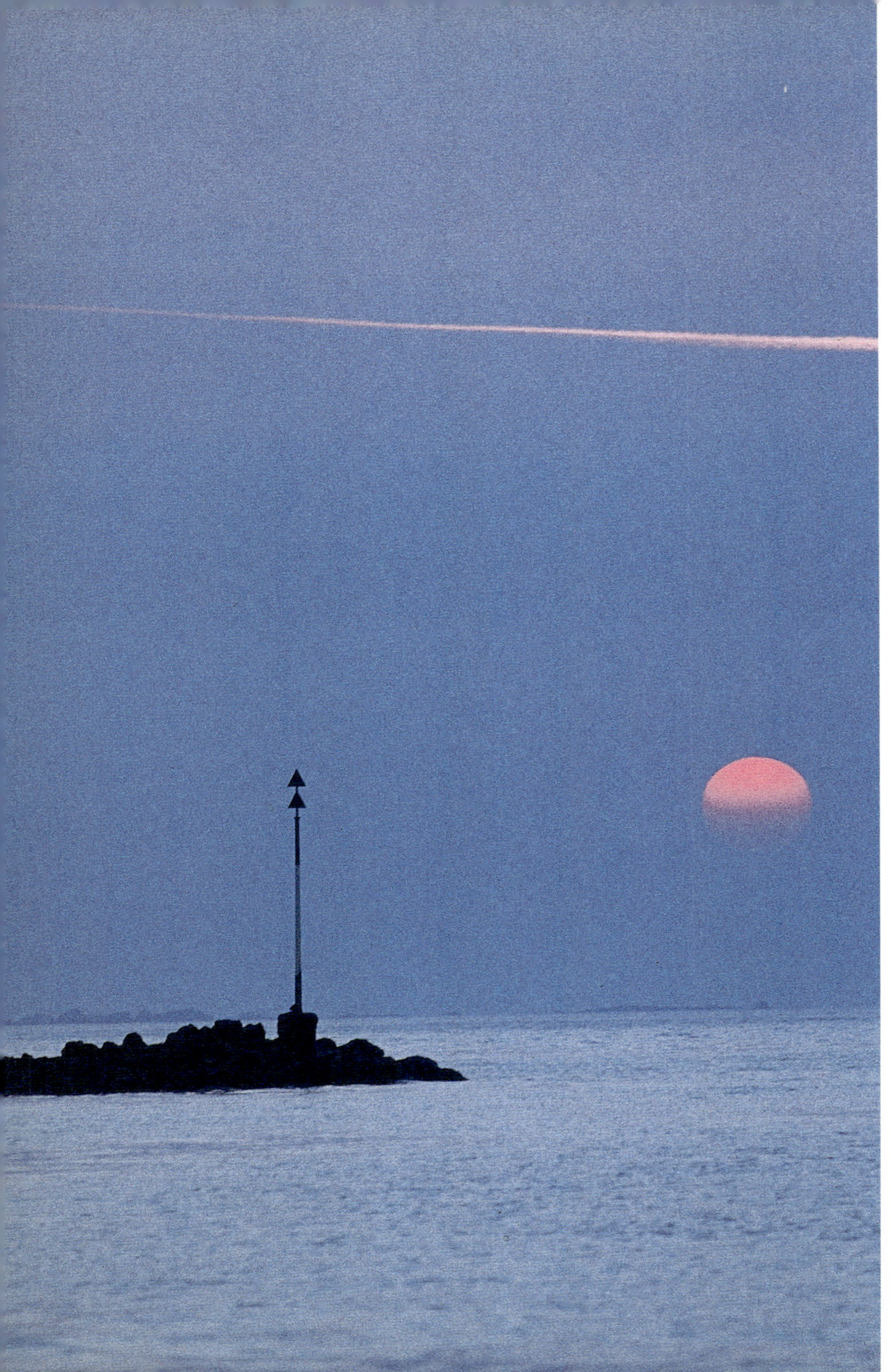

DECEMBER 17

The sea—this truth must be
confessed—has no generosity.
No display of manly qualities—
courage, hardihood, endurance,
faithfulness—has ever been
known to touch its irresponsible
consciousness of power.

Joseph Conrad,
from *The Mirror of the Sea,* 1906

DECEMBER 18

If you are a friend of the captain, you can wipe your hands on the sail.

Arabian proverb

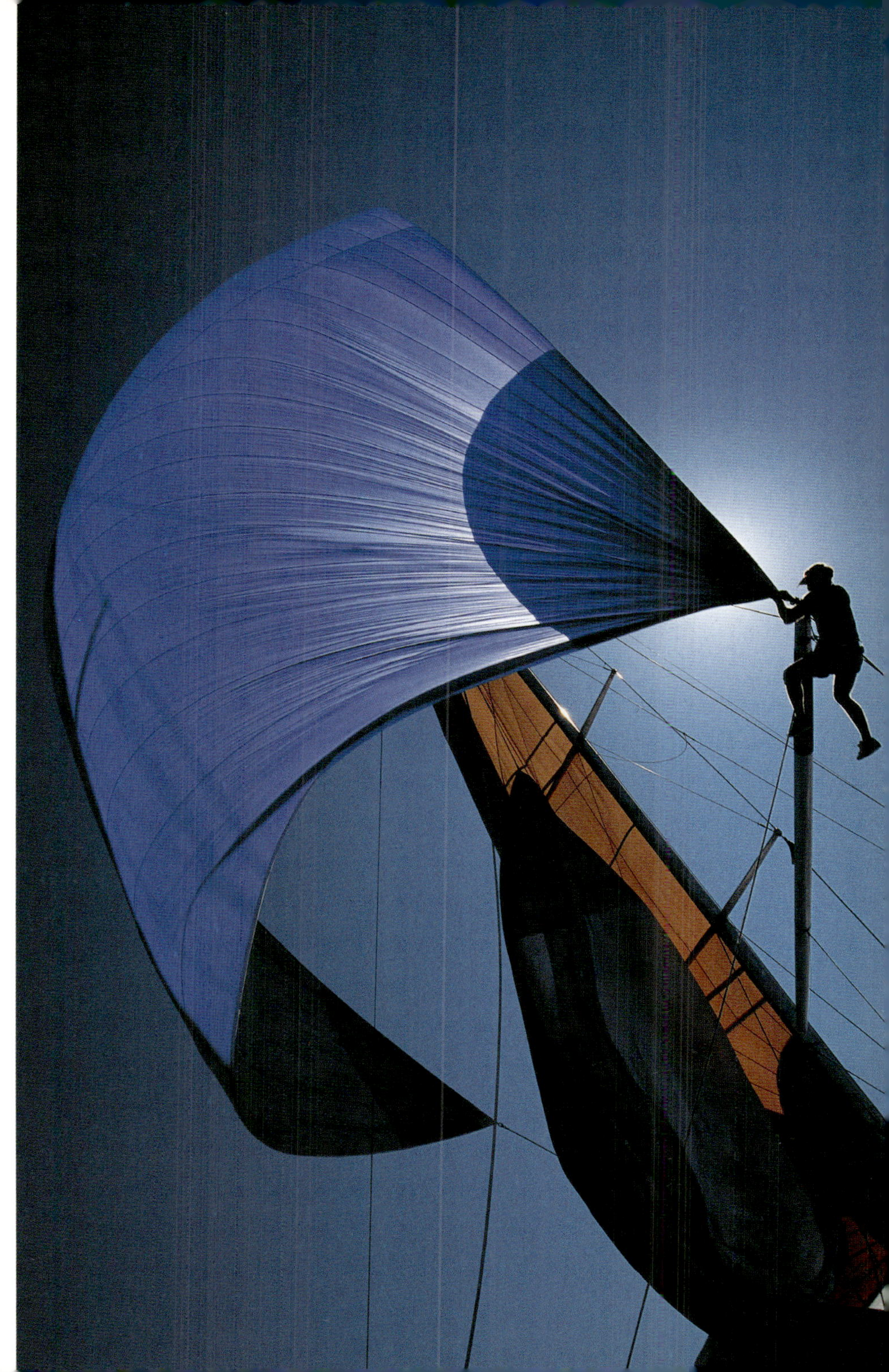

DECEMBER 19

No, no!
Stop scratching at that memory!
Dark lily, shadowy interplay with heaven,
Nor strong enough to wreck a precious vessel...
You were about to reach the ultimate moment...
But who could win a bout with power itself,
Eager to meditate through your eyes on day,
Which chose your forehead as its tower of light?

Paul Valéry,
from *La Jeune Parque,* 1917

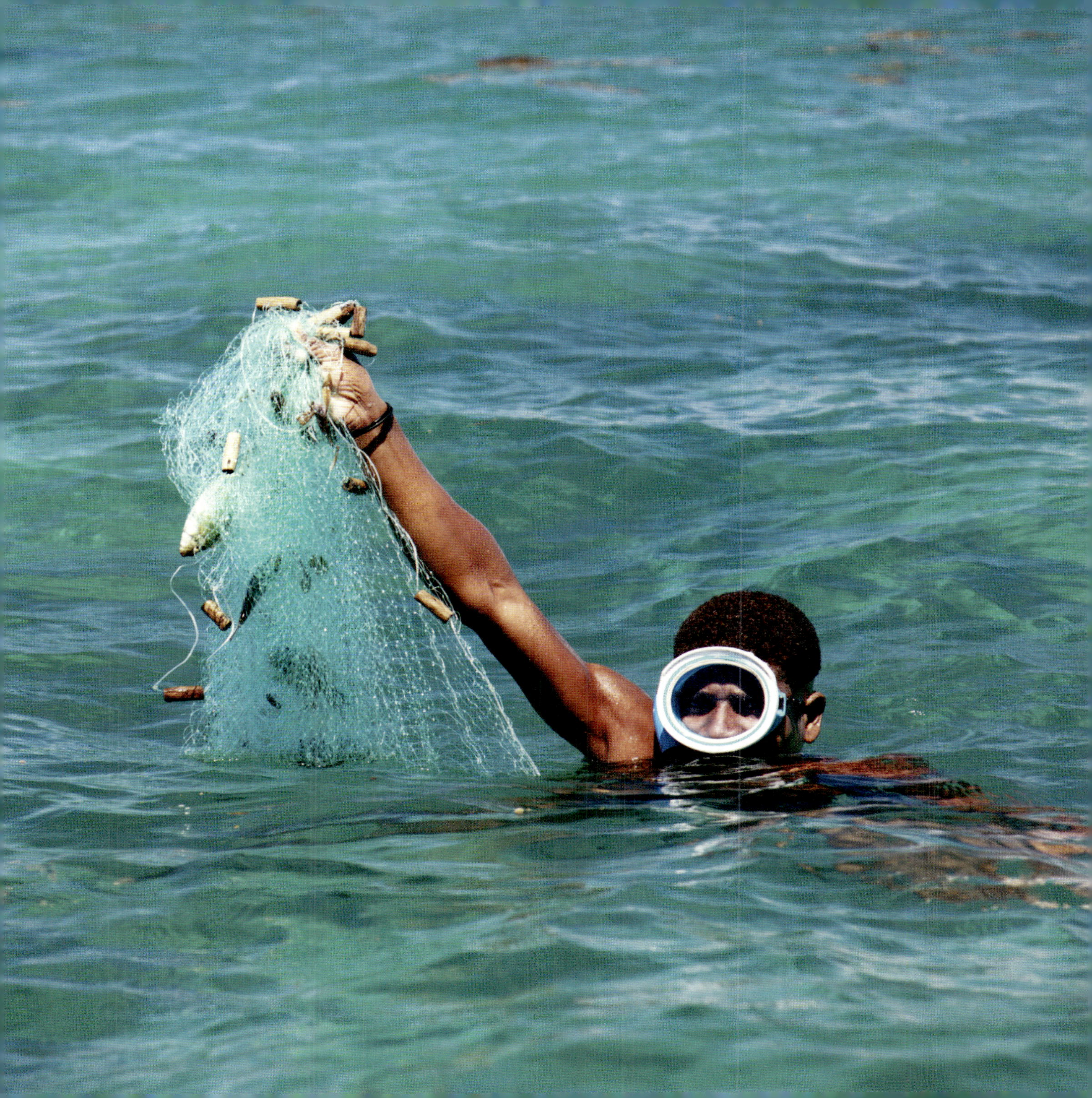

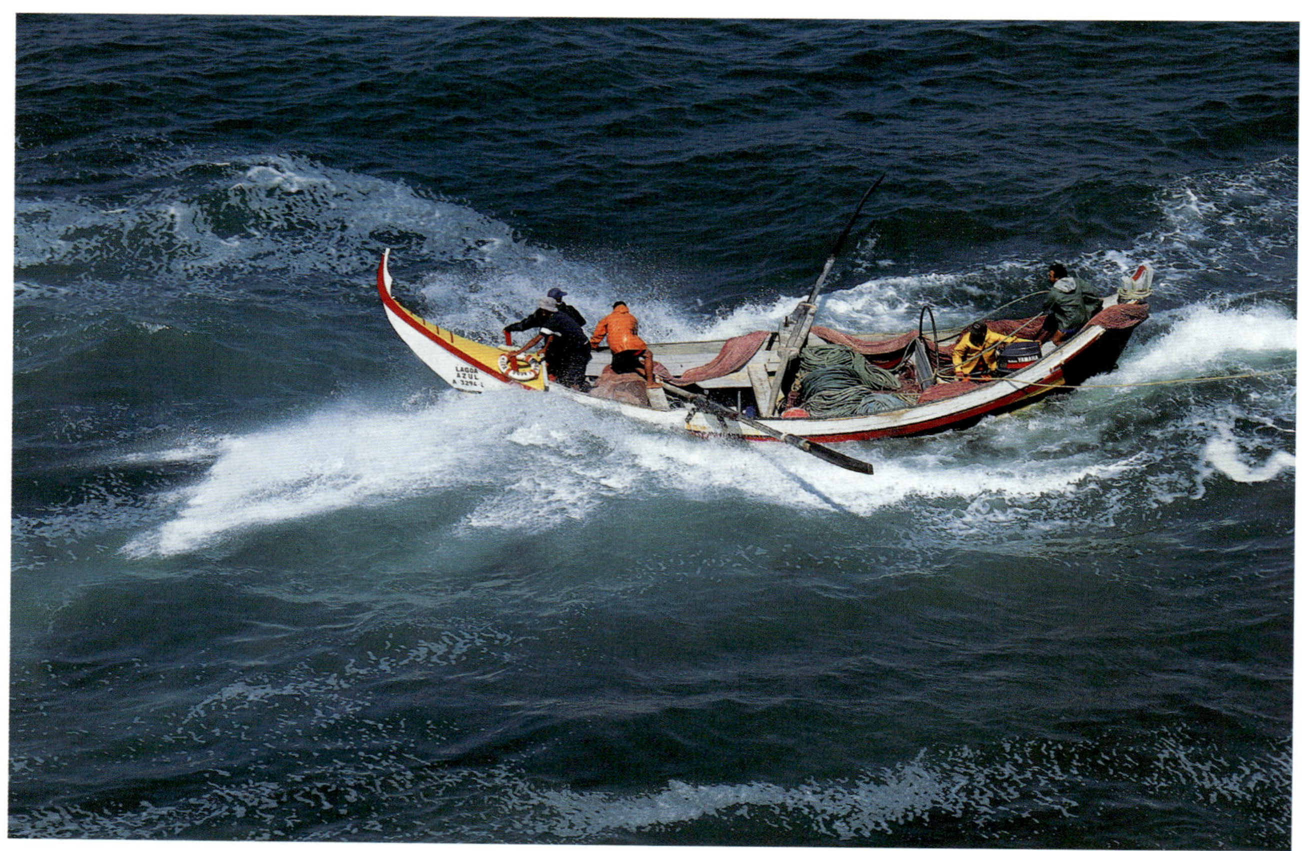

Watchfulness is the law of the ship—watch on watch, for advantage and for life.

Ralph Waldo Emerson, from *English Traits,* 1856

DECEMBER 21

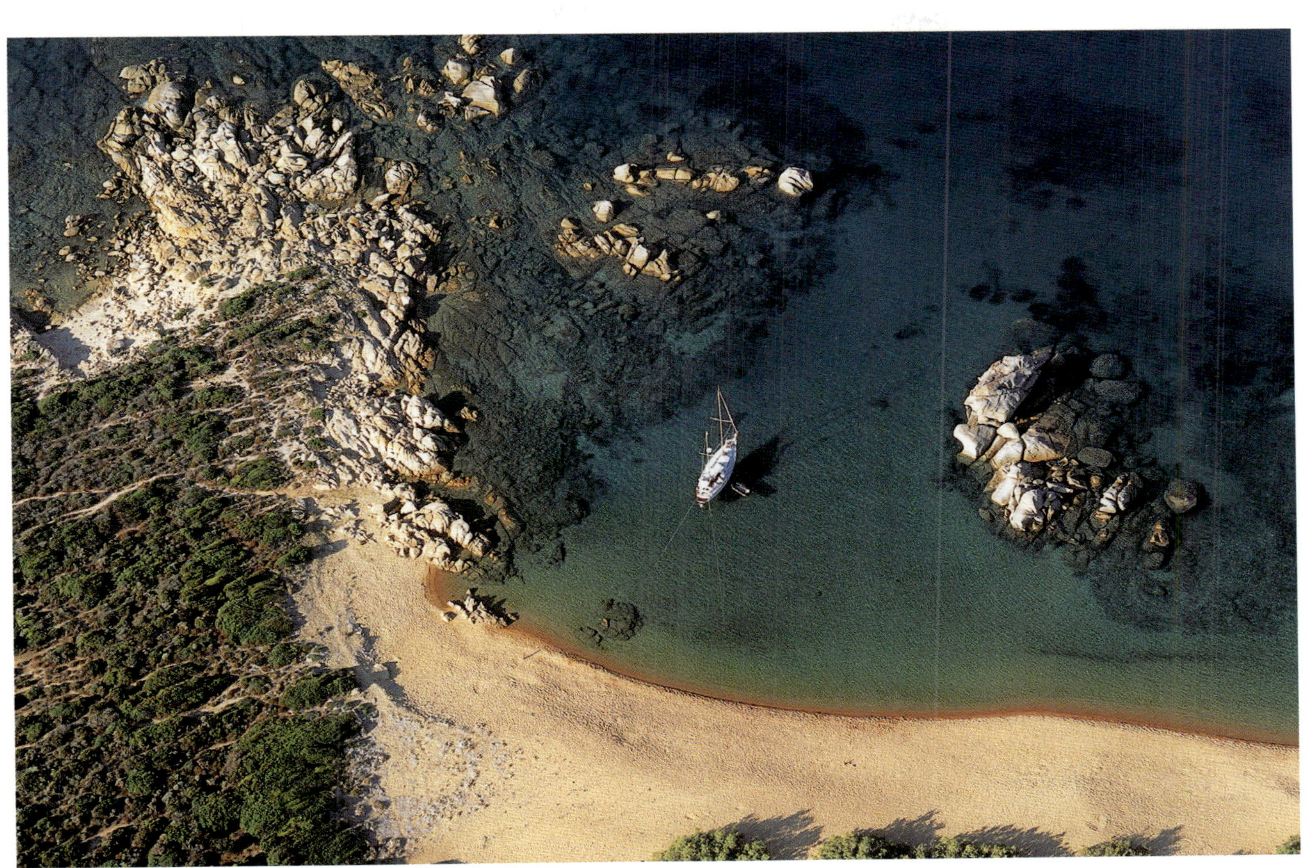

This quiet sail is as a noiseless wing
To waft me from distraction.

Lord Byron, from "Childe Harold's Pilgrimage," 1818

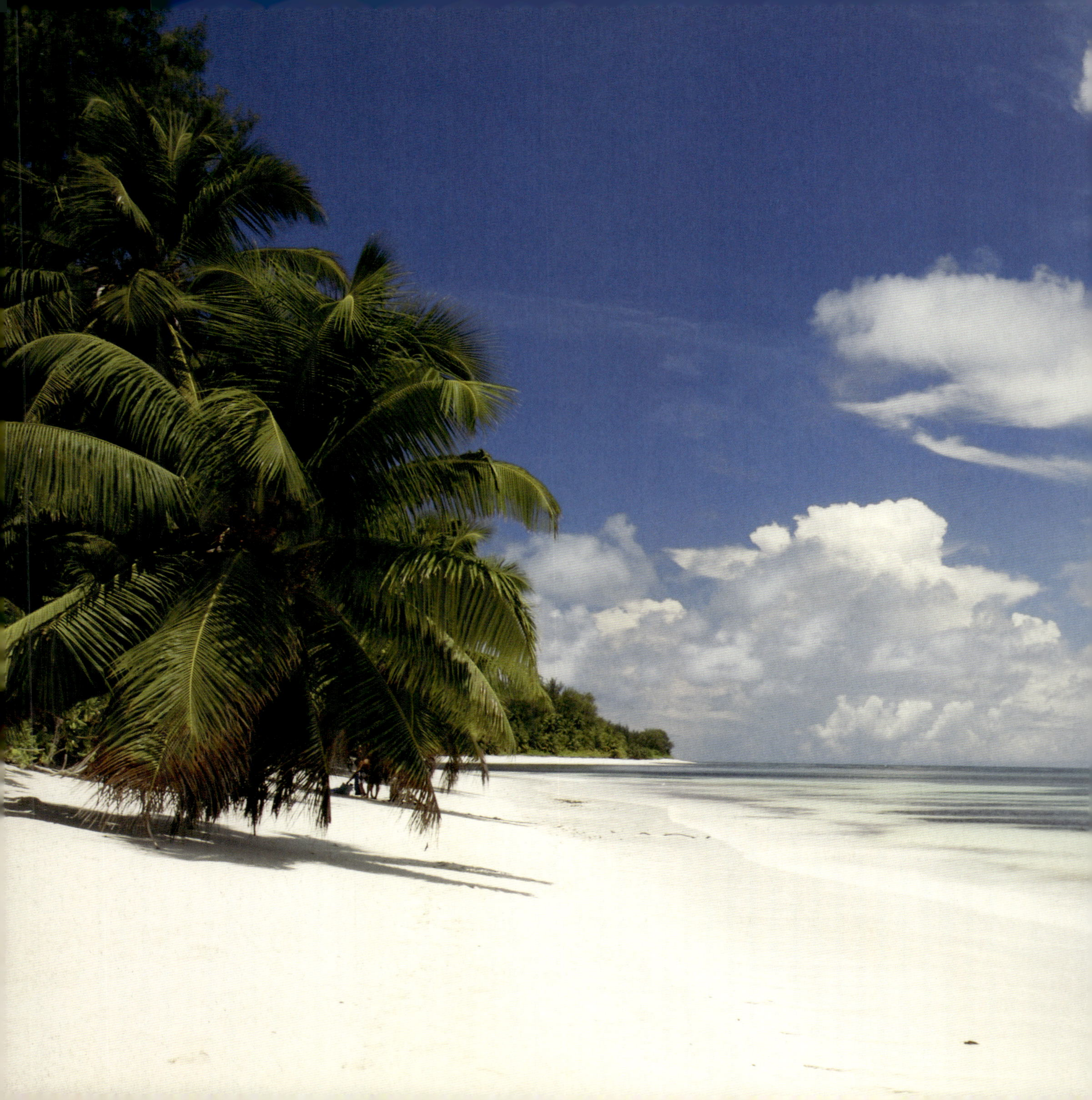

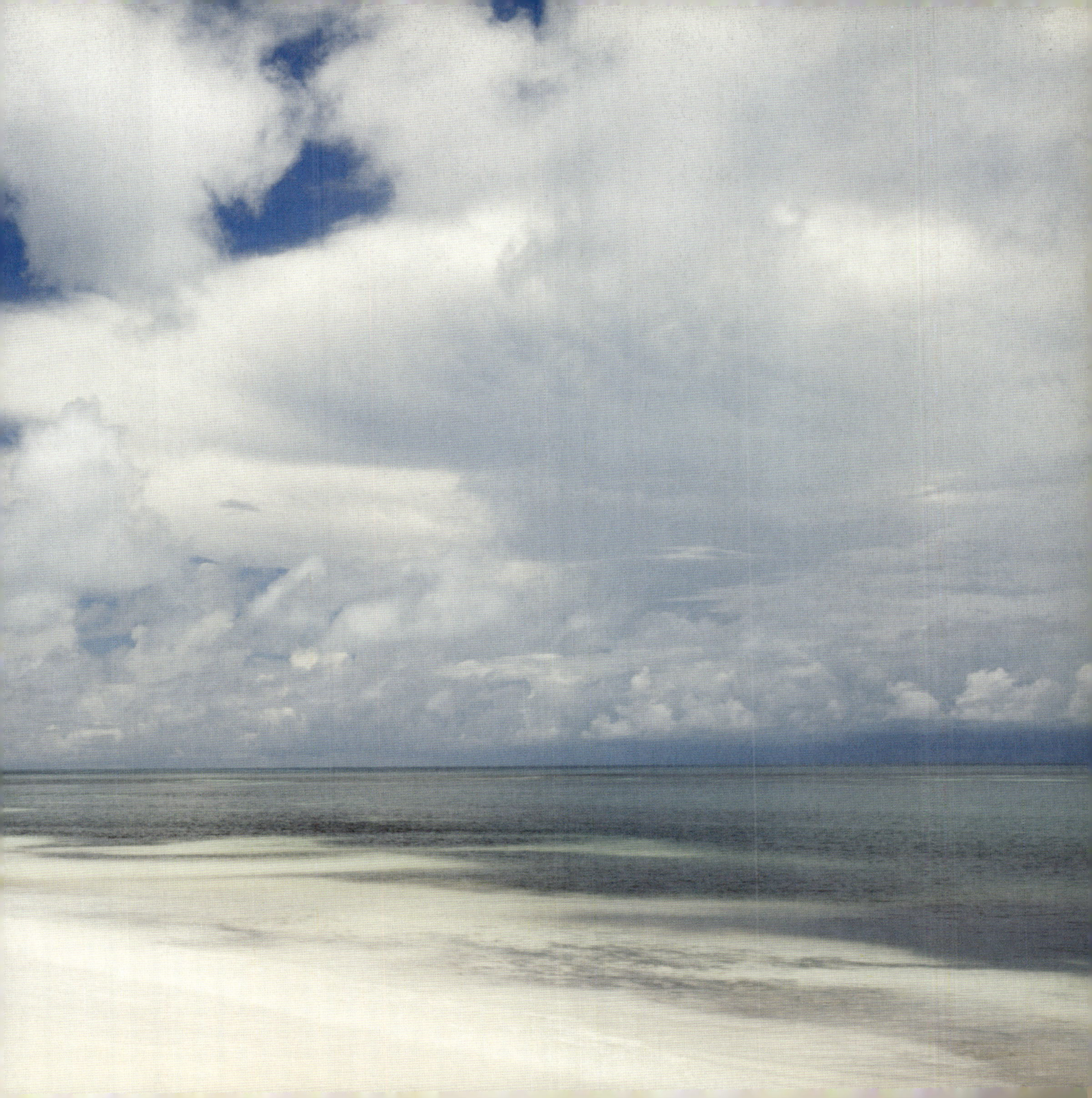

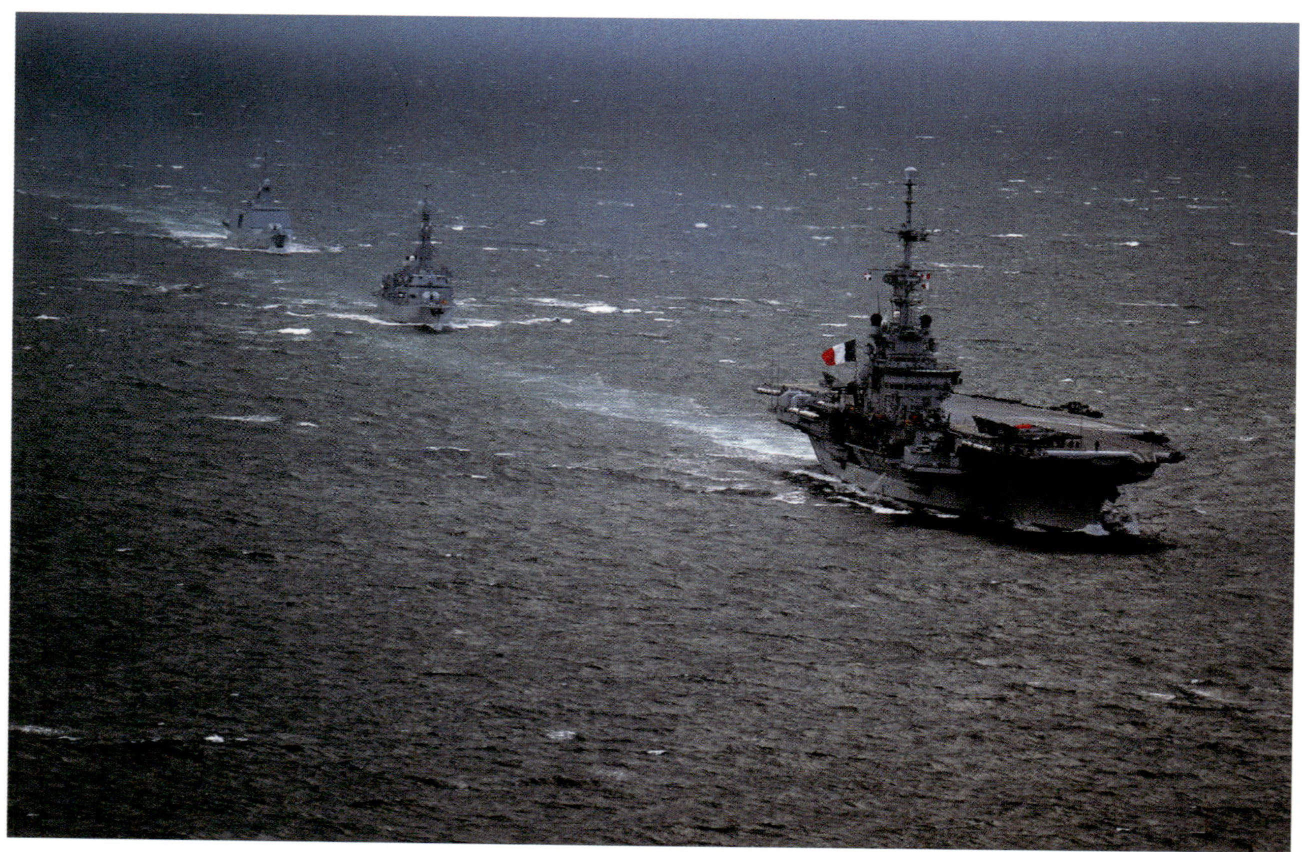

Seamanship is an entirely different matter. It is not learned in a day, nor in many days; it requires years.

Jack London, from *The Cruise of the Snark,* 1913

DECEMBER 23

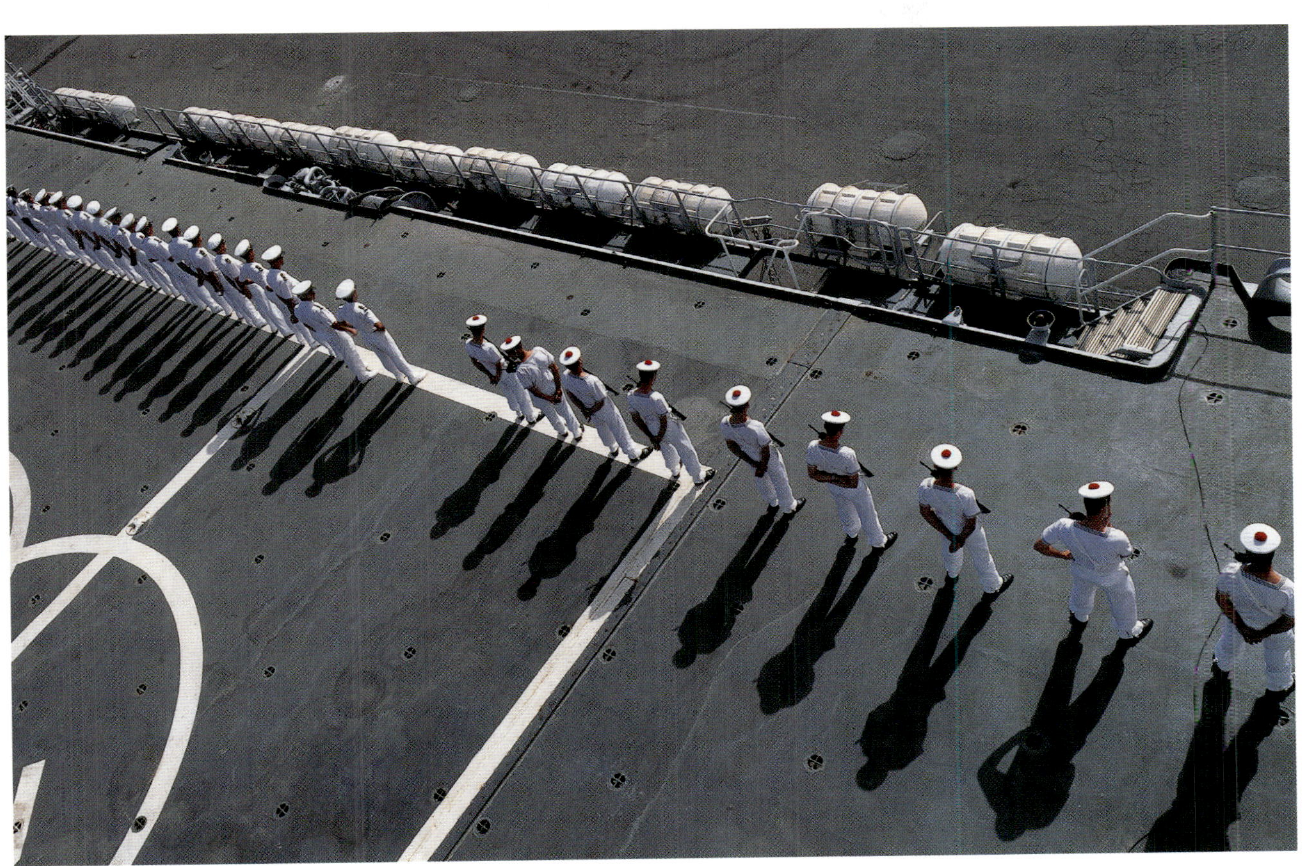

There were gentlemen and there were seamen in the navy...
But the seamen were not gentlemen, and the gentlemen were not seamen.

Lord Macaulay, from *The History of England,* 1848

DECEMBER 24

O lonesome sea-gull, floating far
Over the ocean's icy waste,
Aimless and wide thy wanderings are,
Forever vainly seeking rest:—
Where is thy mate, and where thy nest?

Elizabeth Akers Allen,
from "Sea-Birds," 1868

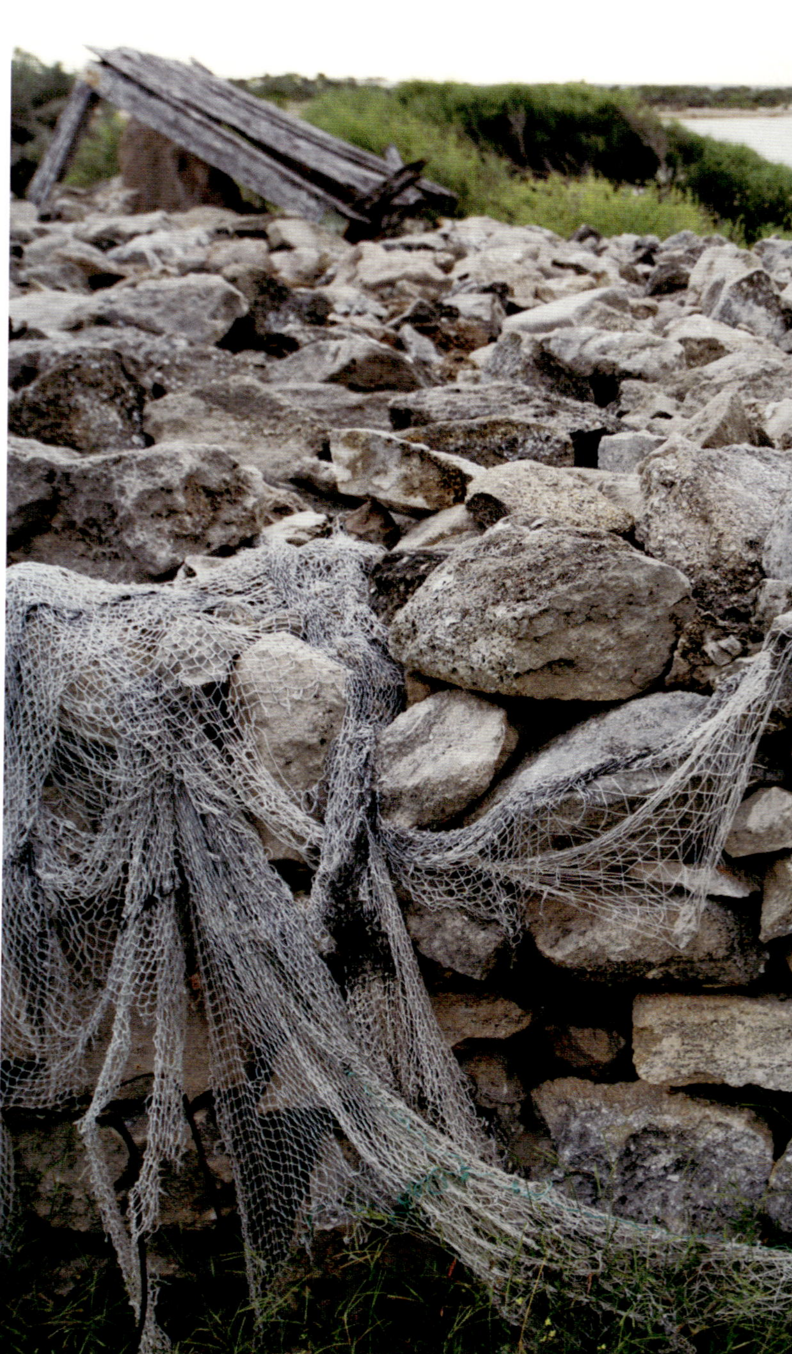

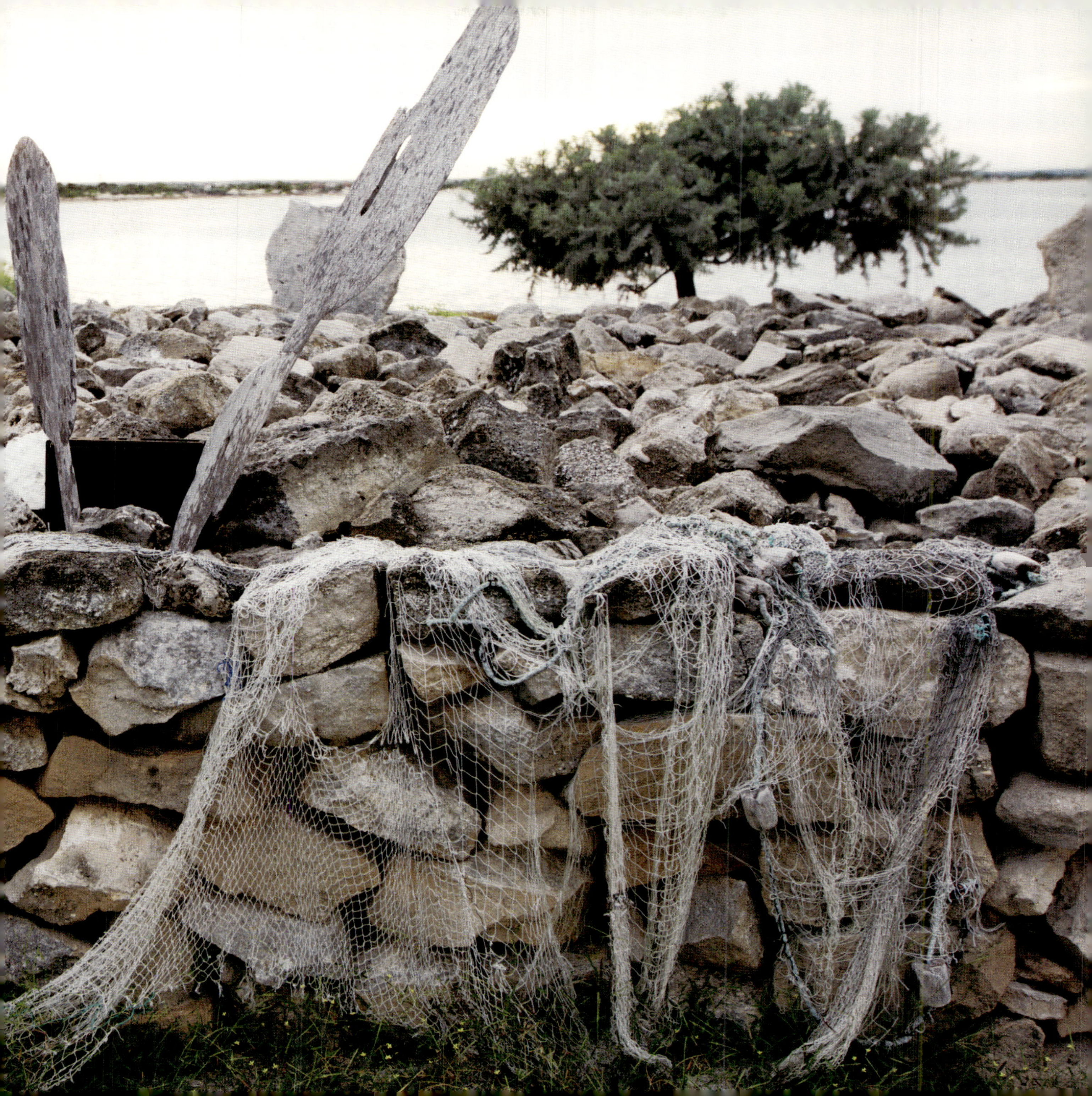

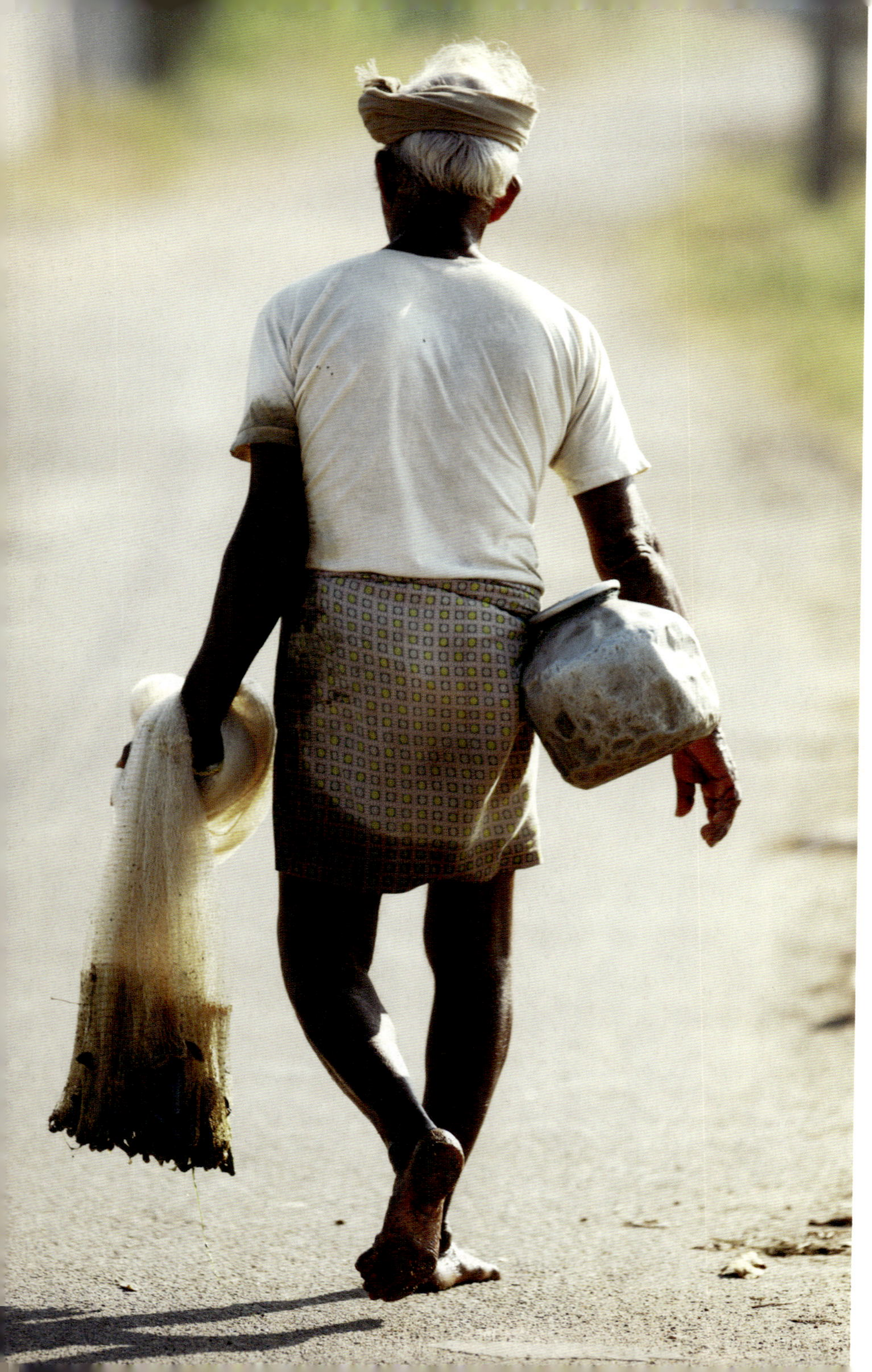

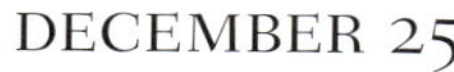

DECEMBER 25

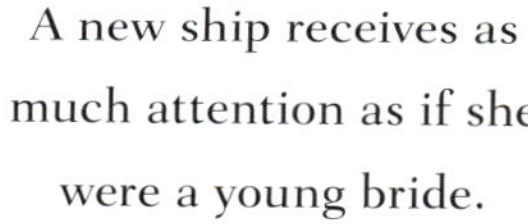

A new ship receives as much attention as if she were a young bride.

Joseph Conrad,
from *The Mirror of the Sea*, 1906

DECEMBER 26

Ay, ay! We sailors sail not in vain. We expatriate ourselves to nationalize with the universe.

Herman Melville,
from *White-Jacket,* 1850

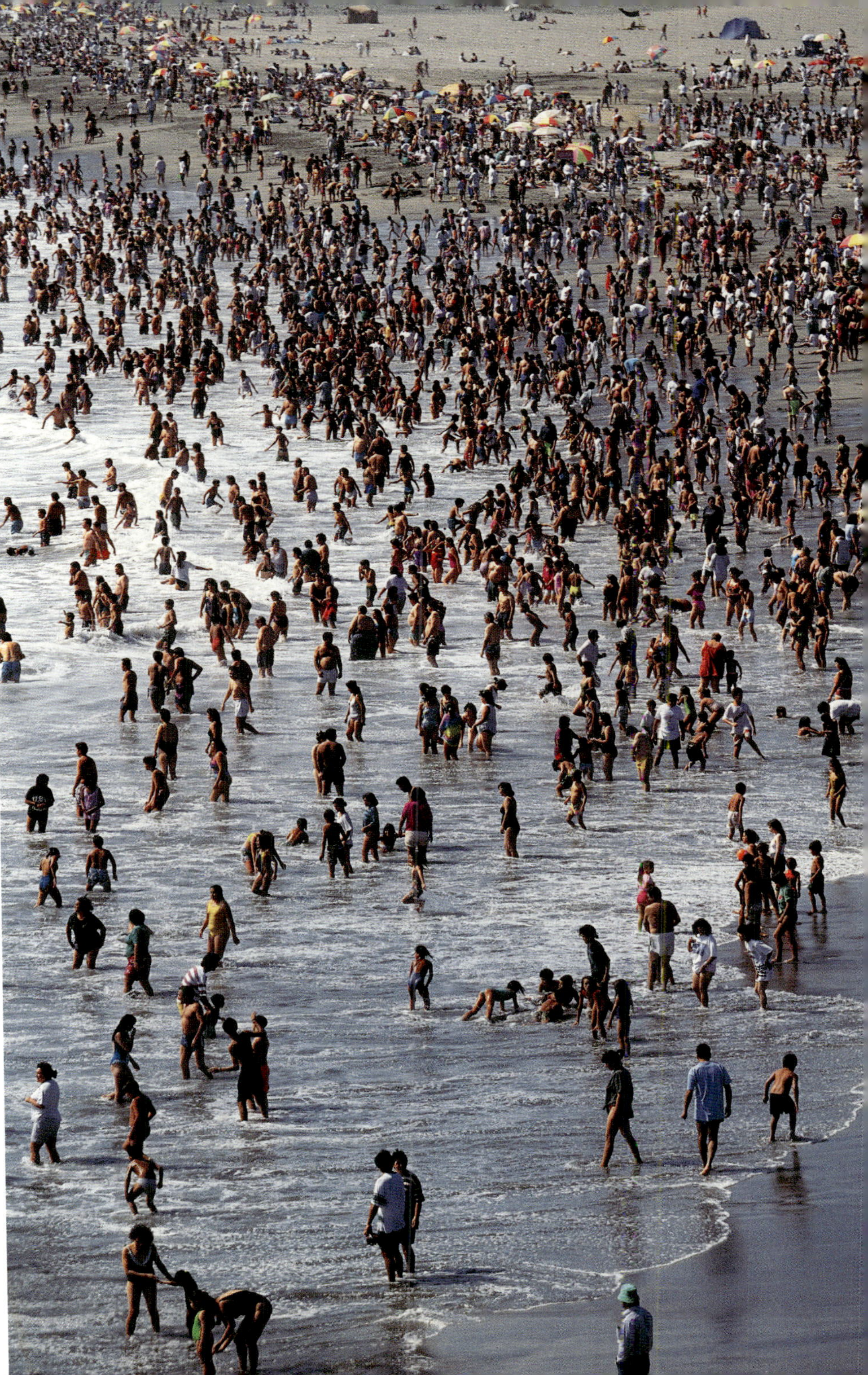

DECEMBER 27

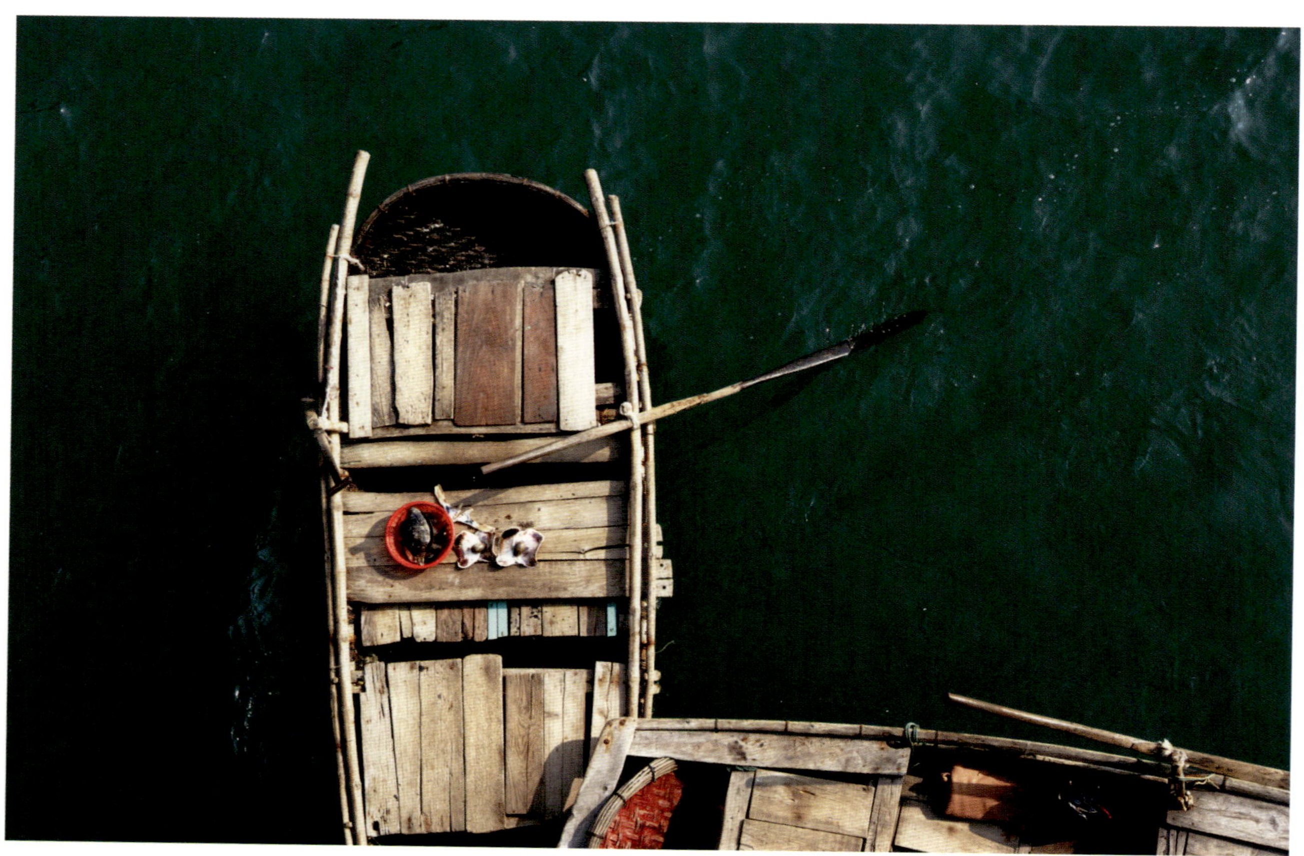

Who can say of a particular sea that it is old? Distilled by the sun, kneaded by the moon, it is renewed in a year, in a day, or in an hour.

Thomas Hardy, from *The Return of the Native,* 1878

DECEMBER 28

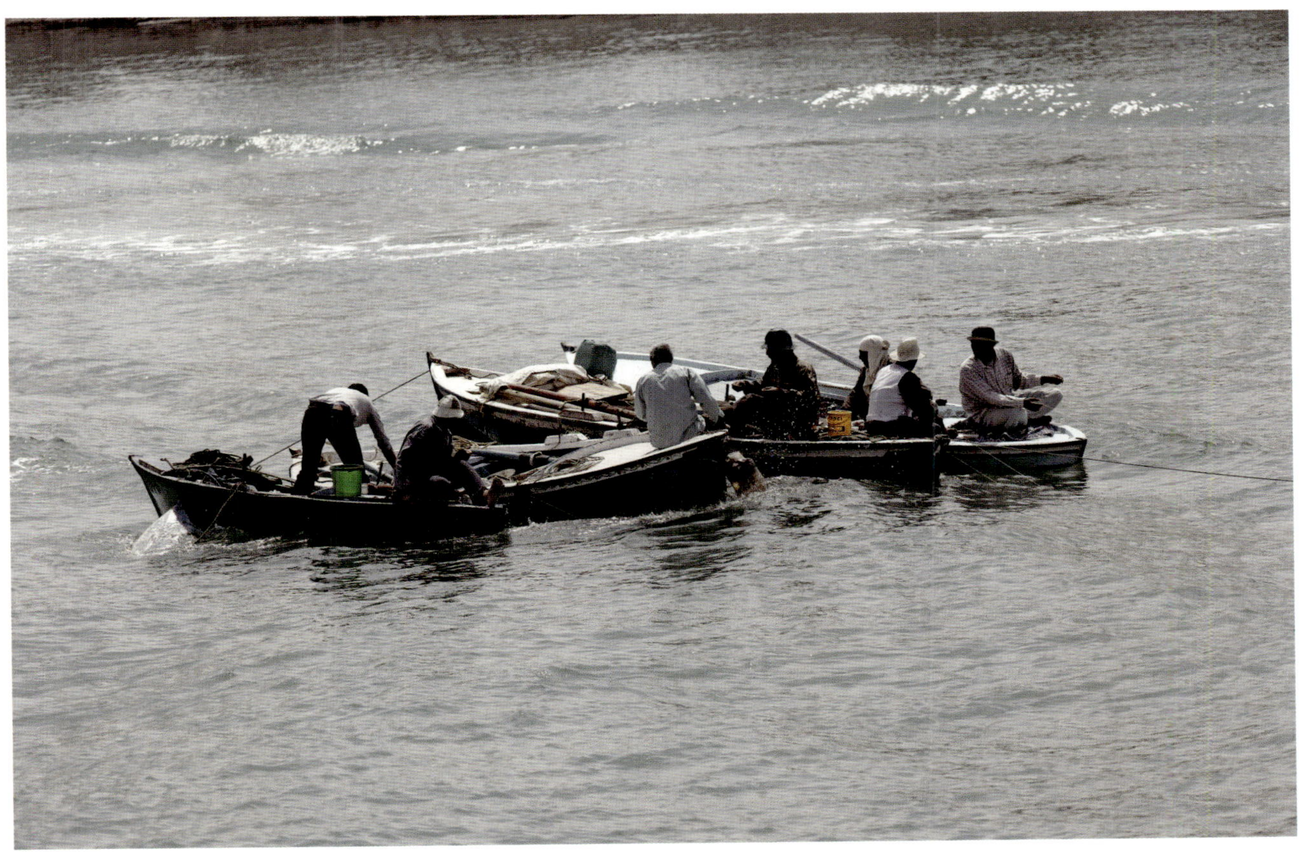

Two bodies of water attack an isthmus with their waves,
And the narrow land hears both seas.

Ovid, from *The Heroïde*

DECEMBER 29

The ocean is but a larger lake. At midsummer you may sometimes see a strip of glassy smoothness on it, a few rods in width and many miles long, as if the surface were covered with a thin pellicle of oil, just as on a country pond... Yet this same placid ocean, as civil now as a city's harbor, a place for ships and commerce, will ere long be lashed into sudden fury, and all its caves and cliffs will resound with tumult.

Henry David Thoreau,
from *Cape Cod,* 1865

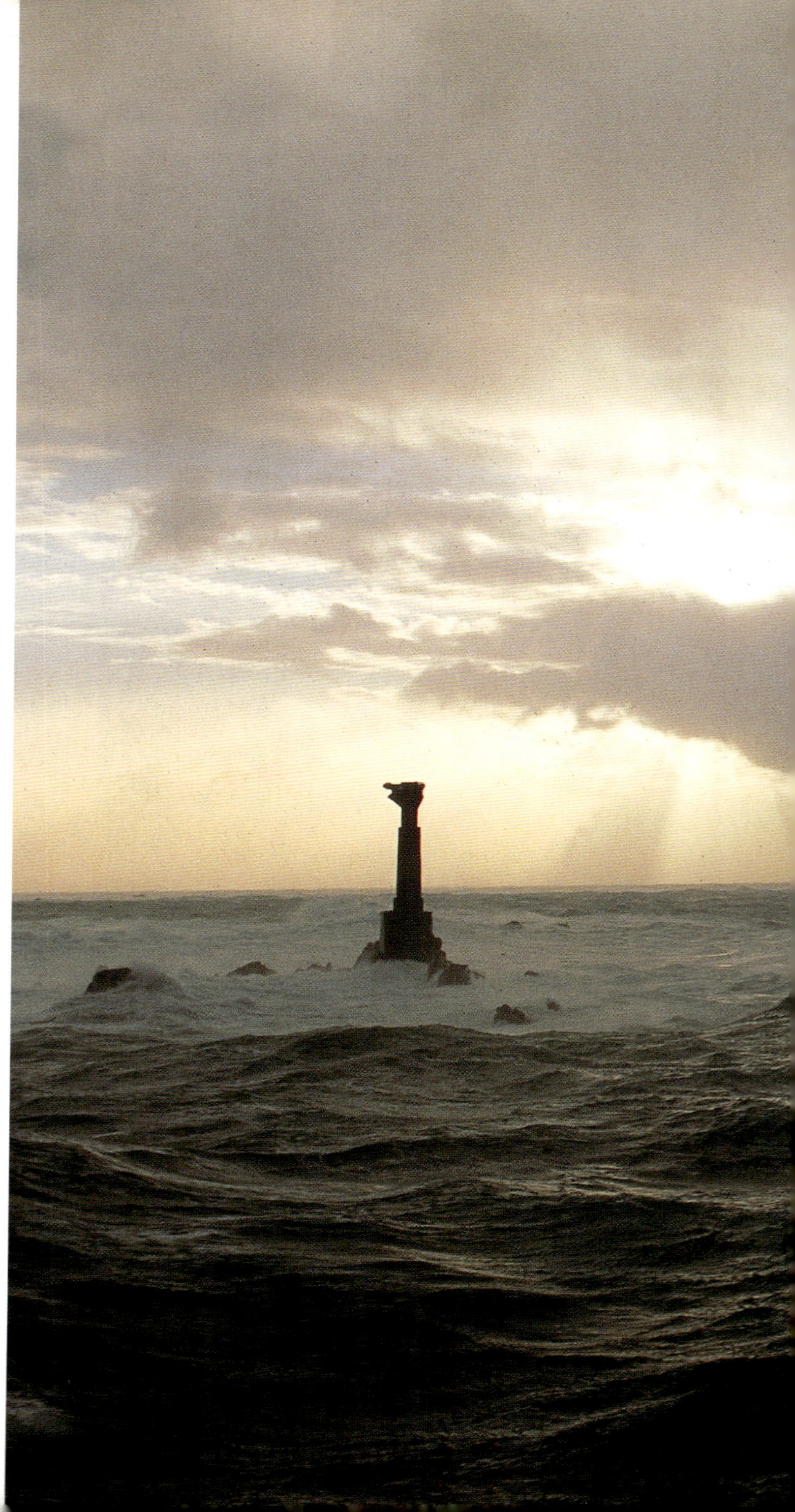

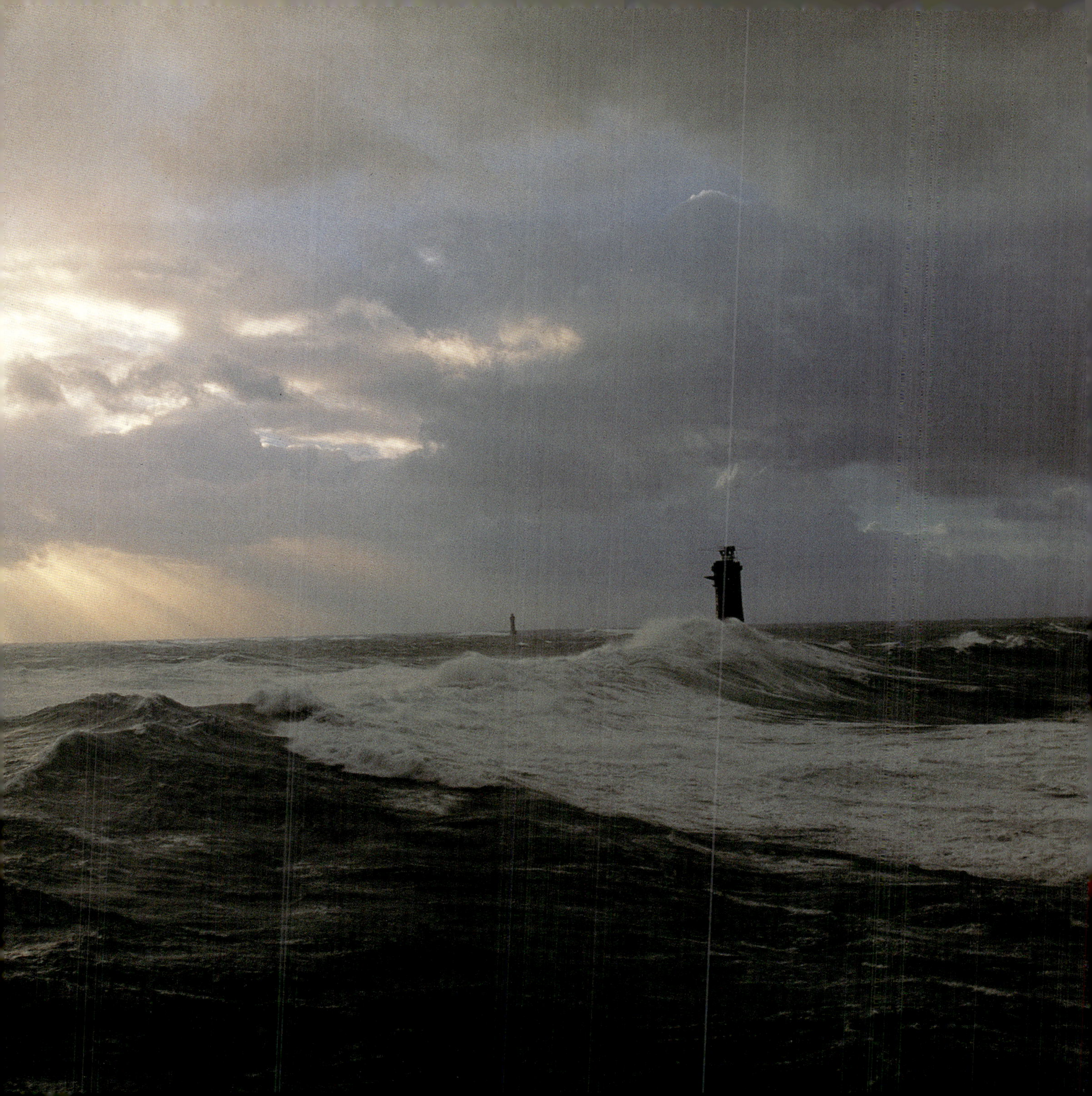

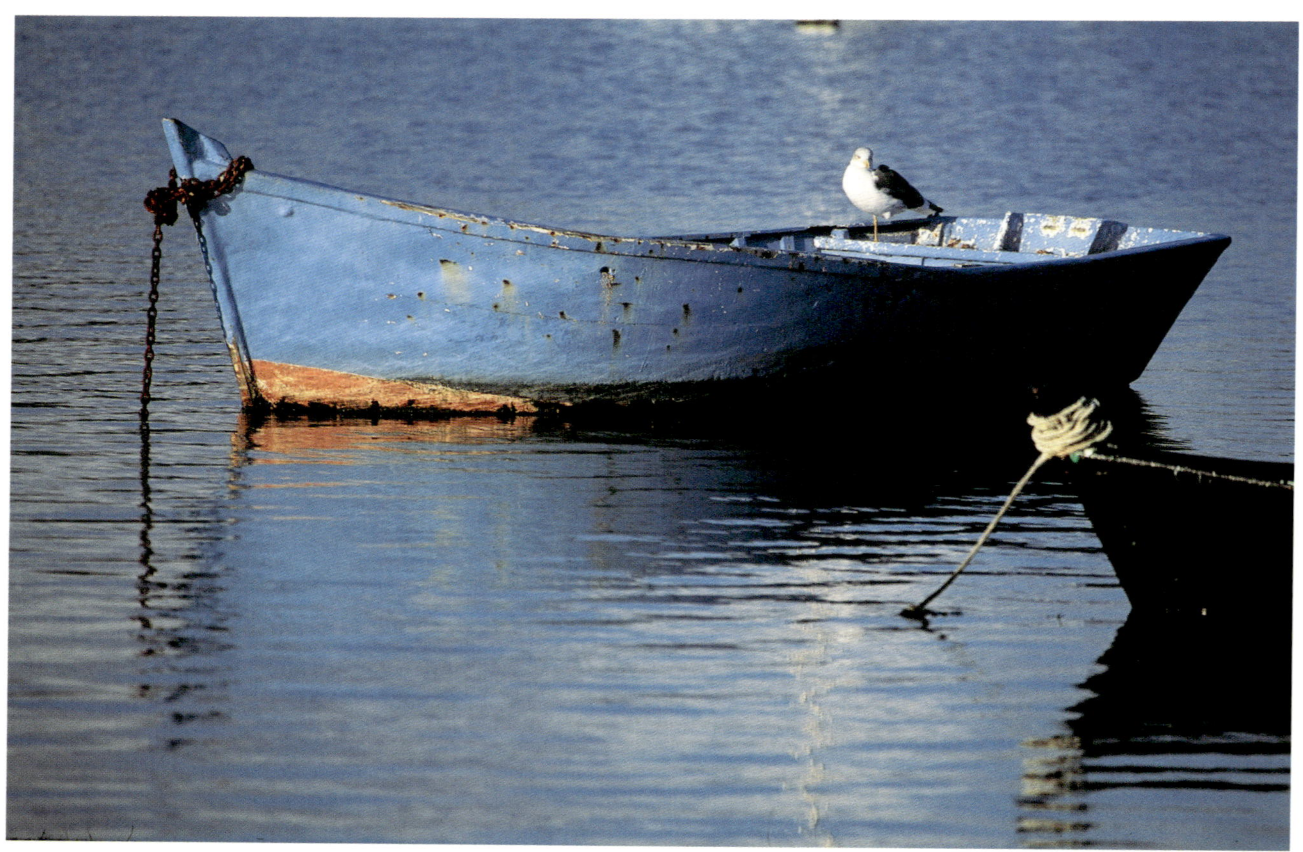

The sea folds away from you like a mystery.

Carl Sandburg, from "North-Atlantic," *Smoke and Steel,* 1920

DECEMBER 31

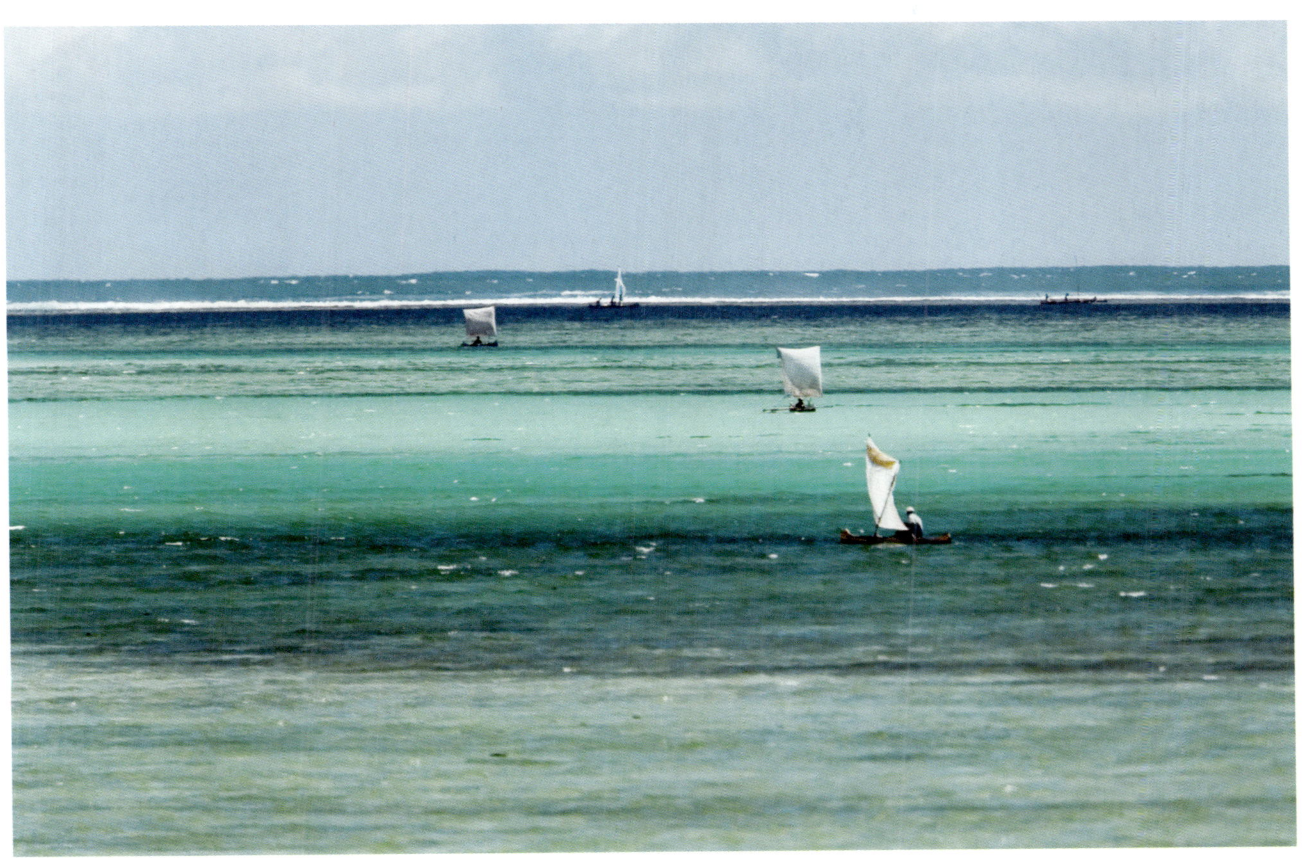

The heart is but the beach beside the sea that is the world.

Chinese proverb

CAPTIONS

JANUARY 1: The end of the day in Venice, Italy

JANUARY 2: An Irish fisherman

JANUARY 3: Béniguets Passage, France

JANUARY 4: Departure of *jangadas* before sunrise, Caponga, Brazil

JANUARY 5: Close-up of the sails of the *Marie Fernand,* France

JANUARY 6: Halyards on the *Belem,* France

JANUARY 7: A lighthouse, Bermuda

JANUARY 8: Mussel farmers, Mont-Saint-Michel Bay, France

JANUARY 9: Essaouira, Morocco

FOLLOWING SPREAD: The *Mariquita* at Les Voiles de Saint-Tropez regatta, France

JANUARY 10: The crew of the *Esmaralda* aloft, France

JANUARY 11: Faial Island of the Azores Archipelago, Portugal

JANUARY 12: A fishing boat, the Auray River, France

JANUARY 13: A jetty in Saint-Jean-de-Luz, France

JANUARY 14: Louet Island, France

JANUARY 15: Mussel beds at the mouth of the Vilaine River, France

JANUARY 16: On Kovalam Beach, India

JANUARY 17: Sailor's knot on the *HMS Rose,* France

FOLLOWING SPREAD: Fishing boat in the Port of Piraeus, Greece

JANUARY 18: Shipyard in Alexandria, Egypt

JANUARY 19: A cargo ship propeller under repair in Brest, France

JANUARY 20: A small trawler in Ireland

JANUARY 21: Fish traps

JANUARY 22: Detail of a fishing boat, Ireland

JANUARY 23: The Port of Essaouira, Morocco

JANUARY 24: Venice, Italy

JANUARY 25: A fisherman, Cochin, India

JANUARY 26: Gathering whelk on the Étel River, France

FOLLOWING SPREAD: On Kovalam Beach, India

JANUARY 27: On a beach in the Vigo Bay, Spain

JANUARY 28: Inshore fishing

JANUARY 29: Coastline of Ceará, Brazil

JANUARY 30: The lighthouse of Quoddy Head, Maine, United States

JANUARY 31: Ventotene Island, Italy

FEBRUARY 1: Calm seas

FEBRUARY 2: A clapboard rowboat, New Zealand

FEBRUARY 3: A reflection of the lighthouse at Saint-Pierre-et-Miquelon, France

FEBRUARY 4: Return to the beach from fishing, Dakar, Senegal

FOLLOWING SPREAD: *Jangadas* fishing, Ceará, Brazil

FEBRUARY 5: A fishing boat

FEBRUARY 6: Fortaleza, Brazil

FEBRUARY 7: Cochin, India

FEBRUARY 8: A punt covered with snow

FEBRUARY 9: Lobster buoys, Maine, United States

FEBRUARY 10: The tugboat *Abeille Bourbon,* France

FEBRUARY 11: Aboard the single-hulled vessel *Phantom,* France

FEBRUARY 12: Fishing nets

FOLLOWING SPREAD: Wreckage at low tide in the Blavet River, France

FEBRUARY 13: Venice, Italy

FEBRUARY 14: Sails of the schooner *Shenandoah,* New Zealand

FEBRUARY 15: A twelve-meter regatta in Newport, Maine, United States

FEBRUARY 16: Tasmania, Australia

FEBRUARY 17: A ship on a path chiseled by an icebreaker to access the Port of Oulu, Finland

FEBRUARY 18: A boat in construction

FEBRUARY 19: Trap fishing, Oman

FEBRUARY 20: *Nan,* launched in 1896, is the oldest remaining yacht built by the Fife family in France

FOLLOWING SPREAD: Port Clyde, Maine, United States

FEBRUARY 21: Fishing boats, Essaouira, Morocco

FEBRUARY 22: A fisherman in his punt

FEBRUARY 23: Navigational marker for Goemoran, Gulf of Morbihan, France

FEBRUARY 24: Saint-Philibert in the morning, France

FEBRUARY 25: The *HMS Rose,* France

FEBRUARY 26: Chenal du Four, France

FEBRUARY 27: Stems of fishing boats, Cochin, India

FEBRUARY 28: A buoy aboard a punt in Horta, the Azores Archipelago, Portugal

MARCH 1: The Cotre lining vessel, *Le Vieux Copain,* Brest, France

MARCH 2: An oyster-farming cabin on the Hudson River, United States

MARCH 3: Early morning in the Port of La Trinité-sur-Mer, France

MARCH 4: The lighthouse of Lost-Pic, France

MARCH 5: A fishing boat, Istanbul, Turkey

MARCH 6: Sailors furling a sail

MARCH 7: Fishing gear on Batz Island in Morlaix Bay, France

MARCH 8: Registration number of a fishing boat, Morbihan, France

MARCH 9: The *Tuiga,* Monaco

MARCH 10: The rescue boat *François Morin* on one of her last missions, Ouessant Island, France

FOLLOWING SPREAD: On the beach of Vizhinjam, India

MARCH 11: San Marco Quay, Venice, Italy

MARCH 12: A floating village, Along Bay, Vietnam

MARCH 13: A whaleboat in training, Faial Island, Portugal

MARCH 14: Les Voiles de Saint-Tropez regatta, France

MARCH 15: The lighthouse of Vierge Island, France

MARCH 16: A pole in the Vilaine River, France

MARCH 17: Small boats, Orkney Islands, Scotland

MARCH 18: The stem of a boat, Malta

FOLLOWING SPREAD: Sunset over Pico Island, Portugal

MARCH 19: A fishing port, Bombay, India

MARCH 20: Fishermen repairing a net

MARCH 21: The Guip shipyard, Île-aux-Moines, France

MARCH 22: On a beach in Massachusetts, United States

MARCH 23: Navigational markers

MARCH 24: On a beach in Camocin, Brazil

MARCH 25: Navigational markers in the sunset

MARCH 26: The *Celtina,* a Monotype 7m50, France

MARCH 27: The Cordouan Lighthouse, France

FOLLOWING SPREAD: The Triagoz Lighthouse, France

MARCH 28: A whaleboat in the Azores Archipelago, Portugal

MARCH 29: The *Tuiga,* Monaco

MARCH 30: Putting a *jangada* to sea, Ceará, Brazil

MARCH 31: The stem of the container ship *CMA CGM Fidelio,* France

APRIL 1: Nuclear submarine missile launcher in the Brest harbor, France

APRIL 2: Wreckage submerging in the Bosphorus Strait, Istanbul, Turkey

APRIL 3: Navigational marker near Saint-Malo, France

APRIL 4: Madeleine Islands, Quebec, Canada

APRIL 5: The islets of Ecrehous in the Anglo-Norman Isles, Great Britain

FOLLOWING SPREAD: A lighthouse in Norway

APRIL 6: Polperro, Cornwall, Great Britain

APRIL 7: The Harbor Master of the Port of Camden, Maine, United States

APRIL 8: A fish market, Istanbul, Turkey

APRIL 9: A dry dock in the Caribbean, Fort-de-France, Martinique

APRIL 10: A fishing boat in Chausey, France

APRIL 11: In the Port of Bangkok, Thailand

APRIL 12: Fishing nets

FOLLOWING SPREAD: The coast of Achill Island, Ireland

APRIL 13: A cargo sailboat

APRIL 14: Painting of the water line of the *Queen Mary 2,* France

APRIL 15: A small fishing boat in front of Faial Island, Portugal

APRIL 16: A gommier boat in the shallows, Martinique

APRIL 17: Harvesting of salt marshes, Guérande, France

APRIL 18: The crew of the *Esmeralda* on the yards during the Rouen Armada, France

APRIL 19: The singled-hulled vessel *Baume & Mercier* at the Route du Rhum race

APRIL 20: A gap in the clouds above a fishing boat

APRIL 21: Point Reyes, California, United States

APRIL 22: A pirogue, Cochin, India

APRIL 23: A regatta in Quiberon Bay, France

APRIL 24: A ship waiting to pass through the Panama Canal in the Port of Colon

APRIL 25: A fishing sailboat returning to port at the end of the day

FOLLOWING SPREAD: A nuclear submarine missile launcher departing from Toulon, France

APRIL 26: Sail detail of the *Pauline,* France

APRIL 27: A boat in construction at the Guip shipyard, Morbihan, France

APRIL 28: Two fishermen on their boat

APRIL 29: A shipyard door, Galicia, Spain

APRIL 30: Aboard the *Candida,* Les Voiles de Saint-Tropez regatta, France

MAY 1: In the Port of Cochin, India

MAY 2: Trap buoys, Maine, United States

MAY 3: Isle of Skye, Scotland

FOLLOWING SPREAD: An oyster-farming pontoon on the Crac'h River, France

MAY 4: Lobster fishermen, Madeleine Islands, Quebec, Canada

MAY 5: A lighthouse in the Florida Keys, United States

MAY 6: The Port of Horta Lighthouse in front of the Pico volcano, the Azores Archipelago, Portugal

MAY 7: A ferry on the Bosphorus Strait, Istanbul, Turkey

MAY 8: The end of the day at the Panama Canal on the Pacific Ocean side

MAY 9: The flagship of the Gendarmerie Maritime prototype, France

MAY 10: Losbter buoys, Cape Cod, United States

MAY 11: A lighthouse in Kollam, India

MAY 12: A fisherman in the Port of Vizhinjam, India

FOLLOWING SPREAD: Net fishing, Cochin, India

MAY 13: Construction of the *Hermione* at the Corderie Royale shipyard, France

MAY 14: Wreckage in a boat cemetery, Portugal

MAY 15: A polluted beach on the Côte d'Amour, France

MAY 16: An oyster-farming pontoon

MAY 17: Reflections of sails in the water

MAY 18: Fishing gear

MAY 19: A fishing boat in the Gulf of Morbihan, France

MAY 20: Essaouira, Morocco

MAY 21: Moonrise over Cap-Ferret in Gironde, France

FOLLOWING SPREAD: Salt marshes in Guérande, France

MAY 22: The Étel River, France

MAY 23: The Port of Sauzon, Belle-Île-en-Mer, France

MAY 24: A pirogue on the Orenoque River, Venezuela

MAY 25: Fishermen at Redcastle, Ireland

MAY 26: A lighthouse near Helsinki, Finland

MAY 27: An oyster-farming pontoon on the Étel River, France

MAY 28: Line fishing gear

MAY 29: Fishing nets

MAY 30: Tuna boat wreckage on the shore of the Étel River, France

MAY 31: A trawler grounded on the Scottish coastline

FOLLOWING SPREAD: A breaking wave in front of Inisheer, Aran Islands, Ireland

JUNE 1: A tugboat near Portland, Maine, United States

JUNE 2: Fishermen, Faial Island, Portugal

JUNE 3: A cargo ship hull in the Port of Piraeus, Greece

JUNE 4: A small shrimp boat off the West coast of Scotland

JUNE 5: Mont-Saint-Michel, France

JUNE 6: A fishing boat in L'Aber-Wrac'h, France

JUNE 7: Repairing fishnets, Madagascar

JUNE 8: The San Blas Archipelago, Panama

JUNE 9: The bow of a scallop-fishing sloop

JUNE 10: Mussel beds in Mont-Saint-Michel Bay, France

FOLLOWING SPREAD: Lampaul Bay, Ouessant Island, France

JUNE 11: Les Voiles de Saint-Tropez regatta, France

JUNE 12: The *Baume & Mercier,* the Route du Rhum race

JUNE 13: A three-masted ship entering the Port of Douarnenez, France

JUNE 14: The frigate *HMS Rose,* France

JUNE 15: A shrimp boat on the Rance River, France

JUNE 16: Taureau, Morlaix Bay, France

JUNE 17: Oyster-farming pontoons on the Trieux River, France

JUNE 18: An icebreaker on the Baltic Sea, the Gulf of Bothnia, Finland

FOLLOWING SPREAD: A small fishing boat at dusk

JUNE 19: The *Moonbeam III* at Les Voiles de Saint-Tropez regatta, France

JUNE 20: Old rigging in Douarnenez, France

JUNE 21: Sunrise over the Tokyo Bay, Japan

JUNE 22: On the bridge of the *Shenandoah,* New Zealand

JUNE 23: The *Shenandoah* in New Zealand waters

JUNE 24: Asturias, Spain

JUNE 25: A fishing boat, Ireland

JUNE 26: SASL (Simple Authentication and Security Layer) of the *Shenandoah*

JUNE 27: Ullapool, the Highlands of Scotland

FOLLOWING SPREAD: The Strait of Messina, Sicily

JUNE 28: The hauling down of a sail on the *Shenandoah*

JUNE 29: Louet Island, France

JUNE 30: Oiseaux Island, Arcachon Basin, France

JULY 1: The stem of a shrimp boat, Maine, United States

JULY 2: An oyster farmer dredging in Morlaix Bay, France

JULY 3: Pilat Dune, Arcachon, France

JULY 4: The mast of the *Belem,* France

JULY 5: Gommier boats on a Martinique beach.

JULY 6: Houses near Bergen, Norway

JULY 7: A fishing cabin, Loire-Atlantique, France

JULY 8: The *Dewaruci,* an Indonesian Navy training ship, at the Rouen Armada, France

JULY 9: The *Mariquita* at Les Voiles de Saint-Tropez regatta, France

JULY 10: A fishing boat in Morlaix Bay, France

JULY 11: Oyster-farming pontoons, Bourgneuf Bay, France

JULY 12: The Goulphar Lighthouse, Morbihan, France

FOLLOWING SPREAD: The three-masted schooner *Shenandoah* in New Zealand

JULY 13: Hauling down the spinnaker on the *Ville de Paris* during the America's Cup

JULY 14: The Madonetta Lighthouse, Corsica, France

JULY 15: The *Queen Mary 2* in Caribbean port of call in Saint Lucia

JULY 16: The *Tuiga* during Les Voiles de Saint-Tropez regatta, France

JULY 17: A reflection of Mont-Saint-Michel, France

JULY 18: A fishing boat leaving from Port-Rhu, France

JULY 19: Reaching under spinnaker, Les Voiles de Saint-Tropez Regatta, France

JULY 20: Cruise sailboat *Le Ponnant* in the Indian Ocean

JULY 21: A small fishing boat, Glénan Islands, France

JULY 22: A small fishing boat in Pays Bigouden, France

JULY 23: Ifaty, Madagascar

JULY 24: Fishing in the Raz de Sein, France

JULY 25: The Yoles Rondes regatta, Martinique

JULY 26: Suez Canal, Egypt

JULY 27: Tuna boats wreckage in the Blavet River, France

JULY 28: Seine fishing in Martinique

JULY 29: Crossing the Atlantic on a prao, from La Rochelle to New Orleans

FOLLOWING SPREAD: Fishing nets on Anakao Beach, Madagascar

JULY 30: Net fishing, Cochin, India

JULY 31: The San Blas Archipelago, Panama

AUGUST 1: Night fishing in the Azores Archipelago, Portugal

AUGUST 2: The Tevennec Lighthouse, Finistère, France

AUGUST 3: A cardinal west spar buoy (navigational marker)

AUGUST 4: A fishing village in Saint Lucia, the Lesser Antilles

AUGUST 5: A house on stilts, Greece

AUGUST 6: A puffin flying

AUGUST 7: The ocean-going tugboat *Abeille Bourbon* offshore Ouessant, France

AUGUST 8: A sea rescue boat

FOLLOWING SPREAD: Pirogues on the Orenoque River, Venezuela

AUGUST 9: A Madagascan boutre sailboat heading to Nosy Be, Madagascar

AUGUST 10: The Le Four Lighthouse, Finistère, France

AUGUST 11: Fair Isle in the north of Scotland

AUGUST 12: Anakao, Madagascar

AUGUST 13: Madagascar

AUGUST 14: Black Sand Beach, French Polynesia

AUGUST 15: Seine fishing on an island facing Anakao, Madagascar

AUGUST 16: The Mexican Navy training ship *Cuauhtémoc* at the Rouen Armada, France

AUGUST 17: The *Cambria* at Les Voiles de Saint-Tropez regatta, France

AUGUST 18: An ocean liner at the port of call in La Valette, Malta

AUGUST 19: The Tower of Hercules, Galicia, Spain

AUGUST 20: The front mast of *Le Ponnant* in the Indian Ocean

AUGUST 21: A fishing boat in Newfoundland, Canada

AUGUST 22: Fishing boats in Essaouira, Morocco

AUGUST 23: Assembly of classic yachts at Les Voiles de Saint-Tropez regatta, France

FOLLOWING SPREAD: The Étel River, France

AUGUST 24: Beagle Canal, Patagonia

AUGUST 25: San Blas Archipelago, Panama

AUGUST 26: A pirogue, French Polynesia

AUGUST 27: Fish crates

AUGUST 28: An Irish coaster leaving Port-Rhu, France

AUGUST 29: Loch Ness, Scotland

AUGUST 30: One of the National Society of Sea Rescue boats, Audierne, France

AUGUST 31: A storm at the Pointe des Poulains Lighthouse, Belle-Île-en-Mer, France

SEPTEMBER 1: The caretaker of the Kereon Lighthouse, France

SEPTEMBER 2: A house decoration in Lofoten, Norway

SEPTEMBER 3: The anchor of the *Queen Mary 2*

SEPTEMBER 4: A fishing party in the Basin of Arcachon, France

SEPTEMBER 5: The *Esmeralda,* France

SEPTEMBER 6: Chinese nets in Cochin, India

SEPTEMBER 7: Béniguets Passage, France

SEPTEMBER 8: The Ram Island Ledge Lighthouse, Maine, United States

SEPTEMBER 9: An outrigger Canoe, Madagascar

FOLLOWING SPREAD: The cruise sailboat *Le Ponnant*

SEPTEMBER 10: A fishing boat returns to port in Saint-Pierre-et-Miquelon, France

SEPTEMBER 11: The seawall in the Port of Horta, the Azores Archipelago, Portugal

SEPTEMBER 12: The Créac'h Lighthouse, Finistère, France

SEPTEMBER 13: Buoys, Finistère, France

SEPTEMBER 14: A fishing ship, Lorient, France

SEPTEMBER 15: A boat haven in the Port of Colon on the Atlantic coast of Panama, where ships wait to pass through the canal

SEPTEMBER 16: A celebration in the port of Marseille at the Louis Vuitton Cup, France

SEPTEMBER 17: Leaving for sardine fishing at sunset, Loire-Atlantique, France

SEPTEMBER 18: Stormy skies over Caponga, Brazil

SEPTEMBER 19: The Lérins Islands in summer at sunrise, France

SEPTEMBER 20: The Port of Horta Lighthouse, the Azores Archipelago, Portugal

SEPTEMBER 21: The *Abri du Marin* in Sainte-Marine, France

SEPTEMBER 22: The coastline of Rockland, Maine, United States

FOLLOWING SPREAD: The Tevennec Lighthouse in the Raz de Sein, France

SEPTEMBER 23: Cloudy skies over Caponga, Brazil

SEPTEMBER 24: Cape Horn, Chile

SEPTEMBER 25: A whaleboat in the Azores Archipelago, Portugal

SEPTEMBER 26: Leaving to go fishing, Caponga, Brazil

SEPTEMBER 27: A lighthouse in Portland, Maine, United States

SEPTEMBER 28: A recreational boating port, Arcachon, France

SEPTEMBER 29: A sailboat under spinnaker

SEPTEMBER 30: *Le Ponnant* in the Indian Ocean

OCTOBER 1: Surfers on Sandy Beach, Cornwall, Great Britain

OCTOBER 2: Mussel beads in Aiguillon Cove, France

OCTOBER 3: Unloading fish in the Port of Newlyn, Cornwall, Great Britain

OCTOBER 4: Seine fishing on the beach, Trivandrum, India

OCTOBER 5: The registration number of a fishing boat, Morbihan, France

OCTOBER 6: Port of Erquy, Côtes-d'Armor, France

OCTOBER 7: Kovalam, India

OCTOBER 8: Fishermen, Madeleine Islands, Quebec, Canada

OCTOBER 9: A pirogue being put to water, Ifaty, Madagascar

OCTOBER 10: Desroches, Seychelles

OCTOBER 11: A ferry and a cargo sailboat

OCTOBER 12: Fishermen at work

OCTOBER 13: Fishing nets spread out on a quay

FOLLOWING SPREAD: Sunrise over Cape Frehel, France

OCTOBER 14: Gondolas in construction, Venice, Italy

OCTOBER 15: Reflections in the Port of Marseille, France

OCTOBER 16: Going out fishing in Vizhinjam, India

OCTOBER 17: The *Endeavour* and the *Shamrock V* racing together in the United Kingdom

OCTOBER 18: The *Prada* under spinnaker at the America's Cup

OCTOBER 19: The mast of the *Belem,* France

OCTOBER 20: The Race Point Lighthouse, Massachusetts, United States

OCTOBER 21: Relieving the caretaker of the Kereon Lighthouse, Finistère, France

OCTOBER 22: The rescue boat *Prince d'Eckhmül,* Finistère, France

OCTOBER 23: An oyster-farming pontoon in Quiberon Bay, France

OCTOBER 24: A fishing cabin in Martinique

OCTOBER 25: A beach in New Zealand

OCTOBER 26: Docking a junk in Along Bay, Vietnam

OCTOBER 27: The end of the day in Shediac, Canada

OCTOBER 28: Aboard a sailing pirogue, Ifaty, Madagascar

OCTOBER 29: Putting up the rigging of a departing pirogue, Madagascar

OCTOBER 30: A day's catch, Vizhinjam, India

FOLLOWING SPREAD: Sunset over Along Bay, Vietnam

OCTOBER 31: A fishing moment, Greece

NOVEMBER 1: Oyster-farming pontoons on the Crac'h River, France

NOVEMBER 2: Mystic Seaport, Connecticut, United States

NOVEMBER 3: Hauling down the spinnaker

NOVEMBER 4: A regatta in front of the Isle of Wight, England

NOVEMBER 5: A small fishing boat, Massachusetts, United States

NOVEMBER 6: Oyster-farming, Vendée, France

NOVEMBER 7: Fishing in Quiberon Bay, France

NOVEMBER 8: The *Queen Mary 2* arriving at Fort-de-France, Martinique

NOVEMBER 9: An evening on the bridge of *Le Ponnant*

NOVEMBER 10: Lobster buoys, Maine, United States

NOVEMBER 11: Aboard a sailing pirogue, Ifaty, Madagascar

NOVEMBER 12: The christening ceremony of *Il Moro de Venezia,* Venice, Italy

FOLLOWING SPREAD: Anchored recreational boats at Cape Ferret, France

NOVEMBER 13: Desroches, Seychelles

NOVEMBER 14: Kollam Beach, India

NOVEMBER 15: Stowing the seine after fishing, Madagascar

NOVEMBER 16: Northern Donegal, Ireland

NOVEMBER 17: Cloudy skies

NOVEMBER 18: A winter storm over Penmarc'h, France

NOVEMBER 19: The Le Four Lighthouse, Finistére, France

NOVEMBER 20: The Le Four Lighthouse submerged, Finistére, France

NOVEMBER 21: A rescue boat from Ouessant in front of the Jument Lighthouse, France

NOVEMBER 22: On a beach in Seychelles

NOVEMBER 23: A monk collecting offerings from inhabitants along the Bangkok Canal, Thailand

NOVEMBER 24: A fishing port, Vizhinjam, India

NOVEMBER 25: Fishing nets in the Port of Istanbul, Turkey

NOVEMBER 26: A schooner

NOVEMBER 27: A boat cemetery, Bono, France

NOVEMBER 28: The Tower of Hercules, Galicia, Spain

NOVEMBER 29: Aboard the *Belem,* France

NOVEMBER 30: The *Orion* at the Cowes Week regatta, Isle of Wight, England

DECEMBER 1: The Cowes Week regatta, Isle of Wight, England

FOLLOWING SPREAD: Stormy skies over Caponga, Brazil

DECEMBER 2: A shipwreck in the Red Sea, Egypt

DECEMBER 3: A shipwreck near Olonne, France

DECEMBER 4: The Port of Sauzon, Belle-Île-en-Mer, France

DECEMBER 5: An oil rig in the North Sea

DECEMBER 6: The bow of the *Belem,* France

DECEMBER 7: Nosy Be, Madagascar

DECEMBER 8: Madagascan Boutre sailboats in the early morning, Anakao, Madagascar

FOLLOWING SPREAD: The *Queen Mary 2* in stormy weather

DECEMBER 8: The Ram Island Ledge Lighthouse, Maine, United States

DECEMBER 10: Going out fishing, Caponga, Brazil

DECEMBER 11: Sunset over Vizhinjam, India

DECEMBER 12: Port Clyde, Maine, United States

DECEMBER 13: Seine fishing in Carbet, France

DECEMBER 14: The Cape Béar Lighthouse, France

DECEMBER 15: The Crac'h River, France

DECEMBER 16: Egrets flying over a reef, Nosy Be, Madagascar

DECEMBER 17: A cardinal north navigational marker

DECEMBER 18: Spinnaker maneuvering

DECEMBER 19: A small catch on the reef, Ifaty, Madagascar

DECEMBER 20: A traditional boat, Portugal

DECEMBER 21: A single-hulled vessel in Figari Bay, Corsica

FOLLOWING SPREAD: Desroches, Seychelles

DECEMBER 22: The aircraft carrier *Clemenceau,* France

DECEMBER 23: Aboard the *Jeanne d'Arc*, France

DECEMBER 24: Vezo Cemetery, Anakao, Madagascar

DECEMBER 25: Net fisherman in the *Backwaters,* Cochin, India

DECEMBER 26: Valparaiso Beach, Chile

DECEMBER 27: Junks in Along Bay, Vietnam

DECEMBER 28: Line fishing in the Suez Canal, Egypt

DECEMBER 29: The Nividic Lighthouse offshore Ouessant, France

DECEMBER 30: A seagull on a fishing dinghy, Morbihan, France

DECEMBER 31: The shallows facing Ifaty, Madagascar

Project Manager, English-language edition: Magali Veillon
Editor, English-language edition: Rachelle Mandik
Designer, English-language edition: Shawn Dahl
Production Manager, English-language edition: Tina Cameron

Library of Congress Control Number: 2007929901
ISBN 10: 0-8109-9448-8
ISBN 13: 978-0-8109-9448-5

Published in 2007 by Abrams, an imprint of Harry N. Abrams, Inc.

Printed and bound in Italy
10 9 8 7 6 5 4 3 2 1

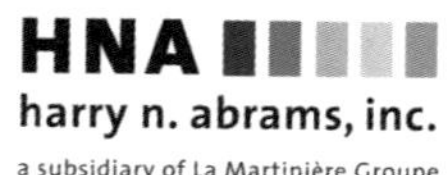

115 West 18th Street
New York, NY 10011
www.hnabooks.com